P9-CJV-840

CONTEMPORARY BUSINESS MATHEMATICS WITH CANADIAN APPLICATIONS

CONTEMPORARY BUSINESS MATHEMATICS WITH CANADIAN APPLICATIONS

S. A. HUMMELBRUNNER

KELLY HALLIDAY
Georgian College

ALI R. HASSANLOU
Kwantlen Polytechnic University

12th Edition

Pearson

Pearson Canada Inc., 26 Prince Andrew Place, North York, Ontario M3C 2H4.

Copyright © 2021, 2018, 2015 Pearson Canada Inc. All rights reserved.

Printed in the United States of America. This publication is protected by copyright, and permission should be obtained from the publisher prior to any prohibited reproduction, storage in a retrieval system, or transmission in any form or by any means, electronic, mechanical, photocopying, recording, or otherwise. For information regarding permissions, request forms, and the appropriate contacts, please contact Pearson Canada's Rights and Permissions Department by visiting www.pearson.com/ca/en/contact-us/permissions.html.

Attributions of third-party content appear on the appropriate page within the text. Cover and Chapter Opener Images: Courtesy of Euan White

PEARSON is an exclusive trademark owned by Pearson Canada Inc. or its affiliates in Canada and/or other countries.

Unless otherwise indicated herein, any third party trademarks that may appear in this work are the property of their respective owners and any references to third party trademarks, logos, or other trade dress are for demonstrative or descriptive purposes only. Such references are not intended to imply any sponsorship, endorsement, authorization, or promotion of Pearson Canada products by the owners of such marks, or any relationship between the owner and Pearson Canada or its affiliates, authors, licensees, or distributors.

If you purchased this book outside the United States or Canada, you should be aware that it has been imported without the approval of the publisher or the author.

9780135285015

3 2021

Library and Archives Canada Cataloguing in Publication

Title: Contemporary business mathematics with Canadian applications / S.A. Hummelbrunner, Kelly Halliday, Georgian College, Ali R. Hassanlou, Kwantlen Polytechnic University.
Names: Hummelbrunner, S. A. (Siegfried August), author. | Halliday, Kelly, author. | Hassanlou, Ali R., author.
Description: 12th edition. | Includes index.
Identifiers: Canadiana 20190126507 | ISBN 9780135285015 (hardcover)
Subjects: LCSH: Business mathematics—Textbooks.
Classification: LCC HF5691 .H85 2019 | DDC 651.01/513—dc23

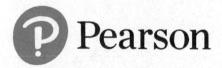

BRIEF CONTENTS

CONTENTS

PREFACE

INTRODUCTION

Contemporary Business Mathematics with Canadian Applications is intended for use in introductory mathematics of finance courses in post-secondary business management, marketing, accounting, and finance programs. It also provides a review of basic mathematics.

The primary objective of the text is to increase the student's knowledge and skill in the solution of practical financial and operational problems encountered in operating a business.

ORGANIZATION

Contemporary Business Mathematics with Canadian Applications is a teaching text using problem-identification and problem-solving approaches. The systematic and sequential development of the material is illustrated by examples that show a step-by-step approach to solving the problem. The detailed solutions are presented in a visually clear and colourful layout that allows learners to monitor their own progress in the classroom or in independent study.

Each topic in each chapter is followed by practice exercises containing numerous drill questions and application problems. At the end of each chapter, Review Exercises, Self-Test, Challenge Problems, and a Case Study integrate the material presented.

The first four chapters and Appendix I (Further Review of Basic Algebra) are intended for students with little or no background in algebra and provide an opportunity to review arithmetic and algebraic processes.

The text is based on Canadian practice, and reflects current trends using available technology—specifically the availability of preprogrammed financial calculators. Students using this book should have access to calculators having a power function and a natural logarithm function. The use of such calculators eliminates the constraints associated with manually calculating results using formulas.

In solving problems involving multiple steps, often values are determined that will be used in further computations. Such values should not be rounded and all available digits should be retained in the calculator. Using the memory functions of the calculator enables the student to retain such non-rounded values.

When using the memory, the student needs to be aware that the number of digits retained in the registers of the calculator is greater than the number of digits displayed. Depending on whether the memory or the displayed digits are used, slight differences may occur.

Students are encouraged to use preprogrammed financial calculators. The use of these preprogrammed calculators facilitates the solving of most financial problems and is demonstrated extensively in Chapters 9 to 16.

NEW TO THIS EDITION

The Twelfth Edition of Hummelbrunner/Halliday/Hassanlou, *Contemporary Business Mathematics with Canadian Applications,* includes updates based on changes in current practices in Canadian finance and business and the needs of students and instructors using this book.

- This edition continues to clarify the consistent approach to rounding rules. The **Student's Reference Guide to Rounding and Special Notations** (pages xix–xxii) gives a clear explanation of the rounding conventions used throughout the text. Additional *Pointers and Pitfalls* boxes are placed in key areas to remind students about the rounding conventions and exceptions in practice.
- The text and solutions manual have been thoroughly technically checked for accuracy and consistency with the rounding approach.
- Tables, charts, and further diagrams have been added to enable the learner to visualize the problems and the solutions.
- Numerous new examples and exercises have been added.
- To help students better understand and solve systems of linear equations, the order of presenting concepts has been changed in Chapter 4. We first introduce an easier concept of graphing linear solutions and continue with algebraic solutions of systems of linear equations with two unknown variables. Finally, solving systems of linear inequalities is presented.
- The cost data in the main example for explaining break-even analysis in Chapter 5 have been revised to eliminate confusion and help students understand various costs of doing business, perform cost-volume-profit analysis, and calculate the break-even point in a business.
- Canadian references have been emphasized in *Business Math News Boxes* and website references.
- Interest rates reflect current investment and borrowing rates.

Many examples and exercises have been updated, rewritten, and expanded. To enhance the building-block approach, exercises are ordered to link the topics and the solved examples. Help references have been expanded to link selected exercises to solved examples.

Specifically, in **Chapter 1** (Review of Arithmetic), prices, salaries, and wages have been updated. Revised rates and calculations for GST/PST/HST have been included to incorporate new legislation for 2018 and property tax terminology and valuations have been updated. Weighted average examples and exercises have been expanded and additional drill questions have been added throughout Chapter 1. The Business Math News Box on National Salary Comparisions has been updated and moved here from Chapter 3.

In **Chapter 2** (Review of Basic Algebra), the chapter-opening vignette emphasizes why business students need algebra, algebra explanations have been expanded, and new diagrams and *Pointers and Pitfalls* clarify these fundamental approaches. Language and math scaffolding strategies have been emphasized in this chapter to improve students' understanding of key concepts and relationships. Calculator solutions have been introduced for several examples and formulas have been simplified.

In **Chapter 3** (Ratio, Proportion, and Percent), a consistent approach for calculating proportions has been introduced, and the percentage-base-rate triangle has been included as a useful aid for determining percentages. Sections in the chapter have been re-ordered to improve student understanding. For example, instructions for calculating the base appear before calculating the percentage rate. Currency conversion rates, prices, CPI numbers, and personal income taxes have been updated. A new Business Math News Box highlights the variability of apartment rental rates in major Canadian cities.

In **Chapter 4** (Linear Systems), the order of the first three subsections has been changed to first introduce graphing linear equations and then explain algebraic solutions to linear systems in two variables. The substitution and elimination methods for solving the point of intersection of two linear systems has been emphasized.

The order of **Chapter 5** and **Chapter 6**, which was switched in the Tenth Edition, is retained to improve the flow of content from Linear Systems (Chapter 4) to Cost-Volume-Profit Analysis and Break-Even (Chapter 5). This chapter has been changed significantly with a comprehensive example that starts at the beginning and continues throughout the chapter. In Chapter 5, a new *Business Math News Box* ties the concepts learned in this chapter to the legalization of marijuana in Canada. The Chapter 5 opening vignette appropriately includes an example that connects with the new *Business Math News Box* presented later in the chapter. The number of formulas has been reduced, and solutions to examples use a simplified approach for calculating break-even.

Chapter 6 (Trade Discounts, Cash Discounts, Markup, and Markdown) explanations and diagrams have been revised to clarify key concepts. *Pointers and Pitfalls* boxes provide tools to help students rearrange formulas, determine the number of days in a discount period, and calculate markup. A sample invoice demonstrates payment terms and cash discounts. EOM and ROG examples, are retained to help students understand the terminology and concepts as they are being used in practice by businesses. Beginning in this chapter, instructions in the text that previously asked students to "find" specific variables have been replaced by more mathematical language such as "solve," "calculate," and "determine."

In **Chapter 7** (Simple Interest), a new Business Math News Box outlining the perils of "buy now, pay later" plans has replaced an outdated box based on the Canada Savings Bond Program. Dates and interest rates have been updated and new exercises have been added, with exercises referenced to examples. Additional tools for choosing focal dates and calculating number of days have been added.

In **Chapter 8** (Simple Interest Applications), a new opening vignette leaves way for a Business Math News Box focused on calculating the annual percentage rate of charge for payday loans. Comments on credit ratings, credit scores, home equity lines of credit, and new exercises calculating unpaid balances have been added. Treasury bill interest rates have been updated to reflect current rates. A new subsection on commercial paper has been included in this edition.

In **Chapter 9** (Compound Interest—Future Value and Present Value), visual explanations for drawing timelines and selecting focal dates have been expanded. The introduction to Future Value, and explanation of the periodic rate of interest, have been simplified. The relationship between n and m has been clarified. Additional examples and questions using weekly and bi-weekly compounding periods have been included, along with questions featuring changing interest rates. A new Business Math News Box using data for fixed- and variable-rate Guaranteed Investment Certificates (GICs) provides examples of escalating interest rates.

In **Chapter 10** (Compound Interest—Further Topics), formula rearrangement is emphasized. A Pointers and Pitfalls box has been added to explain how to calculate the "true cost" of borrowing. Drill questions from previous editions for calculating effective and equivalent interest rates have been added back to the section exercises.

In **Chapter 11** (Ordinary Simple Annuities) and in **Chapter 12** (Ordinary General Annuities), new Pointers and Pitfalls boxes have been added to help students set up equations at the focal date. Advanced questions have been added to the chapter exercises, including changes in interest rates and changes in payment size, as well as calculating the size of the final payment in an annuity. The updated Business Math News Boxes feature credit card minimum payment myths and whether or not it is better to lease or buy a car.

In **Chapter 13** (Annuities Due, Deferred Annuities, and Perpetuities), explanations, diagrams, and calculations for annuities due are simplified. New examples with diagrams have been added, including reference to investments in preferred shares. New Pointers and Pitfalls boxes remind the reader how to calculate the number of payments in an annuity, and how to calculate present value of perpetuities when the size of the payment increases or decreases at a constant rate.

In **Chapter 14** (Amortization of Loans, Including Residential Mortgages), a new section with a diagram develops the skills to calculate the interest, principal, and balance for a period, and bridges between calculating the payment and constructing the amortization schedule. The introduction to residential mortgages has been updated to reflect current legislation on mortgage insurance and stress testing. The "sinking funds" concept covered in this chapter of the Eleventh Edition is now removed from this chapter and included in Chapter 15. Examples and exercises have been reordered and clarified to enhance building-block learning.

In **Chapter 15** (Bond Valuation and Sinking Funds), explanation of basic concepts has been expanded to answer the "why?" and "how?" questions. The order has been changed, with a focus on calculation of bond price under different conditions. An introductory section has been added for concept comprehension. Calculating the purchase price of a bond has been separated into two sections based on whether or not the market rate equals or does not equal the bond rate. Instructions and examples have been provided on how to use the Texas Instrument BA II PLUS calculator to calculate the purchase price of a bond on an interest payment date or between interest payment dates. The "sinking funds" concept that was introduced in Chapter 14 in the Eleventh Edition is now included in this chapter to help students understand how corporations plan to have funds available to pay back their issued bonds on the maturity date.

In **Chapter 16** (Investment Decision Applications), explanations begin the section on Net Present Value, followed by introductory, then more advanced, applications. Repetitive calculator instructions have been eliminated. Computing the Rate of Return by manual methods has been condensed and new visuals have been added. Instructions for using the cash flow analysis of the Texas Instrument BA II PLUS financial calculator and Excel's NPV and IRR functions have been included, with an example for each function to reinforce learning.

COMPREHENSIVE CASE STUDIES

Comprehensive case studies for each part of the book have been created. The questions within each case study have been separated by chapter or group of chapters to facilitate the use of these case studies by those institutions that include only some of the topics in their course syllabus. With the questions separated and identified by chapter, these institutions can use part of the case study in their courses.

Part 1 Mathematics Fundamentals and Business Applications
Til Debt Do Us Part host Gail Vaz-Oxlade has made it her mission to help couples who are headed for disaster get out of debt. Questions for each of Chapters 1–4 are included.

Part 2 Mathematics of Business and Management
A sporting equipment manufacturer and retailer, SportZ Ltd., is based in Alberta. Questions for each of Chapters 5–8 are included.

Part 3 Mathematics of Finance and Investment
Based in Ontario, Lux Resources Group, Inc., rents and sells construction equipment. Questions for each of Chapters 9–16 are included.

In general, interest rates used reflect the current economic climate in Canada. Calculator tips and solutions have been updated or clarified. Spreadsheet instructions and Internet website references have been updated. *Pitfalls and Pointers* have been included to assist in performing tasks and interpreting word problems, and sections have been rewritten to clarify the explanations. Many more word problems have been added and references to solved examples increased. *Business Math News Boxes* and Case Studies have been updated. Examples involving both business and personal situations are included. The pedagogical elements of the previous edition have been retained. In response to requests and suggestions by users of the book, a number of features for this edition have been included. They are described next.

FEATURES

UPDATED!
- A new colourful and student-friendly design has been created for the book, making it more accessible and less intimidating to learners at all levels.

UPDATED!
- Any preprogrammed financial calculator may be used, but this edition includes extensive instructions for using the Texas Instruments BA II PLUS financial calculator. Equivalent instructions are given in Appendix II for the Sharp EL-738C and the Hewlett-Packard 10bII+ financial calculators.

- Each part opens with an introduction to the upcoming chapters and a discussion of the rounding conventions that are relevant to these chapters.

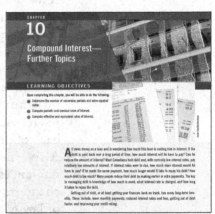

- A set of Learning Objectives is listed at the beginning of each chapter. The corresponding Learning Objectives are also indicated for each Review Exercise, allowing students to see which aspects of the chapter they have mastered.

- Each chapter opens with a description of a situation familiar to students to emphasize the practical applications of the material to follow.

- A **Business Math News Box** is presented in every chapter. This element consists of short excerpts based on material appearing in newspapers, magazines, or websites, followed by a set of questions. These boxes demonstrate how widespread business math applications are in the real world.

- The **Pointers and Pitfalls** boxes emphasize good practices, highlight ways to avoid common errors, show how to use a financial calculator efficiently, or give hints for tackling business math situations to reduce math anxiety.

- Numerous **Examples with worked-out Solutions** are provided throughout the book, offering easy-to-follow, step-by-step instructions.

UPDATED!
- **Programmed solutions** using the Texas Instruments BA II PLUS calculator are offered for most examples in Chapters 9 to 16. Since this calculator display can be pre-set, it is suggested that the learner set the display to show six decimal places to match the mathematical calculations in the body of the text. Both mathematical and calculator solutions

for all Exercises, Review Exercises, and Self-Tests are included in the Instructor's Solutions Manual. An icon highlights information on the use of the BA II PLUS calculator.

- **Key Terms** are introduced in the text in boldface type. A Glossary at the end of each chapter lists each term with its definition and a page reference to where the term was first defined in the chapter.
- Main Equations are highlighted in the chapters and repeated in a Summary of Formulas at the ends of the chapters.
- A list of the Main Formulas can be found on the study card bound into this text.
- An **Exercise set** is provided at the end of each section in every chapter. In addition, each chapter contains a **Review Exercise** set and a **Self-Test**. Answers to all the odd-numbered Exercises, Review Exercises, and Self-Tests are given at the back of the book.
- Also included in this edition are references to solved Examples in several chapters, which are provided at the end of key exercises. Students are directed to specific examples so they can check their work and review fundamental problem types.
- Exercises and Review Exercises that are marked with a 🌐 are also available on MyLab Math. Students have endless opportunities to practise many of these questions with new data and values every time they use MyLab Math.
- A set of **Challenge Problems** is provided in each chapter. These problems give users the opportunity to apply the skills learned in the chapter to questions that are pitched at a higher level than the Exercises.
- Sixteen **Case Studies** are included in the book, at the end of each chapter. They present comprehensive realistic scenarios followed by a set of questions and illustrate some of the important types of practical applications of the chapter material. Sixteen additional case studies can be found on MyLab Math.

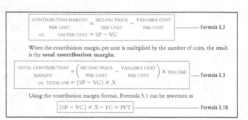

TECHNOLOGY RESOURCES

MyLab Math

MyLab Math from Pearson is the world's leading online resource in mathematics, integrating interactive homework, assessment, and media in a flexible, easy-to-use format. It provides engaging experiences that personalize, stimulate, and measure learning for each student. And, it comes from an experienced partner with educational expertise and an eye on the future.

To learn more about how MyLab Math combines proven learning applications with powerful assessment, visit www.pearsonmylabandmastering.com or contact your Pearson representative.

PEARSON ETEXT

Pearson eText. The Pearson eText gives students access to their textbook anytime, anywhere. In addition to note taking, highlighting, and bookmarking, the Pearson eText offers interactive and sharing features. Instructors can share their comments or highlights, and students can add their own, creating a tight community of learners within the class.

LEARNING SOLUTIONS MANAGERS

Pearson's Learning Solutions Managers work with faculty and campus course designers to ensure that Pearson technology products, assessment tools, and online course materials are tailored to meet and anticipate specific needs. This highly qualified team is dedicated to helping schools take full advantage of a wide range of educational resources, by assisting in the integration of a variety of instructional materials and media formats. Your local Pearson Education sales representative can provide you with more details on this service program.

SUPPLEMENTS

The following instructor supplements are available for downloading from a password-protected section of Pearson Canada's online catalogue (catalogue.pearsoned.ca). Navigate to your book's catalogue page to view a list of the available supplements. See your local sales representative for details and access.

- An **Instructor's Solutions Manual** provides complete mathematical and calculator solutions to all the Exercises, Review Exercises, Self-Tests, *Business Math News Box* questions, Challenge Problems, and Case Studies in the textbook.
- An **Instructor's Resource Manual** includes Chapter Overviews, Suggested Priority of Topics, Chapter Outlines, and centralized information on all the supplements available with the text.
- **PowerPoint® Lecture Slides** present an outline of each chapter in the book, highlighting the major concepts taught. The presentation will include many of the figures and tables from the text and provides the instructor with a visually interesting summary of the entire book.
- Pearson's computerized **test banks** allow instructors to filter and select questions to create quizzes, tests or homework. Instructors can revise questions or add their own, and may be able to choose print or online options. These questions are also available in Microsoft Word format.
- A complete **Answer Key** will contain solutions for all of the exercise and self-test questions.
- **Excel Templates** will allow instructors to assign a selection of Exercises and Review Exercises to be solved using Excel spreadsheets.
- An **Image Library** will provide access to many of the figures and tables in the textbook.

ACKNOWLEDGMENTS

We would like to express our thanks to the many people who offered thoughtful suggestions and recommendations for updating and improving the book, including the following instructors:

Ben Brown, Vancouver Community College

Helen Catania, Centennial College

Margaret Dancy, Fanshawe College

Ana Duff, University of Ontario Institute of Technology

Frances Ford, New Brunswick Community College

Imad Hassan, Algonquin College

Mariana Ionescu, George Brown College

Steve Kopp, Western University

Sylvia A Leskiw, MacEwan University

Deborah Sauer, Capilano College

Marnie Staffen, Cambrian College

Nii Odoi Yemoh, Humber College

We would also like to thank the many people at Pearson Canada Inc. who helped with the development and production of this book, especially to the acquisitions editor, Keriann McGoogan; the content manager, Nicole Mellow; the developmental and media editor, Charlotte Morrison-Reed; the project manager, Pippa Kennard; the copy editor, Susan Bindernagel; and the marketing manager, Euan White.

STUDENT'S REFERENCE GUIDE TO ROUNDING AND SPECIAL NOTATIONS

Developed by Jean-Paul Olivier, based on the textbook authored by Kelly Halliday and Ali Hassanlou

Universal Principle of Rounding: When performing a sequence of operations, never round any interim solution until the final answer is achieved. Only apply rounding principles to the final answer. Interim solutions should only be rounded where common practice would require rounding.

Note: Due to space limitations, the textbook only shows the first 6 decimals (rounded) of any number. Starting in Chapter 11, because the calculator display may not have sufficient space for all 6 decimals, as many decimals as possible will be shown. However, the Universal Principle of Rounding still applies.

Part 1

Section 1.2

1. For repeating decimals, use the notation of placing a period above the repeating sequence. E.g., $\frac{1}{3} = 0.333333\ldots = 0.\overline{3}$

2. For terminating decimals, if they terminate within the first 6 decimal places, then carry all the decimals in your final answer.

3. For non-terminating decimals, round to 6 decimals unless specified or logically sound to do so otherwise. If the final digits would be zeros, the zeros are generally not displayed.

4. Calculations involving money are rounded to 2 decimals as their final answer. Interim solutions may be rounded to 2 decimals if the situation dictates (for example, if you withdraw money from an account). If the calculation does not involve cents, it is optional to display the decimals.

Section 1.3

1. Calculations involving percentages will only involve 4 decimal positions since there are only 6 decimals in decimal format.

Section 1.5

1. Hourly rate calculations for salaried employees require that all the decimals should be carried until the final answer is achieved. If the solution is to express the hourly rate or overtime rate itself, then rounding to 2 decimals is appropriate.

2. Overtime hourly wage rate calculations should carry all decimals of the overtime rate until the final answer is achieved.

Section 3.7

1. Larger sums of money usually are involved in currency exchanges. Therefore, the two decimal rule for money is insufficient. To produce a more accurate result, currency exchange rates need to carry at least four decimals.

2. It needs to be recognized that not all currencies utilize the same decimals when expressing amounts.

   (a) Final currency amounts for the Canadian Dollar, U.S. Dollar, British Pound, Euro, and Swiss Franc should be rounded to the standard two decimal places.

   (b) Final currency amounts for the Japanese Yen should be rounded to the nearest integer, as there are no decimal amounts in their currency.

3. Price per litre of gasoline is generally expressed to three decimal points (129.9¢/L = $1.299/L)

Section 3.8

1. As indexes are similar to percentages, an index will only have 4 decimals.

Part 2

Section 5.1

1. When calculating break-even units, remember that the solution is the *minimum* number of units that must be sold. As such, any decimals must be rounded upwards to the next integer, regardless of the actual value of the decimal. For example, 38.05 units means 39 units must be sold to at least break even.

Section 7.2D

1. t is always an integer. It is important to note in this calculation that in most instances the interest (I) earned or charged to the account has been rounded to two decimals. This will cause the calculation of t to be slightly imprecise. Therefore, when calculating t it is possible that decimals close to an integer (such as 128.998 days or 130.012 days) may show up. These decimals should be rounded to the nearest integer to correct for the rounded interest amount.

Part 3

Section 9.2D

1. In determining when it is appropriate to round, it is important to recognize that if the money remains inside an account (deposit or loan), all of the decimals need to carry forward into the next calculation. For example, if a bank deposit of $2000 earns 6% p.a. compounded monthly for 4 years, and then earns 7% p.a. compounded quarterly for three more years, then the money remained in the account the whole time. We can solve this in one step as follows:

$$FV = 2000.00(1.005)^{48}(1.0175)^{12} = \$3129.06$$

Or two steps as follows:

$$FV = 2000.00(1.005)^{48} = \$2540.978322$$

$$FV = 2540.978322(1.0175)^{12} = \$3129.06$$

Note that the first step is an interim calculation, for which we must carry forward all the decimals to the next step where the solution can then be rounded.

(a) If money is withdrawn/transferred from the account at any time, then only 2 decimals can be carried forward to any further steps (since a currency payout can only involve 2 decimals).

Section 9.4C

1. In promissory notes, the FV solution in the first step must be rounded to 2 decimals before discounting as this is the amount of the debt that will be repaid on the maturity date.

Section 9.5B

1. When calculating equivalent values for more than one payment, each payment is a separate transaction (one could make each payment separate from any other payment) and therefore any equivalent value is rounded to two decimals before summing multiple payments.

Section 10.1

1. When determining the n for non-annuity calculations (lump-sum amounts), generally the solution would not be rounded off since n can be fractional in nature (we can get 4.5632 quarters).

   (a) However, when n is discussed, the n may be simplified to 2 decimals so that it is easier to communicate. For example, if $n = 5.998123$ years this would mean a term of slightly under 6 years. However, when discussed it may be spoken simply as a term of 6.00 years. Alternatively if $n = 17.559876$ months this would mean a little more than half way through the 17th month. However, when discussed it may be spoken as a term of approximately 17.56 months.

   (b) An exception to this rule is when the n gets converted into days. As interest generally is not accrued more than daily, a fraction of a day is not possible. The fraction shows up most likely due to rounding in the numbers being utilized in the calculation. Since we do not know how these numbers were rounded, it is appropriate for our purposes to round n to the nearest integer.

Section 11.5A

1. When determining the n for annuity calculations, remember that n represents the number of payments. Therefore, n must be a whole number and should always be rounded upwards. Whether a partial or full payment is made, it is still a payment. For example, if $n = 21.34$ payments, this would indicate 21 full payments and a smaller last payment (which is still a payment). Therefore, 22 payments are required.

   (a) In most cases, the payment (PMT) has been rounded to two decimals. This may cause insignificant decimals to show up in the calculations. As a result, an exception to this rule would be when n is extremely close to a whole number. This would mean that no significant digits show up in the first two decimals. For example, if $n = 23.001$, it can be reasonably concluded that n is 23 payments since the 0.001 is probably a result of the rounded payment.

Section 13.1E

1. When working with the n for an annuity due, n represents the number of payments and must be a whole number. Therefore, n will always round upward. However, it is important to distinguish whether the question is asking about the term of the annuity due or when the last payment of the annuity due occurs.

   (a) If the term is being asked, n can be used to figure out the timeline. For example, a yearly apartment rental agreement would have $n = 12$ monthly payments, thus the term ends 12 months from now.

   (b) If the last payment is being asked, $n - 1$ can be used to figure out the timeline. In the same example, the last rental payment would occur at the beginning of the 12th month. The last payment would be $12 - 1 = 11$ months from now.

Section 14.1

1. The payment must be rounded to the two decimal standard for currency.

2. When constructing an amortization schedule, it is important to recognize that all numbers in the schedule need to be rounded to two decimals (since it is currency). However, since the money remains in the account at all times, all decimals are in fact being carried forward throughout. As such, calculated numbers may sometimes be off by a penny due to the rounding of the payment or the interest.

Section 15.1

1. When determining the purchase price for a bond, it is important to carry all the decimals until the calculation is complete. When completing the calculation by formula, the present value of the bond's face value and interest payments along with any accrued interest must be calculated. For simplicity, the text shows each of these values rounded to two decimals and then summed to get the purchase price. Remember though that all decimals are being carried forward until the final answer.

Section 15.5

1. A sinking fund schedule has the same characteristics as an amortization schedule and may also experience a penny difference due to the rounding of the payment or the interest.

Section 16.1

1. When making choices between various alternatives, it is sufficient to calculate answers rounded to the nearest dollar. There are two rationales for this. First, in most cases future cash flows are not entirely certain (they are estimates) and therefore may be slightly inaccurate themselves. Second, as cents have little value, most decisions would not be based on cents difference; rather decisions would be based on dollars difference.

Section 16.2

1. In choosing whether to accept or reject a contract using the net present value method, remember that future cash flows are estimates. Therefore, when an NPV is calculated that is within $500 of $0, it can be said that the result does not provide a clear signal to accept or reject. Although the desired rate of return has barely been met (or not), this may be a result of the estimated cash flows. In this case, a closer examination of the estimates to determine their accuracy may be required before any decision could be made.

Section 16.3

1. Performance indexes are generally rounded to one decimal in percentage format.

2. This unknown rate of return (d) is generally rounded to 2 decimals in percentage format.

3. A rate of return is generally rounded to one decimal in percentage format.

For Daryl, Kirkland, and Kealeigh.

— K.H.

To my family for their support and to my two angels, Emma and Elina,
who have brought so much happiness into our lives.

— A.R.H.

The first four chapters and Appendix I call upon students to activate prior knowledge learned in their earlier mathematics courses. As such, Part 1 is intended to provide an opportunity to review arithmetic and algebraic processes and to apply these skills in relevant business situations in fields such as accounting, finance, marketing, human resources, and management.

Chapter 1 covers the basics of arithmetic operations. In this chapter you will learn how to set up equivalent fractions, convert fractions and mixed numbers into decimals and percents, evaluate complex fractions, reduce fractions to lowest terms, and simplify expressions using the rules of the order of operations.

Calculating percents is introduced early because, from a practical standpoint, it is often necessary to convert a percent to a decimal when performing arithmetic calculations or using a calculator.

Applications involving payroll, commissions, GST, PST, HST, and property taxes call upon the use of these basic arithmetical operations and percentages. With respect to payroll, you will be able to calculate regular pay, overtime pay, and total pay. The text illustrates how to calculate straight commission, graduated commission (sliding scale), and salary plus commission as part of a complete discussion on gross earnings.

Chapter 2 reviews the basics of algebra, including simplifying algebraic expressions, evaluating algebraic expressions by substituting numbers into the variables, solving algebraic equations, and creating and solving word problems. Examples show how positive, negative, fractional, and zero exponents are defined. The study of terms involving positive, negative, and zero exponents serves as a prelude to the introduction of logarithms. Logarithms are useful in solving equations in which the unknown is an exponent. These expressions involving exponents appear in the study of compound interest developed later in the text.

Problems involving ratios, proportions, and percents abound in the field of business, and so in Chapter 3 you will learn how to use ratios to solve allocation and equivalence problems. Exchange rate comparisons and the Consumer Price Index (CPI) examples in the chapter demonstrate practical applications of proportions. Discounts, interest rates, growth in earnings, and wages all use percentages.

Chapter 4 deals with linear equations and systems of two simultaneous linear equations in two variables. The algebraic elimination method is demonstrated for solving a system of two linear equations. The rectangular coordinate system is introduced, and an ordered pair is defined. You will learn how to set up a table of ordered pairs that can be used to graph a linear equation. The slope-intercept form of the linear equation is introduced, and special cases are discussed. You will learn how to develop a linear equation to describe a relationship between two variables and how to set up a system of linear equations to solve word problems involving two variables.

The **Universal Principle of Rounding** applies in Part 1 of the textbook. When performing a sequence of operations, never round any interim solution until the final answer is achieved. Apply rounding principles only to the final answer. Interim solutions should only be rounded where common practice would require rounding.

Note, however, that due to space limitations, the textbook shows only the first six decimals (rounded) of any number.

Some specific rounding guidelines for Part 1: Business problems throughout the textbook often involve money values so the rounding for final answers needs to be done to the cent; that is, to two decimal places. However, because larger sums of money usually are involved in currency exchanges, the two-decimal rule is insufficient. To produce a more accurate result, currency exchange rates used in Chapter 3 need to carry at least four decimals. Also, note that in Chapter 3, price per litre of gasoline is generally expressed to three decimal points (129.9 cents = \$1.299/L).

While different methods of rounding are used, for most business purposes the following procedure is suitable:

1. If the first digit in the group of decimal digits that is to be dropped is 5 or greater, the last digit retained is *increased* by 1.

2. If the first digit in the group of decimal digits that is to be dropped is 4 or less, the last digit retained is left *unchanged*.

Review of Arithmetic

LEARNING OBJECTIVES

Objectives are a "roadmap" showing what will be covered and what is especially important in each chapter.

Upon completing this chapter, you will be able to do the following:

❶ Simplify arithmetic expressions using the basic order of operations.

❷ Determine equivalent fractions, and convert fractions to decimals, decimals to percents, and vice versa.

❸ Through problem solving, compute simple arithmetic and weighted averages.

❹ Determine gross earnings for employees remunerated by the payment of salaries, hourly wages, or commissions.

❺ Through problem solving, compute GST, HST, PST, sales taxes, and property taxes.

GROSS

DEDUCTIONS
GOVT PEN
FEDL TAX
OTHRBFTS
TOTAL DEDUCTIONS

NET PAY

Bradcalkins/Fotolia

Each chapter opens with a description of a familiar situation to help you understand the practical applications of the material to follow.

Being able to perform arithmetic calculations is important in today's business environment. Arithmetic is used in planning, forecasting, purchasing, contracting, compensation, and many other aspects of business. Competence in problem solving, including calculation on averages, is essential. When you employ people in operating a business, you must determine the amounts to pay them in the form of salaries or wages, and you must deduct and pay payroll taxes such as Canada Pension Plan, Employment Insurance, and employee income taxes. You are responsible for paying your employees and submitting the tax amounts to the federal government. Operating a business also means that you must determine the amount of goods and services tax (GST) or harmonized sales tax (HST) to collect on almost everything you sell. The amount you must remit to the federal government, or the refund you are entitled to, is calculated on the basis of the GST or HST you pay when you make purchases of goods and services. By using arithmetic and problem-solving approaches in this chapter, you will be able to determine the amounts owed.

INTRODUCTION

The basics of fraction, decimal, and percent conversions are vital skills for dealing with situations you may face, not only as a small-business owner but also as a consumer and investor. Although calculators and computers are commonly used when performing arithmetic operations, to be able to solve more complex business problems modelled using algebra (and calculus), it is important to be skilled at the process of conversion between number forms, the rounding of answers, and the correct order of operations. (Appendix II at the back of the text provides basic operations for three common preprogrammed financial calculator models.)

1.1 BASICS OF ARITHMETIC
A. The basic order of operations

Boldfaced words are Key Terms that are explained here and defined in the Glossary section at the end of the chapter.

To ensure that arithmetic calculations are performed consistently, we must follow the **order of operations**.

If an arithmetic expression contains brackets, exponents, multiplication, division, addition, and subtraction, we use the following procedure:

1. Perform all operations *inside* a bracket first (the operations inside the bracket must be performed in proper order).

2. Perform exponents.

3. Perform multiplication and division.

4. Perform addition and subtraction.

Numerous examples, often with worked-out Solutions, offer you easy-to-follow, step-by-step instructions.

The following "BEDMAS" rule might help you to more easily remember the order of operations:

B	E	D	M	A	S
Brackets	Exponents	Division	Multiplication	Addition	Subtraction

EXAMPLE 1.1A

(i) $(9 - 4) \times 2 = 5 \times 2 = 10$ —————— work inside the bracket first

(ii) $9 - 4 \times 2 = 9 - 8 = 1$ —————— do multiplication before subtraction

(iii) $18 \div 6 + 3 \times 2 = 3 + 6 = 9$ —————— do division and multiplication before adding

(iv) $(13 + 5) \div 6 - 3 = 18 \div 6 - 3$ —————— work inside the bracket first, then do
$\qquad\qquad\qquad = 3 - 3$ division before subtraction
$\qquad\qquad\qquad = 0$

(v) $18 \div (6 + 3) \times 2 = 18 \div 9 \times 2$ —————— work inside the bracket first, then do
$\qquad\qquad\qquad = 2 \times 2$ division and multiplication in
$\qquad\qquad\qquad = 4$ order

(vi) $18 \div (3 \times 2) + 3 = 18 \div 6 + 3$ —————— work inside the bracket first, then
$\qquad\qquad\qquad = 3 + 3$ divide before adding
$\qquad\qquad\qquad = 6$

(vii) $8(9 - 4) - 4(12 - 5) = 8(5) - 4(7)$ —————— work inside the brackets first, then
$\qquad\qquad\qquad = 40 - 28$ multiply before subtracting
$\qquad\qquad\qquad = 12$

(viii) $\dfrac{12-4}{6-2} = (12-4) \div (6-2)$ —————— the fraction line indicates brackets as well as division

$$= 8 \div 4$$
$$= 2$$

(ix) $128 \div (2 \times 4)^2 - 3 = 128 \div 8^2 - 3$ —————— work inside the bracket first, do the exponent, then divide before subtracting

$$= 128 \div 64 - 3$$
$$= 2 - 3$$
$$= -1$$

(x) $128 \div (2 \times 4^2) - 3 = 128 \div (2 \times 16) - 3$ —————— start inside the bracket and do the exponent first, then multiply, then divide before subtracting

$$= 128 \div 32 - 3$$
$$= 4 - 3$$
$$= 1$$

(xi) $12 - 5[8 - 2(9-3)] \div 2 = 12 - 5[8 - 2(6)] \div 2$ — work inside the square bracket first, then multiply before dividing by 2

$$= 12 - 5[8 - 12] \div 2$$
$$= 12 - 5[-4] \div 2$$
$$= 12 + 20 \div 2$$
$$= 12 + 10$$
$$= 22$$

(xii) $8a + 3[10 - (2a+1)] = 8a + 3[10 - (2a+1)]$ —— work inside the square bracket first, then multiply by 3 before combining like terms

$$= 8a + 3[10 - 2a - 1]$$
$$= 8a + 3[9 - 2a]$$
$$= 8a + 27 - 6a$$
$$= 2a + 27$$

EXERCISE 1.1

MyLab Math

Each section in the chapter ends with an exercise that allows you to review and apply what you've just learned. And you can find the solutions to the odd-numbered exercises at the back of the text.

For questions with a globe icon, visit MyLab Math to practise as often as you want. The guided solutions help you determine an answer step by step.

Evaluate each of the following.

 1. $12 + 6 \div 3$

 3. $(7+4) \times 5 - 2$

5. $6(7-2) - 3(5-3)$

7. $4(8-5)^2 - 5(3+2^2)$

9. $250(1 + 0.08)^{10}$

11. $30 \times 600 - 2500 - 12 \times 600$

13. $15 - 7 + 6(2+3) \div 3$

15. $(1 - 0.7) - 4 \times 20 \div 5$

17. $7a - 6[4 - (3a+6)]$

2. $(3 \times 8 - 6) \div 2$

4. $5 \times 3 + 2 \times 4$ ◀———

6. $\dfrac{20 - 16}{15 + 5}$

8. $(3 \times 4 - 2)^2 + (2 - 2 \times 7^2)$

10. $(1 + 0.04)^4 - 1$

12. $1 - [(1 - 0.40)(1 - 0.25)(1 - 0.05)]$

14. $16 \div 2 \times 4 + 6(4+2)$

16. $50[(1 - 0.2)(1 - 0.175)(1 - 0.04)]$

18. $6a + 4b + 2(16 - 2a + b)$

Reference Example 1.1A

References to examples direct you back to the chapter for help in answering the questions.

1.2 FRACTIONS
A. Common fractions

A **common fraction** is used to show a part of the whole. The fraction ⅔ means two parts out of a whole of three. The number written *above* the dividing line is the *part* and is called the **numerator** (or dividend). The number written *below* the dividing line is the *whole* and is called the **denominator** (or divisor). The numbers (in this case the numbers 2 and 3) are called the **terms of the fraction**.

A **proper fraction** has a numerator that is *less* than the denominator. An **improper fraction** has a numerator that is *greater* than the denominator.

EXAMPLE 1.2A

$\dfrac{3}{8}$ ← numerator ─── a proper fraction, since the numerator is less
← denominator ─── than the denominator

$\dfrac{6}{5}$ ← numerator ─── an improper fraction, since the numerator is
← denominator ─── greater than the denominator

B. Equivalent fractions

Equivalent fractions are obtained by changing the *terms* of a fraction without changing the value of the fraction.

Equivalent fractions in higher terms can be obtained by multiplying both the numerator and the denominator of a fraction by the same number. For any fraction, we can obtain an unlimited number of equivalent fractions in higher terms.

EXAMPLE 1.2B

Calculate the missing values that make the following three fractions equivalent.
$$\frac{3}{4} = \frac{?}{8} = \frac{36}{?}$$

SOLUTION

In order to obtain 8 in the denominator of the second equivalent fraction, 4 was multiplied by 2. Therefore, the numerator must also be multiplied by 2.

$$\frac{3}{4} = \frac{(3 \times 2)}{(4 \times 2)} = \frac{6}{8}$$

Similarly, to obtain the numerator 36 in the third equivalent fraction, 6 was multiplied by another 6. The denominator must also be multiplied by 6.

$$\frac{6}{8} = \frac{(6 \times 6)}{(8 \times 6)} = \frac{36}{48}$$

Equivalent fractions in lower terms can be obtained if both the numerator and denominator of a fraction are divisible by the same number or numbers. The process of obtaining such equivalent fractions is called *reducing to lower terms*.

EXAMPLE 1.2C

Reduce $^{210}/_{252}$ to lower terms.

SOLUTION

$$\frac{210}{252} = \frac{210 \div 2}{252 \div 2} = \frac{105}{126}$$

$$= \frac{105 \div 3}{126 \div 3} = \frac{35}{42}$$

$$= \frac{35 \div 7}{42 \div 7} = \frac{5}{6}$$

The fractions $^{105}/_{126}$, $^{35}/_{42}$, and $^5/_6$ are lower-term equivalents of $^{210}/_{252}$.

The terms of the fraction $^5/_6$ cannot be reduced any further. It represents the simplest form of the fraction $^{210}/_{252}$. It is the **fraction in lowest terms**.

ALTERNATIVE SOLUTION

Reduce $^{210}/_{252}$ to lower terms.

$210 = ②×③× 5 ×⑦$ and ——————————— factor the numerator and the
denominator

$252 = 2 ×②×③× 3 ×⑦$

$2 × 3 × 7 = 42$ ——————————————— determine the greatest common
factor

$$\frac{210}{252} = \frac{210 \div 42}{252 \div 42} = \frac{5}{6}$$ ——————— divide both the numerator and the
denominator by the greatest
common factor

The reduced fraction is $^5/_6$.

The **lowest common denominator (LCD)** of two or more fractions is the lowest common multiplier of their denominators. The LCD is helpful because fractions can be added or subtracted from each other only when they have the same denominator. The LCD is also useful for comparing one or more fractions.

POINTERS & PITFALLS

There is a foolproof method of determining the lowest common denominator (LCD) for a given group of fractions:

STEP 1 Divide the given denominators by integers of 2 or greater until they are all reduced to 1. Make sure the integer divides into at least one of the denominators evenly.

STEP 2 Multiply all of the resultant integers (divisors) to determine the LCD.

Pointers and Pitfalls boxes emphasize good practices, highlight ways to avoid common errors, show how to use a financial calculator efficiently, or give hints for business math situations.

EXAMPLE 1.2D

To illustrate, determine the LCD for

(i) $\dfrac{4}{5}$, $\dfrac{7}{9}$, and $\dfrac{5}{6}$

(ii) $\dfrac{3}{4}$, $\dfrac{2}{3}$, $\dfrac{13}{22}$, and $\dfrac{11}{15}$

SOLUTION

(i)
```
              5    9    6  ←——— denominators
÷ 2 ⟹   5    9    3  ←——— 2 divides into 6 evenly
÷ 3 ⟹   5    3    1  ←——— 3 divides into 9 and 3 evenly
÷ 3 ⟹   5    1    1  ←——— 3 divides into 3 evenly
÷ 5 ⟹   1    1    1  ←——— 5 divides into 5 evenly
```
LCD = 2 × 3 × 3 × 5 = 90 ←——— multiply the divisors

(ii)
```
               4    3    22    15  ←——— denominators
÷ 2 ⟹    2    3    11    15
÷ 2 ⟹    1    3    11    15
÷ 3 ⟹    1    1    11     5
÷ 5 ⟹    1    1    11     1
÷ 11 ⟹   1    1     1     1
```
LCD = 2 × 2 × 3 × 5 × 11 = 660 ←——— multiply the divisors

C. Converting common fractions into decimal form

The fraction line is effectively a division sign. Common fractions are converted into decimal form by performing division to the desired number of decimal places or until the decimal terminates or repeats. We place a dot above a decimal number to show that it repeats. For example, $0.\dot{5}$ stands for 0.555….

POINTERS & PITFALLS

For repeating decimals, use the notation of placing a period above the repeating sequence; for example, $0.333333… = 0.\dot{3}$.

Alternatively, use a horizontal bar (or line) over the first occurrence of a repeating digit or sequence of digits; for example $2/11 = 0.181818… = 0.\overline{18}$

EXAMPLE 1.2E

(i) $\dfrac{9}{8} = 9 ÷ 8 = 1.125$

(ii) $\dfrac{1}{3} = 1 ÷ 3 = 0.333333… = 0.\dot{3}$ or $= 0.\overline{3}$

(iii) $\dfrac{7}{6} = 7 ÷ 6 = 1.166666… = 1.1\dot{6}$ or $= 1.1\overline{6}$

D. Converting mixed numbers to decimal form

Mixed numbers consist of a whole number and a fraction, such as $5\frac{3}{4}$. Such numbers represent the *sum* of a whole number and a common fraction and can be converted into decimal form by changing the common fraction into decimal form.

<table>
<tr><td>

EXAMPLE 1.2F

</td><td>

(i) $5\frac{3}{4} = 5 + \frac{3}{4} = 5 + 0.75 = 5.75$

(ii) $6\frac{2}{3} = 6 + \frac{2}{3} = 6 + 0.666\ldots = 6.6666\ldots = 6.\dot{6}$

(iii) $7\frac{1}{12} = 7 + \frac{1}{12} = 7 + 0.083333\ldots = 7.083333\ldots = 7.08\dot{3}$

</td></tr>
</table>

A calculator icon highlights information on the use of the Texas Instruments BA II PLUS calculator.

POINTERS & PITFALLS

Another way to get a mixed number into your calculator is to change the mixed number to an improper fraction. Multiply the fraction's denominator by the whole number and add that value to the numerator. The resulting number then becomes our numerator and the denominator stays the same. Type this new fraction into your calculator.

For example, if you want to get $1\frac{3}{4}$ into your calculator, first multiply 4 by 1. Then, add 3 to get 7 as the new numerator. Keep the denominator unchanged. The resulting fraction is $\frac{7}{4}$.

For example, if you want to get $9\frac{3}{4}$ into your calculator, multiply 4 by 9 to get 36. Then add 3 to get 39. This is the numerator for the improper fraction. Keep the denominator unchanged. The resulting fraction is $39/4$.

E. Rounding

Answers to problems, particularly when obtained with the help of a calculator, often need to be rounded to a desired number of decimal places. In most business problems involving money values, the final rounding needs to be done to the nearest cent; that is, to two decimal places.

While different methods of rounding are used, for most business purposes the following procedure is suitable.

1. If the first digit in the group of decimal digits that is to be dropped is the digit 5 or 6 or 7 or 8 or 9, the last digit retained is *increased* by 1.

2. If the first digit in the group of decimal digits that is to be dropped is the digit 0 or 1 or 2 or 3 or 4, the last digit retained is left *unchanged*.

<table>
<tr><td>

EXAMPLE 1.2G

</td><td>

Round each of the following money values to the nearest cent.

(i) 7.384 $\longrightarrow$ $7.38 $\longrightarrow$ drop the digit 4

(ii) 7.385 $\longrightarrow$ $7.39 $\longrightarrow$ round the digit 8 up to 9

(iii) 12.9448 $\longrightarrow$ $12.94 $\longrightarrow$ drop the 48

(iv) 9.32838 $\longrightarrow$ $9.33 $\longrightarrow$ round the digit 2 up to 3

(v) 24.8975 $\longrightarrow$ $24.90 $\longrightarrow$ round the digit 9 up to 0; this requires rounding 89 to 90

(vi) 1.996 $\longrightarrow$ $2.00 $\longrightarrow$ round the second digit 9 up to 0; this requires rounding 1.99 to 2.00

(vii) 3199.99833 $\longrightarrow$ $3200.00 $\longrightarrow$ round the second digit 9 up to 0; this requires rounding 3199.99 to 3200.00

</td></tr>
</table>

F. Complex fractions

Complex fractions are mathematical expressions containing one or more fractions in the numerator or denominator or both. Certain formulas used in simple discount (Chapter 6) and simple interest calculations (Chapter 7) result in complex fractions. When you encounter such fractions, take care to follow the order of operations properly.

POINTERS & PITFALLS

Calculations involving money are rounded to 2 decimals as their final answer. Interim solutions may be rounded to 2 decimals if the situation dictates (for example, if you withdraw money from a bank account). If the calculation does not involve cents, it is optional to display the decimals.

EXAMPLE 1.2H

(i) $\dfrac{420}{1600 \times \frac{315}{360}} = \dfrac{420}{1600 \times 0.875} = \dfrac{420}{1400} = 0.3$

(ii) $\$500\left(1 + 0.16 \times \dfrac{225}{365}\right)$ ———— calculate the fraction 225/365, then multiply by 0.16

$= 500(1 + 0.098630)$ ———— add inside the bracket

$= 500(1.098630)$

$= \$549.32$

(iii) $\$1000\left(1 - 0.18 \times \dfrac{288}{365}\right) = \$1000(1 - 0.142027)$

$= 1000(0.857973)$

$= \$857.97$

(iv) $\dfrac{\$824}{1 + 0.15 \times \frac{73}{365}} = \dfrac{824}{1 + 0.03} = \dfrac{824}{1.03} = \$800$

(v) $\dfrac{\$1755}{1 - 0.21 \times \frac{210}{365}} = \dfrac{1755}{1 - 0.120822} = \dfrac{1755}{0.879178} = \$1996.18$

POINTERS & PITFALLS

When using a calculator to compute business math formulas involving complicated denominators consider using the reciprocal key $\left(\boxed{\tfrac{1}{x}} \text{ or } \boxed{x^{-1}}\right)$ to simplify calculations. Start by solving the denominator. Enter the fraction first, then multiply, change the sign, and add. Press the reciprocal key and multiply by the numerator. For example, to calculate part (v) of Example 1.2H above, the following calculator sequence would apply:

$$\dfrac{\$1755}{1 - 0.21 \times \frac{210}{365}}$$

210 $\boxed{\div}$ 365 $\boxed{\times}$ 0.21 $\boxed{\pm}$ $\boxed{+}$ 1 $\boxed{=}$ $\boxed{\tfrac{1}{x}}$ $\boxed{\times}$ 1755 $\boxed{=}$

The result is $1996.18.

If your calculator is already pre-programmed with the basic order of operations, the calculator sequence is much more simple:

1755 [/] [( ] 1 [−] 0.21 [×] 210 [÷] 365 [ )]

Notice that the result is the same: $1996.18.

EXERCISE 1.2

MyLab Math

A. Reduce each of the following fractions to lowest terms.

1. $\dfrac{24}{36}$ **2.** $\dfrac{28}{56}$ **3.** $\dfrac{210}{360}$ **4.** $\dfrac{360}{225}$

5. $\dfrac{144}{360}$ **6.** $\dfrac{25}{365}$ **7.** $\dfrac{365}{73}$ **8.** $\dfrac{365}{219}$

B. Convert mixed numbers to improper fractions, and improper fractions to mixed numbers.

1. $6\frac{1}{2}$ **2.** $4\frac{5}{6}$ **3.** $3\frac{3}{4}$ **4.** $8\frac{2}{3}$

5. $\dfrac{23}{2}$ **6.** $\dfrac{51}{10}$ **7.** $\dfrac{31}{4}$ **8.** $\dfrac{19}{7}$

C. Convert each of the following fractions into decimal form. If appropriate, place a dot or horizontal line above a decimal number to show that it repeats.

1. $\dfrac{11}{8}$ **2.** $\dfrac{7}{4}$ **3.** $\dfrac{5}{3}$ **4.** $\dfrac{5}{6}$

5. $\dfrac{11}{6}$ **6.** $\dfrac{7}{9}$ **7.** $\dfrac{13}{12}$ **8.** $\dfrac{19}{15}$

D. Convert each of the following mixed numbers into decimal form.

1. $3\frac{3}{8}$ **2.** $3\frac{2}{5}$ **3.** $8\frac{1}{3}$ **4.** $16\frac{2}{3}$

5. $33\frac{1}{3}$ **6.** $83\frac{1}{3}$ **7.** $7\frac{7}{9}$ **8.** $7\frac{1}{12}$

E. Round each of the following money values to the nearest cent.

1. 5.633 **2.** 17.449 **3.** 18.0046 **4.** 253.4856

5. 57.69875 **6.** 3.09475 **7.** 12.995 **8.** 39.999

F. Simplify each of the following.

1. $25\,000(15 - 8) - 146\,000$

2. $(300 \times 8000) - (180 \times 8000) - 63000$

3. $1 - [(1 - 0.4)(1 - 0.25)(1 - 0.08)]$

4. $1 - [(1 - 0.32)(1 - 0.15)(1 - 0.12)]$

5. $1500 + \dfrac{1500}{0.05}$ **6.** $\dfrac{\$54}{0.12 \times \frac{225}{365}}$

7. $\dfrac{264}{4400 \times \frac{146}{365}}$

8. $\$620\left(1 + 0.14 \times \frac{45}{365}\right)$

9. $\$375\left(1 + 0.16 \times \frac{292}{365}\right)$

10. $\dfrac{\$250\ 250}{1 + 0.15 \times \frac{330}{365}}$

11. $\dfrac{\$2358}{1 + 0.12 \times \frac{146}{365}}$

12. $\$1000\left[\dfrac{(1 + 0.03)^{24} - 1}{0.03}\right]$

13. $\$70(1 + 0.02)\left[\dfrac{(1 + 0.02)^{20} - 1}{0.02}\right]$

14. $\$50\left[\dfrac{1 - (1 + 0.075)^{-8}}{0.075}\right]$

1.3 PERCENT
A. The meaning of percent

Fractions are used to compare the quantity represented by the numerator with the quantity represented by the denominator. The easiest method of comparing the two quantities is to use fractions with denominator 100. The preferred form of writing such fractions is the *percent* form. **Percent** means "per hundred," and the symbol % is used to show "parts of one hundred."

PERCENT means HUNDREDTHS

% means $\dfrac{\quad}{100}$

Accordingly, any fraction involving "hundredths" may be written as follows:

(i) as a common fraction $\dfrac{13}{100}$

(ii) as a decimal $\qquad$ 0.13

(iii) in percent form $\qquad$ 13%

B. Changing percents to common fractions

When speaking or writing, we often use percents in the percent form. However, when computing with percents, we use the corresponding common fraction or decimal fraction. To convert a percent into a common fraction, replace the symbol % by the symbol $\frac{1}{100}$. Then reduce the resulting fraction to lowest terms.

EXAMPLE 1.3A

(i) $24\% = \dfrac{24}{100}$ ——————————— replace % by $\frac{1}{100}$

$= \dfrac{6}{25}$ ——————————— reduce to lowest terms

(ii) $175\% = \dfrac{175}{100} = \dfrac{7 \times 25}{4 \times 25} = \dfrac{7}{4}$

(iii) $6.25\% = \dfrac{6.25}{100}$

$\qquad = \dfrac{625}{10\ 000}$ ——————————— multiply both the numerator and denominator by 100 to change the numerator to a whole number

$\qquad = \dfrac{125}{2000} = \dfrac{25}{400} = \dfrac{5}{80}$ ——————— reduce gradually or in one step

$\qquad = \dfrac{1}{16}$

(iv) $0.025\% = \dfrac{0.025}{100} = \dfrac{25}{100\ 000} = \dfrac{1}{4000}$

(v) $\dfrac{1}{4}\% = \dfrac{\frac{1}{4}}{\frac{100}{1}}$ ——————————— replace % by $\dfrac{100}{1}$

$\qquad = \dfrac{1}{4} \times \dfrac{1}{100}$ ——————————— invert and multiply

$\qquad = \dfrac{1}{400}$

(vi) $33\frac{1}{3}\% = \dfrac{33\frac{1}{3}}{100}$ ——————————— replace % by $\dfrac{}{100}$

$\qquad = \dfrac{\frac{100}{3}}{\frac{100}{1}}$ ——————————— convert the mixed number $33\frac{1}{3}$ into a common fraction

$\qquad = \dfrac{100}{3} \times \dfrac{1}{100} = \dfrac{100}{300}$ ——————— invert and multiply

$\qquad = \dfrac{1}{3}$ ——————————————— reduce to lowest terms

(vii) $216\frac{2}{3}\% = \dfrac{216\frac{2}{3}}{100} = \dfrac{\frac{650}{3}}{\frac{100}{1}} = \dfrac{\overset{13}{\cancel{650}}}{3} \times \dfrac{1}{\underset{2}{\cancel{100}}} = \dfrac{13}{6}$

Alternatively

$216\frac{2}{3}\% = 200\% + 16\frac{2}{3}\%$ ——————— separate the multiple of 100% (i.e., 200%) from the remainder

$\qquad = 2 + \dfrac{\frac{50}{3}}{\frac{100}{1}}$ ——————————— divide both parts of the equation by 100

$\qquad = 2 + \dfrac{50}{3} \times \dfrac{1}{100}$

$\qquad = 2 + \dfrac{1}{6}$

$\qquad = \dfrac{13}{6}$

C. Changing percents to decimals

Replacing the % symbol by $\frac{1}{100}$ indicates a division by 100. Since division by 100 is performed by moving the decimal point *two places to the left*, changing a percent to a decimal is easy to do. Simply drop the % symbol and move the decimal point two places to the left.

EXAMPLE 1.3B

(i) 52% = 0.52 ——————————— drop the percent symbol and move the decimal point two places to the left

(ii) 175% = 1.75

(iii) 6% = 0.06

(iv) 0.75% = 0.0075

(v) $\frac{1}{4}$% = 0.25% ——————————— first change the fraction to a decimal

= 0.0025 ——————————— drop the percent symbol and move the decimal point two places to the left

(vi) $\frac{1}{3}$% = 0.$\dot{3}$ ——————————— change the fraction to a repeating decimal

= 0.00$\dot{3}$ ——————————— drop the percent symbol and move the decimal point two places to the left

POINTERS & PITFALLS

Some calculators, including the Texas Instruments BA II PLUS calculator, have a % key that performs division by 100.

D. Changing decimals to percents

Changing decimals to percents is the inverse operation of changing percents into decimals. It is accomplished by multiplying the decimal by 100. Since multiplication by 100 is performed by moving the decimal point *two places to the right*, a decimal is easily changed to a percent. Move the decimal point two places to the right and add the % symbol.

EXAMPLE 1.3C

(i) 0.36 = 0.36(100)% ——————————— move the decimal point two places to the right and add the % symbol

= 36%

(ii) 1.65 = 165%   (iii) 0.075 = 7.5%

(iv) 0.4 = 40%   (v) 0.001 = 0.1%

(vi) 2 = 200%   (vii) 0.0005 = 0.05%

(viii) 0.$\dot{3}$ = 33.$\dot{3}$%   (ix) 1.1$\dot{6}$ = 116.$\dot{6}$%

(x) $1\frac{5}{6}$ = 1.8$\dot{3}$ = 183.$\dot{3}$%

E. Changing fractions to percents

When changing a fraction to a percent, it is best to convert the fraction to a decimal and then to change the decimal to a percent.

EXAMPLE 1.3D

(i) $\dfrac{1}{4} = 0.25$ ———————————— convert the fraction to a decimal

$\quad\; = 25\%$ ———————————— convert the decimal to a percent

(ii) $\dfrac{7}{8} = 0.875 = 87.5\%$ (iii) $\dfrac{9}{5} = 1.8 = 180\%$

(iv) $\dfrac{5}{6} = 0.8\dot{3} = 83.\dot{3}\%$ (v) $\dfrac{5}{9} = 0.\dot{5} = 55.\dot{5}\%$

(vi) $1\dfrac{2}{3} = 1.\dot{6} = 166.\dot{6}\%$

EXERCISE 1.3   MyLab Math

A.   Change each of the following percents into a decimal.

1. 64%   **2.** 300%   **3.** 2.5%   **4.** 0.1%   **5.** 0.5%

6. 85%   **7.** 250%   **8.** 4.8%   **9.** 7.5%   **10.** 0.9%

11. 6.25%   **12.** 99%   **13.** 225%   **14.** 0.05%   **15.** $8\frac{1}{4}$%

16. $\frac{1}{2}$%   **17.** $112\frac{1}{2}$%   **18.** $9\frac{3}{8}$%   **19.** $\frac{3}{4}$%   **20.** $162\frac{1}{2}$%

21. $\frac{2}{5}$%   **22.** $\frac{1}{4}$%   **23.** $\frac{1}{40}$%   **24.** $137\frac{1}{2}$%   **25.** $\frac{5}{8}$%

26. 0.875%   **27.** $2\frac{1}{4}$%   **28.** $16\frac{2}{3}$%   **29.** $116\frac{2}{3}$%   **30.** $183\frac{1}{3}$%

31. $83\frac{1}{3}$%   **32.** $66\frac{2}{3}$%

B.   Change each of the following percents into a common fraction in lowest terms.

1. 25%   **2.** $62\frac{1}{2}$%   **3.** 175%   **4.** 5%   **5.** $37\frac{1}{2}$%

6. 75%   **7.** 4%   **8.** 8%   **9.** 40%   **10.** $87\frac{1}{2}$%

11. 250%   **12.** 2%   **13.** $12\frac{1}{2}$%   **14.** 60%   **15.** 2.25%

16. 0.5%   **17.** $\frac{1}{8}$%   **18.** $33\frac{1}{3}$%   **19.** $\frac{3}{4}$%   **20.** $66\frac{2}{3}$%

21. 6.25%   **22.** 0.25%   **23.** $16\frac{2}{3}$%   **24.** 7.5%   **25.** 0.75%

26. $\frac{7}{8}$%   **27.** 0.1%   **28.** $\frac{3}{5}$%   **29.** 2.5%   **30.** $133\frac{1}{3}$%

31. $183\frac{1}{3}$%   **32.** $166\frac{1}{3}$%

C.   Express each of the following as a percent.

1. 3.5   **2.** 0.075   **3.** 0.005   **4.** 0.375   **5.** 0.025

6. 2   **7.** 0.125   **8.** 0.001   **9.** 0.225   **10.** 0.008

11. 1.45   **12.** 0.0225   **13.** 0.0025   **14.** 0.995   **15.** 0.09

16. 3   🌐 17. $\frac{3}{4}$ 18. $\frac{3}{25}$ 🌐 19. $\frac{5}{3}$ 20. $\frac{7}{200}$

🌐 21. $\frac{9}{200}$ 22. $\frac{5}{8}$ 23. $\frac{3}{400}$ 24. $\frac{5}{6}$ 25. $\frac{9}{800}$

26. $\frac{7}{6}$ 27. $\frac{3}{8}$ 28. $\frac{11}{40}$ 29. $\frac{4}{3}$ 30. $\frac{9}{400}$

31. $\frac{13}{20}$ 32. $\frac{4}{5}$

1.4 APPLICATIONS—AVERAGES
A. Basic problems

When calculators are used, the number of decimal places used for intermediate values often determines the accuracy of the final answer. To avoid introducing rounding errors, keep intermediate values unrounded.

EXAMPLE 1.4A

A coffee company received $36\frac{3}{4}$ kilograms of coffee beans at $240 per kilogram. Sales for the next five days were as follows:

$3\frac{5}{8}$ kilograms, $4\frac{3}{4}$ kilograms, $7\frac{2}{3}$ kilograms, $5\frac{1}{2}$ kilograms, and $6\frac{3}{8}$ kilograms.

What was the value of inventory at the end of Day 5?

SOLUTION

$$\text{Total sales (in kilograms)} = 3\tfrac{5}{8} + 4\tfrac{3}{4} + 7\tfrac{2}{3} + 5\tfrac{1}{2} + 6\tfrac{3}{8}$$
$$= 3.625 + 4.75 + 7.\dot{6} + 5.5 + 6.375$$
$$= 27.91\dot{6}$$

$$\text{Inventory (in kilograms)} = 36\tfrac{3}{4} - 27.91\dot{6} = 36.75 - 27.91\dot{6} = 8.8\dot{3}$$
$$\text{Value of inventory} = 8.8\dot{3} \times \$240 = \$2120.00$$

Alternatively

Solve using fraction form.

$$\text{Total sales (in kilograms)} = \tfrac{29}{8} + \tfrac{19}{4} + \tfrac{23}{3} + \tfrac{11}{2} + \tfrac{51}{8}$$
$$= \tfrac{87}{24} + \tfrac{114}{24} + \tfrac{184}{24} + \tfrac{132}{24} + \tfrac{153}{24}$$
$$= \tfrac{670}{24}$$

$$\text{Starting inventory (in kilograms)} = 36\tfrac{3}{4} = \tfrac{147}{4} = \tfrac{882}{24}$$
$$\text{Ending inventory (in kilograms)} = \tfrac{882}{24} - \tfrac{670}{24} = \tfrac{212}{24}$$
$$\text{Value of inventory} = \tfrac{212}{24} \times \$240 = \$2120.00$$

EXAMPLE 1.4B

Complete the following excerpt from an invoice.

Quantity	Unit Price	Amount
72	$0.875	$_____
45	$66\frac{2}{3}$¢	_____
54	$83\frac{1}{3}$¢	_____
42	$1.3\dot{3}	_____
32	$1.375	_____
	Total	$_____

SOLUTION

$72 \times \$0.875 =$			$\$63.00$
$45 \times 66\frac{2}{3}\text{¢}$	$= 45 \times 0.\dot{6}$		30.00
$54 \times 83\frac{1}{3}\text{¢}$	$= 54 \times 0.8\dot{3}$		45.00
$42 \times \$1.3\dot{3}$	$= 42 \times 1.\dot{3}$		56.00
$32 \times \$1.375$			44.00
		TOTAL	$\underline{\$238.00}$

POINTERS & PITFALLS

The display on the calculator shows a limited number of decimal places, depending on how the calculator is formatted. By choosing the format function, you can change the setting to show a different number of decimal places. In continuous calculations, the calculator uses unrounded numbers.

It is suggested that you set the display to show six decimal places to match the mathematical calculations in the body of this text.

To format the calculator to six decimal places,

| 2nd | FORMAT | DEC = 6 | Enter | 2nd | QUIT |

B. Problems involving simple arithmetic average

The **arithmetic mean**, also called **arithmetic average**, of a set of values is a widely used calculation, sometimes referred to as simple average. It is calculated by adding the values in the set and then dividing by the number of those values.

EXAMPLE 1.4C

The marks obtained by Byung Kang for the seven quizzes that make up Unit 1 of his Mathematics of Finance course were 82, 68, 88, 72, 78, 96, and 83.

(i) If all quizzes count equally, what was his average mark for Unit 1?

(ii) If his marks for Unit 2 and Unit 3 of the course were 72.4 and 68.9, respectively, and all unit marks have equal value, what was his course average?

SOLUTION

(i) Unit 1 average $= \dfrac{\text{Sum of the quiz marks for Unit 1}}{\text{Number of quizzes}}$

$= \dfrac{82 + 68 + 88 + 72 + 78 + 96 + 83}{7}$

$= \dfrac{567}{7}$

$= 81.0$

$$\text{(ii) Course average} = \frac{\text{Sum of the unit marks}}{\text{Number of units}}$$

$$= \frac{81.0 + 72.4 + 68.9}{3}$$

$$= \frac{222.3}{3}$$

$$= 74.1$$

EXAMPLE 1.4D

Monthly sales of Sheridan Service for last year were:

January	$13 200	July	$13 700
February	11 400	August	12 800
March	14 600	September	13 800
April	13 100	October	15 300
May	13 600	November	14 400
June	14 300	December	13 900

What were Sheridan's average monthly sales for the year?

SOLUTION

Total sales = $164 100

$$\text{Average monthly sales} = \frac{\text{Total sales}}{\text{Number of months}} = \frac{\$164\ 100}{12} = \$13\ 675$$

POINTERS & PITFALLS

Instead of trying to remember the numbers that you have calculated, you may store them in the calculator. After a calculation has been performed, the unrounded number can be stored and later recalled. The Texas Instruments BA II PLUS has the capability of storing 10 different numbers. To perform a calculation, store, and recall the results, follow the steps below:

To calculate $\frac{1}{3} + \frac{1}{7}$

1 $\boxed{\div}$ 3 $\boxed{=}$ Result will show 0.333333 (when set to six decimal places)

To store the results: press $\boxed{\text{STO}}$ 1

1 $\boxed{\div}$ 7 $\boxed{=}$ Result will show 0.142857 (when set to six decimal places)

To store the results: press $\boxed{\text{STO}}$ 2

To recall the results, and to add them together:

$\boxed{\text{RCL}}$ 1 $\boxed{+}$ $\boxed{\text{RCL}}$ 2 $\boxed{=}$ Result will show 0.476190 (rounded to six decimal places)

C. Weighted average

If the items to be included in computing an arithmetic mean are arranged in groups or if the items are not equally important, a **weighted arithmetic average** should be obtained. Multiply each item by the numbers involved or by a weighting factor to represent its importance.

EXAMPLE 1.4E

During last season, Fairfield Farms sold strawberries as follows: 800 boxes at $1.25 per box in the early part of the season; 1600 boxes at $0.90 per box and 2000 boxes at $0.75 per box at the height of the season; and 600 boxes at $1.10 per box during the late season.

(i) What was the average price charged?

(ii) What was the average price per box?

SOLUTION

(i) The average price charged is a simple average of the four different prices charged during the season.

$$\text{Average price} = \frac{1.25 + 0.90 + 0.75 + 1.10}{4} = \frac{4.00}{4} = 1.00$$

(ii) To obtain the average price per box, the number of boxes sold at each price must be taken into account; that is, a weighted average must be computed.

800 boxes @ $1.25 per box	$\longrightarrow$	$1000.00
1600 boxes @ $0.90 per box	$\longrightarrow$	1440.00
2000 boxes @ $0.75 per box	$\longrightarrow$	1500.00
600 boxes @ $1.10 per box	$\longrightarrow$	660.00
5000 boxes $\longleftarrow$ TOTALS	$\longrightarrow$	$4600.00

$$\text{Average price per box} = \frac{\text{Total value}}{\text{Number of boxes}} = \frac{\$4600.00}{5000} = \$0.92$$

EXAMPLE 1.4F

The specialty tea shop creates its house brand by mixing 13 kilograms of tea priced at $7.50 per kilogram, 16 kilograms of tea priced at $6.25 per kilogram, and 11 kilograms of tea priced at $5.50 per kilogram. At what price should the store sell its house blend to realize the same revenue it could make by selling the three types of tea separately?

SOLUTION

13 kg @ $7.50 per kg	$\longrightarrow$	$ 97.50
16 kg @ $6.25 per kg	$\longrightarrow$	100.00
11 kg @ $5.50 per kg	$\longrightarrow$	60.50
40 kg $\longleftarrow$ TOTALS	$\longrightarrow$	$258.00

$$\text{Average value} = \frac{\text{Total value}}{\text{Number of units}} = \frac{\$258.00}{40} = \$6.45$$

The house blend should sell for $6.45 per kilogram.

EXAMPLE 1.4G

The credit hours and grades for Dana's first-term courses are listed here.

Course	Credit Hours	Grade
Accounting	5	A
Economics	3	B
English	4	C
Law	2	D
Marketing	4	A
Mathematics	3	A
Elective	2	D

According to the grading system, A, B, C, and D are worth 4, 3, 2, and 1 grade points, respectively. On the basis of this information, determine

   (i) Dana's average course grade;

  (ii) Dana's grade-point average (average per credit hour).

SOLUTION

   (i) The average course grade is the average grade points obtained:

$$\frac{4 + 3 + 2 + 1 + 4 + 4 + 1}{7} = \frac{19}{7} = 2.71$$

  (ii) The average course grade obtained in part (i) is misleading since the credit hours of the courses are not equal. The grade-point average is a more appropriate average because it is a weighted average allowing for the number of credit hours per course.

Course	Credit Hours	×	Grade Points	=	Weighted Points
Accounting	5	×	4	=	20
Economics	3	×	3	=	9
English	4	×	2	=	8
Law	2	×	1	=	2
Marketing	4	×	4	=	16
Mathematics	3	×	4	=	12
Elective	2	×	1	=	2
	23	←	Totals	→	69

$$\text{Grade-point average} = \frac{\text{Total weighted points}}{\text{Total credit hours}} = \frac{69}{23} = 3.00$$

EXAMPLE 1.4H

Ravi's Business Communications course grades are as follows:

      Assignment 1: 7 out of 10
      Assignment 2: 16 out of 20
      Assignment 3: 37.5 out of 50
      Assignment 4: 39.5 out of 60
      Test 1: 70 out of 84
      Test 2: 82 out of 100

Assignment 1 is worth 5% of his final course grade, assignment 2 and assignment 3 are worth 15% each, and assignment 4 is worth 25%. Both tests are worth 20%. Calculate Ravi's final grade in the course.

SOLUTION

Assessment	Grade	Weight	Weighted Value
A1	7/10	5%	3.5
A2	16/20	15%	12.0
A3	37.5/50	15%	11.25
A4	39.5/60	25%	16.4583̇
T1	70/84	20%	16.6
T2	82/100	20%	16.4
			76.275

Ravi's final grade is 76% in the course.

EXAMPLE 1.4I

A partnership agreement provides for the distribution of the yearly profit or loss on the basis of the partners' average monthly investment balance. The investment account of one of the partners shows the following entries:

Balance, January 1	$25 750
April 1, withdrawal	3 250
June 1, investment	4 000
November 1, investment	2 000

Determine the partner's average monthly balance in the investment account.

SOLUTION

To determine the average monthly investment, determine the balance in the investment account after each change and weigh this balance by the number of months invested.

Date	Change	Balance	×	Months Invested	=	Value
January 1		25 750	×	3	=	$ 77 250
April 1	−3250	22 500	×	2	=	45 000
June 1	+4000	26 500	×	5	=	132 500
November 1	+2000	28 500	×	2	=	57 000
		Totals		12		$311 750

$$\text{Average monthly investment} = \frac{\text{Total weighted value}}{\text{Number of months}} = \frac{\$311\ 750}{12} = \$25\ 979.17$$

EXAMPLE 1.4J

Several shoe stores in the city carry the same make of shoes. The number of pairs of shoes sold and the price charged by each store are shown below.

Store	Number of Pairs Sold	Price per Pair ($)
A	60	$43.10
B	84	$38.00
C	108	$32.00
D	72	$40.50

(i) What was the average number of pairs of shoes sold per store?

(ii) What was the average price per store?

(iii) What was the average sales revenue per store?

(iv) What was the average price per pair of shoes?

SOLUTION

(i) The average number of pairs of shoes sold per store

$$= \frac{60 + 84 + 108 + 72}{4} = \frac{324}{4} = 81 \quad\text{Total number of pairs/Number of stores}$$

(ii) The average price per store

$$= \frac{43.10 + 38.00 + 32.00 + 40.50}{4} = \frac{153.60}{4} = \$38.40 \quad\text{Sum of prices from each store/Number of stores}$$

(iii) The average sales revenue per store

$$60 \times 43.10 = \$\ 2\ 586.00$$
$$84 \times 38.00 = \ \ \ 3\ 192.00$$
$$108 \times 32.00 = \ \ \ 3\ 456.00$$
$$72 \times 40.50 = \ \ \underline{\ 2\ 916.00}$$
$$\$12\ 150.00$$

$$\text{Average} = \frac{\$12\ 150.00}{4} = \$3037.50 \text{ —————— Sum of revenues from each store/Number of stores}$$

(iv) The average price per pair of shoes

$$= \frac{\text{Total sales revenue}}{\text{Total pairs sold}} = \frac{\$12\ 150.00}{324} = \$37.50 \text{ ——— Sum of prices of sold pairs/ Number of pairs sold}$$

EXERCISE 1.4   MyLab Math

A. Answer each of the following questions.

1. Rae sold four pieces of gold when the price was $1569 per ounce. If the pieces weighed, in ounces, $1\frac{1}{3}$, $2\frac{3}{4}$, $1\frac{5}{8}$, and $3\frac{5}{6}$, respectively, what was the total selling value of the four pieces?

2. Five carpenters worked $15\frac{1}{2}$, $13\frac{3}{4}$, $18\frac{1}{2}$, $21\frac{1}{4}$, and $22\frac{3}{4}$ hours, respectively. What was the total cost of labour if the carpenters were each paid $25.75 per hour?

3. A piece of property valued at $56 100 is assessed, or evaluated, for property tax purposes at $\frac{6}{11}$ of its value. If the property tax rate is $3.75 on each $100 of assessed value, what is the amount of tax levied, or payable, on the property?

 4. A retailer was charged the suggested retail price of $0.90 per item, less a discount of $\frac{3}{8}$ of the suggested retail price, by the manufacturer. The retailer returned 2700 defective items to the manufacturer and received a credit for these. What was the amount of the credit received by the retailer?

5. Complete the following invoice.

Quantity	Description	Unit Price	$
64	A	$0.75	_____
54	B	$83\frac{1}{3}$¢	_____
72	C	$0.375	_____
42	D	$1.3\dot{3}$	_____
		Total	_____

6. Complete the following inventory sheet.

Item	Quantity	Cost per Unit	Total
1	96	$0.875	_____
2	330	$16\frac{2}{3}$¢	_____
3	144	$1.75	_____
4	240	$1.6\dot{6}$	_____
		Total	_____

7. Michael's physics professor is taking his best 3 out of 4 quizzes this semester. All quizzes are marked out of 10 points and are worth 5% each. There are also 3 tests in the course. They are all marked out of 50 points and are equally weighted at 20% each. The final exam is worth 25%. Michael's quiz scores were 7, 7.25, 9, and 6.5. His test scores were 38, 41, and 43. His final exam mark was 79%. Calculate Michael's final grade in physics.

B. Solve each of the following problems involving an arithmetic average.

1. Records of Montes Service's fuel oil consumption for the last six-month period show that Montes paid $1.085 per litre for the first 1100 litres, $1.093 per litre for the next 1600 litres, and $1.121 per litre for the last delivery of 1400 litres. Determine the average cost of fuel oil per litre for the six-month period.

2. On a trip, a motorist purchased gasoline as follows: 56 litres at $1.180 per litre; 60 litres at $1.246 per litre; 70 litres at $1.278 per litre; and 54 litres at $1.335 per litre.

    (a) What was the average number of litres per purchase?
    (b) What was the average cost per litre?
    (c) If the motorist averaged 8.75 km per litre, what was the average cost of gasoline per kilometre?

3. The course credit hours and grades for Bill's fall semester are given below. At his college, an A is worth six grade points, a B four points, a C two points, and a D one point.

Credit hours:	3	5	2	4	4	2
Grade:	B	C	A	C	D	A

What is Bill's grade-point average?

4. Kim Blair invested $7500 in a business on January 1. She withdrew $900 on March 1, reinvested $1500 on August 1, and withdrew $300 on September 1. What is Kim's average monthly investment balance for the year?

5. Neuer started a systematic investment program by buying $200.00 worth of mutual funds on the first day of every month starting on February 1. When you purchase mutual funds, you purchase units in the fund. Neuer purchased as many units as he could with his $200.00, including fractions of units. Unit prices for the first six months were $10.00, $10.60, $11.25, $9.50, $9.20, and $12.15, respectively.

    (a) What is the simple average of the unit prices?
    (b) What is the total number of units purchased during the first six months (correct to three decimals)?
    (c) What is the average cost of the units purchased?
    (d) What is the value of Neuer's mutual fund holdings on July 31 if the unit price on that date is $11.90?

1.5 APPLICATIONS—PAYROLL

Employees can be paid for their services in a variety of ways. The main methods of pay, or **remuneration**, are salaries, hourly wage rates, and commission. While the computations involved in preparing employee pay records, or the payroll, are fairly simple, utmost care is needed to ensure that all calculations are accurate.

A. Salaries

Compensation of employees by **salary** is usually on a monthly or a yearly basis. Monthly salaried personnel get paid either monthly or semi-monthly. Personnel on a yearly salary basis may get paid monthly, semi-monthly, every two weeks, weekly, or according to special schedules such as those used by some boards of education to pay their teachers. If salary is paid weekly or every two weeks, the year is assumed to consist of exactly 52 weeks.

POINTERS & PITFALLS

It is easy to confuse the terms semi-monthly and bi-weekly payroll. Semi-monthly payroll refers to paydays that occur 24 times per year, such as paydays that occur on the 15th day and last day of each month. Bi-weekly payroll involves paydays that occur 26 times during the year, such as paydays that occur every other Friday.

Gross earnings or total pay is the amount an employee makes every pay period before the employer deducts any income taxes owed to the government, benefits and pension contributions, labour dues, etc. Calculations of gross earnings per pay period are fairly simple. However, computing overtime for salaried personnel can be problematic, since overtime is usually paid on an hourly basis.

EXAMPLE 1.5A

An employee with an annual salary of $56 264 is paid every two weeks. The regular workweek is 40 hours.

(i) What is the gross (total) pay per pay period?

(ii) What is the hourly rate of pay?

(iii) What are the gross earnings for a pay period in which the employee worked six hours of overtime and is paid one-and-a-half times the regular hourly rate of pay?

SOLUTION

(i) An employee paid every two weeks receives the annual salary over 26 pay periods.

$$\text{Gross pay per two-week period} = \frac{56\ 264}{26} = \$2164$$

(ii) Given a 40-hour week, the employee's compensation for two weeks covers 80 hours.

$$\text{Hourly rate of pay} = \frac{2164}{80} = \$27.05$$

(iii) Regular gross earnings for two-week period $2164
Overtime pay

6 hours at $27.05 × 1.5 = 6 × 27.05 × 1.5 = $243.45

Total gross earnings for pay period $\underline{\$2407.45}$

POINTERS & PITFALLS

Hourly rate calculations for salaried employees require that all decimals should be carried until the final answer is achieved. If the solution is to express the hourly rate or overtime rate itself, then rounding to 2 decimals is appropriate.

Overtime hourly wage rate calculations should carry all decimals of the overtime rate until the final answer is achieved.

EXAMPLE 1.5B

Mike Paciuc receives a monthly salary of $5980 paid semi-monthly. Mike's regular workweek is 37 hours. Any hours worked over 37 hours in a week are overtime and are paid at time-and-a-half regular pay. During the first half of October, Mike worked 7.5 hours overtime.

(i) What is Mike's hourly rate of pay?

(ii) What are his gross earnings for the pay period ending October 15?

SOLUTION

(i) When computing the hourly rate of pay for personnel employed on a monthly salary basis, the correct approach requires that the yearly salary be determined first. The hourly rate of pay may then be computed on the basis of 52 weeks per year.

Yearly gross earnings = Monthly earnings × Number of months per year

$$= 5980 \times 12 = \$71\,760.00$$

$$\text{Weekly gross earnings} = \frac{\text{Yearly gross earnings}}{\text{Number of workweeks in a year}}$$

$$= \frac{71\,760}{52} = \$1380.00$$

$$\text{Hourly rate of pay} = \frac{\text{Weekly gross earnings}}{\text{Number of hours per workweek}}$$

$$= \frac{1380}{37} = \$37.30 \text{ (rounded)}$$

(ii) Regular semi-monthly gross earnings $= \dfrac{5980}{2} = \qquad \$2990.00$

Overtime pay $= 7.5 \times \dfrac{\$1380}{37} \times 1.5 = \qquad 419.59$

Total gross earnings for pay period $\qquad \underline{\$3409.59}$

EXAMPLE 1.5C

Teachers with the Northern Manitoba Board of Education are under contract for 200 teaching days per year. They are paid according to the following schedule:

8% of annual salary on the first day of school
4% of annual salary for each of 20 two-week pay periods
12% of annual salary at the end of the last pay period in June

Alicia Nowak, a teacher employed by the board, is paid an annual salary of $82 700.

(i) What is Alicia's daily rate of pay?

(ii) What is Alicia's gross pay
    (a) for the first pay period?
    (b) for the last pay period?
    (c) for all other pay periods?

(iii) If Alicia takes an unpaid leave of absence for three days during a pay period in April, what is her gross pay for that pay period?

SOLUTION

(i) Daily rate of pay $= \dfrac{82\ 700}{200} = \$413.50$

(ii) (a) First gross pay $= 0.08 \times 82\ 700 = \$6616.00$
    (b) Last gross pay $= 0.12 \times 82\ 700 = \$9924.00$
    (c) All other gross pay $= 0.04 \times 82\ 700 = \$3308.00$

(iii) Gross pay per period in April, $3308.00
Less 3 days of pay $= {}^{3}/_{200}$ of $82 700 = $1240.50
                           Gross pay <u>$2067.50</u>

Explanation: for 3 days of pay

Number of unpaid days ÷ Number of days per year × Annual salary

EXAMPLE 1.5D

Your full-time job pays you a bi-weekly salary of $2455.79.

(i) What is your gross monthly income?

(ii) If residential mortgage payments should not exceed 40% of your total monthly income, what is the maximum monthly payment that you can afford towards the purchase of a house?

SOLUTION

(i) Annual income from work = Pay per pay period × Number of pay periods
                        = $2455.79 × 26 pay periods = $63 850.54

Gross monthly income = $63 850.54 ÷ 12 = $5320.88

(ii) $5320.88 × 0.40 = $2128.35

B. Commission

Persons engaged in the buying and selling functions of a business are often compensated by a **commission**. Of the various types of commission designed to meet the specific circumstances of a particular business, the most commonly encountered are straight commission, graduated (or sliding-scale) commission, and base salary plus commission. The term *commission* is often used for both the commission amount and for commission rate, and can be understood from the context.

Straight commission is usually calculated as a percent of net sales for a given time period. **Net sales** are the difference between the gross sales for the time period and any sales returns and allowances, or sales discounts.

Graduated commission usually involves paying an increasing percent for increasing sales levels during a given time period.

Salary plus commission is a method that guarantees a minimum income per pay period to the salesperson. However, the rate of commission in such cases is either at a lower rate or is not paid until a minimum sales level (called a **quota**) for a time period has been reached.

Sales personnel on commission may be able to receive an advance from a **drawing account** with their employer. The salesperson may withdraw funds from such an account, before making any sales, to meet business and personal expenses. However, any money advanced is deducted from the commission earned when the salesperson is paid.

EXAMPLE 1.5E

Javier receives a commission of 11.5% on his net sales and is entitled to an advance of up to $1500 per month. During August, Javier's gross sales amounted to $25 540 and sales returns and allowances were $360.

  (i) What are Javier's net sales for August?

  (ii) How much is his commission for August?

  (iii) If Javier drew $1400 in August, what is the amount due to him?

SOLUTION

(i)	Gross sales	$25 540.00
	Less sales returns and allowances	360.00
	Net sales	$25 180.00

(ii) Commission = 11.5% of net sales
               = 0.115 × 25 180.00
               = $2895.70

(iii)	Gross commission earned	$2895.70
	Less drawings	1400.00
	Amount due	$1495.70

EXAMPLE 1.5F

Valerie works as a salesperson for the local Minutemen Press. She receives a commission of 7.5% on monthly sales up to $8000, 9.25% on the next $7000, and 11% on any additional sales during the month. If Valerie's September sales amounted to $18 750, what is her gross commission for the month?

SOLUTION

Commission on the first $8000.00 = 0.075 × 8000.00	$ 600.00
Commission on the next $7000.00 = 0.0925 × 7000.00	647.50
Commission on sales over $15 000.00 = 0.11 × 3750.00	412.50
Total commission for September	$1660.00

EXAMPLE 1.5G

Ana is employed as a salesclerk in a sporting goods store. She receives a weekly salary of $625 plus a commission of $6\frac{1}{4}$% on all weekly sales over the weekly sales quota of $5000. Derek works in the shoe store located next door. He receives a minimum of $700 per week or a commission of 12.5% on all sales for the week, whichever is the greater. If both Ana and Derek had sales of $5960 last week, how much compensation did each receive for the week?

SOLUTION		
Ana's compensation		
Base salary		$625.00
plus commission = $6\frac{1}{4}$% on sales over $5000.00		60.00
= 0.0625 × 960.00		
Total compensation		$685.00
Derek's compensation		
Minimum weekly pay		$700.00
Commission = 12.5% of all sales = 0.125 × 5960.00		$745.00

Since the commission is greater than the guaranteed minimum pay of $700, Derek's compensation is $745.00.

C. Wages

The term **wages** usually applies to compensation paid to *hourly* rated employees. Their gross earnings are calculated by multiplying the number of hours worked by the hourly rate of pay, plus any overtime pay. Overtime is most often paid at time-and-a-half the regular hourly rate for any hours exceeding an established number of regular hours per week or per day. This means that each hour worked over regular time will be worth one-and-a-half hours. The number of regular hours is often established by agreement between the employer and employees. The most common regular work-week is 40 hours. If no agreement exists, federal or provincial employment standards legislation provides for a maximum number of hours per week, such as 44 hours for most employers. Any hours over the set maximum must be paid at least at time-and-a-half the regular hourly rate.

When overtime is involved, gross earnings can be calculated by either of the two following methods:

Method A
The most common method, and the easiest for the wage earner to understand, determines total gross earnings by adding overtime pay to the gross pay for a regular workweek.

Method B
In the second method, the additional money to be paid for labour costs (or **overtime premium**) is computed separately and added to gross earnings for all hours (including the overtime hours) at the regular rate of pay. Computation of the excess labour cost due to overtime emphasizes how much extra the overtime costs and provides management with information that is useful for cost control.

EXAMPLE 1.5H	Mario is a machinist with Scott Tool and Die and is paid $23.00 per hour. The regular workweek is 40 hours, and overtime is paid at time-and-a-half the regular hourly rate. If Mario worked $46\frac{1}{2}$ hours last week, what were his gross earnings?

SOLUTION

Method A

Gross earnings for a regular workweek = 40 × 23.00	$ 920.00
Overtime pay = 6.5 × 23.00 × 1.5	224.25
Gross pay	$1144.25

Method B

Earnings at the regular hourly rate = 46.5 × 23.00	$1069.50
Overtime premium = 6.5 × ($\frac{1}{2}$ of 23.00) = 6.5 × 11.50	74.75
Gross pay	$1144.25

EXAMPLE 1.5I

Hasmig works for $18.44 per hour under a union contract that provides for daily overtime for all hours worked over eight hours. Overtime includes hours worked on Saturdays and is paid at time-and-a-half the regular rate of pay. Hours worked on Sundays or holidays are paid at double the regular rate of pay. Use both methods to determine Hasmig's gross earnings for a week in which she worked the following hours:

Monday	9 hours	Tuesday	$10\frac{1}{2}$ hours
Wednesday	7 hours	Thursday	$9\frac{1}{2}$ hours
Friday	8 hours	Saturday	6 hours
Sunday	6 hours		

Day	Mon	Tue	Wed	Thu	Fri	Sat	Sun	Total
Regular hours	8	8	7	8	8			39
Overtime at time-and-a-half	1	2.5		1.5		6		11
Overtime at double time							6	6
Total hours worked	9	10.5	7	9.5	8	6	6	56

SOLUTION

Method A

Gross earnings for regular hours = 39 × 18.44		$718.16
Overtime pay		
at time-and-a-half = 11 × 18.44 × 1.5 = $304.26		
at double time = 6 × 18.44 × 2 = 221.28		525.54
Total gross pay		$1244.70

Method B

Earnings at regular hourly rate = 56 × 18.44		$1032.64
Overtime pay		
at time-and-a-half = 11 ($\frac{1}{2}$ of $18.44)		
= 11 × 9.22	$101.42	
at double time = 6 × 18.44	110.64	212.06
Total gross pay		$1244.70

EXERCISE 1.5

MyLab Math

Answer each of the following questions.

1. R. Burton is employed at an annual salary of $43 056 paid semi-monthly. The regular workweek is 36 hours.
   (a) What is the regular salary per pay period?
   (b) What is the hourly rate of pay?
   (c) What is the gross pay for a pay period in which the employee worked 11 hours overtime at time-and-a-half regular pay?

2. C. Bernal receives a yearly salary of $43 875.00. She is paid bi-weekly and her regular workweek is 37.5 hours.
   (a) What is the gross pay per pay period?
   (b) What is the hourly rate of pay?
   (c) What is the gross pay for a pay period in which she works 8 hours overtime at time-and-a-half regular pay?

3. Carole is paid a monthly salary of $2011.10. Her regular workweek is 35 hours.
   (a) What is Carole's hourly rate of pay?
   (b) What is Carole's gross pay for May if she worked $7^3/_4$ hours overtime during the month at time-and-a-half regular pay?

4. Dimitri receives a semi-monthly salary of $1326.00 and works a regular workweek of 40 hours.
   (a) What is Dimitri's hourly rate of pay?
   (b) If Dimitri's gross earnings in one pay period were $1518.78, for how many hours of overtime was he paid at time-and-a-half regular pay?

5. Mario's wage statement showed 45 hours of work during one week, resulting in $680.20 in gross earnings. What is the hourly rate of pay if the regular workweek is 40 hours and overtime is paid at time-and-a-half the regular rate of pay?

6. An employee of the Board of Education is paid an annual salary in 22 bi-weekly payments of $3942.00 each. If the employee is under contract for 200 workdays of $7^1/_2$ hours each,
   (a) what is the hourly rate of pay?
   (b) what is the gross pay for a pay period in which the employee was away for two days at no pay?

7. Geraldine Moog is paid a commission of $9^3/_4$% on her net sales and is authorized to draw up to $800 a month. What is the amount due to Geraldine at the end of a month in which she drew $720, had gross sales of $12 660, and sales returns of $131.20?

8. What is a salesperson's commission on net sales of $16 244 if the commission is paid on a sliding scale of $8^1/_4$% on the first $6000, $9^3/_4$% on the next $6000, and 11.5% on any additional net sales?

9. A sales representative selling auto parts receives a commission of 4.5% on net sales up to $10 000, 6% on the next $5000, and 8% on any further sales. If his gross sales for a month were $24 250 and sales returns were $855, what was his commission for the month?

10. A salesclerk at a local boutique receives a weekly base salary of $825 on a quota of $8500 per week plus a commission of $6^1/_2$% on sales exceeding the quota.
    (a) What are the gross earnings for a week if sales are $8125?
    (b) What are the gross earnings for a week if sales amount to $10 150?

11. Sandra, working in sales at a clothing store, is paid a weekly salary of $540 or a commission of 6.5% of her sales, whichever is greater. What is her salary for a week in which her sales were
   (a) $5830?
   (b) $8830?

12. Manny's commission was $1590.90 on gross sales of $31 240.00. If returns and allowances were 3% of gross sales, what is his rate of commission based on net sales?

13. For last week, Tony's gross earnings were $566.25. He earns a base salary of $450 per week and has a weekly commission quota of $5000. If his sales for the week were $6550, what is his commission rate?

14. Wilson's commission for March was $2036.88. If his rate of commission is 11.25% of net sales, and returns and allowances were 8% of gross sales, what were Wilson's gross sales for the month?

15. Debra had gross earnings of $837.50 for the week. If she receives a base salary of $664 on a quota of $4800 and a commission of 8.75% on sales exceeding the quota, what were Debra's sales for the week?

16. Kim earns $14.60 per hour. Overtime for the first five days in a week worked is paid at time-and-a-half pay for hours worked greater than 8 in a day. If more than five days are worked in a week, those hours are paid at double the regular rate of pay. Last week, for each day, Kim worked 8 hours, 9 hours, 8 hours, $10\frac{1}{2}$ hours, 8 hours, and 6 hours. Determine Kim's gross wages by each of the two methods.

1.6 APPLICATIONS—TAXES

A **tax** is a fee charged on sales, services, property, or income by a government to pay for services provided by the government. As consumers, we encounter the **provincial sales tax (PST)**, the **goods and services tax (GST)**, or the **harmonized sales tax (HST)**. As homeowners, we encounter property taxes, and as employees and workers, we encounter income taxes. All of these taxes are expressed as a percent of the amount to be taxed. PST, GST, and HST are expressed as a percent of the value of the items or services purchased. Property taxes are determined by a percent of the value of the property. These two types of taxes are discussed in this chapter. Income taxes are also based on percent calculations, and are discussed in Chapter 3.

A. Sales and service taxes

1. Goods and Services Tax (GST)

The goods and services tax (GST) is a federal tax charged on the cost of goods and services that are purchased in Canada, except certain items that are considered *exempt* or free from having to pay tax. Businesses and organizations carrying out commercial activities in Canada must register with the Canada Revenue Agency (CRA) for the purpose of collecting the GST if their total revenue from GST-taxable goods and services exceeds $30 000 in any single calendar quarter or in four consecutive calendar quarters. Below that level of revenue, registration is voluntary.

Since January 1, 2008, GST-taxable goods and services, aside from specific items that are *zero-rated*, are taxed at 5%. Registered businesses and organizations collect tax on behalf of the government by charging the 5% GST on sales of goods and services to their customers, and they must, at the same time, pay the 5% GST on their business purchases. Depending on the volume of taxable sales, each registered business must file a return with the CRA at selected intervals (monthly, quarterly, or annually), showing the amount of tax collected and the amount of tax paid. If the amount of GST collected from customers is more than the amount of GST paid, the difference must be paid or remitted to the CRA. If the amount of GST collected from customers is less than the amount of GST paid for business purchases, the business can claim a refund.

EXAMPLE 1.6A

Suppose you had your car repaired at your local Canadian Tire repair shop. Parts amounted to $165.00 and labour to $246.00. Since both parts and labour are GST-taxable, what is the amount of GST that Canadian Tire must collect from you?

SOLUTION

The GST-taxable amount = $165.00 + $246.00 = $411.00
GST = 5% of $411.00 = 0.05(411.00) = $20.55
Canadian Tire must collect GST of $20.55.

EXAMPLE 1.6B

Canadian Colour Company (CCC) purchased GST-taxable supplies from Polaroid Canada worth $35 000 during 2019. CCC used these supplies to provide prints for its customers. CCC's total GST-taxable sales for the year were $50 000. How much tax must CCC remit to the Canada Revenue Agency?

SOLUTION

GST collected = 0.05($50 000) = $2500
GST paid = 0.05($35 000) = $1750
GST payable = $2500 − $1750 = $750

2. Provincial Sales Tax (PST)

The provincial sales tax (PST) is a provincial tax imposed by certain provinces on the price of most goods. In Manitoba, Saskatchewan, Quebec, and British Columbia, the PST is applied as a percent of the retail price, in the same way as the GST.

NWT	0% PST	Manitoba	7% PST
Nunavut	0% PST	Saskatchewan	6% PST
Yukon	0% PST	Quebec	9.975% PST
Alberta	0% PST	British Columbia	7% PST

3. Harmonized Sales Tax (HST)

For the remaining provinces, the PST and GST are blended to form the Harmonized Sales Tax, or HST.

Prince Edward Island	15% HST
Newfoundland and Labrador	15% HST
New Brunswick	15% HST
Nova Scotia	15% HST
Ontario	13% HST

EXAMPLE 1.6C

Determine the amount of provincial sales tax on an invoice of taxable items totalling $740 before taxes

(i) in Saskatchewan;

(ii) in Quebec.

SOLUTION

(i) In Saskatchewan, the PST = 6% of $740.00 = 0.06(740.00) = $44.40.

(ii) In Quebec, the PST = 9.975% of $740 = 0.09975(740.00) = 73.815 = $73.82.

EXAMPLE 1.6D

In Ontario, restaurant meals are subject to the 13% HST on food items. Alcoholic beverages are also subject to 13% HST. You take your friend out for dinner and spend $60 on food items and $32 on a bottle of wine. You also tip the waiter 15% of the pre-tax cost of food items and wine, for good service. How much do you spend?

SOLUTION

Cost of food items	$60.00
Cost of wine	32.00
Total cost of meal	$92.00

HST on food = 13% of $60.00 = 0.13(60.00) = $7.80
HST on wine = 13% of $32.00 = 0.13(32.00) = $4.16

Total cost including taxes = 92.00 + 7.80 + 4.16 = $103.96
Tip = 15% of $92.00 = 0.15(92.00) = 13.80
Total amount spent = 103.96 + 13.80 = $117.76

B. Property tax

To pay for their services, municipalities charge a **property tax** based on the value they assign to residential and commercial real estate property, called the **assessed value**. Some education taxes are also calculated using this method. The property tax is determined by applying a percent to the assessed value of the property. In some municipalities, the assessed value is divided by 1000, and then the percent is applied.

Property tax rates may also be expressed as a millage rate or mill where a mill is equal to $1.00 of tax for every $1000 of assessed value. For example, a property with an assessed value of $400 000 that is located in a municipality with a mill rate of 15 mills will incur an annual property tax bill of $6000.

EXAMPLE 1.6E

The municipality of Vermeer requires a budget of $650 million to operate next year. Provincial and federal grants, fees, and commercial taxes will cover $450 million, leaving $200 million to be raised by a tax on residential assessments.

(i) Calculate the rate per $1000 to raise the $200 million if the total assessed residential value for taxation purposes is $8 billion.

(ii) Determine the taxes on a building lot in Vermeer if it is assessed at $125 000.

SOLUTION

(i) $\text{Rate} = \dfrac{\text{Tax revenue required from residential assessments}}{\text{Total assessed residential value}}$

$= \dfrac{\$200\,000\,000}{\$8\,000\,000\,000} = 0.025$

0.025 is equivalent to a mill rate of 25 mills. That is, $25 of tax for each $1000 of assessment is required.

(ii) Many municipalities would post a $25 mill rate as 2.5%. To calculate the annual property taxes, multiply this percentage by the current assessed value of the property. Property taxes on the building lot $= 0.025(125\,000) = \$3125.00$

EXAMPLE 1.6F

The municipality of Cranberry lists the following property tax rates for various local services:

Service	Rate per $1000
General city	3.20
Garbage collection	0.99
Schools	10.51
Capital development	1.20

If a homeowner's property has been assessed at $350 000, determine the property taxes payable.

SOLUTION

Total rate per $1000 $= 3.20 + 0.99 + 10.51 + 1.20 = 15.90$

$\text{Tax payable} = \text{Total rate per \$1000} \times \dfrac{\text{Assessed value}}{1000}$

$= 15.90 \times \dfrac{350\,000}{1000} = \$5565.00$

EXERCISE 1.6

MyLab Math

Answer each of the following questions.

1. Cook's Department Store files GST returns monthly. If the figures in the following table represent the store's GST-taxable sales and GST-taxable purchases for the last five months, calculate Cook's monthly GST bills. Determine if Cook's owes the government money or is entitled to a refund.

Month	Sales	Purchases
January	$546 900	$147 832
February	244 000	69 500
March	588 000	866 000
April	650 300	450 000
May	156 800	98 098

2. Riza's Home Income Tax business operates only during tax season. Last season Riza grossed $28 350 including GST. During that season she spent $8000 before GST on her paper and supply purchases. If Riza is voluntarily registered for GST, how much does she owe the Canada Revenue Agency for GST?

3. "Save the GST" is a popular advertising gimmick. How much would you save on the purchase of a TV with a list price of $780 in a Manitoba store during a "Save the GST" promotion?

4. How much would a consumer pay for a T-shirt with a list price of $15 if the purchase was made in Regina, Saskatchewan?

5. During an early season promotion, a weekend ski pass was priced at $214 plus PST and GST at Blackcomb Mountain, B.C., and at $214 plus GST and PST at Mont Tremblant, Quebec. What is the difference in the total price paid by skiers at the two ski resorts?

6. A retail chain sells snowboards for $625 plus tax. What is the price difference for consumers in Toronto, Ontario, and Calgary, Alberta?

7. You purchased two items for a total of $70.56. The first item is GST exempt and it represents 25% of the total purchase price. Assuming that you live in the Northwest Territories, what is the total amount of GST that you paid?

8. Calculate the property taxes on a property assessed at $125 000 if the rate per $1000 is 22.751.

9. The town of Eudora assesses property at market value. How much will the owner of a house valued at $225 000 owe in taxes if this year's property tax rate has been set at 0.019368?

10. The City of Mississauga sent a semi-annual tax bill to a resident who owns a house assessed at $479 000. If the semi-annual tax bill is $2216, what is the annual property tax rate in Mississauga?

11. A town has an assessed residential property value of $500 000 000. The town council must meet the following expenditures:

Education	$3 050 000
General purposes	$2 000 000
Recreation	$250 000
Public works	$700 000
Police and fire protection	$850 000

(a) Suppose 80% of the expenditures are charged against residential real estate. Calculate the total property taxes that must be raised.
(b) What is the tax rate per $1000?
(c) What is the property tax on a property assessed at $375 000?

BUSINESS MATH NEWS — National Salary Comparisons

Knowing how much you are worth in the job market is critical for not being underpaid. Successful salary negotiations are accomplished by having accurate information. In today's electronic age, the Internet offers a variety of websites focusing on salary information.

Three popular job functions along with the respective salaries are listed below by major metropolitan location.

Financial Controller

Responsible for directing an organization's accounting functions. These functions include establishing and maintaining the organization's accounting principles, practices, and procedures. Prepares financial reports and presents findings and recommendations to top management.

Human Resources Manager

Plans, directs, and coordinates the human resource management activities of an organization to maximize the strategic use of human resources and maintain functions such as employee compensation, recruitment, personnel policies, and regulatory compliance.

Marketing Manager

Develops and implements strategic marketing plan for an organization. Generally manages a group of marketing professionals. Typically reports to an executive.

Job Description	Vancouver	Calgary	Toronto	Montreal	National
Financial Controller	$99 500	$106 082	$98 500	$99 758	$99 234
Human Resources Manager	$88 324	$88 611	$83 350	$80 641	$78 669
Marketing Manager	$78 663	$84 836	$77 823	$76 554	$75 450

Source: Payscale.com, retrieved October 26, 2018
www.payscale.com/resources.aspx?nclp_calculator_canada01

QUESTIONS

1. Assuming an employee works a 40-hour week, calculate the hourly rate of each job function by location.
2. Calculate the dollar and percent difference in each city relative to the national average by job description.
3. What might account for the salary differences among the four cities?

Business Math News boxes show you how widely business math applications are used in the real world.

MyLab Math Visit MyLab Math to practise any of this chapter's exercises marked with a 🌐 as often as you want. The guided solutions help you calculate an answer step by step. You'll find a personalized study plan and additional interactive resources to help you master Business Math!

> The Review Exercise provides you with numerous questions that cover all the chapter content. Solutions to the odd-numbered exercises are given at the back of the text.

REVIEW EXERCISE ←

1. LO❶ Simplify each of the following.

(a) $32 - 24 \div 8$

(b) $(48 - 18) \div 15 - 10$

(c) $(8 \times 6 - 4) \div (16 - 4 \times 3)$

(d) $9(6 - 2) - 4(3 + 4)$

(e) $\dfrac{108}{0.12 \times \frac{216}{365}}$

(f) $\dfrac{288}{2400 \times \frac{292}{365}}$

(g) $320\left(1 + 0.10 \times \frac{225}{365}\right)$

(h) $1000\left(1 - 0.12 \times \frac{150}{365}\right)$

(i) $\dfrac{660}{1 + 0.14 \times \frac{144}{365}}$

(j) $\dfrac{1120.00}{1 - 0.13 \times \frac{292}{365}}$

 2. LO❷ Change each of the following percents into a decimal.

(a) 185% (b) 7.5% (c) 0.4%

(d) 0.025% (e) $1\frac{1}{4}\%$ (f) $\frac{3}{4}\%$

(g) $162\frac{1}{2}\%$ (h) $11\frac{3}{4}\%$ (i) $8\frac{1}{3}\%$

(j) $83\frac{1}{3}\%$ (k) $266\frac{2}{3}\%$ (l) $10\frac{3}{8}\%$

3. LO❷ Change each of the following percents into a common fraction in lowest terms.

(a) 50% (b) $37\frac{1}{2}\%$ (c) $16\frac{2}{3}\%$

(d) $166\frac{2}{3}\%$ (e) $\frac{1}{2}\%$ (f) 7.5%

(g) 0.75% (h) $\frac{5}{8}\%$

🌐 **4. LO❷** Express each of the following as a percent.

(a) 2.25 (b) 0.02 (c) 0.009

(d) 0.1275 (e) $\frac{5}{4}$ (f) $\frac{11}{8}$

(g) $\frac{5}{200}$ (h) $\frac{7}{25}$

5. LO❸ Compute each of the following.

(a) 150% of 140 (b) 3% of 240

(c) $9\frac{3}{4}\%$ of 2000 (d) 0.9% of 400

6. LO❷ Sales of a particular make and size of nails during a day were $4\frac{1}{3}$ kg, $3\frac{3}{4}$ kg, $5\frac{1}{2}$ kg, and $6\frac{5}{8}$ kg.

(a) How many kilograms of nails were sold?

(b) What is the total sales value at $1.20 per kilogram?

(c) What was the average weight per sale?

(d) What was the average sales value per sale?

🌐 **7. LO❶** Extend and total the following invoice.

Quantity	Description	Unit Price	Amount
56	Item A	$0.625	?
180	Item B	$83\frac{1}{3}¢$	?
126	Item C	$1.1\dot{6}$	?
144	Item D	$1.75	?
		Total	?

8. LO❸ The basic pay categories, hourly rates of pay, and the number of employees in each category for the machining department of a company are shown below.

Category	Hourly Pay	No. of Employees
Supervisors	$30.45	2
Machinists	20.20	6
Assistants	16.40	9
Helpers	14.50	13

(a) What is the average rate of pay for all categories?

(b) What is the average rate of pay per employee?

🌐 **9. LO❹** Hélène Gauthier invested $15 000 on January 1 in a partnership. She withdrew $2000 on June 1, withdrew a further $1500 on August 1, and reinvested $4000 on November 1. What was her average monthly investment balance for the year?

Reference Example 1.4I

10. LO❹ Brent DeCosta invested $12 000 in a business on January 1 and an additional $2400 on April 1. He withdrew $1440 on June 1 and invested $2880 on October 1. What was Brent's average monthly investment balance for the year?

11. **LO④** Casey receives an annual salary of $34 944.00, is paid monthly, and works 35 regular hours per week. Overtime is paid at time-and-a-half regular pay.

   (a) What is Casey's gross remuneration per pay period?

   (b) What is his hourly rate of pay?

   (c) How many hours overtime did Casey work during a month for which his gross pay was $3387.20?

12. **LO④** Tim is employed at an annual salary of $31 487.04. His regular workweek is 36 hours and he is paid semi-monthly.

   (a) What is Tim's gross pay per period?

   (b) What is his hourly rate of pay?

   (c) What is his gross pay for a period in which he worked 12 hours overtime at time-and-a-half regular pay?

13. **LO④** Artemis is paid a weekly commission of 4% on net sales of $6000, 8% on the next $3000, and 12.5% on all further sales. Her gross sales for a week were $11 160, and sales returns and allowances were $120.

   (a) What were her gross earnings for the week?

   (b) What was her average hourly rate of pay for the week if she worked 43 hours?

14. **LO④** Last week June worked 50.5 hours. She is paid $15.80 per hour for a regular workweek of 44 hours and overtime at time-and-a-half regular pay.

   (a) What were June's gross wages for last week?

   (b) What is the amount of the overtime premium?

15. **LO④** Margit is paid on a weekly commission basis. She is paid a base salary of $540 on a weekly quota of $8000 and a commission of 4.75% on any sales in excess of the quota.

   (a) If Margit's sales for last week were $11 340, what were her gross earnings?

   (b) What were Margit's average hourly earnings if she worked 35 hours?

16. **LO④** Last week Lisa had gross earnings of $541.30. Lisa receives a base salary of $475 and a commission on sales exceeding her quota of $5000. What is her rate of commission if her sales were $6560?

17. **LO④** Costa earned a gross commission of $2101.05 during July. What were his sales if his rate of commission is 10.5% of net sales and sales returns and allowances for the month were 8% of his gross sales?

18. **LO④** Edith worked 47 hours during a week for which her gross remuneration was $779.72. Based on a regular workweek of 40 hours and overtime payment at time-and-a-half regular pay, what is Edith's hourly rate of pay?

19. **LO④** Hong is paid a semi-monthly salary of $1413.75. Regular hours are $37\frac{1}{2}$ per week and overtime is paid at time-and-a-half regular pay.

   (a) What is Hong's hourly rate of pay?

   (b) How many hours overtime did Hong work in a pay period for which his gross pay was $1552.55?

20. **LO④** Silvio's gross earnings for last week were $528.54. His remuneration consists of a base salary of $480 plus a commission of 6% on net sales exceeding his weekly quota of $5000. What were Silvio's gross sales for the week if sales returns and allowances were $136?

21. **LO④** Aviva's pay stub shows gross earnings of $731.92 for a week. Her regular rate of pay is $15.80 per hour for a 35-hour week and overtime is paid at time-and-a-half regular pay. How many hours did she work?

22. **LO⑤** Ramona's Dry Cleaning shows sales revenue of $76 000 for the year. Ramona's GST-taxable expenses were $14 960. How much should she remit to the government at the end of the year?

23. **LO⑤** When Fred of Fred's Auto Repair tallied up his accounts at the end of the year, he found he had paid GST on parking fees of $2000, supplies of $55 000, utilities of $4000, and miscellaneous eligible costs of $3300. During this same time, he found he had charged his customers GST on billings that totalled $175 000 for parts and $165 650 for labour. How much GST must Fred send to the government?

24. **LO⑤** A store located in Kelowna, B.C., sells a laptop computer for $1868 plus GST and PST. If the same model is sold at the same price in a store in Kenora, Ontario, what is the difference in the prices paid by consumers in the two stores?

25. LO❺ Two people living in different communities build houses of the same design on lots of equal size. If the person in Ripley has his house and lot assessed at $350 000 with a rate per $1000 of 10.051, calculate if his taxes be more or less than the person in Amberly with an assessment of $335 000 and a rate per $1000 of 12.124?

26. LO❺ A town has a total residential property assessment of $975 500 000. It is originally esti-mated that $15 567 000 must be raised through residential taxation to meet expenditures.

(a) What tax rate per $1000 must be set to raise $45 567 000 in property taxes?

(b) What is the property tax on a property assessed at $235 000?

(c) The town later finds that it underestimated building costs. An additional $2 000 000 in taxes must be raised. Calculate the increase in the tax rate required to meet these additional costs.

(d) How much more will the property taxes be on the property assessed at $235 000?

SELF-TEST

You can test your under-standing of the chapter content by completing the Self-Test. Again, the solu-tions to the odd-numbered questions are given at the back of the text.

1. Evaluate each of the following.

(a) $4320\left(1 + 0.18 \times \frac{45}{365}\right)$

(b) $2160\left(0.15 \times \frac{105}{365}\right)$

(c) $2880\left(1 - 0.12 \times \frac{285}{365}\right)$

(d) $\dfrac{410.40}{0.24 \times \frac{135}{365}}$

(e) $\dfrac{5124}{1 - 0.09 \times \frac{270}{365}}$

2. Change each of the following percents into a decimal.

(a) 175%

(b) $\frac{3}{8}\%$

3. Change each of the following percents into a common fraction in lowest terms.

(a) $2\frac{1}{2}\%$

(b) $116\frac{2}{3}\%$

4. Express each of the following as a percent.

(a) 1.125

(b) $\dfrac{9}{400}$

5. Extend each of the following and determine the total revenue.

Quantity	Unit Selling Price	Total Revenue
72	$1.25	?
84	$16\frac{2}{3}¢$	?
40	$0.875	?
48	$1.33	?

6. Purchases of an inventory item during the last accounting period were as follows:

No. of Items	Unit Cost	Total Cost
5	$9.00	?
6	$7.00	?
3	$8.00	?
6	$6.00	?

What was the average cost per item?

7. Hazzid Realty sold lots for $25 120 per 1000 square metre. What is the total sales value if the lot sizes, in 1000 square metres, were $5\frac{1}{4}$, $6\frac{1}{3}$, $4\frac{3}{8}$, and $3\frac{5}{6}$?

8. The following information is shown in your investment account for last year: balance on January 1 of $7200; a withdrawal of $480 on March 1; and deposits of $600 on August 1 and $120 on October 1. What was the account's average monthly balance for the year?

9. Carly is paid a semi-monthly salary of $2080. If her regular workweek is 40 hours, what is her hourly rate of pay?

10. A salesperson earned a commission of $806.59 last week on gross sales of $5880. If returns and allowances were 11.5% of gross sales, what is his rate of commission based on net sales?

11. A.Y. receives an annual salary of $52 956.80. She is paid monthly on a 38-hour workweek. What is the gross pay for a pay period in which she works 8.75 hours overtime at time-and-a-half regular pay?

12. J.B. earns $16.60 an hour with time-and-a-half for hours worked over 8 a day. His hours for a week are 8.25, 8.25, 9.5, 11.5, and 7.25. Determine his gross earnings for that week.

13. A wage earner receives a gross pay of $983.15 for 52.5 hours of work. What is his hourly rate of pay if a regular workweek is 44 hours and overtime is paid at time-and-a-half the regular rate of pay?

14. A salesperson receives a weekly base salary of $600 on a quota of $4500. On the next $2000, she receives a commission of 11%. On any additional sales, the commission rate is 15%. Calculate her gross earnings for a week in which her sales total $8280.

15. Mahal of Winnipeg, Manitoba, bought a ring for $6400. Since the jeweller is shipping the ring, she must pay a shipping charge of $20. She must also pay GST and PST on the ring. Determine the total purchase price of Mahal's ring.

16. Suppose you went shopping and bought bulk laundry detergent worth $17.95. You then received a $2.50 trade discount, and had to pay a $1.45 shipping charge. Calculate the final purchase price of the detergent if you lived in New Brunswick.

17. Ilo pays a property tax of $4502.50. In her community the tax rate is 18 per $1000. What is the assessed value of her property, to the nearest dollar?

18. Property valued at $390 000 is assessed at $\frac{2}{3}$ of its value. What is the amount of tax due for this year if the tax rate is $12.50 per $1000 of assessed value?

CHALLENGE PROBLEMS

Challenge Problems give you the opportunity to apply the skills you learned in the chapter at a higher level than the Exercises.

1. Sam purchased two items for a total of $821.40 The first item is GST exempt and it represents 29% of the total purchase price. Assuming that he lives in British Columbia, what is the total amount of GST and PST that Sam paid?

2. Suppose your math grade is based on the results of two tests and one final exam. Each test is worth 30% of your grade and the final exam is worth 40%. If you scored 60% and 50% on your two tests, what mark must you score on the final exam to achieve a grade of 70%?

CASE STUDY   Businesses and the GST/HST

Case Studies present comprehensive, realistic scenarios followed by a set of questions and illustrate some of the important practical applications of the chapter material.

▶ Businesses providing taxable goods and services in Canada must register to collect either GST or HST, depending on where the business is registered. The federal government has set the GST rate at 5%. The HST varies by province. Since July 1, 2010, the province of Ontario has had a rate of 13% HST.

A company must remit its GST/HST collections either on a monthly, quarterly, or annual basis, depending on the amount of annual revenue. At the end of each fiscal year, registrants must file a return summarizing the collection of GST/HST, the GST/HST paid by the registrant (input tax credits or ITCs), and periodic payments made to the Canada Revenue Agency (CRA). The CRA then uses this information to calculate a business's maximum periodic instalment payment for the following year.

The government gives small businesses with annual revenues of under $30 000 the option of registering to collect and remit. If businesses choose not to register, they do not have to charge GST/HST on their goods or services. The disadvantage is that they are then ineligible for a credit on the GST/HST paid on their supplies.

If a business has registered and has annual taxable revenues less than $400 000, the Quick Method can be used to calculate ITCs. When using the Quick Method in Ontario, the registrant charges customers 13% HST on sales of goods and services. The ITCs for the business are calculated by adding all purchases and expenses including the HST, and then subtracting employees' salaries, insurance, and land. The taxable expense amount is then multiplied by 13/113. The result is the amount of ITC.

Under the Quick Method, the numbers in the calculation vary by province.

QUESTIONS

1. Simon operates an HST-registered mobile glass repair service in Ontario. His service revenue for the year is $28 000. His HST-taxable purchases amounted to $4000. Simon does not use the Quick Method for claiming ITCs. By calculating the difference between the HST he collected and the HST he paid, determine Simon's HST remittance to the CRA.

2. Courtney operates a souvenir gift shop in Ontario. Her business is registered for the Quick Method of calculating ITCs. Her HST-taxable sales were $185 000 for the year. HST-taxable purchases of goods for resale were 47% of sales. In addition, Courtney paid $48 000 in purchases and expenses, which included $42 000 for salaries and insurance.
   (a) Calculate how much HST Courtney remitted to the CRA when using the Quick Method.
   (b) If she had not chosen to use the Quick Method of calculating ITCs, how much HST would she have to remit?
   (c) What is the difference in remittances under the two methods?

3. Steve has been operating Castle Creek Restaurant in Ontario for the past several years. On the basis of the information that Steve's accountant filed with the CRA during the prior year, Castle Creek Restaurant must make monthly HST payments of $3120 this year. Steve must complete the Goods and Services Tax/Harmonized Sales Tax (GST/HST) Return for Registrants online, and then make his payment. He has asked his accountant for instructions on how to do this, and was provided with this explanation:

   Line 101 reports amount of GST/HST-taxable revenues.
   Line 103 reports amount of GST/HST collected.

Line 106 reports amount of GST/HST paid.

Line 109 reports amount of net GST/HST payable to the CRA.

Line 110 reports amount of GST/HST payments already made to the CRA this year.

Line 113 reports amount of balance to be paid or to be refunded.

When Steve checked his accounting records, he found the following information for the current fiscal year: HST-taxable revenue of $486 530 and purchases of $239 690. Referring to the form below, help Steve determine the balance of HST to be paid or to be received by calculating each line of this simplified GST/HST return.

Sales and other revenue	101		00

NET TAX CALCULATION

GST and HST amounts collected or collectible	103	
Adjustments	104	

Total GST/HST and adjustments for period (add lines 103 and 104) ⟶ | 105 | |

Input tax credits (ITCs) for the current period	106	
Adjustments	107	

Total ITCs and adjustments (add lines 106 and 107) ⟶ | 108 | |

Net tax (subtract line 108 from line 105) | 109 | |

OTHER CREDITS IF APPLICABLE

Instalment payments and net tax already remitted	110	
Rebates	111	

Total other credits (add lines 110 and 111) ⟶ | 112 | |

Balance (subtract line 112 from line 109) | 113 | |

REFUND CLAIMED | 114 | **PAYMENT ENCLOSED** | 115 |

The Glossary at the end of each chapter lists each key term with its definition and a page reference to where the term was first defined in the chapter.

GLOSSARY ←

Arithmetic average (mean) the average found by adding the values in the set and dividing by the number of those values *(p. 18)*

Arithmetic mean *see* **Arithmetic average**

Assessed value a dollar figure applied to real estate by municipalities to be used in property tax calculations (can be a market value or a value relative to other properties in the same municipality) *(p. 34)*

Commission the term applied to remuneration of sales personnel according to their sales performance *(p. 27)*

Common fraction the division of one whole number by another whole number, expressed by means of a fraction line *(p. 7)*

Complex fraction a mathematical expression containing one or more fractions in the numerator or the denominator or both *(p. 11)*

Denominator the divisor of a fraction (i.e., the number written below the fraction line) *(p. 7)*

Drawing account an accounting record maintained to track money withdrawn from a business *(p. 28)*

Equivalent fractions fractions that have the same value although they consist of different terms *(p. 7)*

Fraction in lowest terms a fraction whose terms cannot be reduced any further (i.e., whose numerator and denominator cannot be evenly divided by the same number except 1) *(p. 8)*

Goods and services tax (GST) a federal tax charged on the price of almost all goods and services *(p. 32)*

Graduated commission remuneration paid as an increasing percent for increasing sales levels for a fixed period of time *(p. 27)*

Gross earnings the amount of an employee's pay before deductions *(p. 25)*

Harmonized sales tax (HST) the merged GST and PST tax used in Prince Edward Island, Newfoundland and Labrador, Nova Scotia, New Brunswick, and Ontario *(p. 32)*

Improper fraction a fraction whose numerator is greater than its denominator *(p. 7)*

Lowest common denominator (LCD) the smallest number that can be used for all denominators of two or more fractions *(p. 8)*

Mixed number a number consisting of a whole number and a fraction, such as $5\frac{1}{2}$ *(p. 9)*

Net sales gross sales less returns and allowances *(p. 27)*

Numerator the dividend of a fraction (i.e., the number written above the fraction line) *(p. 7)*

Order of operations the order in which arithmetic calculations are performed *(p. 5)*

Overtime premium extra labour cost due to overtime *(p. 29)*

Percent % a fraction with a denominator of 100 *(p. 13)*

Proper fraction a fraction whose numerator is less than its denominator *(p. 7)*

Property tax a municipal tax charged on the assessed value of real estate, both commercial and residential *(p. 34)*

Provincial sales tax (PST) a provincial tax charged on the price of most goods (usually a fixed percent of the cost of a good) *(p. 32)*

Quota a sales level required before the commission percent is paid; usually associated with remuneration by base salary and commission *(p. 28)*

Remuneration payment or compensation for services or employment *(p. 24)*

Salary the term usually applied to monthly or annual remuneration of personnel *(p. 25)*

Salary plus commission a method of remunerating sales personnel that guarantees a minimum income per pay period *(p. 28)*

Straight commission remuneration paid as a percent of net sales for a given period *(p. 27)*

Tax a contribution levied on persons, properties, or businesses to pay for services provided by the government *(p. 32)*

Terms of the fraction the numerator and the denominator of a fraction *(p. 7)*

Wages the term usually applied to the remuneration of hourly rated employees *(p. 29)*

Weighted arithmetic average the average found by multiplying each item by the weighting factor and totalling the results *(p. 19)*

2

Review of Basic Algebra

LEARNING OBJECTIVES

Upon completing this chapter, you will be able to do the following:

1. Simplify algebraic expressions using fundamental operations and substitution.

2. Simplify and evaluate powers with positive exponents, negative exponents, and exponent zero.

3. Use an electronic calculator to compute the numerical value of arithmetic expressions involving fractional exponents.

4. Write exponential equations in logarithmic form and use an electronic calculator equipped with a natural logarithm function to determine the value of natural logarithms.

5. Solve basic equations using addition, subtraction, multiplication, and division.

6. Solve equations involving algebraic simplification and formula rearrangement.

7. Solve word problems by creating and solving equations.

Spflaum/Shutterstock

Business managers use algebra every day to calculate values of unknown variables and to describe patterns. Determining how much inventory to buy, what price to set to sell the inventory, how much storage capacity is needed for computer servers, and how much money to borrow to keep the business going can all be solved with algebra. Becoming fluent in using letters and symbols to represent relationships between known and unknown variables will also help you grasp the concepts and calculations used in future courses in accounting, finance, economics, and statistics.

INTRODUCTION

An electronics manufacturer can fit either 8 laptops or 10 tablets into a standard box for shipping. In one shipment he sent a mix of laptops and tablets for a total of 96 items. If there were more laptops than tablets in the shipment, how many full boxes did he ship?

This type of "brain teaser" is an example of the use of basic algebra. We can solve the problem by letting the unknown value be represented by a letter (a variable) and applying the laws of algebraic formula manipulation. Many problems in business and finance can be solved by using predetermined formulas. When these formulas are used, we need the skills of algebraic substitution and simplification to solve them.

Many problems do not fit a predetermined formula. We must then use the basics of algebra to create our own equation, and solve it to answer the problem. An equation is a statement of equality between two algebraic expressions. Any equation that has variables (letter symbols) to only the first power is called a linear equation. Linear equations can often be created to represent business problems. When you solve the equation you solve the business problem. When you finish this chapter you should feel comfortable solving linear equations. (And if you have not already solved the brain teaser above, the electronics manufacturer shipped 11 boxes total: 7 boxes of laptops and 4 boxes of tablets. See Example 2.7F.)

2.1 SIMPLIFICATION OF ALGEBRAIC EXPRESSIONS
A. Addition and subtraction

1. Simplification Involving Addition and Subtraction

In algebra, only **like terms** may be added or subtracted. This is done by *adding* or *subtracting* the **numerical coefficients** of the like terms and *retaining* the common **literal coefficient**. The process of adding and subtracting like terms is called **combining like terms** or **collecting like terms**. In the term $3xy$, the numerical coefficient of xy is 3, and the literal coefficient of 3 is xy.

EXAMPLE 2.1A

(i) $6x + 3x + 7x$ ————————— all three terms are like terms
$= (6 + 3 + 7)x$ ————————— add the numerical coefficients
$= 16x$ ————————— retain the common literal coefficient

(ii) $-5m - (-3m) - (+6m)$ — change the subtraction to addition
$= -5m + (+3m) + (-6m)$ ————— change the addition to subtraction
$= -5m + 3m - 6m$
$= (-5 + 3 - 6)m$
$= -8m$

(iii) $7x - 4y - 3x - 6y$ ————————— the two sets of like terms are $7x$, $-3x$,
$= (7 - 3)x + (-4 - 6)y$ and $-4y$, $-6y$, and are collected
$= 4x - 10y$ separately

(iv) $3x^3 - 2x + 4x^3 + 5x$ ————————— $3x^3$ and $4x^3$ can be combined. Likewise,
$= (3 + 4)x^3 + (-2 + 5)x$ $-2x$ and $5x$ can be combined.
$= 7x^3 + 3x$

(v) $5x^2 - 3x - 4 + 2x - 5 + x^2$
$= (5 + 1)x^2 + (-3 + 2)x + (-4 - 5)$
$= 6x^2 - x - 9$

2. Simplification Involving Brackets

When simplifying **algebraic expressions** involving brackets, remove the brackets according to the following rules and collect like terms.

(a) If the brackets are preceded by a $(+)$ sign or no sign, drop the brackets and retain the terms inside the brackets with their signs unchanged: $(-7a + 5b - c)$ becomes $-7a + 5b - c$, because each term has been multiplied by 1.

(b) If the brackets are preceded by a $(-)$ sign, drop the brackets and change the sign of every term inside the brackets:
$-(-7a + 5b - c)$ becomes $7a - 5b + c$, because each term has been multiplied by -1.

EXAMPLE 2.1B

(i) $(7a - 3b) - (4a + 3b)$
$= 7a - 3b - 4a - 3b$ —————————— $(7a - 3b)$ becomes $7a - 3b$
$= 3a - 6b$ —————————————— $-(4a + 3b)$ becomes $-4a - 3b$

(ii) $-(3x^2 - 8x - 5) + (2x^2 - 5x + 4)$
$= -3x^2 + 8x + 5 + 2x^2 - 5x + 4$
$= -x^2 + 3x + 9$

(iii) $4b - (3a - 4b - c) - (5c + 2b)$
$= 4b - 3a + 4b + c - 5c - 2b$
$= -3a + 6b - 4c$

B. Multiplication

1. Multiplication of Monomials

The product of two or more **monomials** is the product of their numerical coefficients multiplied by the product of their literal coefficients.

EXAMPLE 2.1C

(i) $5(3a)$
$= (5 \times 3)a$ ——————————— obtain the product of the numerical
$= 15a$ ————————————————— coefficients

(ii) $(-7a)(4b)$
$= (-7 \times 4)(a \times b)$ ——————— obtain the product of the numerical
$= -28ab$ ——————————————— coefficients, -7 and 4, and the product of the literal coefficients, a and b

(iii) $(-3)(4x)(-5x)$
$= [(-3)(4)(-5)][(x)(x)]$
$= 60x^2$

---

2. Multiplication of Monomials with Polynomials

The product of a **polynomial** and a monomial is obtained by multiplying each term of the polynomial by the monomial.

EXAMPLE 2.1D

(i) $5(a - 3)$

$= 5(a) + 5(-3)$ ———————————————— multiply 5 by a and 5 by (-3)

$= 5a - 15$

(ii) $-4(3x^2 - 2x - 1)$

$= -4(3x^2) + (-4)(-2x) + (-4)(-1)$ ———— multiply each term of the

$= (-12x^2) + (+8x) + (+4)$ trinomial by (-4)

$= -12x^2 + 8x + 4$

(iii) $3a(4a - 5b - 2c)$

$= (3a)(4a) + (3a)(-5b) + (3a)(-2c)$

$= (12a^2) + (-15ab) + (-6ac)$

$= 12a^2 - 15ab - 6ac$

3. Simplification Involving Brackets and Multiplication

EXAMPLE 2.1E

(i) $3(x - 5) - 2(x - 7)$

$= 3x - 15 - 2x + 14$ ———————————— carry out the multiplication

$= x - 1$ ——————————————————— collect like terms

(ii) $a(3a - 1) - 4(2a + 3)$

$= 3a^2 - a - 8a - 12$

$= 3a^2 - 9a - 12$

(iii) $-4(5a - 3b - 2c) + 5(-2a - 4b + c)$

$= -20a + 12b + 8c - 10a - 20b + 5c$

$= -30a - 8b + 13c$

4. Multiplication of a Polynomial by a Polynomial

The product of two polynomials is obtained by multiplying each term of one polynomial by each term of the other polynomial and collecting like terms.

EXAMPLE 2.1F

(i) $(3a + 2b)(4c - 3d)$ multiply each term of the first

$= 3a(4c - 3d) + 2b(4c - 3d)$ ———————— polynomial by the second polynomial

$= 12ac - 9ad + 8bc - 6bd$ ———————— carry out the multiplication and

                                  remove the brackets

(ii) $(5x - 2)(3x + 4)$

$= 5x(3x + 4) - 2(3x + 4)$

$= 15x^2 + 20x - 6x - 8$

$= 15x^2 + 14x - 8$ ———————————— simplify by combining like terms

(iii) $(4x^2 - 5x - 7)(x + 3)$

$(4x^2 - 5x - 7)(x) + (4x^2 - 5x - 7)(3)$

$= 4x^3 - 5x^2 - 7x + 12x^2 - 15x - 21$

$= 4x^3 + 7x^2 - 22x - 21$

POINTERS & PITFALLS

There is a special method called "FOIL" that is useful for multiplying a two-term polynomial by another two-term polynomial. The letters F-O-I-L stand for the words "first", "outside", "inside", and "last".

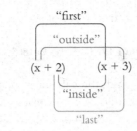

That is, multiply the "first" terms in each polynomial, then multiply the two terms on the "outside" (furthest from each other), then multiply the two terms on the "inside" (closest to each other), and then multiply the "last" terms in each polynomial. The expression is then simplified by combining like terms.

Using the example above, "first": $(x)(x) = x^2$; "outside": $(x)(3) = 3x$; "inside": $(2)(x) = 2x$; "last": $(2)(3) = 6$ so that $(x + 2)(x + 3) = x^2 + 3x + 2x + 6 = x^2 + 5x + 6$

C. Division

1. Division of Monomials

The **quotient** of two monomials is the quotient of their numerical coefficients multiplied by the quotient of their literal coefficients.

EXAMPLE 2.1G

(i) $32ab \div 8b = \left(\dfrac{\overset{4}{\cancel{32}}}{\underset{1}{\cancel{8}}}\right)\left(\dfrac{a\cancel{b}}{\cancel{b}}\right) = 4a$ ——— reduce by dividing by common factors

(ii) $24x^2 \div (-6x) = \left(\dfrac{24}{-6}\right)\left(\dfrac{x^2}{x}\right) = -4x$

2. Division of a Polynomial by a Monomial

To determine the quotient of a polynomial divided by a monomial, divide each term of the polynomial by the monomial.

EXAMPLE 2.1H

(i) $(12a + 8) \div 4 = \dfrac{12a + 8}{4} = \dfrac{12a}{4} + \dfrac{8}{4} = 3a + 2$

(ii) $(18x - 12) \div 6 = \dfrac{18x - 12}{6} = \dfrac{18x}{6} - \dfrac{12}{6} = 3x - 2$

(iii) $(12a^3 - 15a^2 - 9a) \div (-3a)$

$= \dfrac{12a^3 - 15a^2 - 9a}{-3a}$

$= \dfrac{12a^3}{-3a} + \dfrac{-15a^2}{-3a} + \dfrac{-9a}{-3a}$

$= -4a^2 + 5a + 3$

POINTERS & PITFALLS

Many of the solutions for problems such as those below involve repeating and continuous numbers. To standardize, the number of decimal places shown in solutions will be set at six or fewer. The financial calculator can be set to show a maximum of six decimal places by following the steps

[2nd] [Format] DEC = 6 [Enter] [2nd] [QUIT]

It is important to note that even though the calculator display shows six or fewer decimal places, the complete, non-rounded quantity is used in continuous calculations on the calculator.

D. Substitution and evaluation

Evaluating algebraic expressions for given values requires replacing the variables with the given values. The replacement or substitution of the variables takes place each time the variables appear in the expression.

EXAMPLE 2.11

(i) Evaluate $7x - 3y - 5$ for $x = -2$, $y = 3$

$7x - 3y - 5$
$= 7(-2) - 3(3) - 5$ —————— replace x by (-2) and y by 3
$= -14 - 9 - 5$
$= -28$

(ii) Evaluate $\dfrac{2NC}{P(n+1)}$ for N = 12, C = 220, P = 1500, $n = 15$

$\dfrac{2NC}{P(n+1)} = \dfrac{2(12)(220)}{1500(15+1)} = 0.22$

Using a calculator, the key sequence is

[(] 2 [×] 12 [×] 220 [)] [÷] [(] 1500 [×] [(] 15 [+] 1 [)] [)] [=] 0.22

(iii) Evaluate $\dfrac{I}{rt}$ for I = \$126, $r = 0.125$, $t = \dfrac{328}{365}$

$\dfrac{I}{rt} = \dfrac{\$126}{0.125 \times \frac{328}{365}} = \$1121.71$

Using a calculator, the key sequence is

[(] 126 [)] [÷] [(] 0.125 [×] 328 [÷] 365 [)] [=] 1121.7073

(iv) Evaluate $P(1 + rt)$ for P = \$900, $r = 0.15$, $t = \dfrac{244}{365}$

$P(1 + rt) = \$900\left(1 + 0.15 \times \dfrac{244}{365}\right)$
$= \$900(1 + 0.100274)$
$= \$900(1.100274)$
$= \$990.25$

Using a calculator, and following the basic order of operations, you can work from right to left on this question. The key sequence is

244 $\boxed{\div}$ 365 $\boxed{\times}$ 0.15 $\boxed{+}$ 1 $\boxed{=}$ $\boxed{\times}$ 900 $\boxed{=}$ 990.246575

(v) Evaluate $A(1 - dt)$ for A = \$800, $d = 0.135$, $t = \dfrac{292}{365}$

$$A(1 - dt) = \$800\left(1 - 0.135 \times \dfrac{292}{365}\right)$$
$$= \$800(1 - 0.108)$$
$$= \$800(0.892)$$
$$= \$713.60$$

Following the basic order of operations and working from right to left the sequence is

292 $\boxed{\div}$ 365 $\boxed{\times}$ 0.135 $\boxed{\pm}$ $\boxed{+}$ 1 $\boxed{=}$ $\boxed{\times}$ 800 $\boxed{=}$ 713.60

(vi) Evaluate $\dfrac{S}{1 + rt}$ for S = \$1644, $r = 0.16$, $t = \dfrac{219}{365}$

$$\dfrac{S}{1 + rt} = \dfrac{\$1644}{1 + 0.16 \times \frac{219}{365}} = \dfrac{\$1644}{1 + 0.096} = \dfrac{\$1644}{1.096} = \$1500$$

Follow the sequence in the Pointers and Pitfalls example on p. 11 in Chapter 1, starting with the denominator. The sequence is

219 $\boxed{\div}$ 365 $\boxed{\times}$ 0.16 $\boxed{+}$ 1 $\boxed{=}$ $\boxed{\frac{1}{x}}$ $\boxed{\times}$ 1644 $\boxed{\div}$ 1500.00

EXERCISE 2.1

MyLab Math

A. Addition and subtraction. Simplify.

1. $9a + 3a + 7a$ **2.** $6m - 2m - m$

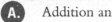 **3.** $-4a - 8 + 3a - 2$ **4.** $2a - 15 - 5a + 1$

5. $2x - 3y - 4x - y$ **6.** $6p + 2q - 3p - q$

7. $12f - 9v + 2f + 5v$ **8.** $9c - 8d - 7c + 5d$

9. $x - 0.2x$ **10.** $x + 0.06x$

11. $x + 0.4x$ **12.** $x - 0.02x$

13. $x + 0.9x + 0.89x$ **14.** $3y + 2.81y - 1.76y$

15. $x^2 - 2x - 5 + x - 3 - 2x^2$ **16.** $3ax - 2x + 1 - 3 + 3x - 4ax$

17. $(2x - 3y) - (x + 4y)$ **18.** $-(4 - 5a) - (-2 + 3a)$

19. $(12b + 4c + 9) + 8 - (8b + 2c + 15)$

20. $(a^2 - ab + b^2) - (3a^2 + 5ab - 4b^2)$

21. $-(3m^2 - 4m - 5) - (4 - 2m - 2m^2)$

22. $6 - (4x - 3y + 1) - (5x + 2y - 9)$

23. $(7a - 5b) - (-3a + 4b) - 5b$

24. $(3f - f^2 + fg) - (f - 3f^2 - 2fg)$

25. $4b^4d + 2ac^7 - (-5b^4d) - 3ac$

26. $(8t^2 - 6t - 9) - (7t^2 - 6t + 7)$

27. $\dfrac{18y}{2} - \dfrac{12}{5} + 3\dfrac{1}{4}y$

28. $1.3x + x^2 + \dfrac{x}{2} - 2x + 4$

29. $\dfrac{k}{(1 + 0.05)} + \dfrac{k}{(1 + 0.05)^2}$

30. $x\left(1 + 0.052 \times \dfrac{142}{365}\right) + \dfrac{x}{\left(1 + 0.052 \times \dfrac{91}{365}\right)}$

B. Multiplication and division. Simplify.

1. $3(-4x)$

2. $-7(8a)$

3. $-5x(2a)$

4. $-9a(-3b)$

5. $-x(2x)$

6. $-6m(-4m)$

7. $-4(5x)(-3y)$

8. $2a(-3b)(-4c)(-1)$

9. $-2(x - 2y)$

10. $5(2x - 4)$

11. $a(2x^2 - 3x - 1)$

12. $-6x(4 - 2b - b^2)$

13. $4(5x - 6) - 3(2 - 5x)$

14. $-3(8a - b) -2(-7a + 9b)$

15. $-3a(5x - 1) + a(5 - 2x) - 3a(x + 1)$

16. $8(3y - 4) - 2(2y - 1) - (1 - y)$

17. $(3x - 1)(x + 2)$

18. $(5m - 2n)(m - 3n)$

19. $(x + y)(x^2 - xy + y^2)$

20. $(a - 1)(a^2 - 2a + 1)$

21. $(5x - 4)(2x - 1) - (x - 7)(3x + 5)$

22. $2(a - 1)(2a - 3) - 3(3a - 2)(a + 1)$

23. $(3x^2 - 4x + 1)(x^2 + 2x - 3)$

24. $5(b^2 + b - 1)(b^3 + 4b + 2)$

25. $20ab \div 5$

26. $30xy \div (-6x)$

27. $(-12x^2) \div (-3x)$

28. $(-42ab) \div (7ab)$

29. $(20m - 8) \div 2$

30. $(14x - 21) \div (-7)$

31. $(10x^2 - 15x - 30) \div (-5)$

32. $(-a^3 - 4a^2 - 3a) \div (-a)$

C. Substitution and evaluation. Evaluate each of the following for the values given.

1. $3x - 2y - 3$ for $x = -4$, $y = -5$

2. $\dfrac{1}{2}(3x^2 - x - 1) - \dfrac{1}{4}(5 - 2x - x^2)$ for $x = -3$

3. $(pq - vq) - f$ for $p = 12$, $q = 2000$, $v = 7$, $f = 4500$

4. F/C for $F = 13\ 000$, $C = 0.65$

5. $(1 - d_1)(1 - d_2)(1 - d_3)$ for $d_1 = 0.35$, $d_2 = 0.08$, $d_3 = 0.02$

6. $C + 0.38C + 0.24C$ for $C = \$25.00$

7. $\dfrac{RP(n + 1)}{2N}$ for $R = 0.21$, $P = \$1200$, $n = 77$, $N = 26$

8. $\dfrac{I}{Pt}$ for I = 63, P = 840, $t = \dfrac{219}{365}$

9. $\dfrac{I}{rt}$ for I = \$198, $r = 0.165$, $t = \dfrac{146}{365}$

🌐 10. $\dfrac{2NC}{P(n+1)}$ for N = 52, C = 60, P = 1800, $n = 25$

11. $P(1 + rt)$ for P = \$880, $r = 0.12$, $t = \dfrac{76}{365}$

12. $FV(1 - rt)$ for FV = \$1200, $r = 0.175$, $t = \dfrac{256}{365}$

13. $\dfrac{P}{1 - dt}$ for P = \$1253, $d = 0.135$, $t = \dfrac{284}{365}$

14. $\dfrac{S}{1 + rt}$ for S = \$1752, $r = 0.152$, $t = \dfrac{228}{365}$

15. $S\left[1 + r \times \dfrac{t}{365}\right]$ for   S = 3240, $r = 0.125$, $t = 290$

16. $(SP \times X) - FC - (VC \times X)$ for   SP = 13, X = 125, FC = 875, VC = 4

17. $(1 + i)^m - 1$ for $i = 0.0275$, $m = 2$

18. $PMT\left[\dfrac{(1 + i)^n - 1}{i}\right]$ for   PMT = 500, $i = 0.025$, $n = 2$

🌐 19. $1 - \left[(1 - d_1)(1 - d_2)\right]$ for $d_1 = 0.15$, $d_2 = 0.04$

20. $\left[\dfrac{(FV)(i)}{(1 + i)^n - 1}\right]$ for   FV = 10,000, $i = 0.0075$, $n = 20$

2.2 INTEGRAL EXPONENTS
A. Basic concept and definition

In mathematics and its applications, we often have a number multiplied by itself several times.

If a number is to be used as a **factor** several times, the mathematical expression can be written more efficiently by using exponents:

$$5 \times 5 \times 5 \times 5 \text{ may be written as } 5^4$$

$$5 \times 5 \times 5 \times 5 = 5^4$$

Note: In the expression 5^4 ⟶ 5 is called the **base**
⟶ 4 is called the **exponent**
⟶ 5^4 is called the **power**

EXAMPLE 2.2A

(i) $7 \times 7 \times 7 \times 7 \times 7 = 7^5$

(ii) $(-4)(-4)(-4) = (-4)^3$

(iii) $(1.01)(1.01)(1.01)(1.01) = (1.01)^4$

(iv) $(a)(a)(a)(a)(a)(a)(a) = a^7$

(v) $(1 + i)(1 + i)(1 + i)(1 + i)(1 + i)(1 + i) = (1 + i)^6$

When the exponent "n" is a positive integer, the notation "a^n" represents the product of "n" equal factors of "a."

$$a^n = (a)(a)(a)(a) \ldots (a) \text{ to } n \text{ factors}$$

a^n is called the power and is referred to as "the nth power of a".

$$\text{POWER} = \text{BASE}^{\text{to the EXPONENT}}$$

Note: If a number is raised to the exponent "1," the power equals the base.

$$5^1 = 5 \text{ and } a^1 = a;$$

$$\text{conversely, } 6 = 6^1 \text{ and } x = x^1.$$

Expressions involving exponents appear in the study of compound interest developed later in the text.

B. Numerical evaluation of powers with positive integral exponents

1. Evaluation When the Base Is a Positive Integer

To evaluate a power, we may rewrite the power in factored form and obtain the product by multiplication.

EXAMPLE 2.2B

(i) 2^5 ——————————————— means that 2 is a factor 5 times

$= (2)(2)(2)(2)(2)$ ——————— power rewritten in factored form

$= 32$ ——————————————— product

(ii) $(5)^3$ ——————————————— 5 is a factor 3 times

$= (5)(5)(5) = 125$

(iii) 1^7 ——————————————— 1 is a factor 7 times

$= (1)(1)(1)(1)(1)(1)(1)$

$= 1$

(iv) Evaluate a^n if $a = 4$, $n = 6$

$$a^n = 4^6$$

$$= (4)(4)(4)(4)(4)(4)$$

$$= 4096$$

2. Evaluation When the Base Is a Negative Integer

If a power has a negative base, the number of equal factors shown by the exponent determines the sign of the product.

(a) If the exponent is an even positive integer, the product is positive.
(b) If the exponent is an odd positive integer, the product is negative.

EXAMPLE 2.2C

(i) $(-4)^3$ ——————————————— (-4) is a factor 3 times

$= (-4)(-4)(-4)$

$= -64$ ——————————————— the answer is negative (exponent is odd)

(ii) $(-2)^8$ ———————————————————— (-2) is a factor 8 times
= $(-2)(-2)(-2)(-2)(-2)(-2)(-2)(-2)$
= 256 ———————————————— the answer is positive (exponent is even)

Note: -2^8 means $-(2)^8 = -(2)(2)(2)(2)(2)(2)(2)(2) = -256$

(iii) $(-1)^{55}$
= $(-1)(-1)(-1)(-1)$ ... to 55 factors
= -1

(iv) Evaluate $3a^n$ for $a = -5, n = 4$
$3a^n = 3(-5)^4$
= $3(-5)(-5)(-5)(-5)$
= $3(625)$
= 1875

3. Evaluation When the Base Is a Common Fraction or Decimal

EXAMPLE 2.2D

(i) $\left(\dfrac{3}{2}\right)^5$ ————————————————— $\frac{3}{2}$ is a factor 5 times

$= \left(\dfrac{3}{2}\right)\left(\dfrac{3}{2}\right)\left(\dfrac{3}{2}\right)\left(\dfrac{3}{2}\right)\left(\dfrac{3}{2}\right)$

$= \dfrac{(3)(3)(3)(3)(3)}{(2)(2)(2)(2)(2)}$

$= \dfrac{243}{32}$

(ii) $(0.1)^4$ ———————————————— 0.1 is a factor 4 times
= $(0.1)(0.1)(0.1)(0.1)$
= 0.0001

(iii) $\left(-\dfrac{1}{3}\right)^3$ ————————————————— $\left(-\frac{1}{3}\right)$ is a factor 3 times

$= \left(-\dfrac{1}{3}\right)\left(-\dfrac{1}{3}\right)\left(-\dfrac{1}{3}\right)$

$= \dfrac{(-1)(-1)(-1)}{(3)(3)(3)}$

$= \dfrac{-1}{27}$

(iv) $(1.02)^2$
= $(1.02)(1.02)$
= 1.0404

(v) Evaluate $(1 + i)^n$ for $i = 0.03, n = 4$
$(1 + i)^n = (1 + 0.03)^4$
= $(1.03)(1.03)(1.03)(1.03)$
= 1.125509

POINTERS & PITFALLS

You can use a calculator's *power function* to evaluate powers. On most financial calculators, the power function is represented by y^x. For example, to evaluate $(-1.03)^5$ using the Texas Instruments BA II PLUS, use the key sequence

$$1.03 \;\boxed{\pm}\;\; \boxed{y^x}\; 5 \;\boxed{=}$$

The answer is -1.159274.

C. Operations with powers

Exponents are handy for making algebra easier because they are compact. In this section we learn some important laws of exponents.

1. Multiplication of Powers

To multiply powers that have the same base, retain the common base and add the exponents.

$$\boxed{a^m \times a^n = a^{m+n}} \text{————————— Formula 2.1}$$

The rule for multiplying three or more powers having the same base follows the same approach.

$$\boxed{a^m \times a^n \times a^p = a^{m+n+p}}$$

EXAMPLE 2.2E

(i) $3^5 \times 3^2$
   $= 3^{5+2}$ ————————————— retain the common base 3
   $= 3^7$ and add the exponents 5 and 2

(ii) $(-4)^3(-4)^7(-4)^5$
   $= (-4)^{3+7+5}$ ————————— retain the common base (-4) and
   $= (-4)^{15}$ add the exponents 3, 7, and 5

(iii) $\left(\dfrac{1}{8}\right)^5\left(\dfrac{1}{8}\right) = \left(\dfrac{1}{8}\right)^{5+1} = \left(\dfrac{1}{8}\right)^6$

(iv) $(x^3)(x^5)(x) = x^{3+5+1} = x^9$

(v) $(1.06)^{16}(1.06)^{14} = (1.06)^{16+14} = 1.06^{30}$

(vi) $(1+i)(1+i)^5(1+i)^{20} = (1+i)^{1+5+20} = (1+i)^{26}$

2. Division of Powers

To divide powers that have the same base, retain the common base and subtract the exponent of the divisor from the exponent of the dividend.

$$\boxed{a^m \div a^n = a^{m-n}} \text{————————— Formula 2.2}$$

EXAMPLE 2.2F

(i) $\quad 2^8 \div 2^5$ ———————————————— retain the common base 2 and subtract
$= 2^{8-5}$ the exponent of the divisor, 5, from the
$= 2^3$ exponent of the dividend, 8

(ii) $\quad (-10)^8 \div (-10)^7$ ———————— retain the common base (-10) and
$= (-10)^{8-7}$ subtract the exponents
$= (-10)^1 \text{ or } -10$

(iii) $\left(-\dfrac{2}{5}\right)^6 \div \left(-\dfrac{2}{5}\right)^2 = \left(-\dfrac{2}{5}\right)^{6-2} = \left(-\dfrac{2}{5}\right)^4$

(iv) $a^{15} \div a^{10} = a^{15-10} = a^5$

(v) $(1.10)^{24} \div 1.10 = (1.10)^{24-1} = 1.10^{23}$

(vi) $(1+i)^{80} \div (1+i)^{60} = (1+i)^{80-60} = (1+i)^{20}$

3. Raising a Power to a Power

To raise a power to a power, retain the base and multiply the exponents.

$$\boxed{\left(a^m\right)^n = a^{mn}}$$ ———————————————— Formula 2.3

EXAMPLE 2.2G

(i) $\quad (3^2)^5$
$= 3^{2 \times 5}$ ———————————————— retain the base 3 and multiply the
$= 3^{10}$ exponents 2 and 5

(ii) $\quad \left[(-4)^5\right]^3$
$= (-4)^{5 \times 3}$ ———————————————— retain the base and multiply the
$= (-4)^{15}$ exponents

(iii) $\left[\left(\dfrac{4}{3}\right)^6\right]^{10} = \left(\dfrac{4}{3}\right)^{6 \times 10} = \left(\dfrac{4}{3}\right)^{60}$

(iv) $(a^7)^3 = a^{7 \times 3} = a^{21}$

(v) $\left[(1.005)^{50}\right]^4 = (1.005)^{50 \times 4} = 1.005^{200}$

(vi) $\left[(1+i)^{75}\right]^2 = (1+i)^{75 \times 2} = (1+i)^{150}$

4. Power of a Product and Power of a Quotient

The power of a product, written in factored form, is the product of the individual factors raised to the exponent.

$$\boxed{(ab)^m = a^m b^m}$$ ———————————————— Formula 2.4

The power of a quotient is the quotient of the dividend and the divisor raised to the exponent.

$$\boxed{\left(\dfrac{a}{b}\right)^m = \dfrac{a^m}{b^m}}$$ ———————————————— Formula 2.5

POINTERS & PITFALLS

Note that ab^2 is not the same as $(ab)^2$ since ab^2 means $(a)(b)(b)$ while $(ab)^2 = (ab)(ab) = (a)(a)(b)(b) = a^2b^2$. For example, when $a = 3$ and $b = 4$, then $ab^2 = 48$ but $(ab)^2 = 144$.

EXAMPLE 2.2H

(i) $(2 \times 3)^5 = 2^5 \times 3^5$; alternatively, $(2 \times 3)^5 = 6^5$

(ii) $(6 \times 2^7)^4 = 6^4 \times (2^7)^4 = 6^4 \times 2^{28}$

(iii) $\left(-\dfrac{5}{7}\right)^3 = \dfrac{(-5)^3}{7^3}$

(iv) $(a^3b)^4 = (a^3)^4 \times b^4 = a^{12}b^4$

(v) $\left[\dfrac{(1 + i)}{i}\right]^3 = \dfrac{(1 + i)^3}{i^3}$

D. Zero exponent

A zero exponent results when applying the law of division of powers to powers with equal exponents.

$$3^5 \div 3^5$$
$$= 3^{5 - 5}$$
$$= 3^0$$

The result may be interpreted as follows.

$$3^5 \div 3^5 = \frac{3^5}{3^5} = \frac{3 \times 3 \times 3 \times 3 \times 3}{3 \times 3 \times 3 \times 3 \times 3} = 1$$

$$\boxed{3^0 = 1}$$

Similarly, $a^6 \div a^6 = a^{6 - 6} = a^0$

and since $a^6 \div a^6 = \dfrac{a^6}{a^6} = \dfrac{(a)(a)(a)(a)(a)(a)}{(a)(a)(a)(a)(a)(a)} = 1$

$$\boxed{a^0 = 1}$$

In general, *any number raised to the exponent zero is 1*, except zero itself. The expression 0^0 has no meaning and is said to be *undefined*.

EXAMPLE 2.2I

(i) $(-4)^0 = 1$

(ii) $(1 + i)^0 = 1$

(iii) $(ax + b)^0 = 1$

(iv) $(a^3b^0c)^2 = a^6c^2$

E. Negative exponents

A negative exponent results when the exponent of the divisor is greater than the exponent of the dividend.

$$4^3 \div 4^5$$
$$= 4^{3-5}$$
$$= 4^{-2}$$

The result may be interpreted as follows.

$$4^3 \div 4^5 = \frac{4^3}{4^5} = \frac{4 \times 4 \times 4}{4 \times 4 \times 4 \times 4 \times 4} = \frac{1}{4 \times 4} = \frac{1}{4^2}$$

$$\boxed{4^{-2} = \frac{1}{4^2}}$$

Similarly, $a^5 \div a^8 = a^{5-8} = a^{-3}$

and since $a^5 \div a^8 = \dfrac{a^5}{a^8} = \dfrac{(a)(a)(a)(a)(a)}{(a)(a)(a)(a)(a)(a)(a)(a)}$

$$= \frac{1}{(a)(a)(a)} = \frac{1}{a^3}$$

$$\boxed{a^{-3} = \frac{1}{a^3}}$$

$$\boxed{a^{-m} = \frac{1}{a^m}} \text{———————————— Formula 2.6}$$

In general, a base raised to a negative exponent is equivalent to "1" divided by the same base raised to the corresponding positive exponent.

EXAMPLE 2.2J

(i) $2^{-3} = \dfrac{1}{2^3} = \dfrac{1}{8}$

(ii) $(-3)^{-2} = \dfrac{1}{(-3)^2} = \dfrac{1}{9}$

(iii) $\left(\dfrac{1}{4}\right)^{-4} = \dfrac{1}{\left(\frac{1}{4}\right)^4} = \dfrac{1}{\frac{1}{256}} = \dfrac{1}{1} \times \dfrac{256}{1} = 256$ ——————— **invert and multiply**

(iv) $(1.05)^{-2} = \dfrac{1}{1.05^2} = \dfrac{1}{1.1025} = 0.907029$

(v) $(1+i)^{-10} = \dfrac{1}{(1+i)^{10}}$

(vi) $(1+i)^{-1} = \dfrac{1}{1+i}$

In general, a fraction raised to a negative exponent is equivalent to the inverse of that fraction raised to the corresponding positive exponent.

$$\boxed{\left(\frac{y}{x}\right)^{-m} = \left(\frac{x}{y}\right)^m} \text{———————————— Formula 2.7}$$

EXAMPLE 2.2K

(i) $\left(-\dfrac{3}{5}\right)^{-3} = \dfrac{1}{\left(-\frac{3}{5}\right)^3} = \dfrac{1}{-\frac{27}{125}} = \dfrac{-125}{27}$

Note: $\dfrac{-125}{27} = \dfrac{(-5)^3}{3^3} = \left(-\dfrac{5}{3}\right)^3$

POINTERS & PITFALLS

Use the ± (change sign) key on your calculator when calculating expressions with negative exponents.

The key sequence for solving $(1 + 0.05)^{-5}$ is:

1 + 0.05 y^x 5 ± = the solution is 0.783526

EXERCISE 2.2

MyLab Math

A. Evaluate each of the following.

1. 3^4 **2.** 1^5 **3.** $(-2)^4$ **4.** $(-1)^{12}$

5. $\left(\dfrac{2}{3}\right)^4$ **6.** $\left(\dfrac{5}{6}\right)^4$ **7.** $\left(-\dfrac{1}{4}\right)^3$ **8.** $\left(-\dfrac{2}{3}\right)^3$

9. $(0.5)^2$ **10.** $(2.2)^6$ **11.** $(-0.1)^3$ **12.** $(-3.2)^5$

13. $(-4)^0$ **14.** m^0 **15.** 3^{-2} **16.** 8^3

17. $(-5)^{-3}$ **18.** $(-3.6)^{-4}$ **19.** $\left(\dfrac{1}{5}\right)^{-3}$ **20.** $\left(\dfrac{2}{3}\right)^{-4}$

21. 1.01^{-1} **22.** $(1.05)^0$ **23.** $1.07^{15} - 1/0.07$ **24.** $\dfrac{1}{(1.07)^0}$

25. $\dfrac{1}{(1 + 0.025)^{10}}$ **26.** $100(1 + 0.0225)^7$ **27.** $425(1 + 0.16)^{-4}$ **28.** $\left(\dfrac{1500}{200}\right)^{0.5} - 1$

29. $\dfrac{(1 + 0.03)^{25}}{0.03}$ **30.** $\left[\dfrac{1 - (1.01)^{-20}}{0.01}\right]$

B. Simplify.

1. $2^5 \times 2^3$ **2.** $(-4)^3 \times (-4)$

3. $4^7 \div 4^4$ **4.** $(-3)^9 \div (-3)^7$

5. $(2^3)^5$ **6.** $\left[(-4)^3\right]^6$

7. $a^4 \times a^{10}$ **8.** $m^{12} \div m^7$

9. $3^4 \times 3^6 \times 3$ **10.** $(-1)^3(-1)^7(-1)^5$

11. $\dfrac{6^7 \times 6^3}{6^9}$ **12.** $\dfrac{(x^4)(x^5)}{x^7}$

🌐 **13.** $\left(\dfrac{3}{5}\right)^4\left(\dfrac{3}{5}\right)^7$ **14.** $\left(\dfrac{1}{6}\right)^5 \div \left(\dfrac{1}{6}\right)^3$

15. $\left(-\dfrac{3}{2}\right)\left(-\dfrac{3}{2}\right)^6\left(-\dfrac{3}{2}\right)^4$ **16.** $\left(-\dfrac{3}{4}\right)^8 \div \left(-\dfrac{3}{4}\right)^7$

17. $(1.025^{80})(1.025^{70})$ **18.** $1.005^{240} \div 1.005^{150}$

19. $\left[1.04^{20}\right]^4$ **20.** $\left[\left(-\dfrac{3}{7}\right)^5\right]^3$

21. $(1+i)^{100}(1+i)^{100}$ 🌐 **22.** $(1-r)^2(1-r)^2(1-r)^2$

23. $\left[(1+i)^{80}\right]^2$ **24.** $\left[(1-r)^{40}\right]^3$

25. $(ab)^5$ **26.** $(2xy)^4$

27. $(m^3n)^8$ 🌐 **28.** $\left(\dfrac{a^3b^2}{x}\right)^4$

29. $2^3 \times 2^5 \times 2^{-4}$ **30.** $5^2 \div 5^{-3}$

🌐 **31.** $\left(\dfrac{a}{b}\right)^{-8}$ 🌐 **32.** $\left(\dfrac{1+i}{i}\right)^{-n}$

2.3 FRACTIONAL EXPONENTS
A. Radicals

When the product of two or more equal factors is expressed in exponential form, one of the equal factors is called the **root of the product**. The exponent indicates the number of equal factors; that is, the **power of the root**.

For example,

$25 = 5^2$ ⟶ 5 is the second power root (square root) of 25
$8 = 2^3$ ⟶ 2 is the third power root (cube root) of 8
$81 = 3^4$ ⟶ 3 is the fourth (power) root of 81
a^5 ⟶ a is the fifth root of a^5
7^n ⟶ 7 is the nth root of 7^n
x^n ⟶ x is the nth root of x^n

The operational symbol for solving the root of an expression is $\sqrt{\ \ }$. This symbol represents the *positive* root only. If the negative root is desired, a minus sign is placed in front of the symbol; that is, the negative root is represented by $-\sqrt{\ \ }$.

The power of a root is written at the upper left of the symbol, as in $\sqrt[3]{\ \ }$ or $\sqrt[n]{\ \ }$.

The indicated root is called a **radical**, the number under the symbol is called the **radicand**, and the power indicated is called the *order* or **index**.

In the radical $\sqrt[5]{32}$, the index is 5 and the radicand is 32.

When the square root is to be found, it is customary to omit the index 2. The symbol $\sqrt{\ \ }$ is understood to mean the positive square root of the radicand.

$\sqrt{49}$ means $\sqrt[2]{49}$ or 7

In special cases, such as those shown in Example 2.3A, the radicand is an integral power of the root. The root can readily be found by expressing the radicand in exponential form; the index of the root and the exponent are the same.

EXAMPLE 2.3A

(i) $\sqrt{64} = \sqrt{8^2}$ —————————— the radicand 64 is expressed in exponential form as a square

$= 8$ —————————— one of the two equal factors 8 is the root

(ii) $\sqrt[5]{32} = \sqrt[5]{2^5}$ —————————— express the radicand 32 as the fifth power of 2

$= 2$ —————————— one of the five equal factors 2 is the root

(iii) $\sqrt[3]{0.125} = \sqrt[3]{0.5^3} = 0.5$

In most cases, however, the radicand cannot be easily rewritten in exponential form. The arithmetic determination of the numerical value of these roots is a laborious process. But computating the root is easily accomplished using electronic calculators equipped with a power function.

To use the power function described in the Pointers and Pitfalls box on page 56, first rewrite the radical so it appears in exponential form. Then, as you will see in Formula 2.8 in the next section, $a^{1/n} = \sqrt[n]{a}$. Use the opposite of this formula to rewrite a radical into exponential form: $\sqrt[n]{a} = a^{1/n}$. For example, $\sqrt[5]{32}$ can be written as $32^{1/5}$. Now use the power function. The key sequence is

32 $\boxed{y^x}$ $\boxed{(}$ 1 $\boxed{\div}$ 5 $\boxed{)}$ $\boxed{=}$ The solution is 2.

Instead of using brackets, you could first calculate $1 \div 5$, save the result in the calculator's memory, and then recall the result from memory after pressing $\boxed{y^x}$.

POINTERS & PITFALLS

The calculator has 10 memory addresses available, numbered 0 through 9. To store a displayed value in a memory address (0 through 9), press $\boxed{\text{STO}}$ and a digit key $\boxed{0}$ through $\boxed{9}$. To recall a value from memory and display it, press $\boxed{\text{RCL}}$ and a digit key $\boxed{0}$ through $\boxed{9}$. The numeric value is displayed but is also retained in that memory address.

The key sequence for solving $32^{1/5}$ using the calculator's store and recall functions is

1/5 $\boxed{=}$ $\boxed{\text{STO}}$ $\boxed{1}$ 32 $\boxed{y^x}$ $\boxed{\text{RCL}}$ $\boxed{1}$ $=$ the solution is 2

The problems in Example 2.3B are intended to ensure that you are able to use the power function. They should be done using an electronic calculator.

EXAMPLE 2.3B

(i) $\sqrt{1425} = 37.749172$ ———— *Check* $37.749172^2 = 1425$

(ii) $\sqrt[5]{12\,960} = 6.645398$ ———— *Check* $6.645398^5 = 12\,960$

(iii) $\sqrt[15]{40\,000} = 2.026768$ ———— *Check* $2.026768^{15} = 40\,000$

(iv) $\sqrt[20]{1\,048\,576} = 2$ ———— *Check* $2^{20} = 1\,048\,576$

(v) $\sqrt{0.005184} = 0.072$ ———— *Check* $0.072^2 = 0.005184$

(vi) $\sqrt[7]{0.038468} = 0.627872$ ———— *Check* $0.627872^7 = 0.038468$

(vii) $\sqrt[45]{1.954213} = 1.015$ ———— *Check* $1.015^{45} = 1.954213$

(viii) $\sqrt[36]{0.022528} = 0.9$ ———— *Check* $0.9^{36} = 0.022528$

(ix) $\sqrt{2^6} = \sqrt{64} = 8$

(x) $\sqrt[3]{5^6} = \sqrt[3]{15\,625} = 25$

EXAMPLE 2.3C

Calculate i in the formula $FV = PV(1 + i)^n$, where $FV = 1102.50$, $PV = 1000.00$, $n = 2$.

SOLUTION

$1102.50 = 1000.00(1 + i)^2$ ——————— divide both sides by 1000.00

$(1 + i)^2 = 1.1025$

$(1 + i) = 1.1025^{0.5}$ ——————— raise both sides to the power 1/2, that is, 0.5

$(1 + i) = 1.05$

$i = 0.05$

B. Fractional exponents

Radicals may be written in exponential form and fractional exponents may be represented in radical form according to the following definitions.

(a) The exponent is a positive fraction with numerator 1.

$$\boxed{a^{\frac{1}{n}} = \sqrt[n]{a}}$$ ——————— Formula 2.8

$$4^{\frac{1}{2}} = \sqrt{4} = 2$$

$$27^{\frac{1}{3}} = \sqrt[3]{27} = \sqrt[3]{3^3} = 3$$

$$625^{\frac{1}{4}} = \sqrt[4]{625} = \sqrt[4]{5^4} = 5$$

(b) The exponent is a negative fraction with numerator 1.

$$\boxed{a^{-\frac{1}{n}} = \frac{1}{a^{\frac{1}{n}}} = \frac{1}{\sqrt[n]{a}}}$$ ——————— Formula 2.9

$$8^{-\frac{1}{3}} = \frac{1}{8^{\frac{1}{3}}} = \frac{1}{\sqrt[3]{8}} = \frac{1}{\sqrt[3]{2^3}} = \frac{1}{2}$$

$$243^{-\frac{1}{5}} = \frac{1}{243^{\frac{1}{5}}} = \frac{1}{\sqrt[5]{243}} = \frac{1}{\sqrt[5]{3^5}} = \frac{1}{3}$$

(c) The exponent is a positive or negative fraction with numerator other than 1.

$$\boxed{a^{\frac{m}{n}} = \sqrt[n]{a^m} = (\sqrt[n]{a})^m}$$ ——————— Formula 2.10

$$\boxed{a^{-\frac{m}{n}} = \frac{1}{a^{\frac{m}{n}}} = \frac{1}{\sqrt[n]{a^m}}}$$ ——————— Formula 2.11

$$16^{\frac{3}{4}} = \sqrt[4]{16^3} = (\sqrt[4]{16})^3 = (\sqrt[4]{2^4})^3 = (2)^3 = 8$$

$$27^{\frac{4}{3}} = \sqrt[3]{27^4} = (\sqrt[3]{27})^4 = (\sqrt[3]{3^3})^4 = (3)^4 = 81$$

$$36^{-\frac{3}{2}} = \frac{1}{(\sqrt{36})^3} = \frac{1}{(\sqrt{6^2})^3} = \frac{1}{6^3} = \frac{1}{216}$$

EXAMPLE 2.3D

(i) $36^{\frac{3}{2}} = 36^{1.5} = 216$

(ii) $3^{\frac{5}{4}} = 3^{1.25} = 3.948222$

(iii) $\sqrt[5]{12} = 12^{\frac{1}{5}} = 12^{0.2} = 1.643752$

(iv) $\sqrt[8]{325^5} = 325^{\frac{5}{8}} = 325^{0.625} = 37.147287$

(v) $\sqrt[6]{1.075} = 1.075^{\frac{1}{6}} = 1.075^{0.16\dot{6}} = 1.012126.$

A. Use an electronic calculator equipped with a power function to compute each of the following, correct to four decimals.

1. $\sqrt{5184}$

2. $\sqrt{205.9225}$

3. $\sqrt[7]{2187}$

4. $\sqrt[10]{1.1046221}$

5. $\sqrt[20]{4.3184}$

6. $\sqrt[16]{0.00001526}$

7. $\sqrt[6]{1.0825}$

8. $\sqrt[12]{1.15}$

B. Compute each of the following.

1. $3025^{\frac{1}{2}}$

2. $2401^{\frac{1}{4}}$

3. $525.21875^{\frac{2}{5}}$

4. $21.6^{\frac{4}{3}}$

5. $\sqrt[12]{1.125^7}$

6. $\sqrt[6]{1.095}$

7. $4^{-\frac{1}{3}}$

8. $1.06^{-\frac{1}{12}}$

9. $\dfrac{1.03^{60} - 1}{0.03}$

10. $\dfrac{1 - 1.05^{-36}}{0.05}$

11. $(1 + 0.08)^{10}$

12. $(1 + 0.045)^{-12}$

13. $26.50(1 + 0.043)\left[\dfrac{(1 + 0.043)^{30} - 1}{0.043}\right]$

14. $350.00(1 + 0.05)\left[\dfrac{(1 + 0.05)^{20} - 1}{0.05}\right]$

15. $133.00\left[\dfrac{1 - (1 + 0.056)^{-12}}{0.056}\right]$

16. $270.00\left[\dfrac{1 - (1 + 0.035)^{-8}}{0.035}\right]$

17. $5000.00(1 + 0.0275)^{-20} + 137.50\left[\dfrac{1 - (1 + 0.0275)^{-20}}{0.0275}\right]$

18. $1000.00(1 + 0.03)^{-16} + 300.00\left[\dfrac{1 - (1 + 0.03)^{-16}}{0.03}\right]$

19. Evaluate the value of i $112.55 = 100.00(1 + i)^4$

20. Evaluate the value of i $380.47 = 300.00(1 + i)^{12}$

21. Evaluate the value of i $3036.77 = 2400.00(1 + i)^6$

22. Evaluate the value of i $1453.36 = 800.00(1 + i)^{60}$

2.4 LOGARITHMS—BASIC ASPECTS
A. The concept of logarithm

In Section 2.2 and Section 2.3, the exponential form of writing numbers was discussed.

$64 = 2^6$ ⟶ the number 64 is represented as a power of 2

$243 = 3^5$ ⟶ the number 243 is represented as a power of 3

$10\ 000 = 10^4 \longrightarrow$ the number 10 000 is represented as a power of 10
$5 = 125^{\frac{1}{3}} \longrightarrow$ the number 5 is represented as a power of 125
$0.001 = 10^{-3} \longrightarrow$ the number 0.001 is represented as a power of 10

Some expressions from mathematics of finance involve solving an equation for the value of the unknown exponent. Logarithms will enable you to do this.

In general, when a number is represented as a base raised to an exponent, the exponent is called a logarithm. A **logarithm** is defined as the *exponent* to which a base must be raised to produce a given number.

Accordingly,

$64 = 2^6 \longrightarrow$ 6 is the logarithm of 64 to the base 2, written $6 = \log_2 64$
$243 = 3^5 \longrightarrow$ 5 is the logarithm of 243 to the base 3, written $5 = \log_3 243$
$10\ 000 = 10^4 \longrightarrow$ 4 is the logarithm of 10 000 to the base 10, written $4 = \log_{10} 10\ 000$
$5 = 125^{\frac{1}{3}} \longrightarrow$ ⅓ is the logarithm of 5 to the base 125, written $⅓ = \log_{125} 5$
$0.001 = 10^{-3} \longrightarrow -3$ is the logarithm of 0.001 to the base 10, written $-3 = \log_{10} 0.001$

The equation $y = 2^x$ is written as $x = \log_2 y$ when written in logarithmic form. This means that if $y = 8$, we ask "what power of 2 gives us 8?" Then knowing that $2^3 = 8$, we determine that $x = 3$, and therefore, $3 = \log_2 8$. (Notice that the base is the same in the exponential and logarithmic forms).

Logarithmic functions are the inverse of exponential functions. Note that the x and y coordinates of inverse functions are interchanged. As a result, the graphs of inverse functions are mirror images of each other in the line $x = y$.

In general, if $N = b^x$ (*exponential* form)

$$\boxed{\text{NUMBER} = \text{BASE}^{\text{to the EXPONENT}}}$$

then $x = \log_b N$ (*logarithmic* form).

$$\boxed{\text{EXPONENT} = \log_{\text{BASE}}{}^{\text{NUMBER}}}$$

$\log_3 81 = 4$ has base 3, exponent 4, and number 81, and therefore $3^4 = 81$.
$\log_7(1/49) = -2$ has base 7, exponent −2, and number 1/49, and therefore $1/49 = 7^{-2}$.

Figure 2.1 For example, if (0,1) is a point on the graph of an exponential function, then (1,0) would be the corresponding point on the graph of the inverse logarithmic function. (© S. A. Hummelbrunner)

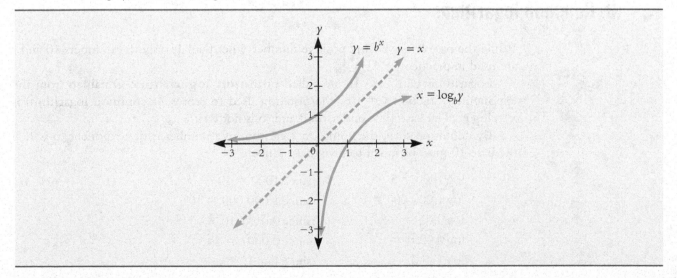

EXAMPLE 2.4A

Write each of the following numbers in exponential form and in logarithmic form using the base indicated.

(i) 32 base 2   (ii) 81 base 3

(iii) 256 base 4   (iv) 100 000 base 10

(v) 6 base 36   (vi) 3 base 27

(vii) 0.0001 base 10   (viii) $\dfrac{1}{8}$ base 2

SOLUTION

Exponential Form   **Logarithmic Form**

(i) Since $32 = 2 \times 2 \times 2 \times 2 \times 2$
$$32 = 2^5 \qquad\qquad\qquad\qquad\qquad 5 = \log_2 32$$

(ii) Since $81 = 3 \times 3 \times 3 \times 3$
$$81 = 3^4 \qquad\qquad\qquad\qquad\qquad 4 = \log_3 81$$

(iii) Since $256 = 4 \times 4 \times 4 \times 4$
$$256 = 4^4 \qquad\qquad\qquad\qquad\qquad 4 = \log_4 256$$

(iv) Since $100\,000 = 10 \times 10 \times 10 \times 10 \times 10$
$$100\,000 = 10^5 \qquad\qquad\qquad\qquad 5 = \log_{10} 100\,000$$

(v) Since $6 = \sqrt{36}$
$$6 = 36^{\frac{1}{2}} \qquad\qquad\qquad\qquad\qquad \frac{1}{2} = \log_{36} 6$$

(vi) Since $3 = \sqrt[3]{327}$
$$3 = 27^{\frac{1}{3}} \qquad\qquad\qquad\qquad\qquad \frac{1}{3} = \log_{27} 3$$

(vii) Since $0.0001 = \dfrac{1}{10\,000} = \dfrac{1}{10^4}$
$$0.0001 = 10^{-4} \qquad\qquad\qquad\qquad -4 = \log_{10} 0.0001$$

(viii) Since $\dfrac{1}{8} = \dfrac{1}{2^3}$
$$\frac{1}{8} = 2^{-3} \qquad\qquad\qquad\qquad\qquad -3 = \log_2 \frac{1}{8}$$

B. Common logarithms

While the base b may be any positive number other than 1, only the numbers 10 and e are used in practice.

Logarithms with base 10 are called **common logarithms**. Obtained from the exponential function $y = 10^x$, the notation used to represent common logarithms is $x = \log y$. (The base 10 is understood and so is not written.)

By definition then, the common logarithm of a number is the exponent to which the base 10 must be raised to give that number.

$$\log 1000 = 3 \qquad\qquad \text{since } 1000 = 10^3$$
$$\log 1\,000\,000 = 6 \qquad \text{since } 1\,000\,000 = 10^6$$
$$\log 0.01 = -2 \qquad\qquad \text{since } 0.01 = 10^{-2}$$
$$\log 0.0001 = -4 \qquad\quad \text{since } 0.0001 = 10^{-4}$$
$$\log 1 = 0 \qquad\qquad\quad\; \text{since } 1 = 10^0$$

Historically, common logarithms were used for numerical calculations that were required in problems involving compound interest. However, with the availability of electronic calculators equipped with a power function, the need for common logarithms as a computational tool has disappeared. Accordingly, this text gives no further consideration to common logarithms.

C. Natural logarithms

The most common exponential function is

$$y = e^x$$

where $e = \underset{n \to \infty}{\text{limit}} \left(1 + \dfrac{1}{n} \right)^n = 2.718282$, approximately.

The logarithmic form of this function is $x = \log_e y$ but is always written as $x = \ln y$ and called the **natural logarithm**.

The symbol e represents a special number (or constant) in mathematics. Like π, it is an irrational number with a non-terminating decimal so we can never know its exact value. e is present when "growth" is involved.

Electronic calculators equipped with the universal power function are generally equipped as well with the e^x function and the ln x function (natural logarithm function). This latter function eliminates any need for common logarithms and can be used when solving equations for which the unknown quantity is an exponent. As you will see in Chapters 9 through 16, the natural logarithm function will be used to solve for n, the number of compounding periods, in mathematics of finance applications using the algebraic method.

POINTERS & PITFALLS

In some calculator models, such as the Texas Instruments BA II PLUS, the natural logarithm function is found *directly* by entering the number and pressing the ⎍LN⎍ key. In other calculators, the natural logarithm function is found *indirectly* by entering the number and pressing combinations of keys.

For the Texas Instruments BA II PLUS calculator, enter the number, and then press the ⎍LN⎍ key.

For the Hewlett-Packard 10bII+ calculator, enter the number, and then press the keys ⎍↓⎍ ⎍2⎍.

For the Sharp EL-738C, press the 2nd key ⎍ln⎍, and then enter the number, and then press ⎍2nd F⎍ ⎍1/x⎍.

EXAMPLE 2.4B   Use an electronic calculator equipped with the natural logarithm key ⎍LN⎍ to determine the value of each of the following.

    (i) ln 2   (ii) ln 3000   (iii) ln 0.5

    (iv) ln 1   (v) ln 0.0125   (vi) ln 2.718282

SOLUTION   (i) To evaluate ln 2 (using the Texas Instruments BA II PLUS),

    1. Key in 2.

    2. Press ⎍LN⎍.

    3. Read the answer in the display.

        ln 2 = 0.693147

(ii) To evaluate ln 3000 (using the Sharp EL-738C), press 2nd F, press 2, key in 3000, press = and read the answer in the display.

$$\ln 3000 = 8.006368$$

(iii) $\ln 0.5 = -0.693147$

(iv) $\ln 1 = 0$

(v) $\ln 0.0125 = -4.382027$

(vi) $\ln 2.718282 = 1$

Note: 1. The natural logarithm of 1 is zero.
   2. The natural logarithm of a number greater than 1 is positive; for example, $\ln 2 = 0.693147$.
   3. The natural logarithm of a number less than 1 is negative; for example, $\ln 0.5 = -0.693147$.

D. Useful relationships

Since a logarithm is an exponent, it follows the laws of exponents. These relationships are helpful when using natural logarithms:

1. The logarithm of a product of two or more positive numbers is the sum of the logarithms of the factors.

$$\boxed{\ln (ab) = \ln a + \ln b} \text{———————— Formula 2.12}$$

By extension,

$$\boxed{\ln (abc) = \ln a + \ln b + \ln c} \text{———————— is true.}$$

2. The logarithm of the quotient of two positive numbers is equal to the logarithm of the dividend (numerator) minus the logarithm of the divisor (denominator).

$$\boxed{\ln \left(\frac{a}{b} \right) = \ln a - \ln b} \text{———————— Formula 2.13}$$

3. The logarithm of a power of a positive number is the exponent of the power multiplied by the logarithm of the number.

$$\boxed{\ln (a^k) = k(\ln a)} \text{———————— Formula 2.14}$$

4.   (i) $\ln e = 1$ since $e = e^1$
     (ii) $\ln 1 = 0$ since $1 = e^0$

EXAMPLE 2.4C   Use an electronic calculator equipped with the natural logarithm function to evaluate each of the following.

(i) $\ln \left[3(15)(36) \right]$

(ii) $\ln \left[\left(\dfrac{5000}{1.045} \right) \right]$

(iii) $\ln\left[1500(1.05^6)\right]$

(iv) $\ln\left[5000(1.045^{-1})\right]$

(v) $\ln\left[\left(\dfrac{4000}{1.07^{12}}\right)\right]$

(vi) $\ln\left[10\,000(1.0125^{-17})\right]$

(vii) $\ln\left[1.00e^7\right]$

(viii) $\ln(2.00e^{-0.6})$

(ix) $\ln\left[600\left(\dfrac{1.04^6 - 1}{0.04}\right)\right]$

(x) $\left[\left(\dfrac{1 - 1.0625^{-12}}{0.0625}\right)\right]$

SOLUTION

(i) $\ln\left[3(15)(36)\right] = \ln 3 + \ln 15 + \ln 36$
$$= 1.098612 + 2.708050 + 3.583519$$
$$= 7.390181$$

Check You can verify the answer by first simplifying.

$\ln 3(15)(36) = \ln 1620 = 7.390181$

(ii) $\ln\left[\left(\dfrac{5000}{1.045}\right)\right] = \ln 5000 - \ln 1.045$
$$= 8.517193 - 0.044017$$
$$= 8.473176$$

(iii) $\ln\left[1500(1.05^6)\right] = \ln 1500 + \ln 1.05^6$
$$= \ln 1500 + 6(\ln 1.05)$$
$$= 7.313220 + 6(0.048790)$$
$$= 7.313220 + 0.292741$$
$$= 7.605961$$

(iv) $\ln\left[5000(1.045^{-1})\right] = \ln 5000 + \ln 1.045^{-1}$
$$= \ln 5000 - 1(\ln 1.045)$$
$$= 8.517193 - 1(0.044017)$$
$$= 8.473176$$

(v) $\ln\left[\left(\dfrac{4000}{1.07^{12}}\right)\right] = \ln 4000 - \ln 1.07^{12}$
$$= 8.294050 - 12(0.067659)$$
$$= 8.294050 - 0.811904$$
$$= 7.482146$$

(vi) $\ln\left[10\,000(1.0125^{-17})\right] = \ln 10\,000 - 17(\ln 1.0125)$
$$= 9.210340 - 17(0.012423)$$
$$= 9.210340 - 0.211183$$
$$= 8.999158$$

(vii) $\ln\left[1.00e^7\right] = \ln 1.00 + \ln e^7$
$$= \ln 1.00 + 7(\ln e)$$
$$= 0 + 7(1)$$
$$= 7$$

(viii) $\ln\left[2.00e^{-0.6}\right] = \ln 2.00 + \ln e^{-0.6}$

$= \ln 2.00 - 0.6(\ln e)$

$= 0.693147 - 0.6$

$= 0.093147$

(ix) $\ln\left[600\left(\dfrac{1.04^6 - 1}{0.04}\right)\right] = \ln 600 + \ln\left(\dfrac{1.04^6 - 1}{0.04}\right)$

$= \ln 600 + \ln(1.04^6 - 1) - \ln 0.04$

$= \ln 600 + \ln(1.265319 - 1) - \ln 0.04$

$= \ln 600 + \ln 0.265319 - \ln 0.04$

$= 6.396930 - 1.326822 - (-3.218876)$

$= 6.396930 - 1.326822 + 3.218876$

$= 8.288984$

(x) $\ln\left[\left(\dfrac{1 - 1.0625^{-12}}{0.0625}\right)\right] = \ln(1 - 1.0625^{-12}) - \ln 0.0625$

$= \ln(1 - 0.483117) - \ln 0.0625$

$= \ln 0.516883 - \ln 0.0625$

$= -0.659939 - (-2.772589)$

$= -0.659939 + 2.772589$

$= 2.112650$

EXERCISE 2.4

MyLab Math

A. Express each of the following in logarithmic form.

1. $2^9 = 512$

2. $3^7 = 2187$

3. $5^{-3} = \dfrac{1}{125}$

4. $10^{-5} = 0.00001$

5. $e^{2j} = 18$

6. $e^{-3x} = 12$

B. Write each of the following in exponential form.

1. $\log_2 32 = 5$

2. $\log_3 \dfrac{1}{81} = -4$

3. $\log_{10} 10 = 1$

4. $\ln e^2 = 2$

C. Use an electronic calculator equipped with a natural logarithm function to evaluate each of the following.

1. $\ln 2$ **2.** $\ln 200$

3. $\ln 0.105$ **4.** $\ln\left[300(1.10^{15})\right]$

5. $\ln\left(\dfrac{2000}{1.09^9}\right)$ **6.** $\ln\left[850\left(\dfrac{1.01^{-120}}{0.01}\right)\right]$

BUSINESS MATH **NEWS**

What Is Dollar-Cost Averaging?

Dollar-cost averaging is an investment strategy that can help smooth out the effect of market fluctuations. It occurs when investors invest a constant dollar amount of money on a regular basis (weekly, bi-weekly, monthly, etc.). The result of dollar-cost averaging is that more shares are purchased when the share price is low and fewer shares are purchased when share prices are high. In theory, the average cost per share should be lower than the average share price over time.

Hypothetical Illustration of Dollar-Cost Averaging

The example below shows that when investing for 12 months, average cost per share is lower than the current cost per share.

Investment Date	Amount invested ($)	Share price ($)	# of shares purchased
January	100	10.00	10.000
February	100	9.78	10.225
March	100	10.40	9.615
April	100	9.62	10.395
May	100	10.50	9.524
June	100	10.75	9.302
July	100	9.87	10.132
August	100	10.75	9.302
September	100	11.10	9.009
October	100	11.50	8.696
November	100	11.30	8.849
December	100	11.25	8.888

The chart above is intended to illustrate the mathematical principle of dollar-cost averaging. This hypothetical example is for illustrative purposes only and doesn't represent any specific type of investment. It doesn't include the impact of expenses or fees, which would have reduced the results of the illustration.

Source: www.desjardinsagent.com

The Royal Bank has identified the following advantages to dollar-cost averaging for the majority of investors:

- Setting up an automatic investment program can help build good financial habits.
- Dollar-cost averaging is an accessible way to get comfortable with investing without making a large financial commitment.
- Investors can start smaller and benefit from market growth over the long-term.

However, investors beware. Dollar-cost averaging does not ensure a profit or protect against loss.

QUESTIONS

1. Calculate the average cost per share in the example above and compare it to the current cost per share.
2. Average cost calculations can also be performed to determine the average share price paid for a security with multiple buys. Compute the average cost per share for the following three purchases:
   (a) 10 shares purchased at $17;
   (b) 15 shares purchased at $16; and
   (c) 20 shares purchased at $16.50.

(Continued)

3. A couple wanted to invest $15 000 over the next three months, and was trying to decide whether to invest it all at once, or to allocate $5 000 at the start of every month. Describe the effect of dollar-cost averaging if the price of the investment rose from $25 per share in the first month, to $32 per share in the second month, and then fell to $20 per share in the third month before returning to its original $25 price at the end of the third month.

4. Studies have shown that lump-sum investments always perform better on average than dollar-cost averaging. Why do you believe this is the case?

Source: https://www.desjardinsagents.com/finances/financial-tools-resources/investing-basics/dollar-cost-averaging, accessed March 17, 2019; https://www6.royalbank.com, accessed March 16, 2019.

2.5 SOLVING BASIC EQUATIONS
A. Basic terms and concepts

1. An **equation** is a statement of equality between two algebraic expressions.

$$7x = 35$$
$$3a - 4 = 11 - 2a$$
$$5(2k - 4) = -3(k + 2)$$

2. If an equation contains only one *variable* and the variable occurs with power 1 only, the equation is said to be a **linear** or **first-degree equation** in one unknown. The three equations listed above are linear equations in one unknown.

3. The two expressions that are equated are called the sides or **members of an equation**. Every equation has a left side (left member) and a right side (right member).

In the equation $3a - 4 = 11 - 2a$,
$3a - 4$ is the left side (left member) and
$11 - 2a$ is the right side (right member).

4. The process of finding a replacement value (number) for the variable, which when substituted into the equation makes the two members of the equation equal, is called *solving the equation*. The replacement value that makes the two members equal is called a *solution* or **root of an equation**. A linear or first-degree equation has only one root and the root, when substituted into the equation, is said to *satisfy* the equation.

The root (solution) of the equation $3a - 4 = 11 - 2a$
is 3 because when 3 is substituted for a
the left side $3a - 4 = 3(3) - 4 = 9 - 4 = 5$ and
the right side $11 - 2a = 11 - 2(3) = 11 - 6 = 5$.

Thus, for $a = 3$, left side = right side and 3 satisfies the equation.

5. Equations that have the same root are called **equivalent equations**. Thus,

$$6x + 5 = 4x + 17, \, 6x = 4x + 12, \, 2x = 12, \text{ and } x = 6$$

are equivalent equations because the root of all four equations is 6; that is, when 6 is substituted for x, each of the equations is satisfied.

Equivalent equations are useful in solving equations. They may be obtained

(a) by multiplying or dividing both sides of the equation by a number other than zero; and

(b) by adding or subtracting the same number on both sides of the equation.

6. When solving an equation, the basic aims in choosing the operations that will generate useful equivalent equations are to

(a) isolate the terms containing the variable on one side of the equation (this is achieved by addition or subtraction); and

(b) make the numerical coefficient of the single term containing the variable equal to $+1$ (this is achieved by multiplication or division).

POINTERS
& PITFALLS

Equations are like balances. When one thing is added, subtracted, multiplied, or divided on one side of the equation, the same must also be done to the other side of the equation to maintain equality. Addition and subtraction are inverse operations, and multiplication and division are inverse operations.

Examples	To isolate for x
$x + 4 = 12$	Subtract 4 from each side—the inverse of addition
$x - 3 = 9$	Add 3 to both sides—the inverse of subtraction
$2x = 10$	Divide both sides by 2—the inverse of multiplication
$x/3 = 12$	Multiply both sides by 3—the inverse of division

B. Solving equations using addition

If the same number is added to each side of an equation, the resulting equation is equivalent to the original equation.

$$x - 5 = 4 \text{ —————————— original equation}$$

add 3 $\quad x - 5 + 3 = 4 + 3$
or add 5 $\quad x - 5 + 5 = 4 + 5$ $\Big\}$ —————————— equivalent equations

Addition is used to isolate the term or terms containing the variable when terms that have a negative coefficient appear in the equation.

EXAMPLE 2.5A

(i) $\quad\quad x - 6 = 4$ ———— add 6 to each side of the equation
$x - 6 + 6 = 4 + 6$ ———— to eliminate the term -6 on the left
$\quad\quad\quad x = 10$ ———— side of the equation

(ii) $\quad\quad -2x = -3 - 3x$
$-2x + 3x = -3 - 3x + 3x$ ———— add $3x$ to each side to eliminate the
$\quad\quad\quad x = -3$ ———— term $-3x$ on the right side

$$(iii) \quad -x - 5 = 8 - 2x \qquad \text{add 5 to eliminate the constant } -5$$
$$-x - 5 + 5 = 8 - 2x + 5 \qquad \text{on the left side}$$
$$-x = 13 - 2x \qquad \text{combine like terms}$$
$$-x + 2x = 13 - 2x + 2x \qquad \text{add } 2x \text{ to eliminate the term } -2x$$
$$x = 13 \qquad \text{on the right side}$$

C. Solving equations using subtraction

If the same number is subtracted from each side of an equation, the resulting equation is equivalent to the original equation.

$$x + 8 = 9 \qquad \text{original equation}$$

subtract 4 $x + 8 - 4 = 9 - 4$ ⎱ — equivalent equations
or subtract 8 $x + 8 - 8 = 9 - 8$ ⎰

Subtraction is used to isolate the term or terms containing the variable when terms having a positive numerical coefficient appear in the equation.

EXAMPLE 2.5B

$$(i) \quad x + 10 = 6$$
$$x + 10 - 10 = 6 - 10 \qquad \text{subtract 10 from each side of the}$$
$$x = -4 \qquad \text{equation}$$

$$(ii) \quad 7x = 9 + 6x$$
$$7x - 6x = 9 + 6x - 6x \qquad \text{subtract } 6x \text{ from each side to eliminate}$$
$$x = 9 \qquad \text{the term } 6x \text{ on the right side}$$

$$(iii) \quad 6x + 4 = 5x - 3$$
$$6x + 4 - 4 = 5x - 3 - 4 \qquad \text{subtract 4 from each side to eliminate}$$
$$\qquad \text{the term 4 on the left side}$$
$$6x = 5x - 7 \qquad \text{combine like terms}$$
$$6x - 5x = 5x - 7 - 5x \qquad \text{subtract } 5x \text{ from each side of the}$$
$$x = -7 \qquad \text{equation to eliminate the term } 5x$$
$$\qquad \text{on the right side}$$

D. Solving equations using multiplication

If each side of an equation is multiplied by the same non-zero number, the resulting equation is equivalent to the original equation.

$$-3x = 6 \qquad \text{original equation}$$

multiply by 2 $-6x = 12$ ⎱ — equivalent equations
or multiply by -1 $3x = -6$ ⎰

Multiplication is used in solving equations containing common fractions to eliminate the denominator or denominators.

EXAMPLE 2.5C

$$(i) \quad \frac{1}{2}x = 3 \qquad \text{original equation}$$

$$2\left(\frac{1}{2}x\right) = 2(3) \qquad \text{multiply each side by 2 to eliminate}$$
$$\qquad \text{the denominator}$$
$$x = 6 \qquad \text{solution}$$

(ii) $-\dfrac{1}{4}x = 2$ —————————— original equation

$$4\left(-\dfrac{1}{4}x\right) = 4(2)$$ —————————— multiply each side by 4 to eliminate the denominator

$$-1x = 8$$
$$(-1)(-x) = (-1)(8)$$ —————————— multiply by (-1) to make the coefficient of the term in x positive
$$x = -8$$

(iii) $-\dfrac{1}{7}x = -2$

$$(-7)\left(-\dfrac{1}{7}x\right) = (-7)(-2)$$ —————————— multiply by (-7) to eliminate the denominator and to make the coefficient of x equal to $+1$

$$x = 14$$

E. Solving equations using division

If each side of an equation is divided by the same non-zero number, the resulting equation is equivalent to the original equation.

$$15x = 45$$ —————————— original equation

divide by 3 $5x = 15$
or divide by 5 $3x = 9$ } —————————— equivalent equations
or divide by 15 $x = 3$

Division is used in solving equations when the numerical coefficient of the single term containing the variable is an integer or a decimal fraction.

EXAMPLE 2.5D

(i) $12x = 36$ —————————— original equation

$$\dfrac{\cancel{12}x}{\cancel{12}} = \dfrac{36}{12}$$ —————————— divide each side by the numerical coefficient 12

$$x = 3$$ —————————— solution

(ii) $-7x = 42$

$$\dfrac{-7x}{-7} = \dfrac{42}{-7}$$ —————————— divide each side by the numerical coefficient 7

$$x = -6$$

(iii) $0.2x = 3$

$$\dfrac{0.2x}{0.2} = \dfrac{3}{0.2}$$

$$x = 15$$

(iv) $x - 0.3x = 14$

$$0.7x = 14$$ —————————— combine like terms

$$\dfrac{0.7x}{0.7} = \dfrac{14}{0.7}$$

$$x = 20$$

F. Using two or more operations to solve equations

When more than one operation is needed to solve an equation, the operations are usually applied as follows.

(a) First, use addition and subtraction to isolate the terms containing the variable on one side of the equation (usually the left side).

(b) Second, after combining like terms, use multiplication and division to make the coefficient of the term containing the variable equal to $+1$.

EXAMPLE 2.5E

(i)
$$7x - 5 = 15 + 3x$$
$$7x - 5 + 5 = 15 + 3x + 5 \quad\text{——— add 5}$$
$$7x = 20 + 3x \quad\text{——— combine like terms}$$
$$7x - 3x = 20 + 3x - 3x \quad\text{——— subtract } 3x$$
$$4x = 20$$
$$x = 5 \quad\text{——— divide by 4}$$

(ii)
$$3x + 9 - 7x = 24 - x - 3$$
$$9 - 4x = 21 - x \quad\text{——— combine like terms}$$
$$9 - 4x - 9 = 21 - x - 9$$
$$-4x = 12 - x$$
$$-4x + x = 12 - x + x$$
$$-3x = 12$$
$$x = -4$$

G. Checking equations

To check the solution to an equation, substitute the solution into each side of the equation and determine the value of each side.

EXAMPLE 2.5F

(i) For $7x - 5 = 15 + 3x$, the solution shown is $x = 5$.

Check that left side of the equation = right side of the equation.
LS $= 7x - 5 = 7(5) - 5 = 35 - 5 = 30$
RS $= 15 + 3x = 15 + 3(5) = 15 + 15 = 30$
Since LS $=$ RS, 5 is the solution.

(ii) For $3x + 9 - 7x = 24 - x - 3$, the solution shown is $x = -4$.

Check
LS $= 3(-4) + 9 - 7(-4) = -12 + 9 + 28 = 25$
RS $= 24 - (-4) - 3 = 24 + 4 - 3 = 25$
Since LS $=$ RS, -4 is the solution.

EXERCISE 2.5

MyLab Math

A. Solve each of the following equations.

 1. $15x = 45$ **2.** $-7x = 35$ **3.** $0.9x = 72$

4. $0.02x = 13$ **5.** $\dfrac{1}{6}x = 3$ **6.** $-\dfrac{1}{8}x = 7$

7. $\dfrac{3}{5}x = -21$ **8.** $-\dfrac{4}{3}x = -32$ **9.** $x - 3 = -7$

10. $-2x = 7 - 3x$ **11.** $x + 6 = -2$ **12.** $3x = 9 + 2x$

13. $4 - x = 9 - 2x$ **14.** $2x + 7 = x - 5$ **15.** $x + 0.6x = 32$

16. $x - 0.3x = 210$ **17.** $x - 0.04x = 192$ **18.** $x + 0.07x = 64.20$

B. Solve each of the following equations and check your solution.

1. $3x + 5 = 7x - 11$ **2.** $5 - 4x = -4 - x$

3. $2 - 3x - 9 = 2x - 7 + 3x$ **4.** $4x - 8 - 9x = 10 + 2x - 4$

5. $3x + 14 = 4x + 9$ **6.** $16x - 12 = 6x - 32$

7. $5 + 3 + 4x = 5x + 12 - 25$ **8.** $-3 + 2x + 5 = 5x - 36 + 14$

9. $x - 50 = 100 + 0.34x + 0.21x$ **10.** $\dfrac{x}{1 + 0.25 \times \dfrac{6}{12}} = \dfrac{2^3}{3^2}x$

2.6 SOLVING EQUATIONS INVOLVING ALGEBRAIC SIMPLIFICATION

A. Solving linear equations involving the product of integral constants and binomials

To solve this type of equation, multiply first, then simplify.

EXAMPLE 2.6A

(i) $3(2x - 5) = -5(7 - 2x)$

$6x - 15 = -35 + 10x$ —————————— expand

$6x - 10x = -35 + 15$ —————————— isolate the terms in x

$-4x = -20$

$x = 5$

Check

$LS = 3[2(5) - 5] = 3(10 - 5) = 3(5) = 15$

$RS = -5[7 - 2(5)] = -5(7 - 10) = -5(-3) = 15$

Since LS = RS, 5 is the solution.

(ii) $x - 4(3x - 7) = 3(9 - 5x) - (x - 11)$

$x - 12x + 28 = 27 - 15x - x + 11$ —————————— expand

$-11x + 28 = 38 - 16x$ —————————— combine like terms

$-11x + 16x = 38 - 28$ —————————— isolate the terms in x

$5x = 10$

$x = 2$

Check

$LS = 2 - 4[3(2) - 7]$ $\qquad\qquad$ $RS = 3[9 - 5(2)] - (2 - 11)$

$= 2 - 4(6 - 7)$ $\qquad\qquad\qquad\quad$ $= 3(9 - 10) - (-9)$

$= 2 - 4(-1)$ $\qquad\qquad\qquad\qquad$ $= 3(-1) + 9$

$= 2 + 4$ $\qquad\qquad\qquad\qquad\quad$ $= -3 + 9$

$= 6$ $\qquad\qquad\qquad\qquad\qquad$ $= 6$

Since LS = RS, 2 is the solution.

B. Solving linear equations containing common fractions

The best approach when solving equations containing common fractions is to first create an equivalent equation without common fractions. Refer to the Pointers and Pitfalls on page 79. Multiply each term of the equation by the lowest common denominator (LCD) of the fractions.

EXAMPLE 2.6B

(i)

$$\frac{4}{5}x - \frac{3}{4} = \frac{7}{12} + \frac{11}{15}x \quad\text{————————— LCD} = 60$$

$$\overset{12}{\cancel{60}}\left(\frac{4}{\cancel{5}}x\right) - \overset{15}{\cancel{60}}\left(\frac{3}{\cancel{4}}\right) = \overset{5}{\cancel{60}}\left(\frac{7}{\cancel{12}}\right) + \overset{4}{\cancel{60}}\left(\frac{11}{\cancel{15}}x\right) \quad\text{————— multiply each term by 60}$$

$$12(4x) - 15(3) = 5(7) + 4(11x) \quad\text{———— reduce to eliminate the}$$

$$\begin{aligned} 48x - 45 &= 35 + 44x \qquad\qquad\qquad\quad \text{fractions} \\ 48x - 44x &= 35 + 45 \\ 4x &= 80 \\ x &= 20 \end{aligned}$$

Check

$$LS = \frac{4}{5}(20) - \frac{3}{4} = 16 - 0.75 = 15.25$$

$$RS = \frac{7}{12} + \frac{11}{15}(20) = 0.58\dot{3} + 14.\dot{6} = 15.25$$

Since LS = RS, 20 is the solution.

(ii)

$$\frac{5}{8}x - 3 = \frac{3}{4} + \frac{5x}{6} \quad\text{————————— LCD} = 24$$

$$24\left(\frac{5x}{8}\right) - 24(3) = 24\left(\frac{3}{4}\right) + 24\left(\frac{5x}{6}\right)$$

$$\begin{aligned} 3(5x) - 72 &= 6(3) + 4(5x) \\ 15x - 72 &= 18 + 20x \\ -5x &= 90 \\ &= -18 \end{aligned}$$

Check

$$LS = \frac{5}{8}(-18) - 3 = -11.25 - 3 = -14.25$$

$$RS = \frac{3}{4} + \frac{5}{6}(-18) = 0.75 - 15 = -14.25$$

Since LS = RS, the solution is −18.

C. Solving linear equations involving fractional constants and multiplication

When solving this type of equation, the best approach is first to eliminate the fractions and then to expand.

EXAMPLE 2.6C

(i)
$$\frac{3}{2}(x-2) - \frac{2}{3}(2x-1) = 5 \quad\text{————— LCD = 6}$$

$$6\left(\frac{3}{2}\right)(x-2) - 6\left(\frac{2}{3}\right)(2x-1) = 6(5) \quad\text{————— multiply each side by 6}$$

$$3(3)(x-2) - 2(2)(2x-1) = 30 \quad\text{————— reduce to eliminate}$$
fractions
$$9(x-2) - 4(2x-1) = 30$$

$$9x - 18 - 8x + 4 = 30 \quad\text{————— expand}$$

$$x - 14 = 30$$

$$x = 44$$

Check

$$\text{LS} = \frac{3}{2}(44-2) - \frac{2}{3}(2 \times 44 - 1) = \frac{3}{2}(42) - \frac{2}{3}(87) = 63 - 58 = 5$$

$$\text{RS} = 5$$

Since LS = RS, 44 is the solution.

(ii)
$$-\frac{3}{5}(4x-1) + \frac{5}{8}(4x-3) = -\frac{11}{10} \quad\text{————— LCD = 40}$$

$$40\left(\frac{-3}{5}\right)(4x-1) + 40\left(\frac{5}{8}\right)(4x-3) = 40\left(\frac{-11}{10}\right) \quad\text{—— multiply each side by 40}$$

$$8(-3)(4x-1) + 5(5)(4x-3) = 4(-11)$$

$$-24(4x-1) + 25(4x-3) = -44$$

$$-96x + 24 + 100x - 75 = -44$$

$$4x - 51 = -44$$

$$4x = 7$$

$$x = \frac{7}{4}$$

Check

$$\text{LS} = -\frac{3}{5}\left[4\left(\frac{7}{4}\right) - 1\right] + \frac{5}{8}\left[4\left(\frac{7}{4}\right) - 3\right]$$

$$= -\frac{3}{5}(7-1) + \frac{5}{8}(7-3)$$

$$= -\frac{18}{5} + \frac{5}{2} = -\frac{36}{10} + \frac{25}{10} = -\frac{11}{10}$$

$$\text{RS} = -\frac{11}{10}$$

Since LS = RS, the solution is $\frac{7}{4}$.

POINTERS

& PITFALLS

When using a lowest common denominator (LCD) to eliminate fractions from an equation involving both fractional constants and multiplication, the LCD must be multiplied by each quantity (on *both* sides of the equation) that is preceded by a + or a − sign *outside of brackets*, as in Example 2.6C above. (Some students multiply the LCD by each quantity inside *and* outside the brackets, which leads to an answer *much* greater than the correct answer.)

D. Formula rearrangement

Formula rearrangement, also known as **formula manipulation**, is the process of rearranging the terms of an equation. To solve for a particular variable, we want the variable to stand alone on the left side of the equation. If it does not already do so, then we have to rearrange the terms. Developing your skill in rearranging formulas is very important because it saves a lot of time in memorization. You need only memorize one form of any particular formula. For example, consider the formula I = P*rt* in Chapter 7. Once we have memorized this formula, there is no need to memorize equivalent forms as long as we are skilled in formula rearrangement. Thus, for example, we need not "memorize" the form P = I/*rt*.

The key to formula manipulation is the concept of *undoing operations.* Addition and subtraction are *inverse operations* (i.e., they *undo* each other). To move a number that has been added on one side of an equation, subtract the number from both sides of the equation. To move a number that has been subtracted on one side of an equation, add the number to both sides of the equation.

Multiplication and division are also inverse operations. To move a number that has been multiplied on one side of an equation, divide by that number on both sides of the equation. To move a number that has been divided on one side of an equation, multiply by that number on both sides of the equation. Powers and roots are inverses too.

Before you begin formula rearrangement, study the formula to see where the variable you wish to isolate is located and what relationship it has with other variables in the formula. Rearrange the formula so that the variable you want is isolated on one side of the equal sign, with all other variables on the other side.

EXAMPLE 2.6D	Given $FV = PV(1 + i)^n$, solve for PV.

$$PV = \frac{FV}{(1 + i)^n}$$ —————— divide both sides by $(1 + i)^n$ and reverse members of the equation

EXAMPLE 2.6E	Given the formula $P = (pq - vq) - F$, solve for q.

$$P = (pq - vq) - F$$

$$P = q(p - v) - F$$ —————— isolate q

$$P + F = q(p - v)$$ —————— add F to both sides

$$q = \frac{P + F}{p - v}$$ —————— divide both sides by $(p - v)$ and reverse members of the equation

EXAMPLE 2.6F	Given $FV = PV(1 + i)^n$, solve for i.

$$FV = PV(1 + i)^n$$

$$\frac{FV}{PV} = (1 + i)^n$$ —————— divide both sides by PV

$$\sqrt[n]{\frac{FV}{PV}} = 1 + i$$ —————— taking a root is the undoing of a power

$$\sqrt[n]{\frac{FV}{PV}} - 1 = i$$ —————— subtract 1 from both sides

$$i = \sqrt[n]{\frac{FV}{PV}} - 1$$ —————— reverse members of the equation

EXERCISE 2.6

MyLab Math

A. Solve each of the following equations and check your solutions.

1. $12x - 4(9x - 20) = 320$

2. $5(x - 4) - 3(2 - 3x) = -54$

3. $3(2x - 5) - 2(2x - 3) = -15$

4. $17 - 3(2x - 7) = 7x - 3(2x - 1)$

5. $4x + 2(2x - 3) = 18$

6. $-3(1 - 11x) + (8x - 15) = 187$

7. $10x - 4(2x - 1) = 32$

8. $-2(x - 4) + 12(3 - 2x) = -8$

9. $x\left(1 + 0.12 \times \dfrac{65}{365}\right) = 1225.64$

10. $x + \dfrac{x}{1.25} + \dfrac{x}{(1.25)^2} = 3148 + \dfrac{1000}{(1.25)^3}$

B. Solve each of the following equations.

1. $x - \dfrac{1}{4}x = 15$

2. $x + \dfrac{5}{8}x = 26$

3. $\dfrac{2}{3}x - \dfrac{1}{4} = -\dfrac{7}{4} - \dfrac{5}{6}x$

4. $\dfrac{5}{3} - \dfrac{2}{5}x = \dfrac{1}{6}x - \dfrac{1}{30}$

5. $\dfrac{3}{4}x + 4 = \dfrac{113}{24} - \dfrac{2}{3}x$

6. $2 - \dfrac{3}{2}x = \dfrac{2}{3}x + \dfrac{31}{9}$

7. $1 - \dfrac{1}{3}x = 15 + \dfrac{2}{3}x$

8. $\dfrac{3x - 2}{5} = \dfrac{2x - 1}{3}$

9. $\dfrac{21}{8} - \dfrac{2}{5}x = \dfrac{11}{4}x - \dfrac{1}{10}$

10. $-\dfrac{2}{3}x - \dfrac{1}{12}x = \dfrac{3}{4} + \dfrac{1}{24}x$

C. Solve each of the following equations.

1. $\dfrac{3}{4}(2x - 1) - \dfrac{1}{3}(5 - 2x) = -\dfrac{55}{12}$

2. $\dfrac{4}{5}(4 - 3x) + \dfrac{53}{40} = \dfrac{3}{10}x - \dfrac{7}{8}(2x - 3)$

3. $\dfrac{2}{3}(2x - 1) - \dfrac{3}{4}(3 - 2x) = 2x - \dfrac{20}{9}$

4. $\dfrac{4}{3}(3x - 2) - \dfrac{3}{5}(4x - 3) = \dfrac{11}{60} + 3x$

5. $\dfrac{2}{3}(5x - 1) = -\dfrac{3}{5}(x + 2)$

D. Solve each of the following equations for the indicated variable.

1. $y = mx + b$ for x

2. $r = \dfrac{M}{S}$ for S

3. $PV = \dfrac{PMT}{i}$ for PMT

4. $I = Prt$ for t

5. $S = P(1 + rt)$ for r

6. $PV = FV(1 + i)^{-n}$ for i

7. $P = \dfrac{S}{(1 + rt)}$ for t

8. $N = L(1 - d)$ for d

9. $f = (1 + i)^m - 1$ for i

10. $FV = PV(1 + i)^n$ for n

2.7 SOLVING WORD PROBLEMS

One of the biggest fears of students is being asked to solve a "word problem." Ironically, word problems are the answer to the "What will I ever need this math for?" question. So think of those dreaded word problems as "practical applications." There are many different types of word problems, from money, to numbers, to mixtures, to when the train will get to the station, to who did the most work. Each type of problem has a specific method of solution, but a series of steps will get you through any word problem.

Before you begin the series of steps, read the problem. Then read the problem again. This is not as strange as it seems. The first reading tells you what type of question you are dealing with. It may involve money, or people, or products. The second reading is done to find out what the question is asking you and what specific information the question is giving you. It is often helpful to draw a diagram or make a chart to sort out the information in the question. To solve problems by means of an algebraic equation, follow the systematic procedure outlined below.

BEFORE STEP 1 *Read the problem* to determine what type of question you are dealing with. Then *read the problem again* to determine the specific information the question is giving you.

STEP 1 *Introduce the variable* to be used by means of a complete sentence. This ensures a clear understanding and a record of what the variable is intended to represent. The variable is usually the item that you are asked to find—the item you do not know until you solve the problem.

STEP 2 *Translate* the information in the problem statement in terms of the variable. Determine what the words are telling you in relationship to the math. Watch for key words such as "more than" or "less than," "reduced by," and "half of" or "twice."

STEP 3 *Set up* an algebraic equation. This usually means matching the algebraic expressions developed in Step 2 to a specific number. Often one side of the equation represents the total number of items described in the word problem.

STEP 4 *Solve* the equation by rearranging the variables, state a conclusion, and check the conclusion against the problem statement.

EXAMPLE 2.7A A TV set was sold during a sale for $575. What is the regular selling price of the set if the price of the set was reduced by $\frac{1}{6}$ of the regular price?

SOLUTION

STEP 1 *Introduce the variable.* Let the regular selling price be represented by $x.

STEP 2 *Translate.* The reduction in price is $\$\frac{1}{6}x$, and the reduced price is $\$\left(x - \frac{1}{6}x\right)$.

STEP 3 *Set up an equation.* Since the reduced price is given as $575,

$$x - \tfrac{1}{6}x = 575$$

STEP 4 *Solve* the equation, state a conclusion, and check.

$$\tfrac{5}{6}x = 575$$

$$x = \frac{6(575)}{5}$$

$$x = 690$$

The regular selling price is $690.

Check	Regular selling price	$690
	Reduction: $\frac{1}{6}$ of 690	115
	Reduced price	$575

EXAMPLE 2.7B

The material cost of a product is $4 less than twice the cost of the direct labour, and the overhead is $\frac{5}{6}$ of the direct labour cost. If the total cost of the product is $157, what is the amount of each of the three elements of cost?

SOLUTION

Three values are needed, and the variable could represent any of the three. However, problems of this type can be solved most easily by representing the proper item by the variable rather than by selecting any of the other items. The *proper* item is the one to which the other item or items are *directly related*. In this problem, direct labour is that item.

Let the cost of direct labour be represented by x; then the cost of material is $(2x - 4)$ and the cost of overhead is $\frac{5}{6}x$.

The total cost is $(x + 2x - 4 + \frac{5}{6}x)$.
Since the total cost is given as $157,

$$x + 2x - 4 + \tfrac{5}{6}x = 157$$
$$3x + \tfrac{5}{6}x = 161$$
$$18x + 5x = 966$$
$$23x = 966$$
$$x = 42$$

TOTAL COST	MATERIAL COST
	LABOUR COST
	OVERHEAD COST

Material cost is $80, direct labour cost is $42, and overhead is $35.

Check	Material cost: $2x - 4 = 2(42) - 4 =$	$80
	Direct labour cost: $x =$	42
	Overhead cost: $\frac{5}{6}x = \frac{5}{6}(42) =$	35
	Total cost	$157

EXAMPLE 2.7C

Nalini invested a total of $24 000 in two mutual funds. Her investment in the Equity Fund is $4000 less than three times her investment in the Bond Fund. How much did Nalini invest in the Equity Fund?

SOLUTION

Although the amount invested in the Equity Fund is required, it is more convenient to represent her investment in the Bond Fund by the variable, since the investment in the Equity Fund is expressed in terms of the investment in the Bond Fund.

Let the amount invested in the Bond Fund be x; then the amount invested in the Equity Fund is $(3x - 4000)$ and the total amount invested is $(x + 3x - 4000)$. Since the total amount invested is $24 000,

$$x + 3x - 4000 = 24\ 000$$
$$4x = 28\ 000$$
$$x = 7000$$

The amount invested in the Equity Fund is $3x - 4000 = 3(7000) - 4000 = \$17\,000$.

Check

Investment in Bond Fund	$7\,000
Investment in Equity Fund	17\,000
Total investment	$24\,000

EXAMPLE 2.7D

The Clarkson Soccer League has set a budget of $3840 for soccer balls. High-quality game balls cost $36 each, while lower-quality practice balls cost $20 each. If 160 balls are to be purchased, how many balls of each type can be purchased to use up exactly the budgeted amount?

SOLUTION

When, as in this case, the items referred to in the problem are not directly related, the variable may represent either item.

Let the quantity of game balls be represented by x; then the quantity of practice balls is $(160 - x)$.

Since the prices of the two types of balls differ, the total value of each type of ball must now be represented in terms of x.

The value of x game balls is $\$36x$;
the value of $(160 - x)$ practice balls is $\$20(160 - x)$;
the total value is $\$\left[36x + 20(160 - x)\right]$.

Since the total budgeted value is given as $3840,

$$36x + 20(160 - x) = 3840$$
$$36x + 3200 - 20x = 3840$$
$$16x = 640$$
$$x = 40$$

The quantity of game balls is 40 and the quantity of practice balls is 120.

Check

Quantity $40 + 120 =$	160
Value of game balls: $36(40) =$	$1440
Value of practice balls: $20(120) =$	$2400
Total value	$3840

EXAMPLE 2.7E

Last year, a repair shop used 1200 small rings. The shop paid $33\frac{1}{3}$ cents per ring for the first shipment and $37\frac{1}{2}$ cents per ring for the second shipment. If the total cost was $430, how many rings did the second shipment contain?

SOLUTION

Let the number of rings in the second shipment be x; then the number of rings in the first shipment was $1200 - x$. The cost of the second shipment was $\$0.37\frac{1}{2}x$ or $\$\frac{3}{8}x$, and the cost of the first shipment was $\$0.33\frac{1}{3}(1200 - x)$ or $\$\frac{1}{3}(1200 - x)$. The total cost is $\$\left[\frac{3}{8}x + \frac{1}{3}(1200 - x)\right]$. Since the total cost is $430,

$$\frac{3}{8}x + \frac{1}{3}(1200 - x) = 430$$

$$24\left(\frac{3}{8}x\right) + 24\left(\frac{1}{3}\right)(1200 - x) = 24(430)$$

$$3(3x) + 8(1200 - x) = 10\,320$$
$$9x + 9600 - 8x = 10\,320$$
$$x = 720$$

The second shipment consisted of 720 rings.

Check   Total number of rings: $720 + 480 = 1200$

$$\text{Total value: } 720\left(\frac{3}{8}\right) + 480\left(\frac{1}{3}\right)$$

$$= 90(3) + 160(1)$$
$$= 270 + 160$$
$$= \$430$$

POINTERS
& PITFALLS

Translating a Word Problem by Identifying Key Words

What are the key words in the problem and what are they asking you to do?

(a) "And" usually means "add." For example,
"Two times a number and three times a number totals $10 000"
would be translated as
$2x + 3x = 10\ 000$.

(b) "Less than" or "fewer than" usually means "subtract." For example,
"$3 less than ten times the amount"
would be translated as
$10x - 3$.

(c) "Reduced by" usually indicates the amount you are to subtract. For example,
"The regular selling price was reduced by 20% to compute the sale price"
would be translated as
$x - 20\%x = $ sales price, where the regular selling price would be x.

(d) "Reduced to" usually indicates the result after a subtraction. For example,
"When a regular selling price of $589 was reduced to $441.75, what was the discount?"
would be translated as
$589 - y\% \times 589 = 441.75$.

EXAMPLE 2.7F

An electronics manufacturer can fit either 8 laptops or 10 tablets into a standard box for shipping. In one shipment he sent a mix of laptops and tablets for a total of 96 items. If there were more laptops than tablets in the shipment, how many full boxes did he ship?

SOLUTION

Two values are needed, the number of boxes of laptops and the number of boxes of tablets, in order to determine the answer.

When, as in this case, we don't have the total number of boxes, we can establish a range for the total and then solve through trial and error, using a table of values for our variables.

Let the number of boxes of laptops be represented by L; let the number of boxes of tablets be represented by T.

The total number of items in the shipment is $8L + 10T = 96$.

Since 96 items were sent and there were more laptops than tablets, establish the high end of the range of boxes. An easy way to do this is to assume no tablets were shipped. Substitute 0 boxes of tablets into the equation for T:

$$8L + 10(0) = 96$$
$$8L + 0 = 96$$
$$L = 12$$

From this, we can conclude that L must be less than 12 (because tablets were indeed shipped). Also note that $8L$ must be greater than $10T$ since more laptops than tablets were shipped.

Using a table to organize our work, and substituting in values for the number of boxes of laptops, L, we find that there is only one solution that results in full boxes of electronics, satisfies our equation, and maintains the fact that $8L$ must be greater than $10T$:

L	$8L + 10T = 96$	$10T$	T
11	$8(11) + 10T = 96$	8	0.8
10	$8(10) + 10T = 96$	16	1.6
9	$8(9) + 10T = 96$	24	2.4
8	$8(8) + 10T = 96$	32	3.2
7	$8(7) + 10T = 96$	40	4.0
6	$8(6) + 10T = 96$	48	4.8

Therefore, the electronics manufacturer shipped 11 boxes in total: 7 boxes of laptops and 4 boxes of tablets.

EXERCISE 2.7  MyLab Math

For each of the following problems, set up an equation with one unknown and solve.

1. Hudson's Bay sold a sweater for $49.49. The selling price included a markup of three-fourths of the cost to the department store. What was the cost?

2. Electronics for Less Canada sold a stereo set during a sale for $576. Determine the regular selling price of the set if the price of the set had been reduced by one-third of the original regular selling price.

3. A client at a hair salon in Alberta paid a total of $36.75 for a haircut. The amount included 5% GST. What was the price of the haircut before the GST was added?

4. Some CDs were put on sale at 40% off. What was the regular price if the sale price was $11.34?

5. This month's commodity index decreased by one-twelfth of last month's index to 176. What was last month's index?

6. After an increase of one-eighth of his current hourly wage, Jean-Luc receives a new hourly wage of $15.75. How much was his hourly wage before the increase?

7. Tai's sales last week were $140 less than three times Vera's sales. What were Tai's sales if together their sales amounted to $940?

8. A metal pipe 90 centimetres long is cut into two pieces so that the longer piece is 15 centimetres longer than twice the length of the shorter piece. What is the length of the longer piece?

9. Jay purchased tickets for a concert over the Internet. To place the order, a handling charge of $18.40 per ticket was charged. GST of 5% was also charged on the ticket price and the handling charges. If the total charge for two tickets was $345.24, what was the cost per ticket?

10. Ken and Martina agreed to form a partnership. The partnership agreement requires that Martina invest $2500 more than two-thirds of what Ken is to invest. If the partnership's capital is to be $55 000, how much should Martina invest?

11. A furniture company has been producing 2320 chairs a day working two shifts. The second shift has produced 60 chairs fewer than four-thirds of the number of chairs produced by the first shift. Determine the number of chairs produced by the second shift.

12. An inventory of two types of floodlights showed a total of 60 lights valued at $2580. If Type A cost $40 each while Type B cost $50 each, how many Type B floodlights were in inventory?

13. A machine requires four hours to make a unit of Product A and 3 hours to make a unit of Product B. Last month the machine operated for 200 hours, producing a total of 60 units. How many units of Product A were produced?

14. Alick has saved $8.80 in nickels, dimes, and quarters. If he has four nickels fewer than three times the number of dimes, and one quarter more than three-fourths the number of dimes, how many coins of each type does Alick have?

15. The Hamilton amateur football club spent $1475 on tickets to a professional football game. If the club bought 10 more 8-dollar tickets than three times the number of 12-dollar tickets; and three fewer 15-dollar tickets than four-fifths the number of 12-dollar tickets, how many of each type of ticket did the club buy?

16. Giuseppi's Pizza had orders for $539 of pizzas. The prices for each size of pizza were as follows: large $18, medium $15, and small $11. If the number of large pizzas was one less than three times the number of medium pizzas, and the number of small pizzas was one more than twice the number of medium pizzas, how many of each size of pizza were ordered?

17. Sai paid Ontario income taxes of $6705.15 plus 22% of the amount by which his taxable income exceeded $44 701. If his tax bill was $7162.53, calculate Sai's taxable income.

18. Danielle invests part of her $3000 savings into a savings account at 3% and part into a GIC at 4.5% simple interest. If she earns $128.25 in interest from her two investments, calculate how much she invested at each rate.

19. Celestica Inc. employs 196 manufacturing employees. There are 3 shifts. Twice as many employees work on the first shift as on the second shift, and 12 fewer work on the third shift than on the second shift. Determine how many employees are on each shift.

20. Your company has introduced a stock option incentive program. A total of 171 000 options are available. Each senior manager will receive twice as many options as each team leader. Each team leader will receive 1.5 times the options of each employee. There are 7 senior managers, 22 team leaders, and 421 employees. How many options will each senior manager receive?

21. The Burnaby Spurs youth basketball organization spent $4320 on practice jerseys for all its teams. Twice as much money was spent on rep players as for recreational players, and the most common size was a Youth Large which cost the organization $10. Smaller sizes cost $8 and larger sizes cost $16. For its recreational players it ordered 50 Youth Small and 50 Youth Medium shirts. For its rep players it ordered no Youth Smalls, 10 fewer Youth Medium size shirts, three times as many Youth Large shirts, as well as an equal number of Adult Small and Adult Large shirts. How many players belong to the organization?

MyLab Math

Visit MyLab Math to practise any of this chapter's exercises marked with a 🌐 as often as you want. The guided solutions help you calculate an answer step by step. You'll find a personalized study plan and additional interactive resources to help you master Business Math!

REVIEW EXERCISE

1. LO❶ Simplify.

(a) $3x - 4y - 3y - 5x$ (b) $2x - 0.03x$

(c) $(5a - 4) - (3 - a)$

(d) $-(2x - 3y) - (-4x + y) + (y - x)$

(e) $(5a^2 - 2b - c) - (3c + 2b - 4a^2)$

(f) $-(2x - 3) - (x^2 - 5x + 2)$

🌐 **2. LO❶** Simplify.

(a) $3(-5a)$ (b) $-7m(-4x)$

(c) $14m \div (-2m)$ (d) $(-15a^2b) \div (5a)$

(e) $-6(-3x)(2y)$ (f) $4(-3a)(b)(-2c)$

(g) $-4(3x - 5y - 1)$ (h) $x(1 - 2x - x^2)$

(i) $(24x - 16) \div (-4)$ (j) $(21a^2 - 12a) \div 3a$

(k) $4(2a - 5) - 3(3 - 6a)$

(l) $2a(x - a) - a(3x + 2) - 3a(-5x - 4)$

(m) $(m - 1)(2m - 5)$

(n) $(3a - 2)(a^2 - 2a - 3)$

(o) $3(2x - 4)(x - 1) - 4(x - 3)(5x + 2)$

(p) $-2a(3m - 1)(m - 4)$
   $-5a(2m + 3)(2m - 3)$

3. LO❶ Evaluate each of the following for the values given.

(a) $3xy - 4x - 5y$ for $x = -2, y = 5$

(b) $-5(2a - 3b) - 2(a + 5b)$ for $a = -\dfrac{1}{4}, b = \dfrac{2}{3}$

(c) $\dfrac{2NC}{P(n + 1)}$ for N = 12, C = 432,
   P = 1800, $n = 35$

(d) $\dfrac{365I}{rP}$ for I = 600, $r = 0.15$, P = 7300

(e) $A(1 - dt)$ for A = \$720, $d = 0.135, t = \dfrac{280}{365}$

(f) $\dfrac{S}{1 + rt}$ for S = 2755, $r = 0.17, t = \dfrac{219}{365}$

🌐 **4. LOs❷ ❸** Simplify.

(a) $(-3)^5$ (b) $\left(\dfrac{2}{3}\right)^4$

(c) $(-5)^0$ (d) $(-3)^{-1}$

(e) $\left(\dfrac{2}{5}\right)^{-4}$ (f) $(1.01)^0$

(g) $(-3)^5(-3)^4$ (h) $4^7 \div 4^2$

(i) $[(-3)^2]^5$ (j) $(m^3)^4$

(k) $\left(\dfrac{2}{3}\right)^3\left(\dfrac{2}{3}\right)^7\left(\dfrac{2}{3}\right)^{-6}$

(l) $\left(-\dfrac{5}{4}\right)^5 \div \left(-\dfrac{5}{4}\right)^3$

(m) $(1.03^{50})(1.03^{100})$

(n) $(1 + i)^{180} \div (1 + i)^{100}$

(o) $[(1.05)^{30}]^5$ (p) $(-2xy)^4$

(q) $\left(\dfrac{a^2b}{3}\right)^{-4}$ (r) $(1 + i)^{-n}$

5. LO❹ Use an electronic calculator to compute each of the following.

(a) $\sqrt{0.9216}$ (b) $\sqrt[6]{1.075}$

(c) $14.974458^{\frac{1}{40}}$ (d) $1.08^{-\frac{5}{12}}$

(e) $\ln 3$ (f) $\ln 0.05$

(g) $\ln(5.1)/\ln(1.015)$ (h) $\ln\left(\dfrac{5500}{1.10^{16}}\right)$

(i) $\ln\left[375(1.01)\left(\dfrac{1 - 1.01^{-72}}{0.01}\right)\right]$

🌐 **6. LO❺** Solve each of the following equations.

(a) $9x = -63$ (b) $0.05x = 44$

(c) $-\dfrac{1}{7}x = 3$ (d) $\dfrac{5}{6}x = -15$

(e) $x - 8 = -5$ (f) $x + 9 = -2$

(g) $x + 0.02x = 255$ (h) $x - 0.1x = 36$

(i) $4x - 3 = 9x + 2$

(j) $9x - 6 - 3x = 15 + 4x - 7$

(k) $x - \dfrac{1}{3}x = 26$ (l) $x + \dfrac{3}{8}x = 77$

7. LO❻ Solve each of the following equations and check your answers.

(a) $-9(3x - 8) - 8(9 - 7x) = 5 + 4(9x + 11)$

(b) $21x - 4 - 7(5x - 6) = 8x - 4(5x - 7)$

(c) $\dfrac{5}{7}x + \dfrac{1}{2} = \dfrac{5}{14} + \dfrac{2}{3}x$

(d) $\dfrac{4x}{3} + 2 = \dfrac{9}{8} - \dfrac{x}{6}$

(e) $\dfrac{7}{5}(6x - 7) - \dfrac{3}{8}(7x + 15) = 25$

(f) $\dfrac{5}{9}(7 - 6x) - \dfrac{3}{4}(3 - 15x) = \dfrac{1}{12}(3x - 5) - \dfrac{1}{2}$

(g) $\dfrac{5}{6}(4x - 3) - \dfrac{2}{5}(3x + 4) = 5x - \dfrac{16}{15}(1 - 3x)$

8. LO❻ Solve each of the following equations for the indicated variable.

(a) $I = Prt$ for r

(b) $S = P(1 + rt)$ for t

(c) $D = rL$ for r

(d) $FV = PMT\left[\dfrac{(1 + p)^n - 1}{p}\right]$ for PMT

LO❼ For each of the following problems, set up an equation and solve.

9. A company laid off one-sixth of its workforce because of falling sales. If the number of employees after the layoff is 690, how many employees were laid off?

10. The current average property value is two-sevenths more than last year's average value. What was last year's average property value if the current average is $346 162.50?

11. The total amount paid for a banquet, including gratuities of one-twentieth of the price quoted for the banquet, was $2457. How much of the amount paid was gratuities?

12. A piece of property with a commercial building is acquired by H & A Investments for $790 000. If the land is valued at $2000 less than one-third the value of the building, how much of the amount paid should be assigned to land?

13. The total average monthly cost of heat, power, and water for Sheridan Service for last year was $2010. If this year's average monthly cost is expected to increase by one-tenth over last year's average monthly cost, and heat is $22 more than three-quarters the cost of power while water is $11 less than one-third the cost of power, how much should be budgeted on average for each month for each item?

14. Remi Swimming Pools has a promotional budget of $87 500. The budget is to be allocated to direct selling, TV advertising, and newspaper advertising; according to a formula. The formula requires that the amount spent on TV advertising be $1000 more than three times the amount spent on newspaper advertising, and that the amount spent on direct selling be three-fourths of the total spent on TV advertising and newspaper advertising combined. How much of the budget should be allocated to direct selling?

15. A product requires processing on three machines. Processing time on Machine A is three minutes less than four-fifths of the number of minutes on Machine B, and processing time on Machine C is five-sixths of the time needed on Machines A and B together. How many minutes of processing time is required on Machine C if the total processing time on all three machines is 77 minutes?

16. Sport Alive sold 72 pairs of ski poles. Superlight poles sell at $130 per pair, while ordinary poles sell at $56 per pair. If the total sales value was $6030, how many pairs of each type were sold?

17. A cash box contains $107 made up of quarters, one-dollar coins, and two-dollar coins. How many quarters are in the box if the number of one-dollar coins is one more than three-fifths of the number of two-dollar coins, and the number of quarters is four times the number of one-dollar coins and two-dollar coins together?

18. Jaime has recently moved into her first appartment. Jaime's monthly income of $1950 comes from her job, her student loan, and scholarships. Half of her income goes towards her tuition, books, school fees, and transportation. She estimates that 30% of what's left over goes toward expenses other than her rent. If Jaime pays $600 per month for rent, how much is left over for savings?

19. Inspire Inc. has a 49% ownership stake in Baldwin Industries. Crown Company has a 24% stake in Baldwin Industries. Inspire Inc. has been offered $19.6 million for 80% of its stake. If Crown Company uses that same valuation to calculate its own position, what is the value of Crown Company's stake in Baldwin Industries?

SELF-TEST

1. Simplify.

   (a) $4 - 3x - 6 - 5x$ (b) $(5x - 4) - (7x + 5)$

   (c) $-2(3a - 4) - 5(2a + 3)$ (d) $-6(x - 2)(x + 1)$

2. Evaluate each of the following for the values given.

   (a) $2x^2 - 5xy - 4y^2$ for $x = -3, y = 5$

   (b) $3(7a - 4b) - 4(5a + 3b)$ for $a = \dfrac{2}{3}, b = -\dfrac{3}{4}$

   (c) $\dfrac{2NC}{P(n + 1)}$ for $N = 12, C = 400, P = 2000, n = 24$

   (d) $\dfrac{I}{Pr}$ for $I = 324, P = 5400, r = 0.15$

   (e) $S(1 - dt)$ for $S = 1606, d = 0.125, t = \dfrac{240}{365}$

   (f) $\dfrac{S}{1 + rt}$ for $S = 1566, r = 0.10, t = \dfrac{292}{365}$

3. Simplify.

   (a) $(-2)^3$ (b) $\left(\dfrac{-2}{3}\right)^2$

   (c) $(4)^0$ (d) $(3)^2(3)^5$

   (e) $\left(\dfrac{4}{3}\right)^{-2}$ (f) $(-x^3)^5$

4. Compute each of the following.

   (a) $\sqrt[10]{1.35}$ (b) $\dfrac{1 - 1.03^{-40}}{0.03}$

   (c) $\ln 1.025$ (d) $\ln\left[3.00e^{-0.2}\right]$

   (e) $\ln\left(\dfrac{600}{1.06^{11}}\right)$ (f) $\ln\left[250\left(\dfrac{1.07^5 - 1}{0.07}\right)\right]$

5. Solve each of the following equations.

   (a) $\dfrac{1}{81} = \left(\dfrac{1}{3}\right)^{n - 2}$ (b) $\dfrac{5}{2} = 40\left(\dfrac{1}{2}\right)^{n - 1}$

6. Solve each of the following equations.

   (a) $-\dfrac{2}{3}x = 24$ (b) $x - 0.06x = 8.46$

   (c) $0.2x - 4 = 6 - 0.3x$ (d) $(3 - 5x) - (8x - 1) = 43$

   (e) $4(8x - 2) - 5(3x + 5) = 18$ (f) $x + \dfrac{3}{10}x + \dfrac{1}{2} + x + \dfrac{3}{5}x + 1 = 103$

   (g) $x + \dfrac{4}{5}x - 3 + \dfrac{5}{6}\left(x + \dfrac{4}{5}x - 3\right) = 77$

   (h) $\dfrac{2}{3}(3x - 1) - \dfrac{3}{4}(5x - 3) = \dfrac{9}{8}x - \dfrac{5}{6}(7x - 9)$

7. Solve each of the following equations for the indicated variable.

(a) $I = Prt$ for P

(b) $S = \dfrac{P}{1 - dt}$ for d

For each of the following problems, set up an equation and solve.

8. After reducing the regular selling price by one-fifth, Star Electronics sold a TV set for $192. What was the regular selling price?

9. The weaving department of a factory occupies 400 square metres more than two times the floor space occupied by the shipping department. The total floor space occupied by both departments is 6700 square metres. Determine the floor space occupied by the weaving department.

10. A machine requires three hours to make a unit of Product A and five hours to make a unit of Product B. The machine operated for 395 hours, producing a total of 95 units. How many units of Product B were produced?

11. You invested a sum of money in a bank certificate yielding an annual return of one-twelfth of the sum invested. A second sum of money invested in a credit union certificate yields an annual return of one-ninth of the sum invested. The credit union investment is $500 more than two-thirds of the bank investment, and the total annual return is $1000. What is the sum of money you invested in the credit union certificate?

CHALLENGE PROBLEMS

1. In checking the petty cash; a clerk counts "t" toonies, "l" loonies, "q" quarters, "d" dimes, and "n" nickles. Later he discovers that x of the nickels were counted as quarters and x of the toonies were counted as loonies. (Assume that x represents the same number of nickels and toonies.) What must the clerk do to correct the original total?

2. Tom and Jerri are planning a 4000-kilometre trip in an automobile with five tires, of which four will be in use at any time. They plan to interchange the tires so that each tire will be used for the same number of kilometres. For how many kilometres will each tire be used?

3. A cheque is written for x dollars and y cents. Both x and y are two-digit numbers. In error, the cheque is cashed for y dollars and x cents, with the incorrect amount exceeding the correct amount by $17.82. Which of the following statements is correct?

(a) x cannot exceed 70.
(b) y can equal $2x$.
(c) The amount of the cheque cannot be a multiple of 5.
(d) The incorrect amount can equal twice the correct amount.
(e) The sum of the digits of the correct amount is divisible by 9.

CASE STUDY   Investing in a Tax-Free Savings Account

▶ At the age of 25, Tasha Fellows obtained her university degree and entered the work-force. She sought the opinion of an investment advisor regarding a tax-free savings account (TFSA). The main recommendations were to start investing early, to invest the maximum allowed each year, and to stay invested. Someone starting a career needs to consider investing as early as possible.

The advisor provided Tasha with scenarios of investing $100 per month at 2% return at different age ranges and calculated the value of her investment at age 65.

Age Started	Total Amount Contributed to Age 65	Total Value of TFSA at Age 65
25	$48 000	$73 566
35	$36 000	$49 355
45	$24 000	$29 529

Source: "TFSA Calculator," Bank of Montreal site, **www.bmo.com**, accessed November 3, 2018.

Tasha was shown that starting to contribute at a later age but still wanting to reach a goal of $73 566 would require larger monthly contributions.

Age Started	Monthly Contributions
35	$150
45	$250

Source: "TFSA Calculator," Bank of Montreal site, **www.bmo.com**, accessed November 3, 2018.

QUESTIONS

1. How much more will Tasha have in her TFSA if she invests the $100 per month starting at age 25 compared to starting at age 35?

2. To reach a goal of $73 566, what is the total amount of contributions necessary if Tasha were to begin investing at age 45?

3. If Tasha begins her contributions at age 45, how much interest will be earned on the contributions if
   (a) her contributions are $100 per month?
   (b) her contributions are $250 per month?

4. Assume Tasha's salary is $48 000 per year. Calculate the percentage of her monthly salary that would go toward her retirement plan goal of $73 566
   (a) if she began investing $150 monthly at age 35?
   (b) if she began investing $250 monthly at age 45?

SUMMARY OF FORMULAS

Formula 2.1

$a^m \times a^n = a^{m+n}$ The rule for multiplying two powers having the same base

Formula 2.2

$a^m \div a^n = a^{m-n}$ The rule for dividing two powers having the same base

Formula 2.3

$$\left(a^m\right)^n = a^{mn}$$

The rule for raising a power to a power

Formula 2.4

$$\left(ab\right)^m = a^m b^m$$

The rule for taking the power of a product

Formula 2.5

$$\left(\frac{a}{b}\right)^m = \frac{a^m}{b^m}$$

The rule for taking the power of a quotient

Formula 2.6

$$a^{-m} = \frac{1}{a^m}$$

The definition of a negative exponent

Formula 2.7

$$\left(\frac{y}{x}\right)^{-m} = \left(\frac{x}{y}\right)^m$$

The rule for a fraction with a negative exponent

Formula 2.8

$$a^{\frac{1}{n}} = \sqrt[n]{a}$$

The definition of a fractional exponent with numerator 1

Formula 2.9

$$a^{-\frac{1}{n}} = \frac{1}{a^{\frac{1}{n}}} = \frac{1}{\sqrt[n]{a}}$$

The definition of a fractional exponent with numerator −1

Formula 2.10

$$a^{\frac{m}{n}} = \sqrt[n]{a^m} = \left(\sqrt[n]{a}\right)^m$$

The definition of a positive fractional exponent

Formula 2.11

$$a^{-\frac{m}{n}} = \frac{1}{a^{\frac{m}{n}}} = \frac{1}{\sqrt[n]{a^m}}$$

The definition of a negative fractional exponent

Formula 2.12

$$\ln\left(ab\right) = \ln a + \ln b$$

The relationship used to calculate the logarithm of a product

Formula 2.13

$$\ln\left(\frac{a}{b}\right) = \ln a - \ln b$$

The relationship used to calculate the logarithm of a quotient

Formula 2.14

$$\ln\left(a^k\right) = k(\ln a)$$

The relationship used to calculate the logarithm of a power

GLOSSARY

Algebraic expression a combination of numbers, variables representing numbers, and symbols indicating an algebraic operation *(p. 47)*

Base one of the equal factors in a power *(p. 53)*

Collecting like terms adding like terms *(p. 46)*

Combining like terms *see* **Collecting like terms**

Common logarithms logarithms with base 10; represented by the notation log x *(p. 66)*

Equation a statement of equality between two algebraic expressions *(p. 72)*

Equivalent equations equations that have the same root *(p. 72)*

Exponent the number of equal factors in a power *(p. 53)*

Factor one of the numbers that, when multiplied with the other number or numbers, yields a given product *(p. 53)*

First-degree equation an equation in which the variable (or variables) appears with power 1 only *(p. 72)*

Formula rearrangement (or formula manipulation) the process of rearranging the terms of an equation *(p. 80)*

Index the power of the root indicated with the radical symbol *(p. 61)*

Like terms terms having the same literal coefficient *(p. 46)*

Linear equation *see* **First-degree equation**

Literal coefficient the part of a term formed with letter symbols *(p. 46)*

Logarithm the exponent to which a base must be raised to produce a given number *(p. 65)*

Members of an equation the two sides of an equation; the left member is the left side; the right member is the right side *(p. 72)*

Monomial an algebraic expression consisting of one term *(p. 47)*

Natural logarithms logarithms with base e; represented by the notation ln y *(p. 67)*

Numerical coefficient the part of a term formed with numerals *(p. 46)*

Polynomial an algebraic expression consisting of more than one term *(p. 47)*

Power a mathematical operation indicating the multiplication of a number of equal factors *(p. 53)*

Power of the root the exponent indicating the number of equal factors *(p. 61)*

Quotient the result of dividing two numbers or expressions *(p. 49)*

Radical the indicated root when using the radical symbol for calculating a root *(p. 61)*

Radicand the number under the radical symbol *(p. 61)*

Root of an equation the solution (replacement value) that, when substituted for the variable, makes the two sides equal *(p. 72)*

Root of the product one of the equal factors in the product *(p. 61)*

Ratio, Proportion, and Percent

Images/Alamy Stock Photo

LEARNING OBJECTIVES

Upon completing this chapter, you will be able to do the following:

1. Use ratios and proportions to solve allocation and equivalence problems.

2. Calculate percents and percent bases to solve business problems.

3. Calculate rates and original quantities for increase and decrease problems.

4. Use proportions and currency cross rate tables to convert currency.

5. Use index numbers and the Consumer Price Index to compute purchasing power of the Canadian dollar.

6. Use federal income tax brackets and tax rates to calculate federal income taxes.

Developing competence with ratios, proportions, and percentages is necessary because these are all widely used in the business world. Business information is often represented as a comparison of related values in the form of ratios or proportions. Ratios are also used in business to allocate expenses and funds.

The discussion of ratios leads into the introduction to proportions, which involve the equality of two ratios. The proportion model is very useful in setting up solutions to problems involving foreign currency exchange rates and the Consumer Price Index (CPI), two applications that are explored in this chapter.

Discounts, interest rates, growth in earnings, and wages all use percentages. The percent of increase or decrease is often mentioned in annual reports and news articles. Percentages also play a significant role in calculating the PST, HST, and GST.

Consumers, like businesses, are particularly interested in lending and income tax rates. Calculation of federal and provincial personal income taxes is explored in this chapter, providing practise in dealing with percentages as well as updates about the Canadian tax system. This exercise may even encourage you to do your own tax returns.

INTRODUCTION

Business information is often based on a comparison of related quantities stated in the form of a ratio. When two or more ratios are equivalent, a proportion equating the ratios can be set up. Allocation problems, such as distribution of costs or profit, generally involve ratios, and many of the physical, economic, and financial relationships affecting businesses may be stated in the form of ratios or proportions.

The fractional form of a ratio is frequently replaced by the percent form because relative amounts are more easily understood as percents. This is routinely done in business reports and articles. Skill in manipulating percents, calculating percents, computing percentage rates, and dealing with problems of increase and decrease is fundamental to solving many business problems.

3.1 RATIOS
A. Setting up ratios

1. A **ratio** is a comparison of the *relative* values of numbers or quantities and may be written in any of the following ways:
   (a) by using the word "to," such as in "5 to 2";
   (b) by using a colon, such as in "5 : 2";
   (c) as a fraction, such as "5/2";
   (d) as a decimal, such as "2.50";
   (e) as a percent, such as "250%."

2. When comparing more than two numbers or quantities, using the colon is preferred.

   To compare the quantities 5 kg, 3 kg, and 2 kg, the ratio is written

$$5 \text{ kg} : 3 \text{ kg} : 2 \text{ kg}$$

3. When using a ratio to compare quantities, the unit of measurement is usually dropped.

   If three items weigh 5 kg, 3 kg, and 2 kg respectively, their weights are compared by the ratio

$$5 : 3 : 2$$

4. The numbers appearing in a ratio are called the **terms of the ratio**. If the terms are in different units, the terms need to be expressed in the same unit of measurement before the units can be dropped.

   The ratio of 1 quarter to 1 dollar becomes 25 cents to 100 cents or 25 : 100. The ratio of 3 hours to 40 minutes becomes 180 min : 40 min or 180 : 40.

5. When, as is frequently done, rates are expressed as ratios, ratios drop the units of measurement, even though the terms of the ratio represent different things.

   100 km/h becomes 100 : 1
   50 m in 5 seconds becomes 50 : 5
   $1.49 for 2 items becomes 1.49 : 2

6. Any statement containing a comparison of two or more numbers or quantities can be used to set up a ratio.

EXAMPLE 3.1A

(i) In a company, the work of 40 employees is supervised by five managers.
The ratio of employees to managers is 40 : 5.

(ii) Variable cost is \$4000 for a sales volume of \$24 000.
The ratio of variable cost to sales volume is 4000 : 24 000.

(iii) The cost of a product is made up of \$30 of material, \$12 of direct labour, and \$27 of overhead.
The costs of material, direct labour, and overhead are in the ratio 30 : 12 : 27.

B. Reducing ratios to lowest terms

When ratios are used to express a comparison, they are usually reduced to *lowest terms*. (This means that the terms of the ratios are integers without a common factor other than 1). Ratios may be rewritten without changing the original relationship between the quantities by using rules similar to the rules for working with fractions. Thus, the procedure used to reduce ratios to lowest terms is the same as that used to reduce fractions to lowest terms. For example, if the cost of a product is made up of \$30 material, \$12 of direct labour, and \$27 of overhead, then the respective cost ratio is 30 : 12 : 27 or, in lowest terms, 10 : 4 : 9. In other words, for each \$10 in cost of material, there are \$4 in direct labour costs, and \$9 in overhead cost. However, when a ratio is expressed by an improper fraction that reduces to a whole number, the denominator "1" must be written to indicate that two quantities are being compared.

EXAMPLE 3.1B

Reduce each of the following ratios to lowest terms.

(i) 80 : 35   (ii) 48 : 30 : 18

(iii) 225 : 45   (iv) 81 : 54 : 27

SOLUTION

(i) Since each term of the ratio 80 : 35 contains a common factor 5, each term can be reduced.
$$80 : 35 = (16 \times 5) : (7 \times 5) = 16 : 7$$
$$\text{or } \frac{80}{35} = \frac{16 \times 5}{7 \times 5} = \frac{16}{7}$$

(ii) The terms of the ratio 48 : 30 : 18 contain a common factor 6.
$$48 : 30 : 18 = (8 \times 6) : (5 \times 6) : (3 \times 6) = 8 : 5 : 3$$

(iii) $225 : 45 = (45 \times 5) : (45 \times 1) = 5 : 1$
$$\text{or } \frac{225}{45} = \frac{5}{1}$$

(iv) $81 : 54 : 27 = (3 \times 27) : (2 \times 27) : (1 \times 27) = 3 : 2 : 1$

C. Equivalent ratios in higher terms

Equivalent ratios in higher terms may be obtained by *multiplying* each term of a ratio by the same number. Higher-term ratios are used to eliminate decimals and fractions from the terms of a ratio.

EXAMPLE 3.1C

State each of the following ratios in higher terms to eliminate the decimals from the terms of the ratios.

(i) 2.5 : 3   (ii) 1.25 : 3.75 : 7.5

(iii) $3 : \dfrac{4}{7} : 1$ (iv) $\dfrac{19.25}{2.75}$

SOLUTION

(i) 2.5 : 3 = 25 : 30 —————————— multiply each term by 10 to eliminate the decimal

$\qquad$ = 5 : 6 ——————————————— reduce to lowest terms

(ii) 1.25 : 3.75 : 7.5

$\qquad$ = 125 : 375 : 750 —————————— multiply each term by 100 to eliminate the decimals

$\qquad$ = $(1 \times 125) : (3 \times 125) : (6 \times 125)$

$\qquad$ = 1 : 3 : 6

(iii) $3 : \dfrac{4}{7} : 1 = \dfrac{21}{7} : \dfrac{4}{7} : \dfrac{7}{7} = 21 : 4 : 7$

(iv) $\dfrac{19.25}{2.75} = \dfrac{1925}{275} = \dfrac{7 \times 275}{1 \times 275} = \dfrac{7}{1}$

D. Allocation according to a ratio

Allocation problems require dividing a whole into a number of parts according to a ratio. The number of parts into which the whole is to be divided is the sum of the terms of the ratio.

EXAMPLE 3.1D

Allocate $480 in the ratio 5 : 3.

SOLUTION

The division of $480 in the ratio 5 : 3 may be achieved by dividing the amount of $480 into (5 + 3) or 8 parts.

$\qquad$ The value of each part = 480 ÷ 8 = 60.

$\qquad$ The first term of the ratio consists of 5 of the 8 parts; that is,

$\qquad$ the first term = 5 × 60 = 300 and the second term = 3 × 60 = 180.

$480 is to be divided into $300 and $180.

Alternatively
$480 in the ratio 5 : 3 may be divided by using fractions.

5 of 8 ——————————→ $\dfrac{5}{8} \times 480 = 300$

3 of 8 ——————————→ $\dfrac{3}{8} \times 480 = 180$

EXAMPLE 3.1E

If net income of $720 000 is to be divided among three business partners in the ratio
4 : 3 : 2, how much should each partner receive?

SOLUTION

Divide the net income into $4 + 3 + 2 = 9$ parts.
Each part has a value of $720 000 ÷ 9 = $80 000.

Partner 1 receives 4 of the 9 parts $4 \times $80 000 = $320 000$
Partner 2 receives 3 of the 9 parts $3 \times $80 000 = $240 000$
Partner 3 receives 2 of the 9 parts $2 \times $80 000 = $160 000$

TOTAL $\underline{$720 000}$

Alternatively

Partner 1 receives $\dfrac{4}{9}$ of 720 000 $= \dfrac{4}{9} \times 720\ 000 = 4 \times 80\ 000 = $320 000$

Partner 2 receives $\dfrac{3}{9}$ of 720 000 $= \dfrac{3}{9} \times 720\ 000 = 3 \times 80\ 000 = $240 000$

Partner 3 receives $\dfrac{2}{9}$ of 720 000 $= \dfrac{2}{9} \times 720\ 000 = 2 \times 80\ 000 = $160 000$

TOTAL $\underline{$720 000}$

EXAMPLE 3.1F

A business suffered a fire loss of $224 640. It was covered by an insurance policy that
stated that any claim was to be paid by three insurance companies in the ratio $\frac{1}{3} : \frac{3}{8} : \frac{5}{12}$.
What is the amount that each of the three companies will pay?

SOLUTION

When an amount is to be allocated in a ratio for which some or all terms are fractions, the ratio can be rewritten in higher terms, without fractions, by converting it into equivalent fractions with the same denominators and then by multiplying the ratio terms with that denominator. The new terms may then be used to allocate the amount.

STEP 1   Convert the ratio to an equivalent ratio with no fraction terms.

$$\frac{1}{3} : \frac{3}{8} : \frac{5}{12} \quad\text{—————— lowest common denominator = 24}$$

$$= \frac{8}{24} : \frac{9}{24} : \frac{10}{24} \quad\text{————— equivalent fractions with the same denominators}$$

$$= 8 : 9 : 10$$

STEP 2   Allocate according to the equivalent ratio without fraction terms.

The ratio is 8 : 9 : 10.

The number of parts is $8 + 9 + 10 = 27$.

The value of each part is $224 640 ÷ 27 = $8320.

First company's share of claim $= 8320 \times\ 8 = $\ 66\ 560$
Second company's share of claim $= 8320 \times\ 9 =\ \ 74\ 880$
Third company's share of claim $= 8320 \times 10 =\ \ 83\ 200$

TOTAL $\underline{$224 640}$

A. Simplify each of the following ratios.

1. Reduce to lowest terms.
   (a) 12 to 32
   (b) 84 to 56
   (c) 15 to 24 to 39
   (d) 21 to 42 to 91

2. Set up a ratio for each of the following and reduce to lowest terms.
   (a) 12 dimes to 5 quarters
   (b) 15 hours to 3 days
   (c) 6 seconds for 50 metres
   (d) $72 per dozen
    (e) $40 per day for 12 employees for 14 days
   (f) 2% per month for 24 months for $5000

3. Use equivalent ratios in higher terms to eliminate decimals and fractions from the following ratios.

    (a) 1.25 to 4   (b) 2.4 to 8.4

   (c) 0.6 to 2.1 to 3.3   (d) 5.75 to 3.50 to 1.25

    (e) $\dfrac{1}{2}$ to $\dfrac{2}{5}$ (f) $\dfrac{5}{3}$ to $\dfrac{7}{5}$

   (g) $\dfrac{3}{8}$ to $\dfrac{2}{3}$ to $\dfrac{3}{4}$ (h) $\dfrac{2}{5}$ to $\dfrac{4}{7}$ to $\dfrac{5}{14}$

   (i) $\dfrac{2}{5}$ to $\dfrac{3}{4}$ to $\dfrac{5}{16}$ (j) $\dfrac{3}{7}$ to $\dfrac{1}{3}$ to $\dfrac{17}{21}$

    (k) $8\dfrac{5}{8}$ to $11\dfrac{1}{2}$ (l) $1\dfrac{3}{4}$ to $3\dfrac{7}{16}$

   (m) $2\dfrac{1}{5}$ to $4\dfrac{1}{8}$ (n) $5\dfrac{1}{4}$ to $5\dfrac{5}{6}$

B. Set up a ratio for each of the following and reduce the ratio to lowest terms.

 1. Deli Delight budgets food costs to account for 40% and beverage costs to account for 35% of total costs. What is the ratio of food costs to beverage costs?

2. At Bargain Upholstery, commissions amounted to $2500, while sales volume was $87 500 for last month. What is the ratio of commissions to sales volume?

 3. A company employs 6 supervisors for 9 office employees and 36 production workers. What is the ratio of supervisors to office employees to production workers?

4. The cost of a unit is made up of $4.25 direct material cost, $2.75 direct labour cost, and $3.25 overhead. What is the ratio that exists between the three elements of cost?

5. The business school at the local college has 8 instructors and 232 students. What is the ratio that exists between the instructors and students?

6. A student spends 20 hours per week in classroom lecture time, 45 hours per week in individual study time, and 5 hours per week travelling to and from school. What is the ratio that exists between the three times?

C. Solve each of the following allocation problems.

1. A dividend of $3060 is to be distributed among three shareholders in the ratio of shares held. If the three shareholders have nine shares, two shares, and one share respectively, how much does each receive?

2. The cost of operating the Maintenance Department is to be allocated to four production departments based on the floor space each occupies. Department A occupies 1000 m²; Department B, 600 m²; Department C, 800 m²; and Department D, 400 m². If the July cost was $21 000, how much of the cost of operating the Maintenance Department should be allocated to each production department?

3. Insurance cost is to be distributed among manufacturing, selling, and administration in the ratio $\frac{5}{8}$ to $\frac{1}{3}$ to $\frac{1}{6}$. If the total insurance cost was $9450, how should it be distributed?

4. Executive salaries are charged to three operating divisions on the basis of capital investment in the three divisions. If the investment is $10.8 million in the Northern Division, $8.4 million in the Eastern Division, and $14.4 million in the Western Division, how should executive salaries of $588 000 be allocated to the three divisions?

5. The cost of warehouse space is allocated to three inventories: raw materials, work-in-process, and finished goods. The inventories use the warehouse space in the ratio of one-third to one-sixth to three-eighths, respectively. If the total warehouse space is 9.6 million square metres, at a cost of $11.55 million, how much of the cost should be allocated to each of the inventories?

6. A vehicle dealership has overhead cost of $480 000. The overhead cost is allocated to new vehicle sales, used vehicle sales, vehicle servicing, and administration. The departments bear overhead cost in the ratio $\frac{1}{8}$ to $\frac{1}{4}$ to $\frac{1}{2}$ to $\frac{1}{16}$. How much of the overhead cost should be allocated to each of the departments?

3.2 PROPORTIONS
A. Solving proportions

When two ratios are equal, they form a **proportion**.

$$2 : 3 = 4 : 6$$
$$x : 5 = 7 : 35$$
$$\frac{2}{3} = \frac{8}{x}$$
$$\frac{a}{b} = \frac{c}{d}$$

— are proportions

Note that each proportion consists of *four terms*. These terms form an equation whose sides are fractions.

If one of the four terms is unknown, the proportions form a linear equation in one variable. The equation can be solved by using the operations discussed in Chapter 2.

EXAMPLE 3.2A

Solve the proportion
2 is to 5 as 8 is to x
$2 \; : \; 5 = 8 \; : \; x$

SOLUTION

$2 : 5 = 8 : x$ ——————————— original form of proportion

$\dfrac{2}{5} = \dfrac{8}{x}$ ——————————— change the proportion into fractional form

$5x\left(\dfrac{2}{5}\right) = 5x\left(\dfrac{8}{x}\right)$ ——————————— multiply by the lowest common denominator = 5x

$2x = 40$

$x = 20$

Check LS $= \dfrac{2}{5}$, RS $= \dfrac{8}{20} = \dfrac{2}{5}$

Note: The two operations usually applied to solve proportions are multiplication and division. These operations permit the use of a simplified technique called *cross-multiplication*, which involves

(a) the multiplication of the numerator of the ratio on the left side with the denominator of the ratio on the right side of the proportion, and
(b) the multiplication of the denominator of the ratio on the left side with the numerator of the ratio on the right side, effectively crossing the terms over.

When the cross-multiplication process is used to solve Example 3.2A, the value of x is obtained as follows:

$$\dfrac{2}{5} \diagdown\!\!\!\!\!\diagup \dfrac{8}{x}$$

$2(x) = 5(8)$ ——————————— cross-multiply

$2x = 40$

$x = 20$

EXAMPLE 3.2B

Solve each of the following proportions.

(i) $x : 5 = 7 : 35$ ——————————— original proportion

$\dfrac{x}{5} = \dfrac{7}{35}$ ——————————— in fractional form

$x(35) = 5(7)$ ——————————— cross-multiply

$35x = 35$

$x = 1$

(ii) $2\tfrac{1}{2} : x = 5\tfrac{1}{2} : 38\tfrac{1}{2}$

$2.5 : x = 5.5 : 38.5$

$\dfrac{2.5}{x} = \dfrac{5.5}{38.5}$

$2.5(38.5) = x(5.5)$ ——————————— cross-multiply

$96.25 = 5.5x$

$x = \dfrac{96.25}{5.5}$

$x = 17.5,\ \text{or}\ 17\tfrac{1}{2}$

(iii) $\dfrac{5}{6} : \dfrac{14}{4} = x : \dfrac{21}{10}$

$\left. \dfrac{\frac{5}{6}}{\frac{14}{4}} = \dfrac{\frac{x}{1}}{\frac{21}{10}} \right\}$ ———————— set up in fractional form

$\left(\dfrac{5}{6}\right)\left(\dfrac{21}{10}\right) = \left(\dfrac{x}{1}\right)\left(\dfrac{14}{4}\right)$ ———————— cross-multiply

$\dfrac{105}{60} = \dfrac{14x}{4}$

$(105)(4) = (60)(14x)$

$420 = 840x$

$x = 0.5, \text{ or } \dfrac{1}{2}$

B. Problems involving proportions

Many problems contain information that permits two ratios to be set up. These ratios are in proportion, but one term of one ratio is unknown. In such cases, a letter symbol for the unknown term is used to complete the proportion statement.

To ensure that the proportion is set up correctly, use the following procedure.

STEP 1 Use a complete sentence to *introduce* the *letter* symbol that you will use to represent the missing term.

STEP 2 Set up the *known ratio* on the *left* side of the proportion. Be sure to retain the units or a description of the quantities in the ratio.

STEP 3 Set up the ratio using the *letter symbol* on the *right* side of the proportion. Make certain that the unit or description of the numerator in the ratio on the right side corresponds to the unit or description of the numerator in the ratio on the left side.

EXAMPLE 3.2C Solve each of the following problems involving a proportion.

(i) If five kilograms of sugar cost $9.20, what is the cost of two kilograms of sugar?

SOLUTION

STEP 1 Introduce the variable.
Let the cost of two kilograms of sugar be x.

STEP 2 Set up the known ratio retaining the units.
5 kg : $9.20

STEP 3 Set up the ratio involving the variable.
2 kg : x

Hence, $\dfrac{5 \text{ kg}}{\$9.20} = \dfrac{2 \text{ kg}}{\$x}$ ————————— make certain the units in the numerators and denominators correspond

$$\dfrac{5}{9.20} = \dfrac{2}{x}$$

$$5(x) = 9.20(2)$$

$$x = \dfrac{18.40}{5}$$

$$x = 3.68$$

Two kilograms of sugar cost $3.68.

(ii) If your car can travel 385 km on 35 L of gasoline, how far can it travel on 24 L?

SOLUTION

Let the distance travelled on 24 L be n km;
then the known ratio is 385 km : 35 L;
the second ratio is n km : 24 L.

$$\dfrac{385 \text{ km}}{35 \text{ L}} = \dfrac{n \text{ km}}{24 \text{ L}}$$

$$\dfrac{385}{35} = \dfrac{n}{24}$$

$$n = \dfrac{385 \times 24}{35}$$

$$n = 264$$

The car can travel 264 km on 24 L.

(iii) Past experience shows that a process requires $17.50 worth of material for every $12 spent on labour. How much should be budgeted for material if the budget for labour is $17 760?

SOLUTION

Let the material budget be $k.

The known ratio is $\dfrac{\$17.50 \text{ material}}{\$12 \text{ labour}}$;

the second ratio is $\dfrac{\$k \text{ material}}{\$17\,760 \text{ labour}}$.

$$\dfrac{\$17.50 \text{ material}}{\$12 \text{ labour}} = \dfrac{\$k \text{ material}}{\$17\,760 \text{ labour}}$$

$$\dfrac{17.50}{12} = \dfrac{k}{17\,760}$$

$$k = \dfrac{17.50 \times 17\,760}{12}$$

$$k = 25\,900$$

The material budget should be $25 900.

EXAMPLE 3.2D

Two contractors agreed to share revenue from a job in the ratio 2 : 3. Contractor A, who received the smaller amount, made a profit of $480 on the job. If contractor A's profit compared to revenue is in the ratio 3 : 8, determine

(i) contractor A's revenue;

(ii) the total revenue of the job.

SOLUTION

(i) We are given two ratios. The first ratio compares the revenues of the two contractors. Both of these are not known, so there are two unknown quantities in the proportion equation.

$$\frac{2}{3} = \frac{\text{A's revenue}}{\text{B's revenue}}$$

The second ratio compares profit and revenue of contractor A, and one of these is known (the profit). This gives us a proportion equation with only one unknown. Therefore we can solve it, giving us the best place to start. Let $x represent contractor A's revenue.

Then $\dfrac{\text{A's profit}}{\text{A's revenue}} = \dfrac{3}{8}$ ─────────────── known ratio

and $\dfrac{\text{A's profit}}{\text{A's revenue}} = \dfrac{\$480}{\$x}$ ─────────────── second ratio

$$\frac{3}{8} = \frac{480}{x}$$

$$3x = 8 \times 480$$

$$x = \frac{8 \times 480}{3}$$

$$x = 1280$$

Contractor A's revenue from the job is $1280.

(ii) Now that we know contractor A's revenue, we can use the first ratio to calculate B's revenue, and then the total revenue. Let $y represent contractor B's revenue.

Then $\dfrac{\text{A's revenue}}{\text{B's revenue}} = \dfrac{2}{3}$ ─────────────── known ratio

and $\dfrac{\text{A's revenue}}{\text{B's revenue}} = \dfrac{\$1280}{\$y}$ ─────────────── second ratio

$$\frac{2}{3} = \frac{1280}{y}$$

$$2y = 3 \times 1280$$

$$y = \frac{3 \times 1280}{2}$$

$$y = 1920$$

Total revenue = $x + y$ = 1280 + 1920 = 3200

Total revenue on the job is $3200.

Alternatively

Apply the allocation process to the revenues ratio to calculate the total revenue. Let total revenue be z.

$$\text{Then } \frac{\text{A's revenue}}{\text{Total revenue}} = \frac{2}{5} = \frac{\$1280}{\$z}$$

$$\frac{2}{5} = \frac{1280}{z}$$

$$2z = 5 \times 1280$$

$$z = 3200$$

EXERCISE 3.2

MyLab Math

A. Calculate the unknown term in the following proportions.

1. $3 : n = 15 : 20$ **2.** $n : 7 = 24 : 42$

3. $3 : 8 = 21 : x$ **4.** $7 : 5 = x : 45$

5. $1.32 : 1.11 = 8.8 : k$ **6.** $2.17 : 1.61 = k : 4.6$

7. $m : 3.4 = 2.04 : 2.89$ **8.** $3.15 : m = 1.4 : 1.8$

9. $t : \dfrac{3}{4} = \dfrac{7}{8} : \dfrac{15}{16}$ **10.** $\dfrac{3}{4} : t = \dfrac{5}{8} : \dfrac{4}{9}$

11. $\dfrac{9}{8} : \dfrac{3}{5} = t : \dfrac{8}{15}$ **12.** $\dfrac{16}{7} : \dfrac{4}{9} = \dfrac{15}{14} : t$

B. Use proportions to solve each of the following problems.

1. Le Point Bookbindery pays a dividend of $1.25 per share every three months. How many months would it take to earn dividends amounting to $8.75 per share?

2. The community of Oakcrest sets a property tax rate of $32 per $1000 of assessed value. What is the assessment if a tax of $3854 is paid on a property?

3. A car requires 9 litres of gasoline for 72 kilometres. At the same rate of gasoline consumption, how far can the car travel if the gas tank holds 75 litres?

4. A manufacturing process requires $85 supervision cost for every 64 labour hours. At the same rate, how much supervision cost should be budgeted for 16 000 labour hours?

5. Suhami Chadhuri has a two-fifths interest in a partnership. She sold five-sixths of her interest for $300 000.
(a) What was the total dollar amount of Ms. Chadhuri's interest before selling?
(b) What is the value of the partnership?

6. Five-eighths of Jesse Black's inventory was destroyed by fire. He sold the remaining part, which was slightly damaged, for one-third of its value and received $13 000.
(a) What was the value of the inventory before the fire?
(b) What was the value of the destroyed part of the inventory?

7. Last year, net profits of Herd Inc. were two-sevenths of revenue. If the company declared a dividend of $128 000 and five-ninths of the net profit was retained in the company, what was last year's revenue?

8. Material cost of a web camera is five-eighths of total cost, and labour cost is one-third of material cost. If labour cost is $15, what is the total cost of the web camera?

3.3 THE BASIC PERCENTAGE PROBLEM
A. Computing percentages

Percentages are used widely in business for determining pay raises, interest amounts, and discounts on sale items.

To determine a percentage of a given number, change the percent to a decimal or a fraction and then multiply by the given number.

$$50\% \text{ of } 60 = \frac{50}{100} \times 60 = 30$$

Note: 50% is called the (percentage) rate.
60 is called the *base* or *original number*.
30 is called the *new number* or percentage (amount).

$$\boxed{\text{PERCENTAGE} = \text{RATE} \times \text{BASE}} \text{————————— Formula 3.1}$$

or

$$\boxed{\text{NEW NUMBER} = \text{RATE} \times \text{ORIGINAL NUMBER}}$$

EXAMPLE 3.3A

(i) 80% of 400 = 0.80 × 400 ————————— **convert the percent into a**
         = 320   **decimal and multiply**

(ii) 5% of 1200 = 0.05 × 1200 = 60

(iii) 240% of 15 = 2.40 × 15 = 36

(iv) 1.8% of $600 = 0.018 × 600 = $10.80

(v) $33\frac{1}{3}$% of $45.60 = $\frac{1}{3}$ × 45.60 = $15.20

(vi) 0.25% of $8000 = 0.0025 × 8000 = $20

(vii) $\frac{3}{8}$% of $1800 = 0.375% of $1800 = 0.00375 × 1800 = $6.75

POINTERS
& PITFALLS

For terminating and non-terminating decimals, carry all the decimals in your final answer unless specified or logically sound to do otherwise. If the final digits are zeros, the zeros are generally not displayed.

B. Computation with commonly used percents

Many of the more commonly used percents can be converted into fractions. These are easy to use when computing manually. The most commonly used percents and their fractional equivalents are listed in Table 3.1.

Table 3.1 Commonly Used Percents and Their Fractional Equivalents (© S. A. Hummelbrunner)

(i)	(ii)	(iii)	(iv)	(v)
$25\% = \frac{1}{4}$	$16\frac{2}{3}\% = \frac{1}{6}$	$12\frac{1}{2}\% = \frac{1}{8}$	$20\% = \frac{1}{5}$	$8\frac{1}{3}\% = \frac{1}{12}$
$50\% = \frac{1}{2}$	$33\frac{1}{3}\% = \frac{1}{3}$	$37\frac{1}{2}\% = \frac{3}{8}$	$40\% = \frac{2}{5}$	$6\frac{2}{3}\% = \frac{1}{15}$
$75\% = \frac{3}{4}$	$66\frac{2}{3}\% = \frac{2}{3}$	$62\frac{1}{2}\% = \frac{5}{8}$	$60\% = \frac{3}{5}$	$6\frac{1}{4}\% = \frac{1}{16}$
	$83\frac{1}{3}\% = \frac{5}{6}$	$87\frac{1}{2}\% = \frac{7}{8}$	$80\% = \frac{4}{5}$	

EXAMPLE 3.3B

(i) 25% of $32 = \frac{1}{4} \times 32 = 8$

(ii) $33\frac{1}{3}\%$ of $150 = \frac{1}{3} \times 150 = 50$

(iii) $87\frac{1}{2}\%$ of $96 = \frac{7}{8} \times \overset{12}{96} = 7 \times 12 = 84$ —————— divide by a common factor of 8

(iv) $83\frac{1}{3}\%$ of $48 = \frac{5}{6} \times 48 = 5 \times 8 = 40$ —————— divide by a common factor of 6

(v) $116\frac{2}{3}\%$ of $240 = (100\% + 16\frac{2}{3}\%)$ of 240

$= \left(1 + \frac{1}{6}\right)(240)$

$= \frac{7}{6} \times 240$

$= 7 \times 40$

$= 280$

(vi) 275% of $64 = \left(2 + \frac{3}{4}\right)(64)$

$= \frac{11}{4} \times 64$

$= 11 \times 16$

$= 176$

POINTERS & PITFALLS

Using the 1% Method

In certain situations one needs to calculate or approximate a percentage amount without access to a calculator (as when required to perform a quick mental calculation or to perform calculations in secure meetings where no digital devices are allowed). In those circumstances, percentages can be computed by determining 1% of the given number and then figuring the value of the given percent. While this method can be used to compute any percentage, it is particularly useful when dealing with *small* percents.

EXAMPLE 3.3C

Use the 1% method to determine each of the following percentages.

(i) 3% of $1800

SOLUTION

1% of $1800 = $18

3% of $1800 = 3 × 18 = $54

(ii) $\frac{1}{2}$% of $960

SOLUTION

1% of $960 = $9.60

$\frac{1}{2}$% of $960 = $\frac{9.60}{2}$ = $4.80

(iii) $\frac{5}{8}$% of $4440

SOLUTION

1% of $4440 = $44.40

$\frac{5}{8}$% of $4440 = (5 × 44.40) ÷ 8 = 222 ÷ 8 = $27.75

(iv) $2\frac{1}{4}$% of $36 500

SOLUTION

1% of $36 500 = $365.00

2% of $36 500 = 2 × 365.00 = $730.00

$\frac{1}{4}$% of $36 500 = $\frac{365.00}{4}$ = 91.25

$2\frac{1}{4}$% of $36 500 = 730 + 91.25 = $821.25

C. Calculating the base

Many business problems involve the relationship from Formula 3.1

> PERCENTAGE = RATE × BASE
> (OR NEW NUMBER = RATE × ORIGINAL NUMBER)

Since three variables are involved, three different problems may be solved using this relationship:

(a) calculating the percentage (see Sections A and B)
(b) calculating the base (see Section C)
(c) calculating the percentage rate (see Section D)

Of the three, the problem of calculating the percentage rate is the most easily recognized. However, confusion often arises in deciding whether the percentage or the base needs to be found. In such cases it is useful to represent the unknown value by a variable and translate the word problem into a mathematical equation. In translating sentences to math equations, typically "of" becomes multiplication and "is" becomes the equal sign.

POINTERS & PITFALLS

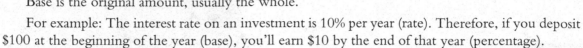

This triangle is a useful aid in determining the variables in Formula 3.1. The percentage (P) is equal to rate (R) multiplied by the base (B).

Percentage is the portion or part, always without a percent sign.
Rate (or percent) has a percent sign. It is the portion in relation to the base.
Base is the original amount, usually the whole.

For example: The interest rate on an investment is 10% per year (rate). Therefore, if you deposit $100 at the beginning of the year (base), you'll earn $10 by the end of that year (percentage).

Rate problems will provide information about 2 of the 3 quantities and you'll need to solve for the third quantity. First, identify the quantities you are given and then rearrange the formula to solve for the other.

For example: During a 20% off sale, Nicole bought a jacket for $125. What was the original price of the jacket?

Solution: The 20% represents the portion that Nicole *saved*. Therefore, we can conclude that the $125 she *paid* was 80% of the original price of the jacket. Using the Percentage-Base-Rate formula, and inputting the percentage or portion ($125) and the rate (80%), we calculate the original price to be $156.25. This answer makes sense in that we expected the base or original price to be larger than $125 sale price.

EXAMPLE 3.3D   Solve each of the following problems by setting up an equation.

(i) What amount is 25% of 84?

SOLUTION   Introduce a variable for the unknown value and write the statement in equation form. Let x be the percentage amount.

What amount is 25% of 84

$$x = 25\% \text{ of } 84$$
$$x = 0.25 \times 84 \qquad \text{change the percent to a fraction or a decimal}$$
$$x = 21$$

The amount is 21.

(ii) 60% of what number is 42?

SOLUTION   Let x be the unknown number.

60% of what number is 42

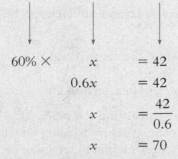

$$60\% \times x = 42$$
$$0.6x = 42$$
$$x = \frac{42}{0.6}$$
$$x = 70$$

The number is 70.

SOLUTION

(iii) How much is $16\frac{2}{3}\%$ of $144?

$x = 16\frac{2}{3}\%$ of 144

$x = \dfrac{1}{6} \times 144$

$x = 24$

The amount is $24.

SOLUTION

(iv) $160 is 250% of what amount?

$160 = 250\%$ of x

$160 = 2.5x$

$x = \dfrac{160}{2.5}$

$x = 64$

The amount is $64.

D. Calculating a percentage rate

Calculating a rate means *comparing* two numbers. This comparison involves a ratio that is usually written in the form of a fraction. When the fraction is converted to a percent, the result is a percentage rate. Note that we often simply say *rate* when we are referring to a percentage rate. In addition, when we say *percentage*, we mean the percentage amount.

When setting up the ratio, the base (or original number) is always the denominator of the fraction, and the percentage (or new number) is always the numerator.

$$\boxed{\text{RATE} = \frac{\text{PERCENTAGE}}{\text{BASE}} \text{ or } \frac{\text{NEW NUMBER}}{\text{ORIGINAL NUMBER}}} \text{────── rearrange Formula 3.1}$$

The problem statement indicating that a percentage rate is to be found is usually in the form
(a) "What percent of x is y?" or
(b) "y is what percent of x?"

This means that y is to be compared to x and requires the setting up of the ratio $y : x$ or the fraction $\frac{y}{x}$ where x is the base (or original number) while y is the percentage (or new number).

A straight-forward approach to solving percentage-related problems is to set up the fundamental relationship between the percentage, the rate and the base, and then solve for the unknown quantity.

$$\text{(some percent) of (original number) is (new number)}$$
$$\text{rate} \quad \times \quad \text{base} \quad = \quad \text{percentage}$$

EXAMPLE 3.3E

Answer each of the following questions.

(i) What percent of 15 is 6?

SOLUTION

$\text{Rate} \times 15 = 6$

$$\text{Rate} = \frac{6}{15} \underline{\hspace{3cm}} \text{percentage (or new number)}$$
$$\phantom{\text{Rate} = \frac{6}{15}} \underline{\hspace{3cm}} \text{base (or original number)}$$

$= 0.40$

$= 40\%$

(ii) 90 is what percent of 72?

SOLUTION

$90 = \text{rate} \times 72$

$$\text{Rate} = \frac{90}{72} \underline{\hspace{3cm}} \text{percentage (or new number)}$$
$$\phantom{\text{Rate} = \frac{90}{72}} \underline{\hspace{3cm}} \text{base (or original number)}$$

$= 1.25$

$= 125\%$

(iii) What percent of $112.50 is $292.50?

SOLUTION

$$\text{Rate} = \frac{292.50}{112.50} = 2.60 = 260\%$$

E. Applications

EXAMPLE 3.3F

Solve each of the following problems.

(i) Variable cost on monthly sales of $48 600 amounted to $30 375. What is the variable cost rate based on sales volume?

SOLUTION

$$\text{Rate} = \frac{\text{Variable cost}}{\text{Sales volume}}$$

$$= \frac{30\ 375}{48\ 600}$$

$= 0.625$

$= 62.5\%$

The variable cost is 62.5% of sales volume.

(ii) A preferred stock or preferred share of a company typically pays out a portion of its earnings, called a dividend, to its shareholders. What is the annual dividend on a $20 preferred share paying 11.5%?

SOLUTION

Let the annual dividend be $x.
Since the annual dividend is 11.5% of $20,

$x = 11.5\%$ of 20

$x = 0.115 \times 20$

$x = 2.30$

The annual dividend is $2.30.

(iii) What was the amount of October sales if November sales of $14 352 were 115% of October sales?

SOLUTION

Let October sales be represented by $x.
Since November sales equal 115% of October sales,

$$14\ 352 = 115\% \text{ of } x$$
$$14\ 352 = 1.15x$$
$$x = \frac{14\ 352}{1.15}$$
$$x = 12\ 480$$

October sales amounted to $12 480.

(iv) The 15% blended sales tax charged on the regular selling price of a computer sold in Halifax, Nova Scotia, amounted to $201.00. What was the total cost of the computer?

SOLUTION

The total cost is regular selling price, which we don't know, plus the tax amount, which we do know.
Let the regular selling price be $x.
Since the sales tax is 15% of the regular selling price,

$$201.00 = 15\% \text{ of } x$$
$$201.00 = 0.15x$$
$$x = \frac{201.00}{0.15}$$
$$x = 1340$$

The regular selling price is	$1340.00
Add 15% of $1340	201.00
TOTAL COST	$1541.00

The total cost of the computer was $1541.00.

EXERCISE 3.3

MyLab Math

A. Compute each of the following.

 1. 40% of 90

2. 0.1% of 950

 3. 250% of 120

4. 7% of 800

5. 3% of 600

6. 15% of 240

7. 0.5% of 1200

8. 300% of 80

9. 0.02% of 2500

 10. $\frac{1}{2}$% of 500

11. $\frac{1}{4}$% of 800

12. $\frac{7}{8}$% of 3600

B. Use fractional equivalents to compute each of the following (round to the highest whole number). Do not convert percentages to decimals.

1. $33\frac{1}{3}\%$ of $48
2. $137\frac{1}{2}\%$ of $400
3. $66\frac{2}{3}\%$ of $72
4. $37\frac{1}{2}\%$ of $24
5. 125% of $160
6. $83\frac{1}{3}\%$ of $720
7. $166\frac{2}{3}\%$ of $90
8. $116\frac{2}{3}\%$ of $42
9. $16\frac{2}{3}\%$ of $54
10. 75% of $180
11. $133\frac{1}{3}\%$ of $45
12. 25% of $440

C. Calculate the percentage rate for each of the following.

1. original amount 60; new amount 36
2. original amount 72; new amount 54
3. base $800; percentage $920
4. base $140; percentage $490
5. new amount $6; original amount $120
6. new amount $11; original amount $440
7. percentage $132; base $22
8. percentage $30; base $45
9. new amount $150; base $90
10. percentage $39; original amount $18

D. Answer each of the following questions.

1. $60 is 30% of what amount?
2. $36 is what percent of $15?
3. What is 0.1% of $3600?
4. 150% of what amount is $270?
5. $\frac{1}{2}\%$ of $612 is what amount?
6. 250% of what amount is $300?
7. 80 is 40% of what amount?
8. $120 is what percent of $60?
9. What is $\frac{1}{8}\%$ of $880?
10. $180 is what percent of $450?

E. Answer each of the following questions.

1. The price of a carpet was reduced by 40%. If the original price was $70, what was the amount by which the price was reduced?

2. Labour content in the production of an article is $37\frac{1}{2}\%$ of total cost. How much is the labour cost if the total cost is $72?

3. If waste is normally 6% of the material used in a production process, how much of $25 000 worth of material will be wasted?

4. If total deductions on a yearly salary of $55 800 amounted to $16\frac{2}{3}\%$, how much was deducted?

5. If the actual sales of $40 500 for last month were 90% of the budgeted sales, how much was the sales budget for the month?

6. The Canada Pension Plan premium deducted from an employee's wages was $106.92. If the premium rate is 4.95% of gross wages, how much were the employee's gross wages?

7. A property was sold for 300% of what the vendors (sellers) originally paid. If the vendors sold the property for $180 000, how much did they originally pay for the property?

8. Gerry's four sons were to share equally in a prize, receiving $280 each. How much was the total prize?

9. Shari's portion of the proceeds of a business was $\frac{1}{2}$%. If the total proceeds, i.e., money received from the business, were $1 200 000, how much would she receive?

10. Mei Jung paid $18 toward a dinner that cost a total of $45. What percent of the total did she pay for?

3.4 PROBLEMS INVOLVING INCREASE OR DECREASE
A. Percent change

Problems involving a *change* (an increase or a decrease) are identifiable by such phrases as

"is 20% *more than*," "is 40% *less than*,"
"is *increased by* 150%," "is *decreased by* 30%."

The amount of change is to be added for an increase to or subtracted for a decrease from the *original number* (*base*) and is usually stated as a percent of the original number.
The existing relationship may be stated as

$$\text{NEW NUMBER} = \text{ORIGINAL NUMBER} \begin{matrix} + \text{INCREASE} \\ - \text{DECREASE} \end{matrix} \quad \text{————— Formula 3.2}$$

where the change (the increase or decrease) is understood to be a *percent of the original number*.

EXAMPLE 3.4A

Answer each of the following questions.

(i) 36 increased by 25% is what number?

SOLUTION

New number is original number increased by a percentage. So
new number = original number + percent of original number.
The original number is 36;
the change (increase) is 25% of 36. ——————— in such problems the change is
Since the original number is known,   a percent of the original number
let x represent the new number.

$36 + 25\%$ of $36 = x$

$36 + \dfrac{1}{4} \times 36 = x$

$36 + 9 = x$

$x = 45$

The number is 45.
Alternatively, multiply 36 by 125%
$36 \times 1.25 = 45$

(ii) What number is 40% less than 75?

SOLUTION

The change (decrease) is 40% of 75.
The original number is 75.
Let x represent the new number.

$$75 - 40\% \text{ of } 75 = x$$
$$75 - 0.40 \times 75 = x$$
$$75 - 30 = x$$
$$x = 45$$

The number is 45.
Alternatively, multiply 75 by $(100\% - 40\%)$
$$75 \times (1.00 - 0.40) = 75 \times (0.60) = 45$$

(iii) A jewellery store purchases watches for \$160 but adds an additional 250% of that amount to the price tag. How much do customers pay?

SOLUTION

The increase is 250% of \$160 and the original number is \$160.
Let the new amount be \$$x$.

$$160 + 250\% \text{ of } 160 = x$$
$$160 + 2.50 \times 160 = x$$
$$160 + 400 = x$$
$$x = 560$$

Customers pay \$560 for the watches (before tax).

B. Calculating the rate of increase or decrease

This type of problem is indicated by such phrases as

(a) "20 is what percent *more than* 15?" or
(b) "What percent *less than* 96 is 72?"

In (a), the increase, which is the difference between 15, the original number, and 20, the number after the increase, is to be compared to the original number, 15.

The rate of increase = (new number − original number) ÷ original number

$$= \frac{(20 - 15)}{15} = \frac{5}{15} = \frac{1}{3} = 33\frac{1}{3}\%$$

In (b), the decrease, which is the difference between 96, the number before the decrease (the original number), and 72, the number after the decrease, is to be expressed as a percent of the original number.

The rate of decrease = (original number − new number) ÷ original number

$$= \frac{(96 - 72)}{96} = \frac{24}{96} = \frac{1}{4} = 25\%$$

In more generalized form, the problem statement is:

$$\text{"}y \text{ is what percent} \begin{Bmatrix} \text{more} \\ \text{less} \end{Bmatrix} \text{than } x\text{?"}$$

This means the difference between x, the number before the change (the original number), and y, the number after the change, is to be expressed as a percent of the original number.

$$\text{RATE OF CHANGE} = \frac{\text{AMOUNT OF CHANGE}}{\text{ORIGINAL NUMBER}}$$ ——————— Formula 3.3

EXAMPLE 3.4B

Answer each of the following questions.
Kristi's parents have increased their contributions to her Education Savings Plan from $125 to $425 per month.

(i) $425 is what percent more than $125?

SOLUTION

The amount before the change (the original number) is $125.
The change (increase) = 425 − 125 = $300.

$$\text{The rate of increase} = \frac{\text{Amount of increase}}{\text{Original amount}}$$

$$= \frac{300}{125} = 2.40 = 240\%$$

A technology stock dropped from $210 to $175 per share in the past six months.

(ii) What percent less than $210 is $175?

SOLUTION

The amount before the decrease is $210.
The decrease is 210 − 175 = $35.

$$\text{The rate of decrease} = \frac{35}{210} = \frac{1}{6} = 16\tfrac{2}{3}\%$$

POINTERS & PITFALLS

You can calculate the percent of increase over a base with your business calculator. The function is labelled [Δ%].

Press [2nd] [Δ%].

OLD is shown on the display. Enter the original value and press [Enter] [↓].

NEW is shown on the display. Enter the next number and press [Enter] [↓].

%CH is shown on the display. Press [CPT].

Example: OLD = 150; NEW = 180; %CH = 20.0.

Press [2nd] [QUIT] to close the worksheet.

Note: Any two of the three values can be entered into the calculator. If the NEW number is greater than the OLD number, the resulting %CH will be a positive number. If the OLD number is greater than the NEW number, the resulting %CH will be a negative number. The fourth input required by the calculator is #PD, indicating how many periods the number changes by the percent indicated. The default for this is 1.

C. Determining the original amount

If the quantity *after* the change has taken place is known, the quantity *before* the change (the original quantity) may be found by using the relationship stated in Formula 3.2.

EXAMPLE 3.4C

Answer each of the following questions.

(i) Ravi wants to pay off his student loan within the next three years, so he has increased his original weekly payment by 60%. His new payment is now $88 per week. How much was his original payment?

SOLUTION

88 is the number after the increase; the number before the increase is unknown.
Let the original number be x; then the increase is 60% of x.

$$x + 60\% \text{ of } x = 88 \text{ ——————————— using Formula 3.2}$$
$$x + 0.6x = 88$$
$$1.6x = 88$$
$$x = \frac{88}{1.6}$$
$$x = 55$$

The original payment was $55 per week.

(ii) Enrolment in the pre-health program dropped 40% in the summer semester to only 75 students. How many students were enrolled before the drop?

SOLUTION

75 is the number after the decrease.
Let the original number be x;
then the decrease is 40% of x.

$$x - 40\% \text{ of } x = 75$$
$$x - 0.4x = 75$$
$$0.6x = 75$$
$$x = \frac{75}{0.6}$$
$$x = 125$$

Thus, 125 students were enrolled before the summer semester.

(iii) What sum of money increased by 175% amounts to $143?

SOLUTION

$143 is the amount after the increase.
Let the original sum of money be x;
then the increase is 175% of x.

$$x + 175\% \text{ of } x = 143$$
$$x + 1.75x = 143$$
$$2.75x = 143$$
$$x = \frac{143}{2.75}$$
$$x = 52$$

The original amount is $52.

(iv) What sum of money when diminished by $33\frac{1}{3}$% is $48?

SOLUTION

$48 is the amount after the decrease.
Let the original sum of money be x;
then the decrease is $33\frac{1}{3}$% of x.

$$x - 33\frac{1}{3}\% \text{ of } x = 48$$

$$x - \frac{1}{3}x = 48, \qquad \text{or} \qquad x - 0.\dot{3}x = 48$$

$$\frac{2}{3}x = 48, \qquad \text{or} \qquad 0.\dot{6}x = 48$$

$$x = \frac{48 \times 3}{2}, \text{ or} \qquad x = \frac{48}{0.\dot{6}}$$

$$x = 72$$

The original sum of money is $72.

EXERCISE 3.4

MyLab Math

A.   Answer each of the following questions.

1. What is 120 increased by 40%?

2. What is 900 decreased by 20%?

3. How much is $1200 decreased by 5%?

4. How much is $24 increased by 200%?

5. What number is $83\frac{1}{3}$% more than 48?

6. What amount is $16\frac{2}{3}$% less than $66?

B.   Solve each of the following.

1. What percent more than 30 is 45?

2. What percent less than $90 is $72?

3. The amount of $240 is what percent more than $80?

4. The amount of $110 is what percent less than $165?

5. What percent less than $300 is $294?

6. The amount of $2025 is what percent more than $2000?

7. After deducting 5% from a sum of money, the remainder is $4.18. What was the original sum of money?

8. After an increase of 7%, the new amount is $749. What was the original amount?

3.5 PROBLEMS INVOLVING PERCENT
A. Summary of useful relationships

Problems involving percents abound in the field of business. The terminology used varies depending on the situation. However, most problems can be solved by means of two basic relationships. In problems related to percent *of* something

$$\boxed{\text{NEW NUMBER} = \text{RATE} \times \text{ORIGINAL NUMBER}} \text{——— Formula 3.1}$$

and in problems related to *more by* a given percent or *less by* a given percent

$$\boxed{\text{NEW NUMBER} = \text{ORIGINAL NUMBER} \begin{array}{l} + \text{INCREASE} \\ - \text{DECREASE} \end{array}} \text{——— Formula 3.2}$$

In the case of calculating a percentage rate by means of the formulas

$$\boxed{\text{RATE} = \frac{\text{NEW NUMBER}}{\text{ORIGINAL NUMBER}}} \text{——— rearrange Formula 3.1}$$

and

$$\boxed{\text{RATE OF CHANGE} = \frac{\text{AMOUNT OF CHANGE}}{\text{ORIGINAL NUMBER}}} \text{——— Formula 3.3}$$

B. Problems involving the computation of a percentage rate

EXAMPLE 3.5A

Solve each of the following problems.

(i) Material content in a lighting fixture is $40. If the total cost of the fixture is $48, what percent of cost is the material cost?

SOLUTION

$$\frac{\text{Material cost}}{\text{Total cost}} = \frac{40}{48} = \frac{5}{6} = 83\frac{1}{3}\%$$

(ii) A cash discount of $3.60 was allowed on an invoice of $120.00. What was the rate of discount?

SOLUTION

$$\text{The rate of discount} = \frac{\text{Amount of discount}}{\text{Invoice amount}}$$

$$= \frac{3.60}{120.00} = \frac{360}{12\ 000} = \frac{3}{100} = 3\%$$

(iii) What percent increase did Nirel Walker receive if her bi-weekly salary rose from $2100 to $2415?

SOLUTION

Salary before the increase (original salary) is $2100;
the raise is $2415 - 2100 = $315

$$\text{The rate of increase} = \frac{\text{Amount of increase}}{\text{Original salary}}$$

$$= \frac{315}{2100} = 0.15 = 15\%$$

(iv) Expenditures for a government program were reduced from $75 000 to $60 000. What percent change does this represent?

SOLUTION

Expenditure before the change is $75 000;
the change (decrease) = 75 000 − 60 000 = $15 000.

$$\text{The rate of change} = \frac{\text{Amount of change}}{\text{Original amount}}$$

$$= \frac{15\ 000}{75\ 000} = 0.20 = 20\%$$

Expenditures were reduced by 20%.

C. Problems involving the basic percentage relationship

EXAMPLE 3.5B

Solve each of the following problems.

(i) An electronic calculator marked $39.95 in an Ontario bookstore is subject to 13% HST (harmonized sales tax). What will it cost you to buy the calculator?

SOLUTION

Cash price = Marked price + HST

= 39.95 + 13% of 39.95

= 39.95 + 5.19 ——————— *rounded to the nearest cent

= 45.14

The calculator will cost $45.14.

(ii) Sales for this year are budgeted at $112\frac{1}{2}\%$ of last year's sales of $360 000. What is the sales budget for this year?

SOLUTION

This year's sales = $112\frac{1}{2}\%$ of 360 000

= 1.125 × 360 000

= 405 000

Budgeted sales for this year are $405 000.

(iii) A commission of $300 was paid to a broker's agent for the sale of a bond. If the commission was $\frac{3}{4}\%$ of the sales value of the bond, how much was the bond sold for?

SOLUTION

The commission paid = $\frac{3}{4}\%$ of the bond sale

$$300 = \frac{3}{4}\% \text{ of } x$$

$$300 = 0.75\% \text{ of } x$$

$$300 = 0.0075x$$

$$x = 40\ 000$$

The bond was sold for $40 000.

(iv) On the basis of past experience, Simcoe District Credit Union estimates uncollectible loans at $1\frac{1}{4}\%$ of the total loan balances outstanding. If, at the end of March, the loans account shows a balance of $3 248 000, how much should the credit union have in reserve for uncollectible loans at the end of March?

SOLUTION

The provision for uncollectible loans = $1\frac{1}{4}\%$ of $3 248 000

1% of $3 248 000 ⎯⎯⎯⎯⎯⎯⎯⎯⎯→ $32 480

$\frac{1}{4}$ of 1% of $3 248 000 ⎯⎯⎯⎯⎯→ 8120

$1\frac{1}{4}\%$ of $3 248 000 ⎯⎯⎯⎯⎯→ $40 600 ⎯⎯⎯⎯⎯ sum

The credit union should have a reserve of $40 600 for uncollectible loans at the end of March.

(v) The Consumer Price Index in July of this year was 125, which is 120% of the index from 10 years ago. What was the index 10 years ago?

SOLUTION

This year's index = 120% of the index 10 years ago

$$125 = 120\% \text{ of } x$$
$$125 = 1.20x$$
$$x = \frac{125}{1.2}$$
$$x = 104.2$$

The index 10 years ago was 104.2.

D. Problems of increase or decrease

EXAMPLE 3.5C

Solve each of the following problems.

(i) Unit sales for August were 5% more than for July. If August unit sales were 76 020, what were the July unit sales?

SOLUTION

Because July is earlier than August, its unit sales are the original number and are not known. Let them be represented by x.

$$x + 5\% \text{ of } x = 76\ 020$$
$$x + 0.05x = 76\ 020$$
$$1.05x = 76\ 020$$
$$x = \frac{76\ 020}{1.05}$$
$$x = 72\ 400$$

Unit sales in July were 72 400.

(ii) The trading price of shares of Northern Gold Mines dropped 40% to $7.20. Determine the trading price before the drop.

SOLUTION

The trading price before the drop is the original value and is not known. Let it be $x.

$$x - 40\% \text{ of } x = 7.20$$
$$x - 0.4x = 7.20$$
$$0.6x = 7.20$$
$$x = \frac{7.20}{0.6}$$
$$x = 12.00$$

The trading price before the drop was $12.00.

(iii) Dorian Guy sold his condo for $316 250. If he sold the condo for $187\frac{1}{2}\%$ more than what he paid for it, how much did he gain?

SOLUTION

The base for the percent gain is the original amount paid for the condo. Since this amount is not known, let it be $x.

$$\text{Original amount paid} + \text{Gain} = \text{Selling price}$$
$$x + 187\tfrac{1}{2}\% \text{ of } x = 316\,250$$
$$x + 1.875x = 316\,250$$
$$2.875x = 316\,250$$
$$x = \frac{316\,250}{2.875}$$
$$x = 110\,000$$

The amount originally paid was $110 000.

$$316\,250 - 110\,000 = \$206\,250$$

He gained $206 250 on the sale.

(iv) The amount paid for an article, including 5% goods and services tax, was $98.70. How much was the marked price of the article?

SOLUTION

The unknown marked price, represented by $x, is the base for the sales tax.

$$\text{Marked price} + \text{GST on marked price} = \text{Amount paid}$$
$$x + 5\% \text{ of } x = 98.70$$
$$x + 0.05x = 98.70$$
$$1.05x = 98.70$$
$$x = \frac{98.70}{1.05}$$
$$x = 94.00$$

The marked price of the article was $94.

(v) After taking off a discount of 5%, a retailer settled an invoice by paying $532.00. How much was the amount of the discount?

SOLUTION

The unknown amount of the invoice, represented by x, is the base for the discount.

Amount of invoice − Discount = Amount paid

$$x - 5\% \text{ of } x = 532$$
$$x - 0.05x = 532$$
$$0.95x = 532$$
$$x = 560$$

5% of 560 = 0.05 × 560 = $28
The discount was $28.

BUSINESS MATH **NEWS**   Canadian Rental Rates Rise at Fastest Pace in 30 Years

According to Statistics Canada, the cost of renting an apartment in Canada increased by 0.9% in a single month—in February 2019. This increase represents the fastest one-month leap experienced in Canada in almost 30 years.

"Asking rates for one-bedroom apartments in Toronto jumped 10.2 percent over the past year, to an average of $2270, while in Vancouver rates rose 4.5 percent, to $2080, and Montreal rents jumped 11.1 percent, to $1500."

However, as per the data compiled by rental site Padmapper in the table below, double-digit annual rental rate increases in 2018 weren't isolated to large expensive markets. Spikes in one- and two-bedroom apartment rental rates occurred in both large and small cities across the country.

Pos.	+/−	City	1 Bedroom			2 Bedrooms		
			Price	M/M%	Y/Y%	Price	M/M%	Y/Y%
1	— 0	Toronto	$2270	0.4	10.2	$2850	0.0	11.8
2	— 0	Vancouver	$2080	−2.3	4.5	$3280	1.5	2.5
3	— 0	Burnaby	$1570	0.0	9.0	$2250	−1.7	5.6
4	— 0	Montreal	$1500	0.0	11.1	$1780	0.0	7.2
5	— 0	Victoria	$1390	0.0	13.0	$1670	5.0	10.6
6	▲ 1	Kelowna	$1340	3.1	15.5	$1600	−4.8	−1.8
7	▼ −1	Barrie	$1330	−1.5	4.7	$1470	5.0	−5.8
8	— 0	Ottawa	$1250	0.0	13.6	$1550	0.0	14.8
9	— 0	Oshawa	$1200	0.0	13.2	$1390	0.0	6.9
10	▲ 1	Hamilton	$1160	−1.7	11.5	$1490	2.8	15.5
11	▲ 1	Kitchener	$1150	0.0	11.7	$1440	2.1	8.3
11	▼ −2	St Catharines	$1150	−4.2	5.5	$1350	−4.3	3.8
13	— 0	Calgary	$1130	2.7	2.7	$1360	0.0	−2.2
14	▲ 2	London	$1070	4.9	15.1	$1210	0.0	8.0
15	▼ −1	Kingston	$1060	0.0	9.3	$1400	0.0	5.3
16	▼ −1	Halifax	$990	−4.8	15.1	$1270	0.0	14.4
17	— 0	Winnipeg	$980	1.0	8.9	$1250	0.8	7.8

| Pos. | +/– | City | 1 Bedroom | | | 2 Bedrooms | | |
			Price	M/M%	Y/Y%	Price	M/M%	Y/Y%
18	— 0	Abbotsford	$950	0.0	11.8	$1080	−1.8	11.3
18	▲ 1	Edmonton	$950	4.4	6.7	$1240	3.3	7.8
20	▲ 1	Regina	$890	3.5	3.5	$1130	4.6	−1.7
21	▼ −1	Quebec	$860	−2.3	14.7	$1050	−5.4	10.5
22	— 0	Saskatoon	$840	1.2	6.3	$1060	5.0	6.0
23	— 0	St John's	$810	0.0	0.0	$890	0.0	6.0
24	— 0	Windsor	$750	2.7	7.1	$990	0.0	15.1

Source: www.huffingtonpost.ca/2019/03/03/canadian-rental-rates-statcan_a_23682881/, accessed March 17, 2019.

QUESTIONS

1. Using the year-over-year% (Y/Y%) information provided in the table above, calculate the base rental rates for a one-bedroom apartment, one year ago, for Toronto, Vancouver, and Montreal.

2. Two-bedroom rental rates actually decreased month-over-month (M/M%) in five cities listed in the table from January to February 2019. Using the M/M% data, calculate the price of a two-bedroom apartment in those cities in January 2019.

3. Many reasons for rental rate increases are cited in the news. Identify three reasons why rental rates are rising in so many Canadian cities.

EXERCISE 3.5

MyLab Math

A. Solve each of the following problems.

1. Out of FasDelivery's 1200 employees, $2\frac{1}{4}\%$ did not report to work last Friday due to an outbreak of the flu. How many employees were absent?

 2. A storekeeper bought merchandise for $1575. If she sells the merchandise at $33\frac{1}{3}\%$ above cost, how much profit does she make?

 3. A clerk whose salary was $740 per week was given a raise of $92.50 per week. What percent increase did the clerk receive?

4. Your hydro bill for March is $174.40. If you pay after the due date, a late payment penalty of $8.72 is added. What is the percent penalty?

5. A sales representative receives a commission of $16\frac{2}{3}\%$ on all sales. How much must his weekly sales be so that he will make a commission of $720 per week?

6. HRH Collection Agency keeps a collection fee of 25% of any amounts collected. How much did the agency collect on a bad debt if the agency forwarded $2490 to a client?

7. A commercial building is insured under a fire policy that has a face value of 80% of the building's appraised value. The annual insurance premium is $\frac{3}{8}\%$ of the face value of the policy and the premium for one year amounts to $675.
   (a) What is the face value of the policy?
   (b) What is the appraised value of the building?

🌐 **8.** A residential property is assessed for tax purposes at 40% of its market value. The residential property tax rate is $3\frac{1}{3}$% of the assessed value and the tax is $1200.
   (a) What is the assessed value of the property?
   (b) What is the market value of the property?

B. Solve each of the following problems.

1. A merchant bought an article for $7.92. For how much did the article sell if he sold it at an increase of $83\frac{1}{3}$%?

2. A retail outlet is offered a discount of $2\frac{1}{2}$% for payment in cash of an invoice of $840. If it accepted the offer, how much was the cash payment?

3. A bicycle shop reduced its selling price on a bicycle by $33\frac{1}{3}$%. If the regular selling price was $195, what was the reduced price?

4. From April 2018 to October 2018, the price of gasoline in Vancouver decreased by 8.7%. If the price in April was $1.619 per litre, what was the price per litre in October?

5. The 13% harmonized sales tax on a pair of shoes amounted to $9.62. What was the total cost of the shoes?

🌐 **6.** Daisy pays $37\frac{1}{2}$% of her monthly salary as rent on a townhouse. If the monthly rent is $1880, what is her monthly salary?

🌐 **7.** The annual interest on a bond is $4\frac{1}{2}$% of its face value and amounts to $225. What is the face value of the bond?

8. A brokerage house charges a fee of $2\frac{1}{4}$%. If its fee on a stock purchase was $432, what was the amount of the purchase?

9. Profit last quarter decreased from $6540 in the previous quarter to $1090. What was the percent decrease in profit?

10. A wage earner's hourly rate of pay increased from $15.50 to $16.12. What was the percent raise?

11. A property purchased for $42 000 is now appraised at $178 500. What is the percent gain in the value of the property?

12. The Bank of Montreal reduced its annual lending rate from 6% to 5.75%. What is the percent reduction in the lending rate?

13. After a reduction of $33\frac{1}{3}$% of the marked price, a fan was sold for $64.46. What was the marked price?

🌐 **14.** A special-purpose index has increased 125% during the past 10 years. If the index is now 279, what was the index 10 years ago?

15. After a cash discount of 5%, an invoice was settled by a payment of $646. What was the invoice amount?

16. Sales in May increased $16\frac{2}{3}$% over April sales. If May sales amounted to $24 535, what were April sales?

🌐 **17.** The working capital at the end of the third quarter was 75% higher than at the end of the second quarter. What was the amount of working capital at the end of the second quarter if the working capital at the end of the third quarter was $78 400?

🌐 **18.** After real estate fees of 8% had been deducted from the proceeds of a property sale, the vendor of the property received $88 090. What was the amount of the real estate fee?

19. A company's employee compensation expense for August, consisting of the gross pay plus 4% vacation pay based on gross pay, was $70 200. How much was the amount of vacation pay expense?

20. In Newfoundland, a car was sold for $16 675, including 15% HST. How much was the harmonized sales tax on the car?

3.6 APPLICATIONS—CURRENCY CONVERSIONS

One practical application of proportions is currency conversion. To perform currency conversions, we use exchange rates. An **exchange rate** is the value of one nation's currency expressed in terms of another nation's currency. In other words, the exchange rate tells us how much of one currency we need to buy one unit of another currency. By using proportions and exchange rate tables (sometimes called *currency cross rate* tables), we can convert easily from one currency to another.

POINTERS & PITFALLS

Larger sums of money are usually involved in currency exchanges. Therefore, the 2 decimal rule for money is insufficient. To produce a more accurate result, currency exchange rates need to carry at least 4 decimals.

A. Using proportions

Suppose we were told that the U.S. dollar is worth $1.2473 Canadian today. How would we calculate the exchange rates between the Canadian dollar and the U.S. dollar? Since there are two currencies involved, we can express the exchange rate in two different ways.

First, we can set up the exchange rate converting U.S. dollars to Canadian dollars. To do so, set up the ratio:

$$\frac{\text{Canadian dollars}}{\text{U.S. dollars}} = \frac{\$1.2473}{\$1.00} = \$1.2473 \qquad \text{\$1.2473 is the exchange rate for converting U.S. dollars to Canadian dollars}$$

To convert U.S. dollars to Canadian dollars, multiply the number of U.S. dollars by $1.2473. Thus, to convert US$10 to Canadian dollars, calculate:
$10.00 \times \$1.2473 = \$12.47$.

Second, we can set up the exchange rate converting Canadian dollars to U.S. dollars. To do so, set up the ratio:

$$\frac{\text{U.S. dollars}}{\text{Canadian dollars}} = \frac{\$1.00}{\$1.2473} = 0.8017 \qquad \text{0.8017 is the exchange rate for converting Canadian dollars to U.S. dollars}$$

To convert Canadian dollars to U.S. dollars, multiply the number of Canadian dollars by 0.8017. Thus, to convert C$10 to U.S. dollars, calculate: $10.00 \times 0.8017 = \$8.02$.

In general, if we know the exchange rate from currency A to currency B (ratio $^B/_A$), then we can calculate the exchange rate from currency B to currency A by taking the reciprocal of the original ratio (i.e., $^A/_B$).

If both rates are known, choosing which exchange rate to use can be confusing. The best way to choose the exchange rate is to express the exchange rate as a proportion of two currencies so that the desired currency is in the numerator of the known ratio.

EXAMPLE 3.6A

Suppose you wanted to convert C$150 into U.S. dollars. You read in the newspaper that one U.S. dollar is worth 1.2473 Canadian dollars, and that one Canadian dollar is worth 0.8017 U.S. dollars. How much would you receive in U.S. dollars?

SOLUTION

Let the number of U.S. dollars be x. The desired currency is U.S. dollars.

Known ratio $\dfrac{\text{US\$0.8017}}{\text{C\$1}}$

Second ratio $\dfrac{\text{US\$}x}{\text{C\$150}}$

Proportion $\dfrac{\text{US\$0.8017}}{\text{C\$1}} = \dfrac{\text{US\$}x}{\text{C\$150}}$

$$\frac{0.8017}{1} = \frac{x}{150}$$

Then cross-multiply:

$$1(x) = 0.8017(150)$$
$$x = 120.255$$

Therefore, C$150 is worth US$120.26.

EXAMPLE 3.6B

While travelling in the United States, you filled your gas tank with 16.6 U.S. gallons of gas at a cost of US$42.00.

(i) How much did the fill-up cost you in Canadian funds if one Canadian dollar costs 0.7644 U.S. dollars?

SOLUTION

Let the amount in Canadian dollars be x.

$$\frac{\text{C\$1}}{\text{US\$0.7644}} = \frac{\text{C\$}x}{\text{US\$42.00}}$$

$$\frac{1}{0.7644} = \frac{x}{42.00}$$

$$1(42.00) = 0.7644(x)$$

$$x = \frac{42.00}{0.7644}$$

$$x = 54.945055$$

The fill-up cost $54.95 in Canadian funds.

(ii) What was the cost of gas per litre in Canadian funds, if one U.S. gallon is equivalent to 3.8 litres?

SOLUTION

Since 1 U.S. gallon = 3.8 litres

16.6 U.S. gallons = 3.8(16.6) = 63.08 litres

From (i), US$42.00 = C$54.95

$$\text{Cost per litre} = \frac{54.95}{63.08} = \text{C\$0.871}$$

The cost per litre in Canadian funds was $0.871/L (or 87.1¢/L).

B. Using cross rate tables

Cross rate tables are commonly found in newspapers and business and travel magazines. They show the exchange rates between a number of currencies. One example is shown in Table 3.2. Notice that exchange rates are often given to more decimal places than the usual two places for dollars and cents. To convert currency A into currency B, first locate currency A in the column headings (along the top of the table). Then find currency B in the row headings (along the left side of the table). The exchange rate is the number where the column and row intersect. For instance, from the table, the exchange rate to convert Canadian dollars to U.S. dollars is 0.7625.

POINTERS & PITFALLS

Not all currencies use the same decimals when expressing amounts.

- Final currency amounts for the Canadian dollar, U.S. dollar, British pound, euro, and Swiss franc should be rounded to the standard 2 decimal places.
- Final currency amounts for the Japanese yen should be rounded to the nearest integer, as there are no decimal amounts in Japanese currency.

EXAMPLE 3.6C   Using the exchange rate in Table 3.2, convert $55 Canadian into Swiss francs.

SOLUTION   First, to find the exchange rate from Canadian dollars to Swiss francs, locate the Canadian dollar column in the table. Move down the Canadian dollar column until you come to the Swiss franc row. The exchange rate is 0.7604.

Conversion = 55.00 × 0.7604

= 41.82 Swiss francs

Table 3.2 Currency Cross Rates (Retrieved October 26, 2018 from x-Rates.com)

| | (converting from) | | | | | | | |
	Canada Dollar	United States Dollar	Europe Euro	United Kingdom Pound	Japan Yen	China Yuan Renminbi	Switzerland Franc	India Rupee
Canada Dollar	1.0000	1.3118	1.4983	1.6832	0.0117	0.1890	1.3160	0.0179
United States Dollar	0.7625	1.0000	1.1417	1.2829	0.0089	0.1440	1.0029	0.0137
Europe Euro	0.6681	0.8761	1.0000	1.1237	0.0078	0.1261	0.8783	0.0120
United Kingdom Pound	0.5944	0.7796	0.8900	1.0000	0.0070	0.1123	0.7818	0.0107
Japan Yen	85.2902	111.8642	127.7273	143.5219	1.0000	16.1130	112.1951	1.5301
China Yuan Renminbi	5.2936	6.9430	7.9270	8.9068	0.0621	1.0000	6.9630	0.0950
Switzerland Franc	0.7604	0.9971	1.1384	1.2792	0.0089	0.1436	1.0000	0.0136
India Rupee	55.7528	73.1157	83.4803	93.8001	0.6536	10.5313	73.3300	1.0000

(converting to)

EXAMPLE 3.6D

Suppose you are taking a trip from Canada to France, and then to Japan. Convert C$100 to euros, then convert the euros to Japanese yen. Use the exchange rates in Table 3.2.

SOLUTION

(i) From the table, the exchange rate for Canadian dollars to euros is 0.6681.

Conversion = 100 × 0.6681

= 66.81 euros

(ii) From the table, the exchange rate for euros to Japanese yen is 127.7273.

Conversion = 66.81 × 127.7273

= 8533 yen

You can check this answer by converting C$100 to Japanese yen. However, the answers may differ slightly due to rounding.

POINTERS & PITFALLS

Price per litre of gasoline is generally expressed to 3 decimal points (129.9 ¢/L = $1.299/L).

EXERCISE 3.6

MyLab Math

A. Answer each of the following questions.

🌐 **1.** How many U.S. dollars can you buy for C$750 if one Canadian dollar is worth US$0.8168?

🌐 **2.** How many Canadian dollars can you buy for US$750 if one Canadian dollar is worth US$0.8168?

🌐 **3.** Suppose the exchange rate was US$1.31 for each Canadian dollar. What is the price, in Canadian dollars, of a flight to Florida costing US$299?

🌐 **4.** What is the price of gasoline per litre in Canadian dollars if a U.S. gallon of gasoline costs US$2.465? One U.S. dollar is worth C$1.2864 and one U.S. gallon is equivalent to 3.8 litres.

B. Use Table 3.2 to make each of the following conversions.

🌐 **1.** Convert US$350 to Canadian dollars.

2. Convert C$200 to euros.

3. Convert US$175 to Swiss francs.

🌐 **4.** Convert 250 United Kingdom pounds to Japanese yen.

5. Convert 550 euros to Canadian dollars.

3.7 APPLICATIONS—INDEX NUMBERS
A. The nature of index numbers

An **index number** results when you compare two values of the same item measured at different points in time. The comparison of the two values is stated as a ratio, and then expressed as a percent. When the percent symbol is dropped, the result is called an index number.

EXAMPLE 3.7A

The price of a textbook was $115 in 2017 and $125.35 in 2019. Compare the two prices to create an index number.

SOLUTION

The change in price over the time period 2017 to 2019 can be measured in relative terms by writing the ratio

$$\frac{\text{Price in 2019}}{\text{Price in 2017}} = \frac{125.35}{115} = 1.09 = 109\%$$

An index number can now be created by dropping the percent symbol. The price index is 109.

To construct an index number, you must select one of the two values as the denominator of the ratio. The point in time at which the denominator was measured is called the **base period**. In Example 3.7A, 2017 was chosen as the base period. The chronologically earlier time period is usually used as the base period.

The index for the base period is always 100. The difference between an index number and 100 indicates the relative change that has taken place. For Example 3.7A, the index number 109 indicates that the price of the book in 2019 was 9% higher than in 2017.

Indexes provide an easy way of expressing changes that occur in daily business. Converting data to indexes makes working with very large or small numbers easier and provides a basis for many types of analysis. Indexes are used in comparing and analyzing economic data and have become a widely accepted tool for measuring changes in business activity. Two of the more common indexes frequently mentioned in the media are the Consumer Price Index (CPI) and the Toronto Stock Exchange S&P/TSX Composite Index.

POINTERS
& PITFALLS

As indexes are similar to percentages, an index will have only 4 decimals.

B. The Consumer Price Index and its uses

The **Consumer Price Index (CPI)** is the most widely accepted indicator of changes in the overall price level of goods and services. In Canada, a fixed "basket" or collection of goods and services is used to represent all Canadian goods and services. The prices of the items in this collection are monitored and are used to represent the price change of all goods and services. The CPI is currently based on 2002 price levels and is published monthly by Statistics Canada. For example, the 2017 CPI of 130.4 indicated that the price level increased 30.4% from 2002 (the base year) to 2017.

You can use the Consumer Price Index to determine the *purchasing power of the Canadian dollar* and to compute *real income*.

The **purchasing power of the dollar** is the reciprocal of the CPI; that is,

$$\text{Purchasing power of the dollar} = \frac{\$1}{\text{Consumer Price Index}}(100)$$

EXAMPLE 3.7B

The CPI was 128.4 for 2016 and 130.4 for 2017. Determine the purchasing power of the Canadian dollar for the two years, and interpret the meaning of the results.

SOLUTION

Purchasing power of the dollar for 2016

$$= \frac{\$1}{128.4}(100) = 0.778816$$

Purchasing power of the dollar for 2017

$$= \frac{\$1}{130.4}(100) = 0.766871$$

This means the dollar in 2016 could purchase only 77.88% of what it could purchase in 2002 (the base year). In 2017, the dollar could purchase even less (about 76.69% of what it could purchase in 2002).

The CPI can be used to eliminate the effect of inflation on income by adjusting **nominal income** (income stated in current dollars) to **real income** (income stated in base-period dollars or inflation-adjusted income).

$$\boxed{\text{REAL INCOME} = \frac{\text{INCOME IN CURRENT DOLLARS}}{\text{CONSUMER PRICE INDEX}}(100)} \quad\text{——— Formula 3.4}$$

EXAMPLE 3.7C

James' income was $65 000 in 2002, $79 500 in 2015, and $84 000 in 2017. The Canadian CPI was 126.6 in 2015 and 130.4 in 2017. The CPI base year is 2002.

(i) Determine James' real income in 2015 and 2017.

(ii) Should James be happy about his increases in salary from 2002 to 2017?

SOLUTION

(i) Real income in 2015 $= \dfrac{\text{Nominal income}}{(\text{CPI in 2015})}(100)$

$\qquad\qquad\qquad = \dfrac{\$79\,500}{126.6}(100) = \$62\,796.21$

Real income in 2017 $= \dfrac{\text{Nominal income}}{(\text{CPI in 2017})}(100)$

$\qquad\qquad\qquad = \dfrac{\$84\,000}{130.4}(100) = \$64\,471.18$

(ii) To compare nominal income with real income, it is useful to determine income changes in absolute and relative terms.

Year	2002	2015	2017
Nominal income	$65 000	$79 500	$84 000
Simple price index	$\frac{65\,000}{(65\,000)}(100)$ $= 100.00$	$\frac{79\,500}{(65\,000)}(100)$ $= 122.3$	$\frac{84\,000}{(65\,000)}(100)$ $= 129.2$
Absolute ($) increase		$14 500	$19 000
Relative (%) increase		22.3%	29.2%
Real income	$65 000	$62 796.21	$64 417.18
Simple price index	$\frac{65\,000}{(65\,000)}(100)$ $= 100.00$	$\frac{62\,796.21}{(65\,000)}(100)$ $= 96.61$	$\frac{64\,417.18}{(65\,000)}(100)$ $= 99.10$
Absolute ($) increase (decrease)		($2 203.79)	($582.82)
Relative (%) increase (decrease)		(3.39%)	(0.90%)

While James' income in 2015 increased 22.3% over his 2002 income, his purchasing power, reflected by his 2015 real income, actually decreased by 3.39% over the thirteen-year period. From 2002 to 2017, his nominal income increased by 29.2% over his 2002 income. His real income decreased by 0.90% during the period 2002 to 2017.

EXERCISE 3.7   MyLab Math

Solve each of the following problems.

1. Using 2015 as a base period, compute a simple price index for each of the following commodities. Interpret your results.

Commodity	Price in 2015	Price in 2017
Bread (loaf)	$2.49	$2.58
Bus pass	$199	$220
Clothing	$1650.00	$1600.00

2. Using 2012 as the base period, compute a series of simple price indexes for the price of gold for the period 2012 to 2017. Interpret your results.

	2012	2013	2014	2015	2016	2017
Gold price per ounce	$1710.55	$1371.87	$1321.52	$1492.85	$1725.60	$1642.10

Source: www.goldbroker.com/charts/gold-price/cad; price of gold on November 1st

3. The Consumer Price Index for 2015 was 126.6 and for 2017 it was 130.4.
   (a) Determine the purchasing power of the dollar in 2015 and 2017 relative to the base year 2002.
   (b) Compute the purchasing power of the dollar in 2017 relative to 2015.

4. Kim's annual incomes for 2013, 2015, and 2017 were $50 000, $60 000, and $65 000, respectively. Given that the Consumer Price Index for the three years was 122.8, 126.6, and 130.4, respectively, compute Kim's real income for 2013, 2015, and 2017.

5. Tamara earned $74 000 in 2016. If the Consumer Price Index in 2016 was 128.4 and in 2017 was 130.4, what did Tamara have to earn in 2017 just to keep up with inflation?

6. The S&P/TSX Composite Index was $15 953.51 on October 26, 2017 and $14 888.26 on October 26, 2018. Josh holds an investment portfolio representative of the stocks in the index. If the value of the portfolio on October 26, 2017 was $279 510, what was the value of the portfolio on October 26, 2018?

3.8 APPLICATIONS—PERSONAL INCOME TAXES

Personal income taxes are taxes imposed by the federal and provincial governments on the earned income of residents of Canada. The federal government collects and refunds income taxes based on the income you calculate on your income tax return each year.

Provincial tax brackets vary by province, and federal tax rates currently range from 15% to 33% of taxable income. The tax rates increase as your income increases. The 2018 federal income tax brackets and tax rates are shown in Table 3.3.

Table 3.3 2018 Federal Income Tax Brackets and Tax Rates (© S. A. Hummelbrunner)

Taxable Income (income tax brackets)	Tax Rates
$46 605 or less	15% of taxable income less than or equal to $46 605; plus
Over $46 605 up to $93 208	20.5% of taxable income greater than $46 605 and less than or equal to $93 208; plus
Over $93 208 up to $144 489	26% of taxable income greater than $93 208 and less than or equal to $144 489; plus
Over $144 489 up to $205 842	29% of taxable income greater than $144 489 and less than or equal to $205 842; plus
Over $205 842	33% of taxable income greater than $205 842

The income tax brackets are adjusted annually for changes in the Consumer Price Index (CPI) in excess of 3%. If the CPI increases by less than 3% during a year, there is no increase in the tax brackets.

The **marginal tax rate** is the rate at which your next dollar of earned income is taxed. Your marginal tax rate increases when your earnings increase and you move from a lower tax bracket to a higher tax bracket. It decreases if your earnings decline and you move into a lower tax bracket. Due to the variety of provincial tax rates and surtaxes, the combined federal-provincial marginal tax rates vary from province to province.

EXAMPLE 3.8A

Use the tax brackets and rates in Table 3.3 to compute the federal tax for Jim, Kulvir, and Lee, who are, respectively, declaring taxable income of

(i) $55 000

(ii) $110 000

(iii) $165 000

(iv) Evaluate the increase in federal tax with respect to the increase in Taxable income of Kulvir and Lee over Jim

SOLUTION

(i) Federal tax for Jim = 15% × $46 605 + 20.5% × (55 000 − 46 605)

= $6990.75 + $1720.98 = $8711.73

(ii) Federal tax for Kulvir = 15% × $46 605 + 20.5% × (93 208 − 46 605) + 26% × (110 000 − 93 208)

= $6990.75 + $9553.62 + $4365.92

= $20 910.29

(iii) Federal tax for Lee = 15% × $46 605 + 20.5% × (93 208 − 46 605) + 26% × (144 489 − 93 208) + 29% × (165 000 − 144 489)

= $6990.75 + $9553.62 + $13 333.06 + $5948.19

= $35 825.62

(iv) Therefore, Jim, Kulvir, and Lee must report federal tax of $8711.73, $20 910.29, and $35 825.62 respectively.

Taxpayer	Taxable Income $	Increase in Income $	Federal Tax $	Increase in Federal Tax $
Jim	55 000		8 711.73	
Kulvir	110 000	55 000 (100%)	20 910.29	12 198.56 (140%)
Lee	165 000	110 000 (200%)	35 825.62	27 113.89 (311%)

For an increase in income of 100%, the federal tax increases 140%. For an increase in income of 200%, the federal tax increases 311%.

EXERCISE 3.8

MyLab Math

Use the 2018 federal income tax brackets and rates in Table 3.3 to answer each of the following questions.

1. Victor calculated his 2018 taxable income to be $49 450. How much federal income tax should he report?

2. Sonja reported a taxable income of $96 300 on her 2018 income tax return. How much federal income tax should she report?

3. How much federal income tax should Aman report if she earned taxable income of $32 920 and $17 700 from her two jobs?

4. In early 2018, Mei Ling's gross pay increased from $87 000 per year to $95 000 per year.
   (a) What was the annual percent increase in Mei Ling's pay before federal income taxes?
   (b) What was the annual percent increase in Mei Ling's pay after federal income taxes were deducted?

MyLab Math Visit MyLab Math to practise any of this chapter's exercises marked with a 🌐 as often as you want. The guided solutions help you calculate an answer step by step. You'll find a personalized study plan and additional interactive resources to help you master Business Math!

REVIEW EXERCISE

1. **LO①** Set up ratios to compare each of the following sets of quantities. Reduce each ratio to its lowest terms.

   (a) twenty-five dimes and three dollars

   (b) five hours to 50 min

   (c) $36.75 for thirty litres of gasoline

   (d) $21 for three-and-a-half hours

   (e) 1440 words for 120 lines for 6 pages

   (f) 90 kg for 24 ha (hectares) for 18 weeks

🌐 2. **LO①** Solve each of the following proportions.

   (a) $5 : n = 35 : 21$

   (b) $10 : 6 = 30 : x$

   (c) $1.15 : 0.85 = k : 1.19$

   (d) $3.60 : m = 10.8 : 8.10$

   (e) $\dfrac{5}{7} : \dfrac{15}{14} = \dfrac{6}{5} : t$

   (f) $\gamma : \dfrac{9}{8} = \dfrac{5}{4} : \dfrac{45}{64}$

🌐 3. **LO③** Use fractional equivalents to compute each of the following.

   (a) $66\frac{2}{3}\%$ of $168

   (b) $37\frac{1}{2}\%$ of $2480

   (c) 125% of $924

   (d) $183\frac{1}{3}\%$ of $720

4. **LO③** Use the 1% method to determine each of the following.

   (a) $\dfrac{1}{4}\%$ of $2664

   (b) $\dfrac{5}{8}\%$ of $1328

   (c) $1\frac{2}{3}\%$ of $5400

   (d) $2\frac{1}{5}\%$ of $1260

🌐 5. **LO③** Answer each of the following questions.

   (a) What is the percentage rate if the base is 88 and the percentage is 55?

   (b) 63 is what percent of 36?

   (c) What is $\frac{3}{4}\%$ of $64?

   (d) 450% of $5 is what amount?

   (e) $245 is $87\frac{1}{2}\%$ of what amount?

   (f) $2\frac{1}{4}\%$ of what amount is $9.90?

   (g) What percent of $62.50 is $1.25?

   (h) $30 is what percent of $6?

   (i) $166\frac{2}{3}\%$ of what amount is $220?

   (j) $1.35 is $\frac{1}{3}\%$ of what amount?

6. **LO④** Answer each of the following questions.

   (a) How much is $8 increased by 125%?

   (b) What amount is $2\frac{1}{4}\%$ less than $2000?

   (c) What percent less than $120 is $100?

   (d) $975 is what percent more than $150?

   (e) $98 is 75% more than what amount?

   (f) After a reduction of 15%, the amount paid for Beats Headphones was $289. What was the price before the reduction?

   (g) What sum of money when increased by 250% will amount to $490?

🌐 7. **LO①** Dale, Evelyn, and Frank own a business jointly and share profits and losses in the same proportion as their investments. How much of a profit of $4500 will each receive if their investments are $4000, $6000, and $5000, respectively?

8. **LO①** Departments A, B, and C occupy floor space of 80 m², 140 m², and 160 m², respectively. If the total rental cost for the floor space is $11 400 per month, how much of the rental cost should each department pay?

🌐 9. **LO①** Four beneficiaries are to divide an estate of $189 000 in the ratio $\frac{1}{3} : \frac{1}{4} : \frac{3}{8} : \frac{1}{24}$. How much should each receive?

10. **LO①** Three insurance companies have insured a building in the ratio $\frac{1}{2}$ to $\frac{1}{3}$ to $\frac{2}{5}$. How much of a fire loss of $185 000 should each company pay?

🌐 11. **LO②** A hot water tank with a capacity of 220 L can be heated in 20 minutes. At the same rate, how many minutes will it take to heat a tank containing 176 L?

12. LO❷ If the variable cost amounts to $130 000 when sales are $250 000, what will the variable cost be when sales are $350 000?

13. LO❸ Gross profit for April was two-fifths of net sales, and net income was two-sevenths of gross profit. Net income was $4200.

  (a) What was the gross profit for April?

  (b) What were net sales for April?

14. LO❸ In a college, $\frac{4}{9}$ of all employees are faculty and the ratio of the faculty to support staff is 5 : 4. How many people does the college employ if the support staff numbers 192?

15. LO❸ In the last municipal election, $62\frac{1}{2}\%$ of the population of 94 800 was eligible to vote. Of those eligible, $33\frac{1}{3}\%$ voted.

  (a) What was the number of eligible voters?

  (b) How many voted?

16. LO❸ An investment portfolio of $150 000 consists of the following: $37\frac{1}{2}\%$ in bonds, $56\frac{1}{4}\%$ in common stock, and the remainder in preferred shares. How much money is invested in each type of investment security?

17. LO❹ A sales representative's orders for May were $16\frac{2}{3}\%$ less than her April orders, which amounted to $51 120.

  (a) How much were the sales rep's orders in May?

  (b) By what amount did her orders decrease?

18. LO❹ The appraised value of a property has increased $233\frac{1}{3}\%$ since it was purchased by the present owner. The purchase price of the property was $120 000, its appraised value at that time.

  (a) How much is the current appraised value?

  (b) How much would the owner gain by selling at the appraised value?

19. LO❸ The direct material cost of manufacturing a product is $103.95, direct labour cost is $46.20, and overhead is $57.75.

  (a) What is the percent content of each element of cost in the product?

  (b) What is the overhead percent rate based on direct labour?

20. LO❸ Inspection of a production run of 2400 items showed that 180 items did not meet specifications. Of the 180 that did not pass inspection, 150 could be reworked. The remainder had to be scrapped.

  (a) What percent of the production run did not pass inspection?

  (b) What percent of the items that did not meet specifications had to be scrapped?

21. LO❹ The price of a stock a week ago was $56.25 per share. Today the price per share is $51.75.

  (a) What is the percent change in price?

  (b) What is the new price as a percent of the old price?

22. LO❹ A wage earner's hourly rate of pay increased from $6.30 to $16.80 during the past decade.

  (a) What was the percent change in the hourly rate of pay?

  (b) What is the current rate of pay as a percent of the rate a decade ago?

23. LO❸ A firm sets aside $2\frac{1}{4}\%$ of sales to cover anticipated bad debt expense. If bad debts were $7875, what were the firm's sales?

24. LO❸ A ski shop lists ski boots at 240% of cost. If the ski shop prices the DX2 Model at $396, what was the cost of the ski boots to the shop?

25. LO❹ A property owner listed his property for 160% more than he paid for it. The owner eventually accepted an offer $12\frac{1}{2}\%$ below his asking price and sold the property for $191 100. How much did the owner pay for the property?

26. LO❹ A marina listed a sailboat at $33\frac{1}{3}\%$ above cost. At the end of the season, the list price was reduced by 22.5% and the sailboat was sold for $15 500. What was the cost of the sailboat to the marina?

27. LO❸ A & E Holdings' profit and loss statement showed a net income of $9\frac{3}{4}\%$ of revenue or $29 250. Fifteen percent of net income was paid in corporation tax and 75% of the net income after tax was paid out as dividends to Alice and Emile, who hold shares in the ratio 5 to 3.

  (a) What was the revenue of A & E Holdings?

  (b) How much was the after-tax income?

  (c) How much was paid out in dividends?

  (d) What percent of net income did Alice receive as a dividend?

28. LO④ A farm was offered for sale at 320% above cost. The farm was finally sold for $770 000, at $8\frac{1}{3}$% below the asking price.

(a) What was the original cost of the farm to the owner?

(b) How much gain did the owner realize?

(c) What percent of the original cost does this gain represent?

29. LO⑤ Suppose it costs C$380 to purchase US$310.61.

(a) What is the exchange rate?

(b) How many U.S. dollars will you receive if you convert C$725 into U.S. dollars?

30. LO⑤ Media Marketing of Atlanta, Georgia, offers a three-day accommodation coupon for a Hilton Head resort in South Carolina at a promotion price of C$316. If the exchange rate is C$1.18 per U.S. dollar, what is the value of the coupon in U.S. dollars?

31. LO⑥ Suppose the Consumer Price Index in 2019 is 131.9, with 2002 as the base year.

(a) What is the purchasing power of the dollar in 2019 compared to 2002?

(b) What is the real income, relative to 2002, of a wage earner whose income amounted to $62 900 in 2019?

32. LO⑦ Abeni calculated her 2018 taxable income to be $102 450. How much federal income tax should she report? Refer Table 3.3.

33. LO⑦ Matt's gross pay had been $68 000 per year, when he received an increase of $6000 per year. Refer Table 3.3.

(a) What was the annual percent increase in Matt's pay before federal income taxes?

(b) What was the annual percent increase in Matt's pay after federal income taxes were deducted?

SELF-TEST

1. Compute each of the following.

(a) 125% of $280

(b) $\frac{3}{8}$% of $20 280

(c) $83\frac{1}{3}$% of $174

(d) $1\frac{1}{4}$% of $1056

2. Solve each of the following proportions.

(a) $65 : 39 = x : 12$

(b) $\frac{7}{6} : \frac{35}{12} = \frac{6}{5} : x$

3. The results of a market survey indicate that 24 respondents preferred Brand X, 36 preferred Brand Y, and 20 had no preference. What percent of the sample preferred Brand Y?

4. Departments A, B, and C occupy floor space of 40 m², 80 m², and 300 m², respectively. If the total rental for the space is $25 200 per month, how much rent should Department B pay?

5. Past experience shows that the clientele of a restaurant spends $9.60 on beverages for every $12 spent on food. If it is expected that food sales will amount to $42 500 for a month, how much should be budgeted for beverage sales?

6. After a reduction of $16\frac{2}{3}$% off the marked price, a pair of boots sold for $60. What was the marked price?

7. A bonus is to be divided among four employees in the ratio $\frac{1}{2} : \frac{1}{3} : \frac{1}{5} : \frac{1}{6}$. What is each employee's share of a bonus of $40 500?

8. Jorjanna Fawcett's hourly rate of pay was increased from $16 to $18.24. What was the percent raise?

9. A bicycle was sold for $282.50. The selling price included 13% harmonized sales tax. Determine the amount of HST on the bike.

10. A microwave oven originally advertised at $220 is reduced to $209 during a sale. By what percent was the price reduced?

11. A special consumer index has increased 100% during the past 10 years. If the index is now 360, what was it 10 years ago?

12. Mr. Braid owned $\frac{3}{8}$ of a racehorse. He sold $\frac{2}{3}$ of his interest in the racehorse for $18 000. What was the value of the racehorse?

13. Suppose it cost C$0.3384 to purchase one Brazilian real.

   (a) How much would it cost in Brazilian reals to purchase one Canadian dollar?

   (b) How many Brazilian reals would you need to buy 500 Canadian dollars?

14. If one Canadian dollar is equivalent to US$0.8150, how much do you need in Canadian funds to buy US$800.00?

15. What is the purchasing power of the dollar relative to the base year of 2002 if the Consumer Price Index is 126.7?

16. Suppose a taxpayer is in the tax bracket in which federal income tax is calculated as $6990.75 plus 20.5% of income over $46 605. How much federal income tax must he report if he earns $48 750?

CHALLENGE PROBLEMS

1. Two consecutive price reductions of the same percent reduced the price of an item from $25 to $16. By what percent was the price reduced each time?

2. Luis ordered four pairs of black socks and some additional pairs of blue socks from a clothing catalogue. The price of the black socks per pair was twice that of the blue. When the order was filled, it was found that the number of pairs of the two colours had been interchanged. This increased the bill by 50% (before taxes and delivery charges). Determine the ratio of the number of pairs of black socks to the number of pairs of blue socks in Luis's original order.

3. Following a 10% decrease in her annual salary, what percent increase would an employee need to receive in future to get back to her original salary level?

CASE STUDY **The Business of Taxes**

▶ Camille operates a child care service from her home. Her gross business income for 2018 amounted to $42 350. Her tax-deductible business expenses consisted of the following:

Advertising	$1700
Dues, memberships, subscriptions	520
Motor vehicle expenses	1115
Supplies	582
Meals and entertainment	495
Other expenses	437

Camille can also deduct home expenses, such as utilities, property taxes, house insurance, mortgage interest, and maintenance for the business use of a workspace in her home. The amount that may be deducted is a proportion of the total annual home expenses allocated to the workspace on a reasonable basis, such as area or number of rooms. Camille's eligible home expenses for the year were:

Heat	$3750
Power	2480
Water	610
House insurance	1420
Maintenance	1930
Mortgage interest	6630
Property taxes	3260
Other expenses	690

The house covers 345 square metres and consists of eight rooms. Camille uses one room with an area of 45 square metres as her business office.

QUESTIONS

1. What portion of her eligible home expenses may Camille claim as tax-deductible expenses if the expenses are allocated on the basis of
   (a) area?   **(b)** number of rooms?

2. What is her net business income if Camille allocates home expenses on the basis of area?

3. For most individuals, basic federal income tax equals the federal tax calculated according to Table 3.3, less non-refundable tax credits. What is Camille's basic federal income tax if she reports a non-refundable tax credit of $12 138?
   Note: Federal tax is reduced by 15% of total non-refundable tax credits.

4. What percent of Camille's business income is basic federal income tax?

5. What percent of Camille's taxable income is basic federal income tax?

SUMMARY OF FORMULAS

Formula 3.1

$$\text{PERCENTAGE} = \text{RATE} \times \text{BASE}$$

or

$$\text{NEW NUMBER} = \text{RATE} \times \text{ORIGINAL NUMBER}$$

$$\text{RATE} = \frac{\text{PERCENTAGE}}{\text{BASE}} \quad \text{or} \quad \frac{\text{NEW NUMBER}}{\text{ORIGINAL NUMBER}}$$

The basic percentage relationship

The formula for calculating the percentage rate when comparing a number (the percentage) to another number (the base or original number)

Formula 3.2

$$\text{NEW NUMBER} = \text{ORIGINAL NUMBER} \begin{array}{l} + \text{ INCREASE} \\ - \text{ DECREASE} \end{array}$$

The relationship to use with problems of increase or decrease (problems of change)

Formula 3.3

$$\text{RATE OF CHANGE} = \frac{\text{AMOUNT OF CHANGE}}{\text{ORIGINAL NUMBER}}$$

The formula for calculating the rate of change (rate of increase or decrease)

Formula 3.4

$$\text{REAL INCOME} = \frac{\text{INCOME IN CURRENT DOLLARS}}{\text{CONSUMER PRICE INDEX}} (100)$$

The formula for eliminating the effect of inflation on income

GLOSSARY

Base period in an index, the period of time against which comparisons are made. The base period is arbitrarily selected, but it always has an index number of 100 *(p. 131)*

Consumer Price Index (CPI) the index that shows the price change for a sample of goods and services that is used to indicate the price change for all goods and services *(p. 131)*

Equivalent ratios in higher terms ratios obtained by multiplying each term of a ratio by the same number *(p. 97)*

Exchange rate the value of one nation's currency expressed in terms of another's currency *(p. 127)*

Index number expresses the relative change in the value of an item at different points in time. One of the points in time is a base period, which is always defined to have a value of 100 *(p. 131)*

Marginal tax rate the rate at which your next dollar of earned income is taxed. Marginal tax rates tend to increase as earnings increase *(p. 134)*

Nominal income income stated in current dollars *(p. 132)*

Personal income tax taxes imposed by the federal and provincial governments on the earned income of Canadian residents *(p. 134)*

Proportion a statement of equality between two ratios *(p. 101)*

Purchasing power of the dollar the reciprocal of the Consumer Price Index *(p. 132)*

Ratio a comparison by division of the relative values of numbers or quantities *(p. 96)*

Real income income stated in base-period dollars or inflation-adjusted income *(p. 132)*

Terms of a ratio the numbers appearing in a ratio *(p. 96)*

4

Linear Systems

LEARNING OBJECTIVES

Upon completing this chapter, you will be able to do the following:

1. Graph linear equalities in two variables.

2. Graph linear systems consisting of two linear relations in two variables.

3. Use graphical solution of systems of linear equations in two variables

4. Solve problems by setting up systems of linear equations in two variables.

5. Solve systems of linear inequalities in two variables using graphical methods.

Frank Coenders/Alamy Stock Photo

Most manufacturing companies produce more than one product. In deciding the quantities of each product to produce, management has to take into account the combination of production levels that will make the most efficient use of labour, materials, and transportation to produce the highest level of profit. In some cases, management has to minimize the cost of producing products just to be able to make enough profits to stay in business. Most companies have so many factors to consider that they need sophisticated methods of evaluation. However, many situations like this can be simplified and solved. Suppose you are in the business of producing children's toys. If you cannot produce all the items because of limited budget or limited manufacturing capacity, you need to consider the relative profitability of each item to determine which combination of items to produce. You can define the variables and then set up a system of linear equations or a system of linear inequalities and solve the system by graphical or algebraic methods to decide how to best allocate your resources to maximize profits or minimize costs to the business.

INTRODUCTION

In many types of problems, the relationship between two or more variables can be represented by setting up linear equations. Graphical as well as algebraic techniques are available to solve such problems.

4.1 GRAPHING LINEAR EQUATIONS
A. Basic concept

Any linear system that consists of two equations in two variables can be solved graphically or algebraically.

Solving a system of two equations requires determining a pair of values for the two variables that satisfies both of the equations. In general, there are three possibilities in solving a system of linear equations;

1. A unique solution exists for the system. Graphically, the lines for the two equations intersect. These systems are called **Consistent and Independent**.

2. No solution exists for the system. Graphically, the lines for the two equations are parallel. These systems are called **Inconsistent systems**.

3. Many solutions exist for the system. The lines for the two equations coincide and the result is an infinite number of solutions for the system. These systems are called **Consistent and Dependent**.

Graphical and algebraic solutions of systems of linear equations in two variables are used extensively when doing break-even analysis. Break-even analysis is explored further in Chapter 5. Graphical solutions include graphing a line for each equation in the system and finding the point of intersection of the two lines, if it exists. Graphical solutions are explained next in this chapter. Algebraic solutions include two important methods of elimination and substitution that will be explored in section 4.2 of this chapter.

B. Graphing in a system of rectangular coordinates

A system of rectangular coordinates, as shown in Figure 4.1, consists of two straight lines that intersect at right angles in a plane. The *horizontal* line is called the **X axis**, while the *vertical* line is called the **Y axis**. The point of intersection of the two axes is called the **origin**.

The two axes are used as number lines. By agreement, on the X axis the numbers are positive to the right of the origin and negative to the left. On the Y axis the numbers are positive above the origin and negative below the origin.

The position of any point relative to the pair of axes is defined by an **ordered pair of numbers** (x, y) such that the first number (the x value or the **x coordinate**) always represents the directed distance of the point from the Y axis. The second number (the y value or the **y coordinate**) always represents the directed distance of the point from the X axis.

The origin is identified by the ordered pair $(0, 0)$; that is, the coordinates of the origin are $(0, 0)$, since the distance of the point from either axis is zero.

As shown in Figure 4.2, the point marked A is identified by the coordinates $(4, 3)$. That is, the directed distance of the point is four units to the right of the Y axis (its x value, or x coordinate, is $+4$), and the directed distance of the point is three units above the X axis (its y value, or y coordinate is $+3$). Note that the point may be found by counting four units to the right along the X axis and then moving three units up, parallel to the Y axis.

Figure 4.1 Rectangular Coordinates (© S. A. Hummelbrunner)

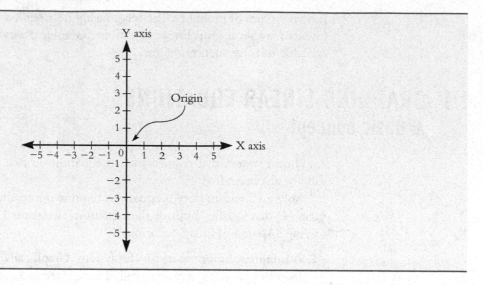

Figure 4.2 Locating a Point (© S. A. Hummelbrunner)

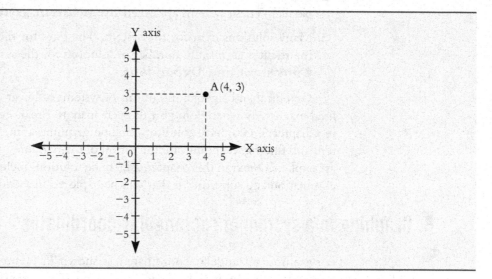

EXAMPLE 4.1A Determine the coordinates of the points A, B, C, D, E, F, G, and H as marked in the following diagram.

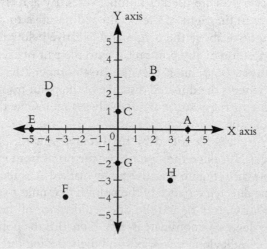

SOLUTION

POINT	COORDINATES	
A	$(4, 0)$	——— 4 units to the right of the origin ($x = 4$) on the X axis ($y = 0$)
B	$(2, 3)$	——— 2 units to the right ($x = 2$) and 3 units up ($y = 3$)
C	$(0, 1)$	——— on the Y axis ($x = 0$) 1 unit up ($y = 1$)
D	$(-4, 2)$	——— 4 units to the left ($x = -4$) and 2 units up ($y = 2$)
E	$(-5, 0)$	——— 5 units to the left ($x = -5$) on the X axis ($y = 0$)
F	$(-3, -4)$	——— 3 units to the left ($x = -3$) and 4 units down ($y = -4$)
G	$(0, -2)$	——— on the Y axis ($x = 0$) 2 units down ($y = -2$)
H	$(3, -3)$	——— 3 units to the right ($x = 3$) and 3 units down ($y = -3$)

To draw the graphs of linear relations, you must plot two or more points in a set of rectangular axes. To *plot* point (x, y), count the number of units represented by x along the X axis (to the right if x is positive, to the left if x is negative) and then count the number of units represented by y up or down (up if y is positive, down if y is negative).

EXAMPLE 4.1B

Plot the following points in a set of rectangular axes.

(i) $A(-3, 4)$ (ii) $B(2, -4)$

(iii) $C(-4, -4)$ (iv) $D(3, 3)$

(v) $E(-3, 0)$ (vi) $F(0, -2)$

SOLUTION

(i) To plot point A, count 3 units to the left (x is negative) and 4 units up (y is positive).

(ii) To plot point B, count 2 units to the right (x is positive) and 4 units down (y is negative).

(iii) To plot point C, count 4 units to the left and 4 units down.

(iv) To plot point D, count 3 units to the right and 3 units up.

(v) To plot point E, count 3 units to the left and mark the point on the X axis since $y = 0$.

(vi) To plot point F, count 2 units down and mark the point on the Y axis since $x = 0$.

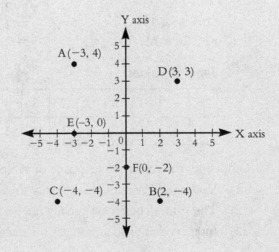

C. Constructing a table of values

To graph linear equations, plot a minimum of two points whose coordinates *satisfy* the equation and then join the points.

A suitable set of points may be obtained by constructing a table of values. Substitute arbitrarily chosen values of x or y in the equation and compute the value of the second variable. The chosen value and the corresponding computed value form an ordered pair (x, y). A listing of such ordered pairs forms a table of values.

EXAMPLE 4.1C

Construct a table of values for

(i) $x = 2y$ for integral values of y from $y = +3$ to $y = -3$;

(ii) $y = 2x - 3$ for integral values of x from $x = -2$ to $x = +4$.

SOLUTION

(i) To obtain the desired ordered pairs, substitute assumed values of y into the equation $x = 2y$.

$$y = +3 \qquad x = 2(3) = 6$$
$$y = +2 \qquad x = 2(2) = 4$$
$$y = +1 \qquad x = 2(1) = 2$$
$$y = 0 \qquad x = 2(0) = 0$$
$$y = -1 \qquad x = 2(-1) = -2$$
$$y = -2 \qquad x = 2(-2) = -4$$
$$y = -3 \qquad x = 2(-3) = -6$$

Listing the obtained ordered pairs gives the following table of values.

Table of values

x	6	4	2	0	−2	−4	−6
y	3	2	1	0	−1	−2	−3

— corresponding computed x values
— chosen y values

(ii) To obtain the desired ordered pairs, substitute assumed values of x into the equation $y = 2x - 3$.

$$x = -2 \qquad y = 2(-2) - 3 = -4 - 3 = -7$$
$$x = -1 \qquad y = 2(-1) - 3 = -2 - 3 = -5$$
$$x = 0 \qquad y = 2(0) - 3 = 0 - 3 = -3$$
$$x = 1 \qquad y = 2(1) - 3 = 2 - 3 = -1$$
$$x = 2 \qquad y = 2(2) - 3 = 4 - 3 = +1$$
$$x = 3 \qquad y = 2(3) - 3 = 6 - 3 = +3$$
$$x = 4 \qquad y = 2(4) - 3 = 8 - 3 = +5$$

Table of values

x	−2	−1	0	1	2	3	4
y	−7	−5	−3	−1	1	3	5

— chosen x values
— corresponding computed y values

Guidelines for constructing a table of values:

(1) Values may be chosen arbitrarily for either x or y.

(2) The values chosen are usually integers.

(3) Integers that yield an integer for the computed value are preferred.

D. Graphing linear equations

To graph a linear equation, you need a minimum of two points. To check for accuracy, a third point may also be plotted. When a line is drawn through the points, the result should be a straight line. To graph linear equations,

(1) *construct* a table of values consisting of at least two (preferably three) ordered pairs (x, y);

(2) *plot* the points in a system of rectangular axes;

(3) *join* the points by a straight line.

EXAMPLE 4.1D

Graph each of the following equations.

   (i) $x + y = 4$

   (ii) $x - y = 5$

   (iii) $x = y$

   (iv) $y = -2x$

   (v) $y = 2x + 100$ for all values of x from $x = 0$ to $x = 200$

SOLUTION

(i) Equation: $x + y = 4$

Table of values

x	0	4	2
y	4	0	2

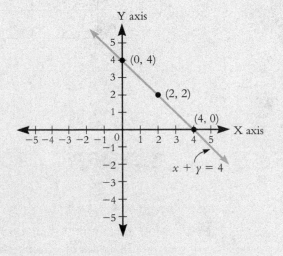

(ii) Equation: $x - y = 5$

Table of values

x	0	5	3
y	-5	0	-2

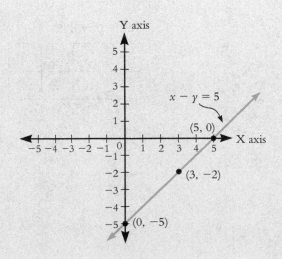

(iii) Equation: $x = y$

Table of values

x	0	3	−3
y	0	3	−3

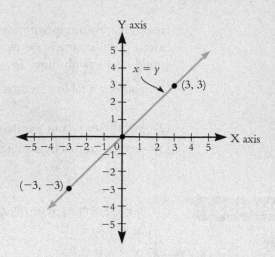

(iv) Equation: $y = -2x$

Table of values

x	0	2	−2
y	0	−4	4

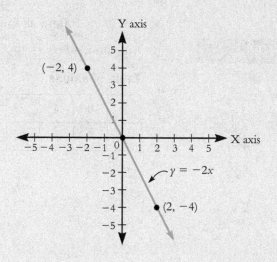

(v) Equation: $y = 2x + 100$ for all values of x from $x = 0$ to $x = 200$

Table of values

x	0	100	200
y	100	300	500

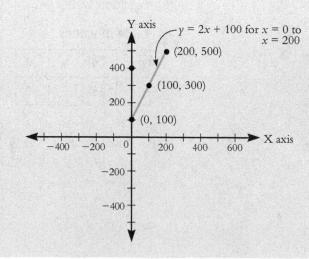

E. Special cases—lines parallel to the axes

1. Lines Parallel to the X Axis

Lines parallel to the X axis are formed by sets of points that all have the *same y* coordinates. Such lines are defined by the equation $y = b$ where b is any real number.

EXAMPLE 4.1E

Graph the lines represented by

(i) $y = 3$ (ii) $y = -2$

SOLUTION

(i) The line represented by $y = 3$ is a line parallel to the X axis and three units above it.

(ii) The line represented by $y = -2$ is a line parallel to the X axis and two units below it.

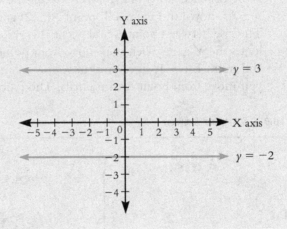

2. Lines Parallel to the Y Axis

Lines parallel to the Y axis are formed by sets of points that all have the same *x* coordinates. Such lines are defined by the equation $x = a$ where a is any real number.

EXAMPLE 4.1F

Graph the lines represented by

(i) $x = 3$ (ii) $x = -5$

SOLUTION

(i) The line represented by $x = 3$ is a line parallel to the Y axis and three units to the right of it.

(ii) The line represented by $x = -5$ is a line parallel to the Y axis and five units to the left of it.

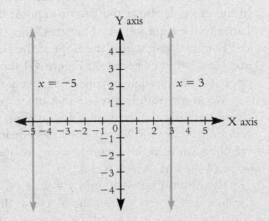

3. The Axes

X axis   The *y* coordinates of the set of points forming the X axis are zero.
Thus the equation $y = 0$ represents the X axis.

Y axis   The *x* coordinates of the set of points forming the Y axis are zero.
Thus the equation $x = 0$ represents the Y axis.

F. The slope–*y*-intercept form of a linear equation

Every line has two important characteristics: its steepness, called the **slope**, and a point
where the line intersects with the Y axis, called the **y-intercept**.

In more technical terms, slope is the ratio of the *rise* of a line to its *run*. The **rise** of
a line is the distance along the Y axis between two points on a line. The **run** of a line
is the distance along the X axis between the same two points on the line.

As shown in Figure 4.3, point A(3, 2) and point B(2, 0) lie on the line $2x - y = 4$.
The rise between point A and point B is −2, since you must move 2 units down, parallel to the Y axis, when you move from point A to point B. The run between point A
and point B is −1, since you must move 1 unit to the left, parallel to the X axis, when
you move from point A to point B. The ratio $^{rise}/_{run}$ is $^{-2}/_{-1}$, or +2.

Figure 4.3 Slope of a Line (© S. A. Hummelbrunner)

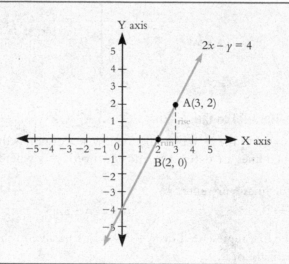

Notice that the slope of a line remains the same if you go from point B to point A.
In the example above, the rise from point B to point A is 2 units up, or +2. The run is
1 unit to the right, or +1. The ratio $^{rise}/_{run}$ is $^{+2}/_{+1}$, or +2, the same as was shown earlier.

For any straight line, the slope is the same for *any* two points on the line because a
line has a constant steepness. Figure 4.4 shows an example of one line having a positive
slope and another line having a negative slope.

We know from Figure 4.3 that the slope of the line representing $2x - y = 4$ is +2.
By rearranging the terms of this equation, we see that the equation of this line can be
written $y = 2x - 4$. We say the line's equation is in the form $y = mx + b$. When a linear equation is in this form, it is easy to see that *m*, the coefficient of *x*, represents the
slope of the line, which is +2.

By substituting $x = 0$ into $y = 2x - 4$, we determine that $y = -4$. You can see that
the line $y = 2x - 4$ crosses the Y axis at the point $(0, -4)$ in Figure 4.3. In the linear
equation $y = mx + b$, *b* is the *y*-intercept of the line. The *y*-intercept of this line is −4.

Figure 4.4 Lines with Positive or Negative Slopes (© S. A. Hummelbrunner)

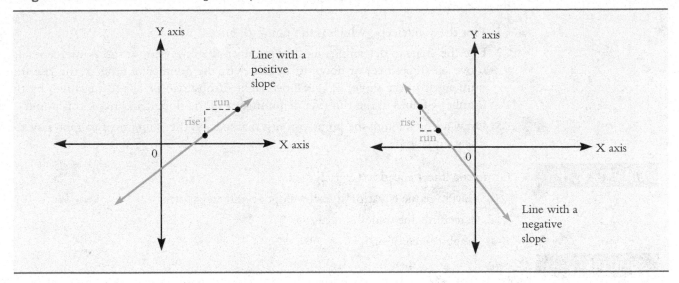

The **slope–y-intercept form of a linear equation** is a linear equation expressed in the form $y = mx + b$.

$$\boxed{y = mx + b}$$ —————————————— Formula 4.1

In any equation in the form of slope–y-intercept $y = mx + b$, m is the slope and b is the y-intercept.

EXAMPLE 4.1G

Using algebra, determine the slope and y-intercept of each of the following equations.

(i) $y = \dfrac{2}{3}x - 7$ (ii) $3x + 4y = -2$

SOLUTION

(i) $y = \dfrac{2}{3}x - 7$ is already in the form $y = mx + b$.

Thus, slope $= \dfrac{2}{3}$, since $m = \dfrac{2}{3}$ in the equation $y = \dfrac{2}{3}x - 7$.

The y-intercept $= -7$, since $b = -7$ in the equation $y = \dfrac{2}{3}x - 7$

(ii) $3x + 4y = -2$ must be expressed in the form $y = mx + b$.

$-3x + 3x + 4y = -3x - 2$ ——————————— subtract 3x from both sides

$4y = -3x - 2$ ——————————— simplify, then divide both sides by 4

$y = -\dfrac{3}{4}x - \dfrac{1}{2}$ ——————————— slope–y-intercept form

Thus, slope $= -\dfrac{3}{4}$, since $m = -\dfrac{3}{4}$ in the equation $y = -\dfrac{3}{4}x - \dfrac{1}{2}$.

The y-intercept $= -\dfrac{1}{2}$, since $b = -\dfrac{1}{2}$ in the equation $y = -\dfrac{3}{4}x - \dfrac{1}{2}$.

Once you have found m and b, you can use the slope and y-intercept to graph a linear equation.

1. Plot the y-intercept, which is the point $(0, b)$.

2. Use the slope to determine another point on the line. Start at the y-intercept and, move up (if positive) or down (if negative) by the number of units in the rise (the numerator of the slope). Then move right (if positive) or left (if negative) by the number of units in the run (the denominator of the slope), and mark this point.

3. Draw a line through the point you just marked and the y-intercept to represent the linear equation.

EXAMPLE 4.1H

Given the linear equation $6x + 2y = 8$,

(i) rearrange the equation into the slope–y-intercept form;

(ii) determine the values of m and b;

(iii) graph the equation.

SOLUTION

(i)
$$6x + 2y = 8$$
$$-6x + 6x + 2y = -6x + 8 \text{ ———————— subtract } 6x \text{ from both side}$$
$$2y = -6x + 8 \text{ ———————— simplify}$$
$$y = -3x + 4 \text{ ———————— slope–}y\text{-intercept form}$$

(ii) $m = -3$, $b = 4$

(iii) Since $b = 4$, the y-intercept is 4, which is represented by the point $(0, 4)$. Since $m = -3$ (or $-^3/_1$), plot a second point on the graph by beginning at the point $(0, 4)$ and moving 3 units down and 1 unit to the right. (You could also move 3 units up and 1 unit to the left if you consider $m = -3$ to be $m = {}^3/_{-1}$.) Draw the line that passes through these two points, as shown below.

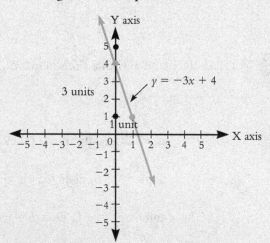

EXAMPLE 4.1I

Graph the equation $x - 2y + 400 = 0$ for all values of x from $x = 0$ to $x = 400$.

SOLUTION

Rearrange the equation into the slope–y-intercept form:

$$-x + x - 2y + 400 - 400 = 0 - x - 400 \text{ ——— subtract } x \text{ and } 400 \text{ from both sides}$$
$$-2y = -x - 400 \text{ ——— simplify}$$
$$y = \frac{1}{2}x + 200$$
$$m = \frac{1}{2}, b = 200$$

Since $b = 200$, the y-intercept is 200, which is represented by the point $(0, 200)$. Since $m = \frac{1}{2}$, the slope is $\frac{1}{2}$. To make plotting points easier, convert $m = \frac{1}{2}$ to the equivalent slope $m = \frac{100}{200}$. Plot a second point on the graph by beginning at the point $(0, 200)$ and moving 100 units up and 200 units to the right.

Draw the line through that point starting at $(0, 200)$ and extend the line to the point where $x = 400$. The graph should indicate that for the last point, $x = 400$ and $y = 400$.

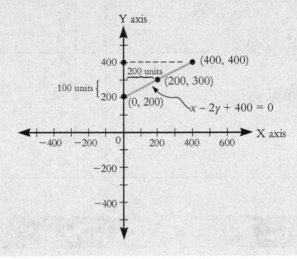

G. Special cases of the slope–y-intercept form of a linear equation

1. Lines Parallel to the X Axis

Recall from Section 4.1E that lines parallel to the X axis are defined by the equation $y = b$, where b is any real number. Since there is no mx in the equation $y = b$, the linear equation $y = b$ represents a line parallel to the X axis that crosses the Y axis at point $(0, b)$ and has a slope of 0.

Figure 4.5 A Line Parallel to the X Axis (© S. A. Hummelbrunner)

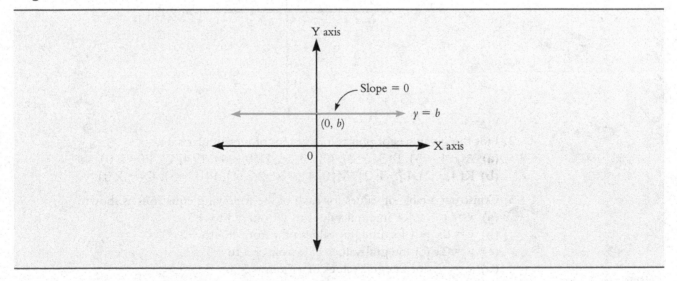

2. Lines Parallel to the Y Axis

Recall from Section 4.1E that lines parallel to the Y axis are defined by the equation $x = a$, where a is any real number. Since there is no y in the equation $x = a$, it cannot be expressed in the form $y = mx + b$. The equation $x = a$ represents a line parallel to the Y axis that crosses the X axis at point $(a, 0)$. Its slope is undefined.

Figure 4.6 A Line Parallel to the Y Axis (© S. A. Hummelbrunner)

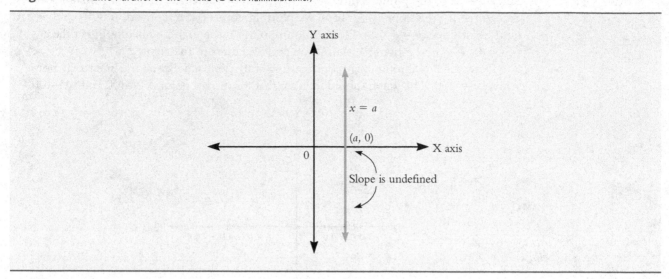

EXERCISE 4.1

MyLab Math

A. Do each of the following.

1. Write the coordinates of the points A, B, C, D, E, F, G, and H marked in the following diagram.

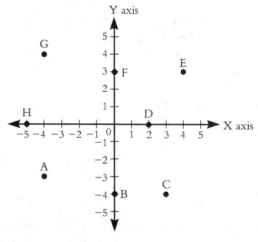

2. Plot the given sets of points in a system of rectangular axes.
   (a) A(-4, -5), B(3, -2), C(-3, 5), D(0, -4), E(4, 1), F(-2, 0)
   (b) K(4, -2), L(-3, 2), M(0, 4), N(-2, -4), P(0, -5), Q(-3, 0)

3. Construct a table of values for each of the following equations as shown.
   (a) $x = y - 2$ for integral values of y from -3 to $+5$
   (b) $y = 2x - 1$ for integral values of x from $+3$ to -2
   (c) $y = 2x$ for integral values of x from $+3$ to -3
   (d) $x = -y$ for integral values of y from $+5$ to -5

4. Using algebra, determine the slope and y-intercept of the lines represented by each of the following equations.
   (a) $4x + 5y = 11$ (b) $2y - 5x = 10$
   (c) $1 - \frac{1}{2}y = 2x$ (d) $3y + 6 = 0$

    (e) $\sqrt{2x - y} = 3$

    (g) $2 - \frac{1}{2}x = 0$

    🌐 **(f)** $0.15x + 0.3y - 0.12 = 0$

    (h) $(x - 2)(y + 1) - xy = 2$

B. Graph each of the following equations.

    1. $x - y = 3$

    3. $y = -x$

    🌐 **5.** $3x - 4y = 12$

    7. $y = -4$

    9. $y = 2x - 3$

    2. $x + 2y = 4$

    4. $x = 2y$

    6. $2x + 3y = 6$

    🌐 **8.** $x = 5$

    10. $y = -3x + 9$

C. Graph each of the following equations for all of the values of x indicated.

    🌐 **1.** $y = 3x + 20$ for $x = 0$ to $x = 40$

    2. $y = -\dfrac{2}{5}x + 40$ for $x = 0$ to $x = 100$

    3. $3x + 4y = 1200$ for $x = 0$ to $x = 400$

    4. $3y - 12x - 2400 = 0$ for $x = 0$ to $x = 300$

4.2 GRAPHING LINEAR SYSTEMS OF EQUATIONS IN TWO VARIABLES

Systems that consist of two linear equations with two variables in each may be solved by drawing the graph of each equation. The graph of the system (or solution, if it exists) is the point where the two lines representing the equations intersect. If the system of linear equations is inconsistent, the lines are parallel and, therefore, they do not intersect (i.e., no solution). If the system of linear equations is consistent and dependent, the lines coincide. In such a system every point on the line will be a solution to the system (i.e., many solutions).

EXAMPLE 4.2A

Graph the linear system $x + y = 5$ and $x - y = 3$.

SOLUTION

Rearrange the first equation into the slope–y-intercept form:

$$x + y = 5$$
$$y = -x + 5$$

Since $b = 5$, the y-intercept is $+5$, represented by the point $(0, 5)$. Since $m = -1$, the slope is -1.

Rearrange the second equation into the slope–y-intercept form:

$$x - y = 3$$
$$y = x - 3$$

Since $b = -3$, the y-intercept is -3, represented by the point $(0, -3)$. Since $m = 1$, the slope is 1.

    The point of intersection is found by setting the two equations for y equal to each other. First, solve for x. This will be the x-coordinate for the point of intersection.

$$-x + 5 = x - 3$$
$$2x = 8$$
$$x = 4$$

Now substitute the value for x into either of the two equations and solve for y. This will be the y coordinate for the point of intersection.

$$x + y = 5$$
$$4 + y = 5$$
$$y = 1$$

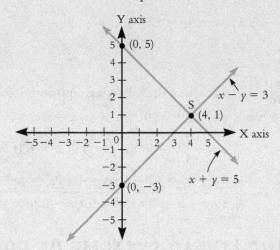

The point $(4, 1)$ satisfies the equation of either line and is the solution of the system.

EXAMPLE 4.2B

Graph the system $x = -2y$ and $y = 3$.

SOLUTION

First equation:

$x = -2y$ can be rearranged to $y = -\dfrac{1}{2}x$

Therefore, when $b = 0$, the y-intercept is 0. Since $m = -\dfrac{1}{2}$, the slope is $-\dfrac{1}{2}$.

Second equation:

$y = 3$

Therefore, when $b = 3$, the y-intercept is 3. Since m is 0, the slope is flat.

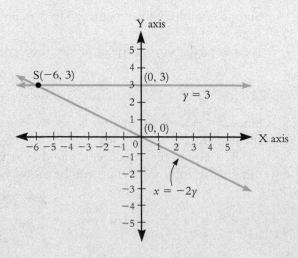

The graph of $y = 3$ is a horizontal line, parallel to the X axis three units above it. The graph of the system is S, the point of intersection of the two lines. In this case, it is easy to substitute $y = 3$ into the first equation in order to determine the point of intersection.

$$x = -2(3)$$
$$x = -6$$

The coordinates of S are $(-6, 3)$ and represent the solution of the system.

EXAMPLE 4.2C

Graph the system $x = y$ and $x - 2y + 2000 = 0$ for all values of x from $x = 0$ to $x = 4000$.

SOLUTION

For the first equation:

$$x = y$$

Since $b = 0$, the y-intercept is 0. Since $m = 1$, the slope is 1.
For the second equation:

$$x - 2y + 2000 = 0$$
$$x - 2y = -2000$$
$$-x + 2y = +2000$$
$$2y = x + 2000$$
$$y = \frac{1}{2}x + 1000$$

Since $b = 1000$, the y-intercept is 1000. Since $m = \frac{1}{2}$, the slope is $\frac{1}{2}$.

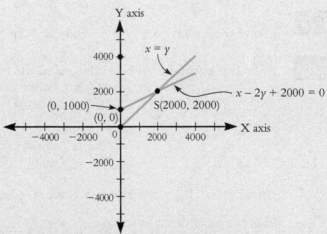

Now substitute $x = y$ into the second equation:

$$y = \frac{1}{2}y + 1000$$

$$\frac{1}{2}y = 1000$$

$$y = 2000$$

The graph of the system is S, the point of intersection of the two lines. The coordinates of S are $(2000, 2000)$ and represent the solution of the system.

Substituting $x = 4000$ into both equations results in points $(4000, 4000)$ and $(4000, 3000)$.

EXAMPLE 4.2D

Solve the system $x + 2y = -3$ and $3x + 6y = 1$.

SOLUTION

The first equation can be rearranged to the form of $y = mx + b$

$$x + 2y = -3$$
$$2y = -x - 3$$
$$y = -\frac{1}{2}x - \frac{3}{2}$$

Since $b = -\frac{3}{2}$, the y-intercept is $-\frac{3}{2}$. Since $m = -\frac{1}{2}$, the slope is $-\frac{1}{2}$.

For the second equation

$$3x + 6y = 1$$

This equation can be rearranged to the form of $y = mx + b$

$$6y = -3x + 1$$
$$y = -\frac{1}{2}x + \frac{1}{6}$$

Since $b = \frac{1}{6}$, the y-intercept is $\frac{1}{6}$. Since $m = -\frac{1}{2}$, the slope is $-\frac{1}{2}$.

Because the slope is the same for both equations, the lines are parallel and parallel lines do not intersect. Therefore, as mentioned before, this is an inconsistent system and there is no solution for this system.

EXAMPLE 4.2E

Solve the system $\frac{1}{2}x - y = -3$ and $-x + 2y = 6$.

SOLUTION

The first equation can be rearranged to the form of $y = mx + b$

$$\frac{1}{2}x - y = -3$$
$$y = \frac{1}{2}x + 3$$

Since $b = 3$, the y-intercept is 3. Since $m = \frac{1}{2}$, the slope is $\frac{1}{2}$.

For the second equation

$$-x + 2y = 6$$

This equation can be rearranged to the form of $y = mx + b$

$$2y = x + 6$$
$$y = \frac{1}{2}x + 3$$

Since $b = 3$, the y-intercept is 3. Since $m = \frac{1}{2}$, the slope is $\frac{1}{2}$.

Because the slopes and y-intercepts for both equations are the same, the lines coincide or they intersect one another. This system is consistent and dependent resulting in an infinite number of solutions.

EXERCISE 4.2

A. Solve each of the following linear systems graphically.

   1. $x + y = 4$ and $x - y = -4$ **2.** $x - y = 3$ and $x + y = 5$

   3. $x = 2y - 1$ and $y = 4 - 3x$ **4.** $2x + 3y = 10$ and $3x - 4y = -2$

   5. $3x - 4y = 18$ and $2y = -3x$ **6.** $4x = -5y$ and $2x + y = 6$

   7. $5x - 2y = 20$ and $y = 5$ **8.** $3y = -5x$ and $x = -3$

B. Graph each of the following systems of equations for all values of x indicated.

   1. $y - 4x = 0$ and $y - 2x - 10\,000 = 0$ for $x = 0$ to $x = 10\,000$

   2. $4x + 2y = 200$ for $x = 0$ to $x = 50$ and $x + 2y = 80$ for $x = 0$ to $x = 80$

   3. $3x + 3y = 2400$ and $x = 500$ for $x = 0$ to $x = 800$

   4. $2y = 5x$ and $y = 5000$ for $x = 0$ to $x = 8000$

C. Solve each of the following systems of linear equations.

   1. $2x - y = 4$ and $2y - 4x = -1$ **2.** $x - 2 = 0$ and $2x + 3 = 0$

   3. $y - 3x - 5 = 0$ and $3y - 9x + 2 = 0$ **4.** $y + x = 3$ and $2y + 2x - 6 = 0$

4.3 ALGEBRAIC SOLUTION OF SYSTEMS OF LINEAR EQUATIONS IN TWO VARIABLES

Two main techniques, elimination and substitution, can be used to solve systems of linear equations. These techniques will be explained next in this section.

A. Solving a system of two linear equations by algebraic elimination

If the coefficients of one variable are the same in both equations, the system can be reduced to one equation by addition or subtraction as follows.

(a) If the coefficients of one variable are numerically equal but opposite in sign, addition will eliminate the variable.

(b) If the coefficients of one variable are numerically equal and have the same sign, subtraction can eliminate the variable. Alternatively, one equation can be multiplied by -1; addition can then be used.

EXAMPLE 4.3A Solve each of the following systems of equations.

   (i) $x + y = 1$ (ii) $5x + 4y = 7$ (iii) $x - 3y = 2$

        $x - y = 7$ $3x - 4y = 17$ $4x - 3y = -10$

SOLUTION (i) $x + y = 1$ ———————————— equation ①

         $\underline{x - y = 7}$ ———————————— equation ②

            $2x = 8$ ———————————— add ① and ② to eliminate y

$x = 4$ ——————————— *Note*: The coefficient of *y* in ① is 1;
the coefficient of *y* in ② is -1. Since
the coefficients are the same but
opposite in sign, adding the two equations
will eliminate the term in *y*.

$4 + y = 1$ ——————————— substitute the value of *x* in ①
$y = -3$

$\boxed{x = 4, y = -3}$ ——————————— solution

Check
in ① LS★ $= 4 + (-3) = 4 - 3 = 1$
   RS† $= 1$
in ② LS $= 4 - (-3) = 4 + 3 = 7$
   RS $= 7$

(ii) $5x + 4y = 7$ ——————————— equation ①
   $3x - 4y = 17$ ——————————— equation ②
   $8x = 24$ ——————————— add ① and ② to eliminate *y*
   $x = 3$
   $5(3) + 4y = 7$ ——————————— substitute 3 for *x* in ①
   $15 + 4y = 7$
   $4y = -8$
   $y = -2$

$\boxed{x = 3, y = -2}$ ——————————— solution

Check
in ① LS $= 5(3) + 4(-2) = 15 - 8 = 7$
   RS $= 7$
in ② LS $= 3(3) - 4(-2) = 9 + 8 = 17$
   RS $= 17$

(iii) $x - 3y = 2$ ——————————— ①
   $4x - 3y = -10$ ——————————— ②

To eliminate the term in *y*, multiply ② by -1.
   $x - 3y = 2$ ——————————— ①
   $-4x + 3y = 10$ ——————————— ② multiplied by -1 to set up addition
   $-3x = 12$ ——————————— add
   $x = -4$
   $-4 - 3y = 2$ ——————————— substitute -4 for *x* in ①
   $-3y = 6$
   $y = -2$

$\boxed{x = -4, y = -2}$ ——————————— solution

Check
in ① LS $= -4 - 3(-2) = -4 + 6 = 2$
   RS $= 2$
in ② LS $= 4(-4) - 3(-2) = -16 + 6 = -10$
   RS $= -10$

★LS Left Side
†RS Right Side

If the coefficients of one variable are not the same in both equations, numerical equality of one pair of coefficients must be *created* before addition or subtraction can be used to eliminate a variable. This equality is usually achieved by multiplying one or both equations by a number or numbers that make the coefficients of the variable to be eliminated numerically equal. Here are some examples demonstrating the elimination method.

EXAMPLE 4.3B

Solve each of the following systems of equations.

(i) $x - 3y = -12$ (ii) $x + 4y = 18$
    $3x + y = -6$ $2x + 5y = 24$

(iii) $6x - 5y + 70 = 0$
     $4x = 3y - 44$

SOLUTION

(i) $x - 3y = -12$ —————————————— equation ①
   $3x + y = -6$ —————————————— equation ②

To eliminate the term in y, multiply ② by 3.
$$x - 3y = -12 \text{ ——————————— ①}$$
$$\underline{9x + 3y = -18} \text{ ——————————— ② multiplied by 3}$$
$$10x = -30 \text{ ——————————— add}$$
$$x = -3$$
$$-3 - 3y = -12 \text{ ——————————— substitute } -3 \text{ for } x \text{ in ①}$$
$$-3y = -9$$
$$y = 3$$
$$\boxed{x = -3, y = 3} \text{ ——————————— solution}$$

(ii) $x + 4y = 18$ —————————————— ①
    $2x + 5y = 24$ —————————————— ②

To eliminate the term in x, multiply ① by 2 and ② by -1.
$$2x + 8y = 36 \text{ ——————————— ① multiplied by 2}$$
$$\underline{-2x - 5y = -24} \text{ ——————————— ② multiplied by } -1 \text{ to set up addition}$$
$$3y = 12 \text{ ——————————— add}$$
$$y = 4$$
$$x + 4(4) = 18 \text{ ——————————— substitute 4 for } y \text{ in ①}$$
$$x + 16 = 18$$
$$x = 2$$
$$\boxed{x = 2, y = 4} \text{ ——————————— solution}$$

(iii) $6x - 5y + 70 = 0$ —————————————— ①
     $4x = 3y - 44$ —————————————— ②

Rearrange the two equations in the same order, so that the constant term is on the right side.
$$6x - 5y = -70 \text{ ——————————— ①}$$
$$4x - 3y = -44 \text{ ——————————— ②}$$

To eliminate the term in y, multiply ① by 3 and ② by -5.
$$18x - 15y = -210 \text{ ——————————— ① multiplied by 3}$$
$$\underline{-20x + 15y = 220} \text{ ——————————— ② multiplied by } -5$$
$$-2x = 10 \text{ ——————————— add}$$

$$x = -5$$
$$6(-5) - 5y = -70 \quad\text{——— substitute } -5 \text{ for } x \text{ in } ①$$
$$-30 - 5y = -70$$
$$-5y = -40$$
$$y = 8$$
$$\boxed{x = -5, y = 8} \quad\text{——— solution}$$

B. Solving a system of two linear equations by algebraic substitution

To solve a system of two linear equations by the substitution method, we choose one of the two equations and solve it for one variable in terms of the second variable. The value of this variable is then substituted into the other equation and solved for the value of the second variable. The value of the second variable is then substituted into the first equation and solved for the value of the first variable.

In this method, the first time that we solve for the first variable, it is in terms of the second variable. The second time that we solve for the first variable, it does not include the second variable in its expression. Here are some examples demonstrating the substitution method.

EXAMPLE 4.3C

Solve each of the following systems of equations.

(i) $2x + 4y = 6$
     $4x + 2y = 6$

(ii) $3x + y = 8$
      $2x - 3y = 9$

(iii) $x + y = 1$
       $x - 3y = 5$

SOLUTION

(i)
$$2x + 4y = 6 \quad\text{——— equation } ①$$
$$4x + 2y = 6 \quad\text{——— equation } ②$$
$$2x = 6 - 4y \quad\text{——— solve } ① \text{ for } x \text{ in terms of } y$$
$$x = 3 - 2y$$
$$4(3 - 2y) + 2y = 6 \quad\text{——— substitute } x \text{ in } ②$$
$$12 - 8y + 2y = 6 \quad\text{——— solve for } y$$
$$-6y = -6$$
$$y = 1$$
$$2x + 4y = 6 \quad\text{——— substitute } y = 1 \text{ in } ① \text{ and solve for } x$$
$$2x = 6 - 4(1)$$
$$2x = 2$$
$$x = 1$$

(ii)
$$3x + y = 8 \quad\text{——— equation } ①$$
$$2x - 3y = 9 \quad\text{——— equation } ②$$
$$3x + y = 8 \quad\text{——— solve } ① \text{ for } y \text{ in terms of } x$$
$$y = 8 - 3x$$
$$2x - 3(8 - 3x) = 9 \quad\text{——— substitute } y \text{ in } ②$$
$$11x - 24 = 9 \quad\text{——— solve for } x$$
$$11x = 33$$
$$x = 3$$
$$3x + y = 8 \quad\text{——— substitute } x = 3 \text{ in } ①$$
$$3(3) + y = 8$$
$$y = -1$$

(iii)

$$x + y = 1$$
$$x - 3y = 5$$
$$x + y = 1 \underline{\hspace{3cm}} \text{solve ① for } x \text{ in terms of } y$$
$$x = 1 - y$$
$$1 - y - 3y = 5 \underline{\hspace{3cm}} \text{substitute } x \text{ in ②}$$
$$1 - 4y = 5 \underline{\hspace{3cm}} \text{solve for } y$$
$$-4y = 4$$
$$y = -1$$
$$x + y = 1 \underline{\hspace{3cm}} \text{substitute } y = -1 \text{ in ① and solve for } x$$
$$x - 1 = 1$$
$$x = 2$$

C. Solving linear systems in two variables involving fractions

When one or both equations contain decimals, it is best to multiply the equation(s) by an appropriate factor of 10 to eliminate the decimals. If one or both equations contain fractions, multiply each equation by its Lowest Common Denominator (LCD) to eliminate the fraction; then solve the system as shown in the previous examples.

EXAMPLE 4.3D

Solve each of the following systems of equations.

(i) $1.5x + 0.8y = 1.2$
$0.7x + 1.2y = -4.4$

(ii) $\dfrac{5x}{6} + \dfrac{3y}{8} = -1$

$\dfrac{2x}{3} - \dfrac{3y}{4} = -5$

SOLUTION

(i) $1.5x + 0.8y = 1.2 \underline{\hspace{2cm}}$ ①

$0.7x + 1.2y = -4.4 \underline{\hspace{2cm}}$ ②

To eliminate the decimals, multiply each equation by 10.

$15x + 8y = 12 \underline{\hspace{2cm}}$ ③

$7x + 12y = -44 \underline{\hspace{2cm}}$ ④

To eliminate the term in y, multiply ③ by 3 and ④ by 2.

$45x + 24y = 36 \underline{\hspace{2cm}}$ ③ multiplied by 3

$\underline{14x + 24y = -88} \underline{\hspace{2cm}}$ ④ multiplied by 2

$31x = 124 \underline{\hspace{2cm}}$ subtract

$x = 4$

$15(4) + 8y = 12 \underline{\hspace{2cm}}$ substitute 4 for x in ③

$60 + 8y = 12$

$8y = -48$

$y = -6$

$\boxed{x = 4, y = -6} \underline{\hspace{2cm}}$ solution

(ii) $\dfrac{5x}{6} + \dfrac{3y}{8} = -1 \underline{\hspace{2cm}}$ ①

$\dfrac{2x}{3} - \dfrac{3y}{4} = -5 \underline{\hspace{2cm}}$ ②

To eliminate the fractions, multiply ① by 24 and ② by 12.

$$\frac{24(5x)}{6} + \frac{24(3y)}{8} = 24(-1) \quad\text{——— ① multiplied by 24}$$

$$4(5x) + 3(3y) = -24$$

$$20x + 9y = -24 \quad\text{——— ③}$$

$$\frac{12(2x)}{3} - \frac{12(3y)}{4} = 12(-5) \quad\text{——— ② multiplied by 12}$$

$$4(2x) - 3(3y) = -60$$

$$8x - 9y = -60 \quad\text{——— ④}$$

To eliminate the term in y, add ③ and ④.

$$20x + 9y = -24 \quad\text{——— ③}$$
$$\underline{8x - 9y = -60} \quad\text{——— ④}$$
$$28x = -84$$
$$x = -3$$
$$20(-3) + 9y = -24 \quad\text{——— substitute } -3 \text{ for } x \text{ in ③}$$
$$-60 + 9y = -24$$
$$9y = 36$$
$$y = 4$$

$$\boxed{x = -3, y = 4} \quad\text{——— solution}$$

POINTERS & PITFALLS

When removing decimals or fractions from linear systems in two variables, remember that each equation can, if necessary, be multiplied by a *different quantity*.

For example,

(i) Solve

$$1.2x + 3.5y = 50 \quad\text{——— multiply by } 10 \text{ to eliminate decimals}$$
$$2.26x - 0.70y = 6.5 \quad\text{——— multiply by } 100 \text{ to eliminate decimals}$$

(ii) Solve

$$\frac{5x}{4} + \frac{4y}{3} = 5$$
$$\frac{3x}{6} + \frac{2y}{2} = 4$$

Multiply the first equation by its LCD of 12 to eliminate fractions: $15x + 16y = 60$
Multiply the second equation by its LCD of 6 to eliminate fractions: $3x + 6y = 24$
Now you can use the elimination method to solve the system.

D. Systems of two linear equations with no solution or many solutions

In the previous examples in this chapter, all systems of linear equations were consistent and independent. Such systems have a unique solution that we could find by using either the elimination or substitution methods. Some systems of linear equations are inconsistent, meaning that there is no solution for them. Other systems are consistent and dependent with many solutions. Let us consider the following examples.

EXAMPLE 4.3E

Solve the following system of linear equations.

(i) $2x + 4y = 6$
$\quad x + 2y = -1$

(ii) $\frac{1}{3}x - y = -2$
$\quad -x + 3y = 6$

SOLUTION

(i)

$$2x + 4y = 6 \text{ ———————————— equation ①}$$
$$x + 2y = -1 \text{ ———————————— equation ②}$$
$$x = -1 - 2y \text{ ———————— solve ② for } x \text{ in terms of } y$$
$$2(-1 - 2y) + 4y = 6 \text{ ————— substitute } x \text{ in ①}$$
$$-2 - 4y + 4y = 6 \text{ ————— solve for } y$$
$$0 = 8 \text{ ———————————— impossible}$$

This result is a contradiction and impossible. Therefore, there is no solution for this system of linear equations. These types of systems are known as inconsistent systems of linear equations.

(ii)

$$\frac{1}{3}x - y = -2 \text{ ———————————— equation ①}$$
$$-x + 3y = 6 \text{ ———————————— equation ②}$$
$$x - 3y = -6 \text{ ———————————— multiply ① by 3}$$
$$x - 3y - x + 3y = 6 - 6 \text{ ———— Add to ②}$$
$$0 = 0$$

The result indicates that the original equations are equivalent and the system is consistent and dependent. Any real number value for x will result in a value for y that satisfies both equations. Therefore, there are many solutions for this system.

EXERCISE 4.3   MyLab Math

A. Solve each of the following systems of equations and check your solutions.

 1. $x + y = -9$
$\quad x - y = -7$

2. $x + 5y = 0$
$\quad x + 2y = 6$

3. $5x + 2y = 74$
$\quad 7x - 2y = 46$

4. $2x + 9y = -13$
$\quad 2x - 3y = 23$

5. $y = 3x + 12$
$\quad x = -y$

6. $3x = 10 - 2y$
$\quad 5y = 3x - 38$

B. Solve each of the following systems of equations and check your solutions.

1. $4x + y = -13$
$\quad x - 5y = -19$

2. $6x + 3y = 24$
$\quad 2x + 9y = -8$

3. $7x - 5y = -22$
$\quad 4x + 3y = 5$

4. $8x + 9y = 129$
$\quad 6x + 7y = 99$

5. $12y = 5x + 16$
$\quad 6x + 10y - 54 = 0$

6. $3x - 8y + 44 = 0$
$\quad 7x = 12y - 56$

C. Solve each of the following systems of equations.

1. $0.4x + 1.5y = 16.8$
$1.1x - 0.9y = 6.0$

2. $6.5x + 3.5y = 128$
$2.5x + 4.5y = 106$

3. $2.4x + 1.6y = 7.60$
$3.8x + 0.6y = 7.20$

4. $2.25x + 0.75y = 2.25$
$1.25x + 1.75y = 2.05$

5. $\dfrac{3x}{4} - \dfrac{2y}{3} = \dfrac{-13}{6}$
$\dfrac{4x}{5} + \dfrac{3y}{4} = \dfrac{123}{10}$

6. $\dfrac{9x}{5} + \dfrac{5y}{4} = \dfrac{47}{10}$
$\dfrac{2x}{9} + \dfrac{3y}{8} = \dfrac{5}{36}$

7. $\dfrac{x}{3} + \dfrac{2y}{5} = \dfrac{7}{15}$
$\dfrac{3x}{2} - \dfrac{7y}{3} = -1$

8. $\dfrac{x}{4} + \dfrac{3y}{7} = \dfrac{-2}{21}$
$\dfrac{2x}{3} + \dfrac{3y}{2} = \dfrac{-7}{36}$

BUSINESS MATH **NEWS**   TFSA Helps Canadians Build Wealth

According to Statistics Canada data, the Household Saving Rate in Canada has been decreasing for more than two decades. The Household Saving Rate is a ratio comparing the amount of money set aside per annum in a saving plan, to the amount of household income per annum. Since 1990, the Household Saving Rate reached a high of 15.40 percent in the second quarter of 1993, and then started to decline to a record low of 0.20 percent in the first quarter of 2005.

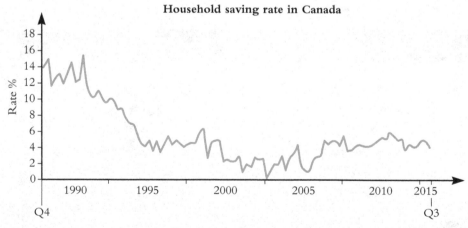

Household saving rate in Canada

Source: Statistics Canada, Canada Household Saving Rate, May of 2016. Reproduced and distributed on an "as is" basis with the permission of Statistics Canada.

In contrast, Household Debt in Canada for the same period has been increasing. The Household Debt Rate is the ratio comparing the amount of household debt, to personal disposable income. According to Statistics Canada data, the Household Debt Rate reached a high of 165.92 percent in the third quarter of 2015 from a record low of about 85.00 percent in the first quarter of 1990.

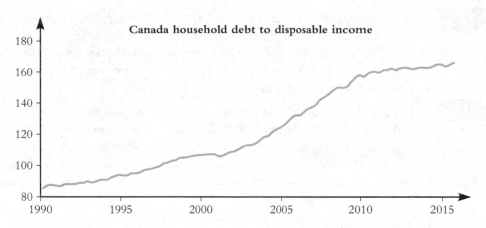

Source: Statistics Canada, Canada Households Debt to Disposable Income, May of 2016. Reproduced and distributed on an "as is" basis with the permission of Statistics Canada.

In an attempt to correct this negative trend and encourage Canadians to save money and build wealth, the Conservative Government of Canada introduced the Tax-Free Savings Account (TFSA) in 2009. The TFSA is a tool designed to help Canadians accumulate wealth. It is a tax-free investment vehicle that allows Canadians over the age of 18 to benefit from holding cash, GICs, stocks, mutual funds, bonds, etc. Under the TFSA umbrella, these investments will grow tax free until the account holder decides to remove them from the investment vehicle. Account holders are not required to pay tax on any capital gains including the interest that the account accumulates.

When the TFSA was first introduced in 2009, the maximum annual contribution was set at $5000. It increased to $5500 in 2013, and then further rose to a maximum annual contribution of $10 000 in 2015. However, after winning a majority government in 2015, the Liberal Government announced a planned reduction in the maximum annual contribution limit back to the 2013 amount of $5500. The government increased the TFSA contribution limit to $6000 for 2019.

There is no penalty if money is withdrawn from a TFSA early. This causes some Canadians to use the TFSA for other immediate needs such as short-term vacation and travel planning, or for a down payment (for a car or home). Notwithstanding, the full benefit of the TFSA is usually realized when the funds are invested in securities for a very long period of time.

QUESTIONS

1. Assuming you were 18 in 2009 when the government introduced the TFSA, how much money could you have in the account by the end of 2019 if you were able to use your maximum contribution each year (not including any interest or other gains)?

2. Assuming the new maximum contribution introduced by the Liberal Government will not change in the future, write an equation of a line that can be used to calculate the maximum amount of money in your TFSA when you turn 71 years old (not including any interest or other gains).

4.4 PROBLEM SOLVING
A. Problems leading to one equation with two variables

In many problems, the relationship between two or more variables can be represented by setting up linear equations. To find the solution to such problems, there must be as many equations as there are variables.

In the case of problems involving two variables, two equations are needed to obtain a solution. If only one equation can be set up, you can represent the relationship between the two variables graphically.

EXAMPLE 4.4A

A manufacturer processes two types of products through the Finishing Department. Each unit of Product A needs 20 minutes in Finishing, while each unit of Product B needs 30 minutes. Per day, 1200 minutes are available. Set up an equation that describes the relationship between the number of units of each product that can be processed daily in Finishing. Graph the relationship.

SOLUTION

Let the number of units of Product A that can be processed daily be represented by x, and let the number of units of Product B be represented by y. Then the number of minutes required per day for Product A is $20x$ and the number of minutes for Product B is $30y$. The total number of minutes per day needed by both products is $20x + 30y$. Since 1200 minutes are available,

$20x + 30y = 1200$

Table of values

x	60	0	30
y	0	40	20

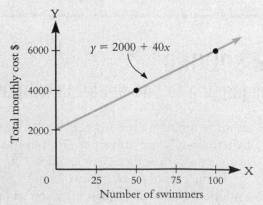

EXAMPLE 4.4B

The Olympic Swim Club rents pool facilities from the city at $2000 per month. Coaching fees and other expenses amount to $40 per swimmer per month. Set up an equation that describes the relationship between the number of swimmers and the total monthly cost of operating the swim club. Graph the relationship.

SOLUTION

Let the number of swimmers be represented by x, and let the total monthly cost be represented by $\$y$. Then the monthly coaching fees and expenses are $\$40x$ and total monthly costs amount to $\$(2000 + 40x)$.

$y = 2000 + 40x$ can be rearranged to $y = 40x + 2000$, where the y-intercept is $(0, 2000)$.

Table of values

x	0	50	100
y	2000	4000	6000

B. Problems leading to systems of equations

The problems in Chapter 2 were solved by using one variable, expressing all the information in terms of that variable, and setting up one equation. To solve many problems, however, using more than one variable and setting up a system of equations is necessary.

EXAMPLE 4.4C

The total enrolment in two classes is 64 students. One class has 10 more students than the other. How many students are enrolled in each class?

SOLUTION

Let the greater number be x and the smaller number be y. Their sum is $x + y$ and their difference is $x - y$.

$$x + y = 64 \quad\text{———————————} ①$$
$$\underline{x - y = 10 \quad\text{———————————} ②}$$
$$2x + 0y = 74$$
$$2x = 74$$
$$x = 37$$
$$37 + y = 64$$
$$y = 27$$

The larger number is 37 and the smaller number is 27.

Check
Sum: $37 + 27 = 64$
Difference: $37 - 27 = 10$

EXAMPLE 4.4D

Kim invested a total of \$24 000 in two mutual funds. Her investment in the Equity Fund is \$4000 less than three times her investment in the Bond Fund. How much did Kim invest in each fund?

SOLUTION

Let the amount invested in the Bond Fund be \$$x$; let the amount invested in the Equity Fund be \$$y$; the total amount invested is

$$x + y = 24\ 000 \quad\text{———————————} ①$$

\$4000 less than three times the investment in the Bond Fund is

$$y = 3x - 4000 \quad\text{———————————} ②$$

Substitute ② in ①

$$x + 3x - 4000 = 24\ 000$$
$$4x = 28\ 000$$
$$x = 7000$$
$$y = 3(7000) - 4000$$
$$y = 17\ 000$$
$$x + y = 24\ 000$$
$$x + 17\ 000 = 24\ 000$$
$$x = 7000$$

The amount invested in the Equity Fund is \$17 000 and the amount invested in the Bond Fund equals \$7000.

EXAMPLE 4.4E

The Clarkson Soccer League has set a budget of $3840 for soccer balls. High-quality game balls cost $36 each, while lower-quality practice balls cost $20 each. If 160 balls are to be purchased, how many balls of each type can be purchased to exactly use up the budgeted amount?

SOLUTION

Let the number of game balls be x;
let the number of practice balls be y;
then the total number of balls is $x + y$.

$$x + y = 160 \text{ —————————————— ①}$$

The value of the x game balls is $36x$;
the value of the y practice balls is $20y$;
the total value of the balls is $(36x + 20y)$.

$$
\begin{aligned}
36x + 20y &= 3840 &&\text{②} \\
-20x - 20y &= -3200 &&\text{① multiplied by } -20 \\
\hline
16x + 0y &= 640 \\
16x &= 640 &&\text{add ② and ①} \\
x &= 40 \\
40 + y &= 160 &&\text{substitute in ①} \\
y &= 120
\end{aligned}
$$

Forty game balls and 120 practice balls can be purchased.

EXAMPLE 4.4F

The Dutch Nook sells two brands of coffee—one for $7.90 per kilogram, and the other for $9.40 per kilogram. If the store owner mixes 20 kilograms and intends to sell the mixture for $8.50 per kilogram, how many kilograms of each brand should she use to make the same revenue as she would if the two brands were sold unmixed?

SOLUTION

Let the number of kilograms of coffee sold for $7.90 be x;
let the number of kilograms of coffee sold for $9.40 be y;
then the number of kilograms of coffee in the mixture is $x + y$.

$$x + y = 20 \text{ —————————————— ① weight relationship}$$

The value of coffee in the mixture selling for $7.90 is $7.90x$;
the value of coffee in the mixture selling for $9.40 is $9.40y$;
the total value of the mixture is $(7.90x + 9.40y)$. Since each kilogram of mixture is to be sold at $8.50, the value is $8.50(20)$, or $170.

$$
\begin{aligned}
7.90x + 9.40y &= 170.00 &&\text{② value relationship} \\
79x + 94y &= 1700.00 &&\text{② multiplied by 10} \\
79x + 79y &= 1580.00 &&\text{① multiplied by 79} \\
\hline
15y &= 120.00 &&\text{subtract} \\
y &= 8 \\
x + 8 &= 20 &&\text{substitute in ①} \\
x &= 12
\end{aligned}
$$

The store owner should mix 12 kilograms of coffee selling for $7.90 per kilogram with 8 kilograms of coffee selling for $9.40 per kilogram.

Check
Weight: $12 + 8 = 20$ kg
Value: $12 \times 7.90 + 8 \times 9.40 = 94.80 + 75.20 = \$170.00$

EXERCISE 4.4 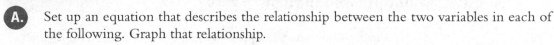   MyLab Math

A. Set up an equation that describes the relationship between the two variables in each of the following. Graph that relationship.

1. A manufacturer makes two types of products. Profit on Product A is $30 per unit, while profit on Product B is $40 per unit. Budgeted monthly profit is $6000.

2. Nakia Company manufactures two products. Product 1 requires three hours of machine time per unit, while Product 2 requires four hours of machine time per unit. There are 120 hours of machine time available per week.

3. U-Save-Bucks tax-consulting service rents space at $200 per week and pays the accounting personnel $4 per completed tax return.

4. Raimi is offered a position as a sales representative. The job pays a salary of $500 per month plus a commission of 10% on all sales.

B. Set up a system of simultaneous equations to solve each of the following problems.

1. Career Printers Ltd. has two locations with a total of 24 employees. If twice the number of employees at the larger location is three more than three times the number of employees at the smaller location, how many employees are at each location?

2. A restaurant is offering two dinner specials. The difference between seven times the orders for the first special and four times the orders for the second special is 12. The sum of three-fourths of the orders for the first special and two-thirds of the orders for the second special is 21. Calculate the number of orders for each special.

3. Loblaws sells two brands of jam. Brand X sells for $2.25 per jar, while the No-Name brand sells for $1.75 per jar. If 140 jars were sold for a total of $290, how many jars of each brand were sold?

4. Nancy's sales last week were $140 less than three times Andrea's sales. Together they sold $940. Determine how much each person sold last week.

5. Kaya and Fred agree to form a partnership. The partnership agreement requires that Fred invest $2500 more than two-thirds of what Kaya is to invest. If the total investment in the partnership is to be $55 000, how much should each partner invest?

6. Best World Places has two locations in eastern Canada with a total number of 240 rooms. If the number of rooms in the larger hotel is 100 less than three times the number of rooms in the smaller hotel, how many rooms does each hotel have?

7. A Brush with Wood has been producing 2320 chairs a day working two shifts. The second shift has produced 60 chairs fewer than four-thirds of the number of chairs produced by the first shift. Determine the number of chairs each shift has produced.

8. An inventory of two types of floodlights showed a total of 60 lights valued at $2580. If Type A cost $40 each and Type B cost $50 each, how many of each type of floodlight were in inventory?

9. A machine requires four hours to make a unit of Product A and three hours to make a unit of Product B. Last month the machine operated for 200 hours, producing a total of 60 units. How many units of each type of product did it produce?

10. Marysia has saved $85.75 in quarters and loonies. If she has one quarter more than three-fourths the number of loonies, how many coins of each type does Marysia have?

11. The local amateur football club spent $675 on tickets to a professional football game. If the club bought three fewer 15-dollar tickets than four-fifths the number of 12-dollar tickets, how many tickets of each type did the club buy?

4.5 GRAPHING INEQUALITIES
A. Basic concepts and method

A straight line drawn in a plane divides the plane into two regions:

(a) the region to the left of the line drawn in the plane;
(b) the region to the right of the line drawn in the plane.

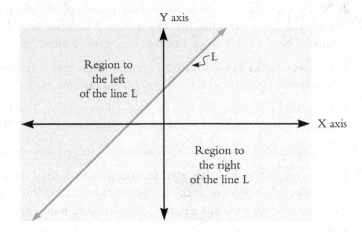

When a system of axes is introduced into the plane, each region consists of a set of points that may be represented by ordered pairs (x, y). Relative to the dividing line, the two sets of ordered pairs (x, y) that represent the points in the regions are defined by the two **inequalities** associated with the equation of the dividing line.

For the equation $x = 5$, the associated inequalities are $x < 5$ (x is less than 5) and $x > 5$ (x is greater than 5). For the equation $y = -3$, the associated inequalities are $y < -3$ and $y > -3$. For the equation $2x + 3y = 6$, the associated inequalities are $2x + 3y < 6$ and $2x + 3y > 6$.

Graphing an inequality means identifying the region that consists of the set of points whose coordinates satisfy the given inequality. To identify this region, use the following method.

1. *Draw* the graph of the equation associated with the inequality.

2. *Test* an arbitrarily selected point that is not a point on the line by substituting its coordinates in the inequality. The preferred point for testing is $(0, 0)$. If $(0, 0)$ is not available because the line passes through the origin, try the points $(0, 1)$ or $(1, 0)$.

3. **(a)** If substituting the coordinates of the selected point in the inequality yields a mathematical statement that is true, the selected point is a point in the region defined by the inequality. Thus, the **feasible region** is identified as the area containing the selected point. This region is called the "feasible region."
   (b) If substituting the coordinates of the selected point in the inequality yields a mathematical statement that is false, the selected point is not a point in the region defined by the inequality. Thus, the region defined by the inequality is the area that does not contain the point tested.

B. Graphing inequalities of the form $ax + by > c$ and $ax + by < c$

EXAMPLE 4.5A	Graph each of the following inequalities.

    (i) $x - y > -3$ (ii) $3x + 2y < -8$

SOLUTION

(i) The equation of the line associated with the inequality $x - y > -3$ is $x - y = -3$.

Table of values

x	0	-3	2
y	3	0	5

Note: To show that the coordinates of the points on the line $x - y = -3$ do not satisfy the inequality, the graph of the equation is drawn as a broken line.

Since the line does not pass through the origin, the point $(0, 0)$ may be used for testing.

$$\text{Substituting } x = 0 \text{ and } y = 0 \text{ in the}$$
$$\text{inequality } x - y > -3 \text{ yields the statement}$$
$$0 - 0 > -3$$
$$0 > -3.$$

Since the statement $0 > -3$ is true, the point $(0, 0)$ is a point in the feasible region. The region defined by the inequality $x - y > -3$ is the area to the right of the line as shown in the following diagram.

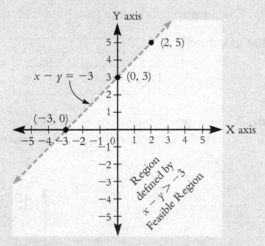

(ii) The equation of the line associated with the inequality $3x + 2y < -8$ is $3x + 2y = -8$.

Table of values

x	0	-2	-4
y	-4	-1	2

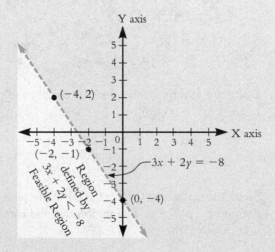

Testing the point $(0, 0)$
$$3(0) + 2(0) < -8$$
$$0 + 0 < -8$$
$$0 < -8.$$

Since the statement $0 < -8$ is false, the point $(0, 0)$ is not a point in the region defined by $3x + 2y < -8$. The region defined by the inequality is the area to the left of the line as shown.

C. Graphing inequalities of the form $ax > by$ or $ax < by$

EXAMPLE 4.5B

Graph each of the following inequalities.

   (i) $y \leq -x$ (ii) $3x < 2y$

SOLUTION

(i) The equation of the line associated with the inequality $y \leq -x$ is $y = -x$.

Table of values

x	0	3	−3
y	0	−3	3

Note: The inequality includes $y = -x$. Because the points on the line meet the condition stated, the graph of the equation is drawn as a solid line.

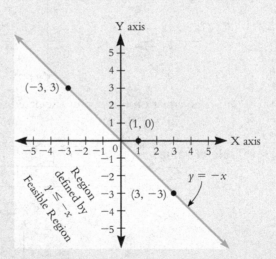

Since the line passes through the origin, the point $(0, 0)$ cannot be used for testing. Instead, we test $(1, 0)$.

Substituting $x = 1$, $y = 0$ in the inequality $y < -x$ yields the statement
$$0 < -1.$$

Since the statement $0 < -1$ is false, the point $(1, 0)$ is not a point in the region defined by $y \leq -x$. The region defined by the inequality is the area to the left of the line *including* the line.

(ii) The equation of the line associated with the inequality $3x < 2y$ is $3x = 2y$.

Table of values

x	0	2	-2
y	0	3	-3

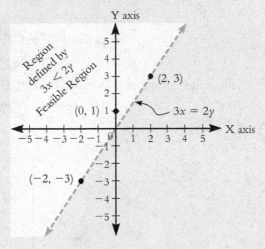

Since $(0, 0)$ is on the line, test $(0, 1)$.
Substituting $x = 0$, $y = 1$ in the
inequality $3x < 2y$ yields the statement
$0 < 2$.

Since the statement $0 < 2$ is true, the point $(0, 1)$ is a point in the region defined by $3x < 2y$. The region defined by the inequality is the area to the left of the line as shown.

D. Graphing inequalities involving lines parallel to the axes

EXAMPLE 4.5C

Graph each of the following inequalities.

(i) $x < 3$ (ii) $y \geq -3$

SOLUTION

(i) The equation of the line associated with the inequality $x < 3$ is $x = 3$. The graph of $x = 3$ is a line parallel to the Y axis three units to the right.

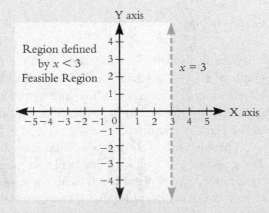

Test $(0, 0)$. Substituting $x = 0$ in the
inequality $x < 3$ yields the statement
$0 < 3$.

Since the statement $0 < 3$ is true, $(0, 0)$ is a point in the region defined by the inequality $x < 3$. The region defined by the inequality is the region to the left of the line as shown.

(ii) The equation of the line associated with the inequality $y \geq -3$ is $y = -3$. The graph of $y = -3$ is a line parallel to the X axis three units below it.

Test $(0, 0)$. Substituting $y = 0$ in the inequality $y > -3$ yields the statement
$$0 > -3.$$

Since the statement $0 > -3$ is true, $(0, 0)$ is a point in the region defined by $y \geq -3$. The region defined by the inequality is the area above the line *including* the line as shown.

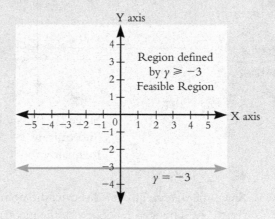

E. Graphing systems of linear inequalities

Systems consisting of two or more linear inequalities in two variables can be drawn by graphing each of the inequalities in the system. The graph of the system is the region *common* to all inequalities.

EXAMPLE 4.5D

Graph the region defined by $x > -2$ and $y > x - 3$.

SOLUTION

The equation of the line associated with the inequality $x > -2$ is $x = -2$. The graph of $x = -2$ is a line parallel to the Y axis and two units to the left of it. The substitution of 0 for x yields the true statement $0 > -2$. The point $(0, 0)$ is a point in the region defined by $x > -2$. The region defined by the inequality is the area to the right of the line.

The equation of the line associated with the inequality $y > x - 3$ is $y = x - 3$. The graph of $y = x - 3$ is a line passing through the points $(3, 0)$ and $(0, -3)$. The substitution of $x = 0$ and $y = 0$ yields the statement $0 > 0 - 3$, or $0 > -3$. Since this statement is true, the point $(0, 0)$ is a point in the region defined by the inequality $y > x - 3$. The region defined by the inequality is the area to the left of the line $y = x - 3$.

The region defined by the two inequalities is the area formed by the intersection of the two regions. The common region is called the **solution region** and is shown in the diagram.

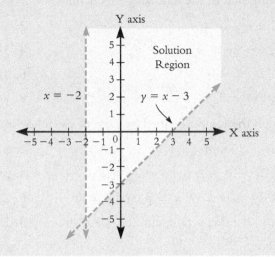

EXAMPLE 4.5E

Graph the region defined by $y \geq 0$, $4x + 5y \leq 20$, and $4x - 3y \geq -12$.

SOLUTION

The equation of the line associated with the inequality $y \geq 0$ is $y = 0$. The graph of $y = 0$ is the X axis. The region defined by the inequality $y \geq 0$ is the area above the X axis and includes the points forming the X axis.

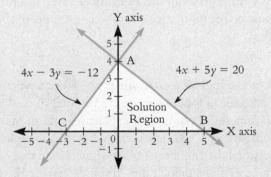

The equation of the line associated with the inequality $4x + 5y \leq 20$ is $4x + 5y = 20$. The graph of the equation is the line passing through the points A(0, 4) and B(5, 0). The true statement $0 < 20$ shows that the origin is a point in the region defined by the inequality. The region defined by $4x + 5y \leq 20$ is the area to the left of the line and includes the line itself.

The equation of the line associated with the inequality $4x - 3y \geq -12$ is $4x - 3y = -12$. The graph of this equation is the line passing through the points A(0, 4) and C(-3, 0). The true statement $0 > -12$ shows that the origin is a point in the region defined by the inequality. The region defined by $4x - 3y \geq -12$ is the area to the right of the line, including the line itself.

The region defined by the three inequalities is the area formed by the intersection of the three regions. The solution region is the triangle ABC shown in the diagram. All the points in the solution region satisfy the three inequalities.

EXERCISE 4.5 — MyLab Math

A. Graph each of the following inequalities.

    1. $x + y > 4$ **2.** $x - y < -2$

    3. $x - 2y \leq 4$ **4.** $3x - 2y \geq -10$

    5. $2x < -3y$ **6.** $4y \geq 3x$

    7. $x \geq -2$ **8.** $y < 5$

B. Graph the region defined by each of the following linear systems.

    1. $y < 3$ and $x + y > 2$ **2.** $x - 2y < 4$ and $x > -3$

    3. $3x - y \leq 6$ and $x + 2y > 8$ **4.** $5x > -3y$ and $2x - 5y \geq 10$

    5. $2y - 3x \leq 9$, $x \leq 3$, and $y \geq 0$ **6.** $2x + y \leq 6$, $x \geq 0$, and $y \geq 0$

    7. $y \geq -3x$, $y \leq 3$, and $2x - y \leq 6$ **8.** $2x \leq y$, $x \geq -3y$, and $x - 2y \geq -6$

4.6 PROBLEM SOLVING
A. Problems leading to one inequality in two variables

In many real-life problems where there are constraints on resources such as material, labour, capacity, budget, etc., the relationship between two variables can be represented by setting up a linear inequality. To find a solution to these problems, a feasible region must be found that satisfies the constraints of the problem.

EXAMPLE 4.6A

A food-processing company processes two types of food in its cooking department. Each unit of food 1 requires 15 minutes of cooking time, and each unit of food 2 needs 25 minutes of cooking time. The maximum time available to operate in the cooking department is 10 hours per day. Set up an inequality describing the relationship between the number of units of each food that can be produced in the cooking department. Using a graphical method, determine the feasible region for the inequality.

SOLUTION

Let the number of units of food 1 processed per day in the cooking department be x, and let the number of units of food 2 processed daily be y. Since each unit of food 1 requires 15 minutes of cooking time, the company can process a maximum of 15x units of food 1 per day. The maximum number of units of food 2 that can be processed per day would be 25y. The maximum time available daily at the cooking department is $(10)(60) = 600$ minutes. Then:

$15x + 25y \leq 600$

To solve this inequality graphically, we first draw the line for the equation $15x + 25y = 600$ and then determine the region that satisfies the inequality (the feasible region). To solve the equation, begin by setting up a table of values:

x	0	40
y	24	0

Next, we chart this data and determine the feasible region for the problem. Draw the line for equation $15x + 25y \leq 600$ and test the coordinates of the origin (0, 0) in the inequality. We will see that the feasible region is on the lower part of the line that satisfies the inequality.

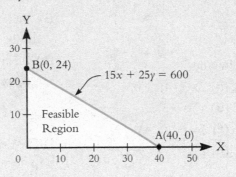

B. Problems leading to systems of linear inequalities in two variables

Many problems require allocating scarce resources to the most profitable products a company produces. Deciding which product to produce in order to maximize profit, or to minimize cost, often requires setting up and solving a system of linear inequalities.

EXAMPLE 4.6B

A car-manufacturing plant makes two types of cars: sedans and SUVs. To paint: each sedan requires 8 minutes and each SUV requires 10 minutes. For assembly: each sedan needs 12 minutes and each SUV needs 14 minutes. The maximum time available in the paint and assembly departments is 240 and 200 hours per month respectively. Formulate a system of linear inequalities for this problem and solve it graphically.

SOLUTION

Let x be the number of sedan cars and y be the number of SUV cars to be produced in one month. The maximum number of sedans to paint is *8x* per month and the maximum number of SUVs to paint is *10y* per month. The maximum number of cars to paint in one month would be $8x + 10y \leq (240)(60)$. In the assembly department, the maximum number of sedans to assemble is *12x* per month and for SUVs it is *14y* per month. The maximum number of cars to assemble in one month would be $12x + 14y \leq (200)(60)$.

First, we graph the equation for each inequality, and then determine the region that satisfies the inequality (the feasible region) for each inequality. The region that is common to both inequalities is the solution region for the problem.

$$8x + 10y = 14\ 400$$

$$12x + 14y = 12\ 000$$

To practise, graph the equations and determine the solution region.

MyLab Math Visit MyLab Math to practise any of this chapter's exercises marked with a as often as you want. The guided solutions help you calculate an answer step by step. You'll find a personalized study plan and additional interactive resources to help you master Business Math!

REVIEW EXERCISE

1. LO❶ Graph each of the following.

(a) $2x - y = 6$

(b) $3x + 4y = 0$

(c) $5x + 2y = 10$

(d) $y = -3$

(e) $5y = -3x + 15$

(f) $5x - 4y = 0$

(g) $x = -2$

(h) $3y = -4x - 12$

2. LO❷ Graphically solve each of the following.

(a) $3x + y = 6$ and $x - y = 2$

(b) $x + 4y = -8$ and $3x + 4y = 0$

(c) $5x = 3y$ and $y = -5$

(d) $2x + 6y = 8$ and $x = -2$

(e) $y = 3x - 2$ and $y = 3$

(f) $y = -2x$ and $x = 4$

(g) $x = -2$ and $3x + 4y = 12$

(h) $y = -2$ and $5x + 3y = 15$

3. LO❸ Using algebra, determine the slope and y-intercept of the line represented by each of the following equations.

(a) $7x + 3y = 6$

(b) $10y = 5x$

(c) $\dfrac{2y - 3x}{2} = 4$

(d) $1.8x + 0.3y - 3 = 0$

(e) $\dfrac{1}{3}x = -2$

(f) $11x - 33y = 99$

(g) $xy - (x + 4)(y - 1) = 8$

(h) $2.5y - 12.5 = 0$

4. LO❹ Solve each of the following systems of equations.

(a) $3x + 2y = -1$
$5x + 3y = -2$

(b) $4x - 5y = 25$
$3x + 2y = 13$

(c) $y = -10x$
$3y = 29 - x$

(d) $2y = 3x + 17$
$3x = 11 - 5y$

(e) $2x - 3y = 13$
$3x - 2y = 12$

(f) $2x = 3y - 11$
$y = 13 + 3x$

(g) $2a - 3b - 14 = 0$
$a + b - 2 = 0$

(h) $a + c = -10$
$8a + 4c = 0$

(i) $3b - 3c = -15$
$-2b + 4c = 14$

(j) $48a - 32b = 128$
$16a + 48b = 32$

(k) $0.5m + 0.3n = 54$
$0.3m + 0.7n = 74$

(l) $\dfrac{3}{4}m + \dfrac{5}{8}n = \dfrac{3}{4}$
$\dfrac{5}{6}n + \dfrac{2}{3}m = \dfrac{7}{9}$

5. LO❹ Write an equation describing the relationship between the two variables in each of the following problems and graph the relationship.

(a) Sun & Ski Travel pays for radio advertising at the fixed rate of $1000 per week plus $75 per announcement during the week.

(b) The Kirkland Company markets two products. Each unit of Product A requires five units of labour, while each unit of Product B requires two units of labour. Two hundred units of labour are available per time period.

6. LO❹ Set up a system of equations to solve each of the following problems.

(a) A tire store sold two types of tires, a sports tire and an all-season tire. The sum of six times the sports tires and five times the all-season tires is 93, and the difference between three-quarters of the sports tires and two-thirds of the all-season tires is zero. For the store manager, calculate the number of each type of tire sold in one day.

(b) The college theatre collected $1300 from the sale of 450 tickets. If the tickets were sold for $2.50 and $3.50, how many tickets were sold at each price?

(c) A jacket and two pairs of pants together cost $175. The jacket is valued at three times the price of one pair of pants. What is the value of the jacket?

(d) Three cases of white Bordeaux and five cases of red Bordeaux together cost $438. Each case of red Bordeaux costs $6 less than twice the cost of a case of white Bordeaux. Determine the cost of a case of each type.

SELF-TEST

1. Graphically solve each of the following systems of equations.

   (a) $y = -x - 2$ and $x - y = 4$ **(b)** $3x = -2y$ and $x = 2$

2. Graph each of the following systems of equations for all values of x indicated.

   (a) $-x = -55 + y$ and $y = 30$ **(b)** $x = 125$ and $3x + 2y = 600$;
   for $x = 0$ to $x = 200$ for $x = 0$ to $x = 200$

3. Using algebra, determine the slope and y-intercept of the line represented by each of the following equations.

   (a) $4y + 11 = y$ **(b)** $\dfrac{2}{3}x - \dfrac{1}{9}y = 1$

   (c) $x + 3y = 0$ **(d)** $-6y - 18 = 0$

   (e) $13 - \dfrac{1}{2}x = 0$ **(f)** $ax + by = c$

4. Solve each of the following systems of equations.

   (a) $6x + 5y = 9$ **(b)** $12 - 7x = 4y$
        $4x - 3y = 25$ $6 - 2y = 3x$

   (c) $0.2a + 0.3b = 0$ **(d)** $\dfrac{4}{3}b - \dfrac{3}{5}c = -\dfrac{17}{3}$
        $0.7a - 0.2b = 250$ $\dfrac{5}{6}b + \dfrac{4}{9}c = \dfrac{5}{9}$

5. Erica Lottsbriner invests $12 000 so that one part of her investment earns interest at 4% per annum and the other part earns 6% per annum. If the total annual interest on the investment is $560, how much has Erica invested at each rate?

6. Eyad and Rahia divide a profit of $12 700. If Eyad is to receive $2200 more than two-fifths of Rahia's share, how much will Rahia receive?

CHALLENGE PROBLEMS

1. Terry invested a total of $4500. A portion was invested at 4% and the rest was invested at 6%. The amount of Terry's annual return on each portion is the same. Calculate the average rate of interest Terry earned on the $4500.

2. In September, Polar Bay Wines had a net revenue of $574.56 from the sale of 3216 new wine bottles less the refund paid for 1824 returned bottles. In October, net revenue was $944.88 from the sale of 5208 bottles less the refund paid on 2232 returned bottles. How much did Polar Bay Wines charge per new wine bottle and how much was the refund for each returned bottle?

3. Ezhno, the owner of AAA College Painting, pays wages totalling $29 760 for a 40-hour workweek to a crew consisting of 16 painters and 24 helpers. To keep their jobs, the painters accepted a wage cut of 10% and the helpers a wage cut of 8%. The wage cut reduces Ezhno's weekly payroll by $2688. What hourly rates of pay does Ezhno pay after the wage cut?

4. In the hotel industry, three important metrics that hotel managers consider to improve their hotel performance are Occupancy Rate, Average Daily Rate (ADR), and Revenue per Available Room (REVPAR), with the last metric being the most important one among all. Occupancy rate is the ratio of rooms sold in a given day divided by the total number of rooms available. ADR is the average of the selling price of all the rooms sold for one day. REVPAR is calculated by multiplying the ADR by the occupancy rate.

You are the hotel manager for a busy downtown hotel that has 120 rooms available to sell.

(a) What is the occupancy rate if you sell 84 rooms on a specific day?

(b) If the average daily rate is $180, calculate the REVPAR.

(c) Write an equation in the form of $y = mx + b$ for this problem so that you can use it to calculate the hotel's total revenue. *Hint*: Let x be the occupancy rate.

(d) If you target a minimum revenue of $15 000 in a given day, how many rooms do you have to sell, assuming the ADR equals $180?

CASE STUDY   Determining the Right Combination

▶ Amarjit was preparing his annual tax return when he noticed that he had a $28 500 unused RRSP contribution limit. Through discussion with his financial advisor, Amarjit realized that he had not fully contributed to his RRSP in past years.

The advisor suggested that Amarjit borrow funds through an RRSP loan to take advantage of his unused contribution limit, as she believed that his RRSP's growth rate would be higher than the interest paid on the loan. The advisor knew of a bank making RRSP loans at a simple interest rate of 4.75% with four end-of-year principal payments required of $7125 each.

Amarjit agreed to this idea, and contemplated being more aggressive with his investments. He asked his advisor to discuss investments in the stock market.

The advisor suggested to him that while investing in the stock market had the potential for higher gains, there was also the possibility of losing money. Investing in equities (stocks) was riskier than his current conservative portfolio of bank savings accounts, treasury bills, and guaranteed investment certificates (GICs).

Details of several leading Canadian companies were provided to Amarjit to consider investing in:

Company	Latest Selling Price per Share	52-Week High/Low Price
Goldcorp	$34.76	$50.17/$32.34
TELUS	$64.92	$65.96/$55.19
International Forest Products	$7.85	$7.89/$3.75
Bank of Montreal	$60.64	$61.29/$53.15

QUESTIONS

1. How many shares of each stock would he get if he used the $28 500 and invested equally in all four companies?

2. Suppose Amarjit decided to buy shares in only TELUS and Goldcorp. How many shares of each would he get if he used the $28 500 and bought three times as many shares of TELUS as he bought of Goldcorp?

3. Suppose Amarjit decided to buy shares in only International Forest Products and the Bank of Montreal. How many shares of each company would he get if he used the $28 500 and bought two shares of the Bank of Montreal for every three shares of International Forest Products?

SUMMARY OF FORMULAS

Formula 4.1

$$y = mx + b$$

Slope–y-intercept form of a linear equation

GLOSSARY

Feasible region a region in the plane whose points satisfy an inequality *(p. 172)*

Inequality a mathematical statement involving relationship between variables described as "greater than" or "less than" *(p. 172)*

Ordered pair of numbers the coordinates of a point (x, y) *(p. 143)*

Origin the point of intersection of the two axes in a system of rectangular coordinates *(p. 143)*

Rise the vertical distance (distance along Y axis) between two points on a line or line segment *(p. 150)*

Run the horizontal distance (distance along X axis) between two points on a line or line segment *(p. 150)*

Slope the measure of the steepness of a line; it is the ratio of the rise of a line to its run *(p. 150)*

Slope–y-intercept form of a linear equation a linear equation expressed in the form $y = mx + b$ *(p. 151)*

Solution region a common region in solving a system of linear inequalities whose points satisfy all inequalities *(p. 177)*

X axis the horizontal reference line in a system of rectangular coordinates *(p. 143)*

x coordinate the first number in an ordered pair of numbers. It describes the position of a point relative to the axes or the directed distance of a point from the vertical axis (Y axis) *(p. 143)*

Y axis the vertical reference line in a system of rectangular coordinates *(p. 143)*

y coordinate the second number in an ordered pair of numbers. It describes the position of a point relative to the axes or the directed distance of a point from the horizontal axis (X axis) *(p. 143)*

y-intercept the y coordinate of the point of intersection of a line and the Y axis *(p. 150)*

Consistent and Dependent systems many solutions exists for these systems *(p. 143)*

Consistent and Independent systems systems of linear equations that have a unique solution *(p. 143)*

Inconsistent systems no solution exists for these systems *(p. 143)*

Til Debt Do Us Part host Gail Vaz-Oxlade has made it her mission to help couples who are headed for disaster to get out of debt. She says that some of the most common mistakes families make are keeping secrets, not having a budget, denying the debt, and failing to plan for emergencies.

Couples who are getting married have many important financial decisions to make. Not only do they have a wedding to pay for, but they also need to decide early on who is going to manage the money and how they will handle household expenses once they come together. This process requires full disclosure from both sides. Young couples, in particular, are prone to disagreements about money, especially if one member of the relationship brings a disproportionate share of the household income or the baggage of large student debt into the marriage. With the wedding fast approaching, Gail's advice to these couples is to start behaving like responsible adults and develop a road map to determine the right balance between their income and their debts. This way they won't end up as "guests" on her show.

Sean and Karen are engaged to be married next year. They are both 26 years old. Karen is a recent graduate, having just completed her MBA, and Sean has been working full-time as a high school teacher in Ontario for two years. Their primary goals for the next three years are to get through the wedding without adding any new debt and to pay off their student loans in full.

1. CHAPTER 1—QUESTIONS

    a. Karen has been offered two similar positions at competing financial firms. One position pays an annual salary of $61 200. The other job guarantees a salary of $2000 per month plus a commission of 2% on all sales. The average monthly sales figure per employee is $120 000.

        (i) If Karen's monthly sales reached $120 000, how much compensation would Karen receive per month?

        (ii) What level of monthly sales is necessary for Karen to consider either job?

b. Karen decides to accept the first position, so Sean takes her out to her favourite restaurant to celebrate. They spend $120 on food items and $27 on a bottle of wine. He also tips the waiter 15% of the combined cost of food items and wine, for good service. Assume Sean must pay 13% HST on food and wine items. How much did he spend?

c. Sean is employed by the Upper Grand District School Board and is under contract for 200 teaching days per year. His annual salary is $63 000. He is paid according to the following schedule:

   8% of annual salary on the first day of school

   4% of annual salary for each of the 20 two-week pay periods

   12% of annual salary at the end of the last pay period in June

   (i) What is Sean's gross pay for the each pay period?

   (ii) What is his gross pay for a regular pay period in which he was away for two days at no pay?

2. CHAPTER 2–QUESTIONS

a. To help pay for her MBA, Karen borrowed $5000 from her parents during her last year of school. The agreement was that Karen would repay the balance plus 3% interest on this personal loan once she started working.

   (i) Compute the amount of annual interest for this loan.

   (ii) If Karen pays back the loan in her first nine months of working, how much interest would she save?

b. Because she has been attending school full time while trying to plan a wedding, Karen has been very careful with her money.

   (i) Karen has set a budget of $700 for flowers for the reception. Roses cost $18 per dozen and daisies cost $10 per dozen. If 50 dozen flowers are to be purchased, how many dozen of each type can be purchased to use up exactly the budgeted amount?

   (ii) Recently, Karen purchased her wedding dress for $900 during a sale. What was the regular selling price of the dress if the price was reduced by $1/4$ of the regular price?

3. CHAPTER 3–QUESTIONS

Sean and Karen sat down months ago and created the following budget for their wedding:

Ceremony (officiator fee, marriage licence)	$400
Reception (location, food, drinks, rentals, cake, favours)	$9800
Clothes (bride's dress, shoes, accessories, hair and makeup, groom's suit, shoes)	$2200
Rings	$800
Flowers (bride's bouquet, bridesmaids' bouquets, corsages and boutonnieres, centrepieces)	$1500
Music (ceremony, DJ)	$1400
Photography	$2500
Transportation	$500
Stationary (invitations, thank you cards, postage, guest book)	$400
Gifts (bridesmaids and groomsmen)	$500
TOTAL	$20 000

a. Each set of parents has offered to contribute to the wedding. Sean already rents a small pickup truck, and now his parents have "gifted" their second vehicle to Karen. The wedding expenses are to be divided among Karen's parents, Sean's parents, and Sean and Karen in the ratio 4:2:2. How much will each party pay for the wedding?

b. Sean and Karen have visited several venues for their dinner and dance reception. They have narrowed the choice down to two locations. The Olympic Club will charge them a $2000 room rental and $65 per guest for dinner. The Fairmont Hotel will charge them $105 per guest.

    (i) If they are planning to host 120 guests at the reception, which venue is more affordable?

    (ii) If Sean and Karen prefer the Fairmont, and Sean's parents offer to pay $2000 more toward the reception, how many guests can attend without pushing Sean and Karen over their new reception budget?

c. When Karen's grandmother passed away she left a small amount of money to be shared equally between Karen and her two sisters for their weddings. Karen's parents invested the $4000 in two mutual funds (an equity fund and a bond). Over the years the investments have grown by 17%, and now the balance in the equity fund is $750 less than three times the amount in the bond. How much money will Karen get from each of these funds toward her wedding?

4. CHAPTER 4—QUESTIONS

Recognizing the importance of planning for their future, Sean and Karen sat down to determine their net worth. They compiled a list of the assets and liabilities each one of them is bringing into the marriage.

	Sean	Karen
Assets		
Chequing/savings account(s)	$3200	$800
Investments	17 000	n/a
Automobile(s)	n/a	3000
Cash value of life insurance	3100	n/a
RRSP(s)	4000	n/a
Other	600	n/a
Liabilities		
Student loans	$7500	$11 000
Car loans	n/a	n/a
Other debts	1350	5000
Line of credit	n/a	n/a
Credit cards	290	475

Then they identified their monthly income and debts as follows:

	Sean	Karen	Total
Monthly Income			
Gross monthly income	$5250	$5100	$10 350
Net Income	$3937	$4080	$8017
Monthly Expenses			
Housing (rent, utilities, cable, phone)	$1700	$780	$2480
Transportation (lease, gas, repairs, insurance, parking)	1140	435	1575
Medical and dental	100	200	300
Living expenses (groceries, clothes, entertainment, miscellaneous)	425	460	885
Credit payments	200	780	980

a. Net worth is calculated as the difference between a person's assets and liabilities. Calculate Sean and Karen's total assets, total liabilities, and individual net worth.

b. Calculate Sean and Karen's total monthly expenses, and determine how much money each one has left over at the end of each month.

c. Sean and Karen are anxious to pay off their student loans so that they can realize their dream of buying a home and starting a family by the time they both turn 30. Currently, Sean is repaying $150 per month on his student loan, and Karen is contributing $350. At these rates, it will take Sean five more years to pay off his student debt and it will take Karen three years.

Using the following formula, calculate the monthly loan payment that will enable Sean to pay off his student debt in only two years. (Assume a fixed interest rate of 3.5%.)

$$Loan\,Amount = Monthly\,Payment\left[\frac{1 - (1 + (fixed\,rate + 5\%/12))^{-24}}{(fixed\,rate + 5\%/12)}\right]$$

d. Although the purchase is still a few years off, Sean and Karen want to estimate now what they'll be able to afford when they go house hunting. One rule of thumb is that couples can afford to spend between 2.5 and 3 times their gross household income. Lenders also ask two key questions to determine whether or not you have the financial ability to carry the costs of a mortgage and of running the home. The two most widely accepted guidelines used are the gross debt service ratio (GDS) and the total debt service ratio (TDS). The GDS should not exceed 35%.

(i) According to the rule of thumb, how much can Sean and Karen afford for their first home?

(ii) Assuming a mortgage payment of $2300 per month, property taxes of $3000 per year, and heating of about $180 per month on equal billing, calculate Sean and Karen's GDS using this formula:

$$GDS = \frac{(Monthly\,mortgage\,Payment + Monthly\,property\,taxes + Monthly\,heating)}{(Gross\,monthly\,income)} \times 100\%$$

(iii) The TDS also needs to be under 42% for lenders to approve a mortgage. Calculate Sean and Karen's TDS if they expect to have paid off their student loans and the loan to Karen's parents, taken on a new car loan of $425 per month, and find themselves paying an average of $9000 per year on their credit payments.

$$TDS = \frac{(Monthly\,mortgage\,Payment + Monthly\,property\,taxes + All\,other\,monthly\,debts)}{(Gross\,monthly\,income)} \times 100\%$$

(iv) If you were a bank manager, would you approve the mortgage for Sean and Karen's home purchase?

Part 2 of the textbook emphasizes the mathematics of business and management and presents a wide range of applications for marketing, production operations, and finance.

Chapter 5 explores the relationships involving level of production, fixed costs, variable costs, total revenue, total cost, and the break-even point. This is called cost-volume-profit analysis. This section ties back to linear systems discussed in Chapter 4.

You will learn to set up linear equations for total revenue and total cost, and will learn how to calculate the break-even point in terms of units, sales dollars, and as a percent of plant capacity.

The concept of contribution margin, used widely in accounting courses, is introduced as an alternative way of viewing and solving the break-even problem.

Linear programming is a tool that can be used to find the product mix, which will maximize profits subject to a set of linear constraints. A linear programming model in two unknowns can be solved by graphing the linear constraints.

Chapter 6 introduces a basic merchandising chain, consisting of manufacturer, wholesaler, distributor, retailer, and consumer. Trade discounts are offered at various points on this chain. The mathematical operations for dealing with trade discounts and cash discounts are covered in detail.

Retailers then mark up a price to cover expenses and earn a profit. The markup may be based on cost or selling price. The mathematical calculations involved in determining the regular sales price, markups, markdowns, and the sales price after a markdown are presented. Problems are provided to give you an opportunity to integrate discounts, markups, and markdowns.

In Chapter 7, you will learn that simple interest is paid on short-term savings certificates and short-term loans. With simple interest, the principal stays the same. The amount of interest, I, earned on short-term savings vehicles is a function of the principal, P (original amount invested); the annual interest rate, r; and the interest period, t, in years.

In Chapter 7, the concept of present value is introduced for the first time. This concept will surface at many places in the text and is crucial to understanding the world of finance. Interest is paid for the use of money; thus, money has time value.

The concepts of present value and future value lead into dated or equivalent values. Examples are provided for finding the equivalent value of a single payment or the value of two or more equivalent payments. A practical application of present value and dated values is the loan repayment problem discussed at the end of the chapter.

Chapter 8 discusses simple interest applications and applies techniques for counting days, finding future value, and finding present value as described in Chapter 7. The promissory note is the first application presented.

Government of Canada T-bills, issued by the federal government, are promissory notes that do not carry an interest rate. Instead of paying interest, the T-bills are sold at a discount. At maturity, the face value of the T-bill is paid. The difference between the maturity value and purchase price is reported as interest income. The discounted price is found by calculating the present value of the maturity value using a current interest rate. The text also shows examples for finding the yield rate.

The nature of demand loans is explained. With a demand loan, all or a portion of the loan may be called in at any time. The borrower also has the right to repay the loan or part of the loan at any time. The interest rate may change over the term of the loan. The method used for counting the days is as follows: count the first day but not the last day. Partial payments are applied to the accumulated interest first when the declining balance approach is used.

Examples of calculating interest charges on a line of credit and credit card loans are shown. An unsecured line of credit in which no assets are pledged to the lender is distinguished from a secured line of credit in which assets are pledged to the lender.

The procedure for setting up an amortization schedule is also introduced in Chapter 8. The schedule shows the principal and interest portions of a blended payment and the outstanding balance at a point in time. This is a critical topic that will be revisited later in the text with mortgages and sinking funds.

The **Universal Principle of Rounding** applies in Part 2 of the textbook. When performing a sequence of operations, never round any interim solution until the final answer is achieved. Apply rounding principles only to the final answer.

Note: Due to space limitations, the textbook shows only the first six decimals (rounded) of any number.

Some specific rounding guidelines for Part 2: Business problems throughout the textbook often involve money values, so the rounding for final answers needs to be done to the cent; that is, to two decimal places. When calculating break-even units in Chapter 5, remember that the solution is the *minimum* number of units that must be sold. As such, any decimals must be rounded upward to the next integer, regardless of the actual value of the decimal. For example, 38.05 units means 39 units must be sold to at least break even. In Chapter 6, interim solutions should be rounded only when common practice would require rounding. Also, keep in mind that in Chapter 7, t is always an integer. It is important to note in this calculation that in most instances the interest (I) earned or charged to the account has been rounded to two decimals. This will cause the calculation of t to be slightly imprecise. Therefore, when calculating t it is possible that decimals close to an integer (such as 128.998 days or 130.012 days) may show up. These decimals should be rounded to the nearest integer to correct for the rounded interest amount.

While different methods of rounding are used, for most business purposes the following procedure is suitable:

1.   If the first digit in the group of decimal digits that is to be dropped is 5 or greater, the last digit retained is *increased* by 1.

2.   If the first digit in the group of decimal digits that is to be dropped is 4 or less, the last digit retained is left *unchanged*.

5

Cost-Volume-Profit Analysis and Break-Even

Agencja Fotograficzna Caro/Alamy Stock Photo

LEARNING OBJECTIVES

Upon completing this chapter, you will be able to do the following:

1. Construct and interpret cost-volume-profit charts.

2. Compute break-even values using cost-volume-profit relationships.

3. Compute break-even values using contribution margin and contribution rate.

4. Compute the effects of changes to cost, volume, and profit.

In business planning, it is useful and necessary to determine the number of units you need to sell to cover costs, or the number of units you need to produce a target profit. Analyzing the relationships among costs, volumes, and profits is an important technique in determining the number of units you need to sell, the price to charge, the costs you may incur, and the profit that results. The Business Math News Box in this chapter (page *214*) provides an interesting example of cost-volume-profit analysis as it relates to the newly legal recreational cannabis industry in Canada. Producers must determine their costs and selling prices to succeed in this new market.

INTRODUCTION

One of the main concerns to owners and managers operating a business is profitability. To achieve or maintain a desired level of profitability, managers must make decisions that determine product quantity, total revenue, and total cost.

Cost-volume-profit analysis is a valuable tool in evaluating the potential effects of decisions on profitability. In this type of analysis, computations of **break-even analysis** may be involved. Further calculations may be performed to determine the effect of changes in one or more components of the break-even analysis. This technique is called **sensitivity** or what-if **analysis**.

5.1 COST-VOLUME-PROFIT ANALYSIS AND BREAK-EVEN CHARTS
A. Cost-volume-profit analysis

Jason is a recent graduate from Kwantlen Polytechnic University's (KPU) horticulture program. KPU Horticulture trains students in three main areas: (1) greenhouse vegetables, flowers, and nursery crops, (2) landscape design, installation, and maintenance, and (3) turf management. According to the university's Website, these three areas of horticulture practice are technology-intensive and knowledge-based, and have a significant impact on the quality of life for urban and suburban society. With the popularity of greenhouse vegetables growing, Jason, who did very well in the first area of the program, is planning to start a business producing vegetables. He has decided he is most interested in growing bell peppers.

Jason's father has a good-sized greenhouse built in his yard that is available for Jason to rent. His father requires $550 per month for the use of his greenhouse. Three important factors in greenhouse growing are lighting, temperature, and humidity. Jason has conducted research on the related cost of these factors and believes they can be managed by upgrading the greenhouse at a cost of $450 per month. In addition, he will need to purchase seeds, fertilizer, net pots, clay pebbles, and some other supplies. Jason estimates that the cost for all the necessary supplies will be 20 cents for each bell pepper he produces. Water and electricity use are expected to cost 10 cents per bell pepper. He thinks he can produce a maximum of 3000 bell peppers every month with the size of the greenhouse he is planning to set up. The local market for bell peppers is $4.20 per pack of 3 bell peppers, but he anticipates he may have to price down each pack and sell his peppers for $3 per pack ($1 for each bell pepper) to be able to compete with the big retailers.

To determine his expected profit, Jason calculated his income based on the number of bell peppers he could produce each month and summarized the information in the table shown below.

Number of Bell Peppers	0	300	1500	3000
Revenue	0	300	1500	3000
Greenhouse rent	550	550	550	550
Greenhouse Upgrade	450	450	450	450
Total cost	1000	1090	1450	1900
Net Income	−$1,000.00	−$790.00	$50.00	$1,100.00

To proceed, Jason took all the above information to a KPU's business school professor. Jason wanted to know if there was a way of determining how many bell peppers he needed to produce and sell to cover his expenses. He also wanted to know how to determine the effects on the net income of changes in the price per bell pepper, the cost of materials, and other costs.

On the basis of his business teaching and practical experiences, the professor would analyze the situation using "break-even analysis." The business professor would need to determine which costs were fixed and which were variable to the number of bell peppers produced and sold. He would use all the information, and then make changes to one part to determine the effect.

A primary function of accounting is the collection of cost and revenue data. These data are then used to examine the existing relationships between cost behaviour and revenue behaviour.

Any analysis, whether algebraic or graphic, makes certain assumptions about the behaviour of costs and revenue. In its simplest form, cost-volume-profit analysis makes the following assumptions:

Cost-Volume-Profit Assumptions

1. Selling price per unit of output is constant. You are operating in a perfectly competitive market, so sellers can produce as much as they want without changing the market price. Total revenue varies directly with volume.

2. Costs are linear and can be classified as either fixed or variable.

   A. **Fixed cost** remains constant over the time period considered for all levels of output. Examples of costs in this category are rent, amortization, property taxes, and supervision and management salaries. Since fixed cost is constant in total, it can be averaged over various numbers of units. When this is calculated, fixed cost appears to vary per unit of output. Fixed cost per unit of output decreases as volume increases because the total cost is spread out over more units.

   B. **Variable cost** is constant per unit of output regardless of volume. It increases or decreases in total amount as volume fluctuates. Examples of costs in this category are direct material costs, direct labour costs, and sales commissions.

3. In manufacturing firms, all units produced in a particular operating period are sold. There is no ending finished goods inventory, and all expenses in one period are incurred against sales in that period.

4. When multiple products are produced within a company, the ratio of various products remains constant.

5. The time value of money is ignored.

With the above assumptions, the real world is viewed in a simplified manner. In most actual situations, fixed cost is not constant across all levels of output; instead, it tends to change in step fashion. Also, per-unit variable cost is not always constant; it is often influenced by economies of scale. Finally, most of the time, costs cannot be rigidly classified as fixed or variable; many costs are semi-variable, with both a fixed and a variable component. However, for purposes of an uncomplicated introductory analysis, these assumptions are useful.

The analysis of cost-volume-profit focuses on profitability. The basic income statement shows that profit results when total cost is subtracted from total revenues. This profit is often named **net income** or operating income.

$$\text{PROFIT} = \text{TOTAL REVENUE} - \text{TOTAL COST}$$

Abbreviated, the equation is

$$\text{PFT} = \text{TR} - \text{TC}$$

The amount of total cost is separated into the amount of fixed cost and the amount of variable cost:

$$\text{TOTAL COST} = \text{FIXED COST} + \text{TOTAL VARIABLE COST}$$

or $$\text{TC} = \text{FC} + \text{TVC}$$

$$\text{TOTAL REVENUE} = \text{FIXED COST} + \text{TOTAL VARIABLE COST} + \text{PROFIT}$$

or $$\text{TR} = \text{FC} + \text{TVC} + \text{PFT}$$

TOTAL REVENUE	PROFIT
	TOTAL VARIABLE COST
	FIXED COST

The approach is specifically concerned with identifying the level of output at which the business neither makes a profit nor sustains a loss—that is, the level of output at which the profit is zero. When the profit is zero, the **break-even point** is the result. Therefore, at the break-even point,

$$\text{PROFIT} = 0$$
$$\text{TOTAL REVENUE} = \text{TOTAL COST}$$
$$\text{TR} = \text{TC}$$

or, $$\text{TOTAL REVENUE} = \text{FIXED COST} + \text{TOTAL VARIABLE COST}$$

Total revenue is determined when the selling price, SP, for a unit is multiplied by the quantity, X, or volume of units sold.

$$\text{TOTAL REVENUE} = \text{SELLING PRICE} \times \text{VOLUME (in units)}$$

or $$\text{TR} = \text{SP} \times X$$

Also, when the variable cost for a unit is multiplied by the quantity of units sold, the result is the total variable cost.

$$\text{TOTAL VARIABLE COST} = \text{VARIABLE COST PER UNIT} \times \text{VOLUME (in units)}$$

or $$\text{TVC} = \text{VC} \times X$$

TOTAL REVENUE (SELLING PRICE × VOLUME)	PROFIT
	TOTAL VARIABLE COST (VARIABLE COST PER UNIT × VOLUME)
	FIXED COST

Thus, the relationship is determined as follows:

$$\text{PROFIT} = (\text{SELLING PRICE} \times \text{VOLUME}) - \text{FIXED COST} - (\text{VARIABLE COST PER UNIT} \times \text{VOLUME})$$

——— Formula 5.1

or, $$\text{PFT} = (\text{SP} \times X) - \text{FC} - (\text{VC} \times X)$$

If the volume of units sold is less than the break-even volume, the negative profit is referred to as a loss.

B. Break-even charts

The relationships among costs, volumes, and profits may be represented graphically by using straight-line diagrams. The following figures show general representations of revenue and cost behaviour.

In graphing these relationships, the horizontal axis (X axis) represents volume of output either as a number of units or as a percent of **capacity**. The highest number of units would be the maximum capacity available, or 100% of capacity. The vertical axis (Y axis) represents dollar values (sales revenue). The origin is at zero–zero, that is zero volume and zero dollars.

The **revenue function** in Figure 5.1 is identified by the equation that represents Selling Price × Volume, TR = SP × X. The total revenue line is drawn by plotting two or more total revenue points (one of which is always the origin) and joining them. While any volume of units may be used, two preferred values represent the two extreme values (minimum and maximum volume) for the example.

The **cost function** in Figure 5.2 is identified by the equation that represents Fixed Cost + Total Variable Cost, or Fixed Cost + (Variable Cost per Unit × Volume), TC = FC + (VC × X). Two lines are drawn: one for the fixed cost, and another for the total cost. Total cost is the sum of the fixed cost and the total variable cost.

Figure 5.1 Revenue Behaviour (© S. A. Hummelbrunner)

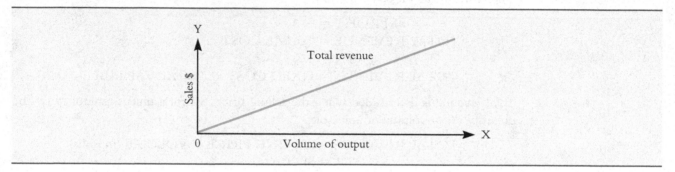

Figure 5.2 Cost Behaviour (© S. A. Hummelbrunner)

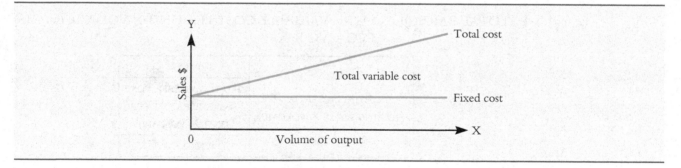

Fixed cost: The fixed cost line is drawn parallel to the horizontal axis from the point on the vertical axis that represents total fixed cost dollars. The *y*-intercept represents the fixed cost in dollars.

Total cost: The total cost line is drawn by plotting two or more total cost points (one of which is always the point at which the fixed cost line starts on the vertical axis, that is the *y*-intercept) and joining them. Assume the two values of the units and compute the corresponding value of total cost. The area between the fixed cost line and the total cost line represents the total variable cost in dollars for all levels of volume of output.

The *break-even approach* to cost-volume-profit analysis focuses on profitability. The relationship between revenue and cost at different levels of output may be portrayed graphically by showing revenue behaviour (Figure 5.1) and cost behaviour (Figure 5.2) on the same graph. The resulting graph shows the break-even point and is known as a **break-even chart** (Figure 5.3).

As shown in (Figure 5.3), the point at which the total revenue line and the total cost line intersect is the *break-even point*. The point of intersection on the horizontal axis of the perpendicular dashed line drawn from the break-even point to the horizontal axis indicates the *break-even volume in units* or as a percent of capacity. The point of intersection on the vertical axis of the perpendicular dashed line drawn from the break-even point to the vertical axis indicates the *break-even volume in dollars* ("Sales $"). The area between the total revenue line and the total cost line to the left of the break-even point represents the *loss area*; that is, where total revenue is less than total cost. The area between the total cost line and the total revenue line to the right of the break-even point represents the *profit area*; that is, where total revenue is greater than total cost.

Figure 5.3 Break-Even Chart (© S. A. Hummelbrunner)

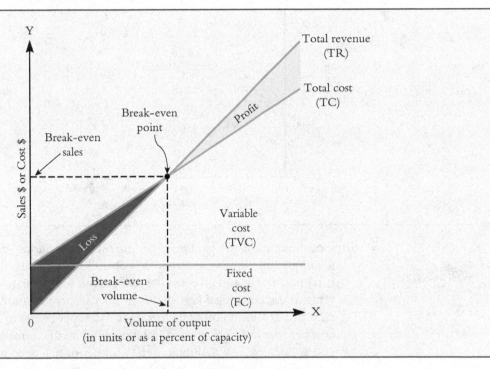

| EXAMPLE 5.1A | For Jason's greenhouse growing business, graph the following cost-volume-profit relationships and determine the break-even point: |

    (i) revenue function;

    (ii) cost function;

    (iii) break-even chart.

| SOLUTION | (i) Revenue function: Since Jason sells each bell pepper for $1, the total revenue is calculated by multiplying the number of bell peppers by the unit price. The revenue function is shown as |

$$TR = 1 \times \text{Number of bell peppers}$$
or, $$TR = 1X$$

This relationship can be graphed (see Figure 5.4) by choosing two points that satisfy the equation. If Jason does not sell any bell peppers, his revenue would be zero. The first point chosen is shown as (0, 0), representing zero units and zero dollars of sales. A second point can be determined by choosing a different number of peppers and multiplying it by 1. For example, if Jason sells 3000 units, his total revenue would be $1 \times 3000 = $3000. The two points are drawn on the chart, and a line is drawn to connect them, becoming the total revenue line. The highest number of units to be shown is the maximum capacity available. In Jason's case, he could produce a maximum of 3000 bell peppers per month.

Figure 5.4 Jason's Greenhouse Growing Revenue (© S. A. Hummelbrunner)

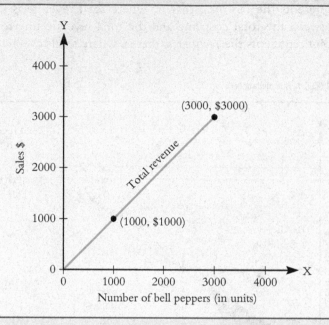

(ii) Cost function: Jason has two types of costs—greenhouse rental of $550 and $450 for upgrading the greenhouse (i.e., controlling humidity, lighting, and temperature) per month and 30 cents per bell pepper for materials and supplies. The rent remains the same regardless of the number of peppers produced, and is therefore classified as a fixed cost. The materials and supplies cost is classified as variable cost because the total amount is determined by the number of units. The total cost is calculated by multiplying the number of bell peppers by the unit variable cost, and adding the fixed cost. The cost function is shown as

TC = Fixed Cost + (0.30 × Number of bell peppers)
or,   TC = 1000 + 0.30X

First, the fixed cost line is drawn as a horizontal line. Second, the total cost is graphed by choosing two points that satisfy the equation. If Jason does not sell any bell peppers, his variable cost would be zero but his fixed cost continues. The total cost at zero volume would be equal to the fixed cost. The first point chosen is shown as (0, 1000), representing zero units and $1000 dollars of cost. A second point can be determined by choosing a different number of bell peppers, multiplying it by 0.30, and adding 1000. For example, if Jason sells 1000 bell peppers, his total cost would be $1000 + ($0.30 × 1000) = $1300. The two points are drawn on the chart, and a line is drawn to connect them, becoming the total cost line. See Figure 5.5.

(iii) Break-even chart: The analysis and labelling of the chart needs to be completed.

1. The break-even point is identified as the point where the total revenue line crosses the total cost line. This indicates that the break-even point is where

TOTAL REVENUE = TOTAL COST

Figure 5.5 Jason's Greenhouse Growing Costs (© S. A. Hummelbrunner)

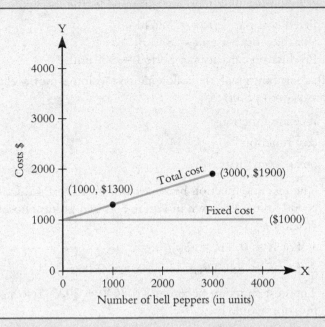

2. The area of loss is identified as the area between the total revenue and total cost lines, below the break-even point.

3. The area of profit is identified as the area between the total revenue and total cost lines, above the break-even point.

To break even, Jason must produce and sell 1429 bell peppers for a total of $1429 in total revenue. If he produces and sells fewer than 1429 bell peppers, he will incur a loss. If he produces and sells more than 1429 bell peppers, he will earn a profit. See Figure 5.6.

Figure 5.6 Break-Even Chart for Jason's Greenhouse Data (© S. A. Hummelbrunner)

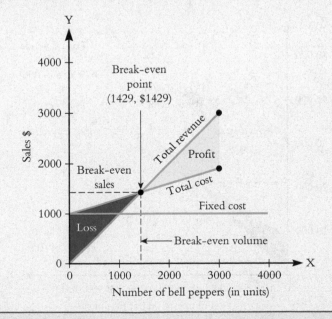

EXAMPLE 5.1B

Market research for a new product called the Scrubby indicates that the product can be sold at $50 per unit. Cost analysis provides the following information.

> Fixed cost per period = $8640
> Variable cost per unit = $30
> Production capacity per period = 900 units

For the Scrubby, graph the following cost-volume-profit relationships and determine the break-even point:

(i) revenue function

(ii) cost function

(iii) break-even chart

SOLUTION

(i) The revenue function becomes TR = 50 X. Production capacity per period is 900 units. As shown in Figure 5.7, two points chosen to graph the function would be:

1. For X = 0, TR = (50)(0) = 0 —————————— **graph point (0, 0)**

2. For X = 900, TR = (50)(900) = 45 000 ————— **graph point (900, 45 000)**

(ii) The cost function becomes TC 8640 + 30X. Two points chosen to graph the function would be

1. For X = 0, TC = 8640 + (30)(0) = 8640 ————— **graph point (0, 8640)**

2. For X = 900, TC = 8640 + (30)(900) = 35 640 — **graph point (900, 35 640)**

(iii) On the break-even chart, identify and label

1. The break-even point: Total revenue is equal to total cost when 432 units are sold, and $21 600 in total revenue is earned.

2. The area of loss is identified as the area between the total revenue and total cost lines, below 432 units or below $21 600 in total revenue.

3. The area of profit is identified as the area between the total revenue and total cost lines, above 432 units or above $21 600 in total revenue.

Figure 5.7 Break-Even Chart for the Scrubby (© S. A. Hummelbrunner)

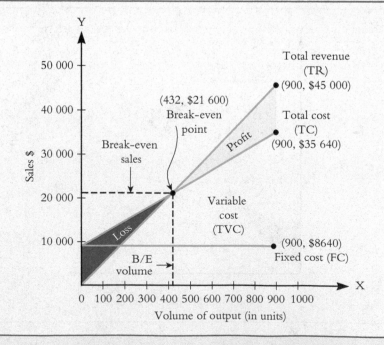

C. Computing break-even using formulas

As mentioned previously, the cost-volume-profit relationship can be analyzed using formulas, starting with Formula 5.1.

$(SP \times X) - FC - (VC \times X) = PFT$ where the volume of units is X.

POINTERS
& PITFALLS

When calculating break-even units, remember that the solution is the *minimum* number of units that must be sold. As such, any decimals must be rounded upward to the next integer.

EXAMPLE 5.1C

Referring to Example 5.1A, for Jason's greenhouse growing business, perform a break-even analysis using Formula 5.1. Provide

 (i) an algebraic statement of the total revenue and the total cost;

 (ii) computation of the break-even point in units;

 (iii) computation of the break-even point in dollars.

SOLUTION

We identify the following:

$$SP = 1; VC = 0.30; FC = \$1000$$

At the break-even point, let the volume in units be X.

 (i) As stated in Example 5.1A,

   Total revenue: $TR = 1X$
   Total cost: $TC = 1000 + 0.30X$

 (ii) $PFT = 0$ at the break-even point, so $TR = TC$

   $1X = 1000 + 0.30X$

   $0.70X = 1000$

   $X = 1428.57$ but we always round up. Therefore, $X = 1429$

 (iii) The break-even point in dollars: Jason will break even when he sells 1429 bell peppers. At that point, his total revenue will equal his total cost. When Jason sells 1429 bell peppers, his total cost is

$$1000 + (\$0.30 \times 1429) = \$1429$$

To cover all of his costs, in order to break even, the revenues needed are also $1429.

EXAMPLE 5.1D

Referring to Example 5.1B, market research for the new product, the Scrubby, indicates that the product can be sold at $50 per unit. Cost analysis provides the following information.

   Fixed cost per period = $8640
   Variable cost per unit = $30
   Production capacity per period = 900 units

Perform a break-even analysis. Provide

   (i) an algebraic statement of the total revenue and the total cost;

  (ii) computation of the break-even point in units;

 (iii) computation of the break-even point in dollars.

SOLUTION

   (i) Let the volume in units be X.

        Total revenue: $TR = 50X$
        Total cost: $TC = 8640 + 30X$

  (ii) $PFT = 0$ at the break-even point, so $TR = TC$

$$50X = 8640 + 30X$$
$$20X = 8640$$
$$X = 432$$

 (iii) The total revenue needed to break even would be
       $50 \times 432 = \$21\ 600$

       Proven by Formula 5.1:
       $(50 \times 432) - 8640 - (30 \times 432) = 0$

D. Calculating break-even when the unit prices and unit costs are unknown

When the sales and variable cost are only available in total dollars, not in the form of dollars per unit, a relationship between total sales and total variable cost can be determined. Note that, in the given information, the net income (or profit) is not zero. This indicates that the given sales amount does not represent a break-even point.

    To determine the break-even point in sales dollars, assume that the price per unit is $1. You can now calculate the variable cost per unit by dividing the total variable cost by the total sales. The break-even point can then be calculated.

EXAMPLE 5.1E

The following information is available about the operations of the King Corporation for the current year.

Sales		$40 000
Fixed cost	$12 600	
Variable cost	16 000	
Total cost		28 600
Net income		$11 400

Capacity is at a sales maximum of $60 000.
Perform a break-even analysis. Provide

   (i) an algebraic statement of
      (a) the revenue function;
      (b) the cost function;

  (ii) computation of
      (a) the break-even point in sales dollars;
      (b) the break-even point as a percent of capacity;

 (iii) a detailed break-even chart

SOLUTION

(i) When the data are in terms of total dollars rather than units, express the functions in terms of sales.

Let X represent the number of units sold.

(a) Assuming that the price per unit is $1, the revenue function, TR, is expressed as $1 × X.

(b) Since variable cost is directly related to sales, it can be expressed as a percent of sales.

In this example, total variable cost is $16 000 for sales of $40 000.

$$\frac{\text{Total variable cost}}{\text{Total revenue}} = \frac{16\ 000}{40\ 000} = 0.4 = 40\%$$

This means that when the price per unit is $1, the variable cost per unit is $0.40.
Total variable cost = $0.40 × Number of units = $0.4X$
The total cost function is TC = 12 600 + 0.4X.

(ii) The break-even point occurs where TR = TC

$$1.00X = 12\ 600 + 0.4X$$
$$0.6X = 12\ 600$$
$$X = 21\ 000$$

(a) The break-even sales in dollars is $21 000.

(b) The break-even point as a percent of capacity is $\frac{21\ 000}{60\ 000} = 0.35 = 35\%$.

(iii) When the accounting data are in terms of total dollars, the horizontal axis represents output in terms of percent of sales capacity. Subdivide the horizontal scale to allow percent sales levels up to 100% (see Figure 5.8). The vertical scale must

Figure 5.8 Break-Even Chart for King Corporation (© S. A. Hummelbrunner)

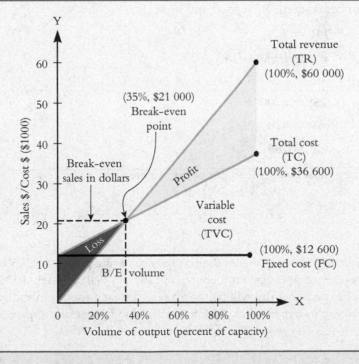

allow for the maximum sales level at a capacity of $60 000. To graph the revenue function, assume at least two different sales volume levels expressed as a percent of capacity.

(a) For $X = 0\%$, TR = $0 $\longrightarrow$ graph point (0%, $0)

(b) For $X = 100\%$, TR = $60 000 $\longrightarrow$ graph point (100%, $60 000)

The line joining the two points represents the revenue function.
To graph the cost function, assume two different sales volume levels and compute TC.

(a) For $X = 0\%$, TC = $12 600 + 0.4(0)$ $\longrightarrow$ graph point (0%, $12 600)

(b) For $X = 100\%$, TC = $12 600 + 0.4(60 000)$

$\qquad$ TC = $36 600 $\longrightarrow$ graph point (100%, $36 600)

EXAMPLE 5.1F

Nia and Jody are planning a student skiing trip for their class. The trip would involve two days of ski passes, with a one-night stay in a local hotel, and round-trip bus transportation to the ski resort. The cost of a two-day ski pass is $99. They estimate the hotel stay would cost $49 per night per person. To rent the bus and to pay for the driver's time would cost $1000 for the two days. The bus can hold a maximum of 40 people, excluding the driver.

If they plan to sell only 25 tickets, how much must they charge each person for the trip?

SOLUTION

$X = 25$

$VC = 99.00 + 49.00 = 148.00$

$FC = 1000.00$

Let the price per unit be SP.

For break-even, PFT $= 0$ and so

$\qquad$ TR = TC

$(SP \times 25) = 1000 + (148 \times 25)$

$(SP \times 25) = 1000 + 3700$

$(SP \times 25) = 4700$

$\qquad SP = 4700/25$

$\qquad SP = 188$

They must charge $188 per person to break even.

EXAMPLE 5.1G

Galaxy Caterers provides dinners for events at a price of $87.50 per contract. The average variable cost for a contract is $62.50. Galaxy catered 112 contracts last month, and expect that this will be the average for each month in the future. The company is wishing to expand, but the kitchen and food preparation space is limited. The owner has located several possible new locations to rent and needs to determine how much extra space she can afford and still stay profitable.

What is the most Galaxy Caterers can spend on rent and other fixed costs to break even?

SOLUTION

SP = 87.50

VC = 62.50

$X = 112$

Let the fixed cost be FC.

To break-even,

$$TR = TC$$
$$(87.50 \times 112) = FC + (62.50 \times 112)$$
$$9800 = FC + 7000$$
$$FC = 9800 - 7000$$
$$FC = 2800$$

Therefore, Galaxy Caterers must pay no more than $2800 in fixed cost to break even.

EXAMPLE 5.1H

Helene and Michel have approached their Uncle Henri for a loan to set up a business. They wish to deliver bouquets of flowers to the people and businesses in their neighbourhood. Uncle Henri has asked them to estimate their revenue and their costs and do a break-even analysis. They need to lease a delivery van at $900 per month including insurance. The cost of advertising would be $300 per month. If they price the bouquets at $35 each, they estimate that they can sell 80 units per month.

What is the most they can spend to purchase each bouquet of flowers to break even?

SOLUTION

SP = 35

FC = 900 + 300 = 1200

$X = 80$

Let the cost of each bouquet be VC.

To break even,

$$TR = TC$$
$$(35 \times 80) = 1200 + (VC \times 80)$$
$$2800 = 1200 + (VC \times 80)$$
$$(VC \times 80) = 1600$$
$$VC = 1600/80$$
$$VC = 20$$

Therefore, to break even, they must pay no more than $20 to purchase each bouquet of flowers.

POINTERS & PITFALLS

You can use the BREAKEVEN function of a Texas Instrument BA II PLUS financial calculator to determine the break-even point. In this function, FC refers to the total fixed cost for the period, VC refers to the unit variable cost, P refers to the unit price, PFT is the resulting profit, and Q is used to input or calculate the quantity or number of units. For example, to solve Example 5.1D using a financial calculator, press:

2nd	Brkevn	FC = 8640.00 Enter	↓
		VC = 30.00 Enter	↓
		P = 50.00 Enter	↓
		PFT = 0 Enter	↓
CPT	Q = 432 units		

Any four of the five variables may be entered. You can then compute a value for the fifth variable.

EXERCISE 5.1   MyLab Math

A. For each of the following, perform a break-even analysis showing

(a) an algebraic statement of
   (i) the revenue function
   (ii) the cost function;

(b) computation of the break-even point
   (i) in units,
   (ii) in sales dollars,
   (iii) as a percent of capacity;

(c) a detailed break-even chart.

1. Engineering estimates show that the variable cost of manufacturing a new product will be $35 per unit. Based on market research, the selling price of the product is to be $120 per unit and variable selling expense is expected to be $15 per unit. The fixed cost applicable to the new product is estimated to be $2800 per period and capacity is 100 units per period.   Reference Example 5.1B

2. A firm manufactures a product that sells for $12 per unit. Variable cost per unit is $8 and fixed cost per period is $1200. Capacity per period is 1000 units.

3. The following data pertain to the operating budget of Matt Manufacturing. Capacity per period is sales of $800 000.

Sales		$720 000
Fixed cost	$220 000	
Total variable cost	324 000	
Total cost		544 000
Net income		$176 000

Reference Example 5.1E

4. Harrow Seed and Fertilizer compiled the following estimates for its operations. Capacity per period is sales of $150 000.

Sales		$120 000
Fixed cost	$43 200	
Total variable cost	48 000	
Total cost		91 200
Net income		$28 800

B. 1. The neighbourhood bookstore sells novels for $6.95 per unit. The cost to purchase one book is $3.95. The store has fixed cost per month of $1800. The store estimates that it can sell 1000 books every month. How many books does it need to sell to break even?
   Reference Example 5.1C

2. Tara makes and sells scarves for children and adults. She is able to sell the scarves for $18 per unit. Materials for the scarves cost $4 each. She has fixed cost per month of $280, and estimates that she can make and sell 80 scarves each month. How many scarves does Tara need to sell to break even?
   Reference Example 5.1D

3. Bargain Toys has just acquired the rights to merchandise the latest video game. It can purchase these games for $16. If Bargain Toys advertises the games at a cost of $630 per month, and sells them for $30 each, how many games does it need to sell each month to break even?

4. Old-Tyme Fashions specializes in hats modelled after fashions from the past. It purchases these hats for $42 each. It can provide a custom service to print the new owner's name on the hatband. The printing machine costs $243 per month to rent. If Old-Tyme sells the hats at a price of $69 each, how many does it need to sell to break even?

5. The operating budget for Packard Machinery Company shows a net income of $469 300. To achieve this, the company is targeting sales of $740 000, variable cost of $259 000, and fixed cost of $11 700. Based on this information, what is the total revenue at the break-even point?

6. The Scarlet Letter bookstore has $85 000 of sales, variable cost of $36 550, and fixed cost of $27 360. What would its sales have to be to break even?

7. Parma is considering the expansion of her picture-framing business to include the printing of oversize pictures. She would need to lease equipment at a cost of $417 per month. To process the pictures, she estimates that she would have supplies expenses of $3 per picture. If she can sell 60 pictures per month, what price should she charge to break even?
   Reference Example 5.1F

8. Jay and his friends have set up a baseball tournament. He can rent a baseball field for a daily charge of $200 and equipment for $150 per day. If he hires independent umpires, he would need to pay $280 for the day. He would arrange to have caps made for each player at a cost of $4 each. If John can get 90 people to participate, what would he have to charge each of them to recover his costs?

9. John wants to earn money this summer by maintaining gardens and lawns. He would have variable cost for each job of $2 for supplies. To be competitive, he can charge $22 per job, and would be able to maintain at least 80 jobs.
   (a) To break even, what is the most he could pay for equipment?
   (b) If John wanted to make $900, what is the most he could pay to purchase his equipment?
   Reference Example 5.1G

10. Melinda and Morris sell soft drinks at basketball tournaments. They charge $2 per can. The cost to purchase the soft drinks is $0.60 per can. They estimate that they can sell at least 200 cans at each game.
   (a) To break even, what is the most that they can pay in fixed cost?
   (b) If they sell 300 cans during a game, how much can they pay in fixed cost?

11. Woody Woodworks makes and sells cedar planter boxes, charging $35 for each box. Woody purchased tools costing $756 to make the planter boxes. Wood and other supplies cost $8 per box if the boxes are unfinished. An additional amount for supplies would be spent if the boxes were painted.

    (a) To break even, how many unfinished boxes must he sell?
    (b) A special order from the City of Langdale for 100 boxes at $30 per box has been negotiated. The city wants the boxes to be painted. To make a profit of $12 per box, how much can be spent on additional painting supplies?

    Reference Example 5.1H

12. Little Hands Daycare charges $40 per day per child. Fixed expenses include $120 per day for wages and $300 per day for space rental and insurance. The daycare can take in up to 20 children each day and is expected to be full.

    (a) To break even, what is the most that can be spent on supplies per child per day?
    (b) To achieve a profit of $200 per day, what is the amount that can be spent on supplies per child per day?

13. To earn some money, John is thinking of starting up a "Back-Yard BBQ" stand at his university campus this summer. The basic "BBQ" equipment will cost $2690 and the variable cost (VC) for each "BBQ Meal" is estimated to be $6.75. He thinks he will be able to sell each "BBQ Meal" for $10.00.

    (a) What is the break-even quantity of "BBQ Meals" for John's "Back-Yard BBQ" stand?
    (b) If John's goal for profit is $2500 for his fall semester tuition, how many "BBQ Meals" would he need to sell in the summer to reach his goal?

5.2 CONTRIBUTION MARGIN AND CONTRIBUTION RATE
A. Contribution margin

As an alternative to using the break-even relationship TOTAL REVENUE = TOTAL COST, we can use the concepts of contribution margin and contribution rate to determine break-even volume and sales.

For Jason's greenhouse growing project, each additional pepper sold increases the revenue by $1. However, at the same time, costs increase by the variable cost (materials and supplies) of $0.30 per pepper. As a result, the profit increases by the difference, which is $1 - 0.30 = 0.70$. This difference of $0.70, which is the selling price of a unit less the variable cost per unit, is the **contribution margin per unit**.

$$\begin{array}{c} \text{CONTRIBUTION MARGIN} \\ \text{PER UNIT} \end{array} = \begin{array}{c} \text{SELLING PRICE} \\ \text{PER UNIT} \end{array} - \begin{array}{c} \text{VARIABLE COST} \\ \text{PER UNIT} \end{array}$$
$$\text{or,} \quad \text{CM PER UNIT} = \text{SP} - \text{VC}$$

———— Formula 5.2

When the contribution margin per unit is multiplied by the number of units, the result is the **total contribution margin**.

$$\begin{array}{c} \text{TOTAL CONTRIBUTION} \\ \text{MARGIN} \end{array} = \left(\begin{array}{c} \text{SELLING PRICE} \\ \text{PER UNIT} \end{array} - \begin{array}{c} \text{VARIABLE COST} \\ \text{PER UNIT} \end{array} \right) \times \text{VOLUME}$$
$$\text{or, TOTAL CM} = (\text{SP} - \text{VC}) \times X$$

———— Formula 5.3

Using the contribution margin format, Formula 5.1 can be rewritten as

$$(\text{SP} - \text{VC}) \times X - \text{FC} = \text{PFT}$$

———— Formula 5.1B

For Jason's greenhouse growing business, if Jason sells zero units, revenue is $0 and variable cost is $0. Total cost then equals fixed cost, which is $1000. His profit is −$1000 (a loss); that is, his loss equals the fixed cost.

If Jason sells one pepper, revenue increases by $1; total cost increases by $0.30 to $1000.30; profit = $1 - 1000.30 = -\$999.30$ (a loss). The sale of one unit decreases the loss by $0.70; that is, the contribution margin of $0.70 has absorbed $0.70 in fixed cost.

If Jason sells 10 peppers, total revenue = $10(\$1) = \$10$; variable cost = $10(\$0.30)$ = $3 and total cost = $1000 + 3 = \$1003$; the loss = $10 - 1003 = \$993$. The reduction in loss is $7. This reduction in loss represents the contribution margin for 10 units, which has absorbed $7 in fixed cost.

The break-even volume is reached when the accumulated contribution margin of a number of units covers the fixed cost. We use Formula 5.4 to compute the break-even volume in units.

$$\text{BREAK-EVEN VOLUME (in units)} = \frac{\text{FIXED COST}}{\text{UNIT CONTRIBUTION MARGIN}} \quad\text{——— Formula 5.4}$$

In Jason's case, since the fixed cost is $1000 and the contribution margin per unit is $0.70, the break-even volume is 1428.57 units.

$$\text{BREAK-EVEN VOLUME (in units)} = \frac{\$1000}{\$0.70} = 1428.57 \text{ units}$$

To prove that 1428.57 units is the break-even point, multiply the number by the contribution margin, $0.70, to equal the fixed cost, $1000.

EXAMPLE 5.2A

Use contribution margin per unit to determine the break-even volume for Example 5.1B.

SOLUTION

Fixed cost = $8640
Selling price per unit = $50
Variable cost per unit = $30
Contribution margin per unit = $50 − $30 = $20

$$\text{Break-even volume} = \frac{\text{FIXED COST}}{\text{CONTRIBUTION MARGIN}}$$

$$= \frac{\$8640}{\$20} = 432 \quad\text{——————————————— using Formula 5.4}$$

Break-even volume is 432 units.

B. Contribution rate

When total revenue is known but the quantity or volume of units is not known, calculation of the contribution rate is needed. We can then compute the break-even sales in dollars. Remember from Formula 5.1 that the price is assumed to be $1.

The contribution rate approach is attractive to decision makers in business because it considers how much the sale of each additional unit (or how each additional sales dollar) contributes to the absorption of fixed cost and increased profit.

In the case of Jason's greenhouse growing business, the contribution margin of $0.70 can be expressed as a fraction of the unit selling price: as $\frac{0.70}{1} = 0.70 = 70\%$. This is called the **contribution rate**.

$$\text{CONTRIBUTION RATE} = \frac{\text{UNIT CONTRIBUTION MARGIN}}{\text{UNIT SELLING PRICE}}$$ ————— Formula 5.5

The break-even sales (in sales dollars) is computed when the overall contribution rate of a number of units covers the fixed cost. We use Formula 5.6 to compute the break-even sales dollars.

$$\text{BREAK-EVEN SALES (in sales dollars)} = \frac{\text{FIXED COST}}{\text{CONTRIBUTION RATE}}$$ ————— Formula 5.6

EXAMPLE 5.2B

Use contribution margin per unit to determine the contribution rate and the break-even volume for Example 5.1E.

SOLUTION

Fixed cost = $12 600

when sales are given in total dollars, the selling price per unit = $1; contribution margin in total = $40 000 − $16 000 = $24 000 and contribution margin per unit is 24 000/40 000 = $0.60

Contribution rate $= \dfrac{\$0.60}{\$1} = 60\%$ ————— using Formula 5.5

Break-even volume $= \dfrac{\$12\ 600}{0.6} = \$21\ 000.$

Break-even sales are $21 000.

EXERCISE 5.2

MyLab Math

A. For each of the following, perform a break-even analysis showing computation of the
  (a) contribution margin;
  (b) contribution rate;
  (c) break-even point in units;
  (d) break-even point in sales dollars.

 1. Rubber and Steel Company is planning to manufacture a new product. The variable cost will be $61 per unit and the fixed cost is estimated to be $5904. To be competitive, the selling price of the product is to be $150 per unit. Variable selling expense is expected to be $17 per unit. Reference Example 5.2A

2. Rosemary is planning to make fancy multi-tiered wedding cakes for the next wedding season. To make the cakes, she must invest $834 in some special baking pans and tools. To get started, she needs to spend $1800 to advertise in the newspaper. She estimates that supplies and materials for each cake will cost $60. She is planning to set the price for each cake at $499.

3. To pay for his academic fees, Tarek, a college student, is selling used cell phones to other students. His cost to purchase each piece is $53, and he is planning to sell the phones for $99 each. Fixed cost for advertising amounts to $500.

4. Lorne is considering working for Part-Time Painters. He would operate as an independent painter, but the jobs would be given to him by the company. In the company's advertisements, $100 would be charged for each room painted. The painter would then receive 80% of the amount billed. For each job, the painter would supply paint and brushes, at a cost of $38. Each painter must have his or her own ladders, drop cloths, and other tools, at a cost of $720.

B. For each of the following, perform a break-even analysis showing computation of the
  (a) contribution margin;
  (b) contribution rate;
  (c) break-even point in sales dollars.

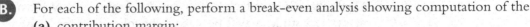 **1.** The following data pertain to the operating budget of Jones Tent Manufacturing.

Sales		$1 020 000
Fixed cost	$160 000	
Total variable cost	581 400	
Total cost		741 400
Net income		$278 600

Reference Example 5.2B

2. Furry Friends Food Manufacturing has compiled the following estimates for operations.

Sales		$765 000
Fixed cost	$152 100	
Total variable cost	497 250	
Total cost		649 350
Net income		$115 650

3. Dave's Lawn Care provides a variety of services for home owners. During the previous month of May, his financial results showed the following:

Sales		$130 000
Fixed cost	$85 000	
Total variable cost	32 500	
Total cost		117 500
Net income		$12 500

For the current year, he is expecting sales to be lower due to the decreased economy.

4. Budget estimates for the parts department of a local car dealership for the month of October showed the following:

Sales		$1 436 000
Fixed cost	$650 000	
Total variable cost	545 680	
Total cost		1 195 680
Net income		$ 240 320

C. **1.** A watchmaker charges $19.99 to replace the battery and clean watches. Variable cost includes a $7 battery and specialized tools that had to be purchased at a cost of $346. How many watches need to be cleaned to break even?   Reference Example 5.2A

2. A vehicle accessory shop is considering buying a new style of wheels for $168 and selling them at $369.60 for each wheel. Fixed cost related to this new style of wheel amounts to $2465. It is estimated that 16 wheels per month could be sold. How much profit will the accessory shop make each month?

3. Slicks Mechanics provides vehicle oil changes for $21.99. For each vehicle, the cost of oil is $6.59 to the shop. Fixed cost for this type of service is $2602.60. How many oil changes need to be completed to break even?

4. Rover's Friends provides dog-washing services. For each dog, supplies cost $3 and wages are $5. To provide this service, a special room and equipment are needed, at a cost of

$300 per month. Rover's Friends maintains an average of 30 dogs washed each month. What must Rover's Friends charge as a price for the dog-washing service to break even?

🌐 5. MacDonald Elementary School needs to raise money for new playground equipment. The students will be selling chocolate bars for $3 each. The chocolate bars will be purchased for $1.25 each. The school budgets $140 for flyers to be distributed to the houses in the school neighbourhood.

(a) How many chocolate bars must the school sell to break even?

(b) How much money will the school make if it achieves its target of selling 1000 chocolate bars?

🌐 6. Tina, an entrepreneurial business student, wants to set up a business completing tax forms for other students. Her price would be $50 for each job. Fixed expenses include $395 for the purchase of tax software, which Tina would need to buy. Tina would hire some accounting students to complete the forms, paying them for two hours at $12 per hour for each job. She would also have paper and supplies costs of $5 per job. How many jobs would she have to generate before she starts to make a profit?

7. The financial statements for the previous year for Empire Inc., a company that sells snowboards online, revealed that sales had been $902 000, total variable cost had been $613 360, and fixed cost amounted to $232 400. Based on the existing cost-volume-profit relationships, what would the sales amount have to be for next year to break even?

🌐 8. The Store on 64, a local convenience store, sells a large variety of snack foods. If the store's budget for the month includes sales of $298 000, total variable cost of $184 760, and fixed cost of $76 660, how much must its sales be to break even?

9. The net income for Abracadabra Magic Store last year was $178 000. If the contribution rate for the store was 27% and the fixed cost was $151 200, what were last years' sales?

10. Fourth Street Lighting shows a net income of $224 000 for the previous year. If the contribution rate for the store was 40.3%, and the fixed cost was $315 000, what were last year's sales?

🌐 11. Henri's business budget included sales of $416 000 and fixed cost of $79 800. If the contribution margin for the business was $145 600, what are the sales needed to break even?

🌐 12. Joy's cupcake business had a budget of $192 000 in sales and $99 840 in total variable cost. What is the most her fixed cost could be for the business to break even?

🌐 13. Peter is thinking of starting up a "Personal Financial Services" consultation in his spare time. The basic office equipment will cost $2285 and the variable cost (VC) for each consultation is estimated to be $14.60. He plans to bill each client $65 per consultation.

(a) What is the break-even quantity of consultations for Peter's "Personal Financial Services" operation?

(b) If Peter's profit goal is $1000, how many consultations would he need to reach his goal?

(c) Briefly explain the concept of a "Contribution Margin" and demonstrate how the Contribution Margin (CM) determined from the information above can be used to determine the same break-even quantity determined in part (a)?

5.3 EFFECTS OF CHANGES TO COST-VOLUME-PROFIT

An understanding of the relationships between cost, volume, and profit makes it possible to determine the effects of changes to any of the variables of the formula. This type of analysis is called "what-if analysis," or sensitivity analysis.

With Jason's greenhouse growing business, he could calculate the effect on profitability if the cost of his supplies changed, if his rent cost changed, if his price changed, if his quantity changed, or if he wished to produce a targeted amount of profit.

EXAMPLE 5.3A

For Jason's greenhouse growing business, recall that the unit price is $1 and the fixed cost is $1000. If variable costs increase to $0.40 for each pepper, what is the new break-even point in units?

SOLUTION

His new variable cost per unit (VC) would be $0.40.

$$TR = TC$$
$$1X = 1000 + 0.40X$$
$$0.60X = 1000$$
$$X = 1666.67$$

Therefore, to break even, he would have to produce 1667 bell peppers.

EXAMPLE 5.3B

For Jason's greenhouse growing business, if the material cost remains at the original $0.30, the rental cost is decreased to $300, and he sold 3000 peppers, what would be the resulting profit?

SOLUTION

Let the profit be PFT and fixed cost FC = 450 + 300 = 750.
Substitute the new values into Formula 5.1.

$$PFT = (1 \times 3000) - 750 - (0.30 \times 3000)$$
$$PFT = 3000 - 750 - 900$$
$$PFT = 1350$$

Therefore, his resulting profit would be $1350.

EXAMPLE 5.3C

Covers Bookstore showed the following operating budget for the next year.

Sales		$1 942 215
Fixed cost	$ 490 000	
Total variable cost	1 210 000	
Total cost		1 700 000
Net income		$ 242 215

Answer each of the following *independent* questions.

(i) How much are the contribution margin and the contribution rate?

(ii) How much does the store need to sell to break even?

(iii) If the store were to spend an additional $20 000 on advertising, how much would the store need to sell to break even?

(iv) If 10% more books were sold, what would be the resulting net income?

SOLUTION

(i) Fixed cost = $490 000
Total revenue (sales) = $1 942 215
Total variable cost = $1 210 000
Contribution margin = $1 942 215 - 1 210 000 = $732 215

$$\text{Contribution rate} = \frac{\$732\ 215}{1\ 942\ 215} = 37.7\%$$

(ii) $$\text{Break-even sales} = \frac{490\ 000}{0.377} = \$1\ 299\ 734.75$$

(iii) Fixed cost = $490 000 + 20 000 = $510 000

$$\text{Break-even sales} = \frac{510\ 000}{0.377} = \$1\ 352\ 785.15$$

(iv) Fixed cost = $490 000
Total revenue (sales) = $1 942 215 × 1.10 = $2 136 436.50
Total variable cost = $1 210 000 × 1.10 = $1 331 000
Contribution margin = $2 136 436.50 − 1 331 000 = $805 436.50
Net income = $805 436.50 − 490 000 = $315 436.50

EXERCISE 5.3　　　　　　　　　　　　　　　　MyLab Math

1. Ingrid is planning to expand her business by taking on a new product. She can purchase the new product at a cost of $8. To market this new product, she would need to spend $984 on advertising each month. The suggested retail price for the product is $14, but she is not sure if she should price her product at this amount. Answer each of the following *independent* questions.

   (a) If she chooses a price of $14, how many units does she need to sell to break even?
   (b) If she chooses a price of $12, how many units does she need to sell to break even?
   (c) If she spends $1500 on advertising, and keeps the price at $14, how many units does she need to sell to break even?
   (d) If she estimates that she can sell 300 units when she spends $1500 for advertising, what is the lowest price she could charge and still break even?

2. Time-For-Us has set up a booth in a shopping mall to sell calendars during the holiday season. The business can purchase the calendars for $2.69 each. It plans to set the unit price at $9.99. During the time it is in business, it must rent equipment for $190 per day, and pay wages of $321 per day. Answer each of the following *independent* questions.

   (a) How many calendars must the business sell each day to break even?
   (b) If it decreases the wages to $240.70 per day, how many must it sell each day to break even?
   (c) If the business puts the calendars "on sale" at 25% off, what would be the profit if it sold 120 units in a day?
   (d) On the last day the business plans to be in the mall, 200 calendars will likely remain on hand. If the wages for the day are $222, what is the lowest price it can charge for each calendar and still break even for that day?

3. Sub Stop, a small sandwich store, is located on a busy corner near many other businesses. The shop's busiest time is during the mid-day period. Rent for the location is $900 per month and wages amount to $2500 per month. Variable cost consists of supplies and sandwich ingredients that cost $2.20 per sub sandwich. The subs are to be sold at a price of $5.69 each. Answer each of the following *independent* questions.

   (a) How many sandwiches must the shop sell to break even?
   (b) If the shop increases variable cost by $0.20 per sandwich, how many sandwiches must it sell to break even?
   (c) If the rent increases by 10%, what would the profit be if the shop sold 1600 units?
   (d) If the sandwich price were reduced by $0.20, how many sandwiches must the shop sell to make $1000 profit?

4. A newsstand sells *Local Business* magazine. The cost to purchase the magazine is the list price of $5 less a discount of 25%. Fixed cost, including rent for the display

space, are $190 per week. The usual price for the magazine is the list price. Answer each of the following *independent* questions.

(a) If the desired profit is $100, how many magazines must the newsstand sell each week?

(b) If the purchase discount is 20% of the list price, how many magazines must the newsstand sell each week to achieve a desired profit of $150?

(c) If the newsstand put the magazine "on sale" at 10% off, how much would the profit be if it sold 300 units in a week?

(d) If the cost to purchase the magazine is 30% off the list price, and 200 magazines are sold, what is the lowest price the newsstand can charge for each magazine and still break even?

5. Projected financial results of a university's cafeteria for meals that will be sold next year are shown below.

Sales		$946 000
Fixed cost	$588 000	
Total variable cost	227 040	
Total cost		815 040
Net income		$130 960

Answer each of the following *independent* questions.

(a) How much are the contribution margin and the contribution rate?

(b) How many meals does the cafeteria need to sell to break even?

(c) If the cafeteria were to spend $23 000 to upgrade its processes, how many meals would the cafeteria need to sell to break even?

(d) If 5% more meals were sold, what would be the resulting net income?

6. Sportsbags Inc. makes and sells backpacks for students. Financial projections for this line of products are revenue of $1 238 000, total variable cost of $841 840, and fixed cost of $218 000.

Answer each of the following *independent* questions.

(a) How much are the contribution margin and the contribution rate?

(b) How much of this product line does the business need to sell to break even?

(c) If the business were to save $56 000 in variable cost by offering fewer colours of backpacks, how much of this product line would the business need to sell to break even?

(d) If a specialized logo were printed on the backpacks, the variable cost would increase by 5%, and the fixed cost would increase by $15 000. If the price of the backpacks were then increased by 10%, what would be the resulting net income?

7. Ace Machinery showed the following operating budget for the next year.

Sales		$2 300 000
Fixed cost	$1 200 000	
Total variable cost	750 000	
Total cost		1 950 000
Net income		$300 000

Answer the following questions:

(a) Calculate the contribution margin and contribution rate.

(b) How much does Ace Machinery need to sell to break even?

(c) If the company has to spend $250 000 on marketing, how much does Ace Machinery need to sell to break even?

(d) If sales increase by 15%, what would the resulting net income be?

BUSINESS MATH **NEWS**   Legalized Marijuana in Canada

After a lengthy process, the legalization of recreational marijuana in Canada came into effect when Bill C-45 was passed by the Senate and received royal assent from the Governor General. Bill C-45, known as the Cannabis Act, became law and came into force on October 17, 2018. With the passage of this law, Canada became the second country in the world that has legalized recreational marijuana. Uruguay was the first country to legalize marijuana in December 2013.

The newness of the cannabis industry in Canada raises a number of concerns in the country. There are concerns from the medical community, law enforcement, and corporate Canada that need to be studied and investigated.

The medical community is concerned about health-related issues that might affect cannabis users. Based on the Cannabis Act, the minimum legal age for the use of marijuana is 19. The medical community is concerned because the brain continues to develop until the age of 25 and cannabis will have adverse effects on brain development if young people use cannabis.

The law-enforcement community believes that it does not have the resources necessary to deal with legalized marijuana. For example, they question the testing equipment and its effectiveness for testing drivers who drive under the influence of marijuana. They also believe that legalization positively affects the tourism industry and people will come to Canada from anywhere in the world searching for legal consumption of marijuana. In addition, they believe that the public is not prepared and lacks training and education that should be provided by the government.

Corporate Canada, on the other hand, is very bullish about the industry and believes that the legalization of cannabis brings huge opportunity to Canada, making it possible for Canada to become a world leader in cannabis production. The players in this industry are concerned that the minimum age requirement will leave a big portion of the market in the hands of the illegal market. According to the Statistics Canada estimates,[1] 4.9 million Canadians older than 15 years consumed cannabis in 2017, and 6 percent of them were 15 to 17 years old.

One of the Canadian players in the cannabis industry is Canopy Growth Corp. "The company, through its subsidiaries, is the licensed producer of medical marijuana in Canada. It grows, produces and sells medical marijuana under various brand names including Tweed, Bedrocan, and Mettrum".[2] In the third quarter of its 2019 fiscal year,[3] the company reported sales revenue of $83.05 million. Total cost of sales for the quarter was $64.8 million. The company's operating expenses for the quarter were $169.7 million, including sales and marketing expenses, general and administrative expenses, and research and development expenses. The company sold 10 102 kilograms and kilogram equivalent of dry cannabis. At the end of the quarter, the company reported a net loss of $75.1 million for the quarter.

QUESTIONS

1. Calculate total contribution margin and contribution rate for the company's third quarter of 2019 operations.

2. Calculate the company's fixed cost.

3. What is the selling price of one gram of cannabis in this operation?

4. How many kilograms and kilogram equivalent of cannabis the company must sell to break even?

[1] Statistics Canada. (2019). Table 36-10-0597-01 Prevalence of cannabis consumption in Canada. Retrieved from https://www150.statcan.gc.ca/t1/tbl1/en/tv.action?pid=3610059701&pickMembers%5B0%5D=2.1&pickMembers%5B1%5D=3.1

[2] TMX Money. (2018). Retrieved from https://web.tmxmoney.com/company.php?qm_symbol=WEED. Accessed on Nov. 6, 2018.

[3] Canopy Growth Corporation. (2018). Canopy Growth Corporation reports first quarter fiscal 2019 financial results. Retrieved from https://www.canopygrowth.com/wp-content/uploads/2018/08/180814-Canopy-Growth-Reports-First-Quarter-Fiscal-Year-2019-Financial-Results_FINAL.pdf.

MyLab Math Visit MyLab Math to practise any of this chapter's exercises marked with a ⊕ as often as you want. The guided solutions help you calculate an answer step by step. You'll find a personalized study plan and additional interactive resources to help you master Business Math!

REVIEW EXERCISE

1. LO①②③ The lighting division of Universal Electric Company plans to introduce a new street light based on the following accounting information:

Fixed cost per period is $3136; variable cost per unit is $157; selling price per unit is $185; and capacity per period is 320 units.

(a) Compute
  (i) the contribution margin;
  (ii) the contribution rate.

(b) Compute the break-even point
  (i) in units;
  (ii) as a percent of capacity;
  (iii) in sales dollars.

(c) Draw a detailed break-even chart.

(d) For each of the following *independent* situations, determine the break-even point as a percent of capacity:
  (i) fixed cost is reduced to $2688;
  (ii) fixed cost increases to $4588 and variable cost is reduced to 80% of the selling price;
  (iii) the selling price is reduced to $171.

2. LO①②③④ The following information is available from the accounting records of Eva Corporation:

Fixed cost per period is $4800. Sales volume for the last period was $19 360, and variable cost was $13 552. Capacity per period is a sales volume of $32 000.

(a) Compute
  (i) the contribution margin;
  (ii) the contribution rate.

(b) Compute the break-even point
  (i) in sales dollars;
  (ii) as a percent of capacity.

(c) Draw a detailed break-even chart.

(d) For each of the following *independent* situations, determine the break-even point:
  (i) fixed cost is decreased by $600;
  (ii) fixed cost is increased to $5670 and variable cost is changed to 55% of sales.

3. LO①②③④ The operating budget of the Bea Company contains the following information:

Sales at 80% of capacity		$400 000
Fixed cost	$105 000	
Variable cost	260 000	
Total cost		365 000
Net income		$35 000

(a) Compute
  (i) the contribution margin;
  (ii) the contribution rate.

(b) Compute the break-even point
  (i) as a percent of capacity;
  (ii) in sales dollars.

(c) Draw a detailed break-even chart.

(d) Determine the break-even point in sales dollars if fixed cost is reduced by $11 200, while variable cost is changed to 72% of sales.

4. LO②③④ A manufacturer of major appliances provides the following information about the operations of the refrigeration division:

Fixed cost per period is $26 880; variable cost per unit is $360; selling price per unit is $640; and capacity is 150 units.

(a) Compute
  (i) the contribution margin;
  (ii) the contribution rate.

(b) Compute the break-even point
  (i) in units;
  (ii) as a percent of capacity;
  (iii) in sales dollars.

(c) Determine the break-even point in sales dollars if fixed cost is increased to $32 200.

(d) Determine the break-even point as a percent of capacity if fixed cost is reduced to $23 808, while variable cost is increased to 60% of sales.

5. LO② Alicia works in a restaurant that has monthly costs of $1500 for rent, $2000 for salaries, and $1700 for other expenses.

On the menu, the restaurant has entrees that sell for $9.99 each. On average, it costs $3.50 in food and materials to serve each of these entrees. How many entrees does the restaurant need to sell to break even?

🌐 **6. LO❷** Quickprint Services operates several franchise where it prints brochures, business cards, and stationery. It plans to sell 80 jobs next week, at an average cost of $52 each. Its weekly expenses are $1840.

(a) How much must Quickprint charge for each job to break even?

(b) If it wishes to make a profit of $1200, what price does it have to charge?

(c) If it sells 90 jobs at the price determined in part (b), how much profit will be realized?

(d) If Quickprint sells 100 jobs through a special promotion, what is the minimum price it could charge to break even?

7. LO❷❸❹ Maritime Insurance projected revenue of $2 995 200, total variable cost of $778 752, and fixed cost of $1 962 000 for the next year.

Answer each of the following *independent* questions, rounding all dollar amounts to the nearest dollar.

(a) How much are the contribution margin and the contribution rate?

(b) How much of this product line does the business need to sell to break even?

(c) As a result of global losses due to hurricanes, the insurance rates have increased. If the business experienced an increase in total variable cost of 45%, and as a result increased its prices by 20% but maintained the same number of insurance contracts, how much of this product line does the business need to sell to break even?

(d) If a new insurance carrier were available and the same number of insurance contracts were projected, variable cost of 7% could be saved, but the fixed cost would increase by $9000. If the price of the insurance contracts stayed the same, what would be the resulting net income?

SELF-TEST

1. The Superior Jumpdrive Company sells jump drives for $10 each. Manufacturing cost is $2.60 per jump drive; marketing costs are $2.40 per jump drive; and royalty payments are 20% of the selling price. The fixed cost of preparing the jump drive is $18 000. Capacity is 15 000 jump drives.

(a) Compute
    (i) the contribution margin;
    (ii) the contribution rate.

(b) Compute the break-even point
    (i) in units;
    (ii) in dollars;
    (iii) as a percent of capacity.

(c) Draw a detailed break-even chart.

(d) Determine the break-even point in units if fixed cost is increased by $1600, while manufacturing cost is reduced by $0.50 per jump drive.

(e) Determine the break-even point in units if the selling price is increased by 10%, while fixed cost is increased by $2900.

2. The management of Lambda Corporation has received the following forecast for the next year.

Sales revenue		$600 000
Fixed cost	$275 000	
Variable cost	270 000	
Total cost		545 000
Net income		$ 55 000

Capacity is a sales volume of $800 000.

(a) Compute
   (i) the contribution margin;
   (ii) the contribution rate.

(b) Compute the break-even point
   (i) in dollars;
   (ii) as a percent of capacity.

(c) Determine the break-even volume in dollars if fixed cost is increased by $40 000, while variable cost is held to 40% of sales.

CHALLENGE PROBLEMS

1. An aluminum company uses a highly mechanized production process to manufacture brackets for the automotive industry. The company's profit function in millions of dollars for x million brackets is $P = 0.7x - 24.5$. The cost function is $C = 0.9x + 24.5$. Calculate the break-even point in millions of units.

2. The Clapton Guitar Company has set a target to sell 1500 units from its new guitar line this year for a suggested retail price of $479 per unit. The company has estimated that its fixed cost that can be attributed to this new line is $3000 per month. The manager also estimates that the variable cost per unit is $190.

   (a) Calculate the break-even volume for the year.

   (b) If the company can produce up to 2000 units per year, compute the break-even point as a percent of capacity.

   (c) How much profit will Clapton Guitar Company earn if it achieves its target sales?

   (d) If an average of only 100 units are sold each month, how much profit will the company realize during the year?

   (e) Describe the impact on expected profit if only 100 units are sold each month.

3. A manufacturer is considering installing new equipment to replace its old hole-punching machine. The equipment will be used for the next 10 years. Two options are being considered. The first piece of equipment uses the latest computer-aided design process. The engineer estimates that the fixed cost for installing this equipment is $125 000 and the variable cost would be $0.15 per unit produced. The second, less-advanced piece of equipment would cost only $75 000 and $0.25 per unit produced. What is the break-even quantity? Which option should the company choose?

CASE STUDY   Segway Tours

▶ Milo is planning to rent out Segway Personal Transporters near a popular park in Vancouver for 90 days this summer. He purchased three Segways for $6500 each. The Segways are battery-powered electric vehicles that will be driven an average of 60 kilometres in a day. By purchasing two additional batteries for $995 each, Milo expects that he'll be able to keep his Segways adequately charged to meet his daily demand. Milo's other expenses will include space rental and utilities for a total of $100 per day, as well as insurance of $15 per Segway per day.

QUESTIONS

1. If Milo charges $35 per half-hour tour (approximately 10 kilometres), how much profit does he expect to make this summer?

2. What is the lowest price he could charge per half-hour tour and still break even?

3. If he wants to realize a profit of $300 per day, how much more should he charge per half-hour tour?

SUMMARY OF FORMULAS

Formula 5.1

PROFIT = (SELLING PRICE × VOLUME) − FIXED COST − (VARIABLE COST PER UNIT × VOLUME)

or, PFT = (SP × X) − FC − (VC × X)   **Formula for calculating profit when separating fixed and variable costs**

or, PFT = (SP − VC) × X − FC

Formula 5.2

CONTRIBUTION MARGIN PER UNIT = SELLING PRICE PER UNIT − VARIABLE COST PER UNIT

or, CM per unit = SP − VC   **Formula for calculating contribution margin per unit**

Formula 5.3

TOTAL CONTRIBUTION MARGIN = (SELLING PRICE PER UNIT − VARIABLE COST PER UNIT) × VOLUME

or, TOTAL CM = (SP − VC) × X **Formula for calculating total contribution margin**

Formula 5.4

$$\text{BREAK-EVEN VOLUME (in units)} = \frac{\text{FIXED COST}}{\text{UNIT CONTRIBUTION MARGIN}}$$

or, $X = \dfrac{\text{FC}}{\text{CM per unit}}$ **Formula for calculating break-even volume in units based on the unit contribution margin**

Formula 5.5

$$\text{CONTRIBUTION RATE} = \frac{\text{UNIT CONTRIBUTION MARGIN}}{\text{UNIT SELLING PRICE}}$$

Formula for calculating contribution rate

Formula 5.6

$$\text{BREAK-EVEN SALES (in sales dollars)} = \frac{\text{FIXED COST}}{\text{CONTRIBUTION RATE}}$$

Formula for calculating break-even sales based on contribution rate

GLOSSARY

Break-even analysis a method of determining the level of output at which a business neither makes a profit nor sustains a loss *(p. 191)*

Break-even chart a graphical representation of cost-volume-profit relationships used to identify the break-even point *(p. 194)*

Break-even point the level of output at which profit is zero *(p. 193)*

Capacity the number of units a facility can hold, receive, store, or produce in a given time *(p. 194)*

Contribution margin per unit the difference between unit selling price and unit variable cost *(p. 206)*

Contribution rate the contribution margin per unit expressed as a fraction of the unit selling price *(p. 207)*

Cost function an algebraic expression stating the relationship between cost and volume *(p. 194)*

Cost-volume-profit analysis a tool used to evaluate the potential effect of decisions on profitability *(p. 191)*

Fixed cost cost that remains constant for the time period for all levels of output considered *(p. 192)*

Net income the amount remaining after total cost and expenses are subtracted from total revenue *(p. 192)*

Revenue function an algebraic expression representing the behaviour of revenue *(p. 194)*

Sensitivity analysis calculations performed to determine the effect of changes in one or more components of analysis *(p. 191)*

Total contribution margin the contribution margin for all units at a given level of output *(p. 206)*

Variable cost cost that is constant per unit of output regardless of volume; it fluctuates in total amount as volume fluctuates *(p. 192)*

Trade Discounts, Cash Discounts, Markup, and Markdown

Steve Estvanik/Fotolia

LEARNING OBJECTIVES

Upon completing this chapter, you will be able to do the following:

1 Solve problems involving trade discounts.

2 Calculate single rates of discount for a discount series.

3 Apply methods of cash discount.

4 Solve problems involving markup based on either cost or selling price.

5 Solve problems involving markdown.

6 Solve integrated problems involving discounts, markup, and markdown.

In a business, traditional accounting profit is calculated by subtracting costs and expenses from sales revenue for a specified period. Determining a suitable selling price for each product or service is crucial for long-term sustainability. Some firms use a *cost-plus* methodology, marking up the cost of each product or service by a certain percentage that is large enough to cover expenses and still leave a respectable profit. Other organizations select their desired profit percentages first, and then work backwards to set their prices.

Suppose you were operating a bicycle shop and selling adult mountain bikes that cost you $200 each from your supplier. Using a cost-plus approach you might add a 20% markup to the cost of bikes sold in the shop in order to cover your additional expenses and make a profit. In this case, you would charge your customers $240 for the bikes, and your resulting profit percentage would be $40 \div \$240 = 16^2/_3\%$. If, however, you wanted to price the bikes in order to earn 20% profit, you would need to charge your customers $250 for the same bicycles ($50 \div \$250 = 20\%$).

INTRODUCTION

The **supply chain** defines the channels or stages that a product passes through as it is converted from a raw material to a finished product purchased by the consumer.

A Supply Chain

Manufacturer → Distributor → Wholesaler → Retailer → Consumer

By the time the product is purchased by the consumer, the raw materials have been converted by the manufacturer, distributed through the wholesaler, and offered for sale by the retailer. In some supply chains, the distributor and wholesaler are separated. In other supply chains, the manufacturer also serves as the wholesaler. Within the supply chain, all of the channels must make a profit on the product to remain in business. Figure 6.1 outlines some of the terminology used in the supply chain.

In order to earn profit, each channel applies a *markup* above its cost to buy the merchandise, which increases the price of the product. Sometimes a manufacturer or supplier sets a *list price* and then offers a *trade discount* or a *series of trade discounts* from that price to sell more product or to promote the product within the supply chain. Also, any of the channels within the supply chain may offer a *cash discount* to encourage prompt payment for the product. When the product is sold to the consumer, the regular selling price may be *marked down* or *discounted* to a sale price in response to competitors' prices or other economic conditions.

Figure 6.1 Terminology Used in the Supply Chain (© S. A. Hummelbrunner)

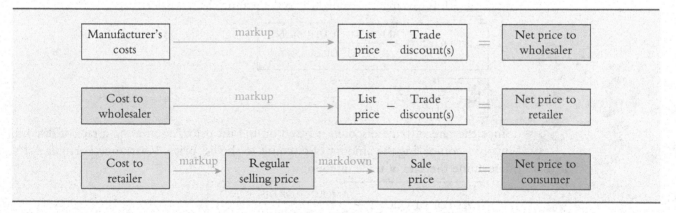

Selling price, cost, and expenses of a product determine the profit for that product. Understanding the relationships between these variables is crucial in maintaining a successful business. In this chapter, we will learn how to calculate the cost of products if trade discounts are offered within the supply chain, as well as how to calculate the amount of cash to be paid when cash discounts are offered for early payment. We will learn how to calculate price and profit when the cost is marked up, and the discounted price and resulting profit or loss when a product is offered "on sale."

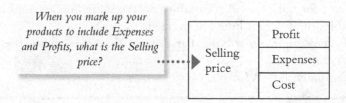

When you mark up your products to include Expenses and Profits, what is the Selling price?

6.1 DETERMINING COST WITH TRADE DISCOUNTS
A. Computing discount amounts, discount rate, net price, and list price

The supply chain is made up of manufacturers, distributors, wholesalers, retailers, and consumers. Merchandise is usually bought and sold among the members of the chain on credit terms. The prices quoted to other members often involve trade discounts. A **trade discount** is a reduction of a **list price** or **manufacturer's suggested retail price (MSRP)** and is usually stated as a percent of the list price or MSRP.

Trade discounts are used by manufacturers, distributors, and wholesalers as pricing tools for several reasons, such as to

(a) determine different prices for different levels of the supply chain;
(b) communicate changes in prices;
(c) enable changes in prices.

When computing a trade discount, keep in mind that the **rate of discount** is based on the list price.

$$\frac{\text{AMOUNT}}{\text{OF DISCOUNT}} = \frac{\text{RATE OF}}{\text{DISCOUNT}} \times \frac{\text{LIST}}{\text{PRICE}}$$

$$A = d \times L \text{ or } A = dL \qquad\text{——————————— Formula 6.1}$$

When the amount of the discount and the discount rate are known, the list price can be determined. Rearrange Formula 6.1 to determine the list price.

$$\text{LIST PRICE} = \frac{\text{AMOUNT OF DISCOUNT}}{\text{RATE OF DISCOUNT}}$$

$$L = \frac{A}{d}$$

Since the rate of trade discount is based on the list price, computing a rate of discount involves comparing the amount of discount to the list price. Rearrange Formula 6.1 to determine the rate of trade discount.

$$\text{RATE OF DISCOUNT} = \frac{\text{AMOUNT OF DISCOUNT}}{\text{LIST PRICE}}$$

$$d = \frac{A}{L}$$

POINTERS & PITFALLS

This diagram is a useful aid in remembering the various forms of the amount of discount formula $A = dL$. Variables on the same line are multiplied together. Variables on different lines are divided.

For example, in solving for d, note that A is above the L. Therefore, $d = A/L$.

Similarly, $L = A/d$.

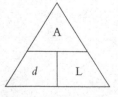

The **net price** is the remainder when the amount of discount is subtracted from the list price. The net price is the price to the supplier, and becomes the cost to the purchaser.

$$\text{NET PRICE} = \text{LIST PRICE} - \text{AMOUNT OF DISCOUNT}$$

$$N = L - A \text{ ————————— Formula 6.2}$$

To compute the amount of the discount and the net price when the list price and discount rate are known, first apply Formula 6.1 to determine the amount of the trade discount, and then apply Formula 6.2 to calculate the net price.

EXAMPLE 6.1A

An item listed at $80.00 is subject to a trade discount of 25%.
Compute

  (i) the amount of discount;

 (ii) the net price.

SOLUTION

  (i) Amount of trade discount = Rate of discount × List price
$$= (0.25)(80.00) = \$20.00$$

 (ii) Net price = List price − Trade discount
$$= 80.00 - 20.00 = \$60.00$$

EXAMPLE 6.1B

A 30% discount on a tennis racket amounts to $89.70.
Compute

  (i) the list price;

 (ii) the net price.

SOLUTION

  (i) List price $= \dfrac{\text{Amount of discount}}{\text{Rate of discount}} = \dfrac{89.70}{0.3} = \$299.00$

 (ii) Net price = List price − Amount of discount
$$= 299.00 - 89.70 = \$209.30$$

EXAMPLE 6.1C

Calculate the rate of discount on

  (i) snowboards listed at $280.00 less a discount of $67.20;

 (ii) snow-sport helmets listed at $129.99 whose net price is $84.49;

(iii) goalie pads whose net price is $368.99 after a discount of $81.00.

SOLUTION

  (i) Rate of discount $= \dfrac{\text{Amount of discount}}{\text{List price}} = \dfrac{67.20}{280.00} = 0.24 = 24\%$

 (ii) Since Net price = List price − Amount of discount (Formula 6.2),

      Amount of discount = List price − Net price = 129.99 − 84.49 = $45.50

      Rate of discount $= \dfrac{\text{Amount of discount}}{\text{List price}} = \dfrac{45.50}{129.99} = 0.350027 = 35\%$

(iii) Since Net price = List price − Amount of discount (Formula 6.2),

      List price = Net price + Amount of discount = 368.99 + 81.00 = $449.99

      Rate of discount $= \dfrac{\text{Amount of discount}}{\text{List price}} = \dfrac{81.00}{449.99} = 0.180004 = 18\%$

B. The net price factor approach

Instead of computing the amount of discount and then deducting this amount from the list price, the net price can be found by using a more efficient net factor approach developed in the following illustration.

Referring back to Example 6.1A, the solution can be restated as follows:

List price	$80.00
Less trade discount 25% of 80.00	20.00
Net price	$60.00

Since the discount is given as a percent of the list price, the three dollar values may be stated as percents of list price:

List price	$80.00 ⟶	100% of list price
Less trade discount	20.00 ⟶	25% of list price
Net price	$60.00 ⟶	75% of list price

Note: The resulting "75%" is called the **net price factor** or **net factor** (in abbreviated form **NPF**) and is obtained by deducting the 25% discount from 100%.

The resulting relationship between net price and list price may be stated generally.

> NET PRICE = LIST PRICE × NET PRICE FACTOR (NPF)

These relationships can be restated in algebraic terms:

Convert the % discount into its decimal equivalent represented by d, and express 100% by its decimal equivalent, 1.

> NET PRICE FACTOR $= 1 - d$

Let the list price be represented by L, and let the net price be represented by N.

$$N = L(1 - d)$$ ——————————————— **Formula 6.3**

Another way to derive the net price formula is to substitute Formula 6.1 into Formula 6.2 and then collect the similar terms. If we substitute amount of discount, $A = dL$, into $N = L - A$, we obtain $N = L - dL$. Since L is a common factor, we can rewrite the formula as $N = L(1 - d)$.

EXAMPLE 6.1D

Calculate the net price for
  (i) list price $36.00 less 15%;
  (ii) list price $86.85 less $33\frac{1}{3}$%.

SOLUTION

(i) Net price = List price × Net price factor ——————— **using Formula 6.3**
        $= (36.00)(1 - 0.15)$
        $= (36.00)(0.85)$
        $= 30.60

(ii) Net price $= (86.85)(1 - 0.\dot{3})$
        $= (86.85)(0.\dot{6})$
        $= $57.90\star$ rounded

EXAMPLE 6.1E

A manufacturer can cover its cost and make a reasonable profit if it sells an article for $63.70. At what price should the article be listed so that a discount of 30% can be allowed?

SOLUTION

Let the list price be represented by $L.
Net price = List price × Net price factor

$$63.70 = L\,(0.7)$$

$$L = \frac{63.70}{0.7} = \$91.00$$

The article should be listed at $91.

C. Discount series

A manufacturer may offer two or more **discounts** to different members of the supply chain. If a list price is subject to two or more discounts, these discounts are called a **discount series**. If the manufacturer wants to encourage large-volume orders or early orders of seasonal items, it may offer additional discounts. For example, a manufacturer might offer a retailer a 5% discount on orders over 1000 items and an additional discount of 6% for ordering Christmas items in April. It may also offer additional discounts to compensate for advertising, promotion, and service costs handled by supply chain members.

When computing the net price, the discounts making up the discount series are applied to the list price successively. The net price resulting from the first discount becomes the list price for the second discount; the net price resulting from the second discount becomes the list price for the third discount; and so on. In fact, determining the net price when a list price is subject to a discount series consists of solving as many discount problems as there are discounts in the discount series.

EXAMPLE 6.1F

An item listed at $150.00 is subject to the discount series 20%, 10%, and 5%. Determine the net price.

SOLUTION

List price	$150.00	⎱ Problem 1
Less first discount 20% of 150.00	30.00	⎰
Net price after first discount	$120.00	⎱ Problem 2
Less second discount 10% of 120.00	12.00	⎰
Net price after second discount	$108.00	⎱ Problem 3
Less third discount 5% of 108.00	5.40	⎰
Net price	$102.60	

Because the solution to Example 6.1F consists of three problems involving a simple discount, the net price factor approach can be used to solve it or any problem involving a series of discounts.

Figure 6. 2 Graphical Representation of Example 6.1F (© S. A. Hummelbrunner)

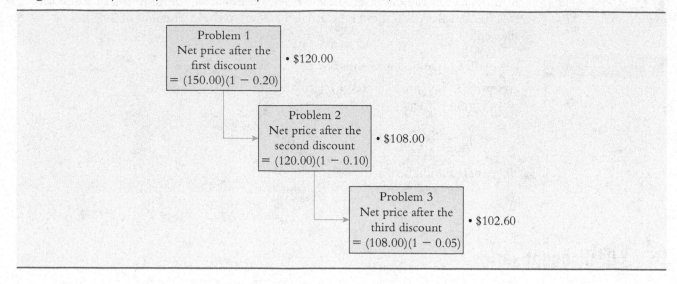

The final net price of $102.60 is obtained from
$$= L (1 - 0.20)(1 - 0.10)(1 - 0.05)$$
$$= 150 (0.80)(0.90)(0.95)$$
$$= \text{Original list price} \times \text{NPF for 20\%} \times \text{NPF for 10\%} \times \text{NPF for 5\%}$$

These relationships can be restated in algebraic terms:

Let the net price be represented by N,
the original list price by L,
the first rate of discount by d_1,
the second rate of discount by d_2,
the third rate of discount by d_3, and
the last rate of discount by d_n.

Then Formula 6.4 can be shown as

$$\text{NET PRICE} = L(1 - d_1)(1 - d_2)(1 - d_3) \ldots (1 - d_n)$$ ———————— **Formula 6.4**

D. Single equivalent rates of discount

For every discount series, a **single equivalent rate of discount** exists.

$$\text{SINGLE EQUIVALENT RATE OF DISCOUNT FOR A DISCOUNT SERIES}$$
$$= 1 - \text{NPF FOR THE DISCOUNT SERIES}$$
$$= 1 - [(1 - d_1)(1 - d_2)(1 - d_3) \ldots (1 - d_n)]$$ ———————— **Formula 6.5**

EXAMPLE 6.1G A manufacturer sells kayaks to dealers at a list price of $2100.00 less 40%, 10%, and 5%. Determine the

(i) net price;

(ii) amount of discount;

(iii) single equivalent rate of discount.

SOLUTION

(i) Net price = List price × NPF
$$= (2100)(1 - 0.40)(1 - 0.10)(1 - 0.05)$$
$$= (2100)(0.60)(0.90)(0.95)$$
$$= \$1077.30 \text{ ——————— using Formula 6.4}$$

(ii) Amount of discount = List price − Net price
$$= 2100.00 - 1077.30$$
$$= \$1022.70$$

(iii) Single equivalent rate of discount $= 1 - \big[(1 - 0.40)(1 - 0.10)(1 - 0.05)\big]$
$$= 1 - \big[(0.60)(0.90)(0.95)\big]$$
$$= 1 - 0.513$$
$$= 0.487$$
$$= 48.7\% \text{ ——————— using Formula 6.5}$$

Note: Taking off a single discount of 48.7% has the *same* effect as using the discount series 40%, 10%, and 5%. That is, the single discount of 48.7% is equivalent to the discount series 40%, 10%, and 5%.
Caution: The sum of the discounts in the series, 40% + 10% + 5% or 55%, is not equivalent to the single discount.

POINTERS
& PITFALLS

The single equivalent rate of discount is not simply the sum of the individual discounts. Proper application of Formula 6.5 will always result in a single equivalent discount rate that is less than the sum of the individual discounts. You can use this fact to check whether the single equivalent discount rate you calculate is reasonable.

An alternative way to calculate the single equivalent rate of discount is by choosing a suitable list price, such as $100, and computing first the amount of discount and then the rate of discount. Remember to carry the decimals until the end.

EXAMPLE 6.1H

Determine the amount of discount for a $100.00 list price subject to the discount series 40%, 12.5%, $8\frac{1}{3}$%, and 2%.

SOLUTION

Net price = List price × NPF
$$= 100\big[(1 - 0.40)(1 - 0.125)(1 - 0.08\dot{3})(1 - 0.02)\big]$$
$$= 100\big[(0.60)(0.875)(0.91\dot{6})(0.98)\big]$$
$$= 47.1625 \text{ ——————— carry the decimals}$$

Amount of discount = List price − Net price
$$= 100 - 47.1625$$
$$= 52.8375 \text{ ——————— carry the decimals}$$

Rate of discount = Amount of discount/List price
$$= 52.8375/100$$
$$= 0.528375$$

The single equivalent rate of discount is 52.84%.

Check

Single equivalent rate of discount $= 1 - \big[(1 - 0.40)(1 - 0.125)(1 - 0.08\dot{3})(1 - 0.02)\big]$
$$= 1 - \big[(0.60)(0.875)(0.91\dot{6})(0.98)\big]$$
$$= 1 - 0.471625$$
$$= 0.528375$$

EXAMPLE 6.1I

A retail kiosk has listed a pair of sunglasses for $136 less 30%. A department store in the shopping mall lists the same model for $126 less 20%, less an additional 15%. What additional rate of discount must the kiosk give to meet the department store price?

SOLUTION

Kiosk net price = 136.00(0.7)	$95.20
Department store price = 126.00(0.8)(0.85)	85.68
Additional discount needed	$ 9.52

Additional rate of discount needed $= \dfrac{9.52}{95.20} = 0.1 = 10\%$

EXAMPLE 6.1J

Redden Distributors bought a shipment of laptops at a net price of $477.36 each, after discounts of 15%, 10%, and 4%. What is the list price?

SOLUTION

Let the list price be $L.
The net price is $477.36. ———————— using Formula 6.4
$N = L(1 - 0.15)(1 - 0.10)(1 - 0.04)$
$477.36 = L(0.85)(0.9)(0.96)$

$$L = \frac{477.36}{(0.85)(0.9)(0.96)} = \$650.00$$

The laptops are listed at $650.00.

Check
$N = \$650.00(0.85)(0.9)(0.96)$
$N = \$477.36$

EXERCISE 6.1

MyLab Math

1. An item with a list price of $125.64 is offered at a discount of 37.5%. What is the net price?
   Reference Example 6.1A

2. An item with a list price of $49.98 is offered at a discount of $16\frac{2}{3}\%$. What is the net price?

3. A 17.5% discount on a flat-screen TV amounts to $560. What is the list price?
   Reference Example 6.1B

4. Golf World sells a set of golf clubs for $762.50 below the suggested retail price. Golf World claims that this represents a 62.5% discount. What is the suggested retail price (or list price)?

5. A $16\frac{2}{3}\%$ discount allowed on a flash drive amounts to $14.82. What was the net price?

6. A store advertises a discount of $44.75 on a pair of running shoes. If the discount represents 25% of the list price, what was the net price (sale price) for the running shoes?

7. The net price of a pair of hockey skates after a discount of $16\frac{2}{3}\%$ is $355. What is the list price?

8. The net price of an article is $63.31. What is the suggested retail price (the list price) if a discount of 35% was allowed?

9. A mountain bike listed at $975 is sold for $820. What rate of discount was allowed?
   Reference Example 6.1C

10. A home theatre system listed at $1136 has a net price of $760. What is the rate of discount?

11. An infrared barbecue grill was originally listed at $769.99. The price was first discounted to $550.54, and then it was discounted to a final price of $449.79. What was the single equivalent rate of discount at the final price?

12. In the original online advertisement, a speciality coffeemaker was listed at a price of $399.99. To promote business to retailers, the appliance was offered at "$120 off" if five or more items were purchased at the same time. If a buyer purchased within three days, a further $42 discount off the price was allowed. Compute the net price and the single equivalent rate of discount if a buyer took advantage of both offers.

13. Compute the single rate of discount for each of the following discount series.

   (a) 30%, 12.5%
   (b) $33\frac{1}{3}$%, 20%, and 3%

14. Determine the single rate of discount for each of the following series of discounts.

   (a) $16\frac{2}{3}$%, 7.5%
   (b) 25%, $8\frac{1}{3}$%, and 2%

15. A camera is listed for $599 less 30%, 20%, and 5%.

   (a) What is the net price?
   (b) What is the total amount of discount allowed?
   (c) What is the exact single rate of discount that was allowed?   Reference Example 6.1G

16. A mobile phone is listed for $174 less $16\frac{2}{3}$%, 10%, and 8%.

   (a) What is the net price?
   (b) What is the total amount of discount allowed?
   (c) What is the exact single rate of discount that was allowed?

17. A home gym is listed for $786.20 less 36%, 10%, and 2%.

   (a) What is the net price?
   (b) What is the total amount of discount allowed?
   (c) What is the exact single rate of discount that was allowed?

18. A racing bike is listed for $1293.44 less $18\frac{1}{3}$%, $9\frac{1}{9}$%, and 3%.

   (a) What is the net price?
   (b) What is the total amount of discount allowed?
   (c) What is the exact single rate of discount that was allowed?

19. An item listed by a wholesaler for $750 less 20%, 5%, and 2% is reduced at a clearance sale to $474.81. What additional rate of discount was offered?   Reference Example 6.1I

20. An office desk listed at $440 less 25% and 15% is offered at a further reduced price of $274.89. What additional rate of discount was offered?

21. An electronic game listed at $180 less 30%, 12.5%, and 5% is offered at a further reduced price of $99.50. What additional rate of discount was offered?

22. A computer listed at $1260 less $33\frac{1}{3}$% and $16\frac{2}{3}$% is offered at a clearance price of $682.50. What additional rate of discount was offered?

23. Arrow Manufacturing offers discounts of 25%, 12.5%, and 4% on a line of products. How much should an item be listed for if it is to be sold for $113.40?

24. What is the list price of an article that is subject to discounts of $33\frac{1}{3}$%, 10%, and 2% if the net price is $564.48?

25. A distributor lists an item for $85 less 20%. To improve lagging sales, the net price of the item is reduced to $57.80. What additional rate of discount does the distributor offer?

26. A hat is listed for $66 less 40%. The net price of the hat is further reduced to $35.64. What additional rate of discount is offered?

🌐 **27.** Galaxy Jewellers sells diamond necklaces for $299 less 25%. Brilliants Jewellers offers the same necklace for $350 less 35% and 10%. What additional rate of discount must Galaxy offer to meet the competitor's price?

28. Polar Bay Wines advertises California Juice listed at $125 per bucket for a discount of 24%. A nearby competitor offers the same type of juice for $87.40 per bucket. What additional rate of discount must Polar Bay Wines give to meet the competitor's price?

6.2 PAYMENT TERMS AND CASH DISCOUNTS
A. Basic concepts

Among each other, manufacturers, distributors, wholesalers, and retailers usually sell goods on credit rather than for cash. An invoice for the goods is sent, and the seller specifies **payment terms** on the invoice. These payment terms indicate when the invoice amount is due for payment and how much is to be paid. The business selling the goods can offer a **cash discount** to encourage prompt payment. This discount reduces the amount to be paid, and is based on the original amount of the invoice, the discount rate, and the timing of the payment or payments.

All payment terms have three things in common:

1. The **rate of discount** is stated as a percent of the net amount of the invoice. The net amount of the invoice is the amount remaining after trade discounts are deducted.

2. The **discount period** is stated, indicating the time period when the cash discount can be applied.

3. The **credit period** is stated, indicating the time period when the invoice must be paid.

The invoice sample in Figure 6.3 is set up for a business in Ontario, where the HST rate is 13%. The payment terms indicate that the invoice amount is due within 30 days. If the invoice is paid in full by May 12, 2022, an additional 3% cash discount will apply.

If payment is not made during the stated discount period, the net amount of the invoice is to be paid by the end of the credit period. The end of the credit period is called the **due date**, and is either stipulated by the payment terms or implied by the prevailing business practice. If payment is not made by the due date, the account is considered overdue and may be subject to a late payment fee or interest charges.

Cash discounts are offered in a variety of ways:

(a) The most commonly used method is **ordinary dating**, where payment terms are based on the invoice date.

(b) Occasionally, **end-of-month dating**, or E.O.M. dating, is used. End-of-month payment terms shift the invoice date to the last day of the month, so that a discount period or credit period starts after the end of the current month.

(c) When the abbreviation R.O.G. (receipt of goods) appears in the terms of payment, the discount and credit periods start the day after the merchandise has been received. **Receipt-of-goods dating** is used when the transportation of the goods takes a long time, possibly due to the distance the goods are being shipped.

Regardless of when the discount and credit periods begin, the mathematics of working with cash discounts is similar to that used in working with trade discounts.

Figure 6.3 A Sample Sales Invoice (© S. A. Hummelbrunner)

Bicycle Locks Supply Inc.
132 Dundas Street
Cambridge, Ontario N1R 5X1

Invoice #: 2274

Sold to:
Spokes and Wheels
1550 Avenue Road
Toronto, Ontario M5M 3Z8

Date: May 2, 2022
Terms: 2/10, n/30

Product Description	Product Number	Quantity	List Price	Discount	Net amount
Evolution Series 4U Lock	ES-4	25	$34.99	25%	$656.06
H-Bar Mount for Series 4U	ES-4H	20	$14.99	20%, 5%	$227.85

Invoice Total: $883.91
Shipping and Handling: $35.00
13%HST: $119.46
Total Amount Due: $1038.37

Overdue accounts subject to 3% interest per month

POINTERS
& PITFALLS

To count the number of days in the discount period, the invoice date is considered "Day 0." For example, if an invoice is dated July 5th with credit terms 2/10, n/30, then July 6th is counted as "Day 1," July 7th as "Day 2," and so on. Payments received up to, and including, July 15th ("Day 10") are entitled to a 2% discount. The balance of the invoice is due on August 4th ("Day 30").

B. Ordinary dating

The most frequently used method of offering a cash discount is ordinary dating, and the most commonly used payment terms are *2/10, n/30* (read "two ten, net thirty").

This payment term means that if payment is made *within* 10 days of the date of the invoice, a discount of 2% may be deducted from the net amount of the invoice. Otherwise, payment of the net amount of the invoice is due within 30 days. (See Figure 6.4.)

Figure 6.4 Interpretation of Payment Terms (© S. A. Hummelbrunner)

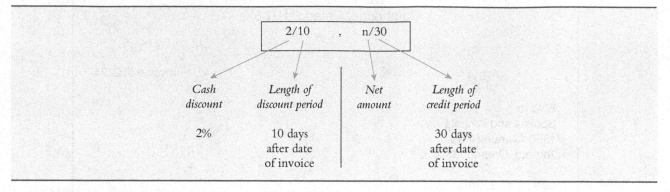

Cash discount	*Length of discount period*	*Net amount*	*Length of credit period*
2%	10 days after date of invoice		30 days after date of invoice

---

EXAMPLE 6.2A   Determine the payment needed to settle an invoice with a net amount of $950, dated September 22, terms 2/10, n/30, if the invoice is paid

(i) on October 10;

(ii) on October 1.

Figure 6.5 Discount and Credit Periods—Example 6.2A, Ordinary Dating (© S. A. Hummelbrunner)

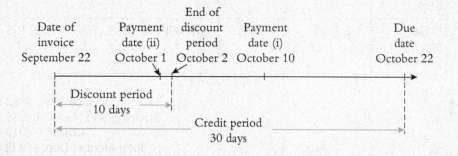

SOLUTION   The terms of the invoice indicate a credit period of 30 days and state that a 2% discount may be deducted from the invoice net amount of $950 if the invoice is paid within 10 days of the invoice date of September 22. The applicable time periods and dates are shown in Figure 6.5.

Ten days after September 22 is October 2. The discount period ends October 2.

(i) Payment on October 10 is beyond the last day for taking the discount. The discount cannot be taken. The full amount of the invoice of $950 must be paid.

(ii) October 1 is within the discount period; the 2% discount can be taken.
Amount paid = Net amount − 2% of the net amount
$$= 950.00 − 0.02(950.00)$$
$$= 950.00 − 19.00$$
$$= \$931.00$$

Alternatively: Using the net price factor approach (Formula 6.3),
Amount paid = Net amount × NPF for a 2% discount
$$= (950.00)(1 − 0.02)$$
$$= (950.00)(0.98)$$
$$= \$931.00$$

EXAMPLE 6.2B

An invoice for $752.84 dated March 25, terms 5/10, 2/30, n/60, is paid in full on April 20. What is the total amount paid to settle the account? (See Figure 6.6.)

Figure 6.6 Discount and Credit Periods—Example 6.2B, Ordinary Dating (© S. A. Hummelbrunner)

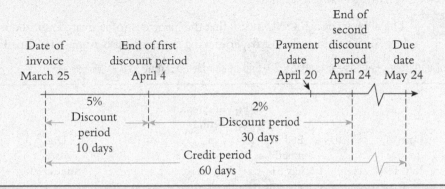

SOLUTION

The payment terms state that

(i) a 5% discount may be taken within 10 days of the invoice date (up to April 4); or

(ii) a 2% discount may be taken within 30 days of the invoice date (after April 4 but no later than April 24); or

(iii) the net amount is due within 60 days of the invoice date if advantage is not taken of the cash discounts offered.

The 5% cash discount is *not* allowed because payment on April 20 is after the end of the discount period for the 5% discount. However, the 2% discount *is* allowed, since payment on April 20 is within the 30-day period for the 2% discount.

Amount paid = 752.84(1 − 0.02) = 752.84(0.98) = $737.78

EXAMPLE 6.2C

Three invoices with terms 5/10, 3/20, and n/60 are paid on November 15. The invoices are for $645 dated September 30, $706 dated October 26, and $586 dated November 7. What is the total amount paid?

SOLUTION

Invoice Dated	End of Discount Period For 5%	For 3%	Discount Allowed on November 15	Amount Paid	
Sept. 30	Oct. 10	Oct. 20	None		$645.00
Oct. 26	Nov. 5	Nov. 15	3%	(706.00)(0.97)	684.82
Nov. 7	Nov. 17	Nov. 27	5%	(586.00)(0.95)	556.70
				Amount paid	$1886.52

C. End-of-the-month dating

End-of-the-month dating is reflected in an invoice with the abbreviation E.O.M., as in 2/10, n/30 E.O.M. The E.O.M. abbreviation has the effect of shifting the invoice date to the last day of the month. This would indicate that the 2% discount may be taken within the first 10 days of the next month.

Commonly, in end-of-the-month dating, the credit period (such as n/30) is not stated. In our example, "2/10, n/30 E.O.M." would be written "2/10 E.O.M." In this case, it is understood that the end of the credit period (the due date) is *twenty* days after the last day for taking the discount.

EXAMPLE 6.2D

An invoice for $1233.95 dated July 16, terms 2/10 E.O.M., is paid on August 10. What is the amount paid?

SOLUTION

The abbreviation E.O.M. means that the invoice is to be treated as if the invoice date were July 31. Therefore, the last day for taking the discount is August 10. (See Figure 6.7).

Figure 6.7 Discount and Credit Periods—Example 6.2D, End-of-the-Month Dating (© S. A. Hummelbrunner)

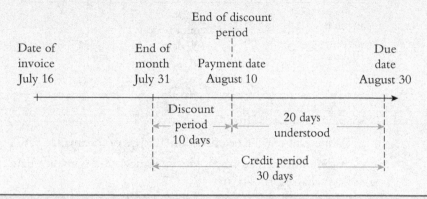

Amount paid = 1233.95(0.98) = $1209.27

D. Receipt-of-goods dating

When the abbreviation R.O.G. (*receipt of goods*) appears in the terms of payment, as in 2/10, n/30 R.O.G., the last day for taking the discount is the stipulated number of days after the date the merchandise is received, rather than the invoice date. This method of offering a cash discount is used when the transportation of the goods takes a long time, as in the case of long-distance overland shipments by rail or truck, or shipments by boat.

EXAMPLE 6.2E

Hansa Import Distributors has received an invoice of $8465.00 dated May 10, terms 3/10, n/30 R.O.G., for a shipment of clocks that arrived on July 15. What is the last day for taking the cash discount and how much is to be paid if the discount is taken?

SOLUTION

The last day for taking the discount is ten days after receipt of the shipment, that is, July 25. (See Figure 6.8).

Figure 6.8 Discount and Credit Periods—Example 6.2E, Receipt-of-Goods Dating (© S. A. Hummelbrunner)

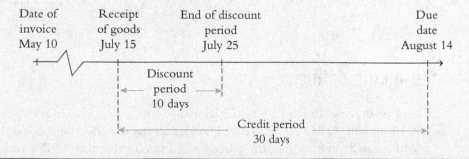

Amount paid = 8465.00(0.97) = $8211.05

E. Partial payments and additional problems

The problem of a cash discount for a **partial payment** arises when a business pays *part* of an invoice within the discount period. In such cases, the purchaser is entitled to the cash discount on the partial amount paid. Each time a partial payment is made, separate the invoice into different parts, and then determine whether the discount applies to each individual part.

EXAMPLE 6.2F

Royal Roads University has received an invoice of $2780 dated August 28, terms 2/10. What payment must be made on September 5 to reduce the debt

(i) by $1000?

(ii) to $1000?

SOLUTION

The last day for taking the cash discount is September 7. Since the payment on September 5 is within the discount period, the discount of 2% may be taken off the partial payment.

(i) Reduce debt *by* $1000

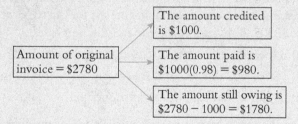

Reducing the debt *by* $1000 requires paying $1000 less the discount. The cash amount paid is $980. Even though less than $1000 has been paid, the debt still owing has been reduced by $1000. This amount is subtracted from the balance to determine the amount owing after the payment. The balance of the debt still owing is now $1780.

(ii) Reduce debt *to* $1000

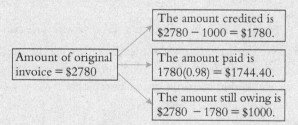

Reducing the debt *to* $1000 requires separating the debt into two parts, the first debt being $1780. The discount is then applied to that amount. The amount paid is $1744.40. The balance of the debt still owing in this case is now $1000.

EXAMPLE 6.2G

Applewood Supplies received a payment of $807.50 from Main Street Service on October 7 on an invoice of $2231.75 dated September 28, terms 5/10.

(i) How much should Applewood credit Main Street Service's account for the payment?

(ii) How much does Main Street Service still owe on the invoice?

SOLUTION

The payment is within the discount period. Main Street Service is entitled to the 5% discount on the partial payment. The amount of $807.50 represents a partial payment already reduced by 5%.

Let the credit allowed be x.

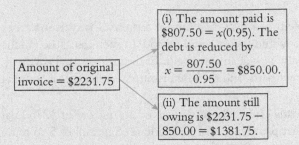

Amount of original invoice = $2231.75

(i) The amount paid is $807.50 = x(0.95)$. The debt is reduced by
$$x = \frac{807.50}{0.95} = \$850.00.$$

(ii) The amount still owing is $2231.75 − 850.00 = \$1381.75$.

   (i) Applewood should credit the account of Main Street Service with $850.

  (ii) Main Street Service still owes ($2231.75 − 850.00$) = $1381.75.

EXAMPLE 6.2H

Thrifty Furniture sells family-room furniture consisting of a couch, loveseat, and two tables for a package price of $2495 if the purchase is financed. The company also advertises "no payments and no interest for one year." Diana buys the furniture and pays $2395.20 in cash at the time of the purchase.

   (i) How much was the discount for paying cash?

  (ii) What was the rate of discount on the cash purchase?

 (iii) Is this actually no interest for one year?

SOLUTION

Since the payment was in cash at the time of purchase, Thrifty Furniture did allow a discount.

   (i) List price − Amount paid = Discount
$$\$2495.00 − 2395.20 = \$99.80$$

Thrifty Furniture allowed a discount of $99.80.

  (ii) Discount rate $= \dfrac{99.80}{2495.00} = 4\%$

Thrifty Furniture allowed a 4% discount rate for this cash payment.

 (iii) No, the advertising is misleading. Since a discount is allowed for early payment, the extra amount paid if the purchase is financed is equivalent to interest on the cash paid at the time of the purchase.

EXERCISE 6.2

MyLab Math

🌐 **1.** Canadian Wheel received an invoice dated May 13 with terms 2/10, n/30. The amount stated on the invoice was $2499.

  (a) What is the last day for taking the cash discount?

  (b) What is the amount due if the invoice is paid on the last day for taking the discount?

Reference Example 6.2A

🌐 **2.** An invoice was received for $6200 dated June 21 with terms 2/10, n/30.

  (a) What is the last day for taking the cash discount?

  (b) What is the amount due if the invoice is paid on the last day for taking the discount?

3. Triton Company received an invoice for $842 dated March 9 with terms 5/10, 2/20, n/60.

   (a) If the invoice is paid on March 19, how much is to be paid?
   (b) If the invoice is paid on March 27, how much is to be paid?
   (c) If the invoice is paid on April 3, how much is to be paid?

   Reference Example 6.2B

4. Manual Company received an invoice for $2412 dated January 22 with terms 3/15, 1/30, n/60.

   (a) If the invoice is paid on January 31, how much is to be paid?
   (b) If the invoice is paid on February 20, how much is to be paid?
   (c) If the invoice is paid on March 22, how much is to be paid?

5. What amount must be remitted if invoices dated July 25 for $929, August 10 for $763, and August 29 for $864, all with terms 3/20, n/40, are paid together on August 30?

6. The following invoices, all with terms 5/10, 2/30, n/60, were paid together on May 15. Invoice No. 234 dated March 30 is for $394.45; Invoice No. 356 dated April 15 is for $595.50; and Invoice No. 788 dated May 10 is for $865.20. What total amount was remitted?

7. An invoice for $5275 dated November 12, terms 4/10, n/30, was received on November 14. What payment must be made on November 20 to reduce the debt to $3000?

8. What payment will reduce the amount due on an invoice of $1940 by $740 if the terms of the invoice are 5/10, n/30 and the payment is made during the discount period?

9. Santucci Appliances received an invoice dated August 12 with terms 3/10 E.O.M. for the items listed below:

   5 GE refrigerators at $980 each less 25% and 5%;

   4 Inglis dishwashers at $696 each less $16\frac{2}{3}$%, 12.5%, and 4%.

   (a) What is the last day for taking the cash discount?
   (b) What is the total amount due if the invoice is paid on the last day for taking the discount?
   (c) What is the total amount of the cash discount if a partial payment is made such that a balance of $2000 remains outstanding on the invoice?

10. Import Exclusives Ltd. received an invoice dated May 20 from Dansk Specialties of Copenhagen with terms 5/20 R.O.G. for

    100 teak trays at $34.30 each;
    25 teak icebuckets at $63.60 each;
    40 teak salad bowls at $54.50 each.

    All items are subject to trade discounts of $33\frac{1}{3}$%, $7\frac{1}{2}$%, and 5%.

    (a) If the shipment was received on June 28, what is the last day of the discount period?
    (b) What is the amount due if the invoice is paid in full on July 15?
    (c) If only a partial payment is made on the last day of the discount period, what amount is needed to reduce the outstanding balance to $2500?

11. Sheridan Service received an invoice dated September 25 from Wolfedale Automotive. The invoice amount was $2540.95, and the payment terms were 3/10, 1/20, n/30. Sheridan Service made a payment on October 5 to reduce the balance

due by $1200, made a second payment on October 15 to reduce the balance to $600, and paid the remaining balance on October 25.

(a) How much did Sheridan Service pay on October 5?

(b) How much did it pay on October 15?

(c) What was the amount of the final payment on October 25?

Reference Example 6.2F

12. The Ski Shop received an invoice for $9600 dated August 11, terms 5/10, 2/30, n/90, for a shipment of skis. The Ski Shop made two partial payments.

(a) How much was paid on August 20 to reduce the unpaid balance to $7000?

(b) How much was paid on September 10 to reduce the outstanding balance by $3000?

(c) What is the remaining balance on September 10?

13. Jelinek Sports received a cheque for $1867.25 in partial payment of an invoice owed by The Ski Shop. The invoice was for $5325 with terms 3/20 E.O.M. dated September 15, and the cheque was received on October 18.

(a) How much should Jelinek Sports credit the account of The Ski Shop?

(b) How much does The Ski Shop still owe Jelinek?

14. Darrigo Grape received an invoice for $13 780 dated September 28, terms 5/20 R.O.G., from Nappa Vineyards for a carload of grape juice received October 20. Darrigo made a partial payment of $5966 on November 8.

(a) By how much did Darrigo reduce the amount due on the invoice?

(b) How much does Darrigo still owe?

15. Highway One Gas sells gas for vehicles at $1.12 per litre. Louis purchases 50 litres of gas for his car. He pays for the purchase in cash, paying a total of $54.04.

(a) How much did he save by paying cash?

(b) What was the rate of discount on the cash purchase?

16. Deals on Wheels advertises a vehicle at $26 465. Marina buys the vehicle, paying $24 877.10 in cash.

(a) How much did she save by paying cash?

(b) What was the rate of discount on the cash purchase?

6.3 MARKUP

A. Basic concepts and calculations

The primary purpose of operating a business is to generate profits. Businesses engaged in merchandising generate profits through their buying and selling activities. The amount of profit depends on many factors, one of which is the pricing of goods. The selling price must cover

1. the cost of buying the goods;

2. the operating expenses (or overhead) of the business;

3. the profit required by the owner to stay in business.

$$\boxed{\text{SELLING PRICE} = \text{COST OF BUYING} + \text{EXPENSES} + \text{PROFIT}}$$

$$\boxed{S = C + E + P} \text{————————} \textbf{Formula 6.6}$$

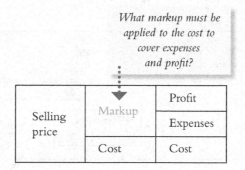

What markup must be applied to the cost to cover expenses and profit?

Selling price	Markup	Profit
		Expenses
	Cost	Cost

EXAMPLE 6.3A

Audio World buys outdoor speakers at a cost of $84.00 each. Operating expenses of the business are 25% of cost and the owner requires a profit of 10% of cost. How much should Audio World sell these speakers for?

SOLUTION

Selling price = Cost of buying + Expenses + Profit
$$= 84.00 + 25\% \text{ of } 84.00 + 10\% \text{ of } 84.00$$
$$= 84.00 + 0.25(84.00) + 0.10(84.00)$$
$$= 84.00 + 21.00 + 8.40$$
$$= \$113.40$$

Audio World should sell the speakers for $113.40 to cover the cost of buying, the operating expenses, and the required profit.

Formula 6.6 can then be rearranged, so that the selling price less the cost equals expenses plus profit.

SELLING PRICE − COST OF BUYING = EXPENSES + PROFIT

$$S - C = E + P$$

In Example 6.3A, the selling price is $113.40 while the cost is $84.00. The difference between selling price and cost = $113.40 - 84.00 = \$29.40$. This difference covers operating expenses of $21.00 and a profit of $8.40 and is known as the **markup**, **margin**, or **gross profit**.

MARKUP = EXPENSES + PROFIT

$$M = E + P$$ —————————— Formula 6.7

Using this relationship between markup, expenses, and profit, the relationship stated in Formula 6.6 becomes

SELLING PRICE = COST OF BUYING + MARKUP

$$S = C + M$$ —————————— Formula 6.8

Figure 6.9 illustrates the relationships among cost of buying (C), markup (M), operating expenses (E), profit (P), and selling price (S) established in Formulas 6.6, 6.7, and 6.8.

Figure 6.9 (© S. A. Hummelbrunner)

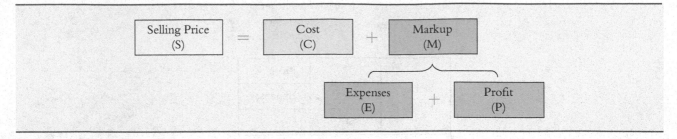

| EXAMPLE 6.3B | Compucorp bought two types of electronic calculators for resale. Model A costs $42.00 and sells for $56.50. Model B costs $78.00 and sells for $95.00. Business overhead is 24% of cost. For each model, determine |

(i) the markup (or gross profit);

(ii) the operating expenses (or overhead);

(iii) the profit.

SOLUTION		

Model A   **Model B**

(i) $S = C + M$ $S = C + M$ ——— using Formula 6.8
    $56.50 = 42.00 + M$ $95.00 = 78.00 + M$
        $M = 56.50 - 42.00$ $M = 95.00 - 78.00$
        $M = 14.50$ $M = 17.00$

The markup on Model A   The markup on Model B is $17.00
is $14.50

(ii) Expenses (or overhead)   Expenses (or overhead)
    $= 24\%$ of 42.00 $= 24\%$ of 78.00
    $= 0.24(42.00)$ $= 0.24(78.00)$
    $= 10.08$ $= 18.72$

Overhead for Model A is $10.08.   Overhead for Model B is $18.72.

(iii) $M = E + P$ $M = E + P$ ——— using Formula 6.7
    $14.50 = 10.08 + P$ $17.00 = 18.72 + P$
        $P = 14.50 - 10.08$ $P = 17.00 - 18.72$
        $P = 4.42$ $P = -1.72$

Profit on Model A is $4.42.   Profit on Model B is $-$1.72,
                                      that is, a loss of $1.72.

| EXAMPLE 6.3C | A ski shop bought 100 pairs of skis for $105.00 per pair and sold 60 pairs at the regular selling price of $295.00 per pair. The remaining skis were sold during a clearance sale for $180.00 per pair. Overhead is 40% of the regular selling price. Determine |

(i) the markup, the overhead, and the profit per pair of skis sold at the regular selling price;

(ii) the markup, the overhead, and the profit per pair of skis sold during the clearance sale;

(iii) the total profit realized.

SOLUTION		

(i) *At regular selling price*   (ii) *At clearance price*
Markup   **Markup**
$S = C + M$ $S = C + M$
$295.00 = 105.00 + M$ $180.00 = 105.00 + M$
$M = \$190.00$ $M = \$75.00$

	Overhead			Overhead	

Overhead

$E = 40\%$ of regular selling price
$= 0.4(295.00)$
$= \$118.00$

Overhead

$E = 40\%$ of regular selling price
$= 0.4(295.00)$
$= \$118.00$

Profit

$M = E + P$
$190.00 = 118.00 + P$
$P = \$72.00$

Profit

$M = E + P$
$75.00 = 118.00 + P$
$P = -\$43.00$

(iii) Profit from sale of 60 pairs
at regular selling price $= 60(72.00)$ $\$4320.00$
Profit from sale of 40 pairs
during clearance sale $= 40(-43.00)$ -1720.00
Total profit $\underline{\$2600.00}$

POINTERS & PITFALLS

It is helpful to organize markup questions in a diagram. S is composed of C and M, or of C, E, and P. Often E and P are expressed as a percentage of C or of S. Enter the values you know (or can calculate) into one of the following diagrams and then solve for the unknown values.

$$S =$$

C	M

$$S =$$

C	E	P

B. Rate of markup

A markup may be stated in one of two ways:

1. as a percent of cost; or

2. as a percent of selling price.

The method used is usually determined by the way in which a business keeps its records. Since most manufacturers keep their records in terms of cost, they usually calculate markup as a percent of cost. Since most department stores and other retailers keep their records in terms of selling price, they usually calculate markup as a percent of selling price.

Computing the rate of markup involves comparing the amount of markup to a base amount. Depending on the method used, the base amount is either the cost or the selling price. Since the two methods produce different results, great care must be taken to note whether the markup is based on the cost or on the selling price.

$$\text{RATE OF MARKUP BASED ON COST} = \frac{\text{MARKUP}}{\text{COST}} = \frac{M}{C} \times 100 \qquad \text{—— Formula 6.9}$$

$$\text{RATE OF MARKUP BASED ON SELLING PRICE} = \frac{\text{MARKUP}}{\text{SELLING PRICE}} = \frac{M}{S} \times 100 \qquad \text{—— Formula 6.10}$$

EXAMPLE 6.3D

A dealer bought personal computers for $1850.00 less 32%, and 17%. They were sold for $1575.00.

a) What was the markup as a percent of cost?
b) What was the markup as a percent of selling price?

SOLUTION

$$Cost = 1850.00(1 - 0.32)(1 - 0.17) = \$1044.14$$
$$M = 1575.00 - 1044.14 = \$530.86$$

a) Rate of markup based on cost = $530.86/1044.14 = 0.508418 = 50.84\%$
b) Rate of markup based on selling price = $530.86/1575.00 = 0.337054 = 33.71\%$

Note: The rate of markup based on cost is higher than the rate of markup based on selling price because the cost amount has a smaller base in the calculations.

C. Calculating the cost or the selling price

When the rate of markup is given and either the cost or the selling price is known, the missing value can be found using Formula 6.8.

$$\boxed{\text{SELLING PRICE} = \text{COST} + \text{MARKUP}} \qquad \boxed{S = C + M}$$

When using this formula, pay special attention to the base of the markup; that is, whether it is based on cost or based on selling price.

EXAMPLE 6.3E

What is the selling price of an article costing $72.00 if the markup is

(i) 40% of cost?

(ii) 40% of the selling price?

SOLUTION

(i) $S = C + M$ ———————— using Formula 6.8
$S = C + 40\%$ of C ———————— replacing M by 40% of C is the crucial
$S = 72.00 + 0.4(72.00)$ step in the solution
$S = 72.00 + 28.80$
$S = 100.80$

When the markup is 40% based on cost, the selling price is $100.80.

(ii) $S = C + M$
$S = C + 40\%$ of S
$S = 72.00 + 0.4S$
$S - 0.4S = 72.00$ ———————— collecting similar terms (of S) to one side
$0.6S = 72.00$ is the crucial step in the solution
$$S = \frac{72.00}{0.6}$$
$S = 120.00$

When the markup is 40% based on selling price, the selling price is $120.00.

POINTERS
& PITFALLS

In problems of this type, replace M by $x\%$ of C or $x\%$ of S before using specific numbers. This approach is used in the preceding problem and in the following worked examples.

EXAMPLE 6.3F

What is the cost of an article selling for $65.00 if the markup is

(i) 30% of selling price?

(ii) 30% of cost?

SOLUTION

(i)   S = C + M
        S = C + 30% of S ——————— replace M by 30% of S
   65.00 = C + 0.3(65.00)
   65.00 = C + 19.50
        C = 65.00 − 19.50
        C = 45.50

When the markup is 30% based on selling price, the cost is $45.50.

(ii)   S = C + M
         S = C + 30% of C ——————— replace M by 30% of C
   65.00 = C + 0.3C
   65.00 = 1.3C
        $C = \frac{65.00}{1.3}$
        C = 50.00

If the markup is 30% based on cost, the cost is $50.00.

EXAMPLE 6.3G

The Beaver Ski Shop sells ski vests for $98.00. The markup based on cost is 75%.

(i) What did the Beaver Ski Shop pay for each vest?

(ii) What is the rate of markup based on the selling price?

SOLUTION

(i)   S = C + M
        S = C + 75% of C
   98.00 = C + 0.75C
   98.00 = 1.75C
        C = 56.00

The Beaver Ski Shop paid $56.00 for each vest.

(ii) Rate of markup based on selling price $= \dfrac{\text{Markup}}{\text{Selling price}}$

$= \dfrac{98.00 - 56.00}{98.00}$

$= \dfrac{42.00}{98.00} = 0.428571 = 42.86\%$

EXAMPLE 6.3H

Main Street Service bought four Michelin tires from a wholesaler for $318.50 and sold the tires at a markup of 35% of the selling price.

(i) For how much were the tires sold?

(ii) What is the rate of markup based on cost?

SOLUTION

(i) $S = C + M$
$S = C + 35\%$ of S
$S = 318.50 + 0.35S$
$0.65S = 318.50$
$S = 490.00$

Main Street Service sold the tires for $490.00.

(ii) Rate of markup based on cost $= \dfrac{\text{Markup}}{\text{Cost}}$

$= \dfrac{490.00 - 318.50}{318.50}$

$= \dfrac{171.50}{318.50} = 0.538462 = 53.85\%$

EXAMPLE 6.31

The markup, or gross profit, on each of two separate articles is $25.80. If the rate of markup for Article A is 40% of cost while the rate of markup for Article B is 40% of the selling price, determine the cost and the selling price of each.

SOLUTION

For Article A
Markup (or gross profit) $= 40\%$ of cost
$25.80 = 0.4C$
$C = 64.50$

The cost of Article A is $64.50.
The selling price is $64.50 + 25.80 = \$90.30$.

For Article B
Markup (or gross profit) $= 40\%$ of selling price
$25.80 = 0.4S$
$S = 64.50$

The selling price of Article B is $64.50.
The cost is $64.50 - 25.80 = \$38.70$.

EXERCISE 6.3 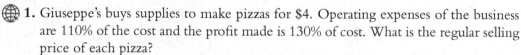 MyLab Math

1. Giuseppe's buys supplies to make pizzas for $4. Operating expenses of the business are 110% of the cost and the profit made is 130% of cost. What is the regular selling price of each pizza?

2. Neptune Dive Shop sells snorkelling equipment for $50. The shop's cost is $25 and the operating expenses are 30% of the regular selling price. How much profit will the shop make on each sale?

3. Mi Casa imports pottery from Mexico. Its operating expenses are 260% of the cost of buying and the profit is 110% of the cost of buying. This business sells a vase for $14.10. What is the cost for each piece?

4. Peninsula Hardware buys cabinet doors for $25 less 40%, 10%, and 4%. The store's overhead expenses are 35% of cost and the required profit is 15% of cost. How much should the cabinet doors be sold for?

5. A merchant buys an item listed at $96 less $33\frac{1}{3}$% from a distributor. Overhead is 32% of cost and profit is 27.5% of cost. For how much should the item be retailed?

6. Tennis racquets were purchased at a price of $55 less 40% (for purchasing more than 100 items), and less a further 25% (for purchasing the racquets in October). They were sold for $54.45.

(a) What is the markup as a percent of cost?
(b) What is the markup as a percent of selling price?

7. A dealer bought computers for $1240 less 50% and 10%. They were sold for $1395.

(a) What was the markup as a percent of cost?
(b) What was the markup as a percent of selling price?

8. The Bargain Bookstore marks up books by $3.42 per book. The store's markup is 15% of cost.

(a) For how much did the bookstore buy each book?
(b) What is the selling price of each book?
(c) What is the rate of markup, based on the selling price?

9. An appliance store sells electric kettles at a markup of 18% of the selling price. The store's margin on a particular model is $6.57.

(a) For how much does the store sell the kettles?
(b) What was the cost of the kettles to the store?
(c) What is the rate of markup based on cost?

10. At Town Lighting, a light fixture is sold at a price of $382.20, including a markup of 40% of cost.

(a) What is the cost of the item?
(b) What is the rate of markup based on the selling price?

11. Sheridan Service sells oil at a markup of 40% of the selling price. If Sheridan paid $0.99 per litre of oil,

(a) What is the selling price per litre?
(b) What is the rate of markup based on cost?

12. Skis & Boards purchased gloves for $20.28 per pair. The gloves are marked up 48% of the selling price.

(a) For how much does Skis & Boards sell a pair of gloves?
(b) What is the rate of markup based on cost?

13. Neal's Photographic Supplies sells a Pentax camera for $444.98. The markup is 90% of cost.

(a) How much does the store pay for this camera?
(b) What is the rate of markup based on selling price?

14. The Cookery buys sets of cookware for $45 and marks them up at $33\frac{1}{3}$% of cost.

(a) What is the selling price of the cookware sets?
(b) What is the rate of markup based on selling price?

15. The Leather Factory buys bags for $84 and marks them up at 40% of selling price

(a) What is the selling price of the bags?
(b) What is the rate of markup based on cost?

16. Four-packs of energy drinks are purchased for $3.24. The store's markup based on selling price is $16\frac{2}{3}$%.

    (a) What is the selling price of the four-packs?
    (b) What is the rate of markup based on cost?

17. It's About Time sells clocks for $23.10. The store's markup based on cost is 37.5%.

    (a) What is the cost of the clocks?
    (b) What is the rate of markup based on selling price?

18. A car accessory is sold for $42.90. The store's markup based on cost is 50%.

    (a) What is the cost of the car accessory?
    (b) What is the rate of markup based on selling price?

19. A gross profit of $289.80 is made on the sale of a treadmill. If the gross profit is 31.5% based on selling price, what was the cost?

20. A nursery bought 100 Christmas trees for $4500.00; 50 trees were sold at a markup of 35% of cost, 40 trees were sold for $52 each, and the remaining trees were sold at 33% below cost. Assume all the trees had the same cost.

    (a) What was the markup realized on the purchase?
    (b) What was the percent markup realized based on cost?
    (c) What was the gross profit realized based on selling price?

21. Lumber Liquidators bought 240 cases of oak hardwood flooring at an auction for $19 200.00. This means that each case had the same cost. Back at the store, the cases were sorted into good quality, seconds, and substandard. The 134 good quality cases were sold at a markup of 105% of cost, the 79 cases classified as seconds were sold at a markup of 28% of cost, and the remaining cases classified as substandard were sold at 65% of their cost.

    (a) What was the unit selling price for each of the three classifications?
    (b) If overhead is 34% of cost, what was the amount of profit realized on the purchase?
    (c) What was the average rate of markup based on the selling price at which the cases were sold?

6.4 MARKDOWN
A. Pricing strategies

Pricing strategies can be based on internal or external influences. Setting a price based on the business' "internal" factors involves examining the actual costs and expenses, as well as a desired profit level. Consideration of the relationship stated in Formula 6.6, Selling price = Cost + Expenses + Profit (or S = C + E + P), is essential in determining how large a markup is needed to cover overhead expenses and to generate a reasonable profit.

    The cost of buying an article plus the overhead represents the **total cost** of the article.

$$\boxed{\text{COST OF BUYING} + \text{EXPENSES} = \text{TOTAL COST}}$$

If an article is sold at a price that *equals* the total cost, the business makes no profit, nor does it suffer a loss. This price occurs at the break-even point and is discussed in Chapter 5. Any business, of course, prefers to sell at a price that is at least the **break-even price**. If the price is insufficient to recover the total cost, the business will suffer an operating loss. If the price does not even cover the cost of buying the item, the business suffers an **absolute loss**.

Often, pricing decisions are determined by the actions of competitors or consumers, changes to economic conditions that affect interest rates and income available for purchases, or other "external" market factors. In response to market changes, marking down selling prices may be required to maintain sales levels.

B. Concepts and calculations

After the price to the retailer has been marked up to determine the regular selling price, the retailer may discount the regular selling price to offer the goods to the consumer at a lower sale price. The reduction from the regular selling price is called a **markdown**. The purpose of a markdown may be for promoting sales, to match competitors' prices, or to clear out inventories that are discontinued or seasonal.

In the merchandising industry, a wide variety of terms are used to identify the price to be reduced, such as regular selling price, selling price, list price, marked price, price tag, or ticket price. The reduced price can be referred to as the sale price or clearance price. The many terms can cause confusion. In this text, we use **regular selling price**, S, to describe the price to be reduced and **sale price**, S_R, to describe the reduced price.

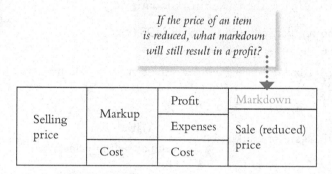

If the price of an item is reduced, what markdown will still result in a profit?

Selling price	Markup	Profit	Markdown
		Expenses	Sale (reduced) price
	Cost	Cost	

Using these standardized terms, a markdown can be calculated as the difference between the regular selling price and the sale price.

> SALE PRICE = REGULAR SELLING PRICE − MARKDOWN

$$S_R = S - MD$$ ——————————— Formula 6.11

The **rate of markdown** or *markdown rate* is the relationship between the amount of the markdown and the regular selling price, and is stated as a percent of the regular selling price.

$$\frac{\text{RATE OF MARKDOWN}}{} = \frac{\text{MARKDOWN}}{\text{REGULAR SELLING PRICE}} = \frac{MD}{S} \times 100$$ ——————— Formula 6.12

Since the markdown is a percent of the regular selling price, the net price factor approach used with discounts is applicable (see Formula 6.3).

> SALE PRICE = REGULAR SELLING PRICE × NPF

$$S_R = S\,(1 - md)$$ ——————————— Formula 6.13

When an article is sold at the sale price, the resulting profit, called the realized profit, can be determined using a variation of Formula 6.6, S − C − E = P. The regular selling price, S, would be replaced with the sale price, S_R. If the sale price of an article does not cover the total cost, the cost of buying, and the overhead expense, the result is a loss.

POINTERS & PITFALLS

It is helpful to organize markdown questions in a diagram. Recall, S is composed of C and M, or of C, E, and P. In the case of markdown (MD), when the original selling price of an item is reduced (S_R), C and E do not change, but profit is impacted (P_R). By definition, the amount of markdown is the difference between S and S_R ($S - S_R = MD$).

$$S =$$

C	E	P

$$S_R =$$

C	E	P_R	MD

EXAMPLE 6.4A

Lund Sporting Goods sold a bicycle regularly priced at $195.00 for $144.30.

   (i) What is the amount of markdown?

  (ii) What is the rate of markdown?

SOLUTION

The regular selling price, S, is $195.00.
The sale price is $144.30.

   (i) Markdown = Regular selling price − Sale price

               = 195.00 − 144.30

               = $50.70

  (ii) Rate of markdown $= \dfrac{\text{Markdown}}{\text{Regular selling price}}$ ──────── **using Formula 6.12**

                   $= \dfrac{50.70}{195.00} = 0.26 = 26\%$

EXAMPLE 6.4B

During its annual Midnight Madness Sale, The Ski Shop sold a pair of ski boots, regularly priced at $245.00, at a discount of 40%. The boots cost $96.00 and expenses are 16% of the regular selling price.

   (i) For how much were the ski boots sold?

  (ii) What was the total cost of the ski boots?

 (iii) What operating profit or loss was made on the sale?

SOLUTION

The regular selling price, S, is $245.00.

   (i) Sale price = S × NPF

             = 245.00 × 0.6 = $147.00

  (ii) Total cost = Cost of buying + Expenses

               = 96.00 + 0.16(245.00)

               = 96.00 + 39.20

               = $135.20

 (iii) Profit = Sale price − Total cost

               = 147.00 − 135.20

               = $11.80 (a profit)

Since the sale price was higher than the cost of the ski boots, The Ski Shop made a profit of $11.80.

EXAMPLE 6.4C

The Cook Nook paid $115.24 for a set of dishes. Expenses are 18% of selling price and the required profit is 15% of selling price. During an inventory sale, the set of dishes was marked down 30%.

(i) What was the regular selling price?

(ii) What was the sale price?

(iii) What was the operating profit or loss?

SOLUTION

(i) Selling price = Cost + Expenses + Profit

$$S = C + 18\% \text{ of } S + 15\% \text{ of } S$$
$$S = C + 0.18S + 0.15S$$
$$S = 115.24 + 0.33S$$
$$0.67S = 115.24$$
$$S = \frac{115.24}{0.67} = \$172.00$$

The regular selling price is $172.00.

(ii) Sale price = Regular selling price − Markdown

$$= S - 30\% \text{ of } S$$
$$= S - 0.3S$$
$$= 0.7S$$
$$= 0.7(172.00)$$
$$= \$120.40$$

The sale price (or revenue) is $120.40.

(iii) Total cost = Cost of buying + Expenses

$$= C + 18\% \text{ of } S$$
$$= 115.24 + 0.18(172.00)$$
$$= 115.24 + 30.96$$
$$= \$146.20$$

Profit = Revenue − Total cost

$$= 120.40 - 146.20$$
$$= -\$25.80$$

Since the total cost was higher than the revenue received from the sale of the dishes, the dishes were sold at an operating loss of $25.80.

EXAMPLE 6.4D

The Winemaker sells Okanagan concentrate for $22.50. The store's overhead expenses are 50% of cost and the owners require a profit of 30% of cost.

(i) For how much does The Winemaker buy the concentrate?

(ii) What is the price needed to cover all of the costs and expenses?

(iii) What is the highest rate of markdown at which the store will still break even?

(iv) What is the highest rate of discount that can be advertised without incurring an absolute loss?

SOLUTION

The regular selling price, S, is $22.50.

(i)
$$S = C + E + P$$
$$S = C + 50\% \text{ of } C + 30\% \text{ of } C$$
$$S = C + 0.5C + 0.3C$$
$$22.50 = 1.8C$$
$$C = \frac{22.50}{1.80} = \$12.50$$

The Winemaker buys the concentrate for $12.50.

(ii)   Total cost $= C + 50\%$ of C

$\qquad\qquad = 1.5C$

$\qquad\qquad = 1.5(12.50)$

$\qquad\qquad = \$18.75$

The price needed to cover costs and expenses is $18.75.

(iii)   To break even, the maximum markdown is $22.50 - 18.75 = \$3.75$.

$$\text{Rate of markdown} = \frac{3.75}{22.50} = 0.16\dot{} = 16.\dot{6}\%$$

The highest rate of markdown to break even is 16.67%. (★rounded)

(iv)   The lowest price at which the concentrate can be offered for sale without incurring an absolute loss is the cost at which the concentrate was purchased; that is, $12.50. The maximum amount of discount is $22.50 - 12.50 = \$10.00$.

$$\text{Rate of discount} = \frac{10.00}{22.50} = 0.\dot{4} = 44.\dot{4}\%$$

The maximum rate of discount that can be advertised without incurring an absolute loss is 44.44%. (★ rounded)

POINTERS & PITFALLS

You may notice that this relationship aligns with income statements used in accounting, in which the selling price or sale price represents revenue for units sold. Once the cost of buying those items and any expenses are subtracted from revenue, the result is either a profit or a loss on the income statement.

EXERCISE 6.4   MyLab Math

1. The Music Store paid $14.95 for a DVD. Expenses are 21% of regular selling price and the required profit is 11% of regular selling price. During an inventory sale, the DVD was marked down 20%.

   (a) What was the regular selling price?
   (b) What was the sale price?
   (c) What was the operating profit or loss on the sale?   Reference Example 6.4A

2. A retail store paid $44 for a microwave oven. Expenses are 27% of regular selling price and the required profit is 18% of regular selling price. During an inventory sale, the microwave was marked down 40%.

   (a) What was the regular selling price?
   (b) What was the sale price?
   (c) What was the operating profit or loss on the sale?

🌐 3. A sports drink was offered for sale at $1.99 at West Store. At East Store, the regular selling price of a similar sports drink was $2.49. What rate of markdown would East Store have to offer to sell the drink at the same price as West Store?   Reference Example 6.4B

🌐 4. An eyeglass company sells frames for $279. If the company wanted to offer the lower price of $239, what rate of markdown would it have to offer?

5. A seminar was advertised at a price of $125 per person. If the tickets were purchased at least two weeks in advance, the price would be lowered to $105 per person. What rate of markdown has been offered?

6. A seven-day Mexican cruise was advertised at a price of $1299 per person based on double occupancy. If the cruise was booked two months in advance, the price would be lowered to $935 per person. What rate of markdown has been offered?

7. Luigi's Restaurant offered a "buy one get one half off" sale for the midweek period. The "one half off" referred to the lesser-priced dinner. A customer ordered a steak dinner, with a regular price of $19, and a chicken dinner, with a regular price of $14.

   (a) What was the overall markdown amount at which the dinners were sold?
   (b) What was the overall rate of markdown at which the dinners were sold?

8. A lakeside resort offered a midweek package at $199 per night for two people. The package included accommodation in a one-bedroom suite, which regularly sold for $225; and breakfast for two, regularly priced at $12 per person.

   (a) What was the markdown at which the packages were sold?
   (b) What was the rate of markdown at which the packages were sold?

9. Par Putters Company sells golf balls for $29 per dozen. The store's overhead expenses are 43% of cost and the owners require a profit of 20% of cost.

   (a) For how much does Par Putters Company buy the golf balls?
   (b) What is the price needed to cover all of the costs and expenses?
   (c) What is the highest rate of markdown at which the store will still break even?
   (d) What is the highest rate of discount that can be advertised without incurring an absolute loss?   Reference Example 6.4D

10. Get-Aways Company sells sightseeing tours of the Ottawa Valley for $3849 per person. Overhead expenses for the company are 31% of cost and the target profit is 17% of cost.

    (a) How much does Get-Aways Company pay for the tours?
    (b) What is the lowest price they can offer while still covering all of the costs and expenses?
    (c) What is the highest rate of markdown at which the company will still break even?

11. A retail store realizes a gross profit of $56.24 if it sells an article at a margin of 37% of the selling price.

    (a) What is the regular selling price?
    (b) What is the cost?
    (c) What is the rate of markup based on cost?
    (d) If overhead is 25% of cost, what is the break-even price?
    (e) If the article is sold at a markdown of 13%, what is the operating profit or loss?

12. Fitness Pro paid $286.99 for a set of PowerBlock weights. Overhead is 23% of the regular selling price and profit is 17% of the regular selling price. During a clearance sale, the set was sold at a markdown of 30%. What was the operating profit or loss on the sale?

13. Mountain Equipment Co-op purchased tents for $334.89 less 27%, 18%, and 6%. The store's overhead is 55% of cost and the normal profit is 21% of cost.

    (a) What is the regular selling price of the tents?
    (b) At what price can the tents be put on sale so that the store incurs an operating loss of no more than 20% of the overhead?
    (c) What is the maximum rate of markdown at which the tents can be offered for sale in part (b)?

6.5 INTEGRATED PROBLEMS

Decisions involving discounts, markups, and markdowns are faced by business owners and managers on a regular basis. To achieve desired profits, prices must be set carefully. With each complex situation, a series of calculations are needed, with one calculation often building upon another. To realize an overall solution, clear steps must be defined and the costs and prices calculated. When presented with an integrated problem, break the problem down into smaller simpler problems.

EXAMPLE 6.5A

Rocky Sports purchased ski bindings for $57.75 that were then marked up 45% of the regular selling price. The store's overhead expenses were 28% of the regular selling price. When the binding was discontinued, it was marked down 40%. What was the sale price of the binding? How much was the operating profit or loss as a result of the sale?

SOLUTION

Consider the given information step by step. First, the regular selling price must be calculated. Next, the sale price can be calculated, and finally, the profit or loss can be calculated.

STEP 1

Since the sale price is based on a markdown from the regular selling price, S, the first step is to determine the regular selling price, S.

$$S = C + M$$
$$S = C + 45\% \text{ of } S$$
$$S = 57.75 + 0.45S$$
$$0.55S = 57.75$$
$$S = \$105.00$$

The regular selling price is $105.00.

STEP 2

Based on the regular selling price, S, determine the sale price.

Sale price = Regular selling price − Markdown
$$S_R = S - MD \text{ ———————————— using Formula 6.11}$$
Sale price = 105.00 − 40% of 105.00
Sale price = 105.00 − 42.00
Sale price = $63.00

Alternatively:

Sale price = Regular selling price × NPF
$$S_R = S (1 - md) \text{ ———————————— using Formula 6.13}$$
Sale price = 105.00 × 0.6
Sale price = $63.00

The sale price is $63.00.

STEP 3

Based on the sale price, determine the profit or loss.

Profit(loss) = Sale price − Cost of buying − Expenses
$$P = 63.00 - 57.75 - 0.28(105.00)$$
$$P = 63.00 - 57.75 - 29.40$$
$$P = -\$24.15$$

With the sale price, the operating loss was $24.15.

In some industries, businesses incorporate a third price into their pricing strategy. In this case, the **marked price** or sticker price is set so that an ongoing discount is deducted to determine the regular selling price. Even though the merchandise is marked with a price, it is seldom sold at that price. When a discount is offered on a regular basis, the discounted price becomes the regular selling price. In addition, the business can apply a markdown to the marked price to determine a sale price. The resulting sale price may be higher or lower than the regular selling price.

EXAMPLE 6.5B

The Cheetah, a fast, sporty, and efficient new vehicle, has just been introduced by Canadian Motors. The local dealer, Andretti's, purchased one of the cars at a list price of $27 685.00 less 30%. Andretti's sets a marked price on all vehicles so that it can offer a regular advertised discount of 10% and maintain a markup of 45% of the cost. During its annual sale, instead of the usual discount, a different markdown was offered by advertising the car at $25 995.00. Determine the cost, the regular selling price, the original marked price, and the sale markdown rate.

SOLUTION

The step-by-step calculations are as follows: determine cost, regular selling price, original marked price, and then the sale markdown rate.

STEP 1
Determine the cost, C, (or purchase price) to the dealer.

Cost = Manufacturer's list price × NPF

$$C = (27\ 685.00)(0.70) = \$19\ 379.50$$

The cost, C, to the business is $19 379.50.

STEP 2
Determine the regular selling price, S, required to maintain the markup based on cost.

S = C + Markup
S = C + 45% of C
S = C + 0.45C
S = 1.45(19 379.50)
S = 28 100.275

The regular selling price, S, is $28 100.28. (★ rounded)

STEP 3
Determine the original marked price to allow a 10% discount.
Let the marked price be MP.

MP − Discount = Regular selling price
MP − 10% of MP = Regular selling price
MP − 0.1MP = 28 100.28
0.9MP = 28 100.28

$$MP = \frac{28\ 100.28}{0.9} = 31\ 222.53$$

The marked price is $31 222.53.

STEP 4
Determine the sale markdown rate.

Markdown = Marked price − Sale price
= 31 222.53 − 25 995.00
= $5 227.53

$$\text{Markdown rate} = \frac{\text{Markdown}}{\text{Marked price}} = \frac{5\ 227.53}{31\ 222.53} = 0.167428 = 16.74\%$$

The markdown is $5227.53, which is 16.74% of the marked price.

EXAMPLE 6.5C

Big Sound Electronics purchased equipment from the manufacturer at a cost of $960.00 less 30% and 15%. According to Big Sound's pricing strategy, all merchandise is marked at a price that allows an ongoing discount of 20% and maintains a profit of 15% of regular selling price. Overhead is 25% of regular selling price. During its annual Boxing Week sale, the usual discount of 20% was replaced by a markdown of 45% on selected models. What operating profit or loss was made during the Boxing Week sale?

SOLUTION

Step-by-step calculations needed: determine cost, regular selling price, marked price, sale price, then profit or loss.

STEP 1

Determine the cost, C, (or purchase price) to the store.

$$\text{Cost} = \text{Manufacturer's list price} \times \text{NPF}$$
$$C = (960.00)(0.70)(0.85) = \$571.20$$

The cost, C, to the store is $571.20.

STEP 2

Determine the regular selling price, S.
Let the regular selling price be S.

$$S = C + E + P$$
$$S = C + 25\% \text{ of } S + 15\% \text{ of } S$$
$$S = C + 0.25S + 0.15S$$
$$S = 571.20 + 0.40S$$
$$0.60S = 571.20$$
$$S = \frac{571.20}{0.6} = \$952.00$$

The regular selling price, S, is $952.00.

STEP 3

Determine the original marked price to allow a 20% discount.
Let the marked price be MP.

$$\text{MP} - \text{Discount} = \text{Regular selling price}$$
$$\text{MP} - 20\% \text{ of MP} = 952.00$$
$$\text{MP} - 0.2\text{MP} = 952.00$$
$$0.8\text{MP} = 952.00$$
$$\text{MP} = \frac{952.00}{0.8} = \$1190.00$$

The marked price is $1190.00.

STEP 4

Determine the Boxing Week sale price.

$$\begin{aligned} \text{Boxing Week sale price} &= \text{Marked price} - \text{Markdown} \\ &= 1190.00 - 45\% \text{ of } 1190.00 \\ &= 1190.00 - 0.45(1190.00) \\ &= \$654.50 \end{aligned}$$

The sale price is $654.50.

STEP 5

Determine the profit or loss.

$$\begin{aligned} \text{Profit} &= \text{Sale price} - \text{Cost of buying} - \text{Expenses} \\ &= 654.50 - 571.20 - 0.25(952.00) \\ &= 654.50 - 809.20 \\ &= -\$154.70 \end{aligned}$$

The merchandise was sold at an operating loss of $154.70 during the Boxing Week sale.

EXAMPLE 6.5D

Magder's Furniture Emporium bought a dining room suite that must be regularly sold for $5250.00 to cover the cost, overhead expenses of 50% of the cost, and a normal net profit of 25% of the cost. The suite is marked at a price so that the store can allow a 20% discount and still receive the required regular selling price.

When the suite remained unsold, the store owner decided to mark the suite down for an inventory clearance sale. To arrive at the rate of markdown, the owner decided that the store's profit would have to be no less than 10% of the normal net profit and that part of the markdown would be covered by reducing the commission paid to the salesperson. The normal commission (which accounts for 40% of the overhead) was reduced by $33\frac{1}{3}$%.

What is the maximum rate of markdown that can be advertised instead of the usual 20%?

The steps required: determine the cost, the normal and required net profits, the normal overhead expense, and the commissions. From these results, the inventory clearance price can be calculated. Determine the marked price and, using the inventory clearance price, calculate the amount of markdown from the marked price. Then calculate the rate of markdown.

SOLUTION

STEP 1 Determine the cost, C.
Let the regular selling price be S.

$$S = C + E + P$$
$$S = C + 50\% \text{ of } C + 25\% \text{ of } C$$
$$S = C + 0.5C + 0.25C$$
$$5250.00 = 1.75C$$
$$C = \frac{5250.00}{1.75} = \$3000.00$$

STEP 2 Determine the required profit.

$$\text{Normal net profit} = 25\% \text{ of cost}$$
$$= 0.25(3000.00)$$
$$= \$750.00$$
$$\text{Required net profit} = 10\% \text{ of normal net profit}$$
$$= 0.1(750.00)$$
$$= \$75.00$$

STEP 3 Determine the amount of overhead expense to be recovered.

$$\text{Normal overhead expense} = 50\% \text{ of cost}$$
$$= 0.5(3000.00)$$
$$= \$1500.00$$
$$\text{Normal commission} = 40\% \text{ of normal overhead expense}$$
$$= 0.4(1500.00)$$
$$= \$600.00$$
$$\text{Reduction in commission} = 33\tfrac{1}{3} \% \text{ of normal commission}$$
$$= 33\tfrac{1}{3}\%(600.00)$$
$$= \$200.00$$

$$\text{Overhead expense to be recovered} = 1500.00 - 200.00 = \$1300.00$$

STEP 4   Determine the inventory clearance price.

$$\text{Inventory clearance price} = \text{Cost} + \text{Reduced overhead} + \text{Reduced profit}$$
$$= 3000.00 + 1300.00 + 75.00$$
$$= \$4375.00$$

STEP 5   Determine the marked price, MP.
Let the marked price be MP.

$$\text{Marked price} - \text{Discount} = \text{Regular selling price}$$
$$\text{MP} - 20\% \text{ of MP} = 5250.00$$
$$\text{MP} - 0.2\text{MP} = 5250.00$$
$$0.8\text{MP} = 5250.00$$
$$\text{MP} = \frac{5250.00}{0.8} = \$6562.50$$

STEP 6   Determine the amount of markdown.

$$\text{Markdown} = \text{Marked price} - \text{Inventory clearance price}$$
$$= 6562.50 - 4375.00$$
$$= \$2187.50$$

STEP 7   Determine the rate of markdown.

$$\text{Rate of markdown} = \frac{\text{Amount of markdown}}{\text{Marked price}}$$
$$= \frac{2187.50}{6562.50}$$
$$= 0.\dot{3}\%$$
$$= 33.\dot{3}\%$$

Instead of the usual 20%, the store can advertise a markdown of 33.33%.

EXERCISE 6.5   MyLab Math

Answer each of the following questions.

1. A telephone set that cost a dealer $240 less 55% and 25% is marked up 230% of cost. The dealer overhead expenses are 25% of the regular selling price. For a sales promotion, the telephone sets were reduced 40%.

   (a) What is the regular selling price?
   (b) What is the sale price?
   (c) At the sale price, what profit or loss was realized?   Reference Example 6.5A

2. A gas barbecue cost a retailer $420 less 33⅓%, 20%, and 5%. Markup is 60% of the regular selling price. During the end-of-season sale, the barbecue is marked down 45%.

   (a) What is the end-of-season sale price?
   (b) What rate of markup based on cost will be realized during the sale?

3. The Stereo Shop sold a radio regularly priced at $125 for $105. The cost of the radio was $120 less 33⅓% and 15%. The store's overhead expense is 12% of the regular selling price.

(a) What was the rate of markdown at which the radio was sold?
(b) What was the operating profit or loss?
(c) What rate of markup based on cost was realized?
(d) What was the rate of markup based on the sale price?

4. An automatic dishwasher cost a dealer $620 less 37½% and 4%. It is regularly priced at $558. The dealer's overhead expense is 15% of the regular selling price and the dishwasher was cleared out for $432.45.

(a) What was the rate of markdown at which the dishwasher was sold?
(b) What is the regular markup based on selling price?
(c) What was the operating profit or loss?
(d) What rate of markup based on cost was realized?

5. A hardware store paid $33.45 for a set of cookware. Overhead expense is 15% of the regular selling price and profit is 10% of the regular selling price. During a clearance sale, the set was sold at a markdown of 15%. What was the operating profit or loss on the sale?

6. Aldo's Shoes bought a shipment of 200 pairs of women's shoes for $42 per pair. The store sold 120 pairs at the regular selling price of $125 per pair, 60 pairs at a clearance sale at a discount of 40%, and the remaining pairs during an inventory sale at a price that equals cost plus overhead (i.e., a break-even price). The store's overhead is 50% of cost.

(a) What was the price at which the shoes were sold during the clearance sale?
(b) What was the selling price during the inventory sale?
(c) What was the total profit realized on the shipment?
(d) What was the average rate of markup based on cost that was realized on the shipment?

7. The Pottery Store bought 600 pans auctioned off for $4950. This means that each pan has the same cost. On inspection, the pans were classified as normal quality, seconds, or substandard. The 360 normal-quality pans were sold at a markup of 80% of cost, the 190 pans classified as seconds were sold at a markup of 20% of cost, and the remaining pans classified as substandard were sold at 20% below their cost.

(a) What was the unit price at which each of the three classifications was sold?
(b) If overhead is 33⅓% of cost, what was the amount of profit realized on the purchase?
(c) What was the average rate of markup based on the selling price at which the pans were sold?

8. A clothing store buys shorts for $24 less 40% for buying over 50 pairs, and less a further 16⅔% for buying last season's style. The shorts are marked up to cover overhead expenses of 25% of cost and a profit of 33⅓% of cost.

(a) What is the regular selling price of the shorts?
(b) What is the maximum amount of markdown in dollars to break even?
(c) What is the rate of markdown if the shorts are sold at the break-even price?

9. Furniture City bought chairs for $75 less 33⅓%, 20%, and 10%. The store's overhead is 75% of cost and net profit is 25% of cost.

   (a) What is the regular selling price of the chairs?
   (b) At what price can the chairs be put on sale so that the store incurs an operating loss of no more than 33⅓% of the overhead?
   (c) What is the maximum rate of markdown at which the chairs can be offered for sale in part (b)?

10. Bargain City clothing store purchased raincoats for $36.75. The store requires a markup of 30% of the sale price. What regular selling price should be marked on the raincoats if the store wants to offer a 25% discount without reducing its markup?

11. A jewellery store paid $36.40 for a watch. Store expenses are 24% of regular selling price and the normal net profit is 20% of regular selling price. During a special bargain day sale, the watch was sold at a discount of 15%. What operating profit or loss was realized on the sale?

12. The Outdoor Shop buys tents for $264 less 25% for buying more than 20 tents. The store operates on a markup of 33⅓% of the sale price and advertises that all merchandise is sold at a discount of 20% of the regular selling price. What is the regular selling price of the tents?

13. Sky Sales Inc. purchased portable communication devices listed at $198 less 60% and 16⅔%. Expenses are 45% of the regular selling price and net profit is 25% of the regular selling price. According to the company's pricing strategy, the merchandise is marked with a price that allows it to advertise a 37.5% discount while still maintaining its usual markup. During the annual inventory sale, the unsold equipment was marked down 55% of the marked price. What operating profit or loss was realized on the devices sold during the sale?

14. Lund's Pro Shop purchased sets of golf clubs for $500 less 40% and 16⅔%. Expenses are 20% of the regular selling price and the required profit is 17.5% of the regular selling price. The store decided to place a marked price on the clubs that allows it to offer a 36% discount without affecting its margin. At the end of the season, the unsold sets were advertised at a discount of 54% of the new regular selling price. What operating profit or loss was realized on the sets sold at the end of the season?

15. Big Boy Appliances bought self-cleaning ovens for $900 less 33⅓% and 5%. Expenses are 15% of the regular selling price and profit is 9% of the regular selling price. For competitive reasons, the store marks all merchandise with a price so that a discount of 25% can be advertised without affecting the margin. To promote sales, the ovens were marked down 40%. What operating profit or loss did the store make on the ovens sold during the sales promotion?

16. Blue Lake Marina sells a make of cruiser for $16 800. This regular selling price covers overhead of 15% of cost and a normal net profit of 10% of cost. The cruisers were marked with a price that allowed the marina to offer a 20% discount while still maintaining its regular gross profit. At the end of the boating season, the cruiser was marked down. The marina made 25% of its usual profit and reduced the usual commission paid to the sales personnel by 33⅓%. The normal commission accounts for 50% of the normal overhead. What was the rate of markdown?

BUSINESS MATH **NEWS**
lululemon athletica inc. Announces Third Quarter Fiscal 2018 Results

lululemon athletica, a high-end retail chain dedicated to yoga and fitness apparel, recently experienced several years of record growth.

Founded and headquartered in Vancouver, British Columbia, lululemon manufactures and sells technical athletic wear aimed primarily at active men and women who are willing to pay premium prices for workout gear. These high prices have allowed the retailer to maintain a gross margin annually above 50% since 2003.

Although the initial goal was to have only one store, consumer demand has resulted in multiple locations. Most stores are located in major cities in Canada, the United States, Australia, New Zealand, and the United Kingdom, as well as in Singapore. lululemon's huge sales growth can be largely attributed to the company's extensive store expansion.

To reach even more customers, lululemon launched a successful e-commerce operation on its company website in 2009. After posting its best-ever first quarter, lululemon said that its priorities were to grow existing stores and to invest more in its thriving online division. On its company website, Lululemon reported a 30% increase in traffic to its e-commerce site in 2018 with its e-commerce efforts netting US $476.9 million in sales, compared to US $421.1 million the year before.

The company offers regular-priced in-store products online. It also offers discounted men's and women's athletic wear under its "we made too much" clearance link.

The following items were recently discounted on the lululemon website:
Women's Wunder Under Pant: $69.00 CAD (was $88.00)
Women's Get Started Jacket: $49 CAD (was $118.00)
Men's Cardio SS Tech Top: $24.00 CAD (was $58.00)
Men's Performance Jacket: $44.00 CAD (was $88.00)

QUESTIONS

1. lululemon athletica inc. reported that its net revenue for the third quarter of 2018 was $747.7 million, an increase of 21% compared to the third quarter of fiscal 2017. Calculate the net revenue for the third quarter of 2017 (rounded to the nearest hundred thousand dollars).

2. Calculate e-commerce revenue as a percentage of total revenue for the period.

3. Calculate the rate of discount for each of the four clearance items listed under the "we made too much" link (rounded to 2 decimal places).

4. Assuming lululemon's overhead is 30% of the regular selling price, and that the cost of the Women's Wonder Under Pant is $36, determine
   (a) the markup, the overhead, and the profit for this item sold at the regular selling price;
   (b) the markup, the overhead, and the profit for this item sold at the clearance price.

Source: lululemon athletica inc., "lululemon athletica inc. Announces Third Quarter Fiscal 2018 Results," press release, December 6, 2018, http://investor.lululemon.com/news-releases/news-release-details/lululemon-athletica-inc-announces-third-quarter-fiscal-2018-0.

MyLab Math Visit MyLab Math to practise any of this chapter's exercises marked with a 🌐 as often as you want. The guided solutions help you calculate an answer step by step. You'll find a personalized study plan and additional interactive resources to help you master Business Math!

REVIEW EXERCISE

1. **LO①** A toolbox is listed for $56 less 25%, 20%, and 5%.

   (a) What is the net price of the toolbox?

   (b) What is the amount of discount?

   (c) What is the single rate of discount that was allowed?

🌐 2. **LO①** Compute the rate of discount allowed on a lawnmower that lists for $168 and is sold for $105.

3. **LO②** Determine the single rate of discount equivalent to the discount series 35%, 12%, and 5%.

🌐 4. **LO①** A 40% discount allowed on an article amounts to $1.44. What is the net price?

5. **LO①** Baton Supplies has been selling skateboard decks for $112 less 15%. What additional discount percent must the company offer to meet a competitor's price of $80.92?

🌐 6. **LO①** A freezer was sold during a clearance sale for $387.50. If the freezer was sold at a discount of $16^2/_3$%, what was the list price?

7. **LO①** The net price of a snow shovel is $20.40 after discounts of 20% and 15%. What is the list price?

🌐 8. **LO③** On May 18, an invoice dated May 17 for $4000 less 20% and 15%, terms 5/10 E.O.M., was received by Aldo Distributors.

   (a) What is the last day of the discount period?

   (b) What is the amount due if the invoice is paid within the discount period?

🌐 9. **LO③** Air Yukon received a shipment of plastic trays on September 2. The invoice amounting to $25 630 was dated August 15, terms 2/10, n/30 R.O.G. What is the last day for taking the cash discount and how much is to be paid if the discount is taken?

🌐 10. **LO③** What amount must be remitted if the following invoices, all with terms 5/10, 2/30, n/60, are paid together on December 8?
Invoice No. 312 dated November 2 for $923.00

Invoice No. 429 dated November 14 for $784.00
Invoice No. 563 dated November 30 for $873.00

11. **LO③** Delta Furnishings received an invoice dated May 10 for a shipment of goods received June 21. The invoice was for $8400.00 less $33^1/_3$% and $12^1/_2$% with terms 3/20, R.O.G. How much must Delta pay on July 9 to reduce its debt

   (a) by $2000?

   (b) to $2000?

🌐 12. **LO③** The Peel Trading Company received an invoice dated September 20 for $16 000 less 25% and 20%, terms 5/10, 2/30, n/60. Peel made a payment on September 30 to reduce the debt to $5000 and a payment on October 20 to reduce the debt by $3000.

   (a) What amount must Peel remit to pay the balance of the debt at the end of the credit period?

   (b) What is the total amount paid by Peel?

13. **LO③** Emco Ltd. received an invoice dated May 5 for $4000 less 15% and $7^1/_2$%, terms 3/15 E.O.M. A cheque for $1595.65 was mailed by Emco on June 15 as part payment of the invoice.

   (a) By how much did Emco reduce the amount due on the invoice?

   (b) How much does Emco still owe?

🌐 14. **LO④** Homeward Hardware buys cat litter for $6 less 20% per bag. The store's overhead is 45% of cost and the owner requires a profit of 20% of cost.

   (a) For how much should the bags be sold?

   (b) What is the amount of markup included in the selling price?

   (c) What is the rate of markup based on selling price?

   (d) What is the rate of markup based on cost?

   (e) What is the break-even price?

   (f) What operating profit or loss is made if a bag is sold for $7.50?

15. **LO④** A retail store realizes a markup of $31.50 if it sells an article at a markup of 35% of the selling price.

   (a) What is the regular selling price?

   (b) What is the cost?

   (c) What is the rate of markup based on cost?

(d) If overhead expense is 28% of cost, what is the total cost?

(e) If the article is sold at a markdown of 24%, what is the operating profit or loss?

16. **LO4** Using a markup of 35% of cost, a store priced a book at $8.91.

(a) What was the cost of the book?

(b) What is the markup as a percent of selling price?

17. **LO4** A bicycle helmet costing $54.25 was marked up to realize a markup of 30% of the regular selling price.

(a) What was the regular selling price?

(b) What was the markup as a percent of cost?

18. **LO4** A bedroom suite that cost a dealer $1800 less 37.5% and 18% carries a price tag with a regular selling price at a markup of 120% of cost. For quick sale, the bedroom suite was marked down 40%.

(a) What was the sale price?

(b) What rate of markup based on cost was realized?

19. **LO4** Gino's purchased men's suits for $195 less $33^1/_3$%. The store operates at a normal markup of 35% of regular selling price. The owner marks all merchandise with prices so that the store can offer a $16^2/_3$% discount while maintaining the same gross profit. What is the marked price?

20. **LO4** An appliance store sold GE coffeemakers for $22.95 during a promotional sale. The store bought the coffeemakers for $36 less 40% and 15%. Overhead is 25% of the regular selling price.

(a) If the store's markup is 40% of the regular selling price, what was the rate of markdown?

(b) What operating profit or loss was made during the sale?

(c) What rate of markup based on cost was realized?

21. **LO5** Billington's buys shirts for $21 less 25% and 20%. The shirts are priced at a regular selling price to cover expenses of 20% of regular selling price and a profit of 17% of regular selling price. For a special weekend sale, shirts were marked down 20%.

(a) What was the operating profit or loss on the shirts sold during the weekend sale?

(b) What rate of markup was realized based on cost?

22. **LO5** A jewellery store paid a unit price of $250 less 40%, $16^2/_3$%, and 8% for a shipment of designer watches. The store's overhead is 65% of cost and the normal profit is 55% of cost.

(a) What is the regular selling price of the watches?

(b) What must the sale price be for the store to break even?

(c) What is the rate of markdown to sell the watches at the break-even price?

23. **LO5** Sight and Sound bought large-screen colour TV sets for $1080.00 less $33^1/_3$% and $8^1/_3$%. Overhead is 18% of regular selling price and required profit is $15^1/_3$% of regular selling price. The TV sets were marked at a price so that the store was able to advertise a discount of 25% while still maintaining its margin. To clear the inventory, the remaining TV sets were marked down $37^1/_2$%.

(a) What operating profit or loss is realized at the clearance price?

(b) What is the realized rate of markup based on cost?

24. **LO1** Ward Fitness lists a treadmill at $1860 less $33^1/_3$% and 15%. To meet competition, Ward wants to reduce its net price to $922.25. What additional percent discount must Ward allow?

25. **LO5** South Side Appliances bought bread makers for $180 less 40%, $16^5/_6$%, and 10%. The store's overhead is 45% of regular selling price and the profit required is $21^1/_4$% of the regular selling price. During a year-end inventory clearance sale, the store marked down the bread makers by 30%.

(a) What was the regular selling price?

(b) What is the sale price?

(c) What is the profit or loss during the clearance sale?

26. **LO6** A merchant realizes a markup of $42 by selling an item at a markup of 37.5% of cost. The merchant's overhead expenses are 17.5% of the

regular selling price. At a promotional sale, the item was reduced in price to $138.95.

(a) What is the regular selling price?

(b) What is the rate of markup based on the regular selling price?

(c) What is the rate of markdown?

(d) What is the profit or loss during the promotional sale?

27. **LO❹** The Knit Shoppe bought 250 sweaters for $3100; 50 sweaters were sold at a markup of

150% of cost and 120 sweaters at a markup of 75% of cost; 60 of the sweaters were sold during a clearance sale for $15 each; and the remaining sweaters were disposed of at 20% below cost. Assume all sweaters had the same cost.

(a) What was the amount of markup realized on the purchase?

(b) What was the percent markup realized based on cost?

(c) What was the percent of gross profit realized based on selling price?

SELF-TEST

1. Determine the net price of an article listed at $590 less 37.5%, 12.5%, and $8\frac{1}{3}$%.

2. What rate of discount has been allowed if an item that lists for $270 is sold for $168.75?

3. Compute the single discount percent equivalent to the discount series 40%, 10%, and $8\frac{1}{3}$%.

4. Discount Electronics lists an article for $1020 less 25% and 15%. A competitor carries the same article for $927 less 25%. What further discount (correct to the nearest $\frac{1}{10}$ of 1%) must the competitor allow so that its net price is the same as Discount's?

5. What total amount must be remitted if the following invoices, all with terms 4/10, 2/30, n/60, are paid on May 10?
   $850 less 20% and 10% dated March 21
   $960 less 30% and $16\frac{2}{3}$% dated April 10
   $1040 less $33\frac{1}{3}$%, 25%, and 5% dated April 30

6. An invoice for $3200, dated March 20, terms 3/10 E.O.M., was received March 23. What payment must be made on April 10 to reduce the debt to $1200?

7. On January 15, Sheridan Service received a shipment with an invoice dated January 14, terms 4/10 E.O.M., for $2592. On February 9, Sheridan Service mailed a cheque for $1392 in partial payment of the invoice. By how much did Sheridan Service reduce its debt?

8. What is the regular selling price of an item purchased for $1270 if the markup is 20% of the regular selling price?

9. The regular selling price of merchandise sold in a store includes a markup of 40% based on the regular selling price. During a sale, an item that cost the store $180 was marked down 20%. For how much was the item sold?

10. An item that cost the dealer $350 less 35% and 12.5% carries a regular selling price on the tag at a markup of 150% of cost. For quick sale, the item was reduced 30%. What was the sale price?

11. An article cost $900 and sold for $2520. What was the percent markup based on cost?

12. Determine the cost of an item sold for $1904 to realize a markup of 40% based on cost.

13. A markup of $90 is made on a sale. If the markup was 45% based on selling price, what was the cost?

14. A surf shop reduces the price of a paddle board for quick sale from $1560 to $1195. Compute the markdown correct to the nearest $\frac{1}{100}$ of 1%.

15. A retailer buys an appliance for $1480 less 25% and 15%. The store prices the merchandise at a regular selling price to cover expenses of 40% of the regular selling price and a net profit of 10% of the regular selling price. During a clearance sale, the appliance was sold at a markdown of 45%. What was the operating profit or loss?

16. Discount Electronics buys stereos for $830 less 37.5% and 12.5%. Expenses are 20% of cost and the required profit is 15% of the regular selling price. All merchandise is marked with a price so that the store can advertise a discount of 30% while still maintaining its regular markup. During the annual clearance sale, the new regular selling price of unsold items is marked down 50%. What operating profit or loss does the store make on items sold during the sale?

CHALLENGE PROBLEMS

1. Rose Bowl Florists buys and sells roses only by the complete dozen. The owner buys 12 dozen fresh roses daily for $117. He knows that 10% of the roses will wilt before they can be sold. What price per dozen must Rose Bowl Florists charge for its saleable roses to realize a 55% markup based on selling price?

2. A merchant bought some goods at a discount of 25% of the list price. She wants to mark them at a regular price so that she can give a discount of 20% of the marked price and still make a markup of 25% of the selling price.

   (a) At what percent of the list price should she mark the regular selling price of the goods?

   (b) Suppose the merchant decides she must make a markup of 25% of the cost price. At what percent of the regular selling price should she mark the price of the goods?

3. On April 13, a stereo store received a new sound system with a list price of $2500 from the manufacturer. The stereo store received a trade discount of 25%. The invoice, with terms 2/10, n/30, arrived on the same day as the sound system. The owner of the store marked up the sound system by 60% of the invoice amount (before cash discount) to cover overhead and profits. The owner paid the invoice on April 20. How much extra profit will be made on the sale, as a percent of the regular selling price, due to the early payment of the invoice?

CASE STUDY   Focusing on Prices

▶ Edward's Electronics is a small electronics store selling a variety of electronics equipment. It has a small but progressive camera department. Since Edward's does not sell very many cameras during the year, it only has a small number in stock. Edward's has just ordered six of the new digital cameras from Nikon. Edward's owner has been told that the cost of each camera will be $170, with terms 2/15, n/30. The manufacturer's suggested retail price (MSRP) of each camera is $400. Edward's owner calculates that the overhead is 15% of the MSRP and that the desired profit is 18% of the MSRP.

Staples Canada has a large camera shop in its store in the mall in the same town. It has ordered 70 of the same cameras from Nikon. Staples has been offered both a cash discount and a quantity discount off the list price of $170. The cash discount is 3/20, n/45, while the quantity discount is 3.5%. Staples estimates its overhead is 25% of the MSRP and it would like to make a profit of 35% of the MSRP.

QUESTIONS

1. What is the cost per camera (ignoring taxes) for Edward's Electronics and for Staples?

2. For each store, what is the minimum selling price required to cover cost, overhead, and desired profits?

3. If Edward's and Staples sell the camera at the MSRP, how much extra profit will each store make
   (a) in dollars?
   (b) as a percent of MSRP?

4. What rate of a markdown from MSRP can Edward's offer to cover its overhead and make its originally intended profit?

SUMMARY OF FORMULAS

Formula 6.1

$$\frac{\text{AMOUNT OF}}{\text{DISCOUNT}} = \frac{\text{RATE OF}}{\text{DISCOUNT}} \times \text{LIST PRICE}$$

or

$$A = dL$$

Calculating the amount of discount when the list price and discount rate are known

Formula 6.2

NET PRICE = LIST PRICE − AMOUNT OF DISCOUNT

or

$$N = L - A$$

Calculating the net amount when the list price and amount of discount are known

Formula 6.3

NET PRICE FACTOR (NPF) = $(1 - d)$

where d = rate of discount in decimal form

$$\text{NET PRICE} = \text{LIST PRICE} \times \frac{\text{NET PRICE}}{\text{FACTOR (NPF)}}$$

or

$$N = L(1 - d)$$

NPF FOR A DISCOUNT SERIES = $(1 - d_1)(1 - d_2)(1 - d_3) \ldots (1 - d_n)$

Calculating the net amount directly without computing the amount of discount

Formula 6.4

$$\text{NET PRICE} = \text{LIST PRICE} \times \frac{\text{NET PRICE FACTOR FOR}}{\text{THE DISCOUNT SERIES}}$$

or

$$\text{NET PRICE} = L(1 - d_1)(1 - d_2)(1 - d_3) \ldots (1 - d_n)$$

Calculating the net amount directly when a list price is subject to a series of discounts

Formula 6.5

SINGLE EQUIVALENT RATE OF DISCOUNT

FOR A DISCOUNT SERIES

$= 1 - $ NPF FOR THE DISCOUNT SERIES

$= 1 - \left[(1 - d_1)(1 - d_2)(1 - d_3) \ldots (1 - d_n) \right]$

Calculating the single rate of discount that has the same effect as a given series of discounts

Formula 6.6

$$\text{SELLING PRICE} = \text{COST OF BUYING} + \text{EXPENSES} + \text{PROFIT}$$

or

$$S = C + E + P$$

Basic relationship between selling price, cost of buying, operating expenses (or overhead), and profit

Formula 6.7

$$\text{MARKUP} = \text{EXPENSES} + \text{PROFIT}$$

or

$$M = E + P$$

Basic relationship between markup, operating expenses (or overhead), and profit

Formula 6.8

$$\text{SELLING PRICE} = \text{COST OF BUYING} + \text{MARKUP}$$

or

$$S = C + M$$

Basic relationship between selling price, cost of buying, and markup

Formula 6.9

$$\frac{\text{RATE OF MARKUP}}{\text{BASED ON COST}} = \frac{\text{MARKUP}}{\text{COST}} = \frac{M}{C} \times 100$$

Calculating the rate of markup as a percent of cost

Formula 6.10

$$\text{RATE OF MARKUP BASED ON SELLING PRICE} = \frac{\text{MARKUP}}{\text{SELLING PRICE}} = \frac{M}{S} \times 100$$

Calculating the rate of markup as a percent of selling price

Formula 6.11

$$\text{SALE PRICE} = \text{REGULAR SELLING PRICE} - \text{MARKDOWN}$$

$$S_R = S - MD$$

Calculating the sale price when the amount of markdown is known

Formula 6.12

$$\frac{\text{RATE OF MARKDOWN}}{} = \frac{\text{MARKDOWN}}{\text{REGULAR SELLING PRICE}} = \frac{MD}{S} \times 100$$

Calculating the rate of markdown

Formula 6.13

$$\text{SALE PRICE} = \text{REGULAR SELLING PRICE} \times \text{NPF}$$

$$S_R = S(1 - md)$$

Calculating the sale price directly without computing the amount of markdown

GLOSSARY

Absolute loss the price does not even cover the cost of buying the item *(p. 246)*

Break-even price the price equals total cost, resulting in zero profit *(p. 246)*

Cash discount a reduction in the amount of an invoice, usually to encourage prompt payment of the invoice *(p. 230)*

Credit period the time period at the end of which an invoice has to be paid *(p. 230)*

Discount a reduction from the original price *(p. 225)*

Discount period the time period during which a cash discount applies *(p. 230)*

Discount series two or more discounts taken off a list price in succession *(p. 225)*

Due date the end of the credit period *(p. 230)*

End-of-month dating (E.O.M.) payment terms based on the last day of the month in which the invoice is dated *(p. 230)*

Gross profit *see* **Markup**

List price price printed in a catalogue or in a list of prices *(p. 222)*

Manufacturer's suggested retail price (MSRP) catalogue or list price that is reduced by a trade discount *(p. 222)*

Margin *see* **Markup**

Markdown a reduction in the price of an article sold to the consumer *(p. 247)*

Marked price the sticker price of an article that is set so than an ongoing discount is deducted to determine the regular selling price *(p. 253)*

Markup the difference between the cost of merchandise and the selling price *(p. 239)*

Net factor *see* **Net price factor (NPF)**

Net price the difference between a list price and the amount of discount *(p. 223)*

Net price factor (NPF) the difference between 100% and a percent discount—the net price expressed as a fraction of the list price *(p. 224)*

Ordinary dating payment terms based on the date of an invoice *(p. 230)*

Partial payment part payment of an invoice *(p. 235)*

Payment terms a statement of the conditions under which a cash discount may be taken *(p. 230)*

Rate of discount a reduction in price expressed as a percent of the original price *(p. 230)*

Rate of markdown the relationship between the amount of the markdown and the regular selling price, stated as a percent of the regular selling price *(p. 247)*

Receipt-of-goods dating (R.O.G.) payment terms based on the date the merchandise is received *(p. 230)*

Regular selling price the price of an article sold to the consumer before any markdown is applied *(p. 247)*

Sale price the price of an article sold to the consumer after a markdown has been applied *(p. 247)*

Single equivalent rate of discount the single rate of discount that has the same effect as a specific series of discounts *(p. 226)*

Supply chain the channels or stages that a product passes through as it is converted from a raw material to a finished product purchased by the consumer *(p. 221)*

Total cost the cost at which merchandise is purchased plus the overhead *(p. 246)*

Trade discount a reduction of a catalogue or list price *(p. 222)*

Nonwarit/123RF

LEARNING OBJECTIVES

Upon completing this chapter, you will be able to do the following:

① Compute the amount of simple interest using the formula
$I = Prt$.

② Compute the principal, interest rate, or time using variations of the formula $I = Prt$.

③ Compute the maturity value (future value) using the formula
$S = P(1 + rt)$.

④ Compute the principal (present value) using the formula
$P = \dfrac{S}{1 + rt}$.

⑤ Compute equivalent or dated values for specified focal dates.

Every day in business, money is lent and borrowed for short periods of time. Businesses lend money when they extend credit to customers or clients, or when they make short-term investments. Businesses borrow money when they purchase on credit from vendors, use a line of credit from a financial institution, or use credit cards to make purchases.

If money is borrowed, interest is charged. If money is invested, interest is earned. The amount of interest earned or charged is a function of the principal (the original amount invested or borrowed). With simple interest, the principal stays constant.

Because interest is paid for the use of money, money has time value. From a practical standpoint, the time value of money is the idea that a particular sum of money in your hand today is worth more than the same sum at some future date. Would you rather have $100 today or $100 a year from now? If you take the money today, you could invest it in a risk-free Guaranteed Investment Certificate (GIC) and earn a return such that your $100 today is worth more than $100 in a year from now. Or, if you didn't invest the $100, but spent it instead, you would still be better off because of inflation. The same bag of groceries purchased today for $100 will likely cost more than $100 in a year. $100 will usually have more buying power today than in the future.

INTRODUCTION

Transactions in business often involve the daily borrowing or lending of money. To compensate the lenders for the use of their money, interest is paid. The amount of interest paid is based on three factors: the amount of money borrowed, the rate of interest at which it is borrowed, and the time period for which it is borrowed.

7.1 CALCULATING THE AMOUNT OF SIMPLE INTEREST
A. Basic concepts and formula

Interest is the fee charged for the use of money. The amount of **simple interest** is determined by the relationship

Interest = Principal × Rate × Time

$$\boxed{I = Prt} \text{————————————————— Formula 7.1}$$

where I is the amount of interest earned, measured in dollars and cents;

P is the principal sum of money earning the interest, measured in dollars and cents;

r is the simple annual (yearly or **nominal) rate** of interest, expressed as a percent, which can be converted into a decimal;

t is the **interest period** in years.

Simple interest is often used in business, through short-term loans to and from financial institutions, vendors, and customers. With simple interest, the principal stays the same throughout the term. The simple interest amount is paid only when the principal is repaid.

B. Matching *r* and *t*

While the time may be stated in days, months, or years, the rate of interest is generally stated as a yearly charge, often followed by "per annum" or "p.a." In using the simple interest formula, it is imperative that the time t correspond to the interest rate r. Time expressed in months or days often needs to be converted into years. The number of days between two dates can be determined manually or by using the DATE function on a financial calculator.

Whenever possible, the time period t should be determined using the *exact* number of days in the term.

EXAMPLE 7.1A

State r and t for each of the following:

(i) rate 6.5% p.a. (per annum); time 6 months;

(ii) rate 5.25% p.a.; time 243 days.

SOLUTION

(i) The annual rate $r = 6.5\% = 0.065$

The time in years $t = \dfrac{6}{12} = 0.5$

Note: To convert months into years, divide by 12.

(ii) The annual rate $r = 5.25\% = 0.0525$

The time in years $t = \dfrac{243}{365}$

Note: To convert days into years, divide by 365.

POINTERS
& PITFALLS

A leap year is a calendar year of 366 days. Leap years occur every four years. Even during a leap year, divide by 365 to convert days into years. Never divide by 366.

A variety of manual techniques can be used for counting the exact number of days between two given dates. For the first method, you need to recall the number of days in each month.

The number of days in each month are listed in Table 7.1.

Table 7.1 The Number of Days in Each Month

Month	Days	Month	Days	Month	Days	Month	Days
January	31	April	30	July	31	October	31
February	28*	May	31	August	31	November	30
March	31	June	30	September	30	December	31

*February has 29 days in leap years. Leap years occur every four years. The year 2000 was a leap year; so was 2004, 2008, 2016 etc.

The "count the first day but not the last day" is a commonly used approach for manual counting. Using this method, we can determine that a three-month loan from April 23 to July 21 is exactly 89 days. The term includes 8 days in April (April 23rd to April 30th inclusive), 31 days in May, 30 days in June, and 20 days in July (July 1st to 20th inclusive). We are not counting the ending date (July 21) because we assume there is a zero balance on the day you repay the loan.

A second method for calculating the number of days is to use Table 7.2. In Table 7.2, the days of the year are appointed sequential serial numbers. The number of days between any two dates in the same calendar year is simply the difference between the serial numbers of the dates.

Table 7.2 The Serial Numbers for Each Day of the Year

Day of Month	Jan	Feb	Mar	Apr	May	Jun	Jul	Aug	Sept	Oct	Nov	Dec
1	1	32	60	91	121	152	182	213	244	274	305	335
2	2	33	61	92	122	153	183	214	245	275	306	336
3	3	34	62	93	123	154	184	215	246	276	307	337
4	4	35	63	94	124	155	185	216	247	277	308	338
5	5	36	64	95	125	156	186	217	248	278	309	339
6	6	37	65	96	126	157	187	218	249	279	310	340
7	7	38	66	97	127	158	188	219	250	280	311	341
8	8	39	67	98	128	159	189	220	251	281	312	342
9	9	40	68	99	129	160	190	221	252	282	313	343
10	10	41	69	100	130	161	191	222	253	283	314	344
11	11	42	70	101	131	162	192	223	254	284	315	345
12	12	43	71	102	132	163	193	224	255	285	316	346
13	13	44	72	103	133	164	194	225	256	286	317	347
14	14	45	73	104	134	165	195	226	257	287	318	348
15	15	46	74	105	135	166	196	227	258	288	319	349
16	16	47	75	106	136	167	197	228	259	289	320	350
17	17	48	76	107	137	168	198	229	260	290	321	351
18	18	49	77	108	138	169	199	230	261	291	322	352
19	19	50	78	109	139	170	200	231	262	292	323	353
20	20	51	79	110	140	171	201	232	263	293	324	354

(Continued)

Day of Month	Jan	Feb	Mar	Apr	May	Jun	Jul	Aug	Sept	Oct	Nov	Dec
21	21	52	80	111	141	172	202	233	264	294	325	355
22	22	53	81	112	142	173	203	234	265	295	326	356
23	23	54	82	113	143	174	204	235	266	296	327	357
24	24	55	83	114	144	175	205	236	267	297	328	358
25	25	56	84	115	145	176	206	237	268	298	329	359
26	26	57	85	116	146	177	207	238	269	299	330	360
27	27	58	86	117	147	178	208	239	270	300	331	361
28	28	59	87	118	148	179	209	240	271	301	332	362
29	29	*	88	119	149	180	210	241	272	302	333	363
30	30		89	120	150	181	211	242	273	303	334	364
31	31		90		151		212	243		304		365

Note: For leap years, *February 29 becomes day number 60 and the serial number for each subsequent day in the table increases by 1.

POINTERS & PITFALLS

Another way to recall the number of days in each month is to make a fist and use the four knuckles on your left hand to determine which months have 31 vs. 30 days. The knuckles correspond to a month with 31 days, and every month that lands on a groove between the knuckles is 30 days (or 28 for February). Moving from the left, and starting with January, January has 31 days, February has 28, March has 31, and so on. When you reach the knuckle of your index finger (July – 31 days) start over. Notice then that the months alternate from long months to short months except for July and August (because both land on knuckles).

EXAMPLE 7.1B

Calculate the term for the following:

(i) a loan that is advanced on February 17, 2021, and repaid on August 11, 2021;

(ii) an investment that starts on December 1, 2022, and matures on March 3, 2023;

(iii) a six-month loan taken on January 25, 2020, and repaid on May 13, 2020.

SOLUTION

(i) Using Table 7.1 to count the number of days in each partial and full month between the dates, the term includes:

12 days in February (February 17th to February 28th inclusive)

31 days in March

30 days in April

31 days in May

30 days in June

31 days in July

10 days in August (August 1st to 10th inclusive)

12 + 31 + 30 + 31 + 30 + 31 + 10 = 175 days

Using Table 7.2, the serial number for February 17th is 48 and the serial number for August 11th is 223. The calculation for the number of days for the loan is 223 − 48 = 175 days.

(ii) Using Table 7.1, the term includes:

31 days in December, 2022 (December 1st to 31st inclusive)

31 days in January, 2023

28 days in February, 2023

2 days in March (March 1st to 2nd inclusive)

31 + 31 + 28 + 2 = 92 days

Using Table 7.2, the serial number for December 1, 2022, is 335 and the serial number for March 3, 2023, is 62. The serial number for December 31, 2022, is also important because the term includes a year-end. The calculation for the number of days for the investment is $(365 - 335) + 62 = 92$ days.

(iii) Using Table 7.1, the term includes:

7 days in January (January 25th to 31st inclusive)

29 days in February (2020 is a leap year)

31 days in March

30 days in April

12 days in May (May 1st to 12th inclusive)

$7 + 29 + 31 + 30 + 12 = 109$ days

When a date occurs after February 29th of a leap year, you must add one day to the serial number in Table 7.2. The serial number for January 25, 2020, is 25 and the serial number for May 13, 2020, is 134 (because it occurs after February 29th). The calculation for the number of days for the loan is $134 - 25 = 109$ days.

POINTERS & PITFALLS

To use the Texas Instruments BA II PLUS financial calculator to determine the number of days between two dates, choose the DATE worksheet by pressing [2nd] [DATE]. The first date, DT1, is usually the earlier date. The date format can be set to show the U.S. format, mm/dd/yy. Enter the date by choosing the one- or two-digit number representing the month, followed by a period, and then enter two digits for the day and the last two digits for the year.

Only one period is entered, between the month and the day. Press [Enter] to save the data. To move to the next label, press the down arrow. The second date, DT2, is usually the later date. Enter the second date in the same manner as the first date, with one or two digits for the number of the month, a period, two digits for the day, and two digits for the year. Following the second date is the "days between dates" (DBD) calculation. Press the down arrow to access this part of the worksheet. To show the exact days, press [CPT] (Compute) to instruct the calculator to perform the calculation. When the first date precedes the second date, the days between dates will appear as a positive number. The fourth label within the worksheet sets the calculator to show the actual number of days between the dates indicated, including adjustments for leap years. Set this label to ACT by pressing [2nd] [SET].

For example, to determine the number of days between April 23, 2022, and July 21, 2022, press

[2nd]	[DATE]	DT1	04.2322	[Enter]	↓
		DT2	07.2122	[Enter]	↓
[CPT]		DBD		Result is 89	

Note that the month is entered first, with one or two digits, followed by a period; the day is entered using two digits; and then the year is entered using two digits.

If only one of the dates and the desired days between the dates are entered, it is possible to determine the second date.

C. Computing the amount of interest

When the principal, rate, and time are known, the amount of interest can be determined by Formula 7.1, where I = Prt.

EXAMPLE 7.1C

Compute the amount of interest for
  (i) $3600 at 6.25% p.a. (per annum) for 1 year;
  (ii) $5240 at 4.5% p.a. for 9 months;
  (iii) $1923.60 at 3% p.a. for 215 days.

SOLUTION

(i) P = $3600.00; r = 6.25% = 0.0625; t = 1
   I = Prt = (3600.00)(0.0625)(1) = $225.00

(ii) P = $5240.00; r = 4.5% = 0.045; t = 9 months = $\frac{9}{12}$

   $I = Prt = (5240.00)(0.045)\left(\frac{9}{12}\right) = \$176.85$

(iii) P = $1923.60; r = 3% = 0.03; t = 215 days = $\frac{215}{365}$

   $I = Prt = (1923.60)(0.03)\left(\frac{215}{365}\right) = \$33.99$

Note: The resulting answers have been rounded to two decimal places, as dollars and cents.

EXAMPLE 7.1D

Compute the amount of interest on $785.95 borrowed at 8% p.a. from January 30, 2022, until March 21, 2022.

SOLUTION

Number of days = 50

   $P = \$785.95;\quad r = 8\% = 0.08;\quad t = \frac{50}{365}$

   $I = (785.95)(0.08)\left(\frac{50}{365}\right) = \$8.61$

EXAMPLE 7.1E

Compute the amount of interest on $1240 earning 6% p.a. from September 30, 2020, to May 16, 2021.

SOLUTION

The starting date is September 30, 2020 (DT1). The ending date is May 16, 2021 (DT2).
Days between dates (DBD) = 228

   $P = \$1240.00;\quad r = 6\% = 0.06;\quad t = \frac{228}{365}$

   $I = (1240.00)(0.06)\left(\frac{228}{365}\right) = \$46.47$

Alternatively, use Table 7.2 to calculate the term.

The year 2020 is a leap year, so add 1 to each serial number for 2020 dates after February 29th. Therefore, the serial number for September 30, 2020, is 274 and the serial number for December 31, 2020, is 366. The serial number for May 16, 2021, is 136. Number of days between dates is (366 − 274) + 136 = 228 days.

D. Using Excel's ACCRINT

If you choose, you can use Excel's ACCRINT function to answer some questions in this section. This function calculates the amount of interest when the time is given in days. Another Excel function, COUPDAYSNC (days between dates), determines the number of days between two dates.

The ACCRINT function in Excel is illustrated in Example 7.1C (iii).

	A	B	C
1	**ACCRINT Function**		
2			
3	**Issue Date**	January 1, 2021	
4	**First Interest Date**	January 1, 2021	
5	**Settlement Date**	August 4, 2021	
6	**Interest Rate**	3%	
7	Value	$1,923.60	
8	**Frequency**	1	
9	Basis	3	
10	Answer	$33.99	
11			

EXERCISE 7.1   MyLab Math

1. On April 1, 2021, Faircloud Variety Company deposited $24 000 into a savings account earning simple interest of 1.5%. How much interest was paid to Faircloud's account on June 30, 2021?

2. On July 17, 2021, Leah deposited $1500 into a savings account that earned simple interest of 1.05%. How much interest was earned and paid into Leah's account on December 1, 2021?   Reference Example 7.1C

3. Kenneth borrowed $8100 to buy a car. If interest was charged on the loan at 7.7%, how much interest would he have to pay in 90 days?

4. Lin Yan borrowed $1800 from her parents to finance a vacation. If interest was charged on the loan at 5.2%, how much interest would she have to pay in 220 days?
Reference Example 7.1D

5. David deposited $1700.00 into a savings account earning interest at 3.4% per annum. After 160 days, how much interest had the deposit earned?

6. Reena had an balance of $200 on her personal loan that charged interest at 8.4% p.a. She paid the balance, plus interest, after 58 days. How much interest did she have to pay?

7. A bank loan of $3000 charged 8% p.a. If the money was borrowed on November 3, and the loan was paid December 1, how much interest was charged?

8. RMB Equipment charged interest at 2% p.a. on overdue accounts. An invoice for $21 000, plus interest, was paid 35 days past the due date. How much interest was paid?

🌐 **9.** Calculate the amount of interest earned on a \$635.00 deposit at 6.5% p.a. between October 2, 2023, and August 4, 2024.

10. Ethan's grandmother deposited \$5000 for him in a savings account on his fifteenth birthday on March 30, 2021. How much interest would he have earned in the account by his eighteenth birthday assuming an interest rate of 2.5% p.a.?

11. Paolo took a loan of \$15 160 on January 26, 2021, at a rate of 8.25%. He repaid the loan on July 8, 2021. What is the interest due on the repayment date?

12. How much interest will you pay on a debt of \$7500 if you are paying the loan off in 13 months? Your loan rate is 6.375%.

13. On May 2, 2019, Seth deposited the \$245 he received in a savings account that had a simple interest rate of 1.4% p.a. How much interest was earned and paid into his account by May 2, 2020?

14. Speed Mobile deposited \$68 450 into an account that had a simple interest rate of 1.9% on December 28, 2019. On January 2, 2021, how much interest had been earned on that deposit?

7.2 CALCULATING THE PRINCIPAL, RATE, OR TIME
A. Formulas derived from the simple interest formula

The simple interest formula $I = Prt$ contains the four variables I, P, r, and t. If any three of the four are given, the value of the unknown variable can be computed by substituting the known values into the $I = Prt$ formula. The formula can also be rearranged in order to isolate the unknown variable P, r or t first, and then solved by substituting the known values into that derived formula.

The three derived formulas are as follows:

(i) To determine the principal P,

$$P = \frac{I}{rt}$$

(ii) To determine the rate of interest r,

$$r = \frac{I}{Pt}$$

(iii) To determine the time period t,

$$t = \frac{I}{Pr}$$

Note:

(a) In (ii), if the time period t is expressed in years, the value of r represents an annual rate of interest in decimal form.

(b) In (iii), if the rate of interest r is an annual rate, the value of t represents years in decimal form.

POINTERS & PITFALLS

This diagram is a useful aid in remembering the various forms of the simple interest formula $I = Prt$. Anything on the same line is multiplied together. Anything on different lines is divided.

For example, in solving for P, note that I is above the r and t. Also note that r and t are on the same line.

Therefore, $P = \dfrac{I}{rt}$.

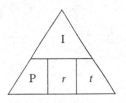

B. Calculating the principal

When the amount of interest, the rate of interest, and the time period are known, the principal can be determined.

EXAMPLE 7.2A   What principal will earn interest of $18.20 at 3.25% in 8 months?

SOLUTION $I = 18.20; \quad r = 3.25\%; \quad t = \dfrac{8}{12}$

(i) Using the formula $I = Prt$,

$18.20 = (P)(0.0325)\left(\dfrac{8}{12}\right)$ —————— by substitution

$18.20 = (P)(0.021\dot{6})$ —————— $(0.0325)\left(\dfrac{8}{12}\right)$

$P = \dfrac{18.20}{0.021\dot{6}}$ —————— divide 18.20 by the coefficient of P

$= \$840.00$

(ii) Using the derived formula $P = \dfrac{I}{rt}$,

$P = \dfrac{18.20}{(0.0325)\left(\frac{8}{12}\right)}$ —————— by substitution

$= \dfrac{18.20}{0.021\dot{6}} = \$840.00$

EXAMPLE 7.2B   Determine the amount of money that must be invested for 245 days at 5.75% to earn $42.46.

SOLUTION $I = 42.46; \quad r = 5.75\% = 0.0575; \quad t = \dfrac{245}{365}$

(i) Using the formula $I = Prt$,

$42.46 = (P)(0.0575)\left(\dfrac{245}{365}\right)$

$42.46 = (P)(0.038596)$

$P = \dfrac{42.46}{0.038596} = \$1100.12$

(ii) Using the derived formula $P = \dfrac{I}{rt}$,

$$P = \frac{42.46}{(0.0575)\left(\frac{245}{365}\right)} = \$1100.12$$

C. Calculating the rate

When the amount of interest, the principal, and the time period are known, the rate of interest can be determined.

EXAMPLE 7.2C   Calculate the annual rate of interest required for $744 to earn $54.25 in 10 months.

SOLUTION $I = 54.25;\quad P = 744.00;\quad t = \dfrac{10}{12}$

(i) Using the formula $I = Prt$,

$$54.25 = (744)(r)\left(\frac{10}{12}\right)$$
$$54.25 = (620)(r)$$
$$r = \frac{54.25}{620} = 0.0875 = 8.75\% \text{—————————— convert to a percent}$$

(ii) Using the derived formula $r = \dfrac{I}{Pt}$,

$$r = \frac{54.25}{(744.00)\left(\frac{10}{12}\right)}$$
$$= \frac{54.25}{620} = 0.0875 = 8.75\%$$

D. Calculating the time

When the amount of interest, the principal, and the rate of interest are known, the time period can be determined.

EXAMPLE 7.2D   Determine the number of years required for $745 to earn $59.60 simple interest at 8% p.a.

SOLUTION $I = 59.60;\quad P = 745.00;\quad r = 8\% = 0.08$

(i) Using the formula $I = Prt$,

$$59.60 = (745.00)(0.08)(t)$$
$$59.60 = (59.60)(t)$$
$$t = \frac{59.60}{59.60}$$
$$= 1 \text{ (year)}$$

(ii) Using the derived formula $t = \dfrac{I}{Pr}$,

$$t = \frac{59.60}{(745.00)(0.08)}$$

$$= 1 \text{ (year)}$$

Note: The value of t in the formula $I = Prt$ will be in years. If the time period is to be stated in months or in days, it is necessary to multiply the initial value of t by 12 for months or 365 for days.

EXAMPLE 7.2E

Determine the number of months required for a deposit of $1320 to earn $16.50 interest at 3.75%.

SOLUTION

$I = 16.50; \quad P = 1320.00; \quad r = 3.75 = 0.0375$

(i) Using the formula $I = Prt$,

$$16.50 = (1320.00)(0.0375)(t)$$

$$16.50 = (49.50)(t)$$

$$t = \frac{16.50}{49.50}$$

$$= 0.\dot{3} \text{ years}$$

$$= (0.\dot{3})(12) \text{ months} \hspace{2cm}\text{— convert to months}$$

$$= 4 \text{ months}$$

(ii) Using the derived formula $t = \dfrac{I}{Pr}$,

$$t = \frac{16.50}{(1320.00)(0.0375)} \text{ years}$$

$$= \frac{16.50}{49.50} \text{ years} = \frac{1}{3} \text{ years}$$

$$= \left(\frac{1}{3}\right)(12) \text{ months} = 4 \text{ months}$$

EXAMPLE 7.2F

For how many days would a loan of $1500 be outstanding to earn interest of $36.16 at 5.5% p.a.?

SOLUTION

$I = 36.16; \quad P = 1500.00; \quad r = 5.5\% = 0.055$

(i) Using the formula $I = Prt$,

$$36.16 = (1500.00)(0.055)(t)$$

$$36.16 = (82.50)(t)$$

$$t = \frac{36.16}{82.50}$$

$$= 0.438\overline{303} \text{ years}$$

$$= (0.438\overline{303})(365) \text{ days} \hspace{2cm}\text{— convert to days}$$

$$= 159.980\overline{6} \text{ days} = 160 \text{ days}$$

(ii) Using the derived formula $t = \dfrac{I}{Pr}$,

$$t = \frac{36.16}{(1500.00)(0.055)} \text{ years}$$
$$= \frac{36.16}{82.50} \text{ years}$$
$$= 0.438303 \text{ years}$$
$$= (0.438303)(365) \text{ days} = 159.9806 \text{ days}$$
$$= 160 \text{ days}$$

POINTERS & PITFALLS

The variable t is always an integer. It is important to note in this calculation that in most instances the interest (I) earned or charged to the account has been rounded to two decimals. This will cause the calculation of t to be slightly imprecise. Therefore, when calculating t, it is possible that decimals close to an integer (such as 128.998 days or 130.012 days) may show up. These decimals should be rounded to the nearest integer to correct for the rounded interest amount.

EXERCISE 7.2   MyLab Math

Determine the value indicated for each of the following:

1. Calculate the principal that will earn $148.32 at 6.75% in eight months.

   Reference Example 7.2A

2. Determine the deposit that must be made to earn $39.27 in 225 days at 2.75%.

   Reference Example 7.2B

3. A loan of $880 can be repaid in 15 months by paying the principal sum borrowed plus $104.50 interest. What was the rate of interest charged?

4. Joan borrowed $650 and is to repay the balance plus interest of $23.70 in seven months. What was the rate of interest charged?   Reference Example 7.2C

5. At what rate of interest will $1387 earn $63.84 in 200 days?

6. A deposit of $2400 will earn $22.74 in 91 days at what rate of interest?

7. In how many months will $1290 earn $100.51 interest at $8\frac{1}{2}$%?

   Reference Example 7.2E

8. Interest of $20.95 is earned at 3.15% on a deposit of $2660 in how many months?

9. Determine the number of days it will take $564 to earn $15.09 at $7\frac{3}{4}$%.

   Reference Example 7.2F

10. How many days will it take $1200 to earn $12.22 interest at 16.9%?

11. What principal will earn $39.96 interest from June 18, 2021, to December 15, 2021, at 9.25%?

12. What rate of interest is required for $740.48 to earn $42.49 interest from September 9, 2022, to March 4, 2023?

🌐 **13.** Philip wants to supplement his pension by $2000 per month with income from his investments. His investments pay him monthly and earn 6% p.a. What value of investments must Philip have in his portfolio to generate enough interest to give him his desired income?

🌐 **14.** Bunny's Antiques received $88.47 interest on a 120-day term deposit of $7800. At what rate of interest was the term deposit invested?

🌐 **15.** Anne's Dress Shop borrowed $3200 to buy material. The loan was paid off seven months later by a lump-sum payment that included $168 of interest. What was the simple rate of interest at which the money was borrowed?

🌐 **16.** Mac's line of credit statement included $360 in cash advances and $3.20 in interest charges. The interest rate on the statement was 13.5%. For how many days was Mac charged interest?

17. Bill filed his income tax return with the Canada Revenue Agency (CRA) after the April 30 deadline. He calculated that he owed the CRA $3448, but did not include a payment for this amount when he sent in his tax return. The CRA's Notice of Assessment indicated agreement with Bill's tax calculation. It also showed that the balance due was $3827.66, which included a 10% late-filing penalty and interest at 9% p.a. For how many days was Bill charged interest?

7.3 COMPUTING FUTURE VALUE (MATURITY VALUE)
A. Basic concept

When you borrow money, you are obligated to repay, at some point in the future, both the sum borrowed (the principal) and any interest due. Therefore, the **future value of a sum of money** (or **maturity value**) is the value obtained by adding the original principal and the interest due. The traditional simple interest symbols P, for principal, and S, for sum, are used in this text for calculating future value.

> FUTURE VALUE (OR MATURITY VALUE) = PRINCIPAL + INTEREST
>
> $$S = P + I$$

———— **Formula 7.2**

EXAMPLE 7.3A Determine the future value (maturity value), principal, or interest as indicated.

(i) The principal is $2200 and the interest is $240. Determine the future value (maturity value).

SOLUTION

P = 2200.00;   I = 240.00

$$S = P + I$$
$$= 2200.00 + 240.00$$
$$= \$2440.00$$

The future value is $2440.

(ii) The principal is $850 and the future value (maturity value) is $920. Compute the amount of interest.

SOLUTION

$$P = 850.00; \quad S = 920.00$$
$$S = P + I$$
$$I = S - P$$
$$I = 920.00 - 850.00$$
$$I = \$70.00$$

The amount of interest is $70.

(iii) The future value (maturity value) is $430 and the interest is $40. Compute the principal.

SOLUTION

$$S = 430.00; \quad I = 40.00$$
$$S = P + I$$
$$P = S - I$$
$$P = 430.00 - 40.00$$
$$P = \$390.00$$

The principal is $390.

B. The future value formula S = P(1 + rt)

To obtain the future value (maturity value) formula for simple interest, the formulas $I = Prt$ and $S = P + I$ are combined.

$$S = P + I$$
$$S = P + Prt \quad \text{———————————— substitute } Prt \text{ for I}$$
$$S = P(1 + rt) \quad \text{———————————— take out the common factor P}$$
$$\boxed{S = P(1 + rt)} \quad \text{———————————— Formula 7.3}$$

POINTERS & PITFALLS

In using the formula $S = P(1 + rt)$, note the order of operations. The product of r and t is found first and 1 is added to this product. Then the value of $(1 + rt)$ is multiplied by P, the principal.

EXAMPLE 7.3B

Determine the future value (maturity value) of an investment of $720 earning 4% p.a. for 146 days.

SOLUTION

$$P = 720.00; \quad r = 4\% = 0.04; \quad t = \frac{146}{365}$$

$$S = P(1 + rt)$$
$$= (720.00)\left[1 + (0.04)\left(\frac{146}{365}\right)\right]$$
$$= (720.00)(1 + 0.016)$$
$$= (720.00)(1.016)$$
$$= \$731.52$$

The future value of the investment is $731.52.

POINTERS
& PITFALLS

When actual dates are provided, as in Example 7.3C, it is helpful to draw a timeline or time graph. Look up the serial numbers for the starting and ending dates in Table 7.2, and write them on the time graph as in Figure 7.1.

EXAMPLE 7.3C

Calculate the maturity value of a deposit of $1250 invested at 2.75% p.a. from October 15, 2021, to May 1, 2022.

SOLUTION

Figure 7.1 Time Graph for Example 7.3C (© S. A. Hummelbrunner)

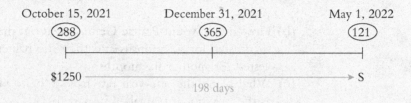

Number of days calculation using Table 7.2:

TIP: *The term of the investment includes a year-end so add December 31 to the time graph. Calculate and add the number of days prior to the year-end to the number of days following the year-end.*

The time period in days = $(365 - 288) + 121 = 198$ days

$$P = 1250.00; \quad r = 2.75\% = 0.0275; \quad t = \frac{198}{365}$$

$$S = P(1 + rt)$$

$$= (1250.00)\left[1 + (0.0275)\left(\frac{198}{365}\right)\right]$$

$$= (1250.00)(1 + 0.014918)$$

$$= (1250.00)(1.014918)$$

$$= \$1268.65$$

The maturity value of the deposit is $1268.65.

EXERCISE 7.3   MyLab Math

1. Paul invested $2500 in a 180-day term deposit at 3.45% p.a. What is the future value of the deposit?   Reference Example 7.3B

2. Suzette invested $800 in a 210-day term deposit at 2.75% p.a. What is the future value of the deposit?

3. On September 30, Red Flag Inn invested $26 750 in a short-term investment of 215 days. An investment of this length earns 1.3% p.a. How much will the investment be worth at maturity?   Reference Example 7.3C

4. Speedy Courier invested $13 500 in a 270-day term deposit. What is the maturity value if the rate of interest is 3.65%?

5. Mishu wants to invest an inheritance of $50 000 for one year. His credit union offers 3.95% for a one-year term or 3.85% for a six-month term.

   (a) How much will Mishu receive after one year if he invests at the one-year rate?
   (b) How much will Mishu receive after one year if he invests for six months at a time at 3.85% each time?
   (c) What would the one-year rate have to be to yield the same amount of interest as the investment described in part (b)?

6. Prairie Grains Cooperative wants to invest $45 000 in a short-term deposit. The bank offers 1.3% interest for a one-year term and 1.1% for a six-month term.

   (a) How much would Prairie Grains receive if the $45 000 is invested for one year?
   (b) How much would Prairie Grains receive at the end of one year if the $45 000 is invested for six months and then the principal and interest earned is reinvested for another six months?
   (c) What would the one-year rate have to be to yield the same amount of interest as the investment described in part (b)?

7. On August 15, 2021, Low Rider Automotive established a line of credit at its bank, with interest at 8.75% p.a. This line of credit was used to purchase $5000 of inventory and supplies. Low Rider paid $5113.87 to satisfy the incurred debt. On what date did Low Rider Automotive honour the line of credit?

8. Nicole will be starting university next fall. She wishes to invest $7000.00 saved from her summer job. Her bank offers 2.75% for a one-year term investment or 2.6% for a six-month term, followed by 2.9% for a second six-month term. Help Nicole investigate her options.

   (a) How much will Nicole receive after one year if she invests at the one-year rate?
   (b) How much will Nicole receive after one year if she invests for six months at a time at 2.6% and then 2.9%?
   (c) What would the one-year rate have to be to yield the same amount of interest as the investment in part (b)?

9. Eastlink Limited has a monthly payroll of $4 million. The payroll manager selects a short-term investment for the money with a 0.6% p.a. rate. At the end of one month, what is the maturity value of Eastlink's investment?

10. On August 26, 2021, Courtney's parents borrowed $4300 from a secured line of credit at their bank in order to pay Courtney's fall tuition, with interest at $4\frac{3}{8}$% p.a. On what date did Courtney's parents repay the line of credit if they ended up paying $4368.55?

11. Pierre registers for a business conference today during an early-bird sale for $449, instead of paying the full price of $499 five months from now. Had he not registered today, he would have invested the money in bonds yielding 7% return. What is his true savings?

12. According to the TD Bank's mortgage calculator, principal of $275 000 on a house that is mortgaged at a rate of 3.84% amortized over a period of 25 years will result in total interest charges of $151 773.99. A private lender is offering simple interest

for customers who do not want to pay compound interest usually associated with traditional mortgages. If the private lender wishes to earn the same amount of interest over the period of 25 years, what rate will the private lender charge its customers, if the loan is paid in equal annual installments?

7.4 CALCULATING THE PRINCIPAL (PRESENT VALUE)
A. Calculating the principal when the maturity value (future value) is known

Any sum of money that is subject to interest will increase over time. This change is called the **time value of money**. It follows a basic financial concept that suggests that money in the present is worth more than the same amount of money to be received in the future, due to its potential earning capacity right now. Money that you have now can be invested to earn interest. As such, the **present value** is the principal you need now in order to grow to that amount over a given period of time at a given rate of interest.

Since the problem of calculating the present value is equivalent to determining the principal when the future value, rate, and time are given, the future value formula $S = P(1 + rt)$ applies. However, because the problem of calculating the present value of an amount is one of the frequently recurring problems in financial analysis, it is useful to rearrange the future value formula and solve for P to obtain the present value formula.

$$S = P(1 + rt) \text{ —————— starting with the future value formula}$$

$$\frac{S}{(1 + rt)} = \frac{P(1 + rt)}{(1 + rt)} \text{ —————— divide both sides by } (1 + rt)$$

$$\frac{S}{(1 + rt)} = P \text{ —————— reduce the fraction } \frac{(1 + rt)}{(1 + rt)} \text{ to 1}$$

This is the present value formula for simple interest.

$$P = \frac{S}{(1 + rt)} \text{ ————————— Formula 7.4}$$

EXAMPLE 7.4A   Compute the value of an investment eight months before the maturity date that earns interest at 6% p.a. and has a maturity value of $884 (see Figure 7.2).

Figure 7.2 Time Graph for Example 7.4A (© S. A. Hummelbrunner)

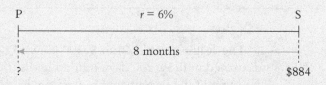

P   r = 6%   S

|———————————————————————————————————————|

|←————————————— 8 months —————————————→|

? $884

SOLUTION

$S = 884.00; \quad r = 6\% = 0.06; \quad t = \dfrac{8}{12}$

$P = \dfrac{S}{(1 + rt)}$ ———————————— use the present value formula when S is known

$P = \dfrac{884.00}{1 + (0.06)\left(\frac{8}{12}\right)}$ ———————— using Formula 7.4

$P = \dfrac{884.00}{1.04}$

$\quad = \$850.00$

The present value of the investment is \$850.00

EXAMPLE 7.4B

What sum of money must have been invested on January 31, 2020, to amount to \$7500 on August 18, 2020, at 5% p.a.?

SOLUTION

Since 2020 was a leap year, the time period in days = 200.

$P = \dfrac{S}{(1 + rt)}$ ———————————— use the present value formula when S is known

$S = 7500.00; \quad r = 5\% = 0.05; \quad t = \dfrac{200}{365}$

$P = \dfrac{7500.00}{1 + (0.05)\left(\frac{200}{365}\right)}$

$P = \dfrac{7500.00}{1.027397}$

$\quad = \$7300.00$

On January 31, 2020, the sum of \$7300.00 should have been invested.

To illustrate the concept of the time value of money, Example 7.4B is represented on the time graph shown in Figure 7.3.

Figure 7.3 Time Graph for Example 7.4B (© S. A. Hummelbrunner)

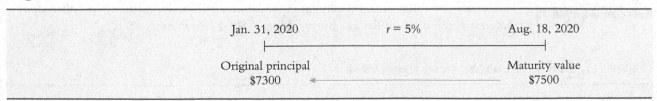

The original principal of \$7300 grew to \$7500 at 5% in 200 days. Interest of \$200 was earned in those 200 days, indicating that the original principal grew by \$1 each day. The value of the investment changed day by day. On January 31, 2020, the \$7300 principal was known as the present value of the August 18, 2020, \$7500.

EXERCISE 7.4   MyLab Math

Solve each of the following.

🌐 **1.** What principal will have a future value of $1241.86 at 3.9% in five months?

🌐 **2.** What amount of money will accumulate to $480.57 in 93 days at 4.6%?

🌐 **3.** Determine the present value of a debt of $1760 due in four months if interest at 9¾% is allowed.

4. Compute the present value of a debt of $708.13 eighty days before it is due if money is worth 5.3%.

5. Compute the amount of money that, deposited in an account on April 1, 2021, will grow to $657.58 by September 10, 2021, at 4.75% p.a.

🌐 **6.** The annual Deerfield Golf Club membership fees of $1750 are due on March 1, 2022. Club management offers reduced membership fees of 18.9% p.a. to members who pay the dues by September 1, 2021. How much must a member pay on September 1 if she chooses to take advantage of the club management's offer?

🌐 **7.** You are the accountant for Peel Credit Union. The lawyer for a member has sent a cheque for $7345.64 in full settlement of the member's loan balance including interest at 6.25% for 11 months. How much of the payment is interest?

🌐 **8.** On March 15, 2024, Ben bought a government-guaranteed short-term investment maturing on September 12, 2024. How much did Ben pay for the investment if he will receive $10 000 on September 12, 2024, and interest is 2.06%?

🌐 **9.** On October 29, 2021, Toddlers' Toys borrowed money with a promise to pay $23 520.18 on March 5, 2022. This loan included interest at 6.5%. How much money did Toddlers' Toys borrow on October 29?

10. On May 28, 2021, Ling purchased a government-guaranteed short-term investment maturing on August 4, 2021. How much did Ling pay for the investment if $10 000 will be received on August 4, 2021, and interest is 1.35% p.a.?

11. An appliance store advertises a sofa for $499.99 with nothing down, no payments, and no interest for six months. Determine the cash value the store would be willing to accept on a six-month investment, if it can earn an interest rate of 3.5%.

12. Monica purchased a government-guaranteed short-term investment for $4965.50 maturing on May 5, 2024. On what date did Monica pay for the investment if she will receive $5000 on the maturity date and interest is 2.45%?

7.5 COMPUTING EQUIVALENT VALUES
A. Dated values

If an amount of money is subject to a rate of interest, it will grow over time. Thus, the value of the amount of money changes with time. This change is known as the time value of money. For example, if you invested $1000 today at 4% p.a. simple interest, your investment has a value of $1000 today, $1010 in three months, $1020 in six months, and $1040 in one year.

The value of the original amount at any particular time is a **dated value**, or **equivalent value**, of that amount. The dated value combines the original sum with the interest earned up to the dated value date. Each dated value at a different time is equivalent to the original amount of money. The following table shows four dated values for $1000 invested at 4% p.a. The longer the time is from today, the greater is the dated value. This is so because interest has been earned on the principal over a longer time period.

Time	Dated Value
Today	$1000.00
3 months from today	$1010.00
6 months from today	$1020.00
1 year from today	$1040.00

Timberwest Company owes Abco Inc. $500 and payment is due today. Timberwest asks for an extension of four months to pay off the obligation. How much should the company expect to pay in four months' time if money is worth 6%?

Since Abco could invest the $500 at 6% p.a., Timberwest should be prepared to pay the dated value. This dated value includes interest for the additional four-month time period. It represents the amount to which the $500 will grow in four months (the future value) and is found using Formula 7.3.

$$S = P(1 + rt)$$

$$= 500.00\left[1 + (0.06)\left(\frac{4}{12}\right)\right]$$

$$= 500.00\,(1 + 0.02)$$

$$= \$510.00$$

In addition, Red Rock Construction owes Abco Inc. $824, due to be paid six months from now. Suppose Red Rock Construction offers to pay the debt today. How much should Red Rock Construction pay Abco Inc. if money is worth 6%?

Since Abco Inc. could invest the payment at 6%, the payment should be the sum of money that will grow to $824 in six months earning 6% p.a. interest. By definition, this amount of money is the present value of the $824. The present value represents today's dated value of the $824 and is found using Formula 7.4.

$$P = \frac{S}{1 + rt}$$

$$= \frac{824.00}{1 + (0.06)\left(\frac{6}{12}\right)}$$

$$= \frac{824.00}{1 + 0.03}$$

$$= \$800.00$$

Because of the time value of money, sums of money given at different times are not directly comparable. For example, imagine you are given a choice between $2000 today and $2200 one year from now. It does not automatically follow, from the point of view of investing money, that either the larger amount of money or the chronologically earlier amount of money is preferable.

To make a rational choice, we must allow for the rate of interest money can earn and choose a comparison date or **focal date** to obtain the dated values of the amounts of money at a specific time.

Equivalent values on the same date are directly comparable and may be obtained for simple interest by using either the maturity value (future value) formula, Formula 7.3, $S = P(1 + rt)$, or the present value formula, Formula 7.4, $P = \dfrac{S}{1 + rt}$.

B. Choosing the appropriate formula

The choice of which formula to use for computing dated values depends on the due date of the sum of money relative to the selected focal (or comparison) date.

(a) If the due date falls before the focal date, use the future value (maturity value) formula.

Figure 7.4 When to Use the Future Value (or Maturity Value) Formula (© S. A. Hummelbrunner)

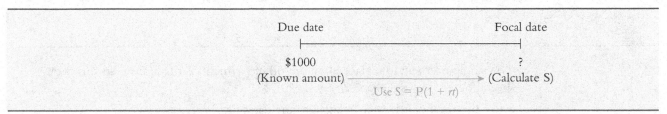

Explanation of Figure 7.4: We are looking for a future value relative to the given value. This future value will be higher than the known value by the interest that accumulates on the known value from the due date to the focal date. Because this is a future value problem (note that the arrow points to the right), the future value (or maturity value) formula $S = P(1 + rt)$ applies.

(b) If the due date falls after the focal date, use the present value formula.

Figure 7.5 When to Use the Present Value Formula (© S. A. Hummelbrunner)

Focal date   Due date
├───┤
? $1000
(Calculate P) ◄──────────────── $\dfrac{S}{1 + rt}$ ──── (Known amount)
                        Use $P = \dfrac{S}{1 + rt}$

Explanation of Figure 7.5: We are looking for an earlier value relative to the given value. This earlier value will be lower than the given value by the amount of interest that would accumulate on the unknown earlier value from the focal date to the due date. We are, in fact, looking for the principal that will grow to the given value. Because this is a present value problem (note that the arrow points to the left), the present value formula $P = \dfrac{S}{1 + rt}$ is appropriate.

C. Calculating the equivalent single payment

A series of two or more payments can be replaced by a single equivalent payment. Do not ignore the time value of money! The economic value of a dollar depends on when it is paid. To get the combined value of the individual payments, add the equivalent values at the same focal date.

EXAMPLE 7.5A

A debt can be paid off by payments of $872 one year from now and $1180 two years from now. Determine the single payment now that would fully repay the debt. Allow for simple interest at 9% p.a.

SOLUTION

See Figure 7.6 for the graphic representation of the dated values. Refer to Figures 7.4 and 7.5 to determine which formula is appropriate.

Figure 7.6 Graphical Representation of the Dated Values (© S. A. Hummelbrunner)

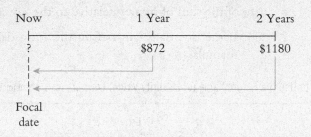

The single payment to replace all of the other payments is made now, so this date should be chosen as the *focal date*.

Since the focal date is *earlier* relative to the dates for the given sums of money (the arrows point to the left), the present value formula $P = \dfrac{S}{1 + rt}$ is appropriate.

(i)   The dated (present) value of the $872.00 at the focal date:

$$P = \frac{872.00}{1 + (0.09)(1)} = \frac{872.00}{1.09} = \$800.00$$

(ii)   The dated (present) value of the $1180.00 at the focal date:

$$P = \frac{1180.00}{1 + (0.09)(2)} = \frac{1180.00}{1.18} = \$1000.00$$

(iii)   Single payment required now = 800.00 + 1000.00 = $1800.00

EXAMPLE 7.5B

Two amounts owing from the past were to be paid today. One debt was $620 from one year ago and the other was $925 from six months ago. Determine the single payment today that would fully repay the debts. Allow for simple interest at 12% p.a.

SOLUTION

See Figure 7.7 for the graphical representation of the dated values. Refer to Figures 7.4 and 7.5 to determine which formula is appropriate.

Figure 7.7 Graphical Representation of the Dated Values (© S. A. Hummelbrunner)

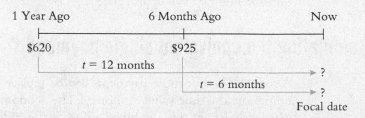

The single payment to replace all of the other payments is made now, so this date should be chosen as the *focal date*.

Since the focal date is *future* relative to the dates for the given sums of money (the arrows point to the right), the future value formula $S = P(1 + rt)$ is appropriate.

(i) The dated (future) value of the $620 at the focal date:

$$S = 620.00\left[1 + (0.12)(1)\right] = \$694.40$$

(ii) The dated (future) value of the $925 at the focal date:

$$S = 925.00\left[1 + (0.12)\left(\frac{6}{12}\right)\right] = \$980.50$$

(iii) Single payment required now $= 694.40 + 980.50 = \$1674.90$

EXAMPLE 7.5C

You are owed payments of $400 due today, $500 due in five months, and $618 due in one year. You have been approached to accept a single payment nine months from now with interest allowed at 12% p.a. How much will the single payment be? (See Figure 7.8.)

Figure 7.8 Graphical Representation of the Dated Values (© S. A. Hummelbrunner)

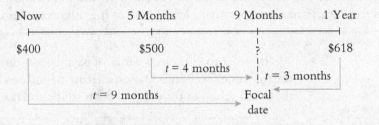

SOLUTION

The single payment to replace all of the other payments is made in nine months, so this date should be chosen as the *focal date*.

Since the focal date is in the *future* relative to the $400 now and the $500 five months from now (the arrows point to the right), the future value formula $S = P(1 + rt)$ is appropriate for these two amounts. However, since the focal date is *earlier* relative to the $618 one year from now (the arrow points to the left), the present value formula $P = \dfrac{S}{1 + rt}$ is appropriate for this amount.

(i) The dated (future) value of $400 at the focal date:

$$P = 400.00; \quad r = 12\% = 0.12; \quad t = \frac{9}{12}$$

$$S = 400\left[1 + (0.12)\left(\frac{9}{12}\right)\right] = 400(1 + 0.09) = 400(1.09) = \$436.00$$

(ii) The dated (future) value of $500 at the focal date:

$$P = 500.00; \quad r = 12\% = 0.12; \quad t = \frac{4}{12}$$

$$S = 500\left[1 + (0.12)\left(\frac{4}{12}\right)\right] = 500(1 + 0.04) = 500(1.04) = \$520.00$$

(iii) The dated (present) value of $618 at the focal date:

$$S = 618.00; \quad r = 12\% = 0.12; \quad t = \frac{3}{12}$$

$$P = \frac{618.00}{1 + (0.12)\left(\frac{3}{12}\right)}$$

$$= \frac{618.00}{1 + 0.03}$$

$$= \frac{618.00}{1.03} = \$600.00$$

(iv) The single payment to be made nine months from now will be $= 436.00 + 520.00 + 600.00 = \$1556.00$.

POINTERS & PITFALLS

A consistent error made by students when solving equivalent payment problems is to miscalculate the number of days between the focal date and the payments. So always draw a timeline. Add the known information to the diagram first and then introduce a variable such as x to represent the information you are being asked to calculate. In the following questions, when you are asked to determine an unknown payment, let the size of the unknown amount be represented by x.

In order to compare a series of payments at different points in time, it is necessary to use the same focal date. The **equation of values** at the focal date is set up by matching the dated values of the original debts to the dated values of the replacement payments.

> THE SUM OF THE DATED VALUES OF THE REPLACEMENT PAYMENTS =
> THE SUM OF THE DATED VALUES OF THE ORIGINAL SCHEDULED PAYMENTS

EXAMPLE 7.5D

Scheduled payments of $400 due now and $700 due in five months are to be settled by a payment of $500 in three months and a final payment in eight months. Determine the amount of the final payment at 6% p.a., using eight months from now as the focal date. (See Figure 7.9.)

SOLUTION

Let the value of the final payment be $x.

(i) Use a time diagram to represent the given data.

Figure 7.9 Graphical Representation of Data (© S. A. Hummelbrunner)

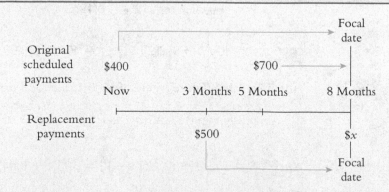

The unknown second replacement payment is made in eight months, so this date should be chosen as the *focal date*.

(ii) Dated value of the original scheduled payments:
   (a) The value at the focal date of the $400 payment due eight months before the focal date is found by using the future value formula.

$$S = 400\left[1 + (0.06)\left(\frac{8}{12}\right)\right] = 400(1 + 0.04) = 400(1.04) = \$416.00$$

   (b) The value at the focal date of the $700 payment due three months before the focal date is found by using the future value formula.

$$S = 700\left[1 + (0.06)\left(\frac{3}{12}\right)\right]$$
$$= 700(1 + 0.015)$$
$$= 700(1.015)$$
$$= \$710.50$$

(iii) Dated value of the replacement payments:
   (a) The value at the focal date of the $500 payment made five months before the focal date is found by using the future value formula.

$$S = 500\left[1 + (0.06)\left(\frac{5}{12}\right)\right]$$
$$= 500(1 + 0.025)$$
$$= 500(1.025)$$
$$= \$512.50$$

   (b) The value at the focal date of the final payment is $x (no adjustment for interest is necessary for an amount of money located at the focal date).

(iv) The equation of values at the focal date is now set up by matching the dated values of the original debts to the dated values of the replacement payments.

$$500\left[1 + (0.06)\left(\frac{5}{12}\right)\right] + x = 400\left[1 + (0.06)\left(\frac{8}{12}\right)\right] + 700\left[1 + (0.06)\left(\frac{3}{12}\right)\right]$$
$$512.50 + x = 416.00 + 710.50$$
$$512.50 + x = 1126.50$$
$$x = 1126.50 - 512.50$$
$$x = 614.00$$

The final payment to be made in eight months is $614.

D. Calculating the value of two or more equivalent payments

Sometimes you might be interested in changing a schedule of payments of irregular amounts to equivalent values at a single date. The equation of values will be used to determine the equivalent values, but to carry out your calculations you need to determine a focal date and the dates of the equivalent values. To make your calculations easier, choose as your focal date the date of one of the equivalent values.

EXAMPLE 7.5E

Jeremy had two equal outstanding loans, one from 63 days ago and one from 105 days ago. He repaid both loans today with the single amount of $3700. If interest is 9% on the loans, what was the size of the equal amounts borrowed? (See Figure 7.10.)

SOLUTION

Let the value of each of the equal loans be $x.

(i) Use a time diagram to represent the given data.

Figure 7.10 Graphical Representation of Data (© S. A. Hummelbrunner)

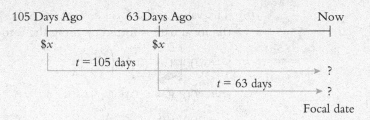

The loans are being repaid by a single payment now, so the *focal date* chosen is today.

(ii) Dated value of the original scheduled payments:
   (a) The value at the focal date of the first $x payment due 105 days before the focal date is found by using the future value formula.

$$S = x\left[1 + (0.09)\left(\frac{105}{365}\right)\right] = x(1 + 0.025890) = 1.025890x$$

   (b) The value at the focal date of the second $x payment due 63 days before the focal date is found by using the future value formula.

$$S = x\left[1 + (0.09)\left(\frac{63}{365}\right)\right] = x(1 + 0.015534) = 1.015534x$$

(iii) Dated value of the replacement payments:
   (a) The value at the focal date of the repayment is $3700 on the focal date.
   (b) The value at the focal date of the two equal loans is

$$1.025890x + 1.015534x = 2.041425x$$

(iv) The equation of values at the focal date is now set up by matching the dated values of the original debts to the dated values of the replacement payment.

$$3700 = 2.041425x$$

$$x = \frac{3700.00}{2.041425}$$

$$x = 1812.46$$

Each of the two equal loans had been $1812.46.

EXAMPLE 7.5F

Clarkson Developments was supposed to pay Majestic Flooring $2000 sixty days ago and $1800 in thirty days. Majestic Flooring agreed to accept three equal payments due today, 60 days from today, and 120 days from today. Compute the size of the equal payments at 10% p.a. Use today as the focal date. (See Figure 7.11.)

SOLUTION

Let the size of the equal payments be $x.

(i) Graphical representation of data:

Figure 7.11 Graphical Representation of Data (© S. A. Hummelbrunner)

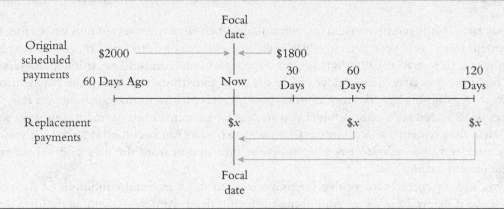

(ii) Dated value of the original scheduled payments at the focal date:
   (a) Because the $2000 payment is due 60 days before the focal date, the future value formula is appropriate.

$$S = 2000\left[1 + (0.10)\left(\frac{60}{365}\right)\right] = 2000(1 + 0.016438) = \$2032.88$$

   (b) Because the $1800 payment is due 30 days after the focal date, the present value formula is appropriate.

$$P = \frac{1800.00}{1 + (0.10)\left(\frac{30}{365}\right)} = \frac{1800.00}{1 + 0.008219} = \$1785.33$$

(iii) Dated value of the replacement payments at the focal date:
   (a) Since the first payment is to be made at the focal date, its value is x.
   (b) Because the second payment is to be made 60 days after the focal date, the present value formula is appropriate.

$$P = \frac{x}{1 + (0.10)\left(\frac{60}{365}\right)} = \frac{x}{1 + 0.016438} = \frac{1(x)}{1.016438} = \$0.983827x$$

   (c) Because the third payment is to be made 120 days after the focal date, the present value formula is appropriate.

$$P = \frac{x}{1 + (0.10)\left(\frac{120}{365}\right)} = \frac{x}{1 + 0.032877}$$

$$= \frac{1(x)}{1.032877} = \$0.968170x$$

(iv) The equation of values (dated value of the replacement payments = dated value of the original scheduled payments):

$$x + 0.983827x + 0.968170x = 2032.88 + 1785.33$$
$$2.951997x = 3818.21$$
$$x = \frac{3818.21}{2.951997}$$
$$x = \$1293.43$$

The size of each of the three equal payments is $1293.43.

The Perils of "Buy Now, Pay Later" Plans

"Buy now, pay later" plans can be convenient, particularly when large unexpected purchases arise. For many years, department stores have been offering "pay later" loans for major home appliances on a simple-interest basis for periods up to one year. Other retailers offer these plans on furniture, electronics, and services.

These "buy now, pay later" plans allow you to purchase something and spread the payment out over a period of time to fit your budget. Borrowers will typically receive a low, promotional interest rate. However, additional fees or increased rates often apply if you are late, or miss, making a payment. Likewise, schemes of no money down, no payments, and no interest for up to two years can become very costly. If you don't pay on time, you may end up having to pay interest on the full amount from the date of purchase rather than simply on the unpaid balance.

Before you sign up, make sure you've carefully reviewed the terms and conditions of the plan. Many companies charge a deferral fee or an administration fee up front. And when you apply for a retail credit card, which works the same way, you are often agreeing to pay an annual credit card fee.

As these types of financing plans become more widely available for smaller purchases such as clothing and jewelry, and when pitched as "try before you buy" in online formats, young consumers, in particular, risk overextending their use and can end up spending more than they can afford. If you default, you could be reported to a credit bureau, which could affect your ability to get credit (such as a car loan, a mortgage, or a bank credit card). A history of bad debt can also impact your capacity to rent an apartment or get a job.

Bottom line: if you're using a "buy now, pay later" plan because you can't afford it now, then you probably can't afford it later.

QUESTIONS

1. Wesley was surprised to find out that the "don't pay a cent" offer that he had accepted on the purchase of a new laptop had actually accrued interest between the purchase date and the date of his first payment. Calculate the amount of interest that had accumulated on his $2300 purchase by the time he went to make his first payment at 6 months. The promotional interest rate for this purchase was 10%.

2. Ari agreed to a "buy now, pay later" plan that called for three equal quarterly payments to begin one year from now on a new $1500 television. Assuming an interest rate of 8%:

   (a) Calculate the size of each payment;
   (b) Determine the amount of interest that Ari paid for his television.

Sources: N. Megawm and C. Cornish, "Buy Now, Pay Later—The New Debt Trap for Millennials?" *Financial Times*, Sept. 21, 2018; https://www.canada.ca/en/financial-consumer-agency/services/loans/buy-now-pay-later.html.

E. Loan repayments

Loans by financial institutions to individuals are usually repaid by **blended payments**, which are equal periodic payments that include payment of interest and repayment of principal. To repay the loan, the sum of the present values of the periodic payments must equal the original principal. The concept of equivalent values is used to determine the size of the blended payments.

EXAMPLE 7.5G   A loan of $2000 made at 8.5% p.a. is to be repaid in four equal payments due at the end of the next four quarters, respectively. Determine the size of the quarterly payments if the agreed focal date is the date of the loan. (See Figure 7.12.)

SOLUTION   Let the size of the equal quarterly payments be represented by $x.

(i) Graphical representation of data:

Figure 7.12 Graphical Representation of Data (© S. A. Hummelbrunner)

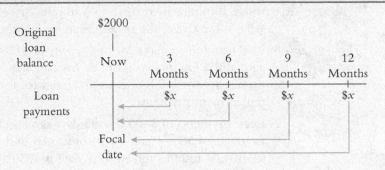

(ii) Dated value of the loan balance at the focal date is $2000.

(iii) Dated value of the loan payments at the focal date:

The payments are due 3, 6, 9, and 12 months after the focal date, respectively. Their values are

(a) $P_1 = \dfrac{x}{1 + (0.085)\left(\frac{3}{12}\right)} = \dfrac{x}{1 + 0.02125} = \dfrac{1(x)}{1.02125} = 0.979192x$

(b) $P_2 = \dfrac{x}{1 + (0.085)\left(\frac{6}{12}\right)} = \dfrac{x}{1 + 0.0425} = \dfrac{1(x)}{1.0425} = 0.959233x$

(c) $P_3 = \dfrac{x}{1 + (0.085)\left(\frac{9}{12}\right)} = \dfrac{x}{1 + 0.06375} = \dfrac{1(x)}{1.06375} = 0.940071x$

(d) $P_4 = \dfrac{x}{1 + (0.085)\left(\frac{12}{12}\right)} = \dfrac{x}{1 + 0.085} = \dfrac{1(x)}{1.085} = 0.921659x$

(iv) $0.979192x + 0.959233x + 0.940071x + 0.921659x = 2000.00$

$$3.800154x = 2000.00$$

$$x = 526.29$$

The size of the quarterly payment is $526.29.

EXERCISE 7.5   MyLab Math

Solve each of the following problems.

1. Scheduled debt payments of $600 each are due three months and six months from now. If interest at 10% is allowed, what single payment today is required to settle the two scheduled payments?   Reference Example 7.5A

2. Debt payments of $700 in two months and $800 in five months are scheduled to be due. If interest at 8.3% is allowed, what single payment today is required to settle the two scheduled payments?

3. A loan payment of $1000 was due 60 days ago, and another payment of $1200 is due 30 days from now. What single payment 90 days from now will pay off the two obligations if interest is to be 8% and the agreed focal date is 90 days from now?
Reference Example 7.5B

4. A loan payment of $2200 was due 91 days ago, and another payment of $1800 is due 45 days from now. What single payment 75 days from now will pay off the two obligations if interest is to be 9% and the agreed focal date is 75 days from now?

5. Jay was due to make loan payments of $500 four months ago, $800 today, and $400 in three months. He has agreed instead to make a single payment one month from today. If money is worth 10.5% and the agreed focal date is one month from today, what is the size of the replacement payment? Reference Example 7.5C

6. Jane was due to make loan payments of $1200 six months ago, $1500 one month ago, and $700 in two months. Instead, she is to make a single payment today. If money is worth 9.8% and the agreed focal date is today, what is the size of the replacement payment?

7. Loan payments of $400 due 95 days ago and $700 due today are to be repaid by a payment of $600 thirty days from today and the balance in 125 days. If money is worth 6% and the agreed focal date is 125 days from today, what is the size of the final payment? Reference Example 7.5D

8. Loan payments of $4000 due 200 days ago and $6000 due 63 days ago are to be replaced by a payment of $5000 today and the balance 92 days from today. If money is worth 8.3% and the agreed focal date is 92 days from today, what is the size of the final payment?

9. Dan borrowed $1100 today and is to repay the loan in two equal payments, one in four months and one in six months. If interest is 8.5% on the loan, what is the size of the equal payments if a focal date of today is used? Reference Example 7.5E

10. When Ruby borrowed $2300, she agreed to repay the loan in two equal payments, to be made 90 days and 135 days from the day the money was borrowed. If interest is 9.25% on the loan, what is the size of the equal payments if a focal date of today is used?

11. Ruben repaid $800, paying back two equal outstanding loans from seven months ago and five months ago. If interest is 11% on the loans, and the agreed focal date is today, what was the size of the equal amounts borrowed?

12. Judy received a payment of $2950 and used it to pay back two equal outstanding loans from 45 days ago and 190 days ago. If interest is 12.5% on the loans, and the agreed focal date is today, what was the size of the equal amounts borrowed?

13. Jessica should have made two payments of $800 each. The first was due 60 days ago and the second payment was due 30 days ago. The two original scheduled payments are to be settled by two equal payments to be made today and 60 days from now. If interest allowed is 7.25% and the agreed focal date is today, what is the size of the equal payments?

14. Krista borrowed $14 000. The loan is to be repaid by three equal payments due in 120, 240, and 260 days from now. Determine the size of the equal payments at 7% with a focal date of today. Reference Example 7.5F

15. Jerry borrowed $4000. The loan is to be repaid by three equal payments due in 4, 8, and 12 months from now. Determine the size of the equal payments at 8.5% with a focal date of today.

16. On March 1, Bear Mountain Tours borrowed $1500. Three equal payments are required, on April 30, June 20, and August 10, as well as a final payment of $400 on September 30 of the same year. If the focal date is September 30, what is the amount of the equal payments at 6.75%? Reference Example 7.5G

17. Debt obligations of $500.00 due on April 27, 2022, and $1625.00 due on September 30, 2022, are to be repaid by a payment of $1200.00 on July 6, 2022, and the balance on January 15, 2023. What is the size of the final payment if interest is 6.25% and the agreed focal date is September 30, 2022?

18. A loan of $1475 taken out on June 7 requires three payments. The first payment is due on July 7. The second payment is twice as large as the first payment and is due on August 19. The final payment due on November 2 is three times as large as the first payment. If the focal date is June 7, what is the size of each of the three payments at an interest rate of 4.6%?

MyLab Math   Visit MyLab Math to practise any of this chapter's exercises marked with a ⊕ as often as you want. The guided solutions help you calculate an answer step by step. You'll find a personalized study plan and additional interactive resources to help you master Business Math!

REVIEW EXERCISE

1. **LO❶** How much interest is owed on a loan of $1975 borrowed at 5.5% for 215 days?

⊕ 2. **LO❷** What principal will earn $34.44 interest at 8.25% from May 30, 2021, to January 4, 2022?

3. **LO❷** What was the rate of interest if the interest on a loan of $675 for 284 days was $39.39?

⊕ 4. **LO❷** If $680 is worth $698.70 after three months, what interest rate was charged?

5. **LO❷** How many days will it take for $2075 to earn $124.29 interest at 8.25% p.a.?

⊕ 6. **LO❷** What principal will earn $24.87 at 4.75% in 156 days?

7. **LO❷** What sum of money will earn $148.57 from September 1, 2021, to April 30, 2022, at 7.5%?

⊕ 8. **LO❷** At what rate of interest must a principal of $1545 be invested to earn interest of $58.93 in 150 days?

9. **LO❷** At what rate of interest will $1500 grow to $1562.04 from June 1, 2022, to December 1, 2022?

⊕ 10. **LO❷** In how many months will $2500 earn $51.04 interest at 3.5%?

11. **LO❷** In how many days will $3100 grow to $3195.72 at 5.75%?

⊕ 12. **LO❸** Compute the accumulated value of $4200 at 4.5% after 11 months.

13. **LO❸** What is the amount to which $1550 will grow from June 10, 2022, to December 15, 2022, at 6.5%?

⊕ 14. **LO❸** What amount of money will accumulate to $1516.80 in eight months at 8%?

15. **LO❹** What principal will amount to $3367.28 if invested at 9% from November 1, 2023, to May 31, 2024?

⊕ 16. **LO❹** What is the present value of $3780 due in nine months if interest is 5%?

17. **LO❸** Compute the present value on June 1, 2022, of $1785 due on October 15, 2022, if interest is 7.5%.

⊕ 18. **LO❺** Payments of $1750 and $1600 are due four months from now and nine months from now, respectively. What single payment is required to pay off the two scheduled payments today if interest is 9% and the focal date is today?

19. **LO❺** A loan payment of $1450 was due 45 days ago and a payment of $1200 is due in 60 days. What single payment made 30 days from now is required to settle the two payments if interest is 7% and the focal date is 30 days from now?

⊕ 20. **LO❺** Scheduled payments of $800 due two months ago and $1200 due in one month are to be repaid by a payment of $1000 today and the balance in three months. What is the amount of the final payment if interest is 7.75% and the focal date is one month from now?

21. **LO❺** An obligation of $10 000 is to be repaid by equal payments due in 90 days and 180 days. What is the amount of the equal payments if money is worth 6.5% and the focal date is today?

⊕ 22. **LO❺** Payments of $4000 each due in four, nine, and eleven months from now are to be settled by two equal payments due today and twelve months from now. What is the amount of the equal payments if interest is 7.35% and the agreed focal date is today?

23. **LO❺** Three debts, the first for $1000 due two months ago, the second for $1200 due in two months, and the third for $1400 due in four months, are to be paid by a single payment today. How much is the single payment if money is worth 8.25% p.a. and the focal date is today?

⊕ 24. **LO❺** Loan payments of $700 due three months ago and of $1000 due today are to be paid by a payment of $800 in two months and a final payment in five months. If 9% interest is allowed, and the focal date is five months from now, what is the amount of the final payment?

25. LO⑤ A loan of $5000 due in one year is to be repaid by three equal payments due today, six months from now, and one year from now. What is the amount of the equal payments if interest is 6.5% and the focal date is today?

26. LO⑤ 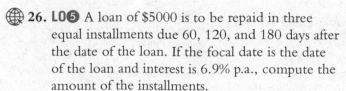 A loan of $5000 is to be repaid in three equal installments due 60, 120, and 180 days after the date of the loan. If the focal date is the date of the loan and interest is 6.9% p.a., compute the amount of the installments.

SELF-TEST

1. Compute the amount of interest earned by $1290 at 3.5% p.a. in 173 days.

2. In how many months will $8500 grow to $8818.75 at 5% p.a.?

3. What interest rate is paid if the interest on a loan of $2500 for six months is $81.25?

4. What principal will have a maturity value of $10 000 at 8.25% p.a. in three months?

5. What is the amount to which $6000 will grow at 3.75% p.a. in 10 months?

6. What principal will earn $67.14 interest at 6.25% for 82 days?

7. What is the present value of $4400 due at 3.25% p.a. in 243 days?

8. What rate of interest is paid if the interest on a loan of $2500 is $96.06 from November 14, 2023, to May 20, 2024?

9. How many days will it take for $8500 to earn $689.72 at 8.25% p.a.?

10. What principal will earn $55.99 interest at 9.75% p.a. from February 4, 2021, to July 6, 2021?

11. What amount invested will accumulate to $7500 at 3.75% p.a. in 88 days?

12. Compute the amount of interest on $835 at 7.5% p.a. from October 8, 2023, to August 4, 2024.

13. Loan payments of $1725 due today, $510 due in 75 days, and $655 due in 323 days are to be combined into a single payment to be made 115 days from now. What is that single payment if money is worth 8.5% p.a. and the focal date is 115 days from now?

14. Scheduled payments of $1010 due five months ago and $1280 due today are to be repaid by a payment of $615 in four months and the balance in seven months. If money is worth 7.75% p.a. and the focal date is in seven months, what is the amount of the final payment?

15. A loan of $3320 is to be repaid by three equal payments due in 92 days, 235 days, and 326 days. Determine the amount of the equal payments at 8.75% p.a. with a focal date of today.

CHALLENGE PROBLEMS

1. Nora borrows $37 500 on September 28, 2023, at 7% p.a. simple interest, to be repaid on October 31, 2024. She has the option of making payments toward the loan before the due date. Nora pays $6350 on February 17, 2024, $8250 on July 2, 2024, and $7500 on October 1, 2024. Compute the payment required to pay off the debt on the focal date of October 31, 2024.

2. A supplier will give Shark Unibase Company a discount of 2% if an invoice is paid 60 days before its due date. Suppose Shark wants to take advantage of this discount but needs to borrow the money. It plans to pay back the loan in 60 days. What is the highest annual simple interest rate at which Shark Unibase can borrow the money and still save by paying the invoice 60 days before its due date?

CASE STUDY   Cost of Financing: Pay Now or Pay Later

▶ Along with licensing, the purchase of auto insurance for vehicles is required in Canada. Benefits of auto insurance are as follows:

- Safeguards the investment in the automobile.
- Pays for medical expenses in case of an accident.
- Covers losses caused by uninsured or underinsured drivers.
- Compensates for damage due to theft, vandalism, or natural disasters.

Quick Courier Service is about to purchase insurance on its new delivery van. Taylor, the manager, has the company's insurance agent outline three payment plans to provide coverage for the next 12 months.

Plan One requires that the full year's premium of $4000 be paid at the beginning of the year.

Plan Two allows payment of the annual premium in two installments. The first installment would have to be paid immediately and would amount to one-half of the annual premium, plus a $60 service charge. The second installment would be paid in six months' time, and would amount to the remaining half of the premium.

Plan Three allows for twelve equal monthly payments of $355 each. These payments would be made on the same date within each month, starting immediately.

Quick Courier Service pays its insurance using Plan One. However, the company realizes that it is missing out on interest it could have earned on this money when it pays the full year's premium at the beginning of the policy term. Taylor considers this to be the "cost" of paying its bill in one lump sum. Taylor is interested in knowing the cost of its insurance payment options.

QUESTIONS

1. Suppose Quick Courier Service could earn 4% p.a. simple interest on its money over the next year. Assume the first premium payment is due today (the first day of the insurance policy term) and the focal date is one year from today. Ignoring all taxes, compute the cost to Quick Courier Service of paying the insurance using each of the three payment plans.

2. Suppose Quick Courier Service expects to earn 2.5% p.a. simple interest on any money it invests in the first three months of this year, and 1.8% p.a. simple interest on any money it invests during the rest of this year. Assume the focal date is one year from today. Which option—Plan One, Plan Two, or Plan Three—will have the least cost for the company?

3. Examine a vehicle insurance policy of your own or of a family member. Calculate what you could earn on your money at today's rates of interest. What is the cost of this insurance policy if you pay the annual premium at the beginning of the policy term? Make the focal date the first day of the policy term.

SUMMARY OF FORMULAS

Formula 7.1

$I = Prt$ — Calculating the amount of interest when the principal, the rate of interest, and the time are known

$P = \dfrac{I}{rt}$ — Calculating the principal directly when the amount of interest, the rate of interest, and the time are known

$r = \dfrac{I}{Pt}$ — Calculating the rate of interest directly when the amount of interest, the principal, and the time are known

$t = \dfrac{I}{Pr}$ — Calculating the time directly when the amount of interest, the principal, and the rate of interest are known

Formula 7.2

$S = P + I$ — Calculating the future value (maturity value) when the principal and the amount of interest are known

Formula 7.3

$S = P(1 + rt)$ — Calculating the future value (maturity value) at simple interest directly when the principal, the rate of interest, and the time are known

Formula 7.4

$P = \dfrac{S}{1 + rt}$ — Calculating the present value at simple interest when the future value (maturity value), the rate of interest, and the time are known

GLOSSARY

Blended payments equal periodic payments that include payment of interest and repayment of principal, usually paid by individuals to financial institutions (p. 294)

Dated value the value of a sum of money at a specific time relative to its due date, including interest (p. 285)

Equation of values the equation obtained when matching the dated values of the original payments at an agreed focal date to the dated values of the replacement payments at the same focal date (p. 290)

Equivalent value see **Dated value**

Focal date a specific time chosen to compare the time value of one or more dated sums of money (p. 286)

Future value of a sum of money the value obtained when the amount of interest is added to the original principal (p. 279)

Interest fee paid for the use of money (p. 268)

Interest period the time period for which interest is charged (p. 268)

Maturity value see **Future value of a sum of money**

Nominal rate the yearly or annual rate of interest charged on the principal of a loan (p. 268)

Present value the principal that grows to a given future value (maturity value) over a given period of time at a given rate of interest (p. 283)

Simple interest the interest calculated on the original principal by the formula $I = Prt$, and paid only when the principal is repaid (p. 268)

Time value of money a concept of money value that allows for a change in the value of a sum of money over time if the sum of money is subject to a rate of interest (p. 283)

8

Simple Interest Applications

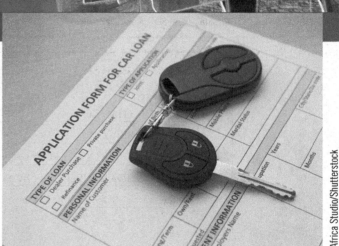

Africa Studio/Shutterstock

LEARNING OBJECTIVES

Upon completing this chapter, you will be able to do the following:

1 Compute maturity value and present value for promissory notes.

2 Compute present values for treasury bills and commercial paper.

3 Compute interest and balances for demand loans.

4 Compute interest and balances for lines of credit and simple interest loans.

5 Construct repayment schedules for loans using blended payments.

Simple interest works in your favour when you are borrowing money because it results in a lower amount of interest than you would pay if your debt were subject to compound interest. It's also fairly easy to calculate simple interest because all you need to know is the principal amount borrowed, the annual interest rate, and the length of the time period. When you invest, however, you will want to seek out compound interest opportunities so that your principal and interest accumulate in every period.

Simple interest is typically used for short periods of borrowing, less than a year. It also applies to open-ended situations, such as lines of credit and credit card balances. Many car loan and consumer loan balances are calculated using simple interest. As the outstanding loan balance diminishes after each payment, the interest payable reduces too and a larger portion of each successive payment goes toward paying down the principal.

Certificates of deposit, private loans, bond interest, and investments in money market funds are good examples of non-compounding interest occurring on the investor side.

INTRODUCTION

Businesses often encounter situations that involve the application of simple interest. Simple interest calculation is usually restricted to financial instruments subject to time periods of less than one year. In this chapter we apply simple interest to short-term promissory notes, treasury bills, demand loans, lines of credit, and other simple interest loans.

8.1 PROMISSORY NOTES

A. Promissory notes and related terms

A **promissory note** is a written promise by one party to pay a certain sum of money, with or without interest, at a specific date or on demand, to another party. (See Figure 8.1.)

Figure 8.1 Promissory Note (© S. A. Hummelbrunner)

$650.00   MISSISSAUGA, ONTARIO   OCTOBER 30, 2022

FOUR MONTHS   after date   I   promise to pay to the order of

VALLEY NURSERY

SIX-HUNDRED-FIFTY and 00/100 ···························· Dollars

at   SHERIDAN CREDIT UNION LIMITED   for value received

with interest at   7.25%   per annum.

Signed   *D. Peel*

This is an **interest-bearing promissory note** because it is a note subject to the rate of interest stated on the face of the note.

The following information is directly available in the promissory note (see items (a) through (f)) or can be determined (see items (g) through (j)).

(a) The **maker** of the note is the party making the promise to pay. ———— (D. Peel)

(b) The **payee** of the note is the party to whom the promise to pay is made. ———————————————————— (Valley Nursery)

(c) The **face value** of the note is the sum of money (principal) specified. ———————————————— ($650.00)

(d) The **rate of interest** is stated as a simple annual rate based on the face value. ———————————————— (7.25%)

(e) The **date of issue** or **issue date** is the date on which the note was made. ———————————— (October 30, 2022)

(f) The **term** of the promissory note is the length of time before the note matures (becomes payable). ———————— (four months)

(g) The **due date** or **date of maturity** is the date on which the note is to be paid. ———————————— (See Example 8.1A)

(h) The **interest period** is the time period from the date of issue to the legal due date. ———————————— (See Example 8.1A)

(i) The **amount of interest** is payable together with the face value on the legal due date. ———————— (See Example 8.1A)

(j) The **maturity value** is the amount payable on the due date (face value plus interest). ———————— (See Example 8.1A)

Canadian law relating to promissory notes allows for a **grace period** to extend a due date that falls on a weekend or statutory holiday. The **legal due date** then becomes the next business day. For example, a promissory note is due for payment on July 1. Because this date is a statutory holiday, the legal due date for the note becomes July 2. When a borrower has 30 days to pay the principal and interest owing after the due date, banks often allow a grace period. During a grace period, interest charges do apply. If payment in full is not made in this time period, the note becomes delinquent and is sent to a collection agency to collect the balance owing. For promissory note examples and exercises in this chapter the grace period will not be included, unless specifically noted.

If a note is outstanding and is sent to a collection agency, this action often negatively affects the borrower's **credit score**, or credit rating. A **credit rating** is a score that reflects the credit history and the repayment reliability of a borrower. If money is borrowed and not repaid on time, the credit score for the borrower is low and the risk for the lender is high. When money is lent to a borrower with a low credit score, the interest rate is often high. The major credit-reporting agencies in Canada are Equifax Canada and TransUnion Canada.

POINTERS & PITFALLS

When the term of a promissory note is specified in months (rather than days), the end of the term is typically on the same "numbered day" of the month as the starting date of issue. A three-month promissory note with an issue date of April 15, for instance, would have a due date of July 15. *(For this reason, the three-month promissory note in Example 8.1E, dated April 30, has a due date of July 30.)*

However, in cases where the expiry month has fewer days than the month in which a promissory note is issued, as in Example 8.1C, the last day of the expiry month is used as the end of the term. A five-month promissory note with an issue date of January 31 would have a due date of June 30.

EXAMPLE 8.1A

For the promissory note illustrated in Figure 8.1, determine

(i) the due date;

(ii) the interest period;

(iii) the amount of interest;

(iv) the maturity value.

SOLUTION

(i) *Determining the due date*
With reference to the promissory note in Figure 8.1,
- the date of issue is October 30, 2022;
- the term of the note is four months;
- the month in which the term ends is February 2023;
- the end of the term is February 28 (since February has no day corresponding to day 30, the last day of the month is used to establish the end of the term of the note).

(ii) *Determining the interest period*
If the note bears interest, the interest period covers the number of days from the date of issue of the note to the legal due date.

October 30 to February 28 = 121 days

(iii) *Computing the amount of interest*

The interest payable on the note is the simple interest based on the face value of the note for the interest period at the stated rate. It is found using the simple interest formula:

$$\boxed{I = Prt}$$ —————————————————————— Formula 7.1

$$I = (650.00)(0.0725)\left(\frac{121}{365}\right) = \$15.62$$

(iv) *Calculating the maturity value of the note*

The maturity value of the promissory note is the total amount payable at the legal due date.

Face value + Interest = 650.00 + 15.62 = \$665.62

B. Maturity value of interest-bearing promissory notes

Since the maturity value of a promissory note is the principal (face value) plus the interest accumulated to the legal due date, the future value formula for simple interest will determine the maturity value directly.

$$\boxed{S = P(1 + rt)}$$ ————————————————— Formula 7.3

S = maturity value of the promissory note
P = the face value of the note
r = the rate of interest on the note
t = the interest period (the number of days between the *date of issue* and the *legal due date*)

EXAMPLE 8.1B

Calculate the maturity value of an \$800, six-month note with interest at 7.5% dated May 31, 2021. Use Table 7.2 to calculate the number of days.

SOLUTION

The date of issue is May 31, 2021;
the term of the note is six months;
the term ends November 30, 2021;
the interest period (May 31 to November 30) has 183 days.

$$P = 800.00; \quad r = 0.075; \quad t = \frac{183}{365}$$

$$S = 800.00\left[1 + (0.075)\left(\frac{183}{365}\right)\right] = 800.00(1 + 0.037603) = \$830.08$$

C. Present value of promissory notes

The present value of a promissory note is its value any time before the due date, allowing for the maturity value, the prevailing interest rate, and the time between the present date and its date of maturity. The prevailing interest rate is called the **rate money is worth**.

The first step in determining the present value is to ascertain whether the note is an interest-bearing or a non-interest-bearing note.

1. **Interest-bearing promissory notes:** When the rate of interest is stated on the note, it is an interest-bearing promissory note. The face value of the note is the principal amount borrowed. The promise or obligation is to repay the principal amount borrowed, plus interest based on the rate of interest *stated* on the face of the note.

   To determine the present value of an interest-bearing note, two steps are required:
   Step 1: Calculate the maturity value of the note, using the *stated interest rate*, then
   Step 2: Calculate the present value of the note, using the *rate money is worth*.

2. **Non-interest-bearing promissory notes:** When there is no rate of interest stated, the promissory note is a **non-interest-bearing promissory note**. Interest on money borrowed may be implied, but is not stated. The face value of the note is the amount to be repaid at maturity.

   To determine the present value of a non-interest-bearing note, only one step is required: Calculate the present value of the non-interest-bearing note, using the *rate money is worth*.

The face value (or principal) of promissory notes can be obtained by solving the future value formula $S = P(1 + rt)$ for P; that is, by using the present value formula

$$P = \frac{S}{(1 + rt)}$$ ———————— **Formula 7.4**

P = the face value (or present value) of the note at the date of issue
S = the maturity value
r = the rate of interest
t = the interest period

EXAMPLE 8.1C

A five-month note dated January 31, 2022, and bearing interest at 8% p.a. (per annum; i.e., per year) has a maturity value of $557.75. Calculate the face value of the note.

SOLUTION

See Figure 8.2.

Figure 8.2 Graphical Representation of Data (© S. A. Hummelbrunner)

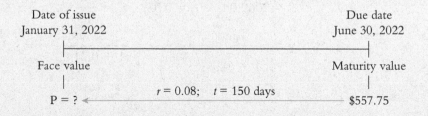

Date of issue
January 31, 2022

Due date
June 30, 2022

Face value

Maturity value

P = ? ← $r = 0.08;$ $t = 150$ days ← $557.75

The term of the note ends June 30;
the interest period (January 31 to June 30) has 150 days.

$$S = \$557.75; \quad r = 0.08; \quad t = \frac{150}{365}$$

$$P = \frac{557.75}{\left[1 + (0.08)\left(\dfrac{150}{365}\right)\right]} = \frac{557.75}{(1 + 0.032877)} = \$540.00$$

EXAMPLE 8.1D   A 180-day note for $2000 with interest at 7% is dated September 18, 2024. Compute the value of the note on December 1, 2024, if money is worth 5%.

SOLUTION   Since the note bears interest at 7%, it is identified as an interest-bearing note. To calculate the present value of the note, two steps are required. Compute the maturity value of the note based on the stated interest rate, 7%. Using the result, compute the present value of the note based on the rate money is worth, 5% (see Figure 8.3).

Figure 8.3 Graphical Representation of Data (© S. A. Hummelbrunner)

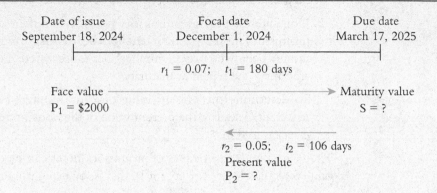

(i) *Compute the maturity value of the note.*
The term of the note is 180 days;
therefore, the term ends March 17, 2025;
the interest rate to be used is 7%.

$$P_1 = 2000; \quad r_1 = 0.07; \quad t_1 = \frac{180}{365}$$

$$S = 2000 \left[1 + (0.07) \left(\frac{180}{365} \right) \right] = 2000(1 + 0.034521) = \$2069.04$$

(ii) *Compute the present value.*
The focal date is December 1, 2024;
the interest period (December 1, 2024, to March 17, 2025) has 106 days:
the interest rate to be used is 5%.

$$S = 2069.04; \quad r_2 = 0.05; \quad t_2 = \frac{106}{365}$$

$$P_2 = \frac{2069.04}{\left[1 + (0.05) \left(\frac{106}{365} \right) \right]} = \frac{2069.04}{(1 + 0.014521)} = \$2039.43$$

POINTERS
& PITFALLS

Example 8.1D involves a leap year. So, using Table 7.2 in Chapter 7, simply add one day to the serial numbers for any dates that occur following February 28th within the leap year. The number of days calculations for this example are:

$$(366 - 262) + 76 = 180 \text{ days}$$

$$(366 - 336) + 76 = 106 \text{ days}$$

EXAMPLE 8.1E

Compute the present value on the date of issue of a non-interest-bearing, $950, three-month promissory note dated April 30, 2022, if money is worth 6.5%.

SOLUTION

This non-interest-bearing note does not state an interest rate. The present value of the note is calculated in one step (see Figure 8.4.).

Figure 8.4 Graphical Representation of Data (© S. A. Hummelbrunner)

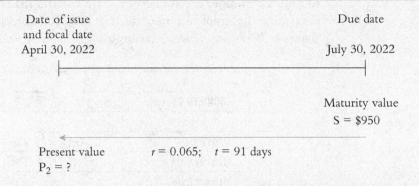

Date of issue
and focal date
April 30, 2022

Due date
July 30, 2022

Maturity value
S = $950

Present value $r = 0.065;$ $t = 91$ days
$P_2 = ?$

(i) Since this is a non-interest-bearing note, the maturity value of the note is the face value, $950.
The term of the note ends July 30, 2022;
the interest period (April 30 to July 30) has 91 days;
the interest rate to be used is 6.5%.

$$S = 950; \quad r = 0.065; \quad t = \frac{91}{365}$$

$$P = \frac{950}{\left[1 + (0.065)\left(\dfrac{91}{365}\right) \right]} = \frac{950}{(1 + 0.016205)} = 934.85$$

EXAMPLE 8.1F

Henry purchased a large-screen TV at a local store that had advertised, "No payment until 2023." He signed the contract on March 14, 2022, agreeing to pay $1995 on January 2, 2023. If money is worth 11%, what is the value of the note on the day of signing?

SOLUTION

The contract serves as a non-interest-bearing promissory note because no interest rate is stated. The maturity value of the contract is its face value, $1995. The present value of the note is calculated in one step. There are 294 days between March 14, 2022, and January 2, 2023. (See Figure 8.5.)

Figure 8.5 Graphical Representation of Data (© S. A. Hummelbrunner)

March 14, 2022   January 2, 2023
                                    $t = 294$ days
$1832.62 $1995

Focal date

$$S = 1995.00; \quad r = 0.11; \quad t = \frac{294}{365}$$

$$P = \frac{1995.00}{\left[1 + (0.11)\left(\dfrac{294}{365}\right) \right]} = \frac{1995.00}{(1 + 0.088603)} = \$1832.62$$

D. Using Excel's ACCRINTM

If you choose, you can use Excel's ACCRINTM function to answer some questions in this section. This function calculates the amount of interest for an investment that has a one-time payment, at maturity. Other Excel functions that could be used to answer the questions in this section are the following: COUPDAYSNC (days between dates) to find the number of days between two dates; YIELDDISC (simple interest yields) to determine the simple interest rate. The ACCRINTM function in Excel is illustrated in Example 8.1A (iii). (Basis 3 means using a 365 day year).

	A	B	C
1	**ACCRINTM Function**		
2			
3	**Issue Date**	October 30, 2022	
4	**Maturity Date**	February 28, 2023	
5	**Interest Rate**	7.25%	
6	Value	$ 650.00	
7	Basis	3	
8	Answer	$ 15.62	
9			

EXERCISE 8.1

MyLab Math

 1. Compute the maturity value for a four-month, 5.25% promissory note for $620 issued May 25, 2023. Reference Example 8.1B

 2. Compute the maturity value for a $350 promissory note issued on October 30, 2022, at 4.5% for 90 days.

3. A 150-day note with interest at 5% is dated June 28, 2022, and has a maturity value of $836.85. Determine the face value of the note. Reference Example 8.1C

4. A seven-month note dated November 1, 2023, earning interest at 7.5%, has a maturity value of $6000. Determine the face value of the note.

 5. A 95-day, 5.81% note for $3600 is issued October 28, 2021. If money is worth 6.27%, calculate the present value on November 30, 2021. Reference Example 8.1D

6. A six-month note for $19 300, with interest at 8%, is issued on April 1, 2022. Calculate the present value on June 20, 2022, if money is worth 7.2%.

7. Calculate the present value of a four-month non-interest-bearing note for $2500 issued June 10, 2021, if money is worth 6.15%, on July 20, 2021. Reference Example 8.1E

8. Determine the maturity date for a 180-day non-interest-bearing note for $7200 issued on February 20, 2024. Then, calculate the present value on June 1, 2024, if money is worth 5.64%.

9. Luigi purchases a new tablet computer during a sale that advertised, "No payment until 2023." The payment contract that he signs states that he has agreed to pay $549 on February 10, 2023. If money is worth 9.8%, what is the equivalent cash price if the purchase date is five months before? Reference Example 8.1F

10. On November 1, 2023, Sonya purchases a leather chair advertised at $1980, including an offer to defer payment for eight months. If she does not agree to the eight-month deferment, and money is worth 19.8%, how much would she have to pay in cash on the date of purchase?

8.2 TREASURY BILLS AND COMMERCIAL PAPER
A. Treasury bills

Treasury bills (or **T-bills**) are promissory notes issued by the federal government and most provincial governments to meet short-term financing requirements.

Government of Canada T-bills are for terms of 91 days, 182 days, and 364 days. T-bills are auctioned by the Bank of Canada on behalf of the federal government. They are available in denominations of $1000, $5000, $25 000, $100 000, and $1 000 000. T-bills are bought at the auction mainly by chartered banks and investment dealers for resale to other investors, such as smaller financial institutions, corporations, mutual funds, and individuals.

T-bills are promissory notes that do not carry an interest rate. The issuing government guarantees payment of the face value at maturity. The investor purchases T-bills at a discounted price reflecting a rate of return that is determined by current market conditions. The discounted price is determined by computing the present value of the T-bills.

| EXAMPLE 8.2A | An investment dealer bought a 91-day Canada T-bill to yield an annual rate of return of 0.99%.

(i) What was the price paid by the investment dealer for a T-bill with a face value of $100 000?

(ii) The investment dealer resold the $100 000 T-bill the same day to an investor to yield 0.95%. What was the investment dealer's profit on the transaction?

| SOLUTION | (i) Determine the purchase price, P_1.
The maturity value is the face value of the T-bill, $100 000.00; the discount period has 91 days (no days of grace are allowed on T-bills).

$$S = 100\ 000.00; \quad r_2 = 0.0099; \quad t_2 = \frac{91}{365}$$

$$P_1 = \frac{100\ 000.00}{1 + 0.0099\left(\dfrac{91}{365}\right)} = \frac{100\ 000.00}{1 + 0.002468} = \$99\ 753.79$$

The investment dealer paid $99 753.79 for a $100 000 T-bill.

(ii) Calculate the resale price, P_2.

$$S = 100\ 000.00; \quad r_1 = 0.0095; \quad t_1 = \frac{91}{365}$$

$$P_2 = \frac{S}{1 + r_1 t_1} = \frac{100\ 000.00}{1 + 0.0095\left(\dfrac{91}{365}\right)} = \frac{100\ 000.00}{1 + 0.002368} = \$99\ 763.71$$

Investment dealer's profit = Resale price − Price paid by dealer
$$= P_2 - P_1$$
$$= 99\ 763.71 - 99\ 753.79 = \$9.92$$

The investment dealer's profit on the transaction was $9.92.

EXAMPLE 8.2B

An investor purchased $250 000 in 364–day T–bills 315 days before maturity to yield 1.12%. He sold the T–bills 120 days later to yield 1.47%.

  (i) How much did the investor pay for the T–bills?

 (ii) For how much did the investor sell the T–bills?

(iii) What rate of return did the investor realize on the investment?

SOLUTION

  (i) Determine the purchase price of the T–bills, P_1.

$$S = 250\ 000.00; \quad r_1 = 0.0112; \quad t_1 = \frac{315}{365}$$

$$P_1 = \frac{250\ 000.00}{1 + 0.0112\left(\dfrac{315}{365}\right)} = \frac{250\ 000.00}{1 + 0.009666} = \$247\ 606.69$$

The investor purchased the T–bills for $247 606.69.

 (ii) Calculate the selling price of the T–bills, P_2.
The time to maturity at the date of sale is 195 days (315 − 120).

$$S = 250\ 000.00; \quad r_2 = 0.0147; \quad t_2 = \frac{195}{365}$$

$$P_2 = \frac{250\ 000.00}{1 + 0.0147\left(\dfrac{195}{365}\right)} = \frac{250\ 000.00}{1 + 0.007853} = \$248\ 051.94$$

The investor sold the T–bills for $248 051.94.

(iii) The investment of $247 606.69 grew to $248 051.94 in 120 days.
To compute the rate of return, use the future value formula (Formula 7.3).

$$P = 247\ 606.69; \quad S = 248\ 051.94; \quad t = \frac{120}{365}$$

$$S = P(1 + rt)$$

$$248\ 051.94 = 247\ 606.69\left[1 + r\left(\frac{120}{365}\right)\right]$$

$$\frac{248\ 051.94}{247\ 606.69} = 1 + \left(\frac{120}{365}\right)r$$

$$1.001798 = 1 + 0.328767r$$

$$0.001798 = 0.328767r$$

$$\frac{0.001798}{0.328767} = r$$

$$r = 0.005470 = 0.5470\%$$

The investor realized a rate of return of 0.5470%.

Alternatively:
The gain realized represents the interest.

$$I = 248\ 051.94 - 247\ 606.69 = \$445.25$$

Using the formula $r = \dfrac{I}{Pt}$,

$$r = \frac{445.25}{247\ 606.69\left(\dfrac{120}{365}\right)} = \frac{445.25}{81\ 404.94} = 0.005470 = 0.5470\%.$$

B. Commercial paper

Commercial paper is a short-term, unsecured form of promissory note. Commercial paper is sold by large banks and corporations who often use the funds to meet their short-term financing obligations such as reducing their accounts payable or making payroll. Similar to treasury bills, commercial paper is usually offered at a discount. The issuing organization promises to pay the buyer the face value specified at maturity.

Commercial paper is typically traded in amounts of $100 000 or more and with terms of 30 days, 60 days, or 90 days. The discounted price, on the date of issue, is determined by calculating the present value of the commercial paper. The commercial paper rate of return can be computed by rearranging the formula I = Prt as in Example 8.2C.

Due to the $100 000 threshold, investment firms, other banks, mutual funds, and wealthy investors have historically been the predominant buyers of commercial paper.

EXAMPLE 8.2C

Pearson Canada Inc. issued 90-day commercial paper with a face value of $100 000 for $99 800. What rate of return was realized upon maturity?

SOLUTION

Interest earned by the buyer = $100 000 − $99 800 = $200;   P = $99 800; t = 90 days

Rearranging the formula I = Prt

$$r = \frac{200}{(99\,800)\left(\dfrac{90}{365}\right)}$$

$r = 0.008127 = 0.81\%$

A 0.81% rate of return was realized upon maturity.

EXERCISE 8.2

MyLab Math

Answer each of the following questions.

1. What is the price of a 364-day, $50 000 Province of British Columbia treasury bill that yields 1.36% per annum? Reference Example 8.2A

2. What is the price of a 91-day, $100 000 Government of Canada treasury bill that yields 0.53% per annum?

3. An investment dealer acquired a $5000, 91-day Province of Alberta treasury bill on its date of issue at a price of $4966.20. What was the annual rate of return?

4. An investment dealer acquired a $10 000, 182-day Province of Quebec treasury bill on its date of issue at a price of $9822.00. What was the annual rate of return?

5. An investor purchased a 91-day, $100 000 T-bill on its issue date for $99 326.85. After holding it for 42 days, she sold the T-bill for a yield of 2.52%.
   (a) What was the original yield of the T-bill?
   (b) For what price was the T-bill sold?
   (c) What rate of return (per annum) did the investor realize while holding this T-bill? Reference Example 8.2B

6. On April 1, $25 000, 364-day treasury bills were auctioned off to yield 2.92%.
   (a) What is the price of each $25 000 T-bill on April 1?
   (b) What is the yield rate on August 15 if the market price is $24 377.64?
   (c) Calculate the market value of each $25 000 T-bill on October 1 if the rate of return on that date is 4.545%.
   (d) What is the rate of return realized if a $25 000 T-bill purchased on April 1 is sold on November 20 at a market rate of 4.625%?

7. Two 182-day, $1 000 000 T-bills were initially issued at a price that would yield the buyer 2.5%. If the yield required by the market remains at 2.5%, how many days before their maturity date will the T-bills' market price first exceed $995 000?

8. The average rate of return on a 182-day Government of Canada treasury bill sold on June 18, 2021, was 0.96%. A client sold the $50 000 T-bill after 53 days. What rate of return (per annum) did the client realize while holding the T-bill, if the short-term interest for this maturity had risen to 1.05% by the date of sale?

9. What was the purchase price of a 30-day commercial paper note issued by Alectra Utilities Corporation with a face value of $750 000 if the current market interest rate was 2.15%?

10. A BMO mutual fund manager purchased commercial paper with a face value of $2 000 000 from Aecon for $1 994 000. If the manager held the paper until its maturity 60 days later, what rate of return did it yield?

8.3 DEMAND LOANS
A. Nature of demand loans

A **demand loan** is a loan for which repayment, in full or in part, may be required at any time, or made at any time. The financial instrument representing a demand loan is called a **demand note**.

When borrowing on a demand note, the borrower receives the full face value of the note. The lender may demand payment of the loan in full or in part at any time. Conversely, the borrower may repay all of the loan or any part at any time without notice and without interest penalty. Interest, based on the unpaid balance, is usually payable monthly. The interest rate on such loans is normally not fixed for the duration of the loan but fluctuates with market conditions. Thus the total interest cost cannot be predicted with certainty. Note that the method of counting days is to count the first day but not the last.

Demand loans and similar debts are sometimes paid off by a series of **partial payments**. The commonly used approach to dealing with this type of loan repayment is the **declining balance approach**, requiring that each partial payment be applied first to the accumulated interest. Any remainder is then used to reduce the outstanding principal. Thus, interest is always calculated on the unpaid balance and the new unpaid balance is determined after each partial payment.

The following step-by-step procedure is useful in dealing with such problems:

(a) Compute the interest due to the date of the partial payment.
(b) Compare the interest due computed in part (a) with the partial payment received, and continue with part (c) if the partial payment is *greater than* the interest due or continue with part (d) if the partial payment is *less than* the interest due.
(c) *Partial payment greater than interest due:*
  (i) Deduct the interest due from the partial payment.
  (ii) Deduct the remainder in part (i) from the principal balance to obtain the new unpaid balance.
(d) *Partial payment less than interest due:*
  In this case, the partial payment is not large enough to cover the interest due.
  (i) Deduct the partial payment from the interest due to determine the unpaid interest due at the date of the principal payment.
  (ii) Keep a record of this balance and apply any future partial payments to this unpaid interest first.

EXAMPLE 8.3A

On April 20, 2022, Bruce borrowed $4000 at 5% on a note requiring payment of principal and interest on demand. Bruce paid $600 on May 10 and $1200 on July 15. What payment is required on September 30 to pay the note in full?

SOLUTION

April 20

Original loan balance ⟶ $4000.00

May 10

Deduct

First partial payment ⟶ $ 600.00

Less interest

April 20–May 10 ⟶ 10.96 ⟶ $(4000)(0.05)\left(\frac{20}{365}\right)$

Amount applied to repay loan   589.04

Unpaid balance ⟶ $3410.96

July 15

Deduct

Second partial payment ⟶ $1200.00

Less interest

May 10–July 15 ⟶ 30.84 ⟶ $(3410.96)(0.05)\left(\frac{66}{365}\right)$

Amount applied to repay loan   1169.16

Unpaid balance ⟶ $2241.80

September 30

Add

Interest

July 15–Sept. 30 ⟶ 23.65 $(2241.80)(0.05)\left(\frac{77}{365}\right)$

Payment required

to pay the note in full ⟶ $2265.45

POINTERS
& PITFALLS

When determining the number of days in any given time period between interest rate changes or between two partial payments, remember to always count the first day and omit the last day. As well, keep in mind that

(a) The date on which there is a change in the interest rate is counted as the first day at the new interest rate.

(b) The date on which a partial payment is made is counted as the first day at the new outstanding principal balance.

EXAMPLE 8.3B

The Provincial Bank lent $20 000 to the owner of the Purple Pelican on April 1, 2023, for commercial improvements. The loan was secured by a demand note subject to a variable rate of interest. This rate was 7% on April 1. The rate of interest was raised to 9% effective August 1 and reduced to 8% effective November 1. Partial payments, applied to the loan by the declining balance method, were made as follows: June 10, $1000; September 20, $400; November 15, $1200. How much interest is due to the Provincial Bank on December 31?

SOLUTION

April 1

Original loan balance ⟶ $20 000.00

June 10

Deduct

First partial payment ———→ $1000.00

Less interest

April 1–June 10 ———→ <u>268.49</u> ——————— $(20000)(0.07)\left(\frac{70}{365}\right)$

Amount applied to repay loan <u>731.51</u>

Unpaid loan balance ———————→ $19 268.49

September 20

Deduct

Second partial payment $400.00

Less interest

June 10–Sept. 20:

June 10–July 31 $192.16 ——————— $(19\,268.49)(0.07)\left(\frac{52}{365}\right)$

(inclusive)

Aug. 1–Sept. 20 <u>237.56</u> <u>429.72</u> ——————— $(19\,268.49)(0.09)\left(\frac{50}{365}\right)$

Unpaid interest to

Sept. 20 ———————→ $29.72

Unpaid loan balance ———————→ $19 268.49

November 15

Deduct

Third partial payment $1200.00

Less interest

Unpaid interest to

Sept. 20 ———→ $29.72 ——————— (see above)

Sept. 20–Oct. 31 ———→ 199.55 ——————— $(19\,268.49)(0.09)\left(\frac{42}{365}\right)$

(inclusive)

Nov. 1–Nov. 15 ———→ <u>59.13</u> ——————— $(19\,268.49)(0.08)\left(\frac{14}{365}\right)$

<u>288.40</u>

Amount applied to repay loan <u>911.60</u>

Unpaid loan balance ———————→ $18 356.89

December 31

Interest due

Nov. 15–Dec. 31 ———————→ <u>$185.08</u> $(18\,356.89)(0.08)\left(\frac{46}{365}\right)$

EXERCISE 8.3

MyLab Math

Answer each of the following.

1. On March 10, Fat Tires Ltd. borrowed $10 000 with an interest rate of 5.5%. The loan was repaid in full on November 15, with payments of $2500 on June 30 and $4000 on September 4. What was the final payment? Reference Example 8.3A

2. Automotive Excellence Inc. borrowed $20 000 on August 12 with an interest rate of 6.75% per annum. On November 1, $7500 was repaid, and on December 15, $9000 was repaid. Automotive Excellence paid the balance of the loan on February 20. What was the final payment?

3. A loan of $6000 made at 11% per annum on March 10 is repaid in full on November 15. Payments were made of $2000 on June 30 and $2500 on September 5. What was the final payment?

4. D. Slipp borrowed $15 000 on August 12. She paid $6000 on November 1, $5000 on December 15, and the balance on February 20. The rate of interest on the loan was 10.5%. How much did she pay on February 20?

5. Erindale Automotive borrowed $8000 from the Bank of Montreal on a demand note on May 10. Interest on the loan, calculated on the daily balance, is charged to Erindale's current account on the 10th of each month. Erindale made a payment of $2000 on July 20, a payment of $3000 on October 1, and repaid the balance on December 1. The rate of interest on the loan on May 10 was 8% per annum. The rate was changed to 9.5% on August 1 and to 8.5% on October 1. What was the total interest cost for the loan?

6. The Tomac Swim Club arranged short-term financing of $12 500 on July 20 with the Bank of Commerce and secured the loan with a demand note. The club repaid the loan by payments of $6000 on September 15, $3000 on November 10, and the balance on December 30. Interest, calculated on the daily balance and charged to the club's current account on the last day of each month, was at 9.5% per annum on July 20. The rate was changed to 8.5% effective September 1 and to 9% effective December 1. How much interest was paid on the loan?

7. The Continental Bank made a loan of $20 000 on March 25 to Dr. Hirsch to purchase equipment for her office. The loan was secured by a demand loan subject to a variable rate of interest that was 7% on March 25. The rate of interest was raised to 8.5% effective July 1 and to 9.5% effective September 1. Dr. Hirsch made partial payments on the loan as follows: $600 on May 15; $800 on June 30; and $400 on October 10. The terms of the note require payment of any accrued interest on October 31. How much must Dr. Hirsch pay on October 31?

8. Dirk Ward borrowed $12 000 for investment purposes on May 10 on a demand note providing for a variable rate of interest and payment of any accrued interest on December 31. He paid $300 on June 25, $150 on September 20, and $200 on November 5. How much is the accrued interest on December 31 if the rate of interest was 7.5% on May 10, 6% effective August 1, and 5% effective November 1?

9. Pamela borrowed $15 000.00 for investment purposes on March 12 on a demand note providing for a variable rate of interest and payment of any accrued interest on December 31. She repaid $1500.00 on June 17, $1850 on September 10, and $3000.00 on November 8. How much is the final payment on December 31 if the rate of interest was 12.5% on March 12, 9.75% effective August 1, and 7.45% effective October 1? Use the declining balance approach.

8.4 LINES OF CREDIT AND SIMPLE INTEREST LOANS

A **line of credit** is a pre-approved loan agreement between a financial institution and a borrower. The borrower may withdraw money, up to an agreed maximum, at any time. Interest is charged only on the amount withdrawn from the line of credit. A minimum repayment may be required each month. The borrower may repay any additional amount at any time without further penalty. The rate of interest charged for money borrowed on a line of credit is often lower than the rate of interest charged on most credit cards. The interest rate can change over time based on market conditions.

An **unsecured line of credit** is a line of credit with no assets promised to the lender to cover non-payment of the loan. Since no security is offered to the lender, the limit of an unsecured line of credit depends on the individual's credit rating and past relationship with the lender.

A **secured line of credit** is a line of credit with assets promised to the lender to cover non-payment of the loan. For example, homeowners might pledge the value of their home—that is, their home equity—to secure a line of credit. In general, the limit of a secured line of credit is higher than the limit of an unsecured one. Furthermore, the interest rate of a secured line of credit is lower than the interest rate of an unsecured one.

Lines of credit secured by home equity are used by some borrowers as an alternative to other types of loans. Home equity lines of credit (HELOC) provide access to larger credit limits.

EXAMPLE 8.4A

Deb secured a line of credit for her business and received the following statement of account for the month of February.

Date	Transaction Description	Deposit	Withdrawal	Balance
Feb. 01	Balance			−600.00
04	Cheque 262		500.00	−1100.00
10	Deposit	2050.00		950.00
16	Cheque 263		240.00	710.00
20	Cheque 264		1000.00	−290.00
22	Cheque 265		80.00	−370.00
27	Cheque 266		150.00	−520.00
28	Interest earned	?		
	Line of credit interest		?	
	Overdraft interest		?	
	Service charge		?	

Note: "−" indicates a negative balance.

The limit on her line of credit is $1000. She receives daily interest of 1.5% p.a. on positive balances and pays daily interest of 7% p.a. on *negative (line of credit) balances*. Overdraft interest is 18% p.a. on the daily amount exceeding her line of credit limit. There is a service charge of $5 for each transaction causing an overdraft or adding to an overdraft.

Determine

(i) the amount of interest earned;

(ii) the amount of interest charged on the line of credit;

(iii) the amount of interest charged on overdrafts;

(iv) the amount of the service charge;

(v) the account balance on February 28.

SOLUTION

(i) Interest earned (on positive balances):

February 10 to February 15 inclusive: 6 days at 1.5% on $950.00

$$I = 950.00(0.015)\left(\frac{6}{365}\right) = \$0.23$$

February 16 to February 19 inclusive: 4 days at 1.5% on $710.00

$$I = 710.00(0.015)\left(\frac{4}{365}\right) = \$0.12$$

Total interest earned = 0.23 + 0.12 = $0.35

(ii) Line of credit interest charged (on negative balances up to $1000.00):
February 1 to February 3 inclusive: 3 days at 7% on $600.00

$$I = 600.00(0.07)\left(\frac{3}{365}\right) = \$0.35$$

February 4 to February 9 inclusive: 6 days at 7% on $1000.00

$$I = 1000.00(0.07)\left(\frac{6}{365}\right) = \$1.15$$

February 20 to February 21 inclusive: 2 days at 7% on $290.00

$$I = 290.00(0.07)\left(\frac{2}{365}\right) = \$0.11$$

February 22 to February 26 inclusive: 5 days at 7% on $370.00

$$I = 370.00(0.07)\left(\frac{5}{365}\right) = \$0.35$$

February 27 to February 28 inclusive: 2 days at 7% on $520.00

$$I = 520.00(0.07)\left(\frac{2}{365}\right) = \$0.20$$

Total line of credit interest charged
$$= 0.35 + 1.15 + 0.11 + 0.35 + 0.20 = \$2.16$$

(iii) Since the line of credit limit is $1000.00, overdraft interest is charged on the amount in excess of a negative balance of $1000.00. The account was in overdraft from February 4 to February 9, inclusive, in the amount of $100.00.

$$\text{Overdraft interest} = 100.00\,(0.18)\left(\frac{6}{365}\right) = \$0.30$$

(iv) There was one transaction causing an overdraft or adding to an overdraft.
Service charge = 1(5.00) = $5.00

(v) The account balance on February 28
$$= -520.00 + 0.35 - 2.16 - 0.30 - 5.00 = -\$527.11$$

EXAMPLE 8.4B

You applied for and received a personal line of credit from your bank. The interest rate charged is 5.75% per annum. You used the line of credit for the following transactions in the month of September.

September 6   Purchased textbooks and supplies for a total of $250.

September 10   Withdrew $500 to purchase a desk

September 30   Received a statement, showing a minimum balance owing of $25. A payment date of October 10 is stated on the statement.

(i) Compute the amount of interest charged on the $500 withdrawal from September 10 until September 30.

(ii) You decide to pay the amount owing, in full, on October 1. How much must you pay?

(iii) Instead of paying the full amount, you decide to pay the minimum, $25, on October 1. What is the balance owing after the payment?

(iv) If there are no further transactions during October, how much is owing at the end of October?

SOLUTION

(i) Interest charged:

September 10 to September 30 inclusive: $500 at 5.75% for 21 days.

$$I = 500(0.0575)\left(\frac{21}{365}\right) = \$1.65$$

(ii) $250 + \$500 + \$750(0.0575)\left(\frac{21}{365}\right) = \$752.48$

(iii) $752.48 - 25 = \$727.48$

(iv) $727.48 + \$727.48(0.0575)\left(\frac{31}{365}\right) = \$731.03$

At the end of October, $731.03 is owing.

EXERCISE 8.4   MyLab Math

1. On June 15, 2020, Jean-Luc borrowed $2500 from his bank secured by a demand loan. He agreed to repay the loan in five equal monthly installments and authorized the bank to collect the interest monthly from his bank account at 6% per annum calculated on the unpaid balance. Determine the total interest on the loan.

2. Jamie borrowed $900 from the Essex District Credit Union. The loan agreement provided for repayment of the loan in four equal monthly payments plus interest at 12% per annum calculated on the unpaid balance. What was the loan balance outstanding after the second payment? How much total interest did Jamie pay on this loan?

3. Grant bought a new lawn tractor on his credit card for $1998. He pays his credit card off in full each month so that he does not incur huge credit card interest on his purchases. This month he was a little short on cash so he paid off the credit card balance using his secured line of credit, which charges him prime (2.75%) plus 1%. If he paid off the line of credit in two equal installments, plus the interest, at 15 days after the purchase and 30 days after the purchase, what was the total amount of interest paid on the purchase of the lawn tractor?

Determine the missing information for each of the following lines of credit.

4. Suppose you have a line of credit and receive the following statement for the month of March.

Date	Transaction Description	Deposit	Withdrawal	Balance
Feb. 28	Balance			−527.71
Mar. 02	Cheque 264		600.00	−1127.71
05	Cheque 265		300.00	−1427.71
10	Deposit	2000.00		572.29
16	Cheque 266		265.00	307.29
20	Cheque 267		1000.00	−692.71
22	Cheque 268		83.50	−776.21
27	Cheque 269		165.00	−941.21
31	Interest earned	?		
	Line of credit interest		?	
	Overdraft interest		?	
	Service charge		?	?

Note: "−" indicates a negative balance.

The limit on the line of credit is $1000. Daily interest of 1.25% p.a. is received on positive balances and daily interest of 8% p.a. is paid on negative (line of credit) balances. Overdraft interest is 18% p.a. on the daily amount exceeding the line of credit limit. There is a service charge of $5 for each transaction causing an overdraft or adding to an overdraft.

(a) Calculate the amount of interest earned.
(b) Calculate the amount of interest charged on the line of credit.
(c) Calculate the amount of interest charged on overdrafts.
(d) Calculate the amount of the service charge.
(e) What is the account balance on March 31?   Reference Example 8.4A

🌐 **5.** Exotic Furnishings Ltd. has a line of credit secured by the equity in the business. The limit on the line of credit is $45 000. Transactions for the period April 1 to September 30 are shown next. Exotic owed $25 960.06 on its line of credit on April 1.

Date	Principal Withdrawal	Principal Payment	Interest Payment	Balance
Apr. 01				−25 960.06
30		200.00	?	
May 23	5 000.00			
31		200.00	?	
June 30		200.00	?	
July 19	5 000.00			
31		200.00	?	
Aug. 05	10 500.00			
31		200.00	?	
Sept. 30		200.00	?	?

Note: "−" indicates a negative balance.

The line of credit agreement requires a regular payment of $200 on the principal plus interest (including overdraft interest) by electronic transfer after closing on the last day of each month. Overdraft interest is 17% p.a. The line of credit interest is variable. It was 6.00% on April 1, 5.50% effective June 20, and 5.00% effective September 10.

(a) Calculate the interest payments on April 30, May 31, June 30, July 31, August 31, and September 30.
(b) What is the account balance on September 30?

8.5 LOAN REPAYMENT SCHEDULES
A. Purpose

In the case of loans repaid in fixed installments (often called **blended payments**), the constant periodic payment is first applied to pay the accumulated interest. The remainder of the payment is then used to reduce the unpaid balance of the principal.

While lenders are obliged to disclose to the borrower the total cost of borrowing as well as the interest rate (see Figure 8.6), a detailed statement of the cost of borrowing as well as the effect of the periodic payments on the principal may be obtained by constructing a **loan repayment schedule**, or an **amortization schedule**.

Figure 8.6 Statement of Disclosure (© S. A. Hummelbrunner)

STATEMENT OF DISCLOSURE

(COST OF LOAN AND ANNUAL INTEREST RATE)   PURSUANT TO THE CONSUMER PROTECTION ACT

Name of Credit Union _____ SHERIDAN _____   Account No. 13465–274

1) Balance of existing loan (if any) $ __2000.00__   4) Cost of Borrowing expressed in dollars and cents
(Interest calculated on full amount of loan (Item 3)) $ __1473.00__

2) Add new amount loaned $ __4000.00__   5) Annual Interest Rate charged (calculated in
accordance with the Consumer Protection Act)   __9__ %

3) Full amount of loan $ __6000.00__

6) If any charge is made to the borrower in addition to interest herein noted, it must be disclosed here. $ _____
(Description)...
Frequency of installments __60 MONTHS__ Amount of installments $ __124.55__ First instalment due _____ 20 __

I, the undersigned, acknowledge receipt of this statement of cost of loan and annual interest rate, prior to the advance of the credit.

DATE _____   X ....
SIGNATURE OF BORROWER

COMPLETE IN DUPLICATE   NOTE: Where more than one maker or co-maker, separate Disclosure Forms should
Original to Borrower   be signed for individually.

The information usually contained in such a schedule includes

(a) the payment number or payment date;
(b) the amount paid at each payment date;
(c) the interest paid by each payment;
(d) the principal repaid by each payment;
(e) the unpaid loan balance after each payment.

Figure 8.7 provides a possible design for such schedules, and the same design is used in the solution to Example 8.5A.

Figure 8.7 Basic Design of a Loan Repayment Schedule (© S. A. Hummelbrunner)

① Payment Number	② Balance Before Payment	③ Amount Paid	④ Interest Paid	⑤ Principal Repaid	⑥ Balance After Payment

B. Construction of loan repayment schedules illustrated

EXAMPLE 8.5A

Great Lakes Marina borrowed $1600 from Sheridan Credit Union at 9% p.a. and agreed to repay the loan in monthly installments of $300 each, over the next year, such payments to cover interest due and repayment of principal. Use the design shown in Figure 8.7 to construct a complete repayment schedule, including the totalling of columns ③, ④, and ⑤ ("Amount Paid," "Interest Paid," and "Principal Repaid").

SOLUTION   See Figure 8.8 and the explanatory notes that follow.

Figure 8.8 Loan Repayment Schedule for Example 8.5A (© S. A. Hummelbrunner)

① Payment Number	② Balance Before Payment	③ Amount Paid (1)	④ Interest Paid (2)	⑤ Principal Repaid (3)	⑥ Balance After Payment (4)
0					1600.00 (5)
1	1600.00	300.00	12.00 (6)	288.00 (7)	1312.00 (8)
2	1312.00	300.00	9.84 (9)	290.16 (10)	1021.84 (11)
3	1021.84	300.00	7.66	292.34	729.50
4	729.50	300.00	5.47	294.53	434.97
5	434.97	300.00	3.26	296.74	138.23 (12)
6	138.23	139.27 (15)	1.04 (14)	138.23 (13)	0.00
Totals (16)		1639.27 (18)	39.27 (19)	1600.00 (17)	

Notes:

(1) The Amount Paid shown in column ③ is the agreed-upon monthly payment of $300.

(2) The Interest Paid shown in column ④ is at 9% per annum. This figure is converted into a periodic (monthly) rate of $\frac{9\%}{12}$ (0.75% per month) to facilitate the computation of the monthly amount of interest paid. (See notes (6) and (9).)

(3) The amount of Principal Repaid each month shown in column ⑤ is found by subtracting the Interest Paid for the month (column ④) from the Amount Paid for the month (column ③). (See notes (7) and (10).)

(4) The Balance After Payment for a month shown in column ⑥ is found by subtracting the Principal Repaid for the month (column ⑤) from the Balance Before Payment for the month (column ②) *or* from the previous Balance After Payment figure (column ⑥). (See notes (8) and (11).)

(5) The original loan balance of $1600 is introduced as the starting amount for the schedule and is the only amount shown in Line 0.

(6) Interest paid in Payment Number 1
= 0.75% of 1600.00 = (0.0075)(1600.00) = $12.00

(7) Principal repaid by Payment Number 1
= 300.00 − 12.00 = $288.00

(8) Balance after Payment Number 1
= 1600.00 − 288.00 = $1312.00

(9) Interest paid in Payment Number 2
= 0.75% of 1312.00 = (0.0075)(1312.00) = $9.84

(10) Principal repaid by Payment Number 2
= 300.00 − 9.84 = $290.16

(11) Balance after Payment Number 2
= 1312.00 − 290.16 = $1021.84

(12) The Balance after Payment Number 5 of $138.23 is smaller than the regular monthly payment of $300. The next payment need only be sufficient to pay the outstanding balance of $138.23 plus the interest due. (See notes (13), (14), and (15).)

(13) Principal repaid in Payment Number 6 must be $138.23 to pay off the outstanding loan balance.

(14) Interest paid in Payment Number 6 is the interest due on $138.23
$$= 0.75\% \text{ of } 138.23 = (0.0075)(138.23) = \$1.04.$$

(15) Amount paid in Payment Number 6
$$= 138.23 + 1.04 = \$139.27.$$

(16) The Totals of columns ③, ④, and ⑤ serve as a check of the arithmetic accuracy of the payment schedule. (See notes (17), (18), and (19).)

(17) Principal Repaid, the total of column 5, must equal the original loan balance of $1600.

(18) Amount Paid, the total of column ③, must equal the total of all the payments made (five payments of $300 each plus the final payment of $139.27).

(19) Interest paid, the total of column ④, must be the difference between the totals of columns ④ and ⑤ = 1639.27 − 1600.00 = $39.27.

C. Computer application—loan repayment schedule

This exercise assumes a basic understanding of spreadsheet applications. However, an individual who has no previous experience with spreadsheets can still complete this task.

Microsoft Excel and other spreadsheet programs allow the user to easily create a flexible loan repayment schedule. The finished repayment schedule will reflect any changes made to the loan amount, the interest rate, or the schedule of payments. (The following example was created in Excel, but most programs work similarly.)

The following Excel application is based on Example 8.5A, which uses six months to repay the loan. An additional row of formulas similar to row 3 would be added for each additional month required to repay the loan.

STEP 1 Enter the labels shown in Figure 8.9 in row 1 and in column A.

STEP 2 Enter the numbers shown in row 2.

Figure 8.9 Workbook 1 (© S. A. Hummelbrunner)

	A	B	C	D	E	F	G
1	Payment	Balance before payment	Amount paid	Interest paid	Principal repaid	Balance	
2	0					1600.00	300.00
3	1	= F2	= $G$2	= $G$4*B3	= C3–D3	= B3–E3	
4	2	= F3	= $G$2	= $G$4*B4	= C4–D4	= B4–E4	= 0.09/12
5	3	= F4	= $G$2	= $G$4*B5	= C5–D5	= B5–E5	
6	4	= F5	= $G$2	= $G$4*B6	= C6–D6	= B6–E6	
7	5	= F6	= $G$2	= $G$4*B7	= C7–D7	= B7–E7	
8	6	= F7	= D8+E8	= $G$4*B8	= B8	= B8–E8	
9	Totals		= SUM(C3:C8)	= SUM(D3:D8)	= SUM(E3:E8)		

STEP 3 Enter only the formulas shown in rows 3, 8, and 9. Make sure that the entry includes the dollar sign ($) as shown in the figure.

STEP 4 The formulas that are entered in row 3 can be copied through the remaining rows.

(a) Select cells B3 to F3, and select Copy.
(b) Select cells B4 to F7, and select Paste.
(c) The formulas are now active in all the cells.

STEP 5 To ensure readability of the spreadsheet, format the numbers to display as two decimal places, and widen the columns to display the full labels.

This spreadsheet can now be used to reflect changes in aspects of the loan and display the effects quickly. Put a new principal amount in cell F2 and a new interest rate in cell G4. The interest rate must be divided by 12 to convert the annual interest rate to a monthly rate. For example, a new annual interest rate of 5% would be entered as $\dfrac{0.05}{12}$.

EXERCISE 8.5   MyLab Math

Use the design shown in Figure 8.7 to construct a complete repayment schedule including the totalling of the Amount Paid, Interest Paid, and Principal Repaid columns for each of the following loans.

1. Carla borrowed $1200 from the Royal Bank at 8.5% per annum calculated on the monthly unpaid balance. She agreed to repay the loan in blended payments of $180 per month.

2. Blended payments on a $3400 loan were $800 per month. Interest was charged at 7.75% per annum calculated on the monthly unpaid balance.

3. On March 15, Julio borrowed $900 from Sheridan Credit Union at 7.5% per annum calculated on the daily balance. He gave the Credit Union six cheques for $135 dated the 15th of each of the next six months starting April 15 and a cheque dated October 15 for the remaining balance to cover payment of interest and repayment of principal.

4. On February 8, Manuel borrowed $700 from his uncle at 6% per annum calculated on the daily balance. He gave his uncle seven cheques for $100 dated the 8th of each of the next seven months starting March 8 and a cheque dated September 8 for the remaining balance to cover payment of interest and repayment of principal.

BUSINESS MATH **NEWS**

What is a payday loan and why do people choose a payday loan? A payday loan is an unsecured loan for a small sum, typically a few hundred dollars, to be repaid after a short period of time—usually no more than two weeks.

Sometimes consumers, even those with steady incomes, find themselves short on cash and can't wait until their next payday. Used responsibly, a small payday loan can be a useful way to finance an emergency shortage of funds due to an unexpected bill or repair. Before obtaining a payday loan, however, you should consider whether a payday loan is a sensible choice that meets your particular financial needs and situation.

How does it work? Payday loans are meant for occasional and unusual use only. Applicants must be at least 18, have a bank account, and prove they have a steady job. Once approved, the funds are either electronically deposited into your bank account or may be picked up at a store location. Your payment is scheduled to be due on your next pay date following the origination of the loan, giving this type of loan its name. Loans must be paid in full on the due date; they cannot be refinanced or rolled over. The payment is withdrawn from your chequing account electronically, so make sure you have enough funds in your account on the due date so that you do not incur any non-sufficient funds (NSF) fees.

How much will it cost you? Payday loans are very high-cost loans. Under the current rules, Nova Scotia lenders can charge fees of up to $25 for every $100 borrowed—the highest rate in the country. By comparison, lenders in British Columbia can charge a maximum fee of $17 per $100. In Ontario, the maximum allowable cost of borrowing is $15 per $100 borrowed (including all fees and charges), which is the lowest in the country.

Like banks, payday loan lenders are required to disclose the "cost" of borrowing in some standardized way as a form of consumer protection. To a consumer who is not trained in the mathematics of finance, equivalent rates can be confusing. The term *annual percentage rate of charge* (APR) describes the interest rate for a whole year (annualized), rather than just a monthly fee/rate, as applied on the loan. The APR is intended to make it easier to compare lenders and loan options.

The effective APR has been called the "mathematically true" interest rate for each year. For instance, the APR on a $300 payday loan for 14 days is a whopping 599.64% (annualized) on a rate of $23.00 per $100.00 borrowed. This means that if your loan was outstanding for a full year, you would pay 6 times the amount you originally borrowed. Note that this amount does not include possible compounding and any late-payment fees!

QUESTIONS

1. The Ontario Payday Loan Act limits the amount an individual may be charged to $15 per $100 borrowed for a two-week period. Calculate the cost of the loan and the annual percentage rate of charge (APR).

2. What is the cost of borrowing $300 for 14 days at a rate of $21 per $100 borrowed, and how much must be paid back on the due date? Calculate the APR.

3. Payday loans are the most expensive form of consumer loan. Before getting a payday loan, you should consider other ways to borrow money. List some possible alternatives.

Source: https://www.canada.ca/en/financial-consumer-agency/services/loans/payday-loans.html

MyLab Math Visit MyLab Math to practise any of this chapter's exercises marked with a ⊕ as often as you want. The guided solutions help you calculate an answer step by step. You'll find a personalized study plan and additional interactive resources to help you master Business Math!

REVIEW EXERCISE

1. **LO①** A four-month promissory note for $1600 dated June 30 bears interest at 6.5%.

   (a) What is the due date of the note?

   (b) What is the amount of interest payable at the due date?

   (c) What is the maturity value of the note?

2. **LO①** Determine the maturity value of a 45-day note for $1250 dated May 23 and bearing interest at 8%.

3. **LO①** Compute the face value of a 120-day note dated September 10 bearing interest at 6.75% whose maturity value is $1533.29.

4. **LO①** The maturity value of a seven-month promissory note issued July 31, 2021, is $3275. What is the present value of the note on the date of issue if interest is 7.75%?

5. **LO①** Compute the maturity value of a 150-day, 6% promissory note with a face value of $5000 dated August 5.

6. **LO①** What is the face value of a three-month promissory note dated June 18, 2022, with interest at 4.5%, if its maturity value is $950.89?

7. **LO①** A 90-day, $800 promissory note was issued July 31 with interest at 8%. What is the value of the note on October 20?

8. **LO①** On June 1, 2021, a four-month promissory note for $1850 with interest at 5% was issued. Compute the proceeds of the note on August 28, 2021, if money is worth 6.5%.

9. **LO①** Determine the value of a $1300 non-interest-bearing note four months before its maturity date of July 13, 2021, if money is worth 7%.

10. **LO①** Compute the proceeds of a five-month, $7000 promissory note dated September 6, 2022, with interest at 5.5% if the note is paid on November 28, 2022, when money is worth 6.5%.

11. **LO①** What is the price of a 183-day, $500 000 Province of Ontario treasury bill that yields 1.05% per annum?

12. **LO②** An investment dealer paid $24 756.25 to acquire a $25 000, 182-day Government of Canada treasury bill at the weekly auction. What was the annual rate of return on this T-bill?

13. **LO③** Government of Alberta 364-day T-bills with a face value of $1 000 000 were purchased on April 7 for $971 578. The T-bills were sold on May 16 for $983 500.

    (a) What was the market yield rate on April 7?

    (b) What was the yield rate on May 16?

    (c) What was the rate of return realized?

14. **LO②** At auction on June 22, 2021, $100 000, 91-day treasury bills were sold for $99 600. An investor purchasing one of these T-bills held it for 40 days, then sold it to yield 1.4%.

    (a) What was the original yield of the T-bill?

    (b) At what price did the investor sell?

    (c) What annual rate of return did the investor realize while holding his T-bill?

15. **LO③** On April 2, Kelly borrowed $15 000 on a demand note with an interest rate of 9% per annum. Payments were made of $2800 on May 14 and $2400 on June 19. How much was the final payment made on August 3?

16. **LO③** Mel's Photography borrowed $15 000 on March 10 on a demand note. The loan was repaid by payments of $4000 on June 20, $3000 on September 1, and the balance on November 15. Interest, calculated on the daily balance and charged to Mel's Photography current account on the last day of each month, was at 5.5% on March 10 but was changed to 6.25% effective June 1 and to 6% effective October 1. How much did the loan cost?

17. **LO③** Quick Print Press borrowed $20 000 from the Provincial Bank on May 25 at 7.5% and secured the loan by signing a promissory note subject to a variable rate of interest. Quick Print made partial payments of $5000 on July 10 and $8000 on September 15. The rate of interest was increased to 8% effective August 1 and to 8.5% effective October 1. What payment must Quick Print make on October 31 if, under the terms of the loan agreement, any interest accrued as of October 31 is to be paid on October 31?

18. LO④ Muriel has a line of credit with a limit of $10 000. She owed $8195 on July 1. Principal withdrawals for the period July 1 to November 30 were $3000 on August 20 and $600 on October 25. The line of credit agreement requires regular payments of $300 on the 15th day of each month. Muriel has made all required payments. Interest (including overdraft interest) is charged to the account on the last day of each month. The interest rate was 8% on July 1, but was changed to 7.5% effective September 15. Overdraft interest is 16% for any balance in excess of $10 000.

(a) Calculate the interest charges on July 31, August 31, September 30, October 31, and November 30.

(b) Calculate the account balance on November 30.

19. LO④ Bryan buys a new washer/dryer set worth $3996. His first option is to pay for the appliances on his personal (unsecured) line of credit and pay it back after 6 months. His second option is to use a secured line of credit and pay it back in 9 months.

The unsecured line of credit charges a rate of prime (3%) plus 2%, and the secured line of credit charges a rate of prime plus 0.5%. What is his best option?

20. LO④ Robin borrowed $3000.00 from HSBC Bank Canada. The line of credit agreement provided for repayment of the loan in three equal monthly payments plus interest at 6.25% per annum calculated on the unpaid balance. Determine the total interest cost.

21. LO⑤ You borrowed $3000 at 9% per annum calculated on the unpaid monthly balance and agreed to repay the principal together with interest in monthly payments of $500 each. Construct a complete repayment schedule.

22. LO⑤ On December 2, 2023, Joan borrowed $2400, agreeing to repay the loan with blended payments of $292 per month, starting on January 2. Interest was charged at 7.8% per annum calculated on the monthly unpaid balance. Construct a complete repayment schedule. (*Hint:* Use the number of days appropriate for each month.)

SELF-TEST

1. The owner of the Wilson Lumber Company signed a promissory note on January 10, 2022, stating that the company was due to pay $565.00 with interest at 8.25% per annum in five months. How much interest is due at maturity of the note?

2. Calculate the maturity value of a $1140, 7.75%, 120-day note dated February 19, 2021.

3. Determine the face value of a four-month promissory note dated May 20, 2022, with interest at 7.5% p.a. if the maturity value of the note is $1190.03.

4. Calculate the present value of a non-interest-bearing, seven-month promissory note for $1800 dated August 7, 2021, on December 20, 2021, if money is then worth 9%.

5. A 180-day note dated September 14, 2021, is made at 5% for $1665. What is the present value of the note on October 18, 2021, if money is worth 6%?

6. What is the price of a 91-day, $25 000 Government of Canada treasury bill that yields 1.28% per annum?

7. An investor purchased a 182-day, $100 000 T-bill on its issue date. It yielded 3.85%. The investor held the T-bill for 67 days, and then sold it for $98 853.84.

(a) What was the original price of the T-bill?
(b) When the T-bill was sold, what was its yield to maturity rate?

8. The owner of Jane's Boutique borrowed $6000 from Halton Community Credit Union on June 5, 2022. The loan was secured by a demand note with interest calculated on the daily balance and charged to the store's account on the 5th day of each month. The loan was repaid by payments of $1500 on July 15, $2000 on October 10, and $2500 on December 30. The rate of interest charged by the credit union was 8.5% on June 5. The rate was changed to 9.5% effective July 1 and to 10% effective October 1. Determine the total interest cost on the loan.

9. Herb's Restaurant borrowed $24 000 on March 1 on a demand note providing for a variable rate of interest. While repayment of principal is open, any accrued interest is to be paid on November 30. Payments on the loan were made as follows: $600 on April 15, $400 on July 20, and $400 on October 10. The rate of interest was 7% on March 1 but was changed to 8.5% effective August 1 and to 7.5% effective November 1. Using the declining balance method to record the partial payments, determine the accrued interest on November 30.

10. Jing has a line of credit from her local bank with a limit of $10 000. On March 1 she owed $7265. From March 1 to June 30, she withdrew principal amounts of $3000 on April 10 and $500 on June 20. According to the line of credit agreement, Jing must make a regular payment of $200 on the 15th of each month. She has made these payments. Interest (including overdraft interest) is charged to the account on the last day of each month. On March 1, the interest rate was 9%, but it was changed to 8.5% effective May 15. Overdraft interest is 18% for any balance in excess of $10 000.

    (a) Calculate the interest charges on March 31, April 30, May 31, and June 30.
    (b) What is the account balance on June 30?

11. Use the design shown in Figure 8.7 to construct a complete repayment schedule, including the totalling of the "Amount Paid," "Interest Paid," and "Principal Repaid" columns, for a loan of $4000 repaid in monthly installments of $750 each including interest of 6.5% per annum calculated on the unpaid balance.

CHALLENGE PROBLEMS

1. Mike Kornas signed a 12-month, 11% p.a. simple interest promissory note for $12 000 with MacDonald's Furniture. After 100 days, MacDonald's Furniture sold the note to the Royal Bank at a rate of 13% p.a. Royal Bank resold the note to Friendly Finance Company 25 days later at a rate of 9% p.a. Determine the gain or loss on this note for each company and bank involved.

2. A father wanted to show his son what it might be like to borrow money from a financial institution. When his son asked if he could borrow $120, the father lent him the money and set up the following arrangements. He charged his son $6 for the loan of $120. The son therefore received $114 and agreed to pay his father 12 installments of $10 a month, beginning one month from today, until the loan was repaid. Calculate the approximate rate of simple interest the father charged on this loan.

CASE STUDY   Debt Consolidation

▶ Shannon and Duncan Fisher were concerned about their level of debt. They had borrowed from their bank to purchase their house, car, and computer. For these three loans, the Fishers must make regular monthly payments. The couple also owe $6000 to MasterCard and $2500 to Visa. Shannon and Duncan decided to meet with a consumer credit counsellor to gain control of their debts.

The counsellor explained to them the details of their loans and credit card debts. Shannon and Duncan were shocked to discover that whereas their computer and car loans had an interest rate of 7.95% p.a., their credit cards had an interest rate of 19.99% p.a. The counsellor pointed out that the interest rate on their three loans was reasonable. However, because the interest rate on the credit cards was so high, she advised Shannon and Duncan to borrow money at a lower interest rate and pay off the credit card debts.

The credit counsellor suggested that they should consider obtaining a home equity line of credit (HELOC). She explained that the rate of interest on the line of credit would likely be a few percentage points higher than the prime rate, but much lower than the rate of interest charged on the credit card balances. Shannon and Duncan would have to make a minimum payment every month, similar to that of a credit card. The payment would then be applied to pay all the interest and a portion of the principal balance owing on the line of credit. The line of credit would allow them to make monthly payments higher than the minimum so that they could pay as much toward the principal balance as they could afford. Due to the much lower interest rate on a line of credit as compared to a typical credit card, the money they would save on interest each month could be paid toward the principal. A line of credit appealed to Shannon and Duncan, as it helped them feel more in control of their finances and gave them the resolve to pay off their credit card debts.

Shannon and Duncan then met with their bank manager and were approved for a $15 000 line of credit. Immediately, they paid off the $6000 owed to MasterCard and the $2500 owed to Visa with money from the line of credit. They then decided to pay off the line of credit over the next ten months by making monthly payments equal to one-tenth of the original line of credit balance plus the simple interest owed on the remaining line of credit balance. The simple interest rate on the line of credit is expected to be 6.25% over the next ten months. Shannon and Duncan agreed to cut up their credit cards and not charge any more purchases until they had paid off their line of credit.

QUESTIONS

1. Suppose Shannon and Duncan pay off their credit cards with their line of credit on April 20. They will make their monthly payments on the 20th of each month, beginning in May. Create a schedule showing their monthly payments for the next ten months. How much interest will they pay using this repayment plan?

2. Suppose Shannon and Duncan had not gotten a line of credit but kept their credit cards. They decided not to make any more credit card purchases. Instead, they borrowed $8500 from Shannon's parents to pay off the MasterCard and Visa and made monthly payments equal to one-tenth of the original credit card debt plus simple interest of 10% p.a. on the remaining monthly balance. They will make their monthly payments on the 20th of each month, beginning in May. Create a schedule showing their monthly payments for the next ten months. How much interest would they have paid using this repayment plan?

3. How much money did Shannon and Duncan save on interest by borrowing from Shannon's parents?

4. What are the requirements for obtaining a line of credit from your financial institution?

SUMMARY OF FORMULAS

Formula 7.1

$I = Prt$ Calculating the amount of interest on promissory notes

Formula 7.3

$S = P(1 + rt)$ Calculating the maturity value of promissory notes directly

Formula 7.4

$P = \dfrac{S}{1 + rt}$ Calculating the present value of promissory notes or treasury bills given the maturity value

GLOSSARY

Amortization schedule see **Loan repayment schedule**

Amount of interest the interest, in dollars and cents, payable to the payee on the legal due date *(p. 302)*

Blended payment the usual method of repaying a personal consumer loan by a fixed periodic (monthly) payment that covers payment of interest and repayment of principal *(p. 319)*

Credit rating a rating that reflects the credit history and the repayment reliability of a borrower *(p. 303)*

Credit score see **Credit rating**

Date of issue the date on which a promissory note is made *(p. 302)*

Date of maturity *see* **Legal due date**

Declining balance approach the commonly used approach to applying partial payments to demand loans whereby each partial payment is first applied to pay the interest due and then applied to the outstanding principal *(p. 312)*

Demand loan a loan for which repayment in full or in part may be required at any time or made at any time *(p. 312)*

Demand note the financial instrument representing a demand loan *(p. 312)*

Due date *see* **Legal due date**

Face value the sum of money specified on the promissory note *(p. 302)*

Grace period the period of time between a statement date and a payment date *(p. 303)*

Interest-bearing promissory note a note subject to the rate of interest stated on the note *(p. 302)*

Interest period the time, in days, from the date of issue to the legal due date for promissory notes *(p. 302)*

Issue date *see* **Date of issue**

Legal due date the date on which the promissory note is to be paid *(p. 303)*

Line of credit a pre-approved loan amount issued by a financial institution for use by an individual or business at any time for any purpose; interest is charged only for the time money is borrowed on the line of credit; a minimum monthly payment is required; the interest rate can change over time *(p. 315)*

Loan repayment schedule a detailed statement of installment payments, interest cost, repayment of principal, and outstanding balance of principal for an installment plan *(p. 320)*

Maker the party making the promise to pay by signing the promissory note *(p. 302)*

Maturity value the amount (face value plus interest) that must be paid on the legal due date to honour the note *(p. 302)*

Non-interest-bearing promissory note a note in which no interest rate is stated *(p. 305)*

Partial payments a series of payments on a debt *(p. 312)*

Payee the party to whom the promise to pay is made *(p. 302)*

Promissory note a written promise to pay a specified sum of money after a specified period of time or on demand, with or without interest as specified *(p. 302)*

Rate of interest the simple annual rate of interest based on the face value *(p. 302)*

Rate money is worth the prevailing rate of interest *(p. 304)*

Secured line of credit a line of credit with assets pledged as security *(p. 316)*

T-bills *see* **Treasury bills**

Term (of a promissory note) the time period for which the note was written (in days or months) *(p. 302)*

Treasury bills promissory notes issued at a discount from their face values by the federal government and most provincial governments to meet short-term financing requirements (the maturity value of treasury bills is the same as their face value) *(p. 309)*

Unsecured line of credit a line of credit in which no assets are pledged by the borrower to the lender to cover non-payment of the line of credit *(p. 315)*

PART 2

Comprehensive Case

SportZ Ltd.

SportZ Ltd. is a manufacturer and retailer of sports equipment based in Calgary, Alberta. Two brothers started the company in 1991. At that time, their children were young and enrolled in pee-wee hockey in the winter and soccer in the summer. They saw a need for sports equipment that was of better quality and more reliable. Since the start-up, the company has expanded into various other sports, with a central manufacturing location and several retail outlet stores in western Canada and Ontario.

One of the items that SportZ Ltd. has manufactured for the past 10 years is a goalie's helmet. Recently, a new mask design has been developed and tested, and the company is ready to start production. The new design has been tested and endorsed by officials connected to the Calgary Flames, the local NHL team. The owners of SportZ Ltd. are excited about the potential offered by the new mask.

In developing and marketing the new mask, costs for the equipment need to be analyzed, with prices and profitability determined. In managing the short-term financial needs, several promissory notes and demand loans are due for payment or renewal. Lines of credit have been established with suppliers and local banks.

You have been asked by the owners to analyze the financial data and to provide answers to several questions.

1. CHAPTER 5 – QUESTIONS

a. SportZ sponsors an evening session of skating at the local arena. A family pass is offered, whereby a parent and up to two children are admitted for $12. Free hot chocolate is provided to those with the family pass. The rental of the arena for each of these sessions costs $1000. Hot chocolate costs $0.50 per person. Estimated capacity for the skating rink is 500 people.

  (i) If only family passes are sold, and each includes a parent and two children, how many family passes must be sold to break even?

  (ii) At break-even, what would be the total revenue?

  (iii) At break-even, what percent of capacity would result?

b. Along with the development of the new helmet for ice hockey, SportZ is also making changes to the street hockey helmets it offers. For one of the most popular models, the cost of the moulds is $49 920 and the selling price would be $39.99. On the basis of sales forecasts, the company estimates that it needs to sell 1600 units to break even.

   (i) What is the maximum variable cost that can be spent to make each helmet, and still break even?

   (ii) If the variable cost per unit changes, and the contribution rate is 85%, how many units need to be sold to break even?

c. To round out its inventory, SportZ outlet store buys and resells sports tape. For a package of eight rolls of standard tape, the store has been paying $3.48 to its supplier. The regular selling price for this package is $7.99. Advertising and promotional material for the product costs $2340.

   (i) How many packages need to be sold to break even?

   (ii) The supplier is offering a special promotional discount of 20% if an order of at least 1000 units is placed for each of the three winter months. If SportZ outlet store were to place this order, what is the minimum sale price it could offer and still break even?

   (iii) What would be the maximum percent discount that could be offered in a sale flyer that would still allow SportZ to break-even?

   (iv) If the packages of tape were ordered with the special promotional discount, a "25% off" sale was offered, and the store sold 950 packages of tape, how much profit or loss would SportZ outlet store make?

2. CHAPTER 6 – QUESTIONS

a. SportZ Ltd. has offered a series of discounts to their retail outlets. The basic wholesale discount is 30% off the suggested retail price. If the retailer purchases more than $5000 from SportZ, a further 20% discount is applied. As an introductory offer on the new mask, if two masks are ordered, a further 5% discount is given for the total order. Lethbridge Sports has placed an order for $9800, at the suggested retail price. How much will Lethbridge Sports have to pay for the order?

b. SportZ has received an invoice from one of its suppliers, dated April 2, for $30 120, terms 2/10. All or part of the amount owing will be paid on April 10.

   (i) How much would have to be paid to fully pay the invoice?

   (ii) How much would have to be paid to reduce the debt by $20 000?

c. A specific type of leather is needed to make gloves for a hockey player. The leather for each glove costs $12.00. To cut and style the leather, expenses of 45% of cost are incurred. The company targets a profit of 60% of cost.

   (i) What is the targeted selling price for the leather glove?

   (ii) What is the resulting markup based on cost?

   (iii) If the profit was reduced to 50% of cost, how much would be the sale price?

d. At their outlet store, SportZ has a supply of soccer balls. To make room for other equipment, the balls are being marked down to sell quickly. The retail price is $22.99, and the store has advertised a sale of 30% off.

   (i) What is the sale price for the balls?

   (ii) Due to a special promotion given to a school nearby, an additional $5.00 discount is given for each ball purchased. What is the resulting markdown rate?

3. CHAPTER 7 – QUESTIONS

SportZ Ltd. purchases materials and services from various vendors. Money has been borrowed from the Bank of Alberta. Payments to the vendors and the bank are being planned.

a. SportZ has invoices for materials purchased from Platinum Steel Inc. The invoices are for $4242 due 60 days ago, $12 567 due in 30 days, and $18 451 due in 140 days. If SportZ pays all of these invoices today, how much cash is needed? Money is worth 6% per annum.

b. Bank of Alberta loan payments of $11 000 due 35 days ago and $16 000 due in 68 days are to be replaced by a payment of $6000 today and a further payment in 90 days. If interest on these loans is 7.2% per annum, what is the size of the final payment?

c. Prairie Plastics Ltd. is owed payments of $18 000 due in 60 days and $16 000 due in 120 days. Instead, SportZ has negotiated a new payment agreement in which three equal payments are to be made in 75 days, 100 days, and 200 days. If interest of 9% is charged, what is the size of the equal payments?

d. Creative Inc., a design company, has sent SportZ an invoice for services provided in the amount of $15 000, due today. Alternatively, they will accept payment of $15 150 in 50 days. What interest rate is being charged?

4. CHAPTER 8–QUESTIONS

a. A 5% promissory note for $10 000 was issued 183 days ago. How much cash is needed today to pay the note?

b. SportZ has secured a line of credit with the Bank of Alberta. The following transactions were made for the last month. The account receives daily interest of 1.5% p.a. on positive balances and pays daily interest of 8% p.a. on negative balances. The limit on the line of credit is $10 000. Overdraft interest of 19% p.a. is charged on the daily amount exceeding the line of credit limit. For each transaction causing an overdraft or adding to an overdraft, a service charge of $10 is applied. Calculate the interest, overdraft interest, service charges, and the month-end balance for the line of credit.

Date	Transaction Description	Deposit	Withdrawal	Balance
March 1	Balance			−4000.00
5	Cheque 437		2185.00	−6185.00
7	Cheque 438		421.00	−6606.00
12	Deposit	6000.00		−606.00
15	Cheque 439		5128.00	−5734.00
21	Cheque 440		6133.00	−11867.00
23	Deposit	2000.00		−9867.00
27	Deposit	5000.00		−4867.00
31	Interest charged		?	
	Overdraft interest		?	
	Service charge		?	

c. SportZ has negotiated a loan of $25 000 with interest at 7.6% per annum, to be paid as month-end payments of $2200.00 over the next year. Construct a loan amortization schedule to answer the following questions.

(i) How much interest is paid over the first two months?

(ii) How much of the principal is paid by the end of the first two months?

(iii) How much interest is paid over the term of the loan?

(iv) What is the amount of the final payment?

PART

3

Mathematics of Finance and Investment

Part 3 of the textbook introduces compound interest mathematics as used in business and develops the concept in applications such as annuities, amortization of loans, bond valuation, and investment decisions.

Chapters 9 and 10 introduce the basic model of compound interest, which you will use to calculate future value, present value, interest rate, and term in the time value of money. These variables are used in typical financial situations, such as calculation of money saved, choosing a credit card, or comparing loan options by determining effective and equivalent interest rates.

In Chapter 11 you will be introduced to annuities through calculation of future value, present value, interest rate, and term for ordinary simple annuities. You will apply these concepts to savings plans and RRSPs, loans, and down payments to purchase property or a vehicle. In Chapter 12 you will continue with these concepts through discussion and development of ordinary general annuities. You will calculate future value, present value, interest rate, and term, with applications such as equipment purchase, contract and business valuations, property mortgages, and insurance payouts. In addition, you will determine and apply constant-growth annuities.

Chapter 13 will introduce variations of annuities. You will calculate simple and general annuities due, for which the payment is made at the beginning of the period. These are illustrated with examples such as rental payments, leases, and membership dues. You will then calculate deferred annuities, for which the start of the payment is deferred to a later period. These are illustrated with examples such as equipment purchase plans, retirement savings, RESPs, and "buy-now-pay-later" purchases. You will also learn how to determine perpetuities and deferred perpetuities for which the payment continues without end. These are illustrated with examples such as scholarships, investments, and benefits of asset purchases.

Chapter 14 expands on loans by introducing the amortization of loans. You will determine payments within loans. As you develop amortization schedules, you will calculate interest paid, principal repaid, and the outstanding principal balance for each period. When necessary, you will calculate the final payment, when different from the other payments. The laws and regulations for various types of residential mortgages in Canada are briefly explained. In this chapter, you will learn about minimum down payment ratios, and the need for mortgage default insurance is also explained. You will calculate effective interest rates, mortgage payments, and balances, for the purpose of comparing these interest rates and renewing or repaying the mortgages.

Chapter 15 applies the mathematics of finance to valuation of bonds. You will discover how to determine the purchase price of a bond when the market rate differs from the bond rate. To construct bond schedules, you will calculate bond premiums or discounts. Also, you will calculate bond yield rates, as well as construct sinking funds and sinking funds schedules.

In Chapter 16, you will employ several commonly used methods of investment decision applications. With the discounted cash flow criterion, you will evaluate capital investments through calculations of net present value and rate of return. Furthermore, you will perform project evaluation involving capital purchases, determining whether replacement or expansion is financially advisable.

The **Universal Principle of Rounding** applies in Part 3 of the textbook. When performing a sequence of operations, never round any interim solution, but apply rounding principles only to the final answer. Interim solutions should be rounded only when common practice would require rounding.

Note: Due to space limitations, the textbook shows only the first six decimals (rounded) of any number. Starting in Chapter 9, because the calculator display may not have sufficient space for all six decimals, as many decimals as possible will be shown. However, the Universal Principle of Rounding still applies.

Some specific rounding guidelines for Part 3: Business problems throughout the textbook often involve money values, so the rounding for final answers needs to be done to the cent—that is, to two decimal places—when the result is a monetary value. Interim solutions should be rounded only when common practice would require rounding. In determining when it is appropriate to round, it is important to recognize that if the money remains inside an account (deposit or loan) all of the decimals need to carry forward into the next calculation. If money is withdrawn or transferred from the account at any time, then only two decimals can be carried forward to any further steps (since a currency payout can involve only two decimals).

When calculating equivalent values for more than one payment, each payment is a separate transaction (one could make each payment separate from any other payment), and therefore any equivalent value is rounded to two decimals before summing multiple payments.

When determining a non-monetary value, such as *n,* it is necessary to determine whether the time period described can reasonably represent a fraction. For non-annuity calculations, generally the solution would not be rounded off, since *n* can be fractional in nature in most cases. If *n* is converted into days, a fraction of a day is not possible. For annuity calculations, *n* represents the number of payments. Therefore, *n* must be a whole number and must always be rounded upward.

For mortgage calculations, the payment, interest, and balance repaid calculations all must be rounded to the two-decimal standard for currency. The final payment made may have to be adjusted by a penny or so, to record the full repayment of the principal.

When determining the purchase price of a bond, it is important to carry all the decimals until the calculation is complete.

Valuation of projects through calculation of net present value and rate of return may be rounded to the nearest dollar or the nearest interest point. If results are close to the same amounts, other non-monetary criteria must be used to choose the best alternative.

While different methods of rounding are used, for most business purposes the following procedure is suitable:

1. If the first digit in the group of decimal digits that is to be dropped is 5 or greater, the last digit retained is *increased* by 1.

2. If the first digit in the group of decimal digits that is to be dropped is 4 or less, the last digit retained is left *unchanged*.

For further details, refer to the Student's Reference Guide to Rounding and Special Notations found on pages xix–xxii of the text.

Compound Interest—Future Value and Present Value

LEARNING OBJECTIVES

Upon completing this chapter, you will be able to do the following:

1. Calculate interest rates and the number of compounding periods.

2. Compute future (maturity) values of investments.

3. Compute present values of future sums of money.

4. Discount long-term promissory notes.

5. Solve problems involving equivalent values.

Marmaduke St. John/Alamy Stock Photo

In preparing for college, Jane needs a car and must borrow money to pay for it. She is trying to decide which method of financing to choose. Before borrowing the money, however, she has many questions that need answering. What is compound interest and how does it work? Does the interest rate make a difference? Does the compounding frequency make a difference? Is it a good option if she borrows now and pays back some of the money in one year? Should she use a credit card or a line of credit? Are these considered consumer loans? If she is given a gift of money, should she pay down some of the car loan? By studying this chapter, Jane should be able to answer these questions, and more, and then buy her car.

INTRODUCTION

Compound interest calculations are used extensively in banking, investing, and business transactions. This type of interest is much more commonly used than simple interest in everyday life, in car loans, mortgages, and long-term planning. With the compound interest method, interest is periodically calculated on a principal, then the interest is added to form a new principal. In the next period, interest is then earned on the new principal. This is what is meant by "earning interest on interest."

We need to understand how compound interest works to decide on interest terms and to perform compound interest calculations. An understanding of exponents is required to use the formulas. Preprogrammed financial calculators and financial functions in computer applications perform calculations to determine future value and present value.

9.1 BASIC CONCEPTS AND CALCULATIONS
A. Basic procedure for calculating compound interest

Compound interest is a procedure whereby interest in earlier periods earns interest in future periods. Interest for a specified time period is calculated based on the original principal plus all interest earned in prior periods. The compound interest method is generally used to calculate interest for long-term investments and loans.

For the first period, the amount of interest for compound interest is the same as the amount of interest for simple interest. In later periods, the amount of interest for compound interest becomes increasingly greater than the amount for simple interest.

Table 9.1 illustrates the basic procedure for computing interest using the simple interest and the compound interest methods, as well as the overall effect of compounding. In this illustration, an original principal of $10 000 is invested at 10% per annum (per year) for five years.

Note that the amount of interest is determined for each interest period on the basis of the previous balance and is then added to that balance. The interest earned on the investment under simple interest is the same amount in each period ($1000 in this case). But, using compound interest calculations, the amount of interest grows with each year (see Figure 9.1).

Table 9.1 Compound Interest Versus Simple Interest Calculations: Principal of $10 000 Invested at 10% per Annum for 5 years
(© S. A. Hummelbrunner)

Year	At Simple Interest			At Compound Interest		
	Interest Calculation	Amount	Balance	Interest Calculation	Amount	Balance
		$10 000.00	$10 000.00			$10 000.00
1	(0.10)(10 000.00)	1 000.00	11 000.00	(0.10)(10 000.00)	1 000.00	11 000.00
2	(0.10)(10 000.00)	1 000.00	12 000.00	(0.10)(11 000.00)	1 100.00	12 100.00
3	(0.10)(10 000.00)	1 000.00	13 000.00	(0.10)(12 100.00)	1 210.00	13 310.00
4	(0.10)(10 000.00)	1 000.00	14 000.00	(0.10)(13 310.00)	1 331.00	14 641.00
5	(0.10)(10 000.00)	1 000.00	$15 000.00	(0.10)(14 641.00)	1 464.10	$16 105.10

Table 9.2 Commonly Used Compounding Frequencies and Periods (© S. A. Hummelbrunner)

Compounding Frequency	Length of Compounding Period	Number of Compounding Periods per Year
Annual	12 months (1 year)	1
Semi-annual	6 months	2
Quarterly	3 months	4
Monthly	1 month	12
Bi-weekly	2 weeks	26
Weekly	1 week	52
Daily	1 day	365

The relationship between the periodic rate of interest and the nominal annual rate of interest can be stated in the form of a formula.

$$\text{PERIODIC RATE OF INTEREST}, i = \frac{\text{NOMINAL (ANNUAL) RATE}}{\text{NUMBER OF COMPOUNDING PERIODS PER YEAR}}$$

Therefore,

$$i = \frac{j}{m}$$ ——————————————— **Formula 9.2**

where i = periodic rate of interest
j = nominal annual rate of interest
m = number of compounding periods per year

EXAMPLE 9.1A

Determine the periodic rate of interest i for
(i) 5% compounded annually;
(ii) 7% compounded semi-annually;
(iii) 12% compounded quarterly;
(iv) 10.5% compounded monthly;
(v) 13% compounded bi-weekly;
(vi) 3.5% compounded weekly;
(vii) 28% compounded daily.

SOLUTION

	Nominal Annual Rate j	Compounding Frequency	Length of Compounding Period	Number of Compounding Periods per Year m	Periodic Rate of Interest $i = \dfrac{j}{m}$
(i)	5%	Annually	12 months	1	$\dfrac{5\%}{1} = 5.0\%$
(ii)	7%	Semi-annually	6 months	2	$\dfrac{7\%}{2} = 3.5\%$
(iii)	12%	Quarterly	3 months	4	$\dfrac{12\%}{4} = 3.0\%$
(iv)	10.5%	Monthly	1 month	12	$\dfrac{10.5\%}{12} = 0.875\%$
(v)	13%	Bi-weekly	2 weeks	26	$\dfrac{13\%}{26} = 0.5\%$
(vi)	3.5%	Weekly	1 week	52	$\dfrac{3.5\%}{52} = 0.0673\%$
(vii)	28%	Daily	1 day	365	$\dfrac{28\%}{365} = 0.0767\%$

D. Determining the number of compounding periods in the term of an investment or loan

Note that n appears as an exponent. The n value keeps track of how many times we apply the interest rate in the given term.

To determine n, the number of compounding periods in the term of an investment or a loan, multiply the number of years in the term by m, the number of compounding periods per year.

$$n = \text{number of years in the term} \times m$$ ———————— Formula 9.3

where n = number of compounding periods in the term

m = number of compounding periods per year

The value n in the compounding factor $(1 + i)^n$ is not restricted to integral values; n may take any fractional value. The future value can be determined by means of the formula $FV = PV(1 + i)^n$ whether the time period contains an integral number of conversion periods or not.

The value of n is determined by multiplying the number of years by m. The time period, or term, must be stated as the number of years. This may be a fraction. When the term is a number of months, divide the number of months by 12 to convert to the number of years. When the term is a number of days, divide by 365.

EXAMPLE 9.1B

Determine the number of compounding periods when

  (i) compounding annually for 14 years;
 (ii) compounding semi-annually for 15 years;
(iii) compounding quarterly for 12.5 years;
 (iv) compounding monthly for 10.75 years;
  (v) compounding quarterly for 32 months;
 (vi) compounding semi-annually for 40 months;
(vii) compounding daily for 183 days;
(viii) compounding bi-weekly for 84 months;
 (ix) compounding weekly for 90 days.

SOLUTION

	Term (in years)	Compounding Frequency	Number of Compounding Periods per Year, m	Number of Compounding Periods in Term, n
(i)	14	annually	1	$14(1) = 14$
(ii)	15	semi-annually	2	$15(2) = 30$
(iii)	12.5	quarterly	4	$12.5(4) = 50$
(iv)	10.75	monthly	12	$10.75(12) = 129$
(v)	$\dfrac{32}{12}$	quarterly	4	$\dfrac{32}{12}(4) = 10.6\dot{6}$
(vi)	$\dfrac{40}{12}$	semi-annually	2	$\dfrac{40}{12}(2) = 6.6\dot{6}$
(vii)	$\dfrac{183}{365}$	daily	365	183
(viii)	$\dfrac{84}{12}$	bi-weekly	26	$\dfrac{84}{12}(26) = 182$
(ix)	$\dfrac{90}{365}$	weekly	52	$\dfrac{90}{365}(52) = 12.821918$

POINTERS
& PITFALLS

Many students have difficulty determining the value of m when compounding is stated as "quarterly." This term means that interest is compounded every quarter of a year. Since there are four quarters in a year, the number of compounding periods per year, m, is 4, each quarter of a year being 3 months in length. The value of m is never 3.

E. Setting up the compounding factor $(1 + i)^n$

The *compounding (accumulation) factor* $(1 + i)^n$ can be set up by first determining i and n and then substituting i and n in the general form of the factor, $(1 + i)^n$. The y^x key on the calculator can be used to calculate the value of $(1 + i)^n$.

EXAMPLE 9.1C

Set up the compounding factor $(1 + i)^n$ for
- (i)   5% compounded annually for 14 years;
- (ii)   7% compounded semi-annually for 15 years;
- (iii)   12% compounded quarterly for 12.5 years;
- (iv)   10.5% compounded monthly for 10.75 years;
- (v)   8% compounded quarterly for 30 months;
- (vi)   9.5% compounded semi-annually for 42 months;
- (vii)   5.8% compounded daily for 2 years.
- (viii)   17% compounded weekly for 6 years.

SOLUTION

	i	m	n	$(1 + i)^n$
(i)	5% = 0.05	1	14(1) = 14	$(1 + 0.05)^{14} = 1.05^{14}$
(ii)	7% ÷ 2 = 0.035	2	15(2) = 30	$(1 + 0.035)^{30} = 1.035^{30}$
(iii)	12% ÷ 4 = 0.03	4	12.5(4) = 50	$(1 + 0.03)^{50} = 1.03^{50}$
(iv)	10.5% ÷ 12 = 0.00875	12	10.75(12) = 129	$(1 + 0.00875)^{129} = 1.00875^{129}$
(v)	8% ÷ 4 = 0.02	4	30/12(4) = 10	$(1 + 0.02)^{10} = 1.02^{10}$
(vi)	9.5% ÷ 2 = 0.0475	2	42/12(2) = 7	$(1 + 0.0475)^{7} = 1.0475^{7}$
(vii)	5.8% ÷ 365 = 0.000159*	365	2(365) = 730	$(1 + 0.058/365)^{730} = (1.000159*)^{730}$
(viii)	17% ÷ 52 = 0.003269*	52	6(52) = 312	$(1 + 0.17/52)^{312} = (1.003269*)^{312}$

*rounded

F. Calculating the numerical value of the compounding factor $(1 + i)^n$

The numerical value of the compounding factor, $(1 + i)^n$, can now be computed using an electronic calculator. For calculators equipped with the exponential function feature $\boxed{y^x}$, the numerical value of the compounding factor can be computed directly.

STEP 1   Enter the numerical value of $(1 + i)$ in the keyboard. Tip: enter i and then add 1.

STEP 2   Press the exponential function key $\boxed{y^x}$.

STEP 3   Enter the numerical value of n in the keyboard.

STEP 4   Press $\boxed{=}$.

STEP 5   Read the answer in the display. Continue calculating or save as needed.

The numerical values of the compounding factors in Example 9.1C are obtained as follows:

		(i)	(ii)	(iii)	(iv)	(v)	(vi)	(vii)
STEP 1	Enter	1 + 0.05	1 + 0.07/2	1 + 0.12/4	1 + 0.105/12	1 + 0.08/4	1 + 0.095/2	1 + 0.058/365
STEP 2	Press	$\boxed{y^x}$	$\boxed{y^x}$	$\boxed{y^x}$	$\boxed{y^x}$	$\boxed{y^x}$	$\boxed{y^x}$	$\boxed{y^x}$
STEP 3	Enter	14	30	50	129	10	7	730
STEP 4	Press	$\boxed{=}$	$\boxed{=}$	$\boxed{=}$	$\boxed{=}$	$\boxed{=}$	$\boxed{=}$	$\boxed{=}$
STEP 5	Read	1.979932	2.806794	4.383906	3.076647	1.218994	1.383816	1.122986

Note: Do not be concerned if your calculator shows a difference in the last decimal. There is no error. It reflects the precision of the calculator and the number of decimal places formatted to show on the display of the calculator.

For example, if your calculator has been set to show only two decimal places, it will automatically round the answer to (i) above to 1.98. If you were to continue calculating without clearing your calculator, it would use the non-rounding number in the further calculations. This is the recommended method for calculating using rounded numbers.

With the increasing use of calculators, computers, and other devices, the two traditional methods of determining the compounding factor $(1 + i)^n$—logarithms and tables—are seldom used. Neither method is used in this text.

EXERCISE 9.1   MyLab Math

A. Determine m, i, and n for each of the following.

1. 12% compounded annually for five years

2. 7.4% compounded semi-annually for eight years

🌐 **3.** 5.5% compounded quarterly for nine years

🌐 **4.** 7% compounded monthly for four years

🌐 **5.** 11.5% compounded semi-annually for 13.5 years

6. 4.8% compounded quarterly for $5^3/_4$ years

7. 8% compounded monthly for 12.5 years

🌐 **8.** 10.75% compounded quarterly for three years and nine months

🌐 **9.** 12.25% compounded semi-annually for 54 months

🌐 **10.** 8.1% compounded monthly for 15.5 years

B. 🌐 **1.** For a sum of money invested at 10% compounded quarterly for 12 years, state
   (a) the nominal annual rate of interest (j);
   (b) the number of compounding periods per year (m);
   (c) the periodic rate of interest (i);
   (d) the number of compounding periods in the term (n);
   (e) the compounding factor $(1 + i)^n$;
   (f) the numerical value of the compounding factor.

2. For a sum of money invested at 4.2% compounded semi-annually for 5.5 years, state
   (a) the nominal annual rate of interest (j);
   (b) the number of compounding periods per year (m);
   (c) the periodic rate of interest (i);
   (d) the number of compounding periods in the term (n);
   (e) the compounding factor $(1 + i)^n$;
   (f) the numerical value of the compounding factor.

3. For a sum of money borrowed at 9.6% compounded monthly for 7 years, state
   (a) the nominal annual rate of interest (j);
   (b) the number of compounding periods per year (m);
   (c) the periodic rate of interest (i);
   (d) the number of compounding periods in the term (n);
   (e) the compounding factor $(1 + i)^n$;
   (f) the numerical value of the compounding factor.

4. For a sum of money borrowed at 16% compounded daily for 2 years, state
   (a) the nominal annual rate of interest (j);
   (b) the number of compounding interest periods per year (m);
   (c) the periodic rate of interest (i);
   (d) the number of compounding periods in the term (n);
   (e) the compounding factor $(1 + i)^n$;
   (f) the numerical value of the compounding factor.

5. For a sum of money borrowed at 7.25% compounded bi-weekly for 84 months, state
   (a) the nominal annual rate of interest (j);
   (b) the number of compounding interest periods per year (m);
   (c) the periodic rate of interest (i);
   (d) the number of compounding periods in the term (n);
   (e) the compounding factor $(1 + i)^n$;
   (f) the numerical value of the compounding factor.

9.2 USING THE FUTURE VALUE FORMULA OF A COMPOUND AMOUNT FV = PV $(1 + i)^n$

A. Calculating the future value (maturity value) of an investment

EXAMPLE 9.2A Calculate the amount to which $6000 will grow if invested at 4% per annum compounded quarterly for five years (see Figure 9.3).

Figure 9.3 Graphical Representation of Data (© S. A. Hummelbrunner)

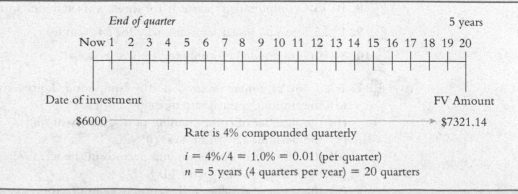

End of quarter   5 years

Now 1 2 3 4 5 6 7 8 9 10 11 12 13 14 15 16 17 18 19 20

Date of investment   FV Amount

$6000 ————————————————————————————————→ $7321.14

Rate is 4% compounded quarterly

$i = 4\%/4 = 1.0\% = 0.01$ (per quarter)
$n = 5$ years (4 quarters per year) = 20 quarters

SOLUTION

The original principal PV = 6000.00;
the nominal annual rate j = 4%;
the number of compounding periods per year m = 4;

the quarterly rate of interest $i = \dfrac{4\%}{4} = 1.0\% = 0.01$

the number of compounding periods (five years of quarterly periods) n = (5)(4) = 20.

$\begin{aligned}
\text{FV} &= \text{PV}(1 + i)^n &&\text{─── using Formula 9.1} \\
&= 6000.00(1.01)^{20} &&\text{─── substituting for P, } i, n \\
&= 6000.00(1.220190) &&\text{─── using a calculator*} \\
&= \$7321.14
\end{aligned}$

*Note that, when recording the result of the calculation above, the number has been rounded to six decimal places. However, to complete the calculations, continue with the number stored in the calculator. If the rounded number is used to complete the calculations, the end result may be different by a small amount.

EXAMPLE 9.2B

What is the future value after 78 months of $2500 invested at 5.25% compounded semi-annually?

SOLUTION

The original principal PV = 2500.00;
the nominal annual rate j = 5.25;
the number of compounding periods per year m = 2;

the semi-annual rate of interest $i = \dfrac{5.25\%}{2} = 2.625\% = 0.02625$;

the number of compounding periods (each period is six months)

$$n = \left(\frac{78}{12}\right)(2) = (6.5)(2) = 13.$$

$\begin{aligned}
\text{FV} &= \text{PV}(1 + i)^n \\
&= 2500.00(1 + 0.02625)^{13} \\
&= 2500.00(1.400526) \\
&= \$3501.32
\end{aligned}$

EXAMPLE 9.2C

What will be the future value of a deposit of $1750 made into a registered retirement saving plan from March 1, 2005, to December 1, 2025, at 4.4% compounded quarterly?

SOLUTION

The original principal PV = 1750.00; j = 4.4; m = 4;

the quarterly rate of interest $i = \dfrac{4.4\%}{4} = 1.1\% = 0.011$;

the time period from March 1, 2005, to December 1, 2025, contains 20 years and 9 months, or 20.75 years: n = (20 9/12)(4) = (20.75)(4) = 83.

$\begin{aligned}
\text{FV} &= \text{PV}(1 + i)^n \\
&= 1750.00(1 + 0.011)^{83} \\
&= 1750.00(2.479396) \\
&= \$4338.94
\end{aligned}$

B. Using preprogrammed financial calculators

 Compound interest calculations, which can become complex, are performed frequently and repeatedly. Doing the calculations algebraically can enhance your understanding and appreciation of the theory, but it can also be time-consuming, laborious, and subject to mechanical and rounding errors. Using preprogrammed financial calculators can save time and reduce or eliminate these errors, assuming the calculators are set up properly and numerical sign conventions are observed when entering data and interpreting results.

Different models of financial calculators vary in their operation and labelling of the function keys and faceplate. Appendix II, "Instructions and Tips for Three Preprogrammed Financial Calculator Models," highlights the relevant variations for students using Texas Instruments BA II PLUS, Sharp EL-738C, and Hewlett-Packard 10bII+ calculators. (Note that Appendix II is intended to help you use one of these three calculators, and merely supplements the instruction booklet that came with your calculator. Refer to the instruction booklet for your particular model.)

Specific function keys on preprogrammed financial calculators correspond to the five variables used in compound interest calculations. Function keys used for the calculator models presented in Appendix II are shown in Table 9.3.

The function keys are used to enter the numerical values of the known variables into the appropriate preprogrammed calculator registers. The data may be entered in any order. The answer is then displayed by using a computation key or by depressing the key representing the unknown variable, depending on the calculator model.

Table 9.3   Financial Calculator Function Keys That Correspond to Variables Used in Compound Interest Calculations
(© S. A. Hummelbrunner)

		Function Key		
Variable	**Algebraic Symbol**	**TI BA II PLUS**	**Sharp EL-738C**	**HP 10bII+**
The number of compounding periods	n	N	N	N
The rate of interest[1]	i	I/Y C/Y	I/Y	I/YR
The periodic annuity payment[2]	PMT	PMT	PMT	PMT
The present value or principal	PV	PV	PV	PV
The future value or maturity value	FV	FV	FV	FV

Notes: 1. The periodic rate of interest, (i) is entered as a percent and not as a decimal equivalent (as it is when using the algebraic method to solve compound interest problems). For example, 8% is entered as "8" not ".08." With some calculators, the rate of interest is the periodic rate. In the case of the BA II PLUS and the Sharp EL-738C, the rate of interest entered is the nominal rate per year I/Y .

2. The periodic annuity payment function key PMT is used only for annuity calculations, which are introduced in Chapter 11.

 Instructions in this text are given for the Texas Instruments BA II PLUS calculator. Refer to Appendix II for instructions for setting up and using the Sharp EL-738C and Hewlett-Packard 10bII+ calculators.

POINTERS & PITFALLS

Before entering the numerical data to complete compound interest calculations, it is important to verify that your calculator has been set up correctly to ensure error-free operation. There are a number of items to check during this "pre-calculation" phase. Specifically, does the calculator require a mode change within a register to match the text presentation? Does the calculator have to be in the financial mode? Are the decimal places set to the correct number to ensure the required accuracy?

Further checks must be made when entering data during the "calculation" phase. For example, have the function key registers been cleared? What numerical data require a minus sign to avoid errors in operation and incorrect answers? How can the data entered be confirmed? Responses to these queries in the "pre-calculation" and "calculation" phases for three preprogrammed financial calculators are provided in Appendix II, along with general information.

Using the Texas Instruments BA II PLUS to Solve Compound Interest Problems

Follow the steps below to compute the future value of a sum of money using the formula $FV = PV(1 + i)^n$ and a Texas Instruments BA II PLUS calculator. Compare your result with that in Example 9.2A.

Pre-calculation Phase (Initial Setup)

STEP 1   The P/Y register, and behind it, the C/Y register, must be set to match the calculator's performance to the text presentation. The P/Y register is used to represent the number of regular payments per year. If the text of the question does not discuss regular payments per year, this should be set to equal the C/Y in the calculator. The C/Y register is used to represent the number of compounding periods per year; that is, the compounding frequency. The description of the compounding frequency is usually contained within the phrase that describes the nominal interest rate. An example would be "8% compounded quarterly." This means that the nominal, or annual, interest rate of 8% is compounded four times each year at 8%/4, or 2%, each period. The compounding frequency of 4 is entered into the C/Y register within the calculator.

Key in	Press	Display shows
	2nd (P/Y)	P/Y = 12 —— checks the P/Y register
4	**ENTER**	P/Y = 4 —— changes the value to "4"
	↓	C/Y = 4 —— changed automatically to match the P/Y
	2nd (QUIT)	0 ———————— returns to the standard calculation mode

STEP 2   Verify that the decimal format is set to the number you require. A setting of "9" represents a floating decimal point format. The default setting is "2."

Key in	Press	Display shows
	2nd (Format)	DEC = 2 — checks the decimal format
6	**ENTER**	DEC = 6 — changes to "6" decimal places shown on the display
	2nd (QUIT)	0 ———————— returns to the standard calculation mode

This calculator is ready for financial calculations in its standard mode.

Calculation Phase

STEP 3   Always clear the function key registers before beginning compound interest calculations. This action resets all values to their default values.

Key in	Press	Display shows	
	2nd (CLR TVM)	0 ——————	clears the function key registers

STEP 4   To solve Example 9.2A, in which PV = $6000, $i = 1.0\%$, and $n = 20$, use the following procedure. Remember that i represents the interest rate per compounding period, and n represents the number of times that interest is compounded. To enter the accurate information into the calculator, you must determine the nominal interest rate for the year, and enter this information into the I/Y register. In this example, the interest rate per year is 4%. The compounding frequency, denoted by the phrase "compounded quarterly," is four times per year. This must be entered into the C/Y register. Also, notice that 6000 is entered as a negative number, since it is cash paid out for an investment. This "cash flow sign convention" is explained below.

If you follow this convention, your calculation will be error-free, and the answer will be accurate and interpreted consistently.

Key in	Press	Display shows	
	2nd (P/Y)	P/Y = 12 ——————	checks the P/Y register
4	ENTER	P/Y = 4 ——————	changes the value to "4"
	↓	C/Y = 4 ——————	changed automatically to match the P/Y
	2nd (QUIT)	0 ——————	returns to the standard calculation mode

The calculator will remember the previously set value. There is no need to re-enter this value unless it changes.

In standard calculation mode, values are keyed in first, followed by pressing the function key.

Key in	Press	Display shows	
6000	± PV	PV = − 6000 ——————	this enters the present value P (principal) with the correct sign convention
4	I/Y	I/Y = 4 ——————	this enters the nominal interest rate as a percent
20	N	N = 20 ——————	this enters the number of compounding periods n
	CPT FV	FV = 7321.140240 ——	this computes and displays the unknown future value S

Since the calculator has been previously set to show six decimal places, the future value shows the final result rounded to six decimal places. The future value is $7321.14.

Cash Flow Sign Convention for Entering Numerical Data

The Texas Instruments BA II PLUS calculator follows the established convention of treating cash inflows (cash received) as positive numbers and cash outflows (cash paid out) as negative numbers. In the calculation above, the present value was considered to be cash paid out for an investment, and so the present value of $6000 was entered as a negative number. The resulting future value was considered to be cash received from the investment and so had a positive value. Note that if the present value had been entered as a positive value, then the future value would have been displayed as a negative number. The *numerical* value would have been correct but the result would have been a negative number. "Error 5" is displayed when calculating I/Y or *n* if both the present value and future value are entered using the same sign. Therefore, to avoid errors, always enter the present value as a negative number for compound interest calculations. Enter all other values as positive numbers. This topic is discussed further in Appendix II and throughout this text as required.

Excel has a FV (future value) function you can use to calculate the future value of an investment subject to compound interest.

EXAMPLE 9.2D

Using a preprogrammed financial calculator, such as the Texas Instruments BA II PLUS, determine the accumulated value of $1000 invested for 2 years and 9 months at 10% compounded annually.

SOLUTION

The entire time period is 2 years and 9 months; the number of whole conversion periods is 2; the fractional conversion period is $\frac{9}{12}$ of a year.

$$PV = 1000.00; I/Y = 10; C/Y = 1; i = 10\%/1 = 0.10; n = 2\frac{9}{12}(1) = 2.75$$

$$FV = 1000.00(1.10)^{2.75} = 1000.00(1.299660) = \$1299.66$$

PROGRAMMED SOLUTION

(Set P/Y, C/Y = 1) 1000 [±] [PV] 10 [I/Y] 2.75 [N] [CPT] [FV] [1299.660393]

POINTERS
& PITFALLS

Calculators have made it easy to compute future values and present values using fractional exponents. You can simply enter the fraction in brackets or convert the fraction to a decimal and proceed as with an integral exponent. Never round the decimal. Instead, use the store and answer recall functions in your calculator.

EXAMPLE 9.2E

Determine the future value amount of $400 invested at 6% compounded quarterly for three years and five months.

SOLUTION

$$PV = 400.00; i = 1.5\% = 0.015$$

$$n = \left(3\frac{5}{12}\right)(4) = \left(\frac{41}{12}\right)(4) = \frac{41}{3} = 13\frac{2}{3} = 13.\dot{6}$$

$$FV = 400.00(1.015)^{13.6} = 400.00(1.225658) = \$490.26$$

PROGRAMMED SOLUTION

(Set P/Y, C/Y = 4) 400 [±] [PV] 6 [I/Y] 13.6 [N] [CPT] [FV] [490.263132]

EXAMPLE 9.2F

A debt of $3500 dated August 31, 2020, is payable together with interest at 9% compounded quarterly on June 30, 2023. Using a preprogrammed financial calculator, determine the amount to be paid.

SOLUTION

PV = 3500.00; I/Y = 9; C/Y = 4; $i = \dfrac{9\%}{4} = 2.25\% = 0.0225$; the time period

August 31, 2020, to June 30, 2023, contains 2 years and 10 months; the number of

quarters $n = 2\dfrac{10}{12}(4) = 11.\dot{3}$.

$FV = 3500.00(1.0225)^{11.\dot{3}}$

$\quad = 3500.00(1.286819)$

$\quad = \$4503.87$

PROGRAMMED SOLUTION

(Set P/Y, C/Y = 4) 3500 $\boxed{\pm}$ $\boxed{PV}$ 9 $\boxed{I/Y}$ 11.$\dot{3}$ $\boxed{N}$ $\boxed{CPT}$ $\boxed{FV}$ $\boxed{4503.867790}$

C. Using Excel's FV or PV

If you choose, you can use Excel's FV (future value) or PV (present value) function to answer the questions in this chapter.

In Example 9.2A, you are required to calculate the future value of an investment. The FV function in Excel is illustrated below.

	A	B	C
1	FV Function		
2			
3	**Interest Rate per Compounding Period**	1.00%	
4	**Total Number of Compounding Periods**	20	
5	Payment or Deposit Per Compounding Period	$0.00	
6	Present Value	−$6,000.00	
7	Type (Ordinary or Due)	0	
8	Answer	$7,321.14	
9			

In Example 9.3A, you are required to calculate the present value of an investment. The PV function in Excel is illustrated below.

	A	B	C
1	PV Function		
2			
3	**Interest Rate per Compounding Period**	10.0%	
4	**Total Number of Compounding Periods**	6	
5	Payment or Deposit Per Compounding Period	0	
6	Future Value	−$17,715.61	
7	Type (Ordinary or Due)	0	
8	Answer	$10,000.00	
9			

D. Applications involving changes in interest rate

A graph or timeline can be set up to outline changes in the interest rate. The break points occur when the interest rate changes. Determine the accumulated value of an investment from the starting point to the time of the first change. This becomes the new principal for calculating the future value with the new interest rate.

EXAMPLE 9.2G

A deposit of $2000 earns interest at 6% compounded monthly for four years. At that time, the interest rate changes to 7% compounded quarterly. What is the value of the deposit three years after the change in the rate of interest?

SOLUTION

The data given can be represented on a time diagram as shown in Figure 9.4.

Separate the entire problem into the time periods during which different interest rates apply.

Figure 9.4 Graphical Representation of Data (© S. A. Hummelbrunner)

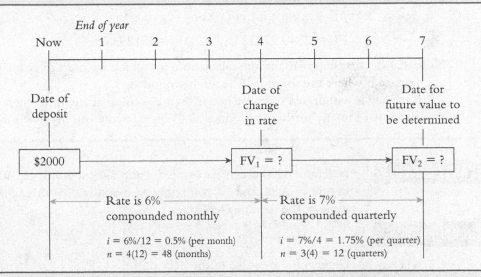

STEP 1   Determine the accumulated value of the original deposit at the time the interest rate changes, that is, after four years.

$$PV = 2000.00; I/Y = 6; C/Y = 12; i = \frac{6\%}{12} = 0.5\% = 0.005; n = 4(12) = 48$$

$$FV_1 = 2000.00(1 + 0.005)^{48} = 2000.00(1.270489) = \$2540.978322$$

Note: Rounding procedures are explained on page 334.

STEP 2   Use the accumulated value after four years as the new principal and calculate its accumulated value three years later using the new rate of interest.

$$PV = 2540.978322; I/Y = 7; C/Y = 4; i = \frac{7\%}{4} = 1.75\% = 0.0175; n = 3(4) = 12$$

$$FV_2 = 2540.978322(1 + 0.0175)^{12} = 2540.978322(1.231439) = \$3129.06$$

PROGRAMMED SOLUTION

(Set P/Y, C/Y = 12) 2000 $\boxed{\pm}$ $\boxed{\text{PV}}$ 6 $\boxed{\text{I/Y}}$ 48 $\boxed{\text{N}}$ $\boxed{\text{CPT}}$ $\boxed{\text{FV}}$ 2540.978322 —answer to Step 1

Do *not* clear your display. Proceed to Step 2

$\boxed{\pm}$ $\boxed{\text{PV}}$ (Set P/Y, C/Y = 4) 7 $\boxed{\text{I/Y}}$ 12 $\boxed{\text{N}}$ $\boxed{\text{CPT}}$ $\boxed{\text{FV}}$ 3129.060604 ——answer to Step 2

After four years, the deposit is worth $2540.98, which then becomes the present value for Step 2. After three further years, the deposit is worth $3129.06.

POINTERS
& PITFALLS

In determining when it is appropriate to round, it is important to recognize that if the money remains inside an account (deposit or loan), all of the decimals need to carry forward into the next calculation. For example, consider a bank deposit of $2000 that earns 6% compounded monthly for four years, and then earns 7% compounded quarterly for three more years, and assume the money remained in the account the entire time. We can solve this in one step as follows:

$$FV = 2000.00(1.005)^{48}(1.0175)^{12} = \$3129.06$$

or, two steps as follows:

$$FV = 2000.00(1.005)^{48} = \$2540.978322$$
$$FV = 2540.978322(1.0175)^{12} = \$3129.06$$

Note that the first step is an interim calculation, for which we must carry forward all the decimals to the next step, where the solution can then be rounded.

If money is withdrawn or transferred from the account at any time, then only 2 decimals can be carried forward to any further steps (since a currency payout can involve only 2 decimals).

EXAMPLE 9.2H

A debt of $500 accumulates interest at 8% compounded quarterly from April 1, 2021, to July 1, 2022, and 9% compounded monthly thereafter. Determine the accumulated value of the debt on December 1, 2023.

SOLUTION

STEP 1

Determine the value of the debt on July 1, 2022.

$PV_1 = 500.00$; I/Y = 8; C/Y = 4; $i = \dfrac{8\%}{4} = 2 = 0.02$;

the period April 1, 2021, to July 1, 2022, contains 15 months: $n = (15/12)(4) = 5$

$FV_1 = 500.00(1.02)^5 = 500.00(1.104081) = \$552.040402$

STEP 2

Use the result of Step 1 as new principal and calculate its accumulated value on December 1, 2023.

$PV_2 = 552.040402$; I/Y = 9; P/Y = 12; $i = \dfrac{9\%}{12} = 0.75 = 0.0075$;

the period July 1, 2022, to December 1, 2023, contains 17 months: $n = (17/12)(12) = 17$

$FV_2 = 552.040402(1.0075)^{17} = 552.040402(1.135445) = \$626.81$

PROGRAMMED SOLUTION

STEP 1 (Set P/Y, C/Y = 4) 500 $\boxed{\pm}$ $\boxed{\text{PV}}$ 8 $\boxed{\text{I/Y}}$ 5 $\boxed{\text{N}}$ $\boxed{\text{CPT}}$ $\boxed{\text{FV}}$ Result: $\boxed{552.040402}$

STEP 2 552.040402 $\boxed{\pm}$ $\boxed{\text{PV}}$ (Set P/Y, C/Y = 12) 9 $\boxed{\text{I/Y}}$ 17 $\boxed{\text{N}}$ $\boxed{\text{CPT}}$ $\boxed{\text{FV}}$ Result: $\boxed{626.811268}$

EXAMPLE 9.21   Midland Credit Union showed that a client deposited $2000 into an investment plan account on February 1, 2015. The client invested an additional $1900 on February 1, 2016, and $1700 on February 1, 2019. What will the balance in the client's investment plan be on August 1, 2025, if the plan earns a fixed rate of interest of 7% compounded semi-annually?

SOLUTION   See Figure 9.5.

Figure 9.5 Graphical Representation of Data (© S. A. Hummelbrunner)

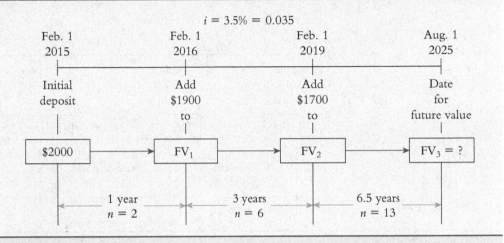

STEP 1   Determine the future value, FV_1, of the initial deposit on February 1, 2016.

$PV_1 = 2000.00$; $I/Y = 7$; $C/Y = 2$; $i = \dfrac{7\%}{2} = 3.5 = 0.035$;

the period February 1, 2015, to February 1, 2016, contains 1 year: $n = 1(2) = 2$
$FV_1 = 2000.00(1.035)^2 = 2000.00(1.071225) = \$2142.45$

STEP 2   Add the deposit of $1900 to the amount of $2142.45 to obtain the new principal as of February 1, 2016, and determine its future value, FV_2, on February 1, 2019.

$PV_2 = 2142.45 + 1900.00 = 4042.45$; $i = 0.035$;

the period February 1, 2016, to February 1, 2019, contains 3 years: $n = 3(2) = 6$
$FV_2 = 4042.45(1.035)^6 = 4042.45(1.229255) = \$4969.203194$

STEP 3   Add the deposit of $1700 to the amount of $4969.203194 to obtain the new principal as of February 1, 2019, and determine its future value, FV_3, on August 1, 2025.

$PV_3 = 4969.203194 + 1700.00 = 6669.203194$; $i = 0.035$;

the period February 1, 2019, to August 1, 2025, contains 6.5 years: $n = 6.5(2) = 13$
$FV_3 = 6669.203194(1.035)^{13} = 6669.203194(1.563956) = \$10\ 430.34$

PROGRAMMED SOLUTION

STEP 1   (Set P/Y, C/Y = 2) 2000 $\boxed{\pm}$ $\boxed{PV}$ 7 $\boxed{I/Y}$ 2 $\boxed{N}$ $\boxed{CPT}$ $\boxed{FV}$ Result: $\boxed{2142.45}$

STEP 2 $\boxed{+}$ 1900 $\boxed{=}$ $\boxed{4042.45}$ $\boxed{\pm}$ $\boxed{PV}$ 6 $\boxed{N}$ $\boxed{CPT}$ $\boxed{FV}$ Result: $\boxed{4969.203194}$

STEP 3 $\boxed{+}$ 1700 $\boxed{=}$ $\boxed{6669.203194}$ $\boxed{\pm}$ $\boxed{PV}$ 13 $\boxed{N}$ $\boxed{CPT}$ $\boxed{FV}$ Result: $\boxed{10430.34075}$

Note: Since the numbers are not being cleared after each step, there is no need to clear and re-enter the interest rate in Steps 2 and 3—it has not changed and is already programmed from Step 1.

EXAMPLE 9.2J

A demand loan of $10 000 is repaid by payments of $5000 in one year, $6000 in four years, and a final payment in six years. Interest on the loan is 10% compounded quarterly during the first year, 8% compounded semi-annually for the next three years, and 7.5% compounded annually for the remaining years. Determine the final payment.

SOLUTION

Figure 9.6 Graphical Representation of Data (© S. A. Hummelbrunner)

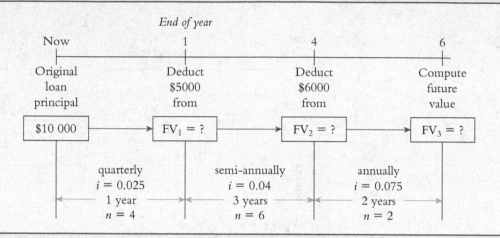

STEP 1 Determine the accumulated value of the debt at the time of the first payment.

$$PV_1 = 10\ 000.00;\ I/Y = 10;\ C/Y = 4;\ i = \frac{10\%}{4} = 2.5\% = 0.025;\ n = 1(4) = 4$$

$$FV_1 = 10\ 000.00(1.025)^4 = 10\ 000.00(1.103813) = \$11\ 038.12891$$

STEP 2 Subtract the payment of $5000 from the accumulated value of $11 038.12891 to obtain the debt balance. Now determine its accumulated value at the time of the second payment three years later.

$$PV_2 = 11\ 038.12891 - 5000.00 = 6038.12891;\ i = 4\% = 0.04;\ n = 3(2) = 6$$

$$FV_2 = 6038.12891(1.04)^6 = 6038.12891(1.265319) = \$7640.159341$$

STEP 3 Subtract the payment of $6000 from the accumulated value of $7640.159341 to obtain the debt balance. Now determine its accumulated value two years later.

$$PV_3 = 7640.159341 - 6000.00 = 1640.159341;\ i = 7.5\% = 0.075;\ n = 1(2) = 2$$

$$FV_3 = 1640.159341(1.075)^2 = 1640.159341(1.155625) = \$1895.41$$

The final payment after six years is $1895.41.

PROGRAMMED SOLUTION

STEP 1 (Set P/Y, C/Y = 4) 10 000 $\boxed{\pm}$ $\boxed{PV}$ 10 $\boxed{I/Y}$ 4 $\boxed{N}$ $\boxed{CPT}$ $\boxed{FV}$ Result: $\boxed{11038.12891}$

STEP 2 $\boxed{-}$ 5000 $\boxed{=}$ $\boxed{6038.128906}$ $\boxed{\pm}$ $\boxed{PV}$ (Set P/Y, C/Y = 2) 8 $\boxed{I/Y}$ 6 $\boxed{N}$ $\boxed{CPT}$ $\boxed{FV}$
Result: $\boxed{7640.159341}$

STEP 3 $\boxed{-}$ 6000 $\boxed{=}$ $\boxed{1640.159341}$ $\boxed{\pm}$ $\boxed{PV}$ (Set P/Y, C/Y = 1) 7.5 $\boxed{I/Y}$ 2 $\boxed{N}$ $\boxed{CPT}$ $\boxed{FV}$
Result: $\boxed{1895.4092139}$

EXERCISE 9.2

1. What is the maturity value of a five-year term deposit of $5000 at 3.5% compounded semi-annually? How much interest did the deposit earn?

2. How much will a registered retirement savings deposit of $1500 be worth in 15 years at 3.45% compounded quarterly? How much of the amount is interest?

3. Reece's parents made a trust deposit of $500 on October 31, 2004, to be withdrawn on Reece's twenty-first birthday on July 31, 2025. What will be the value of the deposit on that date at 7% compounded quarterly?

4. A loan for $5000 with interest at 7.75% compounded semi-annually is repaid after 5 years, 10 months. What is the amount of interest paid?

5. Suppose $4000 can be invested for 4 years and 8 months at 3.83% compounded annually. Then assume the same amount could also be invested for the same term at 3.79% compounded daily. Which investment would earn more interest? What is the difference in the amount of interest?

6. A debt of $8000 is payable in 7 years and 5 months. Determine the accumulated value of the debt at 10.8% compounded annually.

7. The Canadian Consumer Price Index was approximately 98.5 (base year 1992) at the beginning of 1991. If inflation continued at an average annual rate of 3%, what was the index at the beginning of 2020?

8. Peel Credit Union expects an average annual growth rate of 8% for the next five years. If the assets of the credit union currently amount to $2.5 million, what will the forecasted assets be in five years?

9. A deposit of $2000 earns interest at 3% compounded quarterly. After two-and-a-half years, the interest rate is changed to 2.75% compounded monthly. How much is the account worth after six years?

10. An investment of $2500 earns interest at 4.5% compounded monthly for three years. At that time the interest rate is changed to 5% compounded quarterly. How much will the accumulated value be one-and-a-half years after the change?

11. A debt of $800 accumulates interest at 10% compounded semi-annually from February 1, 2021, to August 1, 2023, and 11% compounded quarterly thereafter. Determine the accumulated value of the debt on November 1, 2026.

12. Accumulate $1300 at 8.5% compounded monthly from March 1, 2020, to July 1, 2022, and thereafter at 8% compounded quarterly. What is the amount on April 1, 2025?

13. Patrice opened an RRSP deposit account on December 1, 2016, with a deposit of $1000. He added $1000 on July 1, 2018, and $1000 on November 1, 2020. How much is in his account on January 1, 2024, if the deposit earns 6% compounded monthly?

14. Terri started an RRSP on March 1, 2016, with a deposit of $2000. She added $1800 on December 1, 2018, and $1700 on September 1, 2020. What is the accumulated value of her account on December 1, 2027, if interest is 7.5% compounded quarterly?

15. Gerry the Gardener owed $4000 on his purchase of a new heavy-use lawn mower for his business. He repaid $1500 in 9 months, another $2000 in 18 months, and

the remaining amount owed in 27 months. If interest is 10% compounded quarterly, what is the amount of the final payment?

🌐 **16.** Sheridan Service has a line of credit loan with the bank. The initial loan balance was $6000. Payments of $2000 and $3000 were made after four months and nine months, respectively. At the end of one year, Sheridan Service borrowed an additional $4000. Six months later, the line of credit loan was converted into a collateral mortgage loan. What was the amount of the mortgage loan if the line of credit interest was 9% compounded monthly?

🌐 **17.** A demand loan of $3000 is repaid by payments of $1500 after two years, $1500 after four years, and a final payment after seven years. Interest is 9% compounded quarterly for the first year, 10% compounded semi-annually for the next three years, and 10% compounded monthly thereafter. What is the size of the final payment?

18. A variable rate demand loan showed an initial balance of $12 000, payments of $5000 after 18 months, $4000 after 30 months, and a final payment after 5 years. Interest was 11% compounded semi-annually for the first two years and 12% compounded monthly for the remaining time. What was the size of the final payment?

🌐 **19.** Joan borrowed $15 000 to buy a car. She repaid $2000 two months later and $5000 seven months later. After 12 months, she borrowed an additional $4000, and repaid $3000 after 16 months. She paid the entire balance, including the interest, after 24 months. Interest was 7% compounded monthly for the first year and 7.5% compounded monthly for the remaining time. What was the size of the final payment?

🌐 **20.** A variable rate demand loan showed an initial balance of $9000, payments of $2500 after 6 months, $2500 after 21 months, and a final payment after 4 years. Interest was 8% compounded quarterly for the first 21 months and 7.75% compounded monthly for the remaining time. What was the size of the final payment?

21. You borrowed $3500.00 at 10.4% compounded monthly, and repaid $1000.00 after two years and $750.00 after four years. How much do you owe at the end of five years?

22. You have a line of credit loan with Scotiabank. The initial loan balance was $6000.00. Payments of $2000.00 and $1500.00 were made after five months and ten months, respectively. At the end of one year, you borrowed an additional $3200.00. Eight months later, the line of credit loan was converted into a collateral mortgage loan. What was the amount of the mortgage if the line of credit interest was 6.15% compounded monthly?

9.3 PRESENT VALUE AND COMPOUND DISCOUNT
A. The present value concept and related terms

EXAMPLE 9.3A   Determine the principal that will amount in six years to $17 715.61 at 10% compounded annually.

SOLUTION   The problem may be graphically represented as shown in Figure 9.7.

Figure 9.7 Graphical Representation of Data (© S. A. Hummelbrunner)

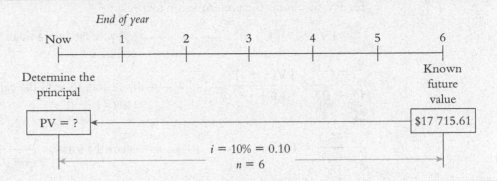

This problem is the inverse of the problem used to illustrate the meaning of compound interest. Instead of knowing the value of the principal and calculating its future value, we know that the future value is $17 715.61. What we want to determine is the value of the principal.

To solve the problem, we use the future value formula $FV = PV(1 + i)^n$ and substitute the known values.

$$FV = 17715.61; I/Y = 10; C/Y = 1; i = \frac{10\%}{1} = 10\% = 0.1; n = 1(6) = 6$$

$17\,715.61 = PV(1.1)^6$ —————————— by substituting in $FV + PV(1 + i)^n$

$17\,715.61 = PV(1.771561)$ —————————— computing $(1.10)^6$

$$PV = \frac{17715.61}{1.771561}$$ —————————— solve for PV by dividing both sides by 1.771561

$$PV = 10\,000.00$$

The principal that will grow to $17 715.61 in six years at 10% compounded annually is $10 000.

This principal is called the **present value** or **discounted value** or **proceeds** of the known future amount.

The difference between the known future amount of $17 715.61 and the computed present value (principal) of $10 000 is the **compound discount** and represents the compound interest accumulating on the computed present value.

The process of computing the present value or discounted value or proceeds is called **discounting**.

B. The present value formula

With compound interest, the present value of an amount at a given time is defined as the principal that will grow to the desired future amount if compounded at a given periodic rate of interest over a given number of conversion periods.

Since the problem of calculating the present value is equivalent to determining the principal when the future value, the periodic rate of interest, and the number of conversion periods are given, the formula for the future value formula, $FV = PV(1 + i)^n$, applies.

However, because the problem of calculating the present value of an amount is frequently encountered in financial analysis, it is useful to solve the future value formula for PV to obtain the present value formula.

$$FV = PV(1 + i)^n$$ —————— start with the future value formula, Formula 9.1

$$\frac{FV}{(1 + i)^n} = \frac{PV(1 + i)^n}{(1 + i)^n}$$ —————— divide both sides by the compounding factor $(1 + i)^n$

$$\frac{FV}{(1 + i)^n} = PV$$ —————— reduce the fraction $\frac{(1 + i)^n}{(1 + i)^n}$ to 1

The present value formula for compound interest is

$$PV = \frac{FV}{(1 + i)^n}$$ —————— Formula 9.4

EXAMPLE 9.3B

Calculate the present value of $6836.56 due in nine years at 6% compounded quarterly.

SOLUTION

$$FV = 6836.56; I/Y = 6; P/Y = 4; i = \frac{6\%}{4} = 1.5\% = 0.015; n = 9(4) = 36$$

$$PV = \frac{FV}{(1 + i)^n}$$ —————— using the present value formula

$$= \frac{6836.56}{(1 + 0.015)^{36}}$$ —————— by substitution

$$= \frac{6836.56}{1.709140}$$

$$= \$4000.003$$

Note: The division of 6836.56 by 1.709140, like any division, may be changed to multiplication by using the reciprocal of the divisor.

$$\frac{6386.56}{1.709140}$$ —————— the division to be changed into a multiplication

$$= 6836.56\left(\frac{1}{1.709140}\right)$$ —————— the reciprocal of the divisor 1.709140 is found by dividing 1 by 1.709140

$$= 6836.56(0.585090)$$ —————— computed value of the reciprocal

$$= \$4000.00$$

 For calculators equipped with the reciprocal function key $\boxed{1/x}$, converting the division into a multiplication is easily accomplished by first computing the compounding factor and then using the $\boxed{1/x}$ key to obtain the reciprocal.

EXAMPLE 9.3C

What principal will amount to $5000 seven years from today if interest is 4.88% compounded monthly?

SOLUTION

Determining the principal that amounts to a future sum of money is equivalent to calculating the present value.

$$FV = 5000.00; \; I/Y = 9; \; C/Y = 12; \; i = \frac{4.88\%}{12} = 0.40\dot{6}6\% = 0.004066\dot{6}; \; n = 7(12) = 84$$

$$PV = \frac{5000.00}{(1.004066\dot{6})^{84}} \text{ ———— using Formula 9.4}$$

$$= \frac{5000.00}{1.406223} \text{ ———— computing the factor } (1.004066\dot{6})^{84}$$

$$= 5000.00(0.711125) \text{ ———— using the reciprocal function key}$$

$$= \$3555.62$$

Using the reciprocal of the divisor to change division into multiplication is reflected in the practice of stating the present value formula with a negative exponent.

$$\frac{1}{a^n} = a^{-n} \text{ ———— negative exponent rule}$$

$$\frac{1}{(1 + i)^n} = (1 + i)^{-n}$$

$$\frac{FV}{(1 + i)^n} = FV(1 + i)^{-n}$$

Formula 9.4, the present value formula, can be restated in multiplication form using a negative exponent.

$$\boxed{PV = FV(1 + i)^{-n}}$$

The factor $(1 + i)^{-n}$ is called the **discount factor** and is the reciprocal of the compounding factor $(1 + i)^n$.

C. Using preprogrammed financial calculators to calculate present value

As explained in Section 9.2B, preprogrammed calculators provide quick solutions to compound interest calculations. Three of the four variables are entered and the value of the fourth variable is retrieved.

To solve Example 9.3C, in which FV = 5000, $i = 0.40\dot{6}6\%$, $n = 84$, and PV is to be determined, use the following procedure. (Remember that the interest rate for the year, 4.88%, must be entered into the calculator as I/Y.)

PROGRAMMED SOLUTION

(Set P/Y, C/Y = 12) 5000 [FV] 4.88 [I/Y] 84 [N] [CPT] [FV] [−3555.6247165]

This calculation retrieves the unknown present value (principal or PV), an investment or cash outflow as indicated by the negative sign.

The present value is $3555.62.

EXAMPLE 9.3D

SOLUTION

Calculate the present value of $2000 due in three years and eight months if money is worth 8% compounded quarterly.

$FV = 2000.00;\ I/Y = 8;\ P/Y = 4;\ i = \dfrac{8\%}{4} = 2\% = 0.02;$

$$n = \left(3\frac{8}{12}\right)(4) = 14\frac{2}{3} = 14.\dot{6}$$

$PV = \dfrac{FV}{(1 + i)^n}$ ———————————— using Formula 9.4

$= \dfrac{2000.00}{(1 + 0.02)^{14.\dot{6}}}$ ———————————— use as many decimals as are available in your calculator

$= 2000.00(0.747936)$ ———————— multiply by the reciprocal

$= \$1495.87$

PROGRAMMED SOLUTION

(Set P/Y, C/Y = 4) 2000 $\boxed{\text{FV}}$ 8 $\boxed{\text{I/Y}}$ 14.6̇ $\boxed{\text{N}}$ $\boxed{\text{CPT}}$ $\boxed{\text{FV}}$ $\boxed{-1495.871001}$

EXAMPLE 9.3E

SOLUTION

Determine the principal that will accumulate to $2387.18 from September 1, 2018, to April 1, 2022, at 5% compounded semi-annually.

Determining the principal that will grow to the given amount of $2387.18 is equivalent to calculating the present value or discounted value of this amount.

The time period September 1, 2018, to April 1, 2022, contains three years and seven months; that is, it consists of seven whole conversion periods of six months each and a fractional conversion period of one month.

Use $PV = \dfrac{FV}{(1 + i)^n}$

$FV = 2387.18;\ I/Y = 5;\ P/Y = 2;\ i = \dfrac{5\%}{2} = 2.5\% = 0.025;$

$$n = \left(3\frac{7}{12}\right)(2) = 7\frac{1}{6} = 7.1\dot{6}$$

$PV = \dfrac{2387.18}{(1.025)^{7.1\dot{6}}}$

$= \dfrac{2387.18}{1.193588}$

$= 2387.18(0.837810)$

$= \$2000.00$

PROGRAMMED SOLUTION

(Set P/Y = 2) 2387.18 $\boxed{\text{FV}}$ 5 $\boxed{\text{I/Y}}$ 7.16̇ $\boxed{\text{N}}$ $\boxed{\text{CPT}}$ $\boxed{\text{FV}}$ $\boxed{-2000.003698}$

POINTERS & PITFALLS

Store all values in the memory of your calculator as positive values. So, when you calculate PV using a preprogrammed calculator, and the final answer shows a negative value, immediately change the sign of this value using the ± key, and then store the positive value in the memory of your calculator.

EXERCISE 9.3

MyLab Math

1. Calculate the present value and the compound discount of $1600 due four-and-a-half years from now if money is worth 4% compounded semi-annually.

2. Calculate the present value and the compound discount of $2500 due in 6 years and 3 months, if interest is 6% compounded quarterly.

3. Determine the principal that will amount to $1250 in five years at 10% compounded quarterly.

4. What sum of money will grow to $2000 in seven years at 9% compounded monthly?

5. A debt of $5000 is due November 1, 2028. What is the value of the obligation on February 1, 2022, if money is worth 7% compounded quarterly?

6. How much would you have to deposit in an account today to have $3000 in a five-year term deposit at maturity if interest is 7.75% compounded annually?

7. What is the principal that will grow to $3000 in 8 years and 8 months at 9% compounded semi-annually?

8. Determine the sum of money that accumulates to $1600 at 5% compounded quarterly in 6 years and 4 months.

9. Calculate the proceeds of $9000 due in 4 years and 11 months discounted at 8.25% compounded bi-weekly.

10. Compute the discounted value of $5000 due in 10 years and 2 months if money is worth 2.75% compounded weekly.

11. You have the choice of receiving $100 000 now, or $60 000 now and another $60 000 five years from now. In terms of today's dollar, which choice is better and by how much? Money is worth 6% compounded annually.

12. In negotiating a contract for your business, you have to decide between receiving $50 000 now, or $20 000 now and $35 000 three years from now. In terms of today's dollar, which choice is better and by how much? Money is worth 4.25% compounded annually.

13. Joe is negotiating the purchase of a sound system for his DJ business. He can either pay $2000 now, or pay $100 now and $2200 in 18 months. Which option is better if money is worth 8% compounded monthly?

14. Jane is purchasing a membership in the local Chamber of Commerce to promote her business. She can pay either $350 now, or pay $130 now, $150 in 12 months, and $170 in 15 months. Which option is better if money is worth 7.5% compounded monthly?

15. John invested part of his inheritance at 3.95% compounded monthly. After two years, the rate changed to 4.0% compounded quarterly. How much money did John originally invest if he currently has $30 000 in his account after seven years?

16. Harpreet's parents deposited a lump sum of money into a savings account for him on his tenth birthday at an interest rate of 5% compounded semi-annually. Three years later, they opened a new account for him. They deposited $5000 to this new account and transferred over the balance from the original account. The new account paid interest at 4.95% compounded daily. How much money was originally invested if Harpreet had $15 000.67 in the account on the day he turned 19?

9.4 APPLICATION—DISCOUNTING NEGOTIABLE FINANCIAL INSTRUMENTS AT COMPOUND INTEREST

A. Discounting long-term promissory notes

When governments or businesses borrow money for terms longer than one year, these long-term promissory notes are usually subject to compound interest. Long-term promissory notes are negotiable and can be bought and sold (*discounted*) at any time before maturity. The principles involved in discounting long-term promissory notes are similar to those used in discounting short-term promissory notes by the simple discount method, *except* that no grace period is considered in determining the legal due date of a long-term promissory note.

The discounted value (or proceeds) of a long-term promissory note is the present value at the date of discount of the maturity value of the note. It is found using the present value formula $PV = \dfrac{FV}{(1 + i)^n}$ or $PV = FV(1 + i)^{-n}$.

For non-interest-bearing notes, the face value is the maturity value. The discounted value is determined in one step—calculating the present value of the discount period.

For interest-bearing notes, determining the discounted value involves two steps. First, the maturity value must be determined by using the future value formula, $FV = PV(1 + i)^n$. The discounted value is determined in the second step by using the future value calculated in the first step and determining the present value of the discount period using the present value formula $PV = FV(1 + i)^{-n}$.

Like promissory notes, long-term bonds promise to pay a specific face value at a specified future point in time. In addition, there is a promise to periodically pay a specified amount of interest. Long-term bonds will be covered in detail in Chapter 15.

B. Discounting non-interest-bearing promissory notes

Since the face value of a non-interest-bearing note is also its maturity value, the proceeds of a non-interest-bearing note are the present value of its face value at the date of discount.

EXAMPLE 9.4A

Determine the proceeds of a non-interest-bearing note for $15 000 discounted two-and-a-quarter years before its due date at 9% compounded monthly (see Figure 9.8).

Figure 9.8 Graphical Representation of Data (© S. A. Hummelbrunner)

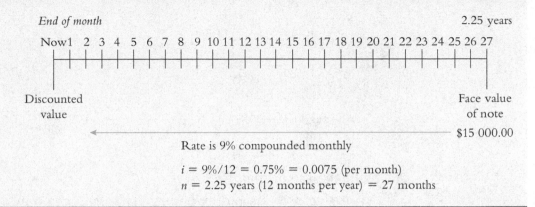

End of month   2.25 years

Now 1 2 3 4 5 6 7 8 9 10 11 12 13 14 15 16 17 18 19 20 21 22 23 24 25 26 27

Discounted   Face value
value   of note

                                                    $15 000.00

Rate is 9% compounded monthly

$i = 9\%/12 = 0.75\% = 0.0075$ (per month)
$n = 2.25$ years (12 months per year) $= 27$ months

SOLUTION

The maturity value FV = 15 000.00;

the rate of discount I/Y = 9; P/Y, C/Y = 12; $i = \dfrac{9\%}{12} = 0.75\% = 0.0075$;

the number of conversion periods $n = (2.25)(12) = 27$.

$PV = FV(1 + i)^{-n}$ ——————————— **using restated Formula 9.4**

$= 15\ 000(1 + 0.0075)^{-27}$

$= 15\ 000(0.817304)$

$= \$12\ 259.5571$

PROGRAMMED SOLUTION

(Set P/Y, C/Y = 12) 15 000 `FV` 9 `I/Y` 27 `N` `CPT` `PV` `−12259.5571`

EXAMPLE 9.4B

A four-year, non-interest-bearing promissory note for $6000 was dated August 31, 2025, and earned interest at 6% compounded quarterly. Determine the proceeds of the note if it was discounted on October 31, 2022 (see Figure 9.9).

Figure 9.9 Graphical Representation of Data (© S. A. Hummelbrunner)

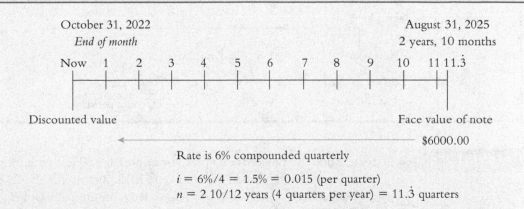

October 31, 2022   August 31, 2025
End of month   2 years, 10 months

Now   1   2   3   4   5   6   7   8   9   10   11 11.3

Discounted value   Face value of note

                                                    $6000.00

Rate is 6% compounded quarterly

$i = 6\%/4 = 1.5\% = 0.015$ (per quarter)
$n = 2\ 10/12$ years (4 quarters per year) $= 11.\dot{3}$ quarters

SOLUTION

The due date of the note is August 31, 2025; the discount period October 31, 2022, to August 31, 2025, contains 2 years and 10 months.

$$FV = 6000.00; I/Y = 6; C/Y = 4; i = \frac{6\%}{4} = 1.5\% = 0.015;$$

$$n = \left(2\frac{10}{12}\right)(4) = 11\frac{1}{3} = 11.\dot{3}$$

$$PV = FV(1 + i)^{-n}$$

$$= 6000.00(1 + 0.015)^{-11.\dot{3}}$$

$$= 6000.00(0.844731)$$

$$= \$5068.39$$

PROGRAMMED SOLUTION

(Set P/Y, C/Y = 4)6000 [FV] 6 [I/Y] 11.$\dot{3}$ [N] [CPT] [PV] -5068.383148

C. Discounting interest-bearing promissory notes

The proceeds of an interest-bearing note are equal to the present value at the date of discount of the value of the note at maturity. Two steps are required:

STEP 1 Determine the maturity value of the note. The calculation of future value is required, using the note's stated interest rate and the entire length of the note.

Note: Rounding procedures are explained on page 334.

STEP 2 Determine the proceeds by discounting the maturity value. The calculation of present value is required, using the prevailing interest rate and the time between the discount date and the maturity date.

POINTERS & PITFALLS

In calculating the proceeds of an interest-bearing note, it is important that the value of n, which is used in the present value formula, is determined from the discount period. The discount period is the time between the date of discount and the due date. The discount period is not the time between the issue date and the discount date. See the diagram below.

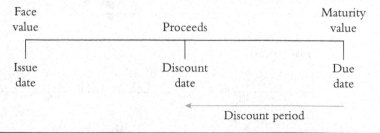

EXAMPLE 9.4C Determine the proceeds of a promissory note for $3600 with interest at 6% compounded quarterly; issued September 1, 2018; due on June 1, 2024; and discounted on December 1, 2020, at 8% compounded semi-annually (see Figure 9.10).

Figure 9.10 Graphical Representation of Method and Data (© S. A. Hummelbrunner)

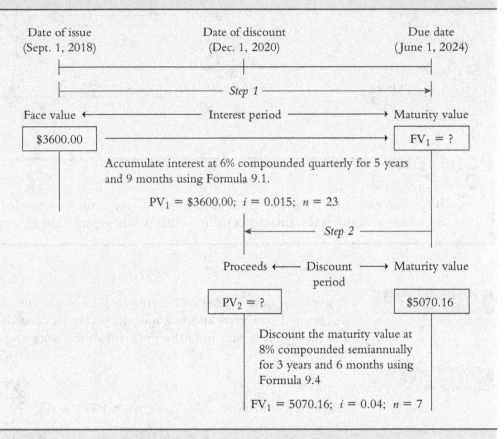

SOLUTION

STEP 1   Calculate the maturity value of the note using Formula 9.1, $FV = PV(1 + i)^n$.

$PV_1 = 3600.00$; $I/Y = 6$; P/Y, $C/Y = 4$; $i = \dfrac{6\%}{4} = 1.5\% = 0.015$; the interest period, September 1, 2018, to June 1, 2024, contains 5 years and 9 months:

$$n = \left(5\frac{9}{12}\right)(4) = 23$$

$$\begin{aligned}FV_1 &= 3600.00(1 + 0.015)^{23} \\ &= 3600.00(1.408377) \\ &= \$5070.16\end{aligned}$$

STEP 2   Calculate the present value at the date of discount of the maturity value found in Step 1 using $PV = FV(1 + i)^{-n}$.

$FV_1 = 5070.16$; $I/Y = 8$; P/Y, $C/Y = 2$; $i = \dfrac{8\%}{2} = 4\% = 0.04$;

the discount period, December 1, 2020, to June 1, 2024, contains 3 years and 6 months:

$$n = \left(3\frac{6}{12}\right)(2) = 7.$$

$$\begin{aligned}PV_2 &= 5070.16(1 + 0.04)^{-7} \\ &= 5070.16(0.759918) \\ &= \$3852.90\end{aligned}$$

The proceeds of the note on December 1, 2020, are $3852.90.

PROGRAMMED SOLUTION

STEP 1   (Set P/Y, C/Y = 4) 3600 [±] [PV] 6 [I/Y] 23 [N] [CPT] [FV] [5070.157757]

The answer to Step 1 is now programmed
as [FV] for Step 2.

STEP 2   (Set P/Y, C/Y = 2) 5070.16 [FV] 8 [I/Y] 7 [N] [CPT] [PV] [−3852.9049]

POINTERS & PITFALLS

In promissory notes, the FV solution in the first step must be rounded to 2 decimals before discounting, as this is the amount of the debt that will be repaid on the maturity date.

EXAMPLE 9.4D

A five-year note for $8000 bearing interest at 6% compounded monthly is discounted two years and five months before the due date at 5% compounded semi-annually. Determine the proceeds of the note and the amount of the discount.

SOLUTION

STEP 1   Calculate the maturity value using $FV = PV(1 + i)^n$.

$PV_1 = 8000.00$; $I/Y = 6$; P/Y, C/Y = 12; $i = \dfrac{6\%}{12} = 0.5\% = 0.005$; $n = 60$

$FV_1 = 8000.00(1.005)^{60}$
$\quad\ = 8000.00(1.348850)$
$\quad\ = \$10\ 790.80$

STEP 2   Calculate the present value of the maturity value found in Step 1 using

$PV_2 = FV(1 + i)^{-n}$.

$FV_1 = 10\ 790.80$; $I/Y = 5$; P/Y = 2; $i = \dfrac{5\%}{2} = 2.5\% = 0.025$;

$n = \left(\dfrac{29}{12}\right)(2) = 4.8\dot{3}$

$PV_2 = 10\ 790.80(1.025)^{-4.8\dot{3}}$
$\quad\ = 10\ 790.80(0.887499)$
$\quad\ = \$9576.83$

PROGRAMMED SOLUTION

STEP 1   (Set P/Y, C/Y = 12) 8000 [±] [PV] 6 [I/Y] 60 [N] [CPT] [FV] [10790.80122]

STEP 2   (Set P/Y, C/Y = 2) 10790.80 [FV] 5 [I/Y] 4.8̇3 [N] [CPT] [PV] [−9576.826669]

The proceeds of the note are $9576.83.

The discount is $9575.25 − 8000 = $1575.25.

EXERCISE 9.4   MyLab Math

1. Determine the proceeds of a non-interest-bearing promissory note for $6000, discounted 54 months before its due date at 6% compounded quarterly.

2. Determine the proceeds of a $4200, non-interest-bearing note due August 1, 2027, discounted on March 1, 2023, at 7.5% compounded monthly.

3. Determine the proceeds of a promissory note with a maturity value of $1800 due on September 30, 2022, discounted at 8.5% compounded semi-annually on March 31, 2019.

4. Determine the proceeds of a 15-year promissory note discounted after 6 years at 9% compounded quarterly with a maturity value of $7500.

5. Determine the proceeds of a 5-year promissory note for $3000 with interest at 8% compounded semi-annually, discounted 21 months before maturity at 9% compounded quarterly.

6. Determine the proceeds of a $5000, seven-year note bearing interest at 8% compounded quarterly, discounted two-and-a-half years after the date of issue at 6% compounded monthly.

7. Determine the proceeds of a six-year, $900 note bearing interest at 10% compounded quarterly, issued June 1, 2017, discounted on December 1, 2022, to yield 8.5% compounded semi-annually.

8. Determine the proceeds of a ten-year promissory note dated April 1, 2017, with a face value of $1300, bearing interest at 7% compounded semi-annually, discounted seven years later when money was worth 9% compounded quarterly.

9. Determine the proceeds of an investment with a maturity value of $10 000 if discounted at 9% compounded monthly 22.5 months before the date of maturity.

10. Compute the discounted value of $7000 due in three years, five months if money is worth 8% compounded quarterly.

11. Calculate the discounted value of $3800 due in 6 years and 8 months if interest is 7.5% compounded annually.

12. Calculate the proceeds of $5500 due in 7 years and 8 months discounted at 4.5% compounded semi-annually.

13. A four-year, non-interest-bearing promissory note for $3750 is discounted 32 months after the date of issue at 5.5% compounded semi-annually. Determine the proceeds of the note.

14. A seven-year, non-interest-bearing note for $5200 is discounted 3 years and 8 months before its due date at 9% compounded quarterly. Determine the proceeds of the note.

15. A non-interest-bearing, eight-year note for $4500 issued August 1, 2019, is discounted April 1, 2023, at 6.5% compounded annually. Calculate the compound discount.

16. A $2800 promissory note issued without interest for five years on September 30, 2019, is discounted on July 31, 2022, at 8% compounded quarterly. Calculate the compound discount.

17. A six-year note for $1750 issued on December 1, 2018, with interest at 6.5% compounded annually, is discounted on March 1, 2021, at 7% compounded semi-annually. What are the proceeds of the note?

18. A 10-year note for $1200, bearing interest at 6% compounded monthly, is discounted at 8% compounded quarterly 3 years, 10 months after the date of issue. Determine the proceeds of the note.

19. Four years and 7 months before its due date, a seven-year note for $2650, bearing interest at 9% compounded quarterly, is discounted at 8% compounded semi-annually. Calculate the compound discount.

20. On April 15, 2023, a 10-year note dated June 15, 2018, is discounted at 10% compounded quarterly. If the face value of the note is $4000 and interest is 8% compounded quarterly, calculate the compound discount.

BUSINESS MATH **NEWS**   Guaranteed Investment Certificates (GICs)

Guaranteed investment vehicles such as Guaranteed Investment Certificates (GICs) are suitable tools to use as part of a balanced personal investment portfolio. GICs are available in many forms to appeal to different types of investors. Unlike stocks and bonds, GICs provide the security of guaranteed interest plus full protection of the principal. Regardless of your age, the size of your investment, or the term, GICs reduce the degree of potential highs and lows and can help to produce steadier investment returns over time.

GICs come in fixed and variable versions, have many different term lengths, and can be either redeemable or non-redeemable. Longer maturity terms tend to yield higher interest rates. Individuals planning to invest for three or five years, who do not need access to their money before maturity, may be interested in purchasing escalating GICs where the interest rates increase each year.

The Canadian Imperial Bank of Commerce (CIBC) offers three- and five-year CIBC Escalating Rate GICs, compounded at the end of every year.

CIBC Escalating Rate TFSA GIC™ (three-year) offers guaranteed premium returns and interest rates that increase each year.

Investment Amount	Year 1	Year 2	Year 3	Effective Yield
$500 to $999 999	1.000%	1.100%	1.650%	1.2496%

CIBC Escalating Rate TFSA GIC™ (five-year) offers guaranteed premium returns and interest rates that increase each year.

Investment Amount	Year 1	Year 2	Year 3	Year 4	Year 5	Effective Yield
$500 to $999 999	1.000%	1.100%	1.150%	1.250%	3.000%	1.4972%

Source: CIBC. Tax Free Savings Account (TFSA) Rates. www.cibc.com/en/interest-rates/tfsa-rates.html, retrieved on March 16, 2019.

QUESTIONS

1. If you invest $10 000 in the stock market, and the market drops 20%, what is the dollar impact on the value of your portfolio?

2. If you invest $6000 in stocks and $4000 in GICs, and the market drops 20%, what are the dollar and percentage impacts on the value of your portfolio?

3. What is the maturity value of a $10 000 three-year GIC with a fixed interest rate of 1.25% compounded annually?

4. Calculate the maturity value using the escalating interest rates based on the terms and amount invested.
   (a) $10 000 invested in a three-year CIBC Escalating Rate TFSA GIC™
   (b) $10 000 invested in a five-year CIBC Escalating Rate TFSA GIC™

5. Demonstrate that the effective yield shown in the CIBC charts are correct for each type of GIC.

9.5 EQUIVALENT VALUES
A. Equations of value

Because of the time value of money, amounts of money have different values at different times, as explained in Chapter 7. When sums of money fall due or are payable at different times, they are not directly comparable. To make such sums of money comparable, a point in time—the **comparison date**—must be chosen. Allowance must be made for interest from the due dates of the sums of money to the selected focal date; that is, the dated equivalent values of the sums of money must be determined.

Any point in time may be chosen as the focal date; the choice does not affect the final answers. It is advisable, however, to choose a date on which an amount is unknown but desired to be known. The choice of date determines which formula is to be used. For compound interest, equations of value need to be set up.

POINTERS & PITFALLS

Choose a convenient focal date—one that can simplify your calculations. When just one payment is unknown, choose a focal date on the due date of this payment. If there is more than one unknown payment, choose *today* as the focal date. (You will be able to see the length of each interval better, and the solutions to equations of value problems at compound interest do not depend on the selection of focal date).

The rules for determining whether to use the FV or PV formula for calculating equivalent values as of the focal date are similar to the rules given for equivalent values in the simple interest rate environment.

Which formula is appropriate depends on the position of the focal date relative to the due dates. The following rules apply:

(a) If the focal date for a payment falls after the due date, use the future value formula, $FV = PV(1 + i)^n$ (see Figure 9.11).

(b) If the focal date for a payment falls before the due date, use the present value formula, $PV = FV(1 + i)^{-n}$ (see Figure 9.12).

B. Calculating the equivalent single payment

Equivalent values are the dated values of an original sum of money.

EXAMPLE 9.5A A sum of $4000 is due for payment three years from now. If money is worth 9% compounded semi-annually, determine the equivalent value

(i) seven years from now;   (ii) now.

Figure 9.11 Graphical Representation of Method and Data (© S. A. Hummelbrunner)

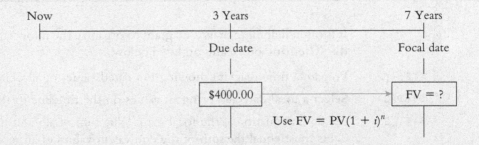

SOLUTION

(i) Using "seven years from now" as the focal date, the method and the data can be represented graphically as shown in Figure 9.11.

Since the focal date falls *after* the due date, use the future value formula.

$$PV = 4000.00; \ I/Y = 9; \ P/Y, \ C/Y = 2; \ i = \frac{9\%}{2} = 0.045; \ n = 4(2) = 8$$

$$FV = 4000.00(1 + 0.045)^8 = 4000.00(1.422101) = \$5688.40$$

The equivalent value of the $4000 seven years from now is $5688.40.

Figure 9.12 Graphical Representation of Method and Data (© S. A. Hummelbrunner)

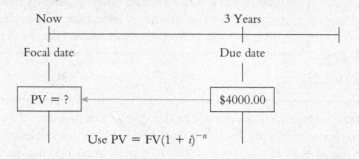

(ii) Using "now" as the focal date, the method and the data can be represented graphically as shown in Figure 9.12.

Since the focal date falls *before* the due date, use the present value formula.

$$FV = 4000.00; \ i = \frac{9\%}{2} = 0.045; \ n = 3(2) = 6$$

$$PV = 4000.00(1 + 0.045)^{-6} = 4000.00(0.767896) = \$3071.58$$

The equivalent value of the $4000.00 now is $3071.58.

PROGRAMMED SOLUTION

(i) (Set P/Y, C/Y = 2) 4000 [±] [PV] 9 [I/Y] 8 [N] [CPT] [FV] [5688.402451]

(ii) 4000 [FV] 9 [I/Y] 6 [N] [CPT] [FV] [−3071.582953]

POINTERS
& PITFALLS

When calculating equivalent values for more than one payment, each payment is a separate transaction (one could make each payment separate from any other payment), and therefore any equivalent value is rounded to two decimals before summing multiple payments.

It is often helpful to draw a diagram to organize the information in the question. Follow the systematic procedure outlined below.

STEP 1 Prepare a time diagram showing the dated values of all obligations.

STEP 2 Select a focal date and bring all values on the timeline to the focal date.

STEP 3 Set up an equation at the focal date. (The sum of all equivalent values of the original debts must equal the sum of the equivalent values of all replacement payments.)

STEP 4 Solve the equation.

EXAMPLE 9.5B

Joanna plans to pay off a debt by payments of $1600 one year from now, $1800 eighteen months from now, and $2000 thirty months from now. Determine the single payment now that would settle the debt if money is worth 8% compounded quarterly.

Figure 9.13 Graphical Representation of Method and Data (© S. A. Hummelbrunner)

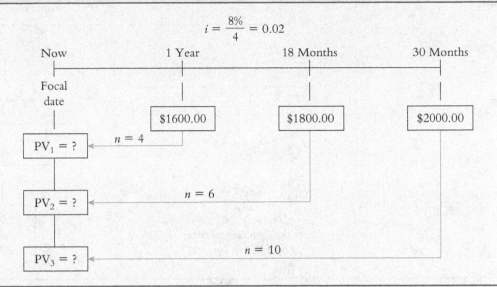

SOLUTION

While any date may be selected as the focal date, a logical choice for the focal date is the time designated "now," since the single payment "now" is wanted. As is shown in Figure 9.13, for the three scheduled payments, the chosen focal date falls before each of the due dates. Therefore, the present value formula $PV = FV(1 + i)^{-n}$ is appropriate for calculating the equivalent values of each of the three scheduled payments.

The equivalents of the three scheduled payments at the selected focal date are

$PV_1 = 1600.00(1 + 0.02)^{-4} = 1600.00(0.923845) = \$1478.15$

$PV_2 = 1800.00(1 + 0.02)^{-6} = 1800.00(0.887971) = \$1598.35$

$PV_3 = 2000.00(1 + 0.02)^{-10} = 2000.00(0.820348) = \$1640.70$

The equivalent single payment to settle the debt now is $4717.20.

PROGRAMMED SOLUTION

PV_1 (Set P/Y, C/Y = 4) 1600 [FV] 8 [I/Y] 4 [N] [CPT] [FV] [−1478.152682]

PV_2 1800 [FV] 8 [I/Y] 6 [N] [CPT] [FV] [−1598.348488]

PV_3 2000 [FV] 8 [I/Y] 10 [N] [CPT] [FV] [−1640.6966]

Note: Remember that the negative sign indicates a cash payment or outflow. Disregard the negative signs when solving equivalent single payments.

1478.15 + 1598.35 + 1640.70 = $4717.20

EXAMPLE 9.5C

Debt payments of $400 due five months ago, $600 due today, and $800 due in nine months are to be combined into one payment due three months from today at 12% compounded monthly.

Figure 9.14 Graphical Representation of Method and Data (© S. A. Hummelbrunner)

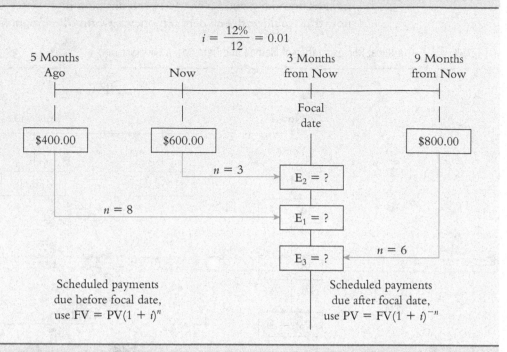

SOLUTION

The logical choice for the focal date is "3 months from now," the date when the equivalent single payment is to be made.

As shown in Figure 9.14, the focal date is after the first two scheduled payments, and therefore, the future value formula $FV = PV(1 + i)^n$ should be used. However, the focal date is before the due date for the third scheduled payment, which means that, for that payment, the present value formula $PV = FV(1 + i)^{-n}$ applies.

The equivalent values (designated E_1, E_2, E_3) of the scheduled debt payments at the selected focal date are

$$E_1 = 400.00(1 + 0.01)^8 \quad = 400.00(1.082857) = \$ 433.14$$
$$E_2 = 600.00(1 + 0.01)^3 \quad = 600.00(1.030301) = \quad 618.18$$
$$E_3 = 800.00(1 + 0.01)^{-6} = 800.00(0.942045) = \quad \underline{753.64}$$

The equivalent single payment to settle the
debt three months from now is $\underline{\$1804.96}$

PROGRAMMED SOLUTION

E_1 (Set P/Y, C/Y = 12) 400 [±] [PV] 12 [I/Y] 8 [N] [CPT] [FV] [433.142682]

E_2 600 [±] [PV] 12 [I/Y] 3 [N] [CPT] [FV] [618.1806]

E_3 800 [FV] 12 [I/Y] 6 [N] [CPT] [PV] [−753.636188]

Remember to treat this payment as a positive amount.

$433.14 + 618.18 + 753.64 = \$1804.96$

EXAMPLE 9.5D

Scheduled debt payments of $1000 due today and $2000 due one year from now are to be settled by a payment of $1500 three months from now and a final payment 18 months from now. Determine the size of the final payment if interest is 10% compounded quarterly.

Figure 9.15 Graphical Representation of Method and Data (© S. A. Hummelbrunner)

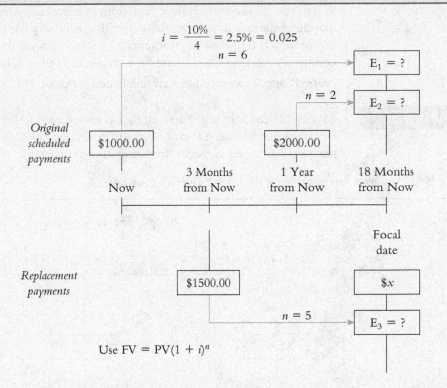

$$i = \frac{10\%}{4} = 2.5\% = 0.025$$

SOLUTION

Let the size of the final payment be x. The logical focal date is the date of the final payment, which is 18 months from now.

As shown in Figure 9.15, the focal date is after the two original scheduled payments and the first replacement payment. The future value formula $FV = PV(1 + i)^n$ applies. Because the final payment is dated on the focal date, its dated value is x.

The equivalent values of the original scheduled debt payments at the selected focal date, designated E_1 and E_2, are matched against the equivalent values of the replacement payments, designated E_3 and x, giving rise to the equation of values.

$$E_1 + E_2 = x + E_3$$
$$1000.00(1.025)^6 + 2000.00(1.025)^2 = x + 1500.00(1.025)^5$$
$$1000.00(1.159693) + 2000.00(1.050625) = x + 1500.00(1.131408)$$
$$1159.693418 + 2101.25 = x + 1697.112319$$
$$x = 1563.83$$

The final payment is $1563.83.

PROGRAMMED SOLUTION

E_1 (Set P/Y, C/Y = 4) 1000 $\boxed{\pm}$ $\boxed{\text{PV}}$ 10 $\boxed{\text{I/Y}}$ 6 $\boxed{\text{N}}$ $\boxed{\text{CPT}}$ $\boxed{\text{FV}}$ $\boxed{1159.693418}$

E_2 2000 $\boxed{\pm}$ $\boxed{\text{PV}}$ 2 $\boxed{\text{N}}$ $\boxed{\text{CPT}}$ $\boxed{\text{FV}}$ $\boxed{2101.25}$

E_3 1500 $\boxed{\pm}$ $\boxed{\text{PV}}$ 5 $\boxed{\text{N}}$ $\boxed{\text{CPT}}$ $\boxed{\text{FV}}$ $\boxed{1697.112319}$

$$1159.69 + 2101.25 = x + 1697.11$$
$$x = 1563.83$$

C. Determining the value of two or more equivalent replacement payments

When two or more equivalent replacement payments are needed, an equation of values matching the dated values of the original scheduled payments against the dated values of the proposed replacement payments on a selected focal date should be set up. This procedure is similar to the one used for simple interest in Chapter 7.

Note: Rounding procedures are explained on page 334.

EXAMPLE 9.5E

Mae is due to make a payment of $1000 now. Instead, she has negotiated to make two equal payments, one year and two years from now. Determine the size of the equal payments if money is worth 8% compounded quarterly.

Figure 9.16 Graphical Representation of Method and Data (© S. A. Hummelbrunner)

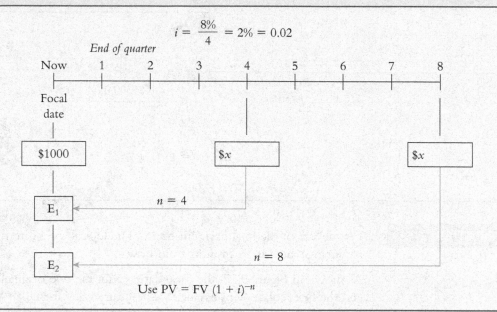

$$i = \frac{8\%}{4} = 2\% = 0.02$$

Use PV = FV $(1 + i)^{-n}$

SOLUTION

Select "now" as the focal date. Let the size of the equal payments be represented as $x and let the dated values of the two payments be represented by E_1 and E_2, as shown in Figure 9.16.

Then the equation of values can be set up.

$1000.00 = E_1 + E_2$

$1000.00 = x(1.02)^{-4} + x(1.02)^{-8}$

$1000.00 = x(0.923845 + 0.853490)$

$1000.00 = 1.777336x$

$\qquad x = \$562.64$

The size of the equal payments is $562.64.

PROGRAMMED SOLUTION

Assume FV = 1x, but use FV = 1 to calculate.

E_1 (Set P/Y = 4) 1 [FV] 8 [I/Y] 4 [N] [CPT] [FV] -0.923845 [±] [STO] 1

E_2 1 [FV] 8 [I/Y] 8 [N] [CPT] [PV] -0.853490 [±] [STO] 2

Remember to treat these payments as positive amounts.

$\boxed{\text{RCL}}\,1\;+\;\boxed{\text{RCL}}\,2 = 1.777336\;\boxed{\text{STO}}\,3$

$0.923845x + 0.853490x = \$1000.00$

$1.777336x = \$1000.00$

$x = \$562.64\,(1000 \div \boxed{\text{RCL}}\,3 =)$

EXAMPLE 9.5F

Olympia owes \$4000 in four years. She wants to repay the debt earlier and plans to make two equal payments in 16 months and in 28 months. Determine the size of the equal payments if money is worth 6% compounded monthly.

Figure 9.17 Graphical Representation of Method and Data (© S. A. Hummelbrunner)

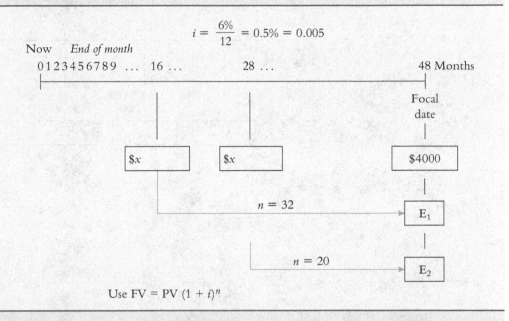

Use FV = PV $(1 + i)^n$

SOLUTION

Select four years from now as the focal date. Let the size of the equal payments be represented as \$x, and let the dated values of the two payments be represented by E_1 and E_2, as shown in Figure 9.17.

The equation of values may be set up.

$4000.00 = E_1 + E_2$

$4000.00 = x(1.005)^{32} + x(1.005)^{20}$

$4000.00 = x(1.173043 + 1.104896)$

$4000.00 = 2.277939x$

$\quad\quad x = 1755.97$

The size of the equal payments is \$1755.97.

PROGRAMMED SOLUTION

E_1 (Set P/Y = 12) 1 $\boxed{\pm}$ $\boxed{\text{PV}}$ 6 $\boxed{\text{I/Y}}$ 32 $\boxed{\text{N}}$ $\boxed{\text{CPT}}$ $\boxed{\text{FV}}$ 1.173043 $\boxed{\text{STO}}$ 1

E_2 1 $\boxed{\pm}$ $\boxed{\text{PV}}$ 6 $\boxed{\text{I/Y}}$ 20 $\boxed{\text{N}}$ $\boxed{\text{CPT}}$ $\boxed{\text{FV}}$ 1.104896 $\boxed{\text{STO}}$ 2

Remember to enter the value "1" as a negative PV amount in both cases.

$\boxed{\text{RCL}}\ 1 + \boxed{\text{RCL}}\ 2 = 2.277939\ \boxed{\text{STO}}\ 3$

$1.173043x + 1.104896x = \$4000.00$

$2.277939x = \$4000.00$

$x = \$1755.97\ (4000 \div \boxed{\text{RCL}}\ 3 =)$

EXAMPLE 9.5G

What is the size of the equal payments that must be made at the end of each of the next five years to settle a debt of \$5000 due in five years, if money is worth 9% compounded annually?

Figure 9.18 Graphical Representation of Method and Data (© S. A. Hummelbrunner)

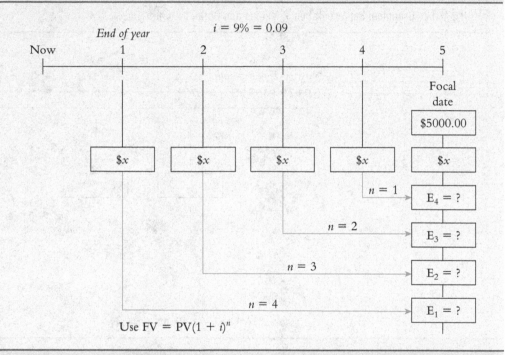

SOLUTION

Select as the focal date "five years from now." Let the equal payments be represented by \$x and let the dated values of the first four payments be represented by E_1, E_2, E_3, and E_4, respectively, as shown in Figure 9.18.

Then the equation of values may be set up.

$5000.00 = x + E_4 + E_3 + E_2 + E_1$

$5000.00 = x + x(1.09) + x(1.09)^2 + x(1.09)^3 + x(1.09)^4$

$5000.00 = x\big[1 + (1.09) + (1.09)^2 + (1.09)^3 + (1.09)^4\big]$

$5000.00 = x(1 + 1.09 + 1.1881 + 1.295029 + 1.411582)$

$5000.00 = 5.984711x$

$x = 835.46$

The size of the equal payments is \$835.46.

PROGRAMMED SOLUTION

(Set P/Y, C/Y = 1) E_1 1 $\boxed{\pm}$ $\boxed{\text{PV}}$ 9 $\boxed{\text{I/Y}}$ 4 $\boxed{\text{N}}$ $\boxed{\text{CPT}}$ $\boxed{\text{FV}}$ 1.411582 $\boxed{\text{STO}}$ 1

E_2 3 $\boxed{\text{N}}$ $\boxed{\text{CPT}}$ $\boxed{\text{FV}}$ 1.295029 $\boxed{\text{STO}}$ 2

E_3 2 $\boxed{\text{N}}$ $\boxed{\text{CPT}}$ $\boxed{\text{FV}}$ 1.1881 $\boxed{\text{STO}}$ 3

E_4 1 $\boxed{N}$ $\boxed{CPT}$ $\boxed{FV}$ $\boxed{1.09}$ $\boxed{STO}$ 4

$\boxed{RCL}$ 1 + $\boxed{RCL}$ 2 + $\boxed{RCL}$ 3 + $\boxed{RCL}$ 4 + 1 = 5.984711 $\boxed{STO}$ 5

or

$$1.411582x + 1.295029x + 1.1881x + 1.09x + x = \$5000.00$$
$$5.984711x = \$5000.00$$
$$x = \$835.46 \; (5000 \div \boxed{RCL}\, 5 =\,)$$

EXAMPLE 9.5H

What is the size of the equal payments that must be made at the end of each of the next five quarters to settle a debt of \$3000 due now if money is worth 12% compounded quarterly?

Figure 9.19 Graphical Representation of Method and Data (© S. A. Hummelbrunner)

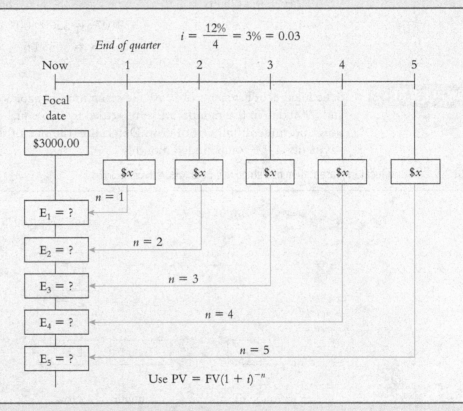

SOLUTION

Select as the focal date "now." Let the size of the equal payments be represented by \$x and let the dated values of the five payments be represented by E_1, E_2, E_3, E_4, and E_5, respectively, as shown in Figure 9.19.

Then the equation of values may be set up.

$$3000.00 = E_1 + E_2 + E_3 + E_4 + E_5$$
$$3000.00 = x(1.03)^{-1} + x(1.03)^{-2} + x(1.03)^{-3} + x(1.03)^{-4} + x(1.03)^{-5}$$
$$3000.00 = x\left[(1.03)^{-1} + (1.03)^{-2} + (1.03)^{-3} + (1.03)^{-4} + (1.03)^{-5}\right]$$
$$3000.00 = x(0.970874 + 0.942596 + 0.915142 + 0.888487 + 0.862609)$$
$$3000.00 = 4.579707x$$
$$x = \frac{3000.00}{4.579707}$$
$$x = \$655.06$$

The size of the equal payments is \$655.06.

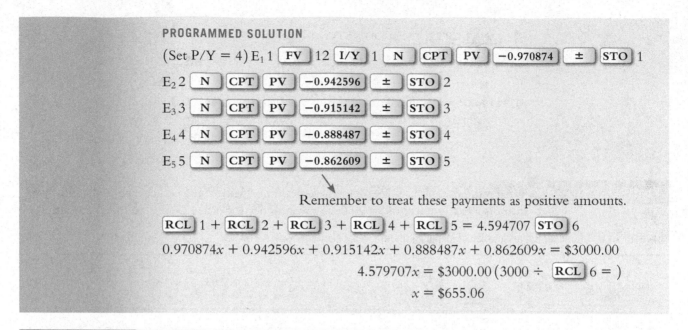

PROGRAMMED SOLUTION

(Set P/Y = 4) E_1 1 | FV | 12 | I/Y | 1 | N | CPT | PV | −0.970874 | ± | STO | 1

E_2 2 | N | CPT | PV | −0.942596 | ± | STO | 2

E_3 3 | N | CPT | PV | −0.915142 | ± | STO | 3

E_4 4 | N | CPT | PV | −0.888487 | ± | STO | 4

E_5 5 | N | CPT | PV | −0.862609 | ± | STO | 5

Remember to treat these payments as positive amounts.

RCL 1 + RCL 2 + RCL 3 + RCL 4 + RCL 5 = 4.594707 STO 6

$$0.970874x + 0.942596x + 0.915142x + 0.888487x + 0.862609x = \$3000.00$$
$$4.579707x = \$3000.00 \ (3000 \div \boxed{RCL} \ 6 \ =\ )$$
$$x = \$655.06$$

EXAMPLE 9.51

Scheduled debt payments of $750 due seven months ago, $600 due two months ago, and $900 due in five months are to be settled by two equal replacement payments due now and three months from now. Determine the size of the equal replacement payments at 9% compounded monthly.

Figure 9.20 Graphical Representation of Method and Data (© S. A. Hummelbrunner)

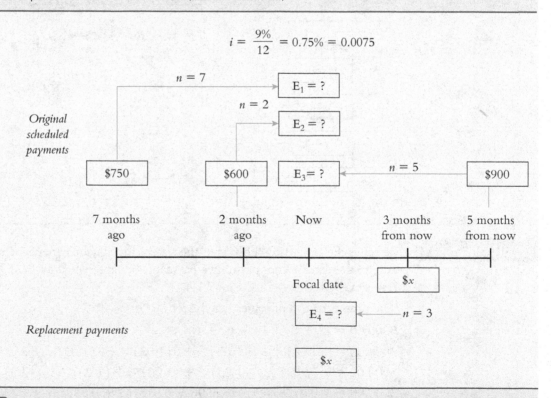

SOLUTION

Let the size of the equal replacement payments be represented by x and choose "now" as the focal date.

I/Y = 9; P/Y, C/Y = 12; $i = \dfrac{9\%}{12} = 0.0075$

Figure 9.20 shows the method and data.

STEP 1   DATED VALUES OF SCHEDULED PAYMENTS
First, consider the dated values of the original scheduled debt payments at the chosen focal date.

 The due dates of the debt payments of $750 and $600 are seven months and two months, respectively, before the focal date. Their equivalent dated values at the focal date are $750.00(1.0075)^7$ and $600.00(1.0075)^2$, represented by E_1 and E_2, respectively.

 The due date of the scheduled payment of $900 is five months after the focal date. Its dated value is $900.00(1.0075)^{-5}$, shown as E_3.

STEP 2   DATED VALUES OF REPLACEMENT PAYMENTS
Second, consider the dated values of the replacement payments at the selected focal date.

 The first replacement payment due at the focal date is $x. The second replacement payment is due three months after the focal date. Its dated value is $x(1.0075)^{-3}$, shown as E_4.

STEP 3   EQUATION OF DATED VALUES
Now equate the dated values of the replacement payments with the equivalent dated values of the original scheduled debt payments to set up the equation of values.

$$x + x(1.0075)^{-3} = 750.00(1.0075)^7 + 600.00(1.0075)^2 + 900.00(1.0075)^{-5}$$
$$x + 0.977833x = 750.00(1.053696) + 600.00(1.015056) + 900.00(0.963329)$$
$$1.977833x = 790.272095 + 609.03375 + 866.996283$$
$$1.977833x = 2266.302128$$
$$x = \frac{2266.302128}{1.977833}$$
$$x = \$1145.85$$

The size of the two equal payments is $1145.85.

For E_1 and E_2, use $FV = PV(1 + i)^n; i = \dfrac{9\%}{12} = 0.0075$

For E_3 and E_4, use $PV = FV(1 + i)^{-n}; i = \dfrac{9\%}{12} = 0.0075$

PROGRAMMED SOLUTION

Note: In $x(1.0075)^{-3}$, $\boxed{FV}$ is not known. To obtain the factor $(1.0075)^{-3}$, use $\boxed{FV} = 1$.

$x + x(1.0075)^{-3}$

(Set P/Y, C/Y = 12) 1 $\boxed{FV}$ 9 $\boxed{I/Y}$ 3 $\boxed{N}$ $\boxed{CPT}$ $\boxed{PV}$ $\boxed{-0.977833}$ $\boxed{\pm}$ (E_4)

$x + 0.977833x$

$750(1.0075)^2$

750 $\boxed{\pm}$ $\boxed{PV}$ 7 $\boxed{N}$ $\boxed{CPT}$ $\boxed{FV}$ $\boxed{790.272095}$ (E_1)

$600(1.0075)^2$

600 $\boxed{\pm}$ $\boxed{PV}$ 2 $\boxed{N}$ $\boxed{CPT}$ $\boxed{FV}$ $\boxed{609.03375}$ (E_2)

$900(1.0075)^{-5}$

900 $\boxed{FV}$ 5 $\boxed{N}$ $\boxed{CPT}$ $\boxed{FV}$ $\boxed{-866.996283}$ $\boxed{\pm}$ (E_3)

$x + (E_4) = (E_1) + (E_2) + (E_3)$

$$x + 0.977833x = 790.272095 + 609.03375 + 866.996283$$
$$1.977833x = 2266.302128$$
$$x = 1145.85$$

EXAMPLE 9.5J

Two scheduled payments, one of $4000 due in 3 months with interest at 9% compounded quarterly and the other of $3000 due in 18 months with a different interest rate of 8.5% compounded semi-annually, are to be discharged by making two equal replacement payments. What is the size of the equal replacement payments if the first is due one year from now, the second two years from now, and money is now worth 10% compounded monthly?

Figure 9.21 Graphical Representation of Method and Data (© S. A. Hummelbrunner)

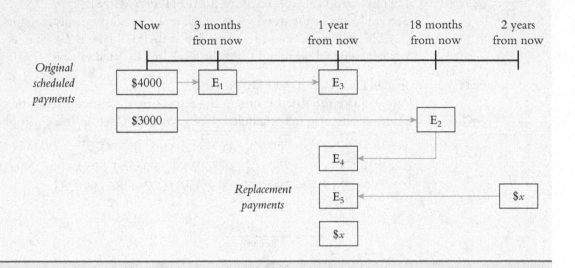

SOLUTION

Let the size of the equal replacement payments be represented by $x. Choose "one year from now" as the focal date. Figure 9.21 illustrates the problem.

STEP 1
MATURITY VALUES OF SCHEDULED PAYMENTS
Since the two scheduled payments are interest-bearing, first determine their maturity value. (Note the different interest rates used for each payment.)
The maturity value of $4000 due in three months at 9% compounded quarterly $= 4000(1.0225)^1 = \$4090.00$, shown as E_1.
The maturity value of $3000 due in 18 months at 8.5% compounded semi-annually $= 3000(1.0425)^3 = 3000(1.132996) = \$3398.98655$, shown as E_2.

STEP 2
DATED VALUES OF SCHEDULED PAYMENTS
Now determine the dated values of the two maturity values at the selected focal date, subject to 10% compounded monthly.
The first scheduled payment matures nine months *before* the selected focal date. Its dated value $= 4090.00(1.008\dot{3})^9 = 4090.00(1.077549) = \$4407.176326$, shown as E_3.
The second scheduled payment matures six months *after* the selected focal date. Its dated value $= 3398.99(1.008\dot{3})^{-6} = 3398.99(0.951427) = \$3233.889239$, shown as E_4.

STEP 3
DATED VALUES OF REPLACEMENTS PAYMENTS
The dated values of the two replacement payments at the selected focal date are $x and $x(1.008\dot{3})^{-12}$, shown as E_5.

STEP 4   EQUATION OF VALUES
Therefore, the equation of values is

$$x + x(1.008333)^{-12} = 4407.176326 + 3233.889239$$
$$x + 0.905212x = 7641.065565$$
$$x = \frac{7641.065565}{1.905212}$$
$$x = \$4010.611714$$

The size of the two equal replacement payments is \$4010.61.

PROGRAMMED SOLUTION

Maturity value of \$4000

(Set P/Y, C/Y = 4) 4000 [±] [PV] 9 [I/Y] 1 [N] [CPT] [FV] [4090] [STO] 1

Maturity value of \$3000

(Set P/Y, C/Y = 2) 3000 [±] [PV] 8.5 [I/Y] 3 [N] [CPT] [FV] [3398.98655]

$x + x(1.008333)^{-12}$

(Set P/Y, C/Y = 12) 1 [FV] 10 [I/Y] 12 [N] [CPT] [PV] [−0.905212] [±] [STO] 2

This gives $x + 0.905212x$.

[RCL] 1 [±] [PV] 9 [N] [CPT] [FV] [4407.176326]

3398.98655 [FV] 6 [N] [CPT] [FV] [−3233.889239]

1 + [RCL] 2 = [STO] 3

4407.176326 + 3233.889239 = [STO] 4

$$x + 0.905212x = 4407.176326 + 3233.889239$$
$$1.905212x = 7641.065565$$
$$x = 4010.611714 \ (\text{[RCL]} 4 \div \text{[RCL]} 3 =)$$

EXERCISE 9.5   MyLab Math

🌐 **1.** A loan of \$4000 is due in five years. If money is worth 7% compounded annually, determine the equivalent payment that would settle the debt
   (a) now; **(b)** in 2 years; **(c)** in 5 years; **(d)** in 10 years.   Reference Example 9.5A

🌐 **2.** A debt payment of \$5500 is due in 27 months. If money is worth 8.4% compounded quarterly, what is the equivalent payment
   (a) now?   **(b)** 15 months from now?
   (c) 27 months from now?   **(d)** 36 months from now?

   3. A debt can be paid by payments of \$2000 scheduled today, \$2000 scheduled in three years, and \$2000 scheduled in six years. What single payment would settle the debt four years from now if money is worth 10% compounded semi-annually?
   Reference Example 9.5C

4. Scheduled payments of $600, $800, and $1200 are due in one year, three years, and six years, respectively. What is the equivalent single replacement payment two-and-a-half years from now if interest is 7.5% compounded monthly?

5. Scheduled payments of $400 due today and $721.28 due in eight months are to be settled by a payment of $500 six months from now and a final payment in 15 months. Determine the size of the final payment if money is worth 6% compounded monthly.

6. Scheduled payments of $1200 due one year ago and $1000 due six months ago are to be replaced by a payment of $800 now, a second payment of $1000 nine months from now, and a final payment 18 months from now. What is the size of the final payment if interest is 10.8% compounded quarterly?

7. Two debts—the first of $800 due six months ago and the second of $1400 borrowed one year ago for a term of three years at 6.5% compounded annually—are to be replaced by a single payment one year from now. Determine the size of the replacement payment if interest is 7.5% compounded quarterly and the focal date is one year from now.

8. Scheduled payments of $2000 due now and $2000 due in four years are to be replaced by a payment of $2000 due in two years and a second payment due in seven years. Determine the size of the second payment if interest is 10.5% compounded annually and the focal date is seven years from now.

9. Scheduled loan payments of $1500 due in 6 months and $1900 due in 21 months are rescheduled as a payment of $2000 due in 3 years and a second payment due in 45 months. Determine the size of the second payment if interest is 7% compounded quarterly and the focal date is 45 months from now. Reference Example 9.5D

10. A loan of $3000 borrowed today is to be repaid in three equal installments due in one year, three years, and five years, respectively. What is the size of the equal installments if money is worth 7.2% compounded monthly? Reference Example 9.5E

11. Savona borrowed $7500 from her aunt today and has agreed to repay the loan in two equal payments to be made in one year and three years from now. What is the size of the equal payments if money is worth 8% compounded quarterly?

12. What is the size of the equal payments that must be made at the end of each of the next four years to settle a debt of $3000 due four years from now and subject to interest at 10% compounded annually?

13. Karina is due to pay $9000 in five years. If she makes three equal payments, in 20 months, 30 months, and 5 years from today, what is the size of the equal payments if money is worth 5.16% compounded monthly?

14. Scheduled payments of $800 due two years ago and $1000 due in five years are to be replaced by two equal payments. The first replacement payment is due in four years and the second payment is due in eight years. Determine the size of the two replacement payments if interest is 12% compounded semi-annually and the focal date is four years from now.

15. Loan payments of $3000 due one year ago and $2500 due in four years are to be replaced by two equal payments. The first replacement payment is due now and the second payment is due in six years. Determine the size of the two replacement payments if interest is 6.9% compounded monthly and the focal date is now. Reference Example 9.5I

16. A payment of $500 is due in six months with interest at 12% compounded quarterly. A second payment of $800 is due in 18 months with interest at 10% compounded semi-annually. These two payments are to be replaced by a single payment nine months from now. Determine the size of the replacement payment if interest is 9% compounded monthly and the focal date is nine months from now.

17. Scheduled payments of $900 due in 3 months with interest at 11% compounded quarterly and $800 due in 30 months with interest at 11% compounded quarterly are to be replaced by two equal payments. The first replacement payment is due today and the second payment is due in three years. Determine the size of the two replacement payments if interest is 9% compounded monthly and the focal date is today.   Reference Example 9.5J

18. Scheduled payments of $1400 due today and $1600 due with interest at 11.5% compounded annually in five years are to be replaced by two equal payments. The first replacement payment is due in 18 months and the second payment is due in 4 years. Determine the size of the two replacement payments if interest is 11% compounded quarterly and the focal date is 18 months from now.

19. Stacy makes monthly payments of $450 to pay off her student loan. Due to unemployment, she defaulted on her last two payments. If she wants to get out of arrears, what amount should she pay for her next payment? Assume the defaulted payments are compounded monthly at a rate of 4%.

20. Scheduled payments of $1500 due today and $1500 due in three years are to be replaced by two payments. The first payment is due in one year and the second payment, which is double the size of the first payment, is due in five years. Determine the size of each payment if interest is 2.9% compounded weekly.

MyLab Math   Visit MyLab Math to practise any of this chapter's exercises marked with a 🌐 as often as you want. The guided solutions help you calculate an answer step by step. You'll find a personalized study plan and additional interactive resources to help you master Business Math!

REVIEW EXERCISE

1. **LO❷** Landmark Trust offers five-year investment certificates at 3.5% compounded semi-annually.
   (a) What is the value of a $2000 certificate at maturity?
   (b) How much of the maturity value is interest?

🌐 2. **LO❷** Western Savings offers three-year term deposits at 2.25% compounded annually while your credit union offers such deposits at 2.0% compounded quarterly. If you have $5000 to invest, what is the maturity value of your deposit
   (a) at Western Savings?   (b) at your credit union?

3. **LO❷** Calculate the future value and the compound interest of
   (a) $1800 invested at 3.7% compounded quarterly for 15.5 years;
   (b) $1250 invested at 2.6% compounded monthly for 15 years.

🌐 4. **LO❷** If $6000 is invested for six years and seven months at 6% compounded semi-annually, what is the interest that the investment earns?

5. **LO❸** Determine the discounted value now of $5200 due in 40 months if money is worth 6.5% compounded quarterly.

🌐 6. **LO❸** Determine the present value and the compound discount of
   (a) $3600 due in 9 years if interest is 8% compounded semi-annually;
   (b) $9000 due in 5 years if money is worth 6.8% compounded quarterly.

🌐 7. **LO❸** Determine the present value and the compound discount of $4000 due in seven years and six months if interest is 8.8% compounded quarterly.

8. **LO❷** A sum of money has a value of $3000 eighteen months from now. If money is worth 6% compounded monthly, what is its equivalent value
   (a) now?
   (b) one year from now?
   (c) three years from now?

9. **LO❹** A non-interest-bearing note for $1500 is due on June 30, 2024. The note is discounted at 10% compounded quarterly on September 30, 2020. What are the proceeds of the note?

🌐 10. **LO❹** Determine the proceeds of a non-interest-bearing promissory note for $75 000 discounted 42 months before maturity at 6.5% compounded semi-annually.

11. **LO❹** A ten-year promissory note for $1750 dated May 1, 2017, bearing interest at 4% compounded semi-annually is discounted on August 1, 2023, to yield 6% compounded quarterly. Determine the proceeds of the note.

🌐 12. **LO❹** A seven-year, $10 000 promissory note bearing interest at 8% compounded quarterly is discounted four years after the date of issue at 7% compounded semi-annually. What are the proceeds of the note?

13. **LO❹** A $40 000, 15-year promissory note dated June 1, 2014, bearing interest at 12% compounded semi-annually is discounted on September 1, 2022, at 11% compounded quarterly. What are the proceeds of the note?

🌐 14. **LO❹** A 15-year promissory note for $16 500 bearing interest at 12% compounded semi-annually is discounted at 9% compounded monthly, 3 years and 4 months after the date of issue. Compute the proceeds of the note.

15. **LO❺** The Ram Company borrowed $20 000 at 10% compounded semi-annually and made payments toward the loan of $8000 after two years and $10 000 after three-and-a-half years. How much is required to pay off the loan one year after the second payment?

🌐 16. **LO❺** Ted deposited $1750 in an RRSP on March 1, 2018, at 3% compounded quarterly. Subsequently, the interest rate was changed to 4% compounded monthly on September 1, 2020, and to 4.5% compounded semi-annually on June 1, 2022. What was the value of the RRSP deposit on December 1, 2024, if no further changes in interest were made?

17. **LO⑤** An investment of $2500 is accumulated at 5% compounded quarterly for two-and-a-half years. At that time, the interest rate is changed to 6% compounded monthly. How much is the investment worth two years after the change in interest rate?

🌐 18. **LO⑤** To ensure that funds are available to repay the principal at maturity, a borrower deposits $2000 each year for three years. If interest is 6% compounded quarterly, how much will the borrower have on deposit four years after the first deposit was made?

19. **LO⑤** Cindy started a registered retirement savings plan on February 1, 2016, with a deposit of $2500. She added $2000 on February 1, 2017, and $1500 on February 1, 2022. What is the accumulated value of her RRSP account on August 1, 2026, if interest is 5% compounded quarterly?

🌐 20. **LO⑤** A demand loan of $8000 is repaid by payments of $3000 after 15 months, $4000 after 30 months, and a final payment after 4 years. If interest was 8% for the first two years and 9% for the remaining time, and compounding is quarterly, what is the size of the final payment?

🌐 21. **LO⑤** Payments of $1000, $1200, and $1500 are due 6 months, 18 months, and 30 months from now, respectively. What is the equivalent single payment two years from now if money is worth 9.6% compounded quarterly?

22. **LO⑤** An obligation of $10 000 is due one year from now with interest at 10% compounded

semi-annually. The obligation is to be settled by a payment of $6000 in 6 months and a final payment in 15 months. What is the size of the second payment if interest is now 9% compounded monthly?

🌐 23. **LO⑤** Waldon Toys owes $3000 due in 2 years with interest at 11% compounded semi-annually and $2500 due in 15 months at 9% compounded, quarterly. If the company wants to discharge these debts by making two equal payments, the first now and the second 18 months from now, what is the size of the two payments if money is now worth 8.4% compounded monthly?

24. **LO⑤** Debt payments of $400 due today, $500 due in 18 months, and $900 due in 3 years are to be combined into a single payment due 2 years from now. What is the size of the single payment if interest is 8% compounded quarterly?

🌐 25. **LO⑤** Debt payments of $2600 due one year ago and $2400 due two years from now are to be replaced by two equal payments due one year from now and four years from now. What is the size of the equal payments if money is worth 9.6% compounded semi-annually?

26. **LO⑤** A loan of $7000 taken out two years ago is to be repaid by three equal installments due now, two years from now, and three years from now. What is the size of the equal installments if interest on the debt is 12% compounded monthly?

SELF-TEST

1. What sum of money invested at 4% compounded quarterly will grow to $3300 in 11 years?

2. Calculate the compound interest earned by $1300 invested at 7.5% compounded monthly for seven years.

3. Determine the maturity value of $1400 due in 71 months compounded annually at 7.75%.

4. What is the present value of $5900 payable in 15 years if the current interest rate is 7.5% compounded semi-annually?

5. Determine the compound discount on $8800 due in 7.5 years if interest is 9.6% compounded monthly.

6. A note dated July 1, 2017, promises to pay $8000 with interest at 7% compounded quarterly on January 1, 2026. Determine the proceeds from the sale of the note on July 1, 2021, if money is then worth 8% compounded semi-annually.

7. Compute the proceeds of a non-interest-bearing note for $1100 three years and seven months before the due date, if money is worth 7.5% compounded annually.

8. Seven years and two months after its date of issue, an 11-year promissory note for $8200 bearing interest at 13.5% compounded monthly is discounted at 10.5% compounded semi-annually. Determine the proceeds of the note.

9. A $10 200 debt will accumulate for five years at 11.6% compounded semi-annually. For how much will the debt sell three years after it was incurred if the buyer of the debt charges 10% compounded quarterly?

10. Five years after Anne deposited $3600 in a savings account that earned interest at 4.8% compounded monthly, the rate of interest was changed to 6% compounded semi-annually. How much was in the account 12 years after the deposit was made?

11. A debt can be repaid by payments of $4000 today, $4000 in five years, and $3000 in six years. What single payment would settle the debt one year from now if money is worth 7% compounded semi-annually?

12. Two debt payments, the first for $800 due today and the second for $600 due in nine months with interest at 10.5% compounded monthly, are to be settled by a payment of $800 six months from now and a final payment in 24 months. Determine the size of the final payment if money is now worth 9.5% compounded quarterly.

13. Adam borrowed $5000 at 10% compounded semi-annually. He repaid $2000 after two years and $2500 after three years. How much will he owe after five years?

14. A debt of $7000 due today is to be settled by three equal payments due 3 months from now, 15 months from now, and 27 months from now. What is the size of the equal payments at 11% compounded quarterly?

CHALLENGE PROBLEMS

1. Jean-Guy Renoir wanted to leave some money to his grandchildren in his will. He decided that they should each receive the same amount of money when they each turn 21. When he died, his grandchildren were 19, 16, and 13 years old. How much will they each receive when they turn 21 if Jean-Guy left a lump sum of $50 000 to be shared among them equally? Assume the interest rate will remain at 7.75% compounded semi-annually from the time of Jean-Guy's death until the youngest grandchild turns 21.

2. Miranda has $1000 to invest. She has narrowed her options to two four-year certificates: A and B. Certificate A pays interest at 8% compounded semi-annually the first year, 8% compounded quarterly the second year, 8% compounded monthly the third year, and 8% compounded daily the fourth year. Certificate B pays 8% compounded daily the first year, 8% compounded monthly the second year, 8% compounded quarterly the third year, and 8% compounded semi-annually the fourth year.

    (a) What is the value of each certificate at the end of the four years?

    (b) How do the values of certificates A and B compare with the value of a third certificate that pays interest at 7% compounded daily for the full four-year term?

▶ Precision Machining Corporation has been growing steadily over the past decade. Demand for the company's products continues to rise, so management has decided to expand the production facility; $2 800 000 has been set aside for this over the next four years.

Management has developed two different plans for expanding over the next four years: Plan A and Plan B. Plan A would require equal amounts of $750 000, one year from now, two years from now, three years from now, and four years from now. Plan B would require $300 000 now, $700 000 one year from now, $900 000 two years from now, and $975 000 four years from now.

The company has decided to fund the expansion with only the $2 800 000 and any interest it can earn on it. Before deciding which plan to use, the company asks its treasurer to predict the rates of interest it can earn on the $2 800 000. The treasurer expects that Precision Machining Corporation can invest the $2 800 000 and earn interest at a rate of 4.5% compounded semi-annually during Year 1, 5.0% compounded semi-annually during Years 2 and 3, and 5.5% compounded semi-annually during Year 4. The company can withdraw part of the money from this investment at any time without penalty.

QUESTIONS

1. **(a)** Could Precision Machining Corporation meet the cash requirement of Plan A by investing the $2 800 000 as described above? (Use "now" as the focal date.)
   (b) What is the exact difference between the cash required and the cash available from the investment?

2. **(a)** Could Precision Machining Corporation meet the cash requirements of Plan B by investing the $2 800 000 as described above? (Use "now" as the focal date.)
   (b) What is the difference between the cash required and the cash available from the investment?

3. **(a)** Suppose Plan A was changed so that it required equal amounts of $750 000 now, one year from now, two years from now, and four years from now. Could Precision Machining Corporation meet the cash requirements of the new Plan A by investing the $2 800 000 as described above? (Use "now " as the focal date.)
   (b) What is the difference between the cash required and the cash available from the investment?

4. Suppose the treasurer found another way to invest the $2 800 000 that earned interest at a rate of 4.9% compounded quarterly for the next five years.

   (a) Could the company meet the cash requirements of the original Plan A with this new investment? (Show all your calculations.)
   (b) Could the company meet the cash requirements of Plan B with this new investment? (Show all your calculations.)
   (c) If the company could meet the cash requirements of both plans, which plan would the treasurer recommend? In other words, which plan would have the lower present value?

SUMMARY OF FORMULAS

Formula 9.1
$$FV = PV(1 + i)^n$$
Calculating the future value (or maturity value) when the original principal, the rate of interest, and the time period are known

Formula 9.2
$$i = \frac{j}{m}$$
Calculating the periodic rate of interest

Formula 9.3
$$n = \text{number of years in the term} \times m$$
Determining the number of compounding (conversion) periods in the term

Formula 9.4
$$PV = \frac{FV}{(1 + i)^n}$$
Determining the present value (or principal, or proceeds, or discounted value) when the future value, the rate of interest, and the time period are known

Can be restated as:
$$PV = FV(1 + i)^{-n}$$
Calculating the present value by means of the discount factor (the reciprocal of the compounding factor)

GLOSSARY

Accumulation factor *see* **Compounding factor**

Comparison date a specific date chosen to compare the time values of one or more dated sums of money *(p. 369)*

Compound discount the difference between a given future amount and its present value (or proceeds or discounted value) at a specified time *(p. 357)*

Compound interest a procedure for computing interest whereby interest earned during an interest period is added onto the principal at the end of the interest period *(p. 337)*

Compounding factor the factor $(1 + i)^n$ found in compound interest formulas *(p. 339)*

Compounding period the time between two successive interest dates *(p. 338)*

Discount factor the factor $(1 + i)^{-n}$; the reciprocal of the compounding factor *(p. 359)*

Discounted value *see* **Present value**

Discounting the process of computing the present value (or proceeds or discounted value) of a future sum of money *(p. 357)*

Equivalent values the dated values of an original sum of money *(p. 369)*

Future value the sum of money to which a principal will grow at compound interest in a specific number of compounding or conversion periods at a specified periodic rate of interest *(p. 338)*

Maturity value *see* **Future value**

Nominal rate the stated rate at which the compounding is done one or more times per year; usually stated as an annual rate *(p. 339)*

Periodic rate the interest rate per compounding period *(p. 339)*

Present value the principal at any time that will grow at compound interest to a given future value over a given number of compounding periods at a given rate of interest *(p. 357)*

Proceeds *see* **Present value**

Jason Cox/Shutterstock

LEARNING OBJECTIVES

Upon completing this chapter, you will be able to do the following:

1 Determine the number of conversion periods and solve equated dates.

2 Compute periodic and nominal rates of interest.

3 Compute effective and equivalent rates of interest.

Ali owes money on a loan and is wondering how much this loan is costing him in interest. If the debt is paid back over a long period of time, how much interest will he have to pay? Can he reduce the amount of interest? Most Canadians hold debt and, with currently low interest rates, pay relatively low amounts of interest. If interest rates were to rise, how much more interest would Ali have to pay? If he made the same payment, how much longer would it take to repay his debt? How much debt is too much? Many people reduce their debt by making earlier or extra payments. The key to managing debt is knowledge of how much is owed, what interest rate is charged, and how long it takes to repay the debt.

Getting out of debt, or at least getting your finances back on track, has many long-term benefits. These include: lower monthly payments, reduced interest rates and fees, getting out of debt faster, and improving your credit rating.

INTRODUCTION

In the previous chapter, we considered future value and present value when using compound interest. In this chapter, we will look at certain aspects of compound interest, including finding the number of conversion periods and computing equated dates, and equivalent and effective rates of interest.

For these calculations we can either manipulate the formulas or use electronic calculators. In this and the following chapters, we will use calculators; in particular, preprogrammed financial calculators such as the Texas Instruments BA II PLUS.

Our calculations will be more accurate and we can save time on our calculations by using the memory feature of the calculator when working with these functions. For the worked examples in this text, we have used the memory in the calculator whenever it was convenient to do so.

10.1 DETERMINING n AND RELATED PROBLEMS
A. Determining the number of conversion periods

If the principal PV, the future value FV, and the periodic rate of interest i are known, the number of conversion periods n can be determined by substituting the known values in Formula 9.1 and solving for n.

$$FV = PV(1 + i)^n \text{————————— Formula 9.1}$$

To solve for n, rearrange Formula 9.1.

$$(1 + i)^n = \frac{FV}{PV}$$

$$n\ln(1 + i) = \ln\left(\frac{FV}{PV}\right) \text{————————}$$ take the natural logarithm of both sides (refer to Section 2.4C)

$$\boxed{n = \frac{\ln\left(\frac{FV}{PV}\right)}{\ln(1 + i)}} \text{———————— Formula 10.1}$$

The value n calculated in Formula 10.1 is the total number of conversion periods. To convert to years, n must be divided by the compounding factor. If compounding semiannually, divide n by 2; if compounding quarterly, divide by 4; if compounding monthly, divide by 12; and if compounding daily, divide by 365.

This method involves the use of logarithms. You can solve the problem using an electronic calculator provided the calculator is equipped with the natural logarithm function (**LN** key).

POINTERS & PITFALLS

If you understand the principles of formula rearrangement, you only have to learn one formula: Formula 9.1. Most of the other formulas in Chapters 9 and 10 are derived from this one formula.

You may also use a financial calculator, such as the TI BA II PLUS, that is preprogrammed with the time value of money (TVM) worksheet. After entering all of the relevant data into the calculator, press CPT N . Note that the units of *n* relate to the payment periods. For example, if you have quarterly payment periods, your answer for *n* indicates the number of quarterly periods in the term.

| EXAMPLE 10.1A | In how many years will $2000.00 grow to $2440.38 at 4% compounded quarterly? |

SOLUTION

$PV = 2000.00; \ FV = 2440.38; \ I/Y = 4; \ P/Y = 4; \ i = \dfrac{4\%}{4} = 1\% = 0.01$

$$FV = PV(1 + i)^n$$

$$n = \frac{\ln\left(\frac{FV}{PV}\right)}{\ln(1 + i)}$$

$2440.38 = 2000.00(1.01)^n$ ———————— substituting in Formula 9.1

$n = \dfrac{\ln\left(\frac{2440.38}{2000.00}\right)}{\ln(1 + 0.01)}$ ———————— substituting in Formula 10.1

$n = \dfrac{0.199007}{0.009950}$ ———————— obtain the numerical values using the LN key

$= 19.999997 = 20 \ (\text{quarters})$

$\text{Number of years} = \dfrac{20}{4} = 5$ ———————— convert the number of periods to years

PROGRAMMED SOLUTION

You can use preprogrammed financial calculators to determine *n* by the same procedure previously used to calculate FV and PV.

(Set P/Y, C/Y = 4) 2000 ±   PV

2440.3 8 FV 4 I/Y   CPT   N   19.999997

At 4% compounded quarterly, $2000 will grow to $2440.38 in 20 quarters or five years.

POINTERS
& PITFALLS

When determining the *n* for non-annuity calculations (lump-sum amounts), generally the solution would not be rounded off, since *n* can be fractional in nature (we can get 4.5632 quarters).

• However, when *n* is discussed, it may be simplified to 2 decimals so that it is easier to communicate. For example, if *n* = 5.998123 years, this would mean a term of slightly under 6 years. However, when discussed it may be referred to simply as a term of 6.00 years. Alternatively, if *n* = 17.559876 months, this would mean a little more than halfway through the 17th month. However, when discussed it may be referred to as a term of approximately 17.56 months.

• An exception to this rule is when *n* is converted into days. As interest generally is not accrued more than daily, a fraction of a day is not possible. The fraction shows up most likely due to rounding in the numbers being used in the calculation. Since we do not know how these numbers were rounded, it is appropriate for our purposes to round *n* to the nearest integer.

EXAMPLE 10.1B

How long does it take for money to double

    (i) at 5% compounded annually?

    (ii) at 10% compounded annually?

SOLUTION

While neither PV nor FV is given, any sum of money may be used as principal. For this calculation, a convenient value for the principal is $100.00.

PV = 100.00; FV = 200.00; I/Y = 5; P/Y = 1

    (i) At 5% compounded annually, $i = 5\% = 0.05$

$$FV = PV(1 + i)^n$$

$$n = \frac{\ln\left(\frac{FV}{PV}\right)}{\ln(1 + i)}$$

$$200.00 = 100.00(1.05)^n$$

$$n = \frac{\ln\left(\frac{200.00}{100.00}\right)}{\ln(1 + 0.05)}$$

$$n = 14.206699 \text{ (years)}$$

PROGRAMMED SOLUTION

(Set P/Y, C/Y = 1) 100.00 $\boxed{\pm}$ $\boxed{PV}$ 200.00 $\boxed{FV}$ 5 $\boxed{I/Y}$

$\boxed{CPT}$ $\boxed{N}$ $\boxed{14.206699}$ (years)

At 5% compounded annually, money doubles in approximately 14.21 years.

    (ii) At 10% compounded annually, I/Y = 10; P/Y = 1; $i = 10\% = 0.10$

$$FV = PV(1 + i)^n$$

$$n = \frac{\ln\left(\frac{FV}{PV}\right)}{\ln(1 + i)}$$

$$200.00 = 100.00(1.10)^n$$

$$n = \frac{\ln\left(\frac{200.00}{100.00}\right)}{\ln(1 + 0.10)}$$

$$n = 7.272541 \text{ (years)}$$

PROGRAMMED SOLUTION

100.00 $\boxed{\pm}$ $\boxed{PV}$ 200.00 $\boxed{FV}$

10 $\boxed{I/Y}$ $\boxed{CPT}$ $\boxed{N}$ $\boxed{7.272541}$ (years)

At 10% compounded annually, money doubles in approximately 7.27 years.

EXAMPLE 10.1C

How many years will it take for $5000, invested at 6% compounded monthly, to grow to $15 000?

SOLUTION

Let PV = 5000; then FV = 15 000; I/Y = 6; P/Y = 12; $i = \frac{6\%}{12} = 0.5\% = 0.005$

$$FV = PV(1 + i)^n$$

$$n = \frac{\ln\left(\frac{FV}{PV}\right)}{\ln(1 + i)}$$

$$15\ 000.00 = 5000.00(1.005)^n$$

$$n = \frac{\ln\left(\frac{15\ 000.00}{5000.00}\right)}{\ln(1 + 0.005)}$$

$$n = \frac{1.098612}{0.004988} = 220.271307 \text{ months}$$

PROGRAMMED SOLUTION

(Set P/Y, C/Y = 12) 5000 $\boxed{\pm}$ $\boxed{\text{PV}}$ 15 000 $\boxed{\text{FV}}$

6 $\boxed{\text{I/Y}}$ $\boxed{\text{CPT}}$ $\boxed{\text{N}}$ $\boxed{220.271307}$ (months)

At 6% compounded monthly, the desired amount will be achieved in approximately 220.27 months or $\frac{220.57}{12} = 18.36$ years.

B. Equated date

The concept of *equivalence* of values when using the compound interest method was discussed in Chapter 9, Section 9.5. In solving problems of equivalence, the unknown value was the size of a payment at the selected focal date. While we often need to determine the size of the payment, occasionally we need to calculate the interest rate on the focal date instead. To determine a specific date to solve your problem, solve for n, and then use the $\boxed{\text{DATE}}$ worksheet within the calculator.

The **equated date** is the date on which a single sum of money is equal to the sum of two or more dated sums of money. An equation of values can be set up by the same technique used in Section 9.5. The method can also be applied to problems in which the single sum of money does not equal the sum of the dated sums of money considered.

EXAMPLE 10.1D

A loan of $2000 taken out today is to be repaid by a payment of $1200 in six months and a final payment of $1000.00. If interest is 12% compounded monthly, when should the final payment be made? Provide your answer in number of days.

SOLUTION

Let the focal point be "now"; I/Y = 12; P/Y = 12; $i = \dfrac{12\%}{12} = 1.0\% = 0.01$.

$$2000.00 = 1200.00(1.01)^{-6} + 1000.00(1.01)^{-n}$$
$$2000.00 = 1200.00(0.942045) + 1000.00(1.01)^{-n}$$
$$2000.00 = 1130.454282 + 1000.00(1.01)^{-n}$$
$$869.545718 = 1000.00(1.01)^{-n}$$

$$n = \frac{\ln\dfrac{1000.00}{869.545718}}{\ln(1.01)}$$

$$-0.009950n = -0.139784$$

$$n = 14.048213 \text{ (months)}$$

PROGRAMMED SOLUTION

$$2000.00 = 1200.00(1.01)^{-6} + 1000.00(1.01)^{-n}$$
$$1200.00(1.01)^{-6}$$

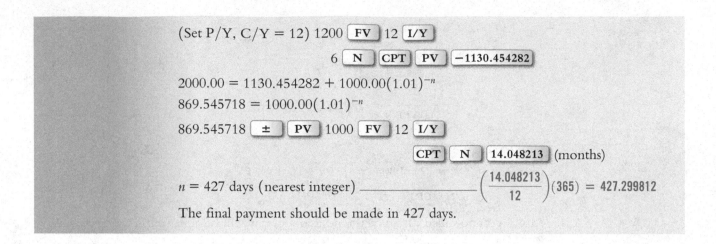

$$(Set\ P/Y, C/Y = 12)\ 1200\ \boxed{FV}\ 12\ \boxed{I/Y}$$

$$6\ \boxed{N}\ \boxed{CPT}\ \boxed{PV}\ \boxed{-1130.454282}$$

$$2000.00 = 1130.454282 + 1000.00(1.01)^{-n}$$

$$869.545718 = 1000.00(1.01)^{-n}$$

$$869.545718\ \boxed{\pm}\ \boxed{PV}\ 1000\ \boxed{FV}\ 12\ \boxed{I/Y}$$

$$\boxed{CPT}\ \boxed{N}\ \boxed{14.048213}\ \text{(months)}$$

$$n = 427\ \text{days (nearest integer)}\ \underline{\hspace{3cm}}\ \left(\frac{14.048213}{12}\right)(365) = 427.299812$$

The final payment should be made in 427 days.

EXAMPLE 10.1E

An existing financial agreement requires three payments: $2000 in 6 months, $3000 in 15 months, and $5000 in 24 months. Alternatively, a single payment equal to the sum of the required payments could be made. If money is worth 9% compounded monthly, when would the single payment have to be made?

SOLUTION

The single payment equal to the sum of the required payments is $2000 plus $3000 plus $5000, or $10 000. Select as the focal date "now." Let the number of compounding periods from the focal date to the equated date be represented by n. Since the compounding is done monthly, n will be a number of months, I/Y = 9, P/Y = 12, and $i = \frac{9}{12}\% = 0.75\% = 0.0075$. The method and data are shown graphically in Figure 10.1.

Figure 10.1 Graphical Representation of Method and Data (© S. A. Hummelbrunner)

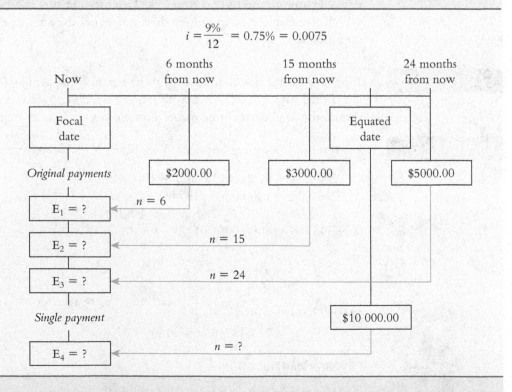

Let E_1, E_2, and E_3 represent the equivalent values of the original payments at the focal date, as shown in Figure 10.1.

Since the focal date falls 6 months before the date of the first payment, the equivalent value E_1 is determined by calculating the present value of $2000. The focal date falls 15 months before the date of the second payment; therefore, E_2 is determined by calculating the present value of $5000. Also, the focal date falls 24 months before the date of the third payment; therefore, E_3 is determined by calculating the present value of $10 000.

Let E_4 represent the equivalent value of the single payment of $10 000 at the focal date.

Since the focal date also falls before the date of the single replacement payment, E_4 represents the present value of the single payment of $10 000. For E_4, the *n* is unknown.

The equation of values can now be set up.

$$E_4 = E_1 + E_2 + E_3$$

$$10\ 000.00(1.0075)^{-n} = 2000.00(1.0075)^{-6} + 3000.00(1.0075)^{-15}$$
$$+ 5000.00(1.0075)^{-24}$$

$$10\ 000.00(1.0075)^{-n} = 2000.00(0.956158) + 3000.00(0.893973)$$
$$+ 5000.00(0.835831)$$

$$10\ 000.00(1.0075)^{-n} = 1912.316036 + 2681.917614 + 4179.157020$$

$$10\ 000.00(1.0075)^{-n} = 8773.39067$$

$$10\ 000.00 = 8773.39067(1.0075)^n$$

$$n = \frac{\ln\left(\frac{10\ 000.00}{8773.39067}\right)}{\ln(1.0075)}$$

$$n = \frac{-0.130861}{-0.007472}$$

$$n = 17.513439$$

The equated date is about 17.5 months from now.

PROGRAMMED SOLUTION

First simplify the equation $E_4 = E_1 + E_2 + E_3$.

$10\ 000.00(1.0075)^{-n} = 2000.00(1.0075)^{-6} + 3000.00(1.0075)^{-15} + 5000.00(1.0075)^{-24}$

$2000.00(1.0075)^{-6}$

(Set P/Y, C/Y = 12) 2000 [FV]

9 [I/Y] 6 [N] [CPT] [PV] [−1912.316036]

$3000.00(1.0075)^{-15}$

3000 [FV] 15 [N] [CPT] [PV] [−2681.917614]

$5000.00(1.0075)^{-24}$

5000 [FV] 24 [N] [CPT] [PV] [−4179.157020]

$10\ 000.00(1.0075)^{-n} = 1912.316036 + 2681.917614 + 4179.157020$

Remember to remove the negative (cash outflow) signs.

$10\ 000.00(1.0075)^{-n} = 8773.39067$

Now solve the simplified equation:

$10\ 000.00(1.0075)^{-n} = 8773.39067$

in which FV = 10 000.00;   PV = 8773.39067;   i = 0.75%

10 000 [FV] 8773.39067

[±] [PV] 9 [I/Y] [CPT] [N] [17.513581]

The equated date is approximately 17.5 months from now.

EXAMPLE 10.1F

When Josh borrowed money, he originally agreed to repay the loan by making three equal payments of $1500, with a payment due now, another payment due two years from now, and the final payment due four years from now. Instead of the original payments, he plans to pay off the loan by making a single payment of $5010. If interest is 10% compounded annually, when will he make the single payment?

SOLUTION

Select as the focal date "now." Let the number of compounding periods from the focal date to the equated date be represented by n. Since the compounding is done annually, n will be a number of years, $I/Y = 10$, $P/Y = 1$, and $i = 10\% = 0.10$.

Let E_1, E_2, and E_3 represent the equivalent values of the original payments at the focal date.

$$E_1 = 1500.00 = 1500.00$$
$$E_2 = 1500.00(1.10)^{-2} = 1500.00(0.826446) = 1239.669421$$
$$E_3 = 1500.00(1.10)^{-4} = 1500.00(0.683013) = \underline{1024.520183}$$
$$E_1 + E_2 + E_3 = \underline{3764.189605}$$

Let E_4 represent the equivalent value of the single payment of $5010 at the focal date.

$$E_4 = 5010.00(1.10)^{-n}$$
$$E_4 = E_1 + E_2 + E_3$$
$$5010.00(1.10)^{-n} = 3764.189605$$
$$n = \frac{\ln\left(\frac{5010.00}{3764.189605}\right)}{\ln(1.10)}$$
$$n = 2.999713 \text{ (years)}$$

The equated date is approximately three years from now.

PROGRAMMED SOLUTION

$E_4 = E_1 + E_2 + E_3$

$5010.00(1.10)^{-n} = 1500.00 + 1500.00(1.10)^{-2} + 1500.00(1.10)^{-4}$

$1500.00(1.10)^{-2}$

(Set P/Y, C/Y = 1) 1500 [FV] 10 [I/Y]

2 [N] [CPT] [PV] [−1239.669421]

$1500.00(1.10)^{-4}$

4 [N] [CPT] [PV] [−1024.520183]

$5010.00(1.10)^{-n} = 1500.00 + 1239.669421 + 1024.520183$

$5010.00(1.10)^{-n} = 3764.189605$

5010 [FV] 3764.189605 [±] [PV]

10 [I/Y] [CPT] [N] [2.999713]

The single payment should be made three years from now.

C. Using Excel's NPER

If you choose, you can use Excel's NPER function to answer the questions in this section.

In Example 10.1A, you are required to calculate the number of compounding periods (NPER) of an investment. The NPER function in Excel is illustrated below.

	B8	*fx* = NPER(B3, B4, B5, B6, B7)	
	A	B	C
1	NPER Function		
2			
3	**Interest Rate per Compounding Period**	1.00%	
4	Payment Size	$0.00	
5	Present Value	−$2,000.00	
6	Future Value	$2,440.38	
7	Type (Ordinary or Due)	0	
8	Answer	20.00	
9			

EXERCISE 10.1   MyLab Math

Answer each of the following questions.

 1. How long will it take $400 to accumulate to $760 at 7% p.a. compounded semi-annually?

2. In how many days will $580 grow to $600 at 4.5% p.a. compounded monthly?

 3. In how many years will money quadruple at 8% compounded quarterly?

 4. If an investment of $800 earned interest of $320 at 6% compounded monthly, for how many years was the money invested?

5. A loan of $2000 was repaid together with interest of $604.35. If interest was 8% compounded quarterly, for how many months was the loan taken out?

 6. If you borrowed $1000 on May 1, 2023, at 10% compounded semi-annually, and interest on the loan amounts to $157.63, on what date is the loan due?

 7. A promissory note for $600 dated May 15, 2021, requires an interest payment of $150 at maturity. If interest is 9% compounded monthly, determine the due date of the note.

8. Joan borrowed $3000 today with the understanding that she would repay the loan in two payments: $1600 in one year and a second payment of $1700. If interest is 8% compounded quarterly, when should the second payment be made?

9. A loan of $5000 taken out today is to be repaid by a payment of $2000 in nine months, a payment of $2500 in two years, and a final payment of $1200. If interest is 9% compounded monthly, when should the final payment be made?

10. Joel's Furniture had a financial agreement whereby two payments were required: $14 000 in 8 months and $15 000 in 14 months. Instead of these two payments, a single payment of $29 000 could be made. If money is worth 10% compounded monthly, when would the single payment have to be made?

11. In purchasing his brother's car, Mahood agreed to take over the payment obligations. Three payments were required: $8000 in 2 months, $1600 in 5 months, and $4500 in 13 months. The current bank borrowing rate is 8.7% compounded monthly. If one payment of $15 000 would replace the three payments, when would that one payment have to be made?

12. A contract requires payments of $4000 today, $5000 in three years, and $6000 in five years. When can the contract be fulfilled by a single payment equal to the sum of the required payments if money is worth 9% p.a. compounded monthly?

13. A financial agreement requires the payment of $1200 in 9 months, $1400 in 18 months, and $1600 in 30 months. When would an alternative single payment of $4000 have to be made if money is worth 7% compounded quarterly?

14. Graham purchased a business by agreeing to make three payments of $12 000 each in one year, two years, and four years. Because of cash flow difficulties in the first year, he renegotiated the payment schedule so that he would pay $16 000 in 18 months, $10 000 in 30 months, and a third payment of $10 000. In how many years should he make the third payment if interest is 7.2% compounded semi-annually?

15. Henrik, a Canadian hockey player, agreed to a contract whereby he was to receive $40 000 in 6 months, $60 000 in 8 months, and $100 000 in 18 months. The deal was renegotiated after 4 months when he received a payment of $30 000. He agreed to accept a payment of $172 000 at a later date. When should Henrik receive the payment if money is worth 6% compounded monthly?

10.2 CALCULATING *i* AND RELATED PROBLEMS
A. Calculating the periodic rate *i* and the nominal annual rate of interest *j*

If the original principal PV, the future value FV, and the number of conversion periods *n* are known, the periodic rate of interest (conversion rate) *i* can be determined by substituting in Formula 9.1, $FV = PV(1 + i)^n$, and solving for *i*.

$$FV = PV(1 + i)^n \text{——————————— Formula 9.1}$$

To solve for *i*, rearrange Formula 9.1.

$$(1 + i)^n = \frac{FV}{PV}$$

$$(1 + i) = \left(\frac{FV}{PV}\right)^{\frac{1}{n}}$$

$$\boxed{i = \left(\frac{FV}{PV}\right)^{\frac{1}{n}} - 1} \text{——————————— Formula 10.2}$$

The value *i* calculated in Formula 10.2 is the periodic interest rate. To calculate the nominal annual rate of interest *j*, multiply the periodic interest rate *i* by the number of conversion periods per year *m*.

Remember, you do not have to memorize this equation if you understand the principles of formula rearrangement.

EXAMPLE 10.2A

What is the annually compounded rate if $200 accumulates to $318.77 in eight years?

SOLUTION

$PV = 200.00; \quad FV = 318.77; \quad C/Y(m) = 1; \quad n = 8$

$i = \left(\dfrac{FV}{PV}\right)^{\frac{1}{n}} - 1$ ———————————————— **Using Formula 10.2**

$i = \left(\dfrac{318.77}{200.00}\right)^{\frac{1}{8}} - 1$

$i = (1.59385)^{\frac{1}{8}} - 1$

$i = 1.060000 - 1$

$i = 0.06 = 6.0\%$ ———————————————— **the desired annual rate**

The annually compounded rate is 6.0%.

PROGRAMMED SOLUTION

You can use preprogrammed financial calculators to calculate *i* by the same procedure used previously to determine FV or PV. That is, select the compound interest mode, enter the given variables FV, PV, and N, and retrieve the fourth variable I/Y.

(Set P/Y, C/Y = 1) 200 ± PV 318.77 FV

8 N CPT I/Y 6.000016 (annual)

Note: In the financial calculator that you use, you must determine whether the interest rate to be entered represents *i*, the periodic rate of interest, or *j*, the nominal rate of interest. For the Texas Instruments BA II PLUS calculator, the I/Y to be used equates to *j* in the formula. Thus, the variables in the formula $i = j/m$ can be translated into $i =$ I/Y C/Y for use in the calculator. The value of I/Y obtained from the calculator is to be expressed as the nominal rate. For example, if C/Y = 4, or quarterly, and the calculator determines that I/Y = 8.5, then the rate is expressed as 8.5% p.a. compounded quarterly.

EXAMPLE 10.2B

Calculate the nominal annual rate of interest compounded monthly if $1200 accumulates to $1618.62 in five years.

SOLUTION

$PV = 1200.00; \quad FV = 1618.62; \quad C/Y(m) = 12; \quad n = 60$

$1618.62 = 1200.00(1 + i)^{60}$ ———————————— *i* is a *monthly* (periodic) rate

$i = \left(\dfrac{FV}{PV}\right)^{\frac{1}{n}} - 1$

$i = \left(\dfrac{1618.62}{1200.00}\right)^{\frac{1}{60}} - 1$

$i = (1.348850)^{\frac{1}{60}} - 1$

$i = 1.005000 - 1$

$i = 0.005 = 0.5\%$

The monthly compounded periodic rate is 0.5%.
The nominal rate is 0.5% × 12 = 6% compounded monthly.

PROGRAMMED SOLUTION

(Set P/Y, C/Y = 12) 1200 [±] [PV]

1618.62 [FV] 60 [N] [CPT] [I/Y] 6.0

The nominal annual rate of interest is 6% per annum compounded monthly. The periodic rate of interest would be $i = j/m = 6\%/12 = 0.5\%$ per month.

EXAMPLE 10.2C

At what nominal rate of interest compounded quarterly will money double in 10 years?

SOLUTION

While neither PV nor FV are given, any sum of money may be used as principal. For this calculation, a convenient value for the principal is $1.00.

$PV = 1; \quad FV = 2; \quad C/Y(m) = 4; \quad n = 40; \quad m = 4$

$2 = 1(1 + i)^{40}$ —————— i is a *quarterly* rate

$i = \left(\dfrac{FV}{PV}\right)^{\frac{1}{n}} - 1$

$i = \left(\dfrac{2}{1}\right)^{\frac{1}{40}} - 1$

$i = (2.00)^{\frac{1}{40}} - 1$

$i = 1.017480 - 1$

$i = 0.017480 = 1.7480\%$

The nominal rate is $1.7480\% \times 4 = 6.9919\%$ compounded quarterly.

PROGRAMMED SOLUTION

(Set P/Y, C/Y = 4) 1 [±] [PV] 2 [FV] 40 [N]

[CPT] [I/Y] 6.991877

The nominal annual rate is 6.99% per annum compounded quarterly. The quarterly rate is $6.99\%/4 = 1.748\%$.

EXAMPLE 10.2D

Suppose $1000 earns interest of $93.81 in one year.
  (i) What is the nominal annual rate of interest compounded annually?
  (ii) What is the nominal annual rate of interest compounded monthly?

SOLUTION

(i) $PV = 1000.00; I = 93.81; FV = PV + I = 1093.81; C/Y(m) = 1; n = 1$

$1093.81 = 1000.00(1 + i)^1$ —————— i is an *annual* rate $(m = 1)$

$1 + i = 1.09381$

$i = 0.09381$

$i = 9.381\%$

PROGRAMMED SOLUTION

(Set P/Y, C/Y = 1) 1000 [±] [PV]

1093.81 [FV] 1 [N] [CPT] [I/Y] 9.381

The annual rate of interest is 9.381%.

Notice that both the nominal rate and the periodic rate of interest are 9.381%, since interest is compounded annually.

(ii)   P/Y = 12

$$1093.81 = 1000.00(1 + i)^{12} \text{\textemdash\textemdash\textemdash\textemdash\textemdash} \textit{i is a monthly rate (m = 12)}$$

$$i = \left(\frac{FV}{PV}\right)^{\frac{1}{n}} - 1$$

$$i = \left(\frac{1093.81}{1000.00}\right)^{\frac{1}{12}} - 1$$

$$i = (1.09381)^{\frac{1}{12}} - 1$$

$$i = 1.007500 - 1$$

$$i = 0.007500 = 0.75\%$$

The nominal rate is 0.7500% × 12 = 9.0003% compounded monthly.

PROGRAMMED SOLUTION

(Set P/Y, C/Y = 12) 1000 $\boxed{\pm}$ $\boxed{\text{PV}}$

1093.81 $\boxed{\text{FV}}$ 12 $\boxed{\text{N}}$ $\boxed{\text{CPT}}$ $\boxed{\text{I/Y}}$ $\boxed{9.0003}$

The nominal annual rate of interest compounded monthly is 9.0003% p.a.
The periodic rate of interest is 9.0003%/12 = 0.7500% per month.

B. Using Excel's RATE Function

If you choose, you can use Excel's RATE function to answer the questions in this section.
    In Example 10.2A, you are required to calculate the RATE of an investment. The RATE function in Excel is illustrated below.

	A	B	C
1	RATE Function		
2			
3	**Total Number of Compounding Periods**	8.00	
4	Payment or Deposit per Compounding Period	$0.00	
5	Present Value	−$200.00	
6	Future Value	$318.77	
7	Type (Ordinary or Due)	0	
8	Answer	6.00%	
9			

EXERCISE 10.2   MyLab Math

Solve each of the following.

🌐 **1.** What is the nominal annual rate of interest compounded quarterly at which $420 will accumulate to $1000 in nine years and six months?

2. A principal of $2000 compounded monthly amounts to $2800 in 7.25 years. What is the nominal annual rate of interest?

3. At what nominal annual rate of interest will money double itself in 6 years and 9 months if compounded quarterly?

4. At what nominal rate of interest will money triple itself in 9 years and 2 months if compounded monthly?

5. What is the nominal annual rate of interest at which money will triple itself in 12 years if compounded annually?

6. Yin Li deposited $800 into a savings account that compounded interest monthly. What nominal annual rate compounded monthly was earned on the investment if the balance was $952.75 in five years?

7. An investment of $4000 earned interest semi-annually. If the balance after $6\frac{1}{2}$ years was $6000, what nominal annual rate compounded semi-annually was charged?

8. Surinder borrowed $1200 and agreed to pay $1400 in settlement of the debt in 3 years and 3 months. What annual nominal rate compounded quarterly was charged on the debt?

9. A debt of $600 was to be repaid in 15 months. If $705.25 was repaid, what was the nominal rate compounded monthly that was charged?

10. A $1000 credit card debt was to be repaid in 12 months. If $1500 was repaid, what was the nominal rate compounded daily that was charged?

10.3 EFFECTIVE AND EQUIVALENT INTEREST RATES
A. Effective rate of interest

In Example 10.2D, compounding at an annual rate of interest of 9.381% has the same effect as compounding at 9.0% p.a. compounded monthly since, in both cases, the interest amounts to $93.81.

The annually compounded rate of 9.381%, in Example 10.2D, is called the **effective rate of interest**. This rate is defined as the rate of interest compounded annually that yields the same amount of interest as a nominal annual rate of interest compounded a number of times per year other than one.

Converting nominal rates of interest to effective rates is the method used for comparing nominal rates of interest. Since the effective rates of interest are the equivalent rates of interest compounded annually, they may be obtained for any set of nominal interest rates by computing the accumulated value of $1 after one year for each of the nominal rates under consideration.

Effective Rates Using the BA II PLUS: Interest Rate Conversion

The BA II PLUS is programmed in the 2nd function to quickly and efficiently calculate effective interest rates by inputting the nominal rate and the number of compounding periods. You can also calculate the nominal rate if you know the effective rate.

To go from the nominal rate to the effective rate, the process is as follows:

1. 2nd (ICONV) (2-key).

2. Enter the nominal rate, NOM = and press Enter.

3. Arrow down to C/Y = and enter the number of times interest compounds in a year. Press [Enter].

4. Arrow up to EFF = and press [CPT].

To go from the effective rate to the nominal rate, the process is as follows:

1. [2nd] (ICONV).

2. Arrow down to EFF = and enter the effective rate. Press [Enter].

3. Arrow down to C/Y = and enter the compounding number relating to the nominal rate you are converting to. Press [Enter].

4. Arrow down to NOM = and press [CPT].

EXAMPLE 10.3A

Assume you are given a choice of a term deposit paying 7.2% compounded monthly or an investment certificate paying 7.25% compounded semi-annually. Which rate offers the higher rate of return?

SOLUTION

The investment certificate offers the higher nominal rate of return while the term deposit offers the higher compounding frequency. Because of the different compounding frequencies, the two nominal rates are not directly comparable. To determine which nominal rate offers the higher rate of return, we need to determine the effective rates for the two given rates.

For the Term Deposit	For the Investment Certificate
I/Y = 7.2; P/Y = 12; $i = 0.6\% = 0.006$; $m = 12$	I/Y = 7.25; P/Y = 2; $i = 3.625\% = 0.03625$; $m = 2$
The accumulated value of $1 after one year,	The accumulated value of $1 after one year,
$FV = 1(1.006)^{12} = 1.074424$	$FV = 1(1.03625)^2 = 1.073814$
Effective rate of interest = 7.4424%.	Effective rate of interest = 7.3814%.

The decimal fraction in each case is the interest earned in one year and represents the effective rate of interest. Since the term deposit has the higher effective rate, it offers the higher rate of return.

PROGRAMMED SOLUTION

For the term deposit
$(1 + i)^{12} = (1.006)^{12} = 1.074424$

(Set P/Y, C/Y = 12) 1 [±] [PV] 7.2 [I/Y]

12 [N] [CPT] [FV] [1.074424]

Alternatively:
[2nd] (IConv) Nom = 7.2; C/Y = 12; Eff = [CPT] 7.4424

For the investment certificate
$(1 + i)^2 = (1.03625)^2 = 1.073814$

(Set P/Y, C/Y = 2) 1 [±] [PV] 7.25 [I/Y]

2 [N] [CPT] [FV] [1.073814]

Alternatively:
[2nd] (IConv) Nom = 7.25; C/Y = 2; Eff = 7.3814

The term deposit offers a higher rate of return. The nominal annual rate is 7.4424% for the term deposit and 7.3814% for the investment certificate.

EXAMPLE 10.3B

Ariel has $1000 to invest and must make a choice between 3.6% compounded monthly and 3.6% compounded semi-annually. Which investment is better and by how much?

SOLUTION

Investment	3.6% Compounded Monthly	3.6% Compounded Semi-annually
I/Y	3.6	3.6
P/Y	12	2
i	$0.003 = 0.3\%$	$0.18 = 1.8\%$
m	12	2
FV after one year	$FV = 1000([1.003])^{12} = 1036.600$	$FV = 1000([1.018])^2 = 1036.324$
Effective rate	3.66%	3.6324%

The amount exceeding the original investment is the interest earned in one year and represents the effective rate of interest.

The investment compounded monthly earns more interest than the investment compounded semi-annually. The difference in the effective rate is 3.66% − 3.6324% = 0.0276%. With the investment of $1000, after one year the difference is $1036.60 − $1036.32 = $0.28.

Alternatively:
For 3.6% compounded monthly
[2nd] (IConv) Nom = 3.6; C/Y = 12; Eff = [CPT] 3.66

For 3.6% compounded semi-annually
[2nd] (IConv) Nom = 3.6; C/Y = 2; Eff = [CPT] 3.6324

The effective rates of interest can also be determined by using Formula 10.3 obtained below (see also the method of calculation used in Examples 10.3A and 10.3B).

The formula is obtained as follows:

Let the nominal annual rate of interest be compounded m times per year, and let the interest rate per conversion period be i.

Then the accumulated amount after one year is $FV_1 = PV(1 + i)^m$.

Let the corresponding effective annual rate of interest be f.

Then the accumulated amount after one year is $FV_1 = PV(1 + f)^1$.

$PV(1 + f)^1 = PV(1 + i)^m$ ————————— the amounts are equal by definition
$1 + f = (1 + i)^m$ ————————————— divide both sides by PV

$$\boxed{f = (1 + i)^m - 1}$$ ————————— Formula 10.3

EXAMPLE 10.3C

Determine the effective rate of interest corresponding to 9% p.a. compounded

(i) annually;

(ii) semi-annually;

(iii) quarterly;

(iv) monthly.

SOLUTION

Calculate the effective rate f using Formula 10.3.

Steps	Annually	Semi-annually	Quarterly	Monthly
I/Y	9.0	9.0	9.0	9.0
P/Y	1	2	4	12
i	$0.09 = 9.0\%$	$0.09/2 = 4.5\%$	$0.09/4 = 2.25\%$	$0.09/12 = 0.75\%$
m	1	2	4	12
f	$f = (1 + .09)^1 - 1$ $= 1.09 - 1$ $= 9\%$	$f = (1 + .045)^2 - 1$ $= 1.092025 - 1$ $= 9.2025\%$	$f = (1 + .0225)^4 - 1$ $= 1.093083 - 1$ $= 9.3083\%$	$f = (1 + .0075)^{12} - 1$ $= 1.093807 - 1$ $= 9.3807\%$

PROGRAMMED SOLUTION: *Calculate Future Value*

Steps	Annually	Semi-annually	Quarterly	Monthly
P/Y C/Y	1	2	4	12
I/Y	9.0	9.0	9.0	9.0
PV	$1 \pm$	$1 \pm$	$1 \pm$	$1 \pm$
n	1	2	4	12
CPT FV	1.09	1.092025	1.093083	1.93807

Alternatively: Use Interest Conversion

Steps	Annually	Semi-annually	Quarterly	Monthly
2nd IConv				
Nom=	9.0	9.0	9.0	9.0
C/Y=	1	2	4	12
Eff = CPT	9.0	9.2025	9.3083	9.3807

POINTERS
& PITFALLS

For nominal annual interest rates and effective rates, the following two points are always true:

1. The effective rate is always larger or equal to the nominal rate. The nominal annual rate is the effective rate of interest *only* if the number of conversion periods per year is 1; that is, if compounding annually.
2. For a given nominal annual rate, the effective rate of interest increases as the number of conversion periods per year increases.

EXAMPLE 10.3D

You have money to invest in interest-earning deposits. Deposits at your bank pay 3.5% compounded semi-annually. Deposits at a local trust company pay 3.625% compounded annually, and deposits at a credit union pay 3.45% compounded monthly. Which institution offers the best rate of interest for your deposit?

SOLUTION

The interest rates given are not directly comparable. To make the rates comparable, determine the effective rates of interest corresponding to the nominal annual rates.

Calculate the effective rate f using Formula 10.3.

Steps	Bank	Trust Company	Credit Union
i	3.5%/2 = 1.75%	3.625%/1 = 3.625%	3.45%/12 = 0.2875%
m	2	1	12
f	$f = (1 + .0175)^2 - 1$	$f = (1 + .03625)^1 - 1$	$f = (1 + .002875)^{12} - 1$
	$= 1.035306$	$= 1.03625 - 1$	$= 1.035051 - 1$
	$= 3.5306\%$	$= 3.625\%$	$= 3.5051\%$

PROGRAMMED SOLUTION: *Use Interest Conversion*

Steps	Bank	Trust Company	Credit Union
2nd IConv			
Nom =	3.5	3.625	3.45
C/Y =	2	1	12
Eff = CPT	3.5306	3.625	3.5051

The trust company offers the best rate of interest for your deposit.

POINTERS & PITFALLS

Banks, credit unions, and credit card companies usually tell you the annual interest rate they charge. By doing so, they are disclosing the effective interest rate or the "true cost" of borrowing. For situations when a lender doesn't disclose the effective rate, it's important to be able to calculate the cost of your debt. Payday lenders charge much higher interest rates than traditional lenders. For example, a payday loan advertised for $15 per $100 loan carries an equivalent annual interest rate ranging between 88% and 391%, depending on the required repayment period!

If you borrow $400 on a credit card that charges 15% in annual interest, it costs you around $5 per month, or $60 per year.

If you borrow $400 from a payday lender who can legally charge up to $60 every 14 days, it costs you around $129 per month. That's over $1500 per year!

Source: www.stepstojustice.ca

B. Equivalent rates

Notice that in Example 10.2D, two different nominal annual rates of interest (9.381% compounded annually and 9% compounded monthly) produced the same future value ($1093.81) for a given principal ($1000.00) after one year. Interest rates that increase a given principal to the same future value over the same period of time are called **equivalent rates**—9.381% compounded annually and 9% compounded monthly are equivalent rates.

EXAMPLE 10.3E

Calculate the future value after one year of a debt of $100 accumulated at
- (i) 12.55% compounded annually;
- (ii) 12.18% compounded semi-annually;
- (iii) 12.00% compounded quarterly;
- (iv) 11.88% compounded monthly.

SOLUTION

	(i)	(ii)	(iii)	(iv)
Principal (PV)	100.00	100.00	100.00	100.00
Nominal rate	12.55%	12.18%	12.00%	11.88%
i	0.1255	0.0609	0.03	0.0099
n	1	2	4	12
Future value (FV)	$100.00(1.1255)^1$ $= 100.00(1.1255)$ $= \$112.55$	$100.00(1.0609)^2$ $= 100.00(1.125509)$ $= \$112.55$	$100.00(1.03)^4$ $= 100.00(1.125509)$ $= \$112.55$	$100.00(1.0099)^{12}$ $= 100.00(1.125487)$ $= \$112.55$

Note: The four different nominal annual rates produce the same future value of $112.55 for the same principal of $100 over the same time period of one year. By definition, the four nominal rates are equivalent rates.

We can compute equivalent rates by equating the accumulated values of $1 for the rates under consideration based on a selected time period, usually one year.

After you become competent in the algebraic method for solving equivalent rates, you may wish to use a programmable financial calculator such as the Texas Instruments BA II PLUS to perform these computations.

Equivalent Rates Using the BA II PLUS

The BA II PLUS can be used to calculate equivalent interest rates by using the effective rate as a constant to make equivalent calculations.

The process is as follows:

1. [2nd] (ICONV).
2. Enter any nominal rate, NOM = Press [Enter].
3. Arrow down to C/Y = and enter the compounds relating to the nominal rate entered in Step 2. Press [Enter].
4. Arrow up to EFF = and press [CPT].
5. Arrow down and change C/Y= to the compounds you want to convert to.
6. Arrow down to NOM = and press [CPT]. Press [Enter].
7. Repeat the process as many times as required to calculate all equivalent rates you are interested in.

EXAMPLE 10.3F

Determine the nominal annual rate compounded semi-annually that is equivalent to an annual rate of 6% compounded annually.

SOLUTION

Let the semi-annual rate of interest be represented by i; P/Y = 2.
For PV = 1, $n = 2$, the accumulated value $FV_1 = (1 + i)^2$.
For the given nominal rate compounded annually the accumulated value
$FV_2 = (1 + 0.06)^1$.
By definition, to be equivalent, $FV_1 = FV_2$.

$$(1 + i)^2 = 1.06$$

$$i = \left(\frac{1.06}{1}\right)^{\frac{1}{2}} - 1$$

$$i = (1.029563) - 1$$

$$i = 0.029563 = 2.9563\% \xrightarrow{\hspace{2cm}} \text{semi-annual rate}$$

The nominal rate is 2.9563% × 2 = 5.9126% compounded semi-annually.

PROGRAMMED SOLUTION

$$1(1 + i)^2 = 1.06$$

PV   FV

(Set P/Y, C/Y = 2) 1 [±] [PV] 1.06 [FV]

2 [N] [CPT] [I/Y] [5.912603]

Alternatively:

[2nd] (IConv) Eff = 6.0; C/Y = 2; Nom = [CPT] 5.9126

The nominal annual rate compounded semi-annually is 5.9126%.

The periodic rate is 5.9126%/2 = 2.9563% per semi-annual period.

EXAMPLE 10.3G

What nominal annual rate compounded quarterly is equivalent to 8.4% p.a. compounded monthly?

SOLUTION

Let the quarterly rate be i; PV = 1; $n = 4$.
The accumulated value of $1 after one year $FV_1 = (1 + i)^4$.

For the given rate I/Y = 8.4; P/Y = 12; $i = \dfrac{8.4\%}{12} = 0.7\% = 0.007$; $n = 12$.

The accumulated value of $1 after one year $FV_2 = (1.007)^{12}$.
To be equivalent, $FV_1 = FV_2$.

$$(1 + i)^4 = (1.007)^{12}$$
$$(1 + i) = (1.007)^{12/4}$$
$$i = (1.021147) - 1$$
$$i = 0.021147 = 2.1147\% \text{──────────── quarterly rate}$$

The nominal rate is 2.1147% × 4 = 8.458937% compounded quarterly.

PROGRAMMED SOLUTION

(Set P/Y, C/Y = 12) 1 [±] [PV] 8.4 [I/Y]

12 [N] [CPT] [FV] [1.087311] [STO] 1

(Set P/Y, C/Y = 4) 1 [±] [PV] [RCL] 1 [FV]

4 [N] [CPT] [I/Y] [8.458937%]

Alternatively:

[2nd] (IConv) Nom = 8.4; C/Y = 12; Eff = [CPT] 8.7311

C/Y = 4; Nom = [CPT] 8.4589

The nominal annual rate compounded quarterly is 8.4589%. The periodic rate is 2.1147% per quarterly period.

Equivalent rate calculations will be used frequently in later chapters once we start Annuities. So to simplify things, equivalent rates of interest, including those involving effective rates, can be determined by using Formula 10.4.

$$i_2 = (1 + i_1)^{m_1/m_2} - 1$$

This formula derivation is similar to Formula 10.3.

Let the nominal rate of interest be compounded m_1 times per year, and let the interest rate per conversion period be i_1.

Then the corresponding equivalent rate of interest can be referred to as i_2, which has a compounded frequency of m_2 times per year.

For equivalent rates, these amounts are equal by definition

$$PV(1 + i_2)^{m_2} = PV(1 + i_1)^{m_1}$$

$$(1 + i_2)^{m_2} = (1 + i_1)^{m_1}$$

$$i_2 = (1 + i_1)^{m_1/m_2} - 1$$

Use your calculator parenthesis or "bracket" keys to handle the calculations for the fractional exponent.

EXAMPLE 10.3H	Roy's bank currently offers 2.4% compounded semi-annually on premium savings deposits. His friend informed him that he would earn more interest if his savings were compounded more frequently. What is the nominal annual rate compounded monthly that would be equivalent to his semi-annual rate?
SOLUTION	Let the monthly rate be i; $P/Y = 12$; $n = 12$; $PV = 1$.

The accumulated value of \$1 after one year $FV_1 = (1 + i)^{12}$.
For the existing rate, $P/Y = 2$; $n = 2$; $i = 0.012$.
The accumulated value of \$1 in one year $FV_2 = (1.012)^2$.
To maintain the same yield, the two rates must be equivalent.

$$(1 + i)^{12} = (1.012)^2$$
$$(1 + i) = (1.012)^{1/6}$$
$$i = (1.001990) - 1$$
$$i = 0.001990 = 0.1990\% \quad\text{————————— monthly rate}$$

The nominal rate is $0.1990\% \times 12 = 2.3881\%$ compounded monthly.

PROGRAMMED SOLUTION

$$(1 + i)^{12} = (1.012)^2$$

$$1(1 + i)^{12} = 1.024144$$

(Set P/Y, C/Y = 2) 1 [±] [PV] 2.4 [I/Y]

2 [N] [CPT] [FV] [1.024144] [STO] 1

(Set P/Y, C/Y = 12) 1 [±] [PV] [RCL] 1 [FV]

12 [N] [CPT] [I/Y] [2.388087]

Alternatively:

[2nd] (IConv) Nom = 2.4; C/Y = 2; Eff = [CPT] 2.4144

C/Y = 12; Nom = [CPT] 2.388087

The nominal rate compounded monthly is 2.388087%. The periodic rate is 2.388087%/12 = 0.199007 per monthly period.

C. Using Excel's EFFECT Function

If you choose, you can use Excel's EFFECT function to answer the questions in this section. The method for using these Excel functions is illustrated below.

In Example 10.3B, you are required to calculate the effective interest rate (EFFECT) of an investment. The EFFECT function in Excel is illustrated below.

	A	B	C	D	E
1	EFFECT Function				
2					
3	**Nominal Annual Interest Rate**	3.60%	3.60%		
4	**Total Compounding Periods**	12	2		
5	Answer	3.6600%	3.6324%	0.0276%	
6					

EXERCISE 10.3

MyLab Math

A. Answer each of the following:

1. Compute the effective annual rate of interest for each of the following:
   (a) 9.5% compounded semi-annually
   (b) 10.5% compounded quarterly
   (c) 5.0% compounded monthly
   (d) 7.2% compounded bi-weekly
   (e) 3.6% compounded daily
   (f) 8.2% compounded weekly

2. Calculate the nominal annual rate compounded
   (a) quarterly that is equivalent to 9% compounded semi-annually;
   (b) monthly that is equivalent to 6.5% compounded quarterly;
   (c) daily that is equivalent to 7.5% compounded semi-annually;
   (d) semi-annually that is equivalent to 4.25% compounded quarterly.

B. Solve each of the following.

1. What is the effective annual rate of interest if $100 grows to $150 in six years compounded quarterly?

2. What is the effective annual rate of interest if $450 grows to $750 in 3 years and 5 months compounded monthly?

 3. If $1100 accumulates to $1350 in 4 years and 6 months compounded semi-annually, what is the effective annual rate of interest?

4. An amount of $2300 earns $500 interest in 3 years and 2 months. What is the effective annual rate if interest compounds monthly?

5. Calculate the nominal annual rate of interest compounded quarterly that is equal to an effective rate of 9.25%.

6. What nominal annual rate of interest compounded semi-annually is equivalent to an effective rate of 6.37%?

7. If the effective rate of interest on an investment is 6.4%, what is the nominal rate of interest compounded monthly?

8. What is the nominal rate of interest compounded quarterly if the effective rate of interest on an investment is 5.3%?

9. The Central Bank pays 7.5% compounded semi-annually on certain types of deposits. If interest is compounded monthly, what nominal rate of interest will maintain the same effective rate of interest?

10. The treasurer of National Credit Union proposes changing the method of compounding interest on premium savings accounts to daily compounding. If the current rate is 6% compounded quarterly, what nominal rate should the treasurer suggest to the board of directors to maintain the same effective rate of interest?

11. Sofia made a deposit of $600 into a bank account that earns interest at 3.5% compounded monthly. The deposit earns interest at that rate for five years.
    (a) Determine the balance of the account at the end of the period.
    (b) How much interest is earned?
    (c) What is the effective rate of interest?

12. Ying invested $5000 into an account earning 2.75% interest compounded daily for two years.
    (a) Determine the balance of the account at the end of the period.
    (b) How much interest is earned?
    (c) What is the effective rate of interest?

13. An RRSP earns interest at 4.25% compounded quarterly. An amount of $1200 is invested into the RRSP and earns interest for 10 years.
    (a) Determine the balance of the account at the end of the period.
    (b) How much interest is earned?
    (c) What is the effective rate of interest?

14. Josef invested $1750 into an RRSP that earned interest at 5% compounded semi-annually for eight years.
    (a) Determine the balance of the account at the end of the period.
    (b) How much interest is earned?
    (c) What is the effective rate of interest?

BUSINESS MATH **NEWS**   Debt Reduction Remains a High Priority for Canadians

"What steps are you taking toward reducing your debt?" Questions like this were asked in an Angus Reid Forum survey conducted for a major Canadian bank, (CIBC). The poll found that 25% of respondents identified debt reduction or elimination as a top priority.

In addition to paying down debt and keeping up with bills, other priorities included saving for retirement or travel, adding to investment portfolios, financial planning for a house or car, establishing an emergency fund, and setting aside resources for a child's education.

The Government of Canada recognizes that the majority of Canadians are in debt. Through the Office of Consumer Affairs, the government offers useful online tools intended to help Canadians map out a plan for managing debt.

One best plan for managing debt is unlikely to work for everyone. Instead, common advice is to consolidate loans, make the minimum payments on all debts by their due dates, and pay down the debt with the highest interest rate first. For many Canadians, this starts with having a more disciplined approach with their credit cards. If you only make your minimum credit card payment each month, it could take you years to pay off your balance.

A prudent approach is to choose the liability (usually your credit card) that is charging you the highest interest, and commit as many resources as possible into paying off this balance first. Once your most expensive debt is paid off, focus the extra payments on your next most expensive liability. Continue this method as you pay down each of your debts.

QUESTIONS

1. Paul recently purchased a new flat screen TV for his first apartment on his Best Buy credit card. Its annual interest rate is 29.90% compounded monthly.
   (a) How many payments will it take him to pay off a $1000 balance if he makes monthly payments of $200? How much interest will he pay overall?
   (b) If he paid for the purchase with a CIBC credit card that charged 19.50% compounded monthly, and kept the payments at $200, how many payments would he have to make? How much interest would he pay with this credit card and how much interest would he save?

2. Many people do not understand the amount of interest they are actually payi ng on their credit cards. What is the effective rate of interest corresponding to a credit card that is advertised at 2% per month?

Source: "Debt Reduction Remains a High Priority for Canadians: CIBC Poll," *The Toronto Star*, December 28, 2017. www.thestar.com

MyLab Math

Visit MyLab Math to practise any of this chapter's exercises marked with a ⊕ as often as you want. The guided solutions help you calculate an answer step by step. You'll find a personalized study plan and additional interactive resources to help you master Business Math!

REVIEW EXERCISE

1. **LO❷** At what nominal rate of interest compounded monthly will $400 earn $100 interest over four years?

⊕ 2. **LO❷** At what nominal rate of interest compounded quarterly will $300 earn $80 interest in six years?

⊕ 3. **LO❶** Determine the equated date at which payments of $500 due six months ago and $600 due today could be settled by a payment of $1300, if interest is 9% compounded monthly.

4. **LO❶** Determine the equated date at which two payments of $600 due four months ago and $400 due today could be settled by a payment of $1100, if interest is 7.25% compounded semi-annually.

5. **LO❶** In what period of time will money triple at 10% compounded semi-annually?

⊕ 6. **LO❶** In how many months will money double at 8% compounded monthly?

7. **LO❸** What nominal rate of interest compounded monthly is equivalent to an effective rate of 6.2%?

⊕ 8. **LO❸** What nominal rate of interest compounded quarterly is equivalent to an effective rate of 5.99%?

9. **LO❷❸** Calculate the nominal annual rate of interest
   (a) at which $2500 will grow to $4000 in eight years compounded quarterly;
   (b) at which money will double in five years if compounded semi-annually;
   (c) if the effective annual rate of interest is 9.2% and compounding is done monthly;
   (d) that is equivalent to 8% compounded quarterly.

⊕ 10. **LO❷❸** Calculate the nominal annual rate of interest
   (a) at which $1500 will grow to $1800 in four years compounded monthly;
   (b) at which money will double in seven years if compounded quarterly;

   (c) if the effective annual rate of interest is 7.75% and compounding is done monthly;
   (d) that is equivalent to 6% compounded quarterly.

11. **LO❷❸** Compute the effective annual rate of interest
   (a) for 4.5% compounded monthly;
   (b) at which $2000 will grow to $3000 in seven years if compounded quarterly.

⊕ 12. **LO❷❸** Compute the effective annual rate of interest
   (a) for 6% compounded monthly;
   (b) at which $1100 will grow to $2000 in seven years if compounded monthly.

13. **LO❸** What is the nominal annual rate of interest compounded monthly that is equivalent to 8.5% compounded quarterly?

⊕ 14. **LO❸** What is the nominal annual rate of interest compounded quarterly that is equivalent to an effective annual rate of 5%?

15. **LO❸** Patrick has $2000 to invest. Which of the following options should he choose?
   (a) 4% compounded annually
   (b) 3.75% compounded semi-annually
   (c) 3.5% compounded quarterly
   (d) 3.25% compounded monthly

⊕ 16. **LO❶ (a)** How many years will it take for $7500 to accumulate to $9517.39 at 3% compounded semi-annually?
   (b) Over what period of time will money triple at 9% compounded quarterly?
   (c) How many years will it take for a loan of $10 000 to amount to $13 684 at 10.5% compounded monthly?

17. **LO❶** Matt agreed to make two payments—a payment of $2000 due in nine months and a payment of $1500 in a year. If Matt makes a payment of $1800 now, when should he make a second payment of $1700 if money is worth 8% compounded quarterly?

18. **LO①** A $4000 debt due in four years was paid with $3885.35 cash. If money is worth 7% compounded monthly, how many months before the due date was the debt paid?

19. **LO①** A financial obligation requires the payment of $2000 now, $2500 in six months, and $4000 in one year. When will a single payment of $9000 discharge the obligation if interest is 6% compounded monthly?

20. **LO①** Girard owes two debt payments—a payment of $5000 due in 6 months and a payment of $6000 due in 15 months. If Girard makes a payment of $5000 now, when should he make a second payment of $6000 if money is worth 11% compounded semi-annually?

21. **LO①** A debt of $12 000 was replaced with two payments. If $7500 was paid in two years, when should a second payment of $7500 be made if interest compounds at 8% quarterly?

22. **LO①** Sasha promised to pay $3000 in $2\frac{1}{2}$ years and $5000 in five years. If she replaces those payments with a payment of $4000 in four years and three months, and money is worth 10% compounded quarterly, when should she make the second payment of $6000?

SELF-TEST

1. An investment with an original value of $11 000 is sold for proceeds of $12 950.00. If the investment yield was 5% compounded semi-annually, for how many years was the money invested?

2. An amount of $1400 was invested for 71 months, maturing to $2177.36. What annually compounded rate was earned?

3. Determine the effective annual rate of interest equivalent to 5.4% compounded monthly.

4. How many months from now can a payment of $1000 due 12 months ago and a payment of $400 due 6 months from now be settled by a payment of $1746.56 if interest is 10.2% compounded monthly?

5. At what nominal rate of interest compounded semi-annually will $6900 earn $3000 interest in five years?

6. In how many years will money double at 7.2% compounded quarterly?

7. What is the nominal rate of interest compounded semi-annually that is equivalent to an effective rate of 10.25%?

8. A financial obligation requires the payment of $1000 in 2 months, $3000 in 8 months, and $4000 in 14 months. Instead, if a payment of $2000 is made now, when should a second payment of $6000 be made if interest is 9% compounded monthly?

9. Sean needs to decide how to invest his savings. He can choose between 3.95% compounded semi-annually, 3.92% compounded quarterly, or 3.90% compounded monthly. Which choice will maximize his return?

CHALLENGE PROBLEMS

1. Olga deposited $800 in an investment certificate paying 9% compounded semi-annually. On the same day, her sister Ursula deposited $600 in an account paying 7% compounded semi-annually. To the nearest day, when will the future value of Olga's investment be equal to twice the future value of Ursula's investment?

2. A financial institution is advertising a new three-year investment certificate. The interest rate is 7.5% compounded quarterly the first year, 6.5% compounded monthly the second year, and 6% compounded daily the third year. What nominal rate of interest compounded semi-annually for three years would a competing institution have to offer to match the interest produced by this investment certificate?

CASE STUDY   Comparing Car Loans

▶ After reading consumer car guides and receiving advice from family and friends, Aysha has chosen the new car she would like to purchase. She now wants to research her financing options to choose the best way to pay for the car.

Aysha knows that with taxes, licence, delivery, and dealer preparation fees, her car will cost $17 650. She has saved $7500 toward the purchase price but must borrow the rest. She has narrowed her financing choices to three options: dealer financing, credit union financing, and bank financing.

- (i)   The car dealer has offered 48-month financing at 4.5% compounded monthly.
- (ii) The credit union has offered 36-month financing at 5% compounded quarterly. It has also offered 48-month financing at 5.3% compounded quarterly.
- (iii) The bank has offered 36-month financing at 4.8% compounded semi-annually. It has also offered 48-month financing at 5.1% compounded semi-annually.

Aysha desires the financing option that offers the best interest rate. However, she also wants to explore the financing options that allow her to pay off her car loan more quickly.

QUESTIONS

1. Aysha wants to compare the 48-month car loan options offered by the car dealer, the credit union, and the bank.
   (a) What is the effective annual rate of interest for each 48-month option?
   (b) How much interest will Aysha save by choosing the best option compared to the worst option?

2. Suppose Aysha wants to pay off her car loan within three years.
   (a) What is the effective annual rate of interest for both of the 36-month options?
   (b) How much interest will Aysha save by choosing the better option?

3. If you wanted to get a car loan today, what are the current rates of interest for 36-month and 48-month terms? Are car dealers offering better interest rates than the banks or credit unions? If so, why?

SUMMARY OF FORMULAS

Formula 9.1

$$FV = PV(1 + i)^n$$

Calculating the future value (or maturity value) when the principal, the rate of interest, and the time period are known

Formula 9.4

$$PV = \frac{FV}{(1 + i)^n}$$

Calculating the present value (or principal, or proceeds, or discounted value) when the future value, the rate of interest, and the time period are known

Formula 9.4 restated as

$PV = FV(1 + i)^{-n}$ **Calculating the present value using negative exponents**

Formula 10.1

$$n = \frac{\ln\left(\frac{FV}{PV}\right)}{\ln(1 + i)}$$ **Determining the number of periods, n, when the present value, the future value, and the rate of interest are known**

Formula 10.2

$$i = \left(\frac{FV}{PV}\right)^{\frac{1}{n}} - 1$$ **Calculating the periodic interest rate, i, when the present value, the future value, and the time period are known**

Formula 10.3

$f = (1 + i)^m - 1$ **Calculating the effective rate of interest, f, for a nominal annual rate compounded m times per year**

Formula 10.4

$i_2 = (1 + i_1)^{m_1/m_2} - 1$ **Calculating the equivalent rate of interest, i_2, for a nominal annual rate compounded m_1 times per year**

GLOSSARY

Effective rate of interest the annual rate of interest that yields the same amount of interest per year as a nominal rate compounded a number of times per year (p. 402)

Equated date the date on which a single sum of money is equal to the sum of two or more dated sums of money (p. 393)

Equivalent rates interest rates that accumulate a given principal to the same future value over the same period of time (p. 406)

Ordinary Simple Annuities

Robert Bird/Alamy Stock Photo

LEARNING OBJECTIVES

Upon completing this chapter, you will be able to do the following:

1. Distinguish between types of annuities based on term, payment date, and conversion period.

2. Compute the future value for ordinary simple annuities.

3. Compute the present value for ordinary simple annuities.

4. Compute the payment for ordinary simple annuities.

5. Compute the number of periods for ordinary simple annuities.

6. Compute the interest rate for ordinary simple annuities.

Having just graduated with his business degree, Emanuel wants to start to develop an investment portfolio. His family has given him some money as a graduation gift. How should he invest the money to grow the value of the investment? If he invests an additional amount from each paycheque, how much should he invest? What will his investments be worth after one year, or after five years? If a dividend is paid from his investments, what equivalent interest rate has been earned? The concepts discussed in this chapter will help Emanuel calculate the effect of investing small but regular amounts.

INTRODUCTION

An annuity is a series of payments, usually of equal size, made at periodic time intervals. The term *annuity* applies to all periodic payment plans, the most frequent of which require annual, semi-annual, quarterly, or monthly payments. Practical applications of annuities are widely encountered in the finances of both businesses and individuals. Periodic contributions to an RRSP, RESP, student loan payments, car loan payments, mortgage payments, and withdrawals from an RRIF are common examples of annuities in personal finance. Businesses may encounter annuities in the form of equipment loans, mortgages, lease contracts, and bond interest payments.

Various types of annuities are identified based on the term of an annuity, the date of payment, and the length of the interest compounding or conversion period. In this chapter, we will deal with ordinary simple annuities, and calculate the future value, present value, payment amount, number of periods, and interest rate.

11.1 INTRODUCTION TO ANNUITIES
A. Basic concepts

In this textbook, an **annuity** is a series of equal payments, made at periodic intervals. The length of time between the successive payments is called the **payment interval** or **payment period**. The length of time from the beginning of the first payment interval to the end of the last payment interval is called the **term of an annuity**. The amount of each of the regular payments is called the **periodic payment**, or **periodic rent**.

When performing annuity calculations, the timing of payments must be considered. Depending on the frequency and regularity of payments, different formulas will be used in annuity calculations. When a payment is made only once, it is treated as either the present value, PV, or the future value, FV, of a calculation. When there are a series of payments, it must be determined if the payments are equal amounts and are paid at the same time within each payment interval of the term. If the payment is equal and periodic, it is treated as the periodic payment, PMT, of an annuity calculation. The types of annuities are described in Section B below.

B. Types of annuities

1. *Ordinary annuities and annuities due*
Annuities are classified by the date of payment. In an **ordinary annuity**, payments are made at the end of each payment period. In an **annuity due**, payments are made at the beginning of each payment period. Loan payments, mortgage payments, and interest payments on bonds are all examples of ordinary annuities. Examples of annuities due include lease rental payments on real estate or equipment. (See Figure 11.1).

2. *Simple and general annuities*
Annuities are classified by the length of the interest compounding or conversion period relative to the payment period (Section 9.1). With a **simple annuity**, the conversion period is the same length as the payment interval. An example is monthly payments on a loan for which the interest is compounded monthly. Since the interest compounding period (C/Y: compounding periods per year) is equal to the payment period (P/Y: payment periods per year), this is a simple annuity.

Figure 11.1 Types of Annuities (© S. A. Hummelbrunner)

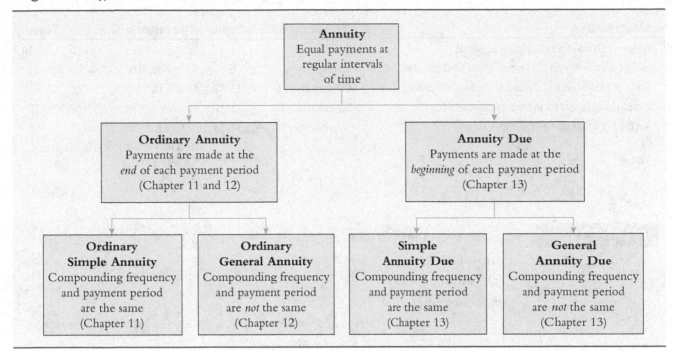

With a **general annuity**, the conversion period and the payment interval are not equal. An example would be a residential mortgage for which interest is compounded semi-annually but payments may be made monthly, semi-monthly, bi-weekly, or weekly. The conversion period, C/Y, does not equal the payment period, P/Y.

3. *Deferred annuities*

A **deferred annuity** occurs when the first payment is delayed for a period of time. For example, a severance amount may be deposited into a fund that earns interest, and then later is converted into another fund that pays out a series of payments until the fund is exhausted.

4. *Perpetuities*

A **perpetuity** is an annuity for which the payments continue forever. When the size of the periodic payment from a fund is equal to the periodic interest earned by the fund, such as an endowment fund to a university or a continuous benefit from a capital investment, a perpetuity is the result.

5. *Annuities certain and contingent annuities*

If both the beginning date and ending date of an annuity are known, indicating a fixed term, the classification is an **annuity certain**. Typical examples of annuities certain include lease payments on equipment, installment payments on loans, and interest payments on bonds.

If the beginning date, the ending date, or both, are unknown, the classification is a **contingent annuity**. Life insurance premiums or pension payments are typical examples of contingent annuities. The ending date is unknown for these annuities, since they terminate with the death of the recipient.

Ordinary simple annuities will be discussed in the current chapter. Ordinary general annuities will be discussed in Chapter 12. Other annuities, such as annuities due, deferred annuities, and perpetuities will be discussed in Chapter 13.

The classification of annuities and the choice of formulas can be clarified if the following questions are asked.

Annuity Questions

Annuity Question	If the answer is YES:	Chapter	If the answer is NO:	Chapter
Is there a series of equal periodic payments?	Annuity	11–13	Not an annuity.	9, 10
Is the conversion period C/Y equal to the payment interval P/Y?	Simple annuity	11	General annuity	12
Is the payment made at the end of the payment period?	Ordinary annuity	11, 12	Annuity due	13
Does the payment start in the first payment period?	Not deferred	11, 12	Deferred annuity	13
Are the beginning and ending dates known?	Annuity certain	11, 13	Perpetuity if infinite term; contingent annuity if dates are not known	13

EXAMPLE 11.1A

Classify each of the following annuities by

(i) term;

(ii) date of payment;

(iii) conversion period.

(a) Deposits of $150 earning interest at 4% compounded quarterly are made at the beginning of each quarter for four years.

(b) Payments of $200 are made at the end of each month for five years. Interest is 7% compounded semi-annually.

(c) A fund of $10 000 is deposited in a trust account earning interest compounded annually. Starting five years from the date of deposit, the interest earned for the year is to be paid out as a scholarship.

(d) In his will, Dr. Chu directed that part of his estate be invested in a trust fund earning interest compounded quarterly. His surviving wife was to be paid, for the remainder of her life, $2000 at the end of every three months starting three months after his death.

SOLUTION

Question (a)

(i) annuity certain (the term is fixed: four years)

(ii) annuity due (payments are made at the beginning of each quarter)

(iii) simple annuity (the quarterly conversion period equals the quarterly payment period)

SOLUTION

Question (b)

(i) annuity certain (the term is fixed: five years)

(ii) ordinary annuity (payments are made at the end of each month)

(iii) general annuity (semi-annual conversion period does not match the monthly payment period)

SOLUTION

Question (c)

(i) perpetuity (the payments can go on forever)

(ii) deferred annuity (the first payment is deferred for five years)

(iii) simple annuity (the annual conversion period equals the annual interest period)

SOLUTION

Question (d)

(i) contingent annuity (both the starting date and the ending date are uncertain)

(ii) ordinary annuity (payments at the end of every three months)

(iii) simple annuity (the quarterly conversion period equals the quarterly payment period)

11.2 ORDINARY SIMPLE ANNUITY—CALCULATING FUTURE VALUE FV
A. Future value of a series of payments—basic computation

EXAMPLE 11.2A

Calculate the future value of five equal deposits of $3000 made at the end of each of five consecutive years at 6% compounded annually, just after the last deposit has been made.

SOLUTION

We first identify the problem as an ordinary simple annuity. This is an annuity because there is a series of equal periodic payments. Since the number of compounding periods per year C/Y and the number of payments per year P/Y are equal, this is simple annuity. This is an ordinary annuity because the payment is made at the end of the payment period.

We choose the focal point as five years from now because we need to calculate the equated value of all deposits at that time. To calculate the future value of a series of deposits, we first need to determine the future value of each of the deposits, including interest, at the focal point. The combined future value is the sum of the individual equivalent future values at the focal date. Each of these calculations can be done using Formula 9.1, $FV = PV(1 + i)^n$.

However, the fact that the deposits are *equal in size* permits a useful mathematical simplification (see Figure 11.2). The equal deposit of $3000 can be taken out as a common factor, and the individual compounding factors can be combined.

Figure 11.2 Graphical Representation of Method and Data (© S. A. Hummelbrunner)

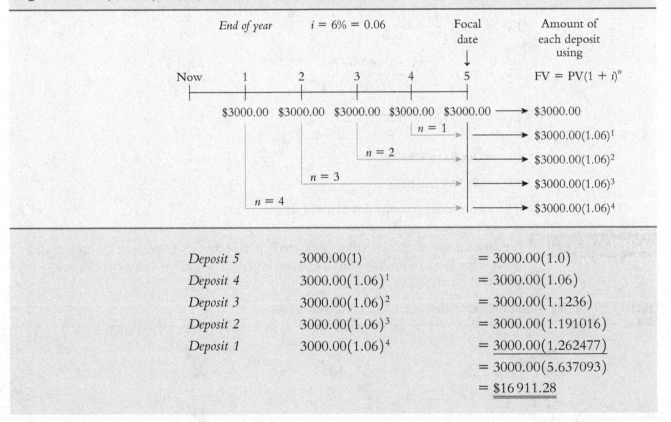

Deposit 5	3000.00(1)	= 3000.00(1.0)
Deposit 4	$3000.00(1.06)^1$	= 3000.00(1.06)
Deposit 3	$3000.00(1.06)^2$	= 3000.00(1.1236)
Deposit 2	$3000.00(1.06)^3$	= 3000.00(1.191016)
Deposit 1	$3000.00(1.06)^4$	= 3000.00(1.262477)
		= 3000.00(5.637093)
		= $16 911.28

POINTERS & PITFALLS

The FV of the individual payments on the focal date are in a geometric series at a common ratio of $(1 + i)$. The formula used for accumulated value of n payments is the sum of this geometric series.

B. Formula for calculating the future value of an ordinary simple annuity

In Example 11.2A, the payments are of equal size and are made periodically (at the end of each year) within the term of five years. By identifying payments as equal and periodic, you can compute the sum of a very large number of terms without having to evaluate each term individually.

The following formula has been developed for calculating the accumulated value of ordinary simple annuities. The notation used conforms to the keys used on a preprogrammed financial calculator.

$$FV_n = PMT\left[\frac{(1 + i)^n - 1}{i}\right] \qquad\text{Formula 11.1}$$

where FV_n = the future value (accumulated value) of an ordinary simple annuity;
$\quad PMT$ = the size of the periodic payment;
$\qquad i$ = the interest rate per conversion period;
$\qquad n$ = the number of periodic payments (which for simple annuities is also the number of conversion periods).

The expression $\left[\dfrac{(1 + i)^n - 1}{i}\right]$ is called the **compounding** or **accumulation factor for annuities** or the **accumulated value of one dollar per period**.

Using Formula 11.1 to solve Example 11.2A, where PMT = 3000.00; i = 0.06; n = 5,

$$FV_n = PMT\left[\frac{(1 + i)^n - 1}{i}\right]$$

$$FV_n = 3000.00\left[\frac{(1 + 0.06)^5 - 1}{0.06}\right]$$

$$FV_n = 3000.00\left[\frac{1.338226 - 1}{0.06}\right]$$

$$FV_n = 3000.00\left[5.637093\right]$$

$$FV_n = \$16\ 911.27888$$

The future value (rounded) is $16 911.28.

EXAMPLE 11.2B   Calculate the accumulated value of quarterly payments of $50 made at the end of each quarter for 10 years just after the last payment has been made if interest is 8% compounded quarterly.

Figure 11.3 Graphical Representation of Method and Data (© S. A. Hummelbrunner)

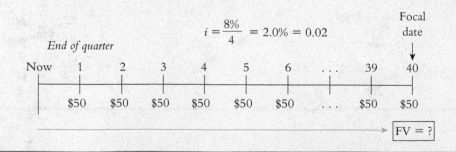

SOLUTION

Since the payments are of equal size made at the end of each quarter and compounding is quarterly, the problem is an ordinary simple annuity.

$$PMT = 50.00; \quad i = \frac{8\%}{4} = 2\% = 0.02;$$

$$n = 10(4) = 40$$

$$FV_n = PMT\left[\frac{(1+i)^n - 1}{i}\right]$$

$$FV = 50.00\left[\frac{(1+0.02)^{40} - 1}{0.02}\right] \text{——————— substituting in Formula 11.1}$$

$$= 50.00\left(\frac{2.208040 - 1}{0.02}\right)$$

$$= 50.00(60.401983)$$

$$= \$3020.10$$

EXAMPLE 11.2C

You deposit $10 at the end of each month for five years in an account paying 6% compounded monthly.

   (i) What will the balance be in your account at the end of the five-year term?

  (ii) How much of the balance will you have contributed?

 (iii) How much is interest?

SOLUTION

   (i) $PMT = 10.00; \quad i = \dfrac{6\%}{12} = 0.5\% = 0.005; \quad n = 12(5) = 60$

$$FV_n = PMT\left[\frac{(1+i)^n - 1}{i}\right]$$

$$FV_n = 10.00\left[\frac{(1.005)^{60} - 1}{0.005}\right]$$

$$= 10.00(69.770031)$$

$$= \$697.70$$

  (ii) Your contribution is $10 per month for 60 months, or $10.00(60) = \$600$.

 (iii) Since your contribution is $600, the interest earned is $697.70 - 600.00 = \$97.70$.

C. Using preprogrammed financial calculators

Preprogrammed financial calculators can be used to perform compound interest calculations involving annuities. As outlined in Section 9.2, function keys correspond to the variables used in annuity calculations. The use of three models of calculators is outlined in Appendix II, "Instructions and Tips for Three Preprogrammed Financial Calculator Models." Relevant highlights are shown in Table 11.1. Instructions in this text are given for the Texas Instruments BA II PLUS calculator.

POINTERS & PITFALLS

Preparation: Before a new calculation is started, remember to clear all previous data. To reset all entries to the default values for each field, press [2nd] [CLR TVM].

Table 11.1 Financial Calculator Function Keys That Correspond to Variables Used in Ordinary Simple Annuity Calculations
(© S. A. Hummelbrunner)

Variable	Algebraic Symbol	Function Key		
		TI BA II PLUS	Sharp EL-738C	HP 10bII +
The periodic rate of interest*	i	[I/Y] and [C/Y]	[I]	[I/YR] and [P/YR]
The number of payment intervals per year	None	[P/Y]	[NONE]	[P/YR]
The number of payment periods in the term	n	[N]	[N]	[N]
The periodic annuity payment	PMT	[PMT]	[PMT]	[I/Y]
The present value or principal	PV	[PV]	[PV]	[PV]
The future value or maturity value	FV	[FV]	[FV]	[FV]

*Note: The periodic rate of interest is entered into the calculator as a percent and not as a decimal equivalent. For example for [I/Y], 8% is entered as "8" not ".08".

To perform calculations for an ordinary simple annuity:

STEP 1   Determine the number of payments per year and enter as the [P/Y]: If the number of payments per year is specified as "monthly," follow the sequence [2nd] [P/Y] 12 [ENTER] [2nd] [QUIT]. Substitute the number for the appropriate number of payments per year in each case. The most common frequencies are monthly, quarterly, semi-annually, and annually.

STEP 2   Enter the other given values in any order. Remember that the value is entered first, then the appropriate button is pressed without the use of the [ENTER] button.

STEP 3   Compute the unknown number: press [CPT] followed by the key representing the unknown variable.

Note: This assumes that the calculator is in the END mode, indicating payment is made at the end of the payment interval. This is the default. To check, look at the upper right corner of the display screen. If no letters are shown in that corner above the numbers, the calculator is in the END mode. If the letters BGN are showing, you must switch modes:

[2nd] [BGN] ([PMT] Key)

[2nd] [SET] (END will now appear.)

[2nd] [QUIT] (Back to standard calculator—upper-right corner is now blank.)

When performing an annuity calculation, usually only one of either the present value PV *or* the future value FV is involved. To avoid incorrect answers, the present value [PV] should be set to zero when determining the future value [FV] and vice versa. In addition, recall that the Texas Instruments BA II PLUS calculator follows the established convention of treating cash inflows (cash received) as positive numbers and cash outflows (cash paid out) as negative numbers. Since periodic annuity payments are considered cash outflows, always enter the periodic payment as a negative number. Also, continue to always enter the present value as a negative number (if the present value is other than 0) to ensure your result has a positive value.

To solve Example 11.2C, in which PMT = 10.00, I/Y = 6, P/Y = 12, and n = 60, use the following procedure.

Key in	Press	Display shows	
		Display shows	
(Set P/Y, C/Y = 12) 0	**PV**	0 —————— a precaution to avoid incorrect answers	
10	**±** **PMT**	−10 —————— this enters the periodic payment, PMT	
6.0	**I/Y**	6.0 —————— this enters the interest rate per year	
60	**N**	60 —————— this enters the number of payments, n	
CPT	**FV**	697.700305 —————— this retrieves the wanted amount, FV	

The future value is $697.70.

D. Applications

EXAMPLE 11.2D

Jim set up a savings plan with TD Canada Trust whereby he deposits $300 at the end of each quarter for eight years. The amount in his account at that time will become a term deposit withdrawable after a further five years. Interest throughout the total time period is 5% compounded quarterly.

   (i) How much will be in Jim's account just after he makes his last deposit?

  (ii) What will be the balance of his account when he can withdraw the deposit?

 (iii) How much of the total at the time of withdrawal did Jim contribute?

 (iv) How much interest is earned?

SOLUTION

As Figure 11.4 shows, problems of this type may be solved in stages. The first stage involves computing the future value of an *ordinary annuity*. This amount becomes the principal or present value for the second stage, which involves calculating the future value of a *single* sum of money invested for five years.

Figure 11.4 Graphical Representation of Method and Data (© S. A. Hummelbrunner)

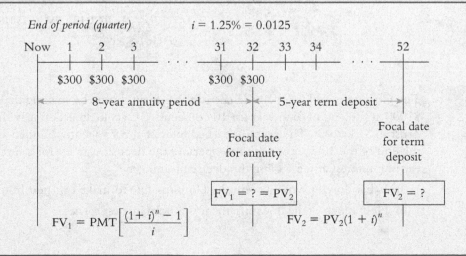

STEP 1 Calculate the accumulated value, FV_1, of the annuity at the end of the 8-year annuity period.

(i) PMT = 300.00; I/Y = 5; P/Y, C/Y = 4; $i = \dfrac{5\%}{4} = 1.25\% = 0.0125$;

$n = 8(4) = 32$

$$FV_1 = 300.00\left[\frac{(1.0125^{32} - 1)}{0.0125}\right] \;\text{————— Formula 11.1}$$

$$= 300.00\left[\frac{(1.488131 - 1)}{0.0125}\right]$$

$$= 300.00(39.050441)$$

$$= \$11\ 715.13$$

STEP 2 Enter the result of Step 1, FV_1, as the present value (deposit), PV_2, for the 5-year term, and compute the accumulated value, FV_2, at the end of the 5-year term. Note that there is no payment amount in this second step, but the account balance continues to grow.

(ii) $PV_2 = FV_1 = 11\ 715.13$; PMT = 0; $i = 0.0125$; $n = 5(4) = 20$
$FV_2 = 11\ 715.13(1.0125)^{20}$ ——— Formula 9.1
$= 11\ 715.13(1.282037)$
$= \$15\ 019.23$

STEP 3 Calculate the total contribution as the payment, PMT, amount made during the 8-year annuity period multiplied by the number of times, n, a contribution was made during that period.

(iii) Jim's contribution = 32(300.00) = \$9600.00.

STEP 4 Calculate the amount of interest earned by subtracting the total contribution from Step 3 from the final future value in Step 2.

(iv) The amount of interest earned = 15 019.23 − 9600.00 = \$5419.23.

PROGRAMMED SOLUTION FOR PARTS (I) AND (II)

(i) (Set P/Y, C/Y = 4) 0 $\boxed{\text{PV}}$ 300 $\boxed{\pm}$ $\boxed{\text{PMT}}$

5 $\boxed{\text{I/Y}}$ 32 $\boxed{\text{N}}$ $\boxed{\text{CPT}}$ $\boxed{\text{FV}}$ $\boxed{11715.132206}$

(ii) 11 715.13 $\boxed{\pm}$ $\boxed{\text{PV}}$ 0 $\boxed{\text{PMT}}$

5 $\boxed{\text{I/Y}}$ 20 $\boxed{\text{N}}$ $\boxed{\text{CPT}}$ $\boxed{\text{FV}}$ $\boxed{15019.235663}$

EXAMPLE 11.2E The Gordons saved for the purchase of their dream home by making deposits of \$1000 at the end of each year for 10 consecutive years in an account with Cooperative Trust in Saskatoon. The account earned interest at 5.75% compounded annually. At the end of the 10-year contribution period, the deposit was left for a further 6 years, earning interest at 5.5% compounded semi-annually.

(i) What down payment were the Gordons able to make on their house?

(ii) How much of the down payment was from interest earned?

SOLUTION

STEP 1   (i) Calculate the accumulated value, FV_1, of the contributions of the ordinary annuity at the end of the 10 years of yearly deposits.

$PMT = 1000.00$; $I/Y = 5.75$; $P/Y = 1$; $i = 5.75\% = 0.0575$; $n = 10$

$$FV_1 = 1000.00\left[\frac{(1.0575^{10} - 1)}{0.0575}\right]$$

$$= 1000.00\left[\frac{1.749056 - 1}{0.0575}\right]$$

$$= 1000.00(13.027064)$$

$$= \$13\,027.06408$$

STEP 2   The future value, FV_1, of the first 10-year period becomes the present value, PV_2, of the next 6-year period. Compute the accumulated value of the savings, FV_2, at the end of the further 6 years.

$PV_2 = FV_1 = 13\,027.06408$; $PMT = 0$; $I/Y = 5.5$; $P/Y = 2$;

$i = \dfrac{5.5\%}{2} = 2.75\% = 0.0275$; $n = 12$

$$FV_2 = 13\,027.06408(1.0275)^{12}$$

$$= 13\,027.06408(1.384784)$$

$$= \$18\,039.67$$

The Gordons made a down payment of \$18 039.67.

(ii) Calculate the amount of interest earned by subtracting the total contribution from the accumulated value at the end of the six years. Since the Gordons contributed $(1000.00)(10) = \$10\,000.00$, the amount of interest in the down payment is \$8039.67.

PROGRAMMED SOLUTION FOR PART (I)

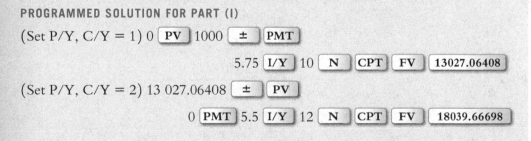

(Set P/Y, C/Y = 1) 0 [PV] 1000 [±] [PMT]

5.75 [I/Y] 10 [N] [CPT] [FV]   13027.06408

(Set P/Y, C/Y = 2) 13 027.06408 [±] [PV]

0 [PMT] 5.5 [I/Y] 12 [N] [CPT] [FV]   18039.66698

EXAMPLE 11.2F   Heather contributed \$1500 at the end of each year for 12 years into a savings account. Interest earned on the savings account was 4.5% compounded annually for the first eight years, then increased to 5.5% compounded annually. How much was the balance in the account five years after her last contribution?

Figure 11.5 Graphical Representation of Method and Data (© S. A. Hummelbrunner)

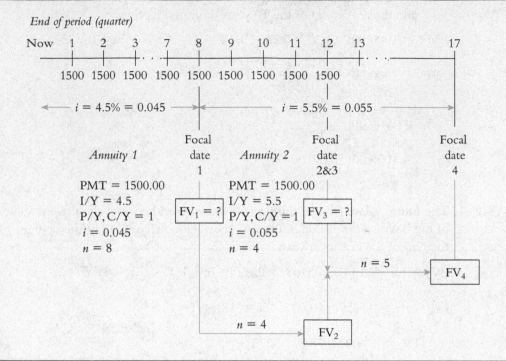

SOLUTION

As Figure 11.5 shows, the problem may be divided into three terms. The first term covers the annuity for the first eight years; the second term covers the annuity for the next four years. These are separated into different calculations because of the differing interest rates. The final term covers the five years during which no further payments are made, but interest continues to increase the balance.

STEP 1

The focal date for the first annuity is at the end of Year 8 (focal date 1). The accumulated value (future value) of this simple annuity is computed by using Formula 11.1.

$$FV_1 = 1500.00\left[\frac{(1.045^8 - 1)}{0.045}\right]$$

$$= 1500.00\left[\frac{(1.422101 - 1)}{0.045}\right]$$

$$= 1500.00(9.380014)$$

$$= \$14\ 070.02043$$

STEP 2

FV_1 then accumulates for four years at 5.5% compounded annually. Focal date 2 is at the end of Year 12.

$$FV_2 = 14\ 070.02043\left[(1.055)^4\right]$$

$$= 14\ 070.02043(1.238825)$$

$$= 17\ 430.288141$$

STEP 3   The focal date for the second annuity is at the end of Year 12 (focal date 3). This part of the annuity earns interest at 5.5% compounded annually. The accumulated value (future value) of this four-year annuity is computed.

$$FV_3 = 1500.00\left[\frac{(1.055^4 - 1)}{0.055}\right]$$

$$= 1500.00\left[\frac{(1.238825 - 1)}{0.055}\right]$$

$$= 1500.00(4.342266)$$

$$= \$6513.399562$$

STEP 4   For the final five years of accumulating interest, the beginning balance is determined by adding the future values of Steps 2 and 3. Then, the future value after the five years is computed.

$$FV_2 + FV_3 = PV_4$$

$$17\ 430.288141 + 6513.399562 = 23\ 943.687703$$

$$FV_4 = 23\ 943.68770\left[(1.055)^5\right]$$

$$= 23\ 943.68770(1.306960)$$

$$= \$31\ 293.44234$$

PROGRAMMED SOLUTION

FV_1

(Set P/Y, C/Y = 1) 0 [PV] 1500 [±] [PMT] 4.5 [I/Y]

8 [N] [CPT] [FV] 14 070.020428

FV_2

(Set P/Y, C/Y = 1) 14 070.020428 [±] [PV] 0 [±] [PMT] 5.5 [I/Y]

4 [N] [CPT] [FV] 17 430.28811 [STO] 1

FV_3

(Set P/Y, C/Y = 1) 0 [PV] 1500 [±] [PMT] 5.5 [I/Y]

4 [N] [CPT] [FV] 6513.399652 [STO] 2

FV_4

[RCL] 1 + [RCL] 2 = 23 943.688770

(Set P/Y, C/Y = 1) 23 943.688770 [±] [PV] 0 [PMT] 5.5 [I/Y]

5 [N] [CPT] [FV] [31 293.44234]

Alternatively
You can simplify the computations and combine Step 2 and 3 on your calculator using the [±] key and the [PV] key immediately following CPT FV_1 and CPT FV_2.

EXERCISE 11.2

If you choose, you can use Excel's FV (future value) function to answer the questions below.

Answer each of the following questions.

1. Calculate the accumulated value of payments of $200 made at the end of every 3 months for 12 years if money is worth 5% compounded quarterly.   Reference Example 11.2B

2. What will deposits of $60 made at the end of each month amount to after six years if interest is 4.8% compounded monthly?

3. An agreement allowed payments of $240 due at the end of each month to be delayed. If interest is 5.4% compounded monthly, how much was owed at the end of 16 months?

4. Monthly payments of $600 were not paid for 19 months. If interest was 19.8% compounded monthly, how much was owed?

5. Monthly payments on a student loan were set at $151.72, with the first payment to be deferred for 6 months. How much was due to be paid immediately after the deferral period if interest was 6.6% compounded monthly?

6. How much interest is included in the future value of an ordinary simple annuity of $1500 paid every 6 months at 7% compounded semi-annually if the term of the annuity is 15 years?   Reference Example 11.2C

7. Joan authorized her bank to withdraw $120 every month. The money was transferred automatically into a savings account. If the savings account earned 2.4% compounded monthly, how much interest will the account have earned after 8 years?

8. Jane Allison made ordinary annuity payments of $15 per month for 16 years, earning 4.5% compounded monthly. How much interest is included in the future value of the annuity?

9. Saving for his retirement 25 years from now, Jimmy Olsen set up a savings plan whereby he will deposit $25 at the end of each month for the next 15 years. Interest is 3.6% compounded monthly.
   (a) How much money will be in Mr. Olsen's account on the date of his retirement?
   (b) How much will Mr. Olsen contribute?
   (c) How much will be interest?   Reference Example 11.2D

10. Aisha contributed $2000 per year for the past 10 years into an RRSP account earning 3.8% compounded annually. Suppose she leaves the accumulated contributions for another five years in the RRSP at the same rate of interest.
    (a) How much will Aisha have in total in her RRSP account?
    (b) How much did Aisha contribute?
    (c) How much interest will have been earned?

11. Cam saved $250 each month for the past five years while he was working. Since he has now gone back to school, his income is lower and he cannot continue to save this amount while studying. He plans to continue with his studies for four years and not withdraw any money from his savings account. Money is worth 4.5% compounded monthly.
    (a) How much will Cam have in total in his savings account when he finishes his studies?
    (b) How much did he contribute?
    (c) How much will be interest?   Reference Example 11.2E

12. Scott has saved $560 per quarter for the past three years in a savings account earning 5.2% compounded quarterly. He plans to leave the accumulated savings for seven years in the savings account at the same rate of interest.
    (a) How much will Scott have in total in his savings account?
    (b) How much did he contribute?
    (c) How much will be interest?

13. To purchase a specialty guitar for his band, for the past two years J.J. Morrison has made payments of $92 at the end of each month into a savings account earning interest at 4.03% compounded monthly. If he leaves the accumulated money in the savings account for another two years at 5.3% compounded monthly, how much will he have saved to buy the guitar? Reference Example 11.2F

14. For the past 6 years Joe Borelli has made deposits of $300 at the end of every 6 months, earning interest at 5% compounded semi-annually. If he leaves the accumulated balance in an account earning 6% compounded quarterly, what will the balance be in Joe's account at the end of another 10 years?

15. Mariana has been saving $200 per month for the past five years at an interest rate of 1.75% compounded monthly. If she continues to save, but she doubles her payment for the next five years, describe the impact of these double payments on her savings account.

16. Calculate the accumulated value in an RRSP account after 15 years under each of the following scenarios:
    (a) $2400 is invested annually at 10% compounded annually;
    (b) $600 is invested quarterly at 10% compounded quarterly;
    (c) $200 is invested monthly at 10% compounded monthly.

17. Grace already has $10 000 accumulated in her RRSP. If she contributes $1200 at the end of each quarter for the next 10 years, how much will she have in the RRSP at the end of the 10-year period if the interest rate is 3.5% compounded quarterly? How much of the total in the RRSP is interest?

18. For two years, while she was a part-time student, Amy deposited $25 at the end of each month into a travel account paying 4% interest compounded monthly. Once she started her first full-time job, she increased her contributions to $200 per month. How much interest did she earn in the account after four years of contributions of $200?

19. Saving for a new home, a man put aside $1500 at the end of every 3 months for five years while he was single. Once he got married, he and his wife increased the quarterly deposits to $1700 for the next two years. How much did they have in the savings account one year after the last deposit, if the account earned 3.6% compounded quarterly?

11.3 ORDINARY SIMPLE ANNUITY—CALCULATING PRESENT VALUE PV
A. Present value of a series of payments—basic computation

The present value of a series of payments has many uses in business. It can be the amount borrowed in a loan or the initial price of a product or service—less a down payment if applicable. It can be the amount invested at the beginning of a term, from which payments are withdrawn over a series of periods. Being able to calculate the present value of a series of payments is essential.

To calculate the present value of a series of payments, we need to determine the combined present value of the payments at the focal point "now." This can be done using Formula 9.4, $PV = FV(1 + i)^{-n}$.

If the problem involves payments that are not equal, individual calculations are needed to determine the present value of each payment; then, these individual present values are summed to determine the overall present value.

When the payments are equal in size, as shown in Example 11.3A and Figure 11.6, mathematical simplification can be used. The equal payments of $3000 can be taken out as a common factor, and the individual discount factors can be added.

EXAMPLE 11.3A

Calculate the present value of five payments of $3000 made at the end of each of five consecutive years if money is worth 6% compounded annually.

SOLUTION

Figure 11.6 Graphical Representation of Method and Data (© S. A. Hummelbrunner)

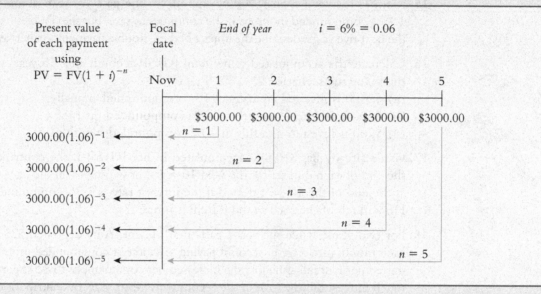

$$\text{Payment 1} \quad 3000.00(1.06)^{-1} = 3000.00(0.943396)$$
$$\text{Payment 2} \quad 3000.00(1.06)^{-2} = 3000.00(0.889996)$$
$$\text{Payment 3} \quad 3000.00(1.06)^{-3} = 3000.00(0.839619)$$
$$\text{Payment 4} \quad 3000.00(1.06)^{-4} = 3000.00(0.792094)$$
$$\text{Payment 5} \quad 3000.00(1.06)^{-5} = \underline{3000.00(0.747258)}$$
$$\text{Sum of the five payments} = 3000.00(4.212363)$$
$$\text{Present value of the five payments} = \$12\ 637.09$$

B. Formula for calculating the present value of an ordinary simple annuity

The present value of an annuity is the sum of the present values of the individual payments using a focal date of $t = 0$. Note that the first payment is made at the end of the first interval. Because annuities are geometric progressions, the following formula for calculating the present value of an ordinary simple annuity has been developed.

$$PV_n = PMT\left[\frac{1 - (1 + i)^{-n}}{i}\right] \text{———— Formula 11.2}$$

where PV_n = the present value (discounted value) of an ordinary simple annuity
  PMT = the size of the periodic payment
    i = the interest rate per conversion period
    n = the number of periodic payments (which for simple annuities equals the number of conversion periods)

The expression $\left[\dfrac{1 - (1 + i)^{-n}}{i}\right]$ is called the present value factor or **discount factor** for annuities, or the **discounted value of one dollar per period**.

EXAMPLE 11.3B   Calculate the present value at the beginning of the first payment period of payments of $50 made at the end of each quarter for 10 years, if interest is 8% compounded quarterly.

SOLUTION   Because the payments are of equal size made at the end of each quarter and compounding is quarterly, the problem is an ordinary simple annuity. Since the focal date is the beginning of the term of the annuity, the formula for calculating the present value of an ordinary simple annuity applies.

Figure 11.7 Graphical Representation of Method and Data (© S. A. Hummelbrunner)

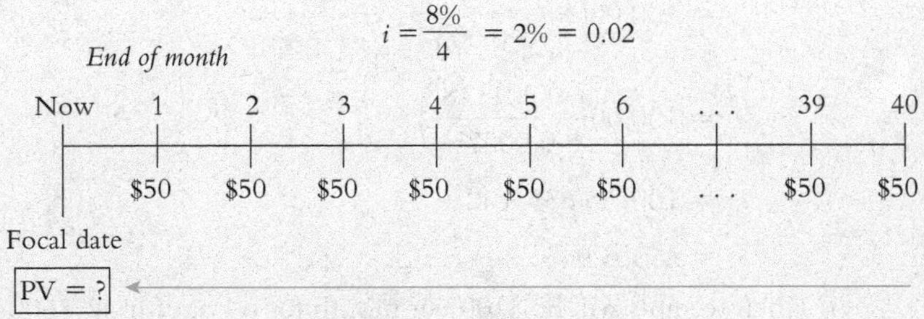

$$i = \frac{8\%}{4} = 2\% = 0.02$$

End of month

Now 1   2   3   4   5   6   . . .   39   40

$50 $50 $50 $50 $50 $50   . . . $50 $50

Focal date

PV = ?

$$PMT = 50.00; \quad I/Y = 8; \quad P/Y, C/Y = 4; \quad i = \frac{8\%}{4} = 2\% = 0.02; \quad n = 10(4) = 40$$

$$PV_n = PMT\left[\frac{1 - (1 + 1)^{-n}}{i}\right] \text{———— Formula 11.2}$$

$$PV = 50.00\left[\frac{1 - (1 + 0.02)^{-40}}{0.02}\right] \text{———— substituting in Formula 11.2}$$

$$= 50.00\left[\frac{1 - 0.452890}{0.02}\right]$$

$$= 50.00(27.355480)$$

$$= \$1367.77$$

EXAMPLE 11.3C   Suppose you want to withdraw $100 at the end of each month for five years from an account paying 4.5% compounded monthly.

  (i) How much must you have on deposit at the beginning of the annuity?

  (ii) How much will you receive in total?

  (iii) How much of what you will receive is interest?

Figure 11.8 Graphical Representation of Method and Data (© S. A. Hummelbrunner)

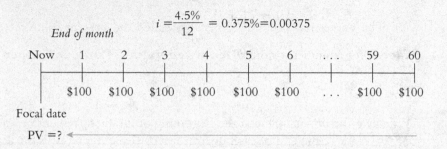

SOLUTION   (i) PMT = 100.00;   I/Y = 4.5;   P/Y, C/Y = 12;

$$i = \frac{4.5\%}{12} = 0.375\% = 0.00375; \quad n = 12(5) = 60$$

$$PV = PMT \left[\frac{1 - (1 + i)^{-n}}{i} \right]$$

$$= 100.00 \left[\frac{1 - (1.00375)^{-60}}{0.00375} \right]$$

$$= 100.00 \left(\frac{0.201148}{0.00375} \right)$$

$$= 100(53.639381)$$

$$= \$5363.94$$

  (ii) Total receipts will be $100 per month for 60 months or $6000.

  (iii) Since the initial balance must be $5363.94, the interest received will be
        6000.00 − 5363.94 = $636.06.

POINTERS
& PITFALLS

The first hurdle in solving future value and present value annuity problems is recognizing *which direction* you are going. Whether you plan to calculate the annuity using formulas or using a financial calculator, you should always start by drawing a timeline diagram showing the payments and payment intervals.

Next, consider the position of the focal date. If you are asked to determine the total amount of principal plus interest that will accumulate *in the future* following a series of regular investments, the focal date is located to the right, after the final payment. Draw an arrow on your diagram indicating that the payments sure accumulating to the right and ending at the point of the focal date. Use the FV annuity formula to calculate the answer.

There tend to be more present value than future value applications in math for finance, and in present value calculations you are asked to determine the value of a series of payments that are yet to come. Common present value applications include determining the original amount of a loan, determining the market value (fair price) of a stream of future payments, and calculating the initial investment required to generate a future withdrawal stream. The focal date is located then to the left, prior to the first payment. Draw an arrow on your diagram indicating that these payments are being discounted to the left at the prevailing interest rate, and ending at the point of the focal date. Use the PV annuity formula to calculate the answer.

C. Present value using preprogrammed financial calculators

To calculate the present value of the ordinary simple annuity in Example 11.3C, in which PMT = 100.00, I/Y = 4.5, P/Y, C/Y = 12, and $n = 60$, proceed as follows.

	Key in	Press	Display shows	
(Set P/Y, C/Y = 12)	0	FV	0	a precaution to clear previous entries
	100	± PMT	−100	
	4.5	I/Y	4.5	
	60	N	60	
	CPT	PV	5363.938035	pressing the PV key retrieves the unknown present value PV_n

You must have $5363.94 on deposit.

POINTERS & PITFALLS

To validate your calculations when using the FV and PV annuity formulas: The value of the accumulation factor in a FV annuity calculation will be larger than the n value whereas the discount factor in a PV annuity calculation will be less than the n value. In Example 11.3C, sixty withdrawals of $100 from an account required an initial deposit of only $5363.94.

D. Applications

When buying a home or vehicle, most people do not have enough money saved to pay the entire price. However, a small initial payment, called a **down payment**, is often accepted in the meantime. A mortgage loan from a financial institution is needed to supply the balance of the purchase price. The larger the down payment, the smaller the amount that needs to be borrowed. Based on the amount borrowed, the rate of interest, and the time to repay, the payments are determined. The amount of the loan is the *present value of the future periodic payments*.

The *cash value* is the price of the property at the date of purchase and represents the dated value of all payments at that date.

CASH VALUE = DOWN PAYMENT + PRESENT VALUE OF THE PERIODIC
(paid now)   PAYMENTS

Analysis of mortgages and amortization of loans is covered in further depth in Chapter 14. Another application of ordinary annuities, interest payments on bonds, is covered in Chapter 15.

EXAMPLE 11.3D

Mr. and Mrs. Hong bought a vacation property, paying $30 000 as a down payment and making further payments of $10 000 every six months for twelve years. If interest is 7% compounded semi-annually, what was the cash value of the property? Calculate the interest paid.

SOLUTION

Since the first ongoing payment is due at the end of the first six-month period and compounding is semi-annual, the present value of an ordinary simple annuity is calculated.

Figure 11.9 Graphical Representation of Method and Data (© S. A. Hummelbrunner)

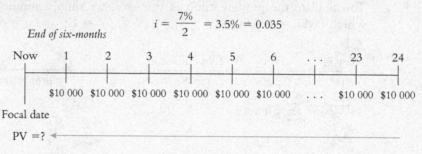

$$PMT = \$10\ 000; \quad I/Y = 7; \quad P/Y, C/Y = 2; \quad i = \frac{7\%}{2} = 3.5\% = 0.035;$$

$$n = 12(2) = 24$$

$$PV = \$10\ 000\left[\frac{(1 - 1.035^{-24})}{0.035}\right]$$

$$= \$10\ 000\left[\frac{(1 - 0.437957)}{0.035}\right]$$

$$= \$10\ 000\left(\frac{0.562043}{0.035}\right)$$

$$= \$10\ 000(16.058368)$$

$$= \$160\ 583.68$$

PROGRAMMED SOLUTION

(Set P/Y, C/Y = 2) 0 [FV] $10 000 [±] [PMT] 7 [I/Y]

24 [N] [CPT] [PV] 160583.6760

The cash value = 30 000 + 160 583.68 = $190 583.68.

Interest paid is the difference between the actual payments and the present value of the annuity. (Interest is charged on the borrowed amount only, not on the down payment.)
Interest = ($10 000)(24) − 160 583.68 = $79 416.32

EXAMPLE 11.3E

Marcello renovated the kitchen in his house to take advantage of a tax rebate program. To pay for the renovations, he arranged a loan whereby he made payments of $288 at the end of every three months for three years. The bank charged interest on the loan at 8.4% compounded quarterly.

(i) How much money was borrowed?

(ii) If the loan was repaid over the three years, how much interest was paid?

SOLUTION

Since the first ongoing payment was due at the end of the first three-month period and compounding was quarterly, the present value of the ordinary simple annuity is calculated.

Figure 11.10 Graphical Representation of Method and Data (© S. A. Hummelbrunner)

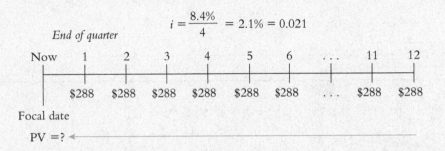

PMT = 288.00;   I/Y = 8.4;   P/Y, C/Y = 4; $i = 8.4\%/4 = 2.1\% = 0.021$; $n = 3(4) = 12$

(i) $PV = 288.00\left[\dfrac{1 - 1.021^{-12}}{0.021}\right] = 288.00(10.510684) = \$3027.08$

PROGRAMMED SOLUTION

(Set P/Y, C/Y = 4) 288 [±] [PMT] 8.4 [I/Y]

12 [N] [CPT] [PV] [3027.077073]

The amount borrowed was $3027.08.

(ii) The interest is the difference between the amount borrowed and the total payments made.

Interest = 288.00(12) − 3027.08 = 3456.00 − 3027.08 = 428.92

The amount of interest paid was $428.92.

EXAMPLE 11.3F

Sheila Davidson borrowed money from her credit union and agreed to repay the loan in blended monthly payments of $161.75 over a four-year period. Interest on the loan was 9% compounded monthly.

(i) How much did she borrow?

(ii) If Sheila did not make the payments in the first year, and if the credit union demanded payment in full, how much money would she need?

(iii) Assuming the situation in part (ii) occurs, what would have been the total cost of the loan?

(iv) If she missed the first 11 payments, how much would she have to pay at the end of the first year to bring her payments up to date?

(v) How much of the total loan cost is additional interest paid on the missed payments?

SOLUTION

(i) The amount borrowed is the present value (or discounted value) of the 48 payments as in the original agreement, as the time diagram shows.

Figure 11.11 Graphical Representation of Method and Data (© S. A. Hummelbrunner)

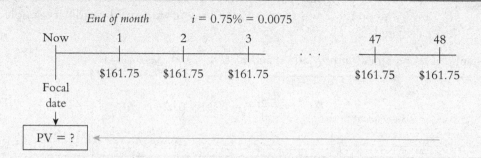

$\text{PMT} = 161.75; \quad \text{I/Y} = 9; \quad \text{P/Y, C/Y} = 12; \quad i = \frac{9\%}{12} = 0.75\% = 0.0075;$

$n = 4(12) = 48$

$\text{PV} = 161.75\left[\frac{(1 - 1.0075^{-48})}{0.0075}\right]$ ———————— using Formula 11.2

$\quad = 161.75\left[\frac{1 - 0.698614}{0.0075}\right]$

$\quad = 161.75(40.184782)$

$\quad = \$6499.89$

PROGRAMMED SOLUTION

Set P/Y, C/Y = 12) 0 [FV] 161.75 [±] [PMT]

9 [I/Y] 48 [N] [CPT] [PV] [6499.898847]

Sheila borrowed $6499.89.

(ii) The sum of money required to pay off the loan in full is the balance owing on the loan after one year. Calculate the future value of the original loan amount, twelve months in the future.

Figure 11.12 Graphical Representation of Method and Data (© S. A. Hummelbrunner)

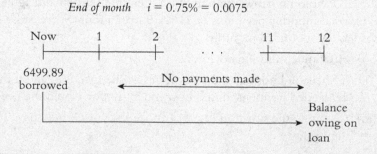

The balance owing can be found using Formula 9.1.

$PV = 6499.89; \quad i = 0.0075; \quad n = 12$

$FV = 6499.89(1 + 0.0075)^{12}$

$\quad = 6499.89(1.0075)^{12}$

$\quad = 6499.89(1.093807)$

$\quad = \$7109.62$

PROGRAMMED SOLUTION

(Set P/Y, C/Y = 12) 6499.89 $\boxed{\text{PV}}$ 0 $\boxed{\text{PMT}}$ 9 $\boxed{\text{I/Y}}$

12 $\boxed{\text{N}}$ $\boxed{\text{CPT}}$ $\boxed{\text{FV}}$ $\boxed{7109.622842}$

The amount of money needed is \$7109.62.

(iii) The total cost of the loan if paid off after one year is the difference between the value of the loan after one year and the original loan balance: $7109.62 - 6499.89 = \$609.73$.

(iv) As the following diagram shows, Sheila Davidson must pay the accumulated value of the first 12 payments to bring her payments up to date after 1 year. Calculate the future value of the first 12 payments.

Figure 11.13 Graphical Representation of Method and Data (© S. A. Hummelbrunner)

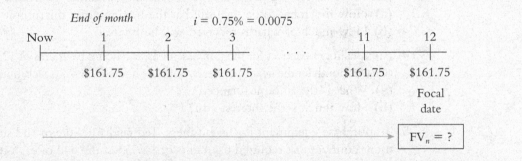

$PMT = 161.75; \quad i = 0.0075; \quad n = 12$

$FV = 161.75\left[\dfrac{(1.0075^{12} - 1)}{0.0075}\right]$ ———————— using Formula 11.1

$\quad = 161.75\left[\dfrac{1.093807 - 1}{0.0075}\right]$

$\quad = 161.75(12.507586)$

$\quad = \$2023.10$

PROGRAMMED SOLUTION

0 $\boxed{\text{PV}}$ 161.75 $\boxed{\pm}$ $\boxed{\text{PMT}}$ 9.0 $\boxed{\text{I/Y}}$ 12 $\boxed{\text{N}}$ $\boxed{\text{CPT}}$ $\boxed{\text{FV}}$ $\boxed{2023.102093}$

She would have to pay \$2023.10.

(v) To bring the payments up to date, \$2023.10 is needed. Since the normal amount paid during the first year would have been $161.75(12) = \$1941.00$, the additional interest paid is $2023.10 - 1941.00 = \$82.10$.

POINTERS & PITFALLS

Calculating the present value when the rate of interest changes during the term of the annuity follows a process similar to Example 11.2F. Divide the problem into multiple terms. The first term covers the annuity during the time of the initial interest rate; the second term covers the annuity during the second interest rate period. Discount the present value of the second annuity as a lump sum, back to the focal date, and then sum these two annuity PVs to determine the total present value.

Similarly, when a payment changes in an annuity, separate the problem into two different annuity calculations, then sum the FV or PV results at the focal date to determine total FV or total PV.

EXERCISE 11.3

MyLab Math

Answer each of the following questions.

1. Calculate the present value of payments of $375 made at the end of every 6 months for 15 years if money is worth 7% compounded semi-annually.   Reference Example 11.3B

2. What is the discounted value of payments of $60 made at the end of each month for nine years if interest is 4.5% compounded monthly?

3. Equipment Inc. agreed to financial terms of $600 payments at the end of every three months for five years. Interest is 7.6% compounded quarterly.
   (a) How much has to be deposited at the beginning of this annuity?
   (b) How much of what is received will be interest?   Reference Example 11.3C

4. An installment contract for the purchase of a car requires payments of $252.17 at the end of each month for the next three years. Suppose interest is 8.4% p.a. compounded monthly.
   (a) What is the amount financed?
   (b) How much is the interest cost?

5. To purchase equipment for his business, Ted paid $400 down and signed an installment contract that required payments of $69.33 at the end of each month for three years. Suppose interest is 10.8% compounded monthly.
   (a) What was the cash price of the equipment?
   (b) How much was the cost of financing?   Reference Example 11.3D

6. New Bread Bakery purchased new equipment by making a down payment of $2000 and agreeing to make payments of $458 at the end of each month for five years. Interest is 9.2% compounded monthly.
   (a) What was the purchase price of the new equipment?
   (b) How much interest will have to be paid?

7. Having earned a bonus at his work, Rick placed the money in an investment earning 4.18% compounded monthly. He withdrew $343 at the end of every month for the next eight years, completely depleting the investment.
   (a) What was the amount of the bonus?
   (b) If he made all of the withdrawals as planned, how much interest was paid?

8. Luisa borrowed funds to buy a piano for her business, Luisa's Music, paying $135 at the end of each month for five years. The bank charges interest on the loan at 8.8% compounded monthly.
   (a) What was the cash price of the piano?
   (b) How much is the cost of financing?   Reference Example 11.3E

9. Wayne borrowed funds to purchase his son's hockey equipment. He made month-end loan payments of $74 for two years on a loan that charges interest at 8.4% compounded monthly. Roberto also borrowed funds to purchase his daughter's hockey equipment. He made loan payments of $244 at the end of each quarter for two years on a loan that charges interest at 6.4% compounded quarterly. What was the cash price of each of the sets of hockey equipment, and which parent paid less?

10. The owners of Cheers in Town, a neighbourhood restaurant, have plans to purchase a new TV. If they finance the purchase through the store's promotional financing option, they will pay $97 at the end of each month for three years, starting with the first month. With the store's promotional financing option, what is the cash price of the TV if the interest rate on the loan is 12.9% compounded monthly?

11. Kimiko signed a loan agreement requiring payments of $234.60 at the end of every month for six years at 7.2% compounded monthly.
   (a) How much was the original loan balance?
   (b) If Kimiko missed the first five payments, how much would she have to pay after six months to bring the payments up to date?
   (c) How much would Kimiko have to pay after six months to pay off the loan (assuming she missed all the payments and there was no late payment penalty)?
   (d) If the loan were paid off after six months, what would the total interest cost be?
   (e) How much of the total interest cost is additional interest because of the missed payments?   Reference Example 11.3F

12. Field Construction agreed to lease payments of $642.79 on construction equipment to be made at the end of each month for three years. Financing is at 9% compounded monthly.
   (a) What is the value of the original lease contract?
   (b) If, due to delays, the first eight payments were deferred, how much money would be needed after nine months to bring the lease payments up to date?
   (c) How much money would be required to pay off the lease after nine months (assuming no payments were made)?
   (d) If the lease were paid off after nine months, what would the total interest be?
   (e) How much of the total interest would be due to deferring the first eight payments?

13. Parth bought an annuity to pay him $2500.00 at the end of every six months for twenty years. How much of the total annuity payments is interest, if interest is 4.5% p.a. compounded semi-annually?

14. A trust fund is set up to make payments of $1000.00 at the end of each quarter for ten years. Interest on the fund is 5% compounded quarterly.
   (a) How much money must be deposited into the fund?
   (b) How much will be paid out of the fund?
   (c) How much interest is earned by the fund?

15. How much will it cost Hitomi to purchase a two-level retirement annuity that will pay $5000 at the end of each month for the first 10 years, and $7000 per month for the following 15 years? The payments include a rate of return to Hitomi of 3% compounded monthly.

16. Calculate the purchase price of an annuity paying $200 per month for 10 years with a lump payment of $2000 on the same day as the last payment of $200, at 6.5% compounded monthly.

17. A loan can be settled by monthly payments of $350 in four years at 5.5% compounded monthly. If the lender sells the loan contract after two years, calculate the selling price if the new buyer's rate of return is:
   (a) 5.5% compounded monthly;
   (b) 5.0% compounded monthly;
   (c) 6.0% compounded monthly.
   (d) Explain the impact on the selling price of a loan contract if the interest rate on the contract increases.

18. Tracey purchased a new car with zero down payment and agreed to make payments of $360 at the end of each month for seven years. After five years, she found she needed a larger vehicle to accommodate her growing family, so she traded the car in to the same dealership for an SUV. Her payments increased to $425 per month. If interest was 4.98% compounded monthly, what was amount she financed?

19. Xavier put $50 000 down on his first condo. He borrowed the rest from his parents at an interest rate of 3.5% compounded weekly. For the first 10 years, he made weekly mortgage payments of $300 before increasing the amount he repaid them to $415 per week for seven more years.
   (a) What was the purchase price of the property?
   (b) How much interest did Xavier pay his parents?

20. The rate of return offered by Sunshine Life Insurance Co. on its 10-year annuity is 4.0% compounded quarterly for the first five years, and 3.75% compounded quarterly for the next five years. What is the purchase price of this annuity if it provides $500 payments at the end of every three months?

21. A grandmother wants to provide an annuity of $2500 payable at the end of every six months during the three years that her grandson attends college. What single deposit must she make today that will finance the annuity, if the grandson will start college in 15 years? Assume she can invest the money at 2.85% compounded semi-annually for the first seven years, and then at 3.0% compounded semi-annually for the next 11 years.

11.4 ORDINARY SIMPLE ANNUITIES—DETERMINING THE PERIODIC PAYMENT PMT
A. Determining the periodic payment PMT when the future value of an annuity is known

If the future value of an annuity, FV_n, the number of conversion periods, n, and the conversion rate, i, are known, you can calculate the periodic payment, PMT, by substituting the given values in the appropriate future value formula and solve algebraically.

For ordinary simple annuities, use Formula 11.1.

$$FV_n = PMT\left[\frac{(1+i)^n - 1}{i}\right]$$ ———— Formula 11.1

As we have emphasized throughout this book, understanding how to rearrange terms in a formula is a very important skill. By knowing how to do this, you can avoid having to memorize equivalent forms of the same formula.

Alternatively:

If you prefer, you can first rearrange the terms of Formula 11.1 to solve for PMT, as shown below.

$$PMT = \left[\frac{FV_n}{\dfrac{(1 + i)^n - 1}{i}} \right]$$

$$\boxed{PMT = \left[\frac{FV_n\, i}{(1 + i)^n - 1} \right]}$$

POINTERS
& PITFALLS

Note that dividing by a fraction is the same as inverting the fraction and multiplying. This can be done using the calculator in two steps. First, calculate the denominator, then press the $\boxed{1/x}$ button to invert the result.

EXAMPLE 11.4A

What deposit made at the end of each quarter will accumulate to $10 000 in four years at 4% compounded quarterly?

SOLUTION

$FV = 10\ 000.00; \ \ I/Y = 4; \ \ P/Y, C/Y = 4; \ \ i = \dfrac{4\%}{4} = 1.0\% = 0.01; \ \ n = 4(4) = 16$

$10\ 000.00 = PMT\left(\dfrac{1.01^{16} - 1}{0.01}\right)$ —————— substituting in Formula 11.1

$10\ 000.00 = PMT\left(\dfrac{1.172579 - 1}{0.01}\right)$

$10\ 000.00 = PMT(17.25786)$

$PMT = \dfrac{10\ 000.00}{17.25786}$

$PMT = \$579.45$

Alternatively:

$FV = 10\ 000.00; \ i = 0.01; \ n = 16$

$PMT = \dfrac{10\ 000.00(0.01)}{1.01^{16} - 1}$ —————— rearranging Formula 11.1 first

$PMT = \$579.45$

When using a preprogrammed financial calculator, you can compute PMT by entering the five known values (FV, N, I/Y, P/Y, and C/Y) and pressing $\boxed{CPT}$ $\boxed{PMT}$.

Recall that the PMT amount will be negative, since payments are considered to be cash outflows.

EXAMPLE 11.4B

If you want to have a $5000 balance in your bank account in three years, how much must you deposit at the end of each month if interest is 4.5% compounded monthly?

SOLUTION

$FV = 5000.00$; $I/Y = 4.5$; $P/Y, C/Y = 12$; $i = \dfrac{4.5}{12} = 0.375\%$; $n = 3(12) = 36$

(Set P/Y = 12) 0 [PV] 5000 [FV]

4.5 [I/Y] 36 [N] [CPT] [PMT] [−129.984622]

The monthly deposit required is $129.98.

B. Determining the periodic payment PMT when the present value of an annuity is known

If the present value of an annuity, PV_n, the number of payment periods, n, and the conversion rate, i, are known and the future value FV equals 0, you can calculate the periodic payment PMT by substituting the given values in the appropriate present value formula and solve algebraically.

For ordinary simple annuities, use Formula 11.2.

$$PV_n = PMT\left[\dfrac{1 - (1 + i)^{-n}}{i}\right] \hspace{2cm} \text{Formula 11.2}$$

Alternatively:

You can first rearrange the terms of Formula 11.2 to solve for PMT.

$$PMT = \left[\dfrac{PV_n}{\dfrac{1 - (1 + i)^{-n}}{i}}\right]$$

$$PMT = \left[\dfrac{PV_n\, i}{1 - (1 + i)^{-n}}\right]$$

When using a preprogrammed financial calculator, you can compute PMT by entering the five known values (PV, N, P/Y, C/Y, and I/Y) and pressing [CPT] [PMT].

EXAMPLE 11.4C

What semi-annual payment at the end of each 6-month period is required to pay off a loan of $8000 in 10 years if interest is 10% compounded semi-annually?

SOLUTION

$PV = 8000.00$; $I/Y = 10$; $P/Y, C/Y = 2$; $i = \dfrac{10\%}{2} = 5\% = 0.05$; $n = 10(2) = 20$

$$8000.00 = PMT\left(\dfrac{1 - 1.05^{-20}}{0.05}\right) \hspace{2cm} \text{substituting in Formula 11.2}$$

$$8000.00 = PMT\left(\dfrac{1 - 0.376889}{0.05}\right)$$

$$8000.00 = PMT(12.462210)$$

$$PMT = \dfrac{8000.00}{12.462210}$$

$$PMT = \$641.94$$

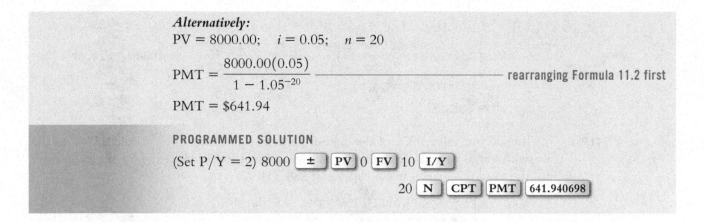

Alternatively:

PV = 8000.00; $i = 0.05$; $n = 20$

$$PMT = \frac{8000.00(0.05)}{1 - 1.05^{-20}}$$ — rearranging Formula 11.2 first

PMT = \$641.94

PROGRAMMED SOLUTION

(Set P/Y = 2) 8000 $\boxed{\pm}$ $\boxed{PV}$ 0 $\boxed{FV}$ 10 $\boxed{I/Y}$

20 $\boxed{N}$ $\boxed{CPT}$ $\boxed{PMT}$ $\boxed{641.940698}$

EXAMPLE 11.4D

Derek bought a new car valued at \$9500.00. He paid \$2000 down and financed the remainder over five years at 9% compounded monthly. How much must Derek pay at the end of each month?

SOLUTION

Remember that the amount financed is the price less the down payment. Therefore, PV = 9500.00 − 2000.00 = 7500.00;   I/Y = 9;   P/Y, C/Y = 12;

$$i = \frac{9\%}{12} = 0.75\%;   n = 60$$

(Set P/Y = 12) 0 $\boxed{FV}$ 7500 $\boxed{\pm}$ $\boxed{PV}$

9 $\boxed{I/Y}$ 60 $\boxed{N}$ $\boxed{CPT}$ $\boxed{PMT}$ $\boxed{155.687664}$

Derek's monthly payment is \$155.69.

EXAMPLE 11.4E

Taylor Marche, now age 37, expects to retire at age 62. To plan for her retirement, she intends to deposit \$1500.00 at the end of each of the next 25 years in a savings plan. After her last contribution, she intends to convert the existing balance into a fund from which she expects to make 20 equal annual withdrawals. If she makes the first withdrawal one year after her last contribution and interest is 6.5% compounded annually, how much is the size of the annual retirement withdrawal?

SOLUTION

As the following time diagram shows, the problem must be separated into two steps.

STEP 1

Compute the *accumulated* value FV_1 of the 25 annual deposits of \$1500.00.

Figure 11.14 Graphical Representation of Method and Data (© S. A. Hummelbrunner)

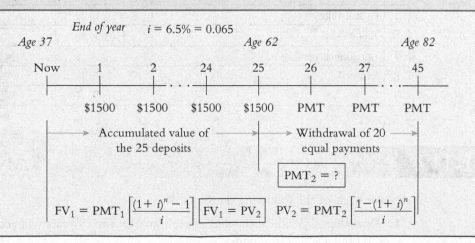

$$PMT_1 = 1500.00; \quad I/Y = 6.5; \quad P/Y = 1; \quad i = 6.5\% = 0.065; \quad n = 25$$

$$FV_1 = 1500.00\left(\frac{1.065^{25} - 1}{0.065}\right) \text{———————— substituting in Formula 11.1}$$

$$= 1500.00(58.887679)$$

$$= \$88\ 331.52$$

STEP 2   The future value, FV_1, of the deposit period becomes the present value, PV_2, of the withdrawal period. Compute the annual payment PMT_2 that can be withdrawn from the fund that has an initial balance of \$88 331.52.

$$FV_1 = PV_2 = 88\ 331.52; \quad i = 0.065; \quad n = 20$$

$$PMT = \left[\frac{88\ 331.52 \times 0.065}{1 - (1 + 0.065)^{-20}}\right] = \frac{5741.5488}{0.716203} = \$8016.65 \text{ ——— using Formula 11.2}$$

PROGRAMMED SOLUTION

STEP 1   (Set P/Y, C/Y = 1) 0 [PV] 1500 [±] [PMT] 6.5 [I/Y]

25 [N] [CPT] [FV] [88331.51788]

STEP 2   88 331.52 [±] [PV] 0 [FV] 6.5 [I/Y] 20 [N] [CPT] [PMT] [8016.650159]

The amount of money that Taylor can withdraw each year is \$8016.65.

(Note: Taylor contributed \$37 500, but she'll be able to withdraw over \$160 000!)

C. Using Excel's PMT Function

If you choose, you can use Excel's PMT (payment) function to answer the questions in this section.

In Example 11.4A, you are required to calculate the periodic deposit. The PMT function in Excel is illustrated below.

	A	B	C
1	PMT Function		
2			
3	**Interest Rate per Compounding Period**	1.00%	
4	**Total Number of Compounding Periods**	16	
5	Present Value	\$0.00	
6	Future Value	−\$10,000.00	
7	Type (Ordinary or Due)	0	
8	Answer	\$579.45	
9			

EXERCISE 11.4   MyLab Math

Answer each of the following questions.

1. What deposit made at the end of each quarter for 15 years will accumulate to
   \$20 000 at 6% compounded quarterly?   Reference Example 11.4B

2. What payment is required at the end of each month for five years to repay a loan of $8000 at 8.4% compounded monthly?

3. A contract can be fulfilled by making an immediate payment of $7500 or equal payments at the end of every 6 months for 10 years. What is the size of the semi-annual payments at 9.6% compounded semi-annually?

4. What payment is required at the end of each month for 12 years to repay a $320 000 mortgage if interest is 6.5% compounded monthly?

5. How much must be deposited at the end of each quarter for nine years to accumulate to $11 000 if interest is 4% compounded quarterly?

6. What payment made at the end of every 6 months for 15 years will accumulate to $18 000 if interest is 5% compounded semi-annually?

7. How much does a depositor have to save at the end of every three months for seven years to accumulate $3500 if interest is 3.75% compounded quarterly?

8. How much would you have to pay into an account at the end of every 6 months to accumulate $10 000 in eight years if interest is 3% compounded semi-annually?

9. Ontario Credit Union entered a lease contract valued at $7200. The contract provides for payments at the end of each quarter for three years. If interest is 6.5% compounded quarterly, what is the size of the quarterly payment?

10. Hunan bought a used car priced at $15 300 for 15% down and equal monthly payments for four years. If interest is 8% compounded monthly, what is the size of the monthly payment?   Reference Example 11.4D

11. Ruben bought a boat valued at $16 500 on the installment plan requiring a $2000 down payment and equal monthly payments for five years. If the first payment is due one month after the date of purchase and interest is 7.5% compounded monthly, what is the size of the monthly payment?

12. Valley Auto sold a used car priced at $10 600 for 10% down and the balance to be paid in equal monthly payments over four years at 7.2% compounded monthly. How much does the buyer have to pay at the end of each month?

13. Watson Properties bought a rental property valued at $250 000 by paying 20% down and mortgaging the balance over 25 years through equal payments at the end of each quarter with interest at 10% compounded quarterly. What was the size of the quarterly payments?

14. Jie & Partners purchased a computer priced at $949.99, financing it by paying $75.12 on the date of purchase, and signing a contract to pay equal monthly payments over the next 15 months. If the terms of the contract state that interest is calculated at 10.8% compounded monthly, how much does Jie & Partners have to pay at the end of each month?

15. George plans to deposit $1200 at the end of every 6 months for 15 years into an RRSP account. After the last deposit, he intends to convert the existing balance into an RRIF and withdraw equal amounts at the end of every 6 months for 20 years. If interest is expected to be 7.5% compounded semi-annually, how much will George be able to collect every 6 months?   Reference Example 11.4E

16. Starting three months after her grandson Robin's birth, Mrs. Devine made deposits of $60 into a trust fund every three months until Robin was 21 years old. The trust fund provides for equal withdrawals at the end of each quarter for four years, beginning three months after the last deposit. If interest is 4.75% compounded quarterly, how much will Robin receive every three months?

17. When his daughter was born, Mr. Dodd started depositing $200 every three months into a trust fund earning 3% compounded quarterly. Following her 18th birthday, Mr. Dodd's daughter is to receive equal payments at the end of each month for four years while she is at university. If interest is to be 3.9% compounded monthly after the daughter's 18th birthday, how much will she receive every month?

18. Mei Li invested $350 at the end of each quarter at 3.2% compounded quarterly. At the end of five years, she was able to withdraw equal amounts at the end of each quarter for nine years. How much is the size of each withdrawal?

19. Mr. Talbot deposits $1500 at the end of every 6 months into his RRSP. He intends to leave the money for 14 years, then transfer the balance into a RRIF and make equal withdrawals at the end of every 6 months for 20 years. If interest is 2.8% compounded semi–annually, what will be the size of each withdrawal?

20. When his aunt died, Ariel inherited an annuity paying $10 000 per year into a savings account for 8 years. The terms of the will state that he cannot withdraw any money for the first 8 years, and then he can withdraw equal amounts at the end of each year for 10 years. If interest is 4.15% compounded annually, what will be the size of each withdrawal?

11.5 DETERMINING THE TERM n OF AN ANNUITY
A. Determining the term n when the future value of an annuity is known

If the future value of an annuity, FV_n, the periodic payment, PMT, and the conversion rate, i, are known, you can determine the term of the annuity, n, by substituting the given values in the appropriate future value formula.

For ordinary simple annuities, use Formula 11.1.

$$FV_n = PMT\left[\frac{(1+i)^n - 1}{i}\right] \text{————————— Formula 11.1}$$

Alternatively:

The procedure for solving for n is more complex in that it requires formula rearrangement and familiarity with logarithms. Therefore, the following formula for solving the term of an annuity has been developed for your use.

$$\frac{FV_n}{PMT} = \frac{(1+i)^n - 1}{i}$$

$$(1+i)^n = \left(\frac{FV_n \times i}{PMT}\right) + 1$$

$$n \ln(1+i) = \ln\left[\left(\frac{FV_n \times i}{PMT}\right) + 1\right]$$

$$n = \frac{\ln\left[\left(\frac{FV_n i}{PMT}\right) + 1\right]}{\ln(1+i)} \text{————————— Formula 11.3}$$

EXAMPLE 11.5A

How long will it take for $200 deposited at the end of each quarter to amount to $5726.70 at 6% compounded quarterly?

SOLUTION

$FV = 5726.70; \ I/Y = 6; \ P/Y, C/Y = 4; \ i = \dfrac{6\%}{4} = 1.5\% = 0.015; \ PMT = 200.00$

$$FV_n = PMT\left[\frac{(1 + i)^n - 1}{i}\right]$$

$5726.70 = 200.00\left[\dfrac{1.015^n - 1}{0.015}\right]$ ——————— substituting in Formula 11.1

$28.6335 = 1.015^n - 1/0.015$ ——————— divide both sides by 200.00

$0.429503 = 1.015^n - 1$ ——————— multiply both sides by 0.015

$1.015^n = 1.429503$ ——————— add 1 to both sides

$n \ln 1.015 = \ln 1.429503$ ——————— solve for n using natural logarithms

$0.014889n = 0.357326$

$n = 0.357326/0.014889 = 23.999985$

$n = 24 \ (\text{quarters})$

Alternatively:

$$n = \frac{\ln\left[\left(\dfrac{FV_n \times i}{PMT}\right) + 1\right]}{\ln(1 + i)}$$

$n = \dfrac{\ln\left[\left(\dfrac{5726.70 \times 0.015}{200.00}\right) + 1\right]}{\ln(1 + 0.015)}$ ——— substituting in Formula 11.3

$n = \dfrac{\ln 1.429503}{\ln 1.015}$

$n = \dfrac{0.357326}{0.014889} = 23.999985$

$n = 24 \ (\text{quarters})$

It will take 24 quarters, or six years, for $200 per quarter to grow to $5726.70.

POINTERS
& PITFALLS

For annuity problems in which the period of investment or loan repayment must be determined, once n has been calculated, round up n and substitute it into Formula 9.3, or simply divide n by m to calculate the period of investment or loan repayment in years. To illustrate, the solution in Example 11.5A is $n = 23.999985$, which is rounded up to $n = 24$. Since $m = 4$ (the question states "at the end of each quarter"), the period of investment is n/m, or $24/4 = 6$ years.

EXAMPLE 11.5B

How many payments will it take for your bank account to grow to $3000 if you deposit $150 at the end of each month and the account earns 9% compounded monthly?

SOLUTION

$FV = 3000.00; \quad PMT = 150.00; \quad I/Y = 9; \quad P/Y, C/Y = 12; \quad i = \dfrac{9\%}{12} = 0.75\%$

(Set P/Y, C/Y = 12) 0 **PV** 3000 **FV**

150 **±** **PMT** 9 **I/Y** **CPT** **N** 18.704720

It will take about 19 payments to accumulate $3000.00.

Interpretation of Result

When FV_n, PMT, and i are known, it is unlikely that n will be a whole number. The fractional time period of 0.7 month indicates that the accumulated value of 18 deposits of $150 will be less than $3000, while the accumulated value of 19 deposits will be more than $3000. This point can be verified by computing FV_{18} and FV_{19}.

$$FV_{18} = 150.00\left(\frac{1.0075^{18} - 1}{0.0075}\right) = 150.00(19.194718) = \$2879.21$$

$$FV_{19} = 150.00\left(\frac{1.0075^{19} - 1}{0.0075}\right) = 150.00(20.338679) = \$3050.80$$

The definition of an annuity does not provide for making payments at unequal time intervals. The appropriate answer to problems in which n is a fractional value is a whole number. The usual approach is to round upward, so in this case $n = 19$.

Rounding upward implies that the deposit made at the end of the 19th month is smaller than the usual deposit of $150.00. The method of computing the size of the final deposit or payment when the term of the annuity is a fractional value rounded upward is considered in Chapter 14 in section 14.3.

POINTERS
& PITFALLS

When determining n for annuity calculations, remember that n represents the number of payments. Therefore, n must be a whole number and should always be rounded upward. Whether a partial or full payment is made, it is still a payment. For example, if $n = 21.34$ payments, this would indicate 21 full payments and a smaller last payment (which is still a payment). Therefore, 22 payments are required.

In most cases, the payment (PMT) has been rounded to 2 decimals. This may cause insignificant decimals to show up in the calculations. As a result, an exception to this rule would be when n is extremely close to a whole number. This would mean that no significant digits show up in the first 2 decimals. For example, if $n = 23.001$, it can be reasonably concluded that n is 23 payments, since the 0.001 is likely a result of the rounded payment.

B. Determining the term n when the present value of an annuity is known

If the present value, PV_n, the periodic payment, PMT, and the conversion rate, i, are known, you can determine the term of the annuity, n, by substituting the given values in the present value formula.

$$FV_n = PMT\left[\frac{1 - (1 + i)^{-n}}{i}\right]$$ ———————— Formula 11.2

Alternatively:

When the present value is known, you can first rearrange the terms of Formula 11.2 to solve for n. A new version of Formula 11.2 is presented here as Formula 11.4.

$$\frac{PV_n}{PMT} = \frac{1 - (1 + i)^{-n}}{i}$$

$$(1 + i)^{-n} = 1 - \left(\frac{PV_n \times i}{PMT}\right)$$

$$-n \ln(1 + i) = \ln\left[1 - \left(\frac{PV_n \times i}{PMT}\right)\right]$$

$$\boxed{n = \frac{\ln\left[1 - \left(\dfrac{PV_n i}{PMT}\right)\right]}{-\ln(1 + i)}} \text{————— Formula 11.4}$$

When using a preprogrammed financial calculator, you can compute n by entering the five known values (PV, PMT, P/Y, C/Y, and I/Y) and pressing $\boxed{\text{CPT}}$ $\boxed{\text{N}}$.

 Note: When using the Texas Instruments BA II PLUS financial calculator, you *must* enter *either* the PV or PMT as a negative amount, *but not both.* Due to the sign conventions used by this calculator, entering *both* PV and PMT as negative amounts or as positive amounts will lead to an *incorrect* final answer. The calculator does *not* indicate that the answer is incorrect or that an entry error was made. (This has not been an issue until now because either PV or PMT was 0 in all the examples previously discussed.) To avoid incorrect answers, *always* enter the PV amount as a negative number and the PMT amount as a positive number when FV = 0 and you are calculating n. However, if PV = 0, enter PMT as a negative number and FV as a positive number. The examples in this text follow these rules. Refer to Appendix II to check whether this step is necessary if you use the Sharp EL-738C or the Hewlett-Packard 10bII+ calculator.

EXAMPLE 11.5C

How many quarterly payments of $600 are required to repay a loan of $5400 at 6% compounded quarterly?

SOLUTION

$PV = 5400.00;\ \ PMT = 600.00;\ \ I/Y = 6;\ \ P/Y, C/Y = 4;\ \ i = \dfrac{6\%}{4} = 1.5\% = 0.015$

$$PV_n = PMT\left[\frac{1 - (1 + i)^{-n}}{i}\right]$$

$$5400.00 = 600.00\left[\frac{1 - 1.015^{-n}}{0.015}\right] \text{————— substituting in Formula 11.2}$$

$$n = \frac{\ln\left[1 - \left(\dfrac{PV_n \times i}{PMT}\right)\right]}{-\ln(1 + i)}$$

$$n = \frac{\ln\left[1 - \left(\dfrac{5400.00 \times 0.015}{600.00}\right)\right]}{-\ln(1.015)} \text{————— substituting in Formula 11.2}$$

$$n = \frac{\ln\left[1 - (0.135)\right]}{-\ln(1.015)}$$

$$n = \frac{\ln 0.865}{-\ln 1.015}$$

$$n = \frac{-0.145026}{-0.014889}$$

$$n = 9.740718$$

$$n = 10 \text{ quarters}$$

To repay the loan, 10 quarterly payments are required.

POINTERS & PITFALLS

By definition, annuity payments or withdrawals occur at regularly scheduled intervals. Rounding up n will adjust the time correctly to the next annuity payment period. If the problem asks you to solve for the term of the annuity (in years and/or months) rather than solving for the number of payments, and you find that once you've converted n to years you have a non-integer value, then you can simply convert the fractional part of that final year to months by multiplying it by 12 (months). Common practice is to allow a full payment period for the final partial payment. For example, if your calculations show $n = 18.704720$ (months), then round up to $n = 19$ payments. In time, that is $19/12 = 1.583$ years or 1 year, 7 months.

EXAMPLE 11.5D

On his retirement, Art received a bonus of $8000 from his employer. Taking advantage of the existing tax legislation, he invested the money in an annuity that provides for semi-annual payments of $1200 at the end of every six months. If interest is 6.25% compounded semi-annually, how long will the annuity exist? What is the amount of Art's final payment?

SOLUTION

$PV = 8000.00$; $PMT = 1200.00$; $I/Y = 6.25$; $P/Y, C/Y = 2$; $i = \dfrac{6.25\%}{2} = 3.125\%$

(Set P/Y, C/Y = 2)0 [FV] 8000 [±] [PV]

1200 [PMT] 6.25 [I/Y] [CPT] [N] [7.591884]

$$n = 7.591884 = 8 \text{ payments} \div 2 = 4 \text{ years}$$

half-year periods

The annuity will be in existence for four years. Art will receive seven half-yearly payments of $1200 and a final payment that will be less than $1200.

Using the PV annuity formula, the PV of the seven half-yearly payments is $7441.24. Therefore the PV of the smaller concluding payment is $558.76 ($8000 − $7441.24). Substituting $558.76 into the lump sum PV formula with $n = 8$ results in a final partial payment of $714.72 at the end of the fourth year.

POINTERS & PITFALLS

In FV annuity calculations, when determining the number of payments required to reach a specific goal (e.g., to save $1 million), we have to check if the *smaller final* contribution is even necessary, particularly if we have a favourable (*high*) interest rate and a large balance following the *last full* contribution. Sometimes the interest after the last full payment will generate enough value to equal or exceed the required balance by the end of the term.

EXERCISE 11.5

Answer each of the following questions.

1. How many months would it take for you to save $4500 by making deposits of $50 at the end of every month into a savings account earning 6% compounded monthly?
   Reference Example 11.5A

2. How many months will it take to save $5000 by making deposits of $60 at the end of every month into an account earning interest at 6% monthly?

3. Suppose $646.56 is deposited at the end of every six months into an account earning 6.5% compounded semi-annually. If the balance in the account four years after the last deposit is to be $20 000, how many deposits are needed?

4. How long does $1000 have to be deposited into a savings account at the end of each month to accumulate to $36 000 if interest is 6.4% compounded monthly?

5. Through a payroll savings plan, Brooke saved $96 at the end of each month. If the account earns interest at 3.6% compounded monthly, how long will it take to save $3600?

6. For how long will Amir need to make payments of $400 at the end of every three months to save a total of $5000 if interest is 1.7% compounded quarterly?

7. Josie borrowed $8000 compounded monthly to help finance her education. She contracted to repay the loan in monthly payments of $300 each. If the payments are due at the end of each month and interest is 4% compounded monthly, how long will Josie have to make monthly payments?

8. A mortgage of $265 000 is to be repaid by making payments of $15 600 at the end of every six months. If interest is 7% compounded semi-annually, what is the term of the mortgage?

9. A car loan of $12 000 is to be repaid with end-of-month payments of $292.96. If interest is 8% compounded monthly, how long is the term of the loan?

10. A deposit of $4000 is made today. For how long can $500 be withdrawn from the account at the end of every three months starting three months from now if interest is 4% compounded quarterly?
    Reference Example 11.5D

11. Lauren deposited $12 000 today. He plans to withdraw $1100 every six months. For how long can he withdraw from the account starting six months from now if interest is 3.9% compounded semi-annually?

12. Cathy placed $7000 into a savings account. For how long can $800 be withdrawn from the account at the end of every month starting one month from now if interest is 4.58% compounded monthly?

13. Rae deposited $5741, the earnings from her part-time job, into a savings account. If she withdraws $650 at the end of each month, how long will the money last if interest is 5.15% compounded monthly?

14. Kaye deposited $6000 into a savings account today. For how long can $730 be withdrawn from the account at the end of every three months starting three months from now if interest is 3.9% compounded quarterly?

15. A car loan of $22 000 is to be repaid with bi-weekly payments of $195. How many payments are required to repay the loan at 4.8% compounded bi-weekly? What is the size of the final payment?

16. If money can earn 4.0% compounded monthly, how long will it take you to accumulate $1 million in your RRSP if you contribute $1440 at the end of each month? What is the size of your last contribution?

BUSINESS MATH **NEWS**
Credit Card Minimum Payment Myths—How to Avoid the Pitfalls

Many Canadian banks and financial institutions have made it fairly easy for patrons to apply for and obtain their first credit card. Credit cards are a popular and convenient method of payment. When used responsibly, credit cards can help new users such as students establish a good credit history, which may benefit them when they need a loan or mortgage in the future.

However, a credit card comes with inherent risks that post-secondary students might not immediately recognize.

Myth #1—Minimum payments will get you out of debt.

Before you apply for your first (or second, or third) credit card, consider the example depicted in the info graphic below.

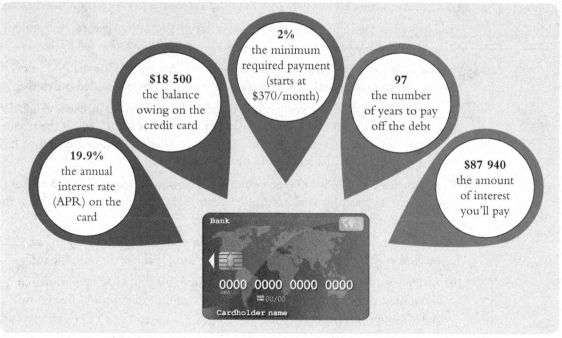

19.9% the annual interest rate (APR) on the card

$18 500 the balance owing on the credit card

2% the minimum required payment (starts at $370/month)

97 the number of years to pay off the debt

$87 940 the amount of interest you'll pay

Source: www.mymoneycoach.ca

Myth #2—A lender will only lend me what I can afford to repay.

Lenders base their calculations on your gross income (before tax), which is typically 20–30% higher than your take-home pay. What about emergencies? *Only you know what you can afford.*

Myth #3—Skipping payments isn't a big deal.

This simply isn't true! Skipping payments breaches the contract and can cause the lender to call out the full amount of the loan. *If you must skip a payment, contact your lender immediately to work out a recovery plan. Ignoring your creditors will make the situation worse. Accepting a credit card is a legal agreement and creditors have the right to sue and collect the amount you owe.*

Let's go back to the original example. If you find you can't pay your credit card off *in full* each month, then making slightly larger *fixed* payments will make a significant difference in terms of how long it will take you to pay off your credit card debt. Given the same $18 500 balance, and the same 19.9% annual interest rate, observe the impact of a $500 *fixed* payment made each month:

- 4.9—the number of years to pay off the debt
- $10 406—the amount of interest you'll pay (that's about $77 500 less than the interest based on the minimum payment!)

QUESTIONS

1. What fixed monthly payment is required to pay off a $5000 credit card balance in three years if the interest rate is 21.1% compounded monthly?

2. What is the amount of interest you will pay?

3. If you were to increase your fixed payment on this same $5000 debt to $500 per month, how much less interest would you pay?

4. How long would it take you to pay off the debt?

Sources: https://www.mymoneycoach.ca, accessed March 18, 2019; https://the province.com, accessed March 18, 2019.

11.6 CALCULATING THE PERIODIC RATE OF INTEREST *i* USING PREPROGRAMMED FINANCIAL CALCULATORS

A. Calculating the periodic rate of interest *i* for simple annuities

Preprogrammed financial calculators are especially helpful when solving for the conversion rate *i*. Determining *i* without a financial calculator is extremely time-consuming. However, it *can* be done by hand using the trial and error method.

When the future value, FV, or present value, PV, the periodic payment, PMT, and the term, *n*, of an annuity are known, the periodic rate of interest, *i*, can be determined by entering the three known values into a preprogrammed financial calculator. (Recall, if both PV and PMT are non-zero, enter PV only as a negative amount.) For ordinary simple annuities, retrieve the answer by pressing $\boxed{\text{CPT}}$ $\boxed{\text{I/Y}}$. This represents the nominal annual rate of interest, *j*. By dividing *j* by the number of compounding periods per year, *m* or C/Y, you can obtain the periodic interest rate, *i*.

EXAMPLE 11.6A

Compute the nominal annual rate of interest compounded monthly at which $100 deposited at the end of every month for 10 years will accumulate to $15 000.

SOLUTION

$FV_n = 15\ 000.00$; $PMT = 100.00$; $P/Y, C/Y = 12$; $n = 120$; $m = 12$

(Set P/Y, C/Y = 12) 0 $\boxed{\text{PV}}$ 15 000 $\boxed{\text{FV}}$ 100 $\boxed{\pm}$ $\boxed{\text{PMT}}$

120 $\boxed{\text{N}}$ $\boxed{\text{CPT}}$ $\boxed{\text{I/Y}}$ $\boxed{\text{4.350057}}$

↑
Allow several seconds
for the computation.

The nominal annual rate of interest is 4.3501% compounded monthly. The monthly conversion rate, *i*, is approximately 4.3501/12 = 0.362505%.

EXAMPLE 11.6B

A loan of $6000 is paid back over five years by weekly payments of $25. What is the nominal annual rate of interest compounded weekly on the loan?

SOLUTION

$PV_n = 6000.00$; $PMT = 25$; $P/Y, C/Y = 52$; $n = 260$; $m = 12$

(Set P/Y, C/Y = 52) 0 $\boxed{\text{FV}}$ 6000 $\boxed{\pm}$ $\boxed{\text{PV}}$ 25 $\boxed{\text{PMT}}$

260 $\boxed{\text{N}}$ $\boxed{\text{CPT}}$ $\boxed{\text{I/Y}}$ $\boxed{\text{3.233816}}$

↑
Allow several seconds
for the computation.

The nominal annual rate of interest is 3.233816% compounded weekly. The weekly compounding rate, *i*, is approximately 3.233816/52 = 0.062189%.

Answer each of the following questions.

1. Compute the nominal annual rate of interest compounded quarterly at which $350 paid at the end of every three months for six years accumulates to $12 239.76.

   Reference Example 11.6A

2. Katrina contributed $2500 at the end of every year into an RRSP for 10 years. What nominal annual rate of interest will the RRSP earn if the balance in Katrina's account just after she made her last contribution was $33 600?

3. What nominal annual rate of interest compounded monthly was paid if contributions of $250 made into an RRSP at the end of every month amounted to $35 000 after 10 years?

4. Compute the nominal annual rate of interest compounded monthly at which $400 paid at the end of the month for eight years accumulates to $45 000.

5. What is the nominal interest rate compounded monthly if a four-year loan of $6000 is repaid by end-of-month payments of $144.23?

   Reference Example 11.6B

6. Rita converted an RRSP balance of $119 875.67 into a RRIF that will pay her $1800 at the end of every month for nine years. What is the nominal annual rate of interest compounded monthly?

7. What is the nominal annual rate of interest compounded quarterly if a loan of $21 500 is repaid over seven years by payments of $1000 made at the end of every three months?

8. A car valued at $11 400 can be purchased for 10% down and end-of-month payments of $286.21 for three-and-a-half years. What is the nominal annual rate of interest compounded monthly?

9. Property worth $50 000 can be purchased for 20% down and mortgage payments of $1000 at the end of each quarter for 25 years. What nominal annual interest rate compounded quarterly is charged?

10. A property worth $35 000 is purchased for 10% down and payments of $2100 at the end of every 6 months for 12 years. What is the nominal annual rate of interest compounded semi-annually?

11. What is the effective annual rate of interest on a loan of $9000.00 repaid in semi-annual installments of $725.00 in nine years?

12. On his retirement, Rob received a lump sum of $300 000 from his employer. Taking advantage of existing tax legislation, he invested his money in an annuity that provides for payments of $20 000 at the end of every 3 months. If interest is 4.25% compounded quarterly, how long will the annuity exist?

13. A $5000 bond that pays 7% semi-annually is redeemable at par in 15 years. Calculate the purchase price if it is sold to yield 5% compounded semi-annually (Purchase price of a bond is equal to the present value of the redemption price plus the present value of the interest payments).

MyLab Math   Visit MyLab Math to practise any of this chapter's exercises marked with a 🌐 as often as you want. The guided solutions help you calculate an answer step by step. You'll find a personalized study plan and additional interactive resources to help you master Business Math!

REVIEW EXERCISE

1. **LO②** Payments of $360 are made into a fund at the end of every 3 months for 12 years. The fund earns interest at 7% compounded quarterly.

   (a) What will be the balance in the fund after 12 years?

   (b) How much of the balance is deposits?

   (c) How much of the balance is interest?

🌐 2. **LO③** Pearson sets up a fund to pay $1000 at the end of each month for 9.5 years. Interest on the fund is 3.9% compounded monthly.

   (a) How much money must be deposited into the fund?

   (b) How much will be paid out of the fund?

   (c) How much interest is earned by the fund?

3. **LO⑤** How long will it take to build up a fund of $10 000 by saving $300 at the end of every 6 months at 4.5% compounded semi-annually?

4. **LO④** Maria has set a goal to save $10 000 in a savings account that earns 2.4% compounded annually. How much must she deposit each year for five years if the deposits are made at the end of each year?

🌐 5. **LO④** A fund of $30 000 has been set up to pay for Edwin's music lessons over the next 12 years. If interest is 6.21% compounded monthly, what is the size of each month-end withdrawal from the fund?

6. **LO②** If you contribute $1500 into a vacation account at the end of every six months for four years and interest on the deposits is 4.26% compounded semi-annually, how much would the balance in the account be six years after the last contribution?

🌐 7. **LO③** Doris purchased a piano with $300 down and end-of-month payments of $124 for two-and-a-half years at 9% compounded monthly. What was the purchase price of the piano?

🌐 8. **LO⑤** A contract valued at $11 500 requires payment of $1450 at the end of every six months. If interest is 10.5% compounded semi-annually, what is the term of the contract?

🌐 9. **LO⑥** What nominal annual rate of interest is paid on RRSP contributions of $1100 made at the end of each quarter for 15 years if the balance just after the last contribution is $106 000?

10. **LO⑥** What nominal annual rate of interest was charged on a loan of $5600 repaid in end-of-month installments of $121.85 in four-and-a-half years?

🌐 11. **LO②④** Glenn has made contributions of $250 at the end of every 3 months into an RRSP for 10 years. Interest for the first 10 years was 4% compounded quarterly.

   (a) What is the amount in the RRSP after the first 10 years?

   (b) After the first 10 years, Glenn stopped making contributions. The interest rate changed to 5% compounded monthly. How much will Glenn have in his RRSP three years after the last contribution?

   (c) Suppose Glenn then decides to withdraw the money from his RRSP. How much will he be able to withdraw in monthly amounts over the next 10 years?

12. **LO③** Avi expects to retire in 12 years. Beginning one month after his retirement he would like to receive $500 per month for 20 years. How much must he deposit into a fund today to be able to do so if the rate of interest on the deposit is 6% compounded monthly?

13. **LO②⑤** The amount of $10 000 is put into a four-year term deposit paying 3.5% compounded semi-annually. After four years the deposit is converted into an ordinary annuity of equal semi-annual payments of $932 each. If the interest rate remains the same, what is the term of the annuity?

🌐 14. **LO②⑥** Harleen has deposited $125 at the end of each month for 13 years at 4.68% compounded monthly. After her last deposit she converted the balance into an ordinary annuity paying $890 every three months for nine years. What is the nominal annual rate of interest compounded quarterly paid by the annuity?

🌐 **15. LO❺❻** Over 14 years, Casey has saved $7200 by authorizing $30 to be deducted at the end of every month through a payroll deduction plan at his work. The money was sent to his savings account to be invested.

(a) What is the nominal annual rate of interest compounded monthly on the savings plan?

(b) If, after the 14 years, he withdraws $135 at the end of each month, what is the term of the annuity?

SELF-TEST

1. You won $100 000 in a lottery and you want to set some of that sum aside for 10 years. After 10 years, you would like to receive $2400 at the end of every 3 months for 8 years. How much of your winnings must you set aside if interest is 5.5% compounded quarterly?

2. A sum of money is deposited at the end of every month for 10 years at 7.5% compounded monthly. After the last deposit, interest for the account is to be 6% compounded quarterly and the account is to be paid out by quarterly payments of $4800 over six years. What is the size of the monthly deposit?

3. Compute the nominal annual rate of interest compounded semi-annually on a loan of $48 000 repaid in installments of $4000 at the end of every 6 months in 10 years.

4. A loan of $14 400 is to be repaid in end-of-the-quarter payments of $600. How many payments are required to repay the loan at 10.5% compounded quarterly?

5. The amount of $574 is invested monthly at 6% compounded monthly for six years. The balance in the fund is then converted into an annuity paying $3600 at the end of every three months. If interest on the annuity is 5.9% compounded quarterly, for how many months is the term of the annuity?

6. A loan was repaid over seven years by end-of-month payments of $450. If interest was 12% compounded monthly, how much interest was paid?

7. Ms. Simms made deposits of $540 at the end of every three months into a savings account. For the first five years interest was 5% compounded quarterly. Since then the rate of interest has been 5.5% compounded quarterly. How much is the account balance after 13 years?

8. How much interest is included in the accumulated value of $3200 paid at the end of every six months for four years if the interest rate is 6.5% compounded semi-annually?

9. What is the size of deposits made at the end of each period that will accumulate to $67 200 after eight years at 6.5% compounded semi-annually?

CHALLENGE PROBLEMS

1. In March 2020, Yves decided to save for a new truck. He deposited $500 at the end of every three months in a bank account earning interest at 5% compounded quarterly. He made his first deposit on June 1, 2020. On June 1, 2022, Yves decided that he needed the money to go to college, so on September 1, 2022, rather than making deposits, he started withdrawing $300 at the end of each quarter until December 1, 2023. How much is left in his account after the last with-

drawal if his bank account interest rate changed to 6.5% compounded quarterly on March 1, 2023?

2. Nicole has just turned 41 and has accumulated $24 500 in her RRSP. She makes month-end contributions of $400 to the plan and intends to do so until she retires at the age of 60. The RRSP will be allowed to continue to accumulate until she reaches the age of 65. If the RRSP earns 6% compounded monthly for the next 24 years, how much will her RRSP contain when she turns 65?

CASE STUDY   # Getting the Picture

▶ Suzanne had a summer job working in the business office of Blast-It TV and Stereo, a local chain of home electronics stores. When Michael Jacobssen, the owner of the chain, heard she had completed one year of business courses, he asked Suzanne to calculate the profitability of two new large-screen televisions. He plans to offer a special payment plan for the two new models to attract customers to his stores. He wants to heavily promote the more profitable TV.

When Michael gave Suzanne the information about the two TVs, he told her to ignore all taxes when making her calculations. The cost of television A to the company is $1950 and the cost of television B to the company is $2160, after all trade discounts have been applied. The company plans to sell television A for a $500 down payment and $230 per month for 12 months, beginning one month from the date of the purchase. The company plans to sell television B for a $100 down payment and $260 per month for 18 months, beginning one month from the date of purchase. The monthly payments for both TVs reflect an interest rate of 15.5% compounded monthly.

Michael wants Suzanne to calculate the profit of television A and television B as a percent of the TV's cost to the company. To calculate profit, Michael deducts overhead (which he calculates as 15% of cost) and the cost of the item from the selling price of the item. When he sells items that are paid for at a later time, he calculates the selling price as the *cash value* of the item. (Remember that cash value equals the down payment plus the present value of the periodic payments.)

Suzanne realized that she could calculate the profitability of each television by using her knowledge of ordinary annuities. She went to work on her assignment to provide Michael with the information he requested.

QUESTIONS

1. (a) What is the cash value of television A? Round your answer to the nearest dollar.
   (b) What is the cash value of television B? Round your answer to the nearest dollar.

2. (a) Given Michael's system of calculations, how much overhead should be assigned to television A?
   (b) How much overhead should be assigned to television B?

3. (a) According to Michael's system of calculations, what is the profit of television A as a percent of its cost?
   (b) What is the profit of television B as a percent of its cost?
   (c) Which TV should Suzanne recommend be more heavily promoted?

4. Three months later, due to Blast-It's successful sales of television A and television B, the suppliers of each model gave the company new volume discounts. For television A, Blast-It received a discount of 9% off its current cost, and for television B one of 6%. The special payment plans for television A and television B will stay the same. Under these new conditions, which TV should Suzanne recommend be more heavily promoted?

SUMMARY OF FORMULAS

Formula 9.1
$$FV = PV(1 + i)^n$$

Calculating the future value of a compound amount (maturity value) when the original principal, the rate of interest, and the time period are known

Formula 9.4
$$PV = FV(1 + i)^{-n}$$

Calculating the present value by means of the discount factor (the reciprocal of the compounding factor)

Formula 11.1
$$FV_n = PMT\left[\frac{(1 + i)^n - 1}{i}\right]$$

Calculating the future value (accumulated value) of an ordinary simple annuity

Can be rearranged to:
$$PMT = \left[\frac{FV_n\, i}{(1 + i)^n - 1}\right]$$

Determining the amount of the payment of an ordinary simple annuity when the future value is known

Formula 11.2
$$PV_n = PMT\left[\frac{1 - (1 + i)^{-n}}{i}\right]$$

Calculating the present value (discounted value) of an ordinary simple annuity

Can be rearranged to:
$$PMT = \left[\frac{PV_n\, i}{1 - (1 + i)^{-n}}\right]$$

Determining the amount of the payment of an ordinary simple annuity when the present value is known

Formula 11.3
$$n = \frac{\ln\left[\left(\dfrac{FV_n\, i}{PMT}\right) + 1\right]}{\ln (1 + i)}$$

Determining the number of payments of an ordinary simple annuity when the future value is known

Formula 11.4
$$n = \frac{\ln\left[1 - \left(\dfrac{PV_n\, i}{PMT}\right)\right]}{-\ln (1 + i)}$$

Determining the number of payments of an ordinary simple annuity when the present value is known

GLOSSARY

Accumulated value of one dollar per period *see* **Accumulation factor for annuities**

Accumulation factor for annuities the expression $\left[\dfrac{(1+i)^n - 1}{i}\right]$ *(p. 422)*

Annuity a series of payments, usually equal in size, made at equal periodic time intervals *(p. 418)*

Annuity certain an annuity for which the term is fixed *(p. 419)*

Annuity due an annuity in which the periodic payments are made at the beginning of each payment interval *(p. 418)*

Compounding factor for annuities *see* **Accumulation factor for annuities**

Contingent annuity an annuity in which the term is uncertain; that is, either the beginning date of the term or the ending date of the term or both are unknown *(p. 419)*

Deferred annuity an annuity in which the first payment is delayed for a number of payment periods *(p. 419)*

Discount factor the expression $\left[\dfrac{1 - (1+i)^{-n}}{i}\right]$

(p. 433)

Discounted value of one dollar per period *see* **Discount factor**

Down payment the portion of the purchase price that is supplied by the purchaser as an initial payment *(p. 435)*

General annuity an annuity in which the conversion (or compounding) period is different from the payment interval *(p. 419)*

Ordinary annuity an annuity in which the payments are made at the end of each payment interval *(p. 418)*

Payment interval the length of time between successive payments *(p. 418)*

Payment period *see* **Payment interval**

Periodic payment the size of the regular periodic payment *(p. 418)*

Periodic rent *see* **Periodic payment**

Perpetuity an annuity for which the payments continue forever *(p. 419)*

Simple annuity an annuity in which the conversion period is the same as the payment interval *(p. 418)*

Term of an annuity the length of time from the beginning of the first payment interval to the end of the last payment interval *(p. 418)*

12

Ordinary General Annuities

LEARNING OBJECTIVES

Upon completing this chapter, you will be able to do the following:

① Compute the future value (or accumulated value) for ordinary general annuities.

② Compute the present value (or discounted value) for ordinary general annuities.

③ Compute the payment for ordinary general annuities.

④ Compute the number of periods for ordinary general annuities.

⑤ Compute the interest rate for ordinary general annuities.

⑥ Compute future value and present value for constant-growth annuities.

Ariel Skelley/Digital Vision/Getty images

A general annuity is defined as an annuity in which the length of the payment interval is not the same as the length of the interest conversion interval. If the payment is made at the end of the period, the annuity is an ordinary general annuity.

A home (residential) mortgage in which there are monthly payments with semi-annual compounding of interest is a common example of a general annuity. Contracts between insurance companies and customers, and investments in income-producing products can also take the form of general annuities.

You are about to make an investment in a company that will pay you an annual amount for the next few years. You plan to deposit this money into an account that pays interest weekly. In this situation, the frequency of interest compounding is not the same as the frequency of the payment in an annuity. To calculate a future value or a present value for this investment, we will have to adjust the interest rate to reflect the rate per annual payment period.

To manage financial obligations and to measure the growth of companies, it is essential to understand the effects of payment and compounding frequencies. Informed decisions result from an understanding of annuities, even when the frequency of interest compounding is not the same as the frequency of payment.

INTRODUCTION

In Chapter 11, we calculated values for ordinary simple annuities. In this chapter, we will calculate the future value, present value, payment, term, and interest rate for ordinary general annuities. The relationship between the payment interval and the interest conversion period will be analyzed. New formulas for ordinary general annuities will be introduced, and rearranged. Alternatively, preprogrammed calculators will be used to determine results.

12.1 ORDINARY GENERAL ANNUITIES—CALCULATING THE FUTURE VALUE FV

A. Basic concepts and computation

With ordinary simple annuities, as in Chapter 11, the payment interval and the interest conversion period are the same length. Often, however, interest is compounded more or less frequently than payments are made. For example, payments may be made weekly or monthly, whereas interest may be compounded less frequently, such as annually.

When the length of the interest conversion period is different from the length of the payment interval, these annuities are called *general annuities*.

To solve compound interest problems, the basic method uses equivalent sets of financial obligations at a selected focal date. The essential tool when dealing with any kind of annuity is the equation of value. This approach is used to make basic computations and develop useful formulas.

EXAMPLE 12.1A

What is the accumulated value of $100 deposited at the end of every six months for three years if interest is 4% compounded annually?

SOLUTION

Since the payments are made semi-annually while the compounding is done annually, this annuity is classified as a general annuity. Furthermore, since the payments are at the end of each payment interval, the annuity is an ordinary general annuity. While the difference in the length of the payment period compared to the length of the compounding period introduces a mathematical complication, the basic approach to calculating the amount of the ordinary general annuity is the same as that used in calculating the amount of an ordinary simple annuity.

The solution and data for the problem are shown graphically in Figure 12.1. Since deposits are made at the end of every six months for three years, there are six deposits of $100 at the times indicated. Because interest is compounded annually, I/Y = 4%, P/Y = 2, C/Y = 1, $i = 4\% = 0.04$ and there are three conversion periods.

The focal point is at the end of Year 3. The last deposit is made at the focal date and has a value of $100 on that date. The fifth deposit is made after 2.5 years and, in terms of conversion periods, has accumulated for a half conversion period ($n = 0.5$); its accumulated value is $100.00(1.04^{0.5}) = \$101.98$ at the focal date.

The fourth deposit made after two years has accumulated for one conversion period ($n = 1.0$); its accumulated value at the focal date is $100.00(1.04^{1.0}) = \$104.00$. Similarly, the accumulated value of the third deposit is $100.00(1.04^{1.5}) = \$106.06$, while the accumulated value of the second deposit is $100.00(1.04^{2.0}) = \$108.16$. Finally, the accumulated value of the first deposit is $100.00(1.04^{2.5}) = \$110.30$. The total accumulated value after three years is $630.50.

Figure 12.1 Graphical Representation of Method and Data (© S. A. Hummelbrunner)

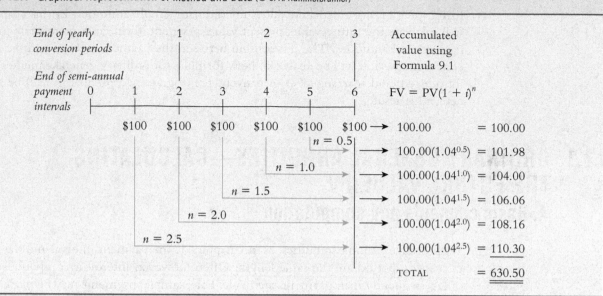

EXAMPLE 12.1B

What is the accumulated value of deposits of $100 made at the end of each year for four years if interest is 4% compounded quarterly?

SOLUTION

Since the deposits are made at the end of every year for four years, there are four payments of $100.00 at the times shown in Figure 12.2. Since interest is compounded quarterly, I/Y = 4, P/Y = 1, C/Y = 4, $i = \frac{4}{4}\% = 1\% = 0.01$, and there are $4(4) = 16$ conversion periods.

Figure 12.2 Graphical Representation of Method and Data (© S. A. Hummelbrunner)

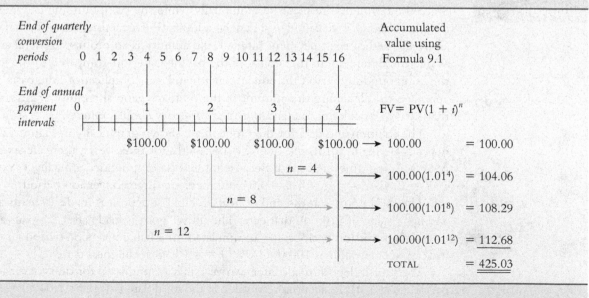

The focal point is the end of Year 4. The last payment is made at the focal point and has a value of $100 at that date. The third payment is made after three years and, in terms of conversion periods, has accumulated for four conversion periods ($n = 4$); its accumulated value is $100.00(1.01^4) = \$104.06$. The second deposit has accumulated for 8 conversion periods ($n = 8$); its accumulated value is $100.00(1.018) = \$108.29$. The first deposit has accumulated for 12 conversion periods ($n = 12$); its accumulated value is $100.00(1.0112) = \$112.68$. The total accumulated value of the deposits after four years is $425.03.

B. Relationship between payment interval and interest conversion period

It is important to understand the relationship between the *payment interval* and the number of *interest conversion periods* per payment interval.

As defined in Chapter 11, the length of time between the successive payments is called the payment interval or payment period. The numbe r of interest conversion periods per payment interval, designated by the letter c, can be determined from the following ratio:

$$c = \frac{\text{THE NUMBER OF INTEREST CONVERSION PERIODS PER YEAR}}{\text{THE NUMBER OF PAYMENT PERIODS PER YEAR}}$$

If the interest conversion period is longer than the payment period, each payment interval contains only a fraction of one conversion period. In this case, c has a fractional value.

If the interest conversion period is shorter than the payment period, each payment interval contains more than one conversion period. In this case, c has a value greater than 1.

Table 12.1 provides a sampling of possible combinations of payment intervals and interest conversion periods you might encounter when dealing with general annuities. One of the most important is the monthly payment interval combined with semi-annual compounding, since this combination is usually encountered with residential mortgages in Canada.

Table 12.1 Some Possible Combinations of Payment Intervals and Interest Conversion Periods

Numerator: Interest Conversion Period	Denominator: Payment Interval	Number of Interest Conversion Periods per Payment Interval
monthly	semi-annually	$c = \frac{12}{2} = 6$
monthly	quarterly	$c = \frac{12}{4} = 3$
quarterly	annually	$c = \frac{4}{1} = 4$
annually	semi-annually	$c = \frac{1}{2} = 0.5$
annually	quarterly	$c = \frac{1}{4} = 0.25$
semi-annually	monthly	$c = \frac{2}{12} = \frac{1}{6}$
quarterly	monthly	$c = \frac{4}{12} = \frac{1}{3}$
annually	monthly	$c = \frac{1}{12}$
semi-annually	bi-weekly	$c = \frac{2}{26}$
semi-annually	weekly	$c = \frac{2}{52}$

C. Computing the equivalent rate of interest per payment period

In Chapter 10 you were introduced to the concept of the effective rate of interest. It was defined as the nominal rate of interest compounded annually and represented by the symbol f. It can readily be determined from the periodic rate of interest i by means of Formula 10.3, $f = (1 + i)^m - 1$, where m is the number of compounding periods per year.

When dealing with general annuities, it is useful to utilize the **equivalent rate of interest per payment period**. Depending on the length of the payment interval, the equivalent interest rate per payment period may be a monthly, quarterly, semi-annual, or annual rate. It can be obtained from the periodic rate of interest i by a formula identical in nature to Formula 10.4.

We distinguish the equivalent rate of interest per payment period from the effective annual rate of interest, f, by using the symbol p for the equivalent rate of interest per payment period. It can be determined by means of Formula 12.1 that

$$\boxed{p = (1 + i)^c - 1}\ \text{———————— Formula 12.1}$$

where $c = \dfrac{\text{THE NUMBER OF INTEREST CONVERSION PERIODS PER YEAR}}{\text{THE NUMBER OF PAYMENT PERIODS PER YEAR}}$

EXAMPLE 12.1C

Jean receives annuity payments at the end of every six months. If she deposits these payments in an account earning interest at 9% compounded monthly, what is the equivalent semi-annually compounded rate of interest?

SOLUTION

Since the payments are made at the end of every six months while interest is compounded monthly

$$c = \dfrac{\text{THE NUMBER OF INTEREST CONVERSION PERIODS PER YEAR}}{\text{THE NUMBER OF PAYMENT PERIODS PER YEAR}} = \dfrac{12}{2} = 6$$

$$i = \dfrac{9\%}{12} = 0.75\% = 0.0075$$

$$p = (1 + i)^c - 1$$

$$p = 1.0075^6 - 1 \ \text{————————————— substituting in Formula 12.1}$$

$$p = 1.045852 - 1$$

$$p = 0.045852 = 4.5852\%$$

The rate of interest is 4.5852% per semi-annual period.

EXAMPLE 12.1D

Peel Credit Union pays 6% compounded quarterly on its Premium Savings Accounts. If Ray Ketch deposits $25 in his account at the end of every month, what is the monthly equivalent compounded rate of interest?

SOLUTION

Since the payments are made at the end of every month while interest is compounded quarterly,

$$c = \dfrac{4}{12} = \dfrac{1}{3}; \qquad i = \dfrac{6\%}{4} = 1.5\% = 0.015$$

$$p = 1.015^{\frac{1}{3}} - 1 \ \text{————————————— substituting in Formula 12.1}$$

$$p = 1.004975 - 1$$

$$p = 0.004975 = 0.4975\%$$

The rate of interest is 0.4975% per month.

POINTERS
& PITFALLS

When the number of interest conversion periods per year is smaller than the number of payment periods per year, c takes the form of a fractional exponent. Either calculate c first and then use the calculator's store and recall functions, or use your calculator's parenthesis or "bracket" keys to handle the calculations for the fractional exponent.

The key sequence for solving p in Example 12.1D using brackets is

0.06 [/] 4 [+] 1 [=] 1.015 [Y^x] [( ] 4 [/] 12 [ )] [=] [−] 1

D. Future value of an ordinary general annuity

Determining the equivalent rate per payment period, p, allows us to treat the ordinary general annuity problem in a similar way to an ordinary simple annuity problem. The following notation will be used for an ordinary general annuity:

FV_g = the future value (or accumulated value) of an ordinary general annuity;
PMT = the size of the periodic payment;
n = the number of periodic payments;
c = the number of interest conversion periods per payment interval;
i = the interest rate per interest conversion period;
p = the equivalent rate of interest per payment period.

Substituting p for i in Formula 11.1, we obtain

$$FV_g = PMT\left[\frac{(1 + p)^n - 1}{p}\right] \text{ where } p = (1 + i)^c - 1 \qquad \text{—— Formula 12.2}$$

POINTERS
& PITFALLS

The word "payment" can be confusing. If the payment indicates equal amounts paid at the same time within each payment interval, this fits the equal and periodic criteria and qualifies as a periodic payment, PMT, in the formula above. If only a single payment is made, this amount would be identified as either the present value, PV, or the future value, FV.

EXAMPLE 12.1E

Determine the accumulated value after 10 years of payments of $2000 made at the end of each year if interest is 6% compounded monthly.

SOLUTION

This problem is an ordinary general annuity. The payments are of equal size, $2000, and are made periodically (at the end of each year). Therefore, they are regular periodic payments. Since there is one payment per year, over the 10 years the number of periodic payments n is 10.

$$PMT = 2000.00; \quad n = 10; \quad c = \frac{12}{1} = 12; \quad i = \frac{6\%}{12} = 0.5\% = 0.005$$

The equivalent annual rate of interest

$$p = 1.005^{12} - 1 = 1.061678 - 1 = 0.061678 = 6.1678\%$$
$$PMT = 2000.00; \, n = 10; \, p = 0.061678$$

$$FV = 2000.00\left(\frac{1.061678^{10} - 1}{0.061678}\right) \quad \text{substituting in Formula 12.2}$$

$$= 2000.00(13.285114)$$

$$= \$26\ 570.23$$

The accumulated value after 10 years is $26 570.23.

EXAMPLE 12.1F

Crestview Farms set aside $1250 at the end of each month for the purchase of machinery. How much money will be available after five years if interest is 6.0% compounded semi-annually?

SOLUTION

This problem involves an ordinary general annuity.

$$PMT = 1250.00; \quad n = 5(12) = 60; \quad c = \frac{2}{12} = \frac{1}{6}; \quad i = \frac{6.0\%}{2} = 3.0\% = 0.03$$

The equivalent monthly rate of interest

$$p = 1.03^{\frac{1}{6}} - 1 = 1.004939 - 1 = 0.004939 = 0.4939\%$$

$$FV = 1250.00\left(\frac{1.004939^{60} - 1}{0.004939}\right) \quad \text{substituting in Formula 12.2}$$

$$= 1250(69.5553)$$

$$= \$87\ 048.66$$

After five years, the amount available is $87 048.66.

E. Using preprogrammed financial calculators to compute the future value of an ordinary general annuity

When using formulas, the use of p rather than i as the rate of interest is the only difference in the solution for a general annuity compared to the solution for a simple annuity.

When using preprogrammed financial calculators, such as the Texas Instruments BA II PLUS, we must identify the following:

[P/Y]: the number of payment periods per year

[N]: the number of payments made during the term of the annuity. Remember that the N is determined by multiplying the number of years in the term by the number of payment periods per year (years × P/Y).

[I/Y]: the annual nominal rate of interest per year

[C/Y]: the number of interest compounding periods per year

In Example 12.1E, the number of payments each year is 2 and there are 20 payments (10 × 2), the annual nominal rate of interest per year is 6% and interest is compounded 4 times per year.

To set the calculator for Example 12.1E, follow these steps:

[2nd] [P/Y] 2 [ENTER] [↓] [C/Y] 4 [ENTER] [2nd] [QUIT]

Note that each time the P/Y is changed, the C/Y automatically changes to match the P/Y. To make the C/Y different from the P/Y, it must be re-entered separately, after the changes to the P/Y have been made.

| EXAMPLE 12.1G | Calculate the future value of $2500 deposited at the end of every 6 months for 10 years if interest is 6% compounded quarterly. |

| SOLUTION | $PMT = 2500.00; \quad n = 2(10) = 20; \quad P/Y = 2; \quad C/Y = 4; \quad c = \dfrac{4}{2} = 2;$ |

$$I/Y = 6; \quad i = \frac{6\%}{4} = 1.5\% = 0.015$$

(Set P/Y = 2; C/Y = 4)

Key in	Press	Display shows
6	I/Y	6
0	PV	0
2500	± PMT	−2500
20	N	20 — the number of payments (number of years × P/Y)
CPT	FV	67 329.89319

The amount on deposit after 10 years will be $67 329.89.

| EXAMPLE 12.1H | Determine the accumulated value of payments of $1250 made at the end of each quarter for eight years if interest is 5.5% compounded annually. |

| SOLUTION | $PMT = 1250.00; \quad n = 8(4) = 32; \quad P/Y = 4; \quad C/Y = 1; \quad c = \dfrac{1}{4} = 0.25;$ |

$$I/Y = 5.5; \quad i = 5.5\% = 0.055$$

(Set P/Y = 4; C/Y = 1) 5.5 I/Y 0 PV

1250 ± PMT 32 N CPT FV 49599.22016

The accumulated value of the payments is $49 599.22.

EXERCISE 12.1   MyLab Math

Answer each of the following questions.

1. Aisha saved $300 at the end of every three months. If interest is 4.10% compounded monthly, how much has she saved after three years?   Reference Example 12.1A

2. To attend school, Sam deposits $1500 at the end of every six months for four and one-half years. What is the accumulated value of the deposits if interest is 6% compounded quarterly?

3. How much will deposits of $25 made at the end of each month amount to after 10 years if interest is 5% compounded quarterly?   Reference Example 12.1B

4. Rex dreams of owning a $18 500 Kawasaki Nomad motorcycle. If he saves $270 at the end of each month for five years and earns interest at 6.2% compounded quarterly, will he have saved enough money, and by how much is he over or short?

5. Mr. Tomas contributed $1000 at the end of each year into an RRSP paying 6% compounded quarterly.
   (a) How much will Mr. Tomas have in the RRSP after 10 years?
   (b) After 10 years, how much of the amount is interest?

6. Kristina saves $20 at the end of each week and deposits the money in an account paying 4% compounded monthly.
   (a) How much will she accumulate in 10 years?
   (b) How much of the accumulated amount is interest?

7. Edwin Ng made deposits of $500 into his savings account at the end of every 3 months for 10 years. If interest is 4.5% compounded semi-annually and if he leaves the accumulated balance for another five years, what will be the balance in his account then?

8. Mrs. Cook made deposits of $950 at the end of every 6 months for 15 years. If interest is 3% compounded monthly, how much will Mrs. Cook have accumulated 10 years after the last deposit?

9. For the past four years, Joely authorized the payroll department at her work to deduct $30 per week to be placed into an RRSP account. If interest is 5.17% compounded monthly, how much has Joely accumulated in her RRSP?

10. Clark's younger brother saved $18 per month from his paper route for the past two years. If interest is 4% compounded quarterly, how much will he have accumulated in his savings account?

11. At the end of each year, Thread Crafts Inc. pays $1000 into a savings account. If interest earned on the account is 3.24% compounded monthly, what would the account balance be in four years?

12. At the end of each quarter, Andrews Machinery pays $4000 into an account to fund a charity event. If interest earned on the account is 1.95% compounded annually, how much would the account balance be in five years?

13. You miss the 13th to 15th payments of a loan. The loan payments are $323.80 each month and the interest rate is 5.45% compounded annually. How much are you behind in your payments on the day that you miss the 15th payment?

14. You are to receive $20 000 from your trust fund in 6.5 years. You negotiate a deal whereby you can withdraw $500 per month starting in 2 years, before you can withdraw the remainder of the funds. You are able to earn 3.12% compounded annually on your money. How much is your trust fund reduced to?

15. Alice invested $100 per month in an RRSP for 20 years. Her sister invested $1200 at the end of each year, also for 20 years. Suppose that both RRSP accounts can earn 4.5% compounded annually. How much larger is the accumulated value in Alice's RRSP than in her sister's RRSP?

16. While Grant was in graduate school, he deposited $100 at the end of each month for five years into an account paying 6% compounded monthly. Once he started his first management job, he increased his contributions to $100 off of every bi-weekly paycheque. What will the balance in the account be after Grant has celebrated his tenth year of working full time as a manager?

12.2 ORDINARY GENERAL ANNUITIES—CALCULATING THE PRESENT VALUE PV

A. Present value of an ordinary general annuity using the equivalent rate of interest per payment period

As with the future value of an ordinary general annuity, we can convert the given periodic rate of interest i into the equivalent rate of interest per payment period.

$$p = (1 + i)^c - 1$$

The use of p converts the ordinary general annuity problem into an ordinary simple annuity problem.

Substituting p for i in Formula 11.2, we obtain

$$PV_g = PMT\left[\frac{1 - (1 + p)^{-n}}{p}\right]$$ ——————————— Formula 12.3

EXAMPLE 12.2A

A loan is repaid by making payments of $2000 at the end of every six months for 12 years. If interest on the loan is 8% compounded quarterly, what was the principal of the loan?

SOLUTION

$PMT = 2000.00$; $n = 12(2) = 24$; $P/Y = 2$; $C/Y = 4$; $c = \dfrac{4}{2} = 2$;

$I/Y = 8$; $i = \dfrac{8\%}{4} = 2\% = 0.02$

The equivalent semi-annual rate of interest

$p = 1.02^2 - 1 = 1.0404 - 1 = 0.0404 = 4.04\%$

$PV = 2000.00\left(\dfrac{1 - 1.0404^{-24}}{0.0404}\right)$ ——————— substituting in Formula 12.3

$= 2000.00(15.184713)$

$= \$30\ 369.43$

The loan principal was $30 369.43.

EXAMPLE 12.2B

A second mortgage requires payments of $370 at the end of each month for 15 years. If interest is 8% compounded semi-annually, what was the amount borrowed?

SOLUTION

$PMT = 370.00$; $n = 15(12) = 180$; $P/Y = 12$; $C/Y = 2$; $c = \dfrac{2}{12} = \dfrac{1}{6}$;

$I/Y = 8$; $i = \dfrac{8\%}{2} = 4\% = 0.04$

The equivalent monthly rate of interest

$p = 1.04^{\frac{1}{6}} - 1 = 1.006558 - 1 = 0.006558 = 0.6558\%$

$PV = 370.00\left(\dfrac{1 - 1.006558^{-180}}{0.006558}\right)$ ——————— substituting in Formula 12.3

$= 370.00(105.468216)$

$= \$39\ 023.24$

The amount borrowed was $39 023.24.

B. Using preprogrammed financial calculators to compute the present value of an ordinary general annuity

STEP 1   Set P/Y as the number of payment periods per year.

STEP 2   Set C/Y as the number of interest compounding periods per year.

STEP 3   Determine the number of payments made during the term of the annuity by multiplying the number of years in the term by the number of payment periods per year (years × P/Y).

STEP 4   Set I/Y as the annual nominal rate of interest per year.

EXAMPLE 12.2C   A contract will be fulfilled by making payments of $8500 at the end of every year for 15 years. If interest is 7% compounded quarterly, what is the current value of the contract?

SOLUTION   PMT = 8500.00; $n = 15$;   P/Y = 1;   C/Y = 4; $c = 4$;   I/Y = 7;

$$i = \frac{7\%}{4} = 1.75\% = 0.0175$$

(Set P/Y = 1; C/Y = 4) 7 $\boxed{\text{I/Y}}$ 0 $\boxed{\text{FV}}$ 8500 $\boxed{\pm}$ $\boxed{\text{PMT}}$

15 $\boxed{\text{N}}$ $\boxed{\text{CPT}}$ $\boxed{\text{PV}}$ $\boxed{76516.37862}$

The current value of the contract is $76 516.38.

EXAMPLE 12.2D   A 25-year mortgage on a house requires payments of $915.60 at the end of each month. If interest is 5.5% compounded semi-annually, what was the mortgage principal?

SOLUTION   PMT = 915.60; $n = 25(12) = 300$;   P/Y = 12;   C/Y = 2; $c = \frac{2}{12} = \frac{1}{6}$;

$$I/Y = 5.5; \quad i = \frac{5.5\%}{2} = 2.75\% = 0.0275$$

(Set P/Y = 12; C/Y = 2) 5.5 $\boxed{\text{I/Y}}$ 0 $\boxed{\text{FV}}$ 915.60 $\boxed{\pm}$ $\boxed{\text{PMT}}$

300 $\boxed{\text{N}}$ $\boxed{\text{CPT}}$ $\boxed{\text{PV}}$ $\boxed{150002.09}$

The mortgage principal was $150 002.09.

EXERCISE 12.2   MyLab Math

Answer each of the following questions.

1. Calculate the present value of payments of $250 made at the end of every 3 months for 12 years if money is worth 3% compounded monthly.   Reference Example 12.2A

2. What is the discounted value of $1560 paid at the end of each year for nine years if interest is 6% compounded quarterly?

3. What cash payment is equivalent to making payments of $825 at the end of every 3 months for 16 years if interest is 7% compounded semi-annually?

Reference Example 12.2B

4. What is the principal from which $175 can be withdrawn at the end of each month for 20 years if interest is 5% compounded quarterly?

5. A property was purchased for $5000 down and payments of $2500 at the end of every six months for six years. Interest is 6% compounded monthly.
   (a) What was the purchase price of the property?
   (b) How much is the cost of financing?

6. A car was purchased for $1500 down and payments of $265 at the end of each month for four years. Interest is 9% compounded quarterly.
   (a) What was the purchase price of the car?
   (b) How much interest will be paid?

7. Corey makes payments of $715.59 at the end of each month to repay a 25-year mortgage. If interest is 5.6% compounded semi-annually, what was the original mortgage principal?

8. Langara Woodcraft borrowed money to purchase equipment. The loan is repaid by making payments of $924.37 at the end of every three months over seven years. If interest is 7.3% compounded annually, what was the original loan balance?

9. Dale purchased a retirement annuity paying $1800 every 6 months for 20 years. If interest is 4.6% compounded monthly, how much did Dale invest in the annuity?

10. For her daughter's education, Georgina Harcourt has invested an inheritance in a fund paying 5.2% compounded quarterly. If ordinary annuity payments of $178 per month are to be made out of the fund for eight years, how much was the inheritance?

11. As a settlement for an insurance claim, Craig was offered one of two choices. He could either accept a lump-sum amount of $5000 now, or accept quarterly payments of $145 for the next 10 years. If the money is placed into a trust fund earning 3.95% compounded semi-annually, which is the better option and by how much?

12. Carl Hightop, a popular basketball player, has been offered a two-year salary deal. He can either accept $2 000 000 now or accept monthly amounts of $100 000 payable at the end of each month. If money can be invested at 5.7% compounded quarterly, which offer is the better option for Carl and by how much?

13. You won $100 000.00 in a lottery and you want to set some of that sum aside for 4 years. After 4 years you would like to receive $2000.00 at the end of every 3 months for 6 years. If interest is 5% compounded semi-annually, how much of your winnings must you set aside?

12.3 ORDINARY GENERAL ANNUITIES—DETERMINING THE PERIODIC PAYMENT PMT

A. Determining the periodic payment PMT when the future value of a general annuity is known

If the future value of a general annuity FV_g, the number of conversion periods n, and the conversion rate i are known, you can determine the periodic payment PMT by substituting the given values in the future value Formula 12.2.

$$FV_g = PMT\left[\frac{(1+p)^n - 1}{p}\right] \text{ where } p = (1+i)^c - 1 \qquad \text{——— Formula 12.2}$$

To calculate PMT, rearrange the terms of the future value formulas as shown below. Then substitute the three known values (FV, n, and i) into the rearranged formula and solve for PMT.

$$FV_g = PMT\left[\frac{(1+p)^n - 1}{p}\right] \quad\text{———— Formula 12.2}$$

$$PMT = \frac{FV_g}{\left[\dfrac{(1+p)^n - 1}{p}\right]} \quad\text{———— divide both sides by } \left[\frac{(1+p)^n - 1}{p}\right]$$

$$\boxed{PMT = \frac{FV_g\, p}{(1+p)^n - 1}} \quad\text{———— dividing by a fraction is the same as inverting the fraction and multiplying}$$

When using a preprogrammed financial calculator, you can compute PMT by entering the five known values (FV, N, I/Y, P/Y, and C/Y) and pressing $\boxed{\text{CPT}}$ $\boxed{\text{PMT}}$.

Recall that the PMT amount will be negative, since payments are considered to be cash outflows.

EXAMPLE 12.3A

What sum of money must be deposited at the end of every three months into an account paying 6% compounded monthly to accumulate to $25 000 in 10 years?

SOLUTION

$FV = 25\ 000.00;\quad n = 10(4) = 40;\quad P/Y = 4;\quad C/Y = 12;\quad c = \dfrac{12}{4} = 3;$

$I/Y = 6;\quad i = 0.5\% = 0.005$

The equivalent quarterly rate of interest

$p = 1.005^3 - 1 = 1.015075 - 1 = 0.015075 = 1.5075\%$

$PMT = \dfrac{FV_g\, p}{(1+p)^n - 1} \quad\text{———— rearranging Formula 12.2}$

$PMT = \dfrac{25\ 000.00(0.015075)}{1.015075^{40} - 1}$

$PMT = \$459.95$

PROGRAMMED SOLUTION

(Set P/Y = 4; C/Y = 12) $\boxed{\text{2nd}}$ (CLR TVM) 6 $\boxed{\text{I/Y}}$ 0 $\boxed{\text{PV}}$

$\qquad\qquad$ 25 000 $\boxed{\text{FV}}$ 40 $\boxed{\text{N}}$ $\boxed{\text{CPT}}$ $\boxed{\text{PMT}}$ $\boxed{-459.945847}$

The required quarterly deposit is $459.95.

B. Determining the periodic payment PMT when the present value of a general annuity is known

If the present value of a general annuity PV_g, the number of conversion periods n, and the conversion rate i are known, you can calculate the periodic payment PMT by substituting the given values in the present value Formula 12.3.

$$\boxed{PV_g = PMT\left[\frac{1 - (1+p)^{-n}}{p}\right]} \quad\text{———— Formula 12.3}$$

To determine PMT rearrange the terms of the present value formulas. Then substitute the three known values (PV, n, and i) into the rearranged formula and solve for PMT.

$$PV_g = PMT\left[\frac{1-(1+p)^{-n}}{p}\right] \text{———— Formula 12.3}$$

$$PMT = \frac{PV_g}{\left[\dfrac{1-(1+p)^{-n}}{p}\right]} \text{———— divide both sides by } \left[\frac{1-(1+p)^{-n}}{p}\right]$$

$$\boxed{PMT = \frac{PV_g\,p}{1-(1+p)^{-n}}} \text{———— dividing by a fraction is the same as inverting the fraction and multiplying}$$

When using a preprogrammed financial calculator, you can compute PMT by entering the five known values (PV, N, I/Y, P/Y, and C/Y) and pressing CPT PMT.

EXAMPLE 12.3B

Mr. and Mrs. White applied to their credit union for a first mortgage of $190 000 to buy a house. The mortgage is to be amortized over 25 years and interest on the mortgage is 4.9% compounded semi-annually. What is the size of the monthly payment if payments are made at the end of each month?

SOLUTION

$$PV = 190\,000.00; \quad n = 25(12) = 300; \quad P/Y = 12; \quad C/Y = 2; \quad c = \frac{2}{12} = \frac{1}{6};$$

$$I/Y = 4.9; \quad i = \frac{4.9\%}{2} = 2.45\% = 0.0245$$

The equivalent monthly rate of interest

$$p = 1.0245^{\frac{1}{6}} - 1 = 1.004042 - 1 = 0.004042 = 0.4042\%$$

$$PMT = \frac{PV_g\,p}{1-(1+p)^{-n}} \text{———— rearranging Formula 12.3}$$

$$PMT = \frac{190\,000.00 \times 0.004042}{1-(1+0.004042)^{-300}}$$

$$PMT^\star = \frac{768.029928}{0.701873} = \$1094.26$$

*Both the numerator and denominator have been rounded for display purposes only. The final number should be determined without mid-calculation rounding.

PROGRAMMED SOLUTION

(Set P/Y = 12; C/Y = 2) 4.9 I/Y 0 FV 190 000 ± PV

300 N CPT PMT 1094.258282

The monthly payment due at the end of each month is $1094.26.

EXERCISE 12.3

MyLab Math

Answer each of the following questions.

1. What payment made at the end of each quarter for 15 years will accumulate to $12 000 at 6% compounded monthly? Reference Example 12.3A

2. What payment is required at the end of each month for five years to repay a loan of $6000 at 7% compounded semi-annually?

3. A contract can be fulfilled by making an immediate payment of $9500 or equal payments at the end of every six months for eight years. What is the size of the semi-annual payments at 7.4% compounded quarterly?

4. What payment made at the end of each year for 18 years will amount to $16 000 at 4.2% compounded monthly?

5. What payment is required at the end of each month for 18 years to amortize a $110 000 mortgage if interest is 5.1% compounded semi-annually? Reference Example 12.3B

6. How much must be deposited at the end of each quarter for 10 years to accumulate to $12 000 at 6% compounded monthly?

7. What payment made at the end of every 3 months for 20 years will accumulate to $20 000 at 7% compounded semi-annually?

8. Derrick bought a car priced at $9300 for 15% down and equal monthly payments for four years. If interest is 8% compounded semi-annually, what is the size of the monthly payment?

9. Harlan made equal payments at the end of each month into his RRSP. If interest in his account is 3.7% compounded annually, and the balance after 15 years is $10 000.28, what is the size of the monthly payment?

10. To finance the development of a new product, a company borrowed $30 000 at 7% compounded monthly. If the loan is to be repaid in equal quarterly payments over seven years and the first payment is due three months after the date of the loan, what is the size of the quarterly payment?

11. To save for future development, a company makes a deposit into a fund that earns interest at 4.44% compounded semi-annually. If the balance after 8 years needs to be $800 000, how much must be deposited at the end of each year?

12. An investment fund that pays quarterly dividends for 10 years yields an annual return of 6.6%. If the initial price of the fund is $200, what is the amount of the dividend?

13. You want to buy a motorcycle for $11 700 plus freight of $165 and other delivery charges of $125. You have already saved 25% of the total purchase price towards a down payment. The bank is willing to finance the remaining balance at 8.76% compounded quarterly. What is the size of your monthly payment if the loan is for 4.25 years?

14. You decide to buy a piece of equipment for $11 500. The equipment is expected to last for 10 years, and you want to have it completely paid off 2.5 years before it becomes unusable. Current loan rates are 6.3% compounded annually. What is the size of your semi-annual payment?

15. Keegan is planning to buy a brand new truck. He plans to keep the truck for 3 years and then trade it in. He borrows $39 000 at 7.4% compounded semi-annually to purchase the truck. What monthly payment will reduce the balance on the loan after 3 years to the expected trade-in value of $17 500?

12.4 ORDINARY GENERAL ANNUITIES—DETERMINING THE TERM n
A. Determining the term n when the future value of a general annuity is known

If the future value of a general annuity FV_g, the periodic payment PMT, and the conversion rate i are known, you can solve the term of the annuity by substituting the given values in the future value Formula 12.2.

$$FV_g = PMT\left[\frac{(1+p)^n - 1}{p}\right] \text{ where } p = (1+i)^c - 1 \quad\text{—— Formula 12.2}$$

To calculate n, rearrange the terms of the future value Formula 12.2. Then substitute the three known values (FV, PMT, and p) into the rearranged formula and solve for n. This procedure is more complex than for isolating PMT. For this reason, we present Formula 12.4 as the rearranged version of Formula 12.2 in order to calculate n.

$$FV_g = PMT\left[\frac{(1+p)^n - 1}{p}\right] \quad\text{—— Formula 12.2}$$

$$\frac{FV_g}{PMT} = \frac{(1+p)^n - 1}{p} \quad\text{———— divide both sides by PMT}$$

$$(1+p)^n = \left(\frac{FV_g\, p}{PMT}\right) + 1 \quad\text{———— multiply both sides by } p \text{ and add 1 to both sides}$$

$$n\ln(1+p) = \ln\left[\left(\frac{FV_g p}{PMT}\right) + 1\right] \quad\text{———— solve for } n \text{ using natural logarithms}$$

$$n = \frac{\ln\left[\left(\dfrac{FV_g p}{PMT}\right) + 1\right]}{\ln(1+p)} \quad\text{———— Formula 12.4: divide both sides by } \ln(1+p)$$

When using a preprogrammed financial calculator, compute n by entering the five known values (FV, PMT, I/Y, P/Y, and C/Y) and press $\boxed{\text{CPT}}$ $\boxed{\text{N}}$.

POINTERS & PITFALLS

ERROR 5: When you see this error message on the display of your calculator, you need to change the sign of one of your inputs, either FV or PMT, when PV = 0. Alternatively, either PV or PMT must be negative, when FV = 0.

Even if there is no error message, to calculate the correct PV (or FV), N, or I/Y, you must enter FV (or PV) as a positive amount and PMT as a negative amount, or the reverse.

EXAMPLE 12.4A

What period of time is required for $125 deposited at the end of each month at 11% compounded quarterly to grow to $15 000?

SOLUTION

FV = 15 000.00;   PMT = 125.00;   P/Y 12;   C/Y = 4;

$$c = \frac{4}{12} = \frac{1}{3}; \quad I/Y = 11; \quad i = \frac{11\%}{4} = 2.75\% = 0.0275$$

The equivalent monthly rate of interest

$$p = 1.0275^{\frac{1}{3}} - 1 = 1.009084 - 1 = 0.009084 = 0.9084\%$$

$$n = \frac{\ln\left[\left(\dfrac{FV_g p}{PMT}\right) + 1\right]}{\ln(1+p)} \quad\text{———— Formula 12.4}$$

$$n = \frac{\ln\left[\dfrac{15\,000.00(0.009084)}{125.00} + 1\right]}{\ln(1 + 0.009084)}$$

$$n = \frac{\ln[2.090068]}{\ln(1.009084)}$$

$$n = \frac{0.737197}{0.009043} = 81.522240 = 82 \text{ months}$$

PROGRAMMED SOLUTION

(Set P/Y = 12; C/Y = 4) 11 [I/Y] 0 [PV] 15 000 [FV]

125 [±] [PMT] [CPT] [N] [81.522240]

It will take 82 months to accumulate $15 000. For the first 81 months, the payment is $125. A smaller amount would be needed for the 82nd payment.

B. Determining the term *n* when the present value of a general annuity is known

If the present value of a general annuity PV_g, the periodic payment PMT, and the conversion rate *i* are known, you can solve the term of the annuity *n* by substituting the given values in the present value Formula 12.3.

$$PV_g = PMT\left[\frac{1 - (1 + p)^{-n}}{p}\right] \hspace{2cm} \text{Formula 12.3}$$

Alternatively, you can first rearrange the terms of Formula 12.3 to solve for *n*.

$$\frac{PV_g}{PMT} = \frac{1 - (1 + p)^{-n}}{p} \hspace{2cm} \text{divide both sides by PMT}$$

$$\left(\frac{PV_g p}{PMT}\right) = 1 - (1 + p)^{-n} \hspace{2cm} \text{multiply both sides by } p \text{ and subtract 1 from both sides}$$

$$(1 + p)^{-n} = 1 - \left(\frac{PV_g p}{PMT}\right) \hspace{2cm} \text{multiply both sides by } -1$$

$$-n \ln(1 + p) = \ln\left[1 - \left(\frac{PV_g p}{PMT}\right)\right] \hspace{2cm} \text{solve for } n \text{ using natural logarithms}$$

$$n = \frac{\ln\left[1 - \left(\frac{PV_g p}{PMT}\right)\right]}{-\ln(1 + p)} \hspace{2cm} \text{Formula 12.5: divide both sides by } -\ln(1 + p)$$

To calculate *n*, rearrange the terms of the present value formulas. Then substitute the three known values (PV, PMT, and *i*) into the rearranged formula and solve for *n*.

When using a preprogrammed financial calculator, compute *n* by entering the five known values (PV, PMT, I/Y, P/Y, and C/Y) and press [CPT] [N].

EXAMPLE 12.4B

A business valued at $96 000 is bought for a down payment of 25% and payments of $4000 at the end of every three months. If interest is 9% compounded monthly, for how long will payments have to be made?

SOLUTION

$PV = 96\,000.00(0.75) = 72\,000.00; \quad PMT = 4000.00; \quad P/Y = 4; \quad C/Y = 12;$

$c = \dfrac{12}{4} = 3; \quad I/Y = 9; \quad i = \dfrac{9\%}{12} = 0.75\% = 0.0075$

The equivalent quarterly rate of interest

$p = 1.0075^3 - 1 = 1.022669 - 1 = 0.022669 = 2.2669\%$

$$n = \dfrac{\ln\left[1 - \left(\dfrac{FV_g\, p}{PMT}\right)\right]}{-\ln(1 + p)} \quad\quad\text{Formula 12.5}$$

$$n = \dfrac{\ln\left[1 - \left(\dfrac{72\,000.00(0.022669)}{4000.00}\right)\right]}{-\ln(1 + 0.022669)}$$

$$n = \dfrac{\ln[1 - (0.408045)]}{-\ln(1 + 0.022669)}$$

$$n = \dfrac{\ln[0.591955]}{-\ln(1.022669)}$$

$$n = \dfrac{-0.524325}{-0.022416} = 23.390604 = 24 \text{ quarters}$$

PROGRAMMED SOLUTION

(Set P/Y = 4; C/Y = 12); 9 [I/Y] 0 [PV] 72 000

[±] [PV] 4000 [PMT] [CPT] [N] 23.390604

Payments will have to be made for 24 quarters or six years. The payment for the last quarter would be a smaller amount.

EXERCISE 12.4   MyLab Math

Answer each of the following questions.

1. How long would it take you to save $5000 by making deposits of $100 at the end of every month into a savings account earning 6% compounded quarterly?

Reference Example 12.4A

2. How long will it take to save $15 000 by making deposits of $90 at the end of every month into an account earning interest at 4% compounded quarterly?

3. In what period of time could you pay back a loan of $3000 by making monthly payments of $90 if interest is 10.5% compounded semi-annually?

Reference Example 12.4B

4. For how many years will Prasad make payments on the $28 000 he borrowed to start his machine shop if he makes payments of $3400 at the end of every three months and interest is 8.08% compounded semi-annually?

5. Mirsad is saving $500 at the end of each month. How soon can he retire if he wants to have a retirement fund of $120 000 and interest is 5.4% compounded quarterly?

6. For how long must contributions of $2000 be made at the end of each year to accumulate to $100 000 at 6% compounded quarterly?

7. For how long can $800 be withdrawn at the end of each month from an account originally containing $16 000, if interest is 6.8% compounded semi-annually?

 8. A mortgage of $120 000 is to be repaid by making payments of $751 at the end of each month. If interest is 5.75% compounded semi-annually, what is the term of the mortgage?

 9. Suppose $370.37 is deposited at the end of every three months into an account earning 6.5% compounded semi-annually. If the balance in the account is to be $20 000, how many deposits are needed?

 10. Mr. Deneau accumulated $100 000 in an RRSP. He converted the RRSP into a RRIF and started to withdraw $4500 at the end of every three months from the fund. If interest is 6.75% compounded monthly, for how long can Mr. Deneau make withdrawals?

11. To repay a loan of $35 000, Airial Company pays out $6000 at the end of each year. If interest on the loan is 8% compounded quarterly, how many payments will it take to repay the loan?

12. Keys Company has a target of establishing a fund of $50 000. If $10 000 is deposited at the end of every six months, and the fund earns interest at 4% compounded quarterly, how long will it take to reach the target?

 13. One month from now, Kelly will make her first monthly contribution of $250 to a Tax-Free Savings Account (TFSA). She expects to earn 6% compounded annually. How long will it take for the contributions and accrued earnings to reach $75 000?

12.5 ORDINARY GENERAL ANNUITIES—CALCULATING THE PERIODIC INTEREST RATE i

A. Calculating the periodic rate of interest i using preprogrammed financial calculators

Preprogrammed financial calculators are especially helpful when solving for the conversion rate i. Determining i without a financial calculator is extremely time-consuming.

When the future value or present value, the periodic payment, PMT, and the term n of a general annuity are known, retrieve the value of I/Y by pressing CPT I/Y.

BUSINESS MATH **NEWS**   Is It Better to Lease or Buy a Car?

Money shouldn't be the only consideration when you are trying to determine whether to lease or buy your first vehicle. But how do you weigh the lifestyle pros of leasing against the financial cons of leasing?

Financing a vehicle is like buying a home. Once you pay off the loan, you own it. Laura Adams says, "Leasing a car is like renting an apartment. Renting gives you monthly payments that may be more manageable . . . but you're just borrowing it."

Some benefits of leasing a car are that

- you make little or no down payment, and monthly payments are lower (because you're only paying for the amount that the car will depreciate during the term of your lease);

- you can't lease used cars, so repair expenses are usually covered by the manufacturer's warranty; and

- you enjoy driving a newer car.

Some benefits of buying a car are that

- each loan payment brings you closer to owning the car, giving you the option to trade it in or sell it at any time;
- there are no limits on annual mileage; and
- the longer you drive it after paying it off, the less it can cost you.

From a financial point of view, the quick answer is to "buy," preferably a relatively new used car with low mileage because, depending on the vehicle, 20% to 40% of its depreciation occurs in the first few years—and you get the advantage of paying a discounted price that reflects this.

How car lease payments are calculated:

Monthly lease payment = Depreciation fee + Finance fee + Sales tax
Depreciation fee = (Selling price − Residual value)/Term
Finance fee = (Selling price + Residual value) × APR/2400
Sales tax = (Depreciation fee + Finance fee) × Sales tax rate

QUESTIONS

1. Calculate the size of your monthly payment (including HST) if you were to lease a $30 000 car in Ontario for three years (with no down payment) at an interest rate of 1.9% APR. Assume that the vehicle's residual value at the end of the term is $17 000.

2. If you were to buy this car instead, and pay it off in three years with 0% financing, what would be the size of your monthly payment (including HST)?

3. What financial benefit do you realize at the end of three years by having bought the car?

Sources: Laura Adams, "Is it better to lease or buy a car?" February 6, 2019, www.goodfinancialcents.com; Erica Alini, "Three numbers you should check before deciding whether to lease or buy a car" April 21, 2017, *Money/Consumer Global News*; www.leaseguide.com.

EXAMPLE 12.5A

Irina deposited $150 in a savings account at the end of each month for 60 months. If the accumulated value of the deposits was $10 000 and interest was compounded semi-annually, what was the nominal annual rate of interest?

SOLUTION

$FV = 10\ 000.00$; $PMT = 150.00$; $n = 60$; $P/Y = 12$; $C/Y = 2$; $c = \dfrac{2}{12} = \dfrac{1}{6}$

(Set P/Y = 12; C/Y = 2) 0 [PV] 10 000 [FV]

150 [±] [PMT] 60 [N] [CPT] [I/Y] [4.25541]

The nominal annual rate of interest was 4.2554% p.a. compounded semi-annually.

EXAMPLE 12.5B

Compute the nominal annual rate of interest compounded monthly at which $500 paid at the end of every 3 months for 10 years will eliminate a debt of $16 000.

SOLUTION

$PV = 16\ 000.00$; $PMT = 500.00$; $n = 40$; $P/Y = 4$; $C/Y = 12$; $c = \dfrac{12}{4} = 3$

(Set P/Y = 4; C/Y = 12) 0 [FV] 16 000 [PV]

500 [±] [PMT] 40 [N] [CPT] [I/Y] [4.528237]

The nominal annual rate is 4.5282% p.a. compounded monthly.

EXERCISE 12.5

Answer each of the following questions.

1. What is the nominal annual rate of interest compounded quarterly if deposits of $253 made each month for 3½ years accumulate to $11 600?   Reference Example 12.5A

2. Victoria saved $416 every six months for eight years. What nominal rate of interest compounded annually is earned if the savings account amounts to $7720 in eight years?

3. What is the nominal annual rate of interest compounded semi-annually if a four-year loan of $6000 is repaid by monthly payments of $144.23?   Reference Example 12.5B

4. A car valued at $11 400 can be purchased for 10% down and monthly payments of $286.21 for three-and-a-half years. What is the nominal rate of interest compounded annually?

5. A property worth $50 000 can be purchased for 20% down and quarterly mortgage payments of $1000 for 25 years. What nominal rate of interest compounded monthly is charged?

6. A vacation property valued at $250 000 was bought for 15 payments of $22 000 due at the end of every 6 months. What nominal annual rate of interest compounded annually was charged?

7. Compute the nominal annual rate of interest compounded monthly at which $400 paid at the end of every three months for eight years accumulates to $20 000.

8. What is the nominal annual rate of interest compounded quarterly if a loan of $21 500 is repaid in seven years by payments of $2000 made at the end of every six months?

9. If Paige has accumulated $4850 by saving $120 every month for 3 years, what nominal annual rate of interest compounded quarterly has been earned?

10. Deanna wants to save $3500 in two years by depositing $420 every three months into a savings account. What nominal rate of interest compounded annually does her savings have to earn?

11. A mortgage of $35 500 is repaid by making payments of $570 at the end of each month for 15 years. What is the nominal annual rate of interest compounded semi-annually?

12. A property worth $35 000 is purchased for 10% down and semi-annual payments of $2100 for 12 years. What is the nominal annual rate of interest if interest is compounded quarterly?

12.6 CONSTANT-GROWTH ANNUITIES

The annuities we have considered so far have the common feature of periodic payments that are equal in size. **Constant-growth annuities** differ from these fixed-payment-size annuities in that the periodic payments change (usually grow) at a constant rate. The assumption of constant growth is often used in sales forecasting and long-term financial planning. It is consistent with the indexing of pensions or annuities.

The types of constant-growth annuities often parallel the different types of fixed payment annuities considered in Chapter 11 and the previous sections of Chapter 12. However, we will deal only with ordinary simple constant-growth annuities.

With ordinary simple constant-growth annuities, the computations may involve determining the size of any periodic payment, the total amount of the periodic payments, the future value and present value of the stream of periodic payments, the amount of interest earned by the periodic payments, and the size of the first payment if either the present value or the future value is known. We will also consider in this section the special case when the constant-growth rate equals the periodic rate of interest.

A. Future value of an ordinary simple constant-growth annuity

To compute the future value of a series of payments growing at a constant rate, the approach is similar to that used in Example 11.2A.

In general, if the first payment is represented by PMT and the constant rate of growth by k, the constant-growth factor for the annuity payments is $(1 + k)$ and the size of the successive payments is as follows:

$$
\begin{aligned}
\text{1st payment} \quad &= \text{PMT} \\
\text{2nd payment} \quad &= \text{PMT}(1 + k) \\
\text{3rd payment} \quad &= \text{PMT}(1 + k)^2 \\
\text{4th payment} \quad &= \text{PMT}(1 + k)^3 \\
&\quad\downarrow \qquad\qquad\quad\downarrow \\
&\quad\downarrow \qquad\qquad\quad\downarrow \\
\text{10th payment} \quad &= \text{PMT}(1 + k)^9
\end{aligned}
$$

$$\boxed{\text{SIZE OF THE } n\text{TH PAYMENT} = \text{PMT}(1 + k)^{n-1}}$$ —————— **Formula 12.6**

The periodic constant-growth payments form an ordinary simple annuity in which PMT is the size of the first payment, k is the periodic compounding rate, and n is the number of payments.

$$\boxed{\begin{array}{l}\text{SUM OF THE PERIODIC CONSTANT-} \\ \text{GROWTH PAYMENTS}\end{array} = \text{PMT}\left[\dfrac{(1 + k)^n - 1}{k}\right]}$$ —————— **Formula 12.7**

Note: Formula 12.7 is similar to Formula 11.1 except that i has been replaced by k. It does not calculate the future value since the interest rate i isn't involved, but it does add up the value of all the contributions made.

The formula for calculating the future value of an ordinary simple constant-growth annuity is also similar in structure to future value Formula 11.1.

$$\boxed{\text{FV} = \text{PMT}\left[\dfrac{(1 + i)^n - (1 + k)^n}{i - k}\right]}$$ —————— **Formula 12.8**

where FV = the future (accumulated) value of an ordinary simple constant-growth annuity;

PMT = the size of the first annuity payment;

$\quad i$ = the interest rate per conversion period;

$\quad k$ = the constant-growth rate of the annuity payments;

$\quad n$ = the number of conversion periods.

The expression $\left[\dfrac{(1 + i)^n - (1 + k)^n}{i - k}\right]$ is the compounding factor for constant-growth annuities. If $k = 0$, which means there is no growth in the periodic payments, the factor becomes the compounding factor used in Formula 11.1. Formula 11.1 is, in fact, a special case of Formula 12.8 the "zero-growth case."

EXAMPLE 12.6A

Five deposits increasing at a constant rate of 2% are made at the end of each of four successive years. The size of the first deposit is $3000 and the fund earns interest at 6% compounded annually.

(i) What is the size of the last deposit?

(ii) How much was deposited in total?

(iii) What is the accumulated value of the deposits?

(iv) What is the interest earned by the deposits?

SOLUTION

The situation is illustrated in Figure 12.3.

Figure 12.3 Graphical Representation of Method and Data (© S. A. Hummelbrunner)

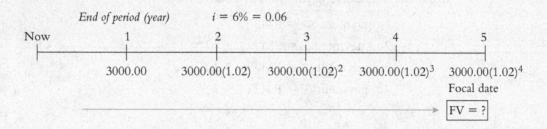

(i) $\text{PMT} = 3000.00;\quad k = 2\% = 0.02;\quad n = 5$

Size of the 5th payment

$= \text{PMT}(1 + k)^{n-1}$ ———————————— using Formula 12.6

$= 3000.00(1.02)^4$

$= 3000.00(1.082432)$

$= \$3247.30$

(ii) $\text{PMT} = 3000.00;\quad k = 2\% = 0.02;\quad n = 5$

Sum of the constant-growth deposits

$= \text{PMT}\left[\dfrac{(1 + k)^n - 1}{k}\right]$ ———————————— using Formula 12.7

$= 3000.00\left[\dfrac{(1.02)^5 - 1}{0.02}\right]$

$= 3000.00\left[\dfrac{1.010408 - 1}{0.02}\right]$

$= 3000.00(5.20404)$

$= \$15\ 612.12$

(iii) $\text{PMT} = 3000.00;\quad k = 2\% = 0.02;\quad n = 5;\quad i = 6\% = 0.06$

Future value of the combined constant-growth deposits

$\text{FV} = \text{PMT}\left[\dfrac{(1 + i)^n - (1 + k)^n}{i - k}\right]$ ———————————— using Formula 12.8

$= 3000.00\left[\dfrac{(1.06)^5 - (1.02)^5}{0.06 - 0.02}\right]$

$$= 3000.00 \left[\frac{1.338226 - 1.104081}{0.04} \right]$$

$$= 3000.00(5.853619)$$

$$= \$17\ 560.86$$

(iv) The interest earned by the deposits
$$= 17\ 560.86 - 15\ 612.12 = \$1948.74.$$

B. Present value of an ordinary simple constant-growth annuity

The approach to determining the present value of a series of payments forming a constant-growth annuity is the same as for calculating the future value of the series of payments except that each payment must be discounted using Formula 9.1, $PV = FV(1 + i)^{-n}$.

$$PV = PMT \left[\frac{1 - (1 + k)^n (1 + i)^{-n}}{i - k} \right] \quad \text{——— Formula 12.9}$$

where PV = the present (discounted) value of an ordinary simple constant-growth annuity;
   PMT = the size of the first annuity payment;
      i = the interest rate per conversion period;
      k = the constant-growth rate of the annuity payments;
      n = the number of conversion periods.

The expression $\left[\dfrac{(1 - (1 + k)^n (1 + i)^{-n}}{i - k} \right]$ is the discount factor for constant-growth annuities. If $k = 0$, which means there is no growth in the periodic payments, the factor becomes the discount factor used in Formula 11.2. Formula 11.2 is, in fact, a special case of Formula 12.9—the "zero-growth case."

Constant-growth annuity formulas are not part of the programming of most financial calculators. Problems involving constant-growth annuities can be solved by substituting in the appropriate formulas, as shown in Examples 12.6A and 12.6B.

EXAMPLE 12.6B

As an alternative to the annual deposits in Example 12.6A, what single amount must be deposited at the beginning of the five years?

SOLUTION

$PMT = 3000.00; \quad k = 2\% = 0.02; \quad n = 5; \quad i = 6\% = 0.06;$

$$PV = 3000.00 \left[\frac{1 - (1.02)^5 (1.06)^{-5}}{0.06 - 0.02} \right] \quad \text{——— using Formula 12.9}$$

$$PV = 3000.00 \left[\frac{1 - (1.104081)(0.747258)}{0.04} \right]$$

$$PV = 3000.00(4.374165)$$

$$PV = \$13\ 122.49$$

Check: Using $PV = FV(1 + i)^n$, \$13 122.49 is the PV of the future value calculated in Example 12.6A(iii). They are economically equivalent.

MyLab Math Visit MyLab Math to practise any of this chapter's exercises marked with a 🌐 as often as you want. The guided solutions help you calculate an answer step by step. You'll find a personalized study plan and additional interactive resources to help you master Business Math!

REVIEW EXERCISE

🌐 **1. LO①** At the end of every three months, Sheila invested $375 into an account earning interest at 3% compounded monthly. What is the accumulated value in the account after eight years?

2. LO① What is the accumulated value after 12 years of monthly deposits of $145 earning interest at 5% compounded semi-annually if the deposits are made at the end of each month?

🌐 **3. LO②** What single cash payment made now is equivalent to 11 years of payments of $4800 made at the end of every 6 months with interest at 4.4% compounded quarterly?

4. LO② What is the principal invested at 6.5% compounded semi-annually from which monthly withdrawals of $240 can be made at the end of each month for 25 years?

5. LO① Contributions of $500 are made at the end of every three months into an RRSP. What is the accumulated balance after 20 years if interest is 6% compounded semi-annually?

6. LO② Kirstie's mortgage is repaid over 20 years by payments of $1055.00 made at the end of each month. If interest is 5.2% compounded semi-annually, what is the mortgage principal?

🌐 **7. LO③** Neena wants to accumulate $18 000 in a fund earning 3.6% compounded semi-annually. How much must she deposit at the end of each year for eight years?

8. LO③ What sum of money can be withdrawn from a fund of $15 750 invested at 4.25% compounded semi-annually

 (a) at the end of every month for 12 years?

 (b) at the end of each year for 15 years?

🌐 **9. LO④** How long will it take for payments of $350 to accumulate to $12 000 at 3% compounded monthly if made

 (a) at the end of every three months?

 (b) at the end of every six months?

10. LO③ A $92 000 mortgage with a 25-year term is repaid by making payments at the end of each month. If interest is 5.8% compounded semi-annually, how much are the payments?

11. LO④ A debt of $14 000 is repaid by making payments of $1500. If interest is 9% compounded monthly, for how long will payments have to be made

 (a) at the end of every six months?

 (b) at the end of each year?

12. LO⑤ What is the nominal rate of interest compounded monthly at which payments of $200 made at the end of every three months accumulate to $9200 in eight years?

13. LO④ A debt of $2290 is repaid by making payments of $198. If interest is 16.95% compounded monthly, for how long will quarterly payments have to be made?

14. LO⑤ A $265 000 mortgage is repaid over 25 years by making monthly payments of $1672. What is the nominal annual rate of interest compounded semi-annually on the mortgage?

15. LO④ The balance in Marc's RRSPs was $148 000 when he converted the RRSPs to an RRIF. The RRIF pays $5000 at the end of each quarter. If interest on the RRIF is 4.3% compounded monthly, for how long will Marc receive quarterly payments?

🌐 **16. LO⑤** Satwinder deposited $145 at the end of each month for 15 years at 7.5% compounded monthly. After her last deposit she converted the balance into an ordinary annuity paying $1200 every 3 months for 12 years. If interest on the annuity is compounded semi-annually, what is the nominal rate of interest paid by the annuity?

17. LO①③ Fred Larsen contributes $345 at the end of every 3 months into an RRSP. Interest on the account is 6% compounded monthly.

 (a) What will be the balance after nine years?

 (b) How much of the balance will be interest?

(c) If Fred converts the balance after nine years into an RRIF earning 5% compounded monthly and makes equal withdrawals at the end of every three months for eight years, what is the size of the withdrawal?

(d) What is the combined interest earned by the RRSP and the RRIF?

18. **LO❸** How much must be contributed into an RRSP at the end of each year for 25 years to accumulate to $100 000 if interest is 8% compounded quarterly?

19. **LO❹** For how long must $75 be deposited at the end of each month to accumulate to $9500 at 6.5% compounded quarterly?

20. **LO❹** A $135 000 mortgage is amortized by making monthly payments of $974.37. If interest is

4.92% compounded semi-annually, for how many years is the term of the mortgage?

21. **LO❻** Toby has opened an RRSP account by making an initial deposit of $1200. She intends to make quarterly deposits for 20 years, increasing at a constant rate of 1.5%. How much of the accumulated value just after the last deposit was made is interest if interest is 7% compounded quarterly?

22. **LO❻** Harry paid $250 000 for a 15-year indexed annuity in which the monthly payments received at the end of each month increase by 0.7% per payment. What is the total amount received by Harry if interest is 8.4% compounded monthly?

SELF-TEST

1. Monthly deposits of $480 were made at the end of each month for eight years. If interest is 4.5% compounded semi-annually, what amount can be withdrawn immediately after the last deposit?

2. A loan was repaid in five years by end-of-quarter payments of $1200 at 9.5% compounded semi-annually. How much interest was paid?

3. A loan of $6000 was repaid by quarterly payments of $450. If interest was 12% compounded monthly, how long did it take to pay back the loan?

4. A mortgage of $95 000 is to be amortized by monthly payments over 25 years. If the payments are made at the end of each month and interest is 8.5% compounded semi-annually, what is the size of the monthly payments?

5. Leo invested $67 250 into an annuity earning 4.4% compounded semi-annually. How much is he able to withdraw from the annuity at the end of every three months for seven years?

6. A $45 000 mortgage is repaid in 20 years by making monthly payments of $387.72. What is the nominal annual rate of interest compounded semi-annually?

7. For how long would you have to deposit $491 at the end of every three months to accumulate $20 000 at 6.0% compounded monthly?

8. What is the size of monthly deposits that will accumulate to $67 200 after eight years at 6.5% compounded semi-annually?

9. Sigrid contributed $200 every month for nine years into an RRSP earning 4.3% compounded annually. She then converted the RRSP into an annuity that pays her monthly for 20 years. If the first payment is due one month after the conversion, and interest on the annuity is 5.4% compounded semi-annually, how much will Sigrid receive at the end of every month?

10. Joy would like to receive $6000 at the end of every 3 months for 10 years after her retirement. If she retires now and interest is 6.5% compounded semi-annually, how much must she deposit into an account?

11. Mira has opened a registered retirement income fund (RRIF) with a starting balance of $250 000. Beginning 6 months later, she plans to make semi-annual withdrawals from the RRIF for 20 years. The withdrawals will increase at a constant rate of 1.75%. If the RRIF earns 8% compounded semi-annually, how much is the amount of interest included in the total withdrawals?

CHALLENGE PROBLEMS

1. After winning some money at a casino, Tony is considering purchasing an annuity that promises to pay him $300 at the end of each month for 12 months, then $350 at the end of each month for 24 months, and then $375 at the end of each month for 36 months. If the first payment is due at the end of the first month and interest is 7.5% compounded annually over the life of the annuity, calculate Tony's purchase price.

2. A loan of $5600 is to be repaid at 9% compounded annually by making payments at the end of the next 10 quarters. Each of the last six payments is two times the amount of each of the first four payments. What is the size of each payment?

CASE STUDY Vehicle Cash-Back Incentives

▶ Karim Soltan is shopping for a new vehicle, and has noticed that many vehicle manufacturers are offering special deals to sell off the current year's vehicles before the new models arrive. Karim's local Ford dealership is advertising 3.9% financing for a full 48 months (i.e., 3.9% compounded monthly) or up to $4000 cash back on selected vehicles.

The vehicle that Karim wants to purchase costs $24 600 including taxes, delivery, licence, and dealer preparation. This vehicle qualifies for $1800 cash back if Karim pays cash for the vehicle. Karim has a good credit rating and knows that he could arrange a vehicle loan at his bank for the full price of any vehicle he chooses. His other option is to take the dealer financing offered at 3.9% for 48 months.

Karim wants to know which option requires the lower monthly payment. He knows he can use annuity formulas to calculate the monthly payments.

QUESTIONS

1. Suppose Karim buys the vehicle on July 1. What monthly payment must Karim make if he chooses the dealer's 3.9% financing option and pays off the loan over 48 months? (Assume he makes each monthly payment at the end of the month and his first payment is due on July 31.)

2. Suppose the bank offers Karim a 48-month loan with the interest compounded monthly and the payments due at the end of each month. If Karim accepts the bank loan, he can get $1800 cash back on this vehicle.

Help Karim work out a method to calculate the bank rate of interest required to make bank financing the same cost as dealer financing. First, calculate the monthly rate of interest that would make the monthly bank payments equal to the monthly dealer payments. Then calculate the effective rate of interest represented by the monthly compounded rate. If the financing from the bank is at a lower rate of interest compounded monthly, choose the bank financing. The reason is that the monthly payments for the bank's financing would be lower than the monthly payments for the dealer's 3.9% financing.

(a) How much money would Karim have to borrow from the bank to pay cash for this vehicle?

(b) Using the method above, calculate the effective annual rate of interest and the nominal annual rate of interest required to make the monthly payments for bank financing exactly the same as for dealer financing.

3. Suppose Karim decides to explore the costs of financing a more expensive vehicle. The more expensive vehicle costs $34 900 in total and qualifies for the 3.9% dealer financing for 48 months or $2500 cash back. What is the highest effective annual rate of interest at which Karim should borrow from the bank instead of using the dealer's 3.9% financing?

SUMMARY OF FORMULAS

Formula 12.1

$$p = (1 + i)^c - 1$$

Calculating the equivalent rate of interest per payment period p for a nominal annual rate of interest compounded c times per payment interval

Formula 12.2

$$FV_g = PMT\left[\frac{(1 + p)^n - 1}{p}\right]$$

Calculating the future value of an ordinary general annuity using the equivalent rate of interest per payment period

where $p = (1 + i)^c - 1$

Can be rearranged as:

$$PMT = \frac{FV_g p}{(1 + p)^n - 1}$$

Determining the payment of an ordinary general annuity using the equivalent rate of interest per payment period when the future value is known

Formula 12.3

$$PV_g = PMT\left[\frac{1 - (1 + p)^{-n}}{p}\right]$$

Calculating the present value of an ordinary general annuity using the equivalent rate of interest per payment period

Can be rearranged as:

$$PMT = \frac{PV_g p}{1 - (1 + p)^{-n}}$$

Determining the payment of an ordinary general annuity using the equivalent rate of interest per payment period when the present value is known

Formula 12.4

$$n = \frac{\ln\left[\left(\dfrac{FV_g p}{PMT}\right) + 1\right]}{\ln(1 + p)}$$

Determining the number of payments of an ordinary general annuity using the equivalent rate of interest per payment period when the future value is known

Formula 12.5

$$n = \frac{\ln\left[1 - \left(\dfrac{PV_g p}{PMT}\right)\right]}{-\ln(1 + p)}$$

Determining the number of payments of an ordinary general annuity using the equivalent rate of interest per payment period when the present value is known

Formula 12.6

SIZE OF THE nTH PAYMENT $= PMT(1 + k)^{n-1}$

Calculating the size of the nth payment of a constant-growth annuity

Formula 12.7

SUM OF THE PERIODIC CONSTANT-GROWTH PAYMENTS $= PMT\left[\dfrac{(1 + k)^n - 1}{k}\right]$

Determining the sum of the periodic payments of a constant-growth annuity.

Formula 12.8

$$FV = PMT\left[\frac{(1 + i)^n - (1 + k)^n}{i - k}\right]$$

Calculating the future value of an ordinary simple constant-growth annuity

Formula 12.9

$$PV = PMT\left[\frac{1 - (1 + k)^n(1 + i)^{-n}}{i - k}\right]$$

Calculating the present value of a series of payments forming a constant-growth annuity

Formula 12.10

$$FV = n(PMT)(1 + i)^{n-1}$$

Calculating the future value of an ordinary simple constant-growth annuity when the constant-growth rate and the periodic interest rate are the same

Formula 12.11

$$PV = n(PMT)(1 + i)^{-1}$$

Calculating the present value of an ordinary simple constant-growth annuity when the constant-growth rate and the periodic interest rate are the same

GLOSSARY

Constant-growth annuity an annuity in which the payments change by the same percentage from one period to the next *(p. 482)*

Equivalent rate of interest per payment period the rate of interest earned during the payment period that yields the same amount of interest as a nominal annual rate compounded c times per year, where c is the number of payment periods per year *(p. 466)*

Annuities Due, Deferred Annuities, and Perpetuities

Ralf Kleemann/Shutterstock

LEARNING OBJECTIVES

Upon completing this chapter, you will be able to do the following:

① Compute the future value, present value, periodic payment, term, and interest rate for simple annuities due.

② Compute the future value, present value, periodic payment, term, and interest rate for general annuities due.

③ Compute the future value, present value, periodic payment, term, and interest rate for ordinary deferred annuities.

④ Compute the future value, present value, periodic payment, term, and interest rate for deferred annuities due.

⑤ Compute the present value, periodic payment, and interest rate for ordinary perpetuities, perpetuities due, and deferred perpetuities.

It is the beginning of the month, and you are planning to make payments that are now due. Anticipated payments include rent for a house, membership dues for fitness classes, fees for school classes, fees for supplies, insurance for vehicles, and RESP savings to finance a child's education. A series of regular, equal payments paid at the beginning of the period represents a type of annuity called an annuity due, whether these payments are made at the beginning of the month, quarter, or beginning of the year.

Previously, in Chapters 11 and 12, you encountered ordinary annuities. These are annuities for which the payment is made at the end of the period, whether a month, quarter, or year. Ordinary annuities typically are loan payments, deposits into savings accounts, and interest paid or earned. Leases often use annuities due or annuities in advance.

You could possibly have an annuity that will be paid on a regular basis, but the payment does not start in the first period. This is a deferred annuity. For example, if someone saved money for your education, but you are not expected to withdraw the payments until a later date, you have a deferred annuity. Deferred annuities are also common in retirement and pension planning.

This chapter explores how to calculate the present value, future value, payment, number of payments, and interest rate for annuities due and deferred annuities.

INTRODUCTION

In the previous chapters, we considered ordinary annuities, both simple and general, in which the payments are made at the end of each payment period.

In this chapter, we will consider other annuities resulting from variations in the payment dates and the length of time that the payments continue. These include annuities due (in which payments are made at the beginning of the period), deferred annuities (in which the first payment is made after the first or several payment intervals have been completed), and perpetuities (in which payments continue indefinitely).

13.1 SIMPLE ANNUITIES DUE
A. Future value of a simple annuity due

When analyzing an annuity, several questions need to be answered. First, how often is a payment made? This determines the payment interval. Next, is the payment made at the beginning or at the end of each payment interval?

If the periodic payment is made at the end of each payment interval, as discussed in Chapters 11 and 12, the annuity is an ordinary annuity. If the periodic payment is made at the beginning of each payment interval, the annuity is an **annuity due**. To determine the future value of an annuity due, we start with the formula used for calculating the future value of an ordinary annuity, and then we adjust it to accommodate for the difference in the timing of the payment.

The future value of an ordinary simple annuity is calculated using Formula 11.1. To calculate the future value of a simple annuity due, the result from Formula 11.1 is multiplied by $(1 + i)$ to account for the additional interest earned by the payment made at the beginning of the first period. (Because the payments in an annuity due start earlier than in an ordinary annuity, each payment will end up earning interest for one more interest conversion period).

$$\begin{matrix} \text{FUTURE VALUE OF} \\ \text{A SIMPLE ANNUITY DUE} \end{matrix} = \begin{matrix} \text{FUTURE VALUE OF AN} \\ \text{ORDINARY SIMPLE ANNUITY} \end{matrix} \times (1 + i)$$

The general notation for simple annuities due is the same as for ordinary simple annuities, except that the accumulated value (future value) or the annuity due is represented by the symbol $FV_n(\text{due})$.

Thus, the formula for the future value of a simple annuity due is

Formula 11.1　Adjustment for payment at beginning of period

$$FV_n(\text{due}) = PMT\left[\frac{(1 + i)^n - 1}{i}\right](1 + i) \qquad\qquad \text{Formula 13.1}$$

The relationship between an annuity due and the corresponding ordinary annuity is graphically illustrated in the comparison of the line diagrams that follow.

The two line graphs show the left shift of the payments by one period. In an annuity due, every payment earns interest for one more period than in an ordinary annuity, and this explains the factor $(1 + i)$.

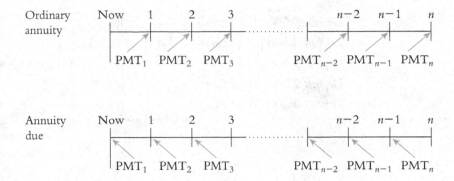

EXAMPLE 13.1A

Calculate the future value at the end date of the last payment period for deposits of $3000 each made at the beginning of five consecutive years with interest at 6% compounded annually.

SOLUTION

As for any problem involving a series of payments, the method of solution and the data can be shown on a time diagram.

Figure 13.1 Graphical Representation of Method and Data (© S. A. Hummelbrunner)

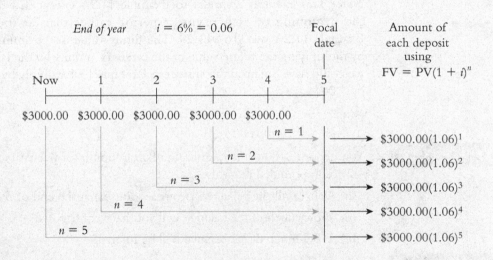

As shown in Figure 13.1, the first deposit is located at the beginning of Year 1, which is the same as "now"; the second deposit is located at the beginning of Year 2, which is the same as the end of Year 1; the third at the beginning of Year 3; the fourth at the beginning of Year 4; and the fifth and last deposit at the beginning of Year 5, which is also the beginning of the last payment period. The focal date, however, is located at the *end* of the last payment period.

The future values of the individual deposits are obtained by using Formula 9.1, $FV = PV(1 + i)^n$. Determining the combined total of the five accumulated values is made easier by taking out the common factors. The common factor 3000.00 is the payment amount. The common factor 1.06 determines the interest earned in the period when the payment is made.

$$
\begin{array}{l}
\textit{Deposit 5 } 3000.00(1.06)^1 \\
\textit{Deposit 4 } 3000.00(1.06)^2 \\
\textit{Deposit 3 } 3000.00(1.06)^3 \quad 3000.00\begin{bmatrix}(1.0)\\(1.06)\\(1.06)^2\\(1.06)^3\\(1.06)^4\end{bmatrix}(1.06) = 3000.00\begin{bmatrix}(1.0)\\(1.06)\\(1.1236)\\(1.191016)\\(1.262477)\end{bmatrix}(1.06) \\
\textit{Deposit 2 } 3000.00(1.06)^4 \\
\textit{Deposit 1 } 3000.00(1.06)^5
\end{array}
$$

$$= 3000.00(5.637093)(1.06)$$
$$= 16\,911.28(1.06)$$
$$= \$17\,925.96$$

The future value can also be found using Formula 13.1.

$$\text{PMT} = \$3000.00; \quad \text{P/Y} = 1; \quad \text{C/Y} = 1; \quad \text{I/Y} = 6.0; \quad i = \frac{0.06}{1} = 0.06; \quad n = 5$$

$$\text{FV}_n(\text{due}) = \text{PMT}\left[\frac{(1+i)^n - 1}{i}\right](1+i) \text{ ———————— Formula 13.1}$$

$$\text{FV}_n(\text{due}) = 3000.00\left[\frac{(1+0.06)^5 - 1}{0.06}\right](1+0.06) = 16\,911.27888(1.06) = \$17\,925.96$$

Note: This example is similar to Example 11.2A except that the deposits are made at the beginning of each payment period rather than at the end. The answer to Example 11.2A was \$16 911.28. The future value of the annuity due can be obtained by multiplying the future value of the ordinary annuity by the factor $(1+i)$. Therefore, we could have obtained the answer to Example 13.1A simply by multiplying \$16 911.28 by 1.06.

EXAMPLE 13.1B

You deposit \$100 at the beginning of each month for five years in an account paying 4.2% compounded monthly.

(i) What will the balance in your account be at the end of five years?

(ii) How much of the balance will you have contributed?

(iii) How much of the balance will be interest?

SOLUTION

(i) PMT = 100.00; P/Y = 12; C/Y = 12; I/Y = 4.2;

$$i = \frac{4.2\%}{12} = 0.35\% = 0.0035; \quad n = 5(12) = 60$$

$$\text{FV(due)} = 100.00\left(\frac{1.0035^{60} - 1}{0.0035}\right)(1.0035)$$

$$= 100.00(66.635949)(1.0035)$$

$$= 6663.5949(1.0035)$$

$$= \$6686.92$$

(ii) Your contribution is the amount of the payment, PMT, multiplied by the number of times you made that payment, N = (100.00)(60) = \$6000.00.

(iii) The interest earned is the difference between the accumulated value and the total contribution 6686.92 − 6000.00 = \$686.92.

POINTERS & PITFALLS

To distinguish between problems dealing with ordinary annuities and annuities due, look for key words or phrases that signal one type of annuity or the other.

Ordinary annuities:	"payments (or deposits) made at the *end* of each (or every) . . ."
	"monthly payments, starting one month from today . . ."
	"interest payments"
Annuities due:	"payments (or deposits) made at the *beginning* of each (or every) . . ."
	"first payment is due on the date of sale (or signing)"
	"payable in advance"
	"monthly payments, starting today . . ."
	"lease or rent payments"

B. Using preprogrammed financial calculators

The future value or the present value of an annuity due can easily be determined by using a preprogrammed financial calculator. One method is to begin by computing the corresponding value for an ordinary simple annuity and multiply it by $(1 + i)$. If you are using the Texas Instruments BA II PLUS, set the calculator in "BGN" mode (since annuity due payments are made at the beginning of each payment period), then solve for the unknown variable the same way as you do for ordinary simple annuities. Follow this key sequence to set the calculator in "BGN" mode:

Key in	Press	Display shows	
2nd	(BGN)	END *or* BGN	—— checks the mode
2nd	(SET)	BGN	—— if previously in "END" mode, BGN will appear in the upper-right corner of the display.
		or	
		END	—— if previously in "BGN" mode, the display will be blank. Press 2nd (SET) again so that BGN appears in the display.
2nd	(QUIT)		—— returns to the standard calculation mode

EXAMPLE 13.1C

Frank deposited $250 at the beginning of each month for four years into a savings account. For the next eight years he made no further deposits but left the money in the account. The savings account paid interest at 4.5% compounded monthly.

(i) What will the balance be after the first four years?

(ii) What will the balance be after the 12 years?

(iii) How much in total was deposited?

(iv) How much interest will have been earned?

SOLUTION

This problem involves two time periods, which must be separated and calculated individually. The time periods are the four years when deposits are being made on a regular monthly basis, and the remaining time period of eight years when no further deposits are being made but the balance continues to earn interest.

Figure 13.2 Graphical Representation of Method and Data (© S. A. Hummelbrunner)

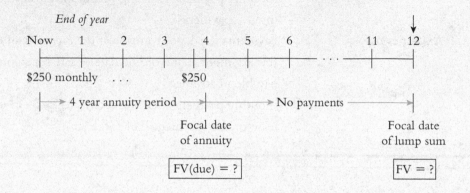

STEP 1

(i) Determine the balance at the end of four years. This problem involves calculating the future value of a simple annuity due.

$$PMT = 250.00; \quad I/Y = 4.5; \quad P/Y, C/Y = 12; \quad i = \frac{4.5\%}{12} = 0.375\%; \quad n = 48$$

$$FV(\text{due}) = 250.00\left(\frac{1.00375^{48} - 1}{0.00375}\right)(1.00375)$$

$$= 250.00(52.483834)(1.00375)$$

$$= 13\ 120.96(1.00375)$$

$$= \$13\ 170.16$$

STEP 2

(ii) Accumulate $13 170.16 for another eight years. Note that the payment is "0" during this period.

$$PV = 13\ 170.16; \quad PMT = 0; \quad i = 0.00375; \quad n = 8(12) = 96$$

$$FV = 13\ 170.16(1.00375)^{96} \underline{\hspace{3cm}} \text{substituting in Formula 9.1}$$

$$= 13\ 170.16(1.432365)$$

$$= \$18\ 864.47$$

PROGRAMMED SOLUTION

("BGN" mode) (Set P/Y, C/Y = 12) 0 [PV] 250 [±] [PMT]

4.5 [I/Y] 48 [N] [CPT] [FV] [13170.162089]

13 170.16209 [±] [PV] 0 [PMT] 4.5 [I/Y]

96 [N] [CPT] [FV] [18864.474664]

The balance in the account after 12 years is $18 864.47.

(iii) The total deposited is 250.00(48) = $12 000.00.

(iv) Interest in the balance is 18 864.47 − 12 000.00 = $6864.47.

C. Solving the terms PMT, *n*, and *i* of a simple annuity due when the FV is known

If the future value of an annuity, FV*n*(due), is known, you can solve the periodic payment, PMT, the term *n*, or the conversion rate *i* by substituting into the future value formula, Formula 13.1, and solve using formula rearrangement.

$$FV_n(\text{due}) = PMT\left[\frac{(1+i)^n - 1}{i}\right](1+i) \text{ ———— Formula 13.1}$$

Solve for PMT by dividing both sides by $\left[\dfrac{(1+i)^n - 1}{i}\right](1+i)$.

$$PMT = \frac{FV_n(\text{due})}{\left[\dfrac{(1+i)^n - 1}{i}\right](1+i)}$$

Note that if you are memorizing formulas, it is more efficient to learn one formula and to understand the method of rearranging this formula to solve for other variables than to memorize multiple connected formulas.

Determining *n* or *i* without a financial calculator is particularly time-consuming. However, this can be done by hand.

Preprogrammed financial calculators are especially helpful when solving for the payment PMT, the term *n*, or the conversion rate *i*. To compute PMT, enter the known values (FV(due), N, I/Y, P/Y, C/Y) into the preprogrammed financial calculator. For simple annuities due, retrieve the answer by being in "BGN" mode and pressing CPT PMT. This is the payment of the annuity. Note that if you have entered FV as a negative amount, the resulting PMT will be positive.

To calculate *n*, enter the known values (FV(due), PMT, I/Y, P/Y, C/Y) into the pre-programmed financial calculator. (Remember, if both FV and PMT are non-zero, enter PMT only as a negative amount.) For simple annuities due, retrieve the answer by being in "BGN" mode and pressing CPT N. This is the term of the annuity.

To calculate the nominal annual rate of interest, I/Y, enter the known values (FV(due), PMT, N, P/Y, C/Y). Press CPT I/Y. This is the nominal annual rate of interest.

EXAMPLE 13.1D

What semi-annual payment must be made into a fund at the beginning of every six months to accumulate to $9600 in 10 years at 7% compounded semi-annually?

SOLUTION

$$FV(\text{due}) = 9600.00; \quad i = \frac{7\%}{2} = 3.5\% = 0.035\%; \quad P/Y, C/Y = 2; \quad I/Y = 7$$

$$n = 10(2) = 20$$

$$PMT = \frac{FV_n(\text{due})}{\left[\dfrac{(1+i)^n - 1}{i}\right](1+i)} \text{ ———— rearranging Formula 13.1}$$

$$PMT = \frac{9600.00}{\left[\dfrac{(1.035)^{20} - 1}{0.035}\right](1.035)}$$

$$PMT = \frac{9600.00}{[28.279682](1.035)}$$

$$PMT = \frac{9600.00}{29.269471}$$

$$PMT = \$327.99$$

PROGRAMMED SOLUTION

("BGN" mode) (Set P/Y, C/Y = 2) 0 [PV] 9600 [FV] 7 [I/Y] 20 [N] [CPT]
[PMT] −327.986799

The semi-annual payment is $327.99.

POINTERS
& PITFALLS

When determining n for annuity calculations, remember that n represents the number of payments. Therefore, n must be a whole number and should always be rounded upward. Whether a partial or full payment is made, it is still a payment. For example, if $n = 21.34$ payments, this would indicate 21 full payments and a smaller last payment (which is still a payment). Therefore, 22 payments are required.

In most cases, the payment (PMT) has been rounded to 2 decimals. This may cause insignificant decimals to show up in the calculations. As a result, an exception to this rule would be when n is extremely close to a whole number. This would mean that no significant digits show up in the first 2 decimals. For example, if $n = 23.001$, it can be reasonably concluded that n is 23 payments, since the 0.001 is likely a result of the rounded payment.

EXAMPLE 13.1E

Atlantic Credit Union intends to accumulate a building fund of $150 000 by depositing $4125 at the beginning of every three months at 7% compounded quarterly. How long will it take for the fund to reach the desired amount?

SOLUTION

FV(due) = 150 000.00; PMT = 4125.00; P/Y = 4; C/Y = 4; I/Y = 7;

$i = \dfrac{7\%}{4} = 1.75\%$

PROGRAMMED SOLUTION

("BGN" mode) (Set P/Y = 4; C/Y = 4) 150 000 [FV]
4125 [±] [PMT] 7 [I/Y] [CPT] [N] 28.000210

It will take 28 quarters, or seven years, to build up the fund.

EXAMPLE 13.1F

Compute the nominal annual rate of interest at which $100 deposited at the beginning of each month for 10 years will amount to $15 000.

SOLUTION

FV(due) = 15 000; PMT = 100.00; P/Y = 12; C/Y = 12; $n = 120$; $m = 12$

("BGN" mode) (Set P/Y = 12; C/Y = 12) 0 [PV] 15 000 [FV]
100 [±] [PMT] 120 [N] [CPT] [I/Y] 4.282801

↑
Allow several seconds for the computation.

The nominal annual rate of interest is 4.2828% compounded monthly.
The monthly conversion rate is 4.2828/12 = 0.3569%.

D. Present value of a simple annuity due

The two formulas to calculate present value for ordinary annuities and annuities due also have a close relationship.

We start with the present value formula for an ordinary annuity, Formula 11.2. The formula is then adjusted to accommodate the difference in the timing of the payment by multiplying by the factor $(1 + i)$.

$$\begin{matrix} \text{PRESENT VALUE OF A SIMPLE} \\ \text{ANNUITY DUE} \end{matrix} = \begin{matrix} \text{PRESENT VALUE OF AN ORDINARY} \\ \text{SIMPLE ANNUITY} \end{matrix} \times (1 + i)$$

The present value of an annuity is represented by the symbol $PV_n(\text{due})$. The formula for the present value of a simple annuity due is

$$\overbrace{\text{Formula 11.2}}\quad \overbrace{\text{Adjustment for payment at beginning of period}}$$

$$PV_n(\text{due}) = PMT\left[\frac{1 - (1 + i)^{-n}}{i}\right](1 + i) \quad\text{——— Formula 13.2}$$

EXAMPLE 13.1G

Calculate the present value of five payments of $3000, each made at the beginning of each of five consecutive years, if money is worth 6% compounded annually.

SOLUTION

As Figure 13.3 shows, the present value of the individual payments is obtained using Formula 9.1, $PV = FV(1 + i)^{-n}$. The sum of the individual present values is easier to calculate when the common factor 3000.00 is taken out.

$$
\begin{array}{l}
\textit{Payment 1 } 3000.00(1.06)^{0} \\
\textit{Payment 2 } 3000.00(1.06)^{-1} \\
\textit{Payment 3 } 3000.00(1.06)^{-2} \\
\textit{Payment 4 } 3000.00(1.06)^{-3} \\
\textit{Payment 5 } 3000.00(1.06)^{-4}
\end{array}
\quad 3000.00
\begin{bmatrix}
(1.0) \\
(1.06)^{-1} \\
(1.06)^{-2} \\
(1.06)^{-3} \\
(1.06)^{-4}
\end{bmatrix}
= 3000.00
\begin{bmatrix}
(1.000000) \\
(0.943396) \\
(0.889996) \\
(0.839619) \\
(0.792094)
\end{bmatrix}
$$

$$= 3000.00(4.465105)$$
$$= \$13\,395.32$$

Figure 13.3 Graphical Representation of Method and Data (© S. A. Hummelbrunner)

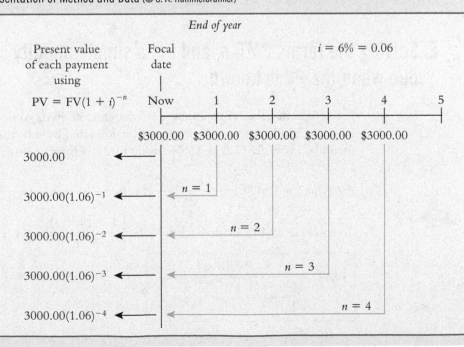

The present value can also be found using Formula 13.2.

$$\text{PMT} = \$3000.00; \quad P/Y = 1; \quad C/Y = 1; \quad I/Y = 6.0; \quad i = \frac{0.06}{1} = 0.06; \quad n = 5$$

$$\text{PV}_n(\text{due}) = \text{PMT}\left[\frac{1 - (1 - i)^{-n}}{i}\right](1 + i) \quad\text{———— Formula 13.2}$$

$$\text{PV}_n(\text{due}) = 3000.00\left[\frac{1 - (1 + 0.06)^{-5}}{0.06}\right](1 + 0.06) = 12\,637.09136(1.06) = \$13\,395.32$$

Example 13.1G is similar to Example 11.3A, except that the payments are made at the beginning of each payment period. The answer to Example 11.3A was $12 637.09. If this amount is multiplied by 1.06, the result is $13 395.32, the answer to Example 13.1G.

This result implies that we could have obtained the present value of the annuity due in Example 13.1G by multiplying the present value of the ordinary annuity in Example 11.3A by the factor 1.06, which is the factor $(1 + i)$.

EXAMPLE 13.1H

What is the cash value of a three-year lease of office facilities renting for $1536.50 payable at the beginning of each month if money is worth 9% compounded monthly?

SOLUTION

Since the payments for the lease are at the beginning of each payment period, the problem involves an annuity due, and since we want the cash value, the present value of the annuity due is required.

$$\text{PMT} = \$1536.50; \quad i = \frac{9\%}{12} = 0.75\% = 0.0075; \quad n = 3(12) = 36$$

$$\text{PV}(\text{due}) = \$1536.50\left[\frac{1 - (1.0075)^{-36}}{0.0075}\right](1.0075)$$

$$= \$1536.50(31.446805)(1.0075)$$

$$= \$48\,318.01627(1.0075)$$

$$= \$48\,680.40$$

The cash value of the lease is $48 680.40.

E. Solving the terms PMT, *n*, and *i* of a simple annuity due when the PV is known

If the present value of an annuity, $\text{PV}_n(\text{due})$, is known, you can determine the periodic payment PMT, the term *n*, or the conversion rate *i* by substituting into the present value formula, Formula 13.2 and solve using formula rearrangement.

$$\text{PV}_n(\text{due}) = \text{PMT}\left[\frac{1 - (1 + i)^{-n}}{i}\right](1 + i) \quad\text{———— Formula 13.2}$$

To solve for PMT, divide both sides by $\left[\dfrac{1 - (1 + i)^{-n}}{i}\right](1 + i)$.

$$\boxed{\text{PMT} = \frac{\text{PV}_n(\text{due})}{\left[\dfrac{1 - (1 + i)^{-n}}{i}\right](1 + i)}}$$

As with Formula 13.1, note that if you are memorizing formulas, it is more efficient to learn one formula and to understand the method of rearranging this formula to solve for other variables than to memorize multiple connected formulas.

Determining n or i, although time-consuming, can be done by hand.

Again, preprogrammed financial calculators are especially helpful when solving for the payment PMT, the term n, or the conversion rate i.

When using the preprogrammed financial calculator, use the same procedures as given in the previous section. To compute PMT, enter the known values (PV(due), N, I/Y, P/Y, C/Y) into the pre-programmed financial calculator. For simple annuities due, retrieve the answer by being in "BGN" mode and pressing CPT PMT . This is the payment of the annuity. Note that if you have entered PV as a negative amount, the resulting PMT will be positive.

To calculate n, enter the known values (PV(due), PMT, I/Y, P/Y, C/Y) into the pre-programmed financial calculator. (Remember, if both PV and PMT are non-zero, enter PMT only as a negative amount.) For simple annuities due, retrieve the answer by being in "BGN" mode and pressing CPT N . This is the term of the annuity.

To calculate the nominal annual rate of interest, I/Y, enter the known values (PV(due), PMT, N, P/Y, C/Y) into the preprogrammed financial calculator. Press CPT I/Y . This is the nominal annual rate of interest.

EXAMPLE 13.11

What monthly rent payment is required at the beginning of each month for four years to fulfill a lease contract worth $7000 if money is worth 7.5% compounded monthly?

SOLUTION

$PV(due) = 7000.00$; $P/Y = 12$; $C/Y = 12$; $I/Y = 7.5$;

$$i = \frac{7.5\%}{12} = 0.625\% = 0.00625; \quad n = 4(12) = 48$$

$$PMT = \frac{PV_n(due)}{\left[\dfrac{1 - (1 + i)^{-n}}{i}\right](1 + i)} \qquad \text{—— rearranging Formula 13.2}$$

$$PMT = \frac{7000.00}{\left[\dfrac{1 - (1.00625)^{-48}}{0.00625}\right](1.00625)}$$

$$PMT = \frac{7000.00}{[41.358371](1.00625)}$$

$$PMT = \frac{7000.00}{41.616861}$$

$$PMT = \$168.20$$

PROGRAMMED SOLUTION

("BGN" mode) (Set P/Y = 12; C/Y = 12) 0 FV 7000 ± PV

7.5 I/Y 48 N CPT PMT 168.201057

The monthly rent payment due at the beginning of each month is $168.20.

EXAMPLE 13.1J

How much will you have to deposit into an account at the beginning of every 3 months for 12 years if you want to have a balance of $100 000 in 20 years and interest is 8% compounded quarterly?

SOLUTION

There are two time periods: the term when no payments are made in the final 8 years (between 12 and 20 years), and the initial 12-year term of annuity payments.

Figure 13.4 Graphical Representation of Method and Data (© S. A. Hummelbrunner)

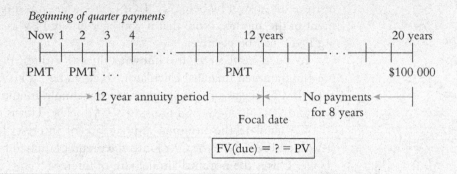

First, determine the balance (PV) at the beginning of the 8-year period. This value is needed to calculate the payments during the initial 12 years.

$FV = 100\ 000.00$; $P/Y = 4$; $C/Y = 4$; $I/Y = 8$; $i = \dfrac{8\%}{4} = 2\% = 0.02$;

$n = 8(4) = 32$

$\quad PV = 100\ 000.00(1.02)^{-32}$

$\qquad = 100\ 000.00(0.530633)$

$\qquad = \$53\ 063.33$

Next, for the initial 12-year annuity period, determine the quarterly payment needed to accumulate to $53 063.33.

$FV(\text{due}) = 53\ 063.33$; $P/Y = 4$; $C/Y = 4$; $I/Y = 8$; $i = \dfrac{8\%}{4} = 0.02$;

$n = 12(4) = 48$

$$PMT = \frac{FV_n(\text{due})}{\left[\dfrac{(1+i)^n - 1}{i}\right](1+i)} \qquad\qquad \text{—— rearranging Formula 13.1}$$

$$PMT = \frac{53\ 063.33}{\left[\dfrac{(1.02)^{48} - 1}{0.02}\right](1.02)}$$

$$PMT = \frac{53\ 063.33}{\left[79.353519\right](1.02)}$$

$$PMT = \$655.58$$

PROGRAMMED SOLUTION

(Set $P/Y = 4$; $C/Y = 4$) 0 [PMT] 100 000 [FV]

8 [I/Y] 32 [N] [CPT] [PV] ⎰−53063.33035⎱

("BGN" mode) $\boxed{\pm}$ 53 063.33035 $\boxed{\text{FV}}$ 0 $\boxed{\text{PV}}$

8 $\boxed{\text{I/Y}}$ 48 $\boxed{\text{N}}$ $\boxed{\text{CPT}}$ $\boxed{\text{PMT}}$ $\boxed{-655.583689}$

The quarterly deposit at the beginning of each payment period is $655.58.

EXAMPLE 13.1K

For how long can you withdraw $480 at the beginning of every three months from a fund of $9000 if interest is 10% compounded quarterly?

SOLUTION

$PV(\text{due}) = 9000.00;$ $PMT = 480.00;$ $P/Y = 4;$ $C/Y = 4;$ $I/Y = 10;$

$i = \dfrac{10\%}{4} = 2.5\% = 0.025$

$9000.00 = 480.00\left(\dfrac{1 - 1.025^{-n}}{0.025}\right)(1.025)$ ———— substituting in Formula 13.2

$9000.00 = 19\ 680.00(1 - 1.025^{-n})$

$\dfrac{9000.00}{19\ 680.00} = 1 - 1.025^{-n}$

$0.457317 = 1 - 1.025^{-n}$

$1.025^{-n} = 1 - 0.457317$

$1.025^{-n} = 0.542683$

$-n \ln 1.025 = \ln 0.542683$

$-n(0.024693) = -0.611230$

$n = \dfrac{0.611230}{0.024693}$

$n = 24.753560$

$n = 25$ (quarterly withdrawals)

PROGRAMMED SOLUTION

(Set P/Y = 4; C/Y = 4) ("BGN" mode) 9000 $\boxed{\pm}$ $\boxed{\text{PV}}$

0 $\boxed{\text{FV}}$ 480 $\boxed{\text{PMT}}$ 10 $\boxed{\text{I/Y}}$ $\boxed{\text{CPT}}$ $\boxed{\text{N}}$ $\boxed{24.753560}$

There will be 24 quarterly withdrawals of $480. The 25th withdrawal will be less than $480. (25 quarterly withdrawals will take 6 1/4 years, or 6 years and 3 months).

POINTERS & PITFALLS

When working with the n for an annuity due, n represents the number of payments and must be a whole number. Therefore, n will always round upward. However, it is important to distinguish whether the question is asking about the term of the annuity due or when the last payment of the annuity due occurs.

- If the term is being asked for, n can be used to figure out the timeline. For example, a yearly apartment rental agreement would have 12 monthly payments; thus the term ends 12 months from now.

- If the last payment is being asked for, n can be used to figure out the timeline. In the same example, the last rental payment would occur at the beginning of the 12th month. The last payment would be $12 - 1 = 11$ months from now.

EXAMPLE 13.1L

A lease agreement valued at $7500 requires payment of $450 at the beginning of every quarter for five years. What is the nominal annual rate of interest charged?

SOLUTION

PV(due) = 7500.00;   PMT = 450.00;   P/Y = 4;   C/Y = 4; $n = 20$; $m = 4$

("BGN" mode) (Set P/Y = 4; C/Y = 4) 0 $\boxed{\text{FV}}$ 7500 $\boxed{\pm}$ $\boxed{\text{PV}}$

450 $\boxed{\text{PMT}}$ 20 $\boxed{\text{N}}$ $\boxed{\text{CPT}}$ $\boxed{\text{I/Y}}$ $\boxed{8.0326}$

Allow several seconds for the computation.

The nominal annual rate of interest is 8.0326% compounded quarterly.
The quarterly compounding rate is 8.0326/4 = 2.0082%.

EXERCISE 13.1

MyLab Math

If you choose, you can use Excel's PV function (present value) or FV function (future value) to answer the questions indicated.

Answer each of the following questions.

1. Calculate the accumulated value of an annuity due of $300 payable at the beginning of every month for seven years at 6% compounded monthly.   Reference Example 13.1A

2. Determine the accumulated value after 12 years of deposits of $360 made at the beginning of every 3 months and earning interest at 7% compounded quarterly.

3. To finance a vacation in four years, Elsie saves $530 at the beginning of every three months in an account paying interest at 3.92% compounded quarterly.
   (a) What will be the balance in her account when she takes the vacation?
   (b) How much of the balance will be interest?
   (c) If she waits an additional year to start her vacation, and continues to save the same amount of money, how much more money does she have to spend?

4. To save for Harman's post-secondary education starting in 18 years, his family deposits $1200 at the beginning of every year into an education fund earning interest at 4.15% compounded annually.
   (a) What will be the balance in the fund after 18 years?
   (b) How much of the balance will be interest?
   (c) If the interest rate increases to 4.65% compounded annually, how much more interest is earned?

5. On an annual renewable lease, the quarterly lease payment on office space is $1600 payable in advance. What equivalent yearly payment made in advance would satisfy the lease if interest is 6.6% compounded quarterly?

6. A washer-dryer combination can be purchased from a department store by making monthly credit card payments of $122.50 for two-and-a-half years. The first payment is due on the date of sale and interest is 21% compounded monthly.
   (a) What is the purchase price?
   (b) How much will be paid in installments?
   (c) How much is the cost of financing?
   (d) If an additional $12.50 per month is added to cover a service contract, what is the new purchase price on the date of sale?

7. Diane Wallace bought a refrigerator on credit, signing an installment contract with a finance company that requires monthly payments of $62.25 for three years. The first payment is made on the date of signing and interest is 24% compounded monthly.
   (a) What was the cash price?
   (b) How much will Diane pay in total?
   (c) How much of what she pays will be interest?
   (d) Based on the cash price calculated in part (a), if the interest rate is changed to 19.9% compounded monthly, what is the new monthly payment?

8. Claude made semi-annual deposits of $3100 at the beginning of a six-month period into a fund earning 6.8% compounded semi-annually for nine years. No further deposits were made.
   (a) How much will be in the account 15 years after the first deposit?
   (b) How much in total was deposited?
   (c) How much interest will have been earned?   Reference Example 13.1C

9. If Gary accumulated $5700 in his savings account over five years, how much did he deposit at the beginning of every month if interest is 4.32% compounded monthly?

10. Elspeth McNab purchased a new motorcycle valued at $12 500 on an installment plan requiring equal monthly payments for four years. If the first payment is due on the date of purchase and interest is 7.5% compounded monthly, what is the size of the monthly payment?   Reference Example 13.1I

11. Payments on a five-year lease valued at $37 750 are to be made at the beginning of every six months. If interest is 9% compounded semi-annually, what is the size of the semi-annual payments?

12. Mr. Clark makes a deposit at the beginning of every three months into a savings account that earns interest at 5.25% compounded quarterly. He saves for 25 years, then converts his savings into an annuity that pays him $900 at the beginning of every 3 months for 20 years. What is the size of the deposit he makes while he is saving?

13. Joey's family wants to save $5000 to finance a vacation trip to a popular amusement park. If they save $240 at the beginning of each month and the fund is invested to earn 5% compounded monthly, how long will it take them to save enough money to take the trip?

14. Ali deposits $450 at the beginning of every quarter. He wants to build up his account so that he can withdraw $1000 every quarter starting 3 months after the last deposit. If he wants to make the withdrawals for 15 years and interest is 10% compounded quarterly, for how long must Ali make the quarterly deposits?

15. If you save $75 at the beginning of every month for 10 years, for how long can you withdraw $260 at the beginning of each month, starting 10 years from now, assuming that interest is 6% compounded monthly?

16. Quarterly payments of $1445 are to be made at the beginning of every three months on a lease valued at $25 000. What should the term of the lease be if money is worth 8% compounded quarterly?

17. What nominal annual rate of interest compounded quarterly was paid if contributions of $250 made into an RRSP at the beginning of every 3 months amounted to $14 559 after 10 years?   Reference Example 13.1L

18. An insurance policy provides a $250 000 benefit 20 years from now. Alternatively, the policy pays $4220 at the beginning of each year for 20 years. What is the effective annual rate of interest paid?

19. A sailboat valued at $25 000 was bought for 15 payments of $2200 due at the beginning of every 6 months. What nominal annual rate of interest was charged?

🌐 **20.** A vehicle can be purchased by paying $27 000 now, or it can be leased by paying $725 per month for the next four years, with the first payment due on the day of signing the lease. What nominal annual rate of interest is charged on the lease?

13.2 GENERAL ANNUITIES DUE
A. Future value of a general annuity due

As with a simple annuity due, the future value of a **general annuity due** is greater than the future value of the corresponding ordinary general annuity by the amount of interest on it for one payment period.

We start with the future value formula for an ordinary general annuity, Formula 12.2. The future value formula for a general annuity due is then adjusted to accommodate the difference in the timing of the payment.

$$\frac{\text{FUTURE VALUE OF A GENERAL}}{\text{ANNUITY DUE}} = \frac{\text{FUTURE VALUE OF AN ORDINARY}}{\text{GENERAL ANNUITY}} \times (1 + p)$$

The interest on a general annuity for one payment period is $(1 + i)^c$, or $(1 + p)$. Use Formula 13.3 to calculate the future value of a general annuity due.

Formula 12.2   Adjustment for payment at beginning of period

$$FV_g(\text{due}) = PMT\left[\frac{(1 + p)^n - 1}{p}\right](1 + p) \text{ —————— Formula 13.3}$$

where $p = (1 + i)^c - 1$

Recall, c represents the number of interest conversion periods per payment interval.

EXAMPLE 13.2A

What is the accumulated value after five years of payments of $20 000 made at the beginning of each year if interest is 7% compounded quarterly?

SOLUTION

$PMT = 20\ 000.00;\quad n = 5;\quad c = 4;\quad P/Y = 1;\quad C/Y = 4;\quad I/Y = 7$

$i = \dfrac{7\%}{4} = 1.75\% = 0.0175$

The equivalent annual rate of interest

$p = 1.0175^4 - 1 = 1.071859 - 1 = 0.071859 = 7.1859\%$

$FV(\text{due}) = 20\ 000.00\left(\dfrac{1.071859^5 - 1}{0.071859}\right)(1.071859)$ ———— substituting in Formula 13.3

$= 20\ 000.00(5.772109)(1.071859)$

$= 115\ 442.1869(1.071859)$

$= \$123\ 737.75$

PROGRAMMED SOLUTION

("BGN" mode) (Set P/Y = 1; C/Y = 4) 7 [I/Y] 0 [PV]

20 000 [±] [PMT] 5 [N] [CPT] [FV] [123737.7535]

The accumulated value after five years is $123 737.75.

B. Solving the terms PMT, *n*, and *i* of a general annuity due when the FV is known

If the future value of an annuity, FV*g*(due), is known, you can calculate the periodic payment PMT by substituting into the future value formula, Formula 13.3.

$$FV_g(\text{due}) = PMT\left[\frac{(1+p)^n - 1}{p}\right](1+p) \quad\quad\text{Formula 13.3}$$
$$\text{where } p = (1+i)^c - 1$$

To calculate PMT, rearrange the terms of Formula 13.3, arriving at the following expression. Substitute the known values (FV(due), *n*, and *i*) and solve for PMT.

$$PMT = \frac{FV_g(\text{due})}{\left[\dfrac{(1+p)^n - 1}{p}\right](1+p)}$$
$$\text{where } p = (1+i)^c - 1$$

To compute PMT, *n*, or I/Y using the preprogrammed financial calculator, follow the procedure outlined in the previous section.

EXAMPLE 13.2B

What deposit made at the beginning of each month will accumulate to $18 000 at 5% compounded quarterly at the end of eight years?

SOLUTION

$$FV(\text{due}) = 18\ 000.00; \quad n = 8(12) = 96; \quad P/Y = 12; \quad C/Y = 4; \quad c = \frac{4}{12} = \frac{1}{3}$$

$$I/Y = 5; \quad i = \frac{5\%}{4} = 1.25\% = 0.0125\%$$

The equivalent monthly rate of interest

$$p = 1.0125^{\frac{1}{3}} - 1 = 1.004149 - 1 = 0.004149 = 0.4149\%$$

$$PMT = \frac{FV_g(\text{due})}{\left[\dfrac{(1+p)^n - 1}{p}\right](1+p)} \quad \text{where } p = (1+i)^c - 1 \quad \begin{array}{l}\text{rearranging}\\ \text{Formula 13.3}\end{array}$$

$$PMT = \frac{18\ 000.00}{\left[\dfrac{(1+0.004149)^{96} - 1}{0.004149}\right](1+0.004149)}$$

$$PMT = \frac{18\ 000.00}{[117.638406](1.004149)}$$

$$PMT = \frac{18\ 000.00}{118.126236}$$

$$PMT = \$152.38$$

PROGRAMMED SOLUTION

("BGN" mode) (Set P/Y = 12; C/Y = 4) 5 [I/Y] 0 [PV]

18 000 [FV] 96 [N] [CPT] [PMT] -152.379359

The monthly deposit is $152.38.

EXAMPLE 13.2C

Ted Davis wants to accumulate $140 000 in an RRSP by making annual contributions of $5500 at the beginning of each year. If interest on the RRSP is 11% compounded quarterly, for how long will Ted have to make contributions?

SOLUTION

$FV(\text{due}) = 140\ 000.00;\quad PMT = 5500.00;\quad P/Y = 1;\quad C/Y = 4;\quad c = 4;$

$I/Y = 11;\quad i = \dfrac{11\%}{4} = 2.75\% = 0.0275$

The equivalent annual rate of interest

$p = 1.0275^4 - 1 = 1.114621 - 1 = 0.114621 = 11.4621\%$

$$140\ 000.000 = 5500.00\left(\frac{1.114621^n - 1}{0.114621}\right)(1.114621) \quad\text{------ using Formula 13.3}$$

$140\ 000.00 = 53\ 484.118(1.114621^n - 1)$

$2.617600 = 1.114621^n - 1$

$1.114621^n = 3.617600$

$n \ln 1.114621 = \ln 3.617600$

$n(0.108515) = 1.285811$

$n = \dfrac{1.285811}{0.108515}$

$n = 11.849188$

$n = 12 \text{ years}$

PROGRAMMED SOLUTION

("BGN" mode) (Set P/Y = 1; C/Y = 4) 11 [I/Y] 0 [PV]

5500 [±] [PMT] 140 000 [FV] [CPT] [N] [11.849188]

Ted will have to contribute for 12 years.

EXAMPLE 13.2D

Compute the nominal annual rate of interest compounded monthly at which $500 deposited at the beginning of every 3 months for 10 years will amount to $30 000.

SOLUTION

$FV(\text{due}) = 30\ 000.00;\quad PMT = 500.00;\quad n = 40;\quad P/Y = 4;\quad C/Y = 12;$

$c = \dfrac{12}{4} = 3$

PROGRAMMED SOLUTION

("BGN" mode) (Set P/Y = 4; C/Y = 12) 0 [PV] 30 000 [FV]

500 [±] [PMT] 40 [N] [CPT] [I/Y] [7.4845]

The nominal annual rate is 7.4845% compounded monthly.

C. Present value of a general annuity due

For a general annuity due, the present value is greater than the present value of the corresponding ordinary general annuity because of the interest earned in the first payment period.

The present value formula for an ordinary general annuity, Formula 12.3, is adjusted to determine the present value formula for a general annuity due.

$$\begin{matrix} \text{PRESENT VALUE OF A} \\ \text{GENERAL ANNUITY DUE} \end{matrix} = \begin{matrix} \text{PRESENT VALUE OF AN ORDINARY} \\ \text{GENERAL ANNUITY} \end{matrix} \times (1 + p)$$

Formula 12.3   Adjustment for payment at beginning of period

$$PV_g(\text{due}) = PMT \left[\frac{1 - (1 + p)^{-n}}{p} \right] (1 + p) \qquad \text{—— Formula 13.4}$$

$$\text{where } p = (1 + i)^c - 1$$

EXAMPLE 13.2E

A three-year lease requires payments of \$1600 at the beginning of every three months. If money is worth 9.0% compounded monthly, what is the cash value of the lease?

SOLUTION

$PMT = 1600.00$; $n = 3(4) = 12$; $P/Y = 4$; $C/Y = 12$; $c = \dfrac{12}{4} = 3$; $I/Y = 9$;

$$i = \frac{9.0\%}{12} = 0.75\% = 0.0075$$

The equivalent quarterly rate of interest

$$p = 1.0075^3 - 1 = 1.022669 - 1 = 0.022669 = 2.2669\%$$

$$PV_g(\text{due}) = PMT \left[\frac{1 - (1 + p)^{-n}}{p} \right] (1 + p) \quad \text{where } p = (1 + i)^c - 1$$

$$PV(\text{due}) = 1600.00 \left(\frac{1 - 1.022669^{-12}}{0.022669} \right) (1.022669) \quad \text{—— substituting in Formula 13.4}$$

$$= 1600.00(10.404043)(1.022669)$$

$$= 16\ 646.46883(1.022669)$$

$$= \$17\ 023.83$$

PROGRAMMED SOLUTION

("BGN" mode) (Set P/Y = 4; C/Y = 12) 9 [I/Y] 0 [FV]

1600.00 [±] [PMT] 12 [N] [CPT] [PV] [17023.83049]

The cash value of the lease is \$17 023.83.

D. Solving the terms PMT, *n*, and *i* of a general annuity due when the PV is known

If the present value of an annuity, $PV_g(\text{due})$, is known, you can calculate the periodic payment PMT by substituting into the present value formula, Formula 13.4.

$$PV_g(\text{due}) = PMT\left[\frac{1 - (1 + p)^{-n}}{p}\right](1 + p) \qquad\text{—— Formula 13.3}$$

where $p = (1 + i)^c - 1$

To calculate PMT, rearrange the terms of Formula 13.4, arriving at the following expression. Substitute the known values (PV(due), *n*, and *i*) and solve for PMT.

$$PMT = \frac{PV_g(\text{due})}{\left[\dfrac{1 - (1 + p)^{-n}}{p}\right](1 + p)}$$

where $p = (1 + i)^c - 1$

When using the preprogrammed financial calculator, use the same procedures as given in the previous section.

To compute *n*, enter the known values (PV(due), PMT, I/Y, P/Y, C/Y) into the pre-programmed financial calculator. (Remember, if both PV and PMT are non-zero, enter PMT only as a negative amount.) For simple annuities due, retrieve the answer by being in "BGN" mode and pressing [CPT] [N]. This is the term of the annuity.

To calculate the nominal annual rate of interest, I/Y, enter the known values (PV(due), PMT, N, P/Y, C/Y) into the preprogrammed financial calculator. Press [CPT] [I/Y]. This is the nominal annual rate of interest.

EXAMPLE 13.2F

What monthly payment must be made at the beginning of each month on a five-year lease valued at $100 000 if interest is 10% compounded semi-annually?

SOLUTION

$PV(\text{due}) = 100\,000.00; \quad n = 5(12) = 60; \quad P/Y = 12; \quad C/Y = 2; \quad c = \dfrac{2}{12} = \dfrac{1}{16};$

$I/Y = 10; \quad i = \dfrac{10\%}{2} = 5\% = 0.05$

The equivalent monthly rate of interest

$p = 1.05^{\frac{1}{6}} - 1 = 1.008165 - 1 = 0.008165 = 0.8165\%$

$$PMT = \frac{PV_g(\text{due})}{\left[\dfrac{1 - (1 + p)^{-n}}{p}\right](1 + p)} \qquad\text{—— rearranging Formula 13.4}$$

$$PMT = \frac{100\,000.00}{\left[\dfrac{(1 - (1 + 0.008165)^{-60}}{0.008165}\right](1 + 0.008165)}$$

$$PMT = \frac{100\,000.00}{\left[47.286470\right](1.008165)}$$

$$PMT = \frac{100\,000.00}{47.672557}$$

$$PMT = \$2097.64$$

PROGRAMMED SOLUTION

("BGN" mode) (Set P/Y = 12; C/Y = 2) 10 $\boxed{\text{I/Y}}$ 0 $\boxed{\text{FV}}$

100 000 $\boxed{\pm}$ $\boxed{\text{PV}}$ 60 $\boxed{\text{N}}$ $\boxed{\text{CPT}}$ $\boxed{\text{PMT}}$ $\boxed{2097.642904}$

The monthly payment due at the beginning of each month is $2097.64.

EXAMPLE 13.2G

Ted Davis, having reached his goal of a $140 000 balance in his RRSP, immediately converts it into an RRIF and withdraws from it $1650 at the beginning of each month. If interest continues at 5.75% compounded quarterly, for how long can he make withdrawals?

SOLUTION

$PV(\text{due}) = 140\,000.00;$ $PMT = 1650.00;$ $P/Y = 12;$ $C/Y = 4;$ $c = \dfrac{4}{12} = \dfrac{1}{3};$

$I/Y = 5.75;$ $i = \dfrac{5.75\%}{4} = 1.4375\% = 0.014375$

The equivalent monthly rate of interest

$p = 1.014375^{\frac{1}{3}} - 1 = 1.004769 - 1 = 0.004769 = 0.4769\%$

$$140\,000.00 = 1650.00\left(\frac{1 - 1.004769^{-n}}{0.004769}\right)(1.004769) \quad\text{——— using Formula 13.4}$$

$$140\,000.00 = 347\,642.59(1 - 1.004769^{-n})$$

$$0.402712 = 1 - 1.004769^{-n}$$

$$1.004769^{-n} = 0.597288$$

$$-n \ln 1.004769 = \ln 0.597288$$

$$-n(0.004758) = -0.515357$$

$$n = 108.32388$$

$$n = 109 \text{ months}$$

PROGRAMMED SOLUTION

("BGN" mode) (Set P/Y = 12; C/Y = 4) 5.75 $\boxed{\text{I/Y}}$ 0 $\boxed{\text{FV}}$

140 000 $\boxed{\pm}$ $\boxed{\text{PV}}$ 1650 $\boxed{\text{PMT}}$ $\boxed{\text{CPT}}$ $\boxed{\text{N}}$ $\boxed{108.323882}$

Ted will be able to make withdrawals for 108 months, or 9 years. His first withdrawal will be now.

EXERCISE 13.2

If you choose, you can use Excel's PV function (present value) or FV function (future value) to answer the questions indicated.

Answer each of the following questions.

1. Bomac Steel sets aside $50 000 at the beginning of every six months in a fund to replace equipment. If interest is 6% compounded quarterly, how much will be in the fund after five years?
 Reference Example 13.2A

2. Jamie Dean contributes $125 at the beginning of each month into an RRSP paying interest at 6.5% compounded semi-annually. What will be the accumulated balance in the RRSP at the end of 25 years?

3. What is the cash value of a lease requiring payments of $750 at the beginning of each month for three years if interest is 8% compounded quarterly?
 Reference Example 13.2E

4. Gerald and Marysia bought a property by agreeing to make semi-annual payments of $12 500 for seven years. If the first payment is due on the date of purchase and interest is 9% compounded quarterly, what is the purchase price of the property?

5. A new owner purchased Alberni Fishing Lodge by contracting to make annual payments of $121 300 for eight years. If the first payment is due on the date of purchase and interest is 3.98% compounded quarterly, what is the purchase price of the property?

6. How much would you have to pay into an account at the beginning of every six months to accumulate $10 000 in eight years if interest is 7% compounded quarterly?
 Reference Example 13.2B

7. Teachers' Credit Union entered a lease contract valued at $5400. The contract provides for payments at the beginning of each month for three years. If interest is 5.5% compounded quarterly, what is the size of the monthly payment?

8. To expand his transmission shop, Hans needs to save $14 000 for new equipment. How much would he have to pay into an account at the beginning of every three months over three years if interest is 7% compounded semi-annually?

9. For its new manufacturing plant, Windsor Windows entered a lease contract valued at $640 000. With the contract, the company must make payments at the beginning of each month for five years. If interest is 5.57% compounded quarterly, what is the size of the monthly payment?

10. Sarah Ling has saved $85 000. If she decides to withdraw $3000 at the beginning of every three months and interest is 6.125% compounded annually, for how long can she make withdrawals?
 Reference Example 13.2G

11. For how long must contributions of $1600 be made at the beginning of each year to accumulate to $96 000 at 10% compounded quarterly?

12. Sadie has subscribed to *Ingenue* magazine through a contract worth $242. If she pays $25 at the beginning of every three months and interest is 21% compounded monthly, for how many months will she receive issues of the magazine?

13. What is the nominal annual rate of interest compounded annually on a lease valued at $21 600 if payments of $680 are made at the beginning of each month for three years?
 Reference Example 13.2D

14. An insurance policy provides for a lump-sum benefit of $50 000 fifteen years from now. Alternatively, payments of $1700 may be received at the beginning of each of the next 15 years. What is the nominal annual rate of interest if interest is compounded quarterly?

BUSINESS MATH NEWS   A Vicious Cycle: Why Tuition Is so High and Will Likely Keep Going Up?

As tuition fees have risen, more students have relied on student loans to help finance their post-secondary education. While post-secondary tuition rises, the government's share of funding has fallen. This shift has put pressure on schools to find more ways to help students with scholarships and student aid. This creates a vicious cycle, as the need to raise funds for scholarships fuels further increases in tuition and fees. According to Statistics Canada, in 2017 the average price tag for an undergraduate degree was $6500 a year for domestic students. Fortunately, studies have shown that post-secondary graduates have fared better in the labour market than those with less education.

With the cost of an undergraduate degree estimated at $60 000, it is essential that parents start to save for their children's education when their kids are young.

Registered Education Savings Plans (RESPs) allow for tax-sheltered growth and, through the Canada Education Savings Grant, the federal government contributes up to $7200 over the life of the plan, depending on your family income. RESPs can be used for tuition at universities, colleges, and trade and technical schools. The original capital can be withdrawn tax-free at any time, but the investment income and the grant are taxable at the beneficiary's (student's) rate of income tax, when withdrawn.

Contributing $100 a month to an RESP can grow to more than $30 000 by the end of 15 years (assuming a 7% annual rate of return).

But if parents have not saved enough, there are other options to help. The federal government offers Canada Student Loans to full- and part-time post-secondary students in most provinces who demonstrate financial need. Alternatively, a student line of credit offers funds at a lower interest rate than a credit card, generally prime plus 1% to 3%. Payments must be made while the student is still in school, but can be spread over many years, and students generally require a cosigner (e.g., a parent or guardian).

The bottom line is that the RESP is likely the best means of accumulating money for post-secondary education, if the contribution is at least $2000 a year per child.

QUESTIONS

1. The advantage of the RESP is that the government will contribute $1 for every $5 parents put in, up to a maximum government grant of $500 per year per child. Assume the Wong family contributes $2000 per year over a 16-year period to an RESP earning 4.85% interest compounded semi-annually.

   (a) Calculate the value the plan would have at the start of the 17th year.
   (b) Calculate the value of annual contributions of $2000 into a non-RESP plan over a 16-year period at 4.85% interest compounded semi-annually.
   (c) Determine the difference in plan values of the RESP plan and those of the non-RESP plan.

2. Assume that $1000 was contributed at the beginning of the year into an RESP plan for 10 years.

   (a) If the rate of interest was 4% per annum compounded annually for the first 5 years, and 5.2% compounded quarterly for the last 5 years, calculate the amount of the plan.
   (b) If the beneficiary's tax rate is 25% and the student uses this amount for a four-year degree, calculate the monthly value that can be used by the student.

Source: Erica Alini, "A vicious cycle: Why tuition is so high and will likely keep going up," September 1, 2018. *Global News*, https://globalnews.ca/news/4414387/canada-tuition-college-resp-2018/.

13.3 ORDINARY DEFERRED ANNUITIES
A. Computation of an ordinary simple deferred annuity

A **deferred annuity** is one in which the first payment is made at a time *later* than the end of the first payment interval. The time period from the time referred to as "now" to the starting point of the term of the annuity is called the **period of deferment**. The number of compounding periods in the period of deferment is designated by the letter symbol d. The future value of a deferred ordinary simple annuity (designated by the symbol $FV_n(\text{defer})$) is the accumulated value of the periodic payments at the end of the term of the annuity.

When a deferred payment amount PMT is to be calculated, and the present value PV of the deferment period is known, first determine the future value of the term of deferment. This value then becomes the present value of the annuity term, and the payment PMT is calculated.

EXAMPLE 13.3A	Determine the size of the payment required at the end of every three months to repay a five-year loan of $25 000 if the payments are deferred for two years and interest is 6% compounded quarterly.
SOLUTION	See Figure 13.5.

Figure 13.5 Graphical Representation of Method and Data (© S. A. Hummelbrunner)

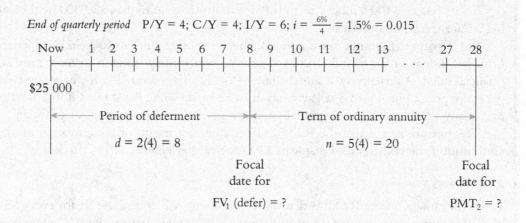

The payments form a deferred ordinary annuity.

$PV(\text{defer}) = 25\ 000.00;$ $P/Y = 4;$ $C/Y = 4;$ $I/Y = 6;$ $i = \dfrac{6\%}{4} = 1.5\% = 0.015;$

$n = 5(4) = 20;$ $d = 2(4) = 8$

STEP 1 Starting with the initial $25 000, focus on the end of the period of deferment (two years from now). Calculate the future value $FV_1(\text{defer})$.

$FV_1 = 25\ 000.00(1.015)^8$ ———————————————— using Formula 9.1

$= 25\ 000.00(1.126493)$

$= \$28\ 162.31466$

STEP 2 Using the future value of the period of deferment as the present value of the term of the ordinary annuity, calculate the payment during the annuity term of five years.

$$28\ 162.31466 = \text{PMT}_2\left(\frac{1 - 1.015^{-20}}{0.015}\right) \qquad \text{substituting in Formula 11.2}$$

$$28\ 162.31466 = (17.168639)\text{PMT}_2$$

$$\text{PMT}_2 = \frac{28\ 162.31466}{17.168639}$$

$$\text{PMT}_2 = \$1640.33$$

PROGRAMMED SOLUTION

(Set P/Y = 4; C/Y = 4) [2nd] (CLR TVM) 25 000 [±] [PV] 0 [PMT]

6 [I/Y] 8 [N] [CPT] [FV] 28160.31466

[±] [PV] 0 [FV] 6 [I/Y] 20 [N] [CPT] [PMT] 1640.334742

The size of the required payment is $1640.33.

When the length of annuity term n is to be calculated, the steps are similar to the method used in solving the periodic payment PMT.

EXAMPLE 13.3B For how long can you pay $500 at the end of each month out of a fund of $10 000 deposited today at 10.5% compounded monthly, if the payments are deferred for nine years?

SOLUTION The payments form a deferred ordinary annuity.

PV(defer) = 10 000.00; PMT = 500.00; P/Y = 12; C/Y = 12; I/Y = 10.5;

$$i = \frac{10.5\%}{12} = 0.875\% = 0.00875; \quad d = 9(12) = 108$$

STEP 1 Determine the value of the $10 000 at the end of the period of deferment. The period of deferment is nine years, or 108 months. There is no payment made during those months and so the initial $10 000 continues to grow.

$$FV = 10\ 000.00(1.00875)^{108}$$
$$= 10\ 000.00(2.562260)$$
$$= 25\ 622.59753$$

STEP 2 Determine the number of monthly payments during the annuity period. The first payment is made at the end of the 109th month.

$$25\ 622.59753 = 500.00\left(\frac{1 - 1.00875^{-n}}{0.00875}\right)$$

$$25\ 622.59753 = 57\ 142.85714(1 - 1.00875^{-n})$$

$$\frac{25\ 622.59753}{57\ 142.85714} = 1 - 1.00875^{-n}$$

$$0.448400 = 1 - 1.00875^{-n}$$

$$1.00875^{-n} = 0.551605$$

$$-n \ln 1.00875 = \ln 0.551605$$

$$-n(0.008712) = -0.594924$$

$$n = \frac{0.594924}{0.008712}$$

$$n = 68.288333$$

$$n = 69 \text{ (months)}$$

PROGRAMMED SOLUTION

(Set P/Y = 12; C/Y = 12) 0 [PMT] 10 000 [±] [PV]

10.5 [I/Y] 108 [N] [CPT] [FV] [25622.59753]

[±] [PV] 0 [FV] 10.5 [I/Y]

500 [PMT] [CPT] [N] [68.288333]

Payments of $500 can be made at the end of each of the first 68 months. For the 69th payment, the amount would be less than $500. (69 months means that the payments occur for 5 years, 9 months.)

In using the financial calculator, the steps to determine the nominal interest rate I/Y during the annuity term when the payments are deferred, are similar to the methods used in computing either the periodic payment PMT or the annuity term n.

EXAMPLE 13.3C

Mr. Dhaliwal wants to receive payments of $800 at the end of each month for 10 years after his retirement in 7 years. If he invests $50 000 now to earn 6% compounded monthly until he retires, what monthly compounded nominal rate of interest must he earn after he retires?

SOLUTION

STEP 1

Calculate the accumulated value of the investment at retirement. The period of deferment is 7 years.

$PV_1 = 50\,000.00$; $PMT = 0$; $P/Y = 12$; $C/Y = 12$; $i = \frac{6\%}{12} = 0.5\% = 0.005$;

$d = 7(12) = 84$

$FV_1 = 50\,000.00(1.005^{84})$

$= 50\,000(1.520370)$

$= \$76\,018.4818$

STEP 2

Calculate the monthly compounded interest rate during the term of the ordinary annuity, the period of 10 years after retirement.

$PV_2 = 76\,018.4818$; $PMT = 800.00$; $P/Y = 12$; $C/Y = 12$; $n = 10(12) = 120$

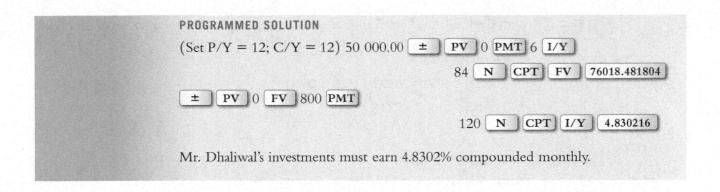

PROGRAMMED SOLUTION

(Set P/Y = 12; C/Y = 12) 50 000.00 [±] [PV] 0 [PMT] 6 [I/Y]

84 [N] [CPT] [FV] 76018.481804

[±] [PV] 0 [FV] 800 [PMT]

120 [N] [CPT] [I/Y] 4.830216

Mr. Dhaliwal's investments must earn 4.8302% compounded monthly.

When the periodic payment amount PMT is known and the payments are deferred, you can work right to left on your timeline, and calculate the present value PV_1 by first determining the present value of the term of the annuity. Then, using the present value of the annuity term as the future value of the deferment period, calculate the present value of the period of deferment PV_2.

EXAMPLE 13.3D

Payments of $500 are due at the end of each year for 10 years. If the annuity is deferred for 4 years and interest is 6% compounded annually, determine the present value of the deferred annuity.

SOLUTION

See Figure 13.6.

STEP 1

Focusing on the date that begins the term of the annuity, calculate the present value of the ordinary annuity of 10 years PV_1.

$$PV_1 = 500.00 \left(\frac{1 - 1.06^{-10}}{0.06} \right) \qquad \text{using Formula 11.2}$$

$$= 500.00(7.360087)$$

$$= \$3680.043526$$

Figure 13.6 Graphical Representation of Method and Data (© S. A. Hummelbrunner)

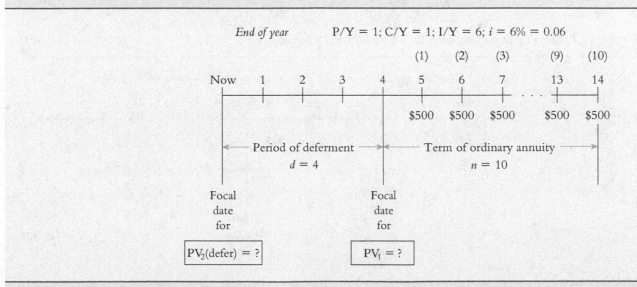

STEP 2 With the focal date "now," and using the present value of the annuity term PV_1 as the future value of the deferment period, calculate the present value of the 4-year period of deferment PV_2.

$$PV_2(\text{defer}) = PV = 3680.043526(1.06^{-4}) \qquad \text{—— using Formula 9.1}$$
$$= 3680.043526(0.792094)$$
$$= \$2914.94$$

PROGRAMMED SOLUTION

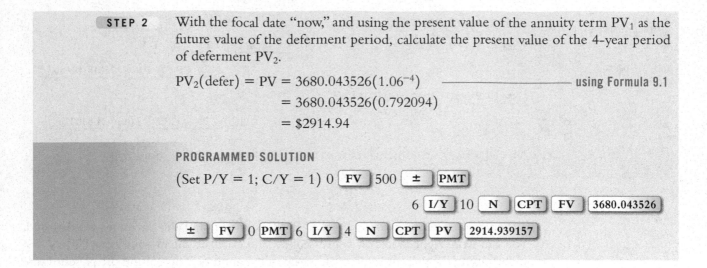

B. Computation of an ordinary general deferred annuity

The same principles apply to an ordinary general deferred annuity as apply to an ordinary simple deferred annuity. If you are dealing with an ordinary general deferred annuity, you calculate the equivalent interest rate per period p and then proceed to solve the future value, present value, payment, term, and interest rate as discussed in previous examples for various forms of a simple deferred annuity.

EXAMPLE 13.3E   Mr. Kovacs deposited a sales bonus of \$31 500 in an income-averaging annuity that will pay \$375 at the end of each month. If payments are deferred for nine months and interest is 6% compounded quarterly, for how many months will Mr. Kovacs receive annuity payments?

SOLUTION   See Figure 13.7.

$$PV(\text{defer}) = 31\,500.00; \quad PMT = 375.00; \quad d = 9; \quad P/Y = 12; \quad C/Y = 4;$$

$$c = \frac{4}{12} = \frac{1}{3}; \quad I/Y = 6; \quad i = \frac{6\%}{4} = 1.5\% = 0.015$$

Figure 13.7 Graphical Representation of Method and Data (© S. A. Hummelbrunner)

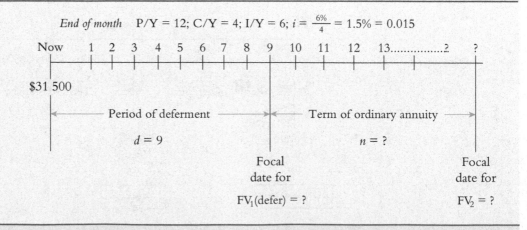

The equivalent monthly rate of interest

$$p = 1.015^{\frac{1}{3}} - 1 = 1.004975 - 1 = 0.004975 = 0.4975\%$$

STEP 1 Calculate the accumulated value at the end of the period of deferment.

$$\begin{aligned} FV &= 31\ 500.00(1.004975)^9 \\ &= 31\ 500.00(1.045678) \\ &= 32\ 938.86881 \end{aligned}$$

PROGRAMMED SOLUTION

(Set P/Y = 12; C/Y = 4) 6 $\boxed{\text{I/Y}}$ 0 $\boxed{\text{PMT}}$

31 500 $\boxed{\pm}$ $\boxed{\text{PV}}$ 9 $\boxed{\text{N}}$ $\boxed{\text{CPT}}$ $\boxed{\text{FV}}$ $\boxed{32938.86881}$

STEP 2 Determine the number of payments for an ordinary annuity with a present value of $32 938.86881.

$$32\ 938.86881 = 375.00\left(\frac{1 - 1.004975^{-n}}{0.004975}\right)$$

$$32\ 938.86881 = 75\ 373.75928(1 - 1.004975^{-n})$$

$$0.437007 = 1 - 1.004975^{-n}$$

$$1.004975^{-n} = 0.562993$$

$$-n \ln 1.004975 = \ln 0.562993$$

$$-n(0.004963) = -0.574488$$

$$n = \frac{0.574488}{0.004963}$$

$$n = 115.757251$$

$$n = 116 \text{ months}$$

PROGRAMMED SOLUTION

32 938.86881 $\boxed{\pm}$ $\boxed{\text{PV}}$ 0 $\boxed{\text{FV}}$ 6 $\boxed{\text{I/Y}}$ 375 $\boxed{\text{PMT}}$ $\boxed{\text{CPT}}$ $\boxed{\text{N}}$ $\boxed{115.757251}$

Mr. Kovacs will receive payments for 116 months.

EXAMPLE 13.3F

Harj and Sukie are considering the purchase of a home theatre system. The purchase price is $2498 if they pay cash now. Alternatively, they can finance the purchase through the store's "Do not pay for 15 months" promotion. If they choose the promotion option and wait 15 months to begin payments, they will then have 20 month-end payments of $175.14. During the first 15 months, the loan charges interest at 7.2% compounded monthly.

(i) What service interest rate compounded monthly is being charged during the payment period?

(ii) What additional interest is paid to finance the purchase?

SOLUTION

STEP 1 Determine the equivalent value of the purchase price at the start of the payment period.

$$PV(\text{defer}) = 2498.00; \quad PMT = 197.25; \quad i = 0.6\%; \quad d = 15$$
$$FV = 2498.00(1.006^{15})$$
$$FV = 2498.00(1.096880)$$
$$FV = 2732.51$$

PROGRAMMED SOLUTION

(Set P/Y = 12; C/Y = 12) 2498 $\boxed{\pm}$ $\boxed{PV}$ 7.2 $\boxed{I/Y}$

15 $\boxed{N}$ $\boxed{CPT}$ $\boxed{FV}$ $\boxed{2732.512421}$

STEP 2 Compute the nominal interest rate for the payment period.

(Set P/Y = 12; C/Y = 12) 2732.51 $\boxed{\pm}$ $\boxed{PV}$ 175.14 $\boxed{PMT}$

20 $\boxed{N}$ $\boxed{CPT}$ $\boxed{I/Y}$ $\boxed{29.896464}$

STEP 3 Interest paid: $20(175.14) - 2498.00 = 3502.80 - 2498.00 = \$1004.80$

(i) Harj and Sukie are paying an interest rate of 29.90% compounded monthly.

(ii) They will have to pay an additional $1004.80 to finance the purchase through the promotion.

EXAMPLE 13.3G Payments of $1000 are due at the end of each year for five years. If the payments are deferred for three years and interest is 10% compounded quarterly, what is the present value of the deferred payments?

SOLUTION

STEP 1 Calculate the present value of the term of the ordinary general annuity.
$$PMT = 1000.00; \quad n = 5; \quad P/Y = 1; \quad C/Y = 4; \quad c = 4; \quad I/Y = 10;$$

$$i = \frac{10\%}{4} = 2.5\% = 0.025$$

The equivalent annual rate of interest

$$p = 1.025^4 - 1 = 1.103813 - 1 = 0.103813 = 10.3813\%$$

$$PV_1 = 1000.00\left(\frac{1 - 1.103813^{-5}}{0.103813}\right) \quad\text{————— substituting in Formula 12.3}$$

$$= 1000.00(3.754149)$$
$$= \$3754.148977$$

PROGRAMMED SOLUTION

(Set P/Y = 1; C/Y = 4) 1000 $\boxed{\pm}$ $\boxed{PMT}$ 0 $\boxed{FV}$ 10 $\boxed{I/Y}$

5 $\boxed{N}$ $\boxed{CPT}$ $\boxed{PV}$ $\boxed{3754.148977}$

STEP 2   Calculate the present value of PV_g at the beginning of the period of deferment.

FV = 3754.148977 is the present value of the general annuity PV_g;

    $d = 3$ is the number of deferred payment intervals;

    $p = 10.3813\%$ is the effective rate of interest per payment interval.

$$PV_2(\text{defer}) = 3754.148977(1.103813^{-3}) \text{ ———————— substituting in Formula 9.1}$$
$$= 3754.148977(0.743556)$$
$$= \$2791.42$$

PROGRAMMED SOLUTION

3754.148977 [FV] 10 [I/Y] 0 [PMT] 3 [N] [CPT] [PV] [−2791.419563]

The present value of the deferred payments is \$2791.42.

EXERCISE 13.3   MyLab Math

If you choose, you can use Excel's PV function (present value) to answer the questions indicated.

Answer each of the following questions.

1. An annuity with a cash value of \$14 500 earns 7% compounded semi-annually. End-of-period, semi-annual payments to the beneficiary are deferred for 7 years, and then continue for 10 years. How much is the amount of each payment?

    Reference Example 13.3A

2. Zheng contracted to write a technical manual for a client. Upon completion of the manual, he agreed to accept \$220.00 at the end of each month for 3 years. If the payments are deferred for 15 months, and interest is 8.10% compounded monthly, what is the current value of the contract?

3. The Omega Venture Group needs to borrow to finance a project. Repayment of the loan involves payments of \$8500 at the end of every three months for eight years. No payments are to be made during the development period of three years. Interest is 9% compounded quarterly.
    (a) How much should the Group borrow?
    (b) What amount will be repaid?
    (c) How much of that amount will be interest?

4. Josie won \$8000 in an essay-writing contest. The money was deposited into a savings account earning 4.2% compounded monthly. She intends to leave the money for five-and-a-half years, then withdraw amounts at the end of each month for the next four years while she studies to become an entrepreneur. What will be the size of each withdrawal?

5. A deposit of \$4000 is made today for a period of five years. For how long can \$500 be withdrawn from the account at the end of every three months starting three months after the end of the five-year term if interest is 4% compounded quarterly?

    Reference Example 13.3B

6. Greg borrowed \$6500 at 6.4% compounded monthly to help finance his education. He contracted to repay the loan in monthly payments of \$300 each. If the payments

are due at the end of each month and the payments are deferred for four years, for how long will Greg have to make monthly payments?

7. Samantha wants to be able to withdraw $500 at the end of each month for two years while she travels, starting three years from now. If she invests $10 000 now to earn 4.68% compounded monthly until she begins to travel, what monthly compounded nominal rate of interest must she earn after she starts to travel?

Reference Example 13.3C

8. Paul is in the process of purchasing a new sound system for his car. The cash price is $1500, or he can sign a contract to "buy now and pay later." During the first year, the loan charges interest at 12.4% compounded monthly. The terms of the contract state that he would start making payments at the end of the month that is 12 months from now, paying $114 per month for 18 months to fulfill the contract.
   (a) What monthly compounded nominal rate of interest would he be paying during the time he would be making payments?
   (b) How much extra would Paul be paying to "buy now and pay later?"

9. On the day of his daughter's birth, Mr. Dornan deposited $2000 in a trust fund with his credit union at 5% compounded quarterly. Following her 18th birthday, the daughter is to receive equal payments at the end of each month for 4 years while she is at college. If interest is to be 6% compounded monthly after the daughter's 18th birthday, how much will she receive every month?

10. Mrs. Bell expects to retire in 7 years and would like to receive $800 at the end of each month for 10 years following the date of her retirement. How much must Mrs. Bell deposit today in an account paying 7.5% compounded semi-annually to receive the monthly payments?

Reference Example 13.3D

11. Calvin Jones bought his neighbour's farm for $100 000 down and payments of $5000 at the end of every 3 months for 10 years. If the payments are deferred for 2 years and interest is 8% compounded quarterly, what was the purchase price of the farm?

12. Arianne borrowed $6200 to buy a vehicle to drive to school. She plans to study for three years, and then start her career using her education. Interest is charged on the loan at 7.64% compounded annually. If she starts making month-end payments of $230 when she begins working, how many payments will she have to make?

Reference Example 13.3E

13. Asa has invested money from the settlement of an insurance claim. She plans to withdraw $600 from her savings account at the end of each month for four years. If the payments are deferred for two years and interest is 6% compounded quarterly, what was the amount of the insurance settlement?

14. Jean inherited $25 000, whereby the terms of the inheritance state that she is to receive $1500 at the end of each quarter, starting in 3 years, until the money is completely withdrawn. If the money is placed in a savings account earning 2.75% compounded monthly, how long will the inheritance last?

15. Amir invested $12 000 in a three-year term investment earning 4.48% compounded semi-annually. He then invested the money in an investment earning 3.82% compounded semi-annually. How many quarterly $1000 withdrawals can he make?

Reference Example 13.3F

16. An annuity purchased for $9000 makes month-end payments for seven years and earns interest at 5% quarterly. If payments do not start for three years, how much is each payment?

17. Ed Ainsley borrowed $10 000 from his uncle to finance his postgraduate studies. The loan agreement calls for equal payments at the end of each month for 10 years. The payments are deferred for 4 years and interest is 8% compounded semi-annually. What is the size of the monthly payments?

18. Thomas is planning to withdraw $8000 from a savings account at the end of each quarter for four years. If the payments are deferred for five years and interest is 5.34% compounded semi-annually, what amount has to be invested now into the savings account?   Reference Example 13.3G

19. At Petruske's Warehouse, the forklift needs major repair. A new forklift can be purchased at a current cost of $28 000. If the new forklift is purchased, month-end payments of $679 would start in two years, and continue for five years. Interest for the first two years is charged at 8.32% compounded annually. What is the monthly compounded interest rate for the payment period?   Reference Example 13.3G

20. Santini Construction is evaluating a project to build a bridge over the Salmon River. The project is currently worth $14 million. In one year, when the construction is 30% complete, there will be a one-time payment of $3 million. Over the next two years, quarterly payments of $1.62 million will be made. The job is scheduled to be completed within the three years. During the first year, money is worth 7.25% compounded annually. What is the annually compounded interest rate for the annuity period?

13.4 DEFERRED ANNUITIES DUE
A. Computation of a simple deferred annuity due

The same principles apply to a simple deferred annuity due as apply to a simple annuity due.

EXAMPLE 13.4A

What payment can be withdrawn at the beginning of each month for 6 years if $5000 is invested today at 12% compounded monthly and the payments are deferred for 10 years?

SOLUTION

The payments form a deferred annuity due.

$PV(\text{defer}) = 5000.00$; $P/Y = 12$; $C/Y = 12$; $I/Y = 12$; $i = \dfrac{12\%}{12} = 1\% = 0.01$;

$n = 6(12) = 72$; $d = 10(12) = 120$

STEP 1

Determine the value of the $5000 at the end of the period of deferment.

$FV = 5000.00(1.01)^{120}$
$\quad = 5000.00(3.300387)$
$\quad = \$16\,501.93447$

STEP 2

Calculate the payment amount of the annuity.

$$PMT = \dfrac{PV_n(\text{due})}{\left[\dfrac{1 - (1 + i)^{-n}}{i}\right](1 + i)} \qquad \text{rearranging Formula 13.2}$$

$$PMT = \frac{16\,501.93447}{\left[\dfrac{1 - (1.01)^{-72}}{0.01}\right](1.01)}$$

$$PMT = \frac{16\,501.93447}{[51.150392](1.01)}$$

$$PMT = \frac{16\,501.93447}{51.661896}$$

$$PMT = \$319.42$$

PROGRAMMED SOLUTION

(Set P/Y = 12; C/Y = 12) 0 PMT 5000 ± PV

12 I/Y 120 N CPT FV 16501.934473

("BGN" mode) 16 501.93447 ± PV 0 FV

12 I/Y 72 N CPT PMT 319.421778

The monthly payment is \$319.42.

EXAMPLE 13.4B

A scholarship of \$2000 per year is to be paid at the beginning of each year from a scholarship fund of \$15 000 invested at 7% compounded annually. How long will the scholarship last if payments are deferred for five years?

SOLUTION

The annual payments form a deferred annuity due.

PV(defer) = 15 000.00; PMT = 2000.00; P/Y = 1; C/Y = 1; I/Y = 7; $i = 7\% = 0.07$; $d = 5$

Determine the value of the \$15 000 at the end of the period of deferment.

STEP 1 $FV = 15\,000.00(1.07)^5$
= 15\,000.00(1.402552)
= 21\,038.27596

STEP 2 $21\,038.27596 = 2000.00\left(\dfrac{1 - 1.07^{-n}}{0.07}\right)(1.07)$ ———— substituting in Formula 13.2

$21\,038.27596 = 30\,571.43(1 - 1.07^{-n})$

$0.688168 = 1 - 1.07^{-n}$

$1.07^{-n} = 0.311832$

$-n \ln 1.07 = \ln 0.311832$

$-0.067659n = -1.165290$

$n = \dfrac{1.165290}{0.067659}$

$n = 17.223081$

$n = 18$ years

PROGRAMMED SOLUTION

(Set P/Y = 1; C/Y = 1) 0 $\boxed{\text{PMT}}$ 15 000 $\boxed{\pm}$ $\boxed{\text{PV}}$

7 $\boxed{\text{I/Y}}$ 5 $\boxed{\text{N}}$ $\boxed{\text{CPT}}$ $\boxed{\text{FV}}$ $\boxed{\text{21038.27596}}$

("BGN" mode) 21 038.27596 $\boxed{\pm}$ $\boxed{\text{PV}}$ 0 $\boxed{\text{FV}}$

7 $\boxed{\text{I/Y}}$ 2000 $\boxed{\text{PMT}}$ $\boxed{\text{CPT}}$ $\boxed{\text{N}}$ $\boxed{\text{17.223081}}$

The scholarship fund will provide 17 payments of $2000 and a final payment of less than $2000.

EXAMPLE 13.4C

George Rich has set up a fund to help pay the expenses for a children's summer camp. The balance in the fund today is $50 000, and it will earn interest at 7% compounded annually. Starting 10 years from now, $10 000 will be withdrawn from the fund at the beginning of every year for 12 years. What is the annually compounded interest rate for the fund during the final 12 years?

SOLUTION

The withdrawals form a simple annuity due.

STEP 1 Calculate the present value of the simple annuity due 10 years from now.

PMT = 0.00; P/Y = 1; C/Y = 1; I/Y = 7; $i = 7\% = 0.07$; $n = 10(1) = 10$;
So PV(due) = $50\,000(1 + 0.07)^{10} = 50\,000(1.967151357289566) = 98\,357.56$.

PROGRAMMED SOLUTION

(Set P/Y = 1; C/Y = 1) 50 000 $\boxed{\pm}$ $\boxed{\text{PV}}$ 0 $\boxed{\text{PMT}}$ 10 $\boxed{\text{N}}$ 7 $\boxed{\text{I/Y}}$ $\boxed{\text{CPT}}$

$\boxed{\text{FV}}$ $\boxed{\text{98357.56786}}$

STEP 2 Compute the nominal interest rate compounded annually during the annuity phase.

(Set P/Y = 1; C/Y = 1) ("BGN" Mode) 98 357.56786 $\boxed{\text{PV}}$ 0 $\boxed{\text{FV}}$ 10000 $\boxed{\pm}$

$\boxed{\text{PMT}}$ 12 $\boxed{\text{N}}$ $\boxed{\text{CPT}}$ $\boxed{\text{I/Y}}$ $\boxed{\text{3.841684}}$

The nominal interest rate for the fund during the final 12 years is 3.8417% compounded annually.

EXAMPLE 13.4D

Mei Willis would like to receive annuity payments of $2000 at the beginning of each quarter for seven years. The annuity term is to start five years from now and interest is 5% compounded quarterly.

  (i) How much must Mei invest today?

  (ii) How much will Mei receive in total from the annuity?

  (iii) How much of what she receives will be interest?

SOLUTION

STEP 1 Calculate the present value of the annuity due (the focal point is five years from now).

  (i) PMT = 2000.00; P/Y = 4; C/Y = 4; I/Y = 5; $i = \dfrac{5\%}{4} = 1.25\% = 0.0125$;

  $n = 7(4) = 28$

$$PV_1(\text{due}) = 2000.00\left[\frac{1 - 1.0125^{-28}}{0.0125}\right](1.0125) \quad\text{——— substituting in Formula 13.2}$$

$$= 2000.00(23.502518)(1.0125)$$

$$= 47\,005.03556(1.0125)$$

$$= \$47\,592.60$$

STEP 2 Calculate the present value of $47\,592.60 (the focal point is "now").

$$FV = 47\,592.598501; \quad i = 1.25; \quad n = 5(4) = 20$$

$$PV_2 = 47\,592.5985(1.0125)^{-20}$$

$$= 47\,592.5985(0.780009)$$

$$= \$37\,122.63$$

PROGRAMMED SOLUTION

("BGN" mode)(Set P/Y = 4; C/Y = 4) 0 [FV] 2000 [±] [PMT]

5 [I/Y] 28 [N] [CPT] [PV] 47592.598501

[FV] 0 [PMT] 5 [I/Y] 20 [N] [CPT] [PV] −37122.633667

Mei will have to invest $37 122.63.

(i) Mei will receive a total of $28(2000.00) = \$56\,000.00$.

(ii) Interest will be $56\,000.00 - 37\,122.63 = \$18\,877.37$.

B. Computation of a general deferred annuity due

The same principles apply to a general deferred annuity due as apply to a simple annuity due. If you are dealing with a general deferred annuity due, first calculate the equivalent interest rate per period p and then proceed to solve the future value, present value, payment, term, and interest rate as discussed in previous examples for various forms of a simple deferred annuity.

EXAMPLE 13.4E A lease contract that has a cash value of $64 000 requires payments at the beginning of each month for seven years. If the payments are deferred for two years and interest is 8% compounded quarterly, what is the size of the monthly payment?

SOLUTION $PV(\text{defer}) = 64\,000.00; \quad n = 7(12) = 84; \quad P/Y = 12; \quad C/Y = 4;$

$$d = 2(12) = 24; \quad c = \frac{4}{12} = \frac{1}{3}; \quad I/Y = 8; \quad i = \frac{8\%}{4} = 2\% = 0.02$$

The equivalent monthly rate of interest

$$p = 1.02^{\frac{1}{3}} - 1 = 1.006623 - 1 = 0.6623\%$$

STEP 1 Determine the accumulated value of the cash value at the end of the period of deferment.

$$FV = 64\,000.00(1.006623)^{24}$$

$$= 64\,000.00(1.171659)$$

$$= \$74\,986.20038$$

PROGRAMMED SOLUTION

(Set P/Y = 12; C/Y = 4) 8 [I/Y] 0 [PMT]

64 000 [±] [PV] 24 [N] [CPT] [FV] [74986.20038]

STEP 2 Determine the periodic payment for the general annuity due whose present value is $74 986.20038.

$$74\ 986.20038 = \text{PMT}\left(\frac{1 - 1.006623^{-84}}{0.006623}\right)(1.006623)$$

$$74\ 986.20038 = \text{PMT}(64.267570)(1.006623)$$

$$74\ 986.20038 = \text{PMT}(64.693195)$$

$$\text{PMT} = \$1159.10$$

PROGRAMMED SOLUTION

("BGN" mode) 74 986.20038 [±] [PV] 0 [FV]

8 [I/Y] 84 [N] [CPT] [PMT] [1159.104917]

The monthly payment is $1159.10.

EXAMPLE 13.4F By age 65, Janice Berstein had accumulated $120 000 in an RRSP by making yearly contributions over a period of years. At age 69, she converted the existing balance into an RRIF from which she started to withdraw $2000 per month. If the first withdrawal was on the date of conversion and interest on the account is 6.5% compounded quarterly, for how many months will Janice Berstein receive annuity payments?

SOLUTION PV(defer) = 120 000.00; PMT = 2000.00; $d = 4(12) = 48$

P/Y = 12; C/Y = 4; $C = \dfrac{4}{12} = \dfrac{1}{3}$; I/Y = 6.5; $I = \dfrac{6.5\%}{4} = 1.625\% = 0.01625$

The monthly effective rate of interest

$p = 1.01625^{\frac{1}{3}} - 1 = 1.005388 - 1 = 0.005388 = 0.5388\%$

Since payments are at the beginning of each month, the problem involves a deferred general annuity due.

STEP 1 Determine the accumulated value at the end of the period of deferment.

$\text{FV} = 120\ 000.00(1.005388)^{48}$

$\quad = 120\ 000.00(1.294222)$

$\quad = \$155\ 306.70$

PROGRAMMED SOLUTION

(Set P/Y = 12; C/Y = 4) 6.5 [I/Y] 0 [PMT]

120 000 [±] [PV] 48 [N] [CPT] [FV] [155306.6971]

STEP 2   Determine the number of payments for an annuity due with a present value of $155 306.70.

$$155\ 306.70 = 2000.00\left(\frac{1 - 1.005388^{-n}}{0.005388}\right)(1.005388)$$

$$155\ 306.70 = 373\ 223.60511(1 - 1.005388^{-n})$$

$$0.416122 = 1 - 1.005388^{-n}$$

$$1.005388^{-n} = 0.583878$$

$$-n \ln 1.005388 = \ln 0.583878$$

$$-n(0.005373) = -0.538064$$

$$n = 100.139801$$

$$n = 101 \text{ months}$$

PROGRAMMED SOLUTION

("BGN" mode) 155 306.70 [±] [PV] 0 [FV]

6.5 [I/Y] 2000 [PMT] [CPT] [N] [100.139801]

Since the first payment is on the conversion date, Janice Berstein will receive payments of $2000 for 100 months. The 101st payment will be less than $2000.

EXAMPLE 13.4G   Tom Casey wants to withdraw $925 at the beginning of each quarter for 12 years. If the withdrawals are to begin 10 years from now and interest is 4.5% compounded monthly, how much must Tom deposit today to be able to make the withdrawals?

SOLUTION   PMT = 925.00; $n = 12(4) = 48$; $d = 10(4) = 40$;   P/Y = 4;   C/Y = 12;

I/Y = 4.5; $c = \dfrac{12}{4} = 3$; $i = \dfrac{4.5\%}{12} = 0.375\% = 0.00375$

The equivalent quarterly rate of interest

$p = 1.00375^3 - 1 = 1.011292 - 1 = 0.011292 = 1.1292\%$

STEP 1   Calculate the present value of the general annuity due.

$$PV_1(\text{due}) = 925.00\left(\frac{1 - 1.011292^{-48}}{0.011292}\right)(1.011292) \quad\text{—— substituting in Formula 13.4}$$

$$= 925.00(36.898160)(1.011292)$$

$$= \$34\ 516.21131$$

PROGRAMMED SOLUTION

(Set P/Y = 4; C/Y = 12)("BGN" mode) 4.5 [I/Y] 0 [FV]

925 [I/Y] [PMT] 48 [N] [CPT] [PV] [34516.21131]

STEP 2   Calculate the present value of $PV_g(\text{due})$ at the beginning of the period of deferment.

FV = 34 516.21131 is the present value of the general annuity $PV_1(\text{due})$

$d = 40$ is the number of deferred payment intervals

$p = 1.1292\%$ is the effective rate of interest per payment interval

$$PV_2(\text{defer}) = 34\ 516.21131(1.011292)^{-40} \quad\text{———— substituting in Formula 9.1}$$
$$= 34\ 516.21131(0.638165)$$
$$= \$22\ 027.04$$

PROGRAMMED SOLUTION

| FV | 4.5 | I/Y | 0 | PMT | 40 | N | CPT | PV | −22027.03920 |

Tom must deposit \$22 027.04 to make the withdrawals.

EXERCISE 13.4

MyLab Math

If you choose, you can use Excel's PV function (present value) to answer the questions indicated.

Answer each of the following questions.

1. To finance the development of a new product, a company borrowed \$50 000 at 7% compounded quarterly. If the loan is to be repaid in equal quarterly payments over seven years and the first payment is due three years after the date of the loan, what is the size of the quarterly payment?   Reference Example 13.4A

2. Mike borrowed \$14 000 at 6.5% compounded semi–annually. If the loan is to be repaid in equal semi-annual payments over three years and the first payment is due four years after the date of the loan, what is the size of the semi-annual payment?

3. Matt's Machine Shop purchased a computer to use in tuning engines. To finance the purchase, the company borrowed \$12 000 at 8% compounded monthly. To repay the loan, equal monthly payments are made over five years, with the first payment due one year after the date of the loan. What is the size of each monthly payment?

4. An RRIF with a beginning balance of \$21 000 earns interest at 10% compounded quarterly. If withdrawals of \$3485 are made at the beginning of every three months, starting eight years from now, how long will the RRIF last?   Reference Example 13.4B

5. A lease valued at \$32 000 requires payments of \$4000 every three months. If the first payment is due three years after the lease was signed and interest is 12% compounded quarterly, what is the term of the lease?

6. For his business, Nicholas leased equipment valued at \$23 000. The terms of the lease required payments of \$1800 every month. If the first payment is due nine months after the lease was signed and interest is 11% compounded monthly, what is the term of the lease?

7. Starting three years from now, Dustin plans to withdraw \$450 at the beginning of every three months for five years. If he has \$7200 now in his savings, and the account earns interest at 4% compounding quarterly during the first three years, what is the nominal interest rate compounded quarterly during the last five years?   Reference Example 13.4C

8. Tina purchases a new computer by financing it on the "no payment until next year" plan. The cash price of the computer is \$1384. The financing agreement requires

equal payments every month for two years. If the first payment of $95 is due at the beginning of the month starting one year after the date of purchase, and interest is 28.8% compounded monthly during the first year, what is the monthly compounded nominal interest rate for the following two years?

9. Nuwan has invested a $30 000 insurance settlement to earn interest at 4.18% compounded semi-annually for the next 10 years. If he then makes withdrawals of $850 at the beginning of every 3 months from the investment for 20 years, what quarterly compounded nominal interest rate is earned during the withdrawal period?

10. Arlene and Mario Dumont want to set up a fund to finance their daughter's university education. They want to be able to withdraw $400 from the fund at the beginning of each month for four years. Their daughter enters university in seven-and-a-half years and interest is 6% compounded monthly.
(a) How much must the Dumonts deposit in the fund today?
(b) What will be the amount of the total withdrawals?
(c) How much of the amount withdrawn will be interest?   Reference Example 13.4D

11. Edmonton Pizza borrowed money to redesign their restaurants. Payments of $1600 would be made at the beginning of each month for 2 years, starting in 18 months. Interest on the loan is 7.12% compounded monthly.
(a) How much must the company borrow today?
(b) What will be the amount of the total payments?
(c) How much of the amount paid will be interest?

12. An investment in a lease offers returns of $2500 per month due at the beginning of each month for five years. What investment is justified if the returns are deferred for two years and the interest required is 12% compounded monthly?

13. Dr. Young bought $18 000 worth of equipment from Medical Supply Company. The purchase agreement requires equal payments every six months for eight years. If the first payment is due two years after the date of purchase and interest is 7% compounded quarterly, what is the size of the payments?   Reference Example 13.4E

14. A business borrows $250 000 to finance an expansion. The loan agreement requires equal payments every three months for nine years. If the first payment is due two years after the date of purchase and interest is 8.3% compounded monthly, what is the size of the payments?

15. Mark and his partners have contracted to purchase the franchise rights, worth $75 000, to open and operate a specialty pizza restaurant called Pepperoni's. With a renewable agreement, the partners have agreed to make payments at the beginning of every six months for five years. To accommodate the renovation period, Pepperoni's corporate office has agreed to allow the payments to start in one year, with interest at 7.82% compounded annually. What is the amount of each payment?

16. Mrs. McCarthy paid a single premium of $22 750 for an annuity, with the understanding that she will receive $385 at the beginning of each month. How long will the annuity last if it earns 5% compounded semi-annually, and the first payment period starts one year from now?   Reference Example 13.4F

17. Bhupinder, who has just had his 55th birthday, invested $3740 on that day for his retirement. The RRIF investment earns 8% compounded monthly. For how long will he be able to withdraw $1100 at the beginning of each year, starting on his sixty-fifth birthday?

18. A property development agreement valued at $45 000 requires annual lease payments of $15 000. The first payment is due five years after the date of the

agreement and interest is 11% compounded semi-annually. For how long will payments be made?

19. New vehicle lift equipment with a value of $82 000 has been purchased by Lockwood Automotive. Starting in 18 months, the company will make payments of $2200 at the beginning of every month over 4 years. If interest is 7.49% compounded quarterly during the first 18 months, what quarterly compounded interest rate is charged during the remaining 4 years?

20. Joe, Henry, and Noela, after graduating together, started a business with a $28 000 investment from their parents. For the first two years, they were charged interest at 6% compounded monthly, but no payments were required during that period. For the next five years, they would make payments of $625 at the beginning of every month, and the interest rate would be changed to semi-annual compounding. What is the nominal interest rate charged for the last five years?

21. A major property developer is concerned about lack of sales due to local economic conditions. To ensure that his condos are occupied, he offers a lease-to-purchase program in which, if people sign a lease by the end of March, they will not have to start making payments until March of the following year. The purchase price of the condo is $189 000. Payments of $1169.51 will be required at the beginning of each month over a 25-year amortization period. If interest is 5.29% compounded semi-annually during the first year, what is the semi-annually compounded interest rate during the payment period?

22. The sale of a property provides for payments of $6000 due at the beginning of every three months for five years. If the payments are deferred for two years and interest is 9% compounded monthly, what is the cash value of the property?

Reference Example 13.4G

23. Emerson developed a new style of camping trailer. He is considering a licensing agreement with Easy-Tow, who will manufacture the new trailer. They are proposing to pay him $30 000 now, and $15 000 at the beginning of each of the 12 years of the licensing agreement, starting in 2 years. If interest is 6.55% compounded semi-annually, what is the agreement worth today?

24. An annuity pays $6000 at the beginning of every year for 12 years. If the payments are deferred for 7 years and interest is 4.38% compounded monthly, what is the cash value of the property?

13.5 PERPETUITIES
A. Basic concepts

A **perpetuity** is an annuity in which the periodic payments begin on a fixed date and continue indefinitely (see Figure 13.8 for a graphical representation). Interest payments on permanently invested sums of money are prime examples of perpetuities. Dividends on preferred shares fall into this category, assuming that the issuing corporation has an indefinite life. Scholarships and trust funds paid perpetually from an endowment fit the definition of perpetuity.

Since there is no end to the term, it is *not* possible to determine the future value of a perpetuity. However, the present value of a perpetuity *is* a definite value. This section deals with the present value of simple perpetuities.

B. Present value of ordinary perpetuities

We will use the following symbols when dealing with perpetuities:

PV = the present value of the perpetuity;
PMT = the periodic rent (or perpetuity payment);
i = the rate of interest per conversion period;
p = the effective rate of interest per payment period.

Figure 13.8 Graphical Representation of an Ordinary Perpetuity (© S. A. Hummelbrunner)

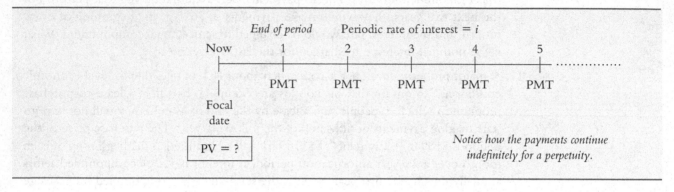

The **perpetuity payment**, PMT, is the interest earned by the present value of the perpetuity in one interest period. The main idea is that only the interest is paid out as PMT; the principal is never touched and so the annuity can continue "forever."

When n is determined, the present value of an ordinary simple annuity was calculated using the formula

$$PV_n = PMT \left[\frac{1 - (1 + i)^{-n}}{i} \right] \qquad \text{Formula 11.2}$$

As n in the formula increases and approaches infinity, the factor $(1 + i)^{-n}$ approaches 0.

Thus, the formula for calculating the present value of an ordinary simple perpetuity is

$$PV = \frac{PMT}{i} \qquad \text{Formula 13.5}$$

POINTERS & PITFALLS

Remember that i represents the periodic interest rate, calculated as the nominal interest rate divided by the number of conversion periods per year. That is, in the terms of the financial calculator, this represents I/Y divided by C/Y.

For an ordinary simple perpetuity, the payment PMT is the interest earned by the present value of the perpetuity in one payment interval. That is,

$$PMT = i \times PV$$

Similarly, the formula for calculating the present value of an ordinary general perpetuity is

$$PV = \frac{PMT}{p}$$
where $p = (1 + i)^c - 1$ ———————————— **Formula 13.6**

where
p = the equivalent rate of interest per payment interval;
c = the number of conversion periods per payment period.

EXAMPLE 13.5A

What sum of money invested today at 5% compounded annually will provide a scholarship of $1500 at the end of every year?

SOLUTION

The payment period is indefinite; therefore the payments form a perpetuity. Also, since the payments are made at the end of the payment period, and the interest conversion is the same length as the payment interval, the problem involves an *ordinary simple perpetuity*.

PMT = 1500.00; $i = 5\% = 0.05$

$PV = \dfrac{1500.00}{0.05} = \$30\ 000.00$ ———————— substituting in Formula 13.5

EXAMPLE 13.5B

The maintenance cost incurred by Northern Railroad for a crossing with a provincial highway is $2000 at the end of each month. Proposed construction of an overpass would eliminate the monthly maintenance cost. If money is worth 6% compounded monthly, how much should Northern be willing to contribute toward the cost of construction?

SOLUTION

The monthly maintenance expense payments form an *ordinary simple perpetuity*.

PMT = 2000.00; $i = \dfrac{6\%}{12} = 0.005$

$PV = \dfrac{2000.00}{0.005} = \$400\ 000.00$

Northern should be willing to contribute $400 000 toward construction.

EXAMPLE 13.5C

What sum of money invested in preferred share dividends at 8% compounded quarterly will provide for payments of $2500 to be paid at the end of each year, indefinitely?

SOLUTION

The payments form an *ordinary general perpetuity*.

PMT = 2500.00; $c = 4$; $i = \dfrac{8\%}{4} = 2\% = 0.02$

The equivalent annual rate of interest
$p = 1.02^4 - 1 = 1.082432 - 1 = 0.082432 = 8.2432\%$

$PV = \dfrac{2500.00}{0.082432} = \$30\ 327.97$ ———————— substituting in Formula 13.6

The required sum of money is $30 327.97.

EXAMPLE 13.5D	Kwantlen Polytechnic University Foundation collected $32 000 to provide a fund for ongoing scholarships. If the money is invested at 7% compounded annually, what is the size of the scholarship that can be paid every six months?
SOLUTION	$PV = 32\ 000.00;\quad c = \dfrac{1}{2};\quad i = 7\% = 0.07$

The equivalent semi-annual rate of interest

$p = 1.07^{0.5} - 1 = 1.034408 - 1 = 0.034408 = 3.4408\%$

By rearranging the terms of Formula 13.6, we get the equation $PMT = pPV$.

$PMT = pPV = 0.034408(32\ 000.00) = \$1101.06$

The size of the scholarship is $1101.06.

EXAMPLE 13.5E	An investment of $50 000 is made in preferred shares that pay dividends of $3000.00 at the end of each year, indefinitely. What annually compounded rate is paid by the shares?
SOLUTION	$PV = 50\ 000.00;\ PMT = \$3000$

By arranging the terms of Formula 13.5, we get the equation $i = \dfrac{PMT}{PV}$.

$i = \dfrac{PMT}{PV} = \dfrac{3000.00}{50\ 000.00} = 0.06 = 6\%$

The investment in the shares pays, or yields, 6% annually.

POINTERS & PITFALLS

For constant growth annuities in Chapter 12, Section 12.6, we introduced k to represent the constant rate of growth or decline in the periodic payment. Applying this concept to perpetuities, whereby the size of the payment changes (increases or decreases) at a constant rate, permits us to calculate present value of these perpetuities using

$PV = PMT/(1 - k)$.

C. Present value of perpetuities due

A **perpetuity due** differs from an ordinary perpetuity only in that the first payment is made at the focal date. Therefore, a simple perpetuity due may be treated as consisting of an immediate payment, PMT, followed by an ordinary perpetuity. The formula for calculating the present value of a simple perpetuity due is

$$PV(\text{due}) = PMT + \frac{PMT}{i}$$ ———————— **Formula 13.7**

A general perpetuity due can also be treated as consisting of an immediate payment, PMT, followed by an ordinary general perpetuity. Using the symbol PV(due) for the present value, the formula for calculating the present value of a general perpetuity due is

$$PV(due) = PMT + \frac{PMT}{p}$$
where $p = (1 + i)^c - 1$ — Formula 13.8

EXAMPLE 13.5F

A tract of land is leased in perpetuity at $1250 due at the beginning of each month. If money is worth 7.5% compounded monthly, what is the present value of the lease?

SOLUTION

$PMT = 1250.00; \quad i = \frac{7.5\%}{12} = 0.625\% = 0.00625$

$PV = 1250.00 + \frac{1250.00}{0.00625}$ — substituting in Formula 13.7

$= 1250.00 + 200\,000.00$

$= \$201\,250.00$

EXAMPLE 13.5G

What is the present value of perpetuity payments of $750 made at the beginning of each month if interest is 8.5% compounded semi-annually?

SOLUTION

$PMT = 750.00; \quad c = \frac{2}{12} = \frac{1}{6}; \quad i = \frac{8.5\%}{2} = 4.25\% = 0.0425$

The equivalent semi-annual rate of interest

$p = 1.0425^{\frac{1}{6}} - 1 = 1.006961 - 1 = 0.006961 = 0.6961\%$

$PV(due) = 750.00 + \frac{750.00}{0.006961} = \$108\,492.18$ — substituting in Formula 13.8

The present value of the perpetuity is $108 492.18.

D. Deferred perpetuities

The payments on a perpetuity may be deferred for a number of payment periods. To perform calculations for a deferred perpetuity, at least two calculations are needed.

To calculate the initial amount invested, first calculate the present value of the perpetuity, then calculate the present value of the amount at the beginning of the deferral period.

EXAMPLE 13.5H

How much money must be invested today in a fund earning 5.5% compounded annually to pay annual scholarships of $2000 starting

(i) at the end of the current year?

(ii) at the end of the year four years from now?

(iii) immediately?

SOLUTION

$PMT = 2000.00; i = 5.5\% = 0.055$

(i) The annual scholarship payments form an ordinary perpetuity.

$PV_1 = \frac{2000.00}{0.055} = \$36\,363.64$

The required sum of money is $36 363.64.

(ii) The annual scholarship payments form an ordinary perpetuity. The first payment is at the end of the fourth year. During the deferral period, there are no payments for the first three years.

$$PV_2(\text{defer}) = PV_1(1.055^{-3})$$
$$= 36\ 363.64(0.851614) \text{ (rounded to six decimals)}$$
$$= \$30\ 967.77$$

The required sum of money is $30 967.77.

(iii) The annual scholarship payments form a perpetuity due.

$$PV = 2000.00 + \frac{2000.00}{0.055}$$
$$= 2000.00 + 36\ 363.64$$
$$= \$38\ 363.64$$

The required sum of money is $38 363.64.

EXAMPLE 13.51

What sum of money invested today in a fund earning 6.6% compounded monthly will provide perpetuity payments of $395 every three months starting

(i) immediately?

(ii) three months from now?

(iii) one year from now?

SOLUTION

$$PMT = 395.00; \quad c = \frac{12}{4} = 3; \quad i = \frac{6.6\%}{12} = 0.55\% = 0.0055$$

The equivalent quarterly rate of interest

$p = 1.0055^3 - 1 = 1.016591 - 1 = 0.016591 = 1.6591\%$ (rounded to six decimals)

(i) Because the perpetuity payments are at the beginning of each payment interval, they form a *perpetuity due*.

$$PV_1(\text{due}) = 395.00 + \frac{395.00}{0.016591} = 395.00 + 23\ 808.21 = \$24\ 203.21$$

The required sum of money is $24 203.21.

(ii) Since the first payment is three months from now, the perpetuity payments form an *ordinary perpetuity*.

$$PV = \frac{395.00}{0.016591} = \$23\ 808.21$$

The required sum of money is $23 808.21.

(iii) If you consider that the payments are deferred for one year, they form a *deferred perpetuity due*.

$$PV_2(\text{defer}) = PV_1(\text{due}) \times (1.0055)^{-12}$$
$$= 24\ 203.21(0.936300)$$
$$= \$22\ 661.47$$

The required sum of money is $22 661.47.

Perpetuities Using a Texas Instruments BA II PLUS

Perpetuities can be treated like any other annuity on the BA II PLUS. While technically there are two missing variables, present value and payments can be calculated using arbitrary values for time and future value. The suggested values to use are a time of at least 300 years when calculating the value of *n*, and 0 for the future value. Using these values will allow the BA II PLUS to mimic annuities and allow you to calculate perpetuity values the same way as you would any other annuity.

The process would be

1. Set the calculator to beginning or end.

2. Set P/Y and C/Y.

3. Input the variables you know.

4. Compute the variable you want to know (present value or payments).

Note: When you are using this method, the answer may be marginally different from the formula due to the approximation used.

EXERCISE 13.5　　　　　　　　　　　　　　　　　　MyLab Math

Answer each of the following questions.

1. Choosing to commute to work by driving a hybrid vehicle will save $32 each month in fuel. If money is worth 4% compounded monthly, how much extra money, over the price of a gas-powered vehicle, should be invested to purchase a hybrid?

    Reference Example 13.5A

2. How much can be paid in scholarships at the end of each year if $150 000 is deposited in a trust fund and interest is 4.5% compounded annually?

3. The Wambat Company pays a dividend of $4.25 every three months per preferred share. What is the expected market price per share if money is worth 8% compounded semi-annually?

    Reference Example 13.5C

4. Transcontinental Pipelines is considering a technical process that is expected to reduce annual maintenance costs by $85 000. What is the maximum amount of money that could be invested in the process to be economically feasible if interest is 7% compounded quarterly?

5. The municipal building for the City of Lethbridge is considering installation of a system of wind-powered generators. With the system, the city can save $13 000 every six months in expenses. If interest is 4.75% compounded quarterly, how much should the city invest to install the system?

6. Alain Dupre wants to set up a scholarship fund for his school. The annual scholarship payment is to be $2500, with the first such payment due four years after his deposit into the fund. If the fund pays 7.25% compounded annually, how much must Alain deposit?

7. Preferred shares of Western Oil paying a quarterly dividend are to be offered at $55.65 per share. If money is worth 6.2% compounded semi-annually, what is the minimum quarterly dividend needed to make investment in such shares economically feasible?

8. Aleena rents a suite and pays $1150 in monthly rent in advance. What is the cash value of the property if money is worth 6.6% compounded monthly?

9. Larry and John purchased a warehouse property for $836 000 that they are going to lease to several businesses, including a computer repair business. The property provides a net income of $3600 at the beginning of every month. What is the monthly compounded annual yield earned by the property?

10. Municipal Hydro offers to acquire a right-of-way from a property owner who receives annual lease payments of $2225 due in advance. What is a fair offer if money is worth 5.5% compounded quarterly?   Reference Example 13.5F

11. What monthly lease payment due in advance should be charged for a tract of land valued at $35 000 if the agreed interest is 8.5% compounded semi-annually?

12. Western Pipelines pays $480 at the beginning of every half-year for using a tract of land. What should the company offer the property owner as a purchase price if interest is 8.6% compounded semi-annually?

13. Carla plans to invest in a property that after three years will yield $1200 at the end of each month, indefinitely. How much should Carla be willing to pay if an alternative investment yields 9% compounded monthly?

14. The faculty of Eastern College collected $14 000 for the purpose of setting up a memorial fund from which an annual award is to be made to a qualifying student. If the money is invested at 7% compounded annually and the first annual award payment is to be made five years after the money was deposited, what is the size of the annual award payment?

15. Barbara Katzman bought an income property for $280 000 three years ago. She has held the property for the three years without renting it. If she rents the property out now, what should be the size of the monthly rent payment due in advance if money is worth 6% compounded monthly?

16. Pharma Manufacturing is considering a medical process that is expected to reduce its annual operating costs by $60 000.00. What is the maximum amount of money that should be invested for the process to be economically feasible if interest is 8.27% compounded quarterly?

17. Georgian College is considering the establishment of a $1 million endowment held in perpetuity for the chair of the Henry Bernick Entrepreneurship Centre. The ongoing cost would be $6500 at the end of each month. What monthly compounded nominal rate of return must be earned to fully fund the endowment?

18. Darcy bought an income property for $238 455.00 three years ago. He held the property for the three years without renting it. If he rents the property now, what size of monthly payment due in advance should he require if money is worth 5.38% compounded monthly?

19. A fund is to be set up for an annual scholarship of $5000.00. If the first payment is due in three years and interest is 6.2% compounded quarterly, what amount must be deposited in the scholarship fund today?

20. What would you be willing to pay for a preferred share of stock that promises to pay you a cash dividend of $25 at the end of each year, which will increase by 1% every year forever? The interest rate is fixed at 4.75%.

21. The purchase of preferred shares in a new software company guarantees a cash dividend of $32 per share at the end of its first year. However, the dividend is expected to decrease by 0.5% per year as the company reinvests its earnings. What is the expected market price per share if money is worth 5.25% compounded annually?

MyLab Math Visit MyLab Math to practise any of this chapter's exercises marked with a ⊕ as often as you want. The guided solutions help you calculate an answer step by step. You'll find a personalized study plan and additional interactive resources to help you master Business Math!

REVIEW EXERCISE

1. LO① What is the future value of monthly payments of $50 each for four years and two months at 4.62% compounded monthly if the payments form an annuity due?

⊕ **2. LO①** Frank makes deposits into his savings account of $225 at the beginning of every three months. Interest earned by the deposits is 3% compounded quarterly.

  (a) What will the balance in Frank's account be after eight years?

  (b) How much of the balance will Frank have contributed?

  (c) How much of the balance is interest?

3. LO② If you save $25 at the beginning of each month, and interest is 4% compounded quarterly, how much will you accumulate in 30 years?

⊕ **4. LO②** What quarterly compounded nominal interest rate is earned on payments of $215 paid at the beginning of every month for 9 years out of an investment of $18 000?

5. LO① Home entertainment equipment can be purchased by making monthly payments of $82 for three-and-a-half years. The first payment is due at the time of purchase and the financing cost is 16.5% compounded monthly.

  (a) What is the purchase price?

  (b) How much will be paid in installments?

  (c) How much is the cost of financing?

⊕ **6. LO①** You have set a goal to save $10 000 in a savings account that earns interest at 2.54% compounded quarterly. How much must you deposit every three months for 5 years if the deposits are made at the beginning of each quarter?

7. LO② Payments of $375 made every 3 months are accumulated at 3.75% compounded monthly. What is their amount after 8 years if the payments are made

  (a) at the end of every 3 months?

  (b) at the beginning of every 3 months?

⊕ **8. LO②** A property was purchased for quarterly payments of $1350 for 10 years. If the first payment was made on the date of purchase and interest is 5.5% compounded annually, what was the purchase price of the property?

9. LO① Arnie will receive payments of $850 at the beginning of every month from a trust account starting on his 30th birthday and continuing for 20 years. Interest is 5.04% compounded monthly.

  (a) What is the balance in the trust account on Arnie's 50th birthday?

  (b) How much interest will be included in the payments he receives?

⊕ **10. LO②** How much must be deposited into an account to accumulate to $32 000 at 7% compounded semi-annually

  (a) at the beginning of each month for 20 years?

  (b) at the end of each year for 15 years?

11. LO② A 6-year lease contract valued at $49 350 requires semi-annual payments. If the first payment is due at the date of signing the contract and interest is 9% compounded monthly, what is the amount of the payment?

⊕ **12. LO①** How long will it take to build up a fund of $10 000 by saving $300 at the beginning of every 6 months at 4.5% compounded semi-annually?

13. LO③ Terry saves $50 at the beginning of each month for 16 years. Beginning 1 month after his last deposit, he intends to withdraw $375 per month. If interest is 6% compounded monthly, for how long can Terry make withdrawals?

⊕ **14. LO①** Debra is considering taking out a membership in her local fitness club. If she pays for a 2-year membership in advance, the cost is $698. If she makes monthly payments over the same 2 years, she would have to pay $34 at the beginning of each month. What is the monthly compounded nominal rate charged for the payment plan?

15. LO③ Alex Sanchez won a $12 500 prize that he deposited in an account paying 5.95% compounded semi-annually for 10 years. At the end of 10 years, he reinvested the balance into an annuity that paid $500 at the beginning of each month starting with the date of reinvestment. If interest on the annuity is 5.16% compounded monthly, for how long will Alex receive monthly payments?

16. **LO②** What is the nominal rate of interest compounded quarterly at which payments of $400 made at the beginning of every six months accumulates to $8400 in eight years?

17. **LO①③** FlexLabs borrowed funds to purchase a new blood analysis machine by signing a loan contract requiring payments of $1630 at the end of every three months for six years.

 (a) How much is the cash value of the contract if money is worth 8.1% compounded quarterly?

 (b) If the first three payments are missed, how much would have to be paid after one year to bring the contract up to date?

 (c) If, because of the missed payments, the contract has to be paid out at the end of one year, how much money is needed?

 (d) How much of the total interest paid is due to the missed payments?

18. **LO②** A debt of $20 000 is repaid by making payments of $3500. If interest is 9% compounded monthly, for how long will payments have to be made?

 (a) at the end of every six months?

 (b) at the beginning of each year?

 (c) at the end of every three months with payments deferred for five years?

 (d) at the beginning of every six months with payments deferred for three years?

19. **LO①** Tomac Swim Club bought electronic timing equipment on a contract requiring monthly payments of $725 for three years beginning eighteen months after the date of purchase. What was the cash value of the equipment if interest is 7.5% compounded monthly?

20. **LO③** Aaron deposited $900 every 6 months for 20 years into a fund paying 5.5% compounded semi-annually. Five years after the last deposit, he converted the existing balance in the fund into an ordinary annuity paying him equal monthly payments for 15 years. If interest on the annuity is 6% compounded monthly, what is the size of the monthly payment he will receive?

21. **LO④** A debt of $40 000 is to be repaid in installments due at the end of each month for seven years. If the payments are deferred for three years and interest is 7% compounded quarterly, what is the size of the monthly payments?

22. **LO③** Ty received a separation payment of $25 000 from his former employer when he was 35 years old. He invested that sum of money at 5.5% compounded semi-annually. When he was 65, he converted the balance into an ordinary annuity paying $6000 every 3 months with interest at 6% compounded quarterly. For how long will the annuity continue to pay him?

23. **LO④** George purchased an annuity that provides payments of $4500 at the end of every 3 months. The annuity is bought for $33 500 and payments are deferred for 12 years. If interest is 4.94% compounded monthly, for how long will payments be received?

24. **LO③** Frank sold an antique car he had inherited, investing the proceeds of $15 000 to earn 4.84% compounded monthly. After 45 months, he converted his investment to an annuity, whereby he withdraws $335 at the end of each month over 5 years. What monthly compounded nominal rate of interest does the annuity earn during the annuity period?

25. **LO③** Reagan O'Brien bought his parents' apple orchards for $200 000. The transfer agreement requires Reagan to make annual year-end payments of $35 000 for 10 years. Money is worth 5.29% compounded annually. If the first payment is due in 3 years, what is the annually compounded nominal interest rate during the next 10 years?

26. **LO④** If the White Rock Fire Department invests now in new ladder systems for several of its trucks, the department would save $3500 every 6 months in repair costs. What single cash investment made now is equivalent to the repair payments if interest is 8% compounded quarterly and the payments are made

 (a) at the end of every 6 months for 15 years?

 (b) at the beginning of every 6 months for 10 years?

 (c) at the end of every 6 months for 8 years but deferred for 4 years?

 (d) at the beginning of every 6 months for 9 years but deferred for 3 years?

(e) at the end of every 6 months in perpetuity?

(f) at the beginning of every 6 months in perpetuity?

27. **LO❸** Bonita contributed $450 at the beginning of every three months to an RRSP. Interest on the account is 6% compounded quarterly.

   (a) What will the balance in the account be after seven years?

   (b) How much of the balance will be interest?

   (c) If Bonita converts the balance after 7 years into an RRIF paying 5% compounded quarterly, and makes equal quarterly withdrawals for 12 years starting 3 months after the conversion into the RRIF, what is the size of the quarterly withdrawal?

   (d) What is the combined interest earned by the RRSP and the RRIF?

28. **LO❹** A church congregation has raised $37 625 for future outreach work. If the money is invested in a fund paying 7% compounded quarterly, what annual payment can be made for 10 years from the fund if the first payment is to be made 4 years from the date of investment in the fund?

29. **LO❷❹** For their marketing class in sales techniques, the business students of Keewaten College raised $16 750 in scholarship donations. What sum of money can be withdrawn from the fund if the money is invested at 6.5% compounded semi-annually

   (a) at the end of every 3 months for 12 years?

   (b) at the beginning of each year for 20 years?

   (c) at the end of each month for 15 years but deferred for 10 years?

   (d) at the beginning of every 3 months for 12 years but deferred for 20 years?

   (e) at the end of each month in perpetuity?

   (f) at the beginning of each year in perpetuity?

30. **LO❶** Niagara Vineyards borrowed $75 000 to update their bottling equipment. The business agreed to make payments of $6000 at the end of every three months. If interest is 7.31% compounded quarterly, how long will the company have to make the payments?

31. **LO❹** Keyes Farms bought a tractor priced at $20 000 and agreed to make payments of $1223 at the end of every three months. If interest is 7.8% compounded quarterly, how long will payments have to be made if the payments are deferred for two years and six months?

32. **LO❺** Pipeline Corporation's preferred share dividend of $1.45 is paid at the end of every six months. If comparable investments yield 5.6% compounded quarterly, what should the selling price of these shares be?

33. **LO❺** Western Railway leases land owned by the City of Regina, paying $11 000 at the beginning of each year. For what amount should Western offer to buy the land if interest is 6.5% compounded annually?

34. **LO❺** A scholarship fund is to be set up to provide annual scholarships of $4000. If the first payment is due in three years and interest is 4.82% compounded quarterly, what sum of money must be deposited in the scholarship fund today?

SELF-TEST

1. To support his handicapped niece, Tony made payments of $1800 into a fund at the beginning of every 3 months. If the fund earns interest at 5.24% compounded quarterly, how much will the balance in the fund be after 18 years?

2. Calculate the present value of payments of $960 made at the beginning of every month for seven years if money is worth 6% compounded monthly.

3. Tim bought a boat valued at $10 104 by agreeing to make semi-annual payments for five years. If the first payment is due on the date of purchase and interest is 8.8% compounded semi-annually, what is the size of the semi-annual payments?

4. Bruce needs construction tools and equipment to start his new job. He has signed a lease contract valued at $5200, and will make payments of $270 at the beginning of

every three months for six years. What is the nominal annual rate of interest compounded quarterly charged on the lease?

5. Through automatic transfer from her bank chequing account to her savings account, Lily has made deposits of $145 at the beginning of each month. The savings account earns interest at 2.12% compounded semi-annually. After 12 years, how much has she accumulated in her savings account?

6. A lease requires monthly payments of $950 due in advance. If interest is 12% compounded quarterly and the term of the lease is five years, what is the cash value of the lease?

7. J.J. deposited $1680 at the beginning of every 6 months for 8 years into a fund paying 5.5% compounded semi-annually. Seven years after the first deposit, he converted the balance into an annuity paying him equal monthly payments for 20 years. If the payments are made at the end of each month and interest on the annuity is 6% compounded monthly, what is the size of the monthly payments?

8. Ken acquired his sister's share of their business by agreeing to make payments of $4000 at the end of each year for 12 years. If the payments are deferred for 3 years and money is worth 5% compounded quarterly, what is the cash value of his sister's share of the business?

9. The amount of $39 600 is invested at 3.5% compounded quarterly. After four years the balance in the fund is converted into an annuity. If payments of $6000 are made at the end of every six months for seven years, what is the nominal rate of interest compounded semi-annually on the annuity?

10. Elsie Shen wants to withdraw $6000 at the beginning of every 3 months for 20 years, starting on the date of her retirement. If she retires in 18 years and interest is 4.68% compounded quarterly, how much must she deposit into an account every quarter for the next 18 years, starting now?

11. An amount of $27 350 is invested at 6% compounded monthly for 6 years. After the initial 6-year period, the balance in the fund is converted into an annuity due paying $1600 every 6 months. If interest on the annuity is 4.96% compounded semi-annually, what is the term of the annuity in years?

12. New Brunswick Bank pays a quarterly dividend of $0.75 per share. If comparable investments yield 4.16% compounded monthly, what is the market value of the shares?

13. Mr. Smart wants to set up an annual scholarship by donating $50 000 to the scholarship fund of his university. If the first payment is to be made in 5 years and interest is 4% compounded annually, what is the amount of the annual scholarship?

14. What is the principal invested at 4.75% compounded semi-annually from which monthly withdrawals of $240 can be made

   (a) at the end of each month for 25 years?
   (b) at the beginning of each month for 15 years?
   (c) at the end of each month for 20 years but deferred for 10 years?
   (d) at the beginning of each month for 15 years but deferred for 12 years?
   (e) at the end of each month in perpetuity?
   (f) at the beginning of each month in perpetuity?

CHALLENGE PROBLEMS

1. A regular deposit of $100 is made at the beginning of each year for 20 years. Simple interest is calculated at i % per year for the 20 years. At the end of the 20-year period, the total interest in the account is $840. Suppose that interest of i % compounded annually had been paid instead. How much interest would have been in the account at the end of the 20 years?

2. Herman has agreed to repay a debt by using the following repayment schedule. Starting today, he will make $100 payments at the beginning of each month for the next two-and-a-half years. He will then pay nothing for the next two years. Finally, after four-and-a-half years, he will make $200 payments at the beginning of each month for one year, which will pay off his debt completely. For the first four-and-a-half years, the interest on the debt is 9% compounded monthly. For the final year, the interest is lowered to 8.5% compounded monthly. Determine the size of Herman's debt. Round your answer to the nearest dollar.

CASE STUDY   Planning for University

▶ Victor and Jasmine Gonzalez were discussing how to plan for their three young sons' university education. Stephen turned 12 years old in April, Jack turned 9 in January, and Danny turned 7 in March. Although university was still a long way off for the boys, Victor and Jasmine wanted to ensure enough funds were available for their studies.

Victor and Jasmine decided to provide each son with a monthly allowance that would cover tuition and some living expenses. Because they were uncertain about the boys' finding summer jobs in the future, Victor and Jasmine decided their sons would receive the allowance at the beginning of each month for four years. The parents also assumed that the costs of education would continue to increase.

Stephen would receive an allowance of $1000 per month starting September 1 of the year he turns 18.

Jack would receive an allowance that is 8% more than Stephen's allowance. He would also receive it at the beginning of September 1 of the year he turns 18.

Danny would receive an allowance that is 10% more than Jack's at the beginning of September of the year he turns 18.

Victor and Jasmine visited their local bank manager to fund the investment that would pay for the boys' allowances for university. The bank manager suggested an investment paying interest of 4.0% compounded monthly, from now until the three boys had each completed their four years of education. Victor and Jasmine thought this sounded reasonable. So on June 1, a week after talking with the bank manager, they deposited the sum of money necessary to finance their sons' post-secondary educations.

QUESTIONS

1. How much allowance will each of the boys receive per month based on their parents' assumptions of price increases?

2. **(a)** How much money must Victor and Jasmine invest for each son on June 1 to provide them the desired allowance?
   (b) Create a timeline of events for each of the sons.
   (c) What is the total amount invested on June 1?

SUMMARY OF FORMULAS

Formula 13.1

$$FV_n(\text{due}) = PMT\left[\frac{(1+i)^n - 1}{i}\right](1+i)$$ Calculating the future value of a simple annuity due

Can be rearranged as:

$$PMT = \frac{FV_n(\text{due})}{\left[\dfrac{(1+i)^n - 1}{i}\right](1+i)}$$ Determining the payment of a simple annuity due when the future value is known

Formula 13.2

$$PV_n(\text{due}) = PMT\left[\frac{1-(1+i)^{-n}}{i}\right](1+i)$$ Calculating the present value of a simple annuity due

Can be rearranged as:

$$PMT = \frac{PV_n(\text{due})}{\left[\dfrac{1-(1+i)^{-n}}{i}\right](1+i)}$$ Determining the payment of a simple annuity due when the present value is known

Formula 13.3

$$FV_g(\text{due}) = PMT\left[\frac{(1+p)^n - 1}{p}\right](1+p)$$ Calculating the future value of a general annuity due using the effective rate of interest per payment period

where $p = (1+i)^c - 1$

Can be rearranged as:

$$PMT = \frac{FV_g(\text{due})}{\left[\dfrac{(1+p)^n - 1}{p}\right](1+p)}$$ Determining the payment of a general annuity due when the future value is known, using the effective rate of interest per payment period

where $p = (1+i)^c - 1$

Formula 13.4

$$PV_g(\text{due}) = PMT\left[\frac{1-(1+p)^{-n}}{p}\right](1+p)$$ Calculating the present value of a general annuity due using the effective rate of interest per payment period

where $p = (1+i)^c - 1$

Can be rearranged as:

$$PMT = \frac{PV_g(\text{due})}{\left[\dfrac{1-(1+p)^{-n}}{p}\right](1+p)}$$ Determining the payment of a general annuity due when the present value is known, using the effective rate of interest per payment period

where $p = (1+i)^c - 1$

Formula 13.5

$$PV = \frac{PMT}{i}$$

Calculating the present value of an ordinary simple perpetuity

Formula 13.6

$$PV = \frac{PMT}{p}$$

Calculating the present value of an ordinary general perpetuity

where $p = (1 + i)^c - 1$

Formula 13.7

$$PV(\text{due}) = PMT + \frac{PMT}{i}$$

Calculating the present value of a simple perpetuity due

Formula 13.8

$$PV(\text{due}) = PMT + \frac{PMT}{p}$$

Calculating the present value of a general perpetuity due

where $p = (1 + i)^c - 1$

GLOSSARY

Annuity due an annuity in which the periodic payments are made at the beginning of each payment interval *(p. 494)*

Deferred annuity an annuity in which the first payment is made at a time later than the end of the first payment interval *(p. 516)*

General annuity due a general annuity in which the payments are made at the beginning of each payment interval *(p. 508)*

Period of deferment the period from the time referred to as "now" to the starting point of the term of the annuity *(p. 516)*

Perpetuity an annuity in which the periodic payments begin at a fixed date and continue indefinitely *(p. 533)*

Perpetuity due a perpetuity in which the first payment is made at the focal date *(p. 536)*

Perpetuity payment the interest earned by the present value of the perpetuity in one interest period *(p. 534)*

Amortization of Loans, Including Residential Mortgages

Andrew Rakoczy Photos/Alamy Stock Photo

LEARNING OBJECTIVES

Upon completing this chapter, you will be able to do the following:

1 Perform computations associated with amortization of debts involving simple annuities, and construct complete or partial amortization schedules.

2 Perform computations associated with amortization of debts involving general annuities, and construct complete or partial amortization schedules.

3 Compute the size of the final payment when all payments except the final payment are equal in size.

4 Compute the periodic interest rate for fixed-rate residential mortgages.

5 Compute the periodic payments for fixed-rate mortgages and for demand mortgages.

6 Create statements for various types of residential mortgages.

You are considering the purchase of your first home. A condominium in your desired neighbourhood is available. You have been saving for a down payment, but do not know if you have enough money. You are very excited, but have many questions. Will you qualify for a mortgage? What will your payments be? How much interest will you have to pay in the first year, or over the life of the mortgage? What if interest rates go up? How will this affect your payments? Will this affect your mortgage balance?

One of the most important financial decisions most of us will have to make is whether to assume a mortgage on a house. Knowledge of how loans and mortgages amortize will give you the potential to make better decisions and save thousands of dollars in repaying your debts.

INTRODUCTION

Amortization of loans refers to the repayment of interest-bearing debts by a series of payments, usually equal in size, made at equal intervals of time. The periodic payments, when equal in size, form an annuity whose present value is equivalent to the original loan principal. Mortgages and many consumer loans are repaid by this method. An amortization schedule shows the allocation of each payment to first cover the interest due and then reduce the principal.

14.1 AMORTIZATION INVOLVING SIMPLE ANNUITIES
A. Computing the periodic payment

What is **amortization**? An interest-bearing debt is *amortized* if both principal and interest are repaid by a series of equal payments made at equal intervals of time.

The basic problem in amortizing a debt is computing the size of the periodic payment. If the payment interval and the interest compounding period are equal in length, the problem involves computing the periodic payment for a simple annuity. Since debts are generally repaid by making payments at the end of the payment interval, the method and formula for ordinary simple annuities apply.

$$PV_n = PMT\left[\frac{1-(1+i)^{-n}}{i}\right] \text{———— Formula 11.2}$$

EXAMPLE 14.1A   A debt of $5000 with interest at 9% compounded annually is to be repaid by equal payments at the end of each year for six years. What is the size of the annual payments?

SOLUTION

Figure 14.1 Graphical Representation of Method and Data (© S. A. Hummelbrunner)

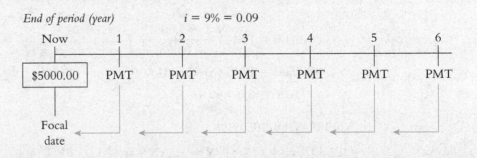

As Figure 14.1 shows, the equal annual payments (designated by PMT) form an ordinary simple annuity in which

$PV = 5000.00$; $FV = 0$; $n = 6$; $P/Y = 1$; $C/Y = 1$; $I/Y = 9$; $i = 9\% = 0.09$

Using "now" as the focal date, you can calculate the value of the annual payment PMT using Formula 11.2.

$$5000.00 = PMT\left(\frac{1-1.09^{-6}}{0.09}\right) \text{———— using Formula 11.2}$$

$$5000.00 = PMT(4.485919)$$

$$PMT = \$1114.60$$

PROGRAMMED SOLUTION

("END" mode) (Set P/Y = 1; C/Y = 1) 0 | FV | 5000 | ± | | PV | 9 | I/Y |

6 | N | | CPT | | PMT | 1114.598916 |

The annual payment is $1114.60.

Rounding

In Example 14.1A, the payment was calculated as $1114.598916. In banking, the actual payment is rounded up to the nearest cent to $1114.60, because the payment must be made with cash, debit, or a transfer of funds from one account to another, all of which have to be made to the nearest cent. Because of this "rounding," an error will eventually occur. This error is taken into account by adjusting the final payment. Thus, the final payment is almost always different from (and slightly smaller than) the other payments. The amount of the actual final payment can be determined by calculating the balance owing at the beginning of the final period and adding the interest charged on this amount for the final interval.

POINTERS & PITFALLS

The payment must be rounded to the 2-decimal standard for currency.

EXAMPLE 14.1B

A loan of $8000 made at 6% compounded monthly is amortized over five years by making equal monthly payments.

(i) What is the size of the monthly payment?

(ii) What is the total amount paid to amortize the loan?

(iii) What is the cost of financing?

SOLUTION

(i) $PV = 8000.00$; $n = 5(12) = 60$; $P/Y = 12$; $C/Y = 12$; $I/Y = 6$;

$$i = \frac{6\%}{12} = 0.5\%$$

$$8000.00 = PMT\left(\frac{1 - 1.005^{-60}}{0.005}\right) \text{————————— using Formula 11.2}$$

$$8000.00 = PMT(51.725561)$$

$$PMT = \$154.66$$

PROGRAMMED SOLUTION

("END" mode) (Set P/Y = 12; C/Y = 12) 0 | FV | 8000 | ± | | PV | 6 | I/Y |

60 | N | | CPT | | PMT | 154.662412 |

The monthly payment is $154.66.

(ii) The total amount paid is 60(154.662412) = $9279.74.

(iii) The cost of financing is 9279.74 − 8000.00 = $1279.74.

B. Calculating the interest, principal, and balance for a period

The interest paid for a given payment period is based on the outstanding principal balance at the beginning of the period. For the first period, the beginning balance is the loan's initial amount. For the second period, the outstanding balance at the end of the first period becomes the outstanding balance at the beginning of the second period. Interest paid in a period is calculated by multiplying the periodic interest rate by the period's beginning balance.

INTEREST IN ANY PERIOD = PERIODIC INTEREST RATE

× BALANCE AT THE BEGINNING OF THE PERIOD

The amount of the payment often exceeds the amount of interest due. The additional amount paid repays the principal of the loan. For a period, subtract the interest paid from the amount paid to determine the principal paid for that period.

PRINCIPAL PAID FOR A PERIOD = PAYMENT FOR THE PERIOD − INTEREST FOR THE PERIOD

The outstanding principal balance is the amount still owing. The balance at the end of a period is determined by subtracting the period's principal repaid from the beginning outstanding balance for that period.

BALANCE AT THE END OF A PERIOD = BALANCE AT THE BEGINNING OF THE PERIOD

− PRINCIPAL PAID FOR THE PERIOD

EXAMPLE 14.1C

To buy a compact car, Howard borrowed $20 000 on a loan that charged 2.4% compounded monthly. He agreed to make end of the month payments for four years.

(i) What is the size of the monthly payment?

(ii) For the first payment, how much of the payment is interest?

(iii) For the first payment, how much of the loan is repaid?

(iv) After the first payment, how much of the loan remains to be paid?

(v) For the second payment, how much of the payment is interest?

(vi) For the second payment, how much of the loan is repaid?

(vii) After the second payment, how much of the loan remains to be paid?

SOLUTION

Figure 14.2 Graphical Representation of Method and Data (© S. A. Hummelbrunner)

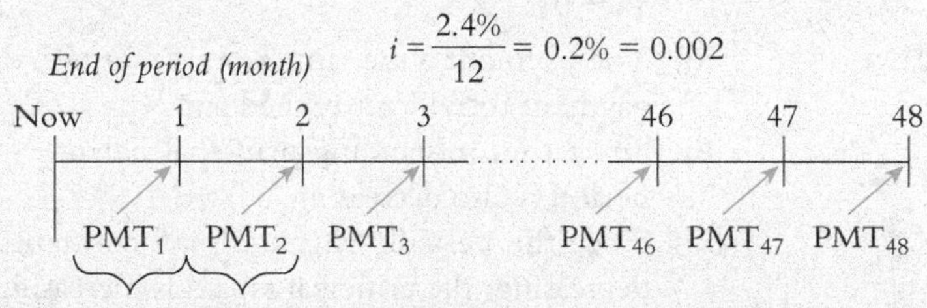

$PV = 20\ 000.00;\quad n = 4(12) = 48;\quad P/Y = 12;\quad C/Y = 12;\quad I/Y = 2.4\%$
$i = 2.4\%/12 = 0.2\% = 0.002$

(i) $20\ 000.00 = PMT\left(\dfrac{1 - 1.002^{-48}}{0.002}\right)$ **using Formula 11.2**

$20\ 000.00 = PMT(45.724442)$

$PMT = 437.402826$

$PMT = \$437.40$

PROGRAMMED SOLUTION

("END" mode) (Set P/Y = 12; C/Y = 12) 0 [FV] 20 000 [±] [PV] 2.4 [I/Y]

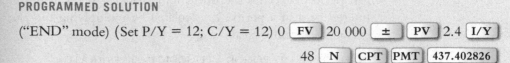

48 [N] [CPT] [PMT] [437.402826]

(ii) The interest for the first period is $20 000.00 × 0.002 = $40.00.

(iii) The principal repaid in the first period is $437.40 − 40.00 = $397.40.

(iv) The balance of the loan after the first period is $20 000.00 − 397.40 = $19 602.60.

(v) The interest for the second period is $19 602.60 × 0.002 = $39.20520, rounded to $39.21.

(vi) The principal repaid in the second period is $437.40 − 39.21 = $398.19.

(vii) The balance at the end of the second period is $19 602.60 − 398.19 = $19 204.41.

C. Constructing amortization schedules

As previously discussed in Section 8.5, **amortization schedules** show in detail how a debt is repaid. Such schedules normally show the payment number (or payment date), the amount paid, the interest paid, the principal repaid, and the outstanding debt balance.

In Example 14.1C, the interest paid, the principal repaid, and the outstanding principal balance for the first two periods of the loan were calculated. An amortization schedule can be constructed to show these details. These amounts can be calculated for the remaining periods to complete the schedule.

Payment Number	Payment	Interest Paid $i = 0.002$	Principal Repaid	Outstanding Principal Balance
0 (Initial balance)				$20 000.00
1	$437.40	$40.00	$397.40	19 602.60
2	437.40	39.21	398.19	19 204.41

Notice that:

(i) The payment is the same amount for every period, but must be adjusted in the last payment to fully repay the loan.

(ii) Since the outstanding principal balance is decreasing, the interest paid in each period is also decreasing.

(iii) Since the periodic payment stays constant and the interest paid in each period is decreasing, the principal repaid is increasing.

(iv) Interest paid in each period is calculated by multiplying periodic interest by the outstanding principal balance of the previous period. For example, interest paid for the second period equals: 0.0002 × 19602.60 = 39.21

1. Amortization Schedule with Blended Payments

When a loan is amortized by making blended payments, the size of the periodic payment must first be determined, as shown in Examples 14.1A, 14.1B, and 14.1C. In most cases, the payment amount must be rounded to the nearest cent. As a result of the rounding, to fully repay the loan, the final payment may be close to but not exactly the same as the other payments. To construct an amortization schedule, follow the procedure explained in the next example.

POINTERS
& PITFALLS

When constructing an amortization schedule, it is important to recognize that all numbers in the schedule need to be rounded to 2 decimals (since it is currency). However, since the money remains in the account at all times, all decimals are in fact being carried forward throughout. As such, calculated numbers may sometimes be off by a penny due to the rounding of the payment or the interest.

EXAMPLE 14.1D

A debt of $5000 is amortized by making equal payments at the end of every 3 months for 2 years. If interest is 8% compounded quarterly, construct an amortization schedule.

SOLUTION

STEP 1 Determine the size of the quarterly payments.

$$PV = 5000.00; \quad n = 4(2) = 8; \quad P/Y = 4; \quad C/Y = 4; \quad I/Y = 8; \quad i = \frac{8\%}{4} = 2\%$$

$$5000.00 = PMT\left(\frac{1 - 1.02^{-8}}{0.02}\right)$$

$$5000.00 = PMT(7.325481)$$

$$PMT = \$682.548996$$

The payment is rounded to the nearest cent, $682.55.

PROGRAMMED SOLUTION

("END" mode) (Set P/Y = 4; C/Y = 4) 0 [FV] 5000 [±] [PV] 8 [I/Y]

8 [N] [CPT] [PMT] 682.548996

STEP 2 Construct the amortization schedule as shown in the following table.

Payment Number	Amount Paid	Interest Paid $i = 0.02$	Principal Repaid	Outstanding Principal Balance
0				$5000.00
1	$682.55	$100.00*	$582.55**	4417.45***
2	682.55	88.35	594.20	3823.25
3	682.55	76.47	606.08	3217.17
4	682.55	64.34	618.21	2598.96
5	682.55	51.98	630.57	1968.39
6	682.55	39.37	643.18	1325.21
7	682.55	26.50	656.05	669.16
8	682.54	13.38	669.16	$0.00
TOTAL	$5460.39	$460.39	$5000.00	

* 5000.0 × 0.02 = $100.00

** 682.55 − 100.00 = $582.55

*** 5000 − 582.55 = $4417.45

Explanations regarding the construction of the amortization schedule

1. Payment 0 is used to introduce the initial balance of the loan.

2. The interest included in the first payment is the periodic interest rate i multiplied by the period's beginning outstanding principal balance, $0.02 \times 5000.00 = \$100.00$. Since the amount paid is \$682.55, the amount available for repayment of principal is $682.55 - 100.00 = \$582.55$. The outstanding principal balance after the first payment is $5000.00 - 582.55 = \$4417.45$.

3. The interest included in the second payment is $0.02 \times 4417.45 = \$88.35$. Since the amount paid is \$682.55, the amount available for repayment of principal is $682.55 - 88.35 = \$594.20$. The outstanding principal is $4417.45 - 594.20 = \$3823.25$.

4. Computation of interest, principal repaid, and outstanding balance for Payments 3 to 7 are made in a similar manner.

5. The last payment of \$682.54 is slightly different from the other payments as a result of rounding in the amount paid or the interest paid. To allow for such rounding errors, the last payment is computed by adding the interest due in the last payment $(0.02 \times 669.16 = \$13.38)$ to the outstanding balance: $669.16 + 13.38 = \$682.54$.

6. The three totals provide useful information and can be used as a check on the accuracy of the schedule.
   (a) The total principal repaid must equal the original outstanding balance;
   (b) The total amount paid is the periodic payment times the number of such payments plus/minus any adjustment in the last payment:

   $$682.55 \times 8 - 0.01 = 5460.40 - 0.01 = \$5460.39;$$

   (c) The total interest paid is the difference between the amount paid and the original principal, $5460.39 - 5000.00 = \$460.39$.

PROGRAMMED SOLUTION

The amortization schedule can also be built by using the Amortization function within the preprogrammed financial calculator. Using the Texas Instruments BA II PLUS, follow these steps:

1. Enter all of the information within the TVM function and compute the payment, PMT, as above. Re-enter the payment, PMT, rounded to the nearest cent.

2. Press 2nd AMORT to start the function.

3. On the calculator display, P1 refers to the number of the first period of the range to be specified. For example, to obtain data for periods 2 through 5, P1 would be entered as "2." Remember to press the Enter key to enter new data.

4. Press the down arrow key ↓ to move to the next cell. P2 refers to the number of the last period of the range to be specified. For example, to obtain data for periods 2 through 5, P2 would be entered as "5."

5. To obtain information for just one period, both P1 and P2 must be entered, as the same number. For example, to obtain data for period 1, both P1 and P2 must be entered as "1," specifying "from" period 1 and "to" period 1. Press the down arrow key ↓ to move to the next cell. BAL is automatically calculated as the loan balance at the end of the period specified in P2. In the given amortization schedule when period 1 is specified, the BAL

calculated is −4417.45. The outstanding balance appears as a negative number because the PV was entered as a negative number.

6. Press the down arrow key ⬇ to move to the next cell. PRN is automatically calculated as the portion of the principal that was repaid. In the given amortization schedule, the PRN is calculated as 582.55.

7. Press the down arrow key ⬇ to move to the next cell. INT is automatically calculated as the portion of the period's payment that was interest on the loan. In the given amortization schedule, the INT is calculated as 100.00.

8. When you get to the last payment, P1 = 8, P2 = 8, BAL = −0.01. This represents an overpayment of one cent which, when subtracted from the equal payment of $682.55, gives a final payment of $682.54.

9. To calculate the total interest paid, set P1 = 1 and P2 = 8. Interest is automatically calculated as $460.39.

   With each method described, the results may be slightly different due to when and where rounding takes place.

EXAMPLE 14.1E   Using the amortization function of the Texas Instruments BA II PLUS, solve Example 14.1C.

SOLUTION

(i) Enter all of the information within the TVM function and compute the payment, PMT:

("END mode) (Set P/Y = 12; C/Y = 12) 0 [FV] 20 000 [±] [PV] 2.4 [I/Y]
48 [N] [CPT] [PMT] 437.402826

(ii) Press [2nd] [AMORT] to start the function. For P1 and P2 enter 1 and 1. Press the arrow down key three times to reach display of interest: INT = 40.

(iii) Press the up arrow key once to reach principal repaid display: PRN = 397.40

(iv) Press the up arrow key once to reach display of balance at the end of the first period: BAL = −19602.597

(v) Press the up arrow key twice to reach the Starting period page. For P1 enter 2 and press down arrow key to reach the ending period page. For P2 enter 2 and press the down arrow key three times to reach display of interest page: INT = 39.20519435.

(vi) Press the up arrow key once to reach principal repaid display: PRN = 398.1976.

(vii) Press the up arrow key once to reach the display of the balance at the end of period 2: BAL = 19204.399.

2. Amortization Schedule When the Payment Is a Convenient Round Figure

When the size of the periodic payment is a convenient round figure instead of a computed blended payment amount, the first step is to determine the number of payments. The size of the final payment will probably be different from the preceding agreed-upon payments. This final payment is obtained in the amortization schedule by adding the interest due on the outstanding balance to the outstanding balance.

This type of loan repayment schedule has been illustrated and explained in Section 8.5. The following example is included for review.

EXAMPLE 14.1F

Bronco Repairs borrowed $15 000 from National Credit Union at 10% compounded quarterly. The loan agreement requires payments of $2500 at the end of every three months. Construct an amortization schedule.

Here we have to determine the number of payments required. Use of the TVM Worksheet determines a value of $n = 6.581682$. This is interpreted as 6 payments of $2500 and a seventh payment of less than $2500.

SOLUTION

$i = \dfrac{10\%}{4} = 2.5\% = 0.025$

Payment Number	Amount Paid	Interest Paid $i = 0.025$	Principal Repaid	Outstanding Principal Balance
0				$15 000.00
1	$2500.00	$375.00	$2125.00	12 875.00
2	2500.00	321.88	2178.12	10 696.88
3	2500.00	267.42	2232.58	8464.30
4	2500.00	211.61	2288.39	6175.90
5	2500.00	154.40	2345.60	3830.30
6	2500.00	95.76	2404.24	1426.06
7	1461.71	35.65	1426.06	$0.00
TOTAL	$16,461.71	$1461.71	$15 000.00	

Note: After Payment 6, the outstanding principal balance is less than the agreed-upon payment. When this happens, the final payment will be the outstanding principal balance plus the interest due on the outstanding principal balance.

$1426.06 + (1426.06 \times 0.025) = 1426.06 + 35.65 = \$1461.71$

Using the Amortization Worksheet in the BA II PLUS, when we enter P1 = 7, P2 = 7, we get BAL = −1038.29. This represents an overpayment, and when subtracted from $2500 leaves a final payment of $1461.71. There is a one-cent error due to rounding.

D. Determining the outstanding principal balance

Often, for various reasons, the borrower or the lender needs to know the outstanding balance or the interest paid in a period before the loan is fully repaid. This may be required because of early repayment, refinancing, or to account for the interest and principal repaid. The outstanding balance and the interest paid can be determined by checking the amortization schedule, if available, or by direct mathematical computation. This computation is also useful for checking the accuracy of the schedule as it is developed.

One of the following two methods can be used to directly calculate the outstanding balance. The **retrospective method** should be used when the original amount financed is known, and the final payment has a different value than the other payments. The retrospective method looks back and considers the loan's original balance and the payments that have been made. This method calculates the outstanding balance by deducting the accumulated value of the payments that have been made from the accumulated value of the original debt. Financial institutions use this method and the balance calculated with financial calculators or any other software is based on the retrospective method.

The **prospective method** can be used when all of the payments have the same known value, including the final payment. The prospective method of computing the outstanding balance looks forward, considering the future prospects of the debt—the payments that remain outstanding. The present value of the remaining outstanding payments is calculated to determine the outstanding balance of the amount financed. When calculating the outstanding balance, both the retrospective method and the prospective method yield the same results.

1. Calculating the Outstanding Balance by the Retrospective Method

The retrospective method determines the outstanding balance at the end of n periods by subtracting the future value of the payments made from the future value of the original debt.

$$\text{OUTSTANDING BALANCE} = \begin{array}{l} \text{FUTURE VALUE OF THE ORIGINAL DEBT} \\ - \text{ FUTURE VALUE OF THE PAYMENTS MADE} \end{array}$$

| EXAMPLE 14.1G | For Example 14.1A, compute the outstanding balance just after the third payment has been made. |

| SOLUTION | The loan history showing the annual payments of $1114.60 can be represented on a time diagram, as shown in Figure 14.3. |

Figure 14.3 Graphical Representation of Loan Payments (© S. A. Hummelbrunner)

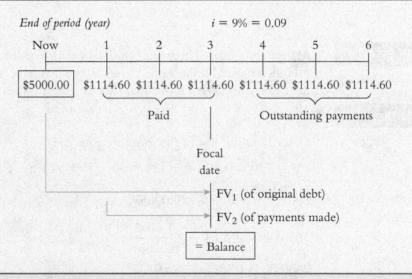

STEP 1   Calculate the future value of the original debt after three periods

$FV_1 = 5000.00(1.09)^3$ ——————————————— using Formula 9.1

$\quad = 5000.00(1.295029)$

$\quad = \$6475.145$

STEP 2   Calculate the future value of the three payments made

$FV_2 = 1114.60 \dfrac{(1.09^3 - 1)}{.09}$ ——————————— using Formula 11.1

$\quad = 1114.60(3.2781)$

$\quad = \$3653.77026$

STEP 3 Subtract the future value of the three payments made from the future value of the original debt

$6475.145 - 3653.77026 = \$2821.37474$

Since the payment is rounded to the nearest cent, a rounding difference may result. With a total of six payments to repay the loan, this difference would be minimal.

The outstanding balance of the loan after three payments is $2821.38.

PROGRAMMED SOLUTION

("END" mode) (Set P/Y = 1; C/Y = 1) 5000.00 $\boxed{\pm}$ $\boxed{\text{PV}}$ 0 $\boxed{\text{PMT}}$

9 $\boxed{\text{I/Y}}$ 3 $\boxed{\text{N}}$ $\boxed{\text{CPT}}$ $\boxed{\text{FV}}$ $\boxed{6745.145}$

1114.60 $\boxed{\text{PMT}}$ 0 $\boxed{\text{PV}}$ 9 $\boxed{\text{I/Y}}$ 3 $\boxed{\text{N}}$ $\boxed{\text{CPT}}$ $\boxed{\text{FV}}$ $\boxed{-3653.77026}$

Note: The programmed solution can be performed in one step, including both the PV and the PMT. The FV is then the outstanding balance.

("END" mode) (Set P/Y = 1; C/Y = 1) 5000.00 $\boxed{\pm}$ $\boxed{\text{PV}}$ 1114.60 $\boxed{\text{PMT}}$

9 $\boxed{\text{I/Y}}$ 3 $\boxed{\text{N}}$ $\boxed{\text{CPT}}$ $\boxed{\text{FV}}$ $\boxed{2821.374740}$

EXAMPLE 14.1H Marisa consolidated her credit card debt with one loan for $7500 at 7.8% compounded monthly. She agreed to repay the loan with month-end payments over the next five years. What is the loan balance after two years?

SOLUTION

STEP 1 Determine the size of the monthly payment.

$\text{PV} = 7500.00; \quad n = 5(12) = 60; \quad \text{P/Y} = 12; \quad \text{C/Y} = 12; \quad \text{I/Y} = 7.8$

$i = \dfrac{0.078}{12} = 0.65\% = 0.0065$

$7500.00 = \text{PMT}\left(\dfrac{1 - 1.0065^{-60}}{0.0065}\right)$

$7500.00 = \text{PMT}(49.552018)$

$\text{PMT} = \$151.356096$

STEP 2 Calculate the future value of the original debt after two years

$\text{FV} = 7500.00(1.0065)^{24}$ ——————————————— using Formula 9.1

$= 7500.00(1.168236)$

$= \$8761.772344$

STEP 3 Calculate the future value of the 24 payments made

$\text{FV}_{24} = 51.356096\left(\dfrac{1.0065^{24} - 1}{0.0065}\right)$ ——————————— using Formula 11.1

$= 151.356096(25.882510)$

$= \$3917.4756$

STEP 4   Subtract the future value of the payments made from the future value of the original debt

$$8761.772344 - 3917.4756 = \$4844.2967$$

Since each of the payments is rounded to the nearest cent, a rounding difference may result. The outstanding balance of the loan after 2 years (24 payments) is \$4844.30.

PROGRAMMED SOLUTION

("END" mode) (Set P/Y = 12; C/Y = 12) 7500.00 $\boxed{\pm}$ $\boxed{\text{PV}}$ 0 $\boxed{\text{FV}}$

7.8 $\boxed{\text{I/Y}}$ 60 $\boxed{\text{N}}$ $\boxed{\text{CPT}}$ $\boxed{\text{PMT}}$ $\boxed{151.356096}$

7500.00 $\boxed{\pm}$ $\boxed{\text{PV}}$ 0 $\boxed{\text{PMT}}$ 7.8 $\boxed{\text{I/Y}}$ 24 $\boxed{\text{N}}$ $\boxed{\text{CPT}}$ $\boxed{\text{FV}}$ $\boxed{8761.772344}$

151.36 $\boxed{\pm}$ $\boxed{\text{PMT}}$ 0 $\boxed{\text{PV}}$ 7.8 $\boxed{\text{I/Y}}$ 24 $\boxed{\text{N}}$ $\boxed{\text{CPT}}$ $\boxed{\text{FV}}$ $\boxed{3917.475612}$

The outstanding balance of the loan after 2 years is $8761.772344 - 3917.475612 = \$4844.30$

2. Determining the Outstanding Balance by the Prospective Method

The original loan principal equals the present value of the payments that are needed to amortize the loan. In the prospective method, the outstanding balance at the end of any payment interval just after a payment has been made is the present value of the remaining outstanding payments.

OUTSTANDING BALANCE = PRESENT VALUE OF THE OUTSTANDING PAYMENTS

EXAMPLE 14.1I   Peyton's Mining purchased office equipment by agreeing to make month-end payments of \$300 for the next 4 years. At the time of the purchase, money was worth 8.22% compounded monthly.

(i) What was the equivalent purchase price?

(ii) Using the prospective method, calculate the outstanding balance of the loan after 6 months.

SOLUTION   See Figure 14.4.

Figure 14.4 Graphical Representation of Method and Data (© S. A. Hummelbrunner)

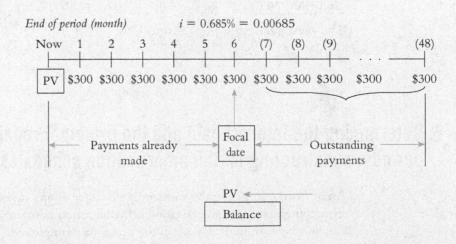

The prospective method is used to calculate the initial purchase price.

(i) Calculate the present value of all of the payments.

$$PMT = 300.00; \quad n = 4(12) = 48; \quad P/Y = 12; \quad C/Y = 12; \quad I/Y = 8.22;$$

$$i = \frac{0.0822}{12} = 0.685\% = 0.00685$$

$$PV_{48} = 300.00\left(\frac{1 - 1.00685^{-48}}{0.00685}\right)$$

$$PV_{48} = 300.00(40.789152)$$

$$PV_{48} = \$12\ 236.75$$

The equivalent purchase price (with 48 remaining payments) is \$12 236.75.

(ii) Using the prospective method, calculate the present value of the remaining payments.

$$PMT = 300.00; \quad n = 48 - 6 = 42; \quad P/Y = 12; \quad C/Y = 12; \quad I/Y = 8.22;$$

$$i = \frac{0.0822}{12} = 0.685\% = 0.00685$$

$$PV_{42} = 300.00\left(\frac{1 - 1.00685^{-42}}{0.00685}\right)$$

$$PV_{42} = 300.00\ (36.390865)$$

$$PV_{42} = \$10\ 917.26$$

The outstanding balance of the loan after six months (with 42 remaining payments) is \$10 917.26. Using the result from (i), the retrospective method yields the same result.

PROGRAMMED SOLUTION

("END" mode) (Set P/Y = 12; C/Y = 12) 300.00 [±] [PMT] 0 [FV]

8.22 [I/Y] 48 [N] [CPT] [PV] 12 236.745533

300.00 [±] [PMT] 0 [FV] 8.22 [I/Y] 42 [N] [CPT] [PV] 10 917.259537

Alternatively, we could use the Amortization Worksheet, which would allow us to calculate the balance after any payment;

[2nd] [AMORT] P1 = 6; P2 = 6; [↓] BAL = 10917.26

The outstanding balance is \$10 917.26.

E. Determining the interest paid and the principal repaid between two periods; constructing partial amortization schedules

Apart from computing the outstanding balance at any one time, all the other information contained in an amortization schedule, such as interest paid and principal repaid, can also be computed. Based on the previous examples, we will be using the retrospective method of calculating an outstanding balance.

EXAMPLE 14.1J

A debt of $5000 is amortized by making equal payments at the end of every three months for two years. If interest is 8% compounded quarterly, compute

(i) the interest paid in the fifth payment period;

(ii) the principal repaid in the fifth payment period.

SOLUTION

(i) To calculate the interest paid by the fifth payment, we need to know the outstanding balance after the fourth payment.

The future value of the original debt after four payments

$$FV = 5000(1.02)^4 = 5412.16$$

The future value of the four payments made

$$FV_4 = 682.55\left(\frac{1.02^4 - 1}{0.02}\right) = 2813.20$$

Balance = 5412.16 − 2813.20 = 2598.96

PROGRAMMED SOLUTION

("END" mode) (Set P/Y = 4; C/Y = 4;) 5000 [±] [PV] 682.55

[PMT] 8 [I/Y] 4 [N] [CPT] [FV] 2598.957260

Interest for Payment Period 5 is 2598.96(0.02) = $51.98.

(ii) Principal repaid = Amount paid − Interest paid

= 682.55 − 51.98

= $630.57

Alternatively, using the Amortization Worksheet

("END" mode) (Set P/Y = 4; C/Y = 4) [2nd] (CLR TVM) 8 [N] 8 [I/Y]

5000 [PV] 682.55 [±] [PMT] 0 [FV]

[2nd] [AMORT] P1 = 5, P2 = 5; [↓] BAL = 1968.39 [↓]

PRN = −630.57 [↓] INT = −51.98

EXAMPLE 14.1K

Jackie Kim borrowed $6000 from her trust company at 9% compounded monthly. She was to repay the loan with monthly payments over five years.

(i) What is the interest included in the 20th payment?

(ii) What is the principal repaid in the 36th payment period?

(iii) Construct a partial amortization schedule showing the details of the first 3 payments, the 20th payment, the 36th payment, and the last 3 payments, and determine the totals of amount paid, interest paid, and principal repaid.

SOLUTION

PV = 6000.00; $n = 5(12) = 60$; P/Y = 12; C/Y = 12; I/Y = 9;

$i = \frac{9\%}{12} = 0.75\% = 0.0075$

$$6000.00 = PMT\left(\frac{1 - 1.0075^{-60}}{0.0075}\right)$$

$$6000.00 = PMT(48.173374)$$

$$PMT = \$124.55$$

PROGRAMMED SOLUTION

("END" mode) (Set P/Y = 12; C/Y = 12) 0 [FV] 6000 [±] [PV] 9 [I/Y]

60 [N] [CPT] [PMT] [124.550131]

(i) The balance after 19 payments

$$FV = 6000(1.0075)^{19} = \$6915.24$$

$$FV_{19} = 124.55\left(\frac{1.0075^{19} - 1}{0.0075}\right) = \$2533.18$$

Balance = 6915.24 − 2533.18 = $4382.06

Interest for Payment Period 20 is 4382.06(0.0075) = $32.87

PROGRAMMED SOLUTION

Alternatively, using the Amortization Worksheet,

("END" mode) (Set P/Y = 12; C/Y = 12) 60 [N]

9 [I/Y] 6000 [PV] 124.55 [±] [PMT] 0 [FV]

[2nd] [AMORT] P1 = 20, P2 = 20; [↓] BAL = 4290.37 [↓]

PRN = −91.68 [↓] INT = −32.87

(ii) The outstanding balance after the 35th payment

$$FV = 6000(1.0075)^{35} = \$7793.42$$

$$FV_{35} = 124.55\left(\frac{1.0075^{35} - 1}{0.0075}\right) = \$4963.79$$

Balance = 7793.42 − 4963.79 = $2829.63

Interest for Payment Period 36 is 2829.63(0.0075) = $21.22

Principal Repaid = 124.55 − 21.22 = $103.33

PROGRAMMED SOLUTION

Alternatively, using the Amortization Worksheet,

[2nd] [AMORT] P1 = 36, P2 = 36; [↓] BAL = 2726.30 [↓]

PRN = −103.33 [↓] INT = −21.22

(iii) We can calculate the first three payments of the amortization table in the usual way, and we have already calculated the values for the 20th and the 36th. We could use the retrospective method to calculate the balance after the 57th payment and use this balance to calculate the values for the last three payments.

Alternatively, we can use the Amortization Worksheet to calculate values:

Partial amortization schedule

Payment Number	P1	P2	Amount Paid	Interest Paid $i = 0.0075$	Principal Repaid	Outstanding Principal Balance
0	-	-	-	-	-	$6000.00
1	1	1	$124.55	$45.00	$79.55	5920.45
2	2	2	124.55	44.40	80.15	5840.30
3	3	3	124.55	43.80	80.75	5759.55
•	•	•	•	•	•	•
19	•	•	•	•	•	4382.06
20	20	20	124.55	32.87	91.68	4290.37
•	•	•	•	•	•	•
35	•	•	•	•	•	2829.63
36	36	36	124.55	21.22	103.33	2726.30
•	•	•	•	•	•	•
57	•	•	•	•	•	368.12
58	58	58	124.55	2.76	121.79	246.33
59	59	59	124.55	1.85	122.70	123.62
60	60	60	124.55	0.93	123.62	$0.00
TOTALS	1	60	$7473.00	$1473.00	$6000.00	

Note: The total principal repaid must be $6000; the total amount paid is $124.55(60) = $7473; the total interest paid is $7473 - 6000 = $1473.

EXAMPLE 14.1L

The Polski Construction Company borrowed $75 000 at 11.20% compounded quarterly to buy construction equipment. Payments of $3500 are to be made at the end of every three months.

(i) How many payments are required?

(ii) Construct a partial amortization schedule showing the details of the last three payments and the totals.

SOLUTION

(i) To show details of the last three payments, we need to know the number of payments required to amortize the loan principal.

$$PV_n = 75\,000.00; \quad PMT = 3500.00; \quad i = 2.8\%$$

$$75\,000.00 = 3500.00\left(\frac{1 - 1.028^{-n}}{0.028}\right)$$

$$0.6 = 1 - 1.028^{-n}$$

$$1.028^{-n} = 0.4$$

$$-n \ln 1.028 = \ln 0.4$$

$$-n(0.027615) = -0.916291$$

$$n = 33.180706$$

PROGRAMMED SOLUTION

0 [FV] 75 000 [±] [PV] 3500 [PMT] 11.20 [I/Y] [CPT] [N] [33.180706]

Thirty-four payments (33 payments of $3500.00 each plus a final payment) are required.

(ii) Since 34 payments are required, with the final payment being an amount less than the regular payment, the amortization schedule should show calculations involving payments 32, 33, and 34. We start by determining the outstanding balance after 31 payments.

The future value of the original loan principal after 31 payments

$$FV = 75\,000.00(1.028)^{31}$$
$$= 75\,000.00(2.353892)$$
$$= \$176\,541.9088$$

The future value of the first 31 payments

$$FV_{31} = 3500.00\left(\frac{1.028^{31} - 1}{0.028}\right)$$
$$= 3500.00(48.353290)$$
$$= \$169\,236.5146$$

The outstanding balance after the 31st payment

$$= 176\,541.9088 - 169236.5146$$
$$= \$7305.39$$

Alternatively, using the Amortization Worksheet

[2nd] [AMORT] P1 = 31, P2 = 31 [↓]

PRN = −7305.39 [↓] INT = 294.31

Note that the calculator shows a negative value for the balance after 31 periods because PV was entered as a negative number. Now a partial amortization schedule can be developed:

Payment Number	P1	P2	Amount Paid	Interest Paid $i = 0.028$	Principal Repaid	Outstanding Principal Balance
31	•	•	•	•	•	$7305.39
32	32	32	$3500.00	$204.55	$3295.45	4009.95
33	33	33	3500.00	112.28	3387.72	622.22
34	34	34	639.64	17.42	622.22	$0
TOTALS	1	34	$116 139.64	$41 139.64	$75 000.00	

When using the calculator's Amortization function, note that for payment 34, BAL = 2860.35, indicating an overpayment, so the actual payment is $3500.00 − 2860.35 = $639.64, INT = $17.42. Also, the final payment has been rounded to result in a balance of 0.

F. Computer application—amortization schedule

The amortization schedule in Example 14.1D displays the manual calculations for the repayment of $5000 with quarterly payments and interest at 8% compounded quarterly. Microsoft Excel and other spreadsheet programs can be used to create a file that will immediately display the results of a change in the principal.

Following are general instructions for creating a file to calculate the amortization schedule in Example 14.1D. The formulas in the spreadsheet file were created using Excel; however, most spreadsheet software works in a similar manner.

This exercise assumes a basic understanding of spreadsheet applications, but an individual who has no previous experience with spreadsheets will be able to complete it.

STEP 1 Enter the labels shown in Figure 14.5 in row 1 and in columns A–E.

Figure 14.5 Amortization Schedule Functions in Excel Spreadsheet (© S. A. Hummelbrunner)

	A	B	C	D	E	F
1	Payment number	Amount paid	Interest paid	Principal repaid	Outstanding principal balance	
2	0				5000	682.55
3	1	=$F$2	=$F$4*E2	=B3–C3	=E2–D3	
4	2	=$F$2	=$F$4*E3	=B4–C4	=E3–D4	0.02
5	3	=$F$2	=$F$4*E4	=B5–C5	=E4–D5	
6	4	=$F$2	=$F$4*E5	=B6–C6	=E5–D6	
7	5	=$F$2	=$F$4*E6	=B7–C7	=E6–D7	
8	6	=$F$2	=$F$4*E7	=B8–C8	=E7–D8	
9	7	=$F$2	=$F$4*E8	=B9–C9	=E8–D9	
10	8	=C10+D10	=$F$4*E9	=E9	=E9–D10	
11	Total	=SUM(B3:B10)	=SUM(C3:C10)	=SUM(D3:D10)		

STEP 2 Enter the principal in cell E2, periodic payment in cell F2 and periodic interest rate i in cell F4. Do not type in the dollar sign or a comma.

STEP 3 Enter only the formulas shown in cells B3, C3, D3, and E3. Make sure that the formula entry includes the dollar ($) signs for correct cell referencing as shown in the figure.

STEP 4 The formulas that were entered in Step 3 can be copied through the remaining cells.
(a) Select and Copy the formulas in cells B3, C3, D3, and E3.
(b) Select cells B4 to E9 and Paste.
(c) The formulas are now active in all the cells.

Alternatively, to copy formulas in Excel you can use the Fill handle, dragging it down the desired range through consecutive cells.

STEP 5 Enter the formulas shown in cells B10, C10, D10, and E10.

STEP 6 Enter the formula shown in cell B11, and then use Copy and Paste to enter the formula into cells C11 and D11.

STEP 7 To ensure readability of the spreadsheet, format the numbers to display with two decimal places, and widen the columns to display the full labels. Figure 14.6 displays the amortization schedule created in Excel for this example.

Figure 14.6 Amortization Schedule Results in Excel Spreadsheet (© S. A. Hummelbrunner)

	A	B	C	D	E	F
1	Payment number	Amount paid	Interest paid	Principal repaid	Outstanding principal balance	
2	0				5000	682.55
3	1	682.55	100.00	582.55	4417.45	
4	2	682.55	88.35	594.20	3823.25	0.02
5	3	682.55	76.46	606.09	3217.16	
6	4	682.55	64.34	618.21	2598.96	
7	5	682.55	51.98	630.57	1968.39	
8	6	682.55	39.37	643.18	1325.20	
9	7	682.55	26.50	656.05	669.16	
10	8	682.54	13.38	669.16	0.00	
11	Total	5460.39	460.39	5000.00		

This spreadsheet can now be used to reflect changes in aspects of the loan and create a new amortization schedule. Use cells E2, F2, and F4 for new principal amounts, periodic payment, and periodic interest rate, respectively.

Using Excel's CUMIPMT function

If you choose, you can use Excel's CUMIPMT function to answer some of the questions in this section. This function calculates the total interest paid in a certain period for a loan.

The CUMIPMT function in Excel for Example 14.1D is illustrated below.

Figure 14.7 Excel's CUMIPMT Function for Example 14.1D (© S. A. Hummelbrunner)

	A	B	C
1	**CUMIPMT Function**		
2			
3	rate	0.02	Periodic interest rate
4	nper	8	Total number of payment periods
5	PV	5000	Present value
6	start_period end_period	1 8	Starting period of calculating interest Ending period of calculating interest
7	type	0	Enter 0 for end of period and 1 for beginning of period payments
8	Answer	−460.39	

In addition to the CUMIPMT function, there are many financial functions available in Excel that you can use to solve numerous finance problems. To access these functions, click on *fx* in Excel and select the financial category. A list of all available functions with a help feature for each one of them will be displayed.

EXERCISE 14.1   MyLab Math

If you choose, you can use Excel's CUMIPMT, CUMPRINC, NPER, PMT, or PV functions to answer the following questions.

A. For each of the following four debts amortized by equal payments made at the end of each payment interval, compute (a) the size of the periodic payments; (b) the interest paid, principal repaid, and the balance for the first period; and (c) the interest paid, principal repaid, and the balance for the second period.

	Debt Principal $	Repayment Period	Payment Period	Interest Rate %	Compounding Period
1.	12 000	8 years	3 months	10	Quarterly
2.	8000	5 years	1 month	12	Monthly
3.	15 000	10 years	6 months	8	Semi-annually
4.	9600	7 years	1 year	6	Annually

B. Answer each of the following questions.

1. Mr. and Mrs. Norman purchased a ski chalet for $36 000. They paid $4000 down and agreed to make equal payments at the end of every 3 months for 15 years. Interest is 8% compounded quarterly.
   (a) What size of payment are the Normans making every 3 months?
   (b) For the first payment period, how much interest is paid, how much of the principal is repaid, and what is the loan balance?
   (c) For the second payment period, how much interest is paid, how much of the principal is repaid, and what is the loan balance?
   (d) How much will they have paid in total after 15 years?
   (e) How much interest will they pay in total?   Reference Example 14.1C

2. A contractor's price for a new building was $96 000. Slade Inc., the buyers of the building, paid $12 000 down and financed the balance by making equal payments at the end of every 6 months for 12 years. Interest is 7.3% compounded semi-annually.
   (a) What is the size of the semi-annual payment?
   (b) For the first payment period, how much interest is paid, how much of the principal is repaid, and what is the loan balance?
   (c) For the second payment period, how much interest is paid, how much of the principal is repaid, and what is the loan balance?
   (d) What is the total cost of the building for Slade Inc.?
   (e) What is the total interest included in the payments?

 3. Leo's Auto Repairs Inc. borrowed $5500 to be repaid by end-of-month payments over four years. Interest on the loan is 9% compounded monthly.
   (a) What is the size of the periodic payment?
   (b) What is the outstanding principal after the 13th payment?
   (c) What is the interest paid in the 14th payment?
   (d) How much principal is repaid in the 14th payment?   Reference Example 14.1G

4. To start their business, Ming and Ling borrowed $24 000 to be repaid by semi-annual payments over 12 years. Interest on the loan is 7% compounded semi-annually.
   (a) What is the size of the periodic payment?
   (b) What is the outstanding principal after the seventh payment?

(c) What is the interest paid in the eighth payment?

(d) How much principal is repaid in the eighth payment?

5. Lynn and Gina purchased a hair-salon business by agreeing to pay $2300 at the end of each month over the next three years. Interest on the "loan to purchase" agreement was 8.04% compounded monthly.

(a) What is the purchase price of the business?

(b) What is the outstanding principal of the loan after the 12th payment?

(c) What is the interest paid in the first year?

(d) How much principal is repaid in the first year?

6. When Dan signed a two-year contract with HardFloors Inc. as a manager, the company allowed reimbursement of $600 at the end of every month for his car expenses. At the time the contract was signed, money was worth 7.68% compounded monthly.

(a) What value did the expense reimbursement provision have when the contract was signed?

(b) What is the outstanding value of the reimbursement after the eighth payment?

7. A loan of $10 000 with interest at 7.75% compounded annually is to be amortized by equal payments at the end of each year for seven years. Calculate the size of the annual payments and construct an amortization schedule. Show the total paid and the cost of financing. *Reference Example 14.1D*

8. A loan of $8000 is repaid by equal payments made at the end of every three months for two years. If interest is 7% compounded quarterly, calculate the size of the quarterly payments and construct an amortization schedule. Show the total paid and the total cost of the loan.

9. Hansco borrowed $9200 paying interest at 11% compounded annually. If the loan is repaid by payments of $2000 made at the end of each year, construct an amortization schedule showing the total paid and the total interest paid.

Reference Example 14.1F

10. Pinto Brothers are repaying a loan of $14 500 by making payments of $2600 at the end of every six months. If interest is 7% compounded semi-annually, construct an amortization schedule showing the total paid and the total cost of the loan.

11. For Question 7, calculate the interest included in the fourth payment. Verify your answer by checking the amortization schedule. *Reference Example 14.1J*

12. For Question 8, calculate the principal repaid in the fifth payment period. Verify your answer by checking the amortization schedule.

13. For Question 9, calculate the principal repaid in the fourth payment period. Verify your answer by checking the amortization schedule.

14. For Question 10, calculate the interest included in the fifth payment. Verify your answer by checking the amortization schedule.

15. Apex Corporation borrowed $85 000 at 8% compounded quarterly for eight years to buy a warehouse. Equal payments are made at the end of every three months.

(a) Determine the size of the quarterly payments.

(b) Compute the interest included in the 16th payment.

(c) Determine the principal repaid in the 20th payment period.

(d) Construct a partial amortization schedule showing details of the first three payments, the last three payments, and totals.

16. Mr. Brabham borrowed $7500 at 6% compounded monthly. He agreed to repay the loan in equal monthly payments over four years.
  (a) What is the size of the monthly payment?
  (b) How much of the 20th payment is interest?
  (c) What is the principal repaid in the 40th payment period?
  (d) Prepare a partial amortization schedule showing details of the first three payments, the last three payments, and totals.

17. Thornhill Equipment Co. borrowed $24 000 at 11% compounded semi-annually. It is to repay the loan by payments of $2500 at the end of every six months.
  (a) How many payments are required to repay the loan?
  (b) How much of the sixth payment is interest?
  (c) How much of the principal will be repaid in the 10th payment period?
  (d) Construct a partial amortization schedule showing details of the first three payments, the last three payments, and totals.

🌐 **18.** Locust Inc. owes $16 000 to be repaid by monthly payments of $475. Interest is 6% compounded monthly.
  (a) How many payments will Locust Inc. have to make?
  (b) How much interest is included in the 18th payment?
  (c) How much of the principal will be repaid in the 30th payment period?
  (d) Construct a partial amortization schedule showing details of the first three payments, the last three payments, and totals.

14.2 AMORTIZATION INVOLVING GENERAL ANNUITIES
A. Determining the periodic payment and constructing amortization schedules

If the length of the payment interval is different from the length of the interest compounding period, the equal debt payments form a general annuity. The amortization of such debts involves the same principles and methods discussed in Section 14.1 except that general annuity formulas are applicable. Provided that the payments are made at the end of the payment intervals, use Formula 12.3.

$$PV_g = PMT\left[\frac{1 - (1 + p)^{-n}}{p}\right]$$ ———— Formula 12.3

where $p = (1 + i)^c - 1$

For a general annuity, interest paid in a period is calculated by multiplying the period's beginning balance by the periodic rate that matches the payment interval, defined as the factor p, as explained in Chapter 12.

To calculate the principal repaid and the balance resulting, use the same methods used for a simple annuity.

EXAMPLE 14.2A

A debt of $30 000 with interest at 9.75% compounded quarterly is to be repaid by equal payments at the end of each year for seven years.

  (i) What is the size of the annual payment?
  (ii) For the first payment, how much of the payment is interest?

(iii) For the first payment, how much of the loan is repaid?

(iv) After the first payment, how much of the loan remains to be paid?

(v) Construct an amortization schedule.

SOLUTION

(i) PV = 30 000.00; $n = 7$;   P/Y = 1;   C/Y = 4; $c = 4$;   I/Y = 9.75;

$$i = \frac{9.75\%}{4} = 2.4375\% = 0.024375$$

$$p = 1.024375^4 - 1 = 1.101123 - 1 = 0.101123 = 10.1123\%$$

$$30\,000.00 = \text{PMT}\left(\frac{1 - 1.101123^{-7}}{0.101123}\right)$$

$$30\,000.00 = \text{PMT}(4.850469)$$

$$\text{PMT} = \$6184.97$$

PROGRAMMED SOLUTION

("END" mode) (Set P/Y = 1; C/Y = 4) 0 [FV] 30 000 [±] [PV] 9.75 [I/Y]

7 [N] [CPT] [PMT] [6184.9769074]

(ii) The interest for the first period is 30 000.00 × 0.101123 = \$3033.69.

(iii) The principal repaid in the first period is 6184.97 − 3033.69 = \$3151.28.

(iv) The balance of the loan after the first period is 30 000.00 − 3151.28 = \$26 848.72.

(v) *Amortization schedule*

Payment Number	Amount Paid	Interest Paid $p = 0.101123$	Principal Repaid	Outstanding Principal Balance
0				\$30 000.00
1	\$6184.97	\$3033.69	\$3151.28	26 848.72
2	6184.97	2715.03	3469.94	23 378.78
3	6184.97	2364.14	3820.83	19 557.95
4	6184.97	1977.76	4207.21	15 350.74
5	6184.97	1552.31	4632.65	10 718.09
6	6184.97	1083.85	5101.12	5616.96
7	6184.96	568.00	5616.96	\$0.00
TOTALS	\$43 294.78	\$13 294.78	\$30 000.00	

Note: The final payment has been rounded to result in a balance of 0.

B. Determining the outstanding principal

1. Calculating the Outstanding Balance by the Retrospective Method

When the payment is calculated and then adjusted or rounded, we know from the previous section that the final payment will also need to be adjusted to compensate for the remaining balance and the interest. Therefore, the final payment may have a different value than the other payments. The retrospective method will be used to calculate the outstanding principal at any point during the repayment of the loan.

Remember that the retrospective method calculates the outstanding balance by subtracting the future value of the payments made from the future value of the original debt at a specific point in time during the repayment of the loan.

$$\text{OUTSTANDING BALANCE} = \frac{\text{FUTURE VALUE OF THE ORIGINAL DEBT}}{-\text{FUTURE VALUE OF THE PAYMENTS MADE}}$$

When this method requires calculating the future value of an ordinary general annuity, Formula 12.2 applies.

$$FV_g = PMT\left[\frac{(1+p)^n - 1)}{p}\right] \quad \text{where } p = (1+i)^c - 1 \quad\text{——— Formula 12.2}$$

EXAMPLE 14.2B

For Example 14.2A, using the retrospective method, compute the outstanding balance after three payments.

SOLUTION

The outstanding balance after three payments is the future value of the loan minus the future value of the three payments.

PMT = 6184.97; $p = 10.1123\%$

FV = 30 000(1.101123)^3 = \$40 052.41959

$FV_2 = 6184.97\left(\dfrac{1.101123^3 - 1}{0.101123}\right)$ = \$20 494.4848

Balance = 40 052.41959 − 20 494.4848 = \$19 557.94

PROGRAMMED SOLUTION

Alternatively, using the Amortization Worksheet,

("END" mode) (Set P/Y = 1;   C/Y = 4) 7 **N** 9.75 **I/Y**

30 000 **PV** 6184.97 **±** **PMT** 0 **FV**

2nd **AMORT** P1 = 3, P2 = 3 **↓** BAL = 19 557.95 **↓**

PRN = −3820.83 **↓** INT = −2364.14

EXAMPLE 14.2C

A loan of \$12 000 with interest at 5% compounded monthly is amortized by payments of \$1500 at the end of every three months.

(i) How many payments must be made to fully repay the loan?
(ii) For the first payment, how much of the payment is interest?
(iii) For the first payment, how much of the loan's principal is repaid?
(iv) After the first payment, how much of the loan remains to be paid?
(v) Construct an amortization schedule.

SOLUTION

(i) $PV_{nc} = 12\,000.00$;   PMT = 1500.00; $i = 0.4167\%$; $c = \dfrac{12}{4} = 3$

$$p = 1.004167^3 - 1 = 1.012552 - 1 = 1.2552\%$$

$$12\,000.00 = 1500.00\left[\frac{1 - 1.012552^{-n}}{0.012552}\right]$$

$$8.00 = \frac{1 - 1.012552^{-n}}{0.012552}$$

$$0.100417 = 1 - 1.012552^{-n}$$

$$1.012552^{-n} = 0.899583$$

$$-n \ln 1.012552 = \ln 0.899583$$

$$-0.012474n = -0.105824$$

$n = 8.48$ quarters, which means we have to make 8 full payments and the 9th payment is less than regular payment.

PROGRAMMED SOLUTION

(Set P/Y = 4; C/Y = 12) 12 000 [±] [PV] 5 [I/Y]

1500 [PMT] [CPT] [N] [8.483563]

(ii) Interest is $12\,000.00 \times 0.012552 = \$150.63$.

(iii) Principal repaid is $\$1500.00 - 150.63 = \$1349.37$.

(iv) Balance is $\$12\,000.00 - 1349.37 = \$10\,650.63$.

(v)

Amortization schedule

Payment Number	Amount Paid	Interest Paid $p = 0.012552$	Principal Repaid	Outstanding Principal Balance
0				$12 000.00
1	$1500.00	$150.63	$1349.37	10 650.63
2	1500.00	133.69	1366.31	9284.31
3	1500.00	116.54	1383.46	7900.85
4	1500.00	99.17	1400.83	6500.03
5	1500.00	81.59	1418.41	5081.61
6	1500.00	63.79	1436.21	3645.40
7	1500.00	45.76	1454.24	2191.16
8	1500.00	27.50	1472.50	718.66
9	727.68	9.02	718.66	-
Total	$12 727.68	$727.68	$12 000.00	

2. Computing the Outstanding Balance by the Prospective Method

We know from Section 14.1 that the original loan principal equals the present value of all payments that are necessary to amortize the loan. Remember that in the prospective method, the outstanding balance at the end of any payment interval just after a payment has been made is the present value of the outstanding payments.

OUTSTANDING BALANCE = PRESENT VALUE OF THE OUTSTANDING PAYMENTS

When this method requires calculating the present value of an ordinary general annuity, Formula 12.3 applies.

$$PV = PMT \left[\frac{1 - (1 + p)^{-n}}{p} \right] \quad \text{where } p = (1 + i)^c - 1 \quad \text{——— Formula 12.3}$$

EXAMPLE 14.2D

Dreamweavers financed an expansion project by agreeing to make payments of $7000 at the end of every three months for the next seven years. At the time of the purchase, money was worth 6.8% compounded annually.

(i) Using the prospective method, compute the equivalent loan value.

(ii) Compute the interest paid and the principal repaid in the 26th payment.

(iii) Using the amortization worksheet of the Texas Instrument BA II PLUS, calculate the amount of interest paid in the 6th year.

(iv) Construct a partial amortization schedule showing the first three payments, the last three payments, and the totals.

SOLUTION

(i) Using the prospective method, calculate the present value of all of the payments.

PMT = 7000.00; $n = 4(7) = 28$; P/Y = 4; C/Y = 1; $c = 1/4$; I/Y = 6.8

$p = (1 + 0.068)^{0.25} - 1 = 0.016583 = 1.6583\%$

$$PV_{28} = 7000.00 \left(\frac{1 - 1.016583^{-28}}{0.016583} \right)$$

$PV_{28} = 7000.00(22.254261)$

$PV_{28} = \$155\ 779.83$

PROGRAMMED SOLUTION

("END" mode) (Set P/Y = 4; C/Y = 1) 7000.00 [±] [PMT] 0 [FV] 6.8 [I/Y]

28 [N] [CPT] [PV] [155779.8282]

(ii) Calculate the present value of the remaining payments, $28 - 25 = 3$

PMT = 7000.00; $n = 3$; P/Y = 4; C/Y = 1; $c = 1/4$; I/Y = 6.8

$p = (1 + .068)^{0.25} - 1 = 0.016583 = 1.6583\%$

$$PV_3 = 7000.00 \left(\frac{1 - 1.016583^{-3}}{0.016583} \right)$$

$PV_3 = 7000.00(2.903186)$

$PV_3 = \$20\ 322.30$

The outstanding balance of the loan after 25 payments (with 3 remaining payments) is $20 322.30.
The interest paid in the 26th payment is $20 322.30(.016583) = 337.00.
The principal repaid in the 26th payment is $7000.00 − 337.00 = $6663.00.

PROGRAMMED SOLUTION

("END" mode)(Set P/Y = 4; C/Y = 1) 7000.00 [±] [PMT] 0 [FV] 6.8 [I/Y]

3 [N] [CPT] [PV] [20322.29592]

(iii) [2nd] [AMORT] P1 = 21, P2 = 24, [↓] BAL = 26 876.61 [↓]
PRN = 25 165.36 [↓] INT = 2834.64

Total interest paid in the 6th year equals $2834.64.

(iv) *Partial amortization schedule*

Payment Number	Amount Paid	Interest Paid $p = 0.016583$	Principal Repaid	Outstanding Principal Balance
0				$155 779.83
1	$7000.00	$2583.29	$4416.71	151 363.11
2	7000.00	2510.04	4489.96	146 873.16
3	7000.00	2435.59	4564.41	142 308.75
•	•	•	•	•
25	•	•	•	20 322.30
26	7000.00	337.00	6663.00	13 659.30
27	7000.00	226.51	6773.49	6885.81
28	7000.00	114.19	6885.81	$0.00
TOTAL	$196 000.00	$40 220.17	$155 779.83	

EXERCISE 14.2

MyLab Math

If you choose, you can use Excel's CUMIPMT, CUMPRINC, EFFECT, NPER, PMT, or PV functions to answer the following questions.

A. For each of the following four debts amortized by equal payments made at the end of each payment interval, compute (a) the size of the periodic payments; (b) the interest paid, principal repaid, and the balance for the first period; and (c) the interest paid, principal repaid, and the balance for the second period.

	Debt Principal $	Repayment Period	Payment Period	Interest Rate %	Compounding Period
1.	36 000	20 years	6 months	8	Quarterly
2.	15 000	10 years	3 months	12	Monthly
3.	8500	5 years	1 month	6	Semi-annually
4.	9600	7 years	1 year	9	Semi-annually

B. Answer each of the following questions.

1. A loan of $16 000 with interest at 9% compounded quarterly is repaid in seven years by equal payments made at the end of each year. Calculate the size of the annual payments and construct an amortization schedule showing the total paid and the total interest. *Reference Example 14.2A*

2. A debt of $12 500 with interest at 7% compounded semi-annually is repaid by payments of $1900 made at the end of every three months. Construct an amortization schedule showing the total paid and the total cost of the debt.

3. A debt of $45 000 is repaid over 15 years with semi-annual payments. Interest is 9% compounded monthly.

(a) What is the size of the periodic payments?

(b) What is the outstanding principal after the 11th payment?

(c) What is the interest paid in the 12th payment?

(d) How much principal is repaid in the 12th payment?   Reference Example 14.2B

4. A debt of $60 000 is repaid over 25 years with monthly payments. Interest is 7% compounded semi-annually.

(a) What is the size of the periodic payments?

(b) What is the outstanding principal after the 119th payment?

(c) What is the interest paid in the 120th payment?

(d) How much principal is repaid in the 120th payment?

5. A loan of $10 000 with interest at 6.72% compounded quarterly is repaid by payments of $950 made at the end of every six months.

(a) How many payments will be required to amortize the loan?

(b) If the loan is repaid in full after six years, what is the payout figure?

(c) If paid out, what is the total cost of the loan?   Reference Example 14.2C

6. The owner of the Blue Goose Motel borrowed $12 500 at 7.1% compounded semi-annually and agreed to repay the loan by making payments of $700 at the end of every three months.

(a) How many payments will be needed to repay the loan?

(b) How much will be owed at the end of five years?

(c) By the end of five years of payments, how much total interest has been paid?

7. Maple Sweets Inc. borrowed at 7.44% compounded monthly to purchase equipment, agreeing to make payments of $2160 at the end of every three months for 14 payments.

(a) What is the equivalent cash price of the equipment?

(b) How much will be owed at the end of two years?

(c) How much of the principal will be repaid within the first two years?

(d) How much interest is paid during the first two years?   Reference Example 14.2D

8. DJR Construction signed a loan contract at 8.36% compounded quarterly, with the provision to pay $765 at the end of each month for 4 years.

(a) What is amount of the loan?

(b) How much will be owed at the end of 14 months?

(c) How much of the principal will be repaid within the first 14 months?

(d) How much interest is paid during the first 14 months?

9. A debt of $32 000 is repaid by payments of $2950 made at the end of every six months. Interest is 8.28% compounded quarterly.

(a) What is the number of payments needed to retire the debt?

(b) What is the cost of the debt for the first five years?

(c) What is the interest paid in the 10th payment period?

(d) Construct a partial amortization schedule showing details of the first three payments, the last three payments, and totals.

10. You would like to purchase a two-bedroom condominium in Vancouver that costs $680 000.00.

(a) Suppose you are able to secure a mortgage for a five-year initial term at 3.34 percent compounded semi-annually and have $70 000 as a down-payment.

What would the required bi-weekly (assume 26 payments per year) payment on this mortgage be if you amortized it over 25 years?

(b) Calculate the total amount of interest that you would pay over the entire 25-year amortization.

(c) Using the following table, construct an amortization table for the payment numbers based on your calculations in part (i).

Payment Number	Payment Amount	Principal Paid	Interest Paid	Remaining Balance
121				
122				
123				

11. You visit the dealer after seeing an advertisement for a sporty Mercedes Benz CLA and negotiate a purchase price of $48 500.00.

(a) What would the monthly payment be with no down-payment, and financing the total with an interest rate of 4.79 percent compounded semi-annually for a six-year term?

(b) If you were able to make payments of $850.00 monthly instead, how many payments would you be required to make?

14.3 DETERMINING THE SIZE OF THE FINAL PAYMENT
A. Three methods for computing the final payment

When all payments except the final payment are equal, three methods are available to compute the size of the final payment.

The first step with all three methods is to compute the value of the term n. Note that the value includes a fractional portion.

METHOD 1   Determine the present value of the final fractional payment. If the payment is made at the end of the payment period, add interest for one payment period to the present value.

METHOD 2   Use the retrospective method to compute the outstanding principal after the last of the equal payments. If the final payment is made at the end of the payment interval, add interest for one payment period to the outstanding principal.

METHOD 3   Assume all payments to be equal, compute the overpayment, and subtract the overpayment from the size of the equal payments. This method must not be used when the payments are made at the beginning of the payment period. This method is used in the Amortization Worksheet in the Texas Instruments BA II PLUS calculator.

EXAMPLE 14.3A   For Example 14.1F, compute the size of the final payment using each of the three methods. Compare the results with the size of the payment shown in the amortization schedule.

SOLUTION

METHOD 1 $PV = 15\ 000.00;\quad PMT = 2500.00;\quad P/Y = 4;\quad C/Y = 4;\quad I/Y = 10;\quad i = 2.5$

$$15\ 000.00 = 2500.00\left(\frac{1 - 1.025^{-n}}{0.025}\right)$$

$$6.00 = \frac{1 - 1.025^{-n}}{0.025}$$

$$0.15 = 1 - 1.025^{-n}$$

$$1.025^{-n} = 0.85$$

$$-n \ln 1.025 = \ln 0.85$$

$$-n(0.024693) = -0.162519$$

$$n = 6.581682$$

PROGRAMMED SOLUTION

("END" mode)(Set P/Y = 4; C/Y = 4) 0 **FV** 15 000 **±** **PV** 2500 **PMT**

10 **I/Y** **CPT** **N** **6.581682**

The fractional value of n for the last payment period is determined by subtracting the whole number from the value of n for the entire loan.

$n_{final} = 6.581682 - 6 = 0.581682$

$$PV = 2500.00\left(\frac{1 - 1.025^{-0.581682}}{0.025}\right)$$

$$= 2500.00(0.570424)$$

$$= \$1426.06$$

PROGRAMMED SOLUTION

0 **FV** 2500 **±** **PMT** 10 **I/Y** 0.581682 **N** **CPT** **PV** **1426.059452**

Interest for one interval is $1426.06(0.025) = \$35.65$.
Final payment is $1426.06 + 35.65 = \$1461.71$. Alternatively, this could be calculated as $1426.06(1 + 0.025) = \$1461.71$.

METHOD 2   Since $n = 6.581682$, the number of equal payments is 6.
The accumulated value of the original principal after six payments

$$FV = 15\ 000.00(1.025)^6$$

$$= 15\ 000.00(1.159693)$$

$$= \$17\ 395.40$$

PROGRAMMED SOLUTION

("END" mode)(Set P/Y = 4; C/Y = 4) 15 000 **±** **PV** 0 **PMT**

10 **I/Y** 6 **N** **CPT** **FV** **17395.40127**

The accumulated value of the first six payments

$$FV_6 = 2500.00\left(\frac{1.025^6 - 1}{0.025}\right)$$

$$= 2500.00(6.387737)$$

$$= \$15\ 969.34$$

PROGRAMMED SOLUTION

0 [PV] 2500 [±] [PMT] 10 [I/Y] 6 [N] [CPT] [FV] [15969.34182]

The outstanding balance after six payments is $17\,395.40 - 15\,969.34 = \$1426.06$.
The final payment = outstanding balance + interest for one period
$$\begin{aligned}
&= \text{the accumulated value of } \$1426.06 \text{ for one year} \\
&= 1426.06(1.025) \\
&= \$1461.71
\end{aligned}$$

METHOD 3   Since $n = 6.581682$, the number of assumed full payments is 7.
The accumulated value of the original principal after seven payments

$$\begin{aligned}
\text{FV} &= 15\,000.00(1.025)^7 \\
&= 5\,000.00(1.188686) \\
&= \$17\,830.29
\end{aligned}$$

PROGRAMMED SOLUTION

("END" mode)(Set P/Y = 4; C/Y = 4) 15 000 [±] [PV] 0 [PMT]

10 [I/Y] 7 [N] [CPT] [FV] [17830.28631]

The accumulated value of seven payments

$$\begin{aligned}
\text{FV}_7 &= 2500.00\left(\frac{1.025^7 - 1}{0.025}\right) \\
&= 2500.00(7.547430) \\
&= \$18\,868.58
\end{aligned}$$

PROGRAMMED SOLUTION

0 [PV] 2500 [±] [PMT] 10 [I/Y] 7 [N] [CPT] [FV] [18868.57535]

Since the accumulated value of seven payments is greater than the accumulated value of the original principal, there is an overpayment.

$18\,868.58 - 17\,830.29 = \$1038.29$

The size of the final payment is $2500.00 - 1038.29 = \$1461.71$.

PROGRAMMED SOLUTION

("END" mode) (Set P/Y = 4; C/Y = 4) 7 [N] 10 [I/Y]

15000 [PV] 2500 [±] [PMT] 0 [FV]

[2nd] [AMORT] P1 = 7, P2 = 7; [↓] BAL = −1038.29, indicating an overpayment.

Note: When using a scientific calculator, Method 1 is preferable; however, we will use Methods 2 and 3 in Subsection B below.

POINTERS & PITFALLS

To calculate the size of the final payment if n has a fractional value, *do not* simply multiply the periodic payment (PMT) by the decimal portion of n (i.e., the non-integral part of n). This will produce an incorrect result. For example, if you had done it *incorrectly*, the final rent payment in Example 14.3A would have shown as $0.581682 \times \$2500.00 = \$1454.21$. Using the *correct* method, the value for the size of the final rent payment in Example 14.3A, Method 1 is $\$1461.71$. The difference is due to interest on the outstanding balance of the loan for the final payment period.

B. Applications

EXAMPLE 14.3B

On his retirement, Art received a bonus of $8000 from his employer. Taking advantage of the existing tax legislation, he invested his money in an annuity that provides for payments of $1200 at the end of every six months. If interest is 6.25% compounded semi-annually, determine the size of the final payment. (See Chapter 11, Example 11.5D.)

SOLUTION

To start, the number of payments must be determined.

$PV = 8000.00;$ $PMT = 1200.00;$ $P/Y = 2;$ $C/Y = 2;$ $I/Y = 6.25;$

$$i = \frac{6.25\%}{2} = 3.125\%$$

$$8000.00 = 1200.00\left(\frac{1 - 1.03125^{-n}}{0.03125}\right)$$

$$0.208333 = 1 - 1.03125^{-n}$$

$$1.03125^{-n} = 0.791667$$

$$-n \ln 1.03125 = \ln 0.791667$$

$$-n(0.030772) = -0.233615$$

$$n = 7.591884 \text{ (half-year periods)}.$$

PROGRAMMED SOLUTION

("END" mode)(Set P/Y = 2; C/Y = 2) 6.25 [I/Y] 8000 [±]

[PV] 1200 [PMT] 0 [FV] [CPT] [N] [7.591884], or eight payments

The annuity will be in existence for eight payments. Art will receive seven payments of $1200.00 and a final payment that will be less than $1200.00.

PROGRAMMED SOLUTION

Balance after seven payments

8000 [±] [PV] 1200 [PMT]

7 [N] 6.25 [I/Y] [CPT] [FV] [693.057863]

Or: [2nd] [AMORT] P1 = 7, P2 = 7; [↓] BAL = −$693.06

Final payment is $693.06(1.03125) = \$714.72$, or
Balance after eight payments

8000 **±** **PV** 1200 **PMT**

8 **N** 6.25 **I/Y** **CPT** **FV** −485.284079

Or: **2nd** **AMORT** P1 = 8, P2 = 8; ↓ BAL = −$485.28, indicating an overpayment, which requires an adjustment by this amount to calculate the final payment.

Final payment is $1200.00 − 485.28 = $714.72.

EXAMPLE 14.3C

A lease contract valued at $7800 is to be fulfilled by payments of $180 due at the beginning of each month. If money is worth 9% compounded monthly, determine the size of the final lease payment.

SOLUTION

PV(due) = 7800.00;   PMT = 180.00;   P/Y = 12;   C/Y = 12;   I/Y = 9;

$i = \dfrac{9\%}{12} = 0.75\%$

PROGRAMMED SOLUTION

("BGN" mode) (Set P/Y = 12; C/Y = 12) 9 **I/Y** 7800 **PV** 180 **±** **PMT**

0 **FV** **CPT** **N** **52.123125** , or 53 payments

$n = 52.123125$

Present value of the final payment

PMT = 180.00; $i = 0.75\%$; $n = 0.123125$

$$\text{PV}_n(\text{due}) = 180.00 \left(\frac{1 - 1.0075^{-0.123125}}{0.0075} \right)(1.0075) \text{————— Formula 13.2}$$

$$= 180.00(0.122609)(1.0075)$$
$$= 180.00(0.123529)$$
$$= \$22.24$$

Final payment is $22.24, or

Balance after 52 payments,

7800 **±** **PV** 180 **PMT** 52 **N** 9 **I/Y** **CPT** **FV** **22.06973**

Or: **2nd** **AMORT** P1 = 52, P2 = 52; ↓ BAL = $22.07

Final payment is $22.07(1.0075) = $22.24, or
Balance after 53 payments,

7800 **±** **PV** 180 **PMT** 53 **N**

9 **I/Y** **CPT** **FV** −157.764717

Or: **2nd** **AMORT** P1 = 53, P2 = 53; ↓ BAL = −$157.76, indicating an overpayment.

Final payment is $180.00 − 157.76 = $22.24.

EXAMPLE 14.3D

Payments of $500 deferred for nine years are received at the end of each month from a fund of $10 000 deposited at 10.5% compounded monthly. Determine the size of the final payment. (See Chapter 13, Example 13.3B.)

SOLUTION

PV(defer) = 10 000.00; PMT = 500.00; $d = 9(12) = 108$; P/Y = 12; C/Y = 12;

I/Y = 10.5; $i = \dfrac{10.5\%}{12} = 0.875\%$

$n = 68.288333$ (see solution to Example 13.3B)

Present value of the final payment

PMT = 500.00; $i = 0.875\%$; $n = 0.288334$

$PV = 500.00\left(\dfrac{1 - 1.00875^{-0.288334}}{0.00875}\right)$

$ = 500.00(0.286720)$

$ = \$143.36$

PROGRAMMED SOLUTION

("END" mode) (Set P/Y = 12; C/Y = 12) 108 $\boxed{N}$ 10.5 $\boxed{I/Y}$ 10000 $\boxed{\pm}$ $\boxed{PV}$

 0 $\boxed{PMT}$ $\boxed{CPT}$ $\boxed{FV}$ $\boxed{25622.59753}$

("END" mode) (Set P/Y = 12; C/Y = 12) 10.5 $\boxed{I/Y}$ 25 622.59753 $\boxed{\pm}$ $\boxed{PV}$

500 $\boxed{PMT}$ 0 $\boxed{FV}$ $\boxed{CPT}$ $\boxed{N}$ $\boxed{68.288}$, or 69 payments

$\boxed{2nd}$ $\boxed{AMORT}$ P1 = 68, P2 = 68; $\boxed{\downarrow}$ BAL = -143.36

Final payment is $\$143.36(1.00875) = \$144.61$, or

P1 = 69, P2 = 69; $\boxed{\downarrow}$ BAL = 355.39, indicating an overpayment.

Final payment is $500.00 - 355.39 = \$144.61$.

EXAMPLE 14.3E

A business valued at $96 000 is purchased for a down payment of 25% and payments of $4000.00 at the end of every three months. If interest is 9% compounded monthly, what is the size of the final payment? (See Chapter 12, Example 12.4B.)

SOLUTION

PV = 96 000.00(0.75) = 72 000.00; PMT = 4000.00; P/Y = 4; C/Y = 12;

I/Y = 9; $c = \dfrac{12}{4} = 3$; $i = \dfrac{9\%}{12} = 0.75\% = 0.0075$; $p = 1.0075^3 - 1 = 2.2669\%$;

$n = 23.390604$ (see solution to Example 12.4B)

PROGRAMMED SOLUTION

("END" mode) (Set P/Y = 4; C/Y = 12) 9 $\boxed{I/Y}$ 72 000 $\boxed{PV}$ 4000 $\boxed{\pm}$ $\boxed{PMT}$

 0 $\boxed{FV}$ $\boxed{CPT}$ $\boxed{N}$ $\boxed{23.391}$, or 24 payments. Set N = 24

Present value of the final payment

PMT = 4000.00; $p = 2.2669\%$; $n = 0.390604$

$PV = 4000.00\left(\dfrac{1 - 1.022669^{-0.390604}}{0.022669}\right)$

$ = 4000.00(0.384556)$

$ = \$1538.23$

PROGRAMMED SOLUTION

[2nd] [AMORT] P1 = 23, P2 = 23; [↓] BAL = 1538.23

Final payment is $1538.23(1.022669) = $1573.10, or

P1 = 24, P2 = 24, [↓] BAL = −2426.90, indicating an overpayment.

Final payment is 4000.00 − 2426.90 = $1573.10.

EXAMPLE 14.3F

Ted Davis, having reached his goal of a $140 000 balance in his RRSP, converts it into a RRIF and withdraws from it $1650 at the beginning of each month. If interest is 5.75% compounded quarterly, what is the size of the final withdrawal? (See Chapter 13, Example 13.2G.)

SOLUTION

PV = 140 000.00;   PMT = 1650.00;   P/Y = 12;   C/Y = 4;   I/Y = 5.75;

$$c = \frac{4}{12} = \frac{1}{3}; \quad i = \frac{5.75\%}{4} = 1.4375\% = 0.014375;$$

$$p = 1.014375^{\frac{1}{3}} - 1 = 1.004769 - 1 = 0.4769\%$$

$$n = 108.323882 \text{ (see solution to Example 13.2G)}$$

PROGRAMMED SOLUTION

("BGN" mode) (Set P/Y = 12; C/Y = 4) 5.75 [I/Y] 140 000 [±] [PV]

  1650 [PMT] 0 [FV] [CPT] [N] yields 108.323882, or 109 payments.

  Set N = 109.

Present value of the final payment

PMT = 1650.00;   p = 0.4769%;   n = 0.323882

$$PV = 1650.00(1.004769)\left(\frac{1 - 1.004769^{-0.323882}}{0.004769}\right)$$

$$= 1650.00(1.004769)(0.322863)$$

$$= 1650.00(0.324403)$$

$$= \$535.27$$

PROGRAMMED SOLUTION

109 [N] 5.75 [I/Y] 140 000 [±] [PV] 1650 [PMT] 0 [FV]

[2nd] [AMORT] P1 = 108, P2 = 108; [↓] BAL = −532.73

Final payment is $532.73(1.004769) = $535.27, or

P1 = 109, P2 = 109, [↓] BAL = 1114.73, indicating an overpayment.

Final payment is 1650.00 − 1114.73 = $535.27.

EXERCISE 14.3

If you choose, you can use Excel's NPER or PV function to answer the following questions.

A. For each of the following six loans, compute the size of the final payment.

	Principal $	Periodic Payment $	Payment Period	Payment Made at:	Interest Rate %	Compounding Period
🌐 1.	17 500	1100	3 months	end	9	quarterly
2.	7800	775	6 months	beginning	7	semi-annually
🌐 3.	9300	580	3 months	beginning	7	quarterly
4.	15 400	1600	6 months	end	8	quarterly
5.	29 500	1650	3 months	end	9	monthly
6.	17 300	425	1 month	beginning	6	quarterly

B. Answer each of the following questions.

🌐 1. A loan of $7200 is repaid by payments of $360 at the end of every three months. Interest is 11% compounded quarterly.
(a) How many payments are required to repay the debt?
(b) What is the size of the final payment? Reference Example 14.3B

🌐 2. Seanna O'Brien receives pension payments of $3200 at the end of every six months from a retirement fund of $50 000. The fund earns 7% compounded semi-annually.
(a) How many payments will Seanna receive?
(b) What is the size of the final pension payment?

3. A loan of $35 000 is repaid by payments of $925 at the end of every month. Interest is 12% compounded monthly.
(a) How many payments are required to repay the debt?
(b) What is the size of the final payment?

🌐 4. An annuity with a cash value of $10 500 pays $900 at the beginning of every three months. The investment earns 11% semi-annually.
(a) How many payments will be paid?
(b) What is the size of the final annuity payment? Reference Example 14.3F

🌐 5. Payments of $1200 are made out of a fund of $25 000 at the end of every three months. If interest is 6% compounded monthly, what is the size of the final payment? Reference Example 14.3E

6. A debt of $30 000 is repaid in monthly installments of $550. If interest is 8% compounded quarterly, what is the size of the final payment?

🌐 7. A lease valued at $20 000 requires payments of $1000 every three months due in advance. If money is worth 7% compounded quarterly, what is the size of the final lease payment? Reference Example 14.3C

8. Eduardo Martinez has saved $125 000. If he withdraws $1250 at the beginning of every month and interest is 4.5% compounded monthly, what is the size of the last withdrawal?

9. Equipment priced at $42 000 was purchased on a contract requiring payments of $5000 at the beginning of every six months. If interest is 9% compounded quarterly, what is the size of the final payment?

10. Noreen Leung has agreed to purchase her partner's share in the business by making payments of $1100 every three months. The agreed transfer value is $16 500 and interest is 10% compounded annually. If the first payment is due at the date of the agreement, what is the size of the final payment?

11. David Jones has paid $16 000 for a retirement annuity from which he will receive $1375 at the end of every 3 months. The payments are deferred for 10 years and interest is 10% compounded quarterly.
    (a) How many payments will David receive?
    (b) What is the size of the final payment?
    (c) How much will David receive in total?
    (d) How much of what he receives will be interest?   Reference Example 14.3D

12. A contract valued at $27 500 requires payments of $6000 every six months. The first payment is due in four years and interest is 11% compounded semi-annually.
    (a) How many payments are required?
    (b) What is the size of the last payment?
    (c) How much will be paid in total?
    (d) How much of what is paid is interest?

13. You fall in love with the perfect vacation property near Little Australia, a neighbourhood near the University of British Columbia. It is listed for $2 799 000.00.
    (a) Suppose you are able to secure a mortgage for a ten-year initial term at 3.99 percent compounded semi-annually and have $298 000 as a down-payment. What would the required monthly payment be on this mortgage if you amortized it over 20 years?
    (b) Calculate the total amount of interest that you would pay over the entire 20-year amortization.
    (c) Using the following table, construct an amortization table for the payment numbers based on your calculations in part (i).

Payment Numbers	Payment Amount	Principal Paid	Interest Paid	Remaining Balance
101				
102				
103				

    (d) Calculate the remaining balance owing on the principal at the end of the ten-year initial mortgage term.
    (e) If you re-finance the remaining balance at 2.99 percent compounded semi-annually for the remaining 10-years, what will your new required monthly payment be?

14.4 RESIDENTIAL MORTGAGES IN CANADA
A. Basic concepts and definitions

A **residential mortgage** is a claim to a residential property given by a borrower to a lender as security for the repayment of a loan. It is often the largest amount of money ever borrowed by an individual. The borrower is called the **mortgagor**; the lender is called the **mortgagee**. The **mortgage contract** spells out the obligations of the borrower and the rights of the lender, including the lender's rights in case of default of payment by the borrower. If the borrower is unable to make the mortgage payments, the lender ultimately has the right to dispose of the property under *power of sale* provisions.

To secure legal claim against a residential property, the lender must register the mortgage against the property at the provincial government's land titles office. A **first mortgage** is the first legal claim against a residential property if the mortgage payments cannot be made and the property must be sold. **Equity** in a property is the difference between the property's market value and the total debts, or mortgages, registered against the property. It is possible to have a **second mortgage** on a residential property that is backed by equity in the property, even if there is a first mortgage already registered against the property. If the borrower defaults on the mortgage payments and the property must be sold, the first mortgagee gets paid before the second mortgagee. For this reason, second mortgages are considered riskier investments than first mortgages. They command higher interest rates than first mortgages to compensate for this risk. Home improvement loans, home equity loans, or home equity lines of credit (HELOCs) are often secured by second mortgages.

The amortization period, part of the mortgage agreement, represents the time that it takes to fully repay the principal of the mortgage. The amortization period is used to calculate the amount of the blended payments. The most common amortization period is 25 years. Other amortization periods may also be used.

Financial institutions offer two types of mortgages—fixed-rate mortgages and variable-rate mortgages. A **fixed-rate mortgage** is a mortgage for which the rate of interest is fixed for a specific period of time, called the *term* of the mortgage. When the term of the mortgage is completed, the mortgage must be *renewed* to determine the conditions of the outstanding loan. At this time, the interest rate, the payment, the payment period, and the term may change, and part or all of the balance may be repaid.

A **variable-rate mortgage** is a mortgage for which the rate of interest changes as money market conditions change. The interest rate change is usually related to a change in the bank's lending rate.

Both types of mortgages are usually repaid by equal payments that blend principal and interest. Payments are usually required to be made monthly, but other payment frequencies are often available, such as semi-monthly, biweekly, and weekly payments.

For fixed-rate mortgages, Canadian law dictates that interest must be calculated semi-annually or annually, not in advance. In this context, "not in advance" means that interest is calculated at the end of each 6-month or 12-month period, not at the beginning. It is Canadian practice to calculate fixed-rate mortgage interest semi-annually, not in advance.

Mortgages can be either open or closed. A **closed mortgage** is a mortgage that restrict the borrower's ability to increase payments, make lump-sum payments, or change the term of the mortgage. Most closed mortgages contain some prepayment privileges. For example, some mortgages allow a lump-sum payment each year of up to 10% of the original mortgage principal, usually on the anniversary date of the mortgage. Changes in the term or transfers are usually subject to prohibitive penalties.

Open mortgages allow prepayment or repayment of the mortgage at any time without penalty. Interest rates on open mortgages are generally significantly higher than interest rates on closed mortgages.

Fixed-rate mortgages and variable-rate mortgages are usually available from financial institutions. Conventional mortgages require the borrower to have at least a 20% down payment for the purchase of a residential property or at least 20% equity in a property. To borrow higher than the 80% level, lending institutions require mortgage default insurance.

Canada Mortgage and Housing Corporation (CMHC), a corporation of the federal government, and several other institutions offer mortgage default insurance. These institutions act as the insurer for the lender in the event that the borrower defaults on the mortgage payments. To qualify for mortgage default insurance, borrowers must qualify within two affordability rules:

- **Gross debt service (GDS) ratio:** monthly housing costs such as mortgage, property tax, and heating cost as a percentage of the gross household monthly income must be no more than 35%.

- **Total debt service (TDS) ratio:** monthly debt load including mortgage, property tax, heating cost, car loan, student loan, and all other monthly debt payments as a percentage of the gross monthly income must be no more than 42%.

Financial institutions normally calculate both ratios for potential home buyers and qualify them for a loan if both ratios are satisfied. Both of these ratios were defined in Chapter 4.

Mortgage Stress Test

In addition to the previous two ratios, which are used to test whether an applicant qualifies for a mortgage, the Office of the Superintendent of Financial Institutions (OFSI)[1] introduced a new rule (Guideline B-20) in July 2017 to protect both banks and borrowers by reducing the risk of foreclosure in case the interest rates go up. This new rule is called the mortgage stress test. Based on this rule, potential homebuyers will be tested for a minimum qualifying rate, which is the higher of the Bank of Canada's five-year benchmark rate[2] (5.34% at the time of writing) and the rate that a lender offers plus 2%. For example, assume that a lender offers interest rate of 3.2% to a home buyer. To test whether the home buyer qualifies for a mortgage, the lender should use the higher rate of 2% added to the offered rate (i.e., in this case 3.2 + 2 = 5.2%) and the five-year bench-mark rate of 5.34%, which in this example is 5.34%, to calculate the monthly payment. Although this rule was initially established to test new home buyers that made down payments of less than 20%, it was revised to include all mortgage applicants as of January 1, 2018. All potential home buyers, even if they make a down payment of 20% or more, as well as those who are renewing a mortgage should undergo a stress test.

B. Computing the periodic rate of interest

For residential mortgages, Canadian legislation requires the rate of interest charged by the lender to be calculated annually or semi-annually, not in advance. The fixed rates advertised, posted, or quoted by lenders are usually nominal annual rates. To meet the legislated requirements, the applicable nominal annual rate of interest must be converted into the equivalent rate of interest per payment period.

This is done as explained in Section 12.1A by using Formula 12.1,

$$p = (1 + i)^c - 1$$

where p = the rate of interest per payment period
where i = the rate per compounding period

$$c = \frac{\text{THE NUMBER OF INTEREST COMPOUNDING PERIODS PER YEAR}}{\text{THE NUMBER OF PAYMENT PERIODS PER YEAR}}$$

---

[1] "The Office of the Superintendent of Financial Institutions (OSFI) is an independent federal government agency that regulates and supervises more than 400 federally regulated financial institutions and 1200 pension plans to determine whether they are in sound financial condition and meeting their requirements." Retrieved from http://www.osfi-bsif.gc.ca/Eng/osfi-bsif/Pages/default.aspx.

[2] *Daily Digest*. Bank of Canada. Retrieved from https://www.bankofcanada.ca/rates/daily-digest/.

Note that when using the TI BA II PLUS financial calculator, this means that the c in the previous formula can be derived by dividing the C/Y by the P/Y.

The prevailing practice is semi-annual compounding and monthly payment for most mortgages. For most mortgages (with semi-annual compounding and monthly payment),

$$c = \frac{2 \text{ (compounding periods per year)}}{12 \text{ (payments per year)}} = \frac{1}{6}$$

EXAMPLE 14.4A

Suppose a financial institution posted the interest rates for closed mortgages shown below. The interest is compounded semi-annually and the mortgages require monthly payments.

Term	Interest Rate
1 year	3.90%
2 years	4.05%
3 years	4.55%
4 years	5.24%
5 years	5.85%
7 years	6.80%
10 years	6.95%

Compute the rate of interest per payment period for:

(i) a three-year term, and

(ii) a five-year term.

SOLUTION

$$c = \frac{1}{6}; \quad p = (1 + i)^{\frac{1}{6}} - 1$$

The three-year term, $i = \dfrac{4.55\%}{2} = 2.275\% = 0.02275$

$$p = (1 + 0.02275)^{\frac{1}{6}} - 1$$
$$= 1.003756 - 1$$
$$= 0.003756, \text{ or } 0.3756\%$$

You can obtain the interest rate per payment period using a preprogrammed financial calculator by using the function keys as follows:

("END" mode) (Set P/Y = 1; C/Y = 1) 1 $\boxed{\pm}$ $\boxed{\text{PV}}$

$\dfrac{1}{6} = 0.166667$ $\boxed{\text{N}}$ 2.275

$\boxed{\text{I/Y}}$ $\boxed{\text{CPT}}$ $\boxed{\text{FV}}$ | **Display Shows** $(1 + p) = 1.00375$, $p = 0.00375$ |

The five-year term, $i = 5.85\%/2 = 2.925\% = 0.02925$;

$$p = (1.02925^{\frac{1}{6}}) - 1$$
$$= 0.004817 = 0.4817\%$$

1 $\boxed{\pm}$ $\boxed{\text{PV}}$ 0.166667 $\boxed{\text{N}}$ 2.925 $\boxed{\text{I/Y}}$ $\boxed{\text{CPT}}$ $\boxed{\text{FV}}$ 1.004817

$p = 0.004817$

(Note that if you perform these calculations in succession, you do not have to key in PV and N each time.)

C. Computing mortgage payments and balances

Blended residential mortgage payments are ordinary general annuities. Therefore, Formula 12.3 applies.

$$PV_g = PMT\left[\frac{1 - (1 + p)^{-n}}{p}\right], \text{ where } p = (1 + i)^c - 1 \hspace{1cm} \text{Formula 12.3}$$

The periodic payment PMT is calculated using the method shown in Section 12.3.

EXAMPLE 14.4B

A mortgage for \$120 000 is amortized over 25 years. Interest is 4.15%, compounded semi-annually, for a 5-year term and payments are monthly.

(i) Compute the monthly payment.

(ii) Compute the balance at the end of the 5-year term.

(iii) Compute the monthly payment if the mortgage is renewed for a 4-year term at 3.95% compounded semi-annually.

SOLUTION

(i) When computing the monthly payment, n is the total number of payments in the amortization period. The term for which the rate of interest is fixed (in this case, 5 years) does *not* enter into this calculation.

PV = 120 000.00; $n = 12(25) = 300$; P/Y = 12; C/Y = 2; I/Y = 4.15; $i = 2.075$; $c = 1/6$

We must first compute the monthly rate of interest, p.

$p = (1.02075)^{\frac{1}{6}} - 1 = 1.003428807 - 1 = 0.003429$

$$120\ 000.00 = PMT\left[\frac{1 - (1.003428807)^{-300}}{0.003429}\right] \hspace{1cm} \text{using Formula 12.3}$$

$120\ 000.00 = PMT\ (187.201658)$

$PMT = \$641.02$

PROGRAMMED SOLUTION

("END" Mode)(Set P/Y = 12; C/Y = 2) 0 $\boxed{\text{FV}}$ 120 000 $\boxed{\pm}$ $\boxed{\text{PV}}$

4.15 $\boxed{\text{I/Y}}$ 300 $\boxed{\text{N}}$ $\boxed{\text{CPT}}$ $\boxed{\text{PMT}}$ $\boxed{641.019931}$

The monthly payment for the original 5-year term is \$641.02.

(ii) The balance at the end of the 5-year term is the future value of the original loan of \$120 000 minus the future value of the payments made.

The number of payments made after 5 years is 60.

PMT = 641.02; $p = 0.03428807$

FV = 120 000$(1.003428807)^{60}$ = \$147 358.4812

$$FV_{60} = 641.019931\left[\frac{(1.003428807)^{60} - 1}{0.003428807}\right] = \$42\ 622.53265$$

Balance is 147 358.4812 − 42 622.53265 = \$104 735.95.

PROGRAMMED SOLUTION

("END" Mode) (Set P/Y = 12; C/Y = 2) 120 000 [±] [PV] 641.02 [PMT]

60 [N] 4.15 [I/Y] [CPT] [FV] [104735.9448]

Or: [2nd] [AMORT] P1 = 60, P2 = 60; [↓] BAL = $104 735.95

The mortgage balance at the end of the first 5-year term is $104 735.95.

(iii) For the renewed term, the starting principal is the balance at the end of the 5-year term. The amortization period is the number of years remaining after the initial term. We must recalculate p for the new interest rate.

PV = 104 735.94; $n = 12(20) = 240$; I/Y = 3.95; $i = 1.975\%$; $c = 1/6$

We must first compute the monthly rate of interest p.

$$p = (1.01975)^{\frac{1}{6}} - 1 = 1.003265 - 1 = 0.003265$$

$$104\ 735.94 = PMT\left[\frac{1 - (1.003265)^{-240}}{0.003265}\right]$$

$$104\ 735.94 = PMT(166.2046)$$

$$PMT = \$630.16$$

PROGRAMMED SOLUTION

("END" mode)(Set P/Y = 12; C/Y = 2) 0 [FV] 104 735.95 [±] [PV]

3.95 [I/Y] 240 [N] [CPT] [PMT] [630.15642]

The monthly payment for the renewed 4-year term is $630.16.

D. Rounded payments

Mortgage payments are sometimes rounded up to an exact cent or dollar value (such as to the next cent, the next dollar, or the next 10 dollars). The payment calculation of $630.15642 might be rounded up to $630.16 or $631 or even $640. Rounded payments up to a higher value will result in a lower balance at the end of the term. In the final renewal term, rounding will affect the size of the final payment.

EXAMPLE 14.4C

A mortgage balance of $17 321.50 is renewed for the remaining amortization period of three years at 4% compounded semi-annually.

(i) Compute the size of the monthly payments.

(ii) Determine the size of the last payment if the payments computed in part (i) have been rounded up to the next dollar.

(iii) Determine the size of the last payment if the payments computed in part (i) have been rounded up to the next-higher 50 dollars.

SOLUTION

(i) PV = 17 321.50; $n = 36$; I/Y = 4; $i = 2.0\%$; $c = 1/6$

$$p = (1.02)^{\frac{1}{6}} - 1 = 1.003306 - 1 = 0.003306$$

$$17\ 321.50 = PMT\left[\frac{1 - (1.003306)^{-36}}{0.003306}\right]$$

$$17\ 321.50 = PMT\ (33.887578)$$

$$PMT = \$511.15$$

PROGRAMMED SOLUTION

("END" Mode)(Set P/Y = 12; C/Y = 2) 0 [FV] 17 321.50 [PV]

4.0 [I/Y] 36 [N] [CPT] [PMT] [−511.145994]

The monthly payment is $511.15.

(ii) If payments are rounded up to $512.00, the last payment will be less than a full payment. To calculate the size of the last payment we need to determine the number of payments of $512.00 that are required to amortize the loan balance.

PV = 17 321.50; PMT = 512.00; $p = 0.003306$

$$17\ 321.50 = 512.00 \left[\frac{1 - (1.003306)^{-n}}{0.003306} \right]$$

$$0.111842 = 1 - 1.003306^{-n}$$

$$1.003306^{-n} = 0.888158$$

$$-n(\ln 1.003306) = \ln 0.888158$$

$$-n(1.003300) = -0.118605$$

$$n = 35.936247$$

PROGRAMMED SOLUTION

0 [FV] 17 321.50 [±] [PV] 512.00 [PMT] 4 [I/Y] [CPT]

[N] [35.936247]

There will be 35 payments of $512.00 and a final payment smaller than 512.00. We need to determine the balance after the 35th payment.

PMT = 512.00; $n = 35$; $p = 0.003306$

FV = 17 321.50(1.003306)^{35} = $19 442.55

$$FV_{35} = 512.00 \left[\frac{(1.003306)^{35} - 1}{0.003306} \right] = \$18\ 964.72$$

Balance is 19 442.55 − 18 964.72 = $477.83.

Final payment is 477.83(1.003306) = $479.41.

PROGRAMMED SOLUTION

("END" mode) (Set P/Y = 12; C/Y = 2) 17 321.50 [±] [PV] 512.00

[PMT] 35 [N] 4 [I/Y] [CPT] [FV] [477.829006]

Or: [2nd] [AMORT] P1 = 36, P2 = 36; [↓] BAL = $32.59, an overpayment

Final payment is 512.00 − 32.59 = $479.41.

(iii) If payments are rounded up to $550.00, the last payment will be less than $550. To calculate the size of the last payment we need to determine the number of payments of $550.00 that are required to amortize the loan balance.

PV = 17 321.50; PMT = 550.00; $p = 0.003306$

$$17\ 321.50 = 550.00 \left[\frac{1 - (1.003306)^{-n}}{0.003306} \right]$$

$$0.104115 = 1 - 1.003306^{-n}$$
$$1.003306^{-n} = 0.895885$$
$$-n(\ln 1.003306) = \ln 0.895885$$
$$-n(1.003300) = -0.109943$$
$$n = 33.311541$$

PROGRAMMED SOLUTION

0 [FV] 17 321.50 [±] [PV] 550.00 [PMT]

4 [I/Y] [CPT] [N] [33.311541]

We need to determine the balance after the 33rd payment.

PMT = 550.00; $n = 33$; $p = 0.003306$

$FV = 17\ 321.50(1.003306)^{33} = \$19\ 314.63$

$$FV_{33} = 550.00 \left[\frac{(1.003306)^{33} - 1}{0.003306} \right] = \$19\ 143.66$$

Balance is $19\ 314.63 - 19\ 143.66 = \$170.97$.

Final payment is $170.97(1.003306) = \$171.54$.

PROGRAMMED SOLUTION

("END" Mode) (Set P/Y = 12; C/Y = 2) 17 321.50 [±] [PV] 550.00 [PMT]

33 [N] 4 [I/Y] [CPT] [FV] [170.97219]

Or: [2nd] [AMORT] P1 = 34, P2 = 34; [↓] BAL = \$378.46, an overpayment

There are 33 payments of \$550 and a final payment of $\$550 - 378.46 = \$171.54$.

BUSINESS MATH NEWS — Pay Down the Mortgage or Top Up the RRSP?

Paying down your mortgage and saving for retirement are two worthy goals. But can you work toward them at the same time? Is it a wise move to make extra mortgage payments or should you put the money into your RRSP instead?

Consider the pros and cons of making larger-than-necessary mortgage payments.

Pros:

- You will pay less interest over the long term.
- You will realize more equity when you sell your home.
- You could get a psychological benefit if you can pay off your mortgage.
- You could be mortgage free by your late 40s or early 50s and still have time to save for retirement.
- Investing in mutual funds or stocks and making double-digit gains might be a good move but these elements will change over time.

Cons:

- Although there is no guarantee on the earnings you will get in your RRSP, your returns will, in effect, be boosted by the RRSP's tax-deferred environment. Furthermore, you get an immediate tax break on your annual contributions.

(Continued)

- You will tie up cash in an illiquid investment. It is more difficult to get money out of your home than it is from your savings and investments for unexpected expenses.
- You will risk being underdiversified. If you put all your money into your house, and the housing market slumps, your net worth might suffer.

Ultimately, the mortgage-versus-retirement question is a highly personal one. Mathematically, you can calculate which alternative is better, given assumptions about mortgage rates and RRSP rates of return. Most analyses conclude that it is better to pay off your mortgage first, assuming the rate of return of the investments in your RRSP does not exceed your mortgage rate. But it is not necessarily an either-or situation. A good solution to this dilemma would be to increase your RRSP contribution and use your tax refund to make an extra mortgage payment each year. Having the discipline to save, paying down the mortgage or topping up the RRSP are both important components of a good financial plan.

QUESTIONS

1. Calculate the monthly payments required to pay off a $250 000 mortgage, assuming the amortization period is 25 years and the interest rate is 5.5% compounded semi-annually.

2. What is the balance at the end of the 5-year term?

3. Assuming a 40% tax refund on RRSP contributions, if the homeowner contributes an extra $500 per month to her RRSP and then uses the tax refund to increase her monthly mortgage payment, how much will she have reduced the balance of her mortgage after 5 years?

4. Assuming that the homeowner uses the tax refund from her RRSP contribution to increase her monthly mortgage payments by $200, how many years will it take to pay off the mortgage?

Sources: 1. Mike Watson, "Do I Pay Down the Mortgage or Invest in RRSPs?" *The Times Colonist,* May 18, 2010. © S. A. Hummelbrunner 2. Robb Engen, "Mortgage or Investments? It's Complicated, and Emotional. But There's a Balanced Approach." *Toronto Star,* October 16, 2018, p. L1.

E. Mortgage statement

Currently, when financial institutions record monthly mortgage payments, they calculate interest for the exact number of days that have elapsed since the last payment. This is done by multiplying the monthly rate of interest by 12 to convert it into a simple annual rate of interest. The annual rate is then multiplied by the number of days expressed as a fraction of 365. For example, $p = 0.6558\%$ becomes the simple annual interest rate $12(0.6558\%) = 7.86984\%$.

This approach takes into account that the number of days elapsed between payments fluctuates depending on the number of days in a particular month. It also allows for fluctuations in receiving payments, and permits semi-monthly, bi-weekly, or weekly payments for mortgages requiring contractual monthly payments.

EXAMPLE 14.4D

A credit union member made the contractual mortgage payment of $725 on May 31, leaving a mortgage loan balance of $75 411.79. The monthly fixed rate was 0.5345%. The member made the contractual payments on June 28, July 31, August 30, September 30, October 29, November 28, and December 30. The credit union agreed to convert the fixed-rate mortgage to a variable-rate mortgage on October 29 at 5.25% compounded annually. This rate was changed to 4.75% on December 2. Determine the mortgage balance on December 30.

SOLUTION

The monthly rate $p = 0.5345\%$ is equivalent to the simple annual rate $12(0.5345\%) = 6.414\%$.

Payment Date	Number of Days	Amount Paid	Interest Paid	Principal	Balance Repaid
May 31	rate is 6.414%				$75 411.79
June 28	28	$725.00	$371.05	$353.95	75 057.84
July 31	33	725.00	435.26	289.74	74 768.10
August 30	30	725.00	394.16	330.84	74 437.26
September 30	31	725.00	405.50	319.50	74 117.76
October 29	29	725.00	377.71	347.29	73 770.47
October 29	rate becomes 5.25%				
November 28	30	725.00	318.32	406.68	73 363.79
December 2	rate becomes 4.75%				
December 30	32	$725.00	$309.54*	$415.46	$72 948.33

*__Note:__ Interest calculation for December is

4 days at 5.25% on $73 363.67	$42.21
28 days at 4.75% on $73 363.67	267.33
TOTAL	$309.54

EXAMPLE 14.4E

A mortgage of $155 000 closed on April 12, amortized over 15 years at 5.29% compounded semi-annually for a 5-year term. It requires contractual monthly payments rounded up to the nearest $10. The lender agreed to accept bi-weekly payments of half the contractual monthly amount starting April 24. The mortgagor's second June payment was 3 days late.

(i) Determine the size of the contractual monthly payment.

(ii) Produce a mortgage statement to June 30.

(iii) Compute the accrued interest on June 30.

SOLUTION

(i) $PV = 155\ 000;\quad n = 12(15) = 180;\quad I/Y = 5.29;\quad i = 0.02645;\quad c = \dfrac{1}{6}$

$p = (1.02645)^{\frac{1}{6}} - 1 = 1.004361 - 1 = 0.004361$

$$155\ 000 = PMT\left[\frac{1 - (1.004361)^{-180}}{0.004361}\right]$$

$155\ 000 = PMT(124.53852)$

$PMT = \$1244.60$

PROGRAMMED SOLUTION

("END" Mode) (Set P/Y = 12; C/Y = 2) 0 [FV] 155 000 [PV]

5.29 [I/Y] 180 [N] [CPT] [PMT] [−1244.594853]

The contractual monthly payment is $1244.60.

(ii) The monthly payment is rounded up to $1250 and therefore, bi-weekly payment would equal to $1250/2 = $625 (this is an accelerated bi-weekly payment when the monthly payment is divided by 2).

The annual rate of interest is 12(0.004360521) = 0.052326 = 5.2326%.

Payment Date	Number of Days	Amount Paid	Interest Paid	Principal Repaid	Balance
April 12					$155 000.00
April 24	12	$625.00	$266.65*	$358.35	154 641.65
May 8	14	625.00	310.37	314.63	154 327.02
May 22	14	625.00	309.74	315.26	154 011.76
June 5	14	625.00	309.11	315.89	153 695.87
June 22	17	$625.00	$374.57	$250.43	$153 445.44

* Interest paid $I = prt = $ 155 000(0.052326)(12/365) = 266.65

The mortgage balance on June 22 is $153 445.44

(iii) On June 30 interest has accrued for 8 days.

The amount of accrued interest = 153 445.44(0.052326)(8/365) = $175.98.

EXERCISE 14.4

MyLab Math

If you choose, you can use Excel's NPER, PMT, PV, or RATE functions to answer the questions that follow.

Answer each of the following questions.

1. When the Littles purchased a home, they borrowed $170 000 as a mortgage to be amortized by making monthly payments for 25 years. Interest is 4.89% compounded semi-annually for a 3-year term.
   (a) Compute the size of the monthly payment.
   (b) Determine the balance at the end of the 3-year term.
   (c) If the mortgage is renewed for a 4-year term at 5.24% compounded semi-annually, what is the size of the monthly payment for the renewal term?

Reference Example 14.4B

2. A variable-rate mortgage of $150 000 is amortized over 20 years by equal monthly payments. After 18 months, the original interest rate of 6% compounded semi-annually was raised to 6.6% compounded semi-annually. Two years after the mortgage was taken out, it was renewed at the request of the mortgagor at a fixed rate of 5.65% compounded semi-annually for a 4-year term.
   (a) Calculate the mortgage balance after 18 months.
   (b) Compute the size of the new monthly payment at the 6.6% rate of interest.
   (c) Determine the mortgage balance at the end of the 4-year term.

3. A $40 000 mortgage is to be repaid over a 10-year period by monthly payments rounded up to the next-higher $50. Interest is 7.15% compounded semi-annually.
   (a) Determine the number of rounded payments required to repay the mortgage.
   (b) Determine the size of the last payment.
   (c) Calculate the amount of interest saved by rounding the payments up to the next-higher $50 increment.

Reference Example 14.4C

4. A mortgage balance of $23 960 is to be repaid over a 7-year term by equal monthly payments at 6.8% compounded semi-annually. At the request of the mortgagor, the monthly payments were set at $440.
   (a) How many payments will the mortgagor have to make?
   (b) What is the size of the last payment?
   (c) Determine the difference between the total actual amount paid through $440 payments and the total amount required through normal amortization at 6.8% to amortize the mortgage by the contractual monthly payments.

5. A mortgage of $180 000 is amortized over 20 years by semi-monthly payments of $611.31. What is the nominal annual rate of interest compounded semi-annually?

6. At what nominal rate of interest compounded semi-annually will a $162 000 variable-rate mortgage be amortized by monthly payments of $1017.31 over 25 years?

7. Interest for the initial 4-year term of a $105 000 mortgage is 4.39% compounded semi-annually. The mortgage is to be repaid by equal weekly payments over 20 years. The mortgage contract permits lump-sum payments at each anniversary date of up to 10% of the original principal.
   (a) What is the balance at the end of the 4-year term if a lump-sum payment of $7000 is made at the end of the third year?
   (b) How many more payments will be required after the 4-year term if there is no change in the interest rate?
   (c) What is the difference in the cost of the mortgage if no lump-sum payment is made?

8. The Berezins agreed to monthly payments rounded up to the nearest $100 on a mortgage of $36 000 amortized over 10 years. Interest for the first 5 years was 8.75% compounded semi-annually. After 30 months, as permitted by the mortgage agreement, the Berezins increased the rounded monthly payment by 10%.
   (a) Determine the mortgage balance at the end of the 5-year term.
   (b) If the interest rate remains unchanged over the remaining term, how many fewer of the increased payments will amortize the mortgage balance?
   (c) How much did the Berezins save by exercising the increase-in-payment option?

9. A $40 000 mortgage, taken out on June 1, is to be repaid by monthly payments rounded up to the nearest $10. The payments are due on the first day of each month starting July 1. The amortization period is 12 years and interest is 5.5% compounded semi-annually for a 6-month term. Construct an amortization schedule for the first 6-month term.   Reference Example 14.4D

10. For Question 9, produce the mortgage statement for the 6-month term. Assume all payments have been made on time. Compare the balance to the balance in Question 9 and explain why there may be a difference.

11. For the mortgage in Question 9, develop a mortgage statement for the first 6-month term if semi-monthly payments equal to one-half of the monthly payment are made on the 1st day and the 16th day of each month. The first payment is due June 16. Compare the balance to the balances in Question 9 and Question 10. Explain why there are differences.

12. For the mortgage in Question 9, develop a mortgage statement for the 6-month term if biweekly payments equal to one-half of the rounded monthly payments are made starting June 16. Compare the balance to the balances in Questions 9, 10, and 11. Explain why it differs significantly from the other three balances.

MyLab Math Visit MyLab Math to practise any of this chapter's exercises marked with a ⊕ as often as you want. The guided solutions help you calculate an answer step by step. You'll find a personalized study plan and additional interactive resources to help you master Business Math!

REVIEW EXERCISE

1. **LO❶** Sylvie Cardinal bought a business for $45 000. She made a down payment of $10 000 and agreed to repay the balance by equal payments at the end of every three months for eight years. Interest is 8% compounded quarterly.

   (a) What is the size of the quarterly payments?

   (b) What will be the total cost of financing?

   (c) How much will Sylvie owe after five years?

   (d) How much interest will be included in the 20th payment?

   (e) How much of the principal will be repaid by the 24th payment?

   (f) Construct a partial amortization schedule showing details of the first three payments, Payments 10, 11, 12, the last three payments, and totals.

2. **LO❶** Angelo Lemay borrowed $8000 from his credit union. He agreed to repay the loan by making equal monthly payments for five years. Interest is 9% compounded monthly.

   (a) What is the size of the monthly payments?

   (b) How much will the loan cost him?

   (c) How much will Angelo owe after 18 months?

   (d) How much interest will he pay in his 36th payment?

   (e) How much of the principal will be repaid by the 48th payment?

   (f) Prepare a partial amortization schedule showing details of the first three payments, Payments 24, 25, 26, the last three payments, and totals.

3. **LO❶** Comfort Swim Limited borrowed $40 000 for replacement of equipment. The debt is repaid in installments of $2000 made at the end of every three months.

   (a) If interest is 7% compounded quarterly, how many payments are needed?

   (b) How much will Comfort Swim owe after two years?

   (c) How much of the 12th payment is interest?

   (d) How much of the principal will be repaid by the 20th payment?

   (e) Construct a partial amortization schedule showing details of the first three payments, the last three payments, and totals.

4. **LO❷** A $198 000 mortgage amortized by monthly payments over 20 years is renewable after 5 years. Interest is 4.65% compounded semi-annually.

   (a) What is the size of the monthly payments?

   (b) How much interest is paid during the first year?

   (c) How much of the principal is repaid during the first 5-year term?

   (d) If the mortgage is renewed for a further 5-year term at 5.24% compounded semi-annually, what will be the size of the monthly payments?

   (e) Construct a partial amortization schedule showing details of the first three payments for each of the two 5-year terms.

5. **LO❷** Pelican Recreational Services owes $27 500 secured by a collateral mortgage. The mortgage is amortized over 15 years by equal payments made at the end of every 3 months and is renewable after 3 years.

   (a) If interest is 7% compounded annually, what is the size of the payments?

   (b) How much of the principal is repaid by the fourth payment?

   (c) What is the balance at the end of the 3-year term?

   (d) If the mortgage is renewed for a further 4 years but amortized over 8 years and interest is 7.5% compounded semi-annually, what is the size of the quarterly payments for the renewal period?

   (e) Construct a partial amortization schedule showing details of the first three payments for each of the two terms.

6. **LO❷** A debt of $17 500 is repaid by payments of $2850 made at the end of each year. Interest is 8% compounded semi-annually.

   (a) How many payments are needed to repay the debt?

   (b) What is the cost of the debt for the first three years?

(c) What is the principal repaid in the fifth year?

(d) Construct an amortization schedule showing details of the first three payments, the last three payments, and totals.

7. LO❸ A debt of $25 000 is repaid by payments of $3500 made at the end of every six months. Interest is 11% compounded semi-annually.

(a) How many payments are needed to repay the debt?

(b) What is the size of the final payment?

8. LO❸ Jane Evans receives payments of $900 at the beginning of each month from a pension fund of $72 500. Interest earned by the fund is 6.3% compounded monthly.

(a) What is the number of payments Jane will receive?

(b) What is the size of the final payment?

9. LO❸ A lease agreement valued at $33 000 requires payment of $4300 every three months in advance. The payments are deferred for three years and money is worth 10% compounded quarterly.

(a) How many lease payments are to be made under the contract?

(b) What is the size of the final lease payment?

10. LO❸ A contract worth $52 000 provides benefits of $20 000 at the end of each year. The benefits are deferred for 10 years and interest is 11% compounded quarterly.

(a) How many payments are to be made under the contract?

(b) What is the size of the last benefit payment?

11. LO❹ A mortgage for $235 000 is amortized over 25 years. Interest is 4.6% p.a., compounded semi-annually, for a 5-year term and payments are monthly.

(a) Compute the monthly payment.

(b) Compute the balance at the end of the 5-year term.

(c) Compute the monthly payment if the mortgage is renewed for a 3-year term at 5% compounded semi-annually.

12. LO❹ A $180 000 mortgage is to be amortized by making monthly payments for 25 years. Interest is 5.62% compounded semi-annually for a 4-year term.

(a) Compute the size of the monthly payment.

(b) Determine the balance at the end of the 4-year term.

(c) If the mortgage is renewed for a 5-year term at 5.30% compounded semi-annually, what is the size of the monthly payment for the renewal term?

13. LO❹ An $80 000 mortgage is to be repaid over a 10-year period by monthly payments rounded up to the next-higher $50 increment. Interest is 4.78% compounded semi-annually.

(a) What is the number of rounded payments required to repay the mortgage?

(b) What is the size of the last payment?

(c) How much interest was saved by rounding the payments up to the next-higher $50 increment?

14. LO❹ A $160 000 mortgage is to be repaid over a 20-year period by monthly payments rounded up to the next-higher $100 increment. Interest is 5.44% compounded semi-annually.

(a) Determine the number of rounded payments required to repay the mortgage.

(b) Determine the size of the last payment.

(c) Calculate the amount of interest saved by rounding the payments up to the next-higher $100 increment.

15. LO❶ A debt of $6500 is repaid in equal monthly installments over four years. Interest is 9% compounded monthly.

(a) What is the size of the monthly payments?

(b) What will be the total cost of borrowing?

(c) What is the outstanding balance after one year?

(d) How much of the 30th payment is interest?

(e) Construct a partial amortization schedule showing details of the first three payments, the last three payments, and totals.

16. LO❶ Milton Investments borrowed $32 000 at 11% compounded semi-annually. The loan is to be repaid by payments of $4500 due at the end of every six months.

(a) How many payments are needed?

(b) How much of the principal will be repaid by the fifth payment?

(c) Prepare a partial amortization schedule showing the details of the last three payments and totals.

17. LO❹ A mortgage of $95 000 is amortized over 25 years by monthly payments of $573.25. What is the nominal annual rate of interest compounded semi-annually?

🌐 **18. LO❹** At what nominal annual rate of interest compounded semi-annually will a $135 000 mortgage be amortized by monthly payments of $1023.12 over 15 years?

19. LO❹ A $28 000 mortgage is amortized by quarterly payments over 20 years. The mortgage is renewable after 3 years and interest is 6% compounded semi-annually.

(a) What is the size of the quarterly payments?

(b) How much interest will be paid during the first year?

(c) What is the balance at the end of the 3-year term?

(d) If the mortgage is renewed for another three years at 7% compounded annually, what will be the size of the quarterly payments for the renewal period?

🌐 **20. LO❸** The Superior Tool Company is repaying a debt of $16 000 by payments of $1000 made at the end of every three months. Interest is 7.5% compounded monthly.

(a) How many payments are needed to repay the debt?

(b) What is the size of the final payment?

SELF-TEST

1. With his financial target to be debt-free, Henrik replaced his credit card debt by borrowing $9000. He is to make equal monthly payments over the next 42 months. What is the outstanding balance of the loan after 22 months if interest is 7.26% compounded monthly?

2. A loan of $15 000 is repaid by quarterly payments of $700 each, at 8% compounded quarterly. What is the principal repaid by the 25th payment?

3. A $50 000 mortgage is amortized by monthly payments over 20 years. If interest is 4.29% compounded semi-annually, how much interest will be paid during the first 3 years?

4. A $190 000 mortgage is to be amortized by making monthly payments for 20 years. Interest is 6.5% compounded semi-annually for a 3-year term.
(a) Compute the size of the monthly payment.
(b) Determine the balance at the end of the 3-year term.
(c) If the mortgage is renewed for a 5-year term at 7.25% compounded semi-annually, what is the size of the monthly payment for the renewal term?

5. A $140 000 mortgage is to be repaid over a 15-year period by monthly payments rounded up to the next-higher increment of $50. Interest is 4.35% compounded semi-annually.
(a) Determine the number of rounded payments required to repay the mortgage.
(b) Determine the size of the last payment.
(c) Calculate the amount of interest saved by rounding the payments up to the next-higher $50.

6. A debt of $24 000 is repaid by quarterly payments of $1100. If interest is 6% compounded quarterly, what is the size of the final payment?

7. A mortgage of $145 000 is amortized over 25 years by monthly payments of $1297. What is the nominal annual rate of interest compounded semi-annually?

8. A loan of $12 000 is amortized over 10 years by equal monthly payments at 7.5% compounded monthly. Construct an amortization schedule showing details of the first three payments, the 40th payment, the last three payments, and totals.

9. A fund of $165 000 is to be accumulated in 6 years by making equal payments at the beginning of each month. If interest is 7.5% compounded monthly, how much interest is earned by the fund in the 20th payment interval?

10. Gillian Armes invested $10 000 in an income fund at 13% compounded semi-annually for 20 years. After 20 years, she is to receive semi-annual payments of $10 000 at the end of every 6-month period until the fund is exhausted. What is the size of the final payment?

CHALLENGE PROBLEMS

1. A debt is amortized by monthly payments of $250. Interest is 8% compounded monthly. If the outstanding balance is $3225.68 just after a particular payment (say, the xth payment), what was the balance just after the previous payment (i.e., the $(x - 1)$th payment)?

2. Captain Sinclair has been posted to Cold Lake, Alberta. He prefers to purchase a condo rather than live on the base. He knows that in 4 years he will be posted overseas. The condo he wishes to purchase will require a mortgage of $130 000, and he has narrowed his choices to two lenders. Trust Company A is offering a 5-year mortgage at 6.75% compounded semi-annually. This mortgage can be paid off at any time but there is a penalty clause in the agreement requiring 2 months' interest on the remaining principal. Trust Company B is offering a 5-year mortgage for 7% compounded semi-annually. It can be paid off at any time without penalty. Both mortgages are amortized over 25 years and require monthly payments. Captain Sinclair will have to sell his condo in 4 years and pay off the mortgage at that time before moving overseas. Given that he expects to earn 3% compounded annually on his money over the next 5 years, which mortgage offer is cheaper? By how much is it cheaper?

CASE STUDY Managing a Mortgage

▶ Malcolm and Shannon purchased their first house with a $180 000 mortgage. Their 5-year mortgage had a 7.5% semi-annually compounded interest rate, and was amortized over 25 years. Payments were made monthly.

After 3 years, interest rates had fallen significantly. In response, Malcolm and Shannon considered paying out the old mortgage (in spite of the interest penalties), and negotiating a new mortgage at the lower rate. They met with the loans officer at their bank, who laid out their options for them.

Interest on mortgages with a 5-year term was 5.5% compounded semi-annually, the lowest rate in many years. The loan officer informed Malcolm and Shannon of the penalty for renegotiating a mortgage early, before the end of the current term. According to their mortgage contract, the penalty for renegotiating the mortgage before the end of the 5-year term is the greater of

A. Three months' interest at the original rate of interest. (Banks generally calculate this as one month's interest on the mortgage principal remaining to be paid, multiplied by three.)

B. The interest differential over the remainder of the original term. (Banks generally calculate this as the difference between the interest the bank would have earned over the remainder of the original term at the original [higher] mortgage rate and at the renegotiated [lower] mortgage rate.)

The loans officer also explained that there are two options for paying the penalty amount: (1) you can pay the full amount of the penalty at the beginning of the new mortgage period, or (2) the penalty amount can be added to the principal when the mortgage is renegotiated, allowing the penalty to be paid off over the term of the new mortgage.

Malcolm and Shannon agreed to look at their options before giving the loans officer their final decision.

QUESTIONS

1. Suppose there were no penalty for refinancing the mortgage after 3 years. How much would Malcolm and Shannon save per month by refinancing their mortgage for a 5-year term at the new rate?

2. Suppose the couple choose to refinance their mortgage for a 5-year term at the new interest rate.
   (a) What is the amount of penalty A?
   (b) What is the amount of penalty B?
   (c) What penalty would Malcolm and Shannon have to pay in this situation?

3. If they pay the full amount of the penalty at the beginning of the new 5-year term, what will Malcolm and Shannon's new monthly payment be?

4. If the penalty amount is added to the principal when the mortgage is renegotiated, what will the new monthly payment be?

SUMMARY OF FORMULAS

No new formulas were introduced in this chapter. However, some of the formulas introduced in Chapters 9 to 13 have been used, namely Formulas 9.1, 11.1, 11.2, 12.1, 12.2, 12.3, and 13.2.

GLOSSARY

Amortization repayment of both interest and principal of interest-bearing debts by a series of equal payments made at equal intervals of time (p. 549)

Amortization schedule a schedule showing in detail how a debt is repaid (p. 552)

Canada Mortgage and Housing Corporation (CMHC) the corporation of the federal government that administers the National Housing Act (NHA) and provides mortgage insurance to lenders (p. 585)

Closed mortgage a mortgage that restricts the borrower's ability to increase payments, make lump-sum payments, or change the term of the mortgage (p. 585)

Equity the difference between the price for which a property could be sold and the total debts registered against the property (p. 585)

First mortgage the first legal claim registered against a property; in the event of default by the borrower, first mortgagees are paid before all other claimants (p. 585)

Fixed-rate mortgage a mortgage for which the rate of interest is fixed for a specific period of time; it can be open or closed *(p. 585)*

Gross debt service (GDS) ratio the percent of gross annual income required to cover such housing costs as mortgage payments, property taxes, and heating costs *(p. 586)*

Mortgage contract a document specifying the obligations of the borrowers and the rights of the lender *(p. 584)*

Mortgagee the lender *(p. 584)*

Mortgagor the borrower *(p. 584)*

Open mortgage mortgage that allows prepayment or repayment at any time without penalty. Interest rates on open mortgages are generally significantly higher than interest rates on closed mortgages. *(p. 585)*

Prospective method a method for computing the outstanding debt balance that considers the payments that remain outstanding *(p. 557)*

Residential mortgage a claim to a residential property given by a borrower to a lender as security for the repayment of a loan *(p. 584)*

Retrospective method a method of computing the outstanding balance of a debt that considers the payments that have been made *(p. 556)*

Second mortgage the second legal claim registered against a property; in the event of default by the borrower, second-mortgage holders are paid only after first-mortgage holders have been paid *(p. 585)*

Total debt service (TDS) ratio the percent of gross annual income required to cover such housing costs as mortgage payments, property taxes, and all other debts and obligations *(p. 586)*

Variable-rate mortgage a mortgage for which the rate of interest changes as money market conditions change *(p. 585)*

LEARNING OBJECTIVES

Upon completing this chapter, you will be able to do the following:

1. Determine the purchase price of a bond when the market rate equals the bond rate, purchased on or between interest dates.

2. Determine the purchase price of a bond when the market rate does not equal the bond rate, purchased on or between interest dates.

3. Construct bond schedules showing the amortization of premiums or accumulation of discounts.

4. Calculate the yield rate for bonds bought on the market by the method of averages.

5. Make sinking fund computations when payments form simple annuities, including the size of the periodic payments, accumulated balance, interest earned, and the time of investment in the fund are known.

6. Construct complete or partial sinking fund schedules.

The Protected Art Archive/Alamy Stock Photo

Many financial planners recommend investment in bonds to balance an investment portfolio. Bond values often do not move in the same direction as stocks and thus add diversification to a financial portfolio. Companies and governments issue bonds to raise large sums of money to spend on various development projects. The contractual obligation is to pay interest on the bond principal and to repay the principal when the bond matures. To have the funds available to pay for the bonds when they mature, companies often create a sinking fund by making periodic equal investments from the outset of the bond issue.

Historically, bonds represent a less risky investment than stocks. Bonds can be purchased and sold in the same way as stocks, often with little or no commission or transaction fee. The price of a bond certificate depends on many factors, including the market valuation of the bond. The annuity formulas learned in previous chapters allow computation of bond values.

INTRODUCTION

Bonds are contracts used to borrow sizeable sums of money, usually from a large group of investors. The indenture, or contract, for most bonds provides for the repayment of the principal at a specified future date, plus periodic payment of interest at a specified percent of the face value. Bonds are negotiable; that is, they can be freely bought and sold. The mathematical issues arising from trading bonds are the topic of this chapter.

15.1 PURCHASE PRICE OF BONDS
A. Basic concepts of bonds

Corporations and governments use bonds to borrow money, usually from a large group of lenders (investors). To deal with the expected large number of investors, the borrower prints up written contracts, called *bonds* or *debentures*, in advance.

The printed bonds specify the terms of the contract, including

(a) the **face value** (also called the **par value** or **denomination**), which is the amount owed to the holder of the bond when it matures, usually a multiple of $100, such as $100, $1000, $5000, $10 000, $25 000, or $100 000;

(b) the **bond rate** (also called the **coupon rate** or **nominal rate**), which is the rate of interest paid, usually semi-annually, based on the face value of the bond;

(c) the **maturity date** (also called the **redemption date** or **due date**), which is the date on which the principal of the bond is to be repaid;

(d) the **principal** (also called the **redemption value** or **maturity value**), which is the amount paid by the issuer to the bondholder at the date of surrender of the bonds.

Most bonds are **redeemable at par**; that is, they are redeemable at their *maturity value*, which is also called their *face value*. However, some bonds have a redemption feature to make the bonds more attractive to investors. These bonds are either *puttable* or *callable* that is, they can be redeemed *before* maturity either by the investor or by the bond issuer. In a puttable bond, the bond holder has the right to return the bond for repayment before the bond matures. The callable bonds will be **redeemable at a premium**; that is, at a price *greater* than their face value. The redemption value in such cases is stated as a percent of the face value. For example, the redemption value of a $5000 bond redeemable at 104 is 104% of $5000, or $5200.

Investors in bonds expect to receive periodic interest payments during the term of the bond from the date of issue to the date of maturity, and they expect to receive the principal at the date of maturity. The bond rate is used to determine the periodic interest payments.

To facilitate the payment of interest, some bonds have dated interest **coupons** attached that can be cashed at any bank on or after the stated interest payment date. For example, a 20-year, $1000 bond bearing interest at 5% payable semi-annually will have attached to it at the date of issue 40 coupons of $25 each. Each coupon represents the semi-annual interest due on each of the 40 interest payment dates.

The issuer may or may not offer security such as real estate, plant, or equipment as a guarantee for the repayment of the principal. Bonds for which no security is offered are called **debentures**.

Bonds are marketable and may be freely bought and sold. When investors acquire bonds, they buy two promises:

1. A promise to be paid the principal of the bond at maturity.

2. A promise to be paid the periodic interest payments according to the rate of interest and the terms stated on the bond.

B. Purchase price of a bond when market rate equals bond rate

When the **market rate**, or **yield rate**, of interest—or the rate money is worth—is equal to the bond rate, the bond is sold at a **market price**, or **quoted price**, that equals the face value. The bond is described as selling *at par*.

For example, a four-year, $1000 bond bearing interest at 6% payable semi-annually, pays interest of $30 eight times, and pays $1000 at maturity. If the bond is purchased at par, at the beginning of its life, and the market rate is 6% when the bond is purchased, the price is $1000.

Bonds are not just purchased and sold on interest payment dates. In practice, most bonds are traded between interest payment dates. In such cases, the buyer and seller split the interest (coupon) at the time of the purchase based on the fractional part of the interest period during which each of them holds ownership of the bond.

Bonds are offered for sale at market price. The total amount paid for the bonds includes the market price plus any interest that has accrued, and is called the **cash price**, or purchase price.

$$\text{CASH PRICE} = \text{MARKET PRICE} + \text{ACCRUED INTEREST}$$

EXAMPLE 15.1A

A $10 000, five-year bond redeemable at par and bearing interest at 6.5% payable semi-annually is purchased at a market price of $10 000 four years and 10 months before maturity. Determine the cash price of the bond.

SOLUTION

Interest has accrued for 5 years less 4 years and 10 months = 2 months

$$\text{CASH PRICE} = \$10\ 000 + (\$10\ 000 \times 2/12 \times 0.065)$$
$$= \$10\ 000 + 108.33 = \$10\ 108.33.$$

Note: The interest is calculated using the bond's face value of $10 000.

15.2 PURCHASE PRICE OF A BOND WHEN MARKET RATE DOES NOT EQUAL BOND RATE
A. Basic concepts—market rate versus bond rate

When the market rate is not equal to the bond rate, the market price of a bond does not equal its face value. The bond is described as selling at a premium or at a discount, depending on whether the bond rate is greater than or smaller than the market rate.

If the purchase price of a bond is greater than its face value, the bond is described as selling at a premium and the difference between the purchase price and the face value is called the **premium**.

$$\text{PREMIUM} = \text{PURCHASE PRICE} - \text{FACE VALUE}$$
where purchase price $>$ face value

If the purchase price of a bond is less than its face value, the bond is described as selling at a discount and the difference between the purchase price and the face value is called the **discount**.

$$\text{DISCOUNT} = \text{FACE VALUE} - \text{PURCHASE PRICE}$$
where purchase price $<$ face value

Whether a bond sells at a premium or at a discount or at par is determined by the relationship between the bond rate *b* and the market rate (or yield rate) *i*.

The bond rate, (*b*), is the per annum rate that is paid to the bondholder. This rate is a percentage of the face value of the bond. This rate is established at the time of issue of the bonds and remains the same throughout the term of the bond. For example, if a $1000 bond has a bond rate of 6% paid semiannually, it receives semiannual interest payment of $30.

On the other hand, the rate at which lenders are willing to provide money fluctuates in response to economic conditions. The combination of factors at work in the capital market at any given time in conjunction with the perceived risk associated with a particular bond determines the market rate (or yield rate) *i* for a bond, and thus, the price at which a bond will be bought or sold.

The bond rate *b* and the market rate *i* are usually *not* equal. If the two rates happen to be equal, then bonds that are redeemable at par will sell at their face value. If the bond rate is *less than* the market rate, the bond will sell at a price less than the face value; that is, at a *discount*. If the bond rate is *greater than* the market rate, the bond will sell at a price above its face value; that is, at a *premium*.

At any time, one of three possible situations exists for any given bond:

1. Bond rate = Market rate $(b = i)$ The bond sells at *par*.

2. Bond rate < Market rate $(b < i)$ The bond sells at *discount*.

3. Bond rate > Market rate $(b > i)$ The bond sells at *premium*.

For example, a $10 000 bond is redeemable at par and bears interest at 10% compounded semi-annually. A comparison of this bond's redemption values and purchase prices 10 years before maturity is shown in Table 15.1.

Table 15.1 Comparison of Principal Values and Purchase Prices for a $10 000 bond. (© S. A. Hummelbrunner)

Principal Value FV	$10 000	$10 000	$10 000
Bond Rate *b*	10%	10%	10%
Market Rate *i*	10%	12%	8%
Purchase Price PV	$10 000	$8853.01	$11 359.03
	Sold at par	Sold below par	Sold above par
		Discount = $1146.99	Premium = $1359.03
b Versus *i*	*b* = *i*	*b* < *i*	*b* > *i*

B. Purchase of a bond on an interest payment date

If a bond is purchased on an interest payment date, the purchase price of the bond is determined by calculating the present value of the redemption price plus the present value of the future interest payments.

THE PURCHASE PRICE OF A BOND PURCHASED ON AN INTEREST PAYMENT DATE	=	THE PRESENT VALUE OF THE REDEMPTION PRICE	+	THE PRESENT VALUE OF THE INTEREST PAYMENTS

First, use Formula 9.4 to calculate the present value of the future redemption price.

$$PV = FV(1 + i)^{-n}$$ ————————— **Formula 9.4**

Second, use Formula 11.2 to calculate the present value of the future interest payments, which form an ordinary annuity.

$$PV_n = PMT \left[\frac{1 - (1 + i)^{-n}}{i} \right] \quad\text{——— Formula 11.2}$$

The two steps involved can be combined, as shown in Formula 15.1.

$$PURCHASE\ PRICE = PV + PV_n = FV(1 + i)^{-n} + PMT \left[\frac{1 - (1 + i)^{-n}}{i} \right] \quad \text{Formula 15.1}$$

Where FV = the principal or face value of the bond;
PMT = the periodic interest payment;
n = the number of outstanding interest payments (or compounding periods);
i = the yield rate per payment interval.

Note: It is important to recognize that two rates of interest are used in determining the purchase price:

1. The bond rate determines the amount of the periodic interest payments;

2. The yield rate is used to determine the present values of the two cash flows.

EXAMPLE 15.2A

A $1000 bond bearing interest at 6% payable semi-annually is due in four years. If money is worth 7% compounded semi-annually, what is the value of the bond if purchased today?

SOLUTION

The buyer of the bond acquires two promises of future cash flows:

1. A promise of $1000 to be paid 4 years from now.

2. A promise of $30 interest due to be paid at the end of every six months. The bond rate is 6% and the periodic interest rate is 6% ÷ 2 = 3%. The interest amount paid is the periodic interest rate stated on the bond multiplied by the face value or maturity value of the bond. This interest of $1000 × 0.03 = $30 will be paid semi-annually for four years, or eight times.

The two cash flows can be represented on a time graph, as Figure 15.1 shows.

Figure 15.1 Graphical Representation of Method and Data (© S. A. Hummelbrunner)

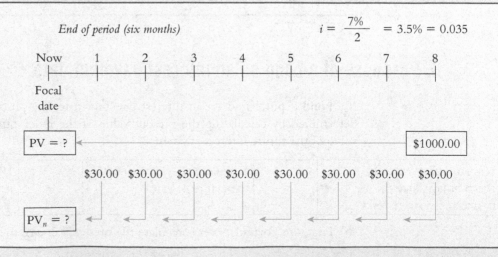

The market rate is 7% compounded semi-annually. To determine the purchase price of the bond, we calculate the present value of the two cash flows, using the market rate.

$$FV = 1000.00; \ n = 4(2) = 8; \ P/Y = 2; \ C/Y = 2; \ I/Y = 7; \ i = \frac{7\%}{2} = 3.5\% = 0.035$$

$$PV = 1000.00(1.035)^{-8} \text{—————————————— using Formula 9.4}$$

$$= 1000.00(0.759412)$$

$$= \$759.41$$

PROGRAMMED SOLUTION

("END" mode) (Set P/Y = 2; C/Y = 2) 1000 [FV] 7 [I/Y]

8 [N] [CPT] [PV] [−759.411556]

$$PMT = \frac{6\% \text{ of } 1000.00}{2} = 30.00; \quad n = 8; \quad i = 3.5\%$$

$$PV_n = 30.00\left(\frac{1 - 1.035^{-8}}{0.035}\right) \text{——————————— using Formula 11.2}$$

$$= 30.00(6.873956)$$

$$= \$206.22$$

PROGRAMMED SOLUTION

("END" mode) (Set P/Y = 2; C/Y = 2) 0 [FV] 30 [PMT] 7 [I/Y] 8 [N]

[CPT] [PV] [−206.218666]

The purchase price of the bond is the sum of the present values of the two promises

$$= PV + PV_n$$

$$= 759.41 + 206.22 = \$965.63 \text{ (the bond is sold at a discount because the bond rate}$$
is smaller than the market rate, thus the purchase price is less than the face value of the bond).

POINTERS & PITFALLS

Always make sure that your calculator is in "END" mode for the payment. Since bonds earn interest, which is paid after a period has finished, the payment of the interest will be at the end of a period.

If you have performed a calculation involving "BGN" mode just before a bond question, change the payment mode to "'END" mode before starting the bond question. To change the BGN to END mode in your Texas Instrument BA II PLUS calculator, press [2nd] and [PMT] buttons to see the current mode on the calculator. If the screen shows BGN, press [2nd] and [Enter] buttons to change the mode of the calculator to END.

Instead of calculating two values and using Formulas 9.4 and 11.2, one calculation using Formula 15.1 can be performed.

POINTERS & PITFALLS

When determining the purchase price of a bond, it is important to carry all the decimals until the calculation is complete. When completing the calculation by formula, the present value of the bond's face value and interest payments along with any accrued interest must be calculated. For simplicity, the text shows each of these values rounded to 2 decimals and then summed to get the purchase price. Remember, though, that all decimals are being carried forward until the final answer.

EXAMPLE 15.2B

A \$5000 bond bearing interest at 6.5% payable semi-annually matures in ten years. If it is bought to yield 5.8% compounded semi-annually, what is the purchase price of the bond?

SOLUTION

PRESENT VALUE OF THE PRINCIPAL $+$ PRESENT VALUE OF THE PERIODIC INTEREST PAYMENTS

$= \text{PV} + \text{PV}_n$

$\text{Periodic Interest Payment} = \$5000 \times \dfrac{0.065}{2} = \$162.5$

$= 5000.00(1.029^{-20}) \quad + 162.50\left(\dfrac{1 - 1.029^{-20}}{0.029}\right)$

$= 5000.00(0.564537) \quad + 162.50(15.015961)$

$= 2822.685609 \quad\quad\quad + 2440.093714$

$= \$5262.78$

PROGRAMMED SOLUTION

("END" mode) (Set P/Y = 2; C/Y = 2) 5000 [FV] 5.8 [I/Y]

20 [N] [CPT] [PV] [−2822.685609]

0 [FV] 162.50 [PMT] 5.8 [I/Y] 20 [N] [CPT] [PV] [−2440.093714]

(These keystrokes can be eliminated, since they are still programmed in the calculator from the previous step.)

The purchase price is 2822.69 + 2440.09 = \$5262.78.

Note: The calculator steps may be combined into one calculation by entering both the future value and the payment as positive numbers, and then computing the present value. The present value will appear as a negative number as shown below:

("END" mode) (Set P/Y = 2; C/Y = 2) 5000 [FV] 5.8 [I/Y] 20 [N] 162.50

[PMT] [CPT] [PV] [−5262.779323]

We can modify Formula 15.1 to allow for a general annuity by using Formula 12.3.

$$\text{PURCHASE PRICE} = \text{PV} + \text{PV}_g = \text{FV}(1 + p)^{-n} + \text{PMT}\left[\dfrac{1 - (1 + p)^{-n}}{p}\right]$$

where $p = (1 + i)^c - 1$

Formula 15.2

EXAMPLE 15.2C

A municipality issues 1000 bond certificates with a face value of $1000 each that mature in 10 years. Interest on the bonds is 3% payable annually. What is the issue price of the bonds if the bonds are sold to yield 4% compounded quarterly?

SOLUTION

The principal of the bonds FV = 1 000 000.00;

the annual interest payment PMT = 1 000 000.00(0.03) = $30 000.00.

Since the interest payment period (annual) is not equal in length to the yield rate conversion period (quarterly), the interest payments form an ordinary general annuity.

$$n = 10; \ P/Y = 1; \ C/Y = 4; \ c = \frac{4}{1} = 4; \ I/Y = 4; \ i = \frac{4\%}{4} = 1.0\% = 0.01;$$

$$p = 1.01^4 - 1 = 1.040604 - 1 = 0.040604 = 4.0604\%$$

For a general annuity

PURCHASE PRICE = PRESENT VALUE OF THE PRINCIPAL
+ PRESENT VALUE OF THE PERIODIC INTEREST
PAYMENTS

$$\text{PURCHASE PRICE} = PV + PV_g$$

$$= 1\,000\,000.00(1.040604)^{-10} \quad + 30\,000.00 \left[\frac{1 - (1.040604)^{-10}}{0.040604} \right]$$

$$= 1\,000\,000.00(0.671653) \qquad + 30\,000.00(8.086562)$$

$$= \$671\,653.14 \qquad\qquad + \$242\,596.87$$

$$= \$914\,250.01.$$

PROGRAMMED SOLUTION

("END" mode) (Set P/Y = 1; C/Y = 4) 1 000 000 [FV] 4

[I/Y] 10 [N] [CPT] [PV] [-671653.13886]

0 [FV] 30 000 [PMT] 4 [I/Y] 10 [N] [CPT] [PV] [242596.872432]

The purchase price is 671 653.14 + 242 596.87 = $914 250.01.

C. Purchase price of a bond between interest payment dates

As discussed in Section 15.1A, bonds are often traded between interest payment dates. To calculate the purchase price of a bond, the first step is to determine the market price of the bond on the interest payment date immediately preceding the date of purchase. For the second step, calculate the accumulated value of the bond (using the compound interest formula) on the date it is traded. To determine the cash price of the bond, add the market price (also called the quoted price) to the accrued interest.

CASH PRICE = MARKET PRICE + ACCRUED INTEREST

EXAMPLE 15.2D

A savings bond with a face value of $1000 bearing interest at 6% payable semi-annually matures on August 1, 2022. What is the purchase price of the bond on April 17, 2020, to yield 5.4% compounded semi-annually?

SOLUTION

STEP 1 Calculate the purchase price on the preceding interest date.
The principal FV = $1000.00;

the semi-annual coupon PMT = $1000.00 \left(\dfrac{0.06}{2} \right) = \$30.00$.

Interest is paid twice a year; on the anniversary of the bond and 6 months later. Since the maturity date is August 1, the semi-annual interest dates are February 1 and August 1. The interest date preceding the date of purchase is February 1, 2020. The time period from February 1, 2020, to the date of maturity is 2.5 years.

$$n = 2.5(2) = 5; \ \ P/Y = 2; \ \ C/Y = 2; \ \ I/Y = 5.4; \ \ i = \frac{5.4\%}{2} = 2.7\% = 0.027$$

The purchase price of the bond on February 1, 2020

$$= 1000.00(1.027^{-5}) + 30.00 \left(\frac{1 - 1.027^{-5}}{0.027} \right)$$
$$= 1000.00(0.875282) + 30.00(4.619201)$$
$$= 875.281566 + 138.576038$$
$$= \$1013.86$$

PROGRAMMED SOLUTION

("END" mode) (Set P/Y = 2; C/Y = 2) 1000 [FV]

5.4 [I/Y] 5 [N] [CPT] [PV] [−875.281566]

0 [FV] 30 [PMT] 5.4 [I/Y] 5 [N] [CPT] [PV] [−138.576038]

The purchase price is 875.28 + 138.58 = $1013.86.

STEP 2 Calculate the accumulated value from February 1 to April 17, 2020.
The number of days from February 1, 2020, to April 17, 2020, is 76; the number of days in the interest interval February 1, 2020, to August 1, 2020, is 182.

$$PV = 1013.86; \ \ \ i = \frac{5.4\%}{2} = 2.7\% = 0.027; \ \ \ n = \frac{76}{182}$$

Purchase Price $= 1013.86(1 + 0.027)^{\left(\frac{76}{182} \right)}$

The purchase price of the bond on April 17, 2020, is $1025.20.

EXAMPLE 15.2E A $5000 bond redeemable at par in seven years and four months, bearing interest at 6.5% payable semi-annually, is bought to yield 7.5% compounded semi-annually. Determine

  (i) the cash price;

  (ii) the accrued interest;

  (iii) the quoted price.

SOLUTION

STEP 1   (i) The redemption price FV = \$5000.00;

the semi-annual coupon PMT $= 5000.00\left(\dfrac{0.065}{2}\right) = \$162.50$.

Since the bond is purchased to yield 7.5% annual interest, the market rate is $\dfrac{0.075}{2} = 0.0375$ every six months.

The interest date preceding the purchase date is 7.5 years before maturity.

$n = 7.5(2) = 15$; P/Y $= 2$; C/Y $= 2$; I/Y $= 7.5$; $i = \dfrac{7.5\%}{2} = 3.75\% = 0.0375$

The purchase price on the interest date preceding the date of purchase

$= 5000.00(1.0375^{-15}) + 162.50\left(\dfrac{1 - 1.0375^{-15}}{0.0375}\right)$

$= 5000.00(0.575676) + 162.50(11.315296)$

$= 2878.381956 + 1838.735638$

$= \$4717.12$

PROGRAMMED SOLUTION

("END" mode) (Set P/Y $= 2$; C/Y $= 2$) 5000 [FV]

7.5 [I/Y] 15 [N] [CPT] [FV]   [−2878.381956]

0 [FV] 162.50 [PMT] 7.5 [I/Y] 15 [N] [CPT] [PV]   [−1838.735638]

The purchase price is 2878.38 + 1838.74 = \$4717.12.

STEP 2   Calculate the accumulated value two months later.

PV $= 4717.12$; $i = 0.0375$; $n = \dfrac{2}{6}$;

Cash Price $= 4717.12\,(1 + 0.0375)^{\left(\frac{2}{6}\right)}$

The cash price two months later is \$4775.36.

(ii) Accrued interest is the fractional payment, $\$162.50\left(\frac{2}{6}\right) = \$54.17$.

(iii) Quoted price $=$ Cash price $-$ Accrued interest $= \$4721.19$.

D. Calculating the purchase price of a bond using the Texas Instrument BA II PLUS "BOND" worksheet

The "BOND" worksheet in the Texas Instrument BA II PLUS calculator is found by pressing the [2nd] button and the number 9 keys (note that "BOND" is shown printed above the number 9 key). This brings up a worksheet into which you can enter all the relevant information regarding a particular bond being priced:

1. SDT - the settlement date, which is the date that the bond is purchased;

2. CPN - the coupon rate or the bond rate that is stated on the bond certificate;

3. RDT - the redemption (or maturity) date of the bond. The redemption date can vary from the maturity date bond those are refinements that are beyond the scope of this text;

4. RV - the redemption value of the bond. This is in percent terms, which is generally 100 percent, unless otherwise stated;

5. ACT - this notes that the "actual number of days" being used. The alternative here is 360 which is instituted by pressing the [2nd] and the [SET] keys;

6. 2/Y - the number of coupon payments per year. The alternate option here would be 1/Y or once per year which is found again by pressing [2nd] and [SET] keys;

7. YLD is the YTM (Yield to Maturity) of the bond;

8. PRI - the price of the bond per $100 of its face value. This is the common way bond prices are indicated in bond markets and in market tables found in newspapers or online;

9. AI - the accrued interest, which is displayed as a percentage of the face value of the bond. To calculate the purchase price of the bond add PRI and AI (note that AI equals zero for bonds that are purchased on an interest payment date).

EXAMPLE 15.2F

Hydro One is Ontario's primary provider of electrical power in the province. In order to fund future electricity generation capacity, they routinely issue bonds. One bond currently on the market has a coupon rate of 7.35 percent payable twice per year with a maturity date of June 03, 2030. Each bond has a face value of $1000.00.

(i) If the current YTM for a bond of this type is 5.45 percent, explain if and why this bond should sell at par, at a premium, or at a discount.

(ii) Determine the purchase price for this bond if the purchase is made on December 03, 2020.

(iii) Determine the cash price for this bond if the purchase is made on January 15, 2021.

SOLUTION

(i) The selling price of a bond depends on the relationship between the coupon or bond rate (the interest that the bond pays) and the bond's YTM. In this case, the coupon rate is 7.35 percent and the YTM is 5.45 percent. Since the coupon rate is higher than the YTM, the bond should sell at a premium.

(ii) Since this bond pays interest twice per year, the interest payment dates would be December 03 and June 03 of each year until maturity. Since we want to determine the purchase price of the bond on December 03, 2020, the calculation is on an interest payment date. Using the **Texas Instrument BA II PLUS Calculator** "Bond" worksheet:

SDT = 12.032 (mm.ddyy)

CPN = 7.35

RDT = 06.0330 (mm.ddyy)

RV = 100

ACT

2/Y

YLD = 5.45

To compute the market price: PRI = press CPT = 113.9449

Note that this calculation is in terms of $100 of face value of the bond. Therefore, multiply this amount by 10 to compute the selling price of a bond with a $1000 face value. The bond should sell for $10 \times \$113.9449 = \$1139.45$ in the market.

From the first part of the question, we expected this bond to sell at a premium or above the face value. Our answer here confirms this expectation. To purchase this $1000.00 bond on December 03, 2020 it would cost $1139.45.

Since this bond was purchased on a coupon payment date, the remaining entries on the worksheet would be:

$$\text{AI or Accrued Interest} = 0$$

Alternatively, the TVM feature of the calculator could be used to calculate the purchase price of the bond on December 03, 2020:

PROGRAMMED SOLUTION

(END mode) (Set P/Y = 2; C/Y = 2)

1000 [FV] 36.75 [PMT] 5.45 [I/Y] 19 [N] [CPT] [PV] [−1139.45]

(iii) Since this settlement date is between payment dates, the next coupon payment must be prorated between the old and new owners of the bond, based on the number of days the bond is held by each of them in the coupon payment period (which in this case is six months).

The first step is to compute the PV of all payments not yet received. This is known as the *CLEAN Price* and it is the price quoted in bond markets. To compute the clean price, we can use the bond worksheet, exactly as before, but we have to change the settlement (or purchase) date to January 15, 2021. The data input now looks like this:

SDT = 01.1521

CPN = 7.35

RDT = 06.0330

RV = 100

ACT

2/Y

YLD = 5.45

To compute the market price: PRI = press CPT = 113.8027. Multiply this number by 10 to obtain a clean price of $1138.03.

However, the actual sale price of the bond, which is known as the *DIRTY Price*, includes both the clean price plus the accrued interest. By scrolling down, you can find the accrued interest amount of 0.868 (which must be multiplied by 10) to obtain $8.68. The dirty price or the cash price is then $1138.03 + $8.68 = $1146.71.

To confirm that these numbers are correct, first calculate the number of days in the coupon payment period – December 03, 2020 to June 03, 2021 = 182 days (found using the "DATE" function on the TI BA II PLUS calculator). The number of days the bond was held by the old owner – December 03, 2020 to January 15, 2021 = 43 days. The new owner held the bond for 139 days in the coupon payment period. The purchase price of the bond on January 15, 2021 is therefore calculated as:

$$FV = PV(1 + i)^n$$

Where:

FV = Future Value (the purchase price of the bond on January 15, 2021)

PV = Present Value of all future payments on December 3, 2020

i = periodic YTM, that is .0545/2 = .02725

n = actual number of days the bond was held by old owner divided by the number of days in a six months period from December 3, 2020 to June 3, 2021, that is 43/182

$$FV = 1139.45(1 + 0.02725)^{43/182} = \$1146.71$$

Note that in the bond worksheet, the YLD (or YTM) is also computable. If you enter the current selling price of the bond (based on $100 of face value) you can compute YLD. For instance, in the bond used in the preceding example, if the selling price on December 03, 2020 was $114.37, the YTM (YLD) would be 5.37825 percent.

E. Using Excel's PRICE function

If you choose, you can use Excel's PRICE function to answer some questions in this section. This function calculates the price per $100 face value of a security that pays periodic interest. Other Excel functions that could be used to answer the questions in this section are as follows: COUPDAYBS (days since last interest date), COUPDAYS (total number of days in the coupon period), and COUPNUM (total number of remaining coupon periods).

The following table illustrates the use of the Excel's PRICE function to calculate the purchase price of a bond in part (ii) of Example 15.2F. Type the given data in column B and in cell B10 enter = PRICE(B3, B4, B5, B6, B7, B8, B9). After pressing enter, Excel provides the purchase price of the bond per each $100 of its face value. Multiply the result by 10 if the face value of the bond is $1000.

	A	B	C
1	Price Function		
2			
3	Settlement Date	December 30, 2020	
4	Maturity Date	June 3, 2030	
5	Annual Bond Interest Rate	0.0735	
6	Annual Market Interest Rate	0.0545	
7	Redemption value per $100	100.00	
8	Compounding Frequency	2	
9	Basis	3	
10	Answer per	$ 113.9448	
11	Maturity Value	$ 1,000.00	
12	Total Purchase Price	$ 1139.45	
13			

F. Direct method of computing the premium or discount— alternative method for calculating the purchase price

EXAMPLE 15.2G   A $5000, 7% bond with semi-annual interest coupons is bought six years before maturity to yield 5.6% compounded semi-annually. Determine the premium or discount.

SOLUTION

$FV = 5000.00;$ $P/Y = 2;$ $C/Y = 2;$ $I/Y = 5.6;$ $b = \dfrac{7\%}{2} = 3.5\% = 0.035;$

$PMT = 5000.00(0.035) = 175.00;$ $i = \dfrac{5.6\%}{2} = 2.8\% = 0.028;$ $n = 6(2) = 12$

Since $b > i$, the bond will sell at a premium.

Purchase price $= 5000.00(1.028^{-12}) + 175.00\left(\dfrac{1 - 1.028^{-12}}{0.028}\right)$

$= 5000.00(0.717931) + 175.00(10.073898)$

$= 3589.65432 + 1762.932101$

$= \$5352.59$ **(due to rounding)**

PROGRAMMED SOLUTION

(Set P/Y = 2; C/Y = 2) 5000 [FV] 5.6 [I/Y]

12 [N] [CPT] [PV] [−3589.65432] [STO] 1

0 [FV] 175 [PMT] 5.6 [I/Y] 12 [N] [CPT] [PV] [−1762.932101] [STO] 2

The purchase price is [RCL] 1 + [RCL] 2 = $5352.59.

The premium is 5352.59 − 5000.00 = $352.59.

While you can always determine the premium by the basic method using Formula 15.1, it is more convenient to determine the premium directly by considering the relationship between the bond rate b and the yield rate i.

As previously discussed, a premium results when $b > i$. When this is the case, the premium is paid because the periodic interest payments received exceed the periodic interest required according to the yield rate.

In Example 15.2G

The semi-annual interest payment	$5000.00(0.035) = \$175.00$
The required semi-annual interest based on the yield rate	$5000.00(0.028) = \underline{140.00}$
The excess of the actual interest received over the required interest to make the yield rate	$= \underline{\$35.00}$

This excess is received at the end of every payment interval; thus, it forms an ordinary annuity whose present value can be computed at the yield rate i.

PMT (the excess interest) = 35.00; $i = 2.8\%;$ $n = 12$

$PV_n = 35.00\left(\dfrac{1 - 1.028^{-12}}{0.028}\right)$

$= 35.00(10.073898)$

$= \$352.59$

PROGRAMMED SOLUTION

(Set P/Y = 2; C/Y = 2) 0 [FV] 35 [PMT] 5.6 [I/Y]

12 [N] [CPT] [PV] [−352.58642]

The premium is $352.59.

The purchase price is 5000.00 + 352.59 = $5352.59.

The premium is the present value of the ordinary annuity formed by the excess of the actual bond interest over the required interest, based on the yield rate. We can obtain the purchase price by adding the premium to the principal.

$$\text{PREMIUM} = (\text{PERIODIC BOND INTEREST} - \text{REQUIRED INTEREST}) \left[\frac{1 - (1 + i)^{-n}}{i} \right]$$

$$= (b \times \text{FACE VALUE} - \text{REDEMPTION PRICE} \times i) \left[\frac{1 - (1 + i)^{-n}}{i} \right]$$

EXAMPLE 15.2H

A $5000, 6% bond with semi-annual interest coupons is bought six years before maturity to yield 8% compounded semi-annually. Determine the premium or discount.

SOLUTION

$\text{FV} = 5000.00; \quad \text{P/Y} = 2; \quad \text{C/Y} = 2; \quad b = \dfrac{6\%}{2} = 3\% = 0.03;$

$\text{PMT} = 5000.00(0.03) = 150.00; \quad \text{I/Y} = 8; \quad i = \dfrac{8\%}{2} = 4\% = 0.04;$

$n = 6(2) = 12$

Since $b < i$, the bond will sell at a discount.

$\text{Purchase price} = 5000.00(1.04^{-12}) + 150.00 \left(\dfrac{1 - 1.04^{-12}}{0.04} \right)$

$\qquad\qquad\qquad = 5000.00(0.624597) + 150.00(9.385074)$

$\qquad\qquad\qquad = 3122.985248 + 1407.761064$

$\qquad\qquad\qquad = \$4530.75$

PROGRAMMED SOLUTION

(Set P/Y = 2; C/Y = 2) 5000 [FV]

$\qquad\qquad$ 8 [I/Y] 12 [N] [CPT] [PV] $\boxed{-3122.985248}$

0 [FV] 150 [PMT] 8 [I/Y] 12 [N] [CPT] [PV] $\boxed{-1407.761064}$

The purchase price is 3122.99 + 1407.76 = $4530.75.

The discount is 5000.00 − 4530.75 = $469.25.

As in the case of a premium, while you can always determine the discount by the basic method using Formula 15.1, it is more convenient to determine the discount directly.

When $b < i$, a discount results. The discount on a bond is received because the periodic interest payments are less than the periodic interest required to earn the yield rate.

In Example 15.2H

The semi-annual interest payment	5000.00(0.03) = $150.00
The required semi-annual interest based on the yield rate	5000.00(0.04) = $\underline{200.00}$
The shortage of the actual interest received compared to the required interest based on the yield rate	= $\underline{\$ 50.00}$

This shortage occurs at the end of every interest payment interval; it forms an ordinary annuity whose present value can be computed at the yield rate i.

PMT = 50.00; $i = 4$; $n = 12$

$$PV_n = 50.00\left(\frac{1 - 1.04^{-12}}{0.04}\right)$$

$$= 50.00(9.385074)$$

$$= \$469.25$$

PROGRAMMED SOLUTION

("END" mode) (Set P/Y = 2; C/Y = 2) 0 $\boxed{\text{FV}}$ 50 $\boxed{\text{PMT}}$ 8 $\boxed{\text{I/Y}}$

$\qquad\qquad\qquad\qquad\qquad\qquad$ 12 $\boxed{\text{N}}$ $\boxed{\text{CPT}}$ $\boxed{\text{PV}}$ $\boxed{-469.253686}$

The discount is \$469.25.

The purchase price is 5000.00 − 469.25 = \$4530.75.

The discount is the present value of the ordinary annuity formed by the shortage of the actual bond interest received as compared to the required interest, based on the yield rate. We can obtain the purchase price by subtracting the discount from the principal.

$$\text{DISCOUNT} = (\text{REQUIRED INTEREST} - \text{PERIODIC BOND INTEREST})\left[\frac{1 - (1 + i)^{-n}}{i}\right]$$

$$= -(\text{PERIODIC BOND INTEREST} - \text{REQUIRED INTEREST})\left[\frac{1 - (1 + i)^{-n}}{i}\right]$$

$$= -(b \times \text{FACE VALUE} - \text{REDEMPTION PRICE} \times i)\left[\frac{1 - (1 + i)^{-n}}{i}\right]$$

Since in both cases the difference between the periodic bond interest and the required interest is involved, the premium or discount on the purchase of a bond can be obtained using the same relationship.

$$\begin{matrix}\text{PREMIUM} \\ \text{or} \\ \text{DISCOUNT}\end{matrix} = (b \times \text{FACE VALUE} - i \times \text{REDEMPTION PRICE})\left[\frac{1 - (1 + i)^{-n}}{i}\right] \quad \text{----- Formula 15.3}$$

EXAMPLE 15.21

A \$1000, 8.5% bond with semi-annual interest coupons redeemable at par in 15 years is bought to yield 7% compounded semi-annually. Determine

(i) the premium or discount;

(ii) the purchase price.

SOLUTION

(i) FV = 1000.00; P/Y = 2; C/Y = 2; $b = \dfrac{8.5\%}{2} = 4.25\% = 0.0425$;

$\qquad$ PMT = 1000.00(0.0425) = 42.50; I/Y = 7; $i = \dfrac{7\%}{2} = 3.5\% = 0.035$;

$\qquad$ $n = 15(2) = 30$

$\qquad$ Since $b > i$, the bond will sell at a premium.

$\qquad$ The required interest based on the yield rate is 1000.00(0.035) = 35.00;
$\qquad$ the excess interest is 42.50 − 35.00 = 7.50.

$\qquad$ The premium is $7.50\left(\dfrac{1 - 1.035^{-30}}{0.035}\right) = 7.50(18.392045) = \$137.94$.

PROGRAMMED SOLUTION

(Set P/Y = 2; C/Y = 2) 0 [FV] 7.50 [PMT] 7 [I/Y]

30 [N] [CPT] [PV] [−137.940341]

(ii) The purchase price is 1000.00 + 137.94 = $1137.94.

EXAMPLE 15.2J

A $50 000, 3.2% bond with quarterly interest coupons redeemable at par in 10 years is purchased to yield 4% compounded quarterly.

(i) What is the premium or discount?

(ii) What is the purchase price?

SOLUTION

(i) FV = 50 000.00; P/Y = 4; C/Y = 4; $b = \dfrac{3.2\%}{4} = 0.8\% = 0.008$;

$n = 10(4) = 40$; $I/Y = 4$; $i = \dfrac{4\%}{4} = 1\% = 0.01$

Since $b < i$, the bond will sell at a discount.

Discount $= (0.008 \times 50\,000.00 - 0.01 \times 50\,000.00)\left(\dfrac{1 - 1.01^{-40}}{0.01}\right)$

——— using Formula 15.3

$= (400.00 - 500.00)(32.834686)$

$= (-100.00)(32.834686)$

$= -\$3283.47$ ——— the negative sign indicates a discount

PROGRAMMED SOLUTION

First compute PMT $= (0.008 \times 50\,000) - (0.01 \times 50\,000) = -100.00$

(Set P/Y = 4; C/Y = 4) 0 [FV] 100 [PMT] 4 [I/Y] 40

[N] [CPT] [PV] [−3283.468611]

(ii) The purchase price is 50 000.00 − 3283.47 = $46 716.53.

EXERCISE 15.2

MyLab Math

Answer each of the following questions.

1. A $500 bond matures on March 1, 2026. Interest is 6% payable semi-annually. Determine the purchase price of the bond on September 1, 2020, to yield 7.5% compounded semi-annually.   Reference Example 15.2A

2. A $15 000, 2.5% bond is purchased six years and six months before maturity to yield 3% semi-annually. If the bond interest is payable semi-annually, what is the purchase price of the bond?

3. A $5000, 6% bond is purchased 13 years before maturity to yield 6.5% semi-annually. If the bond interest is payable semi-annually, what is the purchase price of the bond?

4. A $2000, 5.5% bond is purchased six years before maturity to yield 7.5% semi-annually. If the bond interest is payable semi-annually, what is the purchase price of the bond?

5. A $10 000, 3% bond is purchased nine years and six months before maturity to yield 2% semi-annually. If the bond interest is payable semi-annually, what is the purchase price of the bond?
   Reference Example 15.2B

6. A $25 000, 7% bond is purchased 12 years before maturity to yield 5% compounded semi-annually. If the bond interest is payable semi-annually, what is the purchase price of the bond?

7. A $1000, 5% bond is purchased 8.5 years before maturity to yield 4% compounded semi-annually. If the bond interest is payable semi-annually, what is the purchase price of the bond?

8. A 25-year bond issue of $5 000 000 and bearing interest at 4.25% payable annually is sold to yield 4.5% compounded semi-annually. What is the purchase price of the bond?
   Reference Example 15.2C

9. A $100 000 bond bearing interest at 6.75% payable semi-annually is bought eight years before maturity to yield 7.35% compounded annually. If the bond is redeemable at par, what is the purchase price?

10. Bonds with a maturity value of $40 000 in 7.5 years, bearing interest at 8% payable quarterly, are sold to yield 6.8% compounded semi-annually. Determine the purchase price of the bonds.

11. A $100 000 bond is redeemable at par in 14 years, 10 months. If interest on the bond is 7.5% payable semi-annually, what is the purchase price to yield 8% compounded semi-annually?
    (a) What is the cash price of the bond?
    (b) What is the accrued interest?
    (c) What is the quoted or market price of the bond?
    Reference Example 15.2E

12. A $25 000, 10% bond redeemable at par on December 1, 2030, was purchased on September 25, 2019, to yield 7.6% compounded semi-annually. Bond interest is payable semi-annually.
    (a) What is the cash price of the bond?
    (b) What is the accrued interest?
    (c) What is the quoted price?
    (d) Use TI BA II PLUS calculator to verify your answers to parts a, b, and c.

13. Six $1000 bonds with 2.4% coupons payable semi-annually are purchased three months after a coupon matures, to yield 1.2% compounded monthly. The bonds mature in eight years.
    (a) What is the purchase price of the bonds?
    (b) What is the accrued interest?
    (c) What is the market price of the six bonds?

14. A $100 000 bond redeemable at par on October 1, 2040, is purchased on January 15, 2019. Interest is 5.9% payable semi-annually and the yield is 9% compounded semi-annually.
    (a) What is the purchase price of the bond?
    (b) What is the accrued interest?
    (c) What is the market price?
    (d) Use TI BA II PLUS calculator to verify your answers to parts a, b, and c.

15. A $100 000, 8% bond redeemable at par with quarterly coupons is purchased to yield 6.5% compounded quarterly. Calculate the premium or discount and the purchase price if the bond is purchased
    (a) 15 years before maturity;
    (b) 5 years before maturity.
    Reference Example 15.2G

16. A \$5000, 7.5% bond redeemable at par with semi-annual coupons is purchased to yield 6% compounded semi-annually. What is the premium or discount and the purchase price if the bond is bought
    (a) 10 years before maturity?
    (b) 6 years before maturity?

17. A \$25 000, 4% bond redeemable at par with interest payable annually is bought six years before maturity. Determine the premium or discount and the purchase price if the bond is purchased to yield
    (a) 2% compounded annually;
    (b) 6% compounded annually.   Reference Example 15.2H

18. A \$1000, 8% bond redeemable at par in seven years bears coupons payable annually. Compute the premium or discount and the purchase price if the yield, compounded annually, is
    (a) 6.5%;
    (b) 7.5%;
    (c) 8.5%.

19. A \$5 000 000 issue of 10-year bonds redeemable at par offers 7.25% coupons payable semi-annually. What is the issue price of the bonds to yield 8.4% compounded monthly?

20. A \$3000 issue of nine-year bonds redeemable at par offers 1.5% coupons paid semi-annually. What is the issue price of the bonds to yield 2.0% semi-annually?

21. Twenty \$5000 bonds redeemable at par bearing 8.4% coupons payable quarterly are sold eight years before maturity to yield 8.0% compounded annually. What is the purchase price of the bonds?

22. Sixty \$1000 bonds redeemable at par bearing 4.0% coupons payable semi-annually are sold seven years before maturity to yield 5.5% compounded semi-annually. What is the purchase price of the bonds?

23. Catherine is planning to invest part of the funds she has in her TFSA account into bonds. Suppose she is considering investing in Bell Canada's bonds with a \$10 000 face value maturing on April 17, 2030. The bond's coupon or bond rate is 8.88 percent and interest is paid semi-annually. The current required market rate or yield to market (YTM) for this bond is 4.54 percent compounded semi-annually. Determine the purchase price of this bond if the purchase is made on April 17, 2021.

24. On August 10, 2018, Allison purchased two bond certificates with a face value of \$5000 each issued by Enbridge Pipeline Corp. Bonds from this company currently in the market have a semi-annual coupon rate of 6.5 percent and mature on June 11, 2031. The required market rate for a bond of this type is 4.44 percent. Calculate the cash price of the bond.

BUSINESS MATH **NEWS**

Can the Port Authority and MTA Afford Repairs After Sandy?

Many municipalities, including New York City, suffered infrastructure damage when Hurricane Sandy blasted through the East Coast of North America on October 30, 2012. Subway and railway tunnels, bus garages, bridges, vehicles, roads, and buildings were damaged by flooding and winds from the storm. The Metropolitan Transportation Authority (MTA) for New York City is responsible for funding the capital projects needed to maintain the infrastructure.

Along with repairs and restructuring from the hurricane, capital budget plans include the ongoing upgrade or implementation of capital projects for the next year and for the next 10 years. Capital spending amounts to millions of dollars every year, even without the damage from a hurricane.

What $10 Million in Capital Spending Buys		
Housing	40	units of housing for the homeless
Sanitation	37	dual-bin recycling trucks
Parks	5800	sidewalk trees
Fire	11	ladders trucks
Education	3	classrooms
Transportation	73	lane miles of city resurfacing
Environment	9600	feet of new or reconstructed sewers
Correction	25	jail beds
Parks	9	natural park fields or 5 synthetic ones

Funding can come from many sources. The capital program for New York City is primarily financed by issuing long-term debt in the form of bonds. Annually, the city must service the debt by paying the interest and principal on outstanding debt. While in 2009, $3.6 billion was spent to service general obligations and capital lease obligations, after adjusting for the use of prior surpluses to make prepayments, it is expected to increase to $8.1 billion. The Capital and Expense budgets are closely related.

QUESTIONS

1. New York Series C bonds with a face value of $120 000 mature January 1, 2015, and pay interest at 5% semi-annually. On January 1, 2013, the bonds were sold at a price of 109.007 to yield 0.470%.

   (a) Calculate the amount paid for the bonds.
   (b) For these bonds, how much interest must be paid each year?
   (c) If the bonds had been purchased by the same investor six months earlier for $130 506.40, what would be the market quotation price and the yield rate?
   (d) What yield was realized on this purchase and subsequent sale?

2. New York City Transitional Series S-2 bonds with a face value of $50 000 mature January 1, 2034, with a coupon rate of 4.25% annually. On January 1, 2014, the bonds were sold for a total of $52 998.

   (a) Calculate the market quotation price of the bonds.
   (b) For these bonds, how much interest must be paid each year?
   (c) Calculate the yield for this entire lot of bonds if held to maturity.
   (d) If the investor holds the bonds for one year, then sells them for $53 500, how much money was made on the transaction, and what yield would be realized from the sale?

Source: "Can the Port Authority and MTA afford repairs after Sandy?," **http.blogs.reuters.com/muniland/2012/10/31/can-the-port-authority-and-mta-afford-repairs**, retrieved November 13, 2012; "New York Municipal Bonds Trades," **www.newyork.municipalbonds.com**, retrieved November 27, 2012; "Understanding New York City's Budget—A Guide to the Capital Budget," **www.ibo.nyc.ny.us/iboreports/IBOCBG.pdf**, January, 2010; "Mayor's Preliminary Budget for 2017 and Financial Plan Through 2020," **http://www.ibo.nyc.ny.us/iboreports/analysis-of-the-mayors-2017-preliminary-budget-and-financial-plan-through-2020.pdf**, retrieved May 30, 2016. © S. A. Hummelbrunner

15.3 BOND SCHEDULES
A. Amortization of premium

If a bond is purchased for more than the principal, the resulting premium is not recovered when the bond is redeemed at maturity, so it becomes a capital *loss*. To avoid the capital loss at maturity, the premium is written down or expensed gradually over the period from the date of purchase to the maturity date. The writing down of the premium gradually reduces the bond's book value until it equals the principal at the date of maturity.

The process of writing down the premium is called **amortization of the premium**. The most direct method of amortizing a premium assigns the difference between the interest received (coupon) and the interest required according to the yield rate to write down the premium. The details of writing down the premium are often shown in a tabulation referred to as a *schedule of amortization of premium*.

EXAMPLE 15.3A

A \$1000, 6% bond redeemable at par matures in three years. The coupons are payable semi-annually and the bond is bought to yield 5% compounded semi-annually.

(i) Compute the purchase price.

(ii) Construct a schedule of amortization of premium.

SOLUTION

(i) FV = 1000.00; $n = 3(2) = 6$;   P/Y = 2;   C/Y = 2;

$b = \dfrac{6\%}{2} = 3\% = 0.03$;   I/Y = 5; $i = \dfrac{5\%}{2} = 2.5\% = 0.025$

Since $b > i$, the bond sells at a premium.

$$\text{Premium} = (0.03 \times 1000.00 - 0.025 \times 1000.00)\left(\dfrac{1 - 1.025^{-6}}{0.025}\right)$$

$$= (30.00 - 25.00)(5.508125)$$

$$= (5.00)(5.508125)$$

$$= \$27.54$$

PROGRAMMED SOLUTION

PMT = $(0.03 \times 1000.00) - (0.025 \times 1000.00) = 5.00$

(Set P/Y = 2; C/Y = 2) 0 [FV] 5 [PMT] 5 [I/Y]

6 [N] [CPT] [PV] [−27.540627]

The purchase price is $1000.00 + 27.54 = \$1027.54$

(ii) *Schedule of amortization of premium*

End of Interest Payment Interval	Bond Interest Received (Coupon) $b = 3\%$	Interest on Book Value at Yield Rate $i = 2.5\%$	Amount of Premium Amortized	Book Value of Bond	Remaining Premium
0				\$1027.54	\$27.54
1	\$ 30.00	\$ 25.69	\$ 4.31	1023.23	23.23
2	30.00	25.58	4.42	1018.81	18.81
3	30.00	25.47	4.53	1014.28	14.28
4	30.00	25.36	4.64	1009.64	9.64
5	30.00	25.24	4.76	1004.88	4.88
6	30.00	25.12	4.88	\$1000.00	\$ 0
TOTAL	\$180.00	\$152.46	\$27.54		

Explanations of schedule

1. The original book value shown is the purchase price of $1027.54.

2. At the end of the first interest payment interval, the interest received (coupon) is $1000.00(0.03) = 30.00$; the interest required according to the yield rate is $1027.54(0.025) = 25.69$; the difference $30.00 - 25.69 = 4.31$ is used to write down the premium to 23.23 and reduces the book value from 1027.54 to 1023.23.

3. The coupon at the end of the second interest payment interval is again 30.00. The interest required according to the yield rate is $1023.23(0.025) = 25.58$; the difference $30.00 - 25.58 = 4.42$ reduces the premium to 18.81 and the book value of the bond to 1018.81.

4. Continue in a similar manner until the maturity date, when the principal is reached. If a rounding error becomes apparent at the end of the final interest payment interval, adjust the final interest on the book value at the yield rate to make the premium zero and to obtain a principal exactly the same as the book value.

5. The totals provide useful accounting information showing the total interest received (180.00) and the net income realized (152.46).

B. Accumulation of discount

If a bond is bought at less than the principal, there will be a gain at the time of redemption equal to the amount of discount. It is generally accepted accounting practice that this gain does not accrue in total to the accounting period in which the bond is redeemed. Instead, some of the gain accrues to each of the accounting periods from the date of purchase to the date of redemption.

To adhere to this practice, the discount is decreased gradually so that the book value of the bond increases gradually until, at the date of redemption, the discount is reduced to zero while the book value equals the principal. The process of reducing the discount so as to increase the book value is called **accumulation of discount**.

In the case of a discount, the interest required according to the yield rate is greater than the actual interest received (the coupon). Similar to amortization of a premium, the most direct method of accumulating a discount assigns the difference between the interest required by the yield rate and the coupon to reduce the discount. The details of decreasing the discount while increasing the book value of a bond are often shown in a tabulation called a *schedule of accumulation of discount*.

EXAMPLE 15.3B

A $10 000 bond, redeemable at par in four years, with 5.5% coupons payable semi-annually, is bought to yield 7% compounded semi-annually.

(i) Determine the discount and the purchase price.

(ii) Construct a schedule of accumulation of discount.

SOLUTION

(i) $FV = 10\ 000.00$; $n = 4(2) = 8$; $P/Y = 2$; $C/Y = 2$;

$$b = \frac{5.5\%}{2} = 2.75\% = 0.0275\%;\quad I/Y = 7;\quad i = \frac{7\%}{2} = 3.5\% = 0.035$$

Since $b < i$, the bond sells at a discount.

$$\text{Discount} = (0.0275 \times 10\ 000.00 - 0.035 \times 10\ 000.00)\left(\frac{1 - 1.035^{-8}}{0.035}\right)$$

$$= (275.00 - 350.00)(6.873956)$$

$$= (-75.00)(6.873956)$$

$$= -\$515.55$$

PROGRAMMED SOLUTION

$PMT = (0.0275 \times 10\ 000) - (0.035 \times 10\ 000) = 275.00$

(Set P/Y = 2; C/Y = 2) 0 $\boxed{\text{FV}}$ 75 $\boxed{\text{PMT}}$ 7 $\boxed{\text{I/Y}}$

8 $\boxed{\text{N}}$ $\boxed{\text{CPT}}$ $\boxed{\text{PV}}$ $\boxed{-515.546665}$

The purchase price is 10 000.00 − 515.55 = $9484.45.

(ii) *Schedule of accumulation of discount*

End of Interest Payment Interval	Bond Interest Rate (Coupon) $b = 2.75\%$	Interest on Book Value at Yield Rate $i = 3.5\%$	Amount of Discount Accumulated	Book Value of Bond	Remaining Discount
0				$ 9 484.55	$515.55
1	$ 275.00	$ 331.96	$ 56.96	9 541.41	458.59
2	275.00	333.95	58.95	9 600.36	399.64
3	275.00	336.01	61.01	9 661.37	338.63
4	275.00	338.15	63.15	9 724.52	275.48
5	275.00	340.36	65.36	9 789.88	210.12
6	275.00	342.65	67.65	9 857.53	142.47
7	275.00	345.01	70.01	9 927.54	72.46
8	275.00	347.46	72.46	$10 000.00	$ 0.00
TOTAL	$2200.00	$2715.55	$515.55		

Explanations of schedule

1. The original book value shown is the purchase price of $9484.55.

2. At the end of the first interest payment interval, the coupon is 10 000.00(0.0275) = $275; the interest required according to the yield rate is 9484.55(0.035) = $331.96; the difference used to reduce the discount and to increase the book value is 331.96 − 275.00 = $56.96; the book value is 9484.55 + 56.96 = $9541.41; and the remaining discount is 515.55 − 56.96 = $458.59.

3. The coupon at the end of the second interest payment interval is again $275; the interest required on the book value is 9541.41(0.035) = $333.95; the difference is 333.95 − 275.00 = $58.95; the book value is 9541.41 + 58.95 = $9600.36; and the remaining discount is 458.59 − 58.95 = $399.64.

4. Continue in a similar manner until the maturity date, when the principal is reached. If a rounding error becomes apparent at the end of the final interest payment interval, adjust the final interest on the book value at the yield rate to make the remaining discount equal to zero and obtain the principal exactly equal to the book value.

5. The totals provide useful accounting information showing the total interest received ($2200) and the net income realized ($2715.55).

6. Note that there is always a possibility for small differences due to rounding errors.

C. Book value of a bond—determining the gain or loss on the sale of a bond

EXAMPLE 15.3C

A $10 000, 8% bond redeemable at par with semi-annual coupons was purchased 15 years before maturity to yield 6% compounded semi-annually. The bond was sold 3 years later at 101.25. Calculate the gain or loss on the sale of the bond.

SOLUTION

The market quotation of 101.25 indicates that the bond was sold at 101.25% of its face value. The proceeds from the sale of the bond are 10 000.00(1.0125) = $10 125. To calculate the gain or loss on the sale of the bond, we need to know the book value of the bond at the date of sale. This we can do by determining the original purchase price, constructing a bond schedule, and reading the book value at the time of sale from the schedule.

$FV = 10\ 000.00;\quad n = 15(2) = 30;$

$P/Y = 2;\quad C/Y = 2;\quad I/Y = 6;\quad b = \dfrac{8\%}{2} = 4\% = 0.04;\quad i = \dfrac{6\%}{2} = 3\% = 0.03$

Since $b > i$, the bond was bought at a premium.

$\text{Premium} = (0.04 \times 10\ 000.00 - 0.03 \times 10\ 000.00)\left(\dfrac{1 - 1.03^{-30}}{0.03}\right)$

$= (400.00 - 300.00)(19.600441)$

$= (100.00)(19.600441)$

$= \$1960.04$

PROGRAMMED SOLUTION

$\text{PMT} = (0.04 \times 10\ 000) - (0.03 \times 10\ 000) = 100.00$

(Set P/Y = 2; C/Y = 2) 0 [FV] 100 [PMT] 6 [I/Y] 30 [N]

[CPT] [PV] −1960.044135

The purchase price is 10 000.00 + 1960.04 = $11 960.04.

Schedule of amortization of premium

End of Interest Payment Interval	Coupon $b = 4\%$	Interest on Book Value at Yield Rate $i = 3\%$	Amount of Premium Amortized	Book Value of Bond	Remaining Premium
0				$11 960.04	$1960.04
1	$400.00	$358.80	$41.20	11 918.84	1918.84
2	400.00	357.57	42.43	11 876.41	1876.41
3	400.00	356.29	43.71	11 832.70	1832.70
4	400.00	354.98	45.02	11 787.68	1787.68
5	400.00	353.63	46.37	11 741.31	1741.31
6	$400.00	$352.24	$47.76	$11 693.55	$1693.55
	etc.				

The book value after three years (six semi-annual periods) is $11 693.55. Since the book value is greater than the proceeds, the loss on the sale of the bond is 11 693.55 − 10 125.00 = $1568.55.

We can solve this problem more quickly by computing the book value directly. The book value of a bond at a given time is the purchase price of the bond on that date. We can determine the book value of a bond without constructing a bond schedule by using Formula 15.1 or 15.3. This approach can also be used to verify book values in a bond schedule.

$FV = 10\ 000.00;\quad n = (15 - 3)(2) = 24;\quad b = 4\%;\quad i = 3\%$

$$\text{Premium} = (0.04 \times 10\ 000.00 - 0.03 \times 10\ 000.00)\left(\frac{1 - 1.03^{-24}}{0.03}\right)$$

$$= (100.00)(16.935542) = \$1693.55$$

PROGRAMMED SOLUTION

$PMT = (0.04 \times 10\ 000) - (0.03 \times 10\ 000) = 100.00$

(Set P/Y = 2; C/Y = 2) 0 FV 100 PMT 6 I/Y

24 N CPT PV −1693.554212

The purchase price is $10\ 000.00 + 1693.55 = \$11\ 693.55$.

The loss on the sale is $11\ 693.55 - 10\ 125.00 = \$1568.55$.

EXERCISE 15.3

MyLab Math

A. For each of the following bonds, compute the premium or discount and the purchase price, and construct the appropriate bond schedule.

1. A $5000, 6% bond redeemable at par in three-and-a-half years with semi-annual coupons is purchased to yield 6.5% compounded semi-annually.   Reference Example 15.3B

2. A $25 000 bond with interest at 2.4% payable quarterly, redeemable at par, is bought two years before maturity to yield 2% compounded quarterly.

3. A $1000, 5% bond with semi-annual coupons redeemable at par on September 1, 2023, is bought on March 1, 2020, to yield 4% compounded semi-annually.

4. A $10 000, 7.75% bond with annual coupons redeemable at par in seven years is bought to yield 7.25% compounded annually.

B. Determine the gain or loss on the sale of each of the following bonds without constructing a bond schedule.

1. A $25 000, 6.5% bond redeemable at par with semi-annual coupons bought 10 years before maturity to yield 7% compounded semi-annually is sold 4 years before maturity at 99.25.   Reference Example 15.3C

2. Four $5000, 8.5% bonds with interest payable semi-annually, redeemable at par, were bought 20 years before maturity to yield 7.5% compounded semi-annually. The bonds were sold 3 years later at 103.625.

3. A $5000 bond with 8% interest payable semi-annually redeemable at par on June 1, 2031, was bought on December 1, 2017, to yield 9% compounded semi-annually. The bond was sold on September 22, 2021, at 101.375.

4. Three $10 000, 10.5% bonds with quarterly coupons redeemable at par on August 1, 2025, were bought on May 1, 2011, to yield 12% compounded quarterly. The bonds were sold on January 16, 2019, at 93.5.

15.4 DETERMINING THE YIELD RATE
A. Quoted price of a bond—buying bonds on the market

Bonds are usually bought or sold through a bond exchange, in which agents trade bonds on behalf of their clients. To allow for the different denominations, bonds are offered at a market price stated as a percent of their face value.

It is understood that if the bond is bought between interest dates, such a quoted price does not include any accrued interest. As explained in Section 15.1, the seller of a bond is entitled to the interest earned by the bond to the date of sale, and the interest is added to the quoted price to obtain the cash price.

EXAMPLE 15.4A A $5000, 8% bond with semi-annual coupons payable April 1 and October 1 is purchased on August 25 at 104.75. What is the cash price of the bond?

SOLUTION The quoted price is $5000.00(1.0475) = \$5237.50$.
The time period April 1 to August 25 contains 146 days; the number of days in the interest payment interval April 1 to October 1 is 183.

$$PV = 5000.00; \quad r = i = \frac{8\%}{2} = 4\% = 0.04; \quad t = \frac{146}{183}$$

The accrued interest is $5000.00(0.04)\left(\dfrac{146}{183}\right) = \$159.56$.

The cash price is $5237.50 + 159.56 = \$5397.06$.

B. Determining the yield rate—the average investment method

When bonds are bought on the market, the yield rate is not directly available; it needs to be determined. The simplest method in use is the so-called **method of averages**, which gives a reasonable approximation of the yield rate as the ratio of the average income per interest payment interval to the average book value.

$$\text{APPROXIMATE VALUE OF } i = \frac{\text{AVERAGE INCOME PER INTEREST PAYMENT INTERVAL}}{\text{AVERAGE BOOK VALUE}}$$

where

$$\text{AVERAGE BOOK VALUE} = \frac{1}{2}(\text{QUOTED PRICE} + \text{REDEMPTION PRICE})$$

and

$$\begin{array}{l}\text{AVERAGE INCOME} \\ \text{PER INTEREST} \\ \text{PAYMENT INTERVAL}\end{array} = \frac{\text{TOTAL INTEREST PAYMENTS} \begin{array}{c}- \text{ PREMIUM OR} \\ + \text{ DISCOUNT}\end{array}}{\text{NUMBER OF INTEREST PAYMENT INTERVALS}}$$

Formula 15.4

EXAMPLE 15.4B

A $25 000, 7.5% bond with semi-annual coupons redeemable at par in 10 years is purchased at 103.5. What is the approximate yield rate?

SOLUTION

The quoted price (initial book value) is 25 000.00(1.035) = $25 875.00; the principal is $25 000.00.

The average book value is $\frac{1}{2}$(25 875.00 + 25 000.00) = $25 437.50.

The semi-annual interest payment is 25 000.00$\left(\frac{0.075}{2}\right)$ = $937.50;

the number of interest payments to maturity is 10(2) = 20;
the total interest payments are 20(937.50) = $18 750.00;
the premium is 25 875.00 − 25 000.00 = $875.00.

Average income per interest payment interval = $\frac{18\ 750.00 - 875.00}{20}$ = $893.75.

Approximate value of $i = \frac{893.75}{25\ 437.50}$ = 0.03$\overline{51}$ = 3.$\overline{513}$%.

The yield rate is 2(3.$\overline{513}$) = 7.$\overline{027}$%.

EXAMPLE 15.4C

Eight $1000, 6% bonds with semi-annual coupons redeemable at par in seventeen years are purchased at 97.375. What is the approximate yield rate?

SOLUTION

The quoted price is 8000.00(0.97375) = $7790.00;
the principal is $8000.00;

the average book value is $\frac{(7790.00 + 8000.00)}{2}$ = $7895.00.

The semi-annual interest payment is 8000.00$\left(\frac{0.06}{2}\right)$ = $240.00;

the number of interest payments to maturity is 17(2) = 34;
the total interest payments are 34(240.00) = $8160.00;
the bond discount is 8000.00 − 7790.00 = $210.00.

Average income per interest payment interval = $\frac{(8160.00 + 210.00)}{34}$ = $246.18.

The approximate value of i is $\frac{246.18}{7895.00}$ = 0.031182 = 3.1182%.

The approximate yield rate is 2(3.1182%) = 6.2364%.

EXAMPLE 15.4D

A $5000, 10% bond with semi-annual coupons redeemable at par on July 15, 2030, is quoted on December 2, 2018, at 103.75. What is the approximate yield rate?

SOLUTION

To determine the approximate yield rate for a bond purchased between interest dates, assume that the price was quoted on the nearest interest date. Since the interest dates are January 15 and July 15, the nearest interest date is January 15, 2019, which is 11.5 years before maturity.

The quoted price is 5000.00(1.0375) = $5187.50;

the redemption price is $5000.00;

the average book value is $\frac{(5187.50 + 5000.00)}{2}$ = $5093.75.

The semi-annual interest is $5000.00\left(\dfrac{0.10}{2}\right) = \$250.00$;

the number of interest payments to maturity is $11.5(2) = 23$;
the total interest payments are $23(250.00) = \$5750.00$;
the premium is $5187.50 - 5000.00 = \$187.50$.

The average income per interest payment interval $= \dfrac{(5750.00 - 187.50)}{23} = \$241.85$.

The approximate value of i is $\dfrac{241.85}{5093.75} = 0.047480 = 4.7480\%$.

The approximate yield rate is $2(4.7480\%) = 9.496\%$.

EXERCISE 15.4

MyLab Math

Use the method of averages to determine the approximate yield rate for each of the six bonds shown in the following table. All are redeemed at par.

	Face Value	Bond Rate Payable Semi-annually	Time Before Maturity	Market Quotation
1.	$10 000	6%	15 years	101.375
2.	5 000	10.5	7 years	94.75
3.	25 000	7.5	10 years	97.125
4.	1 000	8.5	8 years	101
5.	50 000	9	5 years, 4 months	98.875
6.	20 000	7	9 years, 8 months	109.25

7. Suppose you are considering investing in a Bombardier Inc. corporate bond with a $7500 face value that matures in 15 years. The bond's coupon or bond rate is 7.350 percent, interest is paid semi-annually, and the market prices this bond at 109.1724. What is the approximate yield rate?

15.5 SINKING FUNDS
A. Determining the size of the periodic payment

Sinking funds are interest-bearing accounts into which payments are made at periodic intervals to provide a desired sum of money at a specified future time. Such funds usually involve large sums of money used by both private and public sectors to repay loans, redeem bonds, finance future capital acquisitions, provide for the replacement of depreciable plant and equipment, and recover investments in depletable natural resources. Therefore, sinking funds are like the reverse of the bond. The issuer has to set up a sinking fund in order to ensure the redemption value of all outstanding bonds is available at the redemption date. To have sufficient funds available to secure a child's future education, parents invest in a Registered Education Savings Plan (RESP), which is a tax-sheltered sinking fund.

The basic problem in dealing with sinking funds is to determine the *size of the periodic payments* that will accumulate to a known future amount. These payments form an annuity in which the accumulated value is known.

Depending on whether the periodic payments are made at the end or at the beginning of each payment period, the annuity formed is an ordinary annuity or an annuity due. Depending on whether the payment interval is equal in length to the interest conversion period, the annuity formed is a simple annuity or a general annuity. However, since sinking funds are normally set up so that the payment interval and the interest conversion period are equal in length, only the simple annuity cases are considered in this text.

(a) For sinking funds with payments at the end of each payment interval,

$$FV_n = PMT\left[\frac{(1 + i)^n - 1}{i}\right] \text{ ————————————— Formula 11.1}$$

(b) For sinking funds with payments at the beginning of each payment interval,

$$FV_n(\text{due}) = PMT\left[\frac{(1 + i)^n - 1}{i}\right](1 + i) \text{ ————————— Formula 13.1}$$

EXAMPLE 15.5A

Western Oil plans to create a sinking fund of $20 000 to replace a pick-up truck by making equal deposits at the end of every six months for four years. Interest is 6% compounded semi-annually.

(i) What is the size of the semi-annual deposit into the fund?

(ii) What is the total amount deposited into the fund?

(iii) How much of the fund will be interest?

SOLUTION

(i) $FV_n = 20\ 000.00$; $P/Y = 2$; $C/Y = 2$; $n = 4(2) = 8$; $I/Y = 6$; $i = \dfrac{6\%}{2} = 3\%$

$$20\ 000.00 = PMT\left(\frac{1.03^8 - 1}{0.03}\right)$$

$$20\ 000.00 = PMT(8.892336)$$

$$PMT = \$2249.13$$

PROGRAMMED SOLUTION

("END" mode)

(Set P/Y = 2; C/Y = 2) 0 [PV] 20 000 [FV] 6 [I/Y]

8 [N] [CPT] [PMT] [−2249.127777]

The size of the semi-annual payment is $2249.13.

(ii) The total deposited into the sinking fund is 8(2249.127777) = $17 993.02

(iii) The amount of interest in the fund is 20 000.00 − 17 993.02 = $2006.98.

EXAMPLE 15.5B

Ace Machinery wants to provide for replacement of equipment seven years from now, estimated to cost $60 000.00. To do so, the company sets up a sinking fund into which it will pay equal sums of money at the beginning of each of the next seven years. Interest paid by the fund is 4.5% compounded annually.

(i) What is the size of the annual payment into the fund?

(ii) What is the total paid into the fund by Ace Machinery?

(iii) How much of the fund will be interest?

SOLUTION

(i) $FV_n(\text{due}) = 60\,000.00;\quad P/Y = 1;\quad C/Y = 1;\quad I/Y = 4.5;\quad n = 7;\quad i = 4.5\%$

$$60\,000.00 = PMT\left(\frac{1.045^7 - 1}{0.045}\right)(1.045)$$

$$60\,000.00 = PMT(8.019152)(1.045)$$

$$PMT = \$7159.89$$

PROGRAMMED SOLUTION

("BGN" mode)

(Set $P/Y = 1; C/Y = 1$) 0 $\boxed{PV}$ 60 000 $\boxed{FV}$ 4.5 $\boxed{I/Y}$

7 $\boxed{N}$ $\boxed{CPT}$ $\boxed{PMT}$ $\boxed{-7159.892899}$

The size of the annual payment is $7159.89.

(ii) The total paid into the fund by Ace Machinery will be $7(7159.892899) = \$50\,119.25$.

(iii) The interest earned by the fund will be $60\,000.00 - 50\,119.25 = \$9\,880.75$.

B. Constructing sinking fund schedules

The details of a sinking fund can be presented in the form of a schedule. Sinking fund schedules normally show the payment number (or payment date), the periodic payment into the fund, the interest earned by the fund, the increase in the fund, and the accumulated balance.

POINTERS & PITFALLS

A sinking fund schedule has the same characteristics as an amortization schedule and may also experience a small difference due to the rounding of the payment or the interest.

EXAMPLE 15.5C

Construct a sinking fund schedule for Example 15.5A.

SOLUTION

$PMT = 2249.13;\quad n = 8;\quad i = 3\% = 0.03$

Sinking fund schedule

Payment Interval Number	Periodic Payment	Interest for Payment Interval $i = 0.03$	Increase in Fund	Balance in Fund at the End of Payment Interval
0				$ 0.00
1	$ 2249.13	$ 0.00	$ 2249.13	2249.13
2	2249.13	67.47	2316.60	4565.73
3	2249.13	136.97	2386.10	6951.83
4	2249.13	208.55	2457.68	9409.51
5	2249.13	282.29	2531.42	11 940.93
6	2249.13	358.23	2607.36	14 548.29
7	2249.13	436.45	2685.58	17 233.87
8	2249.13	517.02	2766.15	$20 000.02
TOTAL	$17 993.04	$2006.98	$20 000.02	

Explanations regarding the construction of the sinking fund schedule

1. The payment number 0 is used to introduce the beginning balance.

2. The first deposit is made at the end of the first payment interval. The interest earned by the fund during the first payment interval is $0 because no money was in the fund until the end of the payment interval, the increase in the fund is $2249.13, and the balance is $2249.13.

3. The second deposit is added at the end of the second payment interval. The interest for the interval is $0.03(2249.13) = \$67.47$. The increase in the fund is $2249.13 + 67.47 = \$2316.60$, and the new balance in the fund is $2249.13 + 2316.60 = \$4565.73$.

4. The third deposit is made at the end of the third payment interval. The interest for the interval is $0.03(4565.73) = \$136.97$, the increase in the fund is $2249.13 + 136.97 = \$2386.10$, and the new balance in the fund is $2386.10 + 4565.73 = \$6951.83$.

5. Calculations for the remaining payment intervals are made in a similar manner.

6. The final balance in the sinking fund will probably be slightly different from the expected value. This difference is a result of rounding. The balance may be left as shown ($20 000.02) or the exact balance of $20 000.00 may be obtained by adjusting the last payment to $2249.11.

7. The three totals shown are useful and should be obtained for each schedule. The total increase in the fund must be the same as the final balance. The total periodic payments are $8(2249.13) = \$17\,993.04$. The total interest is the difference: $20\,000.02 - 17\,993.04 = \$2006.98$.

EXAMPLE 15.5D	Construct a sinking fund schedule for Example 15.5B (an annuity due with payments at the beginning of each payment interval).

SOLUTION

PMT = 7159.89 (made at the beginning); $n = 7$; $i = 4.5\% = 0.045$

Sinking fund schedule for annuity payments at the beginning of payment interval

Payment Interval Number	Periodic Payment	Interest for Payment Interval $i = 0.045$	Increase in Fund	Balance in Fund at the End of Payment Interval
0				$ 0
1	$ 7159.89	$ 322.20	$ 7482.09	7482.09
2	7159.89	658.89	7818.78	15 300.86
3	7159.89	1010.73	8170.62	23 471.49
4	7159.89	1378.41	8538.30	32 009.79
5	7159.89	1762.64	8922.53	40 932.32
6	7159.89	2164.15	9324.04	50 256.35
7	7159.89	2583.73	9743.62	$59 999.98
TOTAL	$ 50 119.23	$9880.75	$59 999.98	

Explanations regarding the construction of the sinking fund schedule

1. The starting balance is $0.

2. The first deposit is made at the beginning of the first payment interval and the interest earned by the fund during the first payment interval is $0.045(7159.89) = \$322.20$. The increase in the fund is $7159.89 + 322.20 = \$7482.09$, and the balance is $7482.09.

3. The second deposit is made at the beginning of the second payment interval, the interest earned is $0.045(7482.09 + 7159.89) = \$658.89$, the increase is $7159.89 + 658.89 = \$7818.78$, and the balance is $7482.09 + 7818.78 = \$15\,300.86$.

4. The third deposit is made at the beginning of the third payment interval, the interest earned is $0.045(15\,300.86 + 7159.89) = \$1010.73$, the increase is $7159.89 + 1010.73 = \$8170.62$, and the balance is $15\,300.86 + 8170.62 = \$23\,471.49$.

5. Calculations for the remaining payment intervals are made in a similar manner. Be careful to add the deposit to the previous balance when computing the interest earned.

6. The final balance of $\$59\,999.98$ is slightly different from the expected balance of $\$60\,000.00$ due to rounding. The exact balance may be obtained by adjusting the last payment to $\$7159.91$.

7. The total increase in the fund must equal the final balance of $\$59\,999.98$. The total periodic payments are $7(7159.89) = \$50\,119.23$. The total interest is $\$59\,999.98 - 50\,119.23 = \$9880.75$.

C. Determining the accumulated balance and interest earned or increase in a sinking fund for a payment interval; constructing partial sinking fund schedules

EXAMPLE 15.5E

In Example 15.5A, Western Oil plans to create a sinking fund of $20 000 to replace a pick-up truck by making equal deposits at the end of every six months for four years. Interest is 6% compounded semi-annually. Compute

(i) the accumulated value in the fund at the end of the third payment interval;

(ii) the interest earned by the fund in the fifth payment interval;

(iii) the increase in the fund in the fifth interval.

SOLUTION

(i) The balance in a sinking fund at any time is the accumulated value of the payments made into the fund.

In this example, payments are made at the end of each payment interval.

$$\text{PMT} = 2249.13; \quad n = 3; \quad i = 3\%$$

$$\text{FV}_n = 2249.13\left(\frac{1.03^3 - 1}{0.03}\right)$$
$$= 2249.13(3.0909)$$
$$= \$6951.83 \text{ ————————— see sinking fund schedule, Example 15.5C}$$

PROGRAMMED SOLUTION

("END" mode)

(Set P/Y = 2; C/Y = 2) 0 [PV] 2249.13 [±] [PMT] 6 [I/Y]

3 [N] [CPT] [FV] [6951.835917]

(ii) The interest earned during any given payment interval is based on the balance in the fund at the beginning of the interval.

The balance at the beginning of the fifth payment interval is equal to the balance at the end of the fourth payment interval.

$$FV_4 = 2249.13\left(\frac{1.03^4 - 1}{0.03}\right)$$

$$= 2249.13(4.183627)$$

$$= \$9409.52$$

PROGRAMMED SOLUTION

("END mode")

(Set P/Y = 2; C/Y = 2) 0 [PV] 2249.13 [±] [PMT]

6 [I/Y] 4 [N] [CPT] [FV] 9409.520995

The interest earned by the fund in the fifth payment interval is
$0.03(9409.52) = \$282.29$.

(iii) The increase in the sinking fund in any given payment interval is the interest earned by the fund during the payment interval plus the periodic payment.

The increase in the fund during the fifth payment interval is
$282.29 + 2249.13 = \$2531.42$.

EXAMPLE 15.5F

The board of directors of National Credit Union decided to establish a building fund of \$130 000 by making equal deposits into a sinking fund at the end of every three months for seven years. Interest is 12% compounded quarterly.

(i) Compute the increase in the fund during the twelfth payment interval.

(ii) Construct a partial sinking fund schedule showing details of the first three deposits, the 12th deposit, the last three deposits, and totals.

SOLUTION

Size of the quarterly deposit:

$$FV_n = 130\,000.00; \quad P/Y = 4; \quad C/Y = 4; \quad I/Y = 12$$

$$n = 7(4) = 28; \quad i = \frac{12\%}{4} = 3\%$$

$$130\,000.00 = PMT\left(\frac{1.03^{28} - 1}{0.03}\right)$$

$$130\,000.00 = PMT(42.930922)$$

$$PMT = \$3028.12$$

PROGRAMMED SOLUTION

("END" mode)

(Set P/Y = 4; C/Y = 4) 0 [PV] 130 000 [FV] 12 [I/Y]

28 [N] [CPT] [PMT] −3028.120347

(i) Balance in the fund at the end of the 11th payment interval

$$FV_n = 3028.12\left(\frac{1.03^{11} - 1}{0.03}\right)$$

$$= 3028.12(12.807796)$$

$$= \$38\ 783.54$$

PROGRAMMED SOLUTION

("END" mode)

(Set $P/Y = 4; C/Y = 4$) 0 PV 3028.12 ± PMT

12 I/Y 11 N CPT FV 38783.54229

The interest earned by the fund during the 12th payment interval is $0.03(38\ 783.54) = \$1163.51$.

The increase in the fund during the 12th payment interval is $1163.51 + 3028.12 = \$4191.63$.

(ii) The last three payments are Payments 26, 27, and 28. To show details of these, we must know the accumulated value after 25 payment intervals.

$$FV_{25} = 3028.12\left(\frac{1.03^{25} - 1}{0.03}\right) = 3028.12(36.459264) = \$110\ 403.03$$

PROGRAMMED SOLUTION

("END" mode)

(Set $P/Y = 4; C/Y = 4$) 0 PV 3028.12 ± PMT

12 I/Y 25 N CPT FV 110403.0275

Partial sinking fund schedule

Payment Interval Number	Periodic Payment Made at End	Interest for Payment Interval $i = 0.03$	Increase in Fund	Balance in Fund at End of Payment Interval
0				$ 0.00
1	$ 3028.12	$ 0.00	$ 3028.12	3028.12
2	3028.12	90.84	3118.96	6147.08
3	3028.12	184.41	3212.53	9359.61
•	•	•	•	•
•	•	•	•	•
11	•	•	•	38 783.54
12	3028.12	1163.51	4191.63	42 975.17
•	•	•	•	•
•	•	•	•	•
25	•	•	•	110 403.03
26	3028.12	3312.09	6340.21	116 743.24
27	3028.12	3502.30	6530.42	123 273.66
28	3028.12	3698.21	6726.33	$129 999.99
TOTAL	$84 787.36	$45 212.63	$129 999.99	

EXAMPLE 15.5G

Laurin and Company want to build up a fund of $75 000 to replace the company's air conditioning system by making payments of $2000 at the beginning of every six months into a sinking fund earning 11% compounded semi-annually. Construct a partial sinking fund schedule showing details of the first three payments, the last three payments, and totals.

SOLUTION

To show details of the last three payments, we need to know the number of payments.

$FV_n(\text{due}) = 75\,000.00; \quad PMT = 2000.00; \quad P/Y = 2; \quad C/Y = 2; \quad I/Y = 11;$

$i = \dfrac{11\%}{2} = 5.5\%$

$75\,000.00 = 2000.00(1.055)\left(\dfrac{1.055^n - 1}{0.055}\right)$

$1.055^n = 2.954976$

$n \ln 1.055 = \ln 2.954976$

$n\,(0.053541) = 1.0834906$

$n = 20.236741 = 21 \text{ payments}$

PROGRAMMED SOLUTION

("BGN" mode)

(Set P/Y = 2; C/Y = 2) 0 [PV] 75 000 [FV] 2000 [±] [PMT]

11 [I/Y] [CPT] [N] [20.236741]

Twenty-one payments are needed. The last three payments are Payments 19, 20, and 21. The balance in the fund at the end of the 18th payment interval

$FV_{18}(\text{due}) = 2000.00(1.055)\left(\dfrac{1.055^{18} - 1}{0.055}\right)$

$= 2000.00(1.055)(29.481205)$

$= \$62\,205.34$

PROGRAMMED SOLUTION

("BGN" mode)

(Set P/Y = 2; C/Y = 2) 0 [PV] 2000 [±] [PMT]

11 [I/Y] 18 [N] [CPT] [FV] [62 205.3422]

Partial sinking fund schedule

Payment Interval Number	Periodic Payment Made at Beginning	Interest for Payment Interval $i = 0.055$	Increase in Fund	Balance in Fund at End of Payment Interval
0				$ 0.00
1	$ 2000.00	$ 110.00	$ 2110.00	2110.00
2	2000.00	226.05	2226.05	4336.05
3	2000.00	348.48	2348.48	6684.53
•	•	•	•	•
•	•	•	•	•
18	•	•	•	62 205.34
19	2000.00	3531.29	5531.29	67 736.63
20	2000.00	3835.51	5835.51	73 572.14
21	1427.86	0.00	1427.86	$75 000.00
TOTAL	$41 427.86	$33 572.14	$75 000.00	

Note: The desired balance in the sinking fund will be reached at the beginning of the 21st payment interval by depositing $1427.86.

D. Computer application—sinking fund schedule

The schedule in Example 15.5C displays the manual calculations for a sinking fund with an interest rate of 3% and eight periodic payments. Microsoft Excel and other spreadsheet programs can be used to create a file that will immediately display the results of a change in the interest rate, the increase in the fund, and the accumulated balance.

The following steps are general instructions for creating a file to calculate the sinking fund schedule in Example 15.5C. The formulas in the spreadsheet file were created using Excel; however, most spreadsheet software works similarly.

Although this exercise assumes a basic understanding of spreadsheet applications, someone without previous experience with spreadsheets will be able to complete it.

STEP 1   Enter the labels shown in Figure 15.2 in row 1 and in columns A through E.

STEP 2   Enter the numbers shown in cells E2, F2, and F4. These are the beginning balance, periodic payment, and periodic interest rate. Do not type in a dollar sign or a comma.

STEP 3   Enter only the formulas shown in cells B3, C3, D3, and E3. Make sure that the formula entry includes the dollar ($) sign as shown in the figure.

STEP 4   The formulas entered in Step 3 can be copied through the remaining cells.
(a) Select and Copy the formulas in cells B3, C3, D3, and E3.
(b) Select cells B4 to D10 and then Paste.
(c) The formulas are now active in all the cells.

STEP 5   Enter the formula shown in cell B11, and then use Copy and Paste to enter the formula in cells C11 and D11.

Figure 15.2 Sinking Fund Schedule Functions in Excel Spreadsheet (© S. A. Hummelbrunner)

	A	B	C	D	E	F
1	Payment number	Amount paid	Interest paid	Principal repaid	Outstanding principal balance	
2	0				0	2249.13
3	1	=$F$2	=$F$4*E2	=B3+C3	=E2+D3	
4	2	=$F$2	=$F$4*E3	=B4+C4	=E3+D4	0.03
5	3	=$F$2	=$F$4*E4	=B5+C5	=E4+D5	
6	4	=$F$2	=$F$4*E5	=B6+C6	=E5+D6	
7	5	=$F$2	=$F$4*E6	=B7+C7	=E6+D7	
8	6	=$F$2	=$F$4*E7	=B8+C8	=E7+D8	
9	7	=$F$2	=$F$4*E8	=B9+C9	=E8+D9	
10	8	=$F$2	=$F$4*E9	=B10+C10	=E9+D10	
11	Total	=SUM(B3:B10)	=SUM(C3:C10)	=SUM(D3:D10)		

STEP 6 To ensure readability of the spreadsheet, format the numbers to display in two decimal places, and widen the columns to display the full labels. This spreadsheet can now be used to reflect changes in aspects of the sinking fund and create a new schedule. Use cell F2 for new payment amounts and cell F4 for new interest rates. Figure 15.3 illustrates the result of formulating Example 15.5C in Excel.

Figure 15.3 Sinking Fund Schedule Results in Excel Spreadsheet (© S. A. Hummelbrunner)

	A	B	C	D	E	F
1	Payment number	Periodic payment	Interest earned	Increase in fund	Balance at end	
2	0				0	2249.1
3	1	2249.13	0.00	2249.13	2249.13	
4	2	2249.13	67.47	2316.60	4565.73	0.03
5	3	2249.13	136.97	2386.10	6951.84	
6	4	2249.13	208.56	2457.69	9409.52	
7	5	2249.13	282.29	2531.42	11940.94	
8	6	2249.13	358.23	2607.36	14548.29	
9	7	2249.13	436.45	2685.58	17233.87	
10	8	2249.13	517.02	2766.15	20000.02	
11	Total	17993.04	2006.98	20000.02		

E. Debt retirement by the sinking fund method

When a sinking fund is created to retire a debt, the debt principal is repaid in total at the due date from the proceeds of the sinking fund while interest on the principal is paid periodically. The payments into the sinking fund are usually made at the same time as the interest payments are made. The sum of the two payments (debt interest payment plus payment into the sinking fund) is called the **periodic cost of the debt**. The difference between the debt principal and the sinking fund balance at any point is called the **book value of the debt**.

POINTERS & PITFALLS

When a debt is retired by the sinking fund method, the borrower is, in effect, paying two separate annuities. Sinking fund installments are made to the fund's trustee, while periodic interest payments are made to the lender. Because of these two payment streams, two interest rates must be quoted in questions involving sinking fund debt retirement. One rate determines the *interest revenue* generated by the sinking fund, and the other rate determines the *interest penalty* paid by the borrower to the lender.

EXAMPLE 15.5H

The City Board of Education borrowed $750 000 for 20 years at 13% compounded annually to finance construction of Hillview Elementary School. The board created a sinking fund to repay the debt at the end of 20 years. Equal payments are made into the sinking fund at the end of each year, and interest earned by the fund is 10.5% compounded annually. Rounding all computations to the nearest dollar,

  (i) determine the annual cost of the debt;

 (ii) compute the book value of the debt at the end of 10 years;

(iii) construct a partial sinking fund schedule showing the book value of the debt, the first three payments, the last three payments, and totals.

SOLUTION

  (i) The annual interest cost on the principal:

$$PV = 750\ 000; \quad P/Y = 1; \quad C/Y = 1; \quad I/Y = 13; \quad i = 13\% = 0.13;$$
$$I = 750\ 000(0.13) = \$97\ 500$$

The annual payment into the sinking fund

$$FV_n = 750\ 000; \quad n = 20; \quad I/Y = 10.5; \quad i = 10.5\%$$

$$750\ 000 = PMT\left(\frac{1.105^{20} - 1}{0.105}\right)$$

$$750\ 000 = PMT(60.630808)$$

$$PMT = \$12\ 369.95 \text{ (Rounded to the nearest dollar, PMT} = \$12\ 370.)$$

PROGRAMMED SOLUTION

("END" mode)

(Set P/Y = 1; C/Y = 1) 0 [PV] 750 000 [FV] 10.5 [I/Y]

20 [N] [CPT] [PMT] [−12369.94895]

The annual cost of the debt is 97 500 + 12 370 = $109 870.

 (ii) The balance in the sinking fund after the 10th payment

$$FV_{10} = 12\ 370\left(\frac{1.105^{10} - 1}{0.105}\right)$$

$$= 12\ 370(16.324579)$$

$$= \$201\ 935.05$$

PROGRAMMED SOLUTION

("END" mode)

(Set P/Y = 1; C/Y = 1) 0 [PV] 12 370 [±] [PMT] 10.5 [I/Y]

10 [N] [CPT] [FV] [201935.0483]

The book value of the debt at the end of the 10th year is 750 000 − 201 935.05 = $548 064.95 (Rounded to the nearest dollar, the book value of the debt at the end of the 10th year equals $548 065.)

(iii) The last three payments are Payments 18, 19, and 20. The balance in the sinking fund at the end of Year 17

$$FV_{17} = 12\,370\left(\frac{1.105^{17} - 1}{0.105}\right) = 12\,370(42.47213) = \$525\,380.24 \quad \text{(Rounded to \$528 380)}$$

PROGRAMMED SOLUTION

("END" mode)

(Set P/Y = 1; C/Y = 1) 0 [PV] 12 370 [±] [PMT]

10.5 [I/Y] 17 [N] [CPT] [FV] [525380.2441]

Partial sinking fund schedule (rounded to the nearest dollar)

Payment Interval Number	Periodic Payment Made at End	Interest for Payment Interval $i = 0.105$	Increase in Fund	Balance in Fund at End of Payment Interval	Book Value of Debt
0				$ 0	$750 000
1	$ 12 370	$ 0	$ 12 370	12 370	737 630
2	12 370	1299	13 669	26 039	723 961
3	12 370	2734	15 104	41 143	708 857
•	•	•	•	•	•
•	•	•	•	•	•
17	•	•	•	525 380	224 620
18	12 370	55 165	67 535	592 915	157 085
19	12 370	62 256	74 626	667 541	82 459
20	12 367	70 092	82 459	$750 000	$ 0
TOTAL	$247 397	$502 603	$750 000		

Note: The last payment has been adjusted to create a fund of exactly $750 000.

EXERCISE 15.5

MyLab Math

If you choose, you can use Excel's Periodic Payment Size (PMT) functions to answer the questions indicated next.

Answer each of the following questions.

1. Hein Engineering expects to expand its plant facilities in six years at an estimated cost of $75 000. To provide for the expansion, a sinking fund has been established

into which equal payments are made at the end of every three months. Interest is 4% compounded quarterly.

(a) What is the size of the quarterly payments?

(b) How much of the maturity value will be payments?

(c) How much interest will the fund contain?

2. To redeem a $100 000 promissory note due in 10 years, Cobblestone Enterprises has set up a sinking fund earning 5.5% compounded semi-annually. Equal deposits are made at the beginning of every six months.

(a) What is the size of the semi-annual deposits?

(b) How much of the maturity value of the fund is deposits?

(c) How much is interest?

3. Equal deposits are made into a sinking fund at the end of each year for seven years. Interest is 5.5% compounded annually, and the maturity value of the fund is $20 000. Calculate the size of the annual deposits and construct a sinking fund schedule showing totals.

4. A sinking fund amounting to $15 000 is to be created by making payments at the beginning of every six months for four years. Interest earned by the fund is 12.5% compounded semi-annually. Determine the size of the semi-annual payments and prepare a sinking fund schedule showing totals.

5. For Question 3, calculate the increase in the fund for the fourth year. Verify your answer by checking the sinking fund schedule.

6. For Question 4, compute the interest earned during the fifth payment interval. Verify your answer by checking the sinking fund schedule.

7. HY Industries Ltd. plans to replace a warehouse in 12 years at an anticipated cost of $45 000. To pay for the replacement, a sinking fund has been established into which equal payments are made at the end of every quarter. Interest is 8% compounded quarterly.

(a) What is the size of the quarterly payments?

(b) What is the accumulated balance just after the 16th payment?

8. To provide for expansion, Champlain Company has established a sinking fund earning 7% semi-annually. The fund is anticipated to reach a balance of $72 000 in 15 years. Payments are made at the beginning of every 6 months.

(a) What is the size of the semi-annual payment?

(b) What is the accumulated balance at the end of the 20th payment period?

9. Winooski Lamp Co. borrowed $95 000 for capital expansion. The company must pay the interest on the loan at the end of every 6 months and make equal payments at the time of the interest payments into a sinking fund until the loan is retired in 20 years. Interest on the loan is 9% compounded semi-annually, and interest on the sinking fund is 7% compounded semi-annually. (Round all answers to the nearest dollar.)

(a) Determine the size of the periodic interest expense of the debt.

(b) Determine the size of the periodic payment into the sinking fund.

(c) What is the periodic cost of the debt?

(d) What is the book value of the debt after 15 years?

10. The City of Chatham borrowed $80 000 to expand a community centre. The city must pay the interest on the loan at the end of every month and make equal payments at the time of the interest payments into a sinking fund until the loan is retired in 12 years. Interest on the loan is 6% compounded monthly and interest on

the sinking fund is 7.5% compounded monthly. (Round all answers to the nearest dollar.)

(a) Determine the size of the periodic interest expense of the debt.

(b) Determine the size of the periodic payment into the sinking fund.

(c) What is the periodic cost of the debt?

(d) What is the book value of the debt after 8 years?

11. Kirk, Klein & Co. requires $100 000 fifteen years from now to retire a debt. A sinking fund is established into which equal payments are made at the end of every month. Interest is 7.5% compounded monthly.

(a) What is the size of the monthly payment?

(b) What is the balance in the sinking fund after five years?

(c) How much interest will be earned by the fund in the 100th payment interval?

(d) By how much will the fund increase during the 150th payment interval?

(e) Construct a partial sinking fund schedule showing details of the first three payments, the last three payments, and totals.

12. The Town of Keewatin issued debentures worth $120 000 maturing in 10 years to finance construction of water and sewer facilities. To redeem the debentures, the town council decided to make equal deposits into a sinking fund at the beginning of every three months. Interest earned by the sinking fund is 6% compounded quarterly.

(a) What is the size of the quarterly payment into the sinking fund?

(b) What is the balance in the fund after six years?

(c) How much interest is earned by the fund in the 28th payment interval?

(d) By how much will the fund increase in the 33rd payment interval?

(e) Prepare a partial sinking fund schedule showing details of the first three payments, the last three payments, and totals.

13. The Township of Langley borrowed $300 000 for road improvements. The debt agreement requires that the township pay the interest on the loan at the end of each year and make equal deposits at the time of the interest payments into a sinking fund until the loan is retired in 20 years. Interest on the loan is 8.25% compounded annually, and interest earned by the sinking fund is 5.5% compounded annually. (Round all answers to the nearest dollar.)

(a) What is the annual interest expense?

(b) What is the size of the annual deposit into the sinking fund?

(c) What is the total annual cost of the debt?

(d) How much is the increase in the sinking fund in the 10th year?

(e) What is the book value of the debt after 15 years?

(f) Construct a partial sinking fund schedule showing details, including the book value of the debt, for the first three years, the last three years, and totals.

14. Ontario Credit Union borrowed $225 000 at 13% compounded semi-annually from League Central to build an office complex. The loan agreement requires payment of interest at the end of every 6 months. In addition, the credit union is to make equal payments into a sinking fund so that the principal can be retired in total after 15 years. Interest earned by the fund is 11% compounded semi-annually. (Round all answers to the nearest dollar.)

(a) What is the semi-annual interest payment on the debt?

(b) What is the size of the semi-annual deposits into the sinking fund?

(c) What is the total annual cost of the debt?

(d) What is the interest earned by the fund in the 20th payment interval?

(e) What is the book value of the debt after 12 years?

(f) Prepare a partial sinking fund schedule showing details, including the book value of the debt, for the first three years, the last three years, and totals.

MyLab Math Visit MyLab Math to practise any of this chapter's exercises marked with a 🌐 as often as you want. The guided solutions help you calculate an answer step by step. You'll find a personalized study plan and additional interactive resources to help you master Business Math!

REVIEW EXERCISE

1. **LO❶❷** A $5000, 4.5% bond with interest payable semi-annually is redeemable at par in 12 years. What is the purchase price to yield

   (a) 3% compounded semi-annually?

   (b) 5% compounded semi-annually?

🌐 2. **LO❶❷** A $10 000, 6% bond with semi-annual coupons is redeemable at par. What is the purchase price to yield 7.5% compounded semi-annually

   (a) 9 years before maturity?

   (b) 15 years before maturity?

3. **LO❷** A $25 000, 9% bond with interest payable quarterly is redeemable at par in six years. What is the purchase price to yield 8.25% compounded annually?

🌐 4. **LO❷** A $1000, 9.5% bond with semi-annual coupons redeemable at par on March 1, 2026, was purchased on September 19, 2017, to yield 7% compounded semi-annually. What was the purchase price?

5. **LO❷** Four $5000, 7% bonds with semi-annual coupons are bought seven years before maturity to yield 6% compounded semi-annually. Calculate the premium or discount and the purchase price if the bonds are redeemable at par.

🌐 6. **LO❶❷** Nine $1000, 8% bonds with interest payable semi-annually and redeemable at par are purchased 10 years before maturity. Calculate the premium or discount and the purchase price if the bonds are bought to yield

   (a) 6%;

   (b) 8%;

   (c) 10%.

7. **LO❷** A $100 000, 5% bond with interest payable semi-annually redeemable at par on July 15, 2031, was purchased on April 18, 2020, to yield 7% compounded semi-annually. Determine

   (a) the premium or discount;

   (b) the purchase price.

🌐 8. **LO❷** Four $10 000 bonds bearing interest at 6% payable quarterly and redeemable at par on September 1, 2028, were purchased on January 23, 2016, to yield 5% compounded quarterly. Determine

   (a) the premium or discount;

   (b) the purchase price.

9. **LO❷** A $5000, 8% bond with semi-annual coupons redeemable at par in 10 years is purchased to yield 10% compounded semi-annually. What is the purchase price?

🌐 10. **LO❷** A $1000 bond bearing interest at 8% payable semi-annually redeemable at par on February 1, 2024, was purchased on October 12, 2017, to yield 7% compounded semi-annually. Determine the purchase price.

11. **LO❸** A $50 000, 11% bond with semi-annual coupons redeemable at par on April 15, 2026, was purchased on June 25, 2019, at 92.375. What was the approximate yield rate?

🌐 12. **LO❸** A $1000, 8.5% bond with interest payable annually is purchased six years before maturity to yield 10.5% compounded annually. Compute the premium or discount and the purchase price, and construct the appropriate bond schedule.

13. **LO❸** A $5000, 4% bond with interest payable annually, redeemable at par in seven years, is purchased to yield 4.75% compounded annually. Calculate the premium or discount and the purchase price, and construct the appropriate bond schedule.

🌐 14. **LO❸** Three $25 000, 11% bonds with semi-annual coupons redeemable at par were bought eight years before maturity to yield 12% compounded semi-annually. Determine the gain or loss if the bonds are sold at 89.375 five years later.

15. **LO❸** A $10 000 bond with 5% interest payable quarterly, redeemable at par on November 15, 2034, was bought on July 2, 2018, to yield 9% compounded quarterly. If the bond sells at 92.75 on September 10, 2024, what would the gain or loss on the sale be?

16. **LO④** A $25 000, 9.5% bond with semi-annual coupons redeemable at par is bought 16 years before maturity at 78.25. What was the approximate yield rate?

17. **LO④** A $10 000, 7.5% bond with quarterly coupons, redeemable at par on October 15, 2032, was purchased on May 5, 2020, at 98.75. What is the approximate yield rate?

18. **LO④** What is the approximate yield realized if the bond in Question 17 sells at 92 on August 7, 2025?

19. **LO④** A 6.5% bond of $50 000 with interest payable quarterly is to be redeemable at par in 12 years.

   (a) What purchase price would yield 8% compounded quarterly?

   (b) What is the book value after 9 years?

   (c) What is the gain or loss if the bond is sold 9 years after the date of purchase at 99.625?

20. **LO④** A $5000, 14.5% bond with semi-annual coupons redeemable at par on August 1, 2030, was purchased on March 5, 2019, at 95.5. What was the approximate yield rate?

21. Suppose the total bond issue by Space Limited Company was $150 000 000 and they set up a sinking fund on December 22, 2021, for 20 years. Sinking funds are accounts that companies establish to ensure certain amounts of money will be available at a given future date (refer to section 15.5 for information about sinking funds). If the rate of interest is 3.49 percent compounded semi-annually and they make annual end of year payments into the fund:

   (a) What is the required annual end-of-year payment for Space Limited Company?

   (b) Complete the following table for the Space Limited Company's sinking fund for each of the payments shown:

Payment Numbers	Payment Amount	Interest Earned on Fund	Total Increase in Fund	Balance in Fund
11				
12				
13				

22. Suppose the total bond issue by Telus Corp. was $155 000 000 and they set up a sinking fund on issue date at July 23, 2015, for 25 years. Sinking funds are accounts that companies establish to ensure certain amounts of money will be available at a given future date (refer to section 15.5 for information about sinking funds). If the rate of interest is 2.85 percent compounded semi-annually and they make annual end of year payments into the fund:

   (a) What is the required annual end-of-year payment for Telus Corp.?

   (b) Complete the following table for the Telus Corp.'s sinking fund for each of the payments shown:

Payment Numbers	Payment Amount	Interest Earned on Fund	Total Increase in Fund	Balance in Fund
17				
18				
19				

23. Suppose you are considering investing in a Telus Corp. corporate bond with a $15 000 face value maturing on July 23, 2024. The bond's coupon or bond rate is 5.05 percent and interest is paid semi-annually. The current required market rate or yield to market (YTM) for a bond of this type is 2.74 percent.

   (a) Carefully explain if and why this bond should sell at par, at a premium, or at a discount.

   (b) Determine the purchase price or "clean price" for this bond if the purchase was made on July 23, 2018.

   (c) Determine the cash price or "dirty price" for this bond if the purchase is instead made on September 28, 2018.

24. Mona is considering investing in a Sun Life Financial Inc. corporate bond with a $25 000 face value maturing on December 22, 2032. The bond's coupon or bond rate is 6.25 percent and interest is paid semi-annually. The current required market rate or yield for a bond of this type is 5.42 percent. Use the bond function of the Texas Instrument BA II PLUS calculator to determine the purchase price of the bond on June 22, 2026.

25. Moji is considering investing in a Manulife Financial corporate bond with a $20 000 face value maturing on December 15, 2034. The bond's coupon or bond rate is 7.25 percent and interest is paid semi-annually. The current required market rate or yield for a bond of this type is 4.55 percent. Use the bond function of the Texas Instrument BA II PLUS calculator to determine the purchase price of the bond on July 22, 2022.

26. **LO7** To provide for the purchase of heavy construction equipment estimated to cost $110 000, Valmar Construction is paying equal sums of money at the end of every six months for five years into a sinking fund earning 7.5% compounded semi-annually.

   (a) What is the size of the semi-annual payment into the sinking fund?

   (b) Compute the balance in the fund after the third payment.

   (c) Compute the amount of interest earned between the fifth and the sixth payments.

   (d) Construct a sinking fund schedule showing totals. Check your answers to parts (b) and (c) with the values in the schedule.

27. **LO7** Alpha Corporation is depositing equal sums of money at the beginning of every three months into a sinking fund to redeem a $65 000 promissory note due eight years from now. Interest earned by the fund is 12% compounded quarterly.

   (a) Determine the size of the equal payments into the sinking fund.

   (b) Compute the balance in the fund after three years.

   (c) Compute the increase in the fund during the 24th payment interval.

   (d) Construct a partial sinking fund schedule showing details of the first three deposits, the last three deposits, and totals.

28. **LO7** The municipality of Kirkfield borrowed $100 000 to build a recreation centre. The debt principal is to be repaid in eight years, and interest at 13.75% compounded annually is to be paid annually. To provide for the retirement of the debt, the municipal council set up a sinking fund into which equal payments are made at the time of annual interest payments. Interest earned by the fund is 11.5% compounded annually.

   (a) What is the annual interest payment?

   (b) What is the size of the annual payment into the sinking fund?

   (c) What is the total annual cost of the debt?

   (d) Compute the book value of the debt after three years.

   (e) Compute the interest earned by the fund in year 6.

   (f) Construct a sinking fund schedule showing the book value of the debt and totals. Verify your computations in parts (d) and (e) against the schedule.

29. **LO7** The Harrow Board of Education financed the acquisition of a building site through a $300 000 long-term promissory note due in 15 years, Interest on the promissory note is 9.25% compounded semi-annually and is payable at the end of every six months. To provide for the redemption of the note, the Board agreed to make equal payments at the end of every six months into a sinking fund paying 8% compounded semi-annually. (Round all answers to nearest dollar.)

   (a) What is the semi-annual interest payment?

   (b) What is the size of the semi-annual payment into the sinking fund?

   (c) What is the annual cost of the debt?

   (d) Compute the book value of the debt after 5 years.

   (e) Compute the increase in the sinking fund in the 20th payment interval.

   (f) Construct a partial sinking fund schedule showing details, including the book value of the debt, for the first three years, the last three years, and totals.

30. **LO8** Northern Flying Service is preparing to buy an aircraft estimated to cost $600 000 by making equal payments at the end of every three months into a sinking fund for five years. Interest earned by the fund is 8% compounded quarterly.

   (a) What is the size of the quarterly payment made to the sinking fund?

   (b) How much of the maturity value of the fund will be interest?

   (c) What is the accumulated value of the fund after two years?

   (d) How much interest will the fund earn in the 15th payment interval?

31. **LO8** A sinking fund of $10 000 is to be created by equal annual payments at the beginning of each year for seven years. Interest earned by the fund is 7.5% compounded annually.

   (a) Compute the annual deposits into the fund.

   (b) Construct a sinking fund schedule showing totals.

32. LO8 Joe Ngosa bought a retirement fund for $150 000. Beginning 25 years from the date of purchase, he will receive payments of $35 000 at the beginning of every six months. Interest earned by the fund is 6% compounded semi-annually.

(a) How many payments will Joe receive?

(b) What is the size of the last payment?

🌐 **33. LO8** The town of Kildern bought firefighting equipment for $96 000. The financing agreement provides for annual interest payments and equal payments into a sinking fund for 10 years. After 10 years the proceeds of the sinking fund will be used to retire the principal. Interest on the debt is 14.5% compounded annually, and interest earned by the sinking fund is 13% compounded annually.

(a) What is the annual interest payment?

(b) What is the size of the annual payment into the sinking fund?

(c) What is the total annual cost of the debt?

(d) What is the book value of the debt after 4 years?

(e) Construct a partial sinking fund schedule showing details, including the book value of the debt for the last three years and totals.

SELF-TEST

1. A $10 000, 10% bond with quarterly coupons redeemable at par in 15 years is purchased to yield 11% compounded quarterly. Determine the purchase price of the bond.

2. What is the purchase price of a $1000, 7.5% bond with semi-annual coupons redeemable at par in 10 years if the bond is bought to yield 6% compounded semi-annually?

3. A $5000, 8% bond with semi-annual coupons redeemable at par is bought six years before maturity to yield 6.5% compounded semi-annually. Determine the premium or discount.

4. A $20 000, 10% bond with semi-annual coupons redeemable at par March 1, 2025, was purchased on November 15, 2018, to yield 9% compounded semi-annually. What was the purchase price of the bond?

5. A $5000, 7% bond with semi-annual coupons redeemable at par on December 15, 2030, was purchased on November 9, 2019, to yield 8.5% compounded semi-annually. Determine the cash price.

6. A $5000, 5.5% bond with semi-annual coupons redeemable at par is bought four years before maturity to yield 7% compounded semi-annually. Construct a bond schedule.

7. A $100 000, 13% bond with semi-annual interest payments redeemable at par on July 15, 2026, is bought on September 10, 2019, at 102.625. What was the approximate yield rate?

8. A $25 000, 6% bond with semi-annual coupons redeemable at par in 20 years is purchased to yield 8% compounded semi-annually. Determine the gain or loss if the bond is sold 7 years after the date of purchase at 98.25.

9. A $10 000, 12% bond with semi-annual coupons redeemable at par on December 1, 2028, was purchased on July 20, 2017, at 93.875. Compute the approximate yield rate.

10. Annual sinking fund payments made at the beginning of every year for six years, earning 9.5% compounded annually, amount to $25 000 at the end of six years. Construct a sinking fund schedule showing totals.

11. Annual sinking fund payments made at the end of every year for six years, earning 4.5% compounded annually, amount to $25 000 at the end of six years. Construct a sinking fund schedule showing totals.

CHALLENGE PROBLEMS

1. A $2000 bond with annual coupons is redeemable at par in five years. If the first coupon is $400, and subsequent annual coupons are each worth 75% of the previous year's coupon, calculate the purchase price of the bond that would yield an interest rate of 10% compounded annually.

2. An issue of bonds, redeemable at par in n years, is to bear coupons at 9% compounded semi-annually. An investor offers to buy the entire issue at a premium of 15%. At the same time, the investor advises that if the coupon rate were raised to 10% compounded semi-annually, he would offer to buy the whole issue at a premium of 25%. At what yield rate compounded semi-annually are these two offers equivalent? (*Hint:* consider a bond certificate of $1000 and use Formula 15.1 to do the calculations for each offer.)

CASE STUDY ▶ Raising Capital Through Bonds

▶ ScanSoft Development Company is developing a new process to manufacture optical disks. The development costs were higher than expected, so ScanSoft required an immediate cash inflow of $5 200 000. To raise the required capital, the company decided to issue bonds. Since ScanSoft had no expertise in issuing and selling bonds, the company decided to work with an investment dealer. The investment dealer bought the company's entire bond issue at a discount, and then planned to sell the bonds to the public at face value or the current market value. To ensure it would raise the $5 200 000 it required, ScanSoft issued 5200 bonds with a face value of $1000 each on January 20, 2020. Interest is paid semi-annually on July 20 and January 20, beginning July 20, 2020. The bonds pay interest at 5.5% compounded semi-annually.

ScanSoft directors realize that when the bonds mature on January 20, 2040, there must be $5 200 000 available to repay the bondholders. To have enough money on hand to meet this obligation, the directors set up a sinking fund (see section 15.5 for a review of sinking funds) using a specially designated savings account. The company earns interest of 1.6% compounded semi-annually on this sinking fund account. The directors began making semi-annual payments to the sinking fund on July 20, 2020.

ScanSoft Development Company issued the bonds, sold them all to the investment dealer, and used the money raised to continue its research and development.

QUESTIONS

1. How much would an investor have to pay for one of these bonds to earn 4.4% compounded semi-annually?

2. **(a)** What is the size of the sinking fund payment?
   (b) What will be the total amount deposited into the sinking fund account would be by January 2040?
   (c) How much of the sinking fund will be interest?

3. Suppose ScanSoft discovers on January 20, 2030, that it can earn 2.5% interest compounded semi-annually on its sinking fund account.
   (a) What is the balance in the sinking fund after the January 20, 2030, sinking fund payment?
   (b) What is the new sinking fund payment if the fund begins to earn 2.5% on January 21, 2030?
   (c) What will be the total amount deposited into the sinking fund account over the life of the bonds?
   (d) How much of the sinking fund will then be interest?

SUMMARY OF FORMULAS

Formula 15.1

$$PP = FV(1 + i)^{-n} + PMT\left[\frac{1 - (1 + i)^{-n}}{i}\right]$$

Basic formula for calculating the purchase price of a bond when the interest payment interval and the yield rate conversion period are equal

Formula 15.2

$$PP = FV(1 + p)^{-n} + PMT\left[\frac{1 - (1 + p)^{-n}}{p}\right]$$

Basic formula for calculating the purchase price of a bond when the interest payment interval and the yield rate conversion period are different

where $p = (1 + i)^c - 1$

Formula 15.3

Direct formula for calculating the premium or discount of a bond (a negative answer indicates a discount)

PREMIUM OR DISCOUNT

$$= (b \times \text{FACE VALUE} - i \times \text{REDEMPTION PRICE})\left[\frac{1 - (1 + i)^{-n}}{i}\right]$$

Formula 15.4

Basic formula for calculating the yield rate using the method of averages

$$\text{APPROXIMATE VALUE OF } i = \frac{\text{AVERAGE INCOME PER INTEREST PAYMENT INTERVAL}}{\text{AVERAGE BOOK VALUE}}$$

where

$$\text{AVERAGE BOOK VALUE} = \frac{1}{2}\left(\text{QUOTED PRICE} + \text{REDEMPTION PRICE}\right)$$

and

$$\begin{matrix}\text{AVERAGE INCOME} \\ \text{PER INTEREST} \\ \text{PAYMENT INTERVAL}\end{matrix} = \frac{\text{TOTAL INTEREST PAYMENTS} \begin{matrix} - \text{ PREMIUM} \\ + \text{ DISCOUNT}\end{matrix}}{\text{NUMBER OF INTEREST PAYMENT INTERVALS}}$$

In addition, Formulas 9.4, 11.1, 11.2, 12.3, and 13.1 were used in this chapter.

GLOSSARY

Accumulation of discount the process of reducing a bond discount *(p. 623)*

Amortization of the premium the process of writing down a bond premium *(p. 622)*

Bond rate the rate of interest paid by a bond, stated as a percent of the face value *(p. 603)*

Book value of a debt the difference at any time between the debt principal and the associated sinking fund balance *(p. 639)*

Cash price the total purchase price of a bond (including any accrued interest) *(p. 604)*

Coupon a voucher attached to a bond to facilitate the collection of interest by the bondholder *(p. 603)*

Coupon rate *see* **Bond rate**

Debentures bonds for which no security is offered *(p. 603)*

Denomination *see* **Face value**

Discount the difference between the purchase price of a bond and its principal when the purchase price is less than the principal *(p. 604)*

Due date *see* **Redemption date**

Face value the amount owed by the issuer of the bond to the bondholder *(p. 603)*

Market price the net price (without accrued interest) at which a bond is offered for sale *(p. 604)*

Market rate the rate of interest that an investor earns on his or her investment in a bond *(p. 604)*

Maturity date *see* **Redemption date**

Maturity value *see* **Redemption value**

Method of averages a method for determining the approximate yield rate *(p. 627)*

Nominal rate *see* **Bond rate**

Par value *see* **Face value**

Periodic cost of a debt the sum of the interest paid and the payment into the sinking fund when a debt is retired by the sinking fund method *(p. 639)*

Premium the difference between the purchase price of a bond and its principal when the purchase price is greater than the principal *(p. 604)*

Principal value *see* **Redemption value**

Quoted price *see* **Market price**

Redeemable at a premium bonds whose principal is greater than the face value *(p. 603)*

Redeemable at par bonds that are redeemed at their face value *(p. 603)*

Redemption date the date at which the bond principal is repaid *(p. 603)*

Redemption value the amount that the issuer of the bond pays to the bondholder upon surrender of the bond on or after the date of maturity *(p. 603)*

Sinking fund a fund into which payments are made to provide a specific sum of money at a future time; usually set up for the purpose of meeting some future obligations *(p. 629)*

Yield rate *see* **Market rate**

Chuck Franklin/Alamy Stock Photo

LEARNING OBJECTIVES

Upon completing this chapter, you will be able to do the following:

1 Determine the discounted value of cash flow and choose between alternative investments on the basis of the discounted cash flow criterion.

2 Determine the net present value of a capital investment project and infer from the net present value whether a project is feasible.

3 Compute the rate of return on investment.

Dharshana, in preparation for her new job, has to decide how she will finance her new car. She can borrow the money to buy her car, she can save up to buy her car, or she can opt to lease it. This is one of many decisions she must make as she moves from a student existence to a working life.

Choices among different investment opportunities often must be made by both individuals and companies. Whether one is deciding between buying or leasing a car or how to increase plant capacity, an understanding of the time value of money is critical. When comparing different ways of achieving the same goal, we should always examine cash flow at the same point in a timeline—usually at the beginning, when a decision must be made. Only then can we know whether it is better to save for, buy, or lease that car, or whether to expand the plant now or wait.

INTRODUCTION

When making investment decisions, all decision makers must consider the comparative effects of alternative courses of action on the cash flow of a business or on an individual. Since cash flow analysis needs to take into account the time value of money (interest), present value concepts are useful and necessary.

When only cash inflow is considered, the value of the discounted cash flow is helpful in guiding management toward a rational decision. If outlays as well as inflows are considered, the net present value concept is applicable in evaluating projects.

The net present value method indicates whether a project will yield a specified rate of return. To be a worthwhile investment, the rate of return on a capital project must be appropriate or meet a desired minimum target. Often required rates of return that tend to be high are more attractive. Knowing the actual rate of return provides useful information to the decision maker. It could be computed using the net present value concept.

16.1 DISCOUNTED CASH FLOW
A. Evaluation of capital expenditures—basic concepts

Projects expected to generate benefits over a period of time longer than one year are called capital investment projects, and they result in capital expenditures. The benefits resulting from these projects may be in either monetary or non-monetary form. The methods of analysis considered in this chapter will deal only with investment projects generating cash flow in monetary form.

While capital expenditures normally result in the acquisition of assets, the primary purpose of investing in capital expenditures is to acquire a future stream of benefits in the form of an inflow of cash. When an investment is being considered, analysis of the anticipated future cash flow aids in the decision to acquire or replace assets, and whether to buy or lease them.

The analysis generally uses the technique of discounted cash flow. This technique involves estimating all anticipated future cash flow arising from an investment or project, projecting an interest rate, and calculating the present value of this cash flow. It is important that the present value be calculated, not the future value, because of the need to make a decision on the investment at the beginning, or in the present, before cash or other resources are invested. The decision to be made might involve determining whether to invest in a project, or choosing which project to invest in.

In some situations, the cash flow estimated may not be certain, or there may be other, non-financial, concerns. The analysis techniques considered in this text are concerned only with the amount and the timing of cash receipts and cash payments under the assumption that the amount and timing of the cash flow are certain.

From a mathematical point of view, the major issue in evaluating capital expenditure projects is the time value of money. This value prevents direct comparison of cash received and cash payments made at different times. The concept of present value, as introduced in Chapter 9 and subsequent chapters, provides the vehicle for making sums of money received or paid at different times comparable at specific points in time.

B. Discounted cash flow

Discounted cash flow is the present value of all cash transactions. When using the discounting technique to evaluate alternatives, two fundamental principles serve as decision criteria:

1. *The cash-in-hand principle*. Given that all other factors are equal, earlier benefits are preferable to later benefits.

2. *The-bigger-the-better principle*. Given that all other factors are equal, bigger benefits are preferable to smaller benefits.

EXAMPLE 16.1A   Suppose you are offered the option of receiving $1000 today or receiving $1000 three years from now. What is the preferred choice?

SOLUTION   Accepting the cash-in-hand principle, you should prefer to receive $1000 today rather than three years from now. The rationale is that $1000 can be invested to earn interest and will accumulate in three years to a sum of money greater than $1000. Stated another way, the present value of $1000 to be received in three years is less than $1000 today.

EXAMPLE 16.1B   Consider a choice of $2000 today or $3221 five years from now. Which alternative is preferable?

SOLUTION   No definite answer is possible without considering interest. A rational choice must consider the time value of money; that is, we need to know the rate of interest. Once a rate of interest is established, we can make the proper choice by considering the present value of the two sums of money and applying the principle of the-bigger-the-better.

If you choose "now" as the focal date, three outcomes are possible.

1. The present value of $3221 is greater than $2000. In this case, the preferred choice is $3221 five years from now.

2. The present value of $3221 is less than $2000. In this case, the preferred choice is $2000 now.

3. The present value of $3221 equals $2000. In this case, either choice is equally acceptable.
   a. *Suppose the rate of interest is 8% compounded annually.*
      FV = 3221.00; i = 8% = 0.08; n = 5
      PV = 3221.00(1.08^{-5}) = 3221.00(0.680583) = $2192.16
      Since at 8% the discounted value of $3221 is greater than $2000, the preferred choice at 8% is $3221 five years from now.
   b. *Suppose the rate of interest is 12% compounded annually.*
      FV = 3221.00; i = 12% = 0.12; n = 5
      PV = 3221.00(1.12^{-5}) = 3221.00(0.567427) = $1827.68
      Since at 12% the discounted value of $3221 is less than $2000, the preferred choice is $2000 now.

c. *Suppose the rate of interest is 10% compounded annually.*
FV = 3221.00; i = 10% = 0.1; n = 5
PV = 3221.00(1.1^{-5}) = 3221.00(0.620921) = $2000
Since at 10% the discounted value is equal to $2000, the two choices are equally acceptable.

PROGRAMMED SOLUTION

("END" mode)
(Set P/Y = 1; C/Y = 1)

(a) 3221 [FV] 8 [I/Y] 5 [N] [CPT] [PV] [−2192.158478]

(b) 3221 [FV] 12 [I/Y] 5 [N] [CPT] [PV] [−1827.681902]

(c) 3221 [FV] 10 [I/Y] 5 [N] [CPT] [PV] [−1999.987582]

EXAMPLE 16.1C

Two investment alternatives are available. Alternative A yields a return of $6000 in two years and $10 000 in five years. Alternative B yields a return of $7000 now and $7000 in seven years. Which alternative is preferable if money is worth

 (i) 11%?   (ii) 15%?

SOLUTION

To determine which alternative is preferable, we need to compute the present value of each alternative and choose the alternative with the higher present value.

Since the decision is to be made immediately, choose a focal point of "now."

 (i) For i = 11%

Alternative A
The present value of Alternative A is the sum of the present values of $6000 in two years and $10 000 in five years.

Present value of $6000 in two years		
= 6000(1.11^{-2}) = 6000(0.811622)	=	$ 4 870
Present value of $10 000 in five years		
= 10 000(1.11^{-5}) = 10 000(0.593451)	=	5 935
The present value of Alternative A	=	$10 805

Alternative B
The present value of Alternative B is the sum of the present values of $7000 now and $7000 in seven years.

Present value of $7000 now	=	$ 7 000
Present value of $7000 in seven years		
= 7000(1.11^{-7}) = 7000(0.481658)	=	3 372
The present value of Alternative B	=	$10 372

PROGRAMMED SOLUTION

Alternative A
("END" mode)
(Set P/Y = 1; C/Y = 1)

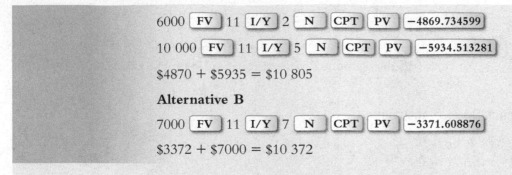

$4870 + $5935 = $10 805

Alternative B

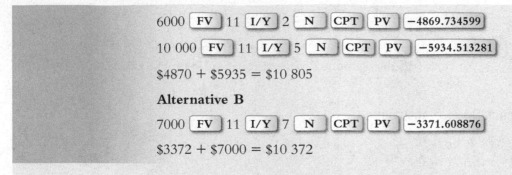

$3372 + $7000 = $10 372

Since at 11% the present value of Alternative A is greater than the present value of Alternative B, Alternative A is preferable.

(ii) For $i = 15\%$

Alternative A

Present value of $6000 in two years
$= 6000(1.15^{-2}) = 6000(0.756144)$ $=$ $4537

Present value of $10 000 in five years
$= 10\,000(1.15^{-5}) = 10\,000(0.497177)$ $=$ <u>4972</u>

The present value of Alternative A $=$ <u>$9509</u>

Alternative B

Present value of $7000 now $=$ $7000

Present value of $7000 in seven years
$= 7000(1.15^{-7}) = 7000(0.375937)$ $=$ <u>2632</u>

The present value of Alternative B $=$ <u>$9632</u>

PROGRAMMED SOLUTION

Alternative A

("END" mode)

(Set P/Y = 1; C/Y = 1)

6000 FV 15 I/Y 2 N CPT PV −4536.862004

10 000 FV 15 I/Y 5 N CPT PV −4971.767353

$4537 + $4972 = $9509

Alternative B

7000 FV 15 I/Y 7 N CPT PV −2631.559279

$2632 + $7000 = $9632

Since at 15% the present value of Alternative B is greater than the present value of Alternative A, Alternative B is preferable.

Note: Applying present value techniques to capital investment problems usually involves estimates of interest rate and cash flow. For this reason, dollar amounts in the preceding example and all following examples may be rounded to the nearest dollar. We suggest that you do the same when working on problems of this nature.

POINTERS & PITFALLS

When making choices between various alternatives, it is sufficient to calculate answers rounded to the nearest dollar. There are two rationales for this. First, in most cases future cash flow is not entirely certain (it is an estimate) and therefore may be slightly inaccurate. Second, as cents have little value, most decisions would not be based on cents difference; rather, decisions would be based on dollars difference.

EXAMPLE 16.1D

An insurance company offers to settle a claim either by making a payment of $50 000 immediately or by making payments of $8000 at the end of each year for 10 years. What offer is preferable for the customer if interest is 8% compounded annually?

The cash inflow for the two alternatives can be represented on a time graph. Note that, in both alternatives, the cash flow represents cash inflow.

Figure 16.1 Graphical Representation of Method and Data (© S. A. Hummelbrunner)

End of period (year)

| Now | 1 | 2 | 3 | 4 | 5 | 6 | 7 | 8 | 9 | 10 |

Alternative 1:
$50 000

Alternative 2:
$8000 $8000 $8000 $8000 $8000 $8000 $8000 $8000 $8000 $8000

The focal date is always "now" in net present value problems. To make a decision now, the customer should compare the present value of the cash flow of the two alternatives.

SOLUTION

Present value of $8000 at the end of each year for 10 years is the present value of an ordinary annuity in which PMT = 8000, $n = 10$, and $i = 8\%$.

$$PV_n = 8000\left(\frac{1 - 1.08^{-10}}{0.08}\right) = 8000(6.710081) = \$53\ 681$$

PROGRAMMED SOLUTION

("END" mode)
(Set P/Y = 1; C/Y = 1)

| 0 | FV | 8000 | PMT | 10 | N | 8 | I/Y | CPT | PV | −53680.65119 |

Since the immediate payment is smaller than the present value of the annual payments of $8000, the annual payments of $8000 are preferable.

EXAMPLE 16.1E

National Credit Union needs to decide whether to buy a high-speed scanner for $6000 and enter a service contract requiring the payment of $45 at the end of every three months for five years, or to enter a five-year lease requiring the payment of $435 at the beginning of every three months. If leased, the scanner can be bought after five years for $600. At 9% compounded quarterly, should the credit union buy or lease?

SOLUTION

To make a rational decision, the credit union should compare the present value of the cash outlays of buying the scanner with the present value of the cash outlays of leasing the scanner.

Present value of the decision to buy

Present value of cash payment for the scanner $=$ $6000

Present value of the service contract involves an ordinary annuity
in which PMT = 45; $n = 20$; P/Y = 4; C/Y = 4; I/Y = 9; i = 2.25%

$$= 45\left(\frac{1 - 1.0225^{-20}}{0.0225}\right) = 45(15.963712) \qquad = \qquad 718$$

Present value of decision to buy $=$ $\underline{\$6718}$

Present value of the decision to lease

Present value of the quarterly lease payments involves an annuity
due: PMT = 435; $n = 20$; i = 2.25%

$$= 435(1.0225)\left(\frac{1 - 1.0225^{-20}}{0.0225}\right) = 435(1.0225)(15.963712) \qquad = \qquad \$7100$$

Present value of purchase price after five years
$= 600(1.0225^{-20}) = 600(0.640816)$ $=$ 384

Present value of decision to lease $=$ $\overline{\$7484}$

PROGRAMMED SOLUTION

Present value of the decision to buy

Present value of cash payment for the scanner is $6000.
Present value of the service contract
("END" mode)
(Set P/Y = 4; C/Y = 4)

0 FV 45 PMT 20 N 9 I/Y CPT PV −718.367057

Present value of decision to buy is $6000 + 718 = $6718.

Present value of the decision to lease

Present value of the quarterly lease payments:
("BGN" mode)

0 FV 435 PMT 20 N 9 I/Y CPT PV −7100.459716

Present value of purchase price after five years:

0 PMT 600 FV 20 N 9 I/Y CPT PV −384.489883

Present value of the decision to lease is $7100 + 384 = $7484.

In the case of costs, the selection criterion follows the principle of the-*smaller*-the-better. Since the present value of the decision to buy is smaller than the present value of the decision to lease, the credit union should buy the scanner.

EXAMPLE 16.1F

Hans Machine Service needs a machine. The machine can be purchased for $4600 and after five years will have a salvage value of $490, or the machine can be leased for five years by making monthly payments of $111 at the beginning of each month. If money is worth 10% compounded annually, should Hans Machine Service buy or lease?

SOLUTION

Alternative 1: Buy machine

Present value of cash price	=	$4600

Less: Present value of salvage value

$= 490(1.1^{-5}) = 490(0.620921)$	=	304
Present value of decision to buy	=	$\underline{\underline{\$4296}}$

Alternative 2: Lease machine

The monthly lease payments form a general annuity due in which

$$PMT = 111; \quad P/Y = 12; \quad C/Y = 1; \quad I/Y = 10; \quad c = \frac{1}{12}; \quad n = 60; \quad i = 10\%;$$

$$p = 1.1^{\frac{1}{12}} - 1 = 1.007974 - 1 = 0.7974\%$$

Present value of the monthly lease payments

$$= 111(1.007974)\left(\frac{1 - 1.007974^{-60}}{0.007974}\right)$$

$$= 111(1.007974)(47.5386866)$$

$$= 5319$$

The present value of the decision to lease is $5319.

PROGRAMMED SOLUTION

Alternative 1: Buy machine

Present value of cash price is $4600.
Less: Present value of salvage value
("END" mode)
(Set P/Y = 1; C/Y = 1)

490 [FV] 5 [N] 10 [I/Y] [CPT] [PV] $\boxed{-304.251448}$

Present value of decision to buy is $4600 - 304 = $4296.

Alternative 2: Lease machine

Present value of the monthly lease payments

("BGN" mode) (Set P/Y = 12; C/Y = 1) 0 [FV] 111 [PMT]

60 [N] 10 [I/Y] [CPT] [PV] $\boxed{-5318.851263}$

Since the present value of the cost to buy is smaller than the present value of the cost to lease, Hans Machine Service should buy the machine.

EXERCISE 16.1

A. For each of the following, compute the present value of each alternative and determine the preferred alternative according to the discounted cash flow criterion (round off to the nearest dollar).

1. The Pet Company must make a choice between two investment alternatives. Alternative 1 will provide returns to the company of $20 000 at the end of three years and $60 000 at the end of six years. Alternative 2 will provide returns to the company of $13 000 at the end of each of the next six years. Which alternative is preferable if money is worth 12 percent?   Reference Example 16.1C

2. The Cap Company has a policy of requiring a rate of return on investments of 16%. Two investment alternatives are available but the company may choose only one. Alternative 1 offers a return of $50 000 after 4 years, $40 000 after 7 years, and $30 000 after 10 years. Alternative 2 will provide returns to the company of $750 at the end of each month for 10 years. Which offer is preferable?

3. An obligation can be settled by making a payment of $10 000 now and a final payment of $20 000 in five years. Alternatively, the obligation can be settled by payments of $1500 at the end of every three months for five years. What offer is preferable if interest is 10% compounded quarterly?   Reference Example 16.1D

4. An unavoidable cost may be met by outlays of $10 000 now and $2000 at the end of every six months for seven years or by making monthly payments of $500 in advance for seven years. At an interest rate of 7% compounded annually, what offer is preferable?   Reference Example 16.1E

5. A company must purchase new equipment costing $2000. The company can pay cash on the basis of the purchase price or make payments of $108 at the end of each month for 24 months. Interest is 7.8% compounded monthly. Should the company purchase the new equipment with cash now or make payments on the installment plan?

6. For less than a dollar a day, Jerri can join a fitness club. She would have to pay $24.99 at the end of each month for 30 months, or she can pay a lump sum of $549 at the beginning. Interest is 16.2% compounded monthly. Should Jerri pay a lump sum or use the monthly payment feature?

B. Solve each of the following questions.

1. A contract offers $25 000 immediately and $50 000 in 5 years or $10 000 at the end of each year for 10 years. If money is worth 6%, which offer is preferable?

2. A professional sports contract offers $400 000 per year paid at the end of each year for six years or $100 000 paid now, $200 000 paid at the end of each of the second and third years, and $800 000 paid at the end of each of the last three years. If money is worth 7.3%, which offer is preferable?

3. Bruce and Carol want to sell their business. They have received two offers. If they accept Offer A, they will receive $15 000 immediately and $20 000 in three years. If they accept Offer B, they will receive $3000 now and $3000 at the end of every six months for six years. If interest is 8%, which offer is preferable?

4. When Peter decided to sell his farm, he received two offers. If he accepts the first offer, he would receive $250 000 now, $750 000 one year from now, and $500 000

two years from now. If he accepts the second offer, he would receive $600 000 now, $300 000 one year from now, and $600 000 two years from now. If money is worth 6.4%, which offer should he accept?

5. A warehouse can be purchased for $90 000. After 20 years the property will have a residual value of $30 000. Alternatively, the warehouse can be leased for 20 years at an annual rent of $10 000 payable in advance. If money is worth 7%, should the warehouse be purchased or leased?

6. A car costs $16 500. Alternatively, the car can be leased for three years by making payments of $360 at the beginning of each month and then bought at the end of the lease for $6750. If interest is 6% compounded semi-annually, which alternative is preferable?

16.2 NET PRESENT VALUE
A. The net present value concept

When the present value of the cash outlays is subtracted from the present value of cash inflows, the resulting difference is called the **net present value**.

$$\begin{array}{|c|}\hline \text{NET PRESENT VALUE} \\ \text{(NPV)} \end{array} = \begin{array}{c}\text{PRESENT VALUE} \\ \text{OF INFLOWS}\end{array} - \begin{array}{c}\text{PRESENT VALUE} \\ \text{OF OUTLAYS}\end{array} \qquad \text{Formula 16.1}$$

Since the net present value involves the difference between the present value of the inflows and the present value of the outlays, three outcomes are possible:

1. If the present value of the inflows is greater than the present value of the outlays, then the net present value is greater than zero.

2. If the present value of the inflows equals the present value of the outlays, then the net present value is zero.

3. If the present value of the inflows is less than the present value of the outlays, then the net present value is less than zero.

$$PV_{IN} > PV_{OUT} \longrightarrow NPV > 0 \, (\text{positive})$$
$$PV_{IN} = PV_{OUT} \longrightarrow NPV = 0$$
$$PV_{IN} < PV_{OUT} \longrightarrow NPV < 0 \, (\text{negative})$$

Criterion rule
At the organization's required rate of return, accept those capital investment projects that have a positive or zero net present value and reject those projects that have a negative net present value.

For a given rate of return:
ACCEPT if $NPV \geq 0$
REJECT if $NPV < 0$.

To distinguish between a negative and a positive present value, use

$$NPV = PV_{IN} - PV_{OUT}.$$

If a company is considering more than one project but can choose only one, the project with the greatest positive net present value is preferable.

Assumptions about the timing of inflows and outlays

The net present value method of evaluating capital investment projects is particularly useful when cash outlays are made and cash inflows received at various times. Since the timing of the cash flow is of prime importance, follow these assumptions regarding the timing of cash inflows and cash outlays.

Unless otherwise stated:

1. All cash inflows (benefits) are assumed to be received at the end of a period.

2. All cash outlays (costs) are assumed to be made at the beginning of a period.

POINTERS & PITFALLS

Calculating Net Present Value Using a Financial Calculator

When using a pre-programmed financial calculator, the net present value (NPV) can be calculated easily. Two steps are involved. First, enter the cash flow of the project to be considered, year by year. Then, in the NPV function, enter the given rate of return, and compute the net present value.

Without the use of a financial calculator, the rate of return must be determined by calculating the present value of each cash flow, and combining the present values to form the net present value.

The following examples; Example 16.2A and Example 16.2B, show solutions found by calculating the present value of each cash flow. Example 16.2C shows solutions calculated with the calculator NPV function.

B. Applications

EXAMPLE 16.2A

Net cash inflows from two ventures are as follows:

End of Year:	1	2	3	4	5
Venture A	12 000	14 400	17 280	20 736	24 883
Venture B	17 000	17 000	17 000	17 000	17 000

Which venture is preferable if the required yield is 20%?

SOLUTION

Present value of Venture A

$$= 12\ 000(1.2^{-1}) + 14\ 400(1.2^{-2}) + 17\ 280(1.2^{-3})$$
$$+ 20\ 736(1.2^{-4}) + 24\ 883(1.2^{-5})$$
$$= 12\ 000(0.8\dot{3}) + 14\ 400(0.69\dot{4}) + 17\ 280(0.578704)$$
$$+ 20\ 736(0.482253) + 24\ 883(0.401878)$$
$$= 10\ 000 + 10\ 000 + 10\ 000 + 10\ 000 + 10\ 000$$
$$= \$50\ 000$$

Present value of Venture B

$$= 17\ 000\left(\frac{1 - 1.20^{-5}}{0.20}\right) = 17\ 000(2.990612) = \$50\ 840$$

PROGRAMMED SOLUTION USING TVM

Present value of Venture A

("END" mode)

(Set P/Y = 1; C/Y = 1)

The present value of Venture A is $10 000 + 10 000 + 10 000 + 10 000 + 10 000 = $50 000.

Present value of Venture B

0 [FV] 17 000 [±] [PMT] 20 [I/Y] 5 [N] [CPT] [PV] −50840.40638

The present value of Venture B is $50 840.

Since at a discount rate of 20%, the present value of Venture B is greater than the present value of Venture A, Venture B is preferable to Venture A.

EXAMPLE 16.2B

Assume for Example 16.2A that Venture A requires an immediate non-recoverable outlay of $9000 while Venture B requires a non-recoverable outlay of $11 000. At 20%, which venture is preferable?

SOLUTION

	Venture A	Venture B
Present value of cash inflows	$50 000	$50 840
Present value of immediate outlay	9 000	11 000
Net present value	$41 000	$39 840

Since the net present value of Venture A is greater than the net present value of Venture B, Venture A is preferable.

EXAMPLE 16.2C

A company is offered a contract promising annual net returns of $36 000 at the end of each year for seven years. If it accepts the contract, the company must spend $150 000 immediately to expand its plant. After seven years, no further benefits are available from the contract and the plant expansion undertaken will have no residual value. Should the company accept the contract if the required rate of return is

    (i) 12%?   (ii) 18%?   (iii) 15%?

SOLUTION

The net inflows and outlays can be represented on a time graph.

Figure 16.2 Graphical Representation of Method and Data (© S. A. Hummelbrunner)

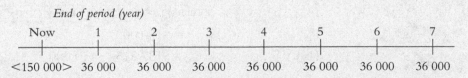

Note: Cash outlays (costs) are identified in such diagrams by a minus sign or by using accounting brackets.

(i) For $i = 12\%$

Since we assume the annual net returns (benefits) are received at the end of a period unless otherwise stated, they form an ordinary annuity in which

$$\text{PMT} = 36\ 000; \quad n = 7; \quad i = 12\%$$

$$\text{PV}_{\text{IN}} = 36\ 000\left(\frac{1 - 1.12^{-7}}{0.12}\right) = 36\ 000(4.563756) \qquad = \qquad \$164\ 295$$

$\text{PV}_{\text{OUT}} = $ Present value of 150 000 now $\qquad = \qquad \underline{150\ 000}$

The net present value (NPV) $= 164\ 295 - 150\ 000 \qquad = \qquad \underline{\$\ 14\ 295}$

Since at 12% the net present value is greater than zero, the contract should be accepted. The fact that the net present value at 12% is positive means that the contract offers a return on investment of more than 12%.

(ii) For $i = 18\%$

$$\text{PV}_{\text{IN}} = 36\ 000\left(\frac{1 - 1.18^{-7}}{0.18}\right) = 36\ 000(3.811528) \qquad = \qquad \$137\ 215$$

$\text{PV}_{\text{OUT}} \qquad = \qquad \underline{150\ 000}$

$\text{NPV} = 137\ 215 - 150\ 000 \qquad = \qquad \underline{-\$\ 12\ 785}$

Since at 18% the net present value is less than zero, the contract should not be accepted. The contract does not offer the required rate of return on investment of 18%.

(iii) For $i = 15\%$

$$\text{PV}_{\text{IN}} = 36\ 000\left(\frac{1 - 1.15^{-7}}{0.15}\right) = 36\ 000(4.16042) \qquad = \qquad \$149\ 775$$

$\text{PV}_{\text{OUT}} \qquad = \qquad \underline{150\ 000}$

$\text{NPV} = 149\ 775 - 150\ 000 \qquad = \qquad \underline{-\$\quad 225}$

The net present value is slightly negative, which means that the net present value method does not provide a clear signal as to whether to accept or reject the contract. The rate of return offered by the contract is almost 15%.

PROGRAMMED SOLUTION USING TVM

(i) For $i = 12\%$

("END" mode)

PV_{IN}: (Set P/Y = 1; C/Y = 1) 0 $\boxed{\text{FV}}$ 36 000 $\boxed{\text{PMT}}$ 7 $\boxed{\text{N}}$

$\qquad\qquad\qquad\qquad\qquad$ 12 $\boxed{\text{I/Y}}$ $\boxed{\text{CPT}}$ $\boxed{\text{PV}}$ $\boxed{-164295.2354}$

$\text{PV}_{\text{OUT}} = $ Present value of 150 000 now $= \$150\ 000$

The net present value (NPV) $= \$164\ 295 - 150\ 000 = \$14\ 295$.

(ii) For $i = 18\%$

("END" mode)

PV_{IN}: 0 $\boxed{\text{FV}}$ 36 000 $\boxed{\text{PMT}}$ 7 $\boxed{\text{N}}$ 18 $\boxed{\text{I/Y}}$ $\boxed{\text{CPT}}$ $\boxed{\text{PV}}$ $\boxed{-137214.9934}$

$\text{PV}_{\text{OUT}} \qquad = \$150\ 000$

(NPV) $\qquad\qquad = \$137\ 215 - 150\ 000 = -\$12\ 785$

(iii) For $i = 15\%$

("END" mode)

PV_{IN}: 0 [FV] 36 000 [PMT] 7 [N] 15 [I/Y] [CPT] [PV] [−149775.1104]

PV_{OUT} = \$150 000

(NPV) = \$149 775 − 150 000 = −\$225

PROGRAMMED SOLUTION USING CASH FLOW AND NPV

STEP 1 Using the cash flow (CF) function of the Texas Instruments BA II PLUS, enter the initial cash outflow, CF0, as a negative number. Press ENTER to save this number, and the down arrow key to access the remaining cash flow. For the next year, enter the first net cash flow after the initial investment as C01, and then the frequency of that cash flow as F01. When the cash flow changes, enter the new numbers as C02 and F02.

[CF] CF0 = 150 000 [±] [ENTER] [↓]   Cash flow at beginning

C01 = 36 000 [ENTER] [↓] F01 = 7 [ENTER]   Cash flow at end of Years 1–7

STEP 2 Press [NVP], enter the required rate of return, and compute.

I = 12 [ENTER] [↓]

[CPT] [NVP] 14 295.235

When I = 12; NPV = 14 295.24

When I = 18; NPV = −12785.01

When I = 15; NPV = −224.89

POINTERS & PITFALLS

In choosing whether to accept or reject a project using the net present value method, remember that future cash flow is an estimates. Therefore, when a NPV is calculated that is close to zero, it can be said that the result does not provide a clear signal to accept or reject the project. Although the desired rate of return has barely been met (or not), this may be a result of the estimated cash flow. In this case, a closer examination of the estimates, to determine their accuracy, may be required before any decision can be made.

EXAMPLE 16.2D

A project requires an initial investment of \$80 000 with a residual value of \$15 000 after six years. It is estimated to yield annual net returns of \$20 000 at the end of each year for six years. Should the project be undertaken at a 16% required rate of return?

SOLUTION

The cash flow is represented in the following diagram.

Figure 16.3 Graphical Representation of Method and Data (© S. A. Hummelbrunner)

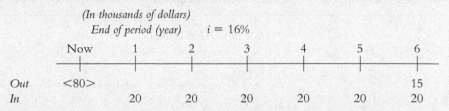

Note: The residual value of \$15 000 is considered to be a reduction in outlays. Its present value should be subtracted from the present value of other outlays.

$$PV_{IN} = 20\,000\left(\frac{1 - 1.16^{-6}}{0.16}\right) = 20\,000(3.684736) \qquad = \quad \$73\,695$$

$$PV_{OUT} = 80\,000 - 15\,000(1.16^{-6})$$
$$= 80\,000 - 15\,000(0.410422) = 80\,000 - 6157 \quad = \quad \underline{73\,843}$$
$$= \text{Net present value (NPV)} \qquad\qquad\qquad = \quad \underline{\$\ -148}$$

PROGRAMMED SOLUTION USING TVM

("END" mode)

PV_{IN}: (Set P/Y = 1; C/Y = 1) 0 [FV] 20 000 [PMT] 6 [N]

16 [I/Y] [CPT] [PV] 73 694.7182

PV_{OUT}: 0 [PMT] 15 000 [FV] 6 [N] 16 [I/Y] [CPT] [PV] −6156.63382

NPV = $73 695 − (80 000 − 6157) = −$148

Since the net present value is negative (the present value of the benefits is smaller than the present value of the costs), the rate of return on the investment is smaller than 16%. The project should NOT be undertaken. However, because the NPV is close to zero, a closer examination of the estimates, to determine their accuracy, may be required before any decision can be made.

PROGRAMMED SOLUTION USING CASH FLOW AND NPV

STEP 1 Enter the initial cash flow, and then the net cash flow for each year.

CF   CF0 = 80 000 [±]   Cash flow at beginning

C01 = 20 000   F01 = 5 Net cash flow at end of Years 1–5

C02 = 35 000   F02 = 1 Net cash flow (15 000 + 20 000) at end of Year 6

STEP 2 Enter the required rate of return, and compute the net present value.

[NPV] I = 16 [↓]

[CPT] NPV = −148.65

EXAMPLE 16.2E The UBA Corporation is considering developing a new product. If undertaken, the project requires the outlay of $100 000 per year for 3 years. Net returns beginning in Year 4 (i.e., end of Year 3) are estimated at $65 000 per year for 12 years. The residual value of the outlays after 15 years is $30 000. If the corporation requires a return on investment of 14%, should it develop the new product?

Figure 16.4 Graphical Representation of Method and Data (© S. A. Hummelbrunner)

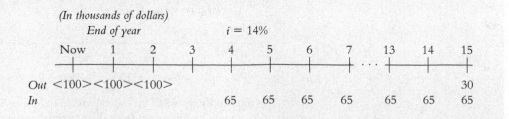

SOLUTION

The net returns, due at the end of Years 4 to 15, form an ordinary annuity deferred for 3 years in which PMT = 65 000, $n = 12$, $d = 3$, $i = 14\%$.

$$PV_{IN} = 65\ 000\left(\frac{1 - 1.14^{-12}}{0.14}\right)(1.14^{-3})$$

$$= 65\ 000(5.660292)(0.674972)$$

$$= \$248\ 335$$

The outlays, assumed to be made at the beginning of each year, form an annuity due in which PMT = 100 000, $n = 3$, $i = 14\%$.

$$PV_{OUT} = 100\ 000(1.14)\left(\frac{1 - 1.14^{-3}}{0.14}\right) - 30\ 000(1.14^{-15})$$

$$= 100\ 000(1.14)(2.321632) - 30\ 000(0.140096)$$

$$= 264\ 666 - 4203$$

$$= \$260\ 463$$

$$NPV = 248\ 335 - 260\ 463 = -\$12\ 128$$

PROGRAMMED SOLUTION USING TVM

("END" mode)

PV_{IN}: (Set P/Y = 1; C/Y = 1) 0 [FV] 65 000 [PMT] 12 [N]

14 [I/Y] [CPT] [PV] [−367918.9882]

0 [PMT] 367 919 [FV] 3 [N] 14 [I/Y] [CPT] [PV] [−248334.853]

("BGN" mode)

PV_{OUT}: 0 [FV] 100 000 [PMT] 3 [N] 14 [I/Y] [CPT] [PV] [−264666.0511]

0 [PMT] 30 000 [FV] 15 [N] 14 [I/Y] [CPT] [PV] [−4202.894462]

$$NPV = \$248\ 335 - (264\ 666 - 4203) = -\$12\ 128$$

Since the net present value is negative, the investment does not offer a 14% return. The corporation should not develop the product.

PROGRAMMED SOLUTION USING CASH FLOW AND NPV

As shown in the diagram, outflows of $100 000 are at the beginning, and then at the end of each of the next 2 years. At the end of Year 3, there is no cash flow. The cash inflows of $65 000 start at the end of Year 4.

[CF] CF0 = 100 000 [±]   Cash flow at beginning

C01 = 100 000 [±]	F01 = 2	Net cash flow at end of Years 1-2
C02 = 0	F02 = 1	Net cash flow at end of Year 3
C03 = 65 000	F03 = 11	Net cash flow at end of Years 4-14
C04 = 95 000	F04 = 1	Net cash flow $(30 + 65)$ at end of Year 15

[NPV] I = 14; [↓] [CPT] NPV = −12 128.32

EXAMPLE 16.2F

A feasibility study concerning a contemplated venture yielded the following estimates:

Initial cost outlay: $1 300 000;
further outlays in Years 2 to 5: $225 000 per year;

residual value after 20 years: $625 000;

net returns: Years 5 to 10: $600 000 per year;

Years 11 to 20: $500 000 per year.

Should the venture be undertaken if the required return on investment is 15%?

Figure 16.5 Graphical Representation of Method and Data (© S. A. Hummelbrunner)

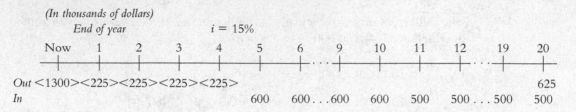

SOLUTION

$$PV_{IN} = 600\,000\left(\frac{1-1.15^{-6}}{0.15}\right)(1.15^{-4}) + 500\,000\left(\frac{1-1.15^{-10}}{0.15}\right)(1.15^{-10})$$

$$= 600\,000(3.784483)(0.571753) + 500\,000(5.018769)(0.247185)$$

$$= \$1\,298\,274 + 620\,281$$

$$= \$1\,918\,555$$

$$PV_{OUT} = 1\,300\,000 + 225\,000\left(\frac{1-1.15^{-4}}{0.15}\right) - 625\,000 \times (1.15^{-20})$$

$$= 1\,300\,000 + 225\,000(2.854978) - 625\,000(0.061100)$$

$$= \$1\,300\,0000 + 642\,370 - 38\,188$$

$$= \$1\,904\,182$$

$$NPV = \$1\,918\,555 - 1\,904\,182 = \$14\,373$$

PROGRAMMED SOLUTION USING TVM

("END" mode)

PV_{IN}: (Set P/Y = 1; C/Y = 1)

0 [FV] 600 000 [PMT] 15 [I/Y] 6 [N] [CPT] [PV] −2270689.616

0 [PMT] 2 270 690 [FV] 15 [I/Y] 4 [N] [CPT] [PV] −1298274.377

0 [FV] 500 000 [PMT] 15 [I/Y] 10 [N] [CPT] [PV] −2509384.313

0 [PMT] 2 509 384 [FV] 15 [I/Y] 10 [N] [CPT] [PV] −620281.3466

PV_{IN} = \$1 298 274 + 620 281 = \$1 918 555

PV_{OUT} 0 [FV] 225 000 [PMT] 15 [I/Y] 4 [N] [CPT] [PV] −642370.1316

0 [PMT] 625 000 [FV] 15 [I/Y] 20 [N] [CPT] [PV] −38187.67434

PV_{OUT} = \$1 300 000 + 642 370 − 38 188 = \$1 904 182

NPV = \$1 918 555 2 − 1 904 182 = \$14 373

Since the net present value is positive, the rate of return on investment is greater than 15%. The venture should be undertaken.

Net present value can be determined by using a preprogrammed financial calculator.

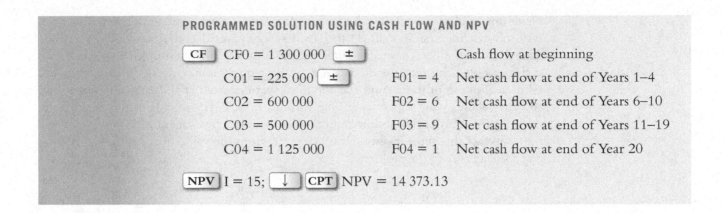

PROGRAMMED SOLUTION USING CASH FLOW AND NPV

CF	CF0 = 1 300 000 ±		Cash flow at beginning
	C01 = 225 000 ±	F01 = 4	Net cash flow at end of Years 1–4
	C02 = 600 000	F02 = 6	Net cash flow at end of Years 6–10
	C03 = 500 000	F03 = 9	Net cash flow at end of Years 11–19
	C04 = 1 125 000	F04 = 1	Net cash flow at end of Year 20

NPV I = 15; ↓ CPT NPV = 14 373.13

C. Using Excel's NPV function

Excel's NPV function can be used to answer some of the questions in this section. The NPV function calculates the net present value for a series of cash flows.

The NPV function in Excel for Example 16.2E is illustrated in Figure 16.6, first by showing the formulas in an Excel worksheet and then in the answer. To formulate the worksheet for NPV function, enter the periodic interest rate in decimals in cell B3.

Figure 16.6 NPV Function is Excel (© S. A. Hummelbrunner)

	A	B
1	**NPV Function in EXCEL**	
2		
3	Interest rate per compounding period	0.14
4	Net cash flow at the end of period 1	–$100000
5	Net cash flow at the end of period 2	–$100000
6	Net cash flow at the end of period 3	$0
7	Net cash flow at the end of period 4	$65000
8	Net cash flow at the end of period 5	$65000
9	Net cash flow at the end of period 6	$65000
10	Net cash flow at the end of period 7	$65000
11	Net cash flow at the end of period 8	$65000
12	Net cash flow at the end of period 9	$65000
13	Net cash flow at the end of period 10	$65000
14	Net cash flow at the end of period 11	$65000
15	Net cash flow at the end of period 12	$65000
16	Net cash flow at the end of period 13	$65000
17	Net cash flow at the end of period 14	$65000
18	Net cash flow at the end of period 15	$95000
19	**NPV, excluding the initial investment**	=NPV(B3,B4:B18)
20	Net Present Value = NPV – Initial investment	=B19 – 100000

	A	B
1	**NPV Function in EXCEL**	
2		
3	Interest rate per compounding period	0.14
4	Net cash flow at the end of period 1	–$100000
5	Net cash flow at the end of period 2	–$100000
6	Net cash flow at the end of period 3	$0
7	Net cash flow at the end of period 4	$65000
8	Net cash flow at the end of period 5	$65000
9	Net cash flow at the end of period 6	$65000
10	Net cash flow at the end of period 7	$65000
11	Net cash flow at the end of period 8	$65000
12	Net cash flow at the end of period 9	$65000
13	Net cash flow at the end of period 10	$65000
14	Net cash flow at the end of period 11	$65000
15	Net cash flow at the end of period 12	$65000
16	Net cash flow at the end of period 13	$65000
17	Net cash flow at the end of period 14	$65000
18	Net cash flow at the end of period 15	$95000
19	**NPV, excluding the initial investment**	$87 871.68
20	Net Present Value = NPV – Initial investment	–$12 128.32

Next, enter a negative number for cash outlays (investments) and a positive number for cash inflows (income) in cells B4 to B18. Excel requires that the cash flow be equally spaced in time, such as annually, quarterly, monthly, etc. and cash inflows should occur at the end of each time interval. Because of this requirement, consider that investments at the beginning of the second and the third year occurred at the end of the first year and the second year, respectively. The formula in cell B19 calculates the net present value for the example but it does not consider the initial investment of $100 000. In cell B20, subtract the initial investment of $100 000 from the value obtained in cell B19 to reach the answer to the problem.

EXERCISE 16.2   MyLab Math

A. For each of the following six investment choices, compute the net present value. Determine which investment should be accepted or rejected according to the net present value criterion.   Reference Example 16.2A and Example 16.2B

1. A contract is estimated to yield net returns of $3500 quarterly for seven years. To secure the contract, an immediate outlay of $50 000 and a further outlay of $30 000 three years from now are required. Interest is 12% compounded quarterly.

2. Replacing old equipment at an immediate cost of $50 000 and an additional outlay of $30 000 six years from now will result in savings of $3000 per quarter for 12 years. The required rate of return is 10% compounded annually.

3. A business has two investment choices. Alternative 1 requires an immediate outlay of $2000 and offers a return of $7000 after seven years. Alternative 2 requires an immediate outlay of $1800 in return for which $250 will be received at the end of every six months for the next seven years. The required rate of return on investment is 17% compounded semi-annually.

4. Suppose you are offered two investment alternatives. If you choose Alternative 1, you will have to make an immediate outlay of $9000. In return, you will receive $500 at the end of every 3 months for the next 10 years. If you choose Alternative 2, you will have to make an outlay of $4000 now and $5000 in two years. In return, you will receive $30 000 ten years from now. Interest is 12% compounded semi-annually.

5. You have two investment alternatives. Alternative 1 requires an immediate outlay of $8000. In return, you will receive $900 at the end of every quarter for the next three years. Alternative 2 requires an immediate outlay of $2000, and an outlay of $1000 in two years. In return, you will receive $300 at the end of every quarter for the next three years. Interest is 7% compounded quarterly. Which alternative would you choose? Why?

6. Your old car costs you $600 per month in gas and repairs. If you replace it, you could sell the old car immediately for $4000. To buy a new car that would last five years, you need to pay out $20 000 immediately. Gas and repairs would cost you only $240 per month on the new car. Interest is 9% compounded monthly. Should you buy a new car? Why?

B. Solve each of the following problems.

1. Teck Engineering normally expects a rate of return of 12% on investments. Two projects are available but only one can be chosen. Project A requires an immediate investment of $4000. In return, a revenue payment of $4000 will be received in four years and a payment of $9000 in nine years. Project B requires an investment of $4000 now and another $2000 in three years. In return, revenue payments will be received in the amount of $1500 per year for nine years. Which project is preferable?   Reference Example 16.2B

2. The owner of a business is presented with two alternative projects. The first project involves the investment of $5000 now. In return, the business will receive a payment of $8000 in 4 years and a payment of $8000 in 10 years. The second project involves an investment of $5000 now and another $5000 three years from now. The returns will be semi-annual payments of $950 for 10 years. Which project is preferable if the required rate of return is 14% compounded annually?   Reference Example 16.2B

3. Northern Track is developing a special vehicle for Arctic exploration. The development requires investments of $60 000 now, and $50 000 and $40 000 for the next 2 years, respectively. Net returns beginning in Year 4 are expected to be $33 000 per year for 12 years. If the company requires a rate of return of 14%, compute the net present value of the project and determine whether the company should undertake the project.   Reference Example 16.2C

4. The Kellogg Company has to make a decision about expanding its production facilities. Research indicates that the desired expansion would require an immediate outlay of $60 000 and an outlay of a further $60 000 in 5 years. Net returns are estimated to be $15 000 per year for the first 5 years and $10 000 per year for the following 10 years. Calculate the net present value of the project. Should the expansion project be undertaken if the required rate of return is 12%?   Reference Example 16.2C

5. Agate Marketing Inc. intends to distribute a new product. It is expected to produce net returns of $15 000 per year for the first four years and $10 000 per year for the following three years. The facilities required to distribute the product will cost $36 000, with a disposal value of $9000 after seven years. The facilities will require a major facelift costing $10 000 each after three years and after five years. If Agate requires a return on investment of 20%, should the company distribute the new product?   Reference Example 16.2E

6. A company is considering a project that will require a cost outlay of $15 000 per year for four years. At the end of the project the salvage value will be $10 000. The project will yield returns of $60 000 in Year 4 and $20 000 in Year 5. There are no returns after Year 5. Alternative investments are available that will yield a return of 16%. Should the company undertake the project?

7. Demand for a product manufactured by Eagle Manufacturing is expected to be 15 000 units per year during the next 10 years. The net return per unit is $2. The manufacturing process requires the purchase of a machine costing $140 000. The machine has an economic life of 10 years and a salvage value of $20 000 after 10 years. Major overhauls of the machine require outlays of $20 000 after 4 years and $40 000 after 7 years. Should Eagle invest in the machine if it requires a return of 12% on its investments?

8. Magnum Electronics Company expects a demand of 20 000 units per year for a special-purpose component during the next six years. Net return (profit) per unit is $4. To produce the component, Magnum must buy a machine costing $250 000 with a life of six years and a salvage value of $40 000 after six years. The company estimates that repair costs will be $20 000 per year during Years 2 to 6. If Magnum requires a return on investment of 18%, should it market the component?

9. Suppose a firm has two business options to choose from and has asked you – a Business Mathematics student – to help them make a decision. Option "A" requires an immediate cost of $20 000 along with "upgrade costs" of $15 000 in year 3 and $17 500 in year 6. The returns from these investments begin in year 2 and are estimated to be $13 000 per year for 3 years, $14 000 per year for the next 3 years, and then $18 000 in years 8 and 9 respectively. The only return in year 10 is a residual value of $5000. Option "B" requires a cost today, and in years 1 and 2 of $19 000 and has estimated returns beginning in year 4 and ending in year 10 of $16 000 per year. There will also be a residual value of $13 000 in year 10. Calculate the NPV (Net Present Value) for each of the two options available to the business based on the information given. Assume the business's required return on investment – the value of money or discount rate – is 15 percent. Explain which, if either, of these two options you would recommend to the business AND why.

BUSINESS MATH **NEWS** Cash for Life Winner Takes $1.5M Payout

A 40-year old man from Bellville, Ontario, Derek Schwager received a great deal of online reaction after he won the Cash For Life draw and decided to take the $1.5 million lump sum payout rather than the alternative of $100 000-a-year for life.

Most of his online commentators diverged into two main camps:

There were those who argued Mr. Schwager is only 40 years old, and noted that as he got older inflation would reduce the real value of his payments. They also pointed out that after Mr. Schwager had received $2 million, he would have to pay tax on the $100 000 in annual payments.

Others agreed he made a good decision in taking the $1.5 million lump sum up front, and offered some creative ways to invest his winnings. Notwithstanding, any interest payments or gains in this case would be subject to market rates and taxation.

QUESTIONS

1. Assume the average life expectancy in Canada is 81 years, and Mr. Schwager lives exactly this long. Using an interest rate of two percent, compounded annually, calculate the present value for Mr. Schwager of $100 000-a-year.

2. At what age will Mr. Schwager have to start paying tax on his annual payments?

3. If Mr. Schwager had decided to take the $100 000-a-year alternative, what interest rate, compounded annually, would be needed for the two alternatives to be equivalent?

4. If Mr. Schwager had been much older (say 65) or much younger (say 20), do you think his decision would have been different and why?

Source: Based on QMI Agency, "Cash for Life Winner takes 1.5 million payout," *Toronto Sun*, February 25, 2013.

16.3 RATE OF RETURN ON INVESTMENT
A. Net present value, profitability index, rate of return

The **return on investment (ROI)** is widely used to measure the value of an investment. This rate of return is often referred to as the **internal rate of return (IRR)**. Since it takes interest into account, knowing the rate of return that results from a capital investment project provides useful information when evaluating a project.

The method of calculating the rate of return that is explained and illustrated in this section uses the net present value concept introduced in Section 16.2. However, instead of being primarily concerned with a specific discount rate and with comparing the present value of the cash inflows and the present value of the cash outlays, this method is designed to determine the rate of return on the investment.

As explained in Section 16.2, three outcomes are possible when using Formula 16.1. These three outcomes indicate whether the rate of return is greater than, less than, or equal to the discount rate used in determining the net present value.

1. If the net present value is greater than zero (positive), then the rate of return is greater than the discount rate used to determine the net present value.

2. If the net present value is equal to zero, then the rate of return is equal to the rate of discount used. As mentioned in the previous pointers and pitfalls, if the net present value is close to zero but not exactly zero, then all the numbers and assumptions must be analyzed before making a decision.

3. If the net present value is less than zero (negative), then the rate of return is less than the discount rate used.

If NPV > 0 (POSITIVE)	ROI $> i$
If NPV $= 0$	ROI $= i$
If NPV < 0 (NEGATIVE)	ROI $< i$

It follows, then, that the rate of return on investment (ROI) is that rate of discount for which the NPV $= 0$, that is, for which $PV_{IN} = PV_{OUT}$.

To compute the rate of return, it is useful to consider a ratio known as the **profitability index** or **discounted benefit–cost ratio**. It is defined as the ratio that results when comparing the present value of the cash inflows with the present value of the cash outlays.

$$\text{PROFITABILITY INDEX (or DISCOUNTED BENEFIT} - \text{COST RATIO)} = \frac{PV_{IN}}{PV_{OUT}}$$

Formula 16.2

Since a division is involved, three outcomes are possible when computing this ratio. Each of these outcomes gives an indication of the rate of return.

1. If the numerator (PV_{IN}) is greater than the denominator (PV_{OUT}), then the profitability index is greater than 1, and the rate of return is greater than the discount rate used.

2. If the numerator (PV_{IN}) is less than the denominator (PV_{OUT}), then the profitability index is less than 1, and the rate of return is less than the discount rate used.

3. If the numerator (PV_{IN}) is equal to the denominator (PV_{OUT}), then the profitability index is equal to 1, and the rate of return equals the discount rate used.

The relationship between the present value of the inflows, the present value of the outlays, the net present value, the profitability index, and the rate of return at a given rate of discount, i, is summarized below.

PV_{IN} Versus PV_{OUT}	Net Present Value (NPV)	Profitability Index	Rate of Return on Investment (ROI)
$PV_{IN} > PV_{OUT}$	NPV > 0	> 1	$> i$
$PV_{IN} = PV_{OUT}$	NPV $= 0$	$= 1$	$= i$
$PV_{IN} < PV_{OUT}$	NPV < 0	< 1	$< i$

POINTERS & PITFALLS

Profitability indices are generally rounded to 1 decimal in percentage format.

B. Procedure for calculating the rate of return

From the relationships noted above, the rate of return on investment can be defined as the rate of discount for which the present value of the inflows (benefits) equals the present value of the outlays (costs). This definition implies that the rate of return is the rate of discount for which the net present value equals zero or for which the profitability index (benefit–cost ratio) equals 1. This conclusion permits us to determine the rate of return.

When using a pre-programmed financial calculator, the rate of return can be calculated easily by using the IRR function. Enter the cash flow of the project to be considered, year by year, and compute the rate of return.

Without the use of the financial calculator, the rate of return must be determined by trial and error. Remember that the purpose is to determine a discount rate that, as closely as possible, results in NPV = 0.

STEP 1   Arbitrarily select a discount rate and compute the net present value at that rate.

STEP 2   From the outcome of Step 1, draw one of the three conclusions.

(a) If NPV > 0, infer that the ROI $> i$.
(b) If NPV $= 0$, infer that the ROI $= i$.
(c) If NPV < 0, infer that the ROI $< i$.

STEP 3   (a) If, in Step 1, NPV > 0 (positive), then we know that ROI $> i$.
Repeat this procedure until the selected rate of discount yields a negative net present value.
(b) If, in Step 1, NPV $= 0$, then ROI $= i$ and the problem is solved.
(c) If, in Step 1, NPV < 0 (negative), then we know that ROI $< i$.
Repeat this procedure until the selected rate of discount yields a positive net present value.

STEP 4   The basic aim of Step 3 is to determine one rate of discount for which the net present value is positive and a second rate for which the net present value is negative. Once this has been accomplished, the rate of return must be a rate between the two rates used to generate a positive and a negative net present value.

You can now obtain a reasonably accurate value of the rate of return by using linear interpolation, which will be explained in section D. To ensure sufficient accuracy in the answer, we recommend that the two rates of discount used when interpolating be no more than two percentage points apart. The worked examples in this section have been solved using successive even rates of discounts when interpolating.

C. Selecting the rate of discount—using the profitability index

While the selection of a discount rate in Step 1 of the procedure is arbitrary, a sensible choice is one that is neither too high nor too low. Since the negative net present value immediately establishes a range between zero and the rate used, it is preferable to be on the high side. Choosing a rate of discount within the range 12% to 24% usually leads to quick solutions.

While the initial choice of rate is a shot in the dark, the resulting knowledge about the size of the rate of return combined with the use of the profitability index should ensure the selection of a second rate that is fairly close to the actual rate of return.

In making the second choice, use the profitability index.

1. Compute the index for the first rate chosen and convert the index into a percent.
2. Deduct 100% from the index and divide the difference by 4.
3. If the index is greater than 1, add the preceding result to obtain the rate that you should use for the second attempt. If, however, the index is smaller than 1, deduct the preceding result from the rate of discount initially used.

To illustrate, assume that the rate of discount initially selected is 16%. The resulting $PV_{IN} = 150$ and the $PV_{OUT} = 120$.

1. The profitability index is $\dfrac{150}{120} = 1.25 = 125\%$.
2. The difference $(125\% - 100\%)$ divided by $4 = 6.25\%$.
3. Since the index is greater than 1, add 6.25% to the initial rate of 16%; the recommended choice is 22.25%, rounded down to 22%.

Assume that the rate of discount initially selected is 20%. The resulting $PV_{IN} = 200$ and the $PV_{OUT} = 250$.

1. The profitability index is $\dfrac{200}{250} = 0.80 = 80\%$.
2. The difference $(80\% - 100\%)$ divided by $4 = 5\%$.
3. Since the index is less than 1, subtract 5% from the initial rate of 20%; the recommended choice is 15%. (If, as in this text, you are using only even rates, try either 14% or 16%.)

D. Using linear interpolation

The method of linear interpolation used in Step 4 of the suggested procedure in section B is illustrated in Example 16.3A.

EXAMPLE 16.3A

Assume that the net present value of a project is $420 at 14% and −$280 at 16%. Use linear interpolation to compute the rate of return correct to the nearest 10th of a percent.

SOLUTION

The data can be represented on a line diagram.

Figure 16.7 Graphical Representation of Method and Data (© S. A. Hummelbrunner)

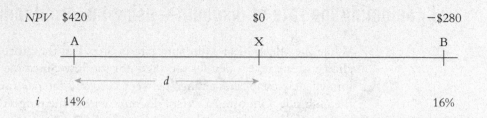

The line segment AB represents the distance between the two rates of discount that are associated with a positive and a negative net present value, respectively.

At Point A,　where $i = 14$, the NPV = 420;
at Point B,　where $i = 16$, the NPV = −280;
at Point X,　where i is unknown, the NPV = 0.

By definition, the rate of return is that rate of discount for which the net present value is zero. Since 0 is a number between 420 and −280, the NPV = 0 is located at a point on AB. This point is marked X.

We can obtain two useful ratios by considering the line segment from the two points of view shown in the diagram.

(i) In terms of the discount rate i,

AB = 2% ————————— 16% − 14%
AX = d% ————————— the unknown percent that must be added to 14% to obtain the rate of discount at which the NPV = 0

$$\frac{\text{AX}}{\text{AB}} = \frac{d\%}{2\%}$$

(ii) In terms of the net present value figures,

AB = 700 ————————— 420 + 280
AX = 420

$$\frac{\text{AX}}{\text{AB}} = \frac{420}{700}$$

Since the ratio AX : AB is written twice, we can derive a proportion statement.

$$\frac{d\%}{2\%} = \frac{420}{700}$$

$$d\% = \frac{420}{700} \times 2\%$$

$$d = 1.2\%$$

Therefore, the rate at which the net present value is equal to zero is 14% + 1.2% = 15.2%. The rate of return on investment is 15.2%.

E. Computing the rate of return

EXAMPLE 16.3B

A project requires an initial outlay of $25 000. The estimated returns are $7000 per year for seven years. Compute the rate of return (correct to the nearest 10th of a percent).

SOLUTION

The cash flow is represented in the following diagram.

The inflows form an ordinary annuity, since inflows are assumed to be received at the end of each year.

Figure 16.8 Graphical Representation of Method and Data (© S. A. Hummelbrunner)

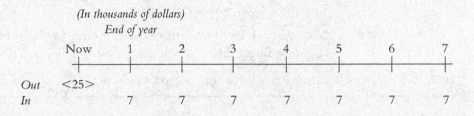

$$PV_{IN} = 7000\left[\frac{1 - (1 + i)^{-7}}{i}\right]$$

The outlays consist of an immediate payment, shown as a negative cash flow on the diagram.

$$PV_{OUT} = 25\ 000$$

To determine the rate of return, we will choose a rate of discount, compute the net present value, and try further rates until we determine two successive even rates. For one, the NPV > 0 (positive); for the other, NPV < 0 (negative).

STEP 1

Try $i = 12\%$.

$$PV_{IN} = 7000\left(\frac{1 - 1.12^{-7}}{0.12}\right) = 7000(4.563757) \qquad = \qquad \$31\ 946$$

$$PV_{OUT} \qquad\qquad = \qquad \underline{25\ 000}$$

$$NPV \text{ at } 12\% \qquad\qquad = \qquad \underline{\$\ 6\ 946}$$

Since the NPV > 0, ROI > 12%.

STEP 2

Compute the profitability index to estimate what rate should be used next.

$$INDEX = \frac{PV_{IN}}{PV_{OUT}} = \frac{31\ 946}{25\ 000} = 1.278 = 127.8\%$$

Since at $i = 12\%$, the profitability index is 27.8% more than 100%, and the rate of discount should be increased by $\frac{27.8\%}{4} = 7\%$ approximately. To obtain another even rate, the increase should be either 6% or 8%. In line with the suggestion that it is better to go too high, increase the previous rate by 8% and try $i = 20\%$.

STEP 3

Try $i = 20\%$.

$$PV_{IN} = 7000\left(\frac{1 - 1.2^{-7}}{0.2}\right) = 7000(3.604592) \qquad = \qquad \$25\ 232$$

$$PV_{OUT} \qquad\qquad = \qquad \underline{25\ 000}$$

$$NPV \text{ at } 20\% \qquad\qquad = \qquad \underline{\$\quad 232}$$

Since the NPV > 0, ROI > 20%.

STEP 4 Since the net present value is still positive, a rate higher than 20% is needed. The profitability index at 20% is $\frac{25\ 232}{25\ 000} = 1.009 = 100.9\%$. The index exceeds 100% by 0.9%; division by 4 suggests an increase of 0.2%. For interpolation, the recommended minimum increase or decrease is 2%. The next try should use $i = 22\%$.

STEP 5 Try $i = 22\%$.

$$PV_{IN} = 7000\left(\frac{1 - 1.22^{-7}}{0.22}\right) = 7000(3.415506) \qquad = \qquad \$23\ 909$$

PV_{OUT}	=	$-\$25\ 000$
NPV at 22%	=	$-\$1\ 091$

Since the NPV $<$ 0, ROI $<$ 22%.
Therefore, 20% $<$ ROI $<$ 22%.

STEP 6 Now that the rate of return has been located between two sufficiently close rates of discount, linear interpolation can be used, as illustrated in Example 16.3A.

Figure 16.9 Graphical Representation of Method and Data (© S. A. Hummelbrunner)

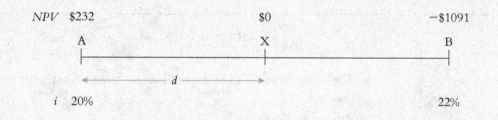

$$\frac{d}{2} = \frac{232}{232 + 1091}$$

$$d = \frac{232(2)}{1323} = 0.35$$

The rate of discount for which the NPV = 0 is approximately 20% + 0.35% = 20.35%. The rate of return is approximately 20.4%. (A more precisely computed value is 20.3382%.)

Present Value of Amounts in General Form	Attempts					
	$i = 12\%$		$i = 20\%$		$i = 22\%$	
	Factor	$	Factor	$	Factor	$
PV_{IN} $7000\left[\dfrac{1 - (1 + i)^{-7}}{i}\right]$	4.563757	31 946	3.604592	25 232	3.415506	23 909
PV_{OUT} 25 000 now				25 000		25 000
NPV		6946		232		$-\$1091$

PROGRAMMED SOLUTION USING CASH FLOW AND IRR

STEP 1 Using the cash flow (CF) function of the Texas Instruments BA II PLUS, enter the initial cash outflow, CF0, as a negative number. Press ENTER to save this number, and the down arrow key to access the remaining cash flow. For the next year, enter the first net cash flow after the initial investment as C01, then the frequency of that cash as F01. When the cash flow changes, enter the new numbers as C02 and F02.

CF CF0 = 25 000 **±** **ENTER** **↓**   Cash flow at beginning

C01 = 7 000 **ENTER** **↓** F01 = 7 **ENTER**   Cash flow at end of Years 1–7

STEP 2   Press IRR and compute.

IRR **CPT** 20.338116

POINTERS & PITFALLS

This unknown rate of return (d) is generally rounded to 2 decimals in percentage format.

EXAMPLE 16.3C

A venture that requires an immediate outlay of $320 000 and an outlay of $96 000 after 5 years has a residual value of $70 000 after 10 years. Net returns are estimated to be $64 000 per year for 10 years. Compute the rate of return.

SOLUTION

The cash flow is represented in the following diagram (in thousands).

Figure 16.10 Graphical Representation of Method and Data (© S. A. Hummelbrunner)

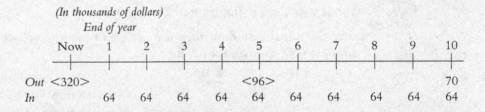

The computations are organized in a chart; explanations regarding the computations follow.

Present Value of Amounts in General Form	Attempts					
	i = 20%		*i* = 14%		*i* = 12%	
PV of benefits	**Factor**	**$**	**Factor**	**$**	**Factor**	**$**
$64\,000\left[\dfrac{1-(1+i)^{-10}}{i}\right]$	4.192	268 288	5.216	333 824	5.650	361 600
PV of costs:						
320 000 now	0.402	320 000	0.519	320 000	0.567	320 000
$96\,000(1+i)^{-5}$	0.162	38 592	0.270	49 824	0.322	54 432
$<70\,000(1+i)^{-10}>$		<11 340>		<18 900>		<22 540>
TOTAL		347 252		350 924		351 892
NPV		<78 964>		<17 100>		9 708

Explanations for computations

STEP 1 Try $i = 20\%$.
Since NPV < 0; ROI $< 20\%$

$$\text{Index at 20\%} = \frac{268\ 288}{347\ 252} = 0.773 = 77.3\%$$

$$\text{Reduction in rate} = \frac{22.7\%}{4} = 5.7\% \longrightarrow 6\%$$

STEP 2 Try $i = 14\%$.
NPV < 0; ROI $< 14\%$

$$\text{Index} = \frac{333\ 824}{350\ 924} = 0.951 = 95.1\%$$

$$\text{Reduction in rate} = \frac{4.9\%}{4} = 1.2\% \longrightarrow 2\%$$

STEP 3 Try $i = 12\%$
NPV > 0; ROI $> 12\%$
$12\% < \text{ROI} < 14\%$

STEP 4 $\dfrac{d}{2} = \dfrac{9708}{9708 + 17\ 100} = \dfrac{9708}{26\ 808} = 0.362131$

$d = 2(0.362131) = 0.72$

The rate of discount at which the net present value is zero is $12\% + 0.72\% = 12.72\%$. The rate of return is 12.7%.

PROGRAMMED SOLUTION USING CASH FLOW AND IRR

STEP 1 Enter the initial cash flow, then the net cash flow for each year. Note that all of the cash flow is in thousands of dollars.

CF	CF0 = 320 $\pm$		Cash flow at beginning
	C01 = 64	F01 = 4	Net cash flow at end of Years 1–4
	C02 = 32 $\pm$	F02 = 1	Net cash flow ($-96 + 64$) at end of Year 5
	C03 = 64	F03 = 4	Net cash flow at end of Years 6–9
	C04 = 134	F04 = 1	Net cash flow ($+70 + 64$) at end of Year 10

STEP 2 Press IRR and compute.

| IRR | CPT | 12.689641 |

EXAMPLE 16.3D A project requires an immediate investment of $33 000 with a residual value of $7000 at the end of the project. It is expected to yield a net return of $7000 in Year 1, $8000 in Year 2, $11 000 per year for the following six years, and $9000 per year for the remaining four years. Calculate the rate of return.

SOLUTION   The cash flow for the project (in thousands) is represented in the following diagram.

Figure 16.11 Graphical Representation of Method and Data

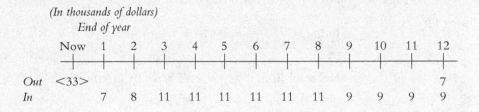

The computations are organized in the chart that follows.

Present Value of Amounts in General Form	Attempts					
	$i = 20\%$		**$i = 28\%$**		**$i = 26\%$**	
PV of returns	**Factor**	**$**	**Factor**	**$**	**Factor**	**$**
$7000(1 + i)^{-1}$	0.833	5831	0.781	5467	0.794	5558
$8000(1 + i)^{-2}$	0.694	5552	0.610	4880	0.630	5040
$11\,000\left[\dfrac{1 - (1 + i)^{-6}}{i}\right]$	3.326		2.759		2.885	
	$\times$	25 391	$\times$	18 513	$\times$	19 993
$\times (1 + i)^{-2}$	0.694		0.610		0.630	
$9000\left[\dfrac{1 - (1 + i)^{-4}}{i}\right]$	2.589		2.241		2.320	
	$\times$	5429	$\times$	2803	$\times$	3278
$\times (1 + i)^{-8}$	0.233		0.139		0.157	
TOTAL PV$_{IN}$		42 203		31 663		33 869
PV of costs 33 000 now		33 000		33 000		33 000
$-7000(1 + i)^{-12}$	0.112	−784	0.052	−364	0.062	−434
TOTAL PV$_{OUT}$		32 216		32 636		32 566
NPV		9987		−973		1303

Explanations for computations

STEP 1   The present value of the returns consists of $7000 discounted for 1 year, $8000 discounted for 2 years, the present value of an ordinary annuity of six payments of $11 000 deferred for 2 years, and the present value of an ordinary annuity of four payments of $9000 deferred for 8 years. The present value of the costs consists of the lump sum of $33 000 less the salvage value of $7000 discounted for 12 years.

STEP 2   The rate of discount chosen for the first attempt is 20%.
For $i = 20\%$, NPV > 0; ROI > 20%

$$\text{Index} = \frac{42\ 203}{32\ 216} = 1.310 = 131.0\%$$

$$\text{Increase in rate} = \frac{31.0}{4} = 7.75\% \text{ or } 8\%$$

STEP 3   For $i = 28\%$, NPV < 0; ROI $< 28\%$

$$\text{Index} = \frac{31\ 663}{32\ 636} = 0.970 = 97.0\%.$$

$$\text{Decrease in rate} = \frac{3}{4} = 0.75\% \text{ or } 2\% \text{ (rounded up)}$$

STEP 4   For $i = 26\%$, NPV > 0; ROI $> 26\%$

$26\% < $ ROI $< 28\%$

STEP 5 $d = \dfrac{1303}{1303 + 973} \times 2 = \dfrac{2606}{2276} = 1.15$

The rate of discount for which the net present value is zero is approximately $26\% + 1.15\% = 27.15\%$. The rate of return, correct to the nearest 10th of a percent, is 27.1%.

PROGRAMMED SOLUTION USING CASH FLOW AND IRR

STEP 1   Enter the initial cash flow, then the net cash flow for each year. Note that all of the cash flow is in thousands of dollars.

CF CF0 = 33 ±			Cash flow at beginning
C01 = 7		F01 = 1	Net cash flow at end of Year 1
C02 = 8		F02 = 1	Net cash flow at end of Year 2
C03 = 11		F03 = 6	Net cash flow at end of Years 3–8
C04 = 9		F04 = 3	Net cash flow at end of Years 9–11
C05 = 16		F05 = 1	Net cash flow $(+7+9)$ at end of Year 12

STEP 2   Press IRR and compute.

IRR   CPT   27.124636

F. Using Excel's IRR function

Excel's IRR function can be used to answer some of the questions in this section. The IRR function calculates the internal rate of return for a series of cash flows.

The IRR function in Excel for Example 16.3D is illustrated in Figure 16.12, first by showing the formulas in an Excel worksheet and then in the answer. To formulate the worksheet for the IRR function, as shown in Figure 16.12 enter the periodic cash flow in order of occurrence in cell B3 to cell B15. Enter a negative number for cash outlay (investment) and a positive number for cash inflow (income). Just below the last entry, enter the IRR formula to calculate the rate of return.

Figure 16.12 Internal Rate of Return (IRR) Function in Excel

	A	B
1	**IRR Function in EXCEL**	
2		
3	Initial cash outflow	−$33000
4	Cash inflow period 1	$7000
5	Cash inflow period 2	$8000
6	Cash inflow period 3	$11000
7	Cash inflow period 4	$11000
8	Cash inflow period 5	$11000
9	Cash inflow period 6	$11000
10	Cash inflow period 7	$11000
11	Cash inflow period 8	$11000
12	Cash inflow period 9	$9000
13	Cash inflow period 10	$9000
14	Cash inflow period 11	$9000
15	Cash inflow period 12	$16000
16	Internal Rate of Return	=IRR(B3:B15)

	A	B
1	**IRR Function in EXCEL**	
2		
3	Initial cash outflow	−$33000
4	Cash inflow period 1	$7000
5	Cash inflow period 2	$8000
6	Cash inflow period 3	$11000
7	Cash inflow period 4	$11000
8	Cash inflow period 5	$11000
9	Cash inflow period 6	$11000
10	Cash inflow period 7	$11000
11	Cash inflow period 8	$11000
12	Cash inflow period 9	$9000
13	Cash inflow period 10	$9000
14	Cash inflow period 11	$9000
15	Cash inflow period 12	$16000
16	Internal Rate of Return	27.124636%

POINTERS
& PITFALLS

Investors should always be aware of the fact that higher rates of return (yield) are accompanied, typically, by higher levels of investment risk. For the most daring investors, high-risk/high-yield investments include derivatives, commodities, precious metals, gemstones, collectible items, common stocks, and growth stocks. For investors more comfortable with moderate risk and moderate yield, investment choices include mutual funds, real estate, corporate bonds, and preferred stocks. Low-risk/low-yield options such as savings accounts, term deposits, guaranteed investment certificates (GICs), and Canada Savings Bonds (CSBs) are designed to appeal to the most conservative investors.

EXERCISE 16.3

MyLab Math

Determine the rate of return for each of the following six situations (correct to the nearest 10th of a percent).

1. The proposed expansion of CIV Electronics' plant facilities requires the immediate outlay of $100 000. Expected net returns are

Year 1: Nil   Year 2: $30 000   Year 3: $40 000

Year 4: $60 000   Year 5: $50 000   Year 6: $20 000

2. The introduction of a new product requires an initial outlay of $60 000. The anticipated net returns from the marketing of the product are expected to be $12 000 per year for 10 years. Reference Example 16.3B

3. Your firm is considering introducing a new product for which net returns are expected to be

Year 1 to Year 3, inclusive:	$2000 per year
Year 4 to Year 8, inclusive:	$5000 per year
Year 9 to Year 12, inclusive:	$3000 per year

The introduction of the product requires an immediate outlay of $15 000 for equipment estimated to have a salvage value of $2000 after 12 years.

4. A project requiring an immediate investment of $150 000 and a further outlay of $40 000 after four years has a residual value of $30 000 after nine years. The project yields a negative net return of $10 000 in Year 1, a zero net return in Year 2, $50 000 per year for the following four years, and $70 000 per year for the last three years. Reference Example 16.3C

5. You are thinking of starting an energy drink business that requires an initial investment of $16 000 and a major replacement of equipment after 10 years, amounting to $8000. From competitive experience, you expect to have a net loss of $2000 the first year, a net profit of $2000 the second year, and, for the remaining years of the first 15 years of operations, net returns of $6000 per year. After 15 years, the net returns will be $3000 per year until the end of 25 years of operations. After 25 years, your lease will expire. The salvage value of equipment at that time is expected to be just sufficient to cover the cost of closing the business. Reference Example 16.3D

6. The Blue Sky Ski Resort plans to install a new chair lift. Construction is estimated to require an immediate outlay of $220 000. The life of the lift is estimated to be 15 years, with a salvage value of $80 000. Cost of clearing and grooming the new area is expected to be $30 000 for each of the first three years of operation. Net cash inflows from the lift are expected to be $40 000 for each of the first 5 years and $70 000 for each of the following 10 years.

7. Suppose a firm has two business options to choose from and has asked you to help them make a decision. Option "A" requires an immediate cost of $25 000 along with "upgrade costs" of $5000 in year 3 and $7500 in year 6. The returns from these investments begin in year 2 and are estimated to be $3000 per year for 3 years, $4000 per year for the next 3 years, and then $8000 in years 8 and 9 respectively. The only return in year 10 is a residual value of $5000. Option "B" requires a cost now, and in years 1 and 2 of $7000 and has estimated returns beginning at the end of year 4 and ending in year 10 of $5000 per year. There will also be a residual value of $4000 in year 10. Using Excel's IRR function, compute the rate of return for each of the two investment options available to the business based on the information given. Assume the business's expected return on investment is 13 percent. Which option would you recommend?

MyLab Math
Visit MyLab Math to practise any of this chapter's exercises marked with a 🌐 as often as you want. The guided solutions help you calculate an answer step by step. You'll find a personalized study plan and additional interactive resources to help you master Business Math!

REVIEW EXERCISE

1. **LO①** Wells Inc. has to choose between two investment alternatives. Alternative A will provide returns to the company of $20 000 after 3 years, $60 000 after 6 years, and $40 000 after 10 years. Alternative B will bring returns of $10 000 per year for 10 years. If the company expects a return of 14% on investments, which alternative should it choose?

🌐 2. **LO①** A piece of property may be acquired by making an immediate payment of $25 000 and payments of $37 500 and $50 000 three and 5 years from now, respectively. Alternatively, the property may be purchased by making quarterly payments of $5150 in advance for 5 years. Which alternative is preferable if money is worth 15% compounded semi-annually?

3. **LO①** An investor has two investment alternatives. If he chooses Alternative 1, he will have to make an immediate outlay of $7000 and will receive $500 every three months for the next nine years. If he chooses Alternative 2, he will have to make an immediate outlay of $6500 and will receive $26 000 after eight years. If interest is 12% compounded quarterly, which alternative should the investor choose on the basis of the net present value criterion?

🌐 4. **LO①** Replacing old equipment at an immediate cost of $65 000 and $40 000 in 5 years will result in a savings of $8000 semi-annually for 10 years. At 14% compounded annually, should the old equipment be replaced?

5. **LO②** A real estate development project requires annual outlays of $75 000 for 8 years. Net cash inflows beginning in Year 9 are expected to be $250 000 per year for 15 years. If the developer requires a rate of return of 18%, compute the net present value of the project.

🌐 6. **LO②** A company is considering a project that will require a cost outlay of $30 000 per year for four years. At the end of the project, the company expects to salvage the physical assets for $30 000. The project is estimated to yield net returns of

$60 000 in Year 4, $40 000 in Year 5, and $20 000 for each of the following five years. Alternative investments are available, yielding a rate of return of 14%. Compute the net present value of the project.

7. **LO③** An investment requires an initial outlay of $45 000. Net returns are estimated to be $14 000 per year for eight years. Determine the rate of return.

🌐 8. **LO③** A project requires an initial outlay of $10 000 and promises net returns of $2000 per year over a 12-year period. If the project has a residual value of $4000 after 12 years, what is the rate of return?

9. **LO③** Compute the rate of return for Question 5.

🌐 10. **LO③** Compute the rate of return for Question 6.

11. **LO③** Superior Jig Co. has developed a new jig for which it expects net returns as follows.

Year 1:	$8000
Years 2 to 6 inclusive:	$12 000 per year
Years 7 to 10 inclusive:	$6000 per year

The initial investment of $36 000 has a residual value of $9000 after 10 years. Compute the rate of return.

🌐 12. **LO③** The owner of a sporting goods store is considering remodelling the store to carry a larger inventory. The cost of remodelling and additional inventory is $60 000. The expected increase in net profit is $8000 per year for the next 4 years and $10 000 each year for the following 6 years. After 10 years, the owner plans to retire and sell the business. She expects to recover the additional $40 000 invested in inventory but not the $20 000 invested in remodelling. Compute the rate of return.

13. **LO①** Outway Ventures evaluates potential investment projects at 20%. Two alternative projects are available. Project A will provide returns to the company of $5800 per year for eight years. Project B will provide returns to the company of $13 600 after one year, $17 000 after five years, and $20 400 after eight years. Which alternative should the company choose according to the discounted cash flow criterion?

14. LO2 Project A requires an immediate investment of $8000 and another $6000 in three years. Net returns are $4000 after two years, $12 000 after four years, and $8000 after six years. Project B requires an immediate investment of $4000, another $6000 after two years, and $4000 after four years. Net returns are $3400 per year for seven years. Determine the net present value at 12%. Which project is preferable according to the net present value criterion?

15. LO2 Net returns from an investment are estimated to be $13 000 per year for 12 years. The investment involves an immediate outlay of $50 000 and a further outlay of $30 000 after 6 years. The investments are estimated to have a residual value of $10 000 after 12 years. Calculate the net present value at 20%.

16. LO3 The introduction of a new product requires an immediate outlay of $45 000. Anticipated net returns from the marketing of the product are expected to be $12 500 per year for 10 years. What is the rate of return on the investment (correct to the nearest 10th of a percent)?

17. LO1 Games Inc. has developed a new electronic game and compiled the following product information.

	Production Cost	Promotion Cost	Sales Revenue
Year 1	$32 000	—	—
Year 2	32 000	$64 000	$ 64 000
Year 3	32 000	96 000	256 000
Year 4	32 000	32 000	128 000
Year 5	32 000		32 000

Should the product be marketed if the company requires a return of 16% on its investment?

18. LO3 Farmer Jones wants to convert his farm into a golf course. He asked you to determine his rate of return on the basis of the following estimates: development cost for each of the first 3 years, $80 000; construction of a clubhouse in Year 4, $240 000; upon his retirement in 15 years, he can sell the golf course for $200 000; net returns from the operation of the golf course will be nil for the first 3 years and $100 000 per year thereafter until his retirement.

19. A small manufacturing firm is planning to either purchase new machinery to add capacity or to outsource part of its business to another company. If they decide to move forward with the first option, they have to make an initial investment of $20 000 to buy the machinery and pay additional maintenance and upgrade cost of $3000 at the beginning of year 2, $5000 at the beginning of year 6 and $8000 at the beginning year 8. The returns from these investments begin at the end of year 2 and are estimated to be $5000 per year for 3 years, $8000 per year for the next 3 years, and then $10 000 in years 8 and 9 respectively. The residual value of the machinery will be $2000 in year 10. The outsourcing option requires a cost $7000 per year for the next 10 years paid at the beginning of each year. They will earn an annual income of $5000 for the first five years and $12 000 every year from year 6 to the end of year 10. Use the cash flow function of your Texas Instrument BAII PLUS to calculate the return on investment (IRR) of these options. Which investment should to company make?

SELF-TEST

1. Opportunities Inc. requires a minimum rate of return of 15% on investment proposals. Two proposals are under consideration, but only one may be chosen. Alternative A offers a net return of $2500 per year for 12 years. Alternative B offers a net return of $10 000 each year after 4, 8, and 12 years. Determine the preferred alternative according to the discounted cash flow criterion.

2. A natural resources development project requires an immediate outlay of $100 000, and $50 000 at the end of each year for 4 years. Net returns are nil for the first 2 years and $60 000 per year thereafter for 14 years. What is the net present value of the project at 14%?

3. An investment of $100 000 yields annual net returns of $20 000 for 10 years. If the residual value of the investment after 10 years is $30 000, what is the rate of return on the investment (correct to the nearest 10th of a percent)?

4. A telephone system with a disposable value of $1200 after five years can be purchased for $6600. Alternatively, a leasing agreement is available that requires an immediate payment of $1500, plus payments of $100 at the beginning of each month for five years. If money is worth 12% compounded monthly, should the telephone system be leased or purchased?

5. A choice has to be made between two investment proposals. Proposal A requires an immediate outlay of $60 000 and a further outlay of $40 000 after 3 years. Net returns are $20 000 per year for 10 years. The investment has no residual value after 10 years. Proposal B requires outlays of $29 000 in each of the first 4 years. Net returns starting in Year 4 are $40 000 per year. The residual value of the investment after 10 years is $50 000. Which proposal is preferable at 20%?

6. Introducing a new product requires an immediate investment in plant facilities of $180 000 with a residual value of $45 000 after seven years. The facilities will require additional capital outlays of $50 000 each after the third and fifth years. Net returns on the investment are estimated to be $75 000 per year for each of the first four years and $50 000 per year for the remaining three years. Determine the rate of return on investment (correct to the nearest 10th of a percent).

CHALLENGE PROBLEMS

1. The owners of a vegetable processing plant can buy a new conveyor system for $85 000. They estimate they can save $17 000 per year on labour and maintenance costs. They can purchase the same conveyor system with an automatic loader for $114 000, and estimate they can save $22 000 per year with that system. If the owners expect both systems to last 10 years and they require at least 14% return per year, should they buy the system with the automatic loader?

2. CheeseWorks owns four dairies in your province and has planned upgrades for all locations. The owners are considering four projects, each of which is independent of the other three projects. The details of each project—A, B, C, and D—are shown below.

Project	Cost at Beginning of Year 1	Revenues and Cost Savings at End of:				
		Year 1	Year 2	Year 3	Year 4	Year 5
A	$300 000	$150 000	$120 000	$120 000	$ 0	$ 0
B	360 000	0	40 000	200 000	200 000	200 000
C	210 000	10 000	10 000	100 000	120 000	120 000
D	125 000	30 000	40 000	40 000	40 000	40 000

The owners of CheeseWorks have $700 000 to invest in these projects. They expect at least 12% return on all of their projects. In which project or combination of multiple projects should the owners of CheeseWorks invest to maximize the return on their investment?

CASE STUDY **To Lease or Not to Lease?**

▶ To travel to her new job, Dharshana needs a car. While reading the newspaper, she notices an ad for an Acura TSX. She thinks that it is her ideal vehicle.

The ad quotes both a cash purchase price of $37 500 and a monthly lease payment option. Since she does not have enough money to pay cash for a car, she would have to finance it from Honda by paying interest of 5.9% compounded monthly on a loan.

The lease option requires payments of $594 a month for 48 months with a $1330 down payment or equivalent trade. Freight and air tax are included. Dharshana does not have a vehicle to offer as a trade-in. If the vehicle is leased, then after 48 months it could be purchased for $16 155. The lease purchase would be based on an interest rate of 3.8%. During the term of the lease, kilometres are limited to 24 000 per year, with an additional charge of $0.08 per kilometre for excess kilometres. The costs include freight and air tax, but exclude taxes, registration, licence, and dealer administration charges. Dharshana is particularly impressed with the "four years or 100 000 kilometre" warranty on the engine and transmission. The manufacturer also offeres 24-hour roadside assistance.

Dharshana must decide whether to buy or lease this car. She lives in a province with a 13% HST tax rate. She realizes that the costs of licence and insurance must be paid, but she will ignore these in her calculations.

QUESTIONS

1. If Dharshana buys the car, what is the total purchase price, including taxes?

2. Since Dharshana has no down payment, she must finance the car if she purchases it.
   (a) Is it cheaper to borrow the money from Honda or to lease?
   (b) The bank is offering a vehicle loan rate of 8% compounded annually. Is it better to buy or to lease the car at this rate?

3. Suppose Dharshana has a $4000 down payment for this car.
   (a) What is the purchase price of the car if she pays cash for it? Assume the down payment is subtracted from the price of the car including tax.
   (b) If the monthly lease payment is $594, is it cheaper to lease or buy the car if Dharshana can get the special dealer rate of 3.8%?

SUMMARY OF FORMULAS

Formula 16.1

$$\text{NET PRESENT VALUE (NPV)} = \text{PRESENT VALUE OF INFLOWS} - \text{PRESENT VALUE OF OUTLAYS}$$

Formula for calculating the difference between the present value of cash inflows and the present value of cash outflows, known as the net present value

Formula 16.2

$$\text{PROFITABILITY INDEX} = \frac{PV_{IN}}{PV_{OUT}}$$

Formula for calculating the profitability index by dividing the present value of cash inflows by the present value of cash outflows

In addition, Formulas 9.4, 11.2, 12.3, 13.2, and 13.4 were used in this chapter.

GLOSSARY

Discounted benefit–cost ratio *see* **Profitability index**

Discounted cash flow the present value of cash payments *(p. 652)*

Internal rate of return (IRR) *see* **Return on investment**

Net present value (NPV) the difference between the present value of the inflows (benefits) and the present value of the outlays (costs) of a capital investment project *(p. 659)*

Profitability index the ratio of the present value of the inflows (benefits) to the present value of the outlays (costs) of a capital investment project *(p. 671)*

Return on investment (ROI) the rate of discount for which the net present value of a capital investment project is equal to zero *(p. 671)*

3

Comprehensive Case

Lux Resources Group, Inc.

Lux Resources Group, Inc., offers equipment rental to the construction and road maintenance industries. The company primarily provides services to Ontario and Manitoba. Started in 1998, the company has steadily expanded geographically outward from its base in Thunder Bay, Ontario. The market has been active, with many projects under construction. Revenues have held steady over the past few years.

The company started with several cranes and large trucks, and has since acquired snow-removal equipment, bobcats, loaders, excavators, utility vehicles, tractors, construction fencing, trailers, and other construction equipment. In the past year, it has come to the company's attention that several pieces of equipment need replacement.

Opportunity beckons for expansion into the northern parts of the provinces, as well as to Windsor, Ontario. To do this, additional equipment is needed. Several pieces of equipment are being considered for purchase at the present time.

In managing the finances of the company, several payments, some loans, and a mortgage need to be rearranged. To finance expansion, additional cash flow is required. The company has decided to issue corporate bonds to raise money and to establish a sinking fund.

Excited about a new opportunity to offer a scholarship, the chief operating officer, Kelsey Bowen, has asked you to analyze the financial data and provide answers to several questions.

1. CHAPTERS 9 AND 10—QUESTIONS

Lux Resources is due to pay one vendor $35 000 in one year, $50 000 in two years, and $30 000 in three years. Instead of making these payments, the company has agreed to make two equal payments, one payment to be made in six months and a second payment in 1½ years. Money is worth 6% compounded monthly. The decision, and therefore the focal date, is to be today.

a. Calculate the equivalent value at the focal date of the original three payments.

b. Calculate the amount of each of the equal payments.

2. CHAPTERS 11 AND 12—QUESTIONS

The company holds a 6-year loan of $230 000, at 7.5% compounded annually. Payments are made quarterly. After 15 months, the terms of the loan are renegotiated at 5.5%, compounded monthly with monthly payments for the remainder of the 6-year term.

a. Calculate the payment amount for the original loan.

b. Calculate the accumulated value of the original loan principal after 15 months.

c. Assuming that payments had been made, calculate the accumulated value of the payments made in the first 15 months.

d. Calculate the outstanding balance of the original loan after 15 months.

e. Calculate the number of payments in the renegotiated term to repay the loan.

3. CHAPTER 13—QUESTIONS

Lux Resources purchased equipment in exchange for a promissory note for $450 000, with the agreement to pay $8000 at the end of each month, starting in eight months. Interest on the loan is 7% compounded annually.

In partnership with the equipment manufacturer, Lux has agreed to establish a scholarship for local business students. A fund of $10 000 has been set up, with the interest earned being paid as the annual scholarship amount. Money is worth 5% compounded annually.

a. Calculate the equivalent value of the equipment loan in eight months.

b. How many month-end payments will have to be made?

c. Calculate the maximum payout of the scholarship, assuming it to be a perpetuity.

4. CHAPTER 14—QUESTIONS

For the company's office and equipment base in Winnipeg, the company holds a 20-year mortgage of $360 000 at 4% compounded semi-annually. The current mortgage contract has a term of 3 years and monthly payments. After the first term is completed, renewal of the mortgage includes monthly payments and interest at 4.8% compounded semi-annually for a term of 5 years.

a. Calculate the monthly payment in the first term.

b. Calculate the balance owing at the end of the first 12 months.

c. Calculate the interest paid in the first 12 months.

d. Calculate the outstanding balance at the end of the 3-year term.

e. Calculate the new payment.

5. CHAPTER 15—QUESTIONS

The company plans to raise $500 000 by issuing 10-year corporate bonds that pay interest at 6% annually. The cash will be used in the expansion of offices and an equipment base in Windsor, Ontario.

a. How much bond interest is to be paid each year?

b. Current financial market conditions have resulted in a bond price to yield 5.4% annually. What is the current market price of the bonds?

c. For an investor, construct a schedule to amortize the premium or discount.

6. CHAPTER 16—QUESTIONS

The purchase of a loader is needed to enable the expansion into Windsor. There are two options to consider. Money is worth 10% compounded annually.

Loader A has a purchase cost of $150 000. Net cash flow would be:

- $30 000 per year for the first 3 years;
- $40 000 for the next year;
- $30 000 for the next 4 years;
- $14 000 for the last 2 years.
- Estimated salvage value: $20 000 at end of 10 years.

Loader B has a purchase cost of $180 000. Net cash flow would be:

- $20 000 per year for the first 2 years;
- $40 000 per year for the next 3 years;
- $30 000 per year for each of the last 5 years.
- Estimated salvage value: $11 000 at end of 10 years.

Calculate for each of the loaders:

a. NPV

b. IRR

c. Profitability index

d. Based on this numerical analysis, what advice would you give to Kelsey Bowen?

I

Further Review of Basic Algebra

I.1 BASIC LAWS, RULES, AND DEFINITIONS

A. The fundamental operations

The fundamental operations of algebra are *addition, subtraction, multiplication,* and *division.* The symbols used to show these operations are the same as the symbols used in arithmetic.

For any two numbers a and b, the fundamental operations are as follows.

1. *Addition* is denoted by $a + b$ and referred to as the sum of a and b.
   If $a = 7$ and $b = 4$, then $a + b = 7 + 4 = 11$.

2. *Subtraction* is denoted by $a - b$ and referred to as the difference between a and b.
   If $a = 7$ and $b = 4$, then $a - b = 7 - 4 = 3$.

3. *Multiplication* is denoted by $a \times b$, $a \star b$, $(a)(b)$ or ab. a and b are called *factors* and ab is referred to as the product of a and b.
   If $a = 7$ and $b = 4$, then $ab = (7)(4) = 28$.

4. *Division* is denoted by $a : b$ or $\dfrac{a}{b}$ or $a \div b$. a is the dividend or numerator, b is the divisor or denominator, and $\dfrac{a}{b}$ is the quotient.
   If $a = 7$ and $b = 4$, then $\dfrac{a}{b} = \dfrac{7}{4}$.

B. Basic laws

The basic laws governing algebraic operations are the same as those used for arithmetic operations.

1. The Commutative Laws for Addition and Multiplication

(a) Commute means "to move from one place to another." When adding two numbers, the commutative property allows you to interchange the two numbers (addends).

$$a + b = b + a$$ ———————— Formula I.1

If $a = 7$ and $b = 4$, then $7 + 4 = 4 + 7 = 11$.

(b) When multiplying two numbers, the two factors may be interchanged.

$$ab = ba$$ ——————————————— Formula I.2

If $a = 7$ and $b = 4$, then $(7)(4) = (4)(7) = 28$.

2. The Associative Laws for Addition and Multiplication

(a) Associate means "to be together." When adding three or more numbers, the numbers (addends) may be combined in any order.

$$a + b + c = (a + b) + c = a + (b + c) = b + (a + c)$$ ——————— Formula I.3

If $a = 7$, $b = 4$, and $c = 2$, then $7 + 4 + 2 = (7 + 4) + 2 = 7 + (4 + 2)$ $= 4 + (7 + 2) = 13$.

(b) When multiplying three or more numbers, the numbers (factors) may be combined in any order.

$$abc = (ab)c = a(bc) = b(ac)$$ ——————————— Formula I.4

If $a = 7$, $b = 4$, and $c = 2$, then $7 \times 4 \times 2 = (7 \times 4) \times 2 = 7 \times (4 \times 2)$ $= 4 \times (7 \times 2) = 56$.

3. The Distributive Law of Multiplication over Addition

(a) Distribute means "to spread around." The product of a times the sum of b and c is equal to the sum of the products ab and ac.

$$a(b + c) = ab + ac$$ ——————————————— Formula I.5

If $a = 7$, $b = 4$, and $c = 2$, then $7(4 + 2) = 7 \times 4 + 7 \times 2 = 42$.

4. Special Properties of 1

(a) $a \times 1 = 1 \times a = a$

When any number a is multiplied by 1, the product is the number a.

If $a = 5$, then $5 \times 1 = 1 \times 5 = 5$.

(b) $\dfrac{a}{1} = a$

When any number a is divided by 1, the quotient is the number a.

If $a = 5$, then $\dfrac{5}{1} = 5$.

(c) $\dfrac{a}{a} = 1$

When any number a is divided by itself, the quotient is 1.

If $a = 5$, then $\dfrac{5}{5} = 1$.

5. Special Properties of 0

(a) *Addition with 0*

$$a + 0 = 0 + a = a$$

When 0 is added to any number a, the sum is the number a.

If $a = 5$, then $5 + 0 = 0 + 5 = 5$.

(b) *Subtraction with 0*

(i) $\boxed{a - 0 = a}$

When 0 is subtracted from any number a, the difference is the number a.

If $a = 5$, then $5 - 0 = 5$.

(ii) $\boxed{0 - a = -a}$

When any number a is subtracted from 0, the difference is the inverse value of a, that is, a with the sign changed.

If $a = 5$, then $0 - 5 = -5$.

(c) *Multiplication with 0*

$$a \times 0 = 0 \times a = 0$$

When 0 is multiplied by any number a, the product is 0.

If $a = 5$, then $5 \times 0 = 0 \times 5 = 0$.

(d) *Division with 0*

(i) $\dfrac{0}{a} = 0$

When 0 is divided by any number a other than 0, the quotient is 0.

(ii) $\dfrac{a}{0} = \text{undefined}$

Division by 0 has no meaning.

If $a = 5$, then $\dfrac{5}{0} = \text{undefined}$.

(e) *0/0 = undefined*

When 0 is divided by itself, the result is undefined.

C. Definitions

1. An **algebraic expression** is a combination of numbers, variables representing numbers, and symbols indicating an algebraic operation.

   $7ab,\ 3a - 5b,\ x^2 - 3x + 4,\ \dfrac{3}{4}x - \dfrac{1}{5}y$ are algebraic expressions.

2. A **term** is a part of an algebraic expression separated from other parts by a positive $(+)$ sign or by a negative $(-)$ sign. The preceding $(+)$ sign or $(-)$ sign is part of the term.

   The terms for the algebraic expressions listed in part (1) are

   $7ab; \quad 3a \text{ and } -5b; \quad x^2, -3x, \text{ and } +4; \quad \dfrac{3}{4}x \text{ and } -\dfrac{1}{5}y$

3. A **monomial** is an algebraic expression consisting of *one* term, such as $7ab$. A **binomial** is an algebraic expression consisting of *two* terms, such as

   $3a - 5b$ or $\dfrac{3}{4}x - \dfrac{1}{5}y$.

   A **trinomial** is an algebraic expression consisting of *three* terms, such as $x^2 - 3x + 4$. A **polynomial** is an algebraic expression consisting of *more than one* term.

4. A **factor** is one of the numbers that when multiplied by another number or other numbers yields a given product.

   The factors of the term $7ab$ are 7, a, and b.

5. A *factor of a term* is called the *coefficient* of the rest of the term.

   In the term $7ab$,   7 is the coefficient of ab,
                              $7a$ is the coefficient of b,
                              $7b$ is the coefficient of a.

6. The **numerical coefficient** is the part of a term formed by *numerals*.

   In the term $7ab$, the numerical coefficient is 7;
   in the term x^2, the numerical coefficient is *understood* to be 1 (1 is usually not written);
   in the term $-\dfrac{1}{5}y$, the numerical coefficient is $-\dfrac{1}{5}$ (the sign is considered to be part of the numerical coefficient).

7. The **literal coefficient** of a term is the part of the term formed with *letter* symbols.

   In the term $7ab$, ab is the literal coefficient;
   in the term $3x^2$, x^2 is the literal coefficient.

8. **Like terms** are terms having the *same* literal coefficients.

   $7a,\ -3a,\ a, -\dfrac{1}{3}a$ are like terms;

   $x^2,\ -2x^2,\ -\dfrac{1}{2}x^2,\ 5x^2$ are like terms.

9. **Combining like terms** or **collecting like terms** means *adding* like terms. Only like terms can be added.

10. **Signed numbers** are numbers preceded by a positive $(+)$ or a negative $(-)$ sign. Numbers preceded by a positive $(+)$ sign are called **positive numbers**, while numbers preceded by a negative $(-)$ sign are called **negative numbers**.

11. **Like signed numbers** are numbers that have the *same* sign, while numbers with *different* signs are called **unlike signed numbers**.

    $+7$ and $+8$ are like signed numbers;
    -7 and -8 are like signed numbers;
    $+7$ and -8 are unlike signed numbers;
    -7 and 8 are unlike signed numbers.

    Note: If no sign is written in front of a number, a plus $(+)$ sign is understood to precede the number.

    6 means $+6$.

12. The **absolute value** of a signed number is the value of the number *without* the sign and is denoted by the symbol $|\ |$ surrounding the number.

    The absolute value of $+5 = |+5| = 5$;
    the absolute value of $-5 = |-5| = 5$.

EXERCISE 1.1

 A. Answer each of the following questions.

1. List the terms contained in each of the following expressions.

(a) $-3xy$　　　　　　　　　　　　　**(b)** $4a - 5c - 2d$

(c) $x^2 - \dfrac{1}{2}x - 2$　　　　　　　　　**(d)** $1.2x - 0.5xy + 0.9y - 0.3$

2. Name the numerical coefficient of each of the following terms.

(a) $-3b$　　　　**(b)** $7c$　　　　**(c)** $-a$　　　　**(d)** x

(e) $12a^2b$　　　**(f)** $-3ax$　　　**(g)** $-\dfrac{1}{2}x^2$　　　**(h)** $\dfrac{x}{5}$

3. Name the literal coefficient of each of the following.

(a) $3x$　　　　**(b)** ab　　　　**(c)** $-4y$　　　　**(d)** $-xy$

(e) $-15x^2y^2$　　**(f)** $3.5abx$　　**(g)** $\dfrac{4}{3}x^3$　　　**(h)** $\dfrac{by}{6}$

1.2　FUNDAMENTAL OPERATIONS WITH SIGNED NUMBERS
A. Additions with signed numbers

1. *Addition of like signed numbers*
To add like signed numbers

(i) add their absolute values, and
(ii) prefix the common sign.

EXAMPLE 1.2A	Add each of the following.

(i) -6 and -8

(ii) $+6$, $+5$, and $+12$

SOLUTION	(i) The absolute values are 6 and 8; the sum of 6 and 8 is 14; the common sign is $(-)$. $(-6) + (-8) = -6 - 8 = -14$

SOLUTION	(ii) The absolute values are 6, 5, and 12; the sum of 6, 5, and 12 is 23; the common sign is $(+)$. $(+6) + (+5) + (+12) = +6 + 5 + 12 = +23$, or 23

(iii) -9, -3, -1, and -15

SOLUTION

The absolute values are 9, 3, 1, and 15;
the sum of the four numbers is 28;
the common sign is $(-)$.
$(-9) + (-3) + (-1) + (-15) = -9 - 3 - 1 - 15 = -28$

2. *Addition of unlike signed numbers*
To add unlike signed numbers,
(i) subtract the smaller absolute value from the larger absolute value, and
(ii) prefix the sign of the *larger* absolute value.

EXAMPLE 1.2B

Add each of the following.

(i) 8 and -5

SOLUTION

The absolute values are 8 and 5;
the difference between the absolute values is 3;
the sign of the larger absolute value is $(+)$.
$(+8) + (-5) = +8 - 5 = +3$, or 3

(ii) 4 and -9

The absolute values are 4 and 9;
the difference between the absolute values is 5;
the sign of the larger absolute value is $(-)$.
$(+4) + (-9) = 4 - 9 = -5$

(iii) -6, $+8$, $+3$, -4, and -5

When more than two numbers are involved and unlike signs appear, two approaches are available.

METHOD 1   Add the first two numbers and then add the sum to the next number and so on.

$(-6) + (+8) + (+3) + (-4) + (-5)$

$= -6 + 8 + 3 - 4 - 5$

$= +2 + 3 - 4 - 5$ ————— add -6 and $+8$, which equals $+2$

$= +5 - 4 - 5$ ————— add $+2$ and $+3$, which equals $+5$

$= +1 - 5$ ————— add $+5$ and -4, which equals $+1$

$= -4$ ————— add $+1$ and -5, which equals -4

METHOD 2   First add the numbers having like signs and then add the two resulting unlike signed numbers.

$(-6) + (+8) + (+3) + (-4) + (-5)$

$= -6 + 8 + 3 - 4 - 5$

$= (-6 - 4 - 5) + (+8 + 3)$

$= (-15) + (+11)$

$= -15 + 11$

$= -4$

B. Subtraction with signed numbers

The subtraction of signed numbers is changed to addition by using the inverse of the **subtrahend**. Thus, to subtract with signed numbers, change the sign of the subtrahend and add.

EXAMPLE 1.2C

Perform each of the following subtractions.

(i) $(+6)$ from (4)

SOLUTION

$(+4) - (+6)$

$= (+4) + (-6)$ ——————— change the subtrahend $(+6)$ to (-6) and change
$= +4 - 6$ ————————— the subtraction to an addition
$= -2$ ——————————— use the rules of addition to add $+4$ and -6

(ii) (-12) from $(+7)$
$(+7) - (-12)$
$= (+7) - (+12)$ ——————— change the subtrahend (-12) to $(+12)$ and add
$= +7 + 12$
$= 19$

(iii) $(+9)$ from (-6)
$(-6) - (+9)$
$= (-6) + (-9)$
$= -6 - 9$
$= -15$

C. Multiplication with signed numbers

The product of two signed numbers is positive or negative according to the following rules.

(a) If the signs of the two numbers are *like*, the product is *positive*.

$(+)(+) = (+)$
$(-)(-) = (+)$

(b) If the signs of the two numbers are *unlike*, the product is *negative*.

$(+)(-) = (-)$
$(-)(+) = (-)$

EXAMPLE 1.2D

(i) $(+7)(+4) = 28$ ———————— the signs are like (both positive); the product is positive

(ii) $(-9)(-3) = 27$ ———————— the signs are like (both negative); the product is positive

(iii) $(-8)(3) = -24$ ———————— the signs are unlike; the product is negative

(iv) $(7)(-1) = -7$ —————————— the signs are unlike; the product is negative

(v) $(-8)(0) = 0$ —————————— the product of any number and 0 is 0

(vi) $(-7)(3)(-4) = (-21)(-4)$ —— (-7) times (3) is (-21)

$\qquad\qquad\qquad\quad = 84$

(vii) $(-2)(-1)(-4)(3) = (2)(-4)(3) = (-8)(3) = -24$

Note: Brackets { } or [ ] or ( ) around one or both numbers indicate multiplication.

D. Division with signed numbers

The quotient of two signed numbers is positive or negative according to the following rules. This is a similar rule to multiplication.

(a) If the signs are *like*, the quotient is *positive*.

$$(+) \div (+) = (+)$$
$$(-) \div (-) = (+)$$

(b) If the signs are *unlike*, the quotient is *negative*.

$$(+) \div (-) = (-)$$
$$(-) \div (+) = (-)$$

EXAMPLE 1.2E

(i) $15 \div (+5) = 3$ —————————— the signs are like; the quotient is positive

(ii) $(-24) \div (-4) = 6$ —————————— the signs are like; the quotient is positive

(iii) $(-18) \div 2 = -9$ —————————— the signs are unlike; the quotient is negative

(iv) $(12) \div (-1) = -12$ —————————— the signs are unlike; the quotient is negative

(v) $0 \div (-10) = 0$ —————————— 0 divided by any number other than 0 is 0

(vi) $(-16) \div 0 = $ undefined —————— division by 0 has no meaning

E. Absolute value of signed numbers

The absolute value of signed numbers, denoted by $|\ |$, is the value of the numbers without the signs.

EXAMPLE 1.2F

(i) $|-7| = 7$

(ii) $|-3 + 8| = |+5| = 5$

(iii) $|4 - 9| = |-5| = 5$

(iv) $|-9 - 4| = |-13| = 13$

(v) $|4(-7)| = |-28| = 28$

(vi) $|(-9)(-3)| = |27| = 27$

(vii) $|(-12) \div (4)| = |-3| = 3$

(viii) $|(-30) \div (-5)| = |+6| = 6$

EXERCISE I.2

A. Simplify.

1. $(+3) + (+7)$	**2.** $(+12) + (+6)$	**3.** $(-5) + (-9)$
4. $(-15) + (-12)$	**5.** $4 + (+5)$	**6.** $(+6) + 8$
7. $-8 + (-7)$	**8.** $(-18) - 7$	**9.** $+3 + 14$
10. $+12 + 1$	**11.** $-6 - 9$	**12.** $-14 - 3$
13. $-8 + 3$	**14.** $-12 + 16$	**15.** $8 - 12$
16. $0 - 9$	**17.** $1 - 0.6$	**18.** $1 - 0.02$

19. $(-4) + (6) + (-3) + (+2)$ **20.** $12 + (-15) + (+8) + (-10)$

21. $-3 - 7 + 9 + 6 - 5$ **22.** $10 - 8 - 12 + 3 - 7$

B. Simplify.

1. $(+9) - (+8)$	**2.** $(+11) - (+14)$	**3.** $(+6) - (-6)$
4. $(+11) - (-12)$	**5.** $(-8) - (-7)$	**6.** $(-9) - (-13)$
7. $(-4) - (+6)$	**8.** $(-15) - (+3)$	**9.** $0 - (-9)$
10. $1 - (-0.4)$	**11.** $1 - (-0.03)$	**12.** $0 - (+15)$

13. $6 - (-5) + (-8) - (+3) + (-2)$ **14.** $-12 - (-6) - (+9) + (-4) - 7$

C. Simplify.

1. $(+5)(+4)$	**2.** $11(+3)$	**3.** $(-4)(-6)$
4. $-7(-3)$	**5.** $(+7)(-1)$	**6.** $10(-5)$
7. $-3(12)$	**8.** $-9(1)$	**9.** $0(-6)$
10. $-12(0)$	**11.** $6(-4)(-3)(2)$	**12.** $-3(5)(-2)(-1)$

D. Simplify.

1. $(+18) \div (+3)$	**2.** $(32) \div (+4)$	**3.** $(+45) \div (-9)$
4. $(63) \div (-3)$	**5.** $(-28) \div (+7)$	**6.** $(-36) \div (+12)$
7. $(-16) \div (-1)$	**8.** $(-48) \div (-8)$	**9.** $0 \div (-5)$
10. $0 \div 10$	**11.** $(+4) \div 0$	**12.** $(-12) \div 0$

E. Simplify.

1. $|-9|$	**2.** $|+4|$	**3.** $|6 - 10|$
4. $|-5 + 12|$	**5.** $|-7 - 8|$	**6.** $|0 - 3|$
7. $|(-3) \times 3|$	**8.** $|4 \times (-5)|$	**9.** $|20 \div (-5)|$
10. $|(-35) \div (7)|$		

I.3   COMMON FACTORING

A. Basic concept

In arithmetic, certain computations, such as multiplication and division involving common fractions, are helped by factoring. Similarly, algebraic manipulation can be made easier by the process of finding the factors that make up an algebraic expression.

Factoring an algebraic expression means writing the expression as a product in component form. Depending on the type of factors contained in the expression, the process of factoring takes a variety of forms. Only the simplest type of factoring applies to the subject matter dealt with in this text. Accordingly, only this type, called *common factoring*, is explained in this section.

A **common factor** is one that is divisible without remainder into each term of an algebraic expression. The factor that is common to each term is usually found by inspection; the remaining factor is then obtained by dividing the expression by the common factor.

B. Examples

EXAMPLE 1.3A

Factor $14a + 21b$.

SOLUTION

By inspection, recognize that the two terms $14a$ and $21b$ are both divisible by 7.

The common factor is 7.
The second factor is now found by dividing the expression by 7.

$$\frac{14a + 21b}{7} = \frac{14a}{7} + \frac{21b}{7} = 2a + 3b$$

Thus the factors of $14a + 21b$ are 7 and $2a + 3b$.

$$14a + 21b = 7(2a + 3b)$$

EXAMPLE 1.3B

Factor $18a - 45$.

SOLUTION

By inspection, the highest common factor is 9;

the second factor is $\dfrac{18a - 45}{9} = 2a - 5$.

$$18a - 45 = 9(2a - 5)$$

Note: If 3 is used as the common factor, the second factor, $6a - 15$, contains a common factor 3 and can be factored again into $3(2a - 5)$.

Thus, $18a - 45 = 3[6a - 15]$
$$= 3[3(2a - 5)]$$
$$= 9(2a - 5)$$

When factoring, the accepted procedure is to always take out the *highest* common factor.

EXAMPLE 1.3C	Factor $mx - my$.
SOLUTION	The common factor is m;

the second factor is $\dfrac{mx - my}{m} = x - y$.

$$mx - my = m(x - y)$$

EXAMPLE 1.3D	Factor $15x^3 - 25x^2 - 20x$.
SOLUTION	The common factor is $5x$.

The second factor is $\dfrac{15x^3 - 25x^2 - 20x}{5x} = 3x^2 - 5x - 4$.

$$15x^3 - 25x^2 - 20x = 5x\,(3x^2 - 5x - 4)$$

EXAMPLE 1.3E	Factor $P + Prt$.
SOLUTION	The common factor is P.

The second factor is $\dfrac{P + Prt}{P} = \dfrac{P}{P} + \dfrac{Prt}{P} + 1 + rt$.

$$P + Prt = P(1 + rt)$$

EXAMPLE 1.3F	Factor $a(x + y) - b(x + y)$.
SOLUTION	The common factor is $(x + y)$.

The second factor is $\dfrac{a(x + y) - b(x + y)}{x + y} = \dfrac{a(x + y)}{x + y} - \dfrac{b(x + y)}{x + y} = a - b$.

$$a(x + y) - b(x + y) = (x + y)(a - b)$$

EXAMPLE 1.3G	Factor $(1 + i) + (1 + i)^2 + (1 + i)^3$.
SOLUTION	The common factor is $(1 + i)$.

The second factor is $\dfrac{(1 + i) + (1 + i)^2 + (1 + i)^3}{(1 + i)}$

$$= \frac{(1 + i)}{(1 + i)} + \frac{(1 + i)^2}{(1 + i)} + \frac{(1 + i)^3}{(1 + i)}$$

$$= 1 + (1 + i) + (1 + i)^2$$

$$(1 + i) + (1 + i)^2 + (1 + i)^3 = (1 + i)\left[1 + (1 + i) + (1 + i)^2\right]$$

EXERCISE I.3

 A. Factor each of the following.

1. $8x - 12$

2. $27 - 36a$

3. $4n^2 - 8n$

4. $9x^2 - 21x$

5. $5ax - 10ay - 20a$

6. $4ma - 12mb + 24mab$

B. Factor each of the following.

1. $mx + my$

2. $xa - xb$

3. $m(a - b) + n(a - b)$

4. $k(x - 1) - 3(x - 1)$

5. $P + Pi$

6. $A - Adt$

7. $r - r^2 - r^3$

8. $(1 + i)^4 + (1 + i)^3 + (1 + i)^2$

SUMMARY OF FORMULAS (LAWS)

Formula I.1

$a + b = b + a$ **The commutative law for addition that permits the addition of two numbers in any order**

Formula I.2

$ab = ba$ **The commutative law for multiplication that permits the multiplication of two numbers in any order**

Formula I.3

$$a + b + c = (a + b) + c$$
$$= a + (b + c)$$
$$= b + (a + c)$$

The associative law for addition that permits the addition of three or more numbers in any order

Formula I.4

$$abc = (ab)c$$
$$= a(bc)$$
$$= b(ac)$$

The associative law for multiplication that permits the multiplication of three or more numbers in any order

Formula I.5

$a(b + c) = ab + ac$ **The distributive law of multiplication over addition that provides the basis for the multiplication of algebraic expressions**

GLOSSARY

Absolute value the value of a number without its sign *(p. 694)*

Algebraic expression a combination of numbers, variables representing numbers, and symbols indicating an algebraic operation *(p. 693)*

Binomial an algebraic expression consisting of two terms *(p. 693)*

Collecting like terms adding like terms *(p. 694)*

Combining like terms *see* **Collecting like terms**

Common factor a factor that is divisible without remainder into each term of an algebraic expression *(p. 700)*

Factor one of the numbers that when multiplied with the other number or numbers yields a given product *(p. 694)*

Like signed numbers numbers having the same sign *(p. 694)*

Like terms terms having the same literal coefficient *(p. 694)*

Literal coefficient the part of a term formed with letter symbols *(p. 694)*

Monomial an algebraic expression consisting of one term *(p. 693)*

Negative numbers signed numbers preceded by a minus (−) sign *(p. 694)*

Numerical coefficient the part of a term formed with numerals *(p. 694)*

Polynomial an algebraic expression consisting of more than one term *(p. 693)*

Positive numbers signed numbers preceded by a plus (+) sign *(p. 694)*

Signed numbers numbers preceded by a plus (+) or by a minus (−) sign *(p. 694)*

Subtrahend a number that is to be subtracted from another number *(p. 697)*

Term a part of an algebraic expression separated from other parts by a plus (+) sign or by a minus (−) sign *(p. 693)*

Trinomial an algebraic expression consisting of three terms *(p. 693)*

Unlike signed numbers numbers having different signs *(p. 694)*

II

Instructions and Tips for Three Preprogrammed Financial Calculator Models

Different models of financial calculators vary in their operation and labelling of the function keys and face plate. This appendix provides you with instructions and tips for solving compound interest and annuity problems with these financial calculators: Texas Instruments BA II PLUS, Sharp EL-738C, and Hewlett-Packard 10bII+. The specific operational details for each of these calculators are given using the following framework:

A. Basic Operations

1. Turning the calculator on and off

2. Operating modes

3. Using the Second function

4. Clearing operations

5. Displaying numbers and display formats

6. Order of operations

7. Memory capacity and operations

8. Operating errors and calculator dysfunction

B. Pre-Calculation Phase (Initial Set-up)

1. Setting to the financial mode, if required

2. Adjusting the calculator's interest key to match the text presentation, if required

3. Setting to the floating-decimal-point format, if required

4. Setting up order of operations, if required

C. Calculation Phase

1. Clearing preprogrammed registers

2. Adjusting for annuities (beginning and end of period), if required

3. Entering data using cash flow sign conventions and correcting entry errors

4. Calculating the unknown variable

D. Example Calculations

1. Compound interest

2. Annuities

E. Checklist for Resolving Common Errors

Go to the section of this appendix that pertains to your calculator. You may want to flag those pages for easy future reference.

II.1 TEXAS INSTRUMENTS BA II PLUS
A. Basic operations

1. Turning the calculator on and off

The calculator is turned on by pressing $\boxed{\text{ON/OFF}}$. If the calculator was turned off using this key, the calculator returns in the standard-calculator mode. If the Automatic Power Down (APD) feature turned the calculator off, the calculator will return exactly as you left it—errors and all, if that was the case. The calculator can be turned off either by pressing $\boxed{\text{ON/OFF}}$ again or by not pressing any key for approximately 10 minutes, which will activate the APD feature.

2. Operating modes

The calculator has two modes: the standard-calculation mode and the prompted-worksheet mode. In the standard-calculation mode, you can perform standard math operations and all of the financial calculations presented in this text. This is the default mode for your calculator. Refer to your calculator's *Guidebook* to learn more about the worksheet mode, since it is not addressed in this appendix.

3. Using the Second function

The primary function of a key is indicated by a symbol on its face. Second functions are marked on the face plate directly above the keys. To access the Second function of a key, press $\boxed{\text{2nd}}$ ("2nd" will appear in the upper-left corner of the display) and then press the key directly under the symbol on the face plate ("2nd" will then disappear from the display).

4. Clearing operations

$\boxed{\longrightarrow}$ clears one character at a time from the display, including decimal points.

$\boxed{\text{CE/C}}$ clears an incorrect entry, an error condition, or an error message from the display.

$\boxed{\text{2nd}}$ (QUIT) clears all pending operations in the standard-calculation mode and returns the display to 0.

CE/C CE/C clears any calculation you have started but not yet completed.

2nd (CLR TVM) sets the financial function registers to 0 and returns to standard-calculation mode.

5. Displaying numbers and display formats

The display shows entries and results up to 10 digits but internally stores numeric values to an accuracy of 13 digits. The default setting in the calculator is 2 decimal places. To change the number of fixed decimal places, press 2nd (FORMAT) along with a number key for the decimal places desired. Then press ENTER to complete the installation. For a floating-decimal-point format, press 2nd (FORMAT) 9 ENTER . Return to standard-calculation mode by pressing 2nd (QUIT).

6. Order of operations

The default for the BA II PLUS is Chn. To change to AOS, which will have the calculator do all mathematical calculations in the proper order according to the rules of mathematics, press 2nd (FORMAT), arrow down four times, and with display on Chn press 2nd SET . Press 2nd (QUIT) to go back to the standard-calculation mode.

7. Memory capacity and operations

The calculator has 10 memory addresses available, numbered 0 through 9. To store a displayed value in a memory address (0 through 9), press STO and a digit key 0 through 9 . To recall a value from memory and display it, press RCL and a digit key 0 through 9 . The numeric value is displayed but is also retained in that memory address.

To clear each memory address individually, store "0" in each selected memory. To clear all of the addresses at the same time, press 2nd (MEM) 2nd (CLR WORK).

Memory arithmetic allows you to perform a calculation with a stored value and then store the result with a single operation. You may add, subtract, multiply, divide, or apply an exponent to the value in the memory. Use this key sequence:

(number in display) STO + (or − or × or ÷ or x^{-1}) and a digit key 0 to 9 for the memory address.

8. Operating errors and calculator dysfunction

The calculator reports error conditions by displaying the message "Error n," where n is a number that corresponds to a particular error discussed in the calculator's *Guidebook*. Errors 4, 5, 7, and 8 are the most common financial calculation errors. A list of possible solutions to calculator dysfunction is given in the *Guidebook*. Generally, if you experience difficulties operating the calculator, press 2nd (RESET) ENTER to clear the calculator, and repeat your calculations.

B. Compound interest and annuity calculations

The BA II PLUS calculator can be used for virtually all compound interest calculations using the third row of the calculator *after* the payment and interest schedules have been set up in the Second function area of the calculator. Each key represents one of the variables in the formula. The variables are:

- N—Represents time. The value is arrived at by taking the number of *years* involved in the transaction and multiplying it by the value set up in P/Y.
- I/Y—The stated or nominal yearly interest rate.
- PV—The amount of money one has at the beginning of the transaction.
- PMT—The amount of money paid on a regular basis.
- FV—The amount of money one has at the end of the transaction.

To perform compound interest or annuity calculations, the process will be to input the variables that are known and to compute the unknown variable.

For compound interest, the process will be:

1. Set up the payment and interest schedules in the Second function of the calculator. This is done by pressing ⌷2nd⌷ (P/Y) and inputting the payment and interest schedules as prompted. Since the transaction will not have any payments, simply make the payment and interest schedules the same. For example, if there are no payments and interest is compounded quarterly, the process would be ⌷2nd⌷ (P/Y), 4, ⌷ENTER⌷ ⌷2nd⌷ (QUIT). This will set up the proper schedules in both P/Y and C/Y and take you back to the calculator mode.

2. Clear out any old information with ⌷2nd⌷ (CLR TVM).

3. Input the variables you know.

4. Compute the variable you need to find.

For annuity calculations, the process will be:

1. Set up the calculator for either an ordinary annuity (payments made at the end) or an annuity due (payments made at the beginning). This is done by hitting ⌷2nd⌷ (BGN) and then setting up the display to END or BGN. ⌷2nd⌷ (SET) will allow you to switch between the two options. ⌷2nd⌷ (QUIT) will take you back to the calculator. Note: if the calculator is in END mode, the display will be clear in the upper-right-hand corner of the display; if it is in BGN mode, the letters BGN will appear in the upper-right-hand corner.

2. Set up the payment and interest schedules in the Second function of the calculator. This is done by pressing ⌷2nd⌷ (P/Y) and inputting the payment and interest schedules as prompted. For example, if the transaction had monthly payments with quarterly compounding, the process would be ⌷2nd⌷ (P/Y) 12, ⌷ENTER⌷ , ⌷↓⌷ , 4, ⌷ENTER⌷ , ⌷2nd⌷ (QUIT). This would set up monthly payments with interest compounded quarterly.

3. Clear out the old information with ⌷2nd⌷ (CLR TVM).

4. Input the variables you know.

5. Compute the variable you need to find.

C. Calculation phase

The steps required to perform calculations and an example calculation appear on pages 347–349 in Chapter 9. The steps required for annuities and sample annuity calculations appear on pages 423–425 and 435 in Chapter 11.

Entering data using cash flow sign conventions and correcting entry errors

Data can be entered in any order, but you *must* observe the cash flow sign conventions. For compound interest calculations, always enter PV as a negative number and all other values (N, I/Y, FV) as positive numbers. An error message will be displayed when calculating I/Y or N if both FV and PV are entered using the same sign. For annuity calculations, enter either PV or PMT as negative numbers and all other values (N, I/Y, FV) as positive numbers. When PV = 0, designate PMT as the negative number and all other values (N, I/Y, FV) as positive numbers. Failure to observe this sign convention will result in either an error message in the display when calculating I/Y values or an incorrect negative number when calculating values of N.

Data entry errors can be corrected one character at a time by using $\boxed{\longrightarrow}$ or the entry, and error messages can be cleared from the display by using $\boxed{\text{CE/C}}$

Calculating the unknown variable

Press $\boxed{\text{CPT}}$ and the financial key representing the unknown variable after all the known variable data are entered (including 0 for PV or FV if required). Successive calculations are possible because numerical values stored in the function key registers remain there until cleared or replaced. The value stored in any of the function key registers can be determined without altering its value by pressing $\boxed{\text{RCL}}$ and the function key.

D. Example calculations

1. Compound interest

See pages 347–349 in Chapter 9 for an example of a compound interest calculation using this calculator.

2. Annuities

See pages 423–425 and 435 in Chapter 11 for examples of annuity calculations using this calculator.

E. Checklist for resolving common errors

1. Confirm that the P/Y and C/Y are properly set.
2. Confirm that the decimal place format is set to a floating decimal point.
3. If attempting annuity calculations, check to see that the calculator is in the appropriate payment mode ("END" or "BGN").
4. Clear all function key registers before entering your data.

5. Be sure to enter a numerical value, using the cash flow sign convention, for all known variables before solving for the unknown variable, even if one of the variables is 0.

II.2 SHARP EL-738C BUSINESS/FINANCIAL CALCULATOR
A. Basic operations

1. Turning the calculator on and off

$\boxed{\text{ON/C}}$ turns the calculator on. $\boxed{\text{2nd F}}$ $\boxed{\text{ON/C}}$ turns the calculator off. To conserve battery life, the calculator will turn itself off automatically 9 to 13 minutes after the last key operation.

2. Operating modes

This calculator has two operational modes statistical (STAT), and Normal (no message). The message STAT or no message appears in the upper right corner of the display to indicate the current mode. Change the mode by pressing $\boxed{\text{MODE}}$ and press either 0 (for normal) or 1 (for STAT) to set the desired mode.

3. Using the Second function

The primary function of a key is indicated by a symbol on the face of the key. Second functions are marked on the face plate directly above the keys. To access the Second function of a key, press $\boxed{\text{2nd F}}$ ("2ndF" will appear in the upper-left corner of the display), and then press the key directly under the symbol on the face plate ("2ndF" will then disappear from the display).

4. Clearing operations

$\boxed{\text{2nd F}}$ (CA) clears the numerical values and calculation commands including data for financial calculations. The contents of memory register storage are not affected.

$\boxed{\text{2nd F}}$ (m→CLR) $\boxed{0}$ $\boxed{0}$ clears the memory.

$\boxed{\text{ON/C}}$ clears the last entry.

$\boxed{\text{DEL}}$ clears the last digit entered.

5. Displaying numbers and display formats

The display shows entries and results up to 10 digits. The default setting in the calculator is the floating decimal. To change the number of fixed decimal places, press $\boxed{\text{SETUP}}$ $\boxed{0}$ $\boxed{0}$ along with a number key for the decimal places desired. For a floating-decimal-point format, press $\boxed{\text{SETUP}}$ $\boxed{0}$ $\boxed{2}$. The number of decimal places is retained even when the power is turned off.

Various messages can appear in the display from time to time. Refer to the *Operation Manual* for a complete list.

6. Memory capacity and operations

This calculator has 11 temporary memory addresses (labelled A–H, X–Z), one independent memory (M) and one last answer memory (ANS). To store a displayed value in memory, press [STO] and a letter key [A] to [H], [M], or [X] to [Z].

To clear the memory of values other than zero, press [2nd F] (m→CLR) [0] [0].

To recall a value from memory and display it, press [RCL] and a letter key [A] to [H], [M], or [X] to [Z].

To add a displayed amount to the value to the independent memory, press [M+]. To subtract a displayed amount to the value to the independent memory, press [2nd F] [M−].

7. Operating errors and calculator dysfunction

Operational errors are indicated by the symbol word Error, followed by a number, across the entire display. Pressing the [←] key or the [→] key returns the cursor to the location of the error. See the *Operation Manual* for a complete description of errors and error conditions that may affect the operation and functioning of your calculator. The error symbol is cleared from the display by pressing [ON/C].

B. Pre-calculation phase

With the calculator on, set the normal mode by pressing [MODE] [0]. Remember, there is no indication in the display area when the calculator is in the normal mode. The calculator requires no change to a register or mode in order to match the text presentation. To set the calculator to the floating-decimal-point format, press [SETUP] [0] [2].

C. Calculation phase

1. Clearing preprogrammed registers

[2nd F] (CA) clears the preprogrammed registers of numerical values and sets them to 0 for financial calculations.

2. Adjusting for annuities (beginning and end of period)

The default mode for annuity calculations is "end of period." If "beginning of period" calculations are required, press [2nd F] (BGN/END). "BGN" will appear in the upper-right corner of the display. To return to "end of period" mode, press [2nd F] (BGN/END) again. "BGN" will disappear from the display.

3. Entering data using cash flow sign conventions and correcting entry errors

Data can be entered in any order but you must observe the cash flow sign conventions to avoid operational errors and incorrect answers. For compound interest calculations, *always* designate PV as a negative number and all other values (N, I/Y, FV) as positive numbers. If you do not observe this sign convention when you enter data, your answer will be the same numerical value but the opposite sign of the answer in the text. An error message will be displayed when calculating I/Y or N if both FV and PV are entered using the same sign. For annuity calculations, when FV = 0, designate PV as a negative number and all other values (N, I/Y, PMT) as positive numbers. When PV = 0, designate PMT as the negative number and all other values (N, I/Y, FV) as positive numbers. Failure to observe this sign convention will result in either an error message in the display when calculating I/Y values or an incorrect negative number when calculating values of N.

4. Calculating the unknown variable

Press COMP and the financial key representing the unknown variable after all the known variable data are entered (including 0 for PV or FV if required). Successive calculations are possible because numerical values stored in the function key registers remain there until cleared or replaced. The value stored in any of the function key registers can be determined without altering its value by pressing RCL and the function key.

D. Example calculations

1. Compound interest (Example 9.2A, page 344)

Key in	Press	Display shows	
	2nd F (CA)	no change	clears all registers
6000	± PV	−6000	this enters the present value P (principal) with the correct sign convention
1.0	I/Y	1.0	this enters the periodic interest rate i as a percent
20	N	20	this enters the number of compounding periods n
	COMP FV	7321.14	this computes and displays the unknown future value S

2. Annuities (Example 11.2D, pages 425–426)

Key in	Press	Display shows	
0	[PV]	0	a precaution to avoid incorrect answers
10	[±] [PMT]	−10	this enters the periodic payment, PMT
6.0	[I/Y]	6.0	this enters the interest rate per year
12	[2nd F] [P/Y] [ENTER] [ON/C]	12	
60	[N]	60	this enters the number of payments, n
	[CPT] [FV]	697.700305	this retrieves the wanted amount, FV

E. Checklist for resolving common errors

1. Check to see that your calculator is in the normal mode.

2. Check to see that the calculator is in the appropriate payment mode (BGN or end mode).

3. Clear all registers before entering your data by pressing [2nd F] (CA).

4. Be sure to enter values for all variables except the unknown variable, before solving for the unknown variable, even if one of the variables is 0.

5. Observe the cash flow sign conventions (discussed previously) when entering the data to avoid unwanted negative signs, display errors, or incorrect answers.

II.3 HEWLETT-PACKARD 10bII+ BUSINESS CALCULATOR
A. Basic operations

1. Turning the calculator on and off

Turn the calculator on by pressing [ON]. Turn the calculator off by pressing the [▬] (SHIFT down) [OFF].

To conserve energy, the calculator turns itself off automatically approximately 10 minutes after you stop using it. The calculator has a continuous memory, so turning it off does not affect the information you have stored in the memory.

2. Operating modes

You can perform all of the financial calculations presented in this text as soon as you turn on the calculator. No mode adjustment is required for financial-, statistical-, or standard-mode calculations.

3. Using the SHIFT function

The primary function of a key is indicated by a symbol on the top face of the key. Secondary functions are marked on the bottom (or beveled) face of the key. To access the secondary function of a key, press ▬ (SHIFT DOWN). ⌊↓⌋ will appear in the lower-left corner of the display, and then press the key with the symbol on the lower face of the key. ⌊↓⌋ will then disappear from the display.

Third-level (or tertiary) functions are marked above the face of the key. To access a third-level function, press the SHIFT UP key (SHIFT UP). ⌊↑⌋ will appear in the lower-left corner of the display, and then press the key with the function above the key (SHIFT UP key will then disappear from the display).

4. Clearing operations

⌊ **SHIFT UP** ⌋ ⌊ **C MEM** ⌋ , followed by a number key, clears the appropriate memory: 0 key (to clear cash flow memory), 1 key (to clear TVM memory, except for P/Y key), 4 key (to clear break-even memory), or 7 key (to clear bond memory).

▬ ⌊ **C ALL** ⌋ (CLEAR ALL) clears all memory, but does not reset the modes.

⌊ ← ⌋ ⌊ **C** ⌋ clears the message and restores the original constants.

⌊ **C** ⌋ clears the entered number to 0.

⌊ ← ⌋ clears the last digit entered.

5. Displaying numbers and display formats

The display shows entries and results up to 12 digits. Brightness is controlled by holding down ⌊ **ON** ⌋ and then pressing ⌊ **+** ⌋ or ⌊ **−** ⌋ . The default setting is 2 decimal places. Regardless of the display format, each number entered is stored with a signed 12-digit number and a signed 3-digit exponent. To change the number of fixed decimal places, press ▬ ⌊ **DSP** ⌋ and a number key for the number of decimal places desired. For a floating decimal point, press ▬ ⌊ **DSP** ⌋ ⌊ **•** ⌋ . To temporarily view all 12 digits, press ▬ ⌊ **DSP** ⌋ and hold ⌊ **=** ⌋ .

Graphics in the display are used to indicate various settings, operating modes, error conditions, and calculator dysfunctions. Refer to the *User's Guide*, Appendix C, for a complete list.

6. Memory capacity and operations

This calculator has 20 numbered registers available to store numbers, a single storage register called the M register, and a constant operation called the K register.

To store a number in the M register, press ⌊ **→ M** ⌋ .

To recall a value from the M register and display it, press ⌊ **RM** ⌋ .

To add a displayed amount to the value in the M register, press ⌊ **M⁺** ⌋ . To subtract a displayed amount to the value in the memory, press ⌊ **±** ⌋ ⌊ **M⁺** ⌋ .

To store a displayed value in a numbered memory register (numbered 0 to 9), press ▬ ⌊ **STO** ⌋ and a digit key ⌊ **0** ⌋ through ⌊ **9** ⌋ . To store a displayed value in a numbered memory register (numbered 10 to 19), press ⌊ **SHIFT DOWN** ⌋ ⌊ **STO** ⌋ and a decimal(period) key and a digit key ⌊ **0** ⌋ through ⌊ **9** ⌋ .

To recall a number from a numbered memory register (0 through 9), press [RCL] and the digit key for the memory register number. To recall a number from a numbered memory register (10 through 19), press RCL key decimal (period) key and the second digit key for the memory register number.

7. Operating errors and calculator dysfunction

Operational errors are indicated by an error message appearing in the display. For a complete description of the error messages, refer to Appendix C of the *User's Guide*. No additional adjustment is required to set the calculator to the financial mode. Begin calculations as soon as you turn on your calculator.

B. Calculation phase

1. Clearing preprogrammed registers

[▬] [CALL] sets all key numerical registers to 0 and momentarily displays the P/YR value.

2. Adjusting for annuities (beginning and end of period)

The default mode for annuity calculations is "end of period." If "beginning of period" calculations are required, press [▬] [BEG/END] . "BEGIN" will appear in the lower middle portion of the display. To return to "end of period" mode, press [▬] [BEG/END] again. "BEGIN" will disappear from the display.

3. Entering data using cash flow sign conventions and correcting entry errors

Data can be entered in any order using the financial function keys. To confirm the values already in the registers or to validate your data entry, press [RCL] and the desired function key.

You must observe the cash flow sign conventions to avoid errors like "no solution" or incorrect answers when calculating N. For compound interest calculations, *always* enter PV as a negative number and the other variables as positive numbers. For annuity calculations, when FV = 0, enter PV as a negative number and all other values (N, I/YR, PMT) as positive numbers. However, when PV = 0, enter PMT as a negative number and all other values (N, I/YR, FV) as positive numbers. If you do not observe the sign convention, the numerical value you calculate will be identical to that of this text except when calculating N (your answer will be incorrect) or when calculating I/YR (an error message may appear in the display).

Data entry errors can be corrected character by character by pressing [←] or the entry can be cleared from the display by pressing [C] .

4. Calculating the unknown variable

Press the financial key representing the unknown variable after all the known variable data are entered (including 0 for PV or FV if required). Successive calculations are possible because numerical values stored in the function key registers remain there until cleared or replaced. The value stored in any of the function key registers can be determined without altering its value by pressing [RCL] and the function key.

C. Example calculations

1. Compound interest (Example 9.2A, page 344)

Key in	Press	Display shows	
	▬ CALL	0	clears the function key registers and confirms the value in the P/YR register
6000	± PV	−6000	this enters the present value P (principal) with the correct sign convention
4	1/YR	4	this enters the periodic interest rate *i* as a percent
4	▬ P/YR	4	
20	N	20	this enters the number of compounding periods *n*
	FV	7321.14	this computes and displays the unknown future value S

2. Annuities (Example 11.2D, pages 425–426)

Key in	Press	Display shows	
	▬ CALL	0	a precaution to avoid incorrect answers
12	SHIFT DOWN P/YR	12	to reset the P/YR value which was not reset in the previous step
10	± PMT	−10	this enters the periodic payment, PMT
6.0	1/YR	6.0	this enters the interest rate per year
60	N	60	this enters the number of payments, *n*
	PV	697.700305	this retrieves the wanted amount, FV

D. Checklist for resolving common errors

1. Confirm that P/YR is properly set.

2. Clear all registers before entering your data by pressing ▬ CALL .

3. Check to see that the calculator is in the appropriate payment mode (BEGIN or END mode).

4. Be sure to enter values for all variables except the unknown variable, before solving for the unknown variable, even if one of the variables is 0.

5. Observe the cash flow sign conventions (discussed previously) when entering the data to avoid unwanted negative signs, display errors, or incorrect answers.

ANSWERS TO ODD-NUMBERED PROBLEMS, REVIEW EXERCISES, AND SELF-TESTS

CHAPTER 1

Exercise 1.1

1. 14
3. 53
5. 24
7. 1
9. 539.73
11. 8300
13. 18
15. -15.7
17. $25a + 12$

Exercise 1.2

A. 1. $\frac{2}{3}$
3. $\frac{7}{12}$
5. $\frac{2}{5}$
7. $\frac{5}{1}$

B. 1. $\frac{13}{2}$
3. $\frac{15}{4}$
5. $11\frac{1}{2}$
7. $7\frac{3}{4}$

C. 1. 1.375
3. $1.\dot{6}$
5. $1.8\dot{3}$
7. $1.08\dot{3}$

D. 1. 3.375
3. $8.\dot{3}$
5. $33.\dot{3}$
7. $7.\dot{7}$

E. 1. $5.63
3. $18.00
5. $57.70
7. $13.00

F. 1. 29 000
3. 0.586
5. 31 500
7. 0.15
9. $423
11. $2250
13. $1734.83

Exercise 1.3

A. 1. 0.64
3. 0.025
5. 0.005
7. 2.5
9. 0.075
11. 0.0625
13. 2.25
15. 0.0825
17. 1.125
19. 0.0075
21. 0.004
23. 0.00025
25. 0.00625
27. 0.0225
29. $1.1\dot{6}$
31. $0.8\dot{3}$

B. 1. $\frac{1}{4}$
3. $\frac{7}{4}$
5. $\frac{3}{8}$
7. $\frac{1}{25}$
9. $\frac{2}{5}$
11. $\frac{5}{2}$
13. $\frac{1}{8}$
15. $\frac{9}{400}$
17. $\frac{1}{800}$
19. $\frac{3}{400}$
21. $\frac{1}{16}$
23. $\frac{1}{6}$
25. $\frac{3}{400}$
27. $\frac{1}{1000}$
29. $\frac{1}{40}$
31. $\frac{11}{6}$

C. 1. 350%
3. 0.5%
5. 2.5%
7. 12.5%
9. 22.5%
11. 145%
13. 0.25%
15. 9%
17. 75%
19. $166.\dot{6}\%$
21. 4.5%
23. 0.75%
25. 1.125%
27. 37.5%
29. $133.\dot{3}\%$
31. 65%

Exercise 1.4

A. 1. $14 970.88
3. $1147.50
5. $ 48.00
   45.00
   27.00
   56.00
   $176.00
7. 80%

B. 1. $1.10
3. 2.9
5. (a) $10.45
   (b) 115.899
   (c) $10.35
   (d) $1379.20

Exercise 1.5

A. 1. (a) $1794.00
   (b) $23.00
   (c) $2173.50
3. (a) $13.26
   (b) $2165.25
5. $14.32
7. $501.56
9. $1421.60
11. (a) $540.00
    (b) $573.95
13. 7.5%
15. $6782.86

Exercise 1.6

1. Cook's owes the government $27 728.50
3. $39.00
5. $6.37
7. $2.52
9. $4357.80
11. (a) $5 480 000
    (b) 10.96
    (c) $4110.00

Review Exercise

1. (a) 29
   (b) -8
   (c) 11
   (d) 8
   (e) $1520.83
   (f) 0.15
   (g) 339.73
   (h) 950.68
   (i) 625.45
   (j) 1250
3. (a) $\frac{1}{2}$
   (b) $\frac{3}{8}$
   (c) $\frac{1}{6}$
   (d) $\frac{5}{3}$
   (e) $\frac{1}{200}$
   (f) $\frac{3}{40}$
   (g) $\frac{3}{400}$
   (h) $\frac{1}{160}$
5. (a) 210
   (b) 7.2
   (c) 195
   (d) 3.6
7. $ 35.00
   $150.00
   $147.00
   $252.00
   $584.00
9. $13 875
11. (a) $2912.00
    (b) $19.20
    (c) 16.5
13. (a) $735
    (b) $17.09
15. (a) $698.65
    (b) $19.96
17. $21 750
19. (a) $17.40
    (b) 5.32
21. 42.55
23. $13 817.50
25. $543.69 more

Self-Test

1. (a) 4415.87
   (b) 93.21
   (c) 2610.15
   (d) 4623.33
   (e) 5489.46

3. (a) $\frac{1}{40}$

(b) $\frac{7}{6}$

5. $203.00

7. $497166.67

9. $24.00

11. $4764.82

13. $17.32

15. $7190.40

17. $250 138.89

CHAPTER 2

Exercise 2.1

A. 1. $19a$

3. $-a - 10$

5. $-2x - 4y$

7. $14f - 4v$

9. $0.8x$

11. $1.4x$

13. $2.79x$

15. $-x^2 - x - 8$

17. $x - 7y$

19. $4b + 2c + 2$

21. $-m^2 + 6m + 1$

23. $10a - 14b$

25. $9b^4d + 2ac^7 - 3ac$

27. $12.25y - 2.4$

29. $1.859410k$

B. 1. $-12x$

3. $-10ax$

5. $-2x^2$

7. $60xy$

9. $-2x + 4y$

11. $2ax^2 - 3ax - a$

13. $35x - 30$

15. $-20ax + 5a$

17. $3x^2 + 5x - 2$

19. $x^3 + y^3$

21. $7x^2 + 3x + 39$

23.
$3x^4 + 2x^3 - 16x^2 + 14x - 3$

25. $4ab$

27. $4x$

29. $10m - 4$

31. $-2x^2 + 3x + 6$

C. 1. -5

3. 5500

5. 0.58604

7. $378

9. $3000

11. $901.99

13. $1400.06

15. 3561.780822

17. 0.055756

19. 0.184

Exercise 2.2

A. 1. 81

3. 16

5. $\frac{16}{81}$

7. $-\frac{1}{64}$

9. 0.25

11. -0.001

13. 1

15. $\frac{1}{9}$

17. $-\frac{1}{125}$

19. 125

21. $\frac{1}{1.01}$

23. -11.526683

25. 0.781198

27. 234.723717

29. 69.792598

B. 1. 2^8

3. 4^3

5. 2^{15}

7. a^{14}

9. 3^{11}

11. 6

13. $\frac{3^{11}}{5^{11}}$

15. $\frac{(-3)^{11}}{2^{11}}$

17. 1.025^{150}

19. 1.04^{80}

21. $(1 + i)^{200}$

23. $(1 + i)^{160}$

25. a^5b^5

27. $m^{24}n^8$

29. 2^4

31. $\frac{b^8}{a^8}$

Exercise 2.3

A. 1. 72.0000

3. 3.0000

5. 1.0759

7. 1.0133

B. 1. 55

3. 12.25

5. 1.071122

7. 0.629961

9. 163.053437

11. 2.158925

13. 1630.176673

15. 1139.915716

17. 5000.00

19. 0.029998

21. 0.04

Exercise 2.4

A. 1. $9 = \log_2 512$

3. $-3 = \log_5 \frac{1}{125}$

5. $2j = \ln 18$

B. 1. $2^5 = 32$

3. $10^1 = 10$

C. 1. 0.693147

3. -2.253795

5. 6.825303

Exercise 2.5

A. 1. $x = 3$

3. $x = 80$

5. $x = 18$

7. $x = -35$

9. $x = -4$

11. $x = -8$

13. $x = 5$

15. $x = 20$

17. $x = 200$

B. 1. $x = 4$

3. $x = 0$

5. $x = 5$

7. $x = 21$

9. $x = 333.\dot{3}$

Exercise 2.6

A. 1. $x = -10$

3. $x = -3$

5. $x = 3$

7. $x = 14$

9. $x = 1200.00$

B. 1. $x = 20$

3. $x = -1$

5. $x = \frac{1}{2}$

7. $x = -14$

9. $x = \frac{109}{126}$

C. 1. $x = -1$

3. $x = \frac{5}{6}$

5. $x = \frac{-8}{59}$

D. 1. $x = \frac{y - b}{m}$

3. $\text{PMT} = \text{PV}i$

5. $r = \frac{S - P}{Pt}$

7. $t = \frac{S - P}{Pr}$

9. $i = (1 + f)^{\frac{1}{m}} - 1$

Exercise 2.7

1. $28.28

3. $35.00

5. 192

7. $670

9. $146.00

11. 1300

13. 20 units

15. 30 $12 tickets, 100 $8 tickets, and 21 $15 tickets.

17. $46 780

19. 104, 52, 40

21. 436

Review Exercise

1. (a) $-2x - 7y$

(b) $1.97x$

(c) $6a - 7$

(d) $x + 3y$

(e) $9a^2 - 4b - 4c$

(f) $-x^2 + 3x + 1$

3. (a) -47

(b) $6\frac{1}{3}$

(c) 0.16

(d) 200

(e) $645.44

(f) 2500

5. (a) 0.96

(b) 1.012126

(c) 1.07

(d) 0.968442

(e) 1.098612

(f) -2.995732

(g) 109.428635

(h) 7.087540

(i) 9.871647

7. (a) $x = -7$

(b) $x = 5$

(c) $x = -3$

(d) $x = -\frac{7}{12}$

(e) $x = 7$

(f) $x = -\frac{1}{3}$

(g) $x = -\frac{1}{2}$

9. 138

11. $117

13. heat = $814; power = $1056; water = $341

15. 35 minutes

17. 164

19. $12 000 000

Self-Test

1. (a) $-2 - 8x$

(b) $-2x - 9$

(c) $-16a - 7$

(d) $-6x^2 + 6x + 12$

3. (a) -8

(b) $\frac{4}{9}$

(c) 1
(d) 2187
(e) $\frac{9}{16}$
(f) $-x^{15}$
5. (a) $n = 6$
  (b) $n = 5$
7. (a) $P = \frac{I}{rt}$
  (b) $d = \frac{S - P}{St}$
9. 4600 square
  metres
11. $4500

CHAPTER 3

Exercise 3.1

A. 1. (a) 3:8
  (b) 3:2
  (c) 5:8:13
  (d) 3:6:13
3. (a) $\frac{5}{16}$
  (b) $\frac{2}{7}$
  (c) 2:7:11
  (d) 23:14:5
  (e) 5:4
  (f) 25:21
  (g) 9:16:18
  (h) 28:40:25
  (i) 32:60:25
  (j) 9:7:17
  (k) 69:92
  (l) 28:55
  (m) 8:15
  (n) 9:10
B. 1. $\frac{8}{7}$
  3. 2:3:12
  5. 1:29
C. 1. $2295
    $ 510
    $ 255
  3. $5250
    $2800
    $1400
  5. $4 400 000
    $2 200 000
    $4 950 000

Exercise 3.2

A. 1. 4
  3. 56
  5. 7.4
  7. 2.4
  9. $\frac{7}{10}$
  11. 1

B. 1. 21
  3. 600 km
  5. (a) $360 000
    (b) $900 000
  7. $1 008 000

Exercise 3.3

A. 1. 36
  3. 300
  5. 18
  7. 6
  9. 0.5
  11. 2
B. 1. $16
  3. $48
  5. $200
  7. $150
  9. $9
  11. $60
C. 1. 60%
  3. 115%
  5. 5%
  7. 600%
  9. $166\frac{2}{3}\%$
D. 1. $200
  3. $3.60
  5. $3.06
  7. 200
  9. $1.10
E. 1. $28
  3. $1500
  5. $45 000
  7. $60 000
  9. $6000

Exercise 3.4

A. 1. 168
  3. $1140
  5. 88
B. 1. 50%
  3. 200%
  5. 2%
  7. $4.40

Exercise 3.5

A. 1. 27
  3. 12.5%
  5. $4320
  7. (a) $180 000
    (b) $225 000

B. 1. $14.52
  3. $130
  5. $83.62
  7. $5000
  9. $83\frac{1}{3}\%$
  11. 325%
  13. $96.69
  15. $680
  17. $44 800
  19. $2700.00

Exercise 3.6

A. 1. US$612.60
  3. C$228.24
B. 1. C$459.13
  3. 174.49 Swiss francs
  5. C$824.07

Exercise 3.7

1. bread, 103.6145
  bus pass, 110.5528
  clothing, 96.9697
3. (a) (i) 2015 relative
      to 2002, 0.7899
    (ii) 2017 relative
      to 2002, 0.7669
  (b) 2017 relative to 2015,
    0.9709
5. $75 152.65

Exercise 3.8

1. $7573.98
3. $7813.83

Review Exercise

1. (a) 5:6
  (b) 6:1
  (c) 147:120
  (d) 6:1
  (e) 240:20:1
  (f) 15:4:3
3. (a) $112
  (b) $930
  (c) $1155
  (d) $1320
5. (a) 62.5%
  (b) 175%
  (c) $0.48
  (d) $22.50
  (e) $280
  (f) $440
  (g) 2%

  (h) 500%
  (i) $132
  (j) $405
7. D: $1200
  E: $1800
  F: $1500
9. First beneficiary: $63 000
  Second beneficiary: $47 250
  Third beneficiary: $70 875
  Fourth beneficiary: $7875
11. 16
13. (a) $14 700
  (b) $36 750
15. (a) 59 250
  (b) 19 750
17. (a) $42 600
  (b) $8520
19. (a) Material cost 50.00%
    Labour cost 22.2%
    Overhead 27.7%
  (b) 125%
21. (a) 8%
  (b) 92%
23. $350 000
25. $84 000
27. (a) $300 000
  (b) $24 862.50
  (c) $18 646.88
  (d) 39.84%
29. (a) C$1 = US$0.817395
  (b) US$592.61
31. (a) 0.758150
  (b) $47 687.64
33. (a) 8.8235%
  (b) 8.424%

Self-Test

1. (a) $350
  (b) $76.05
  (c) $145.00
  (d) $13.20
3. 45%
5. $34 000
7. First bonus: $16 875
  Second bonus: $11 250
  Third bonus: $6750
  Fourth bonus: $5625
9. $32.50
11. 180
13. (a) 1.9573 BRL
  (b) 978.65 BRL
15. 0.789266

CHAPTER 4

Exercise 4.1

A. 1. A(−4,−3)
B(0,−4)
C(3,−4)
D(2,0)
E(4,3)
F(0,3)
G(−4,4)
H(−5,0)

3. (a)

x	−5	−4	−3	−2	−1	0	1	2	3
y	−3	−2	−1	0	1	2	3	4	5

(b)

x	3	2	1	0	−1	−2
y	5	3	1	−1	−3	−5

(c)

x	3	2	1	0	−1	−2	−3
y	6	4	2	0	−2	−4	−6

(d)

x	−5	−4	−3	−2	−1	0	1	2	3	4	5
y	5	4	3	2	1	0	−1	−2	−3	−4	−5

B. 1.

x	0	3	2
y	−3	0	−1

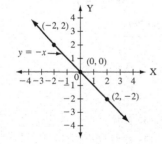

3.

x	0	−2	2
y	0	2	−2

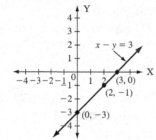

5.

x	0	4	−4
y	−3	0	−6

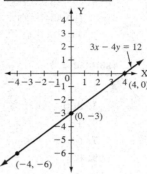

7.

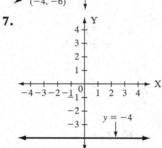

9. For

$y = 2x − 3$

slope, $m = 2$

y-intercept, $b = −3$

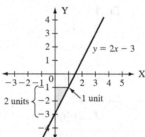

C. 1. For $y = 3x + 20$

x	0	20	40	
y	20	80	140	

or $m = 3$

$b = 20$

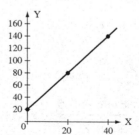

3. For $3x + 4y = 1200$

x	0	200	400	
y	300	150	0	

or $m = -\dfrac{3}{4}$

$b = 300$

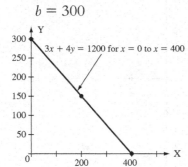

Exercise 4.2

A. 1. $x + y = 4$

x	0	4
y	4	0

$x - y = -4$

x	-4	0
y	0	4

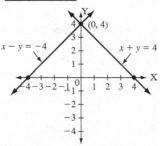

(0, 4) is the solution.

3. $x = 2y - 1$

x	3	-1	-5
y	2	0	-2

$y = 4 - 3x$

x	0	2	1
y	4	-2	1

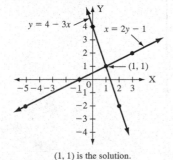

(1, 1) is the solution.

5. $3x - 4y = 18$

x	6	2	-2
y	0	-3	-6

$2y = -3x$

x	0	2	-2
y	0	-3	3

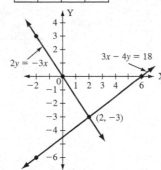

(2, -3) is the solution.

7. $5x - 2y = 20$

x	4	2	6
y	0	-5	5

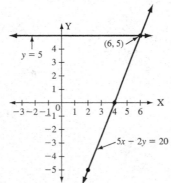

(6, 5) is the solution.

B. 1. For $y - 4x = 0$

x	0	5000	10 000
y	0	20 000	40 000

For $y - 2x - 10\,000 = 0$

x	0	5000	10 000
y	10 000	20 000	30 000

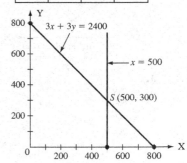

3. For $3x + 3y = 2400$

x	0	400	800
y	800	400	0

C. 1. $0 = 7$

This result is a contradiction and impossible. This is an inconsistent system and therefore, there is no solution for this system of linear equation.

3. $17 = 0$

This result is a contradiction and impossible. This is an inconsistent system and therefore, there is no solution for this system of linear equation.

Exercise 4.3

A. 1. $(x,y) = (-8,-1)$

3. $(x,y) = (10,12)$

5. $(x,y) = (-3,3)$

B. 1. $(x,y) = (-4,3)$

3. $(x,y) = (-1,3)$

5. $(x,y) = (4,3)$

C. 1. $(x,y) = (12,8)$

3. $(x,y) = (1.5,2.5)$

5. $(x,y) = (6,10)$

7. $(x,y) = \left(\dfrac{1}{2},\dfrac{3}{4}\right)$

Exercise 4.4

A. 1.

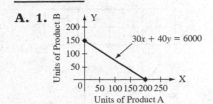

3.

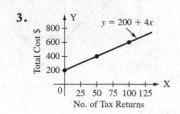

B. 1. The number of employees is 15 at the larger location, and 9 at the smaller one.

3. Sales were 90 jars of Brand X and 50 jars of No-Name brand.

5. Kaya's investment is $31 500 and Fred's investment is $23 500.

7. The first shift produced 1020 chairs and the second shift 1300 chairs.

9. The number of units of Product A is 20, and of Product B is 40.

11. The club bought 30 of $12-tickets and 21 of $15-tickets.

Exercise 4.5

A. 1.

x	0	4
y	4	0

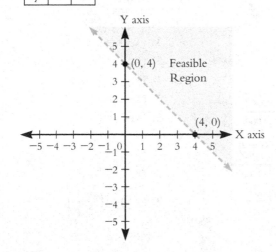

3.

x	0	4
y	−2	0

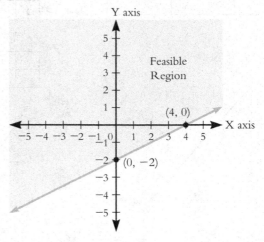

5.

x	0	3
y	0	−2

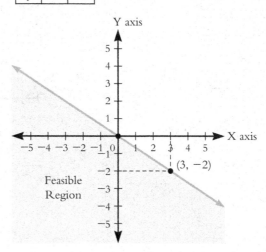

7.

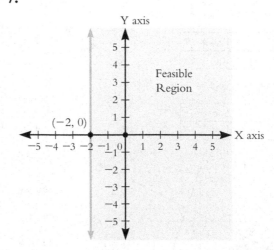

B. 1.

x	0	2
y	2	0

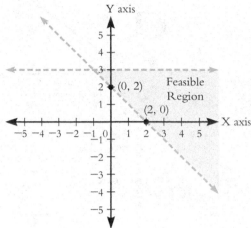

5.

x	0	-3
y	4.5	0

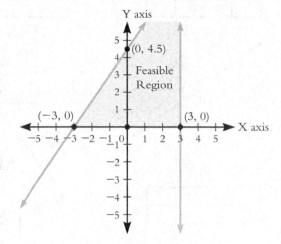

3.

x	0	8
y	4	0

x	0	2
y	-6	0

7.

x	0	1
y	0	-3

x	0	3
y	-6	0

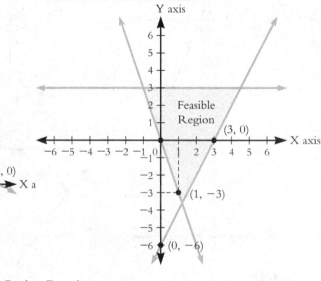

Review Exercise

1. (a) $2x - y = 6$

x	3	0	5
y	0	-6	4

(b) $3x + 4y = 0$

x	0	-4	4
y	0	3	-3

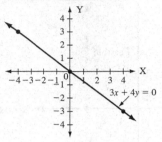

(c) $5x + 2y = 10$

x	0	2	4
y	5	0	-5

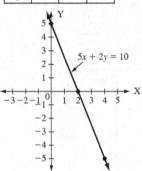

(d) $y = -3$

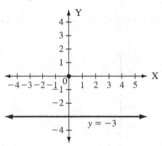

(e) $5y = -3x + 15$

x	0	5	2.5
y	3	0	1.5

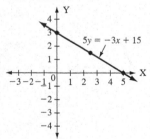

(f) $5x - 4y = 0$

x	0	4	-4
y	0	5	-5

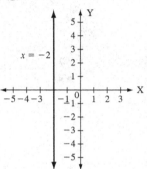

(g) $x = -2$

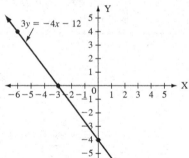

(h) $3y = -4x - 12$

x	-3	0	-6
y	0	-4	4

3. (a) $m = -\dfrac{7}{3}$; $b = 2$

(b) $m = \dfrac{1}{2}$; $b = 0$

(c) $m = \dfrac{3}{2}$; $b = 4$

(d) $m = -6$; $b = 10$

(e) m is undefined.
There is no y-intercept.

(f) $m = \dfrac{1}{3}$; $b = -3$

(g) $m = \dfrac{1}{4}$; $b = -1$

(h) Line is parallel to the x-axis;
$m = 0$; $b = 5$

5. (a)

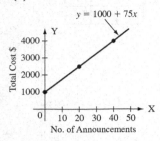

(b)

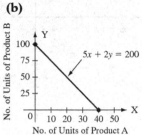

1. (a) $y = -x - 2$

x	0	-2	2
y	-2	0	-4

$x - y = 4$

x	0	4	2
y	-4	0	-2

(b) $3x = -2y$ and $x = 2$

x	0	-2	2
y	0	3	-3

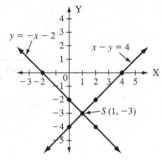

3. (a) $m = 0$; $b = -\dfrac{11}{3}$

(b) $m = 6$; $b = -9$

(c) $m = -\dfrac{1}{3}$; $b = 0$

(d) $m = 0$; $b = -3$

(e) m is undefined; there is no y-intercept

(f) $m = -\dfrac{a}{b}$; $b = \dfrac{c}{b}$

5. The amount invested at 4% is $8000; the amount invested at 6% is $4000.

CHAPTER 5

Exercise 5.1

A. 1. (a) (i)   TR $= 120x$

  (ii)   TC $= 2800 + (35 + 15)x$

 (b) (i)   40 units

  (ii) $4800

  (iii)   40%

 (c)

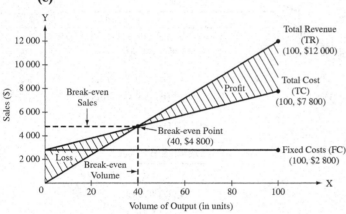

3. (a) (i)   TR $= \$1X$

  (ii)   Total cost $= 220\,000 + 0.45X$

 (b) (i)   400 000 units

  (ii) $400 000

  (iii)   50%

 (c)

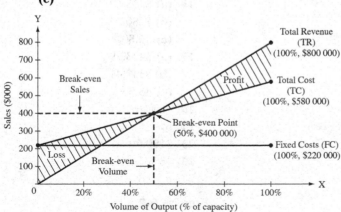

B. 1. 600 books

 3. 45 games

 5. $18 000

 7. $9.95

 9. (a) $1600

  (b) $700

11. (a) 28 unfinished boxes

  (b) $2.44

13. (a) 828 BBQ Meals

  (b) 1597 BBQ Meals

Exercise 5.2

A. 1. (a) $72

  (b) 48%

  (c) 82 units

  (d) $12 300

 3. (a) $46

  (b) 46.47%

  (c) 11 cell phones

  (d) $1089

B. 1. (a) $438 600

  (b) 43%

  (c) 372 094 units; $372 094

 3. (a) $97 500

  (b) 75%

  (c) 113 334 units

C. 1. 27 watches

 3. 169 oil changes

 5. (a) 80 chocolate bars

  (b) $1610.00

 7. $726 250

 9. $1 219 259.26

11. 228 000 units

13. (a) 46 consultations

  (b) 66 consultations

  (c) 45.34

Exercise 5.3

 1. (a) 164 units

  (b) 246 units

  (c) 250 units

  (d) $13

 3. (a) 975 sandwiches

  (b) 1034 sandwiches

  (c) $2094

  (d) 1338 sandwiches

 5. (a) 76%

  (b) 773 685 meals

  (c) 803 948 meals

  (d) $166 908

 7. (a) Fixed cost = $1 200 000

   Total revenue (sales) = $2 300 000

   Total variable cost = $750 000

   Contribution Margin (CM) = $1 550 000

   Contribution rate = 67.39%

  (b) Break-even = $1 780 645.28

  (c) Fixed cost = $1 450 000

   Break-even = $2 151 613.04

(d) Fixed cost = $1 200 000
Total revenue (sales) = $2 645 000
Total variable cost = $862 500
Contribution Margin (CM) = $1 782 500
Net income = $582 500

Review Exercise

1. (a) (i) $28.00
    (ii) 15.14%
  (b) (i) 112 units
    (ii) 35%
   (iii) $20 720
  (c)

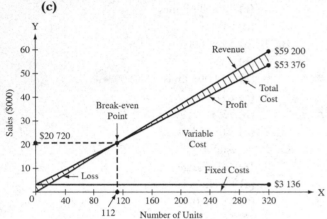

  (d) (i) 30%
    (ii) 38.75%
   (iii) 70%
3. (a) (i) $140 000
    (ii) 35%
  (b) (i) 60%
    (ii) $300 000
  (c)

(d) $335 000
5. 802 meals
7. (a) 74%
  (b) 2 651 352 units
  (c) 2 860 754 units
  (d) $299 960.64

Self-Test

1. (a) (i) $3.00
    (ii) 30%
  (b) (i) 6000 Jump Drives
    (ii) $60 000
   (iii) 40%
  (c)

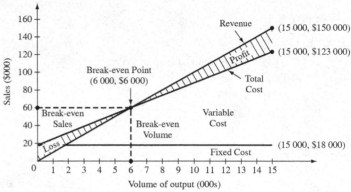

(d) 5600 Units
(e) 5500 Units

CHAPTER 6

Exercise 6.1

1. $78.53
3. $3200.00
5. $74.10
7. $426.00
9. 15.9%
11. 41.58%
13. (a) 38.75%
   (b) 48.27%
15. (a) $318.67
   (b) $280.33
   (c) 46.80%
17. (a) $443.79
   (b) $342.41
   (c) 43.55%
19. 15%
21. 5%
23. $180.00
25. 15%
27. 8.70%

Exercise 6.2

1. (a) May 23
  (b) $2449.02
3. (a) $799.90
  (b) $825.16
  (c) $842.00
5. $2507.19

7. $2184.00
9. (a) September 10
  (b) $5276.85
  (c) $103.20
11. (a) $1164.00
  (b) $733.54
  (c) $600.00
13. (a) $1925.00
  (b) $3400.00
15. (a) $1.96
  (b) 3.5%

Exercise 6.3

1. $13.60
3. $3.00
5. $102.08
7. (a) 150%
  (b) 60%
9. (a) $36.50
  (b) $29.93
  (c) 21.95%
11. (a) $1.65 per litre
  (b) 66.67%
13. (a) $234.20
  (b) 47.37%
15. (a) $140.00
  (b) 66.67%
17. (a) $16.80
  (b) 27.27%
19. $630.20
21. (a) $164.00; $102.40; $52.00
  (b) $5741.60
  (c) 38.99%

Exercise 6.4

1. (a) $21.99
  (b) $17.59
  (c) loss of $1.98
3. 20.08%
5. 16%
7. (a) $7.00
  (b) 21.21%
9. (a) $17.79
  (b) $25.44
  (c) 12.28%
  (d) 38.66%
11. (a) $152.00
  (b) $95.76
  (c) 58.73%
  (d) $119.70
  (e) $12.54 profit

13. (a) $331.65
  (b) $271.35
  (c) 18.18%

Exercise 6.5

1. (a) $267.30
  (b) $160.38
  (c) $12.56
3. (a) 16.00%
  (b) profit of $22.00
  (c) 54.41%
  (d) 35.24%
5. Loss of $2.23
7. (a) $14.85; $9.90; $6.60
  (b) $957.00
  (c) 34.4978%
9. (a) $72.00
  (b) $54.00
  (c) 25%
11. profit of $3.25
13. loss of $6.60
15. loss of $82.50

Review Exercise

1. (a) $31.92
  (b) $24.08
  (c) 43%
3. 45.66%
5. 15%
7. $30.00
9. September 12; $25 117.40
11. (a) $1940.00
  (b) $2813.00
13. (a) $1645.00
  (b) $1500.00
15. (a) $90.00
  (b) $58.50
  (c) 53.85%
  (d) $74.88
  (e) loss of $6.48
17. (a) $77.50
  (b) 42.86%
19. $240.00
21. (a) loss of $0.60
  (b) 26.9841%
23. (a) loss of $13.20
  (b) 25%
25. (a) $239.53
  (b) $167.67
  (c) Loss of $20.96

27. (a) $2152.40
  (b) 69.43%
  (c) 40.98%

Self-Test

1. $295.77
3. 50.5%
5. $1635.04
7. $1450.00
9. $240.00
11. 180%
13. $110.00
15. loss of $660.45

CHAPTER 7

Exercise 7.1

1. $88.77
3. $153.79
5. $25.34
7. $18.41
9. $34.72
11. $558.53
13. $3.44

Exercise 7.2

1. $3296.00
3. 9.5%
5. 8.4%
7. 11 months
9. 126 days
11. $876.00
13. $400 000.00
15. 9%
17. 41 days

Exercise 7.3

1. $2542.53
3. $26 954.84
5. (a) $51 975.00
  (b) $51 943.53
  (c) 3.8871%
7. November 18, 2021
9. $4 002 000
11. $36.90

Exercise 7.4

1. $1222.00
3. $1704.60
5. $644.00
7. $398.04
9. $23 000.00
11. $491.39

Exercise 7.5

1. $1156.80
3. $2248.66
5. $1722.00
7. $519.48
9. $569.45
11. $379.15
13. $811.93
15. $1408.21
17. $937.56

Review Exercise

1. $63.98
3. 7.5%
5. 265 days
7. $3000.17
9. 8.25%
11. 196 days
13. $1601.89
15. $3200.00
17. $1736.47
19. $2664.00
21. $5119.89
23. $3560.00
25. $1614.74

Self-Test

1. $21.40
3. 6.5%
5. $6187.50
7. $4306.81
9. 359 days
11. $7432.80
13. $2910.69
15. $1163.85

CHAPTER 8

Exercise 8.1

1. $630.97
3. $820.00
5. maturity value = $3654.44; present value = $3615.93
7. $2465.93
9. $527.34

Exercise 8.2

1. $49 330.94
3. 2.73%
5. (a) 2.7183%
  (b) $99 662.84
  (c) 2.9397%

7. 73.00 days
9. $748 677

Exercise 8.3

1. $3785.67
3. $1825.63
5. $278.14
7. $178.66
9. $9785.58

Exercise 8.4

1. $37.50
3. $4.62
5. (a) April $128.02;
May $138.67;
June $146.10;
July $151.62;
Aug. $212.57;
Sept. $196.91
(b) −$45 260.06

Exercise 8.5

1. Amount paid,
$1233.69; Interest
paid, $33.69;
Principal repaid,
$1200.00
3. Amount paid,
$922.36; Interest
paid (daily), $22.36;
Principal repaid,
$900.00

Review Exercise

1. (a) October 30
(b) $34.76
(c) $1634.76
3. $1500.00
5. $5123.29
7. $814.17
9. $1270.28
11. $497 381.59
13. (a) 2.93%
(b) 1.88%
(c) 11.48%
15. $10 176.69
17. $79.46
19. The unsecured line
of credit is his best
option because he
will pay less interest.

21. Amount paid, $3081.35;
Interest paid, $81.35;
Principal repaid, $3000.00

Self-Test

1. June 10, 2022; $19.28
3. $1160.69
5. $1666.06
7. (a) $98 116.43
(b) 3.68%
9. Accrued interest, $340.26
11. Amount paid, $4070.41;
Interest paid, $70.41;
Principal repaid, $4000.00

CHAPTER 9

Exercise 9.1

A. 1. $m = 1$; $i = 0.12$; $n = 5$
3. $m = 4$; $i = 0.01375$; $n = 36$
5. $m = 2$; $i = 0.0575$; $n = 27$
7. $m = 12$; $i = 0.006$; $n = 150$
9. $m = 2$; $i = 0.06125$; $n = 9$
B. 1. (a) 10%
(b) 4
(c) 2.5%
(d) 48
(e) $(1 + 0.025)^{48}$
(f) 3.271490
3. (a) 9.6%
(b) 12
(c) 0.80%
(d) 84
(e) $(1 + 0.008)^{84}$
(f) 1.952921
5. (a) 7.25%
(b) 26
(c) 0.2788%
(d) 182
(e) $(1 + 0.002788)^{182}$
(f) 1.65996

Exercise 9.2

1. FV = $5947.22
I = $947.22
3. $2110.21
5. The 3.79% compounded
daily rate earns more
interest. Interest is larger
by $6.97.
7. 232.12
9. $2372.65

11. $1452.78
13. $4126.47
15. $1102.13
17. $1444.24
19. $10 658.73
21. $3677.78

Exercise 9.3

1. $1338.81; $261.19
3. $762.84
5. $3129.97
7. $1398.85
9. $6002.89
11. The two pay-
ments are worth
$4835.49 more
than one payment
now. Choose the
two payments.
13. In terms of today's
dollar, choosing to
pay $2000.00 now
is better by $52.00.
15. $22 721.70

Exercise 9.4

1. $4589.47
3. $1345.06
5. $3800.24
7. $1561.49
9. $8452.52
11. $2346.36
13. $3488.29
15. $1074.71
17. $1972.80
19. $1492.15

Exercise 9.5

1. (a) $2851.94
(b) $3265.19
(c) $4000.00
(d) $5610.21
3. $6805.31
5. $655.02
7. $2464.35
9. $1955.51
11. $4379.98
13. $2707.08
15. $3076.33
17. $978.93
19. $1345.51

Review Exercise

1. (a) $2378.89
(b) $378.89
3. (a) $3185.63; $1385.63
(b) $1845.45; $595.45
5. $4194.33
7. $2082.25; $1917.75
9. $1035.70
11. $2079.94
13. $110 440.03
15. $9791.31
17. $3190.63
19. $9294.86
21. $3841.72
23. $3007.53
25. $3032.54

Self-Test

1. $2129.97
3. $2177.36
5. $4504.29
7. $848.88
9. $14 711.80
11. $9449.31
13. $2425.52

CHAPTER 10

Exercise 10.1

1. 18.66 half-years
3. 17.5 years
5. 40 months
7. November 9, 2023
9. 19.09 months
11. 14.33 months
13. 11.35 months from
now
15. 16.41 months

Exercise 10.2

1. 9.2366% compounded
quarterly
3. 10.4018% compounded
quarterly
5. 9.5873% compounded
annually
7. 6.3362% compounded
semi-annually
9. 12.9997% compounded
monthly

Exercise 10.3

A. 1. (a) 9.7256%
   (b) 10.9207%
   (c) 5.1162%
   (d) 7.4548%
   (e) 3.6654%
   (f) 8.5386%

B. 1. 6.9913%
3. 4.6561%
5. 8.9454% compounded quarterly
7. 6.2196% compounded monthly
9. 7.3854% compounded monthly
11. $714.57; $114.57; 3.5567%
13. $1831.40; $631.40; 4.3182%

Review Exercise

1. 5.592% compounded monthly
3. 19.60 months from now
5. 11.26 years
7. 6.0305% compounded monthly
9. (a) 5.9184% compounded quarterly
   (b) 14.3547% compounded semi-annually
   (c) 8.8334% compounded monthly
   (d) 8.2432% compounded annually
11. (a) 4.5940%
   (b) 5.9634%
13. 8.4405% compounded monthly
15. (a) 4%
   (b) 3.7852%
   (c) 3.5462%
   (d) 3.2989%
17. 22 months from now
19. 18.81 months from now
21. 3.69 years

Self-Test

1. 3.3 years
3. 5.5357%
5. 7.3522% compounded semi-annually
7. 10% compounded semi-annually
9. 3.95% compounded semi-annually

CHAPTER 11

Exercise 11.2

1. $13 045.68
3. $3972.36
5. $922.93
7. $1166.29
9. (a) $8531.12
   (b) $4500.00
   (c) $4031.12
11. (a) $20 090.19
   (b) $15 000.00
   (c) $5090.19
13. $2551.49
15. $38 738.34
17. FV = $71 345.16; Interest = $13 345.16
19. $50 970.11

Exercise 11.3

1. $6897.02
3. (a) $9906.20
   (b) $2093.80
5. (a) $2523.82
   (b) $372.06
7. (a) $27 947.10
   (b) $4980.90
9. $1629.60; $1818.63; Wayne paid less
11. (a) $13 683.13
   (b) $1428.88
   (c) $14 183.17
   (d) $500.04
   (e) $21.28
13. $34 516.19
15. $1 269 011.67
17. (a) $7937.28
   (b) $8016.71
   (c) $7858.68
   (d) Selling price of a loan contract decreases if the interest rate on the contract increases. (A higher interest rate means you'd have to set less aside today in order to earn a specified future amount).

19. (a) $275 983.67
   (b) $34 716.33
21. $9206.90

Exercise 11.4

1. $207.87
3. $591.66
5. $255.36
7. $109.89
9. $665.25
11. $290.55
13. $5462.38
15. $3141.41
17. $428.18
19. $1673.54

Exercise 11.5

1. 75 months
3. 18
5. 3 years
7. 2 years, 4 months
9. 4 years
11. 6 years, 6 months
13. 10 months
15. 127 payments, $121.80

Exercise 11.6

1. 12.5% compounded quarterly
3. 3.0356% compounded monthly
5. 7.1983% compounded monthly
7. 7.685% compounded quarterly
9. 8.8899% compounded quarterly
11. 8.664154%
13. $6046.51

Review Exercise

1. (a) $26 734.60
   (b) $17 280.00
   (c) $9454.60
3. 13 years
5. $296.03
7. $3620.11
9. 6.0185% compounded quarterly
11. (a) $12 221.59
   (b) $14 195.04
   (c) $150.56

13. 7 years
15. (a) 4.860588% compounded monthly
   (b) 5 years, 1 month

Self-Test

1. $35 786.08
3. 10.9002% compounded semi-annually
5. 47 months
7. $40 385.38
9. $3268.62

CHAPTER 12

Exercise 12.1

1. $3810.79
3. $3877.76
5. (a) $13 265.50
   (b) $3265.50
7. $31 293.63
9. $6927.06
11. $4201.67
13. $975.72
15. $770.27

Exercise 12.2

1. $10 041.88
3. $31 736.57
5. (a) $29 829.02
   (b) $5170.98
7. $116 124.78
9. $46 568.95
11. The lump-sum cash offer is $223.27 higher than the quarterly payments offer.
13. $33 885.28

Exercise 12.3

1. $124.41
3. $799.39
5. $776.11
7. $117.26
9. $41.85
11. $85 320.36
13. $211.54
15. $772.99

Exercise 12.4

1. 3 years, 9 months
3. 3 years, 4 months
5. 13 years, 8 months
7. 1 year, 10 months
9. 40 deposits
11. 9 payments
13. 15 years, 6 months

Exercise 12.5

1. 5.0895% compounded quarterly
3. 7.3071% compounded semi-annually
5. 8.8248% compounded monthly
7. 10.7784% compounded monthly
9. 7.856% compounded quarterly
11. 18.6169% compounded semi-annually

Exercise 12.6

1. (a) $1016.40
   (b) $18 229.63
3. (a) $27 748.40
   (b) $35 011.37
   (c) $1413.54
   (d) $7262.97
5. $17 790.55
7. $91 748.66
9. $91 989.41
11. $760 804.04

Review Exercise

1. $13 509.62
3. $82 901.70
5. $75 962.59
7. $1979.24
9. (a) 7 years, 9 months
   (b) 14 years
11. (a) 6 years, 6 months
    (b) 24 years
13. 4 years, 3 months
15. 9 years
17. (a) $16 333.29
    (b) $3913.29
    (c) $622.92
    (d) $7513.44
19. 8 years, 1 month
21. $160 296.97

Self-Test

1. $55 246.47
3. 4 years, 6 months
5. $2801.41
7. 8 years
9. $177.98
11. $302 131.39

CHAPTER 13

Exercise 13.1

1. $31 378.29
3. (a) $9222.21
   (b) $742.21
   (c) $2539.32 more
5. $6245.85
7. (a) $1618.41
   (b) $2241.00
   (c) $622.59
   (d) $59.08
9. $84.97
11. $4565.36
13. 1 year, 8 months
15. 55 monthly withdrawals; since the first withdrawal is immediate, the last withdrawal is 54 months from the first withdrawal, or 4 years, 6 months.
17. 7.0001% compounded quarterly
19. 8.5803% compounded semi-annually

Exercise 13.2

1. $591 131.02
3. $24 111.08
5. $848 279.71
7. $162.26
9. $12 181.57
11. 20 years
13. 9.1776% compounded annually

Exercise 13.3

1. $1651.45
3. (a) $147 329.91
   (b) $272 000
   (c) $124 670.09
5. 2 years 9 months
7. 4.0842% compounded monthly
9. $114.89

11. $216 738.19
13. $22 692.59
15. 15 quarterly withdrawals
17. $165.11
19. 9.1781% compounded monthly

Exercise 13.4

1. $2752.22
3. $261.77
5. 3 years, 6 months
7. 4.4797% compounded quarterly
9. 0.65505% per quarter
11. (a) $32 277.80
    (b) $38 400.00
    (c) $6122.20
13. $1655.40
15. $9523.53
17. 11 yearly payments
19. 7.4885% compounded quarterly
21. 5.1417% compounded semi-annually
23. $143 773.15

Exercise 13.5

1. $9600.00
3. $214.60
5. $343 446.85
7. $0.57
9. 5.1898% compounded monthly
11. $241.95
13. $122 263.83
15. $1667.02
17. 7.80% compounded monthly
19. $69 671.44
21. $556.52

Review Exercise

1. $27 616.11
3. $17 367.79
5. (a) $2638.84
   (b) $3444.00
   (c) $805.16
7. (a) $13 925.54
   (b) $14 056.50
9. (a) $128 905.47
   (b) $75 094.53

11. $5199.99
13. 4 years, 1 month
15. 4 years, 2 months
17. (a) $30 742.57
    (b) $6720.73
    (c) $33 309.38
    (d) $200.73
19. $21 116.58
21. $742.45
23. 3 years, 9 months
25. 9.296% compounded annually
27. (a) $15 749.42
    (b) $3149.42
    (c) $438.32
    (d) $8439.36
29. (a) $503.87
    (b) $1437.96
    (c) $275.12
    (d) $1782.29
    (e) $89.52
    (f) $1037.88
31. 6 years, 6 months
33. $180 230.77

Self-Test

1. $216 115.89
3. $1217.11
5. $23 780.54
7. $244.42
9. 18.927% compounded semi-annually
11. 18.5 years
13. $2339.72

CHAPTER 14

Exercise 14.1

A. 1. (a) $549.22
      (b) $11 750.78
      (c) $11 495.33
   3. (a) $1103.73
      (b) $14 496.27
      (c) $13 972.39
B. 1. (a) $920.58
      (b) $31 719.42
      (c) $31 433.24
      (d) $59 234.80
      (e) $23 234.80
   3. (a) $136.87
      (b) $4199.44
      (c) $31.50
      (d) $105.37

5. (a) $73 353.95
   (b) $50 833.74
   (c) $5079.79
   (d) $22 520.21
7. $1904.33
   Total Paid = $13 330.31
   Cost of Financing = $3330.33
9. Amount paid, $13 534.12;
   Interest paid, $4 334.13;
   Principal repaid, $9200.00
11. $491.56
13. $1351.22
15. (a) $3621.90
   (b) $1035.28
   (c) $2799.85
   (d) $10 445.20
   Total Amount paid =
   $115 900.87;
   Total Interest paid = $30 900.87
17. (a) 14.02 half-years 15 payments
   (b) $957.79
   (c) $1910.53
   (d) $4665.00
   Total Amount paid = $35 057.78;
   Total Interest paid = $11 057.78

Exercise 14.2

A. 1. (a) $1829.69
   (b) Interest paid = $1454.40;
   Principal repaid = $375.29;
   Balance = $35 624.71
   (c) Interest paid = $1439.24;
   Principal repaid = $390.45;
   Balance = $35 234.26
3. (a) $164.04
   (b) Interest paid = $41.97;
   Principal repaid = $122.06;
   Balance = $8377.94
   (c) Interest paid = $41.38;
   Principal repaid = $122.66;
   Balance = $8255.28
B. 1. (a) $3212.01;
   Amount paid = $22 484.09;
   Interest paid = $6484.09;
   Principal repaid = $16 000.00
3. (a) $2790.38
   (b) $34 892.36
   (c) $1599.89
   (d) $1190.49
5. (a) 14 payments
   (b) $1132.35
   (c) $2532.35

7. (a) $26 387.36
   (b) $12 151.69
   (c) $14 235.73
   (d) $3044.27
9. (a) 15 payments
   (b) Balance = $12 478.99;
   Cost of debt = $9978.99
   (c) $619.80
   (d) $7530.57
   Total Amount
   paid = $43 540.28
   Total Interest
   paid = $11 540.28
11. (a) $775.32
   (b) 65 payments

Exercise 14.3

A. 1. $1006.24
3. $348.26
5. $306.39
B. 1. (a) 30 payments
   (b) $157.47
3. (a) 48 payments
   (b) $722.00
5. $234.54
7. $301.40
9. $1152.88
11. (a) 62 payments
   (b) $724.46
   (c) $84 599.46
   (d) $68 599.46
13. (a) $15 099.27
   (b) $1 122 823.63
   (c)

Payment Numbers	Payment Amount	Principle Paid	Interest Paid	Remaining Balance
101	15 099.27	9 523.18	5 576.09	1 681 382.25
102	15 099.27	9 554.58	5 544.68	1 671 827.67
103	15 099.27	9 586.09	5 513.18	1 662 241.58

   (d) $1 494 355.29
   (e) $14 409.99

Exercise 14.4

1. (a) $978.11
   (b) $158 698.67
   (c) $1008.85
3. (a) 109 payments
   (b) $178.13
   (c) $1667.47
5. 5.42% compounded
   semi-annually

7. (a) $83 290.48
   (b) 739 payments
   (c) $7094.23
9. $380.00
11. PMT = 190.00;
   annual rate of
   interest
   = 12 (0.45317%)
   = 5.4380%

Payment date	Number of days	Amount paid	Interest paid	Principal	Balance repaid
June 1					40 000.00
16	15	190.00	89.39	100.61	39 899.39
July 1	15	190.00	89.17	100.83	39 798.56
16	15	190.00	88.94	101.06	39 697.50
Aug 1	16	190.00	94.63	95.37	39 602.13
16	15	190.00	88.50	101.50	39 500.63
Sept 1	16	190.00	94.16	95.84	39 404.79
16	15	190.00	88.06	101.94	39 302.85
Oct 1	15	190.00	87.83	102.17	39 200.68
15	15	190.00	87.61	102.39	39 098.29
Nov 1	16	190.00	93.20	96.80	39 001.49
15	15	190.00	87.16	102.84	38 898.65
Dec 1	15	190.00	86.93	103.07	38 795.58

The mortgage statement balance on December 1 of $38 795.58 differs from the amortization schedule balance of $38 794.01 by $1.57. The difference is reduced from $3.01 in the answer to Question 10 by $1.44 due to making semi-monthly payments.

Review Exercise

1. (a) $1491.37
   (b) $12 723.84
   (c) $15 771.79
   (d) $338.49
   (e) $1247.91
   (f) Total Amount paid =
   $47 723.89;
   Total Interest paid =
   $12 723.89;
   Principal repaid = $35 000.00

3. (a) 25 payments
   (b) $28 940.21
   (c) $426.66
   (d) $1807.58
   (e) Balance after 22
      payments = $5477.30;
      Total Amount paid =
      $49 664.30;
      Total Interest paid =
      $9664.30;
      Principal repaid =
      $40 000.00
5. (a) $735.80
   (b) $280.57
   (c) $23 981.71
   (d) $1000.87
   (e) Total Amount paid =
      $24 843.52;
      Total Interest paid =
      $11 087.46;
      Principal repaid =
      $13 756.06
7. (a) 10 payments
   (b) $1139.87
9. (a) 12 quarters
   (b) $3211.27
11. (a) $1313.76
    (b) $206 661.46
    (c) $1358.02
13. (a) 118 payments
    (b) $736.39
    (c) $389.21
15. (a) $161.75
    (b) $1264.13
    (c) $5086.64
    (d) $21.41
    (e) $478.21
    Total Amount paid =
    $7764.16;
    Total Interest paid =
    $1264.16;
    Principal repaid =
    $6500.00
17. 5.38% compounded
    semi-annually
19. (a) $601.20
    (b) $1650.96
    (c) $25 597.94
    (d) $638.93

Self-Test

1. $4570.18
3. $6070.22

5. (a) 171 payments
   (b) $441.89
   (c) $2911.71
7. 10.0% compounded semi-annually
9. $228.93

CHAPTER 15

Exercise 15.2

1. $466.70
3. $4782.83
5. $10 861.30
7. $1071.46
9. $97 183.63
11. (a) $96 936.04
    (b) $1250.00
    (c) $95 686.04
13. (a) $6565.87
    (b) $36.00
    (c) $6529.87
15. (a) $14 304.00; $114 304.00
    (b) $6359.60; $106 359.60
17. (a) $2800.72; $27 800.72
    (b) $2458.66; $22 541.34
19. $4 569 384.71
21. $103 723.58
23. $13 177.35

Exercise 15.3

A. 1. $77.15; $4922.85
   3. $32.36; $1032.36
B. 1. Gain on Sale = $242.12
   3. Gain on Sale = $387.55

Exercise 15.4

1. 5.8681%
3. 7.901%
5. 9.2566%
7. 4.744%

Exercise 15.5

1. (a) $2780.51
   (b) $65 004.24
   (c) $9995.76
3. $2419.29
5. $2840.83
7. (a) $567.08
   (b) $9598.44
9. (a) $4275.00
   (b) $1124.00
   (c) $5399.00
   (d) $36 976.00

11. (a) $302.01
    (b) $21 903.91
    (c) $257.62
    (d) $764.19
    (e) $97 252.61
13. (a) $24 750.00
    (b) $8604.00
    (c) $33 354.00
    (d) $13 931.00
    (e) $107 196.00
    (f) $232 277.00

Review Exercise

1. (a) $5751.14
   (b) $4776.44
3. $26 174.35
5. Premium = $1129.61;
   Purchase price = $21 129.61
7. (a) Discount = $15 620.41
   (b) Purchase price = $85 892.23
9. $4527.65
11. 12.5685%
13. Discount = $218.97;
    Purchase price = $4781.03
15. Gain on Sale = $1899.18
17. 7.6478%
19. (a) $44 248.79
    (b) $48 017.12
    (c) Gain on Sale = $1795.38
21. (a) $5 293 025.24
    (b)

Payment Numbers	Payment Amount	Interest Earned on Fund	Total Increase in Fund	Balance in Fund
11	5 293 025.235	2 188 075.23	7 481 100.46	69 634 378.42
12	5 293 025.235	2 451 443.65	7 744 468.88	77 378 847.31
13	5 293 025.235	2 724 083.82	8 017 109.06	85 395 956.37

23. (a) The selling price of a bond
       depends on the relationship
       between the coupon or bond rate
       (the interest the bond pays) and
       the bond's YTM. In this case, the
       coupon rate is 5.05 percent and
       the YTM is 2.74 percent. Since
       the coupon rate is higher than
       the YTM, the bond sells at a
       premium.
    (b) $16 905.12
    (c) $16 989.09

25. $25 222.48

27. (a) $1201.97

    (b) $17 570.15

    (c) $2443.36

    (d) $55 982.25

29. (a) $13 875.00

    (b) $5349.00

    (c) $38 448.00

    (d) $235 779.00

    (e) $11 270.00

    (f) $251 853.00

31. (a) $1058.61

    (b) Total Amount paid = $7410.27;
    Total Interest earned = $2589.77;
    Increase in fund = $10 000.04

33. (a) $13 920.00

    (b) $5211.80

    (c) $19 131.80

    (d) $70 723.83

    (e) $54 226.99

Self-Test

1. $9269.43

3. $367.77 (premium)

5. $4607.92

7. 12.4614%

9. 12.9369%

11. $3721.96

CHAPTER 16

Exercise 16.1

A. 1. $44 634; $53 448; Alternative 2 is preferred at 12%.

    3. $22 205; $23 384; Alternative 1 is preferred.

    5. $2000; $2393; Alternative 1 is preferred.

B. 1. $62 363; $73 601; at 6%, Alternative 2 is preferred.

3. $30 876.65; $31 281.27; at 8%, Offer B is preferred because they will receive a higher value for their business today.

5. $82 247.43; $113 355.95; the warehouse should be purchased.

Exercise 16.2

A. 1. −$5367; the investment should be rejected.

    3. $234; $203; Alternative 1 is preferred.

    5. $1666; $352; since the net present value of Alternative 1 is greater than the net present value of Alternative 2, Alternative 1 is preferred.

B. 1. Project B is preferred at 12%.

    3. −$8561; the project will not return 14% on the investment and therefore should not be undertaken.

    5. $5696; the new product provides the required return on investment of 20% and therefore should be distributed.

    7. $5142; the investment will return more than 12% on the investment and should therefore be made.

    9. $18 894.95; −$2906.37; because option A has a positive NPV, it is the preferred option.

Exercise 16.3

1. 19.9%

3. 19.85%

5. 22.2%

7. Both options have an internal rate of return that is smaller than the company's 13 percent expected rate. Therefore, none of these two options is acceptable.

Review Exercise

1. The PV of Alternative B > PV of Alternative A. Therefore, Alternative B is preferred.

3. The NPV of Alternative 1 is greater than the NPV of Alternative 2. Therefore, Alternative 1 is preferred.

5. −$22 227

7. 26.3%

9. 17.4%

11. 25.83%

13. At 20%, the PV of Project B is greater than the PV of Project A. Outway Ventures should choose Project B.

15. −$1215

17. At 16%, the NPV is positive, the return on investment will be greater than 16%. The product should be marketed.

19. Comparing the IRR for each option, we see that investing in new machinery provides a higher return on investment. Therefore, it is the preferred option for the firm.

Self-Test

1. Alternative A is preferred.

3. 16.88%

5. Proposal B is preferred at 20%.

INDEX